P9-CMF-123

U.S. War Dept.

THE

WAR OF THE REBELLION:

A COMPILATION OF THE

OFFICIAL RECORDS

OF THE

UNION AND CONFEDERATE ARMIES.

PUBLISHED UNDER THE DIRECTION OF

The Hon. **DANIEL S. LAMONT**, Secretary of War,

BY

MAJ. GEORGE B. DAVIS, U. S. A.,
MR. LESLIE J. PERRY,
MR. JOSEPH W. KIRKLEY,
Board of Publication.

SERIES I—VOLUME XLIV.

Reports, Correspondence, etc.

WASHINGTON:
GOVERNMENT PRINTING OFFICE.
1893.

PREFACE.

The work of preparing the records of the war for public use was begun under the resolution of Congress of May 19, 1864, by Adjt. Gen. E. D. Townsend, U. S. Army, who caused copies to be made of reports of battles on file in his office and steps to be taken to collect missing records.

Under the provisions of joint resolution No. 91, of 1866, Hon. Peter H. Watson was appointed to supervise the preparation and formulate a plan for the publication of the records, but he did no work and drew no pay under this appointment, which expired July 27, 1868, by limitation of the resolution. This resolution also repealed the former one and work ceased.

The first decisive step taken in this work was the act of June 23, 1874, providing the necessary means "to enable the Secretary of War to begin the publication of the Official Records of the War of the Rebellion, both of the Union and Confederate Armies," and directing him "to have copied for the Public Printer all reports, letters, telegrams, and general orders, not heretofore copied or printed, and properly arranged in chronological order." Appropriations have been made from time to time for continuing such preparation. Under this act the preliminary work was resumed by General Townsend, who first outlined the plan on which the records are printed, though it appears that originally he contemplated publishing to the world only the more important military reports.

Subsequently, under meager appropriations, it was prosecuted in a somewhat desultory manner by various subordinates of the War Department until December 14, 1877, when the Secretary of War, perceiving that the undertaking needed the undivided attention of a single head, detailed Lieut. Col. Robert N. Scott, U. S. Army, to take charge of the bureau and devote himself exclusively to the work.

The act of June 23, 1874, greatly enlarged upon the first crude scheme of publication. On this more comprehensive basis it was determined that the volumes should include not only the battle reports, but also "all official documents that can be obtained by the compiler, and that appear to be of any historical value." Colonel Scott systematized the work and the plan and presented the records in the following order of arrangement, which has been adhered to by his successors:

The first series will embrace the formal reports, both Union and Confederate, of the first seizures of United States property in the Southern States, and of all military operations in the field, with the correspondence, orders, and returns relating specially thereto, and, as proposed, is to be accompanied by an Atlas.

In this series the reports will be arranged according to the campaigns and several theaters of operations (in the chronological order of the events), and the Union reports of any event will, as a rule, be immediately followed by the Confederate accounts. The correspondence, etc., not embraced in the "reports" proper will follow (first Union and next Confederate) in chronological order.

The second series will contain the correspondence, orders, reports, and returns, Union and Confederate, relating to prisoners of war, and (so far as the military authorities were concerned) to State or political prisoners.

The third series will contain the correspondence, orders, reports, and returns of the Union authorities (embracing their correspondence with the Confederate officials) not relating specially to the subjects of the first and second series. It will set forth the annual and special reports of the Secretary of War, of the General-in-Chief, and of the chiefs of the several staff corps and departments; the calls for troops, and the correspondence between the National and the several State authorities.

The fourth series will exhibit the correspondence, orders, reports, and returns of the Confederate authorities, similar to that indicated for the Union officials, as of the third series, but excluding the correspondence between the Union and Confederate authorities given in that series.

The first volume of the records was issued in the early fall of 1880. The act approved June 16, 1880, provided "for the printing and binding, under direction of the Secretary of War, of 10,000 copies of a compilation of the Official Records (Union and Confederate) of the War of the Rebellion, so far as the same may be ready for publication, during the fiscal year;" and that "of said number 7,000 copies shall be for the use of the House of Representatives, 2,000 copies for the use of the Senate, and 1,000 copies for the use of the Executive Departments." Under this act Colonel Scott proceeded to publish the first five volumes of the records.*

---

*All subsequent volumes have been distributed under the act approved August 7, 1882, which provides that:

"The volumes of the Official Records of the War of the Rebellion shall be distributed as follows: One thousand copies to the Executive Departments, as now provided by law. One thousand copies for distribution by the Secretary of War among officers of the army and contributors to the work. Eight thousand three hundred copies shall be sent by the Secretary of War to such libraries, organizations, and individuals as may be designated by the Senators, Representatives, and Delegates of the Forty-seventh Congress. Each Senator shall designate not exceeding twenty-six, and each Representative and Delegate not exceeding twenty-one, of such addresses, and the volumes shall be sent thereto from time to time as they are published, until the publication is completed. Senators, Representatives, and Delegates shall inform the Secretary of War in each case how many volumes of those heretofore published they have forwarded to such addresses. The remaining copies of the eleven thousand to be published, and all sets that may not be ordered to be distributed as provided herein, shall be sold by the Secretary of War for cost of publication with ten per cent. added thereto, and the proceeds of such sale shall be

Col. Robert N. Scott died March 5, 1887, before the completion of the work, which, during a ten years' service, he had come to love so dearly. At his death some twenty-six books only had been issued, but he had compiled a large amount of matter for forthcoming volumes; consequently his name as compiler was retained in all the books up to and including Vol. XXXVI, although his successors had added largely to his compilations from new material found after his demise.

The Secretary of War, May 7, 1887, assigned Lieut. Col. H. M. Lazelle, U. S. Army, to duty as the successor of Colonel Scott. He had continued in charge about two years, when, in the act approved March 2, 1889, it was provided—

> That hereafter the preparation and publication of said records shall be conducted, under the Secretary of War, by a board of three persons, one of whom shall be an officer of the Army, and two civilian experts, to be appointed by the Secretary of War, the compensation of said civilian experts to be fixed by the Secretary of War.

The Secretary of War appointed Maj. George B. Davis, judge-advocate, U. S. Army, as the military member, and Leslie J. Perry, of Kansas, and Joseph W. Kirkley, of Maryland, as the civilian expert members of said board. The board assumed direction of the publication at the commencement of the fiscal year 1889, its first work beginning with Serial No. 36 of Vol. XXIV.

Each volume includes a copious and accurate index, and for the further convenience of investigators there will be, in addition, a general index to the entire set when complete in a volume by itself.

Nothing is printed in these volumes except duly authenticated contemporaneous records of the war. The scope of the board's work is to decide upon and arrange the matter to be published; to correct and verify the orthography of the papers used, and occasionally to add a foot-note of explanation.

GEO. B. DAVIS, *Major and J. A., U. S. A.*,
LESLIE J. PERRY, *Civilian Expert*,
JOSEPH W. KIRKLEY, *Civilian Expert*,
Board of Publication.

Approved:

REDFIELD PROCTOR,
Secretary of War.

WAR DEPARTMENT,
Washington, D. C., August 1, 1891.

---

covered into the Treasury. If two or more sets of said volumes are ordered to the same address, the Secretary of War shall inform the Senators, Representatives, or Delegates who have designated the same, who thereupon may designate other libraries, organizations, or individuals. The Secretary of War shall report to the first session of the Forty-eighth Congress what volumes of the series heretofore published have not been furnished to such libraries, organizations, and individuals. He shall also inform distributees at whose instance the volumes are sent."

CONTENTS.

CHAPTER LVI.

CONTENTS OF PRECEDING VOLUMES.

VOLUME I.

VOLUME II.

VOLUME III.

VOLUME IV.

VOLUME V.

VOLUME VI.

VOLUME VII.

VOLUME VIII.

VOLUME IX.

VOLUME X—IN TWO PARTS.

VOLUME XI—IN THREE PARTS.

VOLUME XII—IN THREE PARTS.

VOLUME XIII.

VOLUME XIV.

VOLUME XV.

VOLUME XVI—IN TWO PARTS.

CHAPTER XXVIII.

Operations in Kentucky, Middle and East Tennessee, North Alabama, and Southwest Virginia. June 10–October 31, 1862.

VOLUME XVII—IN TWO PARTS.

CHAPTER XXIX.

Operations in West Tennessee and Northern Mississippi. June 10, 1862–January 20, 1863.

VOLUME XVIII.

CHAPTER XXX.

VOLUME XIX—IN TWO PARTS.

CHAPTER XXXI.

Operations in Northern Virginia, West Virginia, Maryland, and Pennsylvania. September 3–November 14, 1862.

VOLUME XX—IN TWO PARTS.

CHAPTER XXXII.

Operations in Kentucky, Middle and East Tennessee, North Alabama, and Southwest Virginia. November 1, 1862–January 20, 1863.

VOLUME XXI.

CHAPTER XXXIII.

VOLUME XXII—IN TWO PARTS.

CHAPTER XXXIV.

Operations in Missouri, Arkansas, Kansas, the Indian Territory, and the Department of the Northwest. November 20, 1862–December 31, 1863.

VOLUME XXIII—IN TWO PARTS.

CHAPTER XXXV.

Operations in Kentucky, Middle and East Tennessee, North Alabama, and Southwest Virginia. January 21–August 10, 1863.

VOLUME XXIV—IN THREE PARTS.

CHAPTER XXXVI.

Operations in Mississippi and West Tennessee, including those in Arkansas and Louisiana connected with the Siege of Vicksburg. January 20–August 10, 1863.

VOLUME XXV—IN TWO PARTS.

CHAPTER XXXVII.

Operations in Northern Virginia, West Virginia, Maryland, and Pennsylvania. January 26–June 3, 1863.

VOLUME XXVI—IN TWO PARTS.

CHAPTER XXXVIII.

Operations in West Florida, Southern Alabama, Southern Mississippi, Louisiana, Texas, and New Mexico. May 14–December 31, 1863.

VOLUME XXVII—IN THREE PARTS.

CHAPTER XXXIX.

Operations in North Carolina, Virginia, West Virginia, Maryland, Pennsylvania, and Department of the East. June 3–August 3, 1863.

VOLUME XXVIII—IN TWO PARTS.

CHAPTER XL.

Operations on the coasts of South Carolina and Georgia, and in Middle and East Florida. June 12–December 31, 1863.

VOLUME XXIX—IN TWO PARTS.

CHAPTER XLI.

Operations in North Carolina, Virginia, West Virginia, Maryland, and Pennsylvania. August 4–December 31, 1863.

VOLUME XXX—IN FOUR PARTS.

CHAPTER XLII.

Operations in Kentucky, Southwest Virginia, Tennessee, Mississippi, North Alabama, and North Georgia. August 11-October 19, 1863.

VOLUME XXXI—IN THREE PARTS.

CHAPTER XLIII.

Operations in Kentucky, Southwest Virginia, Tennessee, Mississippi, North Alabama, and North Georgia. October 20-December 31, 1863.

VOLUME XXXII—IN THREE PARTS.

CHAPTER XLIV.

Operations in Kentucky, Southwest Virginia, Tennessee, Mississippi, Alabama, and North Georgia. January 1-April 30, 1864.

VOLUME XXXIII.

CHAPTER XLV.

VOLUME XXXIV—IN FOUR PARTS.

CHAPTER XLVI.

Operations in Louisiana and the Trans-Mississippi States and Territories. January 1-June 30, 1864.

VOLUME XXXV—IN TWO PARTS.

CHAPTER XLVII.

Operations in South Carolina and Florida, and on the Georgia Coast. January 1-November 13, 1864.

VOLUME XXXVI—IN THREE PARTS.

CHAPTER XLVIII.

Operations in Southeastern Virginia and North Carolina. May 1-June 12, 1864.

VOLUME XXXVII—IN TWO PARTS.

CHAPTER XLIX.

Operations in Northern Virginia, West Virginia, Maryland, and Pennsylvania. May 1-August 3, 1864.

VOLUME XXXVIII—IN FIVE PARTS.

CHAPTER L.

The Atlanta, Ga., Campaign. May 1-September 8, 1864.

VOLUME XXXIX—IN THREE PARTS.

CHAPTER LI.

Operations in Kentucky, Southwest Virginia, Tennessee, Mississippi, Alabama, and North Georgia (the Atlanta Campaign excepted). May 1-November 13, 1864.

VOLUME XL—IN THREE PARTS.

CHAPTER LII.

Operations in Southeastern Virginia and North Carolina. June 13-July 31, 1864.

VOLUME XLI—IN FOUR PARTS.

CHAPTER LIII.

Operations in Louisiana and the Trans-Mississippi States and Territories. July 1-December 31, 1864.

VOLUME XLII—IN THREE PARTS.

CHAPTER LIV.

Operations in Southeastern Virginia and North Carolina. August 1–December 31, 1864.

VOLUME XLIII—IN TWO PARTS.

CHAPTER LV.

Operations in Northern Virginia, West Virginia, Maryland, and Pennsylvania. August 4–December 31, 1864.

1864.

	Sunday.	Monday.	Tuesday.	Wednesday.	Thursday.	Friday.	Saturday.
Jan	....	....	....	....	....	1	2
	3	4	5	6	7	8	9
	10	11	12	13	14	15	16
	17	18	19	20	21	22	23
	24	25	26	27	28	29	30
	31	....	....	....	....	....	....
Feb	....	1	2	3	4	5	6
	7	8	9	10	11	12	13
	14	15	16	17	18	19	20
	21	22	23	24	25	26	27
	28	29	....	....	....	....	....
Mar. ...	....	....	1	2	3	4	5
	6	7	8	9	10	11	12
	13	14	15	16	17	18	19
	20	21	22	23	24	25	26
	27	28	29	30	31	....	....
Apr	....	....	....	....	....	1	2
	3	4	5	6	7	8	9
	10	11	12	13	14	15	16
	17	18	19	20	21	22	23
	24	25	26	27	28	29	30
	....	....	....	....	....	....	....
May ...	1	2	3	4	5	6	7
	8	9	10	11	12	13	14
	15	16	17	18	19	20	21
	22	23	24	25	26	27	28
	29	30	31	....	....	....	....
June ...	....	....	....	1	2	3	4
	5	6	7	8	9	10	11
	12	13	14	15	16	17	18
	19	20	21	22	23	24	25
	26	27	28	29	30	....	....

	Sunday.	Monday.	Tuesday.	Wednesday.	Thursday.	Friday.	Saturday.
July ...	....	....	....	....	....	1	2
	3	4	5	6	7	8	9
	10	11	12	13	14	15	16
	17	18	19	20	21	22	23
	24	25	26	27	28	29	30
	31	....	....	....	....	....	....
Aug....	....	1	2	3	4	5	6
	7	8	9	10	11	12	13
	14	15	16	17	18	19	20
	21	22	23	24	25	26	27
	28	29	30	31	....	....	....
Sept ...	....	....	....	....	1	2	3
	4	5	6	7	8	9	10
	11	12	13	14	15	16	17
	18	19	20	21	22	23	24
	25	26	27	28	29	30	....
Oct	....	....	....	....	....	....	1
	2	3	4	5	6	7	8
	9	10	11	12	13	14	15
	16	17	18	19	20	21	22
	23	24	25	26	27	28	29
	30	31	....	....	....	....	....
Nov....	....	....	1	2	3	4	5
	6	7	8	9	10	11	12
	13	14	15	16	17	18	19
	20	21	22	23	24	25	26
	27	28	29	30	....	....	....
Dec	....	....	....	....	1	2	3
	4	5	6	7	8	9	10
	11	12	13	14	15	16	17
	18	19	20	21	22	23	24
	25	26	27	28	29	30	31

CHAPTER LVI.

OPERATIONS IN SOUTH CAROLINA, GEORGIA, AND FLORIDA.

November 14–December 31, 1864.

SUMMARY OF THE PRINCIPAL EVENTS.

Nov. 15–Dec. 21, 1864.—The Savannah (Georgia) Campaign.
16–17, 1864.—Expedition from Barrancas to Pine Barren Bridge, Fla.
29, 1864.—Skirmish near Boyd's Landing, S. C. *
30, 1864.—Engagement at Honey Hill, near Grahamville, S. C.
Dec. 6– 9, 1864.—Demonstrations against the Charleston and Savannah Railroad, S. C.
13–19, 1864.—Expedition from Barrancas, Fla., to Pollard, Ala., and skirmishes.
20, 1864.—Skirmish near the Pocotaligo Road, S. C.

NOVEMBER 15–DECEMBER 21, 1864.—The Savannah (Georgia) Campaign.

SUMMARY OF THE PRINCIPAL EVENTS.

Nov. 15, 1864.—Sherman's army starts from Atlanta.
Skirmish at Jonesborough.
Skirmish near East Point.
Skirmishes near Rough and Ready and Stockbridge.
16, 1864.—Action at Lovejoy's Station.
Skirmish at Bear Creek Station.
Skirmish at Cotton River Bridge.
17, 1864.—Affair at Towaliga Bridge.
19, 1864.—Skirmish at Buck Head Station.
20, 1864.—Skirmish near Clinton.
Skirmish at Walnut Creek.
Skirmish at East Macon.
Skirmish at Griswoldville.
21, 1864.—Skirmish at Griswoldville.
Skirmish near Macon.
Skirmish at Gordon.
Skirmish near Eatonton.
21–23, 1864.—Skirmishes at Clinton.
22, 1864.—Engagement at Griswoldville.
23, 1864.—Skirmish near Milledgeville.
23–25, 1864.—Skirmishes at Ball's Ferry and the Georgia Central Railroad Bridge, Oconee River.
25, 1864.—Skirmish near Sandersville.
26, 1864.—Skirmish at Sandersville.
27, 1864.—Skirmish at Sylvan Grove.
27–28, 1864.—Action at Waynesborough.
28, 1864.—Skirmish near Davisborough.
Skirmish near Waynesborough.

*For mention of this skirmish, see reports of engagement at Honey Hill, pp. 422, 436.

Nov. 28, 1864.—Skirmish at Buck Head Church.
Engagement at Buck Head Creek, or Reynolds' Plantation.
29, 1864.—Skirmish near Louisville.
30, 1864.—Skirmish at Louisville.
Dec. 1, 1864.—Skirmish at Millen's (or Shady) Grove.
2, 1864.—Skirmish at Rocky Creek Church.
Skirmish at Buck Head Creek.
3, 1864.—Skirmish at Thomas' Station.
4, 1864.—Engagement at Waynesborough.
Skirmish near Statesborough.
Skirmish at Station No. 5, Georgia Central Railroad.
Skirmish at the Little Ogeechee River.
Skirmish near Lumpkin's Station.
5, 1864.—Skirmish at the Little Ogeechee River.
7, 1864.—Skirmish at Jenks' Bridge, Ogeechee River.
Skirmish at Buck Creek.
Skirmish at Cypress Swamp, near Sister's Ferry.
8, 1864.—Skirmish at Ebenezer Creek.
Skirmish near Bryan Court-House.
9, 1864.—Skirmish at Ogeechee Canal.
Skirmish between Eden and Pooler Stations.
Skirmish at Cuyler's Plantation.
Skirmish at Monteith Swamp.
10, 1864.—Skirmish near Springfield.
Skirmish near Savannah.
Capture of the C. S. Steamer Ida.
11–21, 1864.—Investment of Savannah.
12, 1864.—Communication established between General Sherman's army and the South Atlantic Blockading Squadron, under Rear-Admiral Dahlgren.
Capture of the C. S. Steamer Resolute.
13, 1864.—Engagement at Fort McAllister.
14–21, 1864.—Naval attack on Forts Rosedew and Beaulieu, Vernon River
16, 1864.—Skirmish at Hinesville.

REPORTS, ETC.*

No. 1.—Maj. Gen. William T. Sherman, U. S. Army, commanding Military Division of the Mississippi.
No. 2.—Organization of the Union Forces.
No. 3.—Itinerary of the Union Forces, November 1–December 31.
No. 4.—Capt. Orlando M. Poe, Corps of Engineers, U. S. Army, Chief Engineer.
No. 5.—Capt. Thomas G. Baylor, U. S. Army, Chief Ordnance Officer.
No. 6.—Col. Amos Beckwith, U. S. Army, Chief Commissary of Subsistence.
No. 7.—Maj. Gen. Oliver O. Howard, U. S. Army, commanding Army of the Tennessee.
No. 8.—Capt. James M. McClintock, U. S. Army, Acting Chief Signal Officer.
No. 9.—Lieut. Col. David Remick, Chief Commissary of Subsistence.
No. 10.—Asst. Surg. David L. Huntington, U. S. Army, Acting Medical Director.
No. 11.—Maj. Gen. Peter J. Osterhaus, U. S. Army, commanding Fifteenth Army Corps.
No. 12.—Lieut. William H. Sherfy, U. S. Army, Signal Officer.
No. 13.—Brig. Gen. Charles R. Woods, U. S. Army, commanding First Division.
No. 14.—Col. Milo Smith, Twenty-sixth Iowa Infantry, commanding First Brigade.

*For Grant's reference to these operations, see Vol. XXXVIII, Part I, p. 29. For reports of naval co-operating forces, see Annual Report of the Secretary of the Navy, December 4, 1865.

No. 15.—Col. Thomas Curly, Twenty-seventh Missouri Infantry, of operations May 1-December 21.
No. 16.—Lieut. Col. Dennis T. Kirby, Twenty-seventh Missouri Infantry, of operations December 4.
No. 17.—Col. Robert F. Catterson, Ninety-seventh Indiana Infantry, commanding Second Brigade, of operations November 22.
No. 18.—Maj. Asias Willison, One hundred and third Illinois Infantry.
No. 19.—Lieut. Col. Isaac N. Alexander, Forty-sixth Ohio Infantry, of operations November 22.
No. 20.—Maj. Edward N. Upton, Forty-sixth Ohio Infantry.
No. 21.—Brig. Gen. William B. Hazen, U. S. Army, commanding Second Division.
No. 22.—Col. Theodore Jones, Thirtieth Ohio Infantry, commanding First Brigade.
No. 23.—Col. James S. Martin, One hundred and eleventh Illinois Infantry, commanding Second Brigade.
No. 24.—Maj. William M. Mabry, One hundred and eleventh Illinois Infantry, of operations October 4, 1864-January 4, 1865.
No. 25.—Lieut. Col. George H. Scott, Eighty-third Indiana Infantry, of operations September 5, 1864-January 2, 1865.
No. 26.—Lieut. Col. Louis von Blessingh, Thirty-seventh Ohio Infantry, of operations November 13, 1864-January 2, 1865.
No. 27.—Col. Augustus C. Parry, Forty-seventh Ohio Infantry, of operations November 15, 1864-January 2, 1865.
No. 28.—Maj. George F. Kili, Fifty-fourth Ohio Infantry.
No. 29.—Col. John M. Oliver, Fifteenth Michigan Infantry, commanding Third Brigade.
No. 30.—Brig. Gen. John E. Smith, U. S. Army, commanding Third Division.
No. 31.—Brig. Gen. John M. Corse, U. S. Army, commanding Fourth Division.
No. 32.—Brig. Gen. Elliott W. Rice, U. S. Army, commanding First Brigade.
No. 33.—Lieut. Col. Jerome D. Davis, Fifty-second Illinois Infantry.
No. 34.—Lieut. Col. Roger Martin, Sixty-sixth Indiana Infantry.
No. 35.—Col. Noel B. Howard, Second Iowa Infantry.
No. 36.—Lieut. Col. James C. Parrott, Seventh Iowa Infantry.
No. 37.—Col. Robert N. Adams, Eighty-first Ohio Infantry, commanding Second Brigade, of operations October 5-December 21.
No. 38.—Maj. Wheelock S. Merriman, Twelfth Illinois Infantry.
No. 39.—Capt. William S. Boyd, Sixty-sixth Illinois Infantry.
No. 40.—Maj. William C. Henry, Eighty-first Ohio Infantry, of operations October 5-December 21.
No. 41.—Lieut. Col. Frederick J. Hurlbut, Fifty-seventh Illinois Infantry, commanding Third Brigade.
No. 42.—Lieut. Col. Hector Perrin, Seventh Illinois Infantry.
No. 43.—Maj. Gen. Frank P. Blair, jr., U. S. Army, commanding Seventeenth Army Corps.
No. 44.—Maj. Gen. Joseph A. Mower, U. S. Army, commanding First Division.
No. 45.—Brig. Gen. Mortimer D. Leggett, U. S. Army, commanding Third Division.
No. 46.—Brig. Gen. Manning F. Force, U. S. Army, commanding First Brigade, of operations December 2.
No. 47.—Brig. Gen. Giles A. Smith, U. S. Army, commanding Fourth Division.
No. 48.—Capt. Henry Duncan, Fifty-third Indiana Infantry, First Brigade.
No. 49.—Maj. Gen. Henry W. Slocum, U. S. Army, commanding Left Wing, of operations September 29-December 21.
No. 50.—Col. George P. Buell, Fifty-eighth Indiana Infantry, commanding Pontoniers.
No. 51.—Lieut. Col. Joseph Moore, Fifty-eighth Indiana Infantry, commanding section of Pontoon Train.
No. 52.—Bvt. Maj. Gen. Jefferson C. Davis, U. S. Army, commanding Fourteenth Army Corps.

No. 53.—Brig. Gen. William P. Carlin, U. S. Army, commanding First Division.
No. 54.—Col. Harrison C. Hobart, Twenty-first Wisconsin Infantry, commanding First Brigade.
No. 55.—Maj. John H. Widmer, One hundred and fourth Illinois Infantry, of operations September 7–December 21.
No. 56.—Lieut. Col. Cyrus E. Briant, Eighty-eighth Indiana Infantry.
No. 57.—Lieut. Col. Joseph H. Brigham, Sixty-ninth Ohio Infantry, commanding Second Brigade.
No. 58.—Lieut. Col. David Miles, Seventy-ninth Pennsylvania Infantry, commanding Third Brigade.
No. 59.—Capt. James H. Low, Thirty-eighth Indiana Infantry.
No. 60.—Lieut. Col. Arnold McMahan, Twenty-first Ohio Infantry, of operations September 3–December 21.
No. 61.—Maj. Robert P. Findley, Seventy-fourth Ohio Infantry.
No. 62.—Maj. Michael H. Locher, Seventy-ninth Pennsylvania Infantry, of operations October 3–December 21.
No. 63.—Brig. Gen. James D. Morgan, U. S. Army, commanding Second Division.
No. 64.—Journal of Second Division.
No. 65.—Col. Robert F. Smith, Sixteenth Illinois Infantry, commanding First Brigade.
No. 66.—Capt. Eben White, Sixteenth Illinois Infantry.
No. 67.—Maj. James H. McDonald, Sixtieth Illinois Infantry.
No. 68.—Capt. Charles H. Richman, Tenth Michigan Infantry.
No. 69.—Lieut. Col. Joel O. Martin, Seventeenth New York Infantry.
No. 70.—Lieut. Col. John S. Pearce, Ninety-eighth Ohio Infantry, commanding Second Brigade.
No. 71.—Lieut. Col. Maris R. Vernon, Seventy-eighth Illinois Infantry.
No. 72.—Capt. James R. McLaughlin, Ninety-eighth Ohio Infantry.
No. 73.—Lieut. Col. James W. Langley, One hundred and twenty-fifth Illinois Infantry, commanding Third Brigade.
No. 74.—Lieut. Col. Charles W. Clancy, Fifty-second Ohio Infantry.
No. 75.—Brig. Gen. Absalom Baird, U. S. Army, commanding Third Division.
No. 76.—Lieut. Joseph R. Channel, Battery C, First Illinois Light Artillery.
No. 77.—Brig. Gen. Alpheus S. Williams, U. S. Army, commanding Twentieth Army Corps.
No. 78.—Brig. Gen. Nathaniel J. Jackson, U. S. Army, commanding First Division.
No. 79.—Surg. Henry Z. Gill, U. S. Army, Surgeon-in-Chief.
No. 80.—Col. James L. Selfridge, Forty-sixth Pennsylvania Infantry, commanding First Brigade.
No. 81.—Lieut. Col. Henry W. Daboll, Fifth Connecticut Infantry, of operations October 21–December 23.
No. 82.—Lieut. Col. James C. Rogers, One hundred and twenty-third New York Infantry, of operations October 21–December 24.
No. 83.—Capt. William Merrell, One hundred and forty-first New York Infantry.
No. 84.—Maj. Patrick Griffith, Forty-sixth Pennsylvania Infantry.
No. 85.—Col. Ezra A. Carman, Thirteenth New Jersey Infantry, commanding Second Brigade.
No. 86.—Col. William Cogswell, Second Massachusetts Infantry.
No. 87.—Maj. Frederick H. Harris, Thirteenth New Jersey Infantry.
No. 88.—Lieut. Col. Allen N. Sill, One hundred and seventh New York Infantry, of operations September 2–December 23.
No. 89.—Maj. Alfred B. Smith, One hundred and fiftieth New York Infantry.
No. 90.—Col. William Hawley, Third Wisconsin Infantry.
No. 91.—Col. James S. Robinson, Eighty-second Ohio Infantry, commanding Third Brigade.
No. 92.—Maj. Ferdinand H. Rolshausen, Eighty-second Illinois Infantry, of operations September 4–December 23.

No. 93.—Lieut. Col. John B. Le Sage, One hundred and first Illinois Infantry, of operations September 2–December 23.
No. 94.—Lieut. Col. Hezekiah Watkins, One hundred and forty-third New York Infantry.
No. 95.—Capt. John Garrett, Sixty-first Ohio Infantry, of operations September 4–December 22.
No. 96.—Lieut. Col. David Thomson, Eighty-second Ohio Infantry.
No. 97.—Col. Francis H. West, Thirty-first Wisconsin Infantry.
No. 98.—Brig. Gen. John W. Geary, U. S. Army, commanding Second Division.
No. 99.—Col. Ario Pardee, jr., One hundred and forty-seventh Pennsylvania Infantry, commanding First Brigade.
No. 100.—Lieut. Col. Robert Kirkup, Fifth Ohio Infantry.
No. 101.—Maj. Myron T. Wright, Twenty-ninth Ohio Infantry, of operations November 15–December 19.
No. 102.—Capt. Jonas Schoonover, Twenty-ninth Ohio Infantry, of operations December 20–24.
No. 103.—Lieut. Col. Eugene Powell, Sixty-sixth Ohio Infantry, of operations September 4–December 21.
No. 104.—Col. John Flynn, Twenty-eighth Pennsylvania Infantry, of operations September 2–December 21.
No. 105.—Lieut. Col. John Craig, One hundred and forty-seventh Pennsylvania Infantry, of operations September 2–December 21.
No. 106.—Col. Patrick H. Jones, One hundred and fifty-fourth New York Infantry, commanding Second Brigade, of operations September 18–December 21.
No. 107.—Col. George W. Mindil, Thirty-third New Jersey Infantry, of operations September 2–December 21.
No. 108.—Col. John T. Lockman, One hundred and nineteenth New York Infantry, of operations September 1–December 21.
No. 109.—Maj. William H. Hoyt, One hundred and thirty-fourth New York Infantry, of operations September 2–December 21.
No. 110.—Maj. Lewis D. Warner, One hundred and fifty-fourth New York Infantry.
No. 111.—Lieut. Col. Charles C. Cresson, Seventy-third Pennsylvania Infantry.
No. 112.—Capt. Walter G. Dunn, One hundred and ninth Pennsylvania Infantry.
No. 113.—Col. Henry A. Barnum, One hundred and forty-ninth New York Infantry, commanding Third Brigade.
No. 114.—Maj. Thomas Elliott, Sixtieth New York Infantry.
No. 115.—Lieut. Col. Harvey S. Chatfield, One hundred and second New York Infantry.
No. 116.—Lieut. Col. Koert S. Van Voorhis, One hundred and thirty-seventh New York Infantry.
No. 117.—Maj. Nicholas Grumbach, One hundred and forty-ninth New York Infantry.
No. 118.—Lieut. Col. Samuel M. Zulich, Twenty-ninth Pennsylvania Infantry.
No. 119.—Lieut. Col. Thomas M. Walker, One hundred and eleventh Pennsylvania Infantry, of operations September 3–December 21.
No. 120.—Brig. Gen. William T. Ward, U. S. Army, commanding Third Division.
No. 121.—Col. Franklin C. Smith, One hundred and second Illinois Infantry, commanding First Brigade, of operations September 23–December 21.
No. 122.—Maj. Hiland H. Clay, One hundred and second Illinois Infantry.
No. 123.—Maj. Henry D. Brown, One hundred and fifth Illinois Infantry.
No. 124.—Col. Henry Case, One hundred and twenty-ninth Illinois Infantry.
No. 125.—Lieut. Col. Samuel Merrill, Seventieth Indiana Infantry.
No. 126.—Col. Daniel Dustin, One hundred and fifth Illinois Infantry, commanding Second Brigade.
No. 127.—Lieut. Col. James E. Burton, Thirty-third Indiana Infantry.
No. 128.—Lieut. Col. Alexander B. Crane, Eighty-fifth Indiana Infantry.

No. 1.

Reports of Maj. Gen. William T. Sherman, U. S. Army, commanding Military Division of the Mississippi.

HDQRS. MILITARY DIVISION OF THE MISSISSIPPI,
In the Field, Savannah, Ga., December 22, 1864.

DEAR GENERAL: I take great satisfaction in reporting that we are in possession of Savannah and all its forts. At first I proposed to extend across the river above the city from Slocum's left, but the enemy had a gun-boat and ram heavily armed that would have made the step extra hazardous; also the submerged rice fields on the northeast bank were impracticable. I then went to Hilton Head to arrange with General Foster to re-enforce his movement from Broad River, but before I had completed the move Hardee got his garrison across and off on the Union plank road. Our troops entered at daylight yesterday, took about 800 prisoners, over 100 guns (some of the heaviest caliber), and a perfect string of forts from Savannah around to McAllister, also 12,000 bales of cotton, 190 cars, 13 locomotives, 3 steam-boats, and an immense supply of shells, shot, and all kinds of ammunition. There is a complete arsenal here, and much valuable machinery. The citizens mostly remain, and the city is very quiet. The river below is much obstructed, but I parted with Admiral Dahlgren yesterday at 4 p. m., and he will at once get about removing them and opening a way. The enemy blew up an iron-clad (Savannah), a good ram, and three tenders, small steamers. As yet we have made but a partial inventory, but the above falls far short of our conquests. I have not a particle of doubt but that we have secured 150 fine guns, with plenty of ammunition. I have now completed my first step, and should like to go on to you, via Columbia and Raleigh, but will prepare to embark as soon as vessels come. Colonel Babcock will have told you all, and you know better than anybody else how much better troops arrive by a land march than when carried by transports. I will turn over to Foster Savannah and all its outposts, with, say, one division of infantry, Kilpatrick's cavalry, and plenty of artillery. Hardee has, of course, moved into South Carolina, but I do not believe his Georgia troops, militia and fancy companies, will work in South Carolina. His force is reported by citizens at from 15,000 to 20,000. The capture of Savannah, with the incidental use of the river, gives us a magnificent position in this quarter; and if you can hold Lee, and if Thomas can continue as he did on the 18th, I could go on and smash South Carolina all to pieces, and also break up roads as far as the Roanoke. But, as I before remarked, I will now look to coming to you as soon as transportation comes. We are all well and confident as ever.

Yours, truly,

W. T. SHERMAN,
Major-General, U. S. Army.

Lieut. Gen. U. S. GRANT,
Commanding Armies of the United States, City Point, Va.

—

HDQRS. MILITARY DIVISION OF THE MISSISSIPPI,
In the Field, Savannah, Ga., January 1, 1865.

GENERAL:*

On the 12th of November my army stood detached and cut off from all communication with the rear. It was composed of four corps—the Fifteenth and Seventeenth, constituting the Right Wing, under Maj. Gen. O. O. Howard; the Fourteenth and Twentieth Corps, constituting the Left Wing, under Maj. Gen. H. W. Slocum—of an aggregate strength of 60,000 infantry; one cavalry division, in aggregate strength 5,500, under Brig. Gen. Judson Kilpatrick, and the artillery, reduced to the minimum, one gun per 1,000 men.

---

*For portion of report (here omitted) relating to operations in North Georgia and North Alabama, see Vol. XXXIX, Part I, p. 580.

The whole force was moved rapidly and grouped about Atlanta on the 14th of November. In the meantime Capt. O. M. Poe had thoroughly destroyed Atlanta, save its mere dwelling-houses and churches, and the Right Wing, with General Kilpatrick's cavalry, was put in motion in the direction of Jonesborough and McDonough, with orders to make a strong feint on Macon, to cross the Ocmulgee about Planters' Mills, and rendezvous in the neighborhood of Gordon in seven days, exclusive of the day of march. On the same day General Slocum moved with the Twentieth Corps by Decatur and Stone Mountain, with orders to tear up the railroad from Social Circle to Madison, to burn the large and important railroad bridge across the Oconee, east of Madison, and turn south and reach Milledgeville on the seventh day, exclusive of the day of march. In person I left Atlanta on the 16th, in company with the Fourteenth Corps (Bvt. Maj. Gen. Jeff. C. Davis), by Lithonia, Covington, and Shady Dale, directly on Milledgeville. All the troops were provided with good wagon trains, loaded with ammunition and supplies, approximating twenty days' bread, forty days' sugar and coffee, a double allowance of salt for forty days, and beef-cattle equal to forty days' supplies. The wagons were also supplied with about three days' forage, in grain. All were instructed, by a judicious system of foraging, to maintain this order of things as long as possible, living chiefly, if not solely, upon the country, which I knew to abound in corn, sweet potatoes, and meats.

My first object was, of course, to place my army in the very heart of Georgia, interposing between Macon and Augusta, and obliging the enemy to divide his forces to defend not only those points, but Millen, Savannah, and Charleston. All my calculations were fully realized. During the 22d [20th] General Kilpatrick made a good feint on Macon, driving the enemy within his intrenchments, and then drew back to Griswoldville, where Walcutt's brigade of infantry joined him to cover that flank, whilst Howard's trains were closing up, and his men scattered, breaking up railroads. The enemy came out of Macon [22d] and attacked Walcutt in position, but was so roughly handled that he never repeated the experiment. On the eighth day after leaving Atlanta (namely, on the 23d [22d]) General Slocum occupied Milledgeville and the important bridge across the Oconee there, and Generals Howard and Kilpatrick were in and about Gordon.

General Howard was then ordered to move eastward, destroying the railroad thoroughly in his progress as far as Tennille Station, opposite Sandersville, and General Slocum to move to Sandersville by two roads. General Kilpatrick was ordered to Milledgeville, and thence move rapidly eastward, to break the railroad which leads from Millen to Augusta, then to turn upon Millen and rescue our prisoners of war supposed to be confined at that place. I accompanied the Twentieth Corps from Milledgeville to Sandersville, approaching which place, on the 25th, we found the bridges across Buffalo Creek burned, which delayed us three hours. The next day we entered Sandersville, skirmishing with Wheeler's cavalry, which offered little opposition to the advance of the Twentieth and Fourteenth Corps, entering the place almost at the same moment.

General Slocum was then ordered to tear up and destroy the Georgia Central Railroad, from Station 13 (Tennille) to Station 10, near the crossing of Ogeechee—one of his corps substantially following the railroad, the other by way of Louisville, in support of Kilpatrick's cavalry. In person I shifted to the Right Wing, and accompanied the Seventeenth Corps (General Blair) on the south of the railroad, till abreast of

Station 9½ (Barton), General Howard, in person, with the Fifteenth Corps, keeping farther to the right, and about one day's march ahead, ready to turn against the flank of any enemy who should oppose our progress. At Barton I learned that Kilpatrick's cavalry had reached the Augusta railroad about Waynesborough, where he ascertained that our prisoners had been removed from Millen, and therefore the purpose of rescuing them, upon which we had set our hearts, was an impossibility. But as Wheeler's cavalry had hung around him, and as he had retired to Louisville to meet our infantry, in pursuance of my instructions not to risk battle unless at great advantage, I ordered him to leave his wagons and all incumbrances with the Left Wing, and moving in the direction of Augusta, if Wheeler gave him the opportunity, to indulge him with all the fighting he wanted. General Kilpatrick, supported by Baird's division of infantry of the Fourteenth Corps, again moved in the direction of Waynesborough, and encountering Wheeler in the neighborhood of Thomas' Station, attacked him in position, driving him from three successive lines of barricades handsomely through Waynesborough and across Brier Creek, the bridges over which he burned; and then, with Baird's division, rejoined the Left Wing, which in the meantime had been marching by easy stages of ten miles a day in the direction of Lumpkin's Station and Jacksonborough. The Seventeenth Corps took up the destruction of the railroad at the Ogeechee, near Station 10, and continued it to Millen, the enemy offering little or no opposition, although preparations had seemingly been made at Millen.

On the 3d of December the Seventeenth Corps, which I accompanied, was at Millen; the Fifteenth Corps (General Howard) was south of the Ogeechee, opposite Station 7 (Scarborough); the Twentieth Corps (General Slocum) on the Augusta railroad, about four miles north of Millen, near Buck Head Church, and the Fourteenth Corps (General Jeff. C. Davis) in the neighborhood of Lumpkin's Station, on the Augusta railroad. All were ordered to march in the direction of Savannah—the Fifteenth Corps to continue south of the Ogeechee, the Seventeenth to destroy the railroad as far as Ogeechee Church—and four days were allowed to reach the line from Ogeechee Church to the neighborhood of Halley's Ferry, on the Savannah River. All the columns reached their destinations on time, and continued to march on their several roads—General Davis following the Savannah River road; General Slocum the middle road, by way of Springfield; General Blair the railroad, and General Howard still south and west of the Ogeechee, with orders to cross to the east bank opposite Eden Station, or Station No. 2.

As we approached Savannah the country became more marshy and difficult, and more obstructions were met in the way of felled trees, where the roads crossed the creek, swamps, or narrow causeways; but our pioneer companies were well organized, and removed these obstructions in an incredibly short time. No opposition from the enemy worth speaking of was encountered until the heads of columns were within fifteen miles of Savannah, where all the roads leading to the city were obstructed more or less by felled timber, with earth-works and artillery. But these were easily turned and the enemy driven away, so that by the 10th of December the enemy was driven within his lines at Savannah. These followed substantially a swampy creek which empties into the Savannah River about three miles above the city, across to the head of a corresponding stream which empties into the Little Ogeechee. These streams were singularly favorable to the enemy as a cover, being very marshy, and bordered by rice fields, which were flooded either by the tide water or by inland ponds, the gates to which were controlled and covered by his heavy artillery. The only approaches to the city were by five narrow causeways—namely, the two railroads, and the Augusta, the Louisville, and the Ogeechee dirt roads—all of which were commanded by heavy ordnance, too strong for us to fight with our light field-guns. To assault an enemy of unknown strength at such a disadvantage appeared to me unwise, especially as I had so successfully brought my army, almost unscathed, so great a distance, and could surely attain the same result by the operation of time. I therefore instructed my army commanders to closely invest the city from the north and west, and to reconnoiter well the ground in their fronts, respectively, whilst I gave my personal attention to opening communications with our fleet, which I knew was waiting for us in Tybee, Wassaw, and Ossabaw Sounds.

In approaching Savannah General Slocum struck the Charleston railroad near the bridge, and occupied the river-bank as his left flank, where he had captured two of the enemy's river boats, and had prevented two others (gun-boats) from coming down the river to communicate with the city; while General Howard, by his right flank, had broken the Gulf railroad at Fleming's and Way's Stations, and occupied the railroad itself down to the Little Ogeechee, near Station 1; so that no supplies could reach Savannah by any of its accustomed channels. We, on the contrary, possessed large herds of cattle, which we had brought along or gathered in the country, and our wagons still contained a reasonable amount of breadstuffs and other necessaries, and the fine rice crops of the Savannah and Ogeechee Rivers furnished to our men and animals a large amount of rice and rice straw. We also held the country to the south and west of the Ogeechee as foraging ground. Still, communication with the fleet was of vital importance; and I directed General Kilpatrick to cross the Ogeechee by a pontoon bridge, to reconnoiter Fort McAllister, and to proceed to Saint Catherine's Sound, in the direction of Sunbery or Kilkenny Bluff, and open communication with the fleet. General Howard had previously, by my direction, sent one of his best scouts down the Ogeechee in a canoe for a like purpose. But more than this was necessary. We wanted the vessels and their contents; and the Ogeechee River, a navigable stream, close to the rear of our camps, was the proper avenue of supply.

The enemy had burned the road bridge across the Ogeechee, just below the mouth of the Cannouchee, known as King's Bridge. This was reconstructed in an incredibly short time, in the most substantial manner, by the Fifty-eighth Indiana (Colonel Buell), under the direction of Captain Reese, of the Engineer Corps, and on the morning of the 13th of December the Second Division of the Fifteenth Corps, under command of Brigadier-General Hazen, crossed the bridge to the west bank of the Ogeechee and marched down with orders to carry by assault Fort McAllister, a strong inclosed redoubt, manned by two companies of artillery and three of infantry, in all about 200 men, and mounting twenty-three guns in barbette and one mortar. General Hazen reached the vicinity of Fort McAllister about 1 p. m., deployed his division about the place, with both flanks resting upon the river, posted his skirmishers judiciously behind the trunks of trees, whose branches had been used for abatis, and about 5 p. m. assaulted the place with nine regiments at three points, all of them successfully. I witnessed the assault from a rice mill on the opposite bank of the river, and can bear testimony to the handsome manner in which it was accomplished.

Up to this time we had not communicated with our fleet. From the signal station at the rice mill our officers had looked for two days over the rice fields and salt marsh in the direction of Ossabaw Sound, but could see nothing of it. But while watching the preparations for the assault on Fort McAllister we discovered in the distance what seemed to be the smoke-stack of a steamer, which became more and more distinct, until about the very moment of the assault she was plainly visible below the fort, and our signal was answered. As soon as I saw our colors fairly planted upon the walls of McAllister, in company with General Howard I went in a small boat down to the fort and met General Hazen, who had not yet communicated with the gun-boat below, as it was shut out to him by a point of timber. Determined to communicate that night, I got another small boat and a crew and pulled down the river till I found the tug Dandelion, Captain Williamson, U. S. Navy, who informed me that Captain Duncan, who had been sent by General Howard, had succeeded in reaching Admiral Dahlgren and General Foster, and that he was expecting them hourly in Ossabaw Sound. After making communications to those officers, and a short communication to the War Department, I returned to Fort McAllister that night, and before daylight was overtaken by Major Strong, of General Foster's staff, advising me that General Foster had arrived in the Ogeechee, near Fort McAllister, and was very anxious to meet me on board his boat. I accordingly returned with him, and met General Foster on board the steamer Nemaha; and after consultation determined to proceed with him down the sound in hopes to meet Admiral Dahlgren. But we did not meet him until we reached Wassaw Sound, about noon. I there went on board the admiral's flag-ship, the Harvest Moon, after having arranged with General Foster to send us from Hilton Head some siege ordnance and some boats suitable for navigating the Ogeechee River. Admiral Dahlgren very kindly furnished me with all the data concerning his fleet and the numerous forts that guarded the inland channels between the sea and Savannah. I explained to him how completely Savannah was invested at all points, save only the plank road on the South Carolina shore, known as the Union Causeway, which I thought I could reach from my left flank across the Savannah River. I explained to him that if he would simply engage the attention of the forts along Wilmington Channel, at Beaulieu and Rosedew, I thought I could carry the defenses of Savannah by assault as soon as the heavy ordnance arrived from Hilton Head. On the 15th the admiral carried me back to Fort McAllister, whence I returned to our lines in the rear of Savannah.

Having received and carefully considered all the reports of division commanders, I determined to assault the lines of the enemy as soon as my heavy ordnance came from Port Royal, first making a formal demand for surrender. On the 17th, a number of 30-pounder Parrott guns having reached King's Bridge, I proceeded in person to the headquarters of Major-General Slocum, on the Augusta road, and dispatched thence into Savannah, by flag of truce, a formal demand for the surrender of the place; and on the following day received an answer from General Hardee refusing to surrender.

In the meantime further reconnaissances from our left flank had demonstrated that it was impracticable or unwise to push any considerable force across the Savannah River, for the enemy held the river opposite the city with iron-clad gun-boats, and could destroy any pontoons laid down by us between Hutchinson's Island and the South Carolina shore, which would isolate any force sent over from that flank.

I therefore ordered General Slocum to get into position the siege guns, and make all the preparations necessary to assault, and to report to me the earliest moment when he could be ready, whilst I should proceed rapidly round by the right, and make arrangements to occupy the Union Causeway from the direction of Port Royal. General Foster had already established a division of troops on the peninsula or neck between the Coosawhatchie and Tullifinny Rivers, at the head of Broad River, from which position he could reach the railroad with his artillery. I went to Port Royal in person, and made arrangements to re-enforce that command by one or more divisions, under a proper officer, to assault and carry the railroad, and thence turn toward Savannah until it occupied the causeway in question. I went on board the admiral's flag-ship, the Harvest Moon, which put to sea the night of the 20th. But the wind was high, and increased during the night, so that the pilot judged Ossabaw Bar impassable, and ran into Tybee, whence we proceeded through the inland channels into Wassaw Sound, and thence through Romney Marsh. But the ebb tide caught the Harvest Moon and she was unable to make the passage. Admiral Dahlgren took me in his barge, and pulling in the direction of Vernon River we met the army tug Red Legs, bearing a message from my adjutant, Captain Dayton, of that morning, the 21st, to the effect that our troops were in possession of the enemy's lines, and were advancing without opposition into Savannah, the enemy having evacuated the place during the previous night.

Admiral Dahlgren proceeded up the Vernon River in his barge, while I transferred to the tug, in which I proceeded to Fort McAllister, and thence to the rice mill, and on the morning of the 22d rode into the city of Savannah, already occupied by our troops.

I was very much disappointed that Hardee had escaped with his garrison, and had to content myself with the material fruits of victory without the cost of life which would have attended a general assault. The substantial results will be more clearly set forth in the tabular statements of heavy ordnance and other public property acquired. And it will suffice here to state that the important city of Savannah, with its valuable harbor and river, was the chief object of the campaign. With it we acquire all the forts and heavy ordnance in its vicinity, with large stores of ammunition, shot and shells, cotton, rice, and other valuable products of the country. We also gain locomotives and cars, which, though of little use to us in the present condition of the railroads, are a serious loss to the enemy; as well as four steam-boats gained, and the loss to the enemy of the iron-clad Savannah, one ram, and three transports, blown up or burned by them the night before.

Formal demand having been made for the surrender, and having been refused, I contend that everything within the line of intrenchments belongs to the United States, and I shall not hesitate to use it, if necessary, for public purposes. But inasmuch as the inhabitants generally have manifested a friendly disposition, I shall disturb them as little as possible consistently with the military rights of present and future military commanders, without remitting in the least our just rights as captors.

After having made the necessary orders for the disposition of the troops in and about Savannah, I ordered Capt. O. M. Poe, chief engineer, to make a thorough examination of the enemy's works in and about Savannah, with a view to making it conform to our future uses. New lines of defenses will be built, embracing the city proper; Forts Jackson, Thunderbolt, and Pulaski retained, with slight modifications in their armament and rear defenses; all the rest of the enemy's forts will be dismantled and destroyed, and their heavy ordnance transferred to Hilton Head, where it can be more easily guarded. Our base of supplies will be established in Savannah as soon as the very difficult obstructions placed in the river can be partially removed. These obstructions at present offer a very serious impediment to the commerce of Savannah, consisting of crib-work of logs and timber heavily bolted together, and filled with the cobble stones which formerly paved the streets of Savannah. All the channels below the city were found more or less filled with torpedoes, which have been removed by order of Admiral Dahlgren. So that Savannah already fulfills the important part it was designed in our plans for the future.

In thus sketching the course of events connected with this campaign, I have purposely passed lightly over the march from Atlanta to the seashore, because it was made in four or more columns, sometimes at a distance of fifteen or twenty miles from each other, and it was impossible for me to attend but one. Therefore, I have left it to the army and corps commanders to describe in their own language the events which attended the march of their respective columns. These reports are herewith submitted, and I beg to refer to them for further details. I would merely sum up the advantages which I conceive have accrued to us by this march.

Our former labors in North Georgia had demonstrated the truth that no large army, carrying with it the necessary stores and baggage, can overtake and capture an inferior force of the enemy in his own country. Therefore no alternative was left me but the one I adopted—namely, to divide my forces, and with the one part act offensively against the enemy's resources, while with the other I should act defensively, and invite the enemy to attack, risking the chances of battle. In this conclusion I have been singularly sustained by the results. General Hood, who, as I have heretofore described, had moved to the westward near Tuscumbia, with a view to decoy me away from Georgia, finding himself mistaken, was forced to choose either to pursue me, or to act offensively against the other part left in Tennessee. He adopted the latter course; and General Thomas has wisely and well fulfilled his part of the grand scheme in drawing Hood well up into Tennessee until he could concentrate all his own troops and then turn upon Hood, as he has done, and destroy or fatally cripple his army. That part of my army is so far removed from me that I leave, with perfect confidence, its management and history to General Thomas.

I was thereby left with a well-appointed army to sever the enemy's only remaining railroad communications eastward and westward, for over 100 miles—namely, the Georgia State Railroad, which is broken up from Fairburn Station to Madison and the Oconee, and the Central Railroad, from Gordon clear to Savannah, with numerous breaks on the latter road from Gordon to Eatonton and from Millen to Augusta, and the Savannah Gulf Railroad. We have also consumed the corn and fodder in the region of country thirty miles on either side of a line from Atlanta to Savannah, as also the sweet potatoes, cattle, hogs, sheep and poultry, and have carried away more than 10,000 horses and mules, as well as a countless number of their slaves. I estimate the damage done to the State of Georgia and its military resources at $100,000,000; at least, $20,000,000 of which has inured to our advantage, and the remainder is simple waste and destruction. This may seem a hard species of warfare, but it brings the sad realities of war home to those who have been directly or indirectly instrumental in involving us in its attendant calamities.

The campaign has also placed this branch of my army in a position from which other great military results may be attempted, besides leaving in Tennessee and North Alabama a force which is amply sufficient to meet all the chances of war in that region of our country.

Since the capture of Atlanta my staff is unchanged, save that General Barry, chief of artillery, has been absent, sick, since our leaving Kingston. Surgeon Moore, U. S. Army, is chief medical director, in place of Surgeon Kittoe, relieved to resume his proper duties as a medical inspector. Major Hitchcock, assistant adjutant-general, has also been added to my staff, and has been of great assistance in the field and office. Captain Dayton still remains as my adjutant-general. All have, as formerly, fulfilled their parts to my entire satisfaction.

In the body of my army I feel a just pride. Generals Howard and Slocum are gentlemen of singular capacity and intelligence, thorough soldiers and patriots, working day and night, not for themselves, but for their country and their men. General Kilpatrick, who commanded the cavalry of this army, has handled it with spirit and dash to my entire satisfaction, and kept a superior force of the enemy's cavalry from even approaching our infantry columns or wagon trains. His report is full and graphic. All the division and brigade commanders merit my personal and official thanks, and I shall spare no efforts to secure them commissions equal to the rank they have exercised so well. As to the rank and file, they seem so full of confidence in themselves that I doubt if they want a compliment from me; but I must do them the justice to say that whether called on to fight, to march, to wade streams, to make roads, clear out obstructions, build bridges, make corduroy, or tear up railroads, they have done it with alacrity and a degree of cheerfulness unsurpassed. A little loose in foraging, they "did some things they ought not to have done," yet, on the whole, they have supplied the wants of the army with as little violence as could be expected, and as little loss as I calculated. Some of these foraging parties had encounters with the enemy which would in ordinary times rank as respectable battles. The behavior of our troops in Savannah has been so manly, so quiet, so perfect, that I take it as the best evidence of discipline and true courage. Never was a hostile city, filled with women and children, occupied by a large army with less disorder, or more system, order, and good government. The same general and generous spirit of confidence and good feeling pervades the army which it has ever afforded me especial pleasure to report on former occasions.

I avail myself of this occasion to express my heartfelt thanks to Admiral Dahlgren and the officers and men of his fleet, as also to General Foster and his command, for the hearty welcome given us on our arrival at the coast, and for their ready and prompt co-operation in all measures tending to the result accomplished.

I send herewith a map* of the country through which we have passed; reports from General Howard, General Slocum, and General Kilpatrick, and their subordinates, respectively, with the usual lists of captured property, killed, wounded, and missing, prisoners of war taken and rescued; as also copies of all papers illustrating the campaign.

All of which is respectfully submitted, by your obedient servant,

W. T. SHERMAN,
Major-General.

Maj. Gen. H. W. HALLECK,
Chief of Staff, Washington City, D. C.

---

* To appear in the Atlas.

Return of casualties and prisoners captured by the army in the field in campaign of Georgia.

Command.	Killed.		Wounded.		Missing.		Aggregate.	Captured.		
	Officers.	Men.	Officers.	Men.	Officers.	Men.		Officers.	Men.	Aggregate.
Right Wing, Army of the Tennessee, Maj. Gen. O. O. Howard commanding.	......	......	......	......	......	......	......	34	632	666
Left Wing, Fourteenth and Twentieth Corps, Maj. Gen. H. W. Slocum commanding.	2	23	6	112	1	258	402	30	409	439
Cavalry Division, Brig. Gen. J. Kilpatrick commanding.	3	35	7	120	......	......	165	13	220	233
Total	5	58	13	232	1	258	567	77	1,261	1,338

Report of casualties in Army of Tennessee not received.
Report of missing in cavalry division not received.

L. M. DAYTON,
Captain and Aide-de-Camp.

[Indorsement.]

This report is not sufficiently accurate to be official, but my command is so scattered that it cannot now be remedied, but will be in due time.

W. T. SHERMAN,
Major-General, Commanding.

ADDENDA.

Abstract from returns showing the effective strength of the army in the field under Maj. Gen. William T. Sherman, November and December, 1864.

NOVEMBER 10.

Command.	Infantry.		Cavalry.		Artillery.	
	Officers.	Men.	Officers.	Men.	Officers.	Men.
ARMY OF THE TENNESSEE.						
Fifteenth Army Corps	724	14,568	......	......	11	376
Seventeenth Army Corps	420	10,667	2	43	5	266
Total	1,144	25,235	2	43	16	642
ARMY OF GEORGIA.						
Fourteenth Army Corps	556	12,397	......	......	11	388
Twentieth Army Corps	602	12,862	......	......	25	607
Total	1,158	25,259	......	......	36	995
Kilpatrick's cavalry	......	......	244	4,672	4	95
Aggregate	2,302	50,494	246	4,715	56	1,732

Abstract from returns showing the effective strength of the army, &c.—Continued.

NOVEMBER 30.

Command.	Infantry.		Cavalry.		Artillery.	
	Officers.	Men.	Officers.	Men.	Officers.	Men.
ARMY OF THE TENNESSEE.						
Fifteenth Army Corps	750	15,144	......	......	17	362
Seventeenth Army Corps	418	11,314	2	30	10	318
Total	1,168	26,458	2	30	27	680
ARMY OF GEORGIA.						
Fourteenth Army Corps	623	13,339	......	......	11	443
Twentieth Army Corps	638	13,103	......	......	22	529
Total	1,261	26,442	......	......	33	972
Kilpatrick's cavalry	......	......	251	4,780	4	96
Aggregate	2,429	52,900	253	4,810	64	1,748

DECEMBER 20.

Command.	Infantry.		Cavalry.		Artillery.	
	Officers.	Men.	Officers.	Men.	Officers.	Men.
ARMY OF THE TENNESSEE.						
Fifteenth Army Corps	753	14,441	......	......	12	367
Seventeenth Army Corps	436	11,293	2	30	7	278
Total	1,189	25,734	2	30	19	645
ARMY OF GEORGIA.						
Fourteenth Army Corps	621	13,170	......	......	11	434
Twentieth Army Corps	631	12,910	......	......	24	526
Total	1,252	26,080	......	......	35	960
Kilpatrick's cavalry	......	......	201	4,351	4	96
Aggregate	2,441	51,814	203	4,381	58	1,701

RECAPITULATION.

Arm.	November 10.	November 30.	December 20.
Infantry	52,796	55,329	54,255
Cavalry	4,961	5,063	4,584
Artillery	1,788	1,812	1,759
Aggregate	59,545	62,204	60,598

SPECIAL FIELD ORDERS, No. 6. } HDQRS. MIL. DIV. OF THE MISSISSIPPI, *In the Field, Savannah, Ga., January 8, 1865.*

The general commanding announces to the troops composing the Military Division of the Mississippi that he has received from the President of the United States, and from Lieutenant-General Grant, letters conveying their high sense and appreciation of the campaign just closed, resulting in the capture of Savannah and the defeat of Hood's army in Tennessee.

In order that all may understand the importance of events it is proper to revert to the situation of affairs in September last. We held Atlanta, a city of little value to us, but so important tc the enemy that Mr. Davis, the head of the rebellious faction in the South, visited his army near Palmetto and commanded it to regain it, as well as to ruin and destroy us by a series of measures which he thought would be effectual. That army, by a rapid march, gained our railroad near Big Shanty, and afterward about Dalton. We pursued it, but it moved so rapidly that we could not overtake it, and General Hood led his army successfully far over toward Mississippi, in hopes to decoy us out of Georgia; but we were not then to be led away by him, and preferred to lead and control events ourselves. Generals Thomas and Schofield, commanding the departments to our rear, returned to their posts and prepared to decoy General Hood into their meshes, whilst we came on to complete the original journey. We quietly and deliberately destroyed Atlanta and all the railroads which the enemy had used to carry on war against us, occupied his State capital, and then captured his commercial capital, which had been so strongly fortified from the sea as to defy approach from that quarter. Almost at the moment of our victorious entry into Savannah came the welcome and expected news that our comrades in Tennessee had also fulfilled nobly and well their part; had decoyed General Hood to Nashville and then turned on him, defeating his army thoroughly, capturing all his artillery, great numbers of prisoners, and were still pursuing the fragments down into Alabama. So complete a success in military operations, extending over half a continent, is an achievement that entitles it to a place in the military history of the world.

The armies serving in Georgia and Tennessee, as well as the local garrisons of Decatur, Bridgeport, Chattanooga, and Murfreesborough, are alike entitled to the common honors, and each regiment may inscribe on its colors at pleasure the words "Savannah" or "Nashville." The general commanding embraces in the same general success the operations of the cavalry column, under Generals Stoneman, Burbridge, and Gillem, that penetrated into Southwest Virginia and paralyzed the efforts of the enemy to disturb the peace and safety of East Tennessee. Instead of being put on the defensive, we have at all points assumed the bold offensive, and completely thwarted the designs of the enemies of our country.

By order of Maj. Gen. W. T. Sherman:

L. M. DAYTON,
Aide-de-Camp.

—

STATE OF CALIFORNIA, EXECUTIVE DEPARTMENT,
Sacramento, January 2, 1865.

Maj. Gen. W. T. SHERMAN,
Savannah:

The series of victories which have attended your army during the past year—the capture of Atlanta, the triumphant march from Atlanta to the sea-coast, and the subsequent capture of Savannah—have filled the hearts of all who love their country with joy, and justly entitles you to the profound gratitude of the nation. For and on behalf of the people of this State I beg to tender to you, and through you to the officers and soldiers under your command, my heartfelt thanks for the signal services your army has rendered to the cause of civilization, liberty, humanity, and good government. To you as their great leader I tender my cordial congratulations, with the prayer that God may preserve and protect you to lead the victorious hosts of the Republic on to still greater victories, even to the conquering of an honorable and permanent peace.

I remain, general, gratefully, your obedient servant,

FRED'K F. LOW,
Governor.

STATE OF NEW YORK, EXECUTIVE DEPARTMENT,
Albany, January 18, 1865.

Maj. Gen. WILLIAM T. SHERMAN:

GENERAL: In compliance with the request made in joint resolutions passed by the senate and assembly of the State of New York commendatory of the conduct and services of certain officers in the Army and Navy of the United States, I take great pleasure in forwarding to you the inclosed resolution referring to yourself and the brave officers and men in your command. I most sincerely join in the expression of thanks for these distinguished services, and, with the loyal people of the nation, acknowledge my deep and heartfelt gratitude.

I am, general, most respectfully, your obedient servant,

R. E. FENTON.

[Inclosure.]

CONCURRENT RESOLUTIONS complimentary to Generals Grant, Sherman, Sheridan, and Thomas, and to Vice-Admiral Farragut and Commodore Winslow.

* * * * * * *

Resolved, That the thanks of the Legislature representing the people of the State of New York are hereby tendered to Maj. Gen. William T. Sherman, and the officers and men of his command, for the series of superb victories culminating in the capture of Atlanta; and for the skillfully executed march from the mountains to the sea, which challenged the admiration of the world, resulted in the capture of Savannah, with many millions of public property, and demonstrated that the so-called Confederacy is indeed but a "shell."

Resolved, That His Excellency the Governor is hereby respectfully requested to transmit a copy of each of the foregoing resolutions to the officers specially named therein.

IN SENATE,
January 5, 1865.

The foregoing resolutions were duly passed.

JAS. TERWILLIGER,
Clerk.

STATE OF NEW YORK,
IN ASSEMBLY,
January 13, 1865.

Resolved, That the assembly concur in the passage of the foregoing resolutions.

By order:

J. B. CUSHMAN,
Clerk.

No. 2.

Organization of the Union Forces, commanded by Maj. Gen. William T. Sherman.

HEADQUARTERS GUARD.

7th Company Ohio Sharpshooters, Lieut. James Cox.

ENGINEERS.

1st Missouri (five companies), Lieut. Col. William Tweeddale.

RIGHT WING.

Maj. Gen. OLIVER O. HOWARD.

ESCORT.

15th Illinois Cavalry, Company K, Lieut. John A. McQueen
4th Company Ohio Cavalry, Capt. John L. King.

FIFTEENTH ARMY CORPS.

Maj. Gen. PETER J. OSTERHAUS.

FIRST DIVISION.

Brig. Gen. CHARLES R. WOODS.

First Brigade.

Col. MILO SMITH.

12th Indiana, Maj. Elbert D. Baldwin.
26th Iowa, Maj. John Lubbers.
27th Missouri, Col. Thomas Curly.
29th Missouri, Lieut. Col. Joseph S. Gage.
31st and 32d Missouri Battalion, Maj. Abraham J. Seay.
76th Ohio, Col. William B. Woods.

Second Brigade.

Brig. Gen. CHARLES C. WALCUTT.*
Col. ROBERT F. CATTERSON.

26th Illinois, Capt. George H. Reed.
40th Illinois, Lieut. Col. Hiram W. Hall.
103d Illinois, Maj. Asias Willison.
97th Indiana:
Col. Robert F. Catterson.
Capt. George Elliott.
100th Indiana, Maj. Ruel M. Johnson.
6th Iowa, Maj. William H. Clune.
46th Ohio, Lieut. Col. Isaac N. Alexander.

Third Brigade.

Col. JAMES A. WILLIAMSON.

4th Iowa, Lieut. Col. Samuel D. Nichols.
9th Iowa, Capt. Paul McSweeney.
25th Iowa, Col. George A. Stone.
30th Iowa, Lieut. Col. Aurelius Roberts.
31st Iowa, Lieut. Col. Jeremiah W. Jenkins.

SECOND DIVISION.

Brig. Gen. WILLIAM B. HAZEN.

First Brigade.

Col. THEODORE JONES.

55th Illinois, Capt. Charles A. Andress.
116th Illinois, Lieut. Col. John E. Maddux.
127th Illinois, Capt. Charles Schryver.
6th Missouri, Lieut. Col. Delos Van Deusen.
8th Missouri (two companies), Capt. John W. White.
30th Ohio, Capt. Emory W. Muenscher.
57th Ohio, Maj. John McClure.

Second Brigade.

Col. WELLS S. JONES.†
Col. JAMES S. MARTIN.

111th Illinois:
Col. James S. Martin.
Maj. William M. Mabry.
83d Indiana, Lieut. Col. George H. Scott.
37th Ohio, Lieut. Col. Louis von Blessingh.
47th Ohio, Col. Augustus C. Parry.
53d Ohio, Capt. David H. Lasley.
54th Ohio, Lieut. Col. Israel T. Moore.

* Wounded November 22.

† Wounded December 13.

Third Brigade.

Col. JOHN M. OLIVER.

48th Illinois, Maj. Edward Adams.
90th Illinois, Lieut. Col. Owen Stuart.
99th Indiana, Lieut. Col. John M. Berkey.
15th Michigan, Lieut. Col. Frederick S. Hutchinson.
70th Ohio, Lieut. Col. Henry L. Philips.

THIRD DIVISION.

Brig. Gen. JOHN E. SMITH.

First Brigade.

Col. JOSEPH B. MCCOWN.

63d Illinois, Lieut. Col. James Isaminger.
93d Illinois,* Lieut. Col. Nicholas C. Buswell.
48th Indiana, Lieut. Col. Edward J. Wood.
59th Indiana, Lieut. Col. Jefferson K. Scott.
4th Minnesota, Col. John E. Tourtellotte.

Second Brigade.

Bvt. Brig. Gen. GREEN B. RAUM.

56th Illinois, Capt. James P. Files.
10th Iowa, Lieut. Col. Paris P. Henderson.
26th Missouri,† Col. Benjamin D. Dean.
80th Ohio, Lieut. Col. Pren Metham.

FOURTH DIVISION.

Brig. Gen. JOHN M. CORSE.

First Brigade.

Brig. Gen. ELLIOTT W. RICE.

52d Illinois:
Maj. Wesley Boyd.
Lieut. Col. Jerome D. Davis.
66th Indiana, Lieut. Col. Roger Martin.
2d Iowa, Lieut. Col. Noel B. Howard.
7th Iowa, Lieut. Col. James C. Parrott.

Second Brigade.

Col. ROBERT N. ADAMS.

12th Illinois, Lieut. Col. Henry Van Sellar.
66th Illinois, Lieut. Col. Andrew K. Campbell.
81st Ohio, Maj. William C. Henry.

Third Brigade.

Lieut. Col. FREDERICK J. HURLBUT.

7th Illinois, Lieut. Col. Hector Perrin.
50th Illinois, Capt. Henry Horn.
57th Illinois, Capt. Frederick A. Battey.
39th Iowa, Maj. Joseph M. Griffiths.

ARTILLERY.

Maj. CHARLES J. STOLBRAND.

1st Illinois Light, Battery H, Capt. Francis De Gress.
1st Michigan Light, Battery B, Capt. Albert F. R. Arndt.
1st Missouri Light, Battery H, Lieut. John F. Brunner.
Wisconsin Light, 12th Battery, Capt. William Zickerick.

* Non-veterans 18th Wisconsin attached.
† Detachment 10th Missouri attached.

SEVENTEENTH ARMY CORPS.

Maj. Gen. FRANK P. BLAIR, Jr.

ESCORT.

11th Illinois Cavalry, Company G, Capt. Stephen S. Tripp.

FIRST DIVISION.

Maj. Gen. JOSEPH A. MOWER.

First Brigade.

Brig. Gen. JOHN W. FULLER.

64th Illinois, Capt. Joseph S. Reynolds.
18th Missouri, Lieut. Col. Charles S. Sheldon.
27th Ohio, Capt. James Morgan.
39th Ohio, Capt. Daniel Weber.

Second Brigade.

Brig. Gen. JOHN W. SPRAGUE.

35th New Jersey, Col. John J. Cladek.
43d Ohio, Col. Wager Swayne.
63d Ohio, Maj. John W. Fouts.
25th Wisconsin, Lieut. Col. Jeremiah M Rusk.

Third Brigade.

Col. JOHN TILLSON.

10th Illinois, Lieut. Col. McLain F. Wood.
25th Indiana, Maj. James S. Wright.
32d Wisconsin, Col. Charles H. De Groat.

THIRD DIVISION.

Brig. Gen. MORTIMER D. LEGGETT.

Provost Guard.

20th Illinois, Capt. Henry King.

First Brigade.

Brig. Gen. MANNING F. FORCE.

30th Illinois, Lieut. Col. William C. Rhoads.
31st Illinois, Lieut. Col. Robert N. Pearson.
45th Illinois, Maj. John O. Duer.
12th Wisconsin, Lieut. Col. James K. Proudfit.
16th Wisconsin, Maj. William F. Dawes.

Second Brigade.

Col. ROBERT K. SCOTT.

20th Ohio, Capt. Lyman N. Ayres.
68th Ohio, Lieut. Col. George E. Welles.
78th Ohio, Col. Greenberry F. Wiles.
17th Wisconsin, Maj. Patrick H. McCauley.

FOURTH DIVISION.

Brig. Gen. GILES A. SMITH.

First Brigade.

Col. BENJAMIN F. POTTS.

14th Illinois } (battalion), Lieut. Alonzo
15th Illinois } J. Gillespie.
41st Illinois (battalion), Maj. Robert H. McFadden.
53d Illinois, Col. John W. McClanahan.
23d Indiana, Lieut. Col. George S. Babbitt.
53d Indiana, Capt. Henry Duncan.
32d Ohio, Lieut. Col. Jefferson J. Hibbets.

Third Brigade.

Brig. Gen. WILLIAM W. BELKNAP.

32d Illinois, Maj. Henry Davidson.
11th Iowa, Capt. Benjamin Beach.
13th Iowa, Capt. Justin C. Kennedy.
15th Iowa, Maj. George Pomutz.
16th Iowa, Capt. Crandall W. Williams.

ARTILLERY.

Maj. ALLEN C. WATERHOUSE.

1st Michigan Light, Battery C, Lieut. Henry Shier.
Minnesota Light, 1st Battery, Lieut. Henry Hurter.
Ohio Light, 15th Battery, Lieut. George R. Caspar.

LEFT WING.

Maj. Gen. HENRY W. SLOCUM.

PONTONIERS.

58th Indiana, Col. George P. Buell.

ENGINEERS.

1st Michigan (detachment), Maj. John B. Yates.

FOURTEENTH ARMY CORPS.

Bvt. Maj. Gen. JEFFERSON C. DAVIS.

FIRST DIVISION.

Brig. Gen. WILLIAM P. CARLIN.

First Brigade.

Col. HARRISON C. HOBART.

104th Illinois, Lieut. Col. Douglas Hapeman.
42d Indiana, Capt. Gideon R. Kellams.
88th Indiana, Lieut. Col. Cyrus E. Briant.
33d Ohio, Capt. Joseph Hinson.
94th Ohio, Lieut. Col. Rue P. Hutchins.
21st Wisconsin, Lieut. Col. Michael H. Fitch.

Second Brigade.

Lieut. Col. JOSEPH H. BRIGHAM.

13th Michigan, Lieut. Col. Theodoric R. Palmer.
21st Michigan, Maj. Benton D. Fox.
69th Ohio, Capt. Lewis E. Hicks.

Third Brigade.

Col. HENRY A. HAMBRIGHT.*
Lieut. Col. DAVID MILES.

38th Indiana, Capt. James H. Low.
21st Ohio, Lieut. Col. Arnold McMahan.
74th Ohio:
Maj. Joseph Fisher.
Maj. Robert P. Findley.
79th Pennsylvania:
Lieut. Col. David Miles.
Maj. Michael H. Locher.

SECOND DIVISION.

Brig. Gen. JAMES D. MORGAN.

First Brigade.

Col. ROBERT F. SMITH.

16th Illinois, Lieut. Col. James B. Cahill.
60th Illinois, Col. William B. Anderson.
10th Michigan, Col. Charles M. Lum.
14th Michigan, Maj. Thomas C. Fitzgibbon.
17th New York, Lieut. Col. Joel O. Martin.

Second Brigade.

Lieut. Col. JOHN S. PEARCE.

34th Illinois, Capt. Peter Ege.
78th Illinois, Lieut. Col. Maris R. Vernon.
98th Ohio, Capt. James R. McLaughlin.
108th Ohio, Maj. Frederick Beck.
113th Ohio, Capt. Toland Jones.
121st Ohio, Maj. Aaron B. Robinson.

* Sick from November 18.

Third Brigade.

Lieut. Col. JAMES W. LANGLEY.

85th Illinois, Maj. Robert G. Rider.
86th Illinois, Lieut Col. Allen L. Fahnestock.
110th Illinois (four companies), Lieut. Col. E. Hibbard Topping.
125th Illinois, Capt. George W. Cook.
22d Indiana, Capt. William H. Snodgrass.
52d Ohio, Lieut. Col. Charles W. Clancy.

THIRD DIVISION.

Brig. Gen. ABSALOM BAIRD.

First Brigade.

Col. MORTON C. HUNTER.

82d Indiana, Lieut. Col. John M. Matheny.
23d Missouri, Lieut. Col. Quin Morton.
17th Ohio, Lieut. Col. Benjamin H. Showers.
31st Ohio, Capt. Michael Stone.
89th Ohio, Lieut. Col. William H. Glenn.
92d Ohio,* Col. Benjamin D. Fearing.

Second Brigade.

Col. NEWELL GLEASON.

75th Indiana, Maj. Cyrus J. McCole.
87th Indiana, Lieut. Col. Edwin P. Hammond.
101st Indiana, Lieut. Col. Thomas Doan.
2d Minnesota, Lieut. Col. Judson W. Bishop.
105th Ohio, Lieut. Col. George T. Perkins.

Third Brigade.

Col. GEORGE P. ESTE.

74th Indiana, Lieut. Col. Thomas Morgan.
18th Kentucky, Lieut. Col. Hubbard K. Milward.
14th Ohio, Lieut. Col. Albert Moore.
38th Ohio, Capt. Charles M. Gilbert.

ARTILLERY.

Maj. CHARLES HOUGHTALING.

1st Illinois Light, Battery C,† Lieut. Joseph R. Channel.
2d Illinois Light, Battery I, Lieut. Alonzo W. Coe.
Indiana Light, 19th Battery, Capt. William P. Stackhouse.
Wisconsin Light, 5th Battery, Lieut. Joseph McKnight.

TWENTIETH ARMY CORPS.

Brig. Gen. ALPHEUS S. WILLIAMS.

FIRST DIVISION.

Brig. Gen. NATHANIEL J. JACKSON.

First Brigade.

Col. JAMES L. SELFRIDGE.

5th Connecticut, Lieut. Col. Henry W. Daboll.
123d New York, Lieut. Col. James C. Rogers.
141st New York, Capt. William Merrell.
46th Pennsylvania, Maj. Patrick Griffith.

Second Brigade.

Col. EZRA A. CARMAN.

2d Massachusetts, Col. William Cogswell.
13th New Jersey, Maj. Frederick H. Harris.
107th New York:
Capt. Charles J. Fox.
Lieut. Col. Allen N. Sill.
150th New York:
Maj. Alfred B. Smith.
Col. John H. Ketcham.
3d Wisconsin, Col. William Hawley.

* Company A, 24th Illinois attached.
† Detachment 11th Ohio Infantry attached.

Third Brigade.

Col. JAMES S. ROBINSON.

82d Illinois, Maj. Ferdinand H. Rolshausen.
101st Illinois, Lieut. Col. John B. Le Sage.
143d New York, Lieut. Col. Hezekiah Watkins.
61st Ohio, Capt. John Garrett.
82d Ohio, Lieut. Col. David Thomson.
31st Wisconsin, Col. Francis H. West.

SECOND DIVISION.

Brig. Gen. JOHN W. GEARY.

First Brigade.

Col. ARIO PARDEE, jr.

5th Ohio, Lieut. Col. Robert Kirkup.
29th Ohio:
Maj. Myron T. Wright.*
Capt. Jonas Schoonover.
66th Ohio, Lieut. Col. Eugene Powell.
28th Pennsylvania, Col. John Flynn.
147th Pennsylvania,† Lieut. Col. John Craig.

Second Brigade.

Col. PATRICK H. JONES.

33d New Jersey, Col. George W. Mindil.
119th New York, Col. John T. Lockman.
134th New York, Lieut. Col. Allan H. Jackson.
154th New York, Maj. Lewis D. Warner.
73d Pennsylvania, Maj. Charles C. Cresson.
109th Pennsylvania, Capt. Walter G. Dunn.

Third Brigade.

Col. HENRY A. BARNUM.

60th New York, Maj. Thomas Elliott.
102d New York, Lieut. Col. Harvey S. Chatfield.
137th New York, Lieut. Col. Koert S. Van Voorhis.
149th New York, Maj. Nicholas Grumbach.
29th Pennsylvania, Lieut. Col. Samuel M. Zulich.
111th Pennsylvania, Lieut. Col. Thomas M. Walker.

THIRD DIVISION.

Brig. Gen. WILLIAM T. WARD.

First Brigade.

Col. FRANKLIN C. SMITH.

102d Illinois, Maj. Hiland H. Clay.
105th Illinois, Maj. Henry D. Brown.
129th Illinois, Col. Henry Case.
70th Indiana, Lieut. Col. Samuel Merrill.
79th Ohio, Lieut. Col. Azariah W. Doan.

Second Brigade.

Col. DANIEL DUSTIN.

33d Indiana, Lieut. Col. James E. Burton.
85th Indiana, Lieut. Col. Alexander B. Crane.
19th Michigan, Lieut. Col. John J. Baker.
22d Wisconsin, Lieut. Col. Edward Bloodgood.

Third Brigade.

Col. SAMUEL ROSS.

20th Connecticut, Lieut. Col. Philo B. Buckingham.
33d Massachusetts, Lieut. Col. Elisha Doane.
136th New York, Lieut. Col. Lester B. Faulkner.
55th Ohio, Lieut. Col. Edwin H. Powers.
73d Ohio, Lieut. Col. Samuel H. Hurst.
26th Wisconsin, Lieut. Col. Frederick C. Winkler.

---

* Wounded December 19.
† Detachment Battery E, Pennsylvania Artillery, attached.

ARTILLERY.

Maj. JOHN A. REYNOLDS.

1st New York Light, Battery I, Capt. Charles E. Winegar.
1st New York Light, Battery M, Lieut. Edward P. Newkirk.
1st Ohio Light, Battery C, Capt. Marco B. Gary,* Lieut. Jerome B. Stephens.
Pennsylvania Light, Battery E, Capt. Thomas S. Sloan.

CAVALRY.

THIRD DIVISION.

Brig. Gen. JUDSON KILPATRICK.

First Brigade.

Col. ELI H. MURRAY.

8th Indiana, Lieut. Col. Fielder A. Jones.
2d Kentucky:
  Capt. Joseph T. Forman.
  Capt. Robert M. Gilmore.
3d Kentucky, Lieut. Col. Robert H. King.
5th Kentucky, Col. Oliver L. Baldwin.
9th Pennsylvania, Col. Thomas J. Jordan.

Second Brigade.

Col. SMITH D. ATKINS.

92d Illinois (mounted infantry), Lieut. Col. Matthew Van Buskirk.
3d Indiana, Capt. Charles U. Patton.
9th Michigan, Col. George S. Acker.
5th Ohio, Col. Thomas T. Heath.
9th Ohio, Col. William D. Hamilton.
10th Ohio, Lieut. Col. Thomas W. Sanderson.
McLaughlin's (Ohio) Squadron, Capt. John Dalzell.

Unattached.

1st Alabama Cavalry,† Col. George E. Spencer.
9th Illinois Mounted Infantry,† Lieut. Col. Samuel T. Hughes.

Artillery.

10th Wisconsin Battery, Capt. Yates V. Beebe.

No. 3.

Itinerary of the Union Forces, November 1–December 31, 1864.‡

RIGHT WING.§

FIFTEENTH ARMY CORPS.‖

November 1.—The First and Second Divisions continued the march from Cave Spring.

November 8.—Reached Smyrna Camp-Ground.

November 13.—Marched to White Hall.

November 15.—Left White Hall, followed up by the Third and Fourth Divisions; from which time the corps continued marching until the end of the month.

*Captured December 12.
†Serving with the Left Wing.
‡From returns of the commands indicated.
§Commanded by Maj. Gen. Oliver O. Howard.
‖Commanded by Maj. Gen. Peter J. Osterhaus.

First Division.

[*November.*]—During the past month this division has marched from Cave Spring, Ga., to this point (near Millen, Ga.), starting November 15 from White Hall, Ga., with the expedition of General Sherman against some, as yet unknown, point in the Southern Confederacy; distance marched thus far about 200 miles. The division has been engaged in destroying parts of the railroad from Macon to Augusta, as well as the line from Savannah to Macon.

November 22.—Part of the division (Second Brigade) was attacked by three brigades of Georgia militia near Griswoldville, some ten miles from Macon. The enemy were repulsed and left the field with dead and wounded in our hands. Loss on the Union side was 13 killed, 69 wounded, and 2 missing. Enemy's acknowledged loss, 614.

December 1.—This division was beyond Scull's Creek, Ga., and on the march.

December 10.—Reached position in rear of Savannah on the right of the Ogeechee Canal.

December 11.—Moved at night to the right, and connected with General Corse's (Fourth) division, Fifteenth Army Corps, with left on the main road from Savannah to King's Ferry.

December 21.—The army entered, this division marching in on the King's Bridge road; took position on the south side of the city.

First Brigade, First Division.

November 1.—The brigade left its camp at Cave Spring, Ga., marching, via Powder Springs, to Smyrna Camp-Ground, near Vining's Station, Ga., at which place we remained in camp six days. Received pay and drew clothing.

November 13.—Marched, via Chattahoochee River railroad bridge, through Atlanta to White Hall.

November 15.—Took up line of march on East Point road, passing via Rough and Ready, McDonough, and Clinton, striking the Savannah and Macon Railroad near Griswold, Ga., destroying about three miles of railroad and burning a bridge, marching the next day toward Gordon and Irwinton, and is yet on the march at this date near the railroad, on Deep Creek, in Emanuel County, Ga. Troops in good health and fine condition for the march.

[*December.*]—Being on the march on the 1st of the month, we continued the march to the Ogeechee River.

December 10.—Crossed the river and marched along the canal which runs from the Ogeechee to the Savannah River. Filing right we struck the King's Bridge road seven miles from Savannah, where we remained from the 13th to the 21st, taking up a position in front of the enemy, near Owen's Bridge, on the plank road, putting up works and having one regiment occupying the works supporting a battery. During that time the Twenty-seventh Missouri Infantry was ordered to report to Major-General Howard, and has been on duty at Doctor Cheves' rice plantation, on the Ogeechee River.

December 21.—It was found that the enemy had evacuated Savannah on the previous night, and the brigade marched inside the inner works about 10 o'clock. The Seventy-sixth Ohio is now on duty as provost guard. The Twenty-seventh Missouri Infantry has been removed from the Ogeechee River and now garrisons Forts Rosedew and Beaulieu, on Wassaw Sound.

The brigade lost no men during the month in action. Health of the troops good. We are now inside the works, one mile from the city.

Second Division.

[*November.*]—During the month the division has marched from Cave Spring, Ga., via Vining's Station, Atlanta, Rough and Ready, McDonough, Indian Springs, Ocmulgee Mills, Hillsborough, Clinton, Larksville, Irwinton, Ball's Ferry, Irwin's Cross-Roads, and Summerville, Ga., and is still marching in a southeasterly direction toward the coast. The division has participated in all the skirmishes in which the corps was engaged. During the month the division has received some 800 recruits.

December 1.—Marched from Summerville, Ga., in a southeasterly direction.

December 9.—Crossed the Cannouchee River in the morning, struck the Gulf railroad near Eden, destroying between six and ten miles of the road.

December 10.—Recrossed the Cannouchee, and moved to a point near the junction of the Cannouchee and Ogeechee, and crossed in good order.

December 13.—In the morning crossed the Ogeechee at King's Bridge and took up our line of march for Fort McAllister; invested the fort at 3.30 o'clock; stormed at 4.30 o'clock. The flags of nine regiments were planted on the fort in ten minutes from the time the order to charge was given. Our loss was 4 commissioned officers and 20 men killed, and 7 commissioned officers and 103 men wounded. The enemy's loss was 14 killed, 21 wounded, and 195 prisoners (unhurt), including 1 officer killed and 17 captured; total, 230. The fort contained 11 siege guns, 1 10-inch mortar, 12 field pieces, and 60 tons of ammunition, and a large amount of commissary stores and liquors.

December 14.—Went into camp on Middleton's plantation, near the fort.

December 17 to 21.—Made a thorough destruction of the Gulf railroad from the Ogeechee River to Walthourville, a distance of thirty miles.

December 21 to 31.—In camp near the fort. All the guns, ammunition, &c., moved out.

The following is a repetition of losses, &c., since December 1: 4 commissioned officers killed, 7 wounded, and 2 captured; 20 enlisted men killed, 111 wounded, and 38 captured.

The division has killed and captured from the enemy 19 officers and 231 men; total, 250. Total number of miles marched during the month, 121.

First Brigade, Second Division.

November 1.—The brigade, with the division, corps, and army, marched from Cave Spring, Ga.

November 4.—Arrived at Smyrna Camp-Ground, where it remained until the 9th, assisting in the destruction of the railroad, receiving pay in the meantime.

November 9.—Moved to Atlanta, where the command was refitted with clothing; thence southward.

November 16 [20?].—Arrived at Clinton, Ga., where a portion of the brigade was engaged with the enemy's cavalry and routed them; since which time it has been constantly on the move.

December 1.—Marched from Summerville, Ga.

December 10.—Arrived in front of Savannah in the afternoon, in which position the brigade remained until the afternoon of the 12th, when we broke camp and marched to King's Bridge, on the Ogeechee River.

December 13.—Crossed the river and marched to Fort McAllister, Ga., arriving at 2 p. m. The brigade took an active part in the assault and capture of the fort, which was carried in gallant style at 5 p. m.

December 14.—Went into camp at White Hall, Ga., assisting in the destruction of the Gulf railroad during the balance of the month.

Third Division.

November 12.—Having concentrated at Cartersville and Allatoona, Ga., and the sick, surplus camp and garrison equipage, baggage, &c., having been sent to the rear, the division started for Atlanta, Ga., to rejoin the corps (Fifteenth), arriving at that place and encamping near White Hall on the 14th. At Atlanta the command was supplied with the necessary quartermaster's stores.

November 15.—The division started south from Atlanta, since which time it has marched via McDonough, Jackson (crossing Ocmulgee River at Seven Islands), Hillsborough, Clinton, and Gordon (at which time the command tore up four miles of railroad), Irwinton (crossing the Oconee River about four miles below the railroad bridge, at Ball's Ferry), and Irwin's Cross-Roads; from thence moving on the extreme right to Summerville.

December 1.—The division started from Summerville and marched via Cannouchee, Statesborough, crossing the Ogeechee River at Jenks' Bridge; thence marching between the Little and Big Ogeechee Rivers to Bethel Church, on the Savannah Canal.

December 10.—The supply train was left in camp, and the division moved up on south side of canal to a point about four miles and a half from Savannah, at which point the enemy were met; skirmished with them during the 10th and 11th; evening of the 11th moved toward the right to Anderson's plantation.

December 12.—Marched to Miller's Station (No. 1), on Gulf railroad, remaining at that place until the 21st, and then, the enemy having evacuated, the command moved into its present camp in the suburbs of the city.

During the campaign the command cut about ten miles of road through the woods, corduroyed over 5,000 yards of impassable roads, and destroyed 800 bales of cotton.

First Brigade, Third Division.

[*November.*]—Brigade continued to do garrison duty at Cartersville and Allatoona, Ga., up to the 12th, when we broke camp and marched for Atlanta, Ga.

November 14.—Arrived at Atlanta at 3 p. m.

November 15.—Left Atlanta at 9.30; marched about fifteen miles.

November 16.—Marched to McDonough.

November 17.—Marched twenty-two miles, passing through Jackson.

November 18.—Marched two miles beyond Ocmulgee Mills, having crossed Ocmulgee River at this point.

November 19.—Marched seventeen miles, passing Hillsborough.

November 20.—Encamped near Clinton.

November 21.—Marched seven miles.

November 22.—Encamped at Gordon.

November 23 and 24.—Remained at Gordon.

November 25.—Marched to Irwinton; twelve miles.

November 26.—Marched eleven miles.

November 27.—Crossed Oconee River; encamped six miles beyond.

November 28 to 30.—Continued marching, and arrived at Summerville; no fighting; plenty to eat, and all in good spirits.

December 1.—Left bivouac near Summerville; marched toward Savannah.

December 9.—Crossed Ogeechee River near Edwin's [Eden?] Station and bivouacked at the Ogeechee Canal, fourteen miles from Savannah; met the enemy strongly intrenched and skirmished until dark.

December 11.—Ordered around to the right; went into camp near Station No. 1, Gulf railroad, on the 12th, where command remained until the 21st, when it moved into Savannah and encamped on the outskirts of the city.

Distance marched during the month, 110 miles. The general health of the command has been excellent throughout the month.

Second Brigade, Third Division.

November 2.—Pursuant to orders from Brig. Gen. John E. Smith, the Tenth Iowa and Twenty-sixth Missouri, stationed at and near Kingston, Ga., on the Atlantic and Western Railroad, marched for Cartersville, headquarters of the division, arriving there on the 3d.

November 7.—The Fifty-sixth Illinois, Eightieth Ohio, and Battalion Tenth Missouri, marched from Resaca en route for Cartersville, arriving there on the 8th.

November 12.—The entire command, under Bvt. Brig. Gen. Green B. Raum, marched for Atlanta, via Allatoona, Acworth, and Marietta.

November 14.—Arrived at Atlanta.

November 15.—The command, after being supplied with quartermaster's stores, started south on campaign, since which time the march has been continued without anything of importance occurring.

December 1.—Marched from Summerville, Ga., at 9 a. m.

December 7.—Encamped near Big Ogeechee River.

December 9.—Crossed Ogeechee and entered first line of rebel defenses; encamped near canal.

December 10.—Marched down south bank of canal; came upon the enemy about five miles from Savannah; found them posted behind an impassable swamp; drove their skirmishers from swamp, and fortified during the night.

December 11.—Moved out from works and marched about two miles to the right; during the night marched still farther to the right and went into bivouac.

December 12.—Marched to near Miller's Station, on Gulf railroad, crossing road, and took up a new position.

December 13.—Demonstrated while the Second Division assaulted Fort McAllister.

December 21.—Enemy evacuated Savannah last night and we marched inside rebel works and went into camp on the south side of city.

December 23.—Changed camp.

December 24.—Army corps reviewed by General Sherman.

Fourth Division.

November 11.—Fortifications at Rome, Ga., were dismantled, and the division took up its line of march to join its corps at Atlanta, Ga., and from there proceeded with General Sherman's army on the campaign then commencing.

The division marched during the month [November] the distance of about 260 miles.

First Brigade, Fourth Division.

[*November.*]—The brigade has taken part in the campaign, leaving Rome, Ga., on the 11th, marching with the army to this place [Slater's Mills].

[*December.*]—The brigade marched with the army of General Sherman from Slater's Mills, Ga., to Savannah, skirmishing with the enemy at Jenks' Bridge and on the Little Ogeechee River, losing 2 men killed and 9 wounded.

Second Brigade, Fourth Division.

[*November.*]—This brigade was engaged doing garrison duty at Rome, Ga., until the 11th, when, with the division, it proceeded to Atlanta, Ga., to join its corps, where it arrived on the 16th.

November 17.—It resumed its line of march in concert with the grand army under Major-General Sherman. The duties performed were such as usually devolve upon troops when engaged in so extensive a campaign.

The distance marched, up to December 1, about 255 miles. In traveling this distance six rivers were crossed and many fatiguing marches were made. The brigade has taken no active part in any engagement during the month.

December 1 found this brigade with the grand army under Major-General Sherman in the interior of Georgia. In concert with its division and corps it moved forward without anything of interest occurring until the day after crossing the Ogeechee Canal (December 9), when, being in advance, it encountered the enemy's pickets about 9 a. m.; skirmished with them nearly all day, finally driving them across the Little Ogeechee River, capturing one piece of artillery and prisoners. The brigade assisted in the investment of Savannah, and after its evacuation by the enemy marched into its present camp near the city.

Artillery Brigade.

November 1.—Marched from Cave Spring to Cedartown, six miles, and encamped.

November 2.—Marched fifteen miles, encamping in the field.

November 3.—Marched sixteen miles; encamped at Pumpkin Vine Creek, Ga.

November 4.—Marched thirteen miles and encamped at Powder Springs.

November 5.—Marched eleven miles and encamped at Smyrna Camp-Ground, near Marietta, Ga.

November 6 to 12.—In camp near Marietta.

November 13.—Marched twelve miles and encamped at White Hall, near Atlanta.

November 15.—Brigade marched with General Sherman's army; commenced campaign through Central Georgia; marched seventeen miles, encamping near Jonesborough.

November 16.—Marched sixteen miles and encamped at McDonough.

November 17.—Marched ten miles and encamped near Jackson.

November 18.—Marched seven miles, encamping at Iron Springs.

November 19.—Marched eleven miles; crossed the Ocmulgee River; encamped at midnight near Hillsborough.

November 20.—Marched nineteen miles, encamping near Clinton.

November 21.—Marched twelve miles; encamped in the field.

November 22.—Marched eight miles and encamped at Gordon. Company B, First Michigan Artillery, engaged in fight near Griswold. Casualties, 7 men wounded.

November 23.—Encamped at Gordon.

November 24.—Marched twelve miles, encamping at Irwinton.

November 25.—Marched thirteen miles and encamped near Oconee River. The Twelfth Wisconsin Battery skirmished with the enemy at the river.

November 26.—Crossed the Oconee River and marched nine miles; encamped at Irwin's Cross-Roads.

November 27.—In camp at Irwin's Cross-Roads.

November 28.—Marched sixteen miles, encamping in the field.

November 29.—Marched eighteen miles; encamped near Sutherland's Mills.

November 30.—Marched sixteen miles and encamped in the field near Ogeechee River.

Miles marched during the month, 257.

December 1.—Marched nine miles; encamped in field.

December 2.—Marched six miles; encamped in field.

December 3.—Remained in camp.

December 4.—Marched fifteen miles; encamped in field.

December 5.—Marched twenty miles; encamped in field.

December 6.—Remained in camp.

December 7.—Marched sixteen miles; encamped at Jenks' Bridge, on Ogeechee River. Company B, First Michigan Artillery, skirmished with the enemy at the river; enemy retired at night.

December 8.—Marched twelve miles; encamped at Eden Court-House.

December 9.—Marched three miles; encamped on Cannouchee River.

December 10.—Marched eighteen miles; encamped on Little Ogeechee River, near enemy's works, nine miles from Savannah, Ga.

December 11.—Batteries took position in rough works and engaged the enemy.

December 12.—Batteries actively engaged against enemy's works from this date until the 21st, when the city of Savannah was evacuated by the enemy; brigade marched nine miles, encamping in the city of Savannah. Battery H, First Missouri Artillery, and Battery H, First Illinois Artillery, had two men wounded.

December 15.—The Twelfth Wisconsin Battery had three men wounded.

December 23.—Brigade reviewed by Maj. Gen. W. T. Sherman.

Brigade remained in camp in the city of Savannah during the balance of the month. Distance marched during the month, 108 miles.

SEVENTEENTH ARMY CORPS.*

First Division.

October 31, division encamped at Cave Spring, Ala. General Sprague was relieved of command by Maj. Gen. Joseph A. Mower. Marched October 31 at 7 a. m. with Army of the Tennessee toward Marietta, Ga.

November 1.—Encamped at night at Cedartown.

November 2.—Encamped at night at Van Wert.

November 3.—Encamped at night at Dallas.

November 4.—Encamped at night at Lost Mountain.

November 5.—Arrived at Marietta, Ga. Remained in camp at Smyrna Camp-Ground, near Marietta, until the 13th, the troops being paid up to August 31 and fully equipped for a winter campaign.

November 12.—The troops were engaged in destroying railroad near Marietta, Ga.

November 13.—Marched at 9 a. m. and encamped at White Hall, near Atlanta.

November 14.—In camp.

November 15.—Marched at 8.30 a. m. on the McDonough road, encamping at Cotton Indian Creek.

November 16.—Marched and encamped on farm of Mr. Walker. two miles north of McDonough.

November 17.—Encamped at Jackson.

November 18.—Crossed Ocmulgee River.

November 19.—Encamped near Hillsborough.

November 20 to 22.—Marched to Gordon, and troops destroyed several miles of the Milledgeville railroad.

November 23.—In camp. At night troops destroyed railroad.

November 24.—Marched at 7 a. m. on the Jackson Ferry road; marched ten miles and destroyed railroad.

November 25.—In camp at Toomsborough.

November 26.—Crossed the Oconee River after dark and encamped on the eastern side.

November 27.—Encamped at ———.

November 28.—Encamped at New Hope Church.

November 29.—Encamped at ———.

November 30.—Crossed the Ogeechee River.

December 1 found this division on east side of the Ogeechee River, having crossed the previous day; marched six miles, troops being engaged in destroying railroad, and encamped on Jones' plantation.

December 2.—Marched twelve miles to Millen (Station No. 8), Georgia Central Railroad, and encamped, having torn up railroad.

December 3.—Marched ten miles to Station No. 7 and encamped.

December 4.—Marched seventeen miles.

December 5.—Marched eight miles; crossed Little Ogeechee River and encamped at Station No. 4½.

December 6.—Troops were engaged in destroying railroad.

December 7.—Marched thirteen miles over bad roads and encamped late in the night.

December 8.—Marched nine miles and encamped near Station No. 2.

December 9.—Marched ten miles; had some skirmishing and artillery-firing, there being several killed and wounded to-day; several torpedoes exploded among our division; encamped at Pooler (Station No. 1).

---

* Commanded by Maj. Gen. Frank P. Blair, jr.

December 10.—Moved about five miles, skirmishing some; fortified in the night.

December 11.—Moved to right, being relieved by Fourteenth Corps.

December 12.—Moved all day and night, encamping near Anderson's plantation; Second Brigade went to Dillon's Bridge.

December 13 to 15.—Lay in camp.

December 16.—In obedience to orders, the division broke camp and marched to King's Bridge and encamped.

December 17.—Marched twenty miles (having no rations); encamped at Midway Church.

December 18.—Destroyed eighteen miles of the Atlantic and Gulf Railroad, including trestle and portions of bridge across the Altamaha River.

December 19.—Continued destroying railroad.

December 20.—Marched back to Midway Church, twenty miles.

December 21.—Reached former camp near Anderson's plantation, having marched twenty miles. Savannah evacuated by the rebels last night and occupied by our army this morning.

December 22.—Removed camp one mile and a half toward the city.

December 23.—In camp.

December 24.—Moved through Savannah to three miles east of city.

December 25 and 26.—In camp.

December 27.—Moved headquarters one mile, to Thunderbolt.

December 28.—Contemplated review postponed on account of rain.

December 29.—General Sherman reviewed Seventeenth Army Corps.

December 30 and 31.—In camp.

The Second Brigade, for the balance of the month after the 12th, was at Dillon's Bridge.

Second Brigade, First Division.

December 1.—The brigade was encamped on the east bank of the Ogeechee, at Station No. 9½, on the Georgia Central Railroad; at 7 a. m. began destruction of railroad and destroyed three miles and a half; went into camp about 2 p. m., having marched six miles.

December 2.—Marched at 7 a. m. and reached Buck Head (or Deep) Creek, at 1 p. m., which we immediately crossed and encamped at Millen.

December 3.—Destroyed railroad south from Millen more thorough and devilish than was ever dreamed of.

December 4.—Marched at 8 a. m.; heard some cannonading in rear about 10 a. m.

December 5.—Marched at 7 a. m., the Second Brigade in the advance, reaching the Little Ogeechee at 12 m.; found the enemy disputing our passage. He was soon dislodged by the Thirty-fifth New Jersey Volunteers and Forty-third Ohio Veteran Volunteers crossing as skirmishers, we encamping east of the stream. The enemy had thrown up works.

December 6.—Destroyed railroad all day, remaining in same camp as yesterday.

December 7.—Marched about 9 a. m., the Second Brigade in rear of trains. Continued march all night over miserable roads through quicksand bottoms.

December 8.—Marched at 9 a. m. and encamped about 10 p. m. twenty-one miles from Savannah, on the farm of Mr. Hines, a rebel quartermaster.

December 9.—Marched at 7 a. m., the Second Brigade in advance; struck the enemy about 10 a. m.; flanked him out of his position and drove him to within ten miles of Savannah, losing some men by the explosion of torpedoes, &c.

December 10.—Marched at 9 a. m. and went into position south of the Ogeechee Canal about noon, losing a few men, having had some sharp skirmishing.

December 11.—Artillery practice and skirmishing to-day; were relieved by the Fourteenth Army Corps after dark, and encamped about three miles in rear.

December 12.—Marched at 7 a. m. toward the right, crossing the Ogeechee Canal late in the p. m., and went into camp near Dillon's Bridge about sunset, with orders to hold the ground between the Great and Little Ogeechee. Remained in camp until date [December 31].

December 19.—Brigade headquarters, with Twenty-fifth Wisconsin and Forty-third Ohio, were moved to King's Bridge by order from Major-General Blair, but returned same day by order of Major-General Sherman.

December 31.—Mustered for pay.

Third Division.

November 1.—Marched from Cave Spring to Cedartown.

November 2.—Marched to Van Wert.

November 3.—Marched to Dallas.

November 4.—Marched to Lost Mountain.

November 5.—Marched to Smyrna Camp-Ground, remaining there until the 13th, destroying four miles of railroad on the 12th.

November 13.—Marched to Atlanta.

November 14.—Remained at Atlanta, loading supplies.

November 15.—Started south, marching to Stockbridge.

November 16.—Marched to near McDonough.

November 17.—Marched to near Jackson.

November 18.—Crossed the Ocmulgee River at Planters' Ferry and bivouacked two miles and a half beyond on Monticello road.

November 19.—Marched to near Hillsborough.

November 20.—Marched to Blountsville.

November 21.—Marched to William Whitley's plantation.

November 22.—Marched to Gordon.

November 23.—Marched to Station No. 16, Georgia Central Railroad.

November 24.—Marched to Station No. 15 (Toomsborough).

November 25.—Marched to Oconee River.

November 26.—Crossed the Oconee to near Station No. 14.

November 27.—Marched to Irwin's Cross-Roads.

November 28.—Marched to New Hope Church.

November 29.—Marched to Mrs. Hauver's plantation, on the old Savannah road.

November 30.—Marched to Station No. 9½, crossing the Ogeechee River.

Number of miles marched, 290; number of miles of railroad destroyed, 22.

December 1.—Moved from Station No. 9½ to near Station No. 9; six miles.

December 2.—Moved to Millen; ten miles.

December 3.—Moved to Station No. 7, or Scarborough Post-Office; ten miles.

December 4.—Moved to Station No. 5½, or Cameron Post-Office; fifteen miles.

December 5.—Moved to Little Ogeechee; ten miles.

December 6.—Laid in camp.

December 7.—Moved to Station No. 3; fifteen miles.

December 8.—Moved to Station No. 2; eleven miles.

December 9.—Moved to Pooler (Station No. 1); ten miles.

December 10.—Moved to enemy's works around Savannah, six miles, and took up position.

December 11.—Moved to the right two miles.

December 12.—Moved farther to the right by a rear and roundabout road; marched twelve miles; took up a position and fortified.

December 13 to 20, inclusive.—Constructed forts and earth-works; also boats and portable bridges with which to cross the rice swamp in front of the enemy's works and make a charge, if possible. Sharp-shooting constantly, and occasionally enlivening the Georgia militia with an artillery duel.

December 21.—At 4 a. m. discovered the enemy were evacuating and pushed for Savannah, Ga., eight miles distant, reaching that place at 6 a. m.

December 22 to 31, inclusive.—Remained in camp.

Total distance marched in month, 115 miles. Aggregate of marches in year: On foot, 1,561 miles; on steam-boat, 1,400 miles; on railroad, 1,200 miles; total, 4,161 miles.

Second Brigade, Third Division.

November 13.—This command left Camp Smyrna, Ga., forming part of the army under General Sherman, and took part in the move through the State of Georgia, destroying railroads, &c.; met with little resistance from the enemy.

[*December.*]—During the past month this command has been on the move until the 10th of the month, at which date it arrived before Savannah, on the Augusta road.

December 11.—Were ordered to take position before the city on the Darien road, which position the command occupied until the surrender of the city, December 21.

During the remainder of the month the command was encamped at Fort No. 3, Savannah, Ga., furnishing regular picket and fatigue parties.

Fourth Division.

November 1.—The division marched on or about this date from Cave Spring with the Army of the Tennessee; arrived at Smyrna Camp-Ground, near Marietta, Ga.

November 6.—Moved to Marietta, Ga. Arriving at that place the Second Brigade, that had been on duty in that vicinity during the summer, joined the division and were consolidated with the First and Third Brigades. We remained at Marietta reorganizing and preparing for the campaign through Georgia until the 13th, when we moved toward Atlanta.

November 14.—Arrived at Atlanta.

November 15.—Started with the army on expedition to Savannah.

November 29.—Arrived at the Ogeechee, and crossed the river opposite Station No. 9½ on the following morning.

December 1.—The division moved from near Station No. 9½, on the Georgia Central Railroad, and continued the march with Major-General Sherman's army toward Savannah, Ga.

December 10.—Drove the enemy in front from two advanced lines of defense across a swamp and into their main line of works, three miles from the city, losing 6 killed and 11 wounded.

December 11.—Changed position to the right.

December 21.—Marched into the city of Savannah; are now [December 31] encamped near the city.

Third Brigade, Fourth Division.

November 1.—Left Cave Spring, and, marching via Cedartown, Van Wert, Dallas, Lost Mountain Post-Office, and Smyrna Camp-Ground, went into camp at Marietta on the 6th; distance marched, sixty-two miles and a half.

November 12.—Marched to Big Shanty, destroying railroad one mile and a half south of it, returning to Marietta that evening; distance, eight miles.

November 13.—Left Marietta, and marched, via Proctor's Creek, Atlanta, Tar Creek, Catawba Creek, Ocmulgee Mills, Monticello, Hillsborough, Gordon Station, Irwinton, and Toomsborough, to within three miles of the M. and A. Railroad bridge over the Oconee River.

November 23.—Went into bivouac; distance, 154 miles.

November 25.—Marched to railroad bridge and skirmished with the enemy; withdrew in the forenoon, and marched, via Toomsborough, to within three miles of Ball's Ferry; distance, fourteen miles.

November 26.—Crossed Ball's Ferry, and marching near Louisville encamped near Ogeechee River; distance, fifty-one miles.

Total distance marched, 289½ miles.

December 1.—Moved from bivouac near Ogeechee River.

December 2 to 4.—Marched to Burton and Millen.

December 5.—Arrived at Ogeechee Church, near Station No. 5½, on Savannah and Augusta Railroad; distance marched, sixty-seven miles and a half; destroyed six miles and a half of the Savannah and Augusta Railroad.

December 7 to 10.—Marched forty-one miles and a half, going into position within two miles and three-quarters of Savannah on the 10th.

December 11.—Being relieved by part of the Fourteenth Army Corps, withdrew and moved to King's Bridge, on Ogeechee Canal; distance marched, four miles.

December 12.—Marched six miles to plank road.

December 13 to 15, inclusive.—In camp.

December 16.—Moved to King's Bridge, on Ogeechee River; distance marched, five miles.

December 17 and 18.—Remained in camp, a portion of the command being engaged in building a wharf on the Ogeechee.

December 19.—Moved nine miles to Lawton's.

December 20.—Had continued skirmishing with the enemy.

December 21.—The enemy having evacuated their position during the night previous, moved into Savannah in the forenoon, and have since been encamped in the outskirts of the city; distance marched on the 21st, seven miles.

Total distance marched during the month, 140 miles.

Capt. E. C. Lawson, Company C, Thirty-second Illinois Volunteers, wounded in groin severely.

*LEFT WING.**

FOURTEENTH ARMY CORPS.†

November 1.—The corps was stationed at Rome, Ga.
November 2.—Marched to Kingston, where preparations for a winter campaign were made.
November 11.—Communication north was given up and the movement south commenced.
November 15.—The corps arrived at Atlanta.
November 16.—Left Atlanta and passed through Decatur.
November 17 to 22.—The march was continued.
November 23.—The corps arrived at Milledgeville.
November 25.—Crossed the Oconee, moving for Sandersville.
November 26.—Arrived at Sandersville.
November 27.—Marched for Louisville.
November 29.—Reached Louisville, at which place the corps remained until December 1.
December 1.—The corps moved from Louisville, the First and Second Divisions on a road running toward Savannah, and the Third Division, in support of Kilpatrick's cavalry, toward Waynesborough. The First and Second Divisions crossed the Augusta railroad at Lumpkin's Station, the Third crossing five miles to the left. The track of the road was thoroughly destroyed to a considerable distance at these points. The Third Division continued moving with Kilpatrick's cavalry, operating on the left flank, until the 5th, arriving on that day at Jacksonborough, near which place the other two divisions arrived and encamped.
December 6.—Continued the march, the whole corps on the Savannah road, until the 11th, when the corps moved forward, following the Twentieth Corps, to a position in front of the enemy's works near Savannah, and formed on the left of the Twentieth Corps, in which position it remained until the evacuation of Savannah, considerable firing being kept up during the time by the artillery and skirmishers.
December 22.—The corps moved to within two miles and a half of Savannah, and remained in camp at this point during the remainder of the month.

First Division.

November 1.—Encamped near Rome, Ga.
November 2.—Marched fifteen miles to Kingston.
November 3.—No change until 11th.
November 11.—Marched eleven miles to Cartersville.
November 13.—Marched to Big Shanty, destroying railroad.
November 14.—Marched to Chattahoochee River.
November 15.—Entered Atlanta.
November 16.—Marched to Lithonia; fifteen miles.
November 17.—Marched to Yellow River; seventeen miles.
November 18.—Marched to Covington; eight miles.
November 19.—Marched toward Shady Dale; twelve miles.
November 20.—Marched to Sparks' house; fifteen miles.
November 21.—Marched six miles.
November 22.—Moved toward Milledgeville; twelve miles.
November 23.—Marched to Milledgeville; eleven miles.

---

* Commanded by Maj. Gen. Henry W. Slocum.
† Commanded by Bvt. Maj. Gen. Jefferson C. Davis.

November 24.—Crossed Oconee River and encamped on Town Creek; ten miles.

November 25.—No changes.

November 26.—Marched ten miles, crossing Buffalo Creek Swamp, to Keg Creek.

November 27.—Marched through Sandersville toward Davisborough; eighteen miles.

November 28.—Passed Davisborough at noon; fourteen miles.

November 29.—Passed through Louisville; three miles.

November 30.—Marched seventeen miles to Mill Creek.

December 1.—On the march from Atlanta to Savannah. The march was continued daily until the 11th.

December 11.—The division was formed on the right of the Second Division, Fourteenth Army Corps, relieving two divisions of the Seventeenth Army Corps, which had thrown up works.

December 12.—The battery opened fire on the enemy's lines about 800 yards distant and continued firing daily. The firing was also kept up steadily on the picket-lines. No changes of importance were made in the lines until the 21st, when two regiments of the Third Brigade entered Savannah and returned to camp the same day.

December 22.—The division marched three miles and encamped near the city, where the troops remain at this date [December 31].

Total distance marched, 125 miles.

Second Brigade, First Division.

November 15.—The Second Brigade was organized at Atlanta, Ga., in obedience to Special Orders, No. 16, from headquarters First Division, Fourteenth Army Corps, and J. H. Brigham, lieutenant-colonel Sixty-ninth Ohio Veteran Volunteer Infantry, placed in command.

November 16.—It left Atlanta, and up to the present time [November 30] marched about 200 miles, passing in its route through Decatur, Lithonia, Conyers, Covington, Sandersville, and Louisville. During the march the brigade was not in any engagement. The general health of the men has been good, only three having died up to the present time.

[*December.*]—During the month the brigade, in conjunction with the Army of Georgia, under General Sherman, marched from the vicinity of Louisville, passing through Sebastopol and Nasworthy, crossing Buck Head Creek, and striking the railroad at Lumpkin's Station, effectually destroying it. From this point the march was continued.

December 4.—Crossed Ebenezer Creek, passing near the remains of old Fort Greene, marching parallel with the Savannah River until within four miles of the city, when, passing to the right of the Twentieth Corps, the brigade, with the First Division, Fourteenth Army Corps, took up position on the 11th instant on the most advanced portion of the entire line, relieving a portion of the Seventeenth Corps. The enemy was in the immediate front, with strong works and an almost impassable swamp intervening. Cannonading and skirmishing was kept up, resulting in the wounding of Lieutenant Trask, Thirteenth Michigan Veteran Volunteer Infantry, and five enlisted men in the whole brigade.

December 19.—The brigade was relieved by the Third Brigade, First Division, Fourteenth Army Corps.

December 21.—The enemy having evacuated, the city was taken possession of.

December 22.—The Fourteenth Army Corps took up position on the outskirts of the city, where it yet remains, active preparations meanwhile being made for another campaign.

December 27.—The Fourteenth Army Corps was reviewed in the streets of Savannah by General Sherman.

Third Brigade, First Division.

November 2.—The brigade marched with the division from Rome to Kingston, at which place it went into camp, doing regular camp and picket duty until the 12th.

November 12.—Marched with the division in direction of Atlanta.

November 15.—Arrived at Atlanta.

November 16.—Marched with the division in the direction of the Atlantic coast, marching through Lithonia, Covington, Milledgeville, Sandersville, and Louisville.

November 30.—Marched to Sebastopol, Ga., on the line of the Macon and Savannah Railroad, at which place went into camp for the night.

During the month the brigade assisted in destroying the Western and Atlantic, Georgia, and the Savannah and Augusta railroads. Distance marched during the month, 247 miles.

December 1.—Marched from Sebastopol.

December 3.—Arrived at Lumpkin's Station, on Augusta and Savannah Railroad.

December 4.—Were engaged for several hours in tearing up the track and destroying the road, and marched the balance of the day as rear guard to the train, and skirmishing with a small body of rebel cavalry, but with no result.

December 11.—Arrived in front of Savannah and went into line of battle and remained there until the 21st, during which time nothing of note occurred but the regular skirmishing, which was kept up by the pickets.

December 21.—Marched into the city at 8 a. m., where we went into camp and remained the balance of the month, doing regular garrison and picket duty.

Distance marched during the month, 140 miles.

Second Division.

November 1.—Left Rome, Ga., for Kingston, Ga.

November 8.—Marched to Cartersville, Ga.

November 13.—Destroyed eight miles of the Chattanooga and Atlanta Railroad.

November 15.—Arrived at Atlanta, Ga.

November 16.—Marched from Atlanta, Ga., via Covington, Milledgeville, Sandersville, Ga., to Louisville, Ga.

November 26.—Skirmished with the enemy at Sandersville, Ga., and drove him. Loss, 1 enlisted man killed and 1 wounded.

November 30.—Enemy attacked picket-line at Louisville, Ga., in which he was repulsed, and left on the field 2 commissioned officers and 4 enlisted men killed and 1 enlisted man wounded.

Distance marched during the month, 252 miles.

December 1.—Division left Louisville, Ga.; marched to within four miles of Savannah.

December 11.—Went into position for offensive operations; remained so until the 21st.

December 20 and 21.—Enemy evacuated his works at night, retreating across Savannah River. Moved into camp at Savannah, Ga., on the 21st; remained to the end of the month.

Number of miles marched, 121.

First Brigade, Second Division.

November 1.—The brigade left Rome, Ga., and marched toward Atlanta, destroying the railroad as they went.

November 16.—Left Atlanta and marched by way of Decatur, Lithonia, Conyers, Covington, Milledgeville, Sandersville, and Fenn's Bridge to Louisville, Ga.

No engagement with the enemy during the month, except at Sandersville, from which town the rebel cavalry was driven out by skirmishers from this brigade and from the Twentieth Army Corps.

December 1.—Left Louisville, Ga., and marched east to the Savannah River.

December 11.—Arrived in front of Savannah. The brigade was posted near the Milledgeville road, only about 400 yards from the rebel batteries, but being covered by an impenetrable swamp and dense woods, suffered but little.

December 21.—After the evacuation of the place by the rebels moved camp nearer the town.

Third Brigade, Second Division.

December 1 found this brigade on the march to Savannah, Ga., which place it reached on or about the 13th. The brigade was not on the line during the investment of the city, but was held as reserve, furnishing all details for fatigue, forage, &c. When the enemy evacuated the city our camp was moved up to within two miles of the city, where we have remained in inactivity ever since.

Third Division.

November 2.—Division moved from camp near Rome, Ga., and arrived at 3 p. m. at Kingston, where it remained until the 12th.

November 12.—Took up the march for Atlanta, encamping first night three miles from Etowah River.

November 13.—Passed through Allatoona Gap; destroyed the railroad from Allatoona Creek to a point one mile beyond Acworth, and went into camp at Big Shanty.

November 14.—Division crossed the Chattahoochee.

November 15.—Marched through and encamped near the city of Atlanta.

November 16.—Passed through Decatur and marched as far as Snapfinger Creek.

November 17.—From this date the march was continued through Lithonia, Conyers, crossing Yellow River, through Covington, over the Ulcofauhachee, through Shady Dale.

November 23.—Reached the city of Milledgeville in the morning.

November 25.—From this place the division marched in the morning; crossed the Oconee and destroyed the bridge.

November 26.—Arrived at Sandersville.

November 27.—Division started for Louisville, taking the road to Fenn's Bridge, the First and Second Divisions, with all the trains of the corps, following the direct route. Head of column reached Rocky Comfort Creek at 8.30 a. m., but the bridge having been destroyed by the enemy, was unable to cross until in the afternoon. Encamped near Louisville, where the division remained until December 1.

December 1.—At 10 a. m. division moved from camp near Louisville, in company with General Kilpatrick's division of cavalry, and went into camp at 5 p. m. on the bank of Buck Head Creek. During the day considerable skirmishing with the enemy's cavalry, with a loss on our side of 3 killed and 2 wounded.

December 2.—Met the enemy again at Rocky Creek at 10 a. m. posted behind strong barricades and disposed to dispute our crossing at the ford. The Seventy-fourth Indiana charged and dispersed them, and the division marched to the farm of Mr. ——— and went into camp.

December 3.—Arrived at Thomas' Station, on the Savannah and Augusta Railroad, and during the night thoroughly destroyed several miles of railroad track.

December 4.—General Kilpatrick attacked the enemy's cavalry one mile from Thomas' Station and drove them in confusion through Waynesborough and two miles beyond. The division followed up and supported General Kilpatrick during the day, and then made a night march to Alexander.

December 5.—Reached Jacksonborough.

December 6.—Crossed Beaver Dam Creek and joined the other divisions of the corps.

December 7.—Late at night reached Sister's Ferry.

December 8.—Remained in camp during the day and had considerable skirmishing with the advance of the enemy's cavalry. Marched at midnight, and crossed Ebenezer Creek at 3 a. m. of the 9th.

December 10.—Encamped within twelve miles of Savannah, making short marches.

December 13.—Division encamped on the Louisville road, six miles from the city, where it remained until the 22d, at which time (the city having been evacuated on the night of the 20th) it was moved to a position still occupied half a mile from the town.

December 27.—Corps reviewed by Major-General Sherman.

First Brigade, Third Division.

November 1.—Brigade remained in camp near Rome, Ga.

November 2.—At 6 a. m. crossed the Etowah River, passing through Rome, marching on Kingston and Rome road; encamped for the night near Kingston.

November 3 to 11.—Remained in camp.

November 12.—Marched at 8 a. m. on Kingston and Marietta road, passing through Cartersville; encamped near Allatoona.

November 13.—Marched at 6.30 a. m., passing through Allatoona; encamped near Big Shanty.

November 14.—Marched at 8 a. m., passing through Marietta; crossed the Chattahoochee River at Turner's Ferry.

November 15.—Marched at 6 a. m.; arriving at Atlanta, encamped for the night.

November 16.—Marched at 11 a. m. to near Little Pine Mountain.

November 17.—Marched at 6 a. m., passing through Lithonia and Conyers, and tearing up one mile and three-quarters of railroad; encamped near Yellow River.

November 18.—At 10 a. m. marched through Covington; encamped for the night one mile south of Covington.

November 19.—Marched at 6.30 a. m., passing through Sandtown; encamped for the night four miles south of Sandtown.

November 20.—Marched at 6.30 a. m. on Covington and Eatonton road.

November 21.—Marched at 6 a. m., passing through Shady Dale; encamped for the night.

November 22.—Marched at 8 a. m.; encamped for the night on Howell Cobb's farm.

November 23.—Marched at 6 a. m.; arriving at Milledgeville, encamped for the night.

November 24.—Remained in position.

November 25.—Marched at 6 a. m., crossing the Oconee River and marching on the Milledgeville and Sandersville road; encamped on Giles' farm.

November 26.—Marched at 6 a. m. on Milledgeville and Sandersville road, passing through Sandersville, and encamped for the night.

November 27.—Marched at 6 a. m. on Fenn's Bridge road, and crossing the Ogeechee, encamped six miles southwest of Louisville.

November 28.—Marched at 6 a. m., building a bridge and crossing Rocky Comfort Creek; passed through Louisville and encamped for the night.

November 29.—Marched at 9 a. m. and took position across Little Rocky Comfort Creek, relieving a brigade of cavalry.

November 30.—Remained in position.

December 1.—Brigade marched on Waynesborough road; arriving at Buck Head Creek, encamped for the night.

December 2.—Marched at 6 a. m. on Waynesborough road five miles, turning south on Savannah road three miles; encamped for the night.

December 3.—Marched at 6 a. m. on Savannah road; turned east on by-road, marching to Thomas' Station, on Augusta and Savannah Railroad; halted for the night, tearing up one mile and three-quarters of road.

December 4.—Supported General Kilpatrick's cavalry in an engagement with rebel General Wheeler's cavalry, driving them beyond Waynesborough; marched from Waynesborough, on Augusta and Savannah Railroad, passing through Alexander; encamped for the night two miles south.

December 5.—Marched same course and road, encamping for the night on Beaver Dam Creek.

December 6.—Marched on same road all night.

December 7.—Formed line of battle; skirmished with the enemy all day.

December 8.—At 1 a. m. withdrew across Sister's Ferry bridge, on Little Ebenezer Creek. At 11 a. m. marched on by-road intersecting Augusta and Savannah road, eighteen miles northwest of Savannah; encamped for the night.

December 9.—Marched on Augusta and Savannah road and took position at Eleven-Mile Post to guard the rear against cavalry.

December 10.—Remained in position.

December 11.—Moved on by-road to Louisville road; took position to guard rear.

December 12 to 21.—Remained in position.

December 20.—The Twenty-third Missouri Volunteer Infantry was detached on fatigue duty at King's Bridge.

December 22.—Marched to within ten miles of Savannah, encamping along Louisville road.

December 23 to 26.—Remained in position.

December 27.—Was reviewed in the streets of Savannah by Major-General Sherman, with balance of Fourteenth Army Corps.

December 28 and 29.—Remained in camp.

December 30.—Moved to Savannah, temporarily relieving Twentieth Corps while on review.

December 31.—Remained in camp.

Second Brigade, Third Division.

November 1.—Encamped at Rome, Ga.

November 2.—Marched to Kingston, Ga., where the brigade lay until the 12th.

November 12.—Marched toward Atlanta.

November 13.—Destroyed railroad and marched to Big Shanty.

November 15.—Reached Atlanta.

November 16.—Marched fifteen miles, passing through Decatur, Ga.

November 17.—Destroyed railroad and encamped near Conyers, Ga., on Augusta and Savannah Railroad.

November 18.—Marched to Covington, Ga.

November 19.—Marched fifteen miles; encamped near Sandtown, Ga.

November 20 to 22.—On the march.

November 23.—Reached Milledgeville, Ga.

November 25.—Marched at daylight; made seventeen miles.

November 26.—Had bad roads through swamps; encamped at Sandersville.

November 27.—Marched eighteen miles, crossing Ogeechee River at Fenn's Bridge.

November 28.—Reached Louisville, Ga.; remained until the close of the month.

Third Brigade, Third Division.

November 1 found this brigade on the march toward Atlanta, Ga., which place it reached on the 15th.

November 16.—Started with the rest of the army to Savannah, Ga.

TWENTIETH ARMY CORPS.*

[*November.*]—The corps remained in Atlanta until the 15th.

November 11.—The Army of Georgia having been organized, Major-General Slocum assumed command of the Left Wing, Brig. Gen. A. S. Williams assumed command of the corps, Brig. Gen. N. J. Jackson assumed command of the First Division.

November 15.—The corps left Atlanta and marched to Stone Mountain.

November 16.—Marched to Yellow River.

November 17.—Marched toward Madison, encamping on Flat Creek.

November 18.—Encamped four miles west of Madison.

November 19.—The Second Division, with one battery, detached from the corps and sent to destroy the railroad from Madison to the Oconee River. The First and Third Divisions marched to Madison, encamping five miles southeast of it.

*Commanded by Brig. Gen. Alpheus S. Williams.

November 20.—The First and Third Divisions marched toward Eatonton, encamping three miles north of it.

November 21.—The First and Third Divisions marched through Eatonton toward Milledgeville, encamping near Dennis Station, on the Eatonton and Milledgeville Railroad.

November 22.—Marched to Milledgeville. The Second Division rejoined the corps, having destroyed the railroad from Madison to Oconee River and the bridge at the river.

November 23.—Corps remained at Milledgeville.

November 24.—Corps marched toward Hebron, encamping near Gum Creek.

November 25.—Marched toward Sandersville, encamping two miles from the town; skirmished with the enemy.

November 26.—Marched to Sandersville; slight skirmishing. The Third Division remained there to guard the trains and artillery. The First and Second Divisions marched to Tennille Station, on the Georgia Central Railroad.

November 27.—The Third Division marched with the train and artillery to Davisborough. The Second Division destroyed the railroad from Tennille Station to within six miles of Davisborough, encamping at the latter place, the First Division on south side of railroad to Davisborough.

November 28.—All the wagon train and artillery of the corps, escorted by the Third Division, marched to Louisville. The First Division destroyed the railroad from Davisborough to Spiers Station, encamping at that place. The Second Division destroyed railroad west of Davisborough; returning, encamped at that place.

November 29.—The First and Second Divisions destroyed the railroad to the Ogeechee River and the railroad bridge there; the Third Division at Louisville.

November 30.—The First and Second Division crossed the Ogeechee River and encamped with the balance of the corps near Louisville.

Casualties, 144.

[*December.*]—During the month the march from Atlanta to Savannah was completed. The daily marches were as follows:

December 1.—Marched from Louisville, Ga., through Birdville; encamped on Bark Camp Creek.

December 2.—Marched to Buck Head Church.

December 3.—Marched toward Sylvania, crossing the Augusta and Millen railroad; destroyed five miles of track; encamped on Horse Creek.

December 4.—Marched to the Little Ogeechee River.

December 5.—Moved forward about five miles on the road to Springfield.

December 6.—Marched to Turkey Creek.

December 7.—Marched to Springfield.

December 8.—Marched toward Monteith. The First and Second Divisions marched thirteen miles. The Third Division, with the corps trains, marched six miles.

December 9.—Marched to Monteith plantation. The Third Division and trains closed up. The enemy at this place, having obstructed the road across a wide swamp and having infantry and artillery in intrenchments on the opposite side, disputed the crossing. They were driven away by a portion of the First Division and their work occupied by us.

December 10.—Marched on the Savannah and Augusta road; found the enemy's intrenched line crossing the road near the Four-Mile Post. After reconnoitering the corps took position in front of the enemy—the left on Savannah River, the right on Georgia Central Railroad. Remained in this position until the 21st, when, the enemy having evacuated, the corps took possession of the city. A small steamer (Ida) was captured in the Savannah River and burned on the 10th.

December 12.—The steamer Resolute was captured.

December 19.—The Second Brigade, First Division, was sent across the river to the South Carolina side, returning upon the occupation of the city. Upon taking possession of the city Brigadier-General Geary was detailed as post commander and the Second Division as guards and patrols. The First and Third Divisions placed in position on west side of city, occupying a line from Savannah River to Georgia Central Railroad.

Positions unchanged at the end of the month. Casualties, 114.

First Division.

[*November.*]—The division remained in camp about Atlanta until the morning of the 15th.

November 10.—An order was received from Major-General Slocum, who had been placed in command of the Left Wing, Army of Georgia, assigning Brig. Gen. A. S. Williams to the command of the Twentieth Corps.

November 11.—Brig. Gen. N. J. Jackson, who had been ordered to report for duty to General Williams, was by him assigned to the temporary command of the First Division, Twentieth Corps.

November 15.—At 7.30 a. m. the division marched out of Atlanta on the Decatur road; passed to the right of Stone Mountain, near which place the Third Brigade destroyed several miles of the Augusta railroad; passed through Social Circle and Madison, and at the latter place took a southeasterly direction, leaving the Augusta railroad and passing through Eatonton; crossed Little River and reached Milledgeville, the capital of Georgia, on the afternoon of the 22d. Remained near the city for one day.

November 24.—Marched in the morning toward Ogeechee River; skirmished with the enemy's cavalry while entering Sandersville.

November 26.—In the afternoon the division struck the Georgia Central Railroad at Tennille Station (No. 13), from which point the division, in connection with the Second Division (General Geary's), tore up the railroad to the Ogeechee River nearly forty miles.

November 30.—Crossed the Ogeechee River in the afternoon four miles south of Louisville.

December 1.—The division was in camp near Louisville, Ga., and at noon resumed the march toward Savannah.

December 2.—Passed through Birdville.

December 3.—Crossed the Waynesborough railroad three miles north of Millen.

December 8.—Passed through Springfield.

December 9.—Came upon a force of the enemy occupying two redoubts, with one piece of artillery commanding the road. While Colonel Selfridge (commanding the First Brigade) occupied the attention of the enemy in front, the Second Brigade (Colonel Carman's) was sent to the enemy's left to get to his rear, if possible, and the Third Brigade (Colonel Robinson's) to his right. Owing to the difficult nature of the ground the Second Brigade did not succeed in reaching the desired position before the movement of the Third Brigade compelled the enemy to evacuate his position.

December 10.—Came upon the enemy, posted in a line of strong works covering the city of Savannah, about four miles from the city. Took position before the enemy's works and remained in position until the 21st, during which time the Second Brigade (Colonel Carman's) was sent to the South Carolina shore.

December 21.—The city was found to have been evacuated by the enemy. The division was brought to the city on the 21st and 22d, its right resting on the Savannah River, and remained in that position during the remainder of the month.

First Brigade, First Division.

[*November.*]—This brigade was encamped near Atlanta, Ga., until the 15th, when it broke camp and marched via Decatur, Madison, and Milledgeville, and reached the vicinity of Louisville on the 30th. On the route the brigade tore up and burned railroad tracks, &c., and subsisted chiefly on the country.

December 1.—Started from Louisville, Ga., and joined the Third Division of this corps, guarding train of that division until the 3d, when the brigade joined the First Division of this corps.

December 9.—Nothing of note occurred up to this date. When about thirteen miles northwest of Savannah, this brigade having the lead, we came to a portion of the road which was completely obstructed by slashed timber, at the end of which the enemy was fortified. The Fifth Connecticut Veteran Volunteers was deployed as skirmishers, supported by the remaining three regiments of this brigade, and, in conjunction with the Second and Third Brigades of this division, drove the enemy from their works, capturing a few prisoners. Three men of the Forty-sixth Pennsylvania Veteran Volunteers were wounded.

December 10.—Marched about nine miles and encamped about four miles from Savannah, where the enemy was strongly fortified. The brigade connected on the left with General Geary's division and on the right with the Third Brigade of this division. Here we remained until the 21st, when it was discovered that the enemy had evacuated. The brigade moved within a mile of the city to its present encampment.

During the whole campaign the brigade subsisted chiefly on the country, destroyed 20 miles of railroad, 73 bales of cotton, 5 cotton gins, picked up about 100 negroes and 40 horses and mules.

Second Brigade, First Division.

November 1.—The brigade still doing duty in Atlanta.

November 15.—Left Atlanta on campaign through Georgia, the Twentieth and Fourteenth Corps forming Left Wing, Army of Georgia; passed through Decatur and Stone Mountain.

November 18.—Marched through Social Circle.

November 19.—Marched through Madison.

November 21.—Marched through Eatonton.

November 22.—Marched through Milledgeville.

November 24.—Crossed Bluff Creek.

November 25.—Crossed Buffalo Creek.

November 26.—Skirmished all day and entered Sandersville; struck the Savannah and Macon Railroad at Station No. 13. Destroyed the railroad until the 30th, when we crossed the Ogeechee and encamped four miles south of Louisville, Ga.

December 1.—Left camp near Louisville, Ga., marching through Birdville, Springfield, and Monteith.

December 10.—Arrived in front of the enemy's works.

December 16.—Moved over to Argyle Island, in the Savannah River, and from there on the South Carolina shore; some skirmishing.

December 22.—Recrossed the river and encamped near the city, it having been evacuated by the enemy.

Third Brigade, First Division.

November 1 to 4.—The brigade remained encamped near Atlanta, Ga.; active preparations made for a campaign; the troops clothed and partially paid; surplus baggage sent to the rear.

November 5.—The brigade ordered to march at 1 p. m; moved out on the McDonough road three miles and encamped at 7 p. m.

November 6.—Marched back to the old camp near Atlanta, Ga., at 1 p. m.

November 7.—The transportation of the brigade inspected.

November 8.—Presidential election held in the Sixty-first and Eighty-second Ohio Veteran, Thirty-first Wisconsin, and One hundred and forty-third New York Volunteers.

November 9.—A detachment of rebel cavalry and artillery, under Iverson, attacked the city at daybreak. The brigade ordered to move out White Hall street to the support of Geary's division. He withdrew before the troops arrived in position, and the brigade returned to its encampment.

November 10 to 13, inclusive.—Preparations for the campaign continued; railroad and other public property in Atlanta destroyed.

November 14.—Brigade ordered to march.

November 15.—Marched at 7 a. m. on the Decatur road. The brigade took in charge the train of the division. During the afternoon encamped near Stone Mountain.

November 16.—Commenced destroying the Georgia Railroad at 7 a. m. Destroyed about two miles of the track by 10 a. m. Marched at 5 p. m. as rear guard of the corps; crossed Stone Mountain Creek at 10.30 and Yellow River at 11.30 p. m.; encamped on left bank of Yellow River.

November 17.—Marched at 12 m. as rear guard; crossed No Business Creek at 1 p. m., Big Haynes Creek at 5 p. m., and Little Haynes at 7 p. m.; passed Sheffield Post-Office at dusk; encamped near Flat Creek one hour after midnight.

November 18.—Marched as rear guard at 8 a. m.; crossed Flat Creek at 10 a. m. and Ulcofauhachee River at 11.30 a. m.; reached Social Circle, on the Georgia Railroad, at 1.30 p. m.; marched from Social Circle at 3 p. m., following the railroad eastward; passed Rutledge at 8 p. m., and encamped five miles west of Madison one hour after midnight.

November 19.—Marched as rear guard of the corps at 7.45 a. m.; passed through Madison at 10 a. m.; marched southward on Eatonton road and encamped at 12 m.

November 20.—Marched at 7.15 a. m; crossed Sugar Creek at 11.30 a. m., and Clark's Fork at 1 p. m.; encamped four miles and a half north of Eatonton at 7 p. m.

November 21.—Weather wet and foggy and roads heavy. Trains commenced moving at 6 a. m.; brigade formed rear guard; rebel cavalry followed closely and encountered the Sixty-first Ohio Veteran Volunteers in rear of the column at 1 p. m; passed through Eatonton at 4 p. m.; trains much impeded by the mud and helped along by the troops; encamped at 11 p. m.

November 22.—Marched at 7.15 a. m., covering rear of the division; crossed Little River at 12.30 p. m.; reached Milledgeville at 7.30 p. m.; crossed the Oconee River and encamped on left bank at 9 p. m.

November 23.—Remained encamped near Oconee River bridge, foraging parties bringing in considerable quantities of supplies.

November 24.—Marched as vanguard at 6 a. m. on the road leading down the left bank of the Oconee; crossed Beaver River at 11 a. m. and Town Creek at 12.15 p. m.; crossed Gum Creek and encamped at 4.30 p. m.

November 25.—Marched as vanguard at 6 a. m.; crossed Bluff Creek at 7 o'clock and reached Hebron at 8 a. m. The column was delayed at this point until 2 p. m. by the destruction of nine bridges by the enemy; march resumed, the advance guard driving before it the rebel cavalry. Advanced three miles, when the enemy, under Wheeler, made a stand, driving back our cavalry; brigade formed line and threw forward skirmishers. The skirmish line advanced directly upon the enemy and drove him precipitately about one mile beyond his position; brigade encamped at 5.30 p. m.

November 26.—Marched at 6.15 a. m. on the road leading to Sandersville; entered Sandersville at 11 a. m.; marched on the road to Tennille Station at 2 p. m.; reached Tennille and commenced destroying railroad at 3.30 p. m.; destroyed one mile of track; encamped at Tennille at 5.30 p. m.

November 27.—Marched at 7.30 a. m. on the Davisborough road; crossed Williamson's Swamp Creek and encamped near Davisborough at 5 p. m.

November 28.—Marched at daybreak, following the railroad, which the troops destroyed as they advanced; encamped at Spiers Turnout at night-fall.

November 29.—Destroyed about one mile of the railroad at 7 a. m.; marched from Spiers at 11 a. m.; crossed Great Coat Creek at 12.30 o'clock and Boggy Girt Creek at 3.30 p. m.; encamped near the Ogeechee River at night-fall.

November 30.—Marched at 8.30 a. m.; crossed Mill Creek at 1 p. m.; crossed the Ogeechee two miles below Louisville at 4.30 p. m.; encamped two miles beyond the river at 5.30 p. m.

December 1.—At this date the brigade was in the midst of the campaign against Savannah from Atlanta, Ga. On the day previous (November 30) it had crossed the Ogeechee River and encamped on the left bank near Louisville. From this point it marched at 12 m., in charge of the First Division trains; line of march on the Birdville road; crossed Big, Dry, Spring, and Bark Camp Creeks, and encamped at 12.30 a. m.; distance marched, twelve miles.

December 2.—Marched at 6 a. m. on the road to Millen; crossed Buck Head Creek at 8 p. m. and encamped at Buck Head Church; marched fourteen miles.

December 3.—Marched at 7 a. m.; crossed Augusta Branch of Georgia Central Railroad near Millen at 12 m.; encamped near Horse Creek at 4.45 p. m.; distance marched, fifteen miles.

December 4.—Marched at 9 a. m.; brigade had in charge the division train, the pontoon train, the corps supply train, and the artillery ammunition train; crossed Little Ogeechee River at 5 p. m. and encamped; distance marched, twelve miles.

December 5.—Marched at 3 p. m.; column greatly retarded by bad roads; encamped at 10 p. m.; distance marched, three miles and a half.

December 6.—Marched at 9.30 a. m. as rear guard to the corps; line of march on the Springfield road; encamped at 9 p. m.; distance marched, thirteen miles.

December 7.—Marched at 8 a. m. in charge of division and cavalry trains; crossed Cowpens Branch Swamp by 1.30 p. m.; encamped one mile above Springfield at 10 p. m.; distance marched, fifteen miles.

December 8.—Marched at 8 a. m.; crossed Jack's Creek and entered Springfield at 10 a. m.; encamped at 5.30 p. m.; marched seventeen miles.

December 9.—Marched at 8.30 a. m. on the road to Monteith; skirmishing and artillery firing soon began at the front; found the enemy in position with artillery at Monteith Swamp at 3.15 p. m. Two regiments of the brigade—the Thirty-first Wisconsin and Sixty-first Ohio Veteran Volunteers—sent to the left to cross the swamp and turn the enemy's right; movement was successful, compelling the enemy to hastily withdraw, evacuating two fine redoubts. Brigade encamped near the captured redoubts at 7 p. m. Distance marched, nine miles.

December 10.—Marched at 7 a. m; struck the Charleston and Savannah Railroad at Monteith Station at 10 a. m.; destroyed one mile of track and resumed the march toward Savannah; came up to the enemy's works, three miles and a quarter from the city, at 2.30 p. m.; brigade went into position in center of division one mile from the Savannah River and encamped; distance marched, ten miles.

December 11.—The brigade shifted its position 400 yards forward and to the left at 4 p. m. and again encamped. Three regiments sent to the rear to guard trains at 11 p. m.

December 12.—No change of position.

December 13.—The remaining three regiments moved to the rear to guard the corps trains. Brigade went into position, covering all the approaches from the rear—center at Cherokee Hill, right near Potter's rice mills on the Savannah, left connecting with line of the Fourteenth Army Corps.

December 14 to 18.—Position unchanged; camps policed and other sanitary regulations instituted.

December 19.—A foraging expedition of twelve companies from the brigade sent four miles beyond Monteith; it encountered and drove in the enemy's pickets, capturing one prisoner.

December 20.—Position unchanged and no demonstrations on the line.

December 21.—The One hundred and forty-third New York Volunteers sent over to Argyle Island at 1 a. m. to cover the flank of the Second Brigade, which had crossed over to the South Carolina shore. Information that the enemy had evacuated Savannah last night received at 6 a. m.

December 22.—The One hundred and forty-third New York Volunteers returned from Argyle Island and resumed its former position; brigade remained in its position to cover the removal of the trains to Savannah.

December 23.—The brigade ordered to move back toward the city; marched at 9.15 a. m.; went into permanent camp one mile above Savannah at 1 p. m. on McAlpin's plantation, right resting on the Savannah River, left joining right of the Second Brigade.

December 24 to 29.—Substantial quarters built and camp policed; drill and parades resumed.

December 30.—Brigade and corps reviewed in the city of Savannah by Major-General Sherman.

December 31.—The Third Division having crossed the Savannah River, the First Division was ordered to occupy its position; brigade changed its position at 11 a. m.; right joined left of the Second Brigade, and left rested on the Charleston and Savannah Railroad.

Second Division.

November 1.—In camp in Atlanta.

November 5.—Moved the entire division two miles out of the city.

November 6.—Moved back to our old camp.

November 9.—An attack was made by Wheeler's cavalry upon the city of Atlanta and was repulsed by us without any loss on our part.

November 15.—Entire army on the move; division moved at 8 a. m. by Decatur road; encamped near Stone Mountain; distance, fifteen miles.

November 16.—Crossed Yellow River, encamping two miles beyond; distance, fifteen miles.

November 17.—Passed through Social Circle; encamped on the Ulcofauhachee River; distance, seventeen miles.

November 18.—Encamped near Madison, Ga.; distance, eighteen miles.

November 19.—Division detached from corps; destroyed railroad to Oconee; encamped at Blue Spring; distance, fourteen miles.

November 20.—Marched down west side of Oconee River; distance, ten miles.

November 21.—Weather and roads very bad; moved on toward Milledgeville; distance, eight miles.

November 22.—Struck Milledgeville railroad; marched through Milledgeville and across Oconee River; distance, twenty miles.

November 23.—Remained in camp; destroyed several miles of railroad.

November 24.—Moved toward Sandersville.

November 25.—Crossed Buffalo Creek; roads bad and swampy; distance, nine miles.

November 26.—Reached Sandersville at noon; from there struck the Georgia Central Railroad at Station No. 13 and continued destroying it; distance, thirteen miles.

November 27.—Destroyed railroad all day; distance, twelve miles.

November 28.—Continued destroying railroad; encamped at Station No. 12.

November 29.—Marched east through Station No. 11 and encamped within three miles and a half of Ogeechee River; distance, twenty-one miles.

November 30.—Marched northward; crossed Ogeechee River and encamped on Big Creek, three miles south of Louisville; distance, ten miles.

December 1.—Marched from near Louisville, Ga., to Bark Camp Creek; distance, thirteen miles.

December 2.—Marched to Buck Head Church; distance, twelve miles.
December 3.—Marched past Millen; distance, ten miles.
December 4.—Marched to Crooked Run; distance, four miles.
December 5.—Crossed Little Ogeechee; distance, twelve miles.
December 6.—Marched seven miles.
December 7.—Marched to Springfield; distance, fifteen miles.
December 8.—Marched toward Monteith; distance, thirteen miles.
December 9.—Marched to Monteith Swamp; distance, six miles.
December 10.—Marched within four miles of Savannah, Ga.; distance, eleven miles.
December 11 to 20.—Siege of Savannah.
December 21.—Entered Savannah before daylight, several hours in advance of any other portions of our army.
December 22 to 31.—Division on post duty, General Geary being commandant of the city.

First Brigade, Second Division.

November 15.—In accordance with orders received the brigade broke camp at Atlanta, Ga., at 7 a. m.; bivouacked for the night near Stone Mountain; distance, thirteen miles.
November 16.—Marched to near Sheffield, Walton County, Ga., and encamped for the night.
November 17.—Marched to near Social Circle; went into camp for the night at 5 p. m.; distance marched, about eighteen miles.
November 18.—Marched to near Madison, Morgan County, passing through the stations of Social Circle and Rutledge, on the Georgia Railroad, destroying the depots and other public property, also tearing up the railroad track on the route.
November 19.—The brigade, in company with the other brigades of the division, was ordered on an expedition down the Georgia Railroad to the Oconee River, to destroy it and the railroad bridge over the above-named stream; went into camp for the night at Blue Spring, Morgan County, Ga., near the Oconee River.
November 20.—Moved at 7 a. m., and marched to Dunham's Tannery, Putnam County, Ga.
November 21.—Moved at 8 a. m., passing by Philadelphia Church, and went into camp for the night.
November 22.—Moved at 6.30 a. m.; struck the Eatonton and Milledgeville Railroad at Dennis Station; marched down the railroad; crossed Little River near railroad bridge, passing through Milledgeville, the capital of the State, and went into camp on the east side of the Oconee River, where the brigade remained in camp until the morning of the 24th.
November 24.—Marched at 7 a. m., and bivouacked on the east side of Gum Creek, Washington County, Ga.
November 25.—Moved at 6.30 a. m.; was delayed several hours in rebuilding bridges over Buffalo Creek, which had been destroyed by the enemy a few days previous, and encamped for the night on the east side of the creek.
November 26.—Moved at 8 a. m.; marched to Sandersville, Washington County, Ga., at which place the division, in connection with the First Division, was detached and ordered to Tennille Station, on the Georgia Central Railroad, to destroy the railroad from that place toward Davisborough. After destroying two miles of track we encamped for the night about three miles east of the last-named place.

November 27.—Marched at 7 a. m.; moved along the railroad, tearing it up as we went. After destroying about four miles of the track we marched to Davisborough, and encamped for the night.

November 28.—Moved at 7 a. m., and commenced destroying the railroad track back toward the place we left off the day previous. After tearing up about three miles of it returned to Davisborough, and encamped for the night.

November 29.—Marched at 7 a. m. to join the corps in the direction of the Ogeechee River; passed through Spiers Station and Bethany, and bivouacked for the night about two miles east of the last-named place.

November 30.—Marched at 7 a. m. toward the Ogeechee River; the bridge being burned over the river was compelled to march toward Louisville, Jefferson County, and cross the river near its headwaters, where we joined the corps and encamped for the night.

December 1.—At Louisville, Jefferson County, Ga.; broke camp at 7 a. m.; marched to Birch Bark Cabin Creek and encamped for the night.

December 2.—Moved at 6 a. m.; passed through Birdville, Burke County, Ga.; was detained several hours by the bridge over Buck Head Creek being partially destroyed; encamped for the night on the east side of the above-named creek.

December 3.—Moved at 2 p. m., this brigade being the rear guard of the corps. The brigade did not go into camp until 6.30 a. m. of the 4th.

December 4.—Moved at 7 a. m. and marched to the east side of Crooked Creek.

December 5.—Moved at 7 a. m.; went into camp for the night at 5 p. m. near the headwaters of the Little Ogeechee River.

December 6.—Moved at 11 a. m. and marched about eleven miles in the direction of Springfield and encamped for the night.

December 7.—Marched at 7 a. m. and moved to near Springfield, Ga.

December 8.—Moved at 7 a. m. in advance of the corps to near Eden; went into camp at 4 p. m.

December 9.—Moved at 8 a. m. in the direction of Monteith, where the advance of the corps had considerable skirmishing with the enemy, but dislodged them from their fortified position a short time before dark, when the whole corps went into camp for the night.

December 10.—Moved at 11 a. m. Our division was left to guard the corps train, while the remainder of the corps pushed forward to destroy the Charleston and Savannah Railroad, after which they pushed forward toward the city of Savannah. We followed close after and encamped for the night at the Five-Mile Post, on the Augusta road.

December 11.—The brigade was ordered to be in readiness to move at 9 a. m., to await the result of a reconnaissance in force by the Third Brigade, which was developing the enemy's lines from the left of the First Division to the Savannah River. The brigade moved about 10 a. m. to a cross-roads about half way between the river and the Savannah road, when one regiment—the Twenty-ninth Ohio Volunteers—was detached to reconnoiter on the left ot the Third Brigade to the river. The brigade was soon after moved in the same direction to the bank of the Savannah River, where we first saw the city of Savannah. The brigade lay in this position until about 4 p. m., when it was moved to the right of the division to relieve the Second Brigade and fill up the line between the left of the First Division and the right of our Third Brigade, which was accomplished by dark in the following order: the

Sixty-sixth Ohio, Twenty-eighth Pennsylvania, Twenty-ninth and Fifth Ohio, and One hundred and forty-seventh Pennsylvania Volunteers. Pickets were taken from the Sixty-sixth Ohio, which were posted along the edge of the wood bordering a field distant from the enemy's skirmishers about 500 yards.

December 12.—Lay in the same position; considerable shelling from the enemy; no injuries received from them; very little firing along the lines.

December 21.—Remained in the same position from the 11th until about 3 a. m. of the 21st, when this brigade received orders to follow the Third Brigade in the direction of Savannah, which brigade was pressing the enemy's pickets. We entered the city of Savannah at sunrise. Two regiments—the Twenty-eighth Pennsylvania and Twenty-ninth Ohio Volunteers—were detached to take possession of Fort Jackson and other fortifications below the city, on the Savannah River. The several regiments of the brigade were then put in camp in several squares or parks, where they remain at the present time [December 31].

Third Brigade, Second Division.

[*November.*]—This brigade lay in camp at Atlanta, Ga., until the 15th.

November 15.—Started on this campaign; marched to Milledgeville via Decatur, Stone Mountain, Madison, Blue Spring, and Oconee River.

November 22.—Reached Milledgeville.

November 24.—Left Milledgeville and marched, via Buffalo Creek and Tennille Station, to Davisborough.

November 27.—Arrived at Davisborough, where we were engaged in destroying the railroad one day; had a skirmish with some of Wheeler's cavalry; marched, via Spiers Station, to Louisville.

December 1.—The brigade broke camp near Louisville, Ga., on the Ogeechee River; marched to Savannah via Millen, Springfield, and Monteith.

December 10.—Arrived within five miles of the city, meeting the enemy.

December 11.—After a brisk skirmish in the morning gained a very good position near the enemy's lines. Remained there until the morning of the 21st.

December 21.—At 2 a. m., finding the enemy had evacuated, the brigade moved directly into the city, since which time it has been doing provost duty. While confronting the enemy near the city the brigade was subject to a severe fire both from artillery and musketry.

Third Division.

November 1 to 14.—The division formed a portion of the garrison of Atlanta, nothing of interest transpiring.

November 15.—Marched from Atlanta via Stone Mountain, Rockbridge, Madison, Eatonton, Milledgeville, Sandersville, Davisborough, and Louisville.

November 30.—Encamped on Big Creek, Jefferson County, Ga.; no skirmishing; lived on the country; forage and supplies abundant.

First Brigade, Third Division.

December 1.—This brigade, part of Major-General Sherman's Army of Georgia, marched from Louisville, Ga., easterly; crossed the railroad to Augusta four miles north of Millen; marched thence southeasterly through Springfield.

December 10.—Arrived before Savannah; constructed a line of earthworks and lay under fire of the enemy's batteries until the 21st.

December 21.—The enemy having evacuated the city, this brigade, with the balance of the Twentieth Corps, occupied it and encamped in the northwest part.

Third Brigade, Third Division.

November 15.—This brigade, part of Major-General Sherman's Army of Georgia, moved from Atlanta, Ga., easterly, through Decatur, Stone Mountain, across Yellow River, through Rockbridge and Social Circle; from the latter place to Rutledge, a distance of seven miles, destroying the Georgia State Railroad at short intervals and railroad buildings. Marched thence to Madison and destroyed a mile of railroad buildings; thence through Eatonton to Milledgeville; crossed the Oconee River and marched through Hebron, Sandersville, and Davisborough; crossed the Ogeechee River and encamped on the 30th four miles east of Louisville.

CAVALRY.

*Third Division.**

November 1.—At Marietta, Ga.

November 14.—Moved to Atlanta, Ga.

November 15.—Took possession of Anthony's Bridge, Flint River.

November 16.—Moved through Jonesborough; found enemy strongly posted at Lovejoy's, under General Cobb. The First Brigade charged and drove him from his position, capturing two 3-inch rifled guns; Tenth Ohio Cavalry charged him again at Bear Creek, when he retreated to Griffin.

November 19.—Crossed the Ocmulgee River at Planters' Factory; reached Clinton, Ga.

November 20.—Moved to Macon, Ga.; drove enemy across Walnut Creek. The Tenth Ohio Cavalry made a charge on enemy's works at East Macon, capturing a battery in position, but were forced to leave it. The command fell back to Griswold Station, destroying railroad track to that point. It here captured a train of cars and destroyed a soap and candle factory and a pistol factory.

November 21 [22].—Wheeler advanced with his cavalry corps and three brigades of infantry against Second Brigade, but was repulsed and compelled to retire.

November 24.—Moved to Milledgeville and crossed the Oconee River; moved on Augusta road and crossed the Ogeechee at the shoals.

November 25 and 26.—Moved through Sylvan Grove, where Wheeler's force attacked us in flank and rear, but was repulsed, with heavy loss.

November 27.—Struck the railroad at Waynesborough, the advance under Captain Estes, assistant adjutant-general, having destroyed the station and train of cars captured day previous, and partly burned the bridge over Brier Creek. Here I learned that our prisoners had been moved from Millen, Ga.; and, after destroying track sufficient to prevent transportation for a few days, deemed it prudent to retire our infantry in direction of Louisville, Ga. Wheeler attacked rear and flank with desperate recklessness whenever opportunity offered, but was easily repulsed.

*Commanded by Brig. Gen. Judson Kilpatrick.

November 28.—Crossed Rocky Creek and waited for the enemy to come up, which he did, with his entire force, charging as he came, but was repulsed again and again; was forced to retire, after losing not less than 600 killed and wounded.

November 29.—Reached Left Wing of the army at Louisville, Ga., where the division encamped for the next few days, resting for the first time.

December 1.—Marched in advance of a division of infantry on the Waynesborough road; found the enemy in position behind barricades. The Fifth Kentucky and Eighth Indiana Cavalry charged, and after a brisk fight compelled them to retire. Marched seven miles and encamped for the night.

December 2.—Marched at early hour; came up and engaged enemy at Rocky Creek, and drove them in confusion toward Waynesborough and Augusta; encamped near Lumpkin's Station.

December 3.—Marched on railroad and encamped at Thomas' Station.

December 4.—Marched out of camp to engage Wheeler's cavalry (encamped at Waynesborough, Ga.), composed of four divisions and two independent brigades. Came upon his advance two miles from town. The Second Brigade, being in advance, charged him in position, and after a fiercely contested struggle of about one hour's duration drove him into town, where he again took up a strong position, determined to hold the town at all hazards. The First Brigade, now having the advance, charged him in the new position, and with equal success. The enemy now fell back in great confusion beyond Bear Creek, closely pursued. They were in this engagement not only defeated, but completely routed and driven in great confusion a distance of eight miles; 200 rebels left in our hands wounded by the saber alone. Encamped for the night at Old Church.

December 5 to 7.—Moved at 7 a. m. on the 5th, in rear of the Fourteenth Army Corps, to Jacksonborough; the 6th, to Rock Head Creek. The 7th encamped near Sister's Ferry.

December 8 to 10.—3 a. m. crossed the Ebenezer Creek and encamped five miles from Springfield. 9th, moved in rear of the Seventeenth Army Corps and encamped at Pooler Station, eleven miles from Savannah, Ga. 10th, encamped five miles from Savannah, Ga.

December 11.—Patrolled the Ogeechee River to find a crossing and encamped near King's Bridge.

December 12.—Crossed the Ogeechee and Cannouchee on pontoons. Encamped four miles of Fort McAllister, which we intended to attack and take on the following morning.

December 13.—Received orders from the general-in-chief not to attack the fort, but try and open communication with our fleet at Saint Catherine's Sound, which was done. Encamped at Kilkenny Bluff.

December 14.—First Brigade encamped at Sunbury; Second Brigade, at Midway. Nothing transpired.

December 15.—In camp.

December 16 and 17.—Marched to vicinity of King's Bridge and went into camp. 17th, 2,000 men, under Colonel Atkins, in conjunction with one division of infantry, moved to Altamaha bridge to destroy it and railroad track. The former being difficult of approach and strongly defended, its destruction was prevented; but the latter was thoroughly destroyed, and the command returned to camp, patrolling the Ogeechee until the 23d, when headquarters and First Brigade crossed and went into camp nine miles from Savannah, where the command is now [December 31] encamped.

No. 4.

Reports of Capt. Orlando M. Poe, Corps of Engineers, U. S. Army, Chief Engineer.

HDQRS. MILITARY DIVISION OF THE MISSISSIPPI,
CHIEF ENGINEER'S OFFICE,
Savannah, Ga., December 26, 1864.

SIR: I have the honor of reporting to the Engineer Department as follows concerning the operations which have just ended in the occupation of Savannah and the opening of complete communications between this army and the forces in the Department of the South:

On the 15th of November the Fifteenth, Seventeenth, and Twentieth Army Corps took up their line of march from Atlanta. Preparatory to the movement, General Sherman directed me to destroy with engineer troops all railroads and property belonging thereto; all storehouses, machine shops, mills, factories, &c., within the lines of the enemy's defenses at Atlanta. The work of destruction was thoroughly done, under my personal supervision, by the Michigan Engineers and Missouri Engineers. About ten miles of track were destroyed by burning the wood-work and twisting each rail, the latter operation being performed by a very simple machine designed by myself. The designated buildings were first burned and the walls afterward razed to the ground. For military purposes the city of Atlanta has ceased to exist, there being no railroad either to or from it. The Chattanooga road was destroyed from Cartersville to Atlanta, the West Point road to Fairburn, and the Macon road to Lovejoy's. On the morning of the 15th of November the march began—the Fifteenth and Seventeenth Corps taking the roads which lead to Griswold and Gordon, on the Macon and Savannah Railroad, and the cavalry moving upon their right flank, threatening Macon; the Twentieth Corps took that passing through Stone Mountain to Social Circle, on the Augusta railroad; the Fourteenth Corps moved on the morning of the 16th of November, taking the road through Lithonia and Covington. The Twentieth Corps destroyed the Augusta railroad from Social Circle to a point near Greensborough, the Fourteenth Corps destroying from Lithonia to Social Circle. The Twentieth Corps then hurried southward through Eatonton to Milledgeville, which place they entered on the evening of the 22d of November. The Fourteenth Corps deflected at Brick [Store] and passed via Shady Dale, Salem, Eatonton Factory, Vaughn's, and Raimoth to Milledgeville, where they arrived early in the morning of the 23d of November. The Fifteenth and Seventeenth destroyed the Georgia Central Railroad from Griswold to Tennille Station, including the Oconee bridge. The cavalry made a strong demonstration on the works at Macon, and afterward destroyed the railroad from Griswold westward, to include Walnut Creek bridge, three miles east of Macon. The cavalry, supported by Walcutt's brigade, of the Fifteenth Army Corps, had a severe fight at Duncan's farm on the 21st [22d] of November, in which our forces gained a complete victory.

On the 24th of November the Fourteenth and the Twentieth Corps and the cavalry moved from Milledgeville, the cavalry taking the road, via Sylvan Grove, to Waynesborough, intending to pass to the eastward of Millen, and, if possible, liberate the prisoners of war at that point. They struck the Augusta and Millen branch railroad near Waynesborough, captured a train of cars, and burned some track and bridges, but learning that the prisoners had been removed from Millen turned back. The Fourteenth Corps marched direct for Sandersville and the

Twentieth Corps took the road, via Hebron, to the same place. At this point some cavalry, under the command of Wheeler, offered resistance, but were quickly dispersed, only the skirmishers of the advanced guard of the two infantry corps being engaged. The court-house in Sandersville, a very substantial brick building, was burned by order of General Sherman, because the enemy had made use of its portico from which to fire upon our troops. The Fifteenth and Seventeenth Corps, which had been destroying railroad, here communicated from Irwin's Cross-Roads, and then left the railroad, the order of march being as follows: The cavalry on the left flank; the Fourteenth Corps direct to Louisville; the Twentieth Corps, via Davisborough, to Ogeechee bridge, destroying the railroad from Tennille Station to and including said bridge; the Seventeenth Corps, by the first road south of the railroad, to Burton Station (No. 9½); and the Fifteenth Corps via Johnson's. The Twentieth Corps, after burning Ogeechee bridge, passed to the northward through Louisville; the Seventeenth Corps crossed the Ogeechee on a pontoon bridge at Station 9½, and thence moved along the railroad to the Five-Mile Post from Savannah; the Twentieth Corps through Springfield; and the Fourteenth Corps close as possible to the Savannah River; the Fifteenth Corps continued on the south side of the Ogeechee to Station 2 (Eden), when three divisions crossed to the north side, while one (Hazen's) moved on down to Fort McAllister, which work was very handsomely carried by assault, capturing the entire garrison, twenty-three guns, and all the stores. The same evening General Sherman personally communicated with the fleet. Orders had been given on the previous day for the investment of the city. No attempt at assault was made, though the opinion universally prevailed that such an attempt would be successful. The general commanding was not willing to sacrifice any lives, feeling certain that the city must soon fall into our hands at any rate.

The line occupied by the enemy was as follows: Beginning at the mouth of the small creek emptying into the Savannah two miles and a half above the city; thence along the southeastern bank of that creek until the headwaters of Salt Marsh Creek were reached; then following along that stream to and along Vernon River to the sea, the lower points being held by detached works behind impassable swamps. All the approaches to this line were rendered very difficult by dams constructed across all small streams. A line was found interior to this, commencing at Laurel Grove Cemetery on the right, and resting on the river between Savannah and Fort Jackson. This was a very heavy line, consisting in part of a continuous bastioned line and in part of a system of detached lunettes in defensive relations. No attempt was made by the enemy to hold this line. They abandoned Savannah and all its dependencies on the night of December 20, and we occupied them on the morning of the 21st, a vast amount of warlike material and many guns (the number not yet definitely known) falling into our hands. I noticed among them one brass 6-pounder having upon it the arms of the State of Georgia and the words "Georgia Military Institute." I suggested to Captain Baylor, chief of ordnance, that he send that gun to the Military Academy at West Point, and he has signified his intention of doing so. The enemy evidently evacuated his position on account of want of supplies. An assault had been ordered, and would have been made in a day or two, which would probably have been successful. I should have said that the enemy, in consequence of our occupation of the city, destroyed his gun-boats and the iron-clad ram Savannah.

A new line of defenses selected by myself and approved by General Sherman has been begun, Captain Reese, Corps of Engineers, being charged with its construction. It will consist of a system of detached lunettes, in defensive relations, which are intended to be connected at our leisure. These works will be principally armed with captured guns. The line will be about two miles and a half in development and is intended for a garrison of about 5,000 men.

On the march, the Engineer Department was constantly engaged in the most arduous duties, repairing roads, building bridges, destroying railroads, and all other matters coming within our province. I think I can safely say that the department is popular in this army, and enjoys the esteem and confidence of all commanders. Not having yet received detailed reports, I cannot specify the amount of labor performed, but it was immense.

Capt. C. B. Reese, chief engineer Department and Army of the Tennessee, was my constant reliance and support. The Corps of Engineers has no more valuable officer in the field. His services are appreciated in the army to which he belongs. First Lieutenant Stickney acted as assistant to Captain Reese and discharged his duty in a satisfactory manner.

First Lieut. William Ludlow acted as chief engineer of the wing commanded by General Slocum, and is highly commended by that officer. He is a dashing young officer.

The pontoon train accompanying the Left Wing was in charge of the Fifty-eighth Indiana Volunteers, Col. George P. Buell commanding; that with the Right Wing was in charge of the First Missouri Engineers, Lieutenant-Colonel Tweeddale. Neither of these trains, though frequently used, failed us at any time. Their efficiency became a subject of remark throughout the army. One of these trains (the one belonging to the Right Wing) has been hauled on wagons all the way from Nashville, Tenn., whence it started in April last, and it is still in an efficient condition—strong evidence of the durability of the "canvas pontoon train."

I am, sir, very respectfully, your obedient servant,

O. M. POE,

Captain of Engineers, Chief Engineer Mil. Div. of the Mississippi.

Brig. Gen. R. DELAFIELD,

Chief of Engineers, U. S. Army.

WASHINGTON, D. C., *October 8, 1865.*

SIR:*

Early in November the preparations for the march to Savannah were completed and everything held in readiness therefor. Under directions from the major-general commanding, engineer orders were issued making the proper assignment of engineer troops and bridge trains.

Meanwhile a freshet in the Chattahoochee carried away all our trestle bridges, and such as were necessary for the passage of the army on its return to Atlanta were relaid from the pontoon trains. They were put down, two at the Chattahoochee railroad bridge and one at Turner's Ferry.

* For portion of report (here omitted) relating to the Atlanta Campaign, etc., see Vol. XXXVIII, Part I, p. 127.

The engineer organization for the march to Savannah was as follows:

First. Engineer troops and troops of the line on engineer duty: (1) First Regiment Michigan Engineers and Mechanics, Col. J. B. Yates, unassigned, receiving orders direct from headquarters Military Division of the Mississippi, ten companies, 1,500 men. (2) First Missouri Engineers, Lieut. Col. William Tweeddale, in charge of pontoon train with Right Wing (Army of the Tennessee), five companies, 500 men. (3) Fifty-eighth Regiment Indiana Volunteer Infantry, Col. George P. Buell, in charge of pontoon train of Left Wing, ten companies, 775 men. Total, 2,775 men.

Second. Pioneers: Left Wing, six divisions, each having a pioneer corps of the average strength of 100 men, 600 men; Right Wing, seven divisions, each having a pioneer corps of the average strength of 100 whites and 70 negroes, 1,200 men; total, 1,800 men.

Recapitulation: Engineer troops and troops of the line doing engineer duty, 2,775 men; pioneers, 1,800 men; aggregate for engineer duty, 4,575 men.

Third. Tools and tool trains: Each of the pioneer corps carried a sufficient number of tools to work their full strength, and in the Right Wing they were supplied with a duplicate set, which were carried in wagons. In the Left Wing each brigade was provided with a tool wagon, loaded with about 350 intrenching tools. A great many axes and shovels were in the hands of the troops, but always within reach in case of emergency. The Michigan Engineers and Mechanics had a train of fifty wagons, of which twenty were loaded with tools, as follows: 1,500 axes and helves, 1,500 shovels, 700 picks and helves, 200 hatchets, and an ample supply of carpenters' and bridge building tools, and extra saws and augers; also, 100 hooks which I had devised for twisting railroad iron. The remainder of the wagons carried subsistence and quartermaster's stores. The Missouri Engineers had a much smaller train, which was somewhat mixed up with the pontoon train of which they had charge. They carried the following intrenching tools: 500 shovels, 500 axes; also, an assortment of carpenters' and blacksmiths' tools.

Fourth. Pontoon trains: Left Wing—pontoniers, Fifty-eighth Regiment Indiana Volunteer Infantry, Col. George P. Buell commanding, 775 men. Materials: 51 canvas pontoon-boats, complete, 15 extra covers, 10 anchors, 2,000 pounds rope, 37 horses, 505 mules, 94 wagons, 3 ambulances, 2 tool wagons, 3 forges, 850 chesses, 196 balks, and the necessary harness, &c., to make the outfit complete. This regiment carried its own supplies of subsistence and forage on the wagons in the above list. The length of bridge which could be built from this train by cutting small timber for the balk was 850 feet. Right Wing—pontoniers, First Missouri Engineers, Lieut. Col. William Tweeddale commanding; strength, 530 men. Materials: 28 canvas pontoon-boats complete, 28 boat wagons, 600 chesses, 15 chess-wagons, 196 claw balks, 1 forge, 1 battery wagon, 2 tool wagons (a general assortment), 7 forage wagons, and a sufficient quantity of harness, rope, &c. Length of bridge, 580 feet; total length of bridges, 1,430 feet.

The foregoing was the engineer organization and equipment which was considered sufficient to make the campaign which I knew would be made to Savannah.

On the 7th of November I received a telegram from General Sherman directing me to take charge of the destruction of the railroads, depots, steam machinery, &c., in the city of Atlanta. On the 9th I telegraphed as follows: "I am all ready to do the work assigned me, and will act the instant I get your order to do so." I had called together the commanding officers of the engineer regiments and explained to them just what I wanted done, and we had selected the buildings and works for destruction. On the morning of the 12th General Sherman directed me to proceed with my work, but to be careful not to use fire, which would endanger other buildings than those set apart for destruction. The engineer regiments were divided into detachments, under picked officers, each of whom received a written order as follows:

You will please take the detachment now under your orders to the first high chimney (stating locality and buildings) and throw it down, and continue the work along (stating the route) until you reach (the point designated as the limit of work for this detachment), being careful not to use fire in doing the work, since it would endanger buildings which it is not intended to destroy.

These orders were faithfully carried out, and neither fire nor powder was used for destroying buildings until after they had been put in ruins by battering down the walls, throwing down smokestacks, breaking up furnace arches, knocking steam machinery to pieces, and punching all boilers full of holes. The railroads within the limits of the old rebel defenses were destroyed by tearing up the iron, piling up the ties, and after putting the rails across them firing the wood which heated the iron and then the rails were twisted. The rails were torn up by using a small but very strong iron "cant hook," devised by myself, and after they were heated were twisted by applying the same hooks at each end of each rail and twisting the iron bar around its horizontal axis, being careful to give the rail at least a half turn. The length of railroad destroyed in this manner, within the limits indicated above, was about ten miles. The depots, car-sheds, machine-shops, and water-tanks were also destroyed.

It was not until the evening of the 15th of November that fire was applied to the heaps of rubbish we had made. I was upon the ground in person to see that the work was done in a proper and orderly manner; and, so far as engineer troops were concerned, this was the case. But many buildings in the business part of the city were destroyed by lawless persons, who, by sneaking around in blind alleys, succeeded in firing many houses which it was not intended to touch.

Three army corps moved on the morning of the 15th of November, striking boldly out toward the sea. On the morning of the 16th the other army corps and the headquarters military division moved. The map* forwarded to the Bureau of Engineers with my letter dated Goldsborough, N. C., April 7, 1865, will indicate the routes pursued by each army corps until our arrival in front of Savannah. During this march the Augusta railroad was destroyed, as described above, to include the Oconee bridge. The Georgia Central was destroyed from Walnut Creek, within three miles of Macon, to the city of Savannah. The Charleston and Savannah Railroad from the Savannah River bridge to Savannah, the Savannah and Gulf Railroad from Savannah to the Altamaha, the branch from Millen to Augusta for several miles from Millen, and the branch from Gordon to Eatonton suffered severely.

Pontoon bridges were built at the following points: Over the Yellow River, at railroad crossing, 100 feet; over the Ulcofauhachee, at road crossing, 80 feet; over the Ocmulgee, at Planters' Factory, 200 feet; over the Little River, at railroad crossing, 250 feet; over the Oconee River, at Ball's Ferry, 300 feet; over the Buffalo Creek, on Sandersville road, 400 feet; over the Buffalo Creek, on upper Sandersville

* To appear in the Atlas.

road, 400 feet; over the Ogeechee River, on Louisville road, 200 feet; over the Ogeechee River, near Burton Station, 200 feet; over the Ogeechee River, Jones' Ferry, 300 feet; over the Buck Head Creek, on Millen road, 100 feet; over the Little Ogeechee, near Station 4½, 80 feet; over the Ogeechee, at Jenks' Ferry, 300 feet; over the Ogeechee, at Dalton's Ferry, 250 feet; over the Ogeechee, at Hilton's Bridge, 300 feet; total, 3,460 feet.

On the 10th of December the army arrived in front of Savannah. Reconnaissances were pushed south of the Cannouchee River, and, fortunately, a plan of Fort McAllister was found. Other reconnaissances were made along the entire extent of the enemy's front, which was found located along the southeastern edge of the chain of swamps running from the Savannah River, opposite King's Island, via the point where the Ogeechee road crosses Salt Marsh Creek, to the junction between Salt Marsh Creek and the Little Ogeechee, and thence through the Vernon, Rosedew, and Beaulieu batteries to Fort McAllister. This line was intrenched in the usual manner, and the defenses were greatly strengthened by closing the sluice gates at the Savannah River and building dams across Salt Marsh Creek, the effect being to make a body of water in front of their entire line.

On the 11th it was decided to attack Fort McAllister, as that was the only obstacle to our free communication with the fleet in Ossabaw Sound. The enemy had destroyed the bridge over the Ogeechee, on the Darien road, commonly known as the "King's Bridge." This was rebuilt by the First Missouri Engineers, under direction of Capt. C. B. Reese, Corps of Engineers, and chief engineer Department and Army of the Tennessee, and on the morning of the 13th the Second Division, Fifteenth Army Corps, crossed over and moved along the south bank of the river, reaching the vicinity of Fort McAllister in the afternoon. As soon as the troops could be properly formed the assault was made, and the fort was carried in handsome style. The same evening the general commanding the military division passed down the river and communicated with the fleet. Fort McAllister stood on the right bank of the Ogeechee River, at the first point of "fast land" met with in ascending that stream, and perfectly commanded the channel. The trace of the fort was irregular, the water front conforming to the shore line and the line of "fast land," while the land front was on a regular bastioned trace. The guns—of which there were twenty-two—were generally mounted in barbette. The fort was provided on its land front with a good ditch, having a row of stout palisades at its bottom, well built glacis, and a row of excellent abatis, exterior to which was planted a row of 8-inch shells arranged to explode when trodden upon. These shells were arranged in a single row just outside the abatis, and were about three feet from center to center. It was impossible to move an assaulting force upon the fort without suffering from the explosion of these shells. The fact that nearly all the guns of the fort were mounted in barbette rendered it much easier to carry it by assault, since our skirmish line advancing at a run readily approached within 200 yards, and by throwing themselves flat on the ground were well concealed by the high grass, and could pick off the rebel gunners at their leisure, readily silencing the fire of the fort, after which our assaulting force was formed in full view of and not more than 500 yards from the parapet.

After the capture of Fort McAllister the obstructions in the river, consisting of a double row of piles and torpedoes, were removed, and steam-boats ascended to the King's Bridge, where was established our depot of supplies. Some of the guns were removed from Fort McAllister and taken there preparatory to placing them in battery along our lines, and six 30-pounder Parrotts were brought down from Hilton Head for the same purpose. We were fast getting ready for another assault, which would this time have been made directly upon their main line, when, on the night of the 20th of December, the enemy, crossing the Savannah River on a bridge of flat-boats, made his escape, having abandoned a large number of guns and other material of war, and blown up his iron-clads. In this case, as in that of Atlanta, no attempt was made to make regular siege approaches. Our lines were thrust forward at all points to the edge of the water defenses of the enemy without any necessity for siege approaches, and beyond that it was useless to attempt anything of the kind. We could only get into the rebel lines by open assault, which was deemed quite practicable, particularly near the crossing of the Ogeechee road over Salt Marsh Creek, and in front of our batteries at Shaw's Bridge, over the Ogeechee Canal. I had closely reconnoitered the latter point and found that the natural obstacles were not very great, but the enemy's works were strongest here. Soon after our occupation of the city of Savannah, the major-general commanding directed me to select a new line, to be intrenched for the defense of such stores, depots, and material as we would leave there in future operations. In company with Captain Reese, I made a careful reconnaissance, and decided upon the location and character of the works. These were, in their main features, a system of large lunettes to be closed at the gorge and to be placed in defensive relations with each other, so that they might be held independently, but to be also connected by curtains of infantry parapet, so as to be used as a continuous line, if that was deemed desirable. The estimated garrison was 5,000 men. The location of the new lines was very nearly the same as those of 1814.

Before leaving Savannah on the campaign through the Carolinas, by request of General Grover, who was left in command at Savannah, I handed him a paper, of which the following is a copy:

HEADQUARTERS MILITARY DIVISION OF THE MISSISSIPPI,
CHIEF ENGINEER'S OFFICE,
Savannah, Ga., January 21, 1865.

Major-General GROVER,
Commanding U. S. Forces, Savannah:

GENERAL: In accordance with your request I have the honor of submitting the following memoranda, with reference to the defense of the city of Savannah:

First. The defense of the city itself: This is accomplished by the line of works now in process of construction, after the plan indicated in my letter to Major-General Sherman, dated December 26, 1864. These works are now ready to receive sixty guns, partly siege and partly field artillery, and in my opinion are in a condition which would warrant their defense by the garrison estimated for. Captain Suter, U. S. Engineers, and chief engineer Department of the South, has been furnished with a trace of this line, on which the several positions of the guns composing the complete armament are indicated. Captain Suter has also been furnished with those maps captured at this city which relate to the defense. Opposite the city, on the main Carolina shore, two small works should be built to command the Union causeway and the Huger causeway. The above contemplates an attack by a much larger force than the garrison, and, in my opinion, will never be made.

Second. The defense of the approaches: Three main roads lead into the city from inland, viz, the Ogeechee plank road (Darien road), the Louisville stage road, the Augusta stage road. The last two join within one mile and a half of the city. The points where the enemy's late lines crossed these roads furnish the best defense. When taken in conjunction with the obstacles formed by opening the sluice gates at high tide the positions are strong. If the bridge across the Ogeechee at King's is destroyed, it effectually cuts off direct approach by that road, and it can only be reached by crossing the river above and getting to it by some of the numerous cross-roads. An enemy would not be likely to do this, unless he were in largely superior force, since he would necessarily put himself in a "pocket."

Third. The defense of the river navigation: This is best accomplished by a force stationed at this city large enough to go out and fight any enemy that would be likely to approach. In order that our opponents might reach any of the points where they could injure us much, they would be compelled to thrust themselves some miles beyond us, leaving whatever garrison there might be in Savannah on their flank and in rear. They could not interrupt navigation without establishing themselves in inclosed works upon the bank of Saint Augustine Creek (we hold Fort Jackson), and a very short time would suffice for the capture of any enemy having temerity enough to do this. With all our great resources of water transportation I regard it impossible for our enemy to make a successful lodgment on Saint Augustine Creek.

I am, general, very respectfully, your obedient servant,

O. M. POE,

Captain, Engineers, Brevet Colonel, U. S. Army,
Chief Engineer Military Division of the Mississippi.

A map* is in course of preparation, under my direction, which will clearly show the topography of Savannah and vicinity, the works of attack and defense, the new lines constructed during our occupation of the city, and the lines of 1814. As soon as completed it will be forwarded to the Engineer Department.†

All of which is respectfully submitted.

O. M. POE,

Captain, U. S. Engineers, Brevet Brigadier-General, U. S. Army.

No. 5.

Report of Capt. Thomas G. Baylor, U. S. Army, Chief Ordnance Officer.

Memorandum list of ordnance and ordnance stores captured from the enemy in the campaign from Atlanta to Savannah, ending December 21, 1864:

Captured and destroyed by the Left Wing at Milledgeville, Ga.

Rifle muskets, caliber .69	2,300
Lances	5,000
Cutlasses	1,500
Small-arm ammunition ... rounds..	30,000
Artillery ammunition ... do....	5,470
Powder ... pounds..	20,000

Captured in Forts McAllister, Beaulieu, Rosedew, Bartow, Thunderbolt, Jackson, Lee, Boggs, Brown, Water Battery opposite Fort Jackson, Lawton Battery, in the lines around the city of Savannah and in the city of Savannah.

ARTILLERY.

For smooth-bore gun	167
For rifled guns	35
For mortars	7
Total	209

---

* See Map 2, Plate LXX of the Atlas.

† For continuation of report, relating to the campaign of the Carolinas, etc., see Vol. XLVII, Part I.

ARTILLERY CARRIAGES.

Barbette	76
Casemate	1
Siege	6
Field	41
Total	124

ARTILLERY AMMUNITION.

	Rounds.
For smooth-bore guns	19,843
For rifled guns	1,903
For mortars	17
Total	21,763

SMALL ARMS.

Various kinds	183

INFANTRY AMMUNITION.

Musket cartridges, caliber .59	8,000
Musket buck and ball cartridges, caliber .69	7,500
Elongated ball cartridges, caliber .57	11,000
Sharps rifle	3,000
Rifled iron balls	18,000
Buck and ball cartridges, caliber .75	4,000
Total	51,500

Expenditures of ammunition during the campaign.

ARTILLERY AMMUNITION.

	Rounds.
For 3-inch guns	2,099
For light 12-pounder guns	1,218
For 30-pounder Parrott guns	30
For 20-pounder Parrott guns	229
Total	3,576

SMALL-ARM AMMUNITION.

	Cartridges.
Elongated ball, caliber .57	950,915
Spencer rifle	141,396
Burnside carbine	56,000
Sharps carbine	62,000
Smith carbine	21,000
Colt army pistol	8,600
Colt navy pistol	4,800
Henry rifle	500
Total	1,245,211

T. G. BAYLOR,
Captain and Chief of Ordnance, Mil. Div. of the Mississippi.

No. 6.

Report of Col. Amos Beckwith, U. S. Army, Chief Commissary of Subsistence.

Statement of cattle on hand at Atlanta and captured while en route to Savannah.

	On hand at Atlanta.	Captured en route.	Slaughtered en route.	On hand when army arrived at Savannah.
Twentieth Corps	429	2,204	889	1,744
Fourteenth Corps	2,047	590	20	2,617
Army of the Tennessee (Fifteenth and Seventeenth Corps).	1,000	10,500	9,000	2,500
Total	3,476	13,294	9,909	6,861

A. BECKWITH,
Colonel, Aide-de-Camp and Commissary of Subsistence.

No. 7.

Report of Maj. Gen. Oliver O. Howard, U. S. Army, commanding Army of the Tennessee.

HDQRS. DEPARTMENT AND ARMY OF THE TENNESSEE,
Savannah, Ga., December 28, 1864.

CAPTAIN: The campaign of Savannah is so closely connected with the campaign into Alabama, just closed, and I have so carefully stated the strength of my army and left it concentrated at Atlanta, where it remained but one day, that I will not weary you with a repetition. General Sherman's Field Orders, Nos. 115 and 119, issued from Kingston, Ga.,* so remarkable for completeness and so explicit that they could not be misunderstood, have been faithfully adhered to. They were the means of initiating preparations fully adequate to the work that has been accomplished.

My command consisted of two army corps—the Fifteenth (Maj. Gen. P. J. Osterhaus), of four divisions, as follows: First Division, Brigadier-General Woods; Second Division, Brig. Gen. W. B. Hazen; Third Division, Brig. Gen. John E. Smith; Fourth Division, Brig. Gen. J. M. Corse; the Seventeenth Army Corps, Maj. Gen. F. P. Blair commanding, consisted of three divisions, as follows: First Division, Maj. Gen. J. A. Mower; Third Division, Brig. Gen. M. D. Leggett; Fourth Division, Brig. Gen. Giles A. Smith—one regiment cavalry (First Alabama), one regiment of engineers (First Missouri), and a bridge train of sufficient capacity to throw two bridges across any stream that we found en route.

At Gordon I made the following report, which I will resubmit without change:

HEADQUARTERS DEPARTMENT AND ARMY OF THE TENNESSEE,
Gordon, Ga., November 23, 1864.

GENERAL: In accordance with Special Field Orders, No. 124, from your headquarters, dated November 14, 1864, my command marched from White Hall, near Atlanta, in two columns. The left column, Major-General Blair commanding, took the direct

* See Vol. XXXIX, Part III, pp. 627, 701.

McDonough road. This column consisted of the Seventeenth Corps, bridge train, engineer regiment, and supply train of General Kilpatrick's cavalry, the whole preceded by the First Alabama Regiment. The right column, of Fifteenth Corps, Major-General Osterhaus commanding, department headquarters train, and the herds of cattle. This column moved via Rough and Ready, turning to the left toward McDonough, about five miles from Jonesborough. Upon the evening of the 15th the command went into camp—Kilpatrick near Jonesborough, the heads of the two infantry columns near Stockbridge. Kilpatrick met the enemy's cavalry skirmishers near East Point, and drove them before him to the crossing of Flint River. Osterhaus met them not far from Rough and Ready, and again in the vicinity of Stockbridge. He found encamped at that point Lewis' brigade of rebel cavalry, reported 900 strong.

November 16, 1864, the command marched to the vicinity of McDonough by three routes. General Osterhaus met the enemy's cavalry at the crossing of Cotton River. They retreated rapidly, setting fire to the bridge. Some mounted infantry that he had in advance drove them from the bridge in time to put out the fire and save everything but the planking. The bridge was immediately repaired, and detained the column just forty minutes. General Kilpatrick crossed the Flint River at the bridge near Jonesborough at 7 a. m. Finding the enemy had left that place, he followed him to Lovejoy's, where he occupied the strong position there, having two brigades of cavalry and two pieces of artillery, and holding the old rebel works. The general charged the works with dismounted cavalry and carried them, driving back the enemy. Subsequently the enemy's artillery was overtaken by another charging column, and captured. He drove the enemy beyond Bear [Creek] Station, capturing over fifty prisoners. He then moved to the left and encamped on the Griffin and McDonough road.

November 17, 1864, moved to Jackson and its vicinity in three columns, encamping, the right near Indian Springs and the left at Hendricks' Mill. General Kilpatrick moved to Towaliga Creek. Some cavalry of the enemy crossed the creek, burning the bridges.

November 18, 1864, the nearest division was pushed to Nutting's (or Planters') Factory early next morning, and a part of it crossed over by the ferry. The bridge arrived at about 10 a. m., was laid, and the troops commenced crossing at 1 p. m. During that day and night, General Blair's corps, Third Division, Fifteenth Army Corps, and all the cavalry, had crossed. The hill on the east side was steep, and the heavy rain during the night rendered the ascent extremely difficult.

On the morning of the 19th instant regiments were detailed in each division to assist the trains in getting up the hill. The Fifteenth Corps, following the cavalry, took country roads to Hillsborough. The Seventeenth Corps moved to the vicinity of Hillsborough via Monticello. The roads now becoming very heavy, the progress was slow. We had two bridges at the point of crossing, and they were kept full all day, yet the crossing was not completed by the rear guard until the morning of the 20th instant.

November 20, 1864, the command moved on Gordon in two columns—General Kilpatrick with his cavalry taking the Clinton road and the river road toward Macon; General Osterhaus, with the bridge train, cavalry train, &c., moved toward Clinton; General Blair with his command via Blountsville. The head of the right column encamped at Clinton, and the left near Fortville. General Kilpatrick waited at Clinton until the arrival of the head of the infantry column, at 12 m., when he moved out toward Macon on the left Macon road. He met the enemy's cavalry about four miles from Macon, drove them in, and charged their works, defended by infantry and artillery. The head of his column got inside the works, but could not hold them. He succeeded in reaching the railroad and destroyed about one mile of the track. The road was struck in two or three places by the cavalry, besides the above, and a train of cars burned. It rained hard during the entire night.

November 21, 1864, the cavalry took up an advanced position covering all the roads debouching from Macon. General Blair continued his march direct on Gordon, reaching that place with his leading division. The right column was subdivided, two divisions, with small trains, taking the road toward Irwinton, and the rest, with headquarters, bridge trains, cattle, &c., moving on the direct Gordon road. The center and left columns met at a point six miles from Gordon, called Pitts' Mill, where the center made a parallel road into Gordon. Only the division of General G. A. Smith, however, reached Gordon on the 21st instant.

November 22, 1864, the troops and trains were closed up toward Gordon, excepting General Woods' division, who was directed to take up a strong position on the Irwinton road, and make a demonstration toward Macon. The demonstration was made by General Walcutt's brigade, in conjunction with the cavalry, on the different roads. The rebel cavalry in force made a charge early in the morning, capturing one of our cavalry picket posts—estimated 45 men killed, wounded, and missing. Quite a little action grew out of it, in which there was charging and counter-charging of cavalry, when finally the enemy were driven from the field in confusion,

Walcutt's infantry, skirmishing, lending a hand. In the afternoon Walcutt had taken up a position two miles in advance of his division toward Macon, having two pieces of artillery, and had thrown up rail barricades, when he was attacked by quite a large body of infantry, accompanied by some artillery, probably a battery of four guns. The assault was made with great vigor, but was met in the usual manner and completely repulsed. The action continued for some three hours. Walcutt was assisted by a regiment of cavalry on either flank. General Woods was present during the action and General Osterhaus part of the time. I regret to say that General Walcutt, than whom there is not a braver or better officer, was wounded, but I hope not seriously. The conduct of the troops, both cavalry and infantry, was highly commended by the general officers present. On my arrival at Gordon, I directed General Blair to send forward the First Alabama Cavalry and General G. A. Smith's division some eight or ten miles toward the Oconee bridge, which he did, with instructions to move forward to-day, and, if possible, to secure that bridge and plank it over for infantry to cross.

November 23, 1864, the Fourth Division, Fifteenth Corps, with bridge train, having roads that were almost impassable, only reached the vicinity of Clinton last night. This morning fifty-five six-mule teams have been sent to assist the pontoon train through. General Woods' division is moving up this way abreast of General Corse; General Hazen moving toward Irwinton; General Blair moving along the railroad and destroying it. I propose, with your sanction, to move across the Oconee River at two points—one six miles below the railroad bridge (at Ball's Ferry), the other two miles and a half above railroad bridge (at Jackson's Ferry). I have already forwarded to you dispatches captured.

Prisoners still estimate the strength of the enemy in our vicinity about 10,000. The attack on Walcutt was made, I think, by militia, mingled with some old troops retained at Macon.

The number of prisoners of war in my hands: In the Seventeenth Corps, 35 enlisted men; in the Fifteenth Corps, 80 enlisted men; total, 115. I believe the cavalry have some 50 or 60 more in addition. We have about 45 wounded of our own men.

The number of bales of cotton reported officially to have been burned is 2,130.

A large cotton factory, known as Ocmulgee Mills, or Planters' Factory, on the map, containing 1,500 spindles and giving employment to 150 hands, and some 20 cotton gins, have also been destroyed.

We have found the country full of provisions and forage, and have almost completely supplied ourselves, drawing but very little upon our rations.

The above estimate is independent of what has been done by the cavalry. I regret to say that quite a number of private dwellings which the inhabitants have left, have been destroyed by fire, but without official sanction; also, many instances of the most inexcusable and wanton acts, such as the breaking open of trunks, taking of silver plate, &c. I have taken measures to prevent it, and I believe they will be effectual. The inhabitants are generally terrified, and believe us a thousand times worse than we are. Having soldiers in the command who have been bitten by bloodhounds, permission has been given to kill them.

Permit me to commend to you Generals Blair and Osterhaus and the officers and men under them, also General Kilpatrick and his command, for their faithfulness, energy, and untiring exertions to make our march a complete success. While the pleasant weather lasted, the marches were easily made; but as soon as the rains came on, the roads became very heavy and the poorer mules broke down, but we have found a number in the country that have more than replaced our losses.

The members of my staff have given me material aid, and I hope to be able to reward them substantially at some time for faithful services.

Very respectfully,

O. O. HOWARD,
Major-General.

P. S.—General Osterhaus reports the enemy's killed on the field yesterday number 300.

O. O. H.,
Major-General.

Maj. Gen. W. T. SHERMAN.

At Irwin's Cross-Roads a second report was made, embracing operations up to that time, as follows:

HEADQUARTERS DEPARTMENT AND ARMY OF THE TENNESSEE,
Irwin's Cross-Roads, Ga., November 27, 1864.

GENERAL: In accordance with instructions from your headquarters, contained in Special Field Orders dated November 23, my command marched from Gordon in two columns—the Fifteenth Corps, via Irwinton, to Ball's Ferry, Seventeenth Corps along the railroad, with instructions to cross at Jackson's Ferry, two miles and a half north of railroad bridge. General Giles A. Smith, who had preceded his column with the First Alabama Cavalry, drove quite a force of the enemy from two stockades and across the bridge. He found that Jackson's Ferry was an old abandoned route through the swamp, completely impracticable. I therefore directed that General Blair's corps move to Ball's Ferry. The two heads of column arrived at Ball's Ferry about the same time on the 25th instant. A detachment of the First Alabama had the day before reconnoitered the ferry. Finding a small force of the enemy, made a raft, crossed the river, and drove the enemy back, but were subsequently themselves forced to recross the river, with some loss. On our arrival at the river, we found the enemy with barricades and quite an extended line of skirmishers. Generals Osterhaus and Blair confronted them with a line which extended beyond the enemy's flanks both up and down the river. The former placed artillery in position and made a demonstration on the front along the road, while the latter, General Blair, sent a detachment some two miles up the river under the direction of Lieutenant-Colonel Kirby, of his staff. Captain Reese, chief engineer, assisted them with boats to cross the river. The current was too swift to get them over by rowing; they were finally swung over after the fashion of a flying ferry. After working through the bayous and swamps till near morning, his men reached the road at a point that was in rear of the enemy's position, but the enemy had retreated. Colonel Kirby came in sight of his rear guard and wagons, but could not overtake them. The Oconee at this place is about as wide as the Ocmulgee at Planters' Ferry, but the current is very swift, and there are some two miles of swampy ground on the right bank, but the immediate approach to the ferry on the left bank is very good. The bridges were laid so that the troops commenced crossing in two columns about 12 m. November 26. Generals Corse and Woods, Fifteenth Army Corps, reached this point between nine and ten miles from the ferry last night. Seventeenth Corps massed near the forks of the roads that leads to Station 14. The rear of the Fifteenth Corps is now crossing. General Blair has sent a division that is destroying the railroad from Oconee bridge to a point near Irwin's Cross-Roads; General Osterhaus has sent a force to destroy the rest to Station 13. I directed the wagon bridges across Commissioner's Creek and the three bridges across Sandy River to be destroyed. The enemy helped me themselves by destroying the one nearest the Oconee. The country this side of the river is thus far quite open and sandy, but there is plenty of forage thus far. Wheeler with his main force passed here the day before yesterday. My headquarters will remain here to-day.

Respectfully, &c.,

O. O. HOWARD,
Major-General.

Maj. Gen. W. T. SHERMAN.

In accordance with instructions from the general-in-chief, dated Sandersville, November 27, 1864, I issued the following order:

SPECIAL FIELD ORDERS, No. 179. } HDQRS. DEPT. AND ARMY OF THE TENNESSEE, *Irwin's Cross-Roads, November 27, 1864.*

* * * * * * *

V. The army will move forward substantially as follows:

First. Major-General Osterhaus will move his left column, of two divisions, by the Louisville road to the intersection of the Johnson road, and thence to Johnson this evening, being careful to clear that intersection at an early hour to-morrow morning. His right column will move by a settlement road directly to Johnson, starting at 7 a. m. to-morrow.

Second. Major-General Blair will move on the Louisville road—starting his column at 7 a. m. to-morrow, or earlier, at his option—till he reaches the nearest parallel road to the railroad on the south side, south of Williamson's Swamp Creek. He will follow this road till abreast of Station No. 10 (or Sebastopol), where it is probable he will cross the Ogeechee. Major-General Sherman proposes to accompany this column in person. Headquarters will be at Johnson to-morrow night, the train moving with the leading division of right column. The herds of cattle (other than those belonging to divisions) will follow the right column to Johnson, a regiment from the rear division of which will remain at this point till everything is passed, and will then follow on to Johnson, carefully guarding all roads leading south.

By order of Maj. Gen. O. O. Howard:

S. L. TAGGART,
Captain and Assistant Adjutant-General.

The above order was literally conformed to, excepting that a portion of General Corse's division bore to the right and entered Wrightsville, the capital of Johnson County. Some considerable difficulty arose from the numerous roads through the pine woods, and from the fact that neither citizens nor negroes knew of such a place as Johnson's Cross-Roads. At night of the 28th the command encamped—the center column near Riddleville, the left abreast on the Sandersville and Savannah roads, and the right (consisting of one brigade and a battery of artillery) at Wrightsville.

The next day (29th) the two lower columns nearly formed a junction, the advance, under General Woods, encamping near Summerville, and the rest along the lower Savannah road and near Sunderland's Mills, some seven miles to the rear of General Woods; the Seventeenth Corps on the upper Savannah road, abreast of Station No. 10 of the Georgia Central Railroad. The character of the country, open pine woods, wire grass, quite a number of swamps along the Ohoopee River and its tributaries, very few clearings or plantations. Quite a number of mules and horses were captured in the swamps, the citizens having run them off, in the hope of escaping our army and Wheeler's cavalry.

November 30, Generals Woods and Corse's divisions pushed on through Summerville northward, until they reached the upper Savannah road, and encamped near Deep Creek. General Blair moved forward to Station No. 9½, effecting a crossing of the Ogeechee. At that point he rebuilt the wagon bridge, partially destroyed, and also laid a pontoon bridge across the river.

December 1, the three columns moved as follows: The lower on the Statesborough road, the middle upon the Savannah road, and the left along the Georgia Central Railroad, destroying it en route. The two right columns encamped opposite Station No. 8, General Woods securing and repairing the wagon bridge across the Ogeechee at that point. A small force crossed over and made a break in the railroad and destroyed the depot. The Seventeenth Corps succeeded in reaching Station No. 9. December 2, the columns preserved the same order of march. General Blair reached Millen, having completely destroyed the railroad up to that point, including the large depot, and considerable lumber, railroad ties, &c. The middle column encamped near Clifton's Ferry, having thrown a bridge over the Ogeechee at that point, and sent a brigade of General Corse's division to assist the Seventeenth Corps in breaking up the railroad. In addition to the above, Scull's Creek, a wide stream too deep to be forded, was carefully bridged in two places. Our scouting parties hurried on to Scarborough, a little below, and seized a mail, which gave us Savannah papers of that day. December 3, the Fifteenth Corps remained in position, excepting that two brigades of General Corse's division crossed the river and aided the Seventeenth Corps in destroying the railroad from Millen to Scarborough. The Seventeenth Corps came up abreast, encamping near Station No. 7. December 4, the central column marched to Wilson's Creek; the left reached Station No. 5½, having continued the destruction of the railroad up to that point; the right proceeded as far as Statesborough, Hazen's division leading encountered a small body of the enemy's cavalry, said to be 400 strong, and had a successful skirmish with them. The road being boggy, he was obliged to corduroy several long stretches during the day. December 5, the two columns of the Fifteenth Corps moved along their respective roads, to a position nearly opposite Station No. 3. I was with the central column, and hearing that some resistance was offered to General Blair near Ogeechee Church, I caused a feint of crossing the Ogeechee to be made at Flat Ford. Some men were thrown over in boats, but no bridge was laid. General Sherman detained General Blair near Station No. 4½ for the Left Wing to come up. December 6, reconnaissances were made toward Wright's Bridge and the bridge at Eden Station (Jenks' Bridge) with a view to saving them, if possible. Colonel Williamson's brigade, of General Woods' division, reached the former in time to save much of the timber, but all the planking and several of the trestles were already burned. He, however, constructed a foot bridge and crossed over a small force, which he pushed forward toward the railroad. A small detachment went as far as the Twenty-Mile Station, and returned skirmishing all the way. This brigade skirmished considerably with the enemy near night. Colonel Oliver's brigade, of Hazen's division, made the reconnaissance to Jenks' Bridge, but found the bridge destroyed. I sent an officer (Lieutenant Harvey) with a select party to strike the Gulf railroad, but he found the bridge across the Cannouchee burned, and the approaches were guarded by rebels, so that he was compelled to return without doing the work. Another party also sent to try for a point higher up the Cannouchee for the same purpose was not yet heard from. December 7, my command moved as follows: The First Division (General Woods) remained at Wright's Bridge, except one brigade of infantry that crossed the foot bridge and marched down the east bank of the Ogeechee toward Eden Station. On the arrival of the pontoon at Jenks' Bridge, the chief engineer (Capt. C. B. Reese), finding the enemy on the other bank, threw over a regiment of Colonel Oliver's brigade and cleared the way. The bridge was immediately laid. General Corse's division had arrived by this time. One brigade (General Rice commanding) crossed over, met the enemy's skirmishers some 500 yards beyond, drove them in, and routed a battalion of rebels behind rail piles in a very handsome manner, capturing 17 prisoners and killing and wounding several more. He lost 2 killed and 2 or 3 wounded. This brigade then formed a junction with General Woods' brigade from Wright's Bridge, at Eden Station. General Hazen's division moved on to Black Creek, sending forward Colonel Oliver's brigade to the Cannouchee. The rest of the corps was encamped near Jenks' Bridge. The Seventeenth Corps encamped in the vicinity of Station No. 3, ceasing to destroy the railroad after leaving Ogeechee Church. December 8, by the map there appeared to be a road between the Big and Little Ogeechee Rivers. As the enemy was reported in some force near the Twelve-Mile Post, having a line of works in his front, I resolved to turn his position by sending two divisions of the Fifteenth Corps down the west bank of the Ogeechee, which were to force a crossing of the Cannouchee and send forward sufficient force to break the Gulf railroad and secure, if possible, King's Bridge, over the Ogeechee, about a mile above the railroad; also, to reconnoiter with one division between the Ogeechee Rivers. The movement on the right bank led; General Osterhaus, in person, conducted it with his First and Second Divisions. I accompanied General Corse, who found a good ridge road on the left bank of the Big Ogeechee. We came upon some carefully constructed works some three miles and a half from Station No. 2, but they were abandoned. The road was obstructed with trees at several points, but the obstructions were so quickly removed by the pioneers that the column did not halt. On reaching the Savannah Canal we found the canal bridge burned. A new one was made in less than half an hour. The Ogeechee bridge near the canal's mouth, called Dillon's, was almost completely destroyed; but Dillon's Ferry, a mile and a half above, I found practicable for a pontoon bridge. General Corse sent forward a reconnaissance, which found the enemy in force at the junction of this road with King's Bridge and Savannah road. General Osterhaus effected a crossing of the Cannouchee with a couple of brigades, as directed. The Seventeenth Corps meanwhile moved up abreast of Station No. 2, having much corduroying to do and many obstructions to clear away. After reaching the canal, I returned to the Station No. 2 and communicated with General Sherman in person. He was glad of the results of the reconnaissance, but directed me to allow General Blair to continue on the Louisville road.

The next day (December 9) the Seventeenth Corps came upon the enemy in rifle-pits three miles and a half from Station No. 2. General Blair drove the rebels from them, but soon came upon an intrenched line with guns in position. At this place the road led through a dense swamp covered with wood and undergrowth peculiar to this region. The swamp was apparently impassable, yet General Blair moved three lines of battle, preceded by a skirmish line, along on the right and left of the road for some two or three miles, occasionally in water knee-deep. He drove the enemy from every position where he made a stand, and encamped for the night near Station No. 1. The Fifteenth Corps marched as follows: The detached brigades succeeded in reaching the Savannah and Gulf Railroad at different points and destroying it. The Third Division (General John E. Smith) closed up on General Corse at the canal. As soon as he was within supporting distance General Corse moved forward toward Savannah. He encountered about 600 rebel infantry with two pieces of artillery near the cross-roads. His advanced brigade quickly dislodged them, capturing one piece of artillery and several prisoners. He followed them up across the Little Ogeechee, and, by my direction, took up a strong position about twelve miles from Savannah, and sent a detachment which broke the Gulf railroad. His advance crossed the Little Ogeechee and halted about eight miles from the city. King's Bridge had been burned by the rebels. All the enemy's force was withdrawn from Osterhaus' front in the morning, except the independent garrison at Fort McAllister, situated on the right bank and near the mouth of the Ogeechee. During the day that section of the pontoon bridge which had been with General Blair's column was sent to Dillon's Ferry, near Fort Argyle, and laid across the Ogeechee, thus substantially uniting my two right columns.

December 10, the entire command closed in on the enemy's works which covered Savannah—General Osterhaus with the right column, consisting of General Corse's division, followed by General Hazen, on the King's Bridge road; the central column, consisting of General John E. Smith's division, followed by General Woods; and the left, General Blair's corps, Major-General Mower's division in advance. These several columns struck the enemy's lines simultaneously with the Left Wing of the army. The nature of the country was such as to render the approaches to that front extremely difficult. By means of the canal and the Little Ogeechee River he was able to flood the country; besides, the great portion of the front was a marsh, with a deep stream winding through it, under the cover of a number of batteries of the enemy. Pursuant to Special Field Orders, No. 130, from your headquarters, the Army of the Tennessee simply gained ground to the right. With regard to opening communication with the fleet, the engineer department, under direction of Capt. C. B. Reese, chief engineer, was instructed to rebuild King's Bridge, which was effected by the morning of the 13th. The work was a remarkable one (being completed in about two days' time), considering there was little left of the old bridge except the posts. The bridge measured 1,000 feet in length. The general-in-chief in the above order had directed General Kilpatrick to aid me in opening communication with the fleet. I therefore sent him across the pontoon bridges near Fort Argyle to reconnoiter Fort McAllister and the inlets in that vicinity, and, if practicable, to take the fort. General Sherman himself subsequently modified these directions, ordering Kilpatrick not to assault the works. General Hazen, of the Fifteenth Corps, was directed to hold his division in readiness to cross King's Bridge the moment it was completed and take Fort McAllister. General Kilpatrick made his reconnaissance on the 12th, drove in the outposts at McAllister, and reported the fort defended by a garrison of some 200 men, with several heavy guns bearing on the land approaches.

The morning of the 13th I accompanied General Sherman to Doctor Cheves' rice mill, where we had McAllister full in view. At the rice mill a section of De Gress' battery was firing occasional shots at the fort opposite, three miles and a half distant, as a diversion, having for its principal object, however, to attract the attention of the fleet. During the day we watched the fort and the bay, endeavoring to catch glimpses of the division moving upon the work and of vessels belonging to the fleet. About midday the rebel artillery at McAllister opened inland, firing occasionally from three or four different guns, and by our glasses we could observe Hazen's skirmishers firing on the fort. About the same time a movable smoke, like that from a steamer, attracted our attention near the mouth of the Ogeechee. Signal communication was established with General Hazen, who gave us notice that he had invested the fort, and also that he observed the steamer. General Sherman signaled him from the top of the old rice mill that it was important to carry the fort by assault to-day. The steamer had now approached near enough to draw the fire of the fort when her signal flag was descried. Captain McClintock, aided by Lieutenant Sampson, signal officers, speedily communicated with the vessel, which proved to be a tug sent by General Foster and Admiral Dahlgren for the purpose of communicating with us. Just as the signal officer of the vessel inquired if the McAllister was ours, we noticed a brisker fire at the fort, and our flags and men passing the abatis, through the ditch and over the parapet, and then we saw the men fire upward in the air, and could distinctly hear their cheer of triumph as they took possession of the fort. It was a gallant assault. General Hazen lost, in killed and wounded, about 90 men; of the garrison, between 40 and 50 killed and wounded, and the rest captured. There were 22 guns of various descriptions, and a large quantity of ammunition, captured in the fort. That night I accompanied General Sherman in a small boat on a visit to General Hazen, to the fort, and thence down the river to the steamer. Here we learned that Captain Duncan and the two scouts that I had sent down the Ogeechee, on arriving at the Savannah canal, had succeeded in passing all obstructions and reached the fleet, and communicated with Admiral Dahlgren. Until now I had been uncertain as to the fate of the party. After the general had written several dispatches, we returned to General Hazen's quarters, feeling that our expedition had been completely successful, our supplies sure, and the possession of Savannah not far distant. It having been intimated that our future plans would be modified by specific instructions from the Commander-in-Chief, General Sherman and his officers became anxious to crown our success by the capture of Savannah. In order to accomplish this every exertion was made. Heavy guns were brought from Hilton Head and McAllister and placed in position, the lines were worked up closer to the enemy, along the dikes, good batteries constructed for small guns, and every part of the front of Generals Osterhaus and Blair thoroughly reconnoitered; light bridges were constructed and fascines made, so as to span the streams and fill up the ditches; in brief, every possible preparation was made to assault the enemy's works. The same was the case along General Slocum's front. Two, at least, of my division commanders felt perfectly confident of success in case the assault should be made. While these preparations were going on, the general-in-chief, having demanded the surrender of Savannah on the 18th instant, and having been refused, had gone to the fleet in order to secure co-operation from the admiral and General Foster in the contemplated attack. He left directions to get ready, but not to strike till his return.

The morning of the 21st, about sunrise, Brigadier-General Leggett reported that the enemy had evacuated his front. Soon the same report came from General Slocum and from other officers. General Slocum moved at once and took possession of Savannah, the enemy having withdrawn to the South Carolina shore. He had abandoned heavy guns in all the works on my front, in town, and at the different forts on the coast. Until now our depot had been at King's Bridge, where the army had built a good wharf and corduroyed the main road thereto from our front for the most of the way. Besides, the railroad between the Ogeechee and the Altamaha was completely destroyed—Brigadier-General Hazen having the eastern and Major-General Mower the western half. This work was completely done, as directed in Special Field Orders, No. 133, from your headquarters.

I have only attempted to touch upon the work really accomplished by the Right Wing of the army, and have purposely abstained from discussing the contemplated objects of the campaign. The former is best told in the accompanying statistical record, and the latter are already evinced in the growing confidence of our army in a speedy and complete success.

I wish to acknowledge my obligations to Major-General Osterhaus, commanding Fifteenth Corps, for his great activity and energy displayed during the entire campaign.

To Major-General Blair, commanding Seventeenth Corps, I feel specially indebted for his hearty co-operation at all times, and for his successful accomplishment of the work allotted to his command.

I here name again the division commanders: Maj. Gen. J. A. Mower, Brig. Gen. C. R. Woods, Brig. Gen. John E. Smith, Brig. Gen. M. D. Leggett, Brig. Gen. W. B. Hazen, Brig. Gen. J. M. Corse, Brig. Gen. Giles A. Smith. I cannot express too high commendation of these officers, who have worked vigorously, early and late, without flagging, to keep their commands in order, to accomplish the marches, to bridge creeks and rivers, to fight battles, destroy railroads; in short, who were ready, without question or hesitation, to set on foot and carry through the varied labors given into their charge.

I wish further to tender to brigade commanders and to other officers and soldiers of this army something of the deep sense of obligation I feel toward them, and commend them to the commander-in-chief, and through him to the country, for cheerfulness, for constancy, for ability, and for distinguished gallantry.

Much praise is due Lieut. Col. William Tweeddale for the aid he afforded the chief engineer in building wagon and foot bridges across the rivers that we met.

I tender my thanks to Admiral Dahlgren and Major-General Foster for their courtesy and the assistance they rendered me in the operations near Savannah.

I wish to bring before the commander-in-chief the names of my staff, who so materially gave me assistance during the campaign:

Lieut. Col. William E. Strong, assistant inspector-general and chief of staff, ever afforded me the most cheerful and ready assistance. He always accompanied one or the other of the columns en route, and used every exertion to have my orders carried out in letter and spirit.

Capt. S. L. Taggart, assistant adjutant-general, aided by Capt. W. Bedford, were never too weary to issue clear and distinct orders after the day's march, and otherwise constantly afforded me aid in bearing dispatches.

Capt. C. B. Reese, chief engineer, with the assistance of Lieutenant Stickney, have always received my warm commendations for their untiring activity, both in engineering and topographical duty. He collated information with regard to different roads, furnished me good maps when needed, and superintended the laying of pontoons, and the rebuilding of bridges over rivers and creeks in our route.

Maj. T. W. Osborn, chief of artillery, aided by Maj. M. V. Z. Woodhull, assistant adjutant-general, and Lieut. W. N. Taylor, aide-de-camp, were constant in their exertions to mobilize the artillery, and keep the animals and material in perfect order. Major Osborn always ably assisted me in using the artillery on the field, and I always found him and his officers able and hearty co-operators, frequently giving me material aid not connected with that special department. Whenever an opportunity has afforded, our batteries have been located, intrenched, and handled in the most skillful manner. Quite brisk artillery duels transpired after our investment of Savannah, where my attention was more particularly called to the artillery of the command, and when I have had occasion to admire the skill and bravery of its officers and men.

Maj. E. Whittlesey, judge-advocate of the department, has afforded me substantial aid by carefully revising all the courts-martial and records of military commissions, besides doing ably other important duties connected with different departments of the service.

Capt. D. H. Buel, chief of ordnance, receives my commendations for his carefulness in regulating the ordnance supplies in such manner as to occasion me no trouble or anxiety.

Capt. E. P. Pearson, jr., commissary of musters, assisted me heartily in various ways during the campaign, and always has performed the duties of his department with fidelity and the clearest apprehension of its requirements.

My chief quartermaster, Col. J. T. Conklin, has performed cheerfully all the duties devolving upon him, omitting no exertion to procure animals and forage as needed.

My chief commissary, Lieut. Col. David Remick, has anticipated the wants of the command and regulated the supply in such manner that no real want has been felt by any soldier of this army during our lengthy campaign. I commend him for cheerfulness, fidelity, and ability, in discharging the duties of his department.

Capt. D. W. Whittle, assistant provost-marshal-general, receives my hearty approbation for his activity in discharging the public duties of his department, for his careful record and disposition of prisoners, and for his unremitting attention to the comfort and interest of myself and staff, while acting in his capacity of commandant of headquarters.

No department of this army has been better conducted on this campaign than the medical. To Asst. Surg. D. L. Huntington, acting medical director, is due great praise for his diligence and eminent success. To him and to Doctor Duncan, the staff surgeons, the officers and soldiers at headquarters of the army are indebted for all the medical aid they required.

Maj. C. H. Howard, senior aide-de-camp, is commended for his diligence, in causing my orders to be executed, in bearing dispatches by perilous and distant routes, and for affording me sympathy and moral support of one who identifies himself completely with the interests of the service.

Capt. W. M. Beebe, jr., additional aide-de-camp, receives my thanks for his generous assistance, being over anxious to undergo any risk, or perform a gallant action.

Capt. F. W. Gilbreth, aide-de-camp, is always at the post of duty, and has spared no pains to carry my orders promptly, and see them executed.

Lieut. E. Blake, staff quartermaster and commissary of subsistence, has shown himself remarkably efficient, and has often received my special thanks.

Capt. E. H. Kirlin, chief of scouts, has carefully reconnoitered the country through Capt. William Duncan and the other scouts, and kept me well advised of the movements of the enemy.

Lieut. J. A. Sladen has cheerfully aided me, writing at my dictation, bearing dispatches, and keeping important records.

My recommendations for the promotion of general and staff officers have already been forwarded and will be found separate in duplicate accompanying this report.

The general-in-chief has been enabled, under a Providential care, not to be mistaken to conduct our noble army thus far to results that one year ago seemed scarcely possible of attainment. He has secured our complete confidence, and, therefore, it may not be improper for me to express the faith that it is our mission, under his direction, to give the finishing blow to this hated rebellion.*

Please find accompanying this a statistical record for the campaigns.

Respectfully,

O. O. HOWARD,
Major-General, Commanding.

Capt. L. M. DAYTON,
Aide-de-Camp.

[Inclosure.]

Statistical report of property captured and destroyed, negroes freed, and prisoners captured, by the Army of the Tennessee during the recent campaigns in Northern and Central Georgia, from October 4 to December 31, 1864.

Negroes set free (estimated number)		3,000
Prisoners captured by Fifteenth Army Corps:		
Commissioned officers	32	
Enlisted men	515	
		547

* For map accompanying this report, see Plate LXIX, Map 5 of the Atlas.

Prisoners captured by Seventeenth Army Corps:		
Commissioned officers	2	
Enlisted men	117	
		119
Total prisoners captured		666
Escaped Federal prisoners:		
Commissioned officers	6	
Enlisted men	43	
		49
Bales of cotton burned *a*		3,523
Subsistence captured (viz, breadstuff, beef, sugar, and coffee), at Government cost of ration in Louisville		$283,202
Command started from Atlanta with head of cattle	1,000	
Took up as captured cattle	10,500	
		11,500
Consumed on the trip		9,000
Balance on hand December 18, 1864		2,500
Horses captured:		
By Fifteenth Army Corps	369	
By Seventeenth Army Corps	562	
		931
Mules captured:		
By Fifteenth Army Corps	786	
By Seventeenth Army Corps	1,064	
		1,850
Corn:		
By Fifteenth Army Corps ....pounds	2,500,000	
By Seventeenth Army Corps ....do	2,000,000	
		4,500,000
Fodder:		
By Fifteenth Army Corps ....pounds	2,500,000	
By Seventeenth Army Corps ....do	2,000,000	
		4,500,000
Miles of railroad destroyed		191

a Ocmulgee Mills (1,500 spindles) and large amount of cotton cloth burned; value not known.

No. 8.

Report of Capt. James M. McClintock, U. S. Army, Acting Chief Signal Officer.

SIGNAL CORPS, U. S. ARMY,
DEPARTMENT AND ARMY OF THE TENNESSEE,
Savannah, Ga., December 24, 1864.

COLONEL: I have the honor to submit the following report of the operations of the detachment under my command during the campaign commencing November 15 and ending in the occupation of Savannah, Ga., December 21, 1864:

On the 15th the detachment moved with the army from Atlanta in the following order, viz: With department headquarters, Lieutenant Sampson, acting adjutant; Lieutenant Ware, acting assistant quartermaster, signal detachment, and myself. With Fifteenth Corps, Lieutenants Sherfy, Weirick, Shellabarger, and Adams; and with Seventeenth Corps, Lieutenants Dunlap, Worley, Allen, and Kelly.

During the time from the departure from Atlanta till the investment of Savannah no line of communication by signals was established or regular signal duty performed, owing principally to the unfavorable country through which we passed, it being densely wooded and quite level. Yet the detachment rendered valuable service upon the march by scouting, carrying information regarding roads, rivers, ferries, &c. In one instance a detachment, of which Lieutenant Sampson and ten men formed the greater part, was sent out by the general commanding to destroy a bridge on the Gulf railroad, but after proceeding some thirty miles was compelled to abandon the project, having met the enemy in greatly superior numbers. A rocket code was also established by Captain Bachtell, chief signal officer military division, for the purpose of transmitting information from the different corps to the general commanding the grand army, and used when occasion required.

On the 10th of December, under orders from the general commanding, I accompanied a party to reconnoiter the country between the Ogeechee Rivers, with a view of opening communication with the fleet, which was supposed to be in the vicinity of Ossabaw Sound, but failed to see anything of our vessels. On the 11th Lieutenant Sampson and myself established a station of observation at a rice mill on the Great Ogeechee two miles and a half north of Fort McAllister. From this point we obtained a good view of the rebel works on the Little Ogeechee, also part of the sound; and to the 13th a strict watch was kept during the day, while rockets were sent up at certain intervals through the night to attract, if possible, the attention of any vessel that might be in the sound near the mouth of the river. The sub-detachments, in charge of Lieutenants Sherfy and Dunlap, also put forth their efforts in a similar manner, but all was apparently of no avail. On the 13th Lieutenant Sherfy and party accompanied the Second Division, Fifteenth Army Corps, Brigadier-General Hazen commanding, which moved across the river and attacked Fort McAllister. Upon arriving near the fort he opened communication with the mill station, and during the engagement several important messages were transmitted. The rice mill being a good position from which to observe the operations at the fort, there were consequently a number of general officers assembled at this point, and among them were Generals Sherman and Howard. About 2 p.m. a vessel was discovered in the sound, which finally moved up the river to within calling distance. We then opened with her, and messages were then exchanged between General Sherman and General Foster and Admiral Dahlgren. After the fall of the fort Lieutenant Sherfy moved his station to it, and again established communication with us. This line, by direction of the general commanding, was to be kept open until further orders. While in communication with Lieutenant Sherfy and the vessel we received great assistance from Lieutenants Ware and Kelly, who had arrived with the general just before the commencement of the fight at the fort.

On the 14th Lieutenant Sampson and myself returned to headquarters, leaving Lieutenants Dunlap and Kelly to work the station. On the 17th I received orders from Captain Bachtell to extend the line to General Sherman's headquarters, due north from the fort. Lieutenant Sherfy was placed in charge, and opened it as soon as practicable. Length of line when completed twelve miles, with three intermediate repeating stations. On the 19th Lieutenant Dunlap reconnoitered the country between the fort and King's Bridge, fifteen miles up the river. At that place supplies for the army were to be landed, and communication between the points was necessary for the benefit of the commissary and quartermaster. On the 20th, having reported favorably regarding the proposed line, he was instructed to open it, but the occupation of the city on the 21st by the Federal forces rendered this line useless. Lieutenant Sherfy, however, was retained, and many important messages transmitted until the evening of the 22d, when, by order of the general commanding, it was broken up and the officers withdrew to their respective detachments.

I have the honor to be, colonel, very respectfully, your obedient servant,

JAMES M. McCLINTOCK,
Captain and Acting Chief Signal Officer.

Lieut. Col. W. J. L. NICODEMUS,
Commanding Signal Corps, U. S. Army, Washington, D. C.

No. 9.

Report of Lieut. Col. David Remick, Chief Commissary of Subsistence.

HDQRS. DEPARTMENT AND ARMY OF THE TENNESSEE,
Near Savannah, Ga., December 18, 1864.

GENERAL: I have the honor to make the following report of subsistence for the Army of the Tennessee:

We took from Atlanta as follows: Hard bread, 15 days; fresh beef, 10 days; sugar, 15 days; coffee, 25 days; salt, 60 days.

It was thirty-four days from the time we left Atlanta until we received stores, which would give the following amount of subsistence taken from the country for 35,000 men:

Stores.	Number of days rations.	Quantity.	Rate per pound.	Total amount.
		Pounds.	*Cents.*	
Bread stuff	19	665,000	7	$46,550 00
Fresh beef	30	1,312,500	15	196,875 00
Sugar	18	89,250	27	24,097 50
Coffee	8	22,400	70	15,680 00
Total cost (Government price)				$283,202 50

Our command started with head of cattle	1,000
Took up as captured cattle	10,500
	11,500
Consumed on the trip	9,000
Balance on hand	2,500

I would respectfully call your attention to the very imperfect coopering of packages containing stores. When they are to be transported over long and rough roads by wagons, the boxes of hard bread should be bound with iron hoops or hickory withes, and sugar should be put in substantial barrels.

Very respectfully, your obedient servant,

D. REMICK,
Lieut. Col. and Chief Com. of Sub. Dept. and Army of the Tenn.

Maj. Gen. O. O. HOWARD.

No. 10.

Report of Asst. Surg. David L. Huntington, U. S. Army, Acting Medical Director.

MEDICAL DIRECTOR'S OFFICE,
HDQRS. DEPARTMENT AND ARMY OF THE TENNESSEE,
Savannah, Ga., December 25, 1864.

GENERAL: I have the honor to submit a brief report of the operations of the Medical Department of the Army of the Tennessee, during the past campaign, terminating in the occupation of Savannah.

Previously to entering upon the campaign such sick and wounded as would not immediately be fit for duty, or who were liable to embarrass the movements of the army, were transferred to the general hospitals at Chattanooga, Nashville, and beyond. The number thus removed was 748, the greater portion of whom were recruits suffering from measles and diseases incident to newly enlisted men. The army has been as well supplied with medical stores as the authorized transportation would allow. No scarcity has been felt, the sick and wounded receiving everything necessary. All preparations being complete, the army left East Point upon the 15th of November, and upon the 21st of December entered the city of Savannah. The average distance marched daily has been ten miles and two-thirds. The sanitary condition of the army has been peculiarly gratifying—the abundance of nutritious food, and particularly of vegetables, the fine weather, good roads, and easy marches, have all proved most salutary to the troops. From an examination of the weekly reports, I find that the average percentage of men unfit for duty from the 15th of November to the week ending December 17 has been scarcely 2 per cent. (in actual figures 1.9), and this including the wounded. During the same period, 32 cases of death from disease have occurred, and 29 men have died from wounds, the greater part of this number dying within three days after the receipt of the injury. On the third day's march one mild case of varioloid was reported. Immediate directions were given to vaccinate all who had been exposed, also all as to whom any doubt existed as to their having been vaccinated. No further case has come to my knowledge. Two cases of fractured thighs were left on the road, it being deemed impracticable to transport them.

On the 22d of November, near Macon, the lines held by troops of the First Division, Fifteenth Army Corps, were attacked by the rebels. After gallantly repelling the assault, our loss was found to be 13 killed and 40 wounded. The wounded were transported in ambulances 190 miles, and have done remarkably well, many of the slighter cases having already returned to duty. At the passages of the Oconee and Ogeechee Rivers skirmishing occurred, but with very trifling injury to us.

On the 13th of December the troops of the Second Division, Fifteenth Army Corps, assaulted and gallantly carried Fort McAllister, with a loss of 12 killed and 80 wounded. The major part of the casualties occurred from the torpedoes which were placed in and about the works. The wounds thus inflicted were generally of a grave nature.

On the 19th of December the hospital transport Cosmopolitan reported, and, in obedience to instructions from the chief medical officer of the military division, I transferred to the hospitals at Beaufort, S. C., 266 cases of sick and wounded.

The casualties in front of Savannah were comparatively few—37 men wounded, 5 deaths from wounds. Fortunately, the season of the year has prevented any considerable increase of sickness while we were detained in the low and swampy grounds environing the city.

On the 23d of December I transferred to hospital at Beaufort, S. C., under directions from Surg. John Moore, U. S. Army, the sick and wounded of General Hazen's division (Second Division, Fifteenth Army Corps), and at the same time the wounded Confederate prisoners of war, amounting in all to 150 cases.

On taking possession of Savannah, directions were given to continue the division hospital organization, the number of the sick hardly warranting, for the present, a greater expansion. Preparations have been made, or are in progress, by which the sick of the different divisions will be comfortably placed in buildings through the city. Abundant supplies, both medical and sanitary, are open to us at Hilton Head, and preparations are now going on for fully equipping the medical department with an ample supply of necessary articles.

RECAPITULATION.

Average percentage of men unfit for duty during the campaign	1.9
Number wounded on campaign	196
Deaths from disease on campaign	32
Deaths from wounds on campaign	29
Left on road from necessity	2
Sick and wounded transferred to hospitals at Beaufort, S. C	386
Wounded Confederate soldiers transferred to hospital at Beaufort	30

At Hillsborough I came into possession of the names of certain soldiers belonging to General Stoneman's command, who had been wounded and left at or near Hillsborough, and afterward died. A list of these men is appended. I am happy to state that I feel convinced that they were well and kindly treated. They have all been buried in or about Hillsborough.

In conclusion, I must bear willing testimony to the zealous, faithful, and untiring care which our sick and wounded have received at the hands of the medical officers of this army. The length of march has made it a difficult, if not hazardous, matter to transport men badly wounded in ambulances; but the result has been most satisfactory, and the admirable condition of the wounded reflects much credit upon those whose industry and skill have so greatly promoted this result.

I am, very respectfully, your obedient servant,

D. L. HUNTINGTON,

Asst. Surg., U. S. Army, Actg. Med. Director, Dept. of the Tenn.

Maj. Gen. O. O. HOWARD,

Commanding Department and Army of the Tennessee.

List of men belonging to General Stoneman's command who died of wounds at or near Hillsborough, Ga.: John Smaltz, private, Company D, Fifth Indiana Volunteer Cavalry; H. L. Ives, sergeant, Company G, Eighth Michigan Volunteer Cavalry; Andrew J. Catron, sergeant, Company L, First Kentucky Volunteer Cavalry; William Farmer, private, Company L, First Kentucky Volunteer Cavalry; Benjamin Sharp, private, Company A, First Kentucky Volunteer Cavalry; Lieutenant Humphrey, First Kentucky Volunteer Cavalry.

No. 11.

Reports of Maj. Gen. Peter J. Osterhaus, U. S. Army, Commanding Fifteenth Army Corps.

HEADQUARTERS FIFTEENTH ARMY CORPS,
Savannah, Ga., December 26, 1864.

CAPTAIN:*

The orders issued regulating the march of the columns from Atlanta south assigned me again to the extreme right, with the privilege of using one or more parallel roads, if it did not interfere with the columns on my left (Seventeenth Army Corps). I respectfully refer the major-general commanding to the accompanying map,† marked B, for the routes taken by and the camps of the different divisions at the end of every day's march.

On November 15, 1864, in pursuance of orders received, the Fifteenth Army Corps left its encampments—Generals Woods, Smith, and Hazen, marching in one column from Atlanta, arrived, via Rough and Ready, in the vicinity of Stockbridge; General Corse, who had on the previous night reached the Chattahoochee River, was necessarily delayed at Atlanta, receiving and issuing quartermaster's stores, which were laid apart for them, and therefore had to halt for the night in the vicinity of Rough and Ready. The head of the former columns (First, Second, and Third Divisions) found near the aforesaid railroad station some rebel pickets, who, evidently surprised at our unexpected appearance, fled. Near Stockbridge the rebel general, Lewis, with about 1,000 mounted troops and one section of artillery, held a position, but he also yielded it after a very feeble show of resistance. This rebel general subsequently indulged merely in the destruction of bridges to oppose our advance, keeping his troops at a very discreet distance. The First, Second, and Third Divisions were encamped in the vicinity of Stockbridge, with a view to prevent a collision with the Seventeenth Army Corps, whose march was also directed toward Stockbridge.

McDonough being the point to be reached on the 16th of November, I directed General Hazen (Second Division) to march on the main road via Stockbridge, while Generals Woods and Smith moved via Lee's Mills, and General Corse was to take a direct road from his camp at Rough and Ready, by Lee's Mills, to McDonough. At McDonough the whole of the Fifteenth Army Corps was for the first time assembled, and the divisions in supporting distance of each other.

The corps marched on November 17 in one column to Locust Grove, where, to facilitate the movement, two columns were formed, moving toward Planters' Factory, on the Ocmulgee River—Generals Woods and Hazen via Indian Springs, Generals Smith and Corse via Jackson. On the same day I succeeded in pushing the Twenty-ninth Missouri Infantry to that river, and secured both banks for the intended bridges. As soon as the pontoon could be laid down at the Ocmulgee Factories, General Smith crossed and took a defensive position on the east side of the Ocmulgee (November 18), the other divisions of the corps remaining in their respective camps until the Seventeenth Corps had crossed.

At 7.30 a. m. November 19 the Seventeenth Corps yielded the bridge to us and we commenced crossing, General Hazen leading. General

---

* For portion of report here omitted, see Vol. XXXIX, Part I, p. 740.

† Not found.

Smith had previously received orders to march on the direct road to Hillsborough, Generals Hazen and Woods were to follow Smith, while General Corse, who brought up the rear, had orders to march, via Monticello, to Hillsborough. This general was also directed to destroy, before leaving the west bank of the Ocmulgee, the cotton factory, &c., which had been used for military purposes by the rebel Government. Rain, very bad roads, and the long trains of the whole Army of the Tennessee, including those of the cavalry, and the pontoon trains and some 4,000 head of beef-cattle, delayed General Corse considerably. His rear could not leave the river before next morning (November 20), and he could march only as far as Monticello, while Woods, Smith, and Hazen reached the vicinity of Clinton that day. General Kilpatrick's cavalry had preceded us to that place and left on our arrival for Macon. Some rebel cavalry kept hovering around Clinton, and repeatedly attacked our pickets without making any impression.

Early on the morning of November 21 I pushed the Twenty-ninth Missouri (mounted) toward the Macon railroad, with orders to destroy the track, and thus prevent the further use of the road for military purposes. Colonel Gage struck and broke the road at 10 a. m. General Smith's division marched the same day from Clinton on the direct road toward Gordon, while Woods and Hazen moved toward Irwinton. A large force of the enemy being reported at Griswoldville, near which place the outer column (Generals Woods and Hazen) had to pass, it was considered prudent to move only the most necessary trains (ordnance) with this exposed column, and give the bulk of the trains, in charge of General Smith, the inner route. The divisions of Woods and Hazen camped for the night in supporting distance of each other near the Macon railroad. The enemy showed, notwithstanding the presence of the large cavalry force of General Kilpatrick, some temerity, and attacked the column of Woods several times. As it appeared impossible for General Corse's division, with the incumbrances clogging his movements, to reach Clinton in time on November 21 to secure that place against rebel assault, I ordered a brigade of Hazen's division (Col. Theodore Jones) to remain there until the arrival of General Corse. Colonel Jones was constantly annoyed by rebel cavalry. When General Corse came up on next day, he considered the remaining of Colonel Jones most desirable, and this zealous officer therefore held his position until all and everything had safely gone by this point of danger, and then followed General Corse on the direct road to Gordon.

Your orders for the 22d of November were to make a demonstration against Griswoldville, while our trains were to be pushed on toward Gordon with all the dispatch the terrible condition of the rutted roads permitted. I consequently ordered one brigade (General Walcutt's) of General Woods' division to move early on the south side of the railroad in the direction of Griswoldville. When I joined General Walcutt to accompany the expedition, I found a brigade of General Kilpatrick's in his front, and a portion of it, which had tried to drive back the rebel advance line, had just come back without having succeeded. General Walcutt was ordered at once to relieve the cavalry, and the advance was sounded. A strong line of skirmishers, supported by two regiments and some cavalry, which General Kilpatrick had kindly furnished, soon struck the rebels, who were in line behind a creek, or rather swamp, in an open pine land, and caused them, with that peculiar spirit of our troops, to look for their horses and run. General Walcutt kept pushing forward, and his men pursued in double-quick with cheers and laughter the fleeing horsemen, waded the creek, marched through the belt of timber beyond until they reached an open prairie-like field, which was in possession of large rebel cavalry forces. General Walcutt halted here just long enough to correct his lines, caution his skirmishers and supports to be prepared for a cavalry dash, and then they emerged into the open field and made for the rebels, who, throwing away the best chance that can be desired by an intrepid cavalry, fled in confusion. General Walcutt followed rapidly, capturing many horses, equipments, &c. When beyond Griswoldville the rebels, who were commanded by General Wheeler in person, took different roads; and as I had some knowledge of Wheeler's way of maneuvering—which is not formidable in the dash of arms, but sometimes successful by great activity and circumspection—I ordered General Woods to have General Walcutt's command rallied and take a defensive position near the open field mentioned above. The position selected was in the edge of the timber and along a slight rise in the ground, at the base of which a kind of marshy swamp formed a natural obstruction to the approach; the right and left of the position was pretty well secured by swamps, &c. Light breast-works, built of rails, were put up to cover our men, and a section of artillery of Captain Arndt's (First Michigan) battery was ordered there. These preparations were considered sufficient to meet any of General Wheeler's reconnaissances, which he might undertake after finding out that he was no longer pressed, but had to stand a more severe trial. In the afternoon the rebel commander brought forward four brigades of infantry and a battery of artillery, supported by a strong cavalry force, to dislodge General Walcutt from his position. For several hours their attempts were repeated with the greatest impetuosity. Their artillery threw a terrific fire into the frail works of Walcutt, while their columns of infantry marched in heroic style to within fifty yards of our line. It was all in vain! Walcutt and his brave brigade proved that superior skill, coolness, and valor made up for the great disparity in numbers. When night came the enemy retired, leaving over 300 dead on the battle-field and a number of wounded, who were taken care of by our medical corps; also a number of prisoners were taken. Our loss was comparatively light. The brave General Walcutt was wounded by a piece of shell during the fight, and Colonel Catterson assumed the command of the brigade.

During these operations at Griswoldville the division of General Hazen had passed behind General Woods and taken a defensive position in his support two miles south of Gordon. General Smith entered Gordon and General Corse passed by Clinton. A portion of General Woods' command during the day was employed in destroying the railroad track from Griswoldville to within three miles of Gordon, and General Smith, immediately after his arrival, put his men to work to meet General Woods' parties. General Smith finished the work of destruction in the next two days.

General Hazen advanced on the 23d within seven miles of Irwinton, and Woods intrenched a line south of Gordon commanding all the approaches from the west and south. Both divisions marched the following day to Irwinton. At last, on November 24, General Corse's division and the brigade of Second Division (Colonel Jones) arrived with all the trains at Gordon, relieving us of a great deal of anxiety. These officers deserve the highest credit for their faithful execution of orders under difficulties almost insurmountable. They brought a train of many hundred wagons fifty miles and over roads whose condition beggars all description. General Corse encamped for the night in the position vacated by General Woods; Colonel Jones joined his division. The corps was to cross Oconee River, at Ball's Ferry, consequently the four divisions marched early on November 25 from their respective camps toward that point. Hazen and Woods arrived at the ferry; Corse and Smith at Milton and Irwinton, respectively. In order to protect the right flank of our column during its crossing of the river against some rebel forces reported to be at Big Sandy Creek, the Twenty-ninth Missouri (mounted) was stationed along that stream, with orders to destroy all bridges and guard all such points where crossing could be effected. They found some opposition at the Light Wood Knot bridge, but succeeded in destroying it, notwithstanding. When I arrived at the Oconee I found there the First Alabama Cavalry, who reported the enemy in position on the east bank. A reconnaissance confirmed the report; but their number was apparently small, and, perceiving that we were preparing in earnest to force a crossing, they left during the night.

Bridges were laid in the morning of November 26, and the corps crossed in the following order: Corse, Woods, Hazen, and Smith. The latter general had orders to remain until the bridge was taken up and the trains all on the way. The two leading divisions marched the same afternoon to Irwin's Cross-Roads, and from there three brigades were detailed on next morning to destroy the Savannah railroad to Station No. 13. The remaining brigades and trains of these divisions (Woods' and Corse's) marched the afternoon (November 27) on the Augusta dirt road to the intersection of the Savannah dirt road, with orders to proceed, on November 28, on the latter road, to a point near railroad station No. 11, and there meet the divisions of Generals Smith and Hazen. These divisions came to Irwin's Cross-Roads on the morning of November 27, and I intended to march with them on next day, by plantation roads, to the point of meeting; consequently all the divisions of the corps encamped the next night (November 28) in supporting distance and within seven miles of Station 11.

On November 29 Woods and Corse followed a very dim road (called the Democrat road) to its intersection with the Swainsborough and old Savannah road. The divisions of Hazen and Smith marched on the main Sandersville and Savannah road until they struck, one mile south of Station No. 11, the Seventeenth Army Corps, who had the right of way. The ground permitting, I ordered a parallel road to be cut for about two miles to a fork which led into a road that ran parallel to that taken by Woods and Corse. The country here is almost a perfect wilderness—long-leaved pines cover the poor sandy soil but sparely, and exclude all other vegetation except where an occasional creek or marsh, lined with narrow skirts of shrub-like undergrowth, breaks this monotony; but what makes the soil almost worthless for agricultural purposes rendered it favorable to our operations. An energetic corps of axmen to corduroy roads across the creeks and marshes opens in a short time enough space for any number of columns. On November 30, when we marched toward the little town of Summerville, the Second, Third, and Fourth Divisions moved part of the way abreast of each other. Generals Woods and Corse reached that day a point within three miles and a half of railroad station No. 9½. Generals Hazen and Smith halted at Summerville. As the accompanying map* shows, there are two roads running substantially parallel to and south of the Ogeechee River and the Savannah railroad; they unite opposite Station No. 2. Both roads were represented practicable, and consequently the corps was

* Not found.

divided into two columns—Hazen and Smith were to march from Summerville, via Statesborough, to No. 2; the left column (Woods and Corse) on the inner route. I took care to regulate the marches daily, so as to have the columns always in supporting distance, and used a portion of the Twenty-ninth Missouri (mounted) to keep up communication and explore the intermediate ground between the columns. The two columns crossed Scull's Creek on December 2, and were ordered to lie over on December 3, to give the columns to our left time to come up with us. The troops of these columns were partly employed in breaking the railroad, and in order to assist this work, detachments of General Woods' troops had crossed the Ogeechee, at Green's Bridge, on December 1 (which we had to repair), and burnt the railroad in the vicinity of Station No. 8.

Next day (December 2) a pontoon was ordered to be laid opposite Station No. 7, and large portions of the divisions of Generals Corse and Woods put to work destroying the railroad there, which they did most effectually for many miles. On the 4th and 5th of December the two columns continued their routes, bringing the left column opposite Guyton (Station No. 3), while the right column camped about four miles off on the headwaters of Black Creek, December 5. General Hazen, who led the right column, fell in on both days with a force of General Wheeler's cavalry; after a lively skirmish at Statesborough, the rebels dispersed and did not make their appearance any more. The next day the corps had to lie over again; but very early in the morning I pushed the Twenty-ninth Missouri forward to secure the crossing of the Ogeechee River, near Station No. 2 (at Wright's and Jenks' Bridges). We found the bridges burnt. I ordered at once a foot bridge to be constructed on the remains of Wright's Bridge, and directed General Woods to send one brigade to the bridge and hold it. The commanding officer of the brigade (Colonel Williamson) threw a regiment across the Ogeechee, and constructed on the east side breast-works, and then pushed a detachment of fifty men, under Captain McSweeney (Ninth Iowa), to the railroad with orders to break it, and thus prevent the enemy from re-enforcing his troops, who opposed the advance of the columns on the east side of the river. Captain McSweeney moved directly for the railroad about two miles off and broke it in plain view of a train coming down loaded with troops. He then fell back pursued by the rebels, but he kept them in check. When in the evening the enemy attempted to drive Colonel Williamson's men from the breast-works thrown up in the afternoon, he was repulsed with some loss. Our appearance on the flank of the rebels drew their attention to the lower crossing, and they sent a detachment of infantry to Jenks' Bridge, three miles below Wright's.

The next morning (December 7) the divisions of Generals Woods, Smith, and Corse were concentrated near Jenks' Bridge. General Hazen was ordered to send, by way of a diversion, the brigade of Colonel Oliver, which had been pushed on the day previous toward Jenks' Bridge, to the Cannouchee and take possession of the bridge near Bryan Court-House; with the rest of his command General Hazen was to follow Colonel Oliver's brigade as far as Black Creek. When Colonel Oliver withdrew in the morning from Jenks' Bridge he left the Ninetieth Illinois (Colonel Stuart) there to watch the rebels on the east side of the river. General Corse on his arrival at Jenks' Bridge found Colonel Stuart behind a line of rifle-pits, livelily disputing the crossing. To re-enforce Colonel Stuart one section of Arndt's battery was brought into position and opened. They succeeded in keeping the rebels under cover while some pontoons were launched, and, manned by the Ninetieth Illinois (Colonel Stuart), crossed the river. As soon as a boat-load of men got a foothold on the other bank the rebels fell back to a line of works at the eastern extremity of a long dam or levee, which formed the connection across the swamp between the river and the high land. The dam is about half a mile long. Our pontoniers could lay the bridge without being molested any further. While this work was going on and the flood-bridges in the dam were repaired, General Corse crossed a portion of his command in boats, and they worked their way through the swamp and the thick woods toward the rebel position. To facilitate their dislodgment General Woods was ordered early in the morning to push Colonel Williamson's whole brigade across Wright's Bridge above and try to strike the enemy's flank. When the pontoons were laid I ordered the advance. The Second Iowa Infantry, of General Rice's brigade (Corse's division), confronted the rebels. They moved up in very good style, pushing sharply on the enemy's wings, and forced them very soon to make for their support, which was intrenched in double line on an elevation where the road from Jenks' Bridge crosses at right angles the Wright's Bridge road. Colonel Williamson's brigade was advancing on the latter road. When I had cause to believe this column in supporting distance, I directed General Rice to attack the rebels in their breast-works. The Second Iowa rushed up to them over an open plain and carried the works, killing and wounding a number and capturing about thirty prisoners. Colonel Williamson arrived at the moment the works were taken, and he dispatched some companies to the railroad, while General Rice advanced on a parallel road to the station. The enemy fled. A portion of Corse's division was stationed at the railroad station, while the remainder of the division and Colonel Williamson's brigade intrenched and occupied a line at the cross-roads mentioned above.

In the evening (December 7) General Hazen reported that Colonel Oliver had arrived at the Cannouchee, but found the bridge partly burnt and strongly defended. The crossing of the river was deemed essential in order to destroy the Gulf railroad, which was largely used by the rebel authorities at Savannah. Under orders from headquarters Department and Army of the Tennessee I moved next morning (December 8) toward Cannouchee River with General Hazen's division and that of General Woods', except Williamson's brigade, which was to occupy Station No. 2 until the arrival of the Seventeenth Army Corps. After reconnoitering the Cannouchee River I brought, however, only General Hazen's division to the bridge near Bryan Court-House, halting Woods' four miles north of it at the forks of the road to Fort Argyle. The enemy's position on the south side of the Cannouchee was naturally very strong. Wide, impassable swamps line both sides of that stream, and there are but very few points where a crossing is practicable. There is none below Bryan Court-House, and parties sent twelve miles upstream could not learn of another above. From the Court-House a good road leads to the bridge, but an impenetrable live-oak swamp is on the other side of it. A levee and three bridges, of an aggregate length of 800 feet, lead through the swamp to the highland; the levee and bridges were swept by a section of artillery and by infantry covered by breast-works. I was, however, informed that there had been an old ferry below the bridge, and thus I hoped to be able to effect a crossing there if the exact spot could be found. By minute inspection of the banks during the night the landing of the old ferry was detected, and an expedition sent in a boat across the river struck high ground and a rebel picket. Our men fired and created the greatest alarm in the rebel camp. They opened with infantry and artillery most vigorously, and, to my astonishment, they left the position by 2 a. m.

The next morning (December 9) showed that the contemplated crossing at the old ferry, which the rebels could not prevent, would have exposed their flanks, and, therefore, their sudden departure. Troops were crossed as fast as possible in boats, while the damaged bridge was being repaired. I ordered General Hazen to send two of his brigades to the railroad, which was in full work yet. One brigade marched toward King's Bridge and Way's Station, the other to Fleming Station; both with orders to destroy the road as effectually as possible. (This work of destruction was afterward completed and extended for twenty miles by General Hazen.) The remaining brigade was placed in reserve at the bridge. The expeditionary brigades returned during the night from their work at the railroad, having, with the assistance of the Twenty-ninth Missouri (mounted), driven everything from the road and taken some prisoners.

On the morning of December 8 General Smith was left in charge of the trains corralled at Jenks' Bridge (west side), and General Corse, who was on the east side of the Ogeechee River, moved his division down the stream toward Dillon's Bridge, which he found burned, however, and had to be replaced by pontoons. On the following day (9th) the general pushed on and met some rebels at the Savannah Canal and drove them back to their main line, which he assaulted and carried, taking 1 piece of rifled artillery and some 60 prisoners. General Corse's report was laid before you, and I respectfully refer to it for the particulars of this brilliant affair. General Corse followed the rebels across Little Ogeechee and to the north fork of it; but was recalled by General Howard behind the Ogeechee, where he threw up a line of defense. General Smith, with the trains of the Third and Fourth Divisions, moved to the canal, and, early on the morning of December 10, from there up the towpath along the canal (south side) abreast of General Corse, who advanced again beyond the Little Ogeechee on the Savannah road.

I left, on December 10, General Hazen, with orders to march by way of a foot bridge constructed at Dillon's Ferry to the support of Corse, while General Woods, with the trains of the First and Second Divisions, moved across the Ogeechee River by the pontoon bridge near Dillon's and closed on Smith's division (the trains were to be left at the canal). General Corse's advance, which I had joined, found no opposition west of the north fork; but behind that stream, which is rather a wide swamp subject to the influence of the tides, the rebel fortifications and camps were stretched out. The rebel troops gathered on and behind the parapets, and with their banners defiantly unfurled awaited the approach of our column. The open and exposed ground, swamps, and stream in front of the rebel works forbade all sudden attacks, and the men of the advance were kept accordingly under cover, while skirmishers probed all along the lines as closely and carefully as possible. I ordered Captain De Gress' 20-pounder Parrott battery to be brought forward in a position from which it could throw an oblique fire into their main works, which covered the Savannah road, without coming under fire of the rebel batteries. With wonted precision De Gress landed his shots and created great commotion in the garrison. The profiles of the works and the traverses were too heavy, however, to inflict any serious damage. A section of Battery H, First Missouri Artillery, opened from an advanced position near the Savannah road, covered only by some trees. It caused the rebels to open at once with six guns and great vehemence; so much so, that it was not considered prudent on our side to continue the fire. The troops of the four divisions were before night in the positions assigned to them and encamped just out of range of the enemy's artillery. In pursuance of orders received during the night, the Fifteenth Army Corps was to occupy the ground on the right of the Savannah road, and accordingly in the morning of the 11th of December General Corse shifted to the right and as near the Gulf railroad as the march would permit, Woods occupying ground between Corse's left and the Savannah road. General Hazen camped *á cheval* of the road about two miles in the rear of the front divisions, and General Smith moved to Station No. 1, on the Gulf railroad, pushing his pickets forward on that road and to the right to cover the approaches from the south. These movements were very difficult to execute owing to the rain which had converted the road through the marshy soil into a sea of mud and quagmire. To prevent serious delays hereafter I ordered the pioneers at once to construct a double corduroy track from our front to the rear.

On the 12th of December I sent, on the general's order, a section of 20-pounder Parrotts and the Twenty-seventh Missouri Infantry (General Woods' division) to Cheves' rice mill, to assist in some movement against Fort McAllister; and in the night the division of General Hazen, with Battery H, First Missouri Artillery, and the remaining section of De Gress' 20-pounder Parrotts, were ordered to march very early on the 13th, via King's Bridge, to the aforesaid fort and take it. Fort McAllister was very strong and apparently well garrisoned. General Hazen arrived before it at 2 o'clock, and at 3.45 p. m. he had completed his arrangements for the assault. They proved to be in keeping with that noble soldier. When the advance sounded the brave men rushed through a line of torpedoes and heavy abatis, jumped into the wide and deep ditch, and climbed in one heroic élan, which secured them the fort after a few minutes' struggle, but not without a heavy loss, mostly occasioned by the explosion of the torpedoes. Twenty-three siege and field guns and 215 men, the entire garrison, were the immediate prize of the capture; but the most important feature of this victory was that it opened communication with the fleet and thus furnished to our armies the necessary supplies, and put beyond doubt the final capture of Savannah, whose garrison and inhabitants were, according to all information, but scantily supplied. The Second Division garrisoned the captured fort. The artillery was ordered back to take a part in the preparation for the contemplated assault on the Ogeechee lines, as General Hardee, the commander of the rebel forces in Savannah, had refused, on December 17, to surrender. Generals Woods and Corse since December 13 had steadily pushed their line forward and were in close proximity to the rebel works. All points which offered a chance for crossing the swamps and the river between our and the rebel works were looked up and most carefully studied; in fact, everything was done to complete our knowledge of the difficult ground before us. I caused a number of substantial batteries to be thrown up. In selecting the sites for these the principal attention was paid to the rebel fort on the Savannah road, where they had a number of heavy siege pieces in position, and which they undoubtedly considered the key of their whole line. The rebels had also a number of batteries farther to their left, and their fire annoyed Generals Smith's and Corse's lines to some extent; however, the guns used in these batteries were light field pieces, and it appeared that the enemy thought their left sufficiently secured by the natural obstructions; at least, its lines of infantry there were weak, and I did not wish to disturb this belief by an ostentatious display of activity. The ground on our side was covered with timber, and thus permitted us to prepare for any operations that might become desirable in perfect concealment.

On the 19th of December I received your orders to prepare everything for an assault on December 21. The closest investigation of the ground before us showed that the stream could be crossed in two places (in addition of the Savannah road), where it is but very narrow and the approaches to it practicable. One of these points was in General Woods', the other in General Corse's front. Both places never had drawn the enemy's attention, and parties of General Woods and General Corse had gone across in boats without being observed by the rebels. Trestles were built and pontoon-boats gotten ready; the rifle-pits were pushed within 150 to 200 yards of the rebel works. Major Stolbrand, chief of artillery, brought ten pieces of artillery on and to the left of the Savannah road, keeping the remaining eight pieces in reserve, and in a convenient place where they could be ordered to any point where the contemplated attack might demand them. On the morning of December 20 an impression was created that the rebels were withdrawing their pieces from the fort on the Savannah road. To prevent such an undertaking I ordered Captain Zickerick (Twelfth Wisconsin) on the Savannah road battery and Captain Arndt on the Cemetery battery to open on the fort. Their practice was splendid. The enemy, who, after considerable work, succeeded in opening his heavy batteries, had to cease firing very soon under the terrific accuracy of our guns. General Woods' advanced line of infantry, which was rather less than 150 yards from the rebel main line, kept the enemy's sharpshooters completely silent and behind their breast-works. This morning's experience gratified the best hope of a successful assault in the coming night, but orders from General Sherman postponed the attack. During the night of the 20th General Woods' pickets kept the enemy closely under their control, always fearing they would get away. Their fears were correct. Leaving their guns and ammunition in the fort, the rebels sneaked away in the darkness of the night, and the Sixth Iowa Infantry entered, before daylight, their fortifications. Savannah was ours. It proved the richest capture of the war. In my immediate front on the Little Ogeechee and in the portion of the lines around Savannah, which was assigned to the Fifteenth Army Corps on the morning of 21st of December, forty-seven guns, with all ammunition, were found, not counting in the armament at McAllister.

In order to recapitulate, I state that since October 4 to December 21, the Fifteenth Army Corps had marched, in forty-six actual marching days, 684 miles; cut, corduroyed, and otherwise constructed thirty-two miles of road, and built 1,502 yards of bridge; while it destroyed most effectually over 60 miles of railroad. Being on an exposed flank, the corps had a large share of the fighting during the campaign, and the actions at Allatoona, Griswoldville, and McAllister will shine as bright stars in the record of the corps.

Our losses in battle were comparatively light, and I am happy to state that, thanks to the very efficient and skillful medical corps under the direction of Doctor Niccolls, surgeon of volunteers, not a single man of our wounded was left behind and given up to the mercies of a prejudiced enemy. All those poor sufferers came with us through the wilderness of Georgia, and are all doing well. It is a consoling thought that even the remains of those noble martyrs are resting in soil which soon will be redeemed from treason and become our country once more. Lists of casualties have been forwarded.

Notwithstanding we were dependent on the country for the subsistence for men and beasts, and large numbers of foragers were necessarily and constantly at large, the system adopted to regulate these parties was efficient enough even in the face of ubiquitous rebel cavalry on our flanks. The troops and animals were more than amply supplied. At times the men fared luxuriously; and while but very few of our men were taken prisoners, our foraging parties captured a considerable number of rebel officers and soldiers; in one instance they secured the bearer of important dispatches from General Hardee to General Wheeler.

I cannot look back on this campaign without feeling under the greatest obligations to the officers under my command. With the assistance of Generals Woods, Hazen, Smith, and Corse, there are but few things which cannot be achieved by such officers and men as the Fifteenth Army Corps is composed of. I had occasion before this to bring the services of the above generals, and of General Walcutt and other officers, officially to the notice of the major-general commanding the army. I here beg to express my high admiration of them.

My thanks are due to the officers of my staff, namely: Colonel Fort, chief quartermaster; Colonel Carpenter, chief commissary of subsistence; Major Gordon, acting senior aide-de-camp; Major Woodworth, medical inspector; Major Gillette, provost-marshal; Captains Whitehead and Wheeler, assistant adjutants-general; Captain Hubbard, acting aide-de-camp; Captain Perkins, acting assistant inspector-general; Lieutenant Dickey, commissary of musters; Lieutenant Perry, acting aide-de-camp; and Lieutenant Mitchell, ordnance officer. They performed their arduous duties with great zeal and proved to be reliable soldiers.

To Major Stolbrand I have to acknowledge important services during the campaign as chief of artillery of the corps. Through his energy and skill that branch of the arms which was under his immediate care was in most excellent condition.

Captain Klostermann, the acting chief engineer, filled the position with marked ability. He did most valuable services in exploring roads through the virgin forests of Johnson, Emanuel, Bulloch, and Bryant Counties, where for miles and miles there is no guide or landmark, and the compass his sole reliance.

I respectfully refer to the inclosed reports of my subordinate commanders.

I remain, your most obedient servant,

P. JOS. OSTERHAUS,
Major-General, U. S. Volunteers.

Capt. SAMUEL L. TAGGART,
Asst. Adjt. Gen., Department and Army of the Tennessee.

HEADQUARTERS FIFTEENTH ARMY CORPS,
Savannah, Ga., December 25, 1864.

CAPTAIN: I have the honor, in compliance with instructions received, to report upon the artillery captured by this command during the investment of Savannah, Ga.:

First Division, Brig. Gen. C. R. Woods commanding:	
32-pounder smooth-bores	12
8-inch sea-coast howitzers	3
24-pounder howitzer	1
Total	16
Third Division, Brig. Gen. John E. Smith commanding:	
32-pounder smooth-bores	10
8-inch howitzers	4
10-pounder columbiad	1
12-pounder howitzer	1
Total	16
Fourth Division, Brig. Gen. John M. Corse commanding:	
Rifled 6-pounder	1
3-inch 10-pounders	2
32-pounders	14
6-inch rifled gun	1
8-inch sea-coast howitzer	1
6-inch smooth-bore	1
12-pounders, brass	3
3-inch guns, iron	2
Total	25

In addition to the above, the Second Division, Brig. Gen. William B. Hazen commanding, captured at Fort McAllister some 23 guns. His report will be duly forwarded when received.

Very respectfully,

P. JOS. OSTERHAUS,
Major-General.

Capt. SAMUEL L. TAGGART,
Asst. Adjt. Gen., Department and Army of the Tennessee.

HEADQUARTERS FIFTEENTH ARMY CORPS,
Savannah, Ga., January 2, 1865.

CAPTAIN: I have the honor to report that, in compliance with paragraph I, Special Field Orders, No. 192, series of 1863, headquarters Department and Army of the Tennessee, an inspection has been made in the several divisions of the corps, and all surplus stock turned over to the division quartermasters and by them branded and regularly taken up on their papers. I would further invite your attention to the following statement, by divisions, of the number of horses and mules actually turned over:

First Division, Brigadier-General Woods commanding	179
Third Division, Brigadier-General Smith commanding	82
Fourth Division, Brigadier-General Corse commanding	212
Total	480

A report has been called for from the Second Division as to the result of the inspection ordered, and as soon as received an extract will be forwarded to department headquarters for the information of the commanding general.

I am, captain, very respectfully, your obedient servant,

P. JOS. OSTERHAUS,
Major-General, Commanding.

Capt. SAMUEL L. TAGGART,
Asst. Adjt. Gen., Department and Army of the Tennessee.

ADDENDA.

HEADQUARTERS FIFTEENTH ARMY CORPS,
Savannah, Ga., January 1, 1865.

Capt. SAMUEL L. TAGGART,
Asst. Adjt. Gen., Department and Army of the Tennessee:

CAPTAIN: In reply to your request for an estimate of the amount of bridging and corduroying done by the pioneer corps of the several divisions of this army corps, I have the honor to invite your attention to the reports of division commanders, herewith transmitted, and a consolidated estimate prepared for the information of the commanding general by the chief engineer of the corps.

I am, captain, very respectfully, your obedient servant,

MAX. WOODHULL,
Major and Assistant Adjutant-General.
(In absence of the major-general.)

[Inclosure No. 1.]

HDQRS. FIRST DIVISION, FIFTEENTH ARMY CORPS,
Savannah, Ga., December 31, 1864.

Major WOODHULL,
Assistant Adjutant-General, Fifteenth Army Corps:

MAJOR: I respectfully offer the following report of the amount of corduroying, &c., done by my command during the campaign just closed, transcribing from the official report of the commanding officer of my pioneer corps:

	Yards.
Amount of corduroying (cut timber)	6,754
Amount of foot bridge (cut timber)	770
Amount of foot bridge (rails)	825
Amount of wagon bridge (cut timber)	2,007
Total	10,356

Nearly six miles.

New road cut, eleven miles, for teams and infantry. Forts erected: One on the Oconee River, 6,844 feet of dirt thrown up; two on Anderson's plantation, 18,854 feet of dirt thrown up; total, 25,698.

I am, major, very respectfully, your obedient servant,

CHARLES R. WOODS,
Brigadier-General, Commanding.

[Inclosure No. 2.]

Report of amount of bridging and corduroying done by Second Division, Fifteenth Army Corps.

Date.	Locality.	Amount of bridging.	Amount of corduroying.
		Feet.	*Feet.*
Nov. 15	Marched from White Hall to Cotton River	....	300
16	Marched through McDonough and camped on Tussahaw Creek	30	250
17	Marched to Liberty Church	....	200
18	Marched to Indian Springs	....	150
19	Marched to Persis' farm	40	500
20	Marched to Dondersberg's place	30	400
21	Marched through Clinton and camped six miles beyond	....	600
22	Marched to Dr. Gibson's place	....	400
23	Marched nine miles; took up position seven miles west of Irwinton	....	100
24	Marched to Irwinton	....	150
25	Marched to Oconee River	....	400
26	Marched to Flucker's farm	....	800
27	Marched to Irwin's Cross-Roads	200	1,200
28	Encamped on the Little Ohoopee	250	2,000
29	Marched to near Sutherland's Mills	100	2,000
30	Marched to Summerville	150	2,500
Dec. 1	Marched to the junction of Jones' farm and old Savannah road	200	3,500
2	Marched to Scull's Creek	250	4,000
3	....	100	2,000
4	Marched to Statesborough	200	4,000
5	Marched to Proctor's farm	200	2,000
6	Marched to Brier Patch	....	1,500
7	Marched to Black Creek	100	1,500
8	Marched to Bryan Court-House	....	1,000
9	Marched across the Cannouchee River	....	200
10	Encamped ten miles from Savannah	....	250
	Total	1,850	31,900

SAVANNAH, GA., *December 31, 1864.*

[Inclosure No. 3.]

HDQRS. THIRD DIVISION, FIFTEENTH ARMY CORPS,
Savannah, Ga., December 31, 1864.

Maj. MAX. WOODHULL,
Assistant Adjutant-General, Fifteenth Army Corps:

MAJOR: In compliance with instructions of date I have the honor to report the following amount of bridging and corduroying done by this division during the past campaign:

Date.	Locality.	Bridging and corduroying.
		Yards.
Nov. 26	Near Ball's Ferry	1,760
27	East of Oconee River	100
28	Between Irwin's Cross-Roads and Savannah road	300
29	Between camp on Savannah road and Sutherland's Mills	700
30	Sutherland's Mills to Summerville	300
Dec. 1	Between Summerville and Cannouchee	350
2	Cannouchee and Scull's Creek	200
4	Between Scull's Creek and Statesborough	300
7	Between Brannon's and Ogeechee River	400
	Ogeechee road	400
	Road to Station No. 1, Georgia railroad	200
	Total	5,010

I am, major, very respectfully, your obedient servant,

JOHN E. SMITH,
Brigadier-General.

[Inclosure No. 4.]

HDQRS. FOURTH DIVISION, FIFTEENTH ARMY CORPS,
Savannah, Ga., December 31, 1864.

Maj. MAX. WOODHULL,
Assistant Adjutant-General, Fifteenth Army Corps:

MAJOR: In compliance with instructions from corps headquarters this evening, I have the honor to forward the inclosed report of bridges built and corduroying done by this division during the recent campaign. This report does not include the foot bridges built or the roads repaired, previously corduroyed by other divisions.

I have the honor to be, very respectfully, your obedient servant,

JOHN M. CORSE,
Brigadier-General. Commanding.

[Sub-inclosure.]

Report of the number of bridges built and the amount of corduroying done by the Fourth Division, Fifteenth Army Corps, on the march from Rome to Savannah, Ga.

No.	Route.	Amount of corduroying done.	Streams.	Number of bridges.
		Yards.		
1	Rome to Kingston	15	Brinley's Creek	1
2	Kingston to Allatoona	100	Two-Run Branch	1
3	Allatoona to Marietta	375	Allatoona Creek	1
4	Marietta to Turner's Ferry	......	......	......
5	Turner's Ferry to East Point	......	......	......
6	East Point to near McDonough	250	Branch Cotton River	1
7	McDonough to near Jackson	50	......	......
8	Jackson to Ocmulgee	25	......	1
9	Ocmulgee to Monticello	500	......	......
10	Monticello to Hillsborough	1,500	Big Muddy Creek	1
11	Hillsborough to near Clinton	1,200	Cedar Creek	1
12	Clinton to Commissioner's Fork	1,000	......	......
13	Commissioner's Fork to Gordon	25	......	......
14	Gordon to Milton	75	......	2
15	Milton to Irwin's Cross-Roads	1,500	......	1
16	Irwin's Cross-Roads to Peacock's	100	......	4
17	Peacock's to Wrightsville	550	......	......
18	Peacock's to Ohoopee	50	......	......
19	Little Ohoopee to Slater's Mills	2,000	......	......
20	Wrightsville to Slater's Mills	1,000	......	4
21	Slater's Mills to near Summerville	500	......	1
22	Summerville to near Millen	500	......	1
23	Near Millen to Scull's Creek	300	Scull's Creek	1
24	Scull's Creek to Hodges' farm	500	......	1
25	Hodges' to near Ogeechee	500	......	1
26	Near Ogeechee to Ogeechee River	100	......	4
27	Bloomingdale to Canal	10	......	1
28	Canal to Little Ogeechee	2,000	......	2
	Total	a14,825	......	31

a 44,475 feet.

[Inclosure No. 5.]

HEADQUARTERS FIFTEENTH ARMY CORPS,
Savannah, Ga., January 1, 1865.

A consolidated estimate of bridges and corduroy road constructed by the pioneer corps of the Fifteenth Army Corps: First Division, 16,915 yards corduroy road, 200 yards bridge; Second Division, 10,630 yards corduroy road, 617 yards bridge; Third Division, 5,010 yards corduroy road; Fourth Division, 14,825 yards corduroy road, 31 bridges; total, 47,380 yards.

H. KLOSTERMANN,
Captain, Engineers, Fifteenth Army Corps.

Report of casualties in the Fifteenth Army Corps during the campaign in pursuit of Hood and the Savannah campaign.

Command.	Commissioned officers.			Enlisted men.			Aggregate.
	Killed.	Wounded.	Missing.	Killed.	Wounded.	Missing.	
First Division	......	6	......	14	72	2	94
Second Division	5	6	1	23	119	49	203
Third Division	......	7	20	39	129	444	641
Fourth Division	6	16	2	100	137	116	477
Artillery Brigade	1	1	......	6	28	1	37
Total*	12	36	25	182	585	612	1,452

List of casualties in the Second Division, Fifteenth Army Corps (Brig. Gen. W. B. Hazen commanding), in the assault on Fort McAllister, December 13, 1864.

Command.	Killed.		Wounded.		Aggregate.
	Officers.	Men.	Officers.	Men.	
70th Ohio	......	6	......	30	36
48th Illinois	1	6	1	15	23
90th Illinois	......	3	......	14	17
6th Missouri	......	1	......	2	3
116th Illinois	1	....	......	7	8
30th Ohio	1	....	......	7	8
53d Ohio	......	....	1	....	1
54th Ohio	......	....	1	4	5
111th Illinois	1	3	3	9	16
47th Ohio	......	1	1	15	17
Total	4	20	7	103	134

All of which I have the honor to submit.

P. JOS. OSTERHAUS,
Major-General.

No. 12.

Report of Lieut. William H. Sherfy, U. S. Army, Signal Officer.

HDQRS. SIGNAL DETACHMENT, FIFTEENTH ARMY CORPS,
Savannah, Ga., December 31, 1864.

CAPTAIN: I have the honor to make the following report of duties performed by the detachment of the Signal Corps serving with the Fifteenth Army Corps during the months of November and December, 1864:

November 1 to 5 I was on the march with the Fifteenth Army Corps, returning from the campaign in North Georgia and Alabama, and had with me the seven enlisted men of my own party. On this march we

---

* The erroneous addition of the third and fifth columns of table is according to the original.

were generally in advance of the infantry column, reconnoitering and scouting, and twice during the five days had successful skirmishes with the enemy. When not in advance I was with the general, doing the duty of a staff officer. The army having gone in camp at Smyrna Camp-Ground, I went to Atlanta with permission to re-equip and collect the detachment, where I remained until the 14th, when I rejoined the corps.

First Lieut. J. H. Weirick was on a signal station on Kenesaw Mountain November 1 to 14. The line this station was on was one of considerable importance, as it was the only rapid means of communication between Atlanta and our base of supplies when the telegraph was interrupted, which was frequently the case; and Lieutenant Weirick's station was the most important one on the line, being, in addition, a station of observation overlooking a considerable portion of country infested by the enemy. Besides this, the lieutenant had no officer to assist him, and was on an exposed and uncomfortable station, but he and the men with him did their duty well. First Lieut. J. L. Shellabarger was at Chattanooga on business for the chief signal officer on the 1st of November, whence he returned to Atlanta on the 3d, reporting to me on the 6th, and remained there until the 14th, awaiting orders. Second Lieut. J. Q. Adams was on a signal station in Marietta until November 14, conducting it creditably and without assistance from the other officers.

Lieutenant Shellabarger and myself with fourteen enlisted men joined the Fifteenth Corps when it started from Atlanta on November 15, and that day we were in a sharp skirmish at Rough and Ready, where, finding a road around the enemy's flank, we assisted in driving them from a fortified position. When the rear of the army had passed Kenesaw Mountain on its march southward, Lieutenants Weirick and Adams abandoned their stations there, coming forward rapidly, and joined the remainder of the detachment on the morning of the 16th. That day we met the enemy at McDonough, and the detachment assisted in a charge in driving a brigade of rebel cavalry from the town, following it up with little support for several miles. There being four officers present with the detachment, one was detailed to accompany the general each day during the remainder of the march to assist in staff duties, or in any other way in which he could make himself useful, while with the remainder of the party, now numbering more than twenty trusty men, mounted and well armed, I was continually reconnoitering and scouting in front and on the flank of the infantry column. In this way we were enabled to obtain much valuable information in regard to the enemy and the roads, and occasionally having a skirmish with or a chase after the rebels. During the march we captured 11 prisoners and nearly 100 horses and mules, not losing a single man or animal out of the detachment. On our arrival opposite Station No. 3, I crossed the Ogeechee River in a little boat with but three men, on the order of General Howard, and reconnoitered through swamps and woods, intending to cut the railroad that night, but was not permitted to do so. The night of our arrival at the Cannouchee River, I crossed that stream in the face of the enemy with but two men and reconnoitered for roads through the swamps until midnight, reporting to General Osterhaus. The following day we swam our horses across, and with the detachment went in advance of the infantry and were the first to reach and destroy the Gulf railroad and telegraph. On our arrival in front of Savannah each of the officers reconnoitered and made himself acquainted with the lines and occasionally directed the fire of our artillery with the aid of our superior glasses. When the Second Division was sent to reduce Fort McAllister, I, with Lieutenant Adams and ten men, went with it, and, taking the advance, charged over torpedoes in the road and captured the picket. While the lines were being formed around the fort we opened communication across the river to a point where General Sherman was, and received through signals his order for the assault, our station being at the time so near as to be under fire that we might be near General Hazen. When the fort was taken we immediately moved to it, and soon after opened communication with the fleet, which was kept up whenever vessels were near us.

December 16, I returned to headquarters of the corps, Lieutenant Weirick taking my place at the fort; and two days afterward I and Lieutenant Shellabarger opened signal communication through from headquarters to the fort, passing a number of important messages, and continuing the line until a day after the fall of Savannah, when it was relieved by order of General Sherman. We then came to the city. On the 24th I was placed in charge of officers of the Seventeenth Corps, and ordered to open communication from the city to Fort McAllister, connecting with the telegraph at Rosedew, which I succeeded in accomplishing the following day. On the 28th Lieutenants Shellabarger and Adams established a signal station on the tower in the river below Fort Jackson, thereby opening communication from the city to Fort Pulaski and Hilton Head, which post they still occupy.

It is but just to say that the officers and men of this detachment have done their duty well and nobly, nor have there been wanting instances of personal bravery well worthy of commendation.

I have the honor to be, very respectfully, your obedient servant,

WM. H. SHERFY,
First Lieutenant, Signal Corps, Commanding Detachment.

Capt. H. N. WHEELER,
Assistant Adjutant-General, Fifteenth Army Corps.

No. 13.

Reports of Brig. Gen. Charles R. Woods, U. S. Army, commanding First Division.

HDQRS. FIRST DIVISION, FIFTEENTH ARMY CORPS,
Massey's Farm, Ga., November 23, 1864.

CAPTAIN: I have the honor to report that the affair of yesterday at Duncan's farm, near Griswold, was of greater magnitude than was at first supposed.

Early in the morning I received orders from Maj. Gen. P. J. Osterhaus, commanding Fifteenth Army Corps, to take up a strong defensive position near the church, and with one brigade to make a demonstration in the direction of Macon. I selected the Second Brigade, commanded by Brig. Gen. C. C. Walcutt, composed of the following regiments: Fortieth Illinois Infantry, Lieut. Col. H. W. Hall commanding, 206 enlisted men; Forty-sixth Ohio Infantry, Lieut. Col. I. N. Alexander commanding, 218 enlisted men; One hundred and third Illinois Infantry, Maj. A. Willison commanding, 219 enlisted men; Sixth Iowa Infantry, Maj. W. H. Clune commanding, 177 enlisted men; Ninety-seventh Indiana Infantry, Col. R. F. Catterson commanding, 366 enlisted men;

One hundredth Indiana Infantry, Maj. R. M. Johnson commanding, 327 enlisted men; total present for duty, 1,513; and one section of Battery B, First Michigan, Captain Arndt commanding. About the time I started, the pickets of Brig. Gen. J. Kilpatrick were driven in by a superior force of the enemy. General Walcutt moved forward about two miles and a half on the Griswold road, with a heavy line of skirmishers, which drove everything in front of them to a point beyond Griswold. The forces met on this reconnaissance were a part of Wheeler's cavalry. I then, by direction of General Osterhaus, drew General Walcutt's brigade back to a strong position on the Duncan farm, and posted it in the edge of the woods, with open fields in front, the flanks resting near a swamp, impassable except at one or two points, and directed temporary works of rails and logs to be thrown up. About 2 o'clock the enemy attacked with infantry (militia), three lines deep, and numbering about 5,000, four pieces of artillery (12-pounder Napoleons), and two brigades of Wheeler's cavalry in reserve. The enemy moved across the open fields in three compact lines and gained a ravine within seventy-five yards of our works, from which they made three assaults, but met each time with a bloody repulse. The fight continued until sundown, when they retired, leaving their dead and wounded on the field. Shortly after dark the brigade was withdrawn to the position near the church. About the middle of the engagement Brig. Gen. C. C. Walcutt was wounded severely in the lower part of the leg; he retired from the field, and Col. R. F. Catterson, Ninety-seventh Indiana Infantry, assumed command of the brigade. He showed marked ability in the manner in which he handled the troops. Shortly after the engagement opened the section of the battery was withdrawn on account of the severe fire from the enemy's lines, then within 100 yards of our position, and very destructive to the men and horses of the battery. About 4 o'clock I sent Major Baldwin, Twelfth Indiana Infantry (First Brigade), to report his regiment to Colonel Catterson, who put him on the right of his lines to prevent the enemy from turning that flank. I also applied to Colonel Murray for some cavalry to cover the flanks; he kindly sent a regiment on each flank, covering and watching the crossing of the swamp.

I cannot speak in too high terms of the coolness and gallantry of Brig. Gen. C. C. Walcutt and Col. R. F. Catterson, Ninety-seventh Indiana Infantry. The skill with which they handled the troops and the results obtained show them to be men of marked ability.

The rebel loss, as near as could be ascertained without actual count, was 300 killed and from 700 to 1,200 wounded. Major-General Philips, Colonel Munn, Fifth Georgia, and Colonel George, are reported by the prisoners taken to have been killed, and Brigadier-General Anderson to have been wounded. Twenty-eight prisoners were captured and turned over to the provost-marshal of the army corps. Fifteen wounded were brought in and left at a house, not having transportation for them. Our loss was 13 killed, 79 wounded, and 2 missing.

Inclosed please find a list of killed and wounded.*

I will forward Colonel Catterson's report as soon as received.

I have the honor to be, captain, your most obedient servant,

CHAS. R. WOODS,
Brigadier-General of Volunteers.

Capt. FREDERICK WHITEHEAD,
Assistant Adjutant-General, Fifteenth Army Corps.

---

* Omitted.

[Indorsement.]

HDQRS. DEPARTMENT AND ARMY OF THE TENNESSEE,
Irwin's Cross-Roads, Ga., November 27, 1864.

Respectfully forwarded.

The within was received subsequent to making my report. The engagement was of a more severe character, and our own loss a little greater than the information led me to suppose, but fortunately the enemy attacked us at the very point where we were prepared, so that with a force only about one-third as large as that of the enemy he was so completely defeated that he has troubled [us] no more in that quarter. I renew my commendations of the brigade commander and others engaged on that day.

Respectfully,

O. O. HOWARD,
Major-General.

HDQRS. FIRST DIVISION, FIFTEENTH ARMY CORPS,
Fort Thunderbolt, Ga., January 15, 1865.

I have the honor to submit the following report of the part taken by this division during the campaign from Atlanta to Savannah:

On the 15th of November last my command started from White Hall, near Atlanta, moving southward on the old Macon road. When the head of the column had arrived in the vicinity of Rough and Ready, indications of the enemy became apparent. However, the rebels steadily withdrew before my skirmishers, as they were from time to time developed. In the afternoon, after having gone into camp, the Twenty-ninth Missouri Mounted Infantry developed a cavalry force of the enemy, some 900 strong, in our front, who made use of two light field pieces. However, they soon withdrew, and the advance, via McDonough and Indian Springs, was continued without interruption until reaching the Ocmulgee River on the 19th. My command crossed the same day on the pontoon and marched to within seven miles of Hillsborough. Passing through Hillsborough and Clinton, the Macon railroad was reached the night of the 21st at a point some thirteen miles east of Macon. The morning of the 22d, in accordance with instructions from the major-general commanding, I promptly ordered two regiments—the Seventy-sixth Ohio Infantry and Ninth Iowa Infantry—at work tearing up the railroad. Some four miles were completely destroyed, in addition to a large trestle-work bridge that was burned by the Seventy-sixth Ohio. Being ordered to make a reconnaissance in the direction of Macon to develop the enemy in that vicinity, I dispatched the Second Brigade, Brig. Gen. C. C. Walcutt commanding, for that purpose. I send herewith my official report of this reconnaissance as made at the time to Major-General Osterhaus.* The morning of the 23d of November the march was resumed, and continued uninterruptedly until reaching the Oconee River, which was crossed on the afternoon of the 26th. November 27, in compliance with orders received from the major-general commanding the corps, I ordered one of my brigades—the Third, Col. J. A. Williamson commanding—to the Macon railroad for the purpose of destroying the rails and ties. Colonel Williamson rejoined the division the same evening at Riddleville, reporting that he had completely destroyed some three miles of the track. From this time until Decem-

---

* See p. 97.

ber 6 nothing worthy of record transpired. The line of march lay through a desolate piney barren, dotted with numberless swamps and sluggish streams, that were a constant hinderance to our advance, often causing delays of three, four, and five hours' duration. I may state, however, that when encamped on Scull's Creek, December 3, I sent one regiment beyond the Ogeechee River for the purpose of destroying the iron and ties on the Central railroad; one mile of the track was torn up and burned. December 6, the Third Brigade, together with one section of my battery (Twelfth Wisconsin), was ordered to Wright's Crossing, for the purpose of securing the crossing over the Ogeechee River at that place. The bridge, however, had been destroyed, but Colonel Williamson managed to cross the Twenty-fifth and part of the Ninth Iowa Infantry, who at once secured a firm foothold on the east side of the river. The rebels here made their appearance in small force, and some considerable skirmishing occurred. Three companies of the Ninth Iowa were advanced as far as Station No. 2 on the railroad; but before they could succeed in tearing up any of the track a superior force of the enemy appeared, and the companies were obliged to return to the river crossing. The next morning, having been directed to send one brigade down on the east side of the river toward Jenks' Bridge, and if possible to Station No. 2, the Third was dispatched with these instructions; and that evening Colonel Williamson reported to me his arrival at the latter place, having met but little opposition. The advance was continued on the 8th, and December 9 I sent one brigade (the First) forward to Eden, where it took position, covering movements being made beyond the Ogeechee River.

December 10, crossed the Ogeechee River at Dillon's Crossing, where I was joined by the First Brigade, and my command at once marched eastward, following the towpath of the Ogeechee Canal. Continuing some nine miles I struck the Augusta and Darien road, and bearing off to the right for the distance of three miles I went into position, throwing up works in my front and connecting my skirmishers with those of the Fourth Division, Fifteenth Army Corps, on my right, while the nature of the ground on my left was such as in itself to afford protection. The night of the 11th my division was moved to the right about twelve miles, to the neighborhood of Anderson's plantation, where I again took position, with my left resting on the Savannah and King's Bridge road, and my right connecting with the Fourth Division of this corps. The enemy was soon developed, strongly posted about one mile to my front, with low, marshy ground and the Little Ogeechee River intervening. This stream, about thirty feet wide and from twelve to fourteen feet deep, followed their line of works from twenty to fifty yards in front of the same. The only approach to the rebel lines was over the main road, which was but a naked causeway, completely swept by artillery admirably posted. From this time I continued to strengthen my works and advance my lines, so that by the 20th of December I was strongly intrenched, with a good earth-work for my guns, and with my skirmishers advanced to within 100 yards of the main line of the rebels. December 21, my division marched with other portions of the army into Savannah, the enemy having evacuated, and camped on the south side of the city.

During the march from Atlanta to Savannah my command built more than four miles of corduroy road, one mile and a half of bridging over the swamps, creeks, and bayous, besides cutting eleven miles of road through the timber for the passage of trains and troops.

I lost in killed 15 enlisted men; in wounded, 8 commissioned officers and 80 enlisted men, with 2 enlisted men missing; making a total of 105.

My division captured during the entire campaign 9 commissioned officers and 45 enlisted men (total, 54), besides killing and wounding a great many.

The rebels abandoned 16 pieces of artillery in my immediate front when they evacuated the works around Savannah.

I am, major, very respectfully, your obedient servant,

C. R. WOODS,
Brevet Major-General.

Maj. MAX. WOODHULL,
Assistant Adjutant-General, Fifteenth Army Corps.

No. 14.

Report of Col. Milo Smith, Twenty-sixth Iowa Infantry, commanding First Brigade.

HDQRS. FIRST BRIG., FIRST DIV., 15TH ARMY CORPS,
Savannah, Ga., January 2, 1865.

CAPTAIN: I have the honor to report that at 6 a. m. of the 15th day of November, 1864, I left camp at White Hall, Ga., with my brigade; marched on the road toward Rough and Ready with the balance of division. My brigade consists of the following regiments: Seventy-sixth Ohio Veteran Volunteers, Col. William B. Woods commanding; Twenty-seventh Missouri Volunteer Infantry, Col. Thomas Curly commanding; consolidated battalion Thirty-first and Thirty-second Missouri, Maj. A. J. Seay commanding; Twelfth Indiana Volunteer Infantry, Maj. E. D. Baldwin commanding; Twenty-sixth Iowa Volunteer Infantry, Maj. John Lubbers commanding; Twenty-ninth Missouri Volunteer Infantry, Lieut. Col. Joseph S. Gage commanding. The latter regiment being mounted and on duty at headquarters Fifteenth Army Corps, I respectfully refer you to the report of Lieut. Col. Joseph S. Gage. I marched, via McDonough and Indian Springs, toward the crossing of the Ocmulgee River at Nutting's Factory, meeting with no resistance on the roads, striking the Georgia Central Railroad about ten miles east of Macon, near Griswoldville, on the evening of the 21st of November, and encamped for the night.

On the morning of the 22d one regiment—the Seventy-sixth Ohio Veteran Volunteer Infantry—was ordered to report to Brig. Gen. C. R. Woods to destroy railroad, which was done by said regiment destroying three miles of railroad, including one large bridge and trestle-work over a stream near Gordon Junction. I moved with the balance of my brigade about three miles and halted; was ordered into position on each side of the road running from Gordon to Griswoldville, where I put up a line of works. The cavalry under Brigadier-General Kilpatrick had been skirmishing with the enemy in our front. Brigadier-General Walcutt, Second Brigade, First Division, Fifteenth Army Corps, was on a reconnaissance toward Griswoldville, when they found the enemy in considerable force, and my brigade was ordered from the line of works to the support of Second Brigade. After moving three-quarters of a mile, I was ordered to return to the works which I had just left, and was ordered to extend them to right and left to cover more than my brigade front. One regiment—the Twelfth Indiana, Major Baldwin—moved on to the support of Second Brigade, and went into position on the right of the line, advanced skirmishers, meeting the enemy's skirmishers just in time to prevent them from flanking the Second Brigade. The Twelfth Indiana had one man slightly wounded. Adjt. Marshall H. Parks had his horse shot from under him while assisting in forming the lines of his regiment. The skirmishers had advanced but a short distance in front of the line when they were engaged, and soon drove the enemy from their front. As soon as it became dark I was called on for one more regiment, which I sent out on the road near where the fighting had been done during the day, and was put in position, forming on the right of the road, and there remained until about 9 o'clock, when the troops were withdrawn and my regiment returned to the line of works I had built during the day. At 12 p. m. the Seventy-sixth Ohio, Colonel Woods commanding, returned from the railroad.

The next day we resumed our march, marching about five miles, and was assigned a position on left of road, where we halted, facing to the rear, and put up a line of works. Marched again about 2 o'clock same day, halting for the night about five miles farther, at Gordon Cross-Roads, and put up another line of works. Next morning at 7 o'clock resumed our line of march and moved on toward Irwinton, crossing the Oconee River at Planter's Ferry, and encamped that night at Irwinton Cross-Roads, where we lay in camp until 12 m. the next day, resuming our march, keeping all the time on the right of Central railroad. Nothing of any importance transpiring; capturing mules and horses and contrabands every day. Moving toward Savannah, we struck the Ogeechee River below Millen, and after crossing Scull's Creek halted for one day, my brigade crossing the river and destroying about one mile of railroad; returned the same day. Marched the next day. My brigade, having the advance, was delayed about one hour in repairing the bridges over Nevil's Creek, this being the 4th day of December. Fifth day we marched about sixteen miles, encamping four miles south of Mill Creek. Lay in camp on the 6th until noon, marched nine miles, and encamped for the night. 7th, lay in camp until 12 m., changed front, and encamped for the night, having three regiments in my front line behind works which I had thrown up. Next day marched seventeen miles, and encamped for the night. About 1 o'clock of the 9th, by order from Brig. Gen. C. R. Woods, my brigade was ordered three miles farther, with instructions to report to Major-General Osterhaus, at Eden Court-House, where we took a position and threw up works. At 12 o'clock that night I received orders from Major-General Osterhaus to move at 4 o'clock on the direct road to Dillon's Bridge, and to take measures to pass the camp of Second Division, Fifteenth Army Corps, by 7 o'clock in the morning, which I did, crossing the Ogeechee River on a foot bridge at Dillon's Crossing, my teams crossing on the pontoon about two miles farther up the river, and moving on the towpath along the canal until we struck a cross-road running to the King's Bridge road, filing right, and encamping for the night near the Little Ogeechee River close in front of the enemy's works.

Next day we tried to get to King's Bridge road, but could not on account of the road being full of cavalry moving. After dark I moved with the balance of the division across the causeway, in front of the enemy's guns, and camped on the King's Bridge road, nine miles from Savannah. Nothing of importance transpired for some days. Remaining in the same camp, and, with a detail from my brigade, put up a line of works and furnished one regiment each day to support the battery by the cemetery from the 13th to 22d [21st], when it was discovered that the enemy had evacuated the night before, and I marched in with the balance of the division to the works just outside the city of Savannah.

The Twenty-seventh Missouri Infantry has been on detached service from 14th of December, guarding the rice mill of Doctor Cheves', on the Ogeechee, and in garrisoning Forts Rosedew and Beaulieu, on Wassaw Sound; the Seventy-sixth Ohio Veteran Volunteer Infantry are on duty as provost guard in the city; the Twenty-ninth Missouri Volunteer Infantry, being yet on duty at corps headquarters, is encamped in the city; the Twelfth Indiana, consolidated battalion Thirty-first and Thirty-second Missouri, and Twenty-sixth Iowa, are encamped on the left of the Ogeechee road, and inside of the inner works.

Our march has been a perfect success.

The loss from my brigade has been 1 man captured and 2 slightly wounded.

We have captured a great number of mules and horses, which have all been either put into teams in place of others which were jaded, taken up, or turned over to provost-marshal or division quartermaster. The men are in much better health than when we started, and our animals have improved at least 25 per cent.

All of which I respectfully submit.

MILO SMITH,
Colonel, Commanding Brigade.

[Capt. FRED. H. WILSON,
Acting Assistant Adjutant-General.]

No. 15.

Report of Col. Thomas Curly, Twenty-seventh Missouri Infantry, of operations May 1–December 21.

HDQRS. TWENTY-SEVENTH MISSOURI VOL. INFANTRY,
Near Savannah, Ga., December 21, 1864.

GENERAL: I have the honor to give you a brief history of this regiment since my last report:

On the 1st day of May, 1864, we left Paint Rock Bridge, Ala., and commenced the great and well-known campaign of Major-General Sherman through Northern Georgia, which lasted four months. The Twenty-seventh Missouri has taken an active part, and has had seven different engagements in the series of great battles that have taken place during the whole campaign, as well as the siege of Atlanta, which lasted one month; in all of which our losses were 1 commissioned officer killed and 1 wounded, and 15 enlisted men killed and 47 wounded. I am proud to say that every officer and soldier has done his duty faithfully and with credit to the great State to which he belongs.

On the 14th [15th] day of November, 1864, we left Atlanta for the Gulf coast, through Southern Georgia, for the purpose of the capture of Savannah. Nothing of any great interest transpired, except occasional skirmishing with the enemy, along our triumphant march to the seacoast, where we opened communication with the fleet of Admiral Dahlgren on the 13th day of December, 1864. The regiment and one section of the First Illinois Artillery, the latter under the command of Captain De Gress, were the first to open fire upon Fort McAllister, which is situated on the Ogeechee River four miles from its mouth.

On the evening of the 13th of December the fort was assaulted and carried at the point of the bayonet by the Second Division, Fifteenth Army Corps, commanded by Brigadier-General Hazen, by which our communications were fully opened and our base established; which has enabled the grand army under the heroic Sherman to completely invest the proud city of Savannah, in which position we rest at the present time, and quietly await the fall of the doomed city before the close of the present year.

The distance marched by the regiment during both campaigns is 800 miles.

Very respectfully, your obedient servant,

THOMAS CURLY,
Colonel, Commanding Twenty-seventh Missouri Volunteers.

Brig. Gen. JOHN B. GRAY,
Adjutant-General of Missouri.

No. 16.

Report of Lieut. Col. Dennis T. Kirby, Twenty-seventh Missouri Infantry, of operations December 4.

HEADQUARTERS SEVENTEENTH ARMY CORPS,
Near Station 5½, Ga., December 4, 1864.

CAPTAIN: In accordance with instructions from the major-general commanding, I proceeded this morning with the First Alabama Cavalry and G Company, Eleventh Illinois Cavalry, on the road to Station 4½. I first struck the enemy's pickets opposite Station 5½, on our left flank, and drove them to Station 5. At this point I found Colonel Gage, Twenty-ninth Missouri Mounted Infantry, retreating, with the enemy in his front and rear. I drove the enemy back, and by directions received from the major-general commanding, sent Colonel Gage and his command to the rear. I continued driving the enemy until I reached the Little Ogeechee River, when I found him in position on the opposite side, with a strong line of skirmishers on this side. He had burned the railroad bridge, but had left the passenger bridge uninjured. I dismounted a company and deployed them as skirmishers, and drove their skirmishers over the river, and found on reaching the banks that they were busily engaged in fortifying on the other side. I skirmished with them a short time for the purpose of developing their force, and I estimate them at from 2,000 to 5,000 strong. I learned from reliable sources that there were four trains came in there to-day loaded with troops, and that they have four pieces of artillery, all under command of General Wayne. The loss was one man mortally wounded, from the First Alabama Cavalry. We captured six of their horses, with equipments and arms complete.

I am, captain, very respectfully, your obedient servant,

D. T. KIRBY,
Lieutenant-Colonel and Picket Officer Seventeenth Army Corps.

Capt. C. CADLE, Jr.

No. 17.

Report of Col. Robert F. Catterson, Ninety-seventh Indiana Infantry, commanding Second Brigade, of operations November 22.

HDQRS. SECOND BRIG., FIRST DIV., 15TH ARMY CORPS,
In the Field, near Gordon, Ga., November 23, 1864.

CAPTAIN: I have the honor to submit the following report of the engagement between this brigade and the enemy, near Griswold, on the 22d instant:

Early on the morning mentioned six regiments of the brigade, General Walcutt commanding—viz, the Forty-sixth Ohio Infantry, Ninety-seventh and One hundredth Indiana Infantry, Sixth Iowa Infantry, the Fortieth and One hundred and third Illinois Infantry—were ordered to move on the road leading to Macon, Ga., for the purpose of feeling the enemy's position in that direction. Proceeding about one mile we met the enemy's cavalry, under Wheeler, and drove them beyond Griswold. The object of the reconnaissance having been accomplished the brigade was retired about one mile and took position at a point known as Duncan's farm. The enemy seeing this move followed up with three brigades of militia, numbering in all between 6,000 and 7,000 men. We had scarcely taken position in the edge of timber skirting the farm on the east when our pickets were fired upon. The brigade, thus posted behind a light barricade of rails hastily prepared after our pickets were driven in, lay anxiously awaiting his appearance. He was soon discovered emerging from the woods about 800 yards from our position, and rapidly running across an open field toward us in three lines of battle, either of which more than covered our brigade front. General Walcutt ordered Captain Arndt, of the First Michigan, Battery B, to open fire upon them, which he did with one section of his battery in position on the road near the center of our line, which was replied to sharply by four guns of the enemy in the open field, at a distance of about 800 yards, to the right and front, the first shot striking and damaging a caisson. On came the enemy, endeavoring to gain possession of a ravine running parallel to and about 100 yards to our front, but the fire was so terrible that ere he reached it many of his number were stretched upon the plain. It was at this moment that General Walcutt received a severe wound and was compelled to leave the field. I immediately assumed command, and discovered the enemy moving to the right. I supposed he contemplated turning my right flank. As I had already disposed of every available man in the brigade, and my left being so strongly pressed that not a man could be spared from it, I sent to the general commanding the division for two regiments. The Twelfth Indiana Infantry was sent, and immediately placed in position on the extreme right; also, a squadron of cavalry to watch the right and left flanks, but the day was already ours, as the enemy had been repulsed and driven from the field. I immediately sent forward a line of skirmishers, who succeeded in capturing about 42 prisoners and 150 small-arms. The battle commenced at 2.30 p. m. and lasted until sunset. During the engagement the enemy made three separate charges, and were as often repulsed with terrible slaughter.

I would gladly notice the many deeds of daring during the action, but to do so of every man who distinguished himself would be to mention each man by name in the brigade; but suffice it to say, the conduct of both officers and men was most superb.

The loss of brigade in killed was 14; in wounded, 42—this number includes only those sent to hospital.

The loss of the enemy in killed and wounded could not have been less than 1,500, about 300 of whom were killed.

The total number of men engaged was 1,300.

I am, respectfully, your obedient servant,

ROBERT F. CATTERSON,
Colonel, Commanding Brigade.

Captain WILSON,
Actg. Asst. Adjt. Gen., First Div., Fifteenth Army Corps.

ADDENDA.

HDQRS. DEPARTMENT AND ARMY OF THE TENNESSEE,
Gordon, Ga., November 23, 1864.

Major-General OSTERHAUS,
Commanding Fifteenth Army Corps:

GENERAL: I take sincere pleasure in congratulating the brigade of General Walcutt, of General Woods' division, of the Fifteenth Corps, on its complete success in the action of yesterday. Officers from other commands who were looking on say that there never was a better brigade of soldiers. I am exceedingly sorry that any of our brave men should fall, and for the sufferings of those that are wounded. The thanks of the army are doubly due to them. I tender my sympathy through you to the brave and excellent commander of the brigade, Brigadier-General Walcutt. It is hoped that his wound may not disable him.

Very respectfully, your obedient servant,

O. O. HOWARD,
Major-General.

P. S.—The loss of the enemy is estimated from 1,500 to 2,000 killed, wounded, and prisoners.

O. O. H.,
Major-General.

No. 18.

Report of Maj. Asias Willison, One hundred and third Illinois Infantry.

HEADQUARTERS 103D ILLINOIS VOLUNTEER INFANTRY,
Greene Square, Savannah, Ga., January 2, 1865.

In compliance with instructions received from brigade headquarters, I have the honor to make the following report of the part taken by the One hundred and third Regiment Illinois Volunteer Infantry in the campaign just ended:

On the morning of November 13, 1864, the regiment moved from camp at Vining's Station, Ga., with the division. At 7 a. m. crossed the Chattahoochee River and passed through the city of Atlanta, and bivouacked one mile and a half west of the city, where we remained until the morning of the 15th of November, when we broke camp and marched with the brigade and division through Rough and Ready Station. Here our advance had a slight skirmish with the enemy. Nothing occurred along the line of our march until the morning of the 22d of November, when, with the brigade, my regiment moved out early on a reconnaissance toward Griswoldville, Ga. We soon found the enemy in force, and deployed Companies A and B on the left of Ninety-seventh Indiana [as] skirmishers. Advanced and had a brisk skirmish, in which the enemy was driven before them through Griswoldville. Here our skirmishers were halted, and were soon withdrawn to an open field where two pieces of artillery were in position on the east side of the field. We took our position to the right of the Sixth Iowa, the Ninety-seventh Indiana on our right. Here we rested, and at 1 p. m. the skirmishers were attacked by the enemy's advance and driven. A strong line was soon seen forming on the west side of the field, and advanced. At this time my regiment had no works for defense, but hastily constructed a small, temporary line of works and awaited the approaching enemy, who was advancing in column by brigades. As soon as they came within range of our muskets a most terrific fire was poured into their ranks, doing fearful execution. Still they moved forward to a ravine which ran in front of the line, within forty-five yards of the works. Here they attempted to reform their line again, but so destructive was our fire that they were compelled to retire. At one time it seemed that they would overcome our thin line, as our ammunition [was] nearly exhausted and none nearer than two miles, but fortunately a sufficient amount was procured, and our boys kept up a continual fire for nearly three hours, when skirmishers were sent forward to capture any of the enemy left on the field. A few prisoners were brought in, besides a number of wounded. In our front were, by actual count, 51 of the enemy killed and wounded; 83 stand of small-arms were left in our hands and turned over to the ordnance officer. Our loss was 4 killed and 8 wounded. At 8 o'clock we received orders to be in readiness to move, and at 9 p. m. moved off the field and rejoined the division.

On the morning of the 23d again resumed the march, and at 12 m. on the 24th camped at Irwinton, Ga. Here we laid over until the 25th, when we moved to the Oconee River, and crossed on the 26th of November.

On the 1st of December, with the command, we halted near the Ogeechee River. My regiment was ordered to the Ogeechee bridge, to hold it and burn the railroad at Station No. 8½. Joined the brigade December 2 and crossed Scull's Creek, where we remained one day. December 3 [4], resumed our march. On the evening of the 6th camped and put up works; here we remained until early in the morning of the 8th of December, and again moved toward the Cannouchee River and camped within six miles of said river. On the 9th was ordered out on a reconnaissance; moved out some six miles to the right, and finding no enemy returned. December 10, moved across the Ogeechee River and up the canal within nine miles of Savannah, and put up works. On the 11th of December heavy cannonading to our right. In the evening moved to the right, and here remained, doing duty with the brigade in supporting the First Wisconsin Battery and skirmishing with the enemy, until the morning of the 21st of December, when the enemy evacuated the city of Savannah, and we marched with the command to the city; since which time we have been on duty in the city.

I am, very respectfully, your obedient servant,

A. WILLISON,

Major, Commanding 103d Illinois Volunteers.

Capt. O. J. FAST,

Actg. Asst. Adjt. Gen., 2d Brig., 1st Div., 15th Army Corps.

No. 19.

Report of Lieut. Col. Isaac N. Alexander, Forty-sixth Ohio Infantry, of operations November 22.

HDQRS. FORTY-SIXTH OHIO VETERAN VOL. INFANTRY,
Near Gordon, Ga., November 25, 1864.

CAPTAIN: I have the honor to report the following as the operations of this regiment in the engagement near Griswoldville on the 22d instant:

The regiment marched from its encampment, being in column next in front of the rear regiment. Proceeded without any occurrence worthy of note until the brigade arrived at a point near where the general engagement occurred, when I was ordered to move the regiment down a road leading to the left. Having advanced a short distance skirmishers were thrown to the front, which had not proceeded more than forty paces in advance of the regiment in column, when they encountered a strong line of rebel cavalry. The skirmishers engaged them, when the cavalry charged them fiercely. In the meantime the regiment was put in line, and to the end that our skirmishers might rejoin the regiment in safety they were allowed to come within thirty yards before orders were given to fire; they were easily repulsed. They left upon the field a number of horses which had been killed and disabled and one prisoner. We then received orders from the general commanding brigade to retire to a position to the rear and on the extreme left of a new line, with the left wing deployed, extending to a swamp, in charge of Major Upton. Shortly after the engagement had commenced, the enemy not appearing in our front, I was ordered to move the regiment to the extreme right, where the enemy was then pressing very closely, and to extend well to the right, which I did under heavy fire, deploying out so as to cover a space equal to about three times my own proper front. In this position, which was hastily fortified, we repulsed the enemy in three or four assaults which he attempted, and remained in it until withdrawn by the brigade commander. There lay in this front about 40 of the enemy's dead and a large number of wounded.

We had engaged 186 men and 13 officers. Our casualties were 5 men wounded.

Very respectfully, your obedient servant,

I. N. ALEXANDER,
Lieut. Col. Forty-sixth Ohio Vet. Vol. Infantry, Comdg. Regt.

Capt. O. J. FAST, *Actg. Asst. Adjt. Gen., Second Brigade.*

No. 20.

Report of Maj. Edward N. Upton, Forty-sixth Ohio Infantry.

HDQRS. FORTY-SIXTH OHIO VETERAN VOL. INFANTRY,
Savannah, Ga., December 24, 1864.

CAPTAIN: In compliance with orders just received from your office, I beg leave to submit the following report of the operations of this regiment on the late campaign through Georgia:

We started with the brigade from our camp, two miles east of Atlanta, November 15, 1864, on the road toward McDonough; passed through McDonough the 17th, and Indian Springs November 18; crossed the Ocmulgee River November 19; passed through Hillsborough the 20th, and Clinton the 21st, and encamped the night of the 21st on the Central Georgia Railroad, about twelve miles from Macon, without any occurrence worthy of note. The next day (November 22) the regiment was sent with the brigade on a reconnaissance toward Macon; met the enemy's cavalry in the forenoon, and were attacked in the afternoon by a heavy force of infantry at Duncan's farm, near Griswoldville, at which time and place occurred the battle of that name, in which the regiment participated. For details of the part which the regiment took in the battle, I would beg leave to refer you to a report forwarded immediately after by the late Lieut. Col. I. N. Alexander, then commanding the regiment.* The casualties of the regiment during the day were six men wounded. The day succeeding the fight we resumed our march toward Savannah, and passed unmolested through Irwinton November 24, Riddleville November 27, and Summerville November 30. At Wright's Bridge, on the Ogeechee River, December 7, the regiment was ordered at 2 p. m. to cross the river with the One hundredth Indiana Infantry, and relieve part of the Third Brigade, which was sent on a reconnaissance. At 12 in the night we were ordered to withdraw, destroy the bridge, and rejoin the brigade. Nothing of importance occurred until we again encountered the enemy eight miles from Savannah, at Anderson's farm, December 11, 1864. Here we remained until the 21st performing our regular tours of duty in the front line of works, where, while lying in support of the Twelfth Wisconsin Battery, December 14, we had one man wounded, the only one with the exception of those at Griswoldville, wounded in the campaign. December 21, we proceeded with the brigade to within one mile and a half of the city (our present encampment), where we have remained ever since.

Before closing this report I would respectfully call your attention to the good conduct of both officers and men, each and all trying to surpass his comrade in soldierly bearing and cheerfulness.

Very respectfully, your obedient servant,

EDWARD N. UPTON,

Major Forty-sixth Ohio Veteran Vol. Infantry, Comdg. Regiment.

[Capt. O. J. FAST.]

No. 21.

Report of Brig. Gen. William B. Hazen, U. S. Army, commanding Second Division.

HDQRS. SECOND DIVISION, FIFTEENTH ARMY CORPS,
Savannah, Ga., January 9, 1865.†

On the 15th of November, every preparation being completed, this division, with the army, broke camp at Atlanta and set out upon its march through Georgia. It then numbered an effective strength of 4,426 officers and men, and was composed of seventeen regimental organizations, the three brigade commanders being Col. John M. Oliver, Fifteenth Michigan; Wells S. Jones, Fifty-third Ohio, and Theodore Jones, Thirtieth Ohio. The troops moved rapidly, passing through McDonough the 16th, Indian Springs the 18th, crossing the Ocmulgee the 19th at Roach's Mills, reaching Hillsborough the 20th, and Clinton the 21st, where Col. Theodore Jones' brigade was left to cover the Macon roads till the next division arrived. Some skirmishing took place here, with a few casualties. On the 22d the Macon and Augusta Railroad

---

* See next, *ante*.

† For portion of report (here omitted) relating to operations in North Georgia and North Alabama, see Vol XXXIX, Part I, p. 745.

was crossed and the march continued, passing Irwinton the 24th and the Oconee River, at Ball's Ferry, the 25th. The enemy was found on the opposite bank, and two regiments deployed to develop them. On the morning of the 26th they had left and preparations were at once made to cross, which was commenced by 11 a. m. The march was resumed without loss of time. Passing Irwin's Cross-Roads the 27th, we moved toward Summerville, through continuous pine forests, crossing several low marshy branches of the Ohoopee, reaching Summerville the 30th. The number of miles marched this month, 275; number of casualties, 11.

On December 1 the march was resumed in the direction of Statesborough, along the right bank of the Ogeechee River. The remainder of the march was impeded by low, broad marshes, which it was invariably found necessary to corduroy. From Summerville to the Cannouchee River, which was reached the 7th, the Third Division, General John E. Smith, with my own, formed a separate column under my command, and was somewhat exposed to annoyances from the enemy endeavoring to reach Savannah from the west before us. On the 3d the Fifty-third Ohio lost by capture a foraging party of 1 officer and 11 men. On the 4th, near Statesborough, the foragers met a brigade of the enemy's cavalry endeavoring to join Wheeler; were attacked by them and driven to the main column, losing by capture 27 and by wounds 8. The enemy lost 2 killed and 2 captured. The enemy defended the crossing of the Cannouchee with infantry and two pieces artillery, having burned the bridge. During the night of the 8th the enemy retired; and the bridge being repaired, at 11 a. m. the 9th the brigades were crossed—one pushed to King's Bridge, the other to a point on the Gulf railroad, about six miles from King's Bridge, which was reached and much of the road destroyed toward the river by night, including the bridge. On the 10th the division recrossed the Cannouchee, moving to and crossing the Ogeechee at Dillon's Ferry, and proceeding to near the Anderson plantation, nine miles from Savannah. On the 12th the division moved back to King's Bridge, it having received orders to cross the Ogeechee there and move down its right bank to Fort McAllister and capture it. At daybreak the 13th the troops were put in motion, reaching the vicinity of McAllister at about 11 a. m. About one mile from the fort a picket was captured, revealing the whereabouts of a line of torpedoes across the road. Some time was lost in safely removing them, when leaving eight regiments at that point, nine were carried forward to about 600 yards from the fort and deployed, with a line of skirmishers thrown sufficiently near the fort to keep the gunners from working their guns with any effect—those firing to the rear being in barbette. The grounds to the right of the fort being marshy, cut through by deep streams, rendered the deployment of that part of the line slow and difficult, and was not completely effected till 4.45 p. m., at which time, every officer and man of the nine regiments being instructed what to do, the bugle sounded the forward, and at precisely 5 o'clock the fort was carried. The troops were deployed in one line as thin as possible, the result being that no man in the assault was struck till they came to close quarters. Here the fighting became desperate and deadly. Just outside the works a line of torpedoes had been placed, many of which were exploded by the tread of the troops, blowing many men to atoms, but the line moved on without checking, over, under, and through abatis, ditches, palisading, and parapet, fighting the garrison through the fort to their bomb-proofs, from which they still fought, and only succumbed as each man was individually overpowered.

Our losses were 24 officers and men killed, and 110 officers and men wounded.

Capt. John H. Groce, Thirtieth Ohio, an officer of many rare and valuable qualities, and who led the first assault on Vicksburg, was killed, and Col. Wells S. Jones, Fifty-third Ohio, commanding brigade, severely wounded.

The regiments most conspicuous in their gallantry were the Seventieth, Forty-seventh, and Thirtieth Ohio; all the rest performed their duty equally well.

After the proper commander of the Second Brigade fell, Col. James S. Martin, One hundred and eleventh Illinois, assumed command of it, led it in the assault, rendering distinguished service.

Col. A. C. Parry, Forty-seventh Ohio, and Lieutenant-Colonel Philips, Seventieth Ohio, were also conspicuous in their performance of duty.

Maj. Thomas T. Taylor, Forty-seventh Ohio, acting judge-advocate of this division, preferring to serve with his regiment on the campaign, was severely wounded while fighting in the fort.

The captures were as follows: The garrison, including killed, 250 men and officers, 24 pieces of ordnance, with their equipment, 40 tons ammunition, a month's supply of food for the garrison, the small-arms of the command, all the animals and equipments of a light battery, the horses of the officers, and a large amount of private stores placed in the fort for safety.

To my entire staff especial praise is due for their faithful and efficient conduct during the campaign.

After the fall of McAllister the division was directed to destroy the Gulf railroad for a distance of twenty miles west of the Ogeechee, which it proceeded to do in the most thorough manner, completing the work December 21.

I would respectfully call attention to accompanying reports of brigade commanders; also, to drawings of Fort McAllister,* and a map of the country passed over.†

The supply train of this division on leaving Atlanta consisted of eighty-three six-mule wagons. I transferred to other commands after reaching the vicinity of this place 22,000 rations.

I am, very respectfully, your obedient servant,

W. B. HAZEN,
Brigadier-General of Volunteers.

ASST. ADJT. GEN., FIFTEENTH ARMY CORPS.

ADDENDA.

SPECIAL FIELD ORDERS, No. 131.

HDQRS. MIL. DIV. OF THE MISS.,
In the Field, near Savannah, Ga.,
December 13, 1864.

The general-in-chief announces with pleasure that to-day at 4.30 p. m. the Second Division, Fifteenth Army Corps, assaulted Fort McAllister and carried the place, capturing its entire garrison and armament, giving him full communication with the fleet and the army of Major-General Foster.

By order of Maj. Gen. W. T. Sherman:

L. M. DAYTON,
Aide-de-Camp.

---

* See p. 112.

† See Plate LXX, Map 1 of the Atlas.

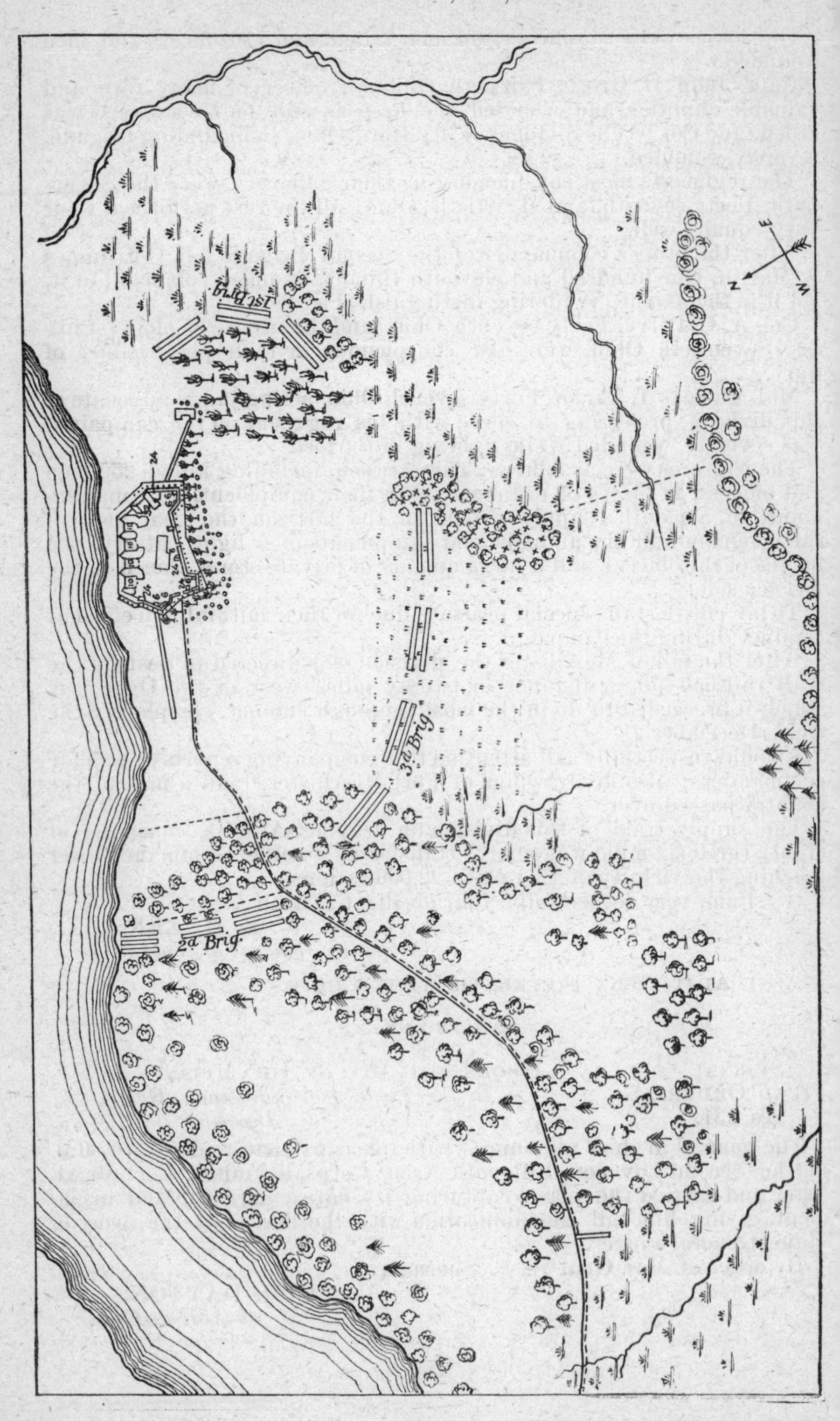
1st Brig.
3d Brig.
2d Brig.
24
24
N
E
W

No. 22.

Report of Col. Theodore Jones, Thirtieth Ohio Infantry, commanding First Brigade.

HDQRS. FIRST BRIG., SECOND DIV., 15TH ARMY CORPS,
Savannah, Ga., January 8, 1865.

CAPTAIN: I have the honor to make the following report of the part taken by this brigade in the campaign from Atlanta to Savannah:

The report of effective force of November 13 was in aggregate 1,163. On November 14 the One hundred and twenty-seventh Illinois Volunteers were detached, and remained so during the whole campaign. On November 15 the brigade, with the division, left its camp near Atlanta, and marched nineteen miles, passing through Rough and Ready. November 16, marched sixteen miles, passing through McDonough. November 17, marched sixteen miles. November 18, marched to Indian Springs; distance, seven miles. November 19, marched twelve miles, crossing the Ocmulgee River at Ocmulgee Mills. November 20, marched twelve miles. November 21, marched to Clinton; distance, six miles. The brigade was left at this place to cover the roads until the Fourth Division passed. Temporary works were thrown up, and remained in this position until the 23d, skirmishing with the enemy most of the time. November 23, moved at 4 p. m. on the main Gordon road, marching nine miles. November 24, marched to Irwinton, distance twenty-three miles, escorting pontoon train from Gordon. November 25, marched to Ball's Ferry, on the Oconee River. Finding the enemy in position on the opposite side, the Fifty-seventh Ohio, Major McClure commanding, and the One hundred and sixteenth Illinois, Lieutenant-Colonel Maddux commanding, were deployed as skirmishers along the river-bank, and opened fire on the enemy across the river. The enemy left during the night. November 26, the brigade crossed the river and marched five miles. November 27, marched seven miles, passing Irwin's Cross-Roads. November 28, marched fourteen miles. November 29, marched sixteen miles. November 30, marched to Summerville; distance, twelve miles.

December 1, marched fourteen miles. December 2, marched ten miles. December 3, marched two miles. December 4, marched to Statesborough; distance, fourteen miles. December 5, marched sixteen miles. December 6, marched one mile and a half. December 7, marched to Black Creek; distance, fifteen miles. December 8, marched to Bryan Court-House; distance, twelve miles. December 9, marched two miles, crossing the Cannouchee River. December 10, recrossed the Cannouchee and crossed the Ogeechee at Dillon's Ferry, and camped nine miles from Savannah on the King's Bridge road; distance, fifteen miles. December 11, remained in the same position. December 12, marched five miles and camped near King's Bridge. December 13, crossed the Ogeechee River and marched to Fort McAllister; distance, thirteen miles. Three regiments of the brigade—viz, the Sixth Missouri Volunteers (Lieutenant-Colonel Van Deusen), the Thirtieth Ohio (Captain Brooks), and the One hundred and sixteenth Illinois (Lieutenant-Colonel Maddux)—were ordered to make a detour to the right and strike the river below the fort, which was with difficulty accomplished, the troops having to move through a deep marsh, and under the fire of the enemy from the fort. At about 5 p. m. the detachment of this brigade moved forward, in conjunction with similar detachments from the Second and Third Brigades of this division, to the assault of the fort, which was carried in a very few moments and in gallant style. Both officers and men of my command behaved in a manner highly creditable to themselves, and deserve all the praise bestowed upon brave and gallant soldiers. December 14, camped at White Hall plantation. December 15 and 16, still in camp. December 17, 18, 19, 20, and 21, the brigade was employed in destroying the Gulf railroad. Having burnt every tie and twisted nearly every rail from the Sunbury River to the Ogeechee, returned to camp on the evening of the 21st, in which position it remained until January 1, 1865.

A report of the losses during the campaign has already been forwarded.

I have the honor to be, very respectfully, your obedient servant,

THEO. JONES,
Colonel, Commanding.

Capt. G. LOFLAND,
Asst. Adjt. Gen., Second Division, Fifteenth Army Corps.

No. 23.

Report of Col. James S. Martin, One hundred and eleventh Illinois Infantry, commanding Second Brigade.

HDQRS. SECOND BRIG., SECOND DIV., 15TH ARMY CORPS,
Savannah, Ga., January 4, 1865.

CAPTAIN:*

Broke camp on the morning of the 15th, and entered upon the great campaign of the war. Our line of march was through McDonough, Hillsborough, Clinton, Irwinton, Summerville, Statesborough, and Eden. Crossed the Cannouchee River on the 9th day of December; marched for and struck the Gulf railroad at 3 p. m., partially destroying about four miles of same; returned and went into camp near the river. On the following morning marched for Savannah, and went into camp at cross-roads, nine miles west of same, making distance marched 340 miles. The march was almost void of the usual hardships, and might be termed a pleasure trip. The men were abundantly supplied, and manifested no reluctance in obeying General Sherman's order to forage liberally off the country. Remained in camp until 4 p. m. of the 12th, when we broke camp and marched in the direction of King's Bridge; bivouacked for the night near same. Broke camp at 6 o'clock on the following morning, and marched for Fort McAllister; halted at 12 m.; formed line, composed of One hundred and eleventh Illinois Volunteers and Fifty-fourth and Forty-seventh Ohio Volunteers, Thirty-seventh and Fifty-third Ohio Volunteers and Eighty-third Indiana Volunteers being held in reserve. Threw out skirmishers and advanced to within 600 yards of the fort, where the main line was halted and skirmishers pushed forward to within range of the fort; remained in this position under fire of the enemy's artillery until 3.30 p. m., when Colonel Jones, commanding brigade, being in advance of the line, was severely wounded and Capt. John H. Groce, acting assistant inspector-general, instantly killed, the same fatal ball killing Captain Groce and wounding Colonel

* For portion of report (here omitted) relating to operations in North Georgia and North Alabama, see Vol. XXXIX, Part I, p. 746.

ones, thereby depriving us of the services of two brave and good officers and casting a gloom over the command. I was ordered to take command and notified to make all necessary preparations for an assault, and at the sound of the bugle to charge the works and take the fort. "Forward" was sounded at 4.30, and within ten minutes the fort was ours.

The conduct of the regiments engaged deserves the highest praise—not a falter, but steadily on under a withering fire, until three starry banners waved from the parapets; the garrison surrendered, and Fort McAllister was ours. The Second Brigade has a right to claim the honor of planting the first flag upon the fort, the Forty-seventh Ohio and One hundred and eleventh Illinois each in good faith claiming the honor. Each regiment having performed their part so nobly, I forbear to make particular mention of any. I entered the fort with the advance of my brigade; and being the first brigade commander in the works, the same was surrendered to me by Major Anderson, and the garrison claimed as our prisoners. No flag was found flying in the fort, and Major Anderson pledged me his word that he had none, though I learn that afterward a garrison flag was found hid in the bomb-proof. This surrender opened up communication with our fleet, and the question of supplies for our army was no longer discussed. Casualties in the assault: Killed, 4; wounded, 34. Marched two miles back and went into camp, where we remained until 17th; received orders to march to McIntosh, on Gulf railroad, with instructions to destroy same from Walthourville to a point two miles east of McIntosh. Reached the road at 1 o'clock on the 18th, went into camp, and commenced work. Destroyed nine miles of track, twisting every rail and burning every tie. Broke camp at 5.30 o'clock on the morning of the 21st; marched to cross-roads near King's Bridge; received orders to report with my brigade to General Osterhaus, commanding corps; halted to issue rations that had been sent me; resumed the march; crossed the river; received official information while on the march that Savannah was evacuated by the enemy and in possession of our troops. I bivouacked for the night, the campaign being closed.

Inclosed you will please find list of casualties.

I have the honor to be, very respectfully, your obedient servant,

JAS. S. MARTIN,
Colonel, Commanding.

Capt. GORDON LOFLAND,
Asst. Adjt. Gen., Second Division, Fifteenth Army Corps.

No. 24.

Report of Maj. William M. Mabry, One hundred and eleventh Illinois Infantry, of operations October 4, 1864–January 4, 1865.

HEADQUARTERS 111TH ILLINOIS VOLUNTEER INFANTRY,
Savannah, Ga., January 4, 1865.

SIR: In compliance with your circular of the 3d instant, I have the honor to report as follows as to the part taken by my command during the past campaign:

Left camp at East Point, Ga., October 4, 1864, and participated in all the marches, skirmishes, &c., of the campaign in Northern Georgia. Occupied the left of our line at the skirmish with Wheeler's cavalry near Turkeytown, Ala., October 25, 1864. No loss. Nothing further of interest occurred during this portion of the campaign.

Left Atlanta, Ga., November 15, 1864, in the expedition through Geo gia to our new base at Savannah. Nothing worthy of particular mentio occurred until our arrival at Fort McAllister, December 13, 1864. Pa ticipated in the successful assault upon the fort, and claim the honor planting our colors on the works of the fort first. Casualties in regimen were 2 killed and 14 wounded in the assault upon the fort. Remained i the vicinity of Fort McAllister until the fall of Savannah, when w moved to within four or five miles of the city; are now encamped or mile from the city on the right of the Atlantic and Gulf Railroad.

Officers and men did their duty so well during the entire campaig that I can make particular mention of none.

Loss during campaign: 2 killed, 14 wounded, 1 missing; total, 17.

Very respectfully, your obedient servant,

W. M. MABRY,
Major 111th Illinois Infantry, Commanding.

Capt. FRANK M. LEWIS,
Actg. Asst. Adjt. Gen., 2d Brig., 2d Div., 15th Army Corps.

No. 25.

Report of Lieut. Col. George H. Scott, Eighty-third Indiana Infant of operations September 5, 1864–January 2, 1865.

HDQRS. EIGHTY-THIRD REGIMENT INDIANA VOLUNTEERS,
Savannah, Ga., January 4, 1865.

CAPTAIN: In accordance with instructions I submit the followi report of the operations of the Eighty-third Regiment Indiana Volu teers from September 5, 1864, up to the occupation of the city of Sava nah, to wit:

Camped at East Point, Ga., until October 4; marched toward Ch tanooga in pursuit of the enemy, via Kingston and Rome, and camp on Little River October 21; distance traveled, 104 miles. Detailed go to Rome to guard supply train; returned October 25; distan eighty-two miles. Marched on the 29th via Powder Springs, a camped near Marietta November 5; distance, 104 miles. Regiment w paid here. November 14 [15], took up line of march south, via Hil borough and Irwinton, toward the coast, meeting with very little oppo tion. Crossed the Ocmulgee, Oconee, Cannouchee, and Ogeech Rivers, and struck the Gulf railroad on the 9th of December and t up several miles of the track. Returned and marched to Fort McAl ter on the 13th. Remained here a few days and marched out on t Gulf railroad, and assisted in destroying about nine miles of the tra Returned and crossed the Ogeechee River on the 21st. Enemy eva ated the city of Savannah on the night of the 21st [20th]. Remain in camp until January 2, and marched into town; went into camp insi the fortifications.

Distance marched since October 4, 1864, 750 miles.

The regiment lost 1 man killed and 2 missing.

I am, sir, very respectfully, your obedient servant,

GEO. H. SCOTT,
Lieut. Col., Comdg. Eighty-third Regiment Indiana Volunteers

Capt. F. M. LEWIS,
Actg. Asst. Adjt. Gen., 2d Brig., 2d Div., 15th Army Corps.

No. 26.

eport of Lieut. Col. Louis von Blessingh, Thirty-seventh Ohio Infantry, of operations November 13, 1864–January 2, 1865.

HDQRS. THIRTY-SEVENTH REGT. OHIO VET. VOL. INFTY.,
Savannah, Ga., January 3, 1865.

History of the Thirty-seventh Regiment Ohio Infantry Veteran olunteers of the late campaign, from November 13, 1864, to Janu-y 2, 1865:

On the 13th day of November, 1864, the regiment marched from Camp nyrna, Ga., to Atlanta, Ga., a distance of twelve miles, and there iving been equipped, marched out of Atlanta on the 15th as a part of e army which, under the command of Major-General Sherman, under-ok the great invasion of the State of Georgia, from the northwestern rt to the southeastern border of said State. The line of march the giment made was over McDonough, Indian Springs, near which place crossed the Ocmulgee River, passing through Hillsborough and Clin-n. At the latter place, November 22, the regiment, with the Fifteenth ichigan Volunteer Infantry, went on picket on the road leading to acon, from where the enemy's cavalry tried to enter Clinton, and cut f the train of the division. The regiment went into line of battle, and e enemy was forced to retreat by our advancing skirmish line. On e 23d the regiment remained near Clinton, covering the rear of the vision, and marched on the same day toward Griswold, and joined s brigade and division near said place, after having crossed the Geor-a Central Railroad; thence passed through Irwinton and marched to e Oconee River, which it crossed on the 26th of November, when it sumed its march through the swamps and arrived at Summerville on e 30th. The regiment, with the brigade, continued its march toward e sea-coast through the low and swampy country of Georgia, and iving passed Emanuel and Bulloch Counties of said State, on the ght (southwest) side of Ogeechee River, it crossed the Cannouchee ver on the 9th of December, marched to the Savannah and Gulf Rail-ad, and destroyed the same, in connection with the other regiments of e Second Brigade, for about five miles. Having returned the same y to the Cannouchee River, it crossed the same the next day, and also e Ogeechee River, the latter near the Ogeechee Canal, then marched ward Savannah, within nine miles of which the regiment bivouacked. On the 12th the regiment returned with the brigade and division to e Ogeechee River, crossed it at King's Bridge on the 13th, and vanced on Fort McAllister, which was invested and carried by sault. The regiment bivouacked near the fort until December 17, ien it marched with the brigade to McIntosh, thirty miles southwest Savannah, on the Savannah and Gulf Railroad, which was reached the 18th, and the regiment being engaged in destroying the railroad mpletely, so that nothing was left but the twisted iron rails, until the ght of the 20th. On the 21st the regiment returned to the Ogeechee ver and crossed it at King's Bridge, in the meantime Savannah ing evacuated by the enemy. The regiment went in bivouac eleven les from Savannah, and marched on the 29th to within four miles of vannah, and went into camp on the southwest side of Savannah, at e Gulf railroad, on the 2d day of January, 1865.

Distance marched from Atlanta November 15, 1864, to January 2, 65, 374 miles.

L. VON BLESSINGH,
Lieut. Col., Comdg. Thirty-seventh Ohio Veteran Vol. Infantry.

No. 27.

Report of Col. Augustus C. Parry, Forty-seventh Ohio Infantry, of operations November 15, 1864–January 2, 1865.

HDQRS. FORTY-SEVENTH REGT. OHIO VET. VOL. INFTY.,
Savannah, Ga., January 4, 1865.

SIR: I have the honor to submit the following report of the part taken by the Forty-seventh Regiment Ohio Veteran Volunteer Infantry in the late expedition through the State of Georgia:

In accordance with orders from superior headquarters, I started with the regiment from camp near Atlanta, Ga., on the 15th day of November, 1864, having received, a few days previous, about 400 drafted men and substitutes, who performed their duties in the subsequent campaign to my entire satisfaction, and better than I had reason to expect. During the whole march nothing remarkable occurred in which the regiment bore a conspicuous part until the morning of the 13th of December, when the division was ordered to march to and assault Fort McAllister, on the Ogeechee River. This day my regiment had the advance, and in the afternoon, when orders for the assault were given, we had the honor of planting the first Stars and Stripes on the parapet of the doomed fort. Four days afterward we participated in the destruction of the Savannah, Gulf, and Albany Railroad. Returned from said expedition on the afternoon of the 21st, and entered the suburbs of the city of Savannah on the 2d of January, 1865.

Inclosed I append a list of casualties during the campaign.*

I have the honor to be, sir, very respectfully, your obedient servant,

AUG. C. PARRY,
Colonel, Comdg. Forty-seventh Regt. Ohio Vet. Vol. Infantry.

Capt. FRANK M. LEWIS,
Acting Assistant Adjutant-General, Second Brigade.

No. 28.

Report of Maj. George F. Kili, Fifty-fourth Ohio Infantry.

HDQRS. FIFTY-FOURTH REGT. OHIO VET. VOL. INFANTRY,
Savannah, Ga., January 4, 1865.

SIR: In obedience to orders, I have the honor to submit the following report of the part taken by the Fifty-fourth Ohio in the late campaign through Georgia:

The Fifty-fourth Ohio joined the brigade from detached service at White Hall, near Atlanta, on the night of November 14. Received orders same evening to be prepared to move next morning (15th) at daylight. Left White Hall about 8 a. m.; marched steadily forward, unmolested by the enemy. On the 16th passed through McDonough; crossed Ocmulgee River at Ocmulgee Mills December 19; 20th, marched through Hillsborough; passed Clinton 21st, and struck the Macon and Augusta Railroad on 22d. 23d, continued march south. 24th, camped near Irwinton. 25th, passed through Irwinton; enemy in our front. 26th, crossed Oconee River at ——— Ferry.

---

* Shows 1 man killed, and 1 officer and 15 men wounded.

December 4, arrived at Statesborough. December 5, leave Statesborough and march south. December 9, crossed Cannouchee River and struck the Gulf railroad, which we destroyed for a distance of four miles. 10th, recrossed Cannouchee River and marched to Ogeechee River, which we crossed, and camped eleven miles from Savannah. 13th, crossed Ogeechee River at King's Bridge, and marched on Fort McAllister, which was in the possession of the rebels and mounting twenty-two heavy guns. Attack was made at 4 p. m., and after a short but stubborn resistance the fort was carried by storm. In this action the Fifty-fourth Ohio lost 5 men wounded, 2 of whom have since died of their wounds. Captain Neff, Company H, received a severe wound in right leg.

The subjoined is a list of the casualties of the Fifty-fourth in the late campaign.*

I have the honor to be, very respectfully,

GEO. F. KILI,
Major, Commanding.

Capt. F. M. LEWIS,
Acting Assistant Adjutant-General, Second Brigade.

No. 29.

Reports of Col. John M. Oliver, Fifteenth Michigan Infantry, commanding Third Brigade.

HDQRS. THIRD BRIG., SECOND DIV., 15TH ARMY CORPS,
Savannah, Ga., January 6, 1865.

SIR: I have the honor to report the following detail of operations of this brigade in the campaign so gloriously concluded by the capture of Fort McAllister and surrender of Savannah:

On the 15th of November, 1864, we left White Hall at 10 a. m., and marched in a southerly direction, passing through Rough and Ready; camped near Tucker's cabin, Henry County, at 5 p. m., having marched fourteen miles. On the 16th left camp at 6 a. m., passing through McDonough. Two miles south of town we reached camp at 5 p. m.; distance marched, sixteen miles. 17th, marched from 3.30 p. m. until 12.30 night. The troops marched on the left side of the road, while the wagon train and artillery took the road. Camped at Liberty Church, having marched seventeen miles. 18th, resumed our march at 8 a. m.; encamped at Indian Springs at 1 p. m.; distance marched, six miles and a half. 19th, left camp at 3 a. m.; marched to the Ocmulgee River and crossed on pontoon bridge; halted for the night near Hillsborough, arrriving in camp at 4.30; distance marched, fifteen miles. 20th, marched at 10 a. m., passing through Hillsborough and encamped five miles south of town, arriving at 7 p. m.; distance marched, twelve miles. 21st, resumed march at 6 a. m.; rained all day; roads in a terrible condition; passed through the town of Clinton and camped within nine miles of Macon; distance marched, thirteen miles. Left Fifteenth Michigan Veteran Volunteer Infantry at Clinton to guard roads leading to Macon until the trains had passed. About 4 p. m. they had a sharp skirmish with Breckinridge's brigade of cavalry, and repulsed them, with a loss of two men wounded. On the 22d broke camp at 8 a. m.;

* Shows 2 men killed, and 1 officer and 4 men wounded.

marched in a southeasterly course, crossing the Macon and Augusta Railroad, which had been destroyed by our troops, and encamped on the Gordon road. The enemy attacked the First Division, and were repulsed. Fifteenth Michigan Veteran Volunteer Infantry reported at 6 p. m. from Clinton. Marched this day ten miles. 23d, marched at 9 a. m. in the direction of Gordon by a circuitous route, reaching camp at 12 m.; took position and fortified; marched five miles. 24th, left camp at 9 a. m., arriving at Irwinton at 3 p. m.; marched five miles. 25th, resumed our march to the Oconee River, passing through the town of Irwinton, arriving at the river at 4 p. m. The enemy, being posted on the opposite bank, prevented our crossing. Artillery was placed in position and opened on their works. The Ninetieth Illinois and Ninety-ninth Indiana Volunteers were detailed to picket the river. The Seventeenth Army Corps joined us at this point. The Fourth Division and pontoon train also arrived. Distance marched, twelve miles. 26th, the enemy evacuated the opposite bank of the Oconee at 12 o'clock (night). At 6 p. m. crossed the river, marched two miles, and encamped. 27th, marched in a northeasterly course and encamped at Irwin's Cross-Roads at 12 m.; distance marched, eight miles. 28th, resumed march and encamped; distance, fifteen miles. 29th, marched eighteen miles; roads in a terrible condition on account of rain. 30th, marched fifteen miles; had to corduroy and bridge the roads continually.

On the 1st of December left camp at 7 a. m., passing through Cannouchee Post-Office, and encamped at the junction of the Jones Ferry and old Savannah roads, arriving at 5 p. m.; marched fourteen miles. 2d, at 8 a. m. marched on the Savannah road, crossing Scull's Creek, and encamped in Bulloch County; distance, ten miles. 3d, marched and encamped on Lott's Creek; distance, five miles. 4th, at 8 a. m. resumed march in a southerly course. At 3 p. m. some mounted foragers of the division were attacked by some 600 cavalry near Statesborough, and driven back, until the enemy encountered the Seventieth Ohio Veteran Volunteer Infantry, who were in advance as guard for pioneers corduroying roads. The Seventieth Ohio gave them one volley, after which the rebels hastily retreated, leaving 6 killed and 1 wounded in our hands. Our loss was slight. We encamped at Statesborough. Distance marched, fourteen miles. 5th, at 9 a. m. marched in an easterly direction, and encamped at 6 p. m.; distance marched, thirteen miles. 6th, I was ordered to march to Jenks' Bridge and secure the crossing. Left camp between 6 and 7 a. m., leaving all my trains but four ambulances, two wagon-loads of ammunition, and the tool wagon. Upon arriving at the river found the bridge destroyed. The Fifteenth Michigan and Seventeenth Ohio Veteran Volunteer Infantry took position on the river-bank; the Forty-eighth Illinois and Ninetieth Illinois and Ninety-ninth Indiana Volunteers were put in position faced to the rear, with a section of artillery from the Third Division on a hill back of the river half a mile. Distance marched, fifteen miles. Stacked arms and went into camp 12 m. The vigor of the troops and their earnest effort to reach the river, secure the bridge, and strike the enemy's cavalry enabled us to make this march with astonishing quickness. When we arrived at the camp of the Third Division, which was one mile and a half nearer Jenks' Bridge than our camp, we waited one hour and a half at least for the artillery, which had not been notified that they were to accompany the expedition. This delay in the outset, and some skirmishing on the way, left the actual marching time less than four hours. 7th, we were ordered to the Cannouchee River to hold and save the bridge across the river if possible. We met the enemy's pickets on Black Creek. Skirmishing commenced and continued for twelve miles, until our mounted force arrived at the bridge, which they found in flames. The officers and men of the command seemed determined to-day to strike the enemy's cavalry, who had some twenty-three prisoners whom they fed on sorghum stalks. At Black Creek the obstructions in the ford were removed, so that our ambulances and ammunition wagons crossed the ford before the troops could get across on the stringers of the still burning bridge. The enemy were pushed so hard that they could not destroy the bridge across Mill Creek at all. At one place, near Bryan County Court-House, the men waded in four ranks through a swamp 300 yards across up to their waists in water. We captured two prisoners and five horses. The mounted force, with one regiment of infantry, remained at the river, and the rest of the brigade encamped at Eden (Bryan County Court-House). Distance marched, twenty miles. Lieutenant-Colonel Berkey, Ninety-ninth Indiana Volunteers, who was in command of the mounted force of the brigade (sixty men), conducted the operations of the advance with great skill and perseverance. 8th, at daylight enemy opened with artillery and shelled the woods fiercely, hurting no one; skirmished with them all day. Sent a detachment of the mounted men to effect a crossing up the river, which they were unable to do. The skirmishing across the river was kept up so fiercely that the enemy in two nights and a day could not destroy the bridges across the two lagoons, which were 600 feet or more across. If they had been destroyed we could not have reached the Gulf railroad or saved any portion of King's Bridge without making a march of thirty miles. The behavior of the officers and men during this expedition was highly praiseworthy. We have no skulkers. The balance of the division and pontoon train joined us here and commenced to put in artillery during the night. 9th, the enemy left during the night, but before leaving opened a brisk fire of artillery and musketry. At daylight was ordered to secure and hold King's Bridge, across the Ogeechee. I at once commenced to cross my brigade over the Cannouchee, by ferrying them in pontoon-boats and swimming the horses. It took us nearly two hours to cross. Pushed rapidly forward for eight miles to King's Bridge, but were unable to save but part of it. We then returned to Way's Station to camp, leaving two companies of Forty-eighth Illinois Volunteers to guard the crossing and prevent further destruction of the bridge. We received orders to destroy all trestles on the railroad; also the railroad bridge across the Ogeechee. We destroyed fourteen trestles, varying from 30 to 150 yards long, and the Gulf railroad bridge across the Ogeechee, a magnificent bridge 500 yards long; took 18 prisoners; finished our work at 9.30 p. m. 10th, left Way's Station at 5 a. m; returned to the Cannouchee River, recrossed, and marched to the Ogeechee River, and crossed at Dillon's Ferry, and encamped within ten miles of Savannah; distance marched, eighteen miles. 11th and 12th, rested in camp. 13th, left camp and marched, crossing the Ogeechee on King's Bridge, to within about one mile of Fort McAllister and formed. The Third Brigade formed the center of division line, the Ninetieth Illinois on the right, Forty-eighth Illinois in the center, and Seventieth Ohio on the left. The Fifteenth Michigan and Ninety-ninth Indiana were in reserve. Advanced half a mile and halted until 5 p. m. to enable other troops to get in position, when the order was given to advance and take the fort. The distance from our line to the fort was about 700 yards through open fields. The taking of this fort was so cheerfully and gallantly done by the troops of this brigade that there is hardly any way to do them full justice. The conduct of Captain Grimes, Forty-eighth Illinois Volunteers, commanding skirmish line, in silencing two of the 10-inch guns bearing on our front, by his sharpshooters, and in his hand-to-hand fight with Captain Clinch, ought to be noticed in general orders. Captain Smith, of the same regiment, who rejoined us on the 27th of November, 1864, after escaping from Columbia, S. C., was the first man in the fort, and was killed inside of it. He was a gallant officer. The flag of the Seventieth Ohio was the first on the fort, though the gallant veterans of the Forty-eighth and Ninetieth Illinois were there with them almost at the same time. Both color bearers of the Forty-eighth were killed with torpedoes. The color bearer of the Seventieth Ohio was also killed just as he handed the flag to a comrade when climbing over the abatis. The men of this command under fire cannot be surpassed. The only order I gave them was that when the "forward" was sounded to march steadily until they reached our skirmishers and then go in. The action lasted twelve minutes. Our loss was 76 officers and men killed and wounded. The results of this action were most important; our communications were at once fully established. Captures in the fort by division were 24 guns, about 200 prisoners, medical stores, quartermaster's stores, a large quantity of ordnance stores, ammunition, and small-arms. A garrison flag was taken by Captain Nelson, of my staff, and sent to your headquarters. On the 14th the Seventieth Ohio Volunteers, on account of the conspicuous part taken by them in the capture of the fort yesterday, was ordered to garrison it. 17th, left camp with three regiments—Ninety-ninth Indiana, Forty-eighth Illinois, and Fifteenth Michigan Volunteers—for the Gulf railroad. Returned on the 21st, having marched forty miles and destroyed seven miles of the road, burning every tie and twisting every rail. On the morning of the 22d our troops entered Savannah. The Third Brigade of this division consists of the Fifteenth Michigan Veteran Volunteer Infantry, Lieutenant-Colonel Hutchinson commanding; Ninetieth Illinois Volunteers, Lieutenant-Colonel Stuart commanding; Seventieth Ohio Veteran Volunteer Infantry, Lieutenant-Colonel Philips commanding; Ninety-ninth Indiana Volunteers, Lieutenant-Colonel Berkey commanding; and Forty-eighth Illinois Veteran Volunteer Infantry, Major Adams commanding. I know of no troops in our army that surpass them in heroism and self-devotion—but few, very few, equal them.

To my staff I have been greatly indebted for success—Captain La Point, acting assistant adjutant-general; Captain Nelson, acting assistant inspector-general; Lieutenant Brown, acting aide-de-camp. I thank them all sincerely for the manner in which they have discharged their duties. Lieut. John Doyle, acting assistant quartermaster of this brigade, deserves special mention. His discharge of duty has been perfect, and I would especially recommend his promotion.

To yourself and other officers of the division staff I offer my hearty thanks for the courtesy and for the many acts which have shown how well and thoroughly you have striven for the success of all in this campaign.

I am, sir, respectfully, your obedient servant,

JOHN M. OLIVER,
Colonel, Commanding.

Capt. G. LOFLAND,
Asst. Adjt. Gen., Second Division, Fifteenth Army Corps.

HDQRS. THIRD BRIG., SECOND DIV., 15TH ARMY CORPS,
Savannah, Ga., January 4, 1865.

SIR: I have the honor to report the following list of casualties in this brigade from November 15, 1864, up to December 22, 1864:

Command.	Killed.			Wounded.			Missing.			Total.
	Officers.	Men.	Aggregate.	Officers.	Men.	Aggregate.	Officers.	Men.	Aggregate.	
15th Michigan Veteran Volunteer Infantry.					3	3		1	1	4
70th Ohio Veteran Volunteer Infantry		7	7	1	35	36		16	16	59
48th Illinois Veteran Volunteer Infantry.	1	6	7		17	17		1	1	25
90th Illinois Volunteers		3	3		14	14				17
99th Indiana Volunteers					2	2		3	3	5
Total	1	16	17	1	71	72		21	21	110

Respectfully, your obedient servant,

JOHN M. OLIVER,
Colonel, Commanding.

[Capt. G. LOFLAND.]

No. 30.

Report of Brig. Gen. John E. Smith, U. S. Army, commanding Third Division.

HDQRS. THIRD DIVISION, FIFTEENTH ARMY CORPS,
Savannah, Ga., January 2, 1865.

MAJOR: I have the honor to submit the following report of my command during the campaign from Atlanta to this place:

In compliance with orders from Maj. Gen. W. T. Sherman, commanding the army, I marched from Cartersville, Ga., on the 12th day of November, 1864. Reported at headquarters Fifteenth Army Corps, at White Hall, near Atlanta, on the 14th of November, at 11 a. m. The necessary clothing and camp and garrison equipage in store for us at Atlanta were issued, and with twenty days' rations and 230 rounds of ammunition per man, was ready to move the same day. The command moved at 11 a. m. on the 15th of November and marched, via Rough and Ready, Stockbridge, McDonough, Jackson, crossing the Ocmulgee River at Seven Islands, Hillsborough and Clinton, to Gordon, at which point my command effectually destroyed four miles of the railroad and about 500 yards of the trestle bridge three miles west of Gordon; thence by way of Irwinton, crossing the Oconee River at Ball's Ferry, four miles below the railroad bridge, Irwin's Cross-Roads, Summerville, Statesborough, crossing the Ogeechee River at Jenks' Bridge; thence marching between the Little and Big Ogeechee Rivers to Bethel Church, on the Savannah Canal. On the 10th of December I left the supply train in camp, guarded by one regiment of infantry, and moved upon the south side of the canal to a point about four miles and a half from Savannah, where the enemy were discovered in position with a battery, covering a small road. Skirmishers were at once deployed, and the

First Brigade, Col. J. B. McCown commanding, promptly formed in line; the Second Brigade, Bvt. Brig. Gen. G. B. Raum commanding, was formed on the right of the First Brigade. These dispositions having been made, it was found impossible for the skirmishers to advance, owing to the low, marshy ground in front having been overflowed from the canal to the depth of from four to six feet, and the road, scarcely ten feet wide, being amply protected by the enemy's guns. During the night a work was thrown up, and three guns of Battery B, First Michigan Artillery, Captain Arndt commanding, were placed in position, which opened upon the enemy's guns about daylight on the morning of the 11th of December. I was ordered to move to the right at 8 a. m. the same morning, when the guns and the line were withdrawn, leaving the skirmishers in position. A brisk fire was kept up by them until the evening of the 11th, when they were relieved by Brig. Gen. G. A. Smith, commanding Fourth Division, Seventeenth Army Corps.

The casualties on the 10th and 11th at this place were as follows: Commissioned officers—slightly wounded, 2. Enlisted men—killed, 1; slightly wounded, 4; severely wounded, 1.

At 9 p. m. December 11 followed the First Division to the right and camped at Anderson's plantation, and on the 12th took up a position near Miller's Station (No. 1) on the Gulf railroad. Owing to the width of the marsh and the Little Ogeechee River, an advance was impracticable. An outpost was stationed at the abutment of the railroad bridge, the only available ground on my front. At this place one man was killed. On the 19th a work was commenced on the railroad for three guns. It was not completed, however, when the enemy evacuated Savannah. On the morning of the 21st the command moved into Savannah, camping in the suburbs between the Gulf railroad and Shell road.

The conduct of the officers and soldiers of this division is worthy of the highest commendation—always cheerful and complying strictly with all orders, which made the march a very pleasant one. I take pleasure in reporting that not a single man was lost by straggling. The commanding officers of brigades and regiments have my thanks for their co-operation.

The weather during the march was pleasant, and supplies of fowls, pigs, and sweet potatoes abundant, with plenty of forage for the animals.

During the march this command cut about ten miles of road through the woods, and made 5,010 yards of corduroy, not including many places where rails were convenient and could be thrown down without detaining the column.

A few prisoners were captured, and 800 bales of cotton destroyed.

I am, major, very respectfully, your obedient servant,

JNO. E. SMITH,
Brigadier-General.

Maj. M. WOODHULL,
Assistant Adjutant-General, Fifteenth Army Corps.

ADDENDA.

CIRCULAR.] HDQRS. THIRD DIV., FIFTEENTH ARMY CORPS,
Savannah, Ga., December 25, 1864.

The general commanding announces with pride and pleasure that the division was highly complimented by Major-General Sherman for their soldierly bearing and the good condition of their arms. The Fifty-ninth Indiana and Sixty-third Illinois Regiments were noticed particularly for their good marching. The general would also take this occasion to thank the officers and soldiers for their prompt execution and compliance with all orders; and the fact that we have lost but one man by straggling during a march of 350 miles is evidence of the good conduct of the command, for which every officer and soldier should be proud, and none more so than the general commanding.

By order of Brig. Gen. John E. Smith:

S. M. BUDLONG,
Assistant Adjutant-General.

No. 31.

Report of Brig. Gen. John M. Corse, U. S. Army, commanding Fourth Division.

HDQRS. FOURTH DIVISION, FIFTEENTH ARMY CORPS,
Savannah, Ga., January 15, 1865.

MAJOR: *

The command by consecutive marches passed through Kingston, Allatoona, and Marietta, and arrived at Atlanta on the morning of the 15th [November], just as the Fifteenth Corps debouched from the town. Twenty days' supplies were loaded on the trains, and the command moved to overtake the corps, and encamped near East Point on the night of the 15th. During the 16th and 17th the column was on the road, and bivouacked near Jackson, Ga., on the 18th. On the night of the 18th the division was put in motion and marched until 10 a. m. of the 19th, when it arrived at the Ocmulgee Mills, where it lay until the entire corps and corps trains had crossed. At noon of the 20th, by direction of the major-general commanding the corps, the division crossed the river. The pontoons were taken up and the train placed under my charge. From the Ocmulgee to Gordon we had continuous wet weather and heavy roads. The command, incumbered by the pontoon train, about 300 wagons belonging to the cavalry division, and a drove of 3,000 head of cattle, struggled through the mud and swamps, making fair progress, and arriving at Gordon, where we for the first time joined our corps after leaving the Ocmulgee River. Here we were relieved of the additional trains, and after one day's rest at Gordon took up our line of march, arriving at the right bank of the Oconee, at Ball's Ferry, November 26, at 10 a. m. The pontoons being speedily laid, the division crossed in advance of the corps and marched to Irwin's Cross-Roads, where we encamped during the 27th.

In accordance with orders from corps headquarters, two brigades (Rice's and Hurlbut's) were sent to the Georgia Central Railroad, at No. 13, to destroy the road between that point and the Oconee River. Six miles were effectually destroyed on the 27th, and the division united again at a point about twelve miles southeast of Wrightsville. The march from here to the point at which we crossed the Ogeechee was through a country well watered, sparsely inhabited, furnishing, however, by means of extensive foraging parties, abundance of vegetables and stock. On the 3d of December we camped on Scull's Creek, near No. 7, to which point Rice's brigade was sent to destroy the railroad, while

* For portion of report (here omitted) relating to operations in North Georgia, see Vol. XXXIX, Part I, p. 767.

Adams' brigade was so disposed as to cover the working party and prevent any sudden dash of cavalry from driving them away. On the 4th the command was again united and put in motion, the head of the column directed toward Jenks' Bridge over the Ogeechee, where the Savannah road crosses and strikes the Georgia Central Railroad. About noon of December 7 the command arrived on the right bank of the Ogeechee River, at the bridge crossing to Bloomingdale, or Station No. 2, on the Savannah and Macon Railroad. The bridge having been destroyed by the enemy on the approach of our forces, was replaced by a pontoon bridge. A force from the Second Division thrown across was skirmishing quite lively on the arrival of the head of my column. By direction of Major-General Osterhaus I crossed the leading brigade (Rice's), which gradually cleared the woods, driving the rebels back across an open field into barricades and rail works they had thrown up for their protection, necessitating the deployment of two regiments (the Second and Seventh Iowa Infantry), which, gallantly charging across the broken fields, entered the rebel works, driving them, capturing, killing, and wounding about 25. Our loss was 2 killed and 4 wounded. Rice's brigade, re-enforced by Williamson's brigade, of the First Division, was then directed to hold the station and remain on the east side of the Ogeechee the night of the 7th, while the rest of the division lay with the corps on the west bank of the river.

The division was again detached from the corps on the 8th, and moved with its transportation to Station No. 2, Bloomingdale. The Seventeenth Corps was distant in our rear about thirteen miles, separated from us by the Little Ogeechee River; the Fifteenth Corps out of supporting distance by noon on the west side of the Ogeechee proper. Leaving the transportation of the division at the station in charge of Williamson's brigade, which was to remain until relieved by the Seventeenth Corps, the head of the column was directed on the road leading to Dillon's Bridge across the Ogeechee, near the mouth of the canal. The first line of works, distant from Bloomingdale about two miles, we found evacuated. The Seventh Illinois Mounted Infantry was thrown out as an advanced guard, and during the day ran into the enemy several times, bringing in five prisoners, among them one commissioned officer. Our flanks were well protected by the two rivers; the ridge between furnished a fine road, occasionally blockaded, not sufficiently serious, however, to occasion much detention. The head of the column arrived at the canal about noon, and discovered the bridge still in flames. A new one was speedily constructed by the pioneer corps, and a portion of the Third Brigade crossed and threw up a tête-de-pont, and the Seventh Illinois Mounted Infantry moved out to reconnoiter the enemy's position. From the citizens we ascertained that a force of the enemy had erected works at the junction of the Dillon's Bridge road with the King's Bridge and Savannah road. The numbers were variously estimated from 1,000 to 5,000. Under the circumstances, our great distance from any supporting columns, the utter destruction of Dillon's Bridge over the Ogeechee, and the absence of pontoons, General Howard deemed it not advisable for me to push any farther. The command was then placed in camp on the north bank of the canal, and intrenched itself for the night. No communication could be effected till late that evening with that portion of the Fifteenth Corps that had moved down the right bank of the Ogeechee. Occasionally we heard their artillery, and learned later that General Osterhaus was forcing a crossing over the Cannouchee. The reconnaissance of the mounted force developed the enemy in force with artillery at the cross-roads above designated, about three miles from our camp.

The transportation arrived during the night of the 8th under guard from the First Brigade, and with two brigades (Adams' and Rice's) and Brunner's battery we moved out about 9 a. m. on the 9th to obtain possession of the cross-roads and try to open communication with the rest of the corps by way of King's Bridge. The trains, with the exception of a few wagons for ordnance, were left with the Third Brigade at the canal. The two brigades moved out, Adams' in advance, covered by a line of skirmishers from the Sixty-sixth Illinois Volunteers, and the flanks well protected by the Seventh Illinois Mounted Infantry. The battery moved in rear of Adams, followed closely by Rice in column. Not until the pickets were driven in and the skirmishers quite warmly engaged did Adams deploy his regiments to their support. The dense undergrowth rendered the movements in line exceedingly difficult, and the advance of the line soon developed the artillery of the enemy, one section of which swept the road on which we were advancing. The reserves were massed on either side where open space could be secured, and one section of artillery under Lieutenant Brunner pushed as near the enemy as the blockaded condition of the road would permit. It was impossible to see through the dense woods, and the enemy's artillery swept the road so as to render it untenable, compelling Brunner to play on their works from a field separated from their position by a dense forest and to fire altogether by the sound of their guns. At this time information was brought that a column of the enemy was moving on my right, and I pushed Rice, with two regiments, toward the King's Bridge road and ordered Adams to push on with vigor. The increased volleys of musketry and sudden cessation of the enemy's artillery, with the significant yelling of our men, indicated that the assault was in progress, and before I could reach the center, or Rice could make the road, our troops were in the enemy's works with quite a squad of prisoners and one piece of artillery as a trophy. The enemy were pursued for four miles, and the Seventh Illinois Mounted Infantry swung around on Adams' right, struck for the Gulf railroad, arriving there in time to tear up a rail and capture a locomotive and eighteen cars, with about forty prisoners. The brigade left at the canal with the supply and ordnance trains was then brought up, and before dark, by order of General Howard, we went into camp near the main branch of the Little Ogeechee River, with a good line of defense. King's Bridge was found in ruins. By means of a boat communication was opened with General Osterhaus, who had crossed the Cannouchee with a portion of the First and Second Divisions and struck the Gulf railroad west of the Ogeechee. The Third Division had arrived at the canal, near Dillon's Bridge, with a pontoon train, and we received information that the pontoon could be thrown across the Ogeechee early, placing again the Fifteenth Corps in close communication.

The morning of the 10th General Osterhaus went with the advanced brigade, commanded by Colonel Hurlbut, until we struck the north branch of the Little Ogeechee, where we found the enemy apparently in heavy force and so separated from us by the swamps and rice fields as to render an assault impracticable till the arrival of re-enforcements. The artillery of the main fort occupied by the enemy mounted guns of so much larger caliber than our light field pieces as to induce the general to order up a battery of 20-pounder Parrotts before opening. The skirmishers were pushed as close as mud and water would permit, and thus we lay until the subsequent day: Colonel Hurlbut's brigade in line, covered by skirmishers; Rice's brigade in column in reserve, and beyond range of the enemy's ordnance. The Second Brigade, Colonel

Adams commanding, was sent to the railroad on our right to create a diversion and also effect a crossing between the Gulf railroad bridge and a point known as the Hermitage, nearer the coast. On the 14th the division was united and placed in position near the forks of the Little Ogeechee, Woods' division on our left, John E. Smith on our right. No effort was made to assault the enemy's lines, which were separated from ours by the north branch of the Little Ogeechee and the rice swamps that abound on either bank of that stream. On the night of the 19th I obtained permission to attempt a lodgment on the other side, which was successfully made by Lieut. William Pittman, Eighty-first Ohio Infantry, with ten men who volunteered for the purpose. Having demonstrated the practicability of crossing a column I desired to push a sufficient force over during the night, and move the division over the following day and assault the enemy. The general commanding, deeming it not expedient, directed me to withdraw my men, which was done without any casualties or without awakening the suspicions of the enemy as to what we were doing. On the morning of the 21st Savannah was found to be evacuated by the enemy, and in accordance with orders I moved my division into the city and went into position on the east side of Savannah, my left resting on the river, my right occupying Fort Brown. The march was in some respects an arduous one, [but] proved on the whole to have been pleasant and even beneficial to the command. The health of the men was never better nor were they ever in better spirits or condition than when they took possession of Savannah.

On reference to memoranda I find that we have obtained on the march, beyond what was necessary for daily issue, 1,000 head of cattle, about 300 head of horses and mules; that nearly seven miles of road were corduroyed and thirty bridges built by the pioneer corps of this division.

The list of casualties is exceedingly small.

I am, very respectfully, your obedient servant,

JNO. M. CORSE,
Brigadier-General.

Maj. MAX. WOODHULL,
Assistant Adjutant-General, Fifteenth Army Corps.

No. 32.

Report of Brig. Gen. Elliott W. Rice, U. S. Army, commanding First Brigade.

HDQRS. FIRST BRIG., FOURTH DIV., 15TH ARMY CORPS,
Savannah, Ga., December 29, 1864.

SIR: I have the honor to submit the following as my report of the recent campaign which resulted in the capture of the city of Savannah, as participated in by the First Brigade, Fourth Division, Fifteenth Army Corps:

In compliance with orders from headquarters Fourth Division, Fifteenth Army Corps, Brig. Gen. J. M. Corse commanding, the brigade destroyed its camp in connection with all property, public and private, for which transportation was not furnished, and left the city of Rome, Ga., at 8 a. m. on the 11th day of November, 1864. From thence I marched the brigade, via Kingston, Allatoona, Big Shanty, Marietta, and Turner's Ferry, to the city of Atlanta. Here I supplied my command with shelter-tents and clothing. This having been hastily done I left the city on the 15th day of November, it being also the date of my arrival, having joined my brigade with the grand army of General Sherman. We passed through Rough and Ready, McDonough, and Jackson, crossing the Ocmulgee River at Seven Islands on the evening of the 19th and morning of the 20th. Here the division took charge of the pontoon train, moving steadily and slowly along over or rather through roads made almost impassable by the incessant rains. Having passed through the towns of Monticello, Hillsborough, and Clinton, the fair weather had greatly improved the roads, and after we had been relieved of the pontoons we moved southward rapidly. We crossed the Georgia Central Railroad at Gordon, and marched on a road south of and parallel to the railroad through the town of Irwinton. Crossing the Oconee River at Ball's Ferry, we camped at Irwin's Cross-Roads during the night.

On the morning of November 22 we struck the Georgia Central Railroad at mile-post 138, and from thence we effectually destroyed the road by burning the ties, bending, twisting, and breaking the rails as far as Station 13, a distance of three or more miles. Moving again on the road south of and parallel to the railroad, we crossed the Ogeechee River, and once more made an effectual destruction of three miles of the same road to Station No. 7. We recrossed the river and struck it again after a long march at a point south of Station No. 2. Here the enemy resisted the crossing, but were easily forced back by the Second Iowa Infantry, which I had deployed as skirmishers, supported by the Seventh Iowa Infantry. The country for nearly three-quarters of a mile was nearly waist deep with water in the swamps and lagoons, through which the troops waded with a good will, driving the enemy into a small rail-work which they had hastily constructed. I endeavored to turn their position and gain the rear of their defenses by throwing a portion of the Second Iowa to their left under cover of a thick woods in that direction, but the troops in their front and on their left could not be held back. They dashed forward with an unparalleled impetuosity, right over the rail-works, capturing 20 prisoners, killing 2, and wounding 4 men. The balance of the rebel force rushed to the railroad, and taking the cars moved off in the direction of Savannah. In this skirmish the Second Iowa Infantry lost 2 men killed and 2 wounded, and the Seventh Iowa Infantry 2 men wounded. The night after the skirmish I threw up a line of works near Station No. 2. On the following morning we took the road north of the Ogeechee River, moved down that stream, crossed the canal and supported the Third Brigade in the skirmish for King's Bridge Cross-Roads on the 9th day of December, 1864. On the 10th day of December the enemy was found occupying a strong position on the north side of the Little Ogeechee River. Here the troops were placed in position. My brigade was assigned the right of the line, which rested on the Anderson plantation one mile west of where the Gulf railroad crosses the Little Ogeechee River. Here we skirmished slightly with the enemy and made demonstrations and reconnaissances until the 21st day of December, when, Savannah being evacuated by the enemy, the brigade marched into the city.

Officers and soldiers conducted themselves remarkably well during the march. Dwelling houses were not entered by soldiers of this brigade; citizens were not molested in their persons or peaceful pursuits.

Forage, cattle, mules, potatoes, rice, and produce of all kinds were freely taken by the proper forage details and carefully distributed to the troops. The command was abundantly supplied until it reached the Little Ogeechee and took up position in front of the enemy, when a scarcity of rations was observed. The health and spirits of the troops were never better than during the campaign just closed.

I have the honor to be, very respectfully, your obedient servant,

E. W. RICE,
Brigadier-General, Commanding.

Capt. A. W. EDWARDS,
Actg. Asst. Adjt. Gen., 4th Div., 15th Corps.

No. 33.

Report of Lieut. Col. Jerome D. Davis, Fifty-second Illinois Infantry.

HDQRS. FIFTY-SECOND ILLINOIS INFANTRY VOLUNTEERS,
Savannah, Ga., December 25, 1864.

LIEUTENANT: In accordance with instructions from your headquarters, I have the honor to submit the following report of the part taken by this regiment in the late campaign:

The regiment broke up camp at Rome, Ga., at 10 a. m. November 11, marched eighteen miles, and bivouacked for the night three miles southeast of Kingston. November 12, the regiment marched at 4 a. m. and bivouacked for the night two miles south of Allatoona, having marched eighteen miles. November 13, the regiment marched fifteen miles and bivouacked for the night two miles north of Marietta. November 14, the regiment marched fourteen miles and bivouacked for the night on the right bank of the Chattahoochee River, five miles below the railroad bridge. November 15, the regiment crossed the Chattahoochee River, and marched twelve miles and bivouacked for the night near East Point. November 16, the regiment marched twenty miles and bivouacked for the night southeast of Jonesborough. November 17, the regiment marched twenty-five miles and bivouacked for the night near Jackson, Ga. November 18, the regiment rested until night, and then marched ten miles and bivouacked until morning. November 19, marched six miles and bivouacked for the night on the right bank of the Ocmulgee River. November 20, the regiment crossed the Ocmulgee River, and marched eight miles and bivouacked for the night near Monticello, Ga. November 21, the regiment marched nine miles and bivouacked for the night near Hillsborough, Ga. November 22, the regiment marched nine miles and bivouacked for the night near Clinton, Ga. November 23, the regiment marched nine miles as rear guard for the division train, and did not bivouac until 2 a. m. the next morning. November 24, the regiment marched ten miles, passed through Gordon, and bivouacked for the night in an advanced position three miles southeast of that place. November 25, the regiment marched eighteen miles and bivouacked for the night eight miles south of Irwinton. November 26, the regiment marched six miles, crossed the Oconee River, and bivouacked for the night at Irwin's Cross-Roads, having marched fourteen miles. November 27, the regiment marched six miles to the Georgia Central Railroad, and took their part with the rest of the Fourth Division in burning the railroad for a distance of four miles to Station No. 13,

November 28, the regiment marched seventeen miles in a southeasterly direction and bivouacked for the night. November 29, the regiment marched eighteen miles and bivouacked for the night near Slater's Mills. November 30, the regiment marched sixteen miles, and bivouacked for the night near Summerville.

December 1, the regiment marched ten miles and bivouacked for the night six miles west of the Ogeechee River. December 2, the regiment marched to the Ogeechee River, and after some delay a pontoon bridge was laid, and the regiment, with the exception of two companies left to picket the right bank of the river, crossed the river and bivouacked for the night on the left bank. December 3, the regiment marched to the Georgia Central Railroad, and, in conjunction with the other regiments of the brigade, burned two miles of the railroad track to Scarborough Station. The regiment recrossed the river at night and bivouacked near the right bank. December 4, the regiment marched twelve miles nearly parallel with the Ogeechee River and bivouacked for the night. December 5, the regiment marched twenty-two miles in a southeasterly direction and bivouacked for the night. December 6, the regiment rested all day. December 7, the regiment marched thirteen miles to Jenks' Bridge, crossed the Ogeechee River, and supported the Seventh Iowa Infantry, which regiment, in conjunction with the Second Iowa Infantry, supported by the Sixty-sixth Indiana Infantry on our left, drove the rebels some distance beyond Station No. 2, on the Georgia Central Railroad. At sunset the regiment returned half a mile, and bivouacked two miles from the bridge for the night, and built a breast-work of rails. December 8, marched fourteen miles in a southeasterly direction, bivouacked for the night near the Ogeechee Canal, and threw up breast-works. December 9, the regiment marched four miles, bivouacked for the night near the Savannah and Gulf Railroad, and threw up breast-works. December 10, the regiment marched slowly a distance of four miles, and bivouacked for the night on the left of the Savannah road, eight miles distant from the city. December 11, the regiment moved two miles to the right and bivouacked. December 12, the regiment remained quiet all day. At night the regiment moved down near the Little Ogeechee River. Companies G and I were deployed as skirmishers, and advanced to the bank of the river without eliciting any shots from the enemy. After lying upon the bank of the river about an hour the skirmishers were withdrawn and the regiment returned to camp. The regiment, with the exception of details for picket, then remained quietly in camp until the morning of December 21, when it marched eight miles and bivouacked near Savannah.

The regiment sustained but one casualty during the campaign, Sergt. T. Busby, Company E, wounded on the picket-line near the Little Ogeechee River, December 14. No men of the regiment were sent to hospital during the campaign. I would also state that there were captured by the regiment during the campaign 17 horses and 13 mules; also, 1 horse was lost and 1 mule died during the campaign.

I have the honor to be, lieutenant, very respectfully, your obedient servant,

J. D. DAVIS,
Lieutenant-Colonel, Commanding.

Lieut. H. J. SMITH,
Aide-de-Camp, Hdqrs. First Brig., Fourth Div., 15th Army Corps.

No. 34.

Report of Lieut. Col. Roger Martin, Sixty-sixth Indiana Infantry.

HDQRS. SIXTY-SIXTH REGT. INDIANA INFANTRY VOLS.,
Savannah, Ga., December 28, 1864.

LIEUTENANT: In compliance with General Orders, No. 11, headquarters First Brigade, Fourth Division, Fifteenth Army Corps, I have the honor to submit the following report of the part taken by this regiment in the late campaign:

The regiment, with the brigade and division, marched from Rome, Ga., at 7 a.m. November 11, and passing through Kingston, encamped near the railroad, two miles south of the town. At 4 a. m. the following day the march was resumed, passing through the towns of Cassville, Cartersville, and Allatoona, also crossing the Etowah River, encamping for the night on Allatoona Creek. The next night bivouacked near the base of Kenesaw Mountain, having passed the towns of Acworth and Big Shanty. On the 14th the regiment marched to the Chattahoochee River, encamping for the night on the west bank of the same, several miles below the railroad bridge. On the 15th Atlanta was reached, and the column halted while the trains were being loaded and clothing and rations issued to the men, after which the march was resumed, halting for the night five miles south of the city on the McDonough road. Early the following morning the command moved, marching by side of the trains, which was very difficult this day, owing to the narrow road and thick undergrowth; bivouacked for the night about five miles southeast of Jonesborough. November 17, marched at 6 a. m. on the Jackson road, passing through McDonough, and encamped ten miles from the Ocmulgee River. The following day did not move until after dark, the Seventeenth Corps having the road during the day. Marched through Jackson and rested until daylight, when the march was resumed, reaching the river in the forenoon. At dark, with the Seventh Iowa, the regiment crossed the river and camped two miles beyond. The following day the march was resumed, the regiment being the rear guard, and the roads very heavy owing to the drenching rain of the night before. Monticello and the camp of the division was not reached until after night. Left Monticello early next morning and arrived at Hillsborough at dark. November 22, marched on the road to Clinton, camping near the town during the night. The heavy roads again delayed us, and but a short distance was marched. At noon the next day the regiment moved and continued the march until 1 o'clock at night. This was probably the most disagreeable march of the campaign, owing to the darkness of the night and roughness of the roads. November 24, marched on the Gordon road, passing the town, and encamped two miles beyond. November 25, passed through Irwinton and camped near the Oconee River, the regiment this day having the advance of the division. November 26, crossed the river and camped at the cross-roads, six miles beyond. November 27, this day the brigade destroyed three miles of the railroad, camping for the night near Tennille. November 28, 29, and 30, the march was continued through a barren and swampy country.

December 1, this day the march was attended with some difficulty, the road being occupied by the Third Division. December 2, the brigade crossed the Ogeechee River; this regiment, with the Fifty-second Illinois, remained at the crossing, and during the night threw up works to protect the same. December 3, the regiment, with the brigade, was engaged in destroying the road to Scarborough Station; later in the afternoon recrossed the river and encamped for the night. December 4 and 5, the march was continued down the right bank of the river, encamping near the same during the night; also during the following day and night. December 7, the regiment, with the brigade, crossed the Ogeechee River again, and the enemy being found, a portion of the Second and Seventh Iowa were deployed as skirmishers, and drove them, the former supported by the Fifty-second Illinois and the latter by this regiment; during the night breast-works of rails and sand were thrown up two miles from the river. December 8, the regiment was this day the rear guard, and when near Eden was fired into by a concealed enemy. Three companies were immediately deployed and pursued the enemy, who fled at once. No casualties occurred. At the railroad crossing the regiment halted and built a barricade, and remained until 8 p. m., when it marched, having charge of the teams of the division, to the Savannah Canal, where it arrived at midnight. December 9, marched in rear of the Second Brigade, who met the enemy early in the morning, but drove them before this regiment, which was deployed on the extreme right, came under fire; built a line of works during the night. December 10, marched on the road leading to Savannah, and found the enemy on the opposite bank of the Little Ogeechee, seven miles from the city; from this time no movement occurred in which this regiment took part until the morning of the 21st, when the city was taken possession of.

There were no casualties in this regiment during the campaign of any kind whatever; the men were in better health and spirits at its close than at its commencement.

Number of public animals lost, 1 horse; number of animals captured, 1 horse and 2 mules.

I have the honor to be, lieutenant, very respectfully, your obedient servant,

ROGER MARTIN,
Lieutenant-Colonel, Commanding.

Lieut. HENRY J. SMITH,
Aide-de-Camp, 1st Brigade, 4th Division, 15th Army Corps.

No. 35.

Report of Col. Noel B. Howard, Second Iowa Infantry.

HEADQUARTERS SECOND IOWA INFANTRY VOLUNTEERS,
Savannah, Ga., December 25, 1864.

SIR: In compliance with General Orders, No. 11, headquarters First Brigade, Fourth Division, Fifteenth Army Corps, December 25, 1864, I have the honor to submit the following report of the part taken by the Second Regiment Iowa Infantry Volunteers, in the campaign just ended:

November 11, the regiment marched from Rome, Ga., on this day with the brigade and division at 7 a. m., passed through Kingston, and camped three miles beyond on the Cassville road. November 12, continued to march, passing through Cassville, Cartersville, and Allatoona, camping two miles beyond the latter place. November 13, the march was resumed at 7 a. m. and Marietta reached, nothing of note occurring. November 14, on this day the regiment was the rear guard of the division, marching behind the train, reaching Turner's Ferry at sunset; the men kept well in ranks. November 15, the regiment moved out with the command on the White Hall road, passed Atlanta, halting beside the road long enough to issue clothing to the men, and encamped four miles beyond the city. November 16, the march was continued on the McDonough road, the command moving alongside the train; the march was rapid and very fatiguing, the weather being warm. November 17, moved at 6 a. m. on the Jackson road and camped four miles from that place, making a tiresome march of twenty-three miles; about one-third of the men fell out of ranks during the day. November 18, on this day the regiment did not leave camp until about 9 p. m., when it moved to the river at Ocmulgee Mills and remained until morning. November 19, did not move, the bridge being occupied by other troops crossing. November 20, the regiment crossed the river at 8 a. m. and, with the Fifty-second Illinois Infantry, remained to protect the pontoons till they were taken up, then marched with the brigade to Monticello, the brigade being the rear guard. November 21, regiment marched at daybreak, passing through Monticello, and camped at Hillsborough; the day was cold and rainy. November 22, the march was continued on this day to within two miles of Clinton and was much delayed by the pontoon train. November 23, the march was resumed at 12 m. on this day and continued till 1 o'clock at night; much confusion existed during the night march on account of the troops marching beside the train. November 24, on this day we marched through Gordon Station, where we reunited with the corps. November 25, passed through Irwinton on a fine road and with fine weather. November 26, on this day the regiment, with the command, passed the Oconee River on pontoons, at 2 p. m., and camped ten miles beyond. The regiment at this place was joined by the three companies of the Third Iowa Infantry, which had been transferred to it. November 27, the regiment, with the remainder of the brigade, was on this day engaged in destroying the railroad, and advanced but a few miles from its last camp. November 28, the march on this day was most of the time through pine barrens over new roads. November 29, about twenty miles were made to-day, through a very poor country. November 30 and December 1, the march was continued on both days with no occurrence worthy of note.

December 2, the Ogeechee River was reached on this day and crossed, and the regiment, with the Seventh Iowa Infantry, tore up one mile of the railroad track below Millen. December 3, the regiment, with the brigade, was engaged all day in destroying the railroad, and recrossed the river at night, camping on the west side. December 4 and 5, marched both days down the river road and camped at the cross-roads opposite Station No. 3. December 7, the regiment marched at 7 a. m. and reached the river at 12 m. at a point opposite Station No. 2, where a crossing was to be effected. The enemy appeared in light force on the opposite side with the evident intention of contesting the passage. Pontoons were laid, and the First Brigade being ordered to cross, my regiment, which had the advance, was thrown across at about 1 p. m. and was deployed as skirmishers as soon as the peculiarities of the ground would admit. The enemy's skirmishers fell back, lightly contesting our advance, to a barricade in an open field one mile and a half from the river. Our skirmishers, supported by the reserve of four companies and the Seventh Iowa, advanced briskly and drove the enemy from his position, killing and wounding several, and taking twenty prisoners. An attempt was made to take the enemy's position in flank by advancing the right of my line, with the reserve, along the timber bordering the field, but the sharpness with which the center attacked and the discovery of the flank movement caused the enemy to retreat in confusion before it could be effected. The station, one mile farther on, was occupied by us without further resistance. The loss in the regiment in this affair was 2 killed and 2 wounded, all belonging to Company E. December 8, on this day we made a rapid and fatiguing march of about twelve miles, to the Savannah Canal. December 9, the regiment moved out suddenly with the brigade on this day. The advance of the division came up with the enemy about three miles out, and after considerable skirmishing drove him from his position, but the regiment was not brought under fire during this affair. December 10, on this day the command marched on the direct Savannah road and found the enemy on the opposite side of the Little Ogeechee. December 11 to December 21, in the operations in front of this place, on and near the Little Ogeechee, the regiment performed its duty as a part of the brigade without becoming at any time directly engaged with the enemy, and entered the city on the 21st instant with the command.

The losses in the regiment are as follows:* Number of public animals lost, 2 mules; number of prisoners captured, 20, all in the affair of the 7th instant; number of animals captured, 10 horses and 8 mules.

Among the losses of the regiment during the march it pains me to enumerate Capt. John A. Duckworth, who died of disease on the 13th instant. He was a veteran actuated by the purest feelings of patriotism, and his loss is one of the greatest the regiment has endured since its organization.

I am, sir, very respectfully, your obedient servant,

N. B. HOWARD,

Colonel Second Iowa Infantry Volunteers, Comdg. Regiment.

Lieut. H. J. SMITH,

Aide-de-Camp, 1st Brigade, 4th Division, 15th Army Corps.

No. 36.

Report of Lieut. Col. James C. Parrott, Seventh Iowa Infantry.

HEADQUARTERS SEVENTH IOWA VETERAN INFANTRY,
Savannah, Ga., December 26, 1864.

LIEUTENANT: In compliance with General Orders, No. 11, dated headquarters First Brigade, Fourth Division, Fifteenth Army Corps, Savannah, Ga., December 25, 1864, I have the honor to make the following report of the part taken by the Seventh Iowa Veteran Infantry in the recent campaign from Rome to Savannah, Ga., during the months of November and December, 1864:

The regiment left Rome, Ga., on the 11th of November, 1864, and camped two miles south of Kingston, having marched a distance of sixteen miles. November 12, marched to Allatoona and camped two miles south of that place; distance, eighteen miles. November 13, marched seventeen miles and camped near the eastern base of Kenesaw Mountain. November 14, marched to the Chattahoochee River, camping at Turner's Ferry; distance, fifteen miles. November 15, marched

* Nominal list (omitted) shows 2 enlisted men killed and 3 wounded.

to Atlanta, drew clothing, rations, &c., then marched five miles and camped in the vicinity of East Point; distance, fourteen miles. November 16, marched on the McDonough road and camped on Indian Cotton Creek; distance, twenty miles. November 17, passed through McDonough and camped near Jackson; distance, twenty miles. November 18, remained in camp all day; broke camp at dark, marched through Jackson and camped in the vicinity of the Ocmulgee River about 12 midnight; distance, ten miles. November 19, left camp early in the morning, and after some delay crossed the Ocmulgee at sunset; marched two miles and went into camp; distance, five miles. November 20, remained in camp till 1 p. m. (detained by pioneer corps, who were taking up pontoons), then marched eight miles and camped in a pine grove. November 21, left camp at 12 m., weather rainy and unpleasant; marched through Hillsborough, camping about dark near said place. November 22, marched at 7 a. m., weather very unpleasent and cold, with snow; marched about ten miles, and, being in advance of the brigade, and owing to the bad condition of the roads which detained the train, camped on a creek some two miles in advance of the brigade. November 23, left camp about 11 a. m., passing through Clinton; marched till 1 a. m. next morning and camped near cross-roads; distance, thirteen miles. November 24, marched to Gordon and went into camp about one mile from town; distance, eight miles. November 25, broke camp at 5.30 a. m., and marched eighteen miles, passing through Irwinton, and camped at Duryea's Store. November 26, left camp at 6 a. m., crossed the Oconee River at 12 m., marched eight miles beyond, making in all fourteen miles. November 27, marched at 6 a. m. in the direction of the Georgia Central Railroad and destroyed one mile of the same, then proceeded to Station No. 13 and camped, having no transportation with the brigade. November 28, marched at 5.30 a. m; at 9 a. m. came in contact with Third Division; camped at 3 p. m. near a large swamp; distance marched, ten miles. November 29, left camp at 5 a. m., crossing the swamp, and marched over bad roads, camping at sunset; distance marched, eighteen miles. November 30, marched at 6.30 a. m., passing through the town of Summerville, and camped four miles from the Ogeechee River; distance, fifteen miles.

December 1, marched at 7 a. m. toward the Ogeechee, then down the river, parallel with it, a distance of fifteen miles. December 2, marched at 6.30 a. m.; crossed Scull's Creek; then crossed the Ogeechee and proceeded to the Georgia Central Railroad, and destroyed one mile of it about four miles east from Millen; camped at dark near railroad. December 3, moved at daylight, and commenced further destruction of the road; at 2 p. m., had destroyed two miles, as far as Station No. 7; then recrossed the Ogeechee and went into camp. December 4, took up our line of march at 6 a. m., and marched twelve miles. December 5, marched at daylight; the Seventh Iowa was soon ordered to the front in support of the Second Brigade, but did not overtake them; camped at dark near the Ogeechee; distance, eighteen miles. December 6, remained in camp all day. December 7, marched at 6.30 a. m. and struck the Ogeechee at 11 a. m.; laid pontoons and crossed about noon. Met the enemy in small force; had a lively skirmish and drove them to Station No. 2, where they went on board a train and left in the direction of Savannah. In this skirmish I had two men slightly wounded. Moved to the rear of Station No. 2 about one mile and camped for the night, leaving Company K on picket guard at the station. December 8, marched at 8 a. m. and struck the Ogeechee and Savannah Canal at 2 p. m., where we went into camp. Here shovels were sent to the front, and we, for the first time on the march, threw up works. December 9, left camp at 9 a. m., crossed the canal, and proceeded in the direction of the Coast Railroad. At 10 a. m. the regiment was formed in line of battle; two companies, commanded by Major Mahon, were deployed as skirmishers and moved obliquely to the right and front. The regiment moved by the right flank on the double-quick till it reached a road leading from the river; then proceeded up said road, but before arriving at the place of action the enemy had fled, leaving a disabled 10-pounder Blakely rifle gun. Camped at 2 p. m. and threw up works. December 10, marched at 9 a. m., and after proceeding a short distance found that the enemy had flooded the country by letting the water out of the canal, which the men were obliged to wade for some distance; but the obstruction was slight, and we soon reached the Little Ogeechee River. The regiment was ordered into line of battle, and moved forward through a heavy-timbered, dense swamp until I came in sight of the rebel works on the opposite side of the Little Ogeechee. In the afternoon I moved the regiment, under orders, about 100 paces to the rear and camped for the night. December 11, moved to the rear and encamped on Anderson's plantation, where we remained encamped until the 21st, keeping up all the time a lively skirmish on the picket-line. On the night of the 19th my regiment was ordered to effect a crossing of the Little Ogeechee. I marched the regiment to the vicinity of the river, Company A being detailed to carry boards for the purpose of crossing sloughs, and Company B was detailed to carry a boat for the purpose of crossing a detachment to reconnoiter the opposite bank. Major Mahon, with four picked men, crossed the river, and from his reconnaissance it was found to be impossible to cross the regiment on account of swamps and morasses on the opposite bank. At 12 midnight the regiment was ordered back to camp. December 20, was quiet all day. December 21, reports were in circulation at an early hour that the enemy had abandoned his stronghold on the Little Ogeechee. The brigade was ordered to move to the front, and at 2 p. m. entered the city of Savannah without firing a gun, the enemy having made a hasty retreat.

During the march my regiment captured 24 horses and mules, 8 of which were turned over to Captain Rattray, acting assistant inspector-general, Fourth Division, at the crossing of the Oconee River. The remaining 16 were turned over to Lieutenant Martin, acting assistant quartermaster, First Brigade, Fourth Division, Fifteenth Army Corps, at Anderson's plantation. My regiment also captured a number of cattle, hogs, &c., and unearthed many bushels of sweet potatoes, all of which were properly disposed of.

My whole casualties on the march were three men wounded, as follows: Job A. Clark, Company B, slight, December 7; Oliver Kneudsen, Company C, slight, December 7; Alexander Krieger, Company D, severely, December 11. Three men are missing since leaving Rome, but whether they are deserters or were captured by the enemy I am unable to say.

My regiment to-day is in fine condition, there being but eight men sick.

I have the honor to be, lieutenant, very respectfully, your obedient servant,

J. C. PARROTT,
Lieutenant-Colonel, Commanding.

Lieut. H. J. SMITH,
Aide-de-Camp, First Brig., Fourth Div., Fifteenth Army Corps.

No. 37.

Report of Col. Robert N. Adams, Eighty-first Ohio Infantry, commanding Second Brigade, of operations October 5–December 21.

HDQRS. SECOND BRIG., FOURTH DIV., 15TH ARMY CORPS,
Savannah, Ga., January 3, 1865.

CAPTAIN: In compliance with orders from headquarters Fourth Division, Fifteenth Army Corps, requiring a report of the operations of this command during the recent campaign, I respectfully submit the following:

From the 5th of October to the 11th of November, 1864, this brigade formed a part of the garrison of Rome, Ga. During this time three reconnaissances were made, in all of which this brigade participated, but without sustaining any loss. On the 29th of October orders were received to make preparation for a "long, arduous, and successful campaign," which was accordingly done, and on the morning of the 11th of November the brigade, with its division, took up the line of march for Atlanta. On the evening of the 14th, after four days' march, reached the Chattahoochee River at Turner's Ferry; crossed to the south side and encamped. 15th, the brigade was ordered as escort to division supply train to Atlanta after clothing and supplies, which being obtained it moved out of the city four miles in the direction of East Point, where it joined the division and went into camp. Leaving the camp near Atlanta on the morning of the 16th, the march was unimpeded until it reached the Ocmulgee River, with the exception of being delayed one day on account of General Kilpatrick's supply train occupying the road, which delay caused us to make a night march of six miles. After crossing the Ocmulgee River our march was very much impeded for four days with the pontoon train, partly on account of the weakness of the teams and partly owing to the bad condition of the roads. On the 24th the brigade, with its division, arrived at Gordon, and, passing two miles southeast of that place, was ordered to occupy the works just evacuated by the First Division, Fifteenth Army Corps. 25th, the brigade, with its division, again took the line of march, and on the 26th crossed the Oconee River; marched seven miles and encamped near Irwin's Cross-Roads.

December 3, the brigade was ordered to cross the Big Ogeechee River as support to General Rice's brigade while engaged in destroying a portion of the Central Georgia Railroad; recrossed the river the same evening, and on the morning of the 4th again took up the line of march on the west side of the river. On the 8th the brigade with its division was again ordered to cross the Ogeechee River, and moved without transportation down on the east side of the river to the Ogeechee Canal, a distance of fifteen miles. Here it was ascertained that two miles and a half in our front the enemy were in some force, and a farther advance was postponed until the following morning. On the morning of the 9th the brigade, with one section of Battery H, First Missouri Light Artillery, Lieutenant Brunner commanding, and two companies of the Seventh Illinois Mounted Infantry, was ordered to cross the Ogeechee Canal and dislodge the enemy from his fortified position at the junction of the old River road and the King's Bridge road, three miles from the canal. The brigade moved out, Seventh Illinois Mounted Infantry in advance. They soon encountered the enemy's pickets, and a brisk skirmish ensued. One company of the Sixty-sixth Illinois Infantry was then deployed as skirmishers. The Seventh Illinois Mounted Infantry were placed on the flanks and ordered to move forward, supported by the Sixty-sixth Illinois Infantry on the right and the Twelfth Illinois Infantry on the left of the road, the Eighty-first Ohio Infantry being held in reserve. After moving forward about half a mile in this manner the skirmish line was strengthened by two companies, one from the Eighty-first Ohio and one from the Sixty sixth Illinois Infantry, and ordered to charge the enemy's works, which was successfully done, resulting in the capture of one 12-pounder rifled gun and twelve prisoners, besides securing for us the important position we desired. We continued, however, to drive the enemy until we reached the west branch of the Little Ogeechee River, the bridge over which he had partially destroyed. Here the brigade was halted and ordered to return to the division. 10th, two regiments of the brigade, Twelfth Illinois and Sixty-sixth Illinois Infantry, were ordered to move to the Gulf railroad bridge, over the Little Ogeechee River, and, if possible, effect a crossing, the Eighty-first Ohio Infantry being left to guard division supply train. Arriving at Station No. 1 on the above-named railroad one company of the Sixty-sixth Illinois Infantry were deployed as skirmishers, supported by one company of the Twelfth Illinois Infantry, and ordered to move forward to the railroad bridge, and the two regiments moved down on the right of the railroad, under cover, to within a quarter of a mile of the bridge. Here the ground became so marshy on either side of the railroad that it was impossible for even the skirmish line to advance farther, except only the few men that were marching on the railroad. It now being ascertained that the bridge could only be reached by the railroad, and that it had been burning for some time, and no enemy having yet been discovered, Capt. James Compton was ordered to move down the railroad with ten men and effect a crossing if possible. He accordingly advanced to the railroad bridge, and was about to make some arrangement by which to cross himself and men, when the enemy suddenly opened upon him from behind the abutment on the opposite side of the river. Here the captain discovered he was confronted by a considerable force of the enemy behind works (both artillery and infantry), and that the only approach to the river was by the railroad. These facts having been reported, an effort was made to find a crossing at some point above the bridge, but without success. The picket-post then at the bridge was strengthened and ordered to open a brisk fire upon the enemy for the purpose of more fully developing his forces. The enemy returned the fire from behind the abutment of the bridge on the opposite side of the river and from his works a few hundred yards from the river, and also used two pieces of artillery. A brisk fire was kept up until dark, when, by direction of the general commanding division, the brigade was withdrawn and encamped on Miller's plantation, at Station No. 1.

On the 11th an effort was made to find a crossing at some point below the bridge. The Twelfth Illinois Infantry was accordingly sent out for this purpose, under command of Lieutenant-Colonel Van Sellar. The colonel spent most of the day in this search, but could not find even an approach to the river. After examining the north shore of the river to within range of the guns of Fort McAllister he returned to camp. The brigade remained in camp on Miller's plantation until the 14th, when it was ordered to join the division then encamped on the Anderson plantation. Here the Eighty-first Ohio Infantry (having been left on the 10th as guard to division supply train) joined the brigade. Previous to this, however, this regiment had been ordered to the front, and while engaged in throwing up a line of breast-works lost one man, mortally wounded by a fragment of a shell. Nothing of importance occurred (the brigade lying quietly in camp) until the night of the 19th, when another attempt was made to cross the Little Ogeechee River. The order was simply to effect a crossing with a few men, to reconnoiter the ground on the south bank preparatory to effecting a crossing in force on the following night. The crossing was successfully made under the immediate supervision of First Lieut. William Pittman, of the Eighty-first Ohio Infantry, with ten men from the Eighty-first Ohio Infantry and Sixty-sixth Illinois Infantry, who volunteered for the purpose. This hazardous movement was accomplished without loss, or without even being discovered by the enemy. Although Lieutenant Pittman is ever first in the line of duty, yet for his conduct on this occasion he deserves special mention, as well as Sergeant Mason and the men who accompanied him. No advantage, however, was obtained from this crossing, the enemy having, on the night of the 20th, evacuated the works in our front, thus leaving us the free passage of the river and in quiet possession of the beautiful city of Savannah.

The casualties of this command during the campaign were 4 enlisted men—1 captured and 3 wounded, 2 severely and 1 mortally.

The campaign, with the exception of a few days, was a pleasant one. Men had an abundance to eat and arrived at Savannah, as they had been during the entire march, in the best spirits and condition possible.

I have the honor to be, very respectfully, your obedient servant,

R. N. ADAMS,

Colonel Eighty-first Ohio Infantry, Comdg. Second Brigade.

Capt. A. W. EDWARDS,

Actg. Asst. Adjt. Gen., Fourth Division, Fifteenth Army Corps.

No. 38.

Report of Maj. Wheelock S. Merriman, Twelfth Illinois Infantry.

HDQRS. TWELFTH REGT. ILLINOIS INFANTRY VOLS.,
Savannah, Ga., January 2, 1865.

SIR:*

November 14, passed through Marietta and marched to Turner's Ferry; fifteen miles. November 15, marched into Atlanta with supply train, and at 5 p. m. moved to East Point, having marched eleven miles. November 16, marched about eighteen miles through a wooded country, leaving Jonesborough to the right. November 17, marched about twenty miles, passing through McDonough. Moved at 5 p. m. on the 18th, and marched ten miles, going through Jackson. November 19, marched nine miles to Ocmulgee River at Seven Islands Factory, and crossed it on the 20th, marching to Monticello; nine miles. On the 21st marched to Hillsborough, ten miles, over bad roads. November 22, marched about ten miles over very bad roads, and on the 23d passed through Clinton, marching about twelve miles; lost one man near Clinton, captured by guerrillas. November 24, passed through Gordon and camped two miles south; distance, seven miles. On the 25th passed through Irwinton; marched eighteen miles and reached Oconee River. Crossed it on the 26th and camped at Irwin's Cross-Roads; seventeen

* For portion of report (here omitted) relating to operations in North Georgia, see Vol. XXXIX, Part I, p. 775.

miles march. Moved at 2 p. m. November 27, and marched five miles. Marched sixteen miles on the 28th, passing through Wrightsville. 29th, marched eighteen miles through a very swampy country, and crossed the headwaters of the Little Ohoopee River. 30th of November, passed Summerville, marching fourteen miles.

December 1, marched ten miles, and on the 2d marched to Scull's Creek and camped near it. December 3, crossed the Ogeechee River; was on picket four miles from Millen, and returned at 5 p. m. 4th, marched down the Ogeechee River fifteen miles. 5th, marched eighteen miles and camped on the bank of the Ogeechee, but finding a bad crossing, lay in camp on the 6th, and on the 7th marched to Jenks' Bridge; eleven miles. On the 8th crossed the Ogeechee and marched to the Ogeechee Canal; fifteen miles. On the 9th marched four miles, and found the enemy in force behind breast-works hastily constructed of logs and rails, though in some places dirt had been thrown up. The Sixty-sixth Illinois deployed across the main road as skirmishers, while the regiment and Eighty-first Ohio marched by the flank until the enemy were driven from their first position, after which they were deployed in line of battle on the left of the road. The enemy retreated to prevent capture by flank movements, and were pursued across Salt-water Creek. On the 10th the regiment and Sixty-sixth Illinois were sent to burn the railroad bridge over the Little Ogeechee, but the enemy burnt it on our approach. We lay in camp on the 12th and 13th, and on the 14th joined the division in line of battle on Anderson's plantation. Lay in camp on the 15th and 16th, and reported to the provost-marshal-general, Fifteenth Army Corps, on the 17th, by order of General Corse. On the 18th started for Fort McAllister with rebel prisoners, and while in camp there, awaiting transportation to Hilton Head, received information of the capture of Savannah. 23d, sent the prisoners on the steamer Ashland (Lieutenant-Colonel Van Sellar taking 100 men with him, as guards, to Hilton Head), and on the 24th rejoined the brigade at this place.

Very respectfully, your obedient servant,

WHEELOCK S. MERRIMAN,
Major, Commanding Twelfth Regiment Illinois Infantry Vols.

Lieut. WILLIAM PITTMAN,
Actg. Asst. Adjt. Gen., 2d Brig., 4th Div., 15th Army Corps.

No. 39.

Report of Capt. William S. Boyd, Sixty-sixth Illinois Infantry.

HDQRS. SIXTY-SIXTH ILLINOIS INFANTRY VOLUNTEERS,
Savannah, Ga., January 2, 1865.

LIEUTENANT:*

The same can be said of our march from Atlanta, commencing on the 15th of November, through the towns of McDonough, Jackson, Monticello, Hillsborough, Clinton, Gordon, Irwinton, and the country intervening, and the pine barrens of Johnson and Emanuel Counties, to the Ogeechee River at Scull's Creek. Here, on the 3d of December, we crossed the river to the east side and lay in the intrenchments

* For portion of report (here omitted) relating to operations in North Georgia, see Vol. XXXIX, Part I, p. 776.

during the day, recrossing at night and resuming our march the next day down the west side of the river. On the 8th crossed the Ogeechee at a point opposite Eden, and moved southward to the Ogeechee Canal, camping on the north side. On the morning of the 9th moved forward in advance of the brigade, across the canal, and down the Eden road. The enemy appearing in our front, Companies A, C, and I were advanced and deployed as skirmishers on both sides of the road, the regiment moving in line of battle in support of the skirmish line. At 11.30 o'clock the skirmishers engaged the enemy, driving him back to his works near the Savannah road, which were stormed and taken by the skirmish line, supported by this regiment and the brigade, the enemy fleeing precipitately after a short but brisk resistance, leaving in our possession one 12-pounder Blakely rifled cannon and 10 or 12 prisoners. Our loss was 1 man severely wounded. Went into camp on the field of action. On the morning of the 10th of December moved in company with the Twelfth Illinois to Station No. 1, on the Gulf railroad, advancing from there along the railroad as near to the bridge over the Little Ogeechee as we could approach. Company E was deployed as skirmishers on the west bank of the river, and engaged the enemy on the opposite side in a brisk skirmish, which was kept up till night, resulting in no loss on our part. Camped on Doctor Miller's plantation till the evening of the 14th of December, when we moved across the west branch of the Little Ogeechee to Anderson's plantation, where we remained till the morning of the 21st of December, nothing in the meantime of importance transpiring. On the morning of the 21st moved forward toward the Little Ogeechee, Companies A and H being deployed as skirmishers. The river was crossed without opposition, and the skirmishers being advanced on the east bank it was soon ascertained that the enemy had evacuated his works, leaving his heavy artillery in our possession. Our march from here to Savannah was unopposed, the city and works having been evacuated on the night of the 20th.

I am, lieutenant, very respectfully, your obedient servant,

WM. S. BOYD,
Captain, Commanding Regiment.

Lieut. WILLIAM PITTMAN,
Actg. Asst. Adjt. Gen., 2d Brig., 4th Div., 15th Army Corps.

No. 40.

Report of Maj. William C. Henry, Eighty-first Ohio Infantry, of operations October 5–December 21.

HDQRS. EIGHTY-FIRST OHIO INFANTRY VOLUNTEERS,
Savannah, Ga., January 2, 1865.

LIEUTENANT: In compliance with circular from headquarters Second Brigade, Fourth Division, Fifteenth Army Corps, I would respectfully submit the following report:

From the 5th of October until the 11th of November, 1864, the regiment was stationed at Rome, Ga., doing garrison duty. During this time the regiment, with its brigade, made several reconnaissances, which were accomplished without loss. On the 29th of October the regiment received orders to prepare for a "long, arduous, and successful campaign," and the necessary preparations were made to place the command in the very best possible condition for active service.

On the morning of the 11th of November the regiment broke up camp at Rome and proceeded, with its brigade and division, to Atlanta, Ga., where it joined Sherman's grand army. The regiment entered Atlanta on the 15th; remained long enough to draw rations and clothing for the command, and the same evening headed southward. The regiment was continually with its brigade throughout the march from Atlanta to the Little Ogeechee River, not participating in any action until the 9th of December, when the regiment, with its brigade, crossed the Ogeechee Canal near the Ogeechee River, and proceeded in the direction of Savannah. The advance of the brigade soon encountered the enemy. The Twelfth and Sixty-sixth Illinois were formed on the right and left of the road, the Eighty-first being held in reserve. One company, F, Lieutenant Pittman commanding, was sent forward as skirmishers. At times the musketry and cannonading was quite brisk, yet the enemy were driven for a considerable distance by our skirmish line. The brigade being very much annoyed by a rebel battery, Colonel Adams ordered the regiment forward with instructions to advance through a wood on the left of the road, and, if possible, get in rear of the battery and capture it. After marching for nearly two miles through a wood, almost impassable on account of the thick underbrush, it was discovered that the enemy had taken the alarm and fled. During the operations of this day the regiment was under fire several times, but did not sustain any loss. Several prisoners were captured by the company on the skirmish line.

From the 10th of December until the capture of Savannah, the regiment was in camp on the Anderson place, near the Little Ogeechee River, doing its share of picket duty, with the loss of one man mortally wounded. Special mention should be made of First Lieut. William Pittman and Sergeant Mason, who, assisted by seven volunteers from the Eighty-first Ohio and three from the Sixty-sixth Illinois, were the first to cross the Little Ogeechee River. Several attempts were made by the division to effect a crossing, but owing to the marshy ground on both sides of the river all the attempts failed, until the night of the 19th of November, when Lieutenant Pittman and party effected a crossing. After they had explored the ground on the opposite side of the river, and had ascertained that troops could be easily thrown across, they were ordered to recross. The enemy evacuated on the night of the 20th, before the necessary preparations could be made to cross a large force, so that no advantage resulted from the crossing effected by Lieutenant Pittman and party; yet they are not deserving of less praise on that account. The undertaking was a hazardous one, and had the enemy remained in our front the information gained by Lieutenant Pittman would have been of great importance to the army. Captain McCain and Lieutenant Harbaugh are also deserving of praise for valuable assistance rendered Lieutenant Pittman.

On the morning of the 21st the regiment, with its brigade, crossed the Little Ogeechee, and proceeded to Savannah, near which place it went into camp.

I am, lieutenant, very respectfully,

WM. CLAY HENRY,
Major Eighty-first Ohio Volunteer Infantry.

Lieut. WILLIAM PITTMAN,
Actg. Asst. Adjt. Gen., 2d Brig., 4th Div., 15th Army Corps.

No. 41.

Report of Lieut. Col. Frederick J. Hurlbut, Fifty-seventh Illinois Infantry, commanding Third Brigade.

HDQRS. THIRD BRIG., FOURTH DIV., 15TH ARMY CORPS,
Savannah, Ga., January 3, 1865.

CAPTAIN:*

On the 15th [November] arrived at Atlanta. Remained at this place a few hours; received some supplies and clothing, and then moved out four miles and a half and camped near East Point. On the 16th, 17th, and 18th passed through the towns of Rough and Ready, McDonough, and Jackson, and arrived at the Ocmulgee River on the morning of the 19th, nothing unusual occurring. The First and Second Divisions were crossing. Here the Seventh Illinois Infantry Veteran Volunteers were ordered to be mounted, and they have succeeded in mounting 4 com missioned officers and 120 enlisted men. At daybreak on the 20th crossed the Ocmulgee. On the 21st passed Monticello and Hillsborough; on the 23d passed Clinton, and on the 24th reached Gordon at 12 m. Left camp at 6 a. m. the 25th, and, passing Irwinton, reached the Oconee River on the 26th at 11 a. m. The bridge being soon completed, the brigade was the first infantry that crossed the river at Ball's Ferry. Received orders on the 27th to move with two days' rations, and proceeded to the Central railroad at Deep Cut, and, in connection with the First Brigade, destroyed the road to Station No. 13, a distance of six miles; camped that night at Tennille, near General Sherman's headquarters. On the 28th broke camp at 5.30 a. m., and marched to Peacock's Cross-Roads, and camped on Little Ohoopee River. Moved at 5 a. m. on the 29th, the First Brigade in the advance, and joined the Second Brigade at 12 m., at cross-roads. 30th, moved at 5.30 a. m., passing Summerville; camped on Scull's Creek.

December 2 and 3, remained in camp; the men cleaned up. An inspection of the command was held, and its condition was found as good as could be expected. The command moved at 6.30 a. m. December 4, nothing unusual occurring, and reached cross-roads, one mile from Jenks' Bridge, over the Ogeechee, on the 7th. At 5.30 a. m. on the 8th the command proceeded forward with two days' rations in haversacks, accompanied by no more train than was necessary; crossed the Ogeechee River at 7, the Seventh Illinois in advance. Moved through Eden Station, and took the right-hand road in the direction of the Ogeechee Canal. Soon after some slight skirmishing took place, and the Seventh Illinois captured one rebel lieutenant and three privates. The roads were obstructed by fallen timber in several places. At noon reached the canal at Dillon's Bridge, and found the bridge, which had been fired by the enemy in the morning, still burning. Two regiments of my command crossed the canal, remained a short time, and were ordered to recross, and the whole went into camp. The mounted portion of the Seventh Illinois, sent in advance, having proceeded to the cross-roads, encountered a rebel force of infantry intrenched. On skirmishing an hour, and finding the enemy well fortified, the mounted Seventh returned to the command, having one man wounded so severely it was impossible to remove him. He was captured by the enemy, but has since escaped. Remained in

*For portion of report (here omitted) relating to operations in North Georgia, see Vol. XXXIX, Part I, p. 782.

camp on the 9th until 11 a. m., and were then ordered forward; moved in a south direction until we entered the main road leading from King's Bridge, over the Ogeechee, direct to Savannah, which we followed for two miles, and went into camp on the left of the same, and, under orders from the general commanding, threw up strong breastworks in our front, the enemy being reported in the immediate vicinity. On this day the mounted portion of the Seventh Illinois, under Colonel Perrin, moved in advance of the Second Brigade, and, on approaching the cross-roads, moved on the flanks of the brigade, skirmishing with the enemy during the engagement that followed; and, after taking possession of the cross-roads, by direction of General Corse, Lieutenant-Colonel Perrin proceeded with one company to the Gulf railroad, which he effectually destroyed for a distance of 200 yards, thereby stopping and capturing a locomotive and train of cars, which he destroyed, and capturing 25 prisoners, whom he turned over to the provost-marshal-general. On the morning of the 10th, at 2 a. m., five companies of the Thirty-ninth Iowa Infantry were ordered to report to Captain Barbour, chief of grand guard of the division; were sent forward by him on the Savannah road. At 7 a. m. the brigade moved forward, being the advance of the division; two miles out crossed Salt Creek, where the road for some distance was submerged by tide water. A little farther on came up with the five companies of the Thirty-ninth Iowa, sent forward as before stated. On moving still farther two companies of the Thirty-ninth Iowa were detailed to rebuild a small bridge that had that morning been destroyed by the enemy. Here the Seventh Illinois were thrown forward and deployed as skirmishers, and exchanged shots with the enemy. It being soon ascertained that the enemy had planted a portion of his artillery so as to command the road, the column was ordered to keep to the right of the road under cover of the timber. On reaching a field the column was ordered to form in line of battle by battalion; did so; moved across the field and halted. The skirmish line was here strengthened, the right by two companies from the Thirty-ninth Iowa, the left by one company from the Fiftieth Illinois and one from the Fifty-seventh Illinois. The command then moved forward three-quarters of a mile until the camp of the enemy was distinctly visible some 1,500 yards distant across open fields and on the east side of the Little Ogeechee, strongly intrenched. By order of the commanding general the battalions in reserve were ordered to halt under cover of timber. I ordered the Seventh Illinois as skirmishers, with strong reserve, to advance across the open field and develop the enemy, which was done most valiantly, under command of Major Johnson, who advanced his skirmishers to within about 400 yards of the works under heavy fire from enemy's artillery. Remaining in present position until 4 p. m., received orders to move the battalion, then in reserve, into camp about three-quarters of a mile to the rear, Major Johnson, holding skirmish line until relieved at night, coming into camp about 7 p. m. December 11, moved to right and rear three-quarters of a mile; was ordered to make permanent camp. Remained in camp until morning of the 21st, in the meantime furnishing men for skirmish or picket duty on our front. No casualties occurred to the men, and but slight firing, while on duty. Moved in town 21st, and bivouacked in suburbs of city. December 22, moved into Fort Brown and ordered to make camp. During the march the men have deported themselves as good soldiers. The march being long and tedious a portion of the time the men were quite short of rations, but expressed no complaint.

Thus ended a march of some 375 miles through the heart of Georgia, a march memorable for the ease and rapidity by which it was accomplished, and the good, soldierly conduct of the men.

My losses were 1 man of the Fifty-seventh and 1 of the Fiftieth Illinois Infantry, died of disease; and 1 of the Fifty-seventh and 1 of the Seventh Illinois Infantry, wounded.

I have the honor to be, captain, very respectfully, your obedient servant,

F. J. HURLBUT,
Lieut. Col. Fifty-seventh Illinois Infantry, Comdg. Brigade.

Capt. A. W. EDWARDS,
Actg. Asst. Adjt. Gen., Fourth Div., Fifteenth Army Corps.

No. 42.

Report of Lieut. Col. Hector Perrin, Seventh Illinois Infantry.

HEADQUARTERS SEVENTH ILLINOIS VOLUNTEERS,
Savannah, Ga., January —, 1865.

SIR:*

On the 19th [November] I was directed by orders from the general commanding division to mount my command, capturing for that purpose stock and equipments in the country. I succeeded during the campaign to mount six companies, numbering in all 5 commissioned officers and 120 enlisted men. On the 27th the dismounted portion of my command, under Maj. Edward S. Johnson, moved with the brigade to the Georgia Central Railroad for the purpose of destroying it. By direction of general commanding division I proceeded with the mounted portion to Station 13, at which place I rejoined the command in the evening of the same day. From that date to the 8th of December the dismounted portion kept its place in line of march with the brigade, and the mounted was sent scouting on the flanks of the column.

On the 9th, the division having crossed the Ogeechee River near Station No. 2, I was directed to take the advance with the mounted men. I proceeded as far as the cross-roads, where I met the enemy in force; had a skirmish of about one hour's duration, when, finding the enemy intrenched, I retired, having had one man severely wounded, whom I left at a house, not being able to take him farther; he was taken to Savannah by the enemy (made his escape since). I then returned to the command, camped on the Ogeechee and Savannah Canal. On the 9th I moved in advance of the Second Brigade with the mounted men, leaving Major Johnson in command of the footmen, within a short distance of the cross-roads. I moved on the flanks of the infantry and skirmished with the enemy during the engagement that followed. After taking possession of the cross-roads, by direction of the general commanding division, I proceeded with one company to the Gulf railroad, which I destroyed effectually for a distance of about 200 yards, thereby stopping and capturing a locomotive and train of cars, which were destroyed by fire; I also captured 25 prisoners, which I turned

---

* For portion of report (here omitted) relating to operations in North Georgia, see Vol. XXXIX, Part I, p. 779.

over to the provost-marshal of the division. On the 10th, in advance on the Little Ogeechee, Major Johnson, with the footmen, was directed to advance and deploy his command as skirmishers on the enemy's position, which was effectually developed on the other side of the Little Ogeechee River, the mounted portion acting as flankers. From that date, December 10, to the occupation of Savannah, December 21, the footmen performed duty with the brigade in front of Little Ogeechee River, and the mounted men were occupied in looking for forage for the division, and on the 16th had a skirmish with some rebel cavalry at Hinesville, in which one rebel was killed. On the 26th Major Johnson was ordered, by order of general commanding division, to proceed to Fort Bonaventure with the footmen of my regiment (four companies) to perform guard duty at that place.

All of which I have the honor to submit.

Very respectfully, your obedient servant,

HECTOR PERRIN,
Lieutenant-Colonel, Commanding.

Lieut. WILLIAM C. GHOST,
Acting Assistant Adjutant-General.

No. 43.

Reports of Maj. Gen. Frank P. Blair, jr., U. S. Army, commanding Seventeenth Army Corps.

HEADQUARTERS SEVENTEENTH ARMY CORPS,
Savannah, Ga., December 31, 1864.

CAPTAIN: I have the honor to make the following report of the operations of this command during the campaign from Atlanta to this point:

The command started from Atlanta on the 15th of November on the McDonough road, and moved, via McDonough and Jackson, to the Ocmulgee River, at Planters' Factory. We crossed the river on the night of the 18th of November, and continued our march, via Monticello and Blountsville, to Gordon, on the Georgia Central Railroad, which point we reached on the 22d of November. On the 23d of November we continued our march along the railroad to the Oconee River, where the enemy were found in some force on the opposite side. Brig. Gen. Giles A. Smith's division (the Fourth) was sent to the railroad bridge, and a battalion of the First Alabama Cavalry to the crossing on the Ball's Ferry road. This battalion succeeded in crossing the Oconee River, but on proceeding a short distance on the other side were attacked by a strong force of the enemy. They succeeded in holding their position until their ammunition was expended, when they were obliged to fall back, with the loss of 21 killed and wounded. On the next morning I moved my entire command to the river and found the enemy intrenched at Ball's Ferry crossing. I succeeded in effecting a crossing above the road, and sent over about 200 men during the night. Upon this force striking the road, about daylight the next morning, they found the enemy just retiring from the river. During the day I crossed my entire command and moved along the railroad to Station 9½, where we crossed the Ogeechee River on the pontoon bridge, meeting no obstructions from the enemy.

On the 2d of December we reached Millen, crossing Buck Head Creek, and using the pontoon bridge. Upon striking the Little Ogeechee River, on December 3, we found the enemy intrenched on the opposite side, their force estimated at 5,000. The next morning I sent a skirmish line of the First Division down to the river, driving the enemy's skirmishers across, and upon crossing a force found the works evacuated. We continued our march, without interruption, until the 9th, when we struck the enemy near Station 1, where they had a force of infantry, cavalry, and artillery. During this day and the next we drove them without difficulty, up to a point within three miles and a half of Savannah, where we found the enemy strongly intrenched. Here I deployed the Fourth Division, Brig. Gen. G. A. Smith commanding, on the Louisville road, and the First Division, General Mower, on their right, on the south side of the canal. On the 11th instant my command was relieved by the Fourteenth Corps and moved to a position on the Ogeechee road, where the Third Division was placed in position on the left of the road, with the right resting on the Fifteenth Corps. The Fourth Division, Brig. Gen. G. A. Smith commanding, was sent to King's Bridge, and furnished details for the building of the wharf on the Ogeechee River and the unloading of vessels. The First Division, Maj. Gen. J. A. Mower commanding, was sent on the Gulf road, and destroyed eighteen miles of the road. I now commenced preparations for the assault on the enemy's works, but on the morning of the 21st of December, as my arrangements were approaching completion, the pickets of the Third Division found the enemy retired from their works, and without opposition we entered the city, where we are now encamped.

The opposition from the enemy throughout our entire march was comparatively nothing. The country marched through was well supplied with provisions, and the forage parties, as organized in accordance with orders from the army commander, kept the troops well supplied. Our transportation, which on starting was very poor, was brought up to a fine condition by the abundance of forage and by animals captured. My command destroyed 93 miles of railroad and marched 285 miles. There was destroyed by this corps during the march, in accordance with orders, 1,735 bales of cotton.

The losses in the command, including 20 of the First Alabama Cavalry, during the campaign were as follows: Killed, 16; wounded, 73; missing, 19.

I forward herewith the reports of my division commanders.

Very respectfully, your obedient servant,

FRANK P. BLAIR, JR.,
Major-General.

Capt. SAMUEL L. TAGGART,
Asst. Adjt. Gen., Department and Army of the Tennessee.

HEADQUARTERS SEVENTEENTH ARMY CORPS,
Savannah, Ga., January 1, 1865.

CAPTAIN: In accordance with a request from Lieutenant Taylor, I have the honor to make the following statement of work done on the campaign: 26,500 yards of corduroy, 700 yards of bridging, 19 miles of road cut through timber, 2,100 yards of obstructions cleared out.

Very respectfully, your obedient servant,

FRANK P. BLAIR, JR.,
Major-General.

Capt. SAMUEL L. TAGGART,
Assistant Adjutant-General, Army of the Tennessee.

No. 44.

Report of Maj. Gen. Joseph A. Mower, U. S. Army, commanding First Division.

HDQRS. FIRST DIVISION, SEVENTEENTH ARMY CORPS,
Near Savannah, Ga., December 31, 1864.

CAPTAIN: In compliance with orders, I have the honor to submit the following report of the operations of my command during the recent campaign:

My division left Marietta, Ga., on the 13th of November, and reached Atlanta the same day. We again took up our line of march on the 15th, crossed the Ocmulgee River on the 18th, and arrived at Gordon (the junction of the Milledgeville with the Georgia Central Railroad) on the 22d of November. Here we destroyed five miles of the Milledgeville Railroad. We again moved on the 24th and destroyed five miles, and on the 25th four miles of the Georgia Central Railroad. On the 26th crossed the Oconee River, and on the 30th the Ogeechee River.

December 1, 1864, destroyed five miles of railroad. December 2, crossed Buck Head Creek, encamping at Millen, Ga. December 3, destroyed two miles and a half. December 4, destroyed three miles of railroad. December 5, crossed the Little Ogeechee. December 6, destroyed six miles of railroad. December 9, my command had the advance. We found the enemy in position behind an earth-work at the end of a causeway leading through a swamp, the swamp extending around on both their flanks. I detached one brigade, Brigadier-General Sprague's, with a section of artillery to engage the enemy in front, whilst I took two brigades (General Fuller's and Colonel Tillson's) around the enemy's right. The troops waded through a cypress swamp to get to the enemy's works. The enemy retired as we approached. We drove them about seven miles, skirmishing with them constantly, artillery being used on both sides. I lost one of my staff officers on that day, killed, Lieut. W. H. Hamrick, acting assistant quartermaster. December 10, I received an order to effect a lodgment on the south side of the canal leading from the Savannah to the Ogeechee River. I succeeded without much opposition, driving a small party of the enemy that were at the canal back to their earth-works, which were about 1,000 yards from the point where I crossed. Skirmishing was kept up during the day; at the same time I sent out reconnoitering parties in every direction, for the purpose of ascertaining whether or not the enemy's works could be approached at any point excepting in front, where we would have been obliged to pass over an open field some half a mile in extent, should we have attacked them there. The field I occupied was found to be bordered with swamps all around excepting in front. I had a staff officer, Lieutenant O'Reilly (aide-de-camp), wounded during the day whilst he was with me, endeavoring to find a position for a battery. That night we threw up a line of works about 400 yards from those of the enemy, and had two redoubts constructed for the artillery, which was placed in one of the redoubts during the night. December 11, skirmishing and artillery firing was kept up during the day, and the embrasures of the enemy's works choked up by the falling sand-bags, so that they were obliged to use their artillery in barbette. I also put the prisoners to work on the morning of the 11th cutting zigzag roads toward a salient of the enemy's works in my rear. Making the road of the brush which was cut down, I felt confident that, if I could succeed in getting roads through the swamp, I should be able to take the enemy by surprise at that point of their works, as they would not be expecting us from that direction, there being from three to ten feet of water in the swamp. I was relieved, however, during the day by General Carlin with his division, before I had completed these roads. December 12, I moved my command to the right, General Sprague's brigade being detached from the division whilst we were en route and ordered to the head of the canal. I went into camp near the King's Bridge and Savannah road, about five miles from the Ogeechee, where I remained until the 16th instant, when I received an order to destroy that portion of the Gulf railroad between the Altamaha River (including the bridge over that stream) and a point twenty miles this side of that river. My time was limited to five days. This limitation of time would make it necessary for me to march twenty miles per day, and give me one day in which to destroy twenty miles of railroad.

I crossed the Ogeechee on the 17th and reached a point on the railroad eight miles from the Altamaha bridge on the 18th. I had previously applied to General Blair for more time, so as to be able to destroy the bridge over the Altamaha. I received a communication in reply, stating that it would be necessary for me to return in five days, and informing me that the First Alabama Cavalry had been directed to report to me and that I could put them to work on the farther end of the road and the bridge. In the meantime Colonel Atkins, commanding a brigade of cavalry, reported to me for orders. I directed him to destroy the bridge and a trestle-work leading to it. He succeeded in destroying the trestle-work, but it was found impracticable to approach the bridge, as the enemy had two redoubts on this side which it was impossible to get at, there being a deep swamp all around them. There were also two 32-pounder rifles on the opposite side of the Altamaha enfilading the bridge, and a locomotive, with a gun on it, which the enemy used at this end of the bridge. My orders being imperative to return in five days I was obliged to desist from the attempt at destroying the bridge, as it was utterly impossible to get at it without occupying at least two more days' time. The destruction of the trestle-work, however, renders the bridge useless to the enemy. I therefore returned to camp, where I arrived on the 21st, having marched eighty miles and destroyed eighteen miles of railroad in five days.

Amount of railroad destroyed in the campaign, fifty-seven miles.

I inclose herewith a list of killed and wounded in the different skirmishes in which my division has been engaged during the campaign.*

Very respectfully, your obedient servant,

JOS. A. MOWER,

Maj. Gen., U. S. Vols., Comdg. First Div., Seventeenth Army Corps.

Capt. C. CADLE, Jr.,

Assistant Adjutant-General, Seventeenth Army Corps.

---

*Nominal list (omitted) shows 1 officer and 2 men killed; 1 officer and 33 men wounded.

SKETCH OF POSITION OCCUPIED BY THE FIRST DIVISION, SEVENTEENTH ARMY CORPS, IN FRONT OF THE ENEMY'S WORKS NEAR SAVANNAH, GA., ON THE 10TH AND 11TH OF DECEMBER, 1864.

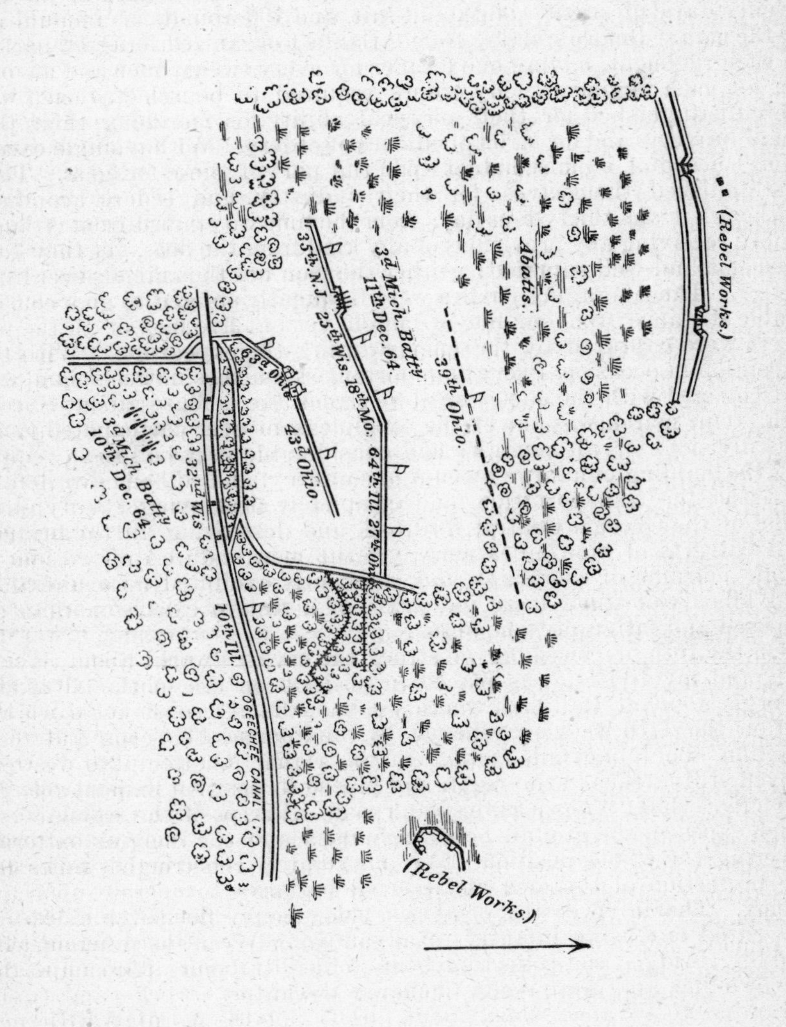

No. 45.

Report of Brig. Gen. Mortimer D. Leggett, U. S. Army, commanding Third Division.

HDQRS. THIRD DIVISION, SEVENTEENTH ARMY CORPS,
Savannah, Ga., December 31, 1864.

CAPTAIN: I have the honor to submit the following as a report of the part taken by my division in the late campaign from Atlanta to this place:

We started from Atlanta, with the balance of the command, on the 15th day of November, with fourteen days' rations of hard bread and twenty days' of sugar, coffee, and salt, and 190 rounds of ammunition to the man. Before starting from Atlanta I organized foraging parties in each regiment, having one forager for every twenty men and an officer for each regiment. My orders required to be selected men who were distinguished for their physical ability for marching, their personal bravery, and for strict obedience of orders. With a single exception, I heard of no misconduct upon the part of these foragers. They distinguished themselves for their industry and orderly conduct. Although it was thirty-four days from the time we started from Atlanta before receiving any provisions of any kind from the fleet, yet they kept the command well supplied; neither the men nor the animals ever lived better. These foraging parties were frequently obliged to go a considerable distance from our line of march, yet but five men of all the foragers were captured by the enemy during the expedition. With the exception of occasional very unimportant skirmishes, my command was not engaged with the enemy until we struck the defenses about Savannah. Our march was one of the most pleasant ever participated in by this division, for, although we had considerable very bad road, requiring the building of a large amount of corduroy, and often heavy details to assist the transportation, and completely destroying twenty-three miles of the Georgia Central Railroad, and destroying all the bridges and culverts of nine miles more, yet the men endured all without a single murmur or complaint, and constantly exhibited an exuberance and hilarity of spirit more indicative of a festive excursion than an exposed and fatiguing campaign.

On the 10th of December we struck the enemy's works about Savannah, and my division was placed in position on the south side of the Georgia Central Railroad, where we immediately constructed works, but on the 11th we were relieved by the Fourteenth Corps and took position about one mile farther to the right. On the 12th we were moved still farther to the right, and placed in position immediately on the left of what is known as the plank road. This position we found very much exposed, the ground being very level and the enemy's batteries covering the whole position. We immediately constructed works for the protection of the men and erected batteries to operate upon the enemy. The intervention of a rice field, deeply flooded with water, prevented our using infantry to advantage. We at once commenced building bridges and collecting boats to facilitate our approach to the enemy's line, and were ready to charge the enemy's works, and awaiting orders to advance, when, about 4 o'clock on the morning of December 21, we discovered the enemy were evacuating. I immediately advanced, but having much farther to march reached Savannah about ten minutes after the advance of the Left Wing had entered the city from another direction.

I must make honorable mention of Brig. Gen. M. F. Force, commanding my First Brigade, and Col. R. K. Scott, commanding the Second Brigade, for the close and soldierly manner in which they have marched and cared for their troops.

My losses during the campaign have been: Killed, 2; wounded, 10; missing, 19.

Of the missing, Privates John O'Lahiff, John Ford, Sanford Failing, Mirion D. Hyland, A Company; John Pelz, B Company; James H. Shannon, C Company; Martin Purcell, F Company; Edward Kelly, H Company, and Edward T. Evans, I Company, Seventeenth Wisconsin Veteran Volunteer Infantry, were captured while straggling in violation of orders. I have issued orders stopping their pay for the whole time they may be prisoners of war, and they will be subject to such additional punishment as may be inflicted by a court-martial when they are returned.

When we started from Atlanta my transportation was in bad condition, the mules being very poor and weak, but during the march many of these mules died or were killed to prevent them from falling into the enemy's hands and their places supplied with captured mules. We reached Savannah with superb transportation—never in better condition.

Very respectfully, your obedient servant,

M. D. LEGGETT,
Brigadier-General.

Capt. C. CADLE, Jr.,
Assistant Adjutant-General, Seventeenth Army Corps.

No. 46.

Report of Brig. Gen. Manning F. Force, U. S. Army, commanding First Brigade, of operations December 2.

HDQRS. FIRST BRIG., THIRD DIV., 17TH ARMY CORPS,
In the Field, Ga., December 2, 1864.

CAPTAIN: I have the honor to report that I struck the railroad at Station 9, at the beginning of dawn this morning, and worked thence to Buck Head Creek, destroying in each mile a section the length of the brigade, all trestles and culverts, burning the depot and tanks, a considerable amount of new ties and prepared timber, and a flat-boat loaded with cord wood. In the sections destroyed the ties and stringers were burned and the rails bent. A pile of rails near the road was also bent by fire. A small section of quadruple track west of Station 9 was also destroyed. No cotton was found. The road was extremely intersected with culverts and small trestles. Some of these were banked up and the track partly excavated, in the hope that rising water might destroy it. I regret to say that the trestle nearest Buck Head Creek may not be thoroughly destroyed. It was reached at the close of the afternoon, and was thought at first to be needed for the crossing of troops. I never saw men work more honestly. They toiled zealously on the track ten hours, with one short respite for coffee.

I am, captain, very respectfully, your obedient servant,

M. F. FORCE,
Brigadier-General, Comdg. First Brigade, Third Division.

Capt. C. CADLE, Jr.,
Assistant Adjutant-General.

No. 47.

Report of Brig. Gen. Giles A. Smith, U. S. Army, commanding Fourth Division.

SAVANNAH, GA., *December 31, 1864.*

SIR: I have the honor to report as follows respecting the movement and operations of the Fourth Division, under my command, during the campaign which closed with the occupation of Savannah:

On Saturday, the 12th day of November, 1864, being encamped at Marietta, Ga., in pursuance of orders received from Major-General Blair I proceeded with my command to destroy the portion of the Atlantic and Western Railroad allotted to me, being from Big Shanty south to near Kenesaw Mountain; and on Sunday, in pursuance of orders, moved toward Atlanta, which place we reached on the following day, and on Monday [Tuesday], the 15th, started with the remainder of the Seventeenth Army Corps in a southeasterly direction toward Savannah or any other place. The command reached Ocmulgee River on the 18th, crossing in the same night on pontoon bridges, and arrived at Gordon on the 21st ultimo, which was occupied after a short skirmish with the enemy by my advance, the First Alabama Cavalry. On Tuesday, the 22d, I was ordered by Major-General Blair to proceed with my division and Colonel Spencer's First Alabama Cavalry to the railroad bridge across the Oconee, between Stations 14 and 15. The cavalry having the advance drove in the enemy's skirmishers from a stockade about two miles from the bridge. The ground near the bridge being very swampy it could only be approached by the railroad. The enemy were posted behind a second stockade, with infantry and artillery. Colonel Potts, commanding First Brigade, was ordered to detach two regiments and drive them across the river. One piece of artillery from Lieutenant Hurter's First Minnesota Battery was taken down the track by hand to assist. After a short skirmish this was accomplished, and two miles of trestle-work destroyed and about three miles of track, but the enemy could not be dislodged from the opposite side on account of the inaccessibility of the swamp. On the 25th the remainder of the corps reached Ball's Ferry, six miles below, where I rejoined them, and the next day crossed the Oconee River on pontoons. On Thursday, December 1, the Ogeechee River was crossed, and the next day the command entered Millen. The next eight days we marched toward Savannah, destroying railroad track and removing obstructions in the roads, and on the 10th of December reached the works of Savannah, forming line across the Georgia Central and Savannah and Charleston railroads, near their junction, three miles from Savannah. The enemy disputed our advance all day, and we met with some loss in gaining our position. On the night of Tuesday, December 20, the enemy evacuated Savannah, and on the 21st our troops took possession, where we are now encamped.

From Atlanta to Savannah this division marched 300 miles, and thoroughly destroyed twenty-four miles and a half of railroad track, including four miles and a half of the Atlantic and Western Railroad, and two miles of trestle-work.

The pioneer corps, Capt. J. H. Davis, Forty-first Illinois Veteran Volunteer Infantry, commanding, constructed seven miles and 300 feet of corduroy road, built 600 feet of bridging, made 150 fascines, built one fort for guns at Oconee River, cut six miles of wagon roads, and removed fallen timber and obstructions from 600 yards of road.

The health and condition of the men at the close of the campaign was excellent.

The following is the amount of stock captured: Horses, 165; mules, 291; total, 456.

The following is the list of casualties during the campaign: Commissioned officers wounded, 2; enlisted men killed, 5; wounded, 12.

Very respectfully, your obedient servant,

GILES A. SMITH,
Brigadier-General of Volunteers.

Capt. C. CADLE, Jr.,
Assistant Adjutant-General, Seventeenth Army Corps.

No. 48.

Report of Capt. Henry Duncan, Fifty-third Indiana Infantry, First Brigade.

HDQRS. FIFTY-THIRD INDIANA VET. VOL. INFANTRY,
Savannah, Ga., January 1, 1865.

LIEUTENANT: In obedience to orders, I hereby submit the following report of the part taken by the Fifty-third Indiana Veteran Volunteer Infantry in the late campaign:

We left camp at Marietta, Ga., with the other regiments composing the First Brigade, Fourth Division, Seventeenth Army Corps, on the 13th day of November, 1864, at 8 a. m., and reached Gordon, the junction of the Milledgeville and Georgia Central railroads, November 21, 1864, where, by order of Col. B. F. Potts, the regiment performed provost guard duty. Left Gordon November 22, 1864, and reached the railroad bridge across the Oconee River November 23, 1864, about 4 p. m., where the enemy were found in position on the opposite side of the river with artillery. On the morning of the 24th I was ordered to relieve the Twenty-third Indiana at the bridge, which I did by deploying three companies as skirmishers or pickets, holding the remainder of the regiment in reserve. The pickets kept up a brisk fire during the day, and at dark were ordered to attempt the destruction of the bridge by fire, but the enemy opened such a terrific fire of canister and musketry that they were compelled to desist. The trestle-work connecting with the bridge, however, had been set on fire in several places and was partially destroyed. The casualty during the affair was one man wounded so as to make amputation of his right leg necessary. November 25, 1864, at 7 a. m., we moved, via Station No. 15, to the Oconee River, which was crossed on pontoons.

We arrived at the Ogeechee River December 1, 1864, which was also crossed on pontoons, and the regiment assisted in destroying railroad track. Again, on the 7th, the regiment was engaged in destroying track at Station No. 7, which, with a few hours' work before crossing the Oconee River, comprised all the work done on railroad, and will, in my opinion, amount to two miles of railroad destroyed by the regiment. On the 10th of December the regiment was the advance of the Seventeenth Army Corps, and encountered the enemy's pickets and drove them within their works three miles from the city. We threw up barricades about 500 yards from the rebel lines, and held them until relieved by a regiment from the Fourteenth Army Corps and moved to a position on the right. December 13, were ordered to escort a forage train, and started about 3 p. m. of that day, crossed the Ogeechee River, and after loading the train twenty-seven miles from the city, returned to King's Bridge and were engaged in unloading steamers until the 24th of December, when we entered the city of Savannah.

In conclusion, I will say that the march was a very pleasant one; our foragers kept us abundantly supplied with potatoes, pork, poultry, &c., and with the exception of a few cases of measles the health of the regiment was remarkably good.

A few days before leaving Marietta we received 185 drafted men from the State of Indiana, and for raw recruits they stood the march far better than I supposed they would.

The following is a list of casualties during the campaign: Died of disease, 4; wounded, 1 (privates).

All of which is respectfully submitted.

I am, sir, very respectfully, your obedient servant,

H. DUNCAN,
Captain, Commanding Regiment.

Lieut. A. S. KINSLOE,
Acting Assistant Adjutant-General.

No. 49.

Report of Maj. Gen. Henry W. Slocum, U. S. Army, commanding Left Wing, of operations September 29–December 21.

HEADQUARTERS LEFT WING, ARMY OF GEORGIA,
Savannah, Ga., January 9, 1865.

CAPTAIN: I have the honor of submitting the following report of operations of the Fourteenth and Twentieth Corps during the recent campaign:

By virtue of Special Field Orders, No. 120, headquarters Military Division of the Mississippi, November 9, 1864, the army, then in the field near Kingston and Atlanta, was divided into wings, the Fourteenth and Twentieth Corps constituting the Left Wing of the army. Prior to this organization these corps had formed a part of the Army of the Cumberland, under Maj. Gen. George H. Thomas, the Fourteenth under command of Bvt. Maj. Gen. J. C. Davis, and the Twentieth Corps under my command. After the capture of Atlanta the Twentieth Corps occupied the city and the line of works constructed by the enemy, and was engaged in the construction of a new line of works designed to enable a small garrison to hold the place. Heavy details were constantly employed in this work from October 5 to November 1. On the 29th of September General Morgan's division of the Fourteenth Corps moved by railroad to Chattanooga and Huntsville, to protect our communications, which were then threatened by General Forrest. The other two divisions moved with the main army in its operations against the enemy under General Hood.

On the 24th of October General Morgan's division rejoined the corps at Gaylesville, Ala. On the 2d of November this corps was concentrated at Kingston, Ga., where preparations were made for the campaign just closed. On the 13th of November it was engaged in the destruction of the railroad from Etowah River to Big Shanty, and on the 14th moved to Atlanta. During this movement the Twentieth Corps was left for the defense of Atlanta. The hospitals of every corps of the army, containing many of our sick and wounded, were located within the line of works constructed by the enemy; and the nature of the movement of our forces operating against General Hood had also compelled the commanders of every corps to leave at this point a portion of their artillery, together with all surplus transportation and stores. In addition to the troops and stores belonging strictly to the Twentieth Corps, there remained at the post 12,700 wounded, sick, and convalescent soldiers, eighty pieces of artillery, and over 5,000 horses and mules, together with much other valuable property. The duty of protecting this property and securing supplies for the garrison and forage for the animals devolved upon the Twentieth Corps. At the time our railroad communication was destroyed at Kingston and Big Shanty, the amount of subsistence stores on hand was deemed amply sufficient to sustain the garrison until communication could be re-established; but it was subsequently found necessary to send a portion of these supplies to the main army at Rome. The supply of forage on hand was not sufficient for the animals for over three days. I was, therefore, compelled not only to reduce the issue of meat to a half ration, but to resort to the country for supplies of subsistence as well as forage. From the 10th of October to the 4th of November foraging expeditions were sent into the country, all of which were completely successful, and conducted with but small loss of life. About 2,000,000 pounds of corn and a large quantity of fodder were collected on these expeditions, together with subsistence for the foraging parties. Great credit is due General Geary, Colonels Robinson, Dustin, and Carman, the officers commanding the several expeditions; also to Colonel Garrard and the brigade of cavalry under his command.

The Twentieth Corps left Atlanta on the morning of November 15, marching via Stone Mountain and Social Circle to Madison, arriving at the latter place on the evening of the 18th. At that point General Geary's division moved to the Oconee and destroyed the railroad bridge over that river, the other divisions moving direct to Milledgeville via Eatonton, Geary's division rejoining the corps at Little River. The corps reached Milledgeville on the 22d of November. Two regiments were sent forward to take possession of the city and establish the necessary guards.

The Fourteenth Corps left Atlanta on the morning of November 16 and moved, via Decatur, Covington, and Shady Dale, to Milledgeville, arriving at the latter place November 23.

The Georgia Railroad was destroyed by the Fourteenth Corps from Lithonia to Yellow River, and from Social Circle to Madison by the Twentieth Corps. It was also broken at several points between Madison and the Oconee River, and the bridge at that river burned by Geary's division of the Twentieth Corps.

On the 24th of November both corps moved from near Milledgeville to Sandersville, the Fourteenth via Black Spring, and the Twentieth via Hebron. The two corps reached Sandersville almost simultaneously on the morning of November 26, driving the enemy's cavalry very rapidly through the town. On the 27th both corps moved toward Louisville, two divisions of the Fourteenth, unencumbered by wagons, going via Fenn's Bridge for the purpose of protecting our left flank and to uncover the crossing of Ogeechee River and Rocky Comfort Creek at a point near Louisville. Two divisions of the Twentieth Corps moved along the Georgia Central Railroad, from Tennille to the Ogeechee River, destroying the road and bridges. The remaining division of each corps, with all the trains, moved on an interior road direct to Louisville. The bridges over the Ogeechee and Rocky Comfort Creek had been destroyed by the enemy, but a pontoon bridge was soon constructed by Colonel Buell, and on the 29th both corps were encamped near Louisville.

Two divisions of the Fourteenth Corps left Louisville December 1, crossing Buck Head Creek five miles above the church, and passing through Habersham, reached Jacksonborough on the 5th. Baird's division moved from Louisville in support of the cavalry, and made a demonstration in the direction of Waynesborough, rejoining the corps at Jacksonborough. The Twentieth Corps left Louisville December 1, crossing Buck Head Creek at the church, and passing through Birdville struck the railroad leading from Millen to Augusta, five miles from Millen, and encamped on the 5th near Hunter's Mills. From Jacksonborough the Fourteenth Corps moved toward Savannah on the Augusta and Savannah road, the Twentieth Corps taking the road through Springfield. On the 10th of December my command reached the main line of the enemy's works in front of Savannah, and took position, the Twentieth Corps on the left, with its left resting on the Savannah River, the Fourteenth on the right and connecting with the Seventeenth Corps beyond the canal near Lawson's plantation. Our line was established as close as possible to that of the enemy, and the time spent in preparation for an assault upon his works. Batteries were established on the river in such positions as prevented any boats from passing. The steamer Ida, while attempting to pass up from Savannah, on the 10th of December, was captured and burned. On the 12th two gun-boats and the steamer Resolute attempted to pass our batteries from above, but both gun-boats were driven back by Winegar's battery, and the steamer was so disabled that she fell into our hands. She was soon repaired, and has since been transferred to the quartermaster's department. On the 18th a brigade of the First Division, Twentieth Corps, was thrown across the river, and established near Izard's plantation, on the South Carolina shore, in a position which threatened the only line of communication still held by the enemy. A bridge in the meantime had been constructed by the enemy from the city to the South Carolina shore, and on the evening of December 20 he commenced the evacuation of the city. The movement was discovered at 3 a. m. on the 21st, and my command was at once moved forward and occupied the city.

For a more detailed account of each day's operations, I respectfully refer you to the reports of Maj. Gen. J. C. Davis, commanding Fourteenth Corps, and Brig. Gen. A. S. Williams, commanding Twentieth Corps, together with the reports of the subordinate commanders, all of which are herewith inclosed. So far as active opposition on the part of the enemy was concerned, there was hardly an event worthy of mention in a report of this nature. The only real annoyance we experienced was from the destruction of bridges, and the obstruction of roads by fallen timber, and these obstacles were very readily overcome.

The conduct of the officers and men on the march is worthy of the highest praise. They endured the fatigues of the march with cheerfulness, and were ever ready, even at the close of a long day's march, to use the ax and spade in removing obstructions and repairing roads and bridges.

The result of the campaign proves conclusively the practicability of subsisting large bodies of troops upon the enemy's country. After leaving the section of country near Atlanta, which had already been foraged upon by both armies, we experienced no difficulty in obtaining supplies for both men and animals. Even the most unproductive sections along our line of march yielded enough for our support so long as the march could be continued from day to day. It was thirty-four days from the date my command left Atlanta to the day supplies were received from the fleet. The total number of rations required during this period was 1,360,000. Of this amount there was issued by the subsistence department 440,900 rations of bread, 142,473 rations of meat, 876,800 of coffee and tea, 778,466 of sugar, 213,500 of soap, and 1,123,000 of salt. As the troops were well supplied at all times, if we deduct the above issues from the amount actually due the soldier, we have the approximate quantities taken from the country, viz, rations of bread, 919,000; meat, 1,217,527; coffee, 483,000; sugar, 581,534; soap, 1,146,500; salt, 137,000. The above is the actual saving to the Government in issue of rations during the campaign, and it is probable that even more than the equivalent of the above supplies was obtained by the soldiers from the country.

Four thousand and ninety valuable horses and mules were captured during the march and turned over to the quartermaster's department. Our transportation was in far better condition on our arrival at Savannah than it was at the commencement of the campaign. The average number of horses and mules with my command, including those of the pontoon train and a part of the Michigan Engineers, was 14,500. We started from Atlanta with four days' grain in wagons. Estimating the amount fed the animals at the regulation allowance, and deducting the amount on hand on leaving Atlanta, I estimate the amount of grain taken from the country at 5,000,000 pounds; fodder, 6,000,000 pounds; beside the forage consumed by the immense herds of cattle that were driven with the different columns.

It is very difficult to estimate the amount of damage done the enemy by the operations of the troops under my command during the campaign; 119 miles of railroad were thoroughly and effectually destroyed, scarcely a tie or rail, a bridge or culvert, on the entire line being left in a condition to be of use again. At Rutledge, Madison, Eatonton, Milledgeville, Tennille, and Davisborough, machine-shops, turn-tables, depots, water-tanks, and much other valuable property were destroyed. The quantity of cotton destroyed is estimated by my subordinate commanders at 17,000 bales. A very large number of cotton gins and presses were also destroyed. Negro men, women, and children joined the column at every mile of our march; many of them bringing horses and mules, which they cheerfully turned over to the officers of the quartermaster's department. I think at least 14,000 of these people joined the two columns at different points on the march, but many of them were too old and infirm, and others too young, to endure the fatigues of the march, and were therefore left in rear. More than one-half of the above number, however, reached the coast with us. Many of the able-bodied men were transferred to the officers of the quartermaster and subsistence departments, and others were employed in the two corps as teamsters, cooks, and servants. Twenty-three hundred stand of small-arms, and a large quantity of powder, were captured at Milledgeville. Fifty-one pieces of artillery were abandoned by the enemy, on his evacuation of Savannah, on the line in front of my command. Thirty-eight pieces in addition to the above were also found in works first entered by the Twentieth Corps. A very large amount of ordnance stores was also found in and about the city.

Bvt. Maj. Gen. J. C. Davis, commanding Fourteenth Corps, and Brig. Gen. A. S. Williams, commanding Twentieth Corps, were during the entire campaign constantly with their troops, and were energetic and zealous in the discharge of every duty.

The Fifty-eighth Indiana Volunteers, under command of Col. George P. Buell, organized as pontoniers, and a portion of the First Michigan Engineers, under Maj. J. B. Yates, accompanied my command, and were at all times most efficient in the discharge of the arduous duties imposed upon them.

I append herewith a statement of casualties, and also a statement of prisoners captured.*

I am, sir, very respectfully, your obedient servant,

H. W. SLOCUM,
Major-General, Commanding Left Wing, Army of Georgia.

Capt. L. M. DAYTON,
Aide-de-Camp.

Report of casualties in Left Wing, Army of Georgia, during the recent campaign.

Corps.	Killed.		Wounded.		Missing.		Aggregate.	Prisoners captured.		Aggregate.
	Officers.	Men.	Officers.	Men.	Officers.	Men.		Officers.	Men.	
Fourteenth	1	12	1	29	.....	94	137	.....	115	115
Twentieth	1	11	5	83	1	164	265	30	294	324
Total	2	23	6	112	1	258	402	30	409	439

No. 50.

Report of Col. George P. Buell, Fifty-eighth Indiana Infantry, commanding Pontoniers.

HDQRS. PONTONIERS, LEFT WING, ARMY OF GEORGIA,
Savannah, Ga., January 7, 1865.

COLONEL: I have the honor to submit the following report of the operations of my command during the campaign from Atlanta to Savannah, Ga.:

November 13, 1864, my command destroyed the railroad bridge over the Chattahoochee River near Atlanta, Ga. 14th, moved my command to and encamped within the city limits, and equipped the same with twenty days' rations and forage. 15th, in accordance with orders, sent one-half of my train (440 feet of bridge complete) and four companies of my regiment, commanded by Lieutenant-Colonel Moore, with the Twentieth Corps. The remainder of my train, with six companies, commanded by myself, marched from Atlanta the morning of the 16th with the Fourteenth Corps, moving on the Decatur road. 17th, after a march of twenty miles threw two bridges (120 feet each) over Yellow River. 18th, in the afternoon took up one of my bridges, moved it forward to the Ulcofauhachee, where it was rethrown; the remaining bridge over Yellow River, being ordered forward under charge of Major

* For map accompanying this report, see Plate LXX, Map 3 of the Atlas.

Downey, reached my camp late in the night. 19th, dismantled the bridge over the Ulcofauhachee and marched eighteen miles during the day. 20th, 21st, and 22d were passed in marching. 23d, reached and encamped in the city of Milledgeville. 24th, marched at 9 a. m., moving on the road to Sandersville. 25th, moved forward a few miles to Buffalo Creek; over this stream we threw a pontoon bridge and also built one small trestle bridge during the night. 26th, took up the pontoon bridge and marched the same day to Sandersville, a distance of ten miles. 27th, sent Major Downey, with two companies and 120 feet of bridge, to report to General Baird, whose division marched on the extreme left flank. The remainder of my command moved on the river road from Louisville with Generals Carlin's and Morgan's divisions of the Fourteenth Corps. 28th, continued our march to Louisville; reached there the same evening; found Colonel Moore's bridge thrown over the large Ogeechee, and Major Downey's thrown over the small Ogeechee River, near Louisville; finished corduroying the swamps on either side of the Ogeechee River. We remained in camp near Louisville until the afternoon of December 1.

December 1, marched at 1 p. m., going a distance of twelve miles on the road to Millen. 2d, continued our march the whole day. 3d, in the morning threw two bridges—one over Buck Head Creek and also one over Rosemary Creek; took the same bridge up in the evening and marched six miles on the road to Jacksonborough. 4th, marched all day and camped near Lumpkin's Station, on the Waynesborough railroad. 5th, marched twelve miles and camped on Beaver Dam Creek, and by 10 o'clock at night we built one trestle bridge over Beaver Dam Creek for Generals Baird and Kilpatrick. 6th, marched seventeen miles. 7th, marched twenty-five miles, reaching Ebenezer Creek; commenced building a trestle bridge over Ebenezer Creek, working my men all night. 8th, finished the trestle bridge in the morning and also threw a pontoon bridge over Lockner's Creek, four miles in advance. 9th, took up both bridges and moved forward during the night toward Savannah. 10th, continued our march. 11th, marched six miles and camped near the Savannah River, within six miles of Savannah City; Lieutenant-Colonel Moore reported and rejoined my command with his detachment. 12th, 13th, 14th, 15th, 16th, and 17th, remained in camp idle. 18th, made 700 fascines during the day, night, and part of the 19th. 20th, received orders to throw a pontoon bridge from Argyle Island to the main South Carolina shore; worked all night, boating my material to the point, and had the bridge half completed when orders were received to take it up and march into Savannah, on the morning of December 21, 1864.

My command, consisting of about 900 men and 600 mules, started from Atlanta with four days' forage and twenty [days'] rations. My men and mules lived well throughout the whole campaign and had been in Savannah several days before we drew rations from the U. S. Government. My entire command was in better condition when it arrived in Savannah than when it left Atlanta.

Before closing this report I desire to tender my thanks to Lieutenant-Colonel Moore and Major Downey, each of whom ably commanded detachments of regiment, displaying a degree of energy and preseverance entitling them to special notice. Capts. James M. Smith and C. C. Whiting rendered very important services in their positions as commanders of pontoon sections. Capt. Woodford Tousey, commissary;

Lieut. Zachariah Jones, aide-de-camp; Lieut. Horace A. Hall, aide-de-camp, and Lieut. Henry Torrence, acting assistant quartermaster, deserve credit for their energy and promptness.

In conclusion, I would state that great credit is due to officers and men of the regiment for the manner in which they conducted themselves throughout the entire campaign. Although many times, after a hard day's march, they have had bridges to build or roads to repair, they were always on hand. Praise is likewise due my officers and men for the good discipline retained throughout the entire march. For the particulars of the operations of Colonel Moore's detachment I refer you to his report, herein inclosed.*

Recapitulation: Corduroyed, 2,000 yards; pontoon bridge by day, 690 feet; trestle bridge by day, 260 feet; trestle bridge by night, 1,030 feet; fascines made, 700; mules, 600; men, 900.

I am, general, very respectfully, your obedient servant,

GEO. P. BUELL,
Colonel, Commanding.

Lieut. Col. H. C. RODGERS,
Assistant Adjutant-General, Left Wing, Army of Georgia.

No. 51.

Report of Lieut. Col. Joseph Moore, Fifty-eighth Indiana Infantry, commanding section of Pontoon Train.

HDQRS. FIFTY-EIGHTH INDIANA VOLUNTEERS (PONTONIERS),
Savannah, Ga., January 6, 1865.

SIR: I have the honor to submit the following report of the amount of bridging done by that portion of the Fifty-eighth Indiana Volunteers under my command during the late campaign from Atlanta, Ga., to this point:

My command consisted of four companies of the Fifty-eighth Indiana Volunteers, effective force 220 men exclusive of teamsters, and a train of forty-one wagons, including baggage and supply train, and hauled about 440 feet of pontoon bridge. November 15, at 7 a. m., in accordance with orders received, I moved my train out on the Decatur road, reporting to Brigadier-General Williams, commanding Twentieth Army Corps. I remained with this corps during the campaign. I had no bridging to do until we reached Little River, twelve miles north of Milledgeville. November 20, we put a pontoon bridge across Little River of ten boats, making 220 feet of bridge during the night of the 20th of November. November 24, we put a pontoon bridge across the channel of Buffalo Creek. This bridge took three boats, and was eighty feet in length. I also repaired five bridges at this point by repairing the trestles that had been burned off, and using balk and chess for covering. These bridges were 360 feet in length. I also repaired two bridges at the same flat or swamp, 120 feet in length, using timber procured from the woods, making the whole length of bridging at this point 560 feet. November 28, we reached Ogeechee River about 1 p. m. and found the bridge across the river burned, and seven others across the swamp, which was near three-quarters of a mile in width. I put a pontoon bridge across the river, using five boats and making 110 feet of bridge. I also set my men at work and cut a

* See next, *post*.

new road across the swamp, which we had to corduroy from the river through the entire swamp. November 29, during the night we built two small trestle bridges, sixty-five feet in length, across Big Creek, three miles south of Louisville. From this on we had no more pontoon bridges to lay, but we traveled through a country that was very level and swampy, and I had 100 of my men daily detailed, under charge of Capt. William E. Chappell, of this regiment, to march in advance as pioneers to corduroy swamps and repair bridges, and clear out the timber which had been felled in the roads at every swamp by the enemy. There were a good many small bridges built, not, however, worth reporting.

On the 10th of December we reached a point five miles from Savannah, and on the 13th I received orders to report to Colonel Buell, then commanding the other section of the train.

Recapitulation: Whole number of pontoon-boats put down, 18, making 410 feet bridges; balk and chess used to build bridges on trestles, 360 feet; trestle bridges built, 185 feet; total, 955 feet.

Respectfully submitted.

JOSEPH MOORE,
Lieutenant-Colonel Fifty-eighth Indiana Volunteers,
Comdg. Section Pontoon Train, Left Wing, Army of Georgia.

Col. GEORGE P. BUELL,
Commanding Pontoon Train.

No. 52.

Report of Bvt. Maj. Gen. Jefferson C. Davis, U. S. Army, commanding Fourteenth Army Corps.

HEADQUARTERS FOURTEENTH ARMY CORPS,
Savannah, Ga., December 31, 1864.

COLONEL:*

On the morning of the 15th [November] the corps reached Atlanta and bivouacked in the suburbs of the city. The remainder of the day and night was spent in issuing clothing to the men, filling up empty wagons with provisions, equalizing and assigning trains to the different commands with a view to rapid marching. On the morning of the 16th the head of the column marched on the road leading to Covington, through Decatur, and made an average march of fifteen miles. On the 17th, moving in the same order of march and destroying the railroad from Lithonia to Yellow River, the corps went into camp on the west bank of the river and vicinity late in the evening. During the night Colonel Buell, commanding pontoon train, laid two excellent bridges across the river, and early on the morning of the 18th the advance was resumed. Passing through Covington the whole command went into camp during the afternoon on the Ulcofauhachee River. The bridges were repaired across the stream, and the march resumed at daylight on the morning of the 19th, in the direction of Eatonton, by the way of Shady Dale, in the vicinity of which place the whole command encamped for the night.

On the 20th the corps marched for and went into camp near Eatonton factories. The advance of the Twentieth Corps from Madisonville,

---

*For portion of report (here omitted) relating to operations in North Georgia and North Alabama, see Vol. XXXIX, Part I, p. 614.

on the main Milledgeville road, required a deflection to the right in the movement of my column in order that the two corps should move on separate roads, and, in compliance with orders from the general-in-chief, whose headquarters moved with my column on this part of our campaign, I ordered the head of the column in the direction of Milledgeville, by the way of Farrar's Mill on Murder Creek. Owing to the heavy rain which had fallen during the night and was still pouring down upon us, the progress of our trains was exceedingly slow, and the night of the 21st was spent in mud and water, crossing Murder Creek. On the 22d the weather partially cleared off, and the corps marched and went into camp in the vicinity of Cedar Creek. On the 23d the weather cleared off, and the roads having dried up so as to be quite passable for trains, the whole command marched and went into camp in the vicinity of Milledgeville by the afternoon. The Twentieth Corps had already reached the city the evening previous, from the direction of Madisonville. On the 24th Carlin's and Morgan's divisions, with their trains, crossed the river and went into camp a few miles beyond the bridge, preparatory to the advance upon Sandersville. This place was reached on the 26th after two days' good marching, the head of the column reaching the town about the same time as did the Twentieth Corps. A part of Wheeler's cavalry was handsomely driven from the town by the advance skirmishers of the two corps.

November 27, the corps trains, under escort of Carlin's division, moved by the way of Davisborough upon Louisville, while Baird's and Morgan's divisions, unembarrassed with trains, moved on the Fenn's Bridge road, thus protecting our left flank from any demonstrations the enemy's cavalry might make from that direction upon our trains. Those two divisions, under command of Brigadier-General Baird, marching on a road between the Ogeechee River and Rocky Comfort Creek, reached Louisville early in the afternoon of the 28th, and immediately laid a pontoon bridge across the creek and commenced the passage of troops. Owing to the movements of the Twentieth Corps and trains occupying the main road from Davisborough to Louisville, Carlin's division and my corps trains moving on that road were only able to reach the Ogeechee about 3 p. m. Colonel Buell's pontoniers immediately commenced laying their bridges and repairing the roads destroyed by the enemy, under the personal supervision of the general commanding the wing, and before night the troops and trains were passing both streams into their camps around Louisville. The road, running as it does here through an immense cypress swamp, required considerable labor to put and keep it in condition for the passage of trains, and it was not until noon the next day that the entire column succeeded in getting into its camps.

Early on the morning of the 29th I received, from a staff officer, a report from General Kilpatrick, commanding the cavalry, that he had succeeded in cutting the road at Waynesborough and burned the railroad bridge across Brier Creek, and that on his return he had been for several days hard pressed by Wheeler. He also reported his command about ten miles from Louisville, on the road leading direct to Buck Head bridge. At his request I immediately sent a brigade of infantry from Baird's division, commanded by Col. Morton C. Hunter, to his support. He, however, experienced less difficulty than was apprehended, and, joining my command during the day, went into camp on the east side of Big Creek, supported by Colonel Hunter's brigade, until the general advance was resumed December 1. November 30, my troops occupied the same position, skirmishing with the enemy's cavalry, who made several pertinacious attempts to drive in our pickets, except General Carlin's division, which, in compliance with orders from wing headquarters, marched to Sebastopol, with a view to uncovering the crossing of the Ogeechee by other troops advancing in that direction.

December 1, in the general advance of the army upon Millen my general instructions required my column to cross Buck Head Creek at some point between Waynesborough and Birdville, for which place the Twentieth Corps was moving. Buck Head bridge, near the church of that name, was designated as my objective point, and Baird, with Kilpatrick's cavalry, was ordered to move in the direction of Waynesborough, and, after crossing Buck Head Creek, to move down the east bank and take position near Reynolds, not far from the church. This Kilpatrick and Baird accomplished by the afternoon of the 2d. Morgan's division, in charge of the whole corps train, moved on the direct road to Buck Head bridge and encamped ten miles from Louisville. On the 2d Carlin's division joined the column from his flank movement in the direction of Sebastopol, and the corps went into camp at the crossing of the Birdville and Waynesborough roads, about two miles from the bridge. The change in the direction of march of the Twentieth Corps again caused a deflection in my line of march, and on the morning of the 3d I caused pontoon bridges to be laid across the creek at a point about five miles higher up the stream, and commenced crossing my troops and trains at 10.30 o'clock. Jacksonborough had by this time been designated by the general commanding as the next objective point for the concentration of my corps, and I ordered Baird and Kilpatrick to move from Reynolds in the direction of Waynesborough, with a view to leading the enemy to believe that our next advance would be upon Augusta. Carlin and Morgan, after a hard day's work upon the roads, went into camp at Lumpkin's Station; Baird and Kilpatrick took position near Thomas' Station, where the enemy was found in considerable force.

December 4, Carlin's and Morgan's divisions, with the corps trains, after destroying three miles of railroad, moved in the direction of Jacksonborough, through Habersham, and encamped on the farm of Mrs. Smith, thirteen miles from Lumpkin's Station. Baird and Kilpatrick, after some fighting with Wheeler's cavalry, drove the enemy from Waynesborough and across Brier Creek. Baird, in the meantime, destroyed three miles of railroad near Thomas' Station. The 5th, after a hard day's march over country roads which required much repairing, the whole corps, with Kilpatrick's cavalry, encamped in the vicinity of Jacksonborough, the advance at Buck Creek Post-Office. During the night the bridge across Beaver Dam Creek at Jacksonborough, which had been destroyed, was rebuilt by Colonel Buell, and early on the morning of the 6th the whole column marched on the river road, and went into camp at and in advance of Hudson's Ferry, making an average march of about twenty miles. December 7, the column moved in the same order of march; Baird and Kilpatrick, unencumbered by the trains, covered the rear. Morgan's division and the pontoon train reached Ebenezer Creek late in the evening, and went immediately to work cutting away the fallen timber which obstructed the roadway through the immense swamp which skirts the creek on both sides at this point. The pontoniers, under Colonel Buell, set to work at once, notwithstanding an exceedingly hard day's march, to reconstruct the bridge, and by noon the next day the column commenced crossing this formidable defile. Notwithstanding the immense amount of labor expended upon the road and bridge to make them passable, much was still required to keep them in condition, and it was not until daylight the 9th that the rear of the column had completed the crossing.

During the 8th the enemy's cavalry made several attempts to drive in our rear pickets, but did not succeed. The loss on our side during these attacks was but slight, although at times the skirmishing was quite animated. On the morning of the 9th, marched from camp at Ebenezer Church to Cuyler's plantation, where General Morgan, who was in the advance, found the enemy occupying a strongly erected field-work, disposed to dispute his advance. General Morgan immediately placed a couple of field pieces in position and opened fire upon the work. His infantry was soon deployed for an attack, but the near approach of night and the impossibility of assaulting the position through the impassable swamp in our front caused me to defer the attack until morning, when it was discovered the enemy had abandoned his position. December 10, advanced Morgan's and Carlin's divisions with trains to the Ten-mile house and went into camp, giving the road to the Twentieth Corps advancing from Monteith and intersecting the Augusta road. Baird's division was ordered to cover the rear and tear up the railroad track in the vicinity of the crossing at the Savannah, and, if possible, to destroy the bridge at that point. December 11, moved down the Augusta road to the position of the Twentieth Corps in front of the enemy's works, and received orders to relieve the Seventeenth Corps in its position on the Louisville road and in the vicinity of the Ogeechee Canal. This was done, and by the 12th the whole corps had taken position in front of the enemy, my left connecting with the Twentieth Corps near the Savannah and Charleston Railroad, and my right connecting with the Seventeenth Corps beyond the canal, near Lawton's plantation.

During the intervening days between the 12th and 21st, at which time the enemy evacuated his position, my troops were assiduously engaged in skirmishing with the enemy, reconnoitering his position, and making general preparations for the attack. Five points in my front had, several days before the evacuation, been well reconnoitered and pronounced accessible to an attacking party. This information was duly forwarded to the general commanding. For further information concerning the position of my troops and the enemy's works and approaches to them I have the honor to refer the general commanding to the accompanying map,* drawn by my chief engineer; it is, I think, perfectly accurate. December 21, it was discovered that the enemy had evacuated his position in our front, and the report of my chief of artillery shows twenty-eight pieces of artillery of different calibers captured. My provost-marshal's report shows 639 able-bodied negroes turned over to the quartermaster's department at King's Bridge, in compliance with special orders from headquarters Military Division of the Mississippi. This number does not include a large number retained in the different commands as officers' servants, pioneers, &c.

I would respectfully submit the following statistics, which have been collected from the reports of the different departments, and are as near correct as can be compiled from such data: Forty-eight miles of railroad track and four large and important bridges upon the Chattanooga and Atlanta, Atlanta and Augusta, Savannah and Augusta, and Georgia Central railroads were thoroughly destroyed. A large amount of cotton, estimated by division commanders at about 12,000 bales, was also destroyed. Seventeen hundred and seventy draft and saddle

---

*Not found; but see Plate LXX, Map 3 of the Atlas.

animals, and, according to the report of the corps commissary, about 1,500 cattle and several hundred sheep were captured. About 1,340 negroes, mostly able-bodied males, followed the column; 115 Confederate prisoners and 34 deserters from the enemy were taken. The corps quartermaster estimates that about 1,000,730 pounds of fodder and about 1,474,834 pounds of grain were obtained from the country. What amounts of provisions for the men were obtained by the foraging parties constantly out from the different brigades of the command it is impossible to state with accuracy. Probably the nearest approximation which can be given will be to state that the corps left Atlanta on the 16th day of November with but seven and one-half days' supplies of the substantial ration. It arrived before Savannah December 11 with about five days' in the wagons, only three and one-half days' having been issued and lost during the march. Of the smaller articles, such as coffee, sugar, and salt, a much larger quantity was issued. For the rest the corps subsisted entirely upon the country through which it passed. Sweet potatoes, which were found by the hundreds of bushels, were the principal and most unfailing article of diet for officers and men; but flour, meal, sorghum, poultry, &c., were found in great abundance.

The list of casualties during the time above reported is as follows: 13 killed, 30 wounded, and 94 missing. (See tabular list appended.)

Considering the active operations of the corps since the beginning of the campaign against Atlanta from Chattanooga the 1st of May last, I am proud to report its excellent condition and efficiency. To the division commanders I desire to express the many obligations I am under for their co-operation throughout the campaigns above described, and to express the hope that the War Department will soon make suitable acknowledgments of their faithful services. Their reports are herewith submitted, and attention asked to them for many details omitted necessarily in this.

Since the entrance of our troops into Savannah the corps has occupied its present camp southwest of the city, making preparations for a resumption of active operations whenever called upon.

I am, colonel, very respectfully, your obedient servant,

JEF. C. DAVIS,
Brevet Major-General, Commanding.

Lieut. Col. H. C. RODGERS,
Chief of Staff, Left Wing.

List of casualties in the Fourteenth Army Corps during the campaign against Savannah, Ga.

Divisions.	Commissioned officers.		Enlisted men.		Missing.
	Killed.	Wounded.	Killed.	Wounded.	
First		1	2	7	37
Second	1		7	16	57
Third *a*			3	6	
Total	1	1	12	29	94

a Missing not given.

Total, 137.

JEF. C. DAVIS,
Brevet Major-General, Commanding.

No. 53.

Report of Brig. Gen. William P. Carlin, U. S. Army, commanding First Division.

HDQRS. FIRST DIVISION, FOURTEENTH ARMY CORPS,
Savannah, Ga., January 6, 1865.

COLONEL:*

On the 15th [November] I reached Atlanta, leaving the Thirteenth Michigan at Chattahoochee bridge, with orders to destroy it after the passage of all our troops and trains. This order was carried out by Lieutenant-Colonel Palmer, commanding the regiment. On the 16th I marched from Atlanta, via Decatur, to Lithonia, twenty miles. On the 21st I marched to Yellow River, destroying five miles of the Georgia Railroad. The march was continued through Covington to Harris' plantation, where we turned southward toward Shady Dale and on to Milledgeville, where we arrived on the 23d. On the 24th we crossed the Oconee, and marched on Sandersville, arriving there on the 27th. On the 28th we arrived at Davisborough. Continuing the march due east through Louisville, we struck the Augusta and Millen Railroad at Lumpkin's Station, and destroyed three miles of railroad, all the buildings, platforms, wood, &c. Marching on eastward we struck the Savannah and Augusta road near the Savannah River, and turned southward.

On the 11th of December I arrived before Savannah and took position on the right of the Louisville road, relieving Mower's, Leggett's, and G. A. Smith's divisions, of the Seventeenth Corps. This position was maintained with more or less skirmishing till the 21st instant [ultimo], when my advance entered the city of Savannah. Several days before the evacuation by Hardee I recommended an attack in front of my division.

My total loss during the campaign in killed, wounded, missing, and deaths by disease is as follows: Commissioned officer, wounded, 1; enlisted men, killed, 2; wounded, 7; missing, 37.

It is impossible to state accurately how much cotton was destroyed by my men, but it would probably amount to 10,000 bales. None was left in the country on our line of march. It is estimated that this division drew from the country on the march at least 120,000 rations, worth to the United States at least $36,000; 116 horses and 204 mules, total 320 head, were seized by this division and used for public purposes. The estimate of rations by the commissary of the division, I am sure, is under the mark.

I have the honor to be, colonel, very respectfully, your obedient servant,

W. P. CARLIN,
Brigadier-General, Commanding.

Lieut. Col. A. C. MCCLURG,
Assistant Adjutant-General, Hdqrs. Fourteenth Army Corps.

---

* For portion of report (here omitted) relating to operations in North Georgia and North Alabama, see Vol. XXXIX, Part I, p. 616.

No. 54.

Report of Col. Harrison C. Hobart, Twenty-first Wisconsin Infantry, commanding First Brigade.

HDQRS. FIRST BRIG., FIRST DIV., 14TH ARMY CORPS,
Near Savannah, Ga., December 31, 1864.

CAPTAIN:*

On the 15th day of November, during the afternoon and night, I clothed my troops and made all possible preparations for the campaign which terminated in the fall of Savannah. On the morning of the 16th my brigade marched in advance of the division. During the day we passed through Decatur, and, taking the upper Covington road, we encamped for the night at Lithonia. On the following morning we resumed our march, and at 12 m. of the 18th I camped my command four miles east of Covington and forty-four miles east of Atlanta. After passing Decatur we found forage in great abundance, a sufficient quantity of which was gathered by my foraging parties to supply my whole command. Near Yellow River the brigade destroyed two miles and a half of railroad. November 19, we again resumed our march, and on the 23d day of November I camped my troops about one mile from Milledgeville. On the morning of the 24th my brigade marched through Milledgeville, and, crossing the Oconee River, we took the Sandersville road and reached Sandersville on the 27th. Here I received orders from General Davis to hold the town until all the trains of the Fourteenth Army Corps and General Kilpatrick's trains had passed, and then follow as an escort. About 7 p. m., the trains having passed, I ordered my pickets to rejoin their commands, and withdrew from the town. From Sandersville my brigade formed the rear guard until we reached Louisville, November 29. At Sandersville the Eighty-eighth Indiana lost one man, captured by a squad of rebel cavalry. On the 30th my brigade, in advance of the division, marched from Louisville on the road leading to Station No. 10, and camped three miles east of Sebastopol. From this point the command marched to Lumpkin's, a station on the Augusta railroad, where we bivouacked during the night. The next morning, December 4, my brigade destroyed one mile and a quarter of railroad, after which we marched in the direction of the Savannah River, and striking the river road, we marched down toward Savannah. Nothing of importance occurred. We reached our first position before the city December 11. Here I relieved a division of the Seventeenth Army Corps, and threw up works along my whole front. About 4 p. m. December 12, by order of General Carlin, I moved my brigade to the right, crossed the Ogeechee Canal, and relieved General Smith's division, Seventeenth Army Corps. While holding this position (with a front of more than two miles) I forwarded 1 prisoner of war captured by the One hundred and fourth Illinois in a light skirmish at the Lawton farm, and 27 deserters, who came through my lines on the night of the 15th of December. During the night of the 20th of December the rebels evacuated the city, and early the next morning my skirmishers crossed the swamps and rice fields in my front, and took possession of their works, capturing 3 prisoners. There were 10 pieces of ordnance left by the rebels in my front, including two 64-pounders. During the day I moved my brigade over on the Lawton farm, and remained until the next morning, when I marched to this camp.

*For portion of report (here omitted) relating to operations in North Georgia and North Alabama, see Vol. XXXIX, Part I, p. 617.

Casualties have been—from the Eighty-eighth Indiana Volunteer Infantry, 1 man captured; Thirty-third Ohio Volunteer Infantry, 1 man wounded and 1 man missing; total, 3.

Number of miles of railroad destroyed, $5\frac{3}{4}$; number of horses and mules captured, 110; number of cattle captured, 500. Forage taken from the country: Corn and oats, 50,000 pounds; long forage, 52,000 pounds; total, 102,000 pounds. Supplies for officers and men: Breadstuffs, 41,000 pounds; potatoes, 55,000 pounds; meat, 47,000 pounds; beans and rice, 4,800 pounds; sugar, 7,200 pounds; molasses (sorghum), 30 barrels; or, subsistence for 1,500 men for forty days.

As the conduct of the brigade during the campaign was constantly under the eye of the general commanding the division, I close this report simply with the foregoing narration of facts.

I have the honor to be, captain, very respectfully, your obedient servant,

H. C. HOBART,
Colonel, Commanding.

Capt. G. W. SMITH,
Actg. Asst. Adjt. Gen., First Div., Fourteenth Army Corps.

No. 55.

Report of Maj. John H. Widmer, One hundred and fourth Illinois Infantry, of operations September 7–December 21.

HEADQUARTERS 104TH ILLINOIS INFANTRY VOLUNTEERS,
Near Savannah, Ga., December 29, 1864.

CAPTAIN: In compliance with circular received to-day, I have the honor to submit the following report:

At the fall of Atlanta this regiment was near Jonesborough, Ga.; thence it moved to White Hall, where it went into camp on the 7th of September, and remained till the 3d of October, during which time its principal operation was resting. From the 3d until the 22d day of October the regiment, with the brigade, was almost constantly on the march in pursuit of General Hood's army through Northwestern Georgia and into Alabama as far as Gaylesville. There it remained until the 28th of October. On the 29th it arrived at Rome, Ga., and on November 2 at Kingston. On the 12th day of November it left Kingston, reaching Atlanta on the 15th. The next morning started for Savannah, arriving in front of the city on the 11th instant and in the city on the 22d, having had a first-rate time on the way here.

From the fall of Atlanta to the fall of Savannah the regiment has been constantly on duty with the brigade. The only time it has been engaged with the enemy since the 3d of October was in a light skirmish at Lawton's farm, in front of Savannah, resulting in the capture of one rebel and driving their pickets across the rice fields in our front. We have not lost a single man since the fall of Atlanta.

On the march from Atlanta to Gaylesville and back the regiment drew from the country seven days' subsistence for 110 men (except sugar and coffee), consisting of meat, flour, meal, beans, and potatoes, and on the march from Atlanta to Savannah drew from the same source not less than twenty-five days' subsistence for 215 men (except sugar and coffee), consisting of fresh beef, pork, poultry, flour, meal, potatoes, turnips, rice, beans, honey, sorghum, and molasses. It has also drawn from the country 75,000 pounds of corn and 75,000 pounds of long forage, captured 14 mules, 9 horses, employed on the march twenty negroes from the country, and destroyed 1,600 yards of railroad.

I am, sir, your most obedient servant,

JOHN H. WIDMER,
Major One hundred and fourth Illinois Infantry.

Capt. JOHN W. FORD,
Actg. Asst. Adjt. Gen., 1st Brig., 1st Div., 14th Army Corps.

No. 56.

Report of Lieut. Col. Cyrus E. Briant, Eighty-eighth Indiana Infantry.

Official report of the part taken by the Eighty-eighth Regiment Indiana Volunteers in the campaign of the Army of Georgia from Atlanta to Savannah:

After clothing my regiment and cutting down the baggage to the least possible compass, I left Atlanta on the 16th day of November, 1864, with 248 guns and 14 officers, in advance of the Fourteenth Army Corps. Passing Decatur about 9 o'clock, we took the upper Covington road, halting for dinner on Snapfinger Creek. Three miles farther brought us to Pole Bridge Creek. From this point the country was more open, but soil apparently poor. Halted for the night at Lithonia. November 17, my regiment train guards. Our route lay along the railroad, passing Conyers, a post village in Newton County. We halted early near Yellow River. Forage plenty, especially corn, sweet potatoes, and sorghum molasses. November 18, crossed Yellow River on pontoons; banks muddy; passed through Covington and halted four miles east on a large plantation about noon; lay in camp till morning. November 19, Second and Third Divisions passed ours (First); marched on the Eatonton road. The first part of our march was through the Ulcofauhachee swamps and was necessarily slow; after noon roads were excellent. Camp for the night one mile east of Sandtown. November 20, moved at daylight; country richer, buildings better, and plantations larger; forage of every description in great abundance. Halted for dinner near Shady Dale. The proprietor of the plantation estimated his individual loss by our army at $50,000. Here we left the Eatonton road to our left, taking a central course between Monticello and Eatonton, halting eight miles from Eatonton; rained all night. November 21, still raining; roads cut up considerably by the advance wagon trains, and by noon we got along very slowly, halting for the night some seventeen miles from Milledgeville. November 22, crossed Murder Creek on a very dilapidated bridge, wagons and horses fording near by; creek up to wagon beds, recent rains having swelled it. My regiment was detached to guard cross-roads at Half Acre, with orders to hold the place until the entire wagon train had crossed the creek. By 2 p. m. I left with my regiment to join the division, going by way of Clopton's Mill. I found them encamped near Cedar Creek; roads passable by evening.

November 23, my regiment train guards to-day. March through an excellent country; forage abundant, especially sweet potatoes and sorghum molasses. By 4 p. m. we were encamped within the fortifications of Milledgeville; roads excellent to-day. November 24, passed through Milledgeville; crossed Oconee River. We took the Sandersville road, crossing Town Creek seven miles from Milledgeville, near where there was a good grist-mill. Marching five miles farther, we encamped about 3 p. m. on Gum Creek, remaining all night. November 25, lay in camp all day; Second and Third Divisions passed us. The forage party from my regiment discovered rebel cavalry near large bridge on Buffalo Creek, but finding enough forage they did not let themselves be known. November 26, marched at 6 a. m., but on the advance wagon train reaching Buffalo Creek we moved but slowly, and by 9 o'clock we had crossed the Big and Little Buffalo Creeks and swamps and were encamped near Keg Creek. November 27, crossed Keg Creek and swamp; passed through Sandersville; my regiment stationed on outpost on Worthen road, where three roads diverge. I sent one company forward on each of these roads. About dark some contrabands [came in] and reported rebel cavalry in our front on the main road, and [that they] had already captured some of our troops. I immediately sent another company in support, but nothing further was heard from them. One of the captured men proved to be William Budd, private of Company G, of my regiment. 7 p. m. I was relieved and took position in rear of division wagon train, halting for the night seven miles east of Sandersville. November 28, my regiment train guards; crossed Macon and Savannah Railroad near Power's Station; crossed Williamson's Creek and swamp on double bridge near Davisborough, halting for the night near Ogeechee River. November 29, crossed Ogeechee River on pontoons; bridge and trestle-work over swamp being burned, the passage was difficult. One mile farther brought us to Comfort Creek and swamp, which we found as difficult to cross as the river. Passing Louisville, we halted about noon on Maryfield road. My foragers had excellent success to-day; meat, potatoes, corn, molasses. November 30, marched on Sebastopol road, crossing Big Creek and swamp; eight miles farther passed Dry and Spring Creeks. 3 p. m. passed Sebastopol Station and camped three miles east on the Millen road, my regiment on picket.

December 1, marched on Sebastopol and Waynesborough road, about one mile from the main road, occupying this position until wagon train all passed. My foraging party, numbering thirty-two men and one officer, were attacked some five miles out by a squad of rebel cavalry, but succeeded in getting off with a goodly supply of forage and no loss. December 2, marched on the Waynesborough road some distance, then east on Millen road, halting near Buck Head Creek. December 3, marched north on Jones' Mill road, thence northeast to Buck Head Creek, the bridge over which being burned, we crossed on pontoons. One mile farther we crossed Rocky Creek, making a detour in a southeast direction. We halted for dinner on Rosemary Creek; from thence to Lumpkin's on the Augusta railroad, where we halted for the night. December 4, my regiment tore up one-quarter mile of track, burning the ties and bending the iron. Crossed the railroad at Lumpkin's, taking an easterly direction through a very poor country, sandy and marshy; toward evening passed Habersham, halting two miles east. December 5, my regiment train guards. Our course lay through the headwaters of Beaver Dam Creek and the Ogeechee River; low places along our route marshy and difficult of passage for wagons. Leaving Jacksonborough to our left we went toward Sylvania. December 6, crossed the Middle Ground road, four miles north of Sylvania, at one of the branches of Buck Creek. The road was blockaded with felled trees which impeded our march some. Passed Black Creek Post-

Office, also Black Creek and swamp, halting for the night fifty miles from Savannah. Forage, which had been scarce since leaving Lumpkin's, was more plentiful in this neighborhood. December 7, our march greatly impeded by fallen timbers and bridges burned across creeks. December 8, more especially at Ebenezer Creek, which the enemy had destroyed, blockading the road across the swamps. While a new bridge was being built the enemy attacked the skirmishers of General Baird's division. My regiment was immediately thrown into position, in the rear line of brigade, and threw up logs, &c. At 11 p. m. my regiment crossed Ebenezer Creek, and halted near the church. December 9, moved from Ebenezer, crossing Ebenezer Creek. Roads blockaded, bridges, sloughways, &c., torn up or burned along our entire march to-day; halted sixteen miles from Savannah. December 10, marched to the main road; passed a rebel redoubt near Fourteen Mile-stone; halted about noon ten miles from Savannah. December 11, marched toward the front, crossing the Charleston and Savannah Railroad, also the Macon and Savannah Railroad, to the Middle Ground road, near which my regiment built breast-works. December 12, moved at 4 p. m., crossing the Ogeechee Canal. I relieved with my regiment the Fifty-second Ohio Volunteers of Seventeenth Army Corps, who were on picket in front of the Lawton farm. I held this position until I was relieved by an Iowa regiment from the same brigade I had relieved. December 19, I moved with my regiment to rear line and camped near canal bridge until morning of December 21, when I moved with my regiment in rear of brigade and encamped with it on the Lawton farm, moving next day into Savannah. Total miles marched, —.

RECAPITULATION.

Casualties: William Budd, private Company G, captured by the enemy, Sandersville, November 26, 1864. I left Atlanta November 16, 1864, with 248 guns and entered Savannah December 22, 1864, with 268 guns. I sent two men to general hospital during the campaign and both were sick before leaving Atlanta. My command captured and turned over during campaign 70 head of cattle, 90 sheep, 20 hogs, 5 horses, and 21 mules. After marching something over 300 miles my regiment entered Savannah in better health, spirits, and condition in every respect, with the exception of clothing and more especially of shoes and stockings.

The saving in supplies to Government during the campaign by my regiment amounts to:

	Pounds.
In forage:	
Corn	8,000
Long forage	8,500
Total	16,500
In rations:	
Breadstuffs	9,300
Meats	7,000
Beans or rice	800
Potatoes	11,100
Sugar	1,400

While the above is a fair estimate of the savings to the Government the loss to the enemy may safely be put down as at least one-third additional in rations and one-half in forage.

I have the honor to be, very respectfully, your obedient servant,

C. E. BRIANT,

Lieut. Col., Commanding Eighty-eighth Indiana Volunteers.

No. 57.

Report of Lieut. Col. Joseph H. Brigham, Sixty-ninth Ohio Infantry, commanding Second Brigade.

HDQRS. SECOND BRIG., FIRST DIV., 14TH ARMY CORPS,
Savannah, Ga., December 30, 1864.

CAPTAIN: In compliance with circular dated headquarters First Division, Fourteenth Army Corps, December 29, 1864, I have the honor to submit the following report:

Miles of railroad destroyed		5½
Cotton gins destroyed		5
Cotton destroyed (300 bales)	pounds	150,000
Horses captured		50
Mules captured		60
Cattle captured		250
Negroes that followed the column		40
Corn captured	pounds	62,000
Rice captured	do	18,000
Oats captured	do	1,400
Fodder captured	do	13,084
Hay captured	do	5,133

From the organization of the brigade up to the fall of Savannah the men were issued five days' rations; the rest of the time they subsisted off the country.

The Second Brigade was organized November 16, 1864, at Atlanta, Ga., and assigned to the First Division, Fourteenth Army Corps, with which it marched to this place, a distance of 293 miles, passing in its route through Decatur, Lithonia, Conyers, Covington, Sandersville, Louisville, Milledgeville, and striking the railroad again at Lumpkin's Station.

I have the honor, captain, to be, your obedient servant,

J. H. BRIGHAM,
Lieutenant-Colonel Sixty-ninth Ohio, Commanding.

Capt. G. W. SMITH,
Actg. Asst. Adjt. Gen., First Div., Fourteenth Army Corps.

No. 58.

Report of Lieut. Col. David Miles, Seventy-ninth Pennsylvania Infantry, commanding Third Brigade.

HDQRS. THIRD BRIG., FIRST DIV., 14TH ARMY CORPS,
Near Savannah, Ga., December 31, 1864.

SIR:*

Arrived at Atlanta the 15th [November]. Here the Sixty-ninth Ohio and Thirteenth Michigan Veteran Volunteer Infantry were taken from the brigade and ordered to the Second Brigade, First Division, Fourteenth Army Corps. Drew clothing, and equipped the unarmed men of the command. November 16, left Atlanta, marching on the Augusta road, and camped at Lithonia Station on the Augusta and Atlanta Railroad. 17th, marched through Conyers Station, and was engaged several hours destroying railroad. November 18, Col. H.

* For portion of report (here omitted) relating to operations in North Georgia and North Alabama, see Vol. XXXIX, Part I, p. 618.

A. Hambright being unfit for duty on account of sickness, Lieut. Col. D. Miles took command of the brigade. November 18 to 23, marched to Milledgeville, capital of the State. November 24 to 27, marched to Davisborough Station, on the Macon and Savannah Railroad. November 28, marched to Louisville. November 30, marched to Sebastopol, on the Macon and Savannah Railroad.

December 1 to 3, marched to Lumpkin's Station, on the Savannah and Augusta Railroad. December 4, part of the day the brigade was engaged destroying railroad; was rear guard to the wagon train, and skirmished with a small body of cavalry who were hovering in the rear, but with no result. December 5 to 8, marched to Ebenezer Swamp, where we formed line of battle to protect the train while crossing the swamp, and at midnight marched two miles and camped on east side of the swamp. December 9, resumed the march, but coming upon a small party of the enemy posted in a small fort protected with artillery, went in line for the night. December 10, the enemy fell back during the night and we resumed our march until the evening of the 11th, when we took up our position in line in front of Savannah, relieving part of the Seventeenth Army Corps. Here we remained until the 21st, during which time nothing of note occurred save regular skirmishing, which was kept up between the pickets but with no loss whatever on our part. December 21, the enemy disappearing from our front, the brigade was ordered forward to discover the whereabouts of the enemy, if possible, but meeting with no opposition whatever, marched into the city at 8 a. m., and, pursuant to orders, returned to our old position, where we remained during the night. December 22, marched forward and went into camp on west side of the city.

During the time mentioned in this report the brigade destroyed about 14 miles of railroad; no cotton nor cotton gins were destroyed; 22 horses, 64 mules, and 200 cattle were captured by the command; 69 negroes followed the column. From the time we left Lithonia until our arrival at Savannah nearly enough forage was gathered by the command to supply them independent of the issues of the commissary.

The loss in the command during the time mentioned in this report is as follows: 1 man wounded; 6 men either killed or captured by the enemy; 10 men captured by the enemy.

I am, captain, very respectfully, your obedient servant,

D. MILES,
Lieutenant-Colonel, Commanding Brigade.

Capt. G. W. SMITH,
Actg. Asst. Adjt. Gen., First Div., Fourteenth Army Corps.

No. 59.

Report of Capt. James H. Low, Thirty-eighth Indiana Infantry.

HDQRS. THIRTY-EIGHTH INDIANA VET. VOL. INFTY.,
Near Savannah, Ga., December 29, 1864.

LIEUTENANT:*

November 16, the regiment, with brigade, marched from Atlanta, moving on road leading to Augusta, bivouacking at Lithonia on the railroad leading from Atlanta to Augusta. The 17th, continued march,

*For portion of report (here omitted) relating to operations in North Georgia and North Alabama, see Vol. XXXIX, Part I, p. 619.

assisting in destroying railroad above mentioned at a point near Yellow River; crossed same and passed through Covington on the 18th, going into camp. On this date, Colonel Hambright having been taken quite sick, the command of the brigade devolved upon Lieut. Col. D. Miles, Seventy-ninth Pennsylvania Veteran Volunteer Infantry, and subsequent operations of the regiment coming under your personal observation, I shall be as brief as possible. November 19, regiment continued march, moving in a southerly direction, passing through Milledgeville November 24. After this place, passed through Sandersville November 27. November 28, crossed Georgia Central Railroad. November 29, passed through Louisville. Continuing march, reached and assisted in destroying Augusta and Savannah Railroad at a point between Waynesborough and Millen.

December 7, came into main Augusta and Savannah road running near and parallel with river, which was followed until arriving near and going into position in front of enemy's works, about four miles northwest of Savannah and south of canal, December 11, 1864, remaining in or near this position until the 17th, when it and brigade relieved the Second Brigade. From this date till the enemy evacuated, the command remained constantly in this position, night of the 20th. The 22d, regiment went into camp in its present position. Besides the railroads which the command assisted in destroying, not to exceed two miles, no other species of property was destroyed. I have no means of ascertaining the number of animals captured, but believe that a rough estimate would include not exceeding 2 horses, 15 mules, and from 5 to 10 head of cattle. Except the servants employed by officers (not exceeding fifteen) I do not know of others being otherwise employed or the number that followed the command. For the campaign, inclusive of the time that the report is made to cover, I believe that not exceeding one month's whole rations were issued, the command subsisting exclusively off the country to supply deficiencies.

Very respectfully, your most obedient,

J. H. LOW,

Captain, Comdg. Thirty-eighth Indiana Veteran Vol. Infantry.

Lieut. L. G. BODIE,

Actg. Asst. Adjt. Gen., 3d Brig., 1st Div., 14th Army Corps.

No. 60.

Report of Lieut. Col. Arnold McMahan, Twenty-first Ohio Infantry, of operations September 3–December 21.

HDQRS. TWENTY-FIRST REGIMENT OHIO INFANTRY VOLS.,

Savannah, Ga., December 30, 1864.

SIR: In compliance with orders dated December 29, 1864, headquarters Third Brigade, First Division, Fourteenth Army Corps, I have the honor to report the operations of the Twenty-first Regiment Ohio Infantry Volunteers, under my command, from the 3d day of September, 1864, to the 21st day of December, 1864:

After the defeat of the enemy before Jonesborough, Ga., September 1, 1864, my command returned to Atlanta and went into camp on the 8th. It remained in camp until the morning of October 3, when it moved with its brigade upon the campaign which resulted in the fall of Savannah on the 21st of the present month. I estimate the distance marched during this time to be at least 630 miles. It was difficult to ascertain the exact distance marched over by-roads and through the country. The regiment exchanged shots with a squad of the enemy on the 4th day of December, near Lumpkin's Station, without any result except to check their attempt to annoy the rear of our column. From the 12th to the night of the 20th of December the pickets of my regiment were engaged with those of the enemy before Savannah. During this campaign the regiment destroyed three miles of railroad, and this was the only structure destroyed by my command. At least 8,000 rations were used by the men from the products of the country, which were necessary in addition to subsistence furnished by the commissary department, but the meat used, which was drawn from the country, was not less than 15,000 rations. This estimate does not include the great waste of meat and other foraged subsistence which could not be transported or was abandoned by the men each morning. I estimate the stores wasted or abandoned equal to the amount used. Twenty-one horses and mules attached to the regiment were supplied with forage taken from the country for twenty days. Twelve negroes accompanied the regiment to Savannah, having joined us on the march. Twelve horses and 13 mules were captured, but many of them were comparatively worthless. Six prisoners of war were captured and turned over to provost-marshal Third Brigade, First Division, Fourteenth Army Corps. The regiment lost 1 enlisted man wounded and 10 enlisted men were captured; 6 enlisted men were either killed or captured straggling. My regiment entered the city of Savannah at 9 a.m. December 21, 1864.

Respectfully submitted.

A. McMAHAN,
Lieutenant-Colonel, Commanding.

Lieut. L. G. BODIE,
Actg. Asst. Adjt. Gen., 3d Brig., 1st Div., 14th Army Corps.

No. 61.

Report of Maj. Robert P. Findley, Seventy-fourth Ohio Infantry.

CAMP SEVENTY-FOURTH OHIO,
Near Savannah Ga., December 30, 1864.

SIR: I have the honor, in absence of Major Fisher, who commanded the Seventy-fourth Ohio from Kingston to Savannah, Ga., to make the following report:

Left Kingston at noon of the 12th [November], marching in rear of wagon train; camped at Cartersville at night. The 13th, marched to Big Shanty, tearing up railroad. On the 15th arrived at Atlanta, halted for the night, and drew rations and clothing. Marched on the 16th to Lithonia, twenty-four miles distant from Atlanta. Our course lay northeast, and nothing of importance transpired until the 23d of November, when we camped near Milledgeville. On the 24th we marched, crossing Oconee River, and making but ten miles, when we camped at 12 m. on account of large swamp in our way. Here the Seventy-fourth was placed on picket, and so remained until the morning of the 26th, when we took up our march in rear of wagon train. Marched that day but about six miles. Thus we marched various distances per day, according to swamps and bad roads, nothing of importance transpiring, and our regiment being engaged in nothing worthy of note, until the ——, when we settled down in front of Savannah, along the Ogeechee River. Lay in line until the morning of the 16th of December, when the regiment received orders to report to Captain Clark, to guard wagon train to King's Bridge on the Ogeechee River. Lay at this post until the 22d, when we returned with train and reported to our brigade. Major Fisher was mustered out on the 18th, and I assumed command on that day.

We drew rations but for two days during the march. Owing to our being in rear we twice had no forage, but when we marched any considerable distance we had more than enough of pork and potatoes. I think it would have been no hardship, so far as the Seventy-fourth was concerned, to have made the march without drawing a cracker or any pork. Certain I am that enough was left in camp almost every day to have subsisted the regiment during the day had it been carried along, but the men argued that "sufficient unto the meal was the evil," and wouldn't carry anything from camp. We destroyed about four miles of railroad since leaving Kingston. Am not sure that the Seventy-fourth set fire to any cotton or gins. Ten negroes came into the regiment and followed along with the column. Captured no cattle, nor horses, and but two mules. All the forage for the Government mules, private horses, and the pack-mules of different companies, was taken from the country, and much more was destroyed than was used.

I am, lieutenant, very respectfully, your obedient servant,

R. P. FINDLEY,
Major Seventy-fourth Ohio.

Lieut. L. G. BODIE,
Actg Asst. Adjt. Gen., 3d Brig., 1st Div., 14th Army Corps.

No. 62.

Report of Maj. Michael H. Locher, Seventy-ninth Pennsylvania Infantry, of operations October 3–December 21.

HDQRS. 79TH REGT. PENNSYLVANIA VET. VOL. INFTY.,
Near Savannah, Ga., December 30, 1864.

SIR: In accordance with circular from headquarters Third Brigade, dated December 29, 1864, I make the following report of operations of the Seventy-ninth Regiment Pennsylvania Veteran Volunteers from the fall of Atlanta until the fall of Savannah, Ga.:

The regiment was encamped at Atlanta, Ga., until October 3, 1864, when we were ordered to move with the corps. Marched with the corps during the 3d, 4th, 5th, 6th, and 7th of October, when I was ordered to report my command to Captain Swift, superintendent of repairs on railroad, of whom I received orders to assist in repairing the railroad between Kenesaw Mountain and Allatoona, at which the command was engaged until October 19, when the repairs were completed. On the 19th rebel cavalry made their appearance outside the picket-lines, cut the telegraph, and captured four enlisted men of the command. I immediately sent out a detachment under Captain McBride, but the enemy had retreated. After the detachment returned to camp, I received orders to report to General Vandever, commanding District of Marietta, at Marietta, to which place the regiment proceeded by railroad. At Marietta the regiment formed part of the garrison, and performed patrol and provost duty until November 13, when we received orders to rejoin the corps on its arrival at that place. On the arrival of the corps I reported my command and accompanied the corps to Atlanta, where we arrived on the 15th instant. On the 16th we moved again, taking the Augusta road, and marched to Lithonia Station, on the Augusta railroad, a distance of eighteen miles. November 17, marched to Yellow River, a distance of thirteen miles, and worked seven hours destroying the railroad. The regiment assisted destroying about two miles of track. November 18, the regiment formed the advance guard of the column, and marched a distance of eight miles, the regiment being on picket during the night. One enlisted man on duty with brigade foraging party captured by the enemy. November 19 to 23, marched to Milledgeville, the capital of Georgia, a distance of fifty-five miles. November 24, marched to Town Creek, a distance of ten miles, where the division encamped until the 26th. November 26 and 27, marched a distance of twenty-four miles to near Davisborough Station, on the Macon and Savannah Railroad. Regiment went on picket. November 28 to December 2, marched to near Buck Head bridge, a distance of fifty-one miles. Regiment on picket duty during night of 2d instant.

December 3, marched to Station No. 1, on the Augusta and Savannah Railroad, a distance of ten miles. December 4, worked three hours destroying railroad and assisted in destroying two miles of track; marched a distance of six miles. December 5 to 7, marched a distance of forty-six miles; during this march the cavalry, covering the rear, were engaged with the enemy. December 8, marched a distance of three miles, and formed line of battle to cover the train until it crossed Ebenezer Swamp; remained until midnight, when we marched to east side of the swamp, a distance of two miles. December 9, marched a distance of seven miles, when we found the enemy posted with artillery and infantry. The regiment was sent out as skirmishers with orders to dislodge the enemy, but the order to advance was countermanded and the regiment remained on picket duty. December 10, the enemy fell back during the night, and to-day we advanced four miles. December 11, marched eight miles and went into position in front of Savannah, relieving a portion of the Seventeenth Army Corps on the Ogeechee Canal, where we remained until the 16th, when we were ordered into camp. On the 16th one man, detailed to drive cattle, was captured by the enemy. December 19, relieved the Twenty-first Michigan, of Second Brigade, in the front line, where we remained until the morning of the 21st, when the regiment was ordered on the skirmish line, relieving the Thirty-eighth Indiana. At daylight it was discovered that the enemy had evacuated their works, and I received orders to advance with the skirmishers as far as possible. I moved immediately and advanced to the city, which my command entered at 8 a. m., capturing on the way one prisoner.

During the campaign my command, independent of the organized foraging parties, captured 2 horses and 4 mules and 25 able-bodied male negroes. During the campaign from Atlanta to Savannah forage and provisions were abundant, as the men subsisted almost entirely off the country.

The total loss of my command from the fall of Atlanta to date is six men captured by the enemy.

I am, very respectfully,

M. H. LOCHER,
Major, Commanding.

Lieut. L. G. BODIE,
Actg. Asst. Adjt. Gen., 3d Brig., 1st Div., 14th Army Corps.

No. 63.

Report of Brig. Gen. James D. Morgan, U. S. Army, commanding Second Division.

HDQRS. SECOND DIVISION, FOURTEENTH ARMY CORPS,
Savannah, Ga., December 29, 1864.

COLONEL: *

November 14, marched at daylight, passing to the right of Kenesaw Mountain and bivouacked at Nickajack Creek, twenty miles. November 15, moved at daylight to Atlanta, twelve miles. November 16, left Atlanta at 11 a. m., passing through Decatur and bivouacking at Snapfinger Creek, marching ten miles. November 17, moved at 7 a. m. through Lithonia to Conyers, seventeen miles, and destroying five miles of railroad. November 18, marched at daylight, crossing Yellow River by Covington to Ulcofauhachee River, fifteen miles, destroying three miles railroad. November 19, marched at daylight, passing through Newborn to Shady Dale, nineteen miles. November 20, left camp at 7 a. m., marching to Eatonton Factory or Little River, fifteen miles. November 21, marched at daylight, crossing Mud Creek and camping at Cedar Creek, marching eighteen miles. November 22, in camp. November 23, moved at daylight and camped near Milledgeville, fifteen miles. November 24, left camp at 10 a. m., passing through Milledgeville and crossing the Oconee River and camping at Town Creek, nine miles. November 25, moved at daylight, crossing Buffalo Creek and camping at Keg Creek, marching twelve miles. 26th, moved at daylight for Sandersville. About four miles west of that place my foragers were met by Wheeler's cavalry, who were disposed to resist their advance. The foragers were soon formed and deployed as skirmishers, and steadily drove the enemy to and through Sandersville, never checking the advance of the column. As a precautionary measure the One hundred and thirteenth Ohio, Captain Jones commanding, of the Second Brigade, were deployed as skirmishers on the left of the road; one division of the Twentieth Corps entered the town simultaneously with my own. 27th, marched at 7 a. m., crossing the Ogeechee River at Fenn's Bridge, camping on Hudson's plantation, marching sixteen miles. 28th, left camp at daylight, crossing Rocky Comfort Creek, camping at Louisville, nine miles. Remained there during the 29th and 30th. While at Louisville six wagons, under charge of Lieutenant Coe, acting assistant quartermaster, were attacked just outside of picket-line by Wheeler's cavalry, and four wagons captured, the remaining two escaping within the lines, followed by the enemy. Captain Dunphy, with Company [G], Tenth Michigan Infantry, waited coolly their approach; when within close range fired, killing 1 lieutenant, 2 privates, and wounding 2 (1 mortally); promptly charging, recaptured the four wagons. The captain is a cool, gallant soldier, and commands brave men. Reports being made that there was a large body of Wheeler's cavalry in my front, Lieutenant-Colonel Pearce, commanding Second Brigade, was ordered forward. The enemy did not wait for a close approach of deployed infantry, but made a rapid retreat. Lieutenant-Colonel Langley, commanding Third Brigade, with two regiments of his command, had previously driven a party of cavalry from his front on the Alabama road, killing a captain and one private. I had no further trouble with Wheeler's command.

---

* For portion of report (here omitted) relating to operations in North Georgia and North Alabama, see Vol. XXXIX, Part I, p. 620.

December 1, leaving my train, in compliance with orders from corps headquarters, marched at 10.30 a. m. on Waynesborough road to Baker's Creek, ten miles. December 2, left camp at 8 a. m., marching ten miles; camped near Buck Head Creek. December 3, left camp at 9 a. m., crossing Buck Head and Rock Creeks, camping near railroad, ten miles. December 4, moved at 6.30, my division in the advance with its own and Third Division trains, crossing railroad at Lumpkin's Station, passing through the town of Habersham to Smith's plantation, marching sixteen miles. December 5, moved at daylight, camping at Buck Creek Post-Office, having marched sixteen miles. December 6, moved at 6.30 a. m., crossing Buck and Black Creeks, camping after a march of eighteen miles; road badly obstructed by fallen trees; removed them during the night. December 7, left camp at 6.30 a. m., and marching fifteen miles camped at ——— plantation, twenty-six miles from Savannah; road badly obstructed by fallen trees, but by heavy details removed them, causing but little delay. The bridge at Ebenezer Creek having been destroyed (two miles in our front), Colonel Buell's command went actively to work to construct a new one. December 8, the bridge having been completed, left camp at 10 a. m., crossing Ebenezer Creek, marched to Little Ebenezer Creek, where, after a delay of several hours for completion of pontoon, moved forward to Kegler's Creek. Just after going into camp received orders from General Davis to return to Little Ebenezer to protect the train of the corps, an attack being apprehended; returned, and the Second and Third Brigades recrossing the creek bivouacked for the night, having marched ten miles. December 9, left camp at 7 a. m., marching eight miles and constructing three bridges. At Doctor Cuyler's plantation, about fourteen miles and a half from Savannah, my advance came within range and fire of a rebel battery. Two regiments of the Third Brigade were at once deployed as skirmishers on the right and left of the road, and one piece of the battery ordered forward. This piece was soon in position and opened fire, which was spiritedly answered by some well-directed shots. Lieutenant Coe, commanding battery, was struck by a shell and instantly killed; a brave, good officer. By order subsequently received from corps commander the First and Third Brigades were placed in position. During the night the works in our front were abandoned. December 10, left camp at 8 a. m., marching four miles; found the Twentieth Corps moving upon our road; went into camp. December 11, received orders to relieve Seventeenth Corps. Left camp at 8 a. m., marching seven miles. Went into position on the right of the Milledgeville road, remaining in this position until the 22d. During this time steady approaches were being made to within 300 yards of the enemy's works. On the night of the 20th succeeded in getting two guns in fine position. Just before daylight my skirmishers entered the abandoned works of the enemy, thus closing a brilliant and successful campaign.

With a few exceptions all have faithfully performed their duties. To Lieutenant-Colonel Pearce, commanding Second Brigade (in the absence of Colonel Mitchell), and Lieutenant-Colonel Langley, commanding Third Brigade (in the absence of Colonel Dilworth), I am under obligations for their promptness in executing all orders. They are good officers, and ought to be promoted.

My staff officers are deserving of all praise for constant and active attention to duty, and I again, as in my former reports, recommend them for promotion, having from long and faithful service earned it.

I close this report with stating: First, that since the fall of Atlanta my division has marched 560 miles, and by railroad, 406; second, captured 189 horses, 586 mules, 6 jacks and 1 jenny, and 418 head of cattle, in addition to the number used during the campaign; third, 17 miles of railroad destroyed; fourth, but three rations of bread and two of salt meat were issued to my command from Atlanta to Savannah, the men always having an abundant supply furnished by forage details; fifth, the mules of my trains and artillery horses were in much finer condition at the end than at the commencement of the campaign; sixth, no cotton gins, cotton, nor other property destroyed by my order.

Casualties: Killed, 8; wounded, 16; missing, 57; total, 81.

All of which is respectfully submitted.

JAMES D. MORGAN,
Brigadier-General, Commanding Second Division.

[Lieut. Col. A. C. McCLURG,
Assistant Adjutant-General.

Consolidated casualty report of Second Division, Fourteenth Army Corps, from September 3 to December 22, 1864.

Command	Killed.		Wounded.		Missing.		Total.		Aggregate.
	Officers.	Men.	Officers.	Men.	Officers.	Men.	Officers.	Men.	
First Brigade	.....	2	.....	3	.....	9	.....	14	14
Second Brigade	.....	1	.....	6	.....	20	.....	27	27
Third Brigade	.....	4	.....	7	.....	28	.....	39	39
Battery I, Second Illinois Artillery	1	.....	.....	.....	.....	.....	1	.....	1
Grand total	1	7	.....	16	.....	57	1	80	81

No. 64.

Journal of Second Division.

November 15.—Division moved at 6 a. m.; crossed the river and arrived at rebel works at 10 a. m.; closed on transportation of First Division; halted until 1.30 p. m., then moved to camp southeast of town. Town on fire at several places, which spread by dark to the main part of town. Orders to move at 12 m. to-morrow, following Twentieth Corps; order from General Sherman announcing the army divided into two wings: General Howard to command the Right (Fifteenth and Seventeenth Corps), General Slocum the Left (Fourteenth and Twentieth Corps); Right Wing gone toward Jonesborough, and Twentieth Corps to the left this morning; quartermaster busy issuing clothing to-night.

November 16.—Division moved at 11 a. m. in the rear of First and Third Divisions; marched ten miles; camped on Snapfinger Creek; headquarters at Lee's house.

November 17.—Division moved at 7 a. m.; marched sixteen miles, passing through Lithonia, destroying four miles of railroad, commencing one mile and a half east of town, camping at Conyers Station, thirty miles from Atlanta by railroad.

November 18.—Division moved at 6 a. m.; marched sixteen miles, crossing Yellow River and Ulcofauhachee; camped half a mile east of latter stream. Troops destroyed three miles of railroad east from Covington; trains passed through town.

November 19.—Division moved at 6 a. m.; marched twenty miles, passing through Sandtown, or Newborn, camping one mile from Shady Grove.

November 20 (Sunday).—Division moved at 7 a. m.; marched fourteen miles, camping one mile west of Little, or Eatonton, Factories, burning them.

November 21.—Division moved at 7 a. m.; marched twelve miles; camped south of Cedar Creek; rained most of the day; roads very heavy; a number of mules brought into camp.

November 22.—In camp; Third and First Divisions and pontoon train passed to our front; General Sherman stopped two hours and a half, and General Davis took dinner with us. Sherman was in fine spirits; told story of the soldier foraging liberally, and that no one could tell where this army would concentrate.

November 23.—Division moved at 6 a. m.; marched fourteen miles, camping two miles from Milledgeville; Twentieth Corps in town; First and Third Divisions in our front.

November 24.—Division moved at 10 a. m.; marched ten miles, passing through Milledgeville, crossing Oconee River and passing Third Division. Band of First Brigade played "Dixie" as the column passed the capitol. Headquarters at Brundage's plantation.

November 25.—Division moved at 6 a. m.; marched twelve miles, crossing Buffalo Creek, which was pontooned; trains late into camp.

November 26.—Division moved at 6 a. m; marched six miles to Sandersville; advance met Wheeler's cavalry one mile and a half from town. Stragglers and foragers put on a skirmish line, with which they were pushed to the edge of town, where one regiment was deployed and the town cleared. One man of the One hundred and eighth Ohio killed and one other wounded. Camped by 10 o'clock in town.

November 27.—Division moved at 7 a. m., following Third Division, leaving main train in charge of Lieutenant Coe, taking the Augusta road; then the right on Louisville road; stopped for dinner at Williamson's Swamp, crossing it at Chickasaw Ford; marched seventeen miles, camping on Hodgson's plantation; 300 negroes; 580 bales of cotton burned; storeroom with books, &c., from Savannah destroyed; crossed Ogeechee River this afternoon.

November 28.—Division moved at 6 a. m.; marched nine miles, crossing Rocky Comfort Creek, over which the bridge was burned. The rear of the division got over a little after dark. General was a long while finding his headquarters; camp at Louisville.

November 29.—Division in camp; Lieutenant Coe, with trains, arrived at 1 p. m.; Twentieth Corps passed to the right on road No. 10; foragers driven in on the left, many of them intoxicated. Discovered in the evening that my trunk had been left at William G. Brown's, at Sandersville.

November 30.—In camp; Wheeler's cavalry in our front drove in our foragers early in the morning. Colonel Langley, with four regiments, sent out on the left, who killed one captain and two men. Lieutenant Coe, with five wagons and five companies, were attacked a short distance from picket-line; Captain Dunphy, Tenth Michigan, drove the enemy back, killing three and wounding four, which broke them, so that he saved the five wagons and companies; wounded rebels reported them two brigades strong.

December 1.—Division moved at 10 a. m., taking charge of Third Division transportation, which passed to our front, then on a road to our left; marched twelve miles, camping on Baker's Creek.

December 2.—Division moved at 8 a. m.; marched ten miles, camping in rear ot Twentieth Corps, two miles northeast of Birdville.

December 3.—Division moved at 8 a. m.; marched ten miles, crossing Buck Head Creek on pontoons; negroes stopped, near 500; Fourteenth Michigan left to come up with Colonel Buell; camped near Lumpkin's Station, Augusta and Millen railroad.

December 4.—Division moved at 6.30 a. m., Second Brigade in advance; took dinner at Hargrove's plantation, eight miles east of railroad; made a day's march of fourteen miles; passed through town of Habersham.

December 5.—Division moved at 6.30 a. m.; marched sixteen miles, camping at Buck Creek Post-Office, six miles from Savannah River, at the mouth of Brier Creek.

December 6.—Division moved at 6.30 a. m.; marched eighteen miles, camping at a swamp, where the road was badly obstructed.

December 7.—Division moved at 6.30 a. m.; marched fifteen miles, camping at Rohrer's plantation, two miles from Ebenezer Creek, three-quarters of a mile from Savannah River, and twenty-six miles from Savannah. Passed two swamps which were badly obstructed by fallen timber.

December 8.—Division moved at 10 a. m.; crossed Large Ebenezer and waited till 3 p. m. for Colonel Buell to pontoon Little Ebenezer; then crossed and marched four miles; at dark were ordered back to Little Ebenezer; Second and Third Brigades encamped north and First Brigade and battery south of creek. Colonel Buell was all night and till 10 a. m. making a bridge over Large Ebenezer; marched twelve miles.

December 9.—Division moved at 7 a. m. from Little Ebenezer; marched eight miles, building two bridges; struck rebel works fourteen miles from Savannah; Lieutenant Coe, commanding battery, killed. Went into camp at dark, one mile from rebel works; headquarters at Cuyler's plantation. Many old papers found in the house; Doctor Watson got a deed dated December 5, 1758; heavy cannonading toward Savannah.

December 10.—Division moved at 7 a. m.; marched four miles, camping at the Ten-Mile house. Rebels left our front last night; Twentieth Corps passed on toward town, road joining at this point. Heavy cannonading most of the day toward Savannah.

December 11.—Received orders at 7.30 a. m. for the division to move to the right of Twentieth Corps. Marched five miles to the front, then passed to the right, crossing Macon railroad, and a mile to the front on Milledgeville road, where we relieved a division of the Seventeenth Corps with First and Second Brigades; Third Brigade, in reserve, save one regiment taken by Captain Munson on picket; Seventeenth Corps moved round to the right.

December 12.—Second Brigade relieved by part of Twentieth Corps and moved to the right of First Brigade, Third Brigade destroying railroad in afternoon. Hospital and supply trains came up during the day; had got into a bad swamp the night before by orders from General Davis. Gun-boat driven up the river and one transport captured by Twentieth Corps.

December 13.—Part of Third Brigade destroying railroad in the forenoon; wagon train sent to the river for rice. General, and Captains Race and Stinson visited a rice plantation and the river this afternoon; first sight of Savannah.

December 14.—General Sherman's order announcing the capture of Fort McAllister and opening of communication with Commodores Farragut and Porter and Foster's army received; no change of troops.

No. 65.

Report of Col. Robert F. Smith, Sixteenth Illinois Infantry, commanding First Brigade.

HDQRS. FIRST BRIG., SECOND DIV., 14TH ARMY CORPS,
Near Savannah, Ga., January 3, 1865.

CAPTAIN:*

After having been furnished with clothing the command broke camp on the day following [November 16], and marched through Decatur, from there to Lithonia Station. Here the work of destroying the railroad was resumed. The track was torn up, the ties burnt, and the rails bent and twisted. From Lithonia to Conyers, and farther to Covington, the Georgia Central Railroad was most effectually destroyed. On the 23d of November the command arrived at Milledgeville. On the following day passed through the town, crossed the Oconee River on the old bridge and the eastern branch on pontoons. On approaching Sandersville, November 26, in the morning, some rebel cavalry tried to oppose our march, but were dislodged and forced back by our advance guard and two companies of the Sixteenth Illinois and Seventeenth New York Infantry, who, having marched ahead of the column for forage, were ordered up on the skirmish line and did good service. The command remained at Sandersville over night, and resumed the march on the following morning. The Ogeechee River and its tributaries were crossed without any considerable difficulty, and in the evening, November 28, the troops passed through Louisville and went into camp. Here the command remained during the following two days. The rebel cavalry annoyed our pickets and came near capturing a foraging party of the Seventeenth Regiment New York Infantry, but for the prompt action of Lieutenant-Colonel Martin, who brought the whole regiment out in time to save the foraging party. Several rebels were killed and wounded by our pickets on November 30.

On the 1st of December the command left Louisville, and after crossing several creeks entered the pine country, passed Habersham and Jacksonborough, and on the 8th of December struck the Savannah River and crossed Ebenezer Creek. Here a rebel gun-boat threw a few shells at our column, doing no damage. In the afternoon, December 9, it was found that the enemy had erected a battery at the point where the Middle Ground and river roads meet. Some cannonading took place in the evening. This brigade was encamped near the rebel works over night. In the morning the position was found evacuated by the enemy, and the column moved on to Monteith Station, on the Charleston and Savannah Railroad and the Milledgeville road, and took up a position between the last-named road and the Ogeechee Canal. In this position the command remained until the evacuation of Savannah. The operations in front of Savannah were, from the nature of the ground, limited to some attempts to push forward sharpshooters to cover the guns of a rebel battery which commanded the Milledgeville road and the Georgia Central Railroad track. A deep swamp in our front was found impassable, and breast-works thrown up in the road proved of little use, as the caliber of their guns enabled the enemy to demolish them in short time. A breast-work for a battery and a rifle-pit constructed by Maj. J. H. McDonald would probably have had sufficient power to resist the rebel balls, but was not completed until the

*For portion of report (here omitted) relating to operations in North Georgia and North Alabama, see Vol. XXXIX, Part I, p. 636.

night before the enemy retreated. The rebel batteries kept up a desultory fire day and night, throwing shot and shell, grape and canister, but the intervening woods prevented them from getting an accurate range of our position, and consequently no harm was done except in one case, where a man of the Seventeenth New York Infantry was struck by a solid shot which tore off one of his legs, causing his death on the following day. A splinter of a tree, cut off by the same ball, slightly wounded another man of the same regiment. For other casualties on this march I beg leave to refer to the report of casualties already forwarded.

With the exception of four days' rations of bread and meal, and about half rations of sugar and coffee, this command drew all its subsistence from the country after leaving Atlanta. The exact amount of supplies of every kind drawn from the country cannot be ascertained, but it may be estimated as equivalent to about 65,000 rations. Of forage not even an approximate estimate can be had, the number of horses and mules in the command varying daily, almost hourly. According to reports from the different regiments of this brigade 110 mules and 61 horses were captured. The number of negroes who followed the column cannot be ascertained with anything like accuracy. It may be safely stated, however, that not less than 100 colored persons were with the brigade on arriving in front of Savannah. The commanding officer of the Tenth Regiment Michigan Infantry reports two cotton gins destroyed by his command, the only instance known to me of such occurrence. At Sandersville three or four bales of cotton were found hidden in a field and destroyed. Of railroad track this command destroyed about twelve miles at nearest computation.

On the 22d of December the army entered the city of Savannah and this brigade was moved to its present location.

Very respectfully, your obedient servant,

R. F. SMITH,
Colonel, Commanding.

Capt. T. WISEMAN,
Asst. Adjt. Gen., Second Division, Fourteenth Army Corps.

No. 66.

Report of Capt. Eben White, Sixteenth Illinois Infantry.

HEADQUARTERS SIXTEENTH ILLINOIS INFANTRY,
*Near Savannah, Ga., January 1, 1865.**

The regiment was here [Atlanta] clothed and equipped, and marched on November 16, following the Georgia railroad to Covington, Ga., from thence to Milledgeville, and from that place in a southeasterly direction to the Savannah River, and down the right bank of that stream to the city of Savannah, which place was invested on the 11th and occupied on the 21st of December, 1864.

Subsistence.—After leaving Atlanta there was issued to the regiment but three days' rations of hard bread and sugar and ten days' rations of coffee. The men obtained all other necessary articles of subsistence and many luxuries in the greatest abundance from the country along the route, which afforded sweet potatoes, chickens, turkeys, and other provisions in larger quantities than could be consumed by the men.

* For portion of report (here omitted) relating to operations in North Georgia and North Alabama, see Vol. XXXIX, Part I, p. 637.

Horses, mules, &c.—The regiment captured on the recent campaign 10 horses and 20 mules, most of which were unusually large and in splendid condition. But few cattle or sheep were taken more than the regiment required for its own use.

Negroes.—There accompanied the regiment to the city of Savannah only six negroes (males), all of whom are used by officers as servants. Large numbers of both sexes and all ages were prohibited from following the command, in obedience to stringent orders issued on that subject from superior headquarters.

Railroads, &c., destroyed.—The regiment on the march from Cartersville to Savannah destroyed about three miles of railroad and one railroad bridge over Pumpkin Vine Creek. Large quantities of fence rails were burned; no cotton gins nor presses were destroyed by the regiment.

Respectfully submitted.

EBEN WHITE,
Captain, Commanding Regiment.

Capt. JOHN P. HOLLERS,
Actg. Asst. Adjt. Gen., 1st Brig., 2d Div., 14th Army Corps.

No. 67.

Report of Maj. James H. McDonald, Sixtieth Illinois Infantry.

HDQRS. SIXTIETH ILLINOIS VETERAN VOL. INFANTRY,
Savannah, Ga., January 3, 1865.

SIR:*

On November 16, 1864, marched from Atlanta on the Augusta road, via Covington, Milledgeville, Sandersville, Louisville, and thence to Savannah, Ga., a distance of 310 miles. Struck the enemy's lines three miles from the city on the 11th of December, 1864. On the march we foraged liberally off the country; subsisted off the country twenty days. Captured 21 mules, 20 horses, and 25 negroes. All property has been turned over to the proper authority. Loss on the entire march, 1 man captured, 1 died of disease. Total distance marched, 551 miles; total distance by railroad, 380 miles; grand total, 931 miles.

Very respectfully, your obedient servant,

J. H. McDONALD,
Major, Comdg. Sixtieth Illinois Veteran Volunteer Infantry.

ACTG. ASST. ADJT. GEN., FIRST BRIGADE, SECOND DIVISION.

No. 68.

Report of Capt. Charles H. Richman, Tenth Michigan Infantry.

HDQRS. TENTH MICHIGAN VETERAN VOL. INFANTRY,
Near Savannah, Ga., January 3, 1865.†

November 14, marched at 5 a. m.; passed Big Shanty at 8.15; moved to the right of Kenesaw Mountain; went into camp five miles from

*For portion of report (here omitted) relating to operations in North Georgia and North Alabama, see Vol. XXXIX, Part I, p. 638.

†For portion of report (here omitted) relating to operations in North Georgia and and North Alabama, see Vol. XXXIX, Part I, p. 638.

Chattahoochee River at 4.30 p. m. November 15, marched at 6 a. m.; reached Atlanta 2 p. m.; went southeast of city and camped; drew clothing and rations. November 16, were ordered to move at 7 a. m., but did not [get] started till 11 a. m.; went on Augusta road to right of Stone Mountain; camped at 7 p. m. November 17, moved at 6.30 a. m.; reached Lithonia 1.15 p. m.; went three miles farther and commenced destruction of railroad; burned about ——; went into camp at Conyers Station at 7 p. m. November 18, marched at 6 a. m.; were train guards; reached Covington 1.15 p. m.; here left the railroad to our left and went toward Eatonton; camped at 4 p. m. November 19, marched at 6 a. m.; rainy; made camp at 4.30 p. m. November 20, marched at 6.45 a. m.; were in advance of the corps; went to one mile of Eatonton Factory. November 21, moved at 6.45 a. m.; camped at sundown at Cedar Creek. November 23, started at 6 a. m.; camped at sundown two miles from Milledgeville. November 24, moved at 9.40 a. m.; reached Milledgeville 10.20; crossed Oconee River and went into camp six miles from town. November 25, marched at 6 a. m.; camped from 7 to 10.30 p. m. six miles from Sandersville; were train guards. November 26, marched at 6.15 a. m.; went into town 9.15; went to east side of town and camped. November 27, marched at 6 a. m.; camped at sundown. November 28, moved at 7 a. m.; camped at 8.30 p. m. one mile east of Louisville; here remained until December 1. The regiment had three companies on grand guard east of camp, when were attacked by about —— mounted infantry. Our men charged and drove them across an open field, where they rallied and tried to drive our men back, but failed. The enemy lost three killed and several wounded. No loss on our side.

December 1, started at 12 m.; went into camp 7.30 p. m. December 2, moved at 9 a. m.; were train guards; halted about sundown. December 3, marched at 10 a. m.; were train guards; went into camp between 11 p. m. and 2 a. m. the 4th. December 4, started about 8 a. m.; crossed the Augusta railroad at 10 a. m.; went into camp at 7 p. m. December 5, moved at 6.30 a. m.; went into camp at Buck Creek, on old River road; regiment on grand guard. December 6, brigade in rear; moved at 10 a. m.; went into camp at 9 p. m. December 7, moved at 7.30; camped near Ebenezer Creek soon after dark. December 8, marched at 10 a. m.; went about seven miles and camped, where remained until 8.30 p. m.; then went back three miles; moved very slow; camped at 11.30 p. m. December 9, moved at 7.30 a. m.; made camp at 4 p. m. December 10, moved at 7.30; went to railroad and remained until 3.30, when went on grand guard on Augusta road. December 11, at 9 a. m. were relieved; went to Conyer's, and on toward Savannah; went to five miles of town; crossed to right of Georgia Central Railroad; went into position near Telfair Station, and about four miles and a half from the city; no calls allowed to be sounded or camp fires at night. December 14, had orders to lay out camp in regular order. December 16 and 20, regiment on grand guard. December 21, had orders to be ready to move at 8 a. m., but did not start until about 9 a. m. the 22d; went about one mile and a half nearer the city and went into camp.

Distance marched during the month of October, 210 miles; November, 233 miles; December, 126 miles; total, 569 miles.

Respectfully submitted.

CHAS. H. RICHMAN,
Captain, Commanding Regiment.

Capt. JOHN P. HOLLERS,
Acting Assistant Adjutant-General, First Brigade, &c.

Amount of forage and subsistence, &c., captured by the Tenth Michigan Infantry Veteran Volunteers during the march from Atlanta to Savannah, Ga.

Flour	pounds	3,300	Long forage ... pounds	6,000
Corn meal	do	5,300	Short forage ... do	5,000
Sugar	do	250	Horses captured	19
Salt	do	450	Mules captured	23
Pork (live hogs)	do	16,000	Negroes that followed regiment	20
Beef (on foot)	do	1,000	Cotton gins burned	2
Rice	do	700	Railroad destroyed ... miles	1½
Sirup	gallons	335		

Respectfully submitted.

CHAS. H. RICHMAN,
Captain, Commanding Regiment.

HEADQUARTERS TENTH MICHIGAN INFANTRY,
Near Savannah, January 3, 1865.

No. 69.

Report of Lieut. Col. Joel O. Martin, Seventeenth New York Infantry.

HDQRS. SEVENTEENTH REGT. NEW YORK VET. VOLS.,
Camp, near Savannah, December 30, 1864.

CAPTAIN:*

Fitted out my command with clothing during the night, and the next morning [November 16] we were ready for another campaign. Left Atlanta at 2 p. m. November 16; worked at tearing up the railroad from Atlanta to Covington. November 17 and 18, without rations or chance to forage. November 24, marched through the city of Milledgeville. November 26, Captain Wilde, Company A, of my regiment, was placed on the skirmish line at Sandersville by General Morgan; had a lively little skirmish with the enemy and were among the first to enter the town. November 28, went into camp near Louisville, where we remained till December 1. On the 30th I sent out a foraging party of forty men under command of Lieutenant Magee. I soon learned that a force of the enemy's cavalry had come between them and our picket and that they were cut off. I endeavored to make my way to them, but was unable to do so. The enemy chased me back to the picket-line, where three of them were killed. I found that my little party of foragers were fighting against a greatly superior force; that their retreat was completely cut off and they were in imminent danger of being captured. There was no time to report these facts to my commanding officer. I was satisfied that my foraging party were lost if they did not have immediate assistance. I moved my regiment out rapidly, sending word to Colonel Smith of my movements. Found the pickets driven back and the enemy occupying their position. Formed line and advanced rapidly upon the enemy. They fell back before us about half a mile, uncovering my foraging party and giving them a chance to join us. Awaited orders from General Morgan and moved back to camp. Nothing of special interest took place on the march from Louisville to the front of Savannah. Reached the latter place December 12. Threw up an earth-work in front of my camp. My command was employed in this work, making fascines, picket duty, &c.,

*For portion of report (here omitted) relating to operations in North Georgia and North Alabama, see Vol. XXXIX, Part I, p. 639.

till the fall of Savannah, December 21. I should judge my command had torn up four or five miles of railroad altogether, captured about 30 mules and 10 horses, no cattle; no cotton gins were destroyed; no negroes were allowed to follow the regiment except those employed as officers' servants.

From the time we left Atlanta, November 16, till December 12 my command received from the Government but four days' rations of bread and meal and about half rations of sugar and coffee. The rest of the food which the men had was picked up by foraging parties along the line of march sent out from the regiment. All the forage for the animals from the time we left Atlanta till the fall of Savannah was gathered in the country.

I had 2 men wounded and 1 killed in front of Savannah.

The regiment left Atlanta September 28 with aggregate strength of 307; arrived in front of Savannah, Ga., December 12 with an aggregate of 356, showing a gain of 49.

I am, captain, very respectfully, your obedient servant,

J. O. MARTIN,
Lieut. Col., Comdg. Seventeenth New York Veteran Vols.

Capt. JOHN P. HOLLERS,
Actg. Asst. Adjt. Gen., 1st Brig., 2d Div., 14th Army Corps.

No. 70.

Report of Lieut. Col. John S. Pearce, Ninety-eighth Ohio Infantry, commanding Second Brigade.

HDQRS. SECOND BRIG., SECOND DIV., 14TH ARMY CORPS,
In Camp, near Savannah, Ga., December 31, 1864.

CAPTAIN:*

November 14, marched twenty miles toward Atlanta, Ga., passing to the right of Marietta, Ga. November 15, arrived in Atlanta after marching twelve miles. Here we remained until the following day, November 16, when, in pursuance of previous orders from the commanding general-in-chief, we took up our line of march at 11 o'clock on the Decatur road for what had been before announced in Special Field Orders, No. 119, headquarters Military Division of the Mississippi, in the field, Kingston, Ga., November 8, 1864—a departure from our present base and a long and difficult march to a new one, and after marching eleven miles encamped for the night three miles southeast of Decatur, passing through that place late in the afternoon. November 17, marching through Lithonia, encamped within a mile of Conyers, distance eighteen miles, destroying three-quarters of a mile of railroad. On the morning of the 18th we crossed Yellow River on pontoons, and passing through Covington, the county seat of Newton County, Ga., we crossed the Ulcofauhachee River, and after destroying half a mile of railroad encamped one mile beyond that river, having marched a distance of eighteen miles. November 19, marched seventeen miles and bivouacked south of Sandtown. November 20, marched eighteen miles and bivouacked within three miles of Eatonton. November 21, marched ten miles, crossing Murder Creek, and went into camp, there remaining until the morning of the 23d; very cold. November 23, passing

---

* For portion of report (here omitted) relating to operations in North Georgia and North Alabama, see Vol. XXXIX, Part I, p. 640.

through one of Howell Cobb's plantations, we marched and bivouacked for the night within one mile and a half of Milledgeville, Ga.; distance marched, fifteen miles. On the following day we passed through Milledgeville and bivouacked for the night eight miles beyond the Oconee River, which stream we crossed about midday. On the following day we marched twelve miles, crossing Buffalo Creek on pontoons, and bivouacked for the night. November 26, marched toward Sandersville, Washington County, Ga., and when within about two miles of that place we met the enemy's cavalry. The brigade having the advance that day I was ordered by General Morgan, commanding the division, to send forward a regiment to support the skirmish line which had been formed from the several foraging parties of the division. The One hundred and thirteenth Ohio Volunteer Infantry, commanded by Captain Jones, being on the right of the brigade, I sent it forward, when the skirmishers advanced, driving the enemy through the town, this regiment following and being the first to enter the place. We marched ten miles this day and encamped a short distance east of Sandersville. November 27, marched sixteen miles and bivouacked for the night within three miles of the Ogeechee River. November 28, resumed march early in the morning, and crossing Rocky Comfort Creek encamped one mile beyond Louisville; distance marched, ten miles. On following day went into camp and here remained until December 1. On November 30 Captain Watson, One hundred and thirteenth Regiment Ohio Volunteer Infantry, having been sent out with six companies of the regiment as train guard, met the enemy's cavalry, and after a lively skirmish with them was driven back to the picket-line, losing 2 wounded and 7 men prisoners. The balance of the brigade having been ordered out by General Morgan to their support, the enemy soon dispersed, when we returned to camp.

December 1, marching eleven miles, encamped for the night. On the following day the brigade was rear guard for the train, and owing to broken bridges, swamps, and bad roads, the command, with the train, did not get into camp until 2 o'clock the following morning; distance marched, twelve miles. On the following day, December 3, marched sixteen miles toward Savannah and bivouacked for the night near Lumpkin's Station, on the Augusta and Waynesborough Railroad. December 4, marched eighteen miles, passing through the town of Habersham, and encamped for the night. December 5, was again train guard and marched sixteen miles, encamping near Buck Head Creek Church. On this march we met with considerable obstructions from the enemy, but they were soon removed by our troops. December 6, marched sixteen miles toward Savannah, and bivouacked for the night on main Savannah and Augusta road. December 7, roads blockaded, obstructions removed, and the brigade marched twelve miles, encamping near Little Ebenezer Creek. On the following day we crossed Little and Big Ebenezer Creeks, and after marching four miles beyond the latter stream, we countermarched and returned to the immediate neighborhood of Ebenezer Church; distance in all marched, fourteen miles. December 9, marched nine miles toward Savannah, encountering rebel artillery. December 10, marched four miles to Charleston and Savannah Railroad and went into camp. On the following morning the brigade marched five miles toward Savannah and relieved a brigade of the Seventeenth Army Corps on the Charleston and Savannah Railroad, where it remained until the evening of the 12th, when, by orders from General Morgan, it relieved the First Brigade, First Division, Fourteenth Army Corps, on the right of the Macon and Savannah Railroad, where we remained until the fall of Savannah, which took place on the morning of the 21st instant. On the following day we moved to our present camp, within one mile and three-quarters of Savannah. During the campaign to Florence, Ala., and to the time of our return to Atlanta—in all, forty-six days—there were regularly issued to the brigade thirty-five days' rations hard bread, corn meal, and flour; thirteen days' rations salt meat; twenty-eight days' rations fresh beef—total meat, forty-one days; thirty-five days' rations coffee; thirty-four days' rations brown sugar; thirty days' rations salt; twenty days' rations desiccated potatoes; five days' rations soap.

The country through which we marched in the North Alabama campaign, as a general thing, and especially that portion lying between Florence and Athens, contained large quantities of meat, breadstuff, and forage of all kinds, but from the fact that the division was reasonably well supplied with Government rations, and the close proximity of the enemy rendering it important that the entire command should be held well together, General Morgan did not permit but little foraging to be done until we arrived at Gaylesville, Ala., where it became necessary, owing to the scarcity of the regular rations. Whilst we did not, for the most of the time, want for enough to eat, yet for the reasons before stated there was much suffering. The general health of the brigade was good, however.

During the campaign from Atlanta to Savannah, and up to the time of the fall of the city—a period of thirty-six days—the brigade received through the commissary five and a half days' rations of bread, five and a half days' rations of salt meat, thirty-one days' rations of coffee, eighteen days' rations of sugar, twenty-four days' rations of salt, seven and three-quarters days' rations of pease, one day's rations of pepper, ten days' rations of soap. These were all the rations that were issued. The balance of the subsistence for the brigade was drawn from the country by regularly organized foraging parties.

On the campaign from Atlanta to Savannah the brigade foraging party consisted of a certain number of mounted and foot soldiers from each regiment. Over each regimental detail was one commissioned officer in charge, and over all was appointed an additional officer, who had general supervision of the foraging for the brigade. The country through which we passed abounding in all kinds of meat—salt, as well fresh—sweet potatoes, turnips, and other vegetables; molasses, corn meal, flour, rice, and an almost inexhaustible quantity of corn, corn fodder, oats—threshed and in the sheaf—it was very seldom, indeed, that the foraging party failed to amply supply the men and animals of the brigade with forage and provisions for each day they had not the regular ration. Large quantities of salt were found on the march, and near Louisville several pounds of green coffee. During the entire march from Atlanta to Savannah the weather was fine: the roads, except when passing through swamps, good, and but seldom obstructed by the enemy, and then, as a general thing, so triflingly that but little delay was occasioned thereby. The health of the command was most excellent and the spirits buoyant, but very few, if any, even speculating of disaster or failure in the accomplishment of that which all felt and believed would be a severe blow against the rebellion. The brigade destroyed in all about five miles of railroad and captured 139 mules and 99 horses. The number of negroes following the brigade was 193. I have no knowledge of the destruction of any cotton gins or cotton by my command or any portion of it. If any were destroyed by any portion of the command it was done without my order, knowledge, or consent, and I am satisfied without the order, knowledge, or consent of the regimental commanders. I at no time received any order from the corps commander (to whom alone was, by Special Field Orders, No. 120, Military Division of the Mississippi, intrusted the power to destroy such) for the destruction of any cotton gin or gins or cotton. I have, therefore, none to report. It would be impossible for me to even approximate to a correct statement of the forage and supplies obtained by the brigade. In order to give some idea of the amount, I have already stated the number of days for which we were fully and regularly rationed, both on the North Alabama campaign and the campaign to Savannah; now I will give the aggregate number of officers and men, horses and mules of the brigade in each campaign, then add that of provisions and forage gathered from the country. The men and animals had at all times abundance. The aggregate number of officers and men of the brigade in the North Alabama campaign was 1,600; horses and mules, 48, for which forage was exclusively drawn from the country. In the latter campaign to Savannah the aggregate of officers and men of the brigade was 1,843; horses and mules, 380, for all of which abundance of forage and provisions was at all times obtained from the country through which we passed.

Accompanying this report you will find a full list of the casualties in the brigade from the 29th of September to the fall of Savannah.* The total number of miles traveled by rail by the brigade on the North Alabama campaign was 334 miles; total number of miles marched on the same campaign up to November 15, when the brigade arrived at Atlanta, 134 miles; total number of miles marched on the campaign from Atlanta to Savannah was 284 miles, making in all a distance of 752 miles.

I would be doing injustice to those who deserve otherwise were I to close this report without acknowledging that the regimental commanders of this brigade—Lieut. Col. M. R. Vernon, Seventy-eighth Illinois Volunteer Infantry; Maj. Frederick Beck, One hundred and eighth Ohio Volunteer Infantry; Maj. A. B. Robinson, One hundred and twenty-first Ohio Volunteer Infantry; Capt. Peter Ege, Thirty-fourth Illinois Veteran Volunteer Infantry; Capt. Toland Jones, One hundred and thirteenth Ohio Volunteer Infantry; Capt. J. R. McLaughlin, Ninety-eighth Ohio Volunteer Infantry—have at all times been most prompt in the execution of all orders intrusted to them, and, in assisting along the trains, removing obstructions, building and repairing bridges, and preserving discipline in their respective commands, displayed a praiseworthy energy and resolution.

The One hundred and eighth Ohio Volunteer Infantry was not with the brigade on the Florence campaign. It rejoined the command on the 17th of November.

Of the members of the brigade staff—Maj. T. B. Williams, One hundred and twenty-first Ohio Volunteer Infantry, surgeon-in-chief; Capt. J. S. Wilson, assistant adjutant-general, U. S. Volunteers; Capt. J. Van Brimer, One hundred and twenty-first Ohio Volunteer Infantry, assistant commissary of subsistence; Capt. Joseph Swisher, One hundred and thirteenth Ohio Volunteer Infantry, acting assistant quartermaster; Capt. Hiram J. Craft, Ninety-eighth Ohio Volunteer Infantry, acting assistant inspector-general; Capt. G. H. Reynolds, Seventy-eighth Illinois, provost-marshal; First Lieut. W. C. Robinson, Thirty-fourth Illinois Veteran Volunteer Infantry, acting aide-de-camp; Sec-

*Not found.

ond Lieut. O. M. Scott, One hundred and twenty-first Ohio Volunteer Infantry, acting ordnance officer—I must say in justice to them they could not have been more faithful, vigilant, prompt, energetic, and courteous in their discharge of their several offices than they have been.

I have the honor to be, captain, very respectfully, your obedient servant,

[J. S. PEARCE,
Lieutenant-Colonel, Commanding.]

[Capt. T. WISEMAN,
Assistant Adjutant-General.]

No. 71.

Report of Lieut. Col. Maris R. Vernon, Seventy-eighth Illinois Infantry.

HDQRS. SEVENTY-EIGHTH REGT. ILLINOIS VOL. INFTY.,
Savannah, Ga., December 30, 1864.

CAPTAIN:*

Reached Atlanta on the 15th [November]; here drew clothing, and on the following day (16th) started upon a new campaign; marched in an easterly course ten miles. 17th, marched seventeen miles in southeast course; destroyed half a mile of railroad, and camped for the night near Conyers Station. 18th, continued the march in an easterly course, passing through Covington, Newton County; destroyed the railroad one mile east of the town; marched seventeen miles and camped for the night on Ulcofauhachee River. 19th, marched southeast twenty miles; camped near Shady Dale. 20th, marched seventeen miles and camped four miles east of Eatonton. 21st, marched eleven miles and camped on Cedar Creek; rained all day. 22d, remained in camp. 23d, marched fourteen miles and camped two miles northwest of Milledgeville. 24th, passed through Milledgeville and camped six miles east of it. 25th, marched in an easterly course nine miles. 26th, marched to Sandersville, county seat of Washington County, distance, six miles, the advance driving enemy's cavalry out of the town. 27th, marched seventeen miles, crossed Ogeechee River, and camped two miles east of it. 28th, marched eight miles, passed through Louisville, county seat of Jefferson County, and went into camp one mile north of the town. 29th, remained in camp. 30th, ordered out on Waynesborough road to the relief of the forage party reported to be surrounded by enemy's cavalry; returned to camp at dark, losing eight men captured by the enemy. In justice to Captain Akins, commanding forage detachment from Seventy-eighth Illinois, I must say it was through no neglect on his part that the men were captured. The enemy, vastly superior in number, charged upon him in front and on flank, and it was with great difficulty he evaded the capture of his whole party. As it was, he reached camp with the loss of but eight men.

December 1, marched in a southeast course nine miles on the flank, guarding wagon trains. 2d, marched east eight miles, guarding train. 3d, marched twelve miles, general course east. 4th, marched sixteen miles, general direction east; crossed Savannah and Augusta Railroad

---

* For portion of report (here omitted) relating to operations in North Georgia and North Alabama, see Vol. XXXIX, Part I, p. 642.

at Lumpkin's Station; still guarding train. 5th, marched in an easterly course seventeen miles. 6th, marched in southeasterly course twenty miles. 7th, marched in southeasterly course fourteen miles, and camped one mile from Savannah River and twenty-seven miles from the city. 8th, moved south five miles; crossed Ebenezer River, enemy demonstrating in front. 9th, moved south seven miles; struck rebel fortifications on main road leading to Savannah. 10th, enemy fell back and we advanced four miles, reaching Savannah and Charleston Railroad. 11th, moved down the railroad and went into position, relieving a part of the Seventeenth Corps, the right of the regiment resting on Savannah and Charleston Railroad some three miles from the city. December 12, relieved by Twentieth Corps and moved with the brigade two miles to the right; went into position with the right of the regiment near the canal, and some four miles from the city; remained in this position until the fall of Savannah.

There was issued to the regiment by the brigade commissary from and including the 16th of November, the date of leaving Atlanta, up to 21st of December the following amount of rations: Six days' rations bread, six days' rations bacon, six days' rations soap, six days' rations salt, twenty-four days' rations coffee, eleven days' rations sugar, nine days' rations beef. The rest required to subsist upon was foraged off the country. I am unable to give the amount brought into the regiment, but I do know the men did not suffer—in fact, they lived well.

The regiment destroyed two miles of railroad, brought in and turned over 23 head of mules, 11 head horses, and 22 head of cattle. Number of negroes that followed the regiment into camp, 23. Cotton and cotton gins destroyed, none.

In conclusion I must say that both officers and men performed the march in fine spirits; none were lost through sickness or fatigue.

I am, captain, with much respect, your obedient servant,

M. R. VERNON,
Lieutenant-Colonel, Commanding Regiment.

Capt. J. S. WILSON,
Actg. Asst. Adjt. Gen., 2d Brig., 2d Div., 14th Army Corps.

No. 72.

Report of Capt. James R. McLaughlin, Ninety-eighth Ohio Infantry.

HDQRS. NINETY-EIGHTH OHIO VOLUNTEER INFANTRY,
Near Savannah, Ga., December 29, 1864.

SIR:*

On the morning of the 16th [November] the Ninety-eighth, with the remainder of the division which formed a part of the Left Wing, Army of Georgia, left Atlanta, moving on the Augusta road. We struck the railroad near Covington, destroying about a quarter of a mile, which is all the railroad destroyed by the Ninety-eighth during the entire trip. The regiment only drew about three days' rations after leaving Atlanta until we arrived outside the defenses of Savannah. With this exception the regiment subsisted entirely off the country.

The captures made by the regiment are as follows: Horses, 20; mules, 30; cattle, 75. Number of darkies following the regiment, 12. During

* For portion of report (here omitted) relating to operations in North Georgia and North Alabama, see Vol. XXXIX, Part I, p. 642.

the entire trip from Atlanta to Savannah there were no casualties occurring in the regiment except one man who was accidentally wounded while foraging.

I have the honor to be, very respectfully, your obedient servant,

J. R. McLAUGHLIN,
Captain, Commanding.

Capt. J. S. WILSON,
Actg. Asst. Adjt. Gen., 2d Brig., 2d Div., 14th Army Corps.

No. 73.

Report of Lieut. Col. James W. Langley, One hundred and twenty-fifth Illinois Infantry, commanding Third Brigade.

HDQRS. THIRD BRIG., SECOND DIV., 14TH ARMY CORPS,
Near Savannah, Ga., January 3, 1865.

CAPTAIN: *

November 14, marched by way of Kenesaw Mountain to within four miles of Chattahoochee River. November 15, resumed march at 6 a. m., crossed the river on pontoon bridge, and reached Atlanta at 1 p. m. This may be said to finish the North Alabama campaign, having been gone from Atlanta forty-eight days instead of four as was expected. Before reaching Atlanta I sent orders to Captain Hall, commanding a small detachment of the brigade at that place, to procure guns, accouterments, and ammunition for every man in his command able to march, and I also had requisitions made by regimental commanders for the amount of such ordnance stores required to perfectly equip their commands. I had also an officer detailed from each regiment to take these requisitions to Atlanta and give them their personal attention. These were sent from Kingston as soon as I received intelligence that we would shortly cut loose from our "old base," but they failed to get the men properly armed in consequence of the surplus ordnance stores having been shipped from Atlanta before their arrival. This left my command on reaching Atlanta short fifty-four guns and accouterments. From Kingston also I directed my brigade quartermaster to proceed to Atlanta and draw his estimate of clothing and allowance of transportation. This he did to my entire satisfaction, having procured a sufficient number of shoes to give every man two pairs, the result of which was that upon our arrival at Savannah I had not a barefooted soldier in my command.

The Third Brigade, comprising 1,721 total commissioned officers and enlisted men present, left Atlanta November 16, at 12 m., and marched on the Decatur road nine miles and camped for the night. November 17, marched at 7 a. m., by way of Lithonia to Conyers Station. During the afternoon of this day we tore up and destroyed three miles railroad track and ties. November 18, marched at 6 a. m. on the Covington road, and camped for the night three miles east of that town. To-day the brigade destroyed two miles and a half of railroad track and ties; to-day also we began to subsist off the country. November 19, marched at 6 a. m.; crossed Ulcofauhachee River, and went into camp at dark near Shady Dale. November 20, marched at 7 a. m. and camped at night near Eatonton Factory. November 21, marched at 6 a. m. and

---

* For portion of report (here omitted) relating to operations in North Georgia and North Alabama, see Vol. XXXIX, Part I, p. 643.

camped at night on east side of Cedar Creek. November 22, laid still to-day and let First and Third Divisions of the corps pass by. November 23, marched at 6 a. m., with two regiments as train guards and two as rear guard. Camped at night within two miles of Milledgeville, the rear guard reaching camp at 9.30 p. m. November 24, marched at 10 a. m. through Milledgeville, with colors displayed and bands playing national airs, and camped at night seven miles beyond, on the Sandersville road. November 25, marched at 6 a. m. to Buffalo Creek, where we found the bridge had been destroyed just before our arrival. My command marching at the head of the division column to-day, upon its reaching this creek I set to work a company of pioneers and two companies of men from the Twenty-second Indiana, and in half an hour had constructed a very good foot bridge, upon which I crossed the Twenty-second Indiana and afterward the entire brigade, and marched a mile beyond, leaving my pioneer party to assist Colonel Buell in putting down a pontoon bridge for the crossing of trains. Camped at night on Keg Creek. November 26, marched at 6 a. m.; crossed Keg Creek and met rebel skirmishers within two miles of Sandersville. My foraging party assisted the troops in the advance to drive the enemy through town. We arrived in town at 10 a. m. and went into camp on the north side. November 27, marched at 7 a. m. on the Louisville road; crossed the Ogeechee River and camped within eight miles of Louisville for the night. November 28, marched at 6 a. m. to within one mile of Louisville, where we found that the bridge across Rocky Comfort Creek had been burned; the Third Division, Fourteenth Corps, was repairing the same. At dusk I crossed my command over, marched through the town, and went into camp on the left of the Augusta road, about one mile and a half beyond. November 29, remained in camp all day. November 30, still in camp at Louisville. To-day I deployed the Eighty-sixth and One hundred and twenty-fifth Illinois as skirmishers, supported by the Fifty-second Ohio and Twenty-second Indiana, and moved forward, covering the Warrenton and Augusta roads. This movement was induced by the presence in our vicinity of small parties of the enemy, who had, for two or three days past, been capturing and murdering foragers and other soldiers who were so unfortunate as to fall into their power. The enemy had, on the night previous to this movement, captured and killed two men of the Eighty-fifth Indiana, one of One hundred and twenty-fifth Illinois. My line advanced at 11 a. m. and drove the enemy in fine style, recapturing a small foraging party, with train, from the Twentieth Corps, that had ventured too far out. Pretty smart skirmishing continued for some minutes, when the enemy attempted to break my line, but were repulsed by the Eighty-sixth Illinois, with the loss of one captain and one private, who were killed outright and left by the flying enemy on the field. At this juncture, by order of General Morgan, I halted and adjusted my line. Everything remained quiet until 3.30 p. m., when I received orders to move forward until my right should connect with the left of the Second Brigade, which was moving across toward the Augusta from the Waynesborough road. In this movement my line advanced at the double-quick across a corn-field, to the woods beyond, driving the enemy out of a line of works about 200 yards in length. It being deemed useless to pursue cavalry with infantry, I was directed, at sundown, to withdraw my brigade and re-establish my picket-line as it had been in the morning, which I did, the enemy following the skirmish line as it retired. In this day's operations a good deal of shooting was done by the enemy, but in driving him more than a mile he did not succeed in wounding one of our men. We recovered the bodies of the enlisted men murdered the night before. I have no hesitancy in saying they were deliberately murdered after they had surrendered, as was evidenced by an examination of the fatal wounds. One man was shot through the head, the ball entering just above the left ear. Surrounding its entrance the hair was singed close to the scalp by the burning powder. The other two were shot through the body; one was shot three times, and the other twice. So close was the weapon held when discharged that in every instance the clothing was scorched and burned. In front of the left of my picket-line stood a cotton gin, containing forty-eight bales of cotton, the property of Asa Hoyt, behind which the enemy had concealed himself and fired upon my men in the morning. Not willing to give him the advantage of that position longer, upon the withdrawal of my troops I detailed Major Holmes, Fifty-second Ohio, with a small party of men, to destroy it, which they accordingly did, and which fact I reported to you in writing while the gin was still burning. This embraces the only property of any kind burned by my order during the campaign.

December 1, marched at 10 a. m. as guard to Third Division train; reached camp at 11 p. m. December 2, marched at 8 a. m.; furnished two regiments to guard the corps reserve artillery and ammunition trains; reached camp at 8 p. m. December 3, marched at 9 a. m. on Augusta road; crossed Buck Head Creek and went into camp at dark on Mill Creek, near Lumpkin's Station. December 4, marched at noon in rear of and as guard to Third Division trains; passed through Habersham and went into camp at 10 p. m. December 5, marched at 7 a. m.; furnished guard of two regiments for corps reserve artillery and ammunition trains; went into camp for night at 7 p. m. December 6, marched at 6.30 a. m.; good roads all day. Marched twenty-one miles and a half on main Savannah road, and went into camp for the night. Road blocked just ahead of this camp for three-quarters of a mile by fallen trees. At night I made a detail of sufficient pioneer force to clear the road, which they accomplished by 9 o'clock. December 7, marched at 11 a. m. in rear and as guards to Third Division trains; reached camp near Ebenezer Creek at 8 p. m. December 8, marched at 7 a. m. Order of march changed. Left all transportation except that belonging to brigade and regimental headquarters. Crossed Ebenezer Creek at 12 m. and awaited the building of a bridge over Little Kegler's Creek, after which we marched four miles beyond and went into camp at 8 p. m. In half an hour afterward I received orders to return and camp for the night between the two creeks. Got into camp at 11 p. m. December 9, marched at 7 a. m.; moved four miles, and built two bridges over creeks. Moved about four miles farther on and encountered a section of a rebel battery planted in the road, well protected by a substantial earth-work. I received orders from General Morgan to send the One hundred and twenty-fifth Illinois Regiment forward, deployed as skirmishers on each side of the road, and develop, if possible, the strength of the enemy. The regiment thus moved to within 100 yards of the rebel works, without drawing a shot from the enemy's musketry, though his artillery played continually upon a piece of our own, posted in the road. The enemy had selected a good position to make a brief stand with a small number of men, having built his works in the center and on either side of the road, just beyond where it divides two swamps. By direction of General Morgan I pushed forward the Eighty-sixth Illinois, six companies deployed as skirmishers, until it joined the right of the One hundred and twenty-fifth Illinois. I then directed Lieutenant-Colonel Fahnestock, commanding the Eighty-sixth Illinois, to wheel gradually to the left, and if possible get his right to the enemy's rear. This he did, so far as it was in his power, but his whole line was in a swamp, where vines, rank weeds, and undergrowth timber were so abundant that his progress was necessarily too slow to reach the desired position before dark, and at dark, by order of General Morgan, the entire line was halted and established as a picket-line for the night. During the night the enemy withdrew, and my skirmishers entered his works at daybreak. In this affair two men of the Eighty-sixth Illinois were wounded. December 10, marched at 7 a. m. Proceeded five miles in the direction of Savannah, when we struck the Twentieth Corps column. Went into camp for the afternoon and night on the left of the road. December 11, marched at 8 a. m. toward the city, as far as the Five-Mile Post, and turned to the right and marched about three-quarters of a mile, when, by the direction of General Morgan, I went into position in three lines, in reserve, facing south. My camp was as comfortable as I could wish, being on high ground and in the midst of a pine grove. December 12, in the afternoon my command tore up and destroyed two miles and a half of track and ties on the Savannah and Macon Railroad. December 13, made the road destroyed yesterday suitable for a wagon road, after which the brigade did no other duties than furnish train and other guards until the 22d of December, the day subsequent to the fall of Savannah, when my command marched to within one mile and a half of the city and went into camp in two lines, facing north, on the left of the canal, where we now are making preparations for such other work as it may be our lot to perform.

This brigade, though small, is perhaps in as good condition for active operations as any. There are many officers and men absent, whom I would be glad to have returned to their commands. While in camp at Atlanta, during the month of September last, there was perfected and forwarded a list of absentees, and efforts were being made to secure their return, but before much could be accomplished in this respect the brigade was put in motion and has only stopped since arriving at this place.

The strength of the command is as follows: Present, commissioned officers, 80; enlisted men, 1,634. Absent, commissioned officers, 58; enlisted men, 1,177. Total, commissioned officers, 138; enlisted men, 2,811.

After two days' marching from Atlanta I found a necessity for a party of pioneers to clear out and repair bad places in the road. To meet this end I detailed thirty enlisted men for whom I could not procure guns, and armed them with spades, picks, and axes. These I put under the command of Lieutenant Groninger, of the Eighty-sixth Illinois, an officer of the proper spirit and energy to make such a party very useful. I required these pioneers to march each day at the head of the brigade column, and build rail or pole bridges over small streams for the safe and speedy passage of troops, and now we well appreciate the utility of such a force in all campaigns. When once drilled to labor they will perform as much work in the same length as three times the number detailed temporarily from the ranks.

On the 18th of November I began to subsist off the country, and to prevent as far as possible pillaging and marauding and all manner of lawlessness, I had details of thirty men and one commissioned officer made daily from each regiment, who reported, at an hour stated, at brigade headquarters, when these details were verified. These I put in charge of a field or acting field officer, whom I made responsible for the conduct of his men on that day. I directed that everything obtained should be reported to officer and by him turned over; if subsistence for the troops to the brigade commissary, or if mules and horses to the brigade quartermaster. By so doing my foragers always obtained plenty, and the troops shared alike in its distribution by the brigade commissary. From a statement submitted to me by Lieutenant Batchelder, acting commissary of subsistence, I find that from November 16 until December 16 inclusive my command drew, per man, of hard bread, nine rations; pease, eight rations; coffee, twenty-six rations; salt, twenty-five rations; sugar, fifteen rations; bacon, four rations; salt pork, six rations; beyond which issues the command subsisted from the country and always had abundance. Besides this tabular statement of issues I left Atlanta with 150 head of beef-cattle, very poor in flesh and already weak from travel. The forage parties supplied the command so bountifully with fresh pork that but little beef was consumed on the march, and before reaching Savannah nearly all those cattle had died along the road or were abandoned on account of being too weak to travel, but still my drove increased daily by acquisitions from the country, and on the 12th of December, when my command took position before this city, it numbered about 230 head, large and small, all of which have since been issued to the troops.

My forage details were frequently annoyed by the enemy, but by always keeping well together they were able to resist or drive away a considerable force. On the 30th of November particularly the foragers of the brigade, under command of Captain Powers, of the Twenty-second Indiana, were attacked, about nine miles from Louisville, by a part of Wheeler's command, and, after a brisk fight, drove the enemy away. Toward night of the same day, as the detail was proceeding to camp at Louisville with four ox-wagon loads of forage, they were suddenly surrounded by three of Wheeler's regiments, and, after some very severe fighting succeeded in getting into camp with the loss of one man killed and four wounded, and were compelled to abandon their provisions and wagons.

On the 29th of November I mounted forty men on captured mules and horses, and placed the party under command of Captain Harbor, of the One hundred and twenty-fifth Illinois, a very brave and efficient officer. These labored to find where subsistence could be obtained, and to aid the infantry details in getting it, as well as for the purpose of capturing stock for the use of the army.

It is not possible for me to state the exact number of horses and mules captured, as such property was frequently taken from my foragers while on their way to camp and informally turned over to Lieutenant Coe, quartermaster for the division. How many were so disposed of I cannot say. The number actually captured and disposed of by orders from these headquarters, together with the number known to have been informally turned over to Lieutenant Coe, were: horses, 104; mules, 160; total, 264. These numbers might have been increased somewhat had I sent parties out to hunt exclusively for stock, but in nearly every instance such captures were the labors of my subsistence details.

The number of negroes that followed my column was 160. Of these 92 were officers' servants and 78 were refugees. The latter have been sent to division headquarters pursuant to orders.

I submit and call your attention to casualty lists of the North Alabama and the Savannah campaigns hereto attached.* A few of these

* Not found.

marked missing deserve the punishment prisoners of war usually get, but it is the misfortune of the service that such men belong to the army and are counted as soldiers. They were doubtless in the act of stealing something when captured. I suppose every command has a few such men; I know this one has, whom to lose from the army is a gain to the Government. Nor can I say much less of some officers in the service, who, in spite of their long experience and in face of positive orders to the contrary, suffer, nay, by their passiveness encourage, their men to throw aside the restrictions of discipline, and become outlaws and brigands. I believe a company commander should be the best disciplinarian in the service, and should feel that his position, so immediately connecting him with the rank and file, makes him a conservator of the peace and good order of the army; and an officer who from incompetency or other cause is not well adapted to teach and maintain a good system of discipline in his command, should be summarily dismissed the service. A few such in my command I could cheerfully recommend for dismissal, and do honestly believe the service would be promoted thereby.

Since the fall of Atlanta the brigade staff has undergone several changes. Most of the old members were absent during the Savannah campaign. Those at present serving on such duty, without specially naming them, have all well and faithfully discharged every trust confided to them. I am also under special obligations to regimental commanders for their efforts to maintain strict discipline throughout the entire campaign. I commend them all to my superior officers.

Number of horses captured, 104; mules, 160; total, 264. Number of negroes that followed the command, 160; rations issued on the Atlanta and Savannah campaigns, per man: hard bread, 9 rations; pease, 8 rations; coffee, 26 rations; salt, 25 rations; sugar, 15 rations; bacon, 4 rations; salt pork, 6 rations; amount of railroad destroyed (track and ties), 11½ miles; cotton destroyed, 48 bales; cotton gins destroyed, 1.

I have the honor to be, very respectfully, your obedient servant,

JAMES W. LANGLEY,

Lieut. Col., 125th Illinois Volunteers, Commanding Brigade.

Capt. T. WISEMAN,

Assistant Adjutant-General, Second Division, Fourteenth Corps.

No. 74.

Report of Lieut. Col. Charles W. Clancy, Fifty-second Ohio Infantry.

HDQRS. FIFTY-SECOND OHIO VOLUNTEER INFANTRY,
Near Savannah, Ga., December 31, 1864.

SIR: I have the honor to submit the following report of the part taken by this command in the late campaign which has resulted in the capture of Savannah:

On the 16th day of November last I took command of the regiment at Atlanta, Ga., and at 9 a.m. received orders to march. In compliance with said order moved at 11 a.m. as guards for division train; marched on a road running parallel with the Augusta and Atlanta Railroad through the town of Decatur; marched near fourteen miles and encamped with the train at 9 p.m. 17th, moved with the brigade at 7 a.m., following the One hundred and tenth Illinois; assisted in destroying a portion of the Augusta railroad; encamped at Conyers Station with the brigade at 7 p. m. 18th, marched with the brigade at 5 a. m. in the direction of Covington, reaching the same at 12 m.; spent three hours in the destruction of railroad southeast of the town, then concluded a march of fifteen miles and encamped with the brigade. 19th, marched at 6 a. m. with the brigade in the direction of Eatonton, and at 6 p. m. encamped with the same near said place, having marched near eighteen miles. 20th, moved at 7 a. m. in the direction of Milledgeville and west of Eatonton; encamped with the brigade at 3 p. m. 21st, marched with the brigade at 6 a.m. and encamped at 4 p.m. on the west bank of Cedar Creek, where we remained until 6 a. m. of the 23d, when, with the Eighty-sixth Illinois, the command marched as rear guard for the division and encamped with the brigade near Milledgeville at 11 p.m. 24th, moved at 10 a.m., passing through Milledgeville; encamped with the brigade six miles southeast. 25th, marched at 6 a. m. and encamped with the brigade east of Buffalo Creek. 26th, marched with the brigade at 6 a. m., passing through the town of Sandersville; encamped near and east of it at 12 m. 27th, marched with the brigade at 7 a. m., crossing the Ogeechee River at Fenn's Bridge; encamped near Rocky Comfort Creek, having marched fifteen miles. Companies A, F, D, I, and B were detailed for picket. 28th, picket companies were brought in at 6 a. m., and the command moved with the brigade and encamped two miles east of Louisville at 5 p. m. In this camp the command remained until the 30th, when, at 2 p. m., I was ordered to move to a road about one mile to the right and support the pickets while their line advanced; light skirmishing ensued, but no loss was sustained. At this point, by order of brigade commander, Major Holmes, with a detail of men, burned one cotton gin, including — bales of cotton. Moving a short distance to the right the entire regiment was placed on picket, relieving the Eighty-sixth Illinois.

December 1, at 7 a. m. I was ordered to return to the camp occupied the previous day, and at 10 a. m. marched with the brigade and encamped at 11 p. m. 2d, moved at 9 a. m. as train guards; marched twelve miles and encamped with the brigade at 10 p. m. 3d, marched with the brigade at 8 a. m., following the Twenty-second Indiana; encamped at 7 p. m., having marched twelve miles. 4th, moved with the brigade at 10 a. m., crossing the railroad at Lumpkin's Station, and encamped at 7 p. m. 5th, marched at 7 a. m. as train guard; encamped with the brigade at 9 p. m. near Buck Head Creek Post-Office. 6th, marched at 6.20 a. m., leading the division; encamped with the brigade at 5 p. m., having marched seventeen miles; Companies C, E, and K were detailed for picket. 7th, moved with the brigade at 7 a. m., and encamped near Ebenezer Creek. 8th, moved with the brigade and encamped after a march of six miles. 9th, marched with the brigade on a road leading to Savannah at 2 p. m. The enemy opened fire on the head of the column from a battery in position on the road. I was ordered to take position on the right of the road and in rear of the Twenty-second Indiana. About 5 p. m. the command was moved near one mile to the right and encamped for the night. 10th, marched as rear guard for the division, encamping with the brigade at 2 p. m. 11th, marched with the brigade in the direction of Savannah, and when within five miles of the city encamped. 12th and 13th, destroyed a portion of the Macon railroad, returning to the same camp, which we occupied until the morning of the 22d, when the command moved, with the brigade, to its present camp.

During the entire campaign only three days' rations were issued to this regiment. A detail of thirty men, in charge of a commissioned officer, was made each day to forage for the command, supplying it bountifully with meat and potatoes, and occasionally with flour and meal. This was done without molestation by the enemy until the 26th of November, when, on entering the town of Sandersville, a lively skirmish was kept up for near an hour between the enemy's cavalry and the foraging parties of the division, the detail from this command, in charge of Lieutenant Summers, participating. No casualties occurred in his command.

Again, on the 30th, the detail in charge of Lieutenant McIntire was attacked by the enemy in considerable force near Louisville, resulting in a loss of 5 men—1 wounded and 4 missing. Added to this 1 man missing at Fenn's Bridge (on the 29th), and the list of casualties is complete.

I have no correct means of ascertaining the number of horses and mules captured, from the fact that foraging parties report to the brigade commander. I can only state that there are at present four horses and twelve mules in this command, the property of the Government, all of which, I believe, have been accounted for.

Inclosed* will be found accurate notes of the part taken by the command in rear of Atlanta from the 28th of September to the 15th day of November, while in command of Major Holmes.

In conclusion, it is my duty to say, in commendation of both officers and men, that all did their duty promptly, under all circumstances, adhering strictly to that good order and soldierly bearing that had hitherto characterized them.

Very respectfully, your obedient servant,

CHAS. W. CLANCY,
Lieutenant-Colonel, Commanding Regiment.

Lieut. M. W. TANNER,
Actg. Asst. Adjt. Gen., 3d Brig., 2d Div., 14th Army Corps.

No. 75.

Report of Brig. Gen. Absalom Baird, U. S. Army, commanding Third Division.

HDQRS. THIRD DIVISION, FOURTEENTH ARMY CORPS,
Savannah, Ga., January 7, 1865.

COLONEL:†

November 15, marched through and camped near the city of Atlanta. November 16, passed through Decatur and marched as far as Snapfinger Creek. From the 17th the march was continued through Lithonia, Conyers, crossing Yellow River, through Covington, over the Ulcofauhachee, through Shady Dale, and reaching the city of Milledgeville. On the morning of the 25th crossed the Oconee, and destroyed the bridge. On the 26th arrived at Sandersville. November 27, division started for Louisville, taking the road to Fenn's Bridge, the First and Second Divisions, with all the trains of the corps, following the direct road. Head of column reached Rocky Comfort Creek at 8.30 a. m., but the

---

* Not found.

† For portion of report (here omitted) relating to operations in North Georgia and North Alabama, see Vol. XXXIX, Part I, p. 646.

bridge having been destroyed by the enemy, was unable to cross till late in the afternoon. Encamped near Louisville, where the division remained until December 1, 1864.

December 1, at 10 a. m. division moved from camp near Louisville, Ga., in company with General Kilpatrick's division of cavalry, and went into camp at 5 p. m., on the bank of Buck Head Creek. During the day considerable skirmishing with the enemy's cavalry, with a loss on our side of 3 men killed and 10 wounded. December 2, met the enemy again at Rocky Creek, at 10 a. m., posted behind strong barricades and disposed to dispute our crossing at the ford. The Seventy-fourth Indiana charged and dispersed them, and the division marched to the farm of Mr. Gisholm and went into camp. December 3, arrived at Thomas' Station, on the Savannah and Augusta road, and during the night thoroughly destroyed several miles of railroad track. December 4, General Kilpatrick attacked the enemy's cavalry one mile from Thomas' Station, and drove them in confusion through Waynesborough and two miles beyond. Division followed up and supported General Kilpatrick during the day, and then made a night march to Alexander. December 5, reached Jacksonborough. December 6, arrived at Beaver Dam Creek, and joined the other two divisions of the corps. December 7, late at night, reached Sister's Ferry. December 8, remained in camp during the day and had considerable skirmishing with the advance of the enemy's cavalry. Marched at midnight, and crossed Ebenezer Creek at 3 a. m. December 9. December 10, encamped within twelve miles of Savannah, making short marches. Division encamped, December 13, on the Louisville road, six miles from the city, where it remained until the 22d, at which time, the city having been evacuated on the night of the 20th, it was moved to a position (still occupied) half a mile from the town. December 27, corps reviewed by Major-General Sherman. The division entered upon the campaign organized as it had hitherto been into three brigades of infantry, commanded respectively by Col. George P. Este, Fourteenth Ohio Volunteers, Col. Morton C. Hunter, Eighty-second Indiana Volunteers, and Col. N. Gleason, Eighty-seventh Indiana Volunteers. The Fifth Wisconsin Battery, four guns, Capt. Joseph McKnight, was likewise attached to it.

Our effective force of fighting men during the whole march was, upon an average, a little under 5,000; the number of mouths which we had to feed, including teamsters and servants, somewhat over 6,000.

We cut loose from our connections at Atlanta to march to this point with the following supplies: 57,000 rations bread (about nine and a half days), 161,000 rations coffee (about twenty-seven days), 117,000 rations sugar (about nineteen days), 30,000 rations salt meat (about five days), and an abundance of salt, with some candles and soap. We also started with 550 head of beef-cattle, and have yet remaining seventy-five head. On these supplies, together with what was drawn from the country, the division subsisted from the 16th of November to the 16th of December. The amount of sweet potatoes, hogs, cattle, and poultry taken in the country and consumed by the troops cannot be estimated, but it must have been very large, the men living well.

The division destroyed quite effectually eighteen miles of railroad and two large bridges, that over Rocky Comfort Creek, on the Augusta road, and that over the Oconee River at Milledgeville, as well as the State magazine at that place. It destroyed, I feel quite sure, 1,000 bales of cotton, and probably less than 2,000 bales.

The amount of forage and other minor articles consumed and destroyed cannot be estimated. The command foraged liberally. The number of drafted and saddle animals captured was about 597. Some of them were used to replace those in our trains already worn out; others were worthless, and my quartermaster has still about 400 head to turn over.

Negroes to the number of about 668 joined or followed our column on the march, and have since our arrival here either been employed or turned over to the provost-marshal. A large number was probably with the column or near it at certain times, but as no notice was taken of any of them and no restraint exercised over those simply passing along the road, many doubtless disappeared without any account being had of them.

The division captured 16 prisoners, and its loss in action was 8 men wounded, 3 of whom afterward died. The list of casualties by name is appended.

In closing this report I have again to commend to the notice of my superior commanders the ability and meritorious services of Col. George P. Este, Fourteenth Ohio; Col. Morton C. Hunter, Eighty-second Indiana, and Col. N. Gleason, Eighty-seventh Indiana, who commanded my three brigades, and to ask for their promotion, at least by brevet, to the rank of brigadier-general. I have also to request that Col. B. D. Fearing, Ninety-second Ohio Volunteers, an officer of surpassing merit and the only other full colonel who made the campaign with the division, may be promoted to the same grade.

To my staff officers I am again deeply indebted, and I beg to renew the recommendations which I have heretofore given for their promotion.

I am, sir, very respectfully,

A. BAIRD,
Brigadier-General, Commanding Division.

Lieut. Col. A. C. McCLURG,
Assistant Adjutant-General, Fourteenth Army Corps.

No. 76.

Report of Lieut. Joseph R. Channel, Battery C, First Illinois Light Artillery.

HEADQUARTERS BATTERY C, FIRST ILLINOIS ARTILLERY,
Near Savannah, Ga., December 30, 1864.

CAPTAIN: In obedience to circular received I have the honor to submit the following report:

While in camp near Atlanta, Ga., I received orders, on the 2d of October, to prepare to march next morning with thirteen days' rations and three days' forage, and to report to Brigadier-General Carlin, commanding First Division. I joined the division as directed, and marched with it throughout the entire campaign north of Atlanta, returning to that point on the 15th of November, 1864. During the campaign I drew about sixteen days' full rations and fifteen days' forage; the remainder of the forage and subsistence I obtained from the country along the line of march. After remaining in Atlanta, Ga., one night I again joined the First Division, Fourteenth Army Corps (in obedience to orders), with three days' rations and three days' forage, and marched with it to a point near Savannah, Ga., where I took up position in line of battle on the 12th of December; was engaged lightly by the enemy's batteries on the 12th, 13th, 14th, 15th, 16th, 17th, 19th, and 20th, during which time I expended 283 rounds of ammunition without any loss, except one wheel belonging to a gun carriage. On the 22d I moved into camp near the city of Savannah, Ga., the enemy having evacuated the night before. During the march from Atlanta I drew three days' full rations and one day's forage; the remainder of forage and subsistence I obtained along the line of march. During the entire campaign the officers and men of the battery performed their duty well in every respect.

Very respectfully, your obedient servant,

JOSEPH R. CHANNEL,

First Lieutenant, Comdg. Battery C, First Illinois Artillery.

No. 77.

Report of Brig. Gen. Alpheus S. Williams, U. S. Army, commanding Twentieth Army Corps.

HEADQUARTERS TWENTIETH CORPS,
Savannah, Ga., January 9, 1865.

COLONEL:*

Changes in the principal commands of the corps since the last campaign left the organization as follows: First Division, Brig. Gen. N. J. Jackson commanding—three brigades, commanded, respectively, by Colonels Selfridge, Carman, and Robinson; Second Division, Brig. Gen. J. W. Geary commanding—three brigades, commanded by Colonels Pardee, Jones, and Barnum; Third Division, Brig. Gen. W. T. Ward commanding—three brigades, commanded by Colonels Smith, Dustin, and Ross. A list of the regiments composing the brigades will be found in reports of subordinate commanders. The artillery was reduced to four batteries of four guns each, two of 3-inch Rodmans and two of 12-pounder Napoleons, under charge of Maj. J. A. Reynolds, chief of artillery; the horses were increased to eight to a carriage. The Ninth Illinois Infantry (mounted), Lieutenant-Colonel Hughes commanding, joined the command on the second day and remained with it through to Savannah, and performed excellent service throughout. One battalion of Fifty-eighth Indiana Volunteers, Lieutenant-Colonel Moore commanding, with pontoon train, was also attached to the corps, and was very useful during the march.

On the morning of the 15th of November the corps marched from Atlanta, taking the road east through Decatur. We encamped on 15th near the Georgia railroad, south of Stone Mountain; on evening of the 16th near Rock Bridge Post-Office; on 17th near Cornish Creek, and on the 18th three miles west of Madison. The country for the first three days' march was very hilly, and the crossing at Yellow River, Little Haynes River, and other streams very bad. The condition of the teams was not good, and delays to the rear of our long column were consequently vexatious and protracted. Geary's division was detached unencumbered on the morning of the 19th, with orders to destroy the Georgia railroad bridge over the Oconee River and such wagon bridges as he might find on that river toward Milledgeville. The purpose was

*For portion of report (here omitted) relating to operations about Atlanta, see Vol. XXXIX, Part I, p. 649.

fully accomplished, and several miles of railroad, as well as the long railroad bridge over the Oconee, were destroyed. A wagon bridge over that river and several mills and factories were also burned. The division rejoined the column on the 21st before reaching Little River; the other two divisions, with the trains of the corps, moved through Madison and encamped four miles beyond. About six miles of railroad were destroyed by Ward's division. Supplies for man and beast became abundant on third day after leaving Atlanta. On 20th moved forward and encamped near Eatonton. The afternoon was rainy and the roads heavy. On 21st marched through Eatonton, encamping near Little River. Two or three miles of the Eatonton Branch Railroad were destroyed on the march. On 22d, having laid the pontoon bridge over Little River, the corps crossed and moved forward to the suburbs of Milledgeville. Two regiments under Colonel Hawley, Third Wisconsin Volunteers, appointed commandant of the post, were sent to occupy the town. The First and Second Divisions were encamped on the east side of the Oconee and the Third Division on the west side, near the bridge. Large quantities of arms, ammunition, and accouterments were found and destroyed, as well as salt and other public property. The report of Colonel Hawley, commander of post, forwarded herewith,* will give the details of this property. The railroad depot, two arsenals, a powder magazine, and other public buildings and shops, were burned. The railroad track for five miles toward Gordon was destroyed. On 24th the march was resumed and the divisions encamped near Gum Creek, and on the 25th, after some delay to rebuild the bridge over Buffalo Creek and swamp, the head of the column encamped about seven miles from Sandersville. Some skirmishing was had, and the enemy's cavalry was driven away by Colonel Robinson's brigade just as we were going into camp. On the following morning, 26th, two regiments of Carman's brigade, Jackson's division, drove away the rebel cavalry and the corps moved rapidly into Sandersville, entering simultaneously with the Fourteenth Corps upon a road on our left. In the afternoon the First and Second Divisions were moved down to Tennille Station (No. 13), the Third Division being left to cover the trains. The First Michigan Engineers reported for duty with the corps. On 27th, 28th, and 29th the Central railroad and all wagon bridges over Williamson's Swamp Creek were destroyed from Tennille Station to the Ogeechee River, including the long railroad bridge over that stream, by the First and Second Divisions and Michigan Engineers. The Third Division marched with the trains, via Davisborough, across the Ogeechee and Rocky Comfort Rivers, and encamped near Louisville. On the 30th the First and Second Divisions moved up the Ogeechee to Coward's Bridge, which was found partly destroyed but easily repaired. The whole corps encamped about three miles south of Louisville, between the Oconee and the Ogeechee. The roads, excepting at the river and swamp crossings, were good, the country very level, and the weather during the march superb; supplies of all kinds were very abundant.

From the 1st to the 8th of December our line of march was down the peninsula between the Ogeechee and Savannah Rivers, following the Louisville and Savannah road, encamping on the 1st on Baker's Creek, on the 2d at Buck Head Church, on 3d at Horse Creek, on 4th at Little Ogeechee, on 5th at Sylvania Cross-Roads, on 6th near Cowpens Creek, on 7th on Jack's Branch, near Springfield, and on 8th near Eden Cross-Roads. As we approached the coast the surface of the country became flat and swampy. Large ponds or pools were met every mile

* See p. 248.

or so, and the creeks spread out into several miry branches. The roads between the creeks and ponds, though apparently of sandy and substantial character, proved to be upon a thin crust, which was soon cut through by our long trains into the deep quicksand, requiring miles of corduroy. At several of the swamps the enemy had attempted to obstruct our march by felling timber. The supplies continued good and the weather excellent. On the 9th our direction of march was changed to the east, taking the road from Eden to Monteith Post-Office, on the Charleston railroad. At the large Monteith swamp we found that the enemy, besides obstructing the road for nearly a mile by felling trees, had built two small earth-works, and, with a single gun and about 400 infantry, was making a show of stopping our march. Jackson's division being in advance, he was ordered to throw out several regiments on each flank, while a brigade in the center should make a feint to engage attention and enable the pioneers to clear the obstructions. Our hope of capturing the whole party did not succeed, but their pretentious defenses were speedily abandoned as soon as a portion of Robinson's brigade, under Colonel West, Thirty-first Wisconsin Volunteers, could cross the swamp. The fugitives left behind a considerable quantity of new clothing and accouterments. Our loss was one man killed and four wounded. Much praise was awarded to Colonel West for his conduct on this occasion.

On the following morning (10th of December) the corps moved down to Monteith Station, on the Charleston railroad, and, after destroying some miles of the road, marched to near the Five-Mile post on the Augusta and Savannah Railroad. At this point, meeting with the enemy's strong line of defenses behind swamps and artificial ponds, the corps was ordered to encamp for the night. During the afternoon a party of foragers, with some cavalry, succeeded in bringing to and capturing, near the foot of Argyle Island, a rebel dispatch boat, called the Ida, having on board Colonel Clinch, of General Hardee's staff, with dispatches for gun-boats above. The boat was unfortunately set on fire and burned. On the 11th Geary's division was moved to the left, encountering some opposition from rebel pickets. They were, however, driven back into the main works, and our line was established from the Savannah River, near Williamson's plantation, in advance of Pipemaker's Creek, across the Charleston railroad to the Central railroad, a few hundred yards from the junction of the two roads, connecting with the Fourteenth Corps (Third Division on the right, First Division in center, and Second Division on the left). On the 12th Winegar's battery (four 3-inch guns), which had been placed in position at Tweedside to command the channel between Argyle Island and the Georgia shore, drove back two gun-boats attempting to descend the river, and so crippled the tender Resolute as to drive her aground, in which position she was taken possession of by Colonel Hawley, Third Wisconsin Volunteers, whose regiment was on duty on Argyle Island. Five naval officers and nineteen men were captured, besides a quantity of ordnance and subsistence stores. The boat, which was without armament, was subsequently turned over to the quartermaster's department, and is now in our service.

From the 13th to the 20th several changes were made in the positions of the troops: Robinson's brigade, of the First Division, was sent back to Cherokee Hill to cover the roads in our rear; two regiments from Geary's division occupied the upper end of Hutchinson's Island; Carman's brigade, First Division, was sent to Argyle Island and subsequently across to the Carolina shore with a section of Battery I, First New York Artillery. He took up a strong position on the 19th in advance of Izard's house, and made several demonstrations and reconnaissances toward Clydesdale Creek and the Union causeway road from Savannah to Hardeeville. The enemy opposed these movements in strong force. The nature of the country for miles back (being rice plantations crossed by dikes and canals) effectually prevented anything beyond a menace. These threatening movements, however, undoubtedly hastened the evacuation of Savannah. In the meantime our main line was pushed toward the enemy's works, and preparations for assault made by close reconnaissances, construction of light bridges, and experiments with balks of the pontoon train and fascines of straw and cane for bridging canals. Strong field-works were constructed for the heavy guns and for the field guns, some of them masked on the road within 150 yards of the enemy's line. These preparations were completed on the 20th. The assailable points in our front were very few; almost every foot was covered deep by artificial ponds from the irrigating canals, behind which and upon the approaches were strong earthworks for artillery, connected throughout by rifle-pits well constructed. The confidence of the troops in carrying these works was, however, perfect and earnest.

During the day of the 20th the fire from the enemy's works and gunboats was unusually heavy and continuous. Reports from Carman's brigade indicated that large columns were crossing to the Carolina shore, either to cover their only line of communication or preparatory to a final evacuation of the city. In the night General Geary reported to me that the movements across the river were apparently still going on. Division commanders were instructed to keep on the alert and press their pickets closer to the rebel works, but the enemy, intending to abandon his heavy guns, kept up a fire until the moment of quitting their defenses. At 3.30 o'clock on the morning of the 21st Geary reported that Barnum's brigade was in the rebel main line. Orders were sent him and General Ward to advance the picket-lines and follow with their divisions into the city. By 6 a. m. Geary's division without opposition had entered the city. Patrols were sent out to preserve order. Two regiments were ordered to occupy Fort Jackson and other works below the city. General Geary was temporarily assigned to the command of the post and his division placed within the city. The retreating rebels had disconnected the pontoon bridge to Hutchinson's Island and set fire to that connecting with the Carolina shore. The ram Savannah still lay off Screven's Ferry, two miles or so away, and occasionally fired a shot toward the town. She was evidently covering the removal of supplies up the causeway road. There were no means of reaching her, and our guns, though well served, plainly did her no damage. At night she was destroyed, as had been all the other rebel public vessels the day previous.

The troops of the corps while in front of the rebel works suffered a number of casualties. Among those killed was Lieut. C. A. Ahreets, One hundred and thirty-fourth New York Volunteers, assistant to Lieutenant-Colonel Asmussen, inspector-general of the corps, an excellent and faithful young officer. Among the severely wounded was Col. John H. Ketcham, One hundred and fiftieth New York Volunteers, an officer of superior intelligence and worth. Major Wright, Twenty-ninth Ohio Volunteers, an excellent officer, also received a painful wound.

I append hereto a series of campaign maps,* prepared by Captain McDowell, chief topographical engineer for the corps, showing the positions of the several divisions at each camp during the march from Atlanta to Savannah. These positions were laid down and the notes accompanying the maps kept by Lieutenant-Colonel Asmussen, inspector-general of the corps. The faithful and skillful manner in which this work is done presents a complete and accurate view of the daily marches of the corps.

Tabular statement marked A shows the casualties of the corps by divisions during the campaign—an aggregate of 12 killed, 88 wounded, 165 missing. Of the missing the greater part were stragglers and small parties of foragers captured. Some few were deserting bounty-jumpers, who had reached us just before marching from Atlanta. In the case of Captain Reid, One hundred and seventh New York Volunteers, missing with a detail of forty-three men, foraging, I have ordered a special report of the statements made by a rebel cavalry officer who was of the capturing party. If these statements are true, Captain Reid behaved in a most shameful and cowardly manner, and should be dismissed in disgrace. As both officer and men are still prisoners of war no proper investigation can now be made.

We captured, on the march and before Savannah, 30 officers (13 of whom were naval), 135 privates, and 14 seamen; 122 deserters came into our ranks. A tabular statement and list of officers captured prepared by Major Parks, provost-marshal, is attached hereto, marked B.† A very considerable number of prisoners were taken on entering the city, all of whom are in the hands of the post commandant and will be the subject of report by him.

I make the following estimates of public property destroyed and supplies taken from the country, upon information from commanders and staff officers, approved by my own observation and judgment:

Miles marched by the troops	305
Miles trains moved (as per odometer)	281.35
Miles of railroad destroyed	71

Besides railroad destroyed, more than a million feet of timber for the largest sized bridges and thousands of cords of wood were burned.

Number of animals taken from country:	
Horses, reported by Captain Whittelsey, chief quartermaster	410
Horses, reported by Major Reynolds, chief of artillery	40
Horses, put into teams and not reported (estimated)	150
	600
Mules, reported by Captain Whittelsey	1,020
Mules, reported by Major Reynolds	100
Mules, put into trains in exchange for poor animals and never reported (estimated)	600
	1,720
Total animals	2,320

	Pounds.
Forage—	
By Captain Whittelsey's report:	
Corn taken en route	1,227,984
Corn taken east of Atlanta	1,932,468
By Major Reynolds' report	130,000
Total corn	3,290,452

* See Plate LXXI, Maps 1 to 11 of the Atlas.
† Omitted.

Forage—

	Pounds.
By Captain Whittelsey's report:	
Fodder taken en route	1,091,619
Fodder taken near Atlanta	138,200
Total fodder	1,229,819
Rice fodder:	
By Captain Whittelsey's report	550,694
By Major Reynolds' report	20,000
Total rice fodder	570,694

There was with the corps an average of over 7,000 animals. At the regulation allowance these animals would have consumed, in twenty-days, 2,100,000 pounds corn; hay or fodder, 2,450,000 pounds.

I estimate that at least this quantity was taken from the country on the march and exclusive of that taken before marching from Atlanta. Upon this basis estimates made on actual returns to Captain Whittelsey and Major Reynolds will be increased over 700,000 pounds of corn and 800,000 pounds of fodder. The waste of this, as of other articles, was enormous.

Subsistence taken from the country, as per report of Lieutenant-Colonel Balloch, chief commissary of subsistence.

Fresh beef	pounds..	400,000
Fresh pork and mutton	do....	150,000
Rice	do....	110,000
Flour	do....	20,000
Sweet potatoes	bushels..	6,500
Sorghum sirup	gallons..	4,000

Of the quantities of turkeys, geese, ducks, and poultry of all kinds taken, no approximate estimate can be made. For at least 200 miles of our route these articles were in great abundance, and were used lavishly and wastefully. So of the other articles above mentioned, it would be safe to say that the amount might be doubled for waste and subsistence of the thousands of refugee slaves who followed our march.

Cotton.—I estimate the quantity of cotton burned by the corps at 5,000 bales, or 2,500,000 pounds. The estimate is probably low, as our line of march was through some of the best cotton-growing portions of Georgia, and we swept, with our foragers and flankers, a belt of six to eight miles in width of all the cotton and most of the gins and presses. No large accumulations were found except at Milledgeville, reported 1,800 bales, bonded by order of General Sherman; near Sandersville, where about 100 bales were destroyed; at Lee Jordan's plantation, 280 bales destroyed by General Geary, and at Tennille Station, on Central railroad, where between 300 and 400 bales were burned; other lots ranging from ten to thirty bales were frequently found.

Fugitive slaves.—Negroes of all ages and of every variety of physical condition, from the infant in its mother's arms to the decrepid old man, joined the column from plantations and from cross-roads, singly and in large groups, on foot, on horseback, and in every description of vehicles. The vehicles were discarded, as obstructing the progress of our very long column. Beyond this no effort was made to drive away the fugitives. The decrepid, the aged, and the feeble were told of the long journey before them, and advised to remain behind. I estimate that at from 6,000 to 8,000 slaves, at different points in the campaign, joined the march of this corps, of whom something over 2,500 reached our camp before Savannah. About 1,700, of whom one-third were able-bodied, were, on account of scarcity of subsistence, placed in colony on the Coleraine plantation, on the Savannah River, and plentifully supplied with rice, and occasionally with beef. The able-bodied men were employed in transporting rice from the islands and in working rice mills. When communication was opened by way of the Ogeechee the whole colony was turned over to the chief quartermaster and chief commissary. Four hundred to 500, not of the colony, found employment as officers' servants and teamsters for the Government.

Ordnance and ordnance stores destroyed in Milledgeville, per report of Colonel Hawley, commanding post.

Muskets (caliber .69)		2,300
Accouterments (sets)		300
Lances		5,000
Cutlasses		1,500
Ammunition (caliber .69)	rounds..	10,000
Ammunition (fixed artillery)	boxes..	170
Powder	kegs..	200

Destroyed at Milledgeville by Lieutenant Shepherd, ordnance officer, artillery, as per report of Major Reynolds, chief of artillery.

Fixed ammunition:		
Artillery	rounds..	3,500
Infantry	do....	20,000
Sharps primers	boxes..	2
Powder	pounds..	2,000

Major Reynolds reports the number of guns of all calibers found in and around Savannah in works first taken possession of by the Twentieth Corps at 89. Of these, 23 of calibers from 6-pounder smooth-bores to 42-pounder carronades were found in position in front of the line occupied by the corps before Savannah. Major Reynolds' report, forwarded herewith, will furnish details.* On entering the city General Geary took possession of a large quantity of ordnance stores and materials of war, details of which will be found in his report to these headquarters. They are not recapitulated, as the chief ordnance officer has doubtless already received schedules of them.

Notwithstanding repeated instances of wanton pillage occurred on the march, the general conduct of the men was orderly, contented, and faithful to duty. The nature of the march was calculated to relax discipline, and yet, after all, it was comparatively but the few (ever found in large bodies of men) who were disorderly and vicious. The labor, especially of those in guard of the trains, was very arduous, often extending through the night. I calculate our average daily marches for each marching day exceeded thirteen miles. Two of the divisions rested but one entire day without marching.

The division commanders deserve my cordial acknowledgments for zealous, cheerful, and intelligent co-operation at all times. I desire also to acknowledge the valuable services of Major Yates and the officers and men of the First Michigan Mechanics and Engineers, who, while temporarily attached to the corps, were indefatigable, as well as skillful, in assisting in the destruction of railroads, in constructing bridges, and repairing roads.

From the length of the column, often from ten to fifteen miles, the duties which fell upon several officers of the staff were often very laborious and fatiguing, but were always executed with cheerfulness and zeal. I desire, in an especial report hereafter, to bring to the notice of the

* See p. 356.

major-general commanding, and through him to the Government, the names of such of these officers whose meritorious services on this and previous campaigns entitle them, I think, to promotion.

I forward herewith the reports of division commanders and such subordinate reports as have been received, also reports and statements of staff officers covering estimates of property destroyed and supplies taken from the country.

I am, colonel, very respectfully, your obedient servant,

A. S. WILLIAMS,
Brigadier-General, Commanding.

Lieut. Col. H. C. RODGERS,
Assistant Adjutant-General.

A.

Report of casualties in the Twentieth Corps from October 28 to December 27, 1864, inclusive.

Division.	Killed.		Wounded.		Missing.		Aggregate.
	Officers.	Men.	Officers.	Men.	Officers.	Men.	
Headquarters Twentieth Corps	1	......	......	......	......	......	1
First Division	......	2	2	17	......	88	109
Second Division	......	8	2	58	......	46	114
Third Division	......	1	1	7	......	28	37
Artillery	......	......	......	1	1	2	4
Total	1	11	5	83	1	164	265

Journal accompanying campaign maps, showing positions of the Twentieth Army Corps on the march from Atlanta to Savannah, November 15 to December 21, 1864, submitted with report of Bvt. Maj. Gen. A. S. Williams, U. S. Army, dated January 9, 1865.*

November 15.—Order of march: First, Second, and Third Divisions. The Third Division did not arrive at the place of destination until 8 a. m. next day. No supplies gathered. Weather fine. Road good, but hilly. No important bridges on streams were crossed. Distance, sixteen miles.

November 16.—Order of march: Second, Third, and First Divisions. Weather fine. Road good, but hilly. The crossing of the Yellow River at Rock Bridge bad and easily disputed. Supplies scanty, except some forage and live stock. Distance, eight miles.

November 17.—Order of march: Second, Third, and First Divisions. Weather fine. Road good, but very hilly, particularly at the crossing of Little Haynes Creek. Supplies more plenty. Distance, sixteen miles.

November 18.—Order of march: Second, Third, and First Divisions. Weather fine. Rain during the night. Road excellent. Water scarce after leaving the Ulcofauhachee River. Supplies scarce. Poor country. Distance, fifteen miles.

---

* See Plate LXXI, Maps 1 to 11 of the Atlas.

November 19.—Order of march: Cavalry, First and Third Divisions, the Second Division detached. Railroad destroyed to Madison. Weather rainy. Roads good, but muddy. Supplies more plenty. Distance, seven miles.

November 20.—Order of march: Cavalry, Third and First Divisions, Second Division detached. Weather cloudy. Commenced raining 5 p. m. Road good, but heavy. Supplies not so plenty. Distance, twelve miles.

November 21.—Order of march: Cavalry, Third and First Divisions, Second Division detached. Pontoons laid across Little River. Weather very rainy. Road very muddy and worn. The condition of the road caused the Third Brigade, First Division, to encamp two miles to the rear. Supplies more plenty. Distance, thirteen miles.

November 22.—Order of march: Cavalry, First, Second, and Third Divisions. Weather cold, clear, but windy. Road good. Supplies plenty. Distance, fifteen miles.

November 23.—The troops remained in camp.

November 24.—Order of march: Cavalry, First, Second, and Third Divisions. Weather fine. Road excellent. Supplies not so plenty. Distance thirteen miles.

November 25.—Order of march: Cavalry, First, Second, and Third Divisions. The cavalry had a skirmish with Wheeler's cavalry. Weather fine. Road good, except the crossing of Buffalo Creek, the bridges of the dam being destroyed. Supplies not so plenty. Poor country. Distance, eight miles.

November 26.—Order of march: First, Second, Third Divisions, cavalry on the flanks. The troops entered Sandersville simultaneously with Fourteenth Corps, skirmishing with enemy's cavalry. After entering town the First and Second Divisions, preceded by the cavalry, went to Tennille Station to destroy the railroad. The Michigan Engineers reported for duty and accompanied the column to said Station No. 13. Third Division covered trains at Sandersville. Weather clear. Road excellent. Supplies plenty. Distance, twelve miles.

November 27.—Order of march: First Division, preceded by the cavalry, moved south of Georgia Central Railroad, while Second Division and Michigan Engineers destroyed the same to within five miles of Davisborough. The Third Division and trains moved from Sandersville to Davisborough. Weather fine. Road excellent. The bridge at Davisborough over Williamson's Swamp Creek was not destroyed. Supplies plenty. Distance, fifteen miles.

November 28.—Order of march: The Cavalry, Third Division, and train moved toward Louisville and encamped on Ogeechee River. The First Division destroyed railroad to Spiers Station. The Michigan Engineers and Second Division destroyed railroad at and west of Davisborough, the Second Brigade, Second Division, covering part of the train to Spiers Station. Weather fine. Road excellent. Supplies abundant. Distance, twelve miles.

November 29.—Order of march: Cavalry, Third Division, and train crossed the Ogeechee and Rocky Comfort Creek on pontoons and encamped southeast of Louisville. The First and Second Brigades, First Division, destroyed railroad from Spiers Station to Station $10\frac{1}{2}$; the Second Brigade, Second Division, from $10\frac{1}{2}$ to Ogeechee River; the remainder of Second Division and Michigan Engineers moved up from Davisborough, Third Brigade, First Division, protecting part of train. Weather fine. Road good. Supplies plenty. Distance, nine miles.

November 30.—Order of march: Finding Ragford's Bridge destroyed, the First and Second Divisions and Michigan Engineers crossed the

Ogeechee at Coward's Bridge after repairing it, and encamped on the right of the Third Division. Weather warm. Road swampy. Supplies scarce. Poor country. Distance, ten miles.

December 1.—Order of march: Cavalry, Second Division, Michigan Engineers, First and Third Divisions. Weather warm. Road swampy. Supplies more plenty. Distance, thirteen miles.

December 2.—Order of march: Cavalry, Second Division, Michigan Engineers, First and Third Divisions. The cavalry drove in the rebel pickets near Buck Head Church. Weather cloudy. Road good, except the crossing Buck Head Creek, the bridges across the swamp being partially destroyed. Supplies abundant. Distance, eleven miles.

December 3.—Order of march: Cavalry, First Division, Michigan Engineers, Third and Second Divisions. Weather cloudy. Clear in the afternoon. Road good. Supplies plenty. Distance, fifteen miles.

December 4.—Order of march: Cavalry, First Division, Michigan Engineers, Third and Second Divisions. Weather fine. Road swampy. Supplies not so plenty. Distance, fifteen miles.

December 5.—Order of march: Third, Second, and First Divisions. Cavalry sent to communicate with Fourteenth Corps. Michigan Engineers ordered to army headquarters. Weather fine. Road fair. Supplies plenty. Distance, six miles.

December 6.—Order of march: Cavalry, Third, Second, and First Divisions. Weather good. It rained during the night. Road fair—swampy. Supplies plenty. Distance, thirteen miles.

December 7.—Order of march: Cavalry, Third, Second, and First Divisions. Weather, raining in the morning, cloudy in the afternoon. Road fair, but swampy. The crossing of Jacks Creek, near Springfield, was very bad. Supplies abundant. Distance, ten miles.

December 8.—Order of march: Cavalry, Second, First, Third Divisions, and train. Weather fine. Road good until the troops struck the Eden Cross-Road, which was very swampy. Supplies plenty. Distance, ten miles.

December 9.—Order of march: Cavalry, First, Second, and Third Divisions. The First Division repulsed the enemy near Monteith. Weather cloudy. Road, good pike. Supplies plenty. Distance, nine miles.

December 10.—Order of march: Cavalry, First, Third, and Second Divisions. First Division destroyed Charleston railroad. The troops captured steamer Ida and burnt it. Weather cloudy. Road, good pike. Distance, ten miles.

December 11.—The troops moved into position in front of the enemy's works. The Third Division established connection with Seventeenth Corps, which was that day relieved by the Fourteenth Corps. Breastworks thrown up. Twenty-second Wisconsin and Battery I, First New York Artillery, moved to the Savannah River. Eighty-second and One hundred and first Regiments Illinois Volunteers, and Sixty-first Regiment Ohio Volunteers stationed at Cherokee Hill. Weather fine, but cold. Supplies scanty. A quantity of rice was found and a mill set to running to prepare it for the troops.

OPERATIONS BEFORE SAVANNAH.

December 12.—Third Regiment Wisconsin Volunteers crossed to Argyle Island. Steamer Resolute captured.

December 13.—The remainder of the Third Brigade, First Division, moved to Cherokee Hill to protect the rear, and formed connection on its left with portion of Fourteenth Corps.

December 14.—Two regiments of Second Division pushed over on to Hutchinson's Island.

December 15.—Second Regiment Massachusetts Volunteers re-enforced Third Regiment Wisconsin Volunteers on Argyle Island.

December 16.—Second Brigade, Third Division, relieved remainder of Second Brigade, First Division, the latter crossing over to Argyle Island.

December 19.—The regiments of the Second Brigade, First Division, crossed over to the South Carolina shore and intrenched themselves between Clydesdale Creek and the house of Mr. Izard.

December 21.—Savannah having been evacuated by the enemy, the Second Division took possession of the city early in the morning. The Third and First Divisions arrived during the day.

No. 78.

Report of Brig. Gen. Nathaniel J. Jackson, U. S. Army, commanding First Division.

HEADQUARTERS FIRST DIVISION, TWENTIETH CORPS,
Savannah, Ga., December 31, 1864.

COLONEL: I have the honor to submit the following report of the operations of this division from the time at which I was placed in command to the time of the occupation of Savannah:

November 11, pursuant to Special Orders, No. 124, headquarters Twentieth Corps, I assumed command of the First Division, Twentieth Corps. November 13, the Second Brigade (Col. E. A. Carman commanding) was ordered to proceed to a point on the Chattanooga railroad, midway between the Chattahoochee bridge and the city of Atlanta, and destroy the railroad track each way. Colonel Carman reported that he destroyed three miles and a half. November 15, pursuant to orders previously received, the division, having the advance of the corps, moved out of Atlanta at 7 a. m., taking the road through Decatur and encamping at night one mile and a half southeast of Stone Mountain. The Second Massachusetts Volunteers (Colonel Cogswell commanding) remained behind to destroy the public property in the city and accompany the Fourteenth Corps until such time as it could rejoin its command. Marched sixteen miles. November 16, the division, being ordered to march in the rear, did not break camp until 2 p. m. In the meantime the Third Brigade (Colonel Robinson commanding) moved to the Georgia railroad and destroyed two miles of the track. The road was hilly and rough, and the march consequently impeded by the several trains of the corps; crossed Yellow River and encamped at 10 p. m. near Rock Bridge Post-Office; marched ten miles. November 17, marched at 10 a. m. in the rear; crossed No Business, Big Haynes, and Little Haynes Creeks and encamped for the night near Flat Creek, the rear of the division not getting up until after midnight; distance, thirteen miles. November 18, marched at 7 a. m., still having the rear of the corps; passed through Social Circle at noon, where we crossed to the south side of the Georgia railroad; after passing Social Circle the road was good, and at 10 p. m. the whole division was in camp within five miles of Madison, having marched nineteen miles. November 19, the division had charge of the entire wagon train of the corps, the other two divisions having been assigned to other duty; marched at 7 a. m., passing through Madison, and encamped four miles south of that place; marched nine miles.

November 20, broke camp at 8 a. m., the division being in the rear and guarding one-half of the trains of the Second Division. Considerable rain had fallen, which retarded the movement of the trains so that the rear did not get into camp until 11 p. m. Encamped within four miles and a half of Eatonton, having marched fourteen miles. November 21, marched at 7 a. m., still in the rear, and having the same number of wagons to guard. Passed through Eatonton at 12 m. On account of continued rain the roads were extremely muddy, and it was with the greatest labor that a portion of the trains could be got along; marched twelve miles. November 22, crossed Little River at 9 a. m., the division having the advance. The head of the column arrived within one mile of Milledgeville at 2 p. m., having met with no opposition. Here the command was halted, and, pursuant to orders from Major-General Slocum, commanding Left Wing, Army of Georgia, the Third Wisconsin and One hundred and seventh New York Volunteers were sent forward to occupy, as provost guard, the city, Colonel Hawley, commanding Third Wisconsin Volunteers, being appointed post commander. The remainder of the division was then marched through the city across the Oconee River, where it encamped, with right resting on that river; marched fourteen miles. November 23, pursuant to orders from headquarters of the corps, I ordered the First Brigade (Colonel Selfridge commanding) to proceed to the Gordon and Milledgeville Railroad and destroy the track. Colonel Selfridge reported that he effectually destroyed five miles of the track. The remainder of my command remained in camp, resting after their tedious marches. November 24, moved at 7 a. m., having the advance; roads good; encamped at 4 p. m., having marched fifteen miles. November 25; moved at 6 a. m., having again the lead. Reached Buffalo Swamp at 8 a. m. Found that the bridges (nine in number) had been destroyed by enemy's cavalry, which delayed the column until 2 p. m. Encamped at 4 p. m. Cavalry skirmishing in front; distance, nine miles. November 26, marched at 6 a. m., the division still having the advance. Entered Sandersville at 11 a. m., having driven out the enemy's cavalry with my skirmish line. Leaving the wagon trains to be guarded by the Third Division, my command marched to the Georgia Central Railroad at Tennille Station and destroyed six miles of track, the railroad depot, Government warehouses, and 342 bales of cotton; marched nine miles. November 27, marched to Davisborough, sixteen miles. November 28 and 29, destroyed the Georgia Central Railroad from Davisborough to Bostwick Station, a distance of twenty miles, together with the depots and Government buildings along that portion of the road; also two saw mills and lumber yards and four large bridges, framed and ready for use, estimated to contain 1,500,000 feet of lumber. November 30, crossed the Ogeechee River and joined the trains near Louisville, having marched eleven miles.

December 1, moved at 11.30 a. m., being the center division in column; portion of the road very bad. The First Brigade (Colonel Selfridge commanding) was, by order of Brigadier-General Williams, commanding corps, directed to report to General Ward to assist in guarding the trains of the cavalry. Encamped at 11 p. m.; marched ten miles. December 2, marched through Birdville to Buck Head Church, thirteen miles; the First Brigade reported back to the command. December 3, crossed the Waynesborough railroad three miles north of Millen. The enemy having destroyed the bridges, the column was somewhat delayed. Encamped on Horse Creek at 4 p. m., having marched fifteen miles and a half, the division being in advance. December 4, division again in advance; crossed several streams; country low; marched fourteen miles. December 5, marched at 3 p. m., having waited in camp for the other divisions to pass; the road was extremely bad and but three miles was made at 11 p. m., at which time the division went into camp. December 6, marched at 7 a. m., still in the rear; roads very hard; marched fourteen miles. December 7, moved at 7 a. m., still in rear, and encamped at 10 p. m. near Springfield; country low and swampy, and roads bad; marched fifteen miles. December 8, leaving the wagon trains in charge of Third Division my command moved through Springfield in rear of Second Division; marched sixteen miles. December 9, my command moved in advance, coming into the main Savannah road shortly after leaving camp. On arriving at Monteith Swamp, about noon, the road was found very much obstructed by felled trees. Beyond the portion of the road obstructed the enemy had thrown up two redoubts, and in the more advanced one had posted a piece of artillery, which commanded the road and prevented the removal of the obstructions. Having ordered Colonel Selfridge (commanding First Brigade) to occupy the attention of the enemy in front, I sent the Second Brigade (Colonel Carman commanding) to the right of the road, with instructions to advance well around the enemy's left and endeavor to get in his rear. At the same time I ordered Colonel Robinson (commanding Third Brigade) to send three regiments to the left of the road to come up on the right flank of the enemy. Owing to the nature of the ground (a rice swamp), Carman's brigade was unable to reach the desired position before the regiments of the Third Brigade had debouched from the woods on the right of the enemy's works. The enemy fled, after firing one volley, leaving their knapsacks and camp equipage, but succeeded in removing the piece of artillery. Four prisoners were captured. My loss was one man killed and seven wounded. The distance marched was nine miles.

December 10, struck the Charleston and Savannah Railroad at Monteith Station, ten miles from Savannah. After destroying three miles of the track, my command advanced toward Savannah, following the Third Division. When within five miles of the city, the enemy having been found in an intrenched position, by direction of the brigadier-general commanding the corps I placed my command in position, with right resting on Savannah road. I then ordered Colonel Selfridge, whose brigade was on the left, to send a regiment with instructions to go if possible to the river. Afterward, it having been reported that this regiment was meeting with resistance, I ordered Selfridge to re-enforce it with another regiment. Owing, however, to the lateness of the hour at which the expedition started it did not succeed in reaching the river. On the 11th I ordered a reconnaissance to be made in front of my line, consisting of two regiments of Carman's brigade, under command of Colonel Cogswell, Second Massachusetts Volunteers, which developed the enemy's position, and the nature of the intervening ground. On the same day, by direction of the brigadier-general commanding the corps, I directed Colonel Carman to send one regiment to Argyle Island to secure the stores and hold the rice mills upon the island. Pursuant to orders from headquarters of the corps, I also directed Colonel Robinson, commanding Third Brigade, to send three regiments to the rear to protect the trains, and on the 13th Colonel Robinson was directed to take the remainder of his brigade to the same position. On the 15th the Second Massachusetts Volunteers, Colonel Cogswell commanding, was ordered to report with his regiment to Colonel Hawley on Argyle Island, and on the next day, pursuant to orders from headquarters of the corps, I directed Colonel Carman to move the remaining regiments of his brigade to Argyle Island and from thence to the South Carolina shore. Owing to the want of boats the passage to the South Carolina shore was made with great difficulty, and it was not until the 19th instant that the whole brigade had effected a landing on the Carolina shore, where it took up a position threatening the Charleston and Savannah road. Understanding that the object of this movement was merely to threaten the enemy's only line of communications, and thereby cause him to withdraw his troops from his main line in front of Savannah, I directed Colonel Carman to present a bold front and sent out frequent reconnaissances. On the morning of the 21st, the enemy having evacuated the city of Savannah during the afternoon and night previous, I received orders from the brigadier-general commanding the corps to move the First and Second Brigades to a position nearer the city. The First Brigade was moved at once to the position assigned to it, but owing to the high winds which prevailed during this and the following day, and the activity of the enemy, quite a force of which still remained in his front, Colonel Carman was unable to cross his entire brigade to the Georgia shore until the afternoon of the 22d. During the crossing, Col. John H. Ketcham, commanding One hundred and fiftieth New York Volunteers, a brave and efficient officer, was wounded severely in the thigh. In the evening of the 22d the Second Brigade was brought to its present camp, and on the following morning the Third Brigade, which had remained in its old position until the trains could be moved to the vicinity of the city, was also brought up and encamped, with right resting on Savannah River.

During the march, which from time of leaving Atlanta to the arrival before Savannah occupied twenty-six days, the troops of my command subsisted mostly upon provisions taken from the country through which we passed, and were abundantly supplied. After arriving in front of Savannah a large supply of rice was found on the plantations in the vicinity, upon which, with the beef-cattle on hand, the command subsisted until supplies were obtained from the fleet.

The following supplies were taken from the country by the foraging parties which were sent out daily:

Item	Unit	Quantity	Item	Unit	Quantity
Beef-cattle		560	Meal and flour	pounds	1,500
Sheep		300	Bacon	do	1,000
Hogs		500	Fresh meat	do	95,000
Corn	pounds	298,472	Sugar	do	1,000
Fodder	do	399,051	Tobacco	do	1,500
Rice (in sheaf)	do	20,000	Molasses	barrels	26
Rice (threshed)	do	38,800	Whisky	do	3
Sweet potatoes	do	164,200	Salt	do	6

In addition to the foregoing, on the 10th of December a foraging party of Carman's brigade, commanded by Captain Gildersleeve, One hundred and fiftieth New York Volunteers, captured the dispatch steamer Ida from the enemy, taking thirteen prisoners, among whom was Colonel Clinch, of General Hardee's staff. On account of the approach of rebel gun-boats, Captain Gildersleeve burned the steamer after removing the prisoners. On the 12th Colonel Hawley, commanding Third Wisconsin, on Argyle Island, took possession of the steamer Resolute, which had been driven on the Argyle shore by Captain Winegar's battery. The boat and stores captured upon her, as well as prisoners, were turned over by Colonel Hawley directly to corps headquarters.

One hundred and fifty horses and 175 mules were captured during the march. Of these 130 horses were turned over to the provost-marshal of the corps, and the remainder of the horses and the mules were put into the different trains of the division. Twenty-two cotton gins and 1,028 bales of cotton were destroyed by my command; 1,800 bales of cotton were also turned over by Colonel Hawley, Third Wisconsin Volunteers, while commanding post of Milledgeville, by order of Major-General Sherman. My command also destroyed 36 miles of railroad.

About 900 negroes joined and followed the column to our position in front of Savannah, where all except those who had been taken for teamsters and officers' servants were turned over to the provost-marshal of the corps.

My aggregate effective force on leaving Atlanta was 5,363, and on arriving at Savannah the report of effective force showed an aggregate of 5,174, making a loss of 189. Of this number 157 were killed, wounded, or missing, and are accounted for by name in the report of casualties appended to this report. The remaining number, 32, were taken from the effective force by sickness.

The organization of my command is as follows: First Brigade, Colonel Selfridge, Forty-sixth Pennsylvania Volunteers, commanding, composed of the following regiments, One hundred and twenty-third New York Volunteers, Fifth Connecticut Veteran Volunteers, Forty-sixth Pennsylvania Veteran Volunteers, and One hundred and forty-first New York Volunteers. Second Brigade, Col. E. A. Carman, Thirteenth New Jersey Volunteers, commanding, composed of the Third Wisconsin Veteran Volunteers, Second Massachusetts Volunteers, One hundred and seventh New York Volunteers, Thirteenth New Jersey Volunteers, and One hundred and fiftieth New York Volunteers. Third Brigade, Col. J. S. Robinson, Eighty-second Ohio Volunteers, commanding, composed of the Thirty-first Wisconsin Volunteers, Eighty-second Ohio Volunteers, Eighty-second Illinois Volunteers, One hundred and first Illinois Volunteers, One hundred and forty-third New York Volunteers, and Sixty-first Ohio Volunteers.

My staff was composed of the following-named officers:

1. Maj. James Francis, Second Massachusetts Volunteers, acting assistant inspector-general.
2. Surg. H. Z. Gill, surgeon, U. S. Volunteers, surgeon-in-chief.
3. Capt. George B. Cadwalader, assistant quartermaster.
4. Capt. John C. Livezey, commissary of subsistence.
5. Capt. E. A. Wickes, One hundred and fiftieth New York Volunteers, assistant commissary of musters.
6. Capt. S. A. Bennett, One hundred and seventh New York Volunteers, acting topographical engineer.
7. Capt. M. P. Whitney, Fifth Connecticut Volunteers, provost-marshal.
8. Capt. William J. Augustine, Twenty-ninth Pennsylvania Volunteers, ordnance officer.
9. First Lieut. George Robinson, aide-de-camp to Brigadier-General Williams, acting assistant adjutant-general.
10. First Lieut. E. B. Benedict, Forty-sixth New York Volunteers, aide-de-camp.

Accompanying this report I forward reports of brigade and regimental commanders.

Very respectfully, your obedient servant,

N. J. JACKSON,
Brigadier-General, Commanding.

Lieut. Col. H. W. PERKINS,
Assistant Adjutant-General, Twentieth Corps.

No. 79.

Report of Surg. Henry Z. Gill, U. S. Army, Surgeon-in-Chief.

HDQRS. FIRST DIVISION, TWENTIETH ARMY CORPS,
SURGEON'S OFFICE,
Savannah, Ga., December 31, 1864.

GENERAL: I have the honor to make the following report of First Division, Twentieth Army Corps, during the campaign and siege of Savannah, commencing at Atlanta, Ga., November 15, and closing with the capture of the city of Savannah, Ga., December 21, 1864, embracing a period of thirty-seven days:

The Twentieth Corps formed the right of the Left Wing of the Army of Georgia. The division was commanded by Brig. Gen. N. J. Jackson, and was composed of three brigades, commanded respectively by—First Brigade (four regiments), Col. J. L. Selfridge, Forty-sixth Pennsylvania Veteran Volunteers; Second Brigade (five regiments), Col. E. A. Carman, Thirteenth New Jersey Volunteers; Third Brigade (six regiments), Col. J. S. Robinson, Eighty-second Ohio Volunteers, giving a total present strength of 5,829. (See Appendix, Table I.*) The men were generally in good condition, having had for some weeks the advantage of foraging expeditions, and were well clothed before leaving Atlanta, having received issues of new clothing. There were in the command about 300 recruits. The transportation of the division comprised 177 six-mule army wagons, thirty-eight of which carried ammunition. The transportation of the division hospital consisted of three army wagons and one medicine wagon, carrying sixteen tent-flies and the usual monthly allowance of the most useful medical supplies. The transportation for the sick and wounded consisted of thirty two-mule ambulances, under the supervision of a captain and one lieutenant from each brigade, to which were added, near the close of the march, three army wagons for carrying knapsacks and equipments of men in regiments—such cases as were not proper for hospital and who would return to the regiments at night. The supplies consisted of twelve days' rations of hard bread, fifteen days' rations of coffee, fifteen days' rations of sugar, sixty days' rations of salt, and one day's ration of salt meat. The ambulances carried 200 pounds of hard bread for the hospital, which was much needed after the commissary's supply was exhausted and before the communication was opened with the fleet; also, a quantity of beef essence. The sick and wounded of the command had been mainly sent to the rear before we left Atlanta, the credit for which is partly due to the foresight and energy of Surgeon Kittoe, medical inspector, U. S. Army. The hospital report of November 15 showed but one remaining. There were at the same date fifty-one in the regiments excused from duty. (See Table I.*) On the march men were admitted to ambulance or hospital with passes signed by the regimental medical officers. (See Form, Table III*a*.*) One medical officer of the hospital corps and one steward accompanied the ambulance train each day to regulate admissions and attend to the wants of the sick. The number of sick and wounded admitted to hospital during the campaign was: (see Table IV†; also list of casualties). At the close of the siege the number in hospital was only 1 per cent. of the command. The regiments were supplied in most cases with a pack-mule and a pannier set to each, and no regiment in the command was

---

* Omitted.

† Shows 668 sick and 72 wounded; total, 740.

without a medical officer. The Ninth Illinois Mounted Infantry was attached to the corps until we reached the defenses of the city. The wounded of the regiment were admitted to hospital of the First Division. (See Table II.*)

GENERAL REMARKS.

The weather was unusually fine during the campaign, there being but three rainy days, though there were also a few light showers. The roads were good most of the time, with the exception of the few days mentioned above, and in the latter part of the route where the road led through swampy country some difficulty was experienced on that account. Had the weather been rainy it would have necessitated the abandoning of a portion, at least, of our train. The fact of but one corps moving on one road was of the greatest advantage, which was demonstrated in the moving of the rear division, whichever that happened to be. Sometimes it would be till midnight, sometimes till nearly morning, getting into camp. At one time the First Division was in the rear, and it required five hours' hard work to make a distance of two miles. The supplies were taken mainly from the country through which we passed, and though comparatively thinly settled, it usually furnished an abundance of beef-cattle, hogs, sheep, poultry of all kinds, sweet potatoes in abundance for the men, and plenty of forage for the horses and mules. The water was, generally speaking, very good and sufficient for this season of the year. The animals were in very bad condition at the time of leaving Atlanta, on account of the destruction of the railroad between that point and Chattanooga, by General Hood, in October. A portion of the time there had been no forage issued; at other times only half rations of grain, with no hay at all. We started with four days' forage of grain only. Had we not been able to capture a large number of mules and horses during the first week it would have been impossible to have brought the train with us. Many of the mules we started with died or were killed and their places filled with fine stock from the farms on the route. At the end of the campaign the teams were in splendid condition, much of the stock, especially the mules, being first class.

The command marched about 350 miles and passed through the following towns: Decatur, November 15; Social Circle, November 18; Madison, November 19; Eatonton, November 21; Milledgeville, the capital of Georgia, November 22; Sandersville and Tennille Station, November 26; Davisborough, November 27; Spiers Turnout, November 28; Springfield, December 7. The battle of Monteith Swamp occurred on December 9, at which the division captured two forts, with a loss of 1 killed and 5 wounded. We reached the main works for the defense of the city of Savannah on the 10th of December and commenced the siege. On the same day the division captured one steam-boat in the Savannah River, Ida, and on the 12th another, Resolute. One brigade crossed the river and intrenched on the South Carolina side December 19. The city was evacuated by the enemy on the night of the 20th, and was formally surrendered by the civil authorities at 3 a. m. December 21, 1864, to Brig. Gen. J. W. Geary, Second Division, Twentieth Army Corps. On the route we had two skirmishes—one at Sandersville November 26; the other at Monteith Swamp December 9. The campaign is said to be the most extensive, the most rapid, and the most successful of the war, with the least loss to us, while it accomplished

* Shows 6 wounded and 15 sick.

the destruction of most of the railroad from Atlanta on the west to the Savannah River on the east, the destruction of vast quantities of cotton, the capture of a large amount of valuable stock, and finally of the city of Savannah and surrounding forts.

I am, general, very respectfully, your obedient servant,

H. Z. GILL,
Surgeon, U. S. Volunteers, Chief First Div., 20th Army Corps.

Brig. Gen. J. K. BARNES,
Surgeon-General, U. S. Army.

No. 80.

Report of Col. James L. Selfridge, Forty-sixth Pennsylvania Infantry, commanding First Brigade.

HDQRS. FIRST BRIG., FIRST DIV., 20TH ARMY CORPS,
Savannah, Ga., December 26, 1864.

LIEUTENANT: *

On the morning of November 15 we started from Atlanta en route for Savannah. My brigade was the leading one of the corps and moved from Decatur at 7 a. m., passed through that town, and after traveling about fourteen miles in an easterly direction, encamped for the night near Stone Mountain. November 16, moved from camp this afternoon at 1 p. m. and after a march of about ten miles encamped for the night near Rock Bridge. November 17, moved from near Rock Bridge at 9 a. m., traveled about fifteen miles toward Social Circle, and encamped at 12 midnight. November 18, started from encampment at 10 a. m., reached Social Circle at 2 p. m., where my brigade halted for dinner. The brigade was in the extreme rear of the corps, acting as rear guard. Marched about nineteen miles, and encamped near Rutledge at 10 p. m. November 19, started from near Rutledge at 9 a. m., passed through Madison at 11 a. m., and encamped at 5 p. m. a few miles south of that place on the Milledgeville road, after marching about eight miles. November 20, moved toward Eatonton this morning at 9 a. m. and encamped about five miles from Eatonton, after marching ten miles. This day's march was a very severe one, owing to the muddy nature of the roads; more or less rain during the entire day and evening. November 21, moved from our encampment at 9 a. m. and passed through Eatonton about noon; roads in very bad condition. Traveled twelve miles and encamped, at 12 midnight, fourteen miles from Milledgeville. November 22, my brigade entered Milledgeville at 4 p. m. without opposition, crossed the Oconee River, and encamped close to the city at 5 p. m. November 23, pursuant to orders from division headquarters this brigade marched through the city of Milledgeville at 1 p. m. to the Milledgeville and Gordon Railroad, five miles of which we completely destroyed by burning and bending the rails; returned to camp about 9 p. m. November 24, resumed our march this morning at 7 o'clock, and after traveling about fourteen miles went into camp near Hebron at 4 p. m.; roads very much improved; weather cold and clear. November 25, started this morning promptly at 6 o'clock; reached Buffalo Swamp at 8 a. m.; found that the bridges, nine in number, had been destroyed

---

* For portion of report (here omitted) relating to operations about Atlanta, see Vol. XXXIX, Part I, p. 653.

by the enemy's cavalry; were detained here until 2 p. m., by which time the bridges were rebuilt, and we passed quietly over the swamp, and after marching about five miles encamped at 5 p. m. November 26, entered Sandersville this morning at 11 o'clock. Moved to Tennille Station at 2 p. m., and destroyed about two miles of railroad, together with large Government warehouses, the railroad depot, and sixty-two bales of cotton. November 27, marched toward Davisborough at 6 a. m. and reached that place at 4 p. m., where we encamped, after marching about twelve miles. November 28, brigade moved to the Georgia Central Railroad and assisted in destroying the track, &c., from Davisborough to Spiers Station, a distance of twelve miles. Arrived at Spiers and encamped at 7 p. m. November 29, continued destroying the railroad at 7 a. m. and reached Bostwick Station about 6 p. m., after having destroyed eight miles of road. November 30, started this morning toward Louisville at 9 o'clock, and after marching ten miles encamped within two miles of Louisville.

December 1, pursuant to orders from division headquarters I reported with my brigade to Brigadier-General Ward, commanding Third Division, Twentieth Corps, who placed my brigade as guard alongside his wagon train, which was in rear of the corps; after traveling about five miles we encamped with the Third Division. December 2, started at daylight in the same order as yesterday; marched about twelve miles and got into camp at 6 p. m.; received orders from General Jackson to join the First Division at 6 o'clock the following morning. December 3, brigade started at 5.30 a. m. and joined the First Division, which was two miles in advance, at 6 a. m.; traveled about fourteen miles and encamped near Horse Creek at 4 p. m. December 4, started this morning at 6 o'clock, and after marching through a desolate, piney country for fifteen miles, encamped near Little Ogeechee River at 4 p. m. December 5, did not move till 4 p. m.; very bad roads; marched four miles and encamped about midnight. December 6, started at 6 a. m.; marched about ten miles, and encamped near Smoke's house 6 p. m. December 7, resumed our march at 10 a. m., having the rear of the corps; passed through one continuous swamp twelve miles in length, and reached camp near Springfield on the following morning at 2 o'clock; the most tedious and unpleasant march during the campaign; rained during the entire day. December 8, resumed our march at 7 a. m., and after marching twelve miles through a flat, swampy country, encamped at dark about twenty miles northwest of Savannah. December 9, brigade moved at 7 a. m. in advance of the corps; after traveling about seven miles we came to a portion of the road which had been most effectually obstructed by slashed timber which extended about 200 yards, at the end of which was an open field, and in the field, completely commanding the road, were two forts occupied by the enemy, and from which position they prevented our pioneers from clearing the road of the obstructions referred to. In accordance with orders from division headquarters I sent forward the Fifth Regiment Connecticut Veteran Volunteers, Lieut. Col. H. W. Daboll commanding, as skirmishers, and shortly afterward sent the Forty-sixth Pennsylvania Veteran Volunteers, One hundred and twenty-third New York Volunteers, and One hundred and forty-first New York Volunteers, all that remained of my brigade, to support the Fifth Connecticut Veteran Volunteers. In a short time they opened fire, and in conjunction with the Second and Third Brigades, which had been sent around on their flanks, drove the enemy in great confusion from both forts and captured two prisoners. Lieutenant-Colonel Daboll, commanding the Fifth Connecticut Veteran Volunteers, is entitled to much credit for the gallant manner in which he charged and drove the enemy from their works, as he was directly under fire of their guns and exposed to much danger. He is a brave officer and worthy of promotion. I moved on beyond the forts in line of battle for a distance of about one mile and a half, when I was ordered to return, and encamped for the night. In this little affair I only lost 3 men in my brigade, all from the Forty-sixth Regiment Pennsylvania Veteran Volunteers—1 man wounded in the leg (afterward amputated), 1 man wounded severely in the head, and 1 other slightly in the shoulder. There was supposed to be about 1,000 of the enemy in the forts, with two pieces of artillery.

December 10, traveled about nine miles, and encamped four miles from Savannah. Five of the enemy's soldiers surrendered near General Harrison's plantation to Capt. A. W. Selfridge, acting commissary of subsistence of this brigade, while the latter was foraging in advance of my troops. The Fifth Connecticut Veteran Volunteers, of my command, captured a wagon loaded with ammunition. The road at the point where we encamped for the night was obstructed by slashed timber, and just beyond the slashing the enemy were strongly fortified. Pursuant to orders from Brig. Gen. N. J. Jackson, I sent the Forty-sixth Regiment Pennsylvania Veteran Volunteers about half a mile to the left on a road running parallel with the enemy's works and about 400 yards from them. In endeavoring to reach the river this regiment met the enemy's skirmishers, and after a brisk fire of fifteen or twenty minutes were obliged to fall back about 200 yards. While here seven deserters from the enemy gave themselves up and were forwarded to division headquarters. On the following day I removed the remainder of my brigade to the road upon which the Forty-sixth Pennsylvania Veteran Volunteers were stationed, my left connecting with General Geary's line and my right connecting with the left of the Third Brigade of this division. Here I remained until the morning of the 21st instant, when it was discovered that the enemy had evacuated his works. In accordance with orders from division headquarters I moved my brigade at 6 a. m. and occupied the rebel works. Shortly afterward I moved my troops to within one mile of the city of Savannah, where they are encamped. During the time we were encamped in front of Savannah my troops were within close range of the enemy's guns, and although they kept up a vigorous fire upon our lines, strange to say, only one man of my command was struck by their missiles. He was a member of the Forty-sixth Pennsylvania Veteran Volunteers, and was slightly wounded by a piece of shell.

During the whole campaign the foraging was all that could be desired. The troops of my command subsisted principally from the captures of regimental foraging parties, which were sent out daily by each regimental commander. Besides this, my acting commissary of subsistence obtained the following supplies and issued them to this command during the march: 12 wagon-loads sweet potatoes, averaging 1,600 pounds per load; 100 head of beef-cattle, averaging 2,000 pounds each; 100 sheep; 50 hogs; 2 half-barrels of sorghum molasses. The brigade captured about 40 horses and mules, destroyed 5 cotton gins and 73 bales of cotton, picked up about 100 negroes, and destroyed 20 miles of railroad. During the march the quartermaster of this brigade obtained from the country 36,094 pounds of corn and 75,231 pounds of fodder. Our stock was in much better condition when we entered Savannah than it was at the commencement of the campaign.

The health of the command was never better, and both officers and men were in excellent spirits and seemed to have the most perfect confidence in the success of our enterprise. When I left Atlanta, on the 15th of November, the effective force of this brigade was 63 commissioned officers and 1,448 enlisted men. At the close of the campaign I had 64 officers and 1,380 enlisted men, making an increase of 1 officer and a decrease of 68 enlisted men. Twenty-three of the above are supposed to have been captured by the enemy and 4 of them were wounded. The remainder (41) were taken from the effective force of the command on account of sickness.

In closing my report, duty requires that I should make a few comments upon the conduct of line and non-commissioned officers, many of whom seem to forget the responsibility of their positions and did but little toward preserving that discipline for which this command has ever been renowned. Regimental commanders exerted themselves to have their men together and endeavored to prevent straggling, but, owing to the indifference of line and non-commissioned officers, were unable to prevent their men from taking liberties which could and might have been remedied by their subordinates.

To my regimental commanders I wish to tender my warmest thanks for the cheerful manner in which they discharged each and every duty imposed upon them. Capt. William Merrell, commanding One hundred and forty-first New York Volunteers, is entitled to especial praise for the zealous manner in which he performed the duties which devolved upon him as a regimental commander, having but a short time been in command and with but very few company officers to assist him.

To Capt. D. W. Palmer, assistant adjutant-general; Capt. William C. Rockwell, acting assistant inspector-general; Capt. A. W. Selfridge, acting commissary of subsistence; First Lieut. George Tubbs, topographical engineer; First Lieut. R. Cruikshank, provost-marshal; First Lieut. A. L. Crawford, acting assistant quartermaster; and Lieut. W. F. Martin, aide-de-camp, members of my staff, I wish to offer my grateful appreciation of their efforts at all times to assist me in performing the several duties devolving upon them in a cheerful and soldier-like manner.

Just previous to leaving Atlanta my aide-de-camp, Lieutenant Martin, received a leave of absence for twenty days, and although without proper equipments for a campaign (having just made his escape from Charleston prison), when he learned that we were likely to start southward before the expiration of his leave of absence, refused to avail himself of the same, and has been ever at his post, ready and willing to perform whatever service I required of him.

Accompanying this report you will please find reports of my regimental commanders.

All of which is most respectfully submitted.

I have the honor to be, lieutenant, very respectfully, your obedient servant,

JAS. L. SELFRIDGE,
Colonel Forty-sixth Pennsylvania Vet. Vols., Comdg. First Brig.

Lieut. GEORGE ROBINSON,
Actg. Asst. Adjt. Gen., First Division, Twentieth Army Corps.

No. 81.

Report of Lieut. Col. Henry W. Daboll, Fifth Connecticut Infantry, of operations October 21–December 23.

HDQRS. FIFTH REGIMENT CONNECTICUT VET. VOLS.,
Near Savannah, Ga., December 26, 1864.

CAPTAIN: I have the honor to submit the following report of movements of this regiment since the occupation of Atlanta, Ga., September 2, 1864:

October 21, we received orders to march as a portion of guard to a wagon train of some 800 teams; we moved in the direction of Flat Shoals, eighteen miles; assisted in loading the train with corn, and returned to Atlanta on the 24th. October 29, moved with the First Brigade to Decatur, and formed portion of rear guard to a forage train coming in same day. November 5, moved out of the city three miles; encamped for the night and returned to the city next day. November 15, regiment marched, as advance guard of Twentieth Army Corps, in direction of Stone Mountain. We continued our march with the main column each day, nothing worthy of note occurring until November 20, when a small party of rebel cavalry made a dash on our rear, capturing some eight stragglers, three of them being members of this regiment. November 22, reached Milledgeville, the capital of the State. November 23, at work all day destroying the Gordon and Milledgeville Railroad, the regiment tearing up about two miles and a half of track. Moved with the main column until the 26th, when we were again at work on the railroad, tearing up about a mile of track and destroying four large warehouses at Tennille Station, on the Macon road. November 28, again at work destroying railroad. November 29, at work on the railroad all day, reaching a point near the Ogeechee River; we left the railroad here, and rejoined the main column.

Nothing of importance occurred until December 9; the regiment, having the advance of the corps, came upon a small body of rebel infantry with one piece of artillery intrenched on the road near Monteith. The regiment was quickly deployed, and advancing through a deep marsh soon developed the force of the enemy. The First Division, Twentieth Corps, making a concentrated movement on them, they retreated at double-quick. Some portion of this regiment, being the first to enter the rebel fort, captured two prisoners. Our casualties were none. December 10, the regiment moved at an early hour, with four wagons belonging to First Brigade commissary department, to General Harrison's plantation; loaded the wagons with sweet potatoes and meat, and obtained some three days' rations besides. Lieutenant Kellum, proceeding down a by-road with two companies, came upon two wagons loaded with ammunition and supplies which had been abandoned by the rebels; they were brought in, and accounted for. Same day we moved within three miles and a half of Savannah. Brigade formed line of battle on the left of railroad, the regiment in reserve in close column by division. The evening of December 15 the regiment was ordered to accompany a train of 165 wagons to King's Bridge, for the purpose of getting a mail and bringing up supplies; remained at King's Bridge until the 22d; returned with the train to Savannah. December 23, took position on left of the brigade, where the regiment remains at present.

During our march from Atlanta the regiment has mainly subsisted on the country. At no time have the men been without meat or potatoes—articles not furnished by the subsistence department. The animals picked up have all been accounted for by the quartermaster of the regiment.

Very respectfully, your obedient servant,

HENRY W. DABOLL,
Lieutenant-Colonel, Commanding Regiment.

No. 82.

Report of Lieut. Col. James C. Rogers, One hundred and twenty-third New York Infantry, of operations October 21–December 24.

HEADQUARTERS 123D NEW YORK VOLUNTEERS,
Savannah, Ga., December 24, 1864.

CAPTAIN: I have the honor to submit the following report of the operations of this regiment from the occupation of Atlanta by the U. S. forces to the present time:

Shortly after the occupation of Atlanta by our forces, the Twentieth Army Corps having been assigned to the duty of garrisoning the city, this regiment went into camp on the northeast of the town. The troops built themselves comfortable and commodious quarters, and stringent measures were adopted for preserving the health of the men, somewhat impaired by the protracted campaign and defective diet. With the exceptions hereafter noted, the regiment remained here in camp until the 15th of November following, engaged in the customary duties of the garrison, viz, drills, picket guards, and fatigue upon the fortifications. On the 21st day of October this regiment, in connection with other forces and a large number of wagons, the whole under the command of Colonel Dustin, went upon a foraging expedition into the Snapfinger Creek and South River Valleys. A large amount of corn and fodder was gathered here, but I have no definite knowledge or official information of the amount. The expedition returned, without being molested, on the 24th of October. On the 29th of October this regiment, with the other regiments of the brigade, went to Decatur in aid of a foraging party under command of Brigadier-General Geary, and returned the same day without having seen the enemy. On the 5th day of November this regiment, in connection with the other regiments of the Twentieth Army Corps, broke camp and moved out upon the McDonough road, and encamped for the night. It returned the next day and reoccupied its old camp.

These movements comprise all the field operations of this regiment during its stay in Atlanta. During this time attention was paid to perfecting discipline, which was somewhat relaxed by a long and arduous campaign. The men were fully clothed and equipped, convalescents called in from hospitals, the returns of company officers completed and sent in, and every effort made to bring the command to a condition for active service. The regiment here received eight of their ten months' pay then due. Forty-three recruits were received here, but so shortly before moving from the city that but little instruction in drill could be imparted. They are, however, a good class of men, and have, in the main, proved themselves good soldiers. The elective franchise, conferred by an act of the New York Legislature at its last session, was here exercised, and it is believed with less of partisan heat and undue influence than ordinarily occurs at elections held in communities free from military authority.

Every preparation having been made in obedience to orders which had been previously received, on the 15th of November the regiment, together with the other troops composing the Twentieth Army Corps, moved out of the city on the Decatur road, taking the route, via Stone Mountain, Rock Bridge, and Social Circle, to Madison, which we entered on the 19th of November. Thence taking the Milledgeville road, we passed through Eatonton, and on the 22d of November passed through Milledgeville, crossed the Oconee, and encamped on the east bank. On the 23d the regiment destroyed one mile of the railroad leading to the Georgia Central. On the 24th of November we moved from Milledgeville, via Hebron, Sandersville, to Tennille, where we encamped the night of 26th of November. Near Sandersville there was some skirmishing, and the regiment was moved forward on the double-quick with aid of Colonel Robinson's brigade, but the enemy fled, and the regiment was not engaged. On the 27th of November we moved to Davisborough. The 28th and 29th of November, in connection with other troops, we destroyed all the Georgia railroad from Davisborough to Bostwick, with trifling exceptions. This regiment effectually destroyed three miles of road, tearing up and burning the ties and twisting the rails. November the 30th the Ogeechee was crossed without opposition, and we encamped for the night about four miles south of Louisville. Pushing southeasterly we passed through Springfield on the 8th of December. The march was much impeded near this place by the marshy nature of the ground, rendering it very difficult to move the trains of wagons and artillery.

On the 9th day of December the First Brigade, First Division, being in advance, at a point near Harrison's plantation, about four miles from the Savannah and Charleston Railroad and fourteen miles from Savannah, where the road passed through a difficult marsh, the road was found blockaded by felled trees and a redoubt with a piece of artillery planted to command the defile. The regiment, with the rest of the brigade, forced its way through a dense jungle and marshy ground to the left of the road, and as soon as it could be formed on solid ground the brigade advanced in line upon the enemy's works. Alarmed by our near approach, or that of the co-operating forces, the enemy fled and we encamped for the night. On the 10th of December we moved upon Savannah, and meeting the enemy, we went into position about four miles and a half from the city, between the Savannah and Augusta pike and the river, having a flooded rice swamp and canal in our front, with a narrow belt of timber intervening. With exception of slight alteration in position, we remained here until the 21st of December, subjected at all hours of the day and night to a heavy fire from the enemy's batteries, but, thanks to fortune or their unskillful artillerists, nearly every shell flew harmlessly over our heads. As the day dawned on the 21st, it was discovered that the enemy had evacuated the works in our front. The regiment was at once placed under arms and soon after crossed the swamp and entered the enemy's works, and later in the day went into the camp assigned it on the banks of the Savannah River just outside the city, where it is now resting from its labors.

During this movement the subsistence stores have been gathered almost exclusively from the country. Sweet potatoes have supplied the place of bread, and beef and pork gathered in the country have supplied the usual army rations of meat. Besides what was consumed at the time, twenty-odd beef-cattle were turned over by the regiment to the commissary of subsistence of the brigade, and a number of fine mules and horses to the brigade quartermaster. During the ten days before the city, rice was issued instead of bread and potatoes. Ten days' rations of hard bread and three and a half days' of salt meat were the only issues of those rations brought from Atlanta up to the time of entering Savannah.

Fourteen officers and seventy-three men having been detached for various duties in the corps, the regiment left Atlanta on the 15th of November with 18 officers and 447 men, and entered Savannah on the 21st of December with 18 officers and 446 men, the only loss during the campaign being 1 man (Edward Phair), a private of Company B, who, straggling from the regiment near Madison, was probably captured by the enemy's cavalry.

The health and physical vigor of the command have not only been preserved but greatly improved during the campaign, and the troops are now, with the exception of clothing, of which they are in great need, better fitted for active service than when they left Atlanta.

While the highest state of discipline could not be preserved from the peculiar character of the movement, I take pleasure in saying that under circumstances of extraordinary temptation this command has, in a great measure, been preserved from the vices of straggling and marauding. Both officers and men have always exhibited a cheerful willingness to perform every duty imposed on them, and a large share of that unquestioning confidence in the leader of this army which is so important an element in the success of military movements.

I have the honor to be, very respectfully, your obedient servant,

JAS. C. ROGERS,
Lieutenant-Colonel, Commanding.

Capt. D. W. PALMER,
Asst. Adjt. Gen., 1st Brig., 1st Div., 20th Army Corps.

No. 83.

Report of Capt. William Merrell, One hundred and forty-first New York Infantry.

HDQRS. 141ST REGIMENT NEW YORK VOLUNTEERS,
Savannah, Ga., December 26, 1864.

SIR: I have the honor to submit the following report of the operations of this command during the recent campaign:

From the occupation of Atlanta, Ga., the regiment was engaged in building quarters and the usual duties of camp life until the 30th instant, when we were ordered to report to Col. N. M. Crane, commanding a provisional brigade doing guard duty in the city; here we remained until the commencement of the recent campaign; on the morning of November 15 we broke camp and joined the First Brigade on the Decatur road; marching fifteen miles, we halted near Stone Mountain and camped for the night. 16th, marched across Yellow River, guarding ammunition train; halted at 11.30 p. m. for the night. 17th, commenced the march at 10 a. m., guarding train; camped at 12.30 p. m. 18th, marched at 9 a. m.; halted at Social Circle at 2 p. m. for dinner; afternoon resumed the march, passing through Rutledge, and encamped at 11 p. m. 19th, marched at 9 a. m. on train guard; passed through Madison at 2 p.m.; taking the Milledgeville road at that place, we camped four miles from the town. 20th, marched at 9 a. m., camping near Eatonton for the night. 21st, marched at 9 a. m.; passed through Eatonton; camped at 1 a. m., 22d, four miles from that place. 22d, marched at daylight; crossed Little River; reached Milledgeville at sunset; went into camp about one mile east of the town. 23d, was ordered out in light marching order at 1 p. m.; marched to the Milledgeville and Eatonton Railroad; we were engaged in destroying that road until after dark, when we returned to camp. 24th, marched at daylight from Milledgeville; camped about 4 p. m. 25th, marched at 6.30 a. m.; made about eight miles. 26th, marched at 6.15 a. m.; reached Sandersville at 10 a. m., where we halted for dinner; we then marched to Tennille Station, on the Georgia Central Railroad, and halted for the night. 27th, marched at 6 a. m. from Tennille Station to Davisborough, fifteen miles; captured during the afternoon twelve head of cattle and two mules; went into camp for the night. 28th, marched at 7 a. m. to the railroad, destroying it to Spiers Station; encamped for the night at that place. 29th, moved at 6.30 a. m. on the railroad; destroyed it to Bostwick Station, a distance of eight miles, and camped for the night. 30th, marched at 9.30 a. m.; crossed the Ogeechee River two miles from Louisville and camped for the night.

Nothing of importance occurred until the 9th of December, when the road was found to be obstructed by fallen timber, rendering it impossible to advance. The pioneers were ordered forward, but as soon as the work began the rebels opened a piece of artillery upon the advance, which had halted in the road. After a short time the balance of our brigade were ordered to advance and support the Fifth Connecticut Volunteers, which were on the skirmish line, while two brigades were sent on the flanks. The First Brigade advanced as fast as the nature of the ground would permit, and after getting within range the Fifth Connecticut Volunteers opened a terrific fire on the enemy's battery, driving them in great confusion from their works, which we soon occupied; here we halted for the night. 10th, marched at 7.30 a. m., striking the Charleston and Savannah Railroad at 10 a. m.; after a halt of three hours we again advanced in direction of Savannah and within four miles of the city, when it was discovered that a large force of the enemy was in our front, when we halted and formed a line of battle to the left of the road; after sending out pickets we encamped for the night. 11th, advanced about one-quarter of a mile, constructed works, and remained until the morning of the 21st, when it was discovered that the enemy had evacuated, when we immediately advanced our lines, moved within one mile of the city, where we are now encamped.

There were issued during the campaign eleven days' rations; the balance of rations were foraged from the country. There were twenty-five negroes brought along by this command.

I have the honor to be, captain, very respectfully, your obedient servant,

WILLIAM MERRELL,
Captain, Comdg. 141st Regiment New York Volunteers.

Capt. D. W. PALMER,
Assistant Adjutant-General.

No. 84.

Report of Maj. Patrick Griffith, Forty-sixth Pennsylvania Infantry.

HDQRS. FORTY-SIXTH REGT. PENNSYLVANIA VET. VOLS.,
Savannah, Ga., December 26, 1864.

SIR:*

November 15, left Atlanta, Ga., nothing of importance transpiring; camped near Stone Mountain at 4 p. m. 16th, nothing of importance

*For portion of report (here omitted) relating to operations about Atlanta, see Vol. XXXIX, Part I, p. 654.

transpiring; camped at Yellow River at 12 p. m. 17th, nothing of importance transpiring; camped five miles from Hot Creek at 12 p. m.; roads bad; forage plenty. 18th, rear guard left camp at 7.50 a. m.; passed through Social Circle at noon; crossed the ——— River; camped five miles from Rutledge at 2 p. m. 19th, left camp at 6 a. m.; train guard; raining, weather warm; passed through Madison at 1 p. m.; camped four miles from Madison on the Milledgeville road at 5 p. m. 20th, rainy all night; First Brigade rear guard; passed through Eatonton at noon; roads almost impassable; camped at 2 a. m. 21st, rain; roads worse than yesterday; camped at 2 a. m. 22d, left camp at 7 a. m.; weather very cold; crossed Little River at 10 a. m.; arrived in Milledgeville, Ga., at 4 p. m.; crossed Oconee River to camp. 23d, left camp to burn railroad; First Brigade destroyed five miles of road; returned to camp at 10 p. m. 24th, left Milledgeville at 7 a. m.; weather clear and cold; roads good; passed through several canebrakes, and camped near Hebron at 4 p. m. 25th, left camp at 6 a. m.; delayed at Buffalo Creek on account of bridges having been destroyed; moved to near Sandersville; cavalry had a severe skirmish with the enemy; camped in line for the night. 26th, left camp at 7 a. m.; the advance skirmishing to Sandersville; enemy retreating; moved to Tennille Station, three miles and a half; destroyed immense amounts of cotton, both raw and manufactured; destroyed one mile and a half of railroad and large warehouses used by the rebel Government to store provisions. 27th, marched from Tennille to Davisborough; camped at 4 p. m. 28th, destroyed railroad from Davisborough to Spiers Station, a distance of eleven miles; camped before night. 29th, resumed destroying the railroads, and after destroying eight miles encamped at dark near Bostwick. 30th, left camp at 8.30 a. m., course due north; camped near Louisville at dark.

December 1, left camp at daylight, and camped at 8 p. m., nothing of import transpiring. December 2, left camp at 6.30 a. m.; camped at Buck Head Creek at 8 p. m. December 3, left camp at 5.30 a. m.; marched eighteen miles, and encamped at 4 p. m.; weather cloudy. December 4, showers during the night; nothing of importance transpiring. December 5, left camp at dark; camped at 12 p. m.; forage plenty. December 6, left camp at 9 a. m.; camped at dark. December 7, left camp near Sylvania at 10 a. m.; rain all night; passed through the worst kind of swamps; on the road until daylight. December 8, resumed the march at 8.30 a. m.; weather good; camped at dark. December 9, left camp at 8 a. m.; advance engaged with the enemy; First Division in advance; found the enemy strongly posted in earth-works at Cypress Swamp; First Brigade moved forward in the center, Second Brigade on the right, and Third Brigade on the left; charged and took the enemy's works in fine style; loss in regiment, three wounded; camped on the captured ground at dark. December 10, left camp at 8 a. m.; came on the enemy's works four miles from Savannah, when I was ordered by Col. James L. Selfridge, commanding First Brigade, First Division, Twentieth Corps, to move my regiment about half a mile to the left on the road leading from the main road to the river. About half an hour after I received an order from Brigadier-General Jackson, commanding division, directing me to push my command to the river, if I could do so safely. I moved on to within a quarter of a mile of the river, where we met the enemy's skirmishers, and exchanged shots with them about twenty minutes. Finding the enemy's line strong, and my flanks entirely exposed, I deemed it prudent to fall back a distance of 200 yards, where I remained in line of battle during the night, having at the same time thrown out a strong skirmish line covering my front and left, my right connecting with the Third Brigade skirmishers, who were thrown forward during the evening. During the night I received seven deserters from the enemy, whom I forwarded to brigade headquarters under guard. On the 12th was ordered into camp near the road occupied by my regiment the night previous, threw up breastworks, and remained until the 23d, when it was found that the enemy had evacuated his works, when we advanced to within two miles of the city, and went into our present camp.

From the 15th of November (date of leaving Atlanta) until the 23d of December, we drew about ten days' full rations of crackers, sugar, and coffee. The balance of our supplies were foraged from the country through which we passed.

During the campaign I captured 15 or 20 negroes, whom I directed to report to Captain Cadwalader, division quartermaster; also some mules and horses, which were turned in to Captain Whittelsey, corps quartermaster. My command captured 4 Prussian rifled muskets, which were turned in to the division ordnance department.

The officers of my command behaved well during the campaign. The enlisted men of my regiment, with one or two exceptions, obeyed orders promptly. Those who failed to observe them were punished at the time.

When the regiment left Atlanta the effective strength was 16 officers and 415 enlisted men.

I have the honor to be, very respectfully, your obedient servant,

P. GRIFFITH,
Major, Commanding Regiment.

Capt. D. W. PALMER,
Assistant Adjutant-General, First Brigade.

No. 85.

Report of Col. Ezra A. Carman, Thirteenth New Jersey Infantry, commanding Second Brigade.

HDQRS. SECOND BRIG., FIRST DIV., TWENTIETH CORPS,
Near Savannah, Ga., December 27, 1864.

SIR:*

November 15, the brigade, with the exception of the Second Massachusetts Volunteer Infantry which was left to destroy the public property in the city and accompany the Fourteenth Corps until such time as it could rejoin its brigade, took up its line of march with the division and corps to which it belongs, marched to Stone Mountain and encamped for the night. November 16 it crossed Yellow River and Rock Bridge, and encamped two miles from east bank. November 17, crossed Big and Little Haynes Creeks, and encamped near Sheffield. November 18, in compliance with orders issued from Major-General Sherman previous to starting on this campaign, I detailed a forage party consisting of two companies from each regiment, with directions to proceed along each side of the road, keeping within half a mile of the column, and collect what subsistence they could find for the use of the brigade. One detachment of forty-three men, under command of

* For portion of report (here omitted) relating to operations about Atlanta, see Vol. XXXIX, Part I, p. 655.

Capt. G. W. Reid, all from the One hundred and seventh New York Volunteers, did not return. I have since learned they were captured by the enemy five or six miles from the column. Passed through Social Circle and Rutledge this day, and encamped four miles from Madison. November 19, the brigade marched through Madison and encamped four miles east of that place. November 20, it marched to within four miles of Eatonton. November 21, it passed through Eatonton and marched to Little River. November 22, marched to Milledgeville, the capital of Georgia. When within one mile of the city the Third Wisconsin and One hundred and seventh New York Volunteers were sent forward as guard to the city, Col. William Hawley, Third Wisconsin Volunteers, being appointed post commander. The brigade then marched through the city, crossed the Oconee River, encamping near it. The State arsenal and a large amount of public property was destroyed at this place, for particulars of which I respectfully refer to report of Colonel Hawley, commanding Third Wisconsin Volunteer Infantry, and also to appendix to this report, marked C. November 23, remained in camp in Milledgeville; Second Massachusetts Volunteers joined the brigade here. November 24, the brigade marched to within three miles of Hebron Post-Office. November 25, it crossed Buffalo Creek and marched to within four miles of Sandersville. November 26, the brigade this day had the advance; moved out of camp at 6.30 a. m., and after marching two miles, the Ninth Illinois Cavalry* in our front encountered the enemy, who were posted on a small creek, the road through which had been obstructed by fallen trees. The enemy were soon dislodged and pursued to Sandersville, at which place they made a stand, driving back our cavalry. I then deployed six companies of the Thirteenth New Jersey Volunteers as skirmishers, with four companies in reserve, and advanced on them, the Ninth Illinois being disposed on the flanks. The enemy gave way before my skirmishers, and I entered town at the same time as did the Fourteenth Corps, who came in on another road to the left. Moving to the right I followed the enemy through town and one mile beyond, skirmishing a little. My loss was two men wounded, belonging to the Thirteenth New Jersey Volunteers. I was then recalled and ordered with the rest of the division to Tennille Station, on the Georgia Central Railroad, where I destroyed about three miles of track and encamped for the night. November 27, marched to Davisborough Station, No. 22; crossed Williamson's Swamp Creek. November 28, destroyed three miles of railroad track and marched to Spiers Station. November 29, destroyed four miles of railroad track of Georgia Central, two saw-mills and lumber yards, and the timber for four large bridges ready for use. One of the bridges was marked Strawberry Plains, one Chattanooga Creek; the other two names have escaped my memory. This timber has been gotten out and made ready for use, even to having the pegs to unite it turned, and was intended, as I afterward learned from a citizen, for future operations of the enemy in East Tennessee. I should estimate the number of feet in this pile of timber to be 1,500,000. November 30, crossed the Ogeechee and encamped three miles southeast of Louisville.

December 1, crossed Jones' Mill Creek, Dry, Spring, Baker's, and Camp Creeks, camping near Jones' Mill Creek. December 2, passed through Birdville and encamped at Buck Head Church. December 3, crossed Waynesborough railroad and marched three miles to Millen. December 4, crossed Little Ogeechee Creek at Hunter's Mills and encamped

* Mounted infantry.

six miles southeast of Sylvania. December 5, marched two miles southeast. December 6, marched seventeen miles in same direction. December 7, marched to Springfield. December 8, camped near Eden. December 9, moved out to the Monteith road, reaching the Monteith Swamp about noon, where the enemy had erected two earth-works across the road and felled the timber for some distance in front. Received orders to move up on the right of the road and endeavor to flank these works. I moved through the wood about three-quarters of a mile, where I found a rice field extending up to the left of their battery (our right). I formed the brigade in two lines across this field, advanced skirmishers, and moved forward. The enemy opened one piece of artillery on my skirmishers, but soon ceased and evacuated their fort. The ground being a rice swamp my progress was necessarily very slow, and they escaped, with the exception of three men captured by the Third Wisconsin Volunteers; encamped for the night. December 10, moved down to the Charleston and Savannah Railroad, and destroyed about two miles of the track, and moved on to within five miles of Savannah, where the enemy were found strongly intrenched. Formed line of battle on left of Third Division, right resting on the Savannah turnpike. A forage party under command of Captain Gildersleeve, One hundred and fiftieth New York Volunteers, this day captured the rebel dispatch steamer Ida on the Savannah River, taking thirteen prisoners, among whom was Colonel Clinch, of General Hardee's staff. The steamer was burned by Captain Gildersleeve, he not being able to hold it on account of the rebel gun-boats on the river. Decem- 11, the brigade in same position; under orders from the brigadier-general commanding the division, the Second Massachusetts and One hundred and seventh New York, under command of Colonel Cogswell, Second Massachusetts, made a reconnaissance of the enemy's position and reported directly to division headquarters. Later in the day I was directed to send one regiment to report to the brigadier-general commanding the corps for special service. The Third Wisconsin, Colonel Hawley commanding, was selected, and received orders from Brigadier-General Williams, commanding Twentieth Corps, to cross to Argyle Island in the Savannah River, secure such property as he might find there, and also to make a reconnaissance to the South Carolina shore. Two companies of this regiment crossed to Argyle Island this night and six companies the following morning, leaving two companies to guard the Georgia shore and take charge of a rice mill and contraband camp. December 12, while crossing the river Colonel Hawley discovered three steamers descending. Winegar's battery, on the Georgia shore, immediately opened fire upon them, driving two gun-boats, Macon and Sampson, back. One, the armed steam tender Resolute, was driven on the island and captured with all the crew, consisting of 5 officers and 19 men, by Colonel Hawley. There was a quantity of ordnance and subsistence stores on board, a list of which is given in appendix C. Colonel Hawley also secured a quantity of stores and animals upon the island, which will be found enumerated in appendix C to this report. The brigade remained in same position until December 15, when the Second Massachusetts Volunteers was ordered by Brigadier-General Williams to report to Colonel Hawley at once upon Argyle Island. December 16, received orders from Brigadier-General Williams to move my brigade over Argyle Island, and from thence to the South Carolina shore. At 7 a. m., being relieved by Colonel Dustin's brigade, of Third Division, I proceeded with the remainder of the brigade to Argyle Island, and took up position on the eastern point and near South Carolina shore. Two pieces of artillery, Battery I, First New York, were ordered to report to me, and were put into position. During the night received orders from Brigadier-General Williams, commanding corps, to cross my brigade to the South Carolina shore, and take up position near the river, threatening the Savannah and Charleston pike. Later in the evening this order was countermanded, and an order given to send 100 men only and cross them in small boats. December 17, I found it impossible to cross 100 men in small boats, not having enough for the purpose, and the low state of the tide not warranting the use of the large barges. Nothing special occurred during the day, save a desultory fire on our position by a light battery of General Wheeler's cavalry command, which had now taken up position on the South Carolina shore opposite us. December 18, remained in same position on Argyle Island, with slight shelling from General Wheeler's guns. December 19, under orders from the brigadier-general commanding division, the Third Wisconsin, Second Massachusetts, and Thirteenth New Jersey, all under command of Colonel Hawley, were sent over to the South Carolina shore at daybreak. They landed without opposition, and, advancing to and beyond Izard's Mill, succeeded, after a slight skirmish, in securing a good position. Deeming the force too inadequate to maintain its ground against the accumulating force of the enemy, the One hundred and seventh New York was sent over in the afternoon and succeeded in gaining an important point on the line. So important did the enemy consider this position that they charged our forces with their cavalry, but were speedily driven off. I then moved the remaining regiment of the brigade, One hundred and fiftieth New York Volunteers, to the South Carolina shore, and established there my headquarters at Izard's Mill. The position occupied by the brigade was strong for defense, but the nature of the ground was such that an advance was difficult. It was a rice plantation, cut up by numerous dikes and canals, and the enemy had burned all the bridges over the canals and overflowed the whole plantation to a depth of eight to eighteen inches water, thus necessitating all our movements by the flank up these dikes, and they stood well prepared at these places to resist our advance. During the night I transported the two pieces of artillery across the river and put them in position in the center of the line. The line, as then formed and held by my brigade, was two miles and a quarter long, the left resting on the Savannah River near Izard's Mill, the right on an inlet near Clydesdale Creek. During the night I caused earth-works to be thrown up at all the prominent points along the line, making my position as strong as possible. December 20, in obedience to orders from the brigadier-general commanding division to determine the position of Clydesdale Creek with reference to my line, I detailed twelve companies of the brigade, under immediate command of Colonel Hawley, Third Wisconsin Volunteers, and accompanied them myself. The force succeeded in reaching Clydesdale Creek with the loss of one man killed, and after erecting works for one regiment and posting therein two companies of Thirteenth New Jersey Volunteers, an effort was made to strike the Savannah and Hardeeville road, but the enemy, anticipating the movement, had thrown a strong force in our front. Having a canal to cross under their fire if we advanced I ordered the detachment to withdraw. During the day a great number of vehicles of all descriptions were seen passing our front, moving from Savannah toward Hardeeville, which fact was reported to the headquarters of the division. In the afternoon a rebel gun-boat came up the river in our rear and threw about thirty shells in my brigade, killing one man of One hundred and fiftieth New York. I could not reach it with my artillery. At 4 p. m. the enemy were re-enforced by three regiments of infantry from Savannah. From 7 p. m. until 3 a. m. the noise of the retreating enemy could plainly be heard as they crossed the bridges from Savannah to the South Carolina shore. December 21, at 7 a. m. I received orders from the brigadier-general commanding division, through Captain Bennett, topographical engineer, to recross my brigade to the Georgia shore as rapidly as possible and march into Savannah, which place had surrendered to us at 5 a. m. The enemy were still in my front, and I made dispositions to cross by sending the One hundred and fiftieth New York, Colonel Ketcham commanding, across to Argyle Island and put into position behind the dike so as to cover the withdrawal of the rear guard down a dike on the Carolina shore to a lower landing opposite Gibbon's Mill. The Second Massachusetts Volunteers and the two pieces of artillery were then withdrawn, the Second Massachusetts landing on Argyle Island, and the artillery, loaded on a barge, being ordered to land on the island. On account of the high wind the artillery could not be landed as desired. The enemy perceiving our movements advanced their skirmishers rapidly, but were checked by the bold front and steadiness of our own skirmishers. It was 2 o'clock before the artillery and stores could be got far enough away to warrant the withdrawal of the balance of the brigade; then it was withdrawn, followed by our skirmishers, the enemy pressing hard. The One hundred and seventh New York Volunteers crossed; then the enemy grew more bold, advancing at all points, but under cover of the numerous dikes they were held in check. At sunset the Thirteenth New Jersey Volunteers crossed, and Colonel Hawley, commanding Third Wisconsin, with the skirmish line, was left to the delicate task of withdrawing under cover of darkness. At 11 p. m. the skirmish line crossed and without the loss of a man captured. During the severe skirmishing of the afternoon Col. John H. Ketcham, commanding One hundred and fiftieth New York Volunteers, a valuable officer, was severely wounded in the thigh. He had but two days before joined his command while we lay on Argyle Island. December 22, crossed from Argyle Island to mainland and took position on the right of the First Brigade of the division, about two miles north of the city of Savannah. On withdrawing from South Carolina and Argyle Island about 150 negroes came with my brigade.

In closing this report I cannot forbear to say that in my opinion the position taken and held by this brigade on the South Carolina side of the river had much to do in accelerating the evacuation of the city of Savannah.

During the entire march from Atlanta to this place the brigade has subsisted entirely upon the country (for statement of stores captured see appendix C). We have traveled 323 miles, have not lost a man by sickness, and have now only 11 on the sick list, or less than 1 per cent.

For list of casualties see appendix A; for list of prisoners captured see appendix B; for list of property captured and destroyed see appendix C.

Accompanying this report I submit the reports of my regimental commanders.

I am, very respectfully, your obedient servant,

E. A. CARMAN,
Colonel, Commanding Brigade.

Lieut. GEORGE ROBINSON,
Actg. Asst. Adjt. Gen., First Division, Twentieth Corps.

RECAPITULATION.

APPENDIX A.

Command.	Killed.			Wounded.			Captured and missing.			Aggregate.		
	Officers.	Men.	Total.	Officers.	Men.	Total.	Officers.	Men.	Total.	Officers.	Men.	Total.
107th New York Volunteers	....	....	....	....	6	6	1	52	53	1	58	59
150th New York Volunteers *a*	....	2	2	1	5	6	....	12	12	1	19	20
13th New Jersey Volunteers	....	....	....	....	3	3	....	3	3	....	6	6
2d Massachusetts Veteran Volunteers	....	....	....	....	2	2	....	17	17	....	19	19
3d Wisconsin Veteran Volunteers	....	1	1	1	3	4	....	9	9	1	13	14
Total	....	3	3	2	19	21	1	93	94	3	115	118

a One committed suicide.

APPENDIX B.—*List of rebel prisoners captured.*

Date.	Location.	Officers.	Men.
December 9	Monteith Swamp	....	3
10	Steamer Ida	1	12
11	Steamer Resolute	5	19
	Total	6	34

APPENDIX C.

Property captured and appropriated for use of the brigade.

Horses	5
Mules	44
Corn ..... pounds	177,118
Fodder ..... do	205,500
Sweet potatoes ..... do	95,000
Fresh meat, including poultry ..... pounds	95,000
Rice (in the sheaf) ..... do	20,000
Rice (threshed) ..... bushels	500
Sirup ..... barrels	13
Sugar ..... pounds	1,000
Salt ..... barrels	6
Bacon ..... pounds	1,000
Meal and flour ..... do	1,500
Whisky ..... barrels	2
Tobacco ..... pounds	1,500

Property captured and turned over.

Cotton (taken by Col. William Hawley at Milledgeville and disposed of by Major-General Sherman) ..... bales .. 1,800

Steamer Resolute, of C. S. Navy, with the following cargo, turned over to Captain Whittelsey, assistant quartermaster Twentieth Corps:

Short Whitney rifled muskets (accouterments complete)	10
Short Whitney rifled muskets (accouterments complete)	10
Flour ..... barrels	5
Beef ..... do	6
Sirup ..... do	½
Vinegar ..... do	½
Rice ..... do	½
Coffee ..... bags	6
Candles ..... box	1
Bread ..... boxes	3
Bacon ..... pounds	500

Taken on Argyle Island and turned over to Captain Whittelsey, assistant quartermaster Twentieth Corps:

Horses	2
Mules	14

Property destroyed.

Item	Unit	Quantity
Railroad track between Atlanta and Chattahoochee River	miles	3½
Georgia Central Railroad	do	9
Charleston and Savannah Railroad	do	1½
Ordnance and ordnance stores destroyed at Milledgeville:		
Muskets (smooth-bore, caliber .69) burned		2,300
Ammunition for the same burned	rounds	10,000
Infantry accouterments burned	sets	300
Lances, or John Brown pikes, burned		5,000
Cutlasses burned		1,500
U. S. standard weights and measures burned	boxes	15
Fixed artillery ammunition thrown in the river	boxes	170
Kegs of powder thrown in the river		200
Also a quantity of saddles, harness, &c.		
Destroyed during the march:		
Cotton gins		5
Cotton	bales	400
Steam saw-mills		2
Railroad bridges framed and ready for use (1,500,000 feet)		4

Captured on the Savannah River by Captain Gildersleeve, One hundred and fiftieth New York Volunteers, and burned, Confederate steamer Ida.

No. 86.

Report of Col. William Cogswell, Second Massachusetts Infantry.

HEADQUARTERS SECOND MASSACHUSETTS INFANTRY,
In the Field, December 25, 1864.

CAPTAIN: I have the honor to report that on the occupation of Atlanta by the Twentieth Corps, September 2, the Second Massachusetts Infantry was assigned to duty in the city as provost guard, in which position it remained until November 16, when it started on the march in rear of the Fourteenth Corps, being the last of the army to leave town. Camped at night about five miles beyond Decatur. November 17, marched in rear of Fourteenth Corps wagon train to Conyers; foraged about eight head of cattle. November 18, followed Fourteenth Corps train across Yellow River; foraged two days' rations of potatoes. November 19, marched through Covington; crossed the Ulcofauhachee River, destroying the bridge, and camped at Newborn. November 20, marched in rear of Fourteenth Corps train about sixteen miles; foraged a wagon-load of sweet potatoes. November 21, left the Fourteenth Corps at Eatonton Factory; crossed Little River and camped. November 22, marched through Eatonton; crossed Little River on pontoon, and camped at Meriweather. November 23, marched through Milledgeville; crossed the Oconee River; joined the brigade and went into camp. November 24, marched with brigade to Hebron. November 25, crossed Buffalo Creek and camped about three miles beyond. November 26, marched through Sandersville; skirmished with cavalry; marched to Tennille Station and destroyed half a mile of railroad track. November 27, marched to Davisborough Station. November 28, marched on railroad to Spiers Turnout; destroyed about one mile of track. November 29, marched on railroad about seven miles; destroyed about two miles of track. November 30, crossed the Ogeechee and camped about three miles beyond.

December 1, marched with wagons about ten miles through bad swamps. December 2, marched with wagons. December 3, marched about eleven miles. December 4, marched to near Hunter's Mills.

December 5, marched in rear of train. December 6, marched. December 7, crossed Turkey Branch; camped near Springfield. December 8, marched about ten miles. December 9, marched to about fifteen miles from Savannah; encountered a small force of the enemy in a small work with two guns; got on their flank and they left. December 10, marched across the Charleston and Savannah Railroad; partially destroyed a bridge, and at night went into position about five miles from Savannah, about one mile from the enemy's works. December 11, the regiment, with the One hundred and seventh New York, made a reconnaissance toward the enemy's works. December 12, advanced with the brigade and took position near the enemy's works. December 13 and 14, lay in the same position. December 15, crossed the Savannah River on flat-boats and camped on a rice plantation on Argyle Island, near the Third Wisconsin. December 16, were shelled from the South Carolina shore and from a rebel gun-boat. December 17, lay in same position; threw up some slight defensive works. December 18, lay in same position. December 19, crossed at daylight on flat-boats to the Carolina shore; the Third Wisconsin in advance; drove in the enemy's skirmishers and established a line of battle about a mile from the river; advanced a short distance about noon to a small hill and threw up works; were shelled by the enemy. December 20, had works built for two guns which were crossed in the night; were shelled by gun-boat and field battery. December 21, received orders to cross to Argyle Island, which was effected without loss to our regiment. Companies A and C and our pickets were hard pressed by the enemy, but crossed late at night with a loss of one man wounded. The regiment attempted to cross to the mainland, but, a heavy wind prevailing, were blown down river to King's Island and recrossed the regiment to Argyle Island in small boats with much difficulty. December 22, the whole day spent in crossing the brigade to the Georgia shore. At night marched about seven miles to the present camp of the command.

I have the honor to be, very respectfully, your obedient servant,

WM. COGSWELL,
Colonel, Commanding Second Massachusetts Infantry.

Capt. J. R. LINDSAY,
Acting Assistant Adjutant-General, Second Brigade.

No. 87.

Report of Maj. Frederick H. Harris, Thirteenth New Jersey Infantry.

HDQRS. THIRTEENTH NEW JERSEY VOLUNTEERS,
Near Savannah, Ga., December 24, 1864.

SIR:*

November 15, marched seventeen miles in a southeasterly direction to foot of Stone Mountain, passing through Decatur and into De Kalb County, where our brigade did picket duty. November 16, marched ten miles in a northeasterly direction to two miles east of Yellow River; crossed river at Rock Bridge and passed into Gwinnett County. November 17, marched thirteen miles east, to three miles beyond Sheffield, and into Newton and Walton Counties; crossed Big and Little

---

*For portion of report (here omitted) relating to operations about Atlanta, see Vol. XXXIX, Part I, p. 656.

Haynes Creeks. November 18, marched twenty-one miles southeast to five miles east of Rutledge, passing through Social Circle and Rutledge to within four miles of Madison. November 19, marched four miles east to Madison, passing through the town; thence south four miles toward Eatonton, and passed into Morgan County. November 20, marched thirteen miles south to five miles north of Eatonton, county town of Putnam County. November 21, marched eighteen miles south to Little River, passing through Eatonton. November 22, marched twelve miles to Milledgeville, the capital of Georgia, which was surrendered to our forces without opposition. Our brigade marched through the city on the advance, crossed the Oconee River, and encamped about a mile from the city, in Baldwin County. November 23, rested near Milledgeville. November 24, marched fifteen miles to within three miles of Hebron Post-Office, crossed Town, Gum, and Bluff Creeks and entered Washington County. November 25, marched four miles east to Buffalo Creek, passing through Hebron Post-Office; thence four miles east of Buffalo Creek; were delayed at creek some little time by burning of bridge across it and camped four miles from Sandersville. November 26, started at 6 a. m., our regiment being on the right of the division, the Ninth Illinois Cavalry* being the advance guard. We had not proceeded far before the cavalry were fired upon by the enemy. Our regiment was then deployed as skirmishers, with four companies in reserve. We then advanced, crossing a creek which the enemy had made impassable for our cavalry by fallen timber and other obstructions. We commenced skirmishing with the rebels at this point, but drove them rapidly for about four miles, and entered the town of Sandersville a little in advance of the skirmishers of the Fourteenth Corps. Two of our men were severely wounded, one slightly. We then resumed our march south to Tennille Station, No. 13; skirmishers thrown out on both sides of road; here we commenced tearing up the track of the Georgia Central Railroad; we tore up about half a mile, and then were sent out as pickets for the brigade, after which we returned to Tennille, where we encamped for the night. November 27, marched eighteen miles east to Davisborough Station, No. 12, Georgia Central Railroad; crossed Williamson's Swamp Creek. November 28, marched eleven miles east to Spiers Station, No. 11, tearing up and destroying about half a mile of track; passed into Jefferson County. November 29, marched eight miles east to Bostwick, tearing up and destroying about half a mile of track; also destroyed a large lumber yard of bridge timber; thence one mile to camp. November 30, marched eight miles northwest to near Louisville; crossed Ogeechee River, and encamped three miles southeast of the town of Louisville.

December 1, marched thirteen miles east to near Jones' Mill Creek, crossing Dry, Spring, Baker's, and Camp Creeks; passed into Burke County. December 2, marched fifteen miles east to Buck Head Church; crossed Jones' Mill and Buck Head Creeks; passed through Birdville. December 3, marched sixteen miles east to three miles north of Millen; passed Camp Lawton and into Screven County; crossed Little Buck Head Creek and Waynesborough railroad. December 4, marched sixteen miles east to six miles southeast of Sylvania; crossed Little Ogeechee River at Hunter's Mills. December 5, marched two miles southeast and camped eight miles southeast of Sylvania. December 6, marched eleven miles southeast to sixteen miles northwest of Springfield; passed into Effingham County. December 7, marched fifteen

* Mounted infantry.

miles southeast to one mile northwest of Springfield; crossed Turkey Branch Creek. December 8, marched twelve miles southwest to near Eden; passed through Springfield. December 9, marched three miles south to the Monteith road, thence along this road southeast to the Monteith Swamp, which the road crosses fourteen miles from Savannah. Here we found the rebels had built two forts across the road, which was also obstructed by felled timber. Our brigade was sent to the right of the forts; formed in two lines in a rice swamp. The rebels opened on us with one piece of artillery. A charge was then made upon the fort, which the rebels evacuated before we reached; encamped near it for the night, having marched nine miles. December 10, marched on the Monteith pike about five miles; struck the Charleston and Savannah Railroad; tore up and burned a quarter of a mile of it; then moved to within about five miles of Savannah, when our regiment was placed in reserve in rear of the One hundred and fiftieth New York Volunteers, and about a mile from the rebel works. December 11, moved at 7 p. m. from the second line to the front; encamped in line of battle. December 12, took position in line of battle to left of and between Savannah turnpike and river and to the north of Pipe-Maker's Creek. December 13, threw up breast-works in front of regiment. December 16, crossed Savannah River at Cumming's Ferry to Argyle Island in flat-boats; we threw up breast-works on the northeast side of island. December 19, according to order this regiment, together with the Second Massachusetts and Third Wisconsin Volunteers, crossed to the South Carolina shore, at 7 a. m., in flat-boats. Skirmishers were thrown out. The regiment took position to protect the right; the right, resting on Hog Island Creek, landed on South Carolina shore near Izard's Mill. Our regiment was then moved farther to the left to Smith's house, Beech Hill, where it threw up breast-works, one company being sent to Colonel Hawley to assist in capturing a hill. December 20, three companies joined with other detachments, under command of Colonel Hawley, to make reconnaissance. Late in afternoon was severely shelled by gun-boat in river. During night heard much noise as of moving of troops in our front, which was afterward found to be the evacuation of Savannah. December 21, crossed river to Argyle Island and part of regiment over to Georgia shore. December 22, crossed balance of regiment to Georgia shore and marched seven miles south to two miles from Savannah, taking position near river and opposite Hutchinson's Island.

I am, sir, with much respect, your obedient servant,

FRED. H. HARRIS,
Major, Commanding Thirteenth New Jersey Volunteers.

Capt. J. R. LINDSAY,
Actg. Asst. Adjt. Gen., 2d Brig., 1st Div., 20th Army Corps.

No. 88.

Report of Lieut. Col. Allen N. Sill, One hundred and seventh New York Infantry, of operations September 2–December 23.

HEADQUARTERS 107TH NEW YORK VOLUNTEERS,
Near Savannah, Ga., December 24, 1864.

CAPTAIN: I have the honor to submit the following report as the part taken by this regiment in this campaign:

On the 2d of September, 1864, this regiment entered Atlanta as part of a reconnoitering party sent from division headquarters under command of Col. N. M. Crane. After passing through the city we took position in the rebel breast-works fronting toward Decatur. Remained in camp until the morning of the 5th of September, when orders were received for this regiment to report to Col. A. Beckwith, chief commissary of subsistence, in the city for duty. Remained on duty in the city, guarding subsistence and quartermaster's stores, until ordered to join the brigade on the 15th of November preparatory to this campaign; joined the brigade and marched to Stone Mountain and camped for the night; resumed the march on the 16th and camped near Sheffield at 12 midnight. On the 17th marched twenty miles and camped for the night near Social Circle. On the 18th marched twenty miles; sent out two companies (D and K) foraging by direction from brigade headquarters, under command of Capt. George W. Reid, with instructions to keep near the road and bring the stores gathered up to the road to be loaded into wagons, but not returning we afterward learned that Reid's company, comprising 27 enlisted men and 16 men belonging to Company D, had been captured near Social Circle; the whole number captured, including the captain, was 44 men. Camped near Madison on the 18th. On the 19th broke camp at 6 a. m. and resumed the march, passing through Madison about noon; camped at 4 p. m. six miles east of Madison. November 20, broke camp at 9 a. m.; marched eighteen miles; camped at 9 p. m. four miles north of Eatonton; rained quite hard during the night. Resumed the march on the 21st, at 7 a. m.; found the roads very heavy and in some places almost impassable; rained very hard during the forenoon; passed through Eatonton about 11 a. m; camped for the night twelve miles from Milledgeville. November 22, found the air clear and cold; ground frozen. This regiment, with the brigade, moved in advance of the train and came up to the capital of Georgia about 3 p. m.; this regiment, with the Third Wisconsin Volunteers, was ordered to enter the city; we met with no opposition; marched to the square about the capitol and camped; guards were at once stationed about all public works, arsenal, armory, &c., under direction of Colonel Hawley, Third Wisconsin Volunteers, and all Government property taken account of; remained here until the morning of the 24th of November, when the march was resumed; crossed the Oconee River, camping for the night near Hebron Post-Office, having traveled fifteen miles. November 25, marched ten miles; camped six miles from Sandersville. On the 26th moved at 6 a. m.; had proceeded but about two miles when skirmishing was heard ahead. The enemy was soon driven back and we passed on to Sandersville; having passed through the village this regiment was formed in line of battle on the right of the Second Massachusetts Volunteers; advanced but a short distance when the halt was sounded; returned to the village and resumed the march on another road; crossed the Macon and Savannah Railroad at Station No. 13; proceeded down the track about one mile and destroyed the track for some distance; went into camp near the station. Resumed the march on the 27th instant, at 6 a. m.; marched fifteen miles and camped near Davisborough. November 28, moved out on the railroad at 6 a. m.; followed the track for two days, destroying both ties and rails. On the 30th left the railroad, moving up the Ogeechee River, on the south side, until near Louisville, where we crossed the river and joined our train.

December 1, broke camp at 8 a. m.; found the roads very bad, running through an almost impassable swamp; camped at midnight ten miles from where we started. December 2, broke camp at 6 a. m.; camped at 11 p. m. in the woods. December 3, resumed the march at

8 a. m.; reached the Millen and Augusta Railroad about noon; camped near Millen. December 4, broke camp at daylight and marched fifteen miles and went into camp. Remained in camp December 5 until 6 p. m. waiting for the wagon trains to pass; moved two miles and camped. December 6, resumed the march, guarding the rear of the trains; made a distance of twelve miles and camped. December 7, broke camp at 7 a. m.; marched thirteen miles; roads very bad; rained during most of the forenoon; camped at 9 p. m. December 8, resumed the march at 7 a. m.; passed through Springfield at 9 a. m.; marched nine miles and camped. December 9, broke camp at 9 a. m. and marched at 10; at 2 p. m. reached Monteith Swamp, where we found the First Brigade skirmishing with the enemy; halted for dinner. At 3 p. m. moved to the right of the road and formed line of battle in a swamp where the water was knee deep. This regiment went into position on the left of the Third Wisconsin Volunteers and on the right of the One hundred and fiftieth New York Volunteers. Moved forward and soon our skirmishers were engaged and uncovered a redoubt, when the enemy opened on us with artillery. The line halted, when soon after the First Brigade opened on the redoubt from the opposite side and the enemy left their works and retreated in haste, taking with them, however, their artillery. Our line moved forward and halted near the redoubt and camped for the night. December 10, resumed the march at 6.30 a. m.; crossed the Savannah and Charleston Railroad at Monteith Station; halted and destroyed the track for some distance, when orders came to move on; camped at 2 p. m. four miles from Savannah. December 11, this regiment, with the Second Massachusetts, was ordered out on a reconnaissance; did not proceed far before we found the enemy in strong works; returned to camp at 11 a. m. December 12, moved into line of battle on the left of the Second Massachusetts Volunteers and on the right of the Thirteenth New Jersey Volunteers, where breast-works were erected. December 13, 14, and 15, remained in camp without any change. December 16, broke camp at 6 a. m.; marched to the Savannah River and crossed to Argyle Island with the brigade, a distance of four miles, where we camped and remained without accident until the 19th, when this regiment changed position and occupied the camp of the Thirteenth New Jersey Volunteers, but at 2 p. m. crossed the east branch of the river to South Carolina to join the brigade. This regiment was divided and four companies ordered to report to Colonel Cogswell, Second Massachusetts Volunteers, and two companies to report to Colonel Hawley, Third Wisconsin Volunteers, and two companies were left to guard the landing; five companies (A, E, G, H, and I) were moved upon by the enemy, and the enemy were repulsed, when the five companies were ordered back by Colonel Hawley, and took position in rear and fortified; two men only were slightly wounded. December 20, were joined by the remaining companies and lay in works all day. December 21, received news that Savannah was occupied by our troops; orders were received at 8 a. m. to recross the river; this regiment moved down to the landing but was returned to the support of the line; remained in works until 2 p. m., during which time the enemy made movements in front as if to attack, but nothing occurred but slight skirmishing; at 2 p. m. we were again ordered to retire to the river; recrossed safely to Argyle Island and remained during the night. December 22, remained in works on the island, unable to recross the west branch of the river on account of the strong wind; about 12 m. the enemy moved down to the river and annoyed the troops by sharpshooters; we had one man severely wounded in the leg; crossed to

the Georgia shore at 4 p. m. and marched to within one mile of Savannah; went into camp at 10 p. m. December 23, received orders to go into camp and erect comfortable quarters.

I am, captain, very respectfully, your obedient servant,

A. N. SILL,
Lieutenant-Colonel, Commanding.

Capt. J. R. LINDSAY,
Actg. Asst. Adjt. Gen., 2d Brig., 1st Div., 20th Army Corps.

No. 89.

Report of Maj. Alfred B. Smith, One hundred and fiftieth New York Infantry.

HEADQUARTERS 150TH NEW YORK VOLUNTEERS,
Near Savannah, Ga., December 24, 1864.

SIR:*

November 15, marched at 5.30 a. m. toward Decatur; made Stone Mountain, a distance of sixteen miles. November 16, ready to march at 6.30 a. m., and marched at 4 p. m. a distance of eight miles, and got into camp on the east side of the Yellow River. November 17, marched at 8 a. m.; difficult roads; made seventeen miles, and halted at Rock Bridge at 12 midnight. November 18, marched at 8 a. m., guarding and assisting sixty wagons over all bad places in the roads. Passed through Social Circle and Rutledge, and encamped four miles from Madison; marched nineteen miles. Sent out two companies foraging; procured 1,530 pounds of fresh pork and 10 sheep, and 6 head of fat cattle—average weight dressed, 300 pounds a head; aggregate, 1,800 pounds—and 42 bushels of sweet potatoes, about 64 gallons of sirup; the cattle were turned over to the brigade commissary. November 19, started at 7 a. m.; roads very heavy; helped sixty wagons through; passed through Madison; made nine miles, and got into camp at 3 p. m. November 20, marched sixteen miles, over bad roads, toward Eatonton and encamped; rainy day. November 21, marched at 7 a. m.; roads very bad; built 100 rods of corduroy road of rails at the side of the road, and helped 120 wagons over them; advanced nine miles and encamped late in the night. November 22, marched at 6 a. m.; crossed Little River on pontoon bridge; reached Milledgeville at 1 p. m., and went into camp east of the city across the river, having marched thirteen miles. November 23, remained in same camp; collected forage in large quantities; picked up and turned in 4 large serviceable mules, 40 bushels of sweet potatoes, 2,000 pounds fresh pork, 200 pounds bacon, 60 gallons molasses or sirup, 100 pounds meal. November 24, marched at 6.30 a. m.; advanced fifteen miles, to within two miles of Hebron, and encamped at dusk; 50 bushels of sweet potatoes procured for the regiment and 1,000 pounds fresh pork. November 25, marched at 6.30 a. m.; advanced ten miles and found a bridge destroyed six miles from Sandersville; halted for the night; some skirmishing in front with rebel cavalry. November 26, marched at 6 a. m.; crossed a creek and through a bad swamp, and moved rapidly toward Sandersville. Heard brisk firing in front; formed line of battle, One hundred and fiftieth Regiment on left of the road. Advanced in line half a mile, then by the flank to within half a mile of the town; then formed line and supported the

---

* For portion of report (here omitted) relating to operations about Atlanta, see Vol. XXXIX, Part 1, p. 657.

skirmish line through the town in line of battle. At 12 m. moved south to Tennille, having marched ten miles, destroyed half a mile of railroad, burning the ties and bending the rails, and went into camp at Tennille. November 27, marched at 7 a. m. along the south side of the railroad by a circuitous route, and reached Davisborough Station at dusk, having marched eighteen miles. November 28, marched at 6 a. m. to tear up railroad; destroyed three miles of railroad, burning ties and twisting rails; also burned 1,000 new railroad ties; made eleven miles; procured 1,000 pounds fresh meat and 20 bushels of sweet potatoes; reached Spiers Station at dark; captured and turned over to brigade commissary 17 head of cattle; average weight, 300 pounds. November 29, marched at 6.30 a. m.; tore up and destroyed one mile and a half of railroad, burned a large quantity of framed bridge timber, and got into camp at 7 p. m.; then reported to General Jackson and went on picket with the regiment, holding the road on which we were to advance. Made eleven miles this day. November 30, marched at 9 a. m. up the Ogeechee River to Blake's plantation; crossed on a repaired bridge; marched three miles, and encamped on a high plain near our wagon train and not far from Louisville, having marched eleven miles.

December 1, marched at 8 a. m.; made thirteen miles; procured 40 bushels sweet potatoes and 400 pounds fresh pork. December 2, marched at 7 a. m.; guarded ninety wagons and made eleven miles. December 3, marched at 6.30 a. m.; passed the pen where the rebels kept our prisoners; made sixteen miles toward Sylvania; obtained an abundance of sweet potatoes and pork—about 40 bushels sweet potatoes and 1,000 pounds fresh pork—and turned in to brigade commissary 24 head of cattle—average weight 275 pounds, dressed—100 pounds sugar, and 60 gallons of molasses. December 4, marched at 6 a. m.; crossed Little Ogeechee River; made fifteen miles; foraging party from brigade, under command of Captain Cogswell, procured three wagon-loads of sweet potatoes, 150 pounds of bacon, and 17 head of cattle, average weight dressed, 250 pounds. December 5, ready to march at daylight; marched at 7 p. m.; passed a very bad swamp; made two miles and went into camp at 1 o'clock in the night; the men procured 40 bushels of sweet potatoes and 600 pounds fresh meat. December 6, marched at 9 a. m.; made twelve miles; some bad swamps passed; got into camp at dark; men supplied themselves with sweet potatoes, 40 bushels, and 400 pounds fresh pork. December 7, marched at 7 a. m.; very bad roads; helped fifty wagons through the swamp, and took out of the road a large number of felled trees; went into camp near Springfield, having marched eleven miles. December 8, marched at 7 a. m., leaving wagons and pack-mules at Springfield; made ten miles southwest and southeast, gaining but little; regiment procured plenty of sweet potatoes, 40 bushels, and 200 pounds of pork; men had all to march with wet feet; roads bad, swamps flooding them. December 9, marched at 8 a. m.; halted at 10 a. m.; road obstructed by fallen trees and a rebel gun playing down the road through the swamp; passed with the brigade around to the right of the road, through a bad swamp. The One hundred and fiftieth was at first ordered and deployed in third line of battle, in a rice swamp covered with water from one to three feet deep, then ordered to the left of the first line, adjoining the Third Wisconsin, then ordered farther to the left, through an almost impenetrable swamp and thicket, to give room between the One hundred and fiftieth and Third Wisconsin for the One hundred and seventh Regiment New York Volunteers. This regiment halted on this line, but seeing the other regiments advancing and the rebels running away, advanced to the fort.

The men and officers executed all orders on this difficult maneuver with most commendable alacrity and promptness. Marched about eight miles. December 10, marched at 6 a. m., the One hundred and fiftieth Regiment in advance of the corps; advanced three miles to the Savannah and Charleston Railroad, and at 8 a. m. commenced tearing up the railroad. Advanced again at 9 a. m. to within four miles of Savannah and formed line of battle, and sent out the right wing of the One hundred and fiftieth Regiment as skirmishers and established the picket-line. Captain Gildersleeve with his company went out foraging and came upon the rebel dispatch boat Ida; captured and burned it. They took 13 prisoners, 1 of them a Confederate colonel, Clinch by name. December 11, remained in same position. December 12, advanced the line 500 yards and erected breast-works, the One hundred and fiftieth on the right of the brigade next the road. December 13, 14, and 15, remained in same position; men very destitute of food, rice and fresh meat the only articles, and ten pounds of rice to 100 men. December 16, moved at 6 a. m. up the river about four miles; crossed over the river to Argyle Island, near the south end of the island. The soldiers procured plenty of unhulled rice, and, pounding it out, supplied themselves bountifully. Crossed the river in scows. December 17 and 18 remained in same position. December 19, relieved the Third Wisconsin Regiment in the works on the island at daylight, and crossed to the South Carolina shore at 3 p. m. to support the balance of the brigade. Sent out two companies on picket. The rebel gun-boat shelled us vigorously and killed one man on the island. December 20, the line was extended to the right by a reconnaissance, in which three companies of the One hundred and fiftieth were engaged, to a creek opposite Savannah; established line and threw up rifle-pits or breast-works, and retired, losing only one man killed. December 21, received orders at 7 o'clock to recross the river, as Savannah was ours. Commenced recrossing to Argyle Island. The One hundred and fiftieth crossed first and then took position on the extreme southeasterly point of the island, to cover the crossing of the balance of the brigade. The rebels pressed our rear guard, and Companies C and I of the One hundred and fiftieth opened fire upon them with good effect, checking their advance and enabling the rear of the brigade to cross safely. The wind was very high, rendering the boats unmanageable, and the day was consumed in crossing to Argyle Island. Our noble colonel, who had returned but two days before and assumed command of his regiment, was severely wounded in this skirmish. The country can ill afford to lose the services, even for a time, of one so devoted to his regiment, and so competent, faithful, and energetic in the discharge of every duty. The regiment crossed to the south side of Argyle Island, and remained on the dike all night awaiting an opportunity to cross. December 22, commenced crossing the river in small boats at 9 a. m. By crossing to the sand-bar and walking across it, and thence to the main shore the regiment was all over the river at 12 m. Marched at 4 o'clock to Savannah and encamped about two miles out of the city, near the Savannah River, second regiment from the left of our brigade.

As an approximate estimate of the amount of provisions secured on this march by the One hundred and fiftieth Regiment, I would say two pounds potatoes per day per man from November 18 to and including December 8, twenty days.

Gross amount of potatoes	pounds	20,200
Fresh meat, aside from issue	do	15,000
Sirup	gallons	640

Honey	pounds..	300
Bacon and salt meat	do...	3,000
Salt	do...	500
Sugar	do...	1,000
Flour	do...	1,000
Corn meal	do...	1,000
Forage for public and private horses and mules:		
Corn	pounds..	11,340
Fodder	do...	13,860

There have been, as above stated, 47 head of cattle captured by the regiment and turned over to the brigade commissary, the net weight of which would be about 14,000 pounds.

Casualties from September 2 to December 22 inclusive.*

The conduct of the men and officers of this regiment in this campaign deserves the highest commendation.

I am, most respectfully, your obedient servant,

A. B. SMITH,
Major, Commanding Regiment.

Capt. J. R. LINDSAY,
Acting Assistant Adjutant-General.

No. 90.

Reports of Col. William Hawley, Third Wisconsin Infantry.

HDQRS. THIRD WISCONSIN VETERAN VOLUNTEER INFTY.,
Near Savannah, Ga., December 25, 1864.

CAPTAIN:†

November 15, started with the balance of the army on the expedition to this city; passed through Decatur and went into camp on railroad near Stone Mountain; distance marched, fourteen miles. November 16, marched seven miles and went into camp near Yellow River. November 17, marched fourteen miles and went into camp near Gum Creek. November 18, marched eighteen miles and camped near Social Circle. November 19, marched twelve miles, passing through Madison, and arriving in camp at an early hour. Here I was directed by the colonel commanding brigade to conduct an expedition into the country for supplies, furnishing me for this purpose four wagons. On this expedition I marched eight miles and loaded my wagons with molasses, hogs, bacon, and potatoes. These supplies were turned over to the brigade commissary. November 20, marched ten miles toward Eatonton. November 21, marched twelve miles, passing through Eatonton, and went into camp at Dennis Station. November 22, marched thirteen miles to Milledgeville. Arriving near the city the corps was halted, and by direction of major-general commanding Left Wing, I entered the place at the head of my own regiment and the One hundred and seventh New York Volunteer Infantry, and assumed command of the post. During my short stay in Milledgeville I received orders direct from the major-general commanding Left Wing of the army. My duties mainly consisted in patrolling the streets, ascertaining the amount of public and other property captured and guarding the same, and maintaining—so far as my limited means would allow—good order in the city. The following is a list of the property seized, with the disposition made of the same: Burned—2,300 muskets, smooth-bore, cali-

---

*Nominal list (here omitted) shows 2 enlisted men killed, and 1 committed suicide, 1 commissioned officer and 3 enlisted men wounded, and 12 enlisted men missing.

†For portion of report (here omitted) relating to operations about Atlanta, see Vol. XXXIX, Part I, p. 658.

ber .69; 10,000 rounds cartridges, caliber .69; 300 sets accouterments; 5,000 lances; 1,500 cutlasses; 15 boxes U. S. standard weights and measures. Thrown into the river—170 boxes fixed artillery ammunition; 200 kegs powder; 16 hogsheads salt. A large amount of cotton, say 1,800 bales, was disposed of by General Sherman; the manner of disposition was not made known to me. About 1,500 pounds tobacco was taken by my order and distributed among the troops generally. Besides the property above enumerated, a large lot of miscellaneous articles, such as harness, saddles, canteens, tools for repairing war materials, caps, &c., was burned in the building situated in the square near the State House. I remained in command of the post until November 24, when, by order of Major-General Slocum, I rejoined my brigade, being relieved by colonel commanding Nineteenth Kentucky Volunteers, name not known. Marched same day fourteen miles to near Bluff Creek. November 25, marched to Hebron; on this march the command was delayed six hours by the burning of the bridge over Buffalo Creek by the enemy; whole distance marched, nine miles. November 26, marched to Tennille Station, on the Savannah and Macon Railroad, via Sandersville, the advance of the brigade skirmishing slightly with the enemy. Although my regiment advanced in line of battle for several miles, the enemy retreated so rapidly before the advance guard that my regiment did not come up with him. At Tennille my regiment was placed directly on the railroad without going into camp and destroyed the road until dark; amount destroyed, say half a mile. November 27, marched twelve miles to Davisborough. November 28, commenced the destruction of the railroad in the morning. Marched thirteen miles, passing through Key West, and went into camp at Spiers Station. November 29, marched eight miles, destroying railroad track, going into camp near Bostwick. On this day's march my regiment destroyed at least two miles of track, besides burning a large lumber and timber yard, situated on both sides of the track, and extending a quarter of a mile. This yard contained the worked timber for four complete railroad bridges, besides a large quantity of sawed ties and boards. The whole lot is variously estimated at from 1,000,000 to 5,000,000 feet; I think 3,000,000 feet a fair estimate. November 30, marched eight miles, crossing the Ogeechee River, and went into camp three miles beyond.

December 1, marched ten miles, crossing Dry Creek, going into camp at an early hour. December 2, marched fifteen miles and went into camp near Jones' Mill Creek. December 3, marched fourteen miles, crossing the Millen and Augusta Railroad. December 4, marched twelve miles, and went into camp near Hunter's Mills. December 5, marched three miles and went into camp. December 6, marched ten miles toward Springfield. December 7, marched eleven miles, and went into camp one mile southeast of Springfield. December 8, marched ten miles, and went into camp. December 9, changed the direction of our march, and took the direct Savannah road. After marching about four miles the enemy were found, strongly intrenched and occupying two small forts directly in our front, entirely covering the road over which we had to pass. At this point the First Division, being in the advance, was halted and formed for the attack in the following order: Second Brigade, Col. E. A. Carman, on the right; First Brigade, Colonel Selfridge, in the center; Third Brigade, Colonel Robinson, on the left. The Second Brigade, in order to gain the rear of the enemy, if possible, made a detour to the right, moving by the flank a distance of one mile, gaining a position in a rice swamp, through which the rear of the forts could be reached. My regiment, with the Second Massachusetts

Infantry on its right, was formed in line of battle in the rice swamp; the balance of the brigade was formed on the left, in the woods. An advance was then made, in the above order, for nearly one mile, when the skirmish line became engaged, and the brigade was halted. I remained in this position without orders to advance until the enemy, being hard pressed by the Third Brigade, who had gained the right flank of his position, began to retreat. I then moved on rapidly without orders, but the swamp was so deep, and the enemy having a good road at his command, it was impossible for us to overtake him. After following him a distance of two miles, I returned, by your order, and went into camp near the enemy's deserted works. The only casualty on this day was one officer, Captain Buck, wounded. Three of the enemy were captured by my skirmish line. Distance marched this day, six miles. December 10, marched at daylight; reached the Charleston and Savannah Railroad; halted and destroyed a portion of the road. The march was resumed until the enemy's works were reached in front of Savannah, when I took up a position with the brigade in line of battle about three-quarters of a mile from the enemy's outer line of works. Distance marched this day, ten miles. December 11, at 3 o'clock, by your order, I reported to brigadier-general commanding corps, from whom I received instructions to take my command to Argyle Island, in the Savannah River, secure the rice and other public property there, and to make a reconnaissance on the South Carolina shore. I succeeded in crossing two companies that night. December 12, crossed the balance of my command this morning. While crossing I discovered three rebel steamers coming down the river. Two of them proved to be gun-boats by almost immediately becoming engaged with our battery on shore. I immediately deployed two companies to intercept them if possible, and pick off their gunners. Before the skirmishers could reach a position where their fire could be effective, the two gun-boats had retreated, making their escape up the river. While changing their positions the two gun-boats had both run into the third vessel—which afterward proved to be the armed tender Resolute—which had so disabled her that her wheels could not revolve. When my troops came up to her, the officers and crew had lowered the small boats and were busily engaged in getting in their baggage and other personal property, and would have succeeded in making their escape in a few minutes more. After one volley from my men, resulting in the wounding of the executive officer of the boat, the vessel was surrendered, immediately boarded by my troops, and brought to the Georgia shore. The following is a list of the arms and supplies found on board, which, with the boat, were turned over to Captain Whittelsey, corps quartermaster, by order of Brigadier-General Williams, commanding corps: 10 short Whitney rifled muskets, saber bayonets, accouterments complete; 10 Whitney rifled muskets with bayonets, and accouterments; 5 barrels flour; 6 barrels beef; one-half barrel molasses; one-half barrel vinegar; one-half barrel rice; 6 bags coffee; 3 boxes bread; 1 box candles; 500 pounds bacon. The prisoners, except the wounded officer who was left on board in care of the surgeon of the boat, consisting of 5 officers and 19 men, were turned over to Maj. W. Parks, provost-marshal of corps, by order of brigadier-general commanding corps. December 13 and 14, the entire time was occupied in collecting boats, reconnoitering the island, and securing the rice and such other property as could be found, of which the following is a partial list: 5 large barge loads of rice in sheaf; 260 bushels threshed rice; 9 barrels sirup; 14 mules and 2 horses. The mules, horses, and sheaf rice were turned over to corps quartermaster and the balance of the stores were used in subsisting the negroes, and otherwise disposed of by the corps quartermaster. In addition to the above, about 2,000 bushels of rice was threshed and left in the mill on the island. December 15, in compliance with previous orders from brigadier-general commanding corps, I crossed five companies of my regiment to the South Carolina shore, driving the enemy from the plantation known as Izard's, and made a reconnaissance in the country for about two miles, gaining much valuable information respecting the country and roads. After a stay of about one hour the enemy made their appearance in my front in strong force. Being entirely isolated from the balance of the army, with limited means of transportation, I deemed it prudent to withdraw my small force and return to the island. This I accomplished successfully, although vigorously pressed by the enemy. I immediately reported to the brigadier-general commanding corps, and applied for a force sufficient to enable me to recross to the South Carolina shore in safety, and to occupy the plantation, if thought necessary or desirable. The Second Massachusetts Infantry was sent me, but before I could effect a recrossing the boats were ordered to the Georgia shore to transport your entire brigade to the island and South Carolina shore. The arrival of the balance of the brigade with the colonel commanding relieved me of the command and responsibility of the expedition. December 19, I recrossed my regiment with the balance of the brigade, under the orders of the colonel commanding, to the South Carolina shore and occupied my original position. December 20, skirmished all day with the enemy. December 21, the brigade recrossed to the island, my regiment guarding the rear; the enemy pressed my regiment hard at times, but we finally succeeded in gaining the island, late at night, without loss. December 22, crossed from the island to the main Georgia shore, marched seven miles, and went into camp in my present position.

My casualties in this expedition were 1 man killed and 3 wounded. The total number of casualties during the campaign are as follows: Killed, 1 man; wounded, 1 officer and 3 men.

I beg leave to report, in conclusion, that so excellent have been the arrangements adopted by the colonel commanding brigade for foraging, and so ample the facilities given the men while on the road to gather potatoes, turnips, and other vegetables at the resting places, that I have experienced no difficulty during the entire march in subsisting my men and animals on the country, obtaining all that was needed, excepting coffee and sugar.

I beg leave also to report that on the march twelve bales of cotton were discovered, which had been secreted in the woods, and were burned by my orders.

Respectfully submitted.

WILLIAM HAWLEY,

Colonel Third Regiment Wisconsin Veteran Volunteer Infantry.

Capt. J. R. LINDSAY,

Actg. Asst. Adjt. Gen., 2d Brig., 1st Div., 20th Army Corps.

HDQRS. THIRD WISCONSIN VETERAN VOLUNTEER INFTY.,

Near Savannah, Ga., December 12, 1864.

COLONEL: I have the honor to transmit the following report of the operations of my command, resulting in the capture of the C. S. steamer Resolute:

At 7.30 o'clock this morning I received information that two rebel gun-boats, with their tender, the Resolute, were steaming down the river. I had previously crossed over to the island with four companies of my command, and immediately on hearing the firing between the boats and the battery on shore, deployed two companies for the purpose of intercepting the boats and picking off the gunners. Before we reached the bank, however, the gun-boats had made their escape. On reaching the bank I found the Resolute aground on the island and in a disabled condition, caused by coming in contact with the gun-boats, both of which struck her while changing position. The captain of the Resolute was making every effort to escape with the small boats, and would have succeeded had we been fifteen minutes later. I called out for them to surrender, when the captain surrendered the boat and all on board as prisoners of war. I put the two companies on board, and used every means to bring her to the landing. On making an examination of the boat I found that she had received two shots from Battery I, First New York Artillery, resulting in no material injury, one having passed through the wheel-house and the other through the mess room. I also found a quantity of stores and small-arms, an inventory ot which will be forwarded with this report. I examined the baggage belonging to the prisoners, and allowed them to retain all that was of a private nature. The executive officer of the boat was wounded by my command before the surrender, and was left in charge of the surgeon on board.

On receiving your order I turned over the boat, with all its stores, to Captain Whittelsey, assistant quartermaster Twentieth Army Corps, and the prisoners, consisting of 5 officers and 19 men, to Maj. W. Parks, provost-marshal Twentieth Army Corps.

Inventory of stores and arms captured on board the C. S. steamer Resolute December 12, 1864, by Col. William Hawley, commanding Third Wisconsin Veteran Volunteer Infantry: 5 barrels flour, 6 barrels beef, half a barrel molasses, half a barrel vinegar, half a barrel rice, 6 bags coffee, 3 boxes bread, 1 box candles, 500 pounds bacon, 10 short Whitney rifled muskets, with saber bayonets and accouterments complete, and 10 Whitney rifled muskets, with bayonets and accouterments.

Very respectfully, your obedient servant,

WILLIAM HAWLEY,

Colonel Third Regiment Wisconsin Veteran Volunteer Infantry.

Lieut. Col. H. W. PERKINS,

Assistant Adjutant-General, Twentieth Army Corps.

No. 91.

Report of Col. James S. Robinson, Eighty-second Ohio Infantry, commanding Third Brigade.

HDQRS. THIRD BRIG., FIRST DIV., TWENTIETH CORPS,

Near Savannah, Ga., December 28, 1864.

LIEUTENANT:*

On the 15th [November], at 7 a. m., my brigade filed out of its encampments and made its final exit from the city of Atlanta. Behind us all means of communication and supply had been utterly destroyed, and the town itself was a blazing ruin, abandoned alike by citizens and

*For portion of report (here omitted) relating to operations about Atlanta, see Vol. XXXIX, Part I, p. 659.

soldiers to the harsh fortunes of war. Before us lay a vast stretch of country, containing no organized army, yet thoroughly infested with enemies clear to its natural boundary, the ocean. There was nothing left for us to rely upon but ourselves, our leader, and the God of battles. Moving out on the Decatur road, my brigade passed the village of Decatur at 2 p. m. Our first day's march terminated near Stone Mountain, about fifteen miles from Atlanta. Early on the morning of the 16th I was directed by General Jackson, commanding division, to take my brigade and commence destroying the Georgia railroad at a point about half a mile beyond my encampment. Extending my brigade along the track, I succeeded in thoroughly destroying about two miles of it by 10 a. m. After this was accomplished, having been assigned as rear guard of the corps, my command awaited the passage of the troops and trains. This was not completed until 5 p. m., at which hour my brigade marched from Stone Mountain. My column crossed Stone Mountain Creek at 10 and Yellow River at 11.30 p. m. It encamped on the left bank of Yellow River, near Rock Bridge Post-Office, about midnight, having marched about seven miles. My brigade, still the rear guard of the corps, marched from its camp near Rock Bridge at noon on the 17th. It crossed No Business Creek at 1, Big Haynes Creek at 5, and Little Haynes Creek, at Summers' Mills, at 7 p. m. My column was greatly detained by the trains, which moved very slowly, owing to the heavy loads carried in the wagons and the difficult places in the road. My command did not get into camp until one hour after midnight, when it reached a point near Flat Creek. The distance marched on this day was about thirteen miles. My brigade marched, following the Second Brigade of the First Division, and charged with the protection of about 100 wagons, at 8 a. m. on the 18th; it passed Alcovy Mountain at 11, and crossed Alcovy or Ulcofauhachee River at 11.30 a. m. At 1.30 p. m. it reached Social Circle, on the Georgia railroad. Here it emerged into a fine, level, open country with a good road which enabled us to move along briskly. At 8 p. m. my command passed through Rutledge Station, and at 10 p. m. encamped five miles west of Madison.

My brigade marched at 7.45 a. m. on the ensuing morning, November 19, leading the division and corps, and unencumbered with wagons. At 10 a. m. it passed through the village of Madison and marched in a southward course on the Eatonton road. At 12 m. it encamped three miles south of Madison. The aggregate distance marched on this and the preceding day was about twenty-five miles. On the 20th my command resumed its march at 7.15 a. m. It moved in rear of the division and was charged with the protection of about 300 wagons, including the pontoon and a large portion of the Second Division train. Considerable rain had fallen, which rendered the road heavy and retarded the movement of the column. It crossed Sugar Creek at 11.30 a. m., and Clark's Fork at 1 p. m. The country now being traversed was quite fertile, and afforded an abundance of all kinds of supplies. A considerable number of fine horses and mules were also brought in. By this means the transportation of my brigade was greatly improved. At 7 p. m. my command reached a point about four miles and a half from Eatonton and encamped. The distance marched this day was about twelve miles. On the 21st the morning dawned dark and lowering, with occasional gusts of rain. My brigade was again assigned to duty as rear guard of the corps. A battery of artillery accompanied my command, which was unencumbered with wagons. Our march commenced at 11 a. m. At 1 p. m., the column being temporarily delayed by the breaking of a tongue in an artillery carriage, the rebel cavalry appeared in our rear and made a slight demonstration. It was driven off precipitately by the Sixty-first Ohio Veteran Volunteers, which constituted my rear guard. At 4 p. m. my command marched through the village of Eatonton. At 9 p. m., the column having been tediously delayed, I discovered, upon investigation, that about sixty wagons had become almost hopelessly stalled in a sort of quagmire. My troops were at once put to work lightening out these wagons and were thus employed for about two hours, when the march was resumed. My brigade encamped six miles from Eatonton at midnight, having marched ten miles and a half. At 7.15 a. m. on the 22d my march was continued. My command moved in the rear of the division and was charged with the protection of about 400 wagons. The weather had now cleared up, but the column still moved slowly. My brigade did not cross Little River until 12.30 p. m. From that point the march was resumed again at 3 p. m. on the direct road to Milledgeville. My brigade marched into Milledgeville at 7.30 p. m. Passing through the town, and crossing the Oconee River on a wooden bridge, it encamped on the left bank at 9 p. m., having marched seventeen miles. On the 23d my brigade remained in camp near the Oconee bridge. This day's rest enabled the foraging parties to collect a considerable quantity of provisions and a number of horses and mules.

At 6 a. m. on the 24th my brigade resumed its march, leading the division and corps. Being charged with the duty of advance guard it was unencumbered by the trains. Our line of march pursued the Oconee through a sparsely settled, broken, piney country. My column crossed Beaver Dam at 11 a. m., and at 12.15 p. m. crossed Town Creek. At 3 p. m. my brigade crossed Gum Creek and at 4.30 p. m. encamped on the ridge beyond. The distance marched on this day was about fifteen miles. On the 25th, at 6 a. m., my brigade continued its march, again being the vanguard of the division and corps. Bluff Creek was passed at 7, and the column reached Hebron Post-Office at 8 and Buffalo Creek at 9 a. m. Over Buffalo Creek, a wide, swampy stream, was a series of bridges, nine in number, all of which had been destroyed by the enemy. According to directions, I detailed a regiment, the One hundred and first Illinois Volunteers, to assist in their reconstruction. While this work was going on, the rebel cavalry made a demonstration on the pickets on the left bank of the stream. At the instance of the general commanding division, I at once dispatched five companies of the One hundred and first Illinois Volunteers to re-enforce the picket-line. The enemy at once withdrew, and the bridges were completed without further annoyance. The remainder of my brigade crossed Buffalo Creek at 3.30 p. m., and the entire command, excepting the five companies of the One hundred and first Illinois Volunteers left to cover a side road, pursued its march toward Sandersville. Having ascended a plateau three miles from the creek lively skirmishing was overheard toward the front, which proved to be the cavalry advance engaging the rebel forces under Wheeler. As the enemy appeared to be charging down the road I was directed by the general commanding division to throw my command immediately forward into line, extending across and covering the road. My troops came up promptly on the double-quick, and were in a very short space of time advancing in a steady line of battle. Contemporaneously with this movement a line of skirmishers, consisting of two companies from the Thirty-first Wisconsin Volunteers and two from the Eighty-second Ohio Veteran Volunteers, had been thrown forward, covering the front of the brigade. My line of battle had not advanced but a short distance when, it not being deemed necessary to push it any farther, it was, by direction of the general commanding division, halted and the troops put in camp. My skirmish line, however, under direction of two officers of my staff, Capt. A. E. Lee, acting assistant adjutant-general, and Capt. Cyrus Hearrick, acting aide-de-camp, steadily advanced, and without hesitation and without loss drove the enemy from a commanding position from which he had charged our cavalry half an hour previously. Not content with this my skirmish line pursued the enemy and drove him through woods and open fields one mile farther, when it was, by my order, halted and withdrawn.

On the ensuing day, the 26th, my brigade resumed the march at 6.15 a. m., following the Second Brigade, which was in advance of the division and corps. This brigade at 7 a. m. commenced skirmishing with the enemy's cavalry at the point where it had been left by my skirmishers on the evening previous. Soon afterward a detachment of rebels having been discovered observing our movements on a side road leading to our right, I was directed to send a regiment to drive them off. I immediately dispatched the One hundred and first Illinois Volunteers, Lieutenant-Colonel Le Sage. This regiment charged the enemy and drove him precipitately to the woods, capturing one prisoner, and discovering about 100 bales of cotton, which were burned, including the cotton gin. The regiment then rejoined the brigade, which had by this time resumed its march toward Sandersville. My column reached that village without any further opposition at 11 a. m. Here the trains being left in charge of the Third Division, the troops of the First Division, including my brigade, marched unencumbered toward the Georgia Central Railroad, three miles distant. My command struck the road at Tennille Station at 3.30 p. m. and immediately began the destruction of the track. About one mile was thoroughly destroyed by my brigade by sundown. My troops were then encamped near the station. The entire distance marched on this day was nine miles. On the 27th my brigade marched in the center of the division at 7 a. m. The route from Tennille pursued a secluded, untraveled road on the south side of the railroad. The troops being unencumbered, marched rapidly and made Jackson's Church by 11 a. m. At 4.30 p. m. my command crossed Williamson's Swamp Creek and arrived at Davisborough. Here the troops were encamped for the night, having marched about seventeen miles. At daylight the next morning, November 28, my brigade marched down the railroad track three miles and commenced its destruction. Inasmuch as the track bed for the most part ran through a difficult swamp much of it was composed of trestle-work and bridges, all of which were effectually destroyed. When the track was laid upon a road bed the rail upon one side, with the stringer attached, was unfastened by means of levers and lifted over against the rail on the other side. Rails and dry wood were then piled on top and the whole set on fire. The heat would soon spring the rails, still attached to the wooden stringers, into a variety of contortions, and the work of destruction was completed. Thus my brigade, in connection with the other brigades of the division and alternating with them, proceeded down the track, destroying mile after mile. At night-fall my command reached Spiers Turnout, and there encamped, having marched eleven miles and destroyed four miles of track during the day.

At 7 a. m. on the 29th my brigade returned about two miles up the track and completed its destruction down as far as Spiers. The station house and other railroad fixtures were then burned or otherwise effectually destroyed. At 11 a. m. my command marched singly on the wagon road from Spiers. The corps and division headquarters trains were placed in its charge, but it was otherwise unencumbered. My column crossed Great Coat Creek at 12.30, and arrived at Bethany at 1.30 p. m. At 3.30 p. m. it crossed Boggy Girt Creek, and at nightfall encamped two miles and a half from the Ogeechee River. By direction of the general commanding division, I sent forward a regiment (the Eighty-second Ohio Veteran Volunteers) with orders to proceed as far as the Ogeechee, and there encamp for the night, picketing well the bank of the river. On the morning of the 30th the regiment sent forward to the river was withdrawn and rejoined the brigade, which marched up the right bank at 8.30 a. m. At 1 p. m. the column crossed Mill Creek and halted for dinner on Blake's plantation. At 4.30 p. m. my command crossed the Ogeechee River, at a point two miles below Louisville. The bridge here had been ineffectually destroyed by the enemy, and was repaired by my pioneer corps. My brigade pushed forward and encamped two miles beyond the river at nightfall. It marched on this day about fifteen miles.

On the morning of December 1 the march was resumed in the direction of Birdville. My brigade moved in the center of the division and in charge of the division train. However, it did not leave its encampment near Louisville until noon. During the afternoon it crossed Big, Dry, Spring, and Bark Camp Creeks, all small, swampy streams of clear water. The march was very much retarded by the boggy places in the road. My command did not get into camp until half an hour after midnight, when it reached a point about four miles from Birdville, having marched thirteen miles. On the 2d my brigade resumed its march at 9.45 a. m., leading its division and following the Second Division, which was in advance. At noon it reached Birdville, and at 8 p. m. crossed Buck Head Creek at Buck Head Church, and there encamped. The distance marched on this day was about fifteen miles. Shortly after passing Birdville, having received reliable information that a planter named Bullard, living in that neighborhood, had made himself conspicuous for his zeal in recapturing and securing prisoners from our army escaped from the rebel authorities, I dispatched an officer with authority to destroy his outbuildings and cotton. He accordingly set fire to the corn cribs, cotton gin, cotton presses, and a warehouse containing $50,000 worth of cotton. These were all consumed, and the owner admonished that a repetition of his offense would bring a similar fate upon his dwelling at the next visitation of our army. On the 3d my brigade marched at 7 a. m. on the Sylvania road; my command occupied the center of the division, and was unencumbered with wagons. My brigade crossed the Augusta branch of the Central railroad at noon. The Michigan Engineers having been charged with the destruction of this road, my command pressed forward and encamped near Horse Creek at 4.45 p. m. The distance marched on this day was about fifteen miles. On the 4th my brigade, having in charge the entire division train, the pontoon trains, the corps supply train, and the artillery ammunition train, marched at 9 a. m. The column crossed a number of small, swampy streams, and passed through a sterile, sandy country, bountifully timbered with groves of pine. At 12.30 p. m. it crossed Little Horse Creek, and at 5 p. m. Little Ogeechee Creek. At 6 p. m. my troops encamped one mile beyond the Little Ogeechee, having marched thirteen miles. On the 5th the First Division, which had previously been in advance, dropped to the rear, allowing the other two divisions to go ahead; this consumed most of the day. My brigade marched at 5 p. m.; the road was very sloughy, greatly detaining the trains. The column advanced only about three miles and a half, when it encamped at 10.30 p. m.

On the 6th my brigade, with a battery of artillery, was detailed as a rear guard for the corps. It marched at 9.30 a. m., unencumbered with wagons. The line of march pursued the Springfield road through a moderately fertile country. My foraging parties, which were now kept out daily, were enabled to obtain a considerable quantity of sweet potatoes and fresh meat. Ample supplies of forage were also obtained along the road. My command marched on this day about twelve miles, and encamped at a point about six miles from the Ogeechee River, six from the Savannah, and sixteen from Springfield. On the 7th our march was resumed at 8 a. m. My brigade had charge of about 300 wagons, consisting of the division and the cavalry trains. The road soon entered the Cowpens Branch Swamp, a low, flat, boggy surface, about three miles in width. The wagons easily cut through the surface and many of them became completely mired. In the meantime a drizzling rain set in, which had no tendency to improve the roads. In many instances the animals had to be entirely removed from the wagons and the vehicles drawn out of the slough by the troops. By 1.30 p. m. the trains were all gotten safely through the swamp and the column moved slowly on. At 8 p. m. it reached Turkey Creek and Swamp, and at 10 p. m. encamped one mile above Springfield. The distance marched on this day was fifteen miles. At 8 a. m. on the morning of the 8th my brigade crossed Jack's Creek and arrived at Springfield. My command was now unencumbered and marched in advance of the division, following the Second Division. Our course followed the Monteith road about nine miles, then turned to the right and pursued a southwesterly direction for a distance of six miles, which brought us to our encampment, having marched in the aggregate fifteen miles.

The march was resumed at 8.30 a. m. on the 9th. My brigade followed the Second, the First being in the advance. At 10 a. m. the column struck the main road leading to Savannah. Cannonading and musketry were now occasionally heard in the advance. It began to be evident that a considerable force of the enemy had gathered in our front and meant to oppose our onward march to Savannah. At 3 p. m. my brigade reached Monteith Swamp, where the First and Second Brigades had already encountered a considerable force of the enemy. The rebel forces were so disposed as to completely command the only practicable passage of the swamp, which was by the main road. Their artillery, which they were disposed to use freely, was so posted as to completely sweep the road, and was covered by earth-works. The advance of the First Brigade against the enemy's front, together with that of the Second Brigade against his left flank, having failed to dislodge him, I was instructed by the general commanding division to send two regiments around the left, with directions to push through the swamp if possible and turn the enemy's right. I immediately dispatched the Thirty-first Wisconsin and Sixty-first Ohio Veteran Volunteers, the whole commanded by Colonel West, of the Thirty-first Wisconsin Volunteers, to whom I gave the instructions above repeated. Making a detour of about one mile to the left Colonel West formed his command in line of battle and plunged into the almost impenetrable swamp. It was found impossible to get a horse over the miry surface, and officers and men were alike compelled to go on foot. The swamp, which was about 400 yards in width, was finally passed and the troops emerged into an open field skirted on the farther side by timber, in which the enemy lay concealed. The point at which he was struck was far in the rear of his main position, which was completely turned, yet he was not wholly unprepared to meet Colonel West's forces, upon whom he opened fire at their first appearance. The fire was returned with a good will, but only three volleys were needed to complete the overthrow and effect the precipitate retreat of the enemy. Colonel West now cautiously advanced his line, fearing an ambush. He soon discovered that the rebel forces were all gone, and quietly occupied two fine redoubts, containing eighty abandoned knapsacks, well packed with clothing, &c. The remainder of my brigade, except the Eighty-second Ohio Veteran Volunteer Infantry, which had been sent to the support of Colonel West, now crossed the swamp by the main road, and the whole encamped near the rebel redoubts. This little affair, in my judgment, reflects great credit upon those concerned in it, and I take this occasion to express my appreciation of the skill and promptitude with which Colonel West handled his troops. I regret to say, however, that this affair cost us one man killed and four wounded.

My brigade marched again at 7 a. m. on the 10th, in the center of the division, the Second Brigade leading. The road was excellent, and devoid of all obstructions. My brigade struck the Charleston and Savannah Railroad at Monteith Station at 10 a. m., and soon afterward commenced destroying the track. By 11.30 a. m. half a mile of the track was thoroughly destroyed by the brigade, and the column resumed its march, now on the direct road to the city of Savannah. By 2.30 p. m. my command reached the fifth mile-post from the city. About one mile in advance of this the enemy had already been encountered, strongly intrenched, with artillery in position. It was evident that this was the main line of the defenses of the city. My brigade immediately went into position on the left of the Second Brigade, which had already formed in the dense forest on the left of the road. My left flank joined the right of the First Brigade. Pickets covering the line were at once thrown forward, but no demonstration was made upon the enemy. My troops encamped in the position thus taken. On the 11th my command was thrown forward and to the left about 400 yards, and the troops again encamped in their position. At 11 p. m., by direction of the general commanding division, I detached the One hundred and first and Eighty-second Illinois and Sixty-first Ohio Veteran Volunteers, the whole under the command of Lieutenant-Colonel Le Sage, of the One hundred and first Illinois Volunteers, and sent them to the rear, to be used in guarding the trains of the corps. On the 13th I was directed to move the remainder of my brigade to the rear, to cover the approaches to the trains. At 3 p. m. my entire command was posted, covering the different roads coming from the rear. My line was about three miles in extent, joining the pickets of the Twenty-second Wisconsin Volunteers on the right, near the Savannah River, and those of the Fourteenth Army Corps on the left. The One hundred and forty-third New York Volunteers was placed near the junction of the Tweedside, the Potter's plantation, and the Savannah roads. The Eighty-second Ohio Veteran Volunteers was placed about three-quarters of a mile farther to the right, on the Potter's plantation road. The One hundred and first Illinois Volunteers and Sixty-first Ohio Veteran Volunteers covered the Savannah road, near Cherokee Hill. The Eighty-second Illinois Volunteers covered the line of the Charleston and Savannah Railroad. The Thirty-first Wisconsin Volunteers was placed three-quarters of a mile south of Cherokee Hill, on a road leading in that direction. The positions thus chosen, excepting those of the two regiments first named, were covered by substantial breast-works. A section of artillery, which reported to me on the 14th, was posted on the Savannah road and was covered by a redoubt. My brigade remained in the position just described without incident worthy of note until the 19th. On that date, by permission of the general commanding division, I sent out a foraging expedition, consisting of twelve companies of infantry, two from each regiment, and eight wagons. My instructions to Lieutenant-Colonel Le Sage, commanding the detachment, were to proceed about four miles north of Monteith Station, to obtain all the forage and supplies he could, and to develop the strength and position of a hostile force reported to be in that neighborhood. The party returned at 3 p. m. without having obtained either provisions or forage. It had encountered the enemy's outposts and driven them back to within one mile and a half of his main camp, capturing one prisoner. During the night of the 20th, according to direction, I detailed a regiment, the One hundred and forty-third New York Volunteers, to cross to Argyle Island and there go into position, covering the flank of the Second Brigade, which had crossed to the South Carolina shore. On the morning of the 21st it was discovered that the enemy had evacuated the city and defenses of Savannah. The One hundred and forty-third New York Volunteers therefore rejoined the brigade on the morning of the 22d. On the 23d my command moved back toward the city and encamped on McAlpin's plantation, on the right bank of the Savannah River. The position assigned me was on the right of the Second Brigade and one mile above the city of Savannah. Here my troops erected comfortable quarters, in which they still remain.

During the extraordinary campaign which has terminated, my command marched over 350 miles, completely destroyed 9 miles of railroad track, burned a station-house, several water-tanks, and a large quantity of wood and railroad lumber; burned 12 cotton-gins and presses, and 250 bales of cotton; captured 5 serviceable horses, 42 serviceable mules, 460 head of cattle, 200 sheep, 500 hogs, 12 barrels of molasses, 1 barrel of whisky, 50,000 pounds of sweet potatoes, 10,800 pounds of rice, besides a vast quantity of flour, meal, bacon, poultry, and other promiscuous kinds of provisions. The quantity of forage captured it is difficult to estimate, but it is safe to say that it amounted to not less than 130,000 pounds. Excepting the articles of bread, coffee, and sugar, my troops subsisted almost entirely from the country. The animals also were fed almost exclusively upon what was obtained from the same source.

I take pleasure in expressing my hearty commendation of the soldierly behavior of the officers and men of my command during this long and arduous campaign. The fatigues and privations of the march were borne with cheerfulness. The heavy labor of assisting trains, destroying railroads, building bridges, repairing roads, &c., was performed with alacrity, and when the voice of danger summoned, every soldier sprang to his post with enthusiasm. The commanders of my regiments and the officers of my staff deserve and are tendered my sincere thanks for their ready co-operation in every laudable undertaking, and their earnest zeal in carrying out my orders. But the soldiers and officers of my command need no praise from me. Their own achievements are their highest encomium, and the united admiration of their countrymen their best reward. These are already theirs, and neither my pen nor voice can add anything to them.

In conclusion I have the honor to add the following list of the regiments composing my brigade and the officers commanding them during the campaign: Thirty-first Wisconsin Volunteers, Col. Francis H. West;

Eighty-second Ohio Veteran Volunteers, Lieut. Col. David Thomson; One hundred and forty-third New York Volunteers, Lieut. Col. Hezekiah Watkins; One hundred and first Illinois Volunteers, Lieut. Col. John B. Le Sage; Eighty-second Illinois Volunteers, Maj. F. H. Rolshausen; Sixty-first Ohio Veteran Volunteers, Capt. John Garrett.

The officers of my staff were as follows: Capt. A. E. Lee, acting assistant adjutant-general; Capt. Benjamin Reynolds, acting assistant inspector-general; Capt. F. S. Wallace, topographical engineer; Capt. Charles Saalmann, acting commissary of subsistence; Capt. W. T. George, acting assistant quartermaster; Surg. H. K. Spooner, surgeon-in-chief; Capt. Cyrus Hearrick, acting aide-de-camp; Capt. Myron H. Lamb, acting aide-de-camp; Lieut. Charles M. Lockwood, acting assistant provost-marshal.

The following casualties and losses occurred in my brigade during the campaign: One enlisted man killed in action, 4 deserted, 1 missing in action, 4 injured in destroying railroad, 2 captured while foraging, making an aggregate loss of 16 [12] enlisted men.

Respectfully, your obedient servant,

J. S. ROBINSON,
Colonel, Commanding.

Lieut. GEORGE ROBINSON,
Acting Assistant Adjutant-General, First Division.

No. 92.

Report of Maj. Ferdinand H. Rolshausen, Eighty-second Illinois Infantry, of operations September 4–December 23.

HDQRS. EIGHTY-SECOND ILLINOIS VOLUNTEER INFANTRY,
Near Savannah, Ga., December 26, 1864.

SIR: I have the honor to submit to you the report of operations of my regiment since the entrance of Atlanta up to the present moment.

On the 4th of September, 1864, we did strike tents at the Chattahoochee River and entered Atlanta at 11 a. m., where we pitched camp on the north side of the city, at the old inner rebel works, where we stopped until September 12, when we were detailed to take charge of the military Confederate prisoners till October 4, 1864. During October 16, 17, 18, and 19 we were ordered to go on a foraging expedition in charge of Colonel Robinson. On the same we loaded all wagons taken along with corn and straw; also eatables, as sweet potatoes, pork, and beef. Another foraging expedition we participated in, under the command of Brigadier-General Geary, commanding Second Division, Twentieth Corps, on the 26th, 27th, 28th, and 29th, at which there was a similar result. We laid up till we received (by an order from General Sherman) marching orders.

It was on the morning of the 15th of November when we started on (as we know now) for Savannah. We encamped this night on the other side of Decatur, a little town on the Atlanta and Augusta railroad, where we arrived at 8 p. m. On the 16th we left at 8 a. m., and commenced to tear up and burn the railroad until 4 p. m.; arrived in camp at 12 p. m. Marched November 17 and 18. On November 19 we passed Madison, and camped at 1 p. m. Marched 20th, 21st, and 22d, and arrived at Milledgeville, the capital of Georgia, at 9 p. m. Laid up November 23, and marched November 24, 25, and 26, and destroyed here Station No. 13 of the Augusta and Macon Railroad. November 27, marched to Davisborough, Station No. 12. November 28, marched and tore up railroad for ten miles, and camped at Station No. 11. November 29, marched and tore up two miles of railroad.

Marched from December 1 to 8, inclusive. On December 9 marched two miles, and had to reconnoiter the surrounding country and flank a small body of the enemy hovering around our front; arrived in camp at 6 p. m. On the 10th we struck the Savannah and Charleston Railroad, destroyed and burned it up near the bridge over the Savannah River, and encamped four miles and a half from Savannah. December 11, took position, but were withdrawn again at 10 o'clock that night to protect the trains from the rear. Remained here from December 12 to 22, inclusive. December 23, we left this camp and moved into Savannah, where we arrived at 1 p. m. and are now encamped on the west side of Savannah. Here I must remark, yet, that during the last campaign our foraging parties have supplied the regiment with a plentiness of sweet potatoes, poultry, fresh and salt pork, beef, forage, and other eatables for men and animals. We obtained about ten horses and sixteen mules, with which we completed our regimental teams and turned over the rest to the provost-marshal of the brigade. At the same time we picked up eleven negroes, which supplied the places of officers' servants and company cooks on the latter end of the campaign; so my command has never lived any better since in service as while this tramp was made. Cotton and cotton presses were also destroyed whenever found and an order from a superior officer was given.

Officers and enlisted men behaved themselves, and were as obedient to orders as usual.

F. H. ROLSHAUSEN,
Major, Commanding Eighty-second Illinois Volunteers.

Col. JAMES S. ROBINSON,
Comdg. Third Brigade, First Division, Twentieth Corps.

No. 93.

Report of Lieut. Col. John B. Le Sage, One hundred and first Illinois Infantry, of operations September 2–December 23.

HDQRS. 101ST REGT. ILLINOIS VOLUNTEER INFANTRY,
Savannah, Ga., December 25, 1864.

CAPTAIN: I have the honor to submit the following report of the operations of the One hundred and first Regiment of Illinois Volunteers from the occupation of Atlanta by the U. S. forces to the capture of the city of Savannah:

From the 2d of September, when Atlanta fell into the hands of the Union Army, until the 21st of September, the regiment which I have the honor to command remained quietly in camp. On the 21st it was detailed on duty in the fire department, and remained on that duty during the whole time that Atlanta was occupied by our forces.

On the 15th of October the regiment went with the brigade on a foraging expedition to Flat Shoals, on which expedition the regiment was gone four days and loaded thirty-two wagons with forage. Again, on the 26th of October, the regiment went with the brigade on a foraging expedition to Berkshire Post-Office, remaining four days, and, in conjunction with the Eighty-second Ohio Veteran Volunteers, loading sixty wagons with forage. During the remainder of the time until the commencement of the recent expedition the regiment remained quietly in camp.

On the morning of the 15th of November the regiment left the city of Atlanta, or rather what was left of the city of Atlanta, and started on the great raid through Georgia, and marched on that day to Stone Mountain, a distance of about fourteen miles. On the 16th, during the morning, it tore up and destroyed about half a mile of the railroad track on the Atlanta and Augusta road, and then marched to the Yellow River, about fifteen miles, reaching camp about 2 a. m. On the 17th we marched about fifteen miles, encamping in the country about 1 a. m. On the 18th we marched, passing through Social Circle about noon, and proceeding nearly to Madison, making in all about fifteen miles. On the 19th we marched through Madison and proceeded on the Eatonton road, making about ten miles. On the 20th we marched toward Eatonton about ten miles, reaching a point about four miles from Eatonton. On the 21st we marched through Eatonton and on toward Milledgeville, making about fifteen miles. On the 22d we marched about eleven miles, to Milledgeville, and on the 23d remained there. On the 24th marched toward Hebron, about fifteen miles. On the 25th the regiment was the leading regiment of the corps. We marched about four miles until we reached Buffalo Creek, where the series of bridges were found to have been destroyed. The regiment was engaged for awhile in repairing these bridges. About noon a party of rebel cavalry having been stirred up across the creek the right wing of the regiment was sent across to attend to them. About 2 o'clock, the bridges being completed, we crossed over, where one of the companies rejoined us, and the other four were left to guard the crossing until the Second Division of the corps should come over. With six companies we marched ahead about two miles farther, when a brisk cavalry skirmish was stirred up in front, and a large number of "bummers" made a rapid retreat from the front. The regiment was promptly formed in line of battle to the right of the road, and then advanced about 200 yards, when we were ordered to encamp for the night. On the 26th we marched toward Sandersville. After proceeding about two miles the regiment was sent to the right about half a mile, to dislodge some guerrillas, which we did; and we also destroyed a gin and about 100 bales of cotton, after which we rejoined the column and marched to Sandersville, and thence to Power's, on the Macon and Savannah Railroad, where we encamped for the night, having marched about twelve miles. On the 27th we marched to Davisborough, a distance of about twenty miles, having to make a detour to avoid a swamp. On the 28th we marched along the railroad to Spiers, tearing up the track to within three miles of that place. I am unable to state how much the regiment tore up during the day, but should say that of eleven regiments engaged in the destruction of seven miles it did its full proportion. On the 29th we went back about three miles and finished the destruction of the railroad to Spiers, doing about one-sixth of the destruction. We then marched in the direction of Louisville, about twelve miles. On the 30th we marched to where the Third Division was in camp, about two miles and a half east of Louisville on the eastern side of the Ogeechee River, having made a march of about eighteen miles.

On the 1st of December we marched in the direction of Millen, about fifteen miles, reaching camp about 1 a. m. On the 2d we marched about fifteen miles to Buck Head Church. On the 3d we marched about fifteen miles, passing about three miles north of Millen, and marching in the direction of Sylvania. On the 4th we marched about twelve miles. On the 5th marched two miles and a half and went into camp about 11 p. m. On the 6th marched about eight or ten miles toward Springfield. On the 7th seven companies were detached to go back after forage, with — wagons, which they loaded, and rejoined the regiment that night, which had marched about ten miles toward Springfield. On the 8th we marched to Springfield, four miles, and from there toward Monteith, about twelve miles. On the 9th we marched toward Monteith Station, on the Savannah and Charleston Railroad. About 2 p. m. we reached a swamp where the rebels had obstructed the road with felled timber, and commanded the road with artillery placed in a couple of redoubts on the other side. The Sixty-first Ohio Veteran Volunteers and Thirty-first Wisconsin Volunteers of our brigade were sent to the left to wade the swamp and flank the rebel position. This they did splendidly. At the first fire, which they opened, the rest of the brigade rushed forward to their assistance, but they had completed the task and held the forts, the rebels, unfortunately, making good their retreat. We camped for the night around the forts, having marched about eight miles. On the 10th we marched to Monteith Station, where we tore up the railroad, completely destroying about twice the length of the regiment, and then marched to where the rebel line of works around the city of Savannah confronted us—a distance of about nine miles. Here we went into position. Late in the evening the regiment was sent out to hold a road, while the Forty-sixth Pennsylvania Veteran Volunteers proceeded to the river on a reconnaissance. On the 11th we changed position, moving farther to the left. About 9 p. m. I was ordered, with my own regiment and the Eighty-second Illinois Volunteers and Sixty-first Ohio Veteran Volunteers, to proceed to the rear of the train, and guard the train, against which the rebel cavalry under Wheeler were said to be demonstrating. I reached the point designated about 1 a. m. and went into position. We remained here until the 13th, when the rest of the brigade came out, and, with a slight change of position, we went into camp, building a strong line of breast-works. Here we remained until the 23d, when we moved to our present position.

As to the number of horses, mules, and cattle captured by the regiment, I have no very correct idea. We captured no horses, probably three or four mules, and as to cattle, I have no idea. We foraged a great deal of beef. We captured and turned into the brigade commissary about twenty head of cattle, and in addition to that I should estimate the number of cattle foraged by the regiment for their own use at about fifty head; but it is mere guesswork. We captured large numbers of hogs, sheep, and various kinds of poultry. We lived almost wholly upon what we foraged, excepting sugar and coffee and occasional issues of hard bread. We lived wholly upon the country and, with but one or two days' exception, fared, I might say, for soldiers, sumptuously. As to forage, our horses were subsisted wholly from what we gathered on the march, and they have grown fat from it, for they had all they could eat. As to negroes, I should place the number picked up by the regiment at about forty.

In conclusion, I would state that so far as the regiment is concerned the whole expedition was a splendid affair. I feel glad to say that I have not lost a man, killed or captured, and only three wounded by the accidental falling of railroad iron upon them while engaged in tearing up the track—one of them seriously, the others only slightly. And I would take this occasion to return my thanks to all, both officers and men, for their ready obedience to my orders and for their good, soldierly conduct on the whole march.

I have the honor to remain, very respectfully, your obedient servant,

JOHN B. LE SAGE,
Lieutenant-Colonel, Comdg. 101st Regiment Illinois Volunteers.

Capt. A. E. LEE,
Actg. Asst. Adjt. Gen., 3d Brig., 1st Div., 20th Army Corps.

No. 94.

Report of Lieut. Col. Hezekiah Watkins, One hundred and forty-third New York Infantry.

HDQRS. 143D REGIMENT NEW YORK VOL. INFANTRY,
Near Savannah, Ga., December 26, 1864.

CAPTAIN:*

On the morning of November 15 the regiment broke camp and started on the campaign just ended. The effective force at this time was 19 commissioned officers and 244 muskets, also 14 unarmed recruits for whom arms could not be procured previous to starting. The effective force at present, 19 commissioned officers and 243 muskets. One enlisted man supposed to be captured while out with a foraging detail.

The number of animals captured is as follows: 11 horses, 12 mules, and about 100 cattle. There were also about 25 negroes picked up on the march.

During the time from starting from Atlanta, November 15 to December 21, there were issued to the command of Government rations, viz, 13 days' hard bread, 20 days' coffee, 15 days' sugar, 26 days' salt. There was also issued 1,000 pounds of grain for the animals, the remainder needed by the regiment being foraged from the country.

Very respectfully, your obedient servant,

H. WATKINS,
Lieutenant-Colonel, Commanding Regiment.

Capt. A. E. LEE,
Acting Assistant Adjutant-General.

No. 95.

Report of Capt. John Garrett, Sixty-first Ohio Infantry, of operations September 4–December 22.

HDQRS. SIXTY-FIRST OHIO VOLUNTEER INFANTRY,
Near Savannah, Ga., December 26, 1864.

CAPTAIN: I have the honor to submit the following report of the operations of the Sixty-first Ohio Volunteers from the occupation of Atlanta to the capture of Savannah by the National forces:

Entered Atlanta September 4 and occupied the intrenchments of the enemy.

On October 6 was assigned to a position on Peach Tree Creek road. During our stay at this place accompanied two foraging expeditions,

---

* For portion of report (here omitted) relating to operations about Atlanta, see Vol. XXXIX, Part I, 661.

the first, under command of Colonel Robinson, to Flat Rock, Ga., and the second, under command of Brigadier-General Geary, to Stone Mountain, the object being to procure subsistence for the men and animals of the corps.

Started on the recent campaign November 15, following the line of the Augusta railroad as far as Madison, where we turned southward and struck the Milledgeville railroad at Eatonton, and entered Milledgeville November 22. Resumed the march November 24, and on the 26th struck the Georgia Central Railroad and destroyed a portion of the track near Station No. 13. November 27, moved eastward along the line of the Georgia Central Railroad, and on the 28th assisted in destroying the track and bridges between Davisborough and Spiers Station. Resumed the march on the 29th, and on the 30th crossed the Ogeechee River.

No incident of importance transpired till December 9, when I was ordered to assist Colonel West, Thirty-first Wisconsin Volunteers, to capture two small forts of the enemy, erected to command the road at a point where it passed through a dense swamp fourteen miles from Savannah. We penetrated the swamp to the left of the road, and when within 100 yards of the enemy they opened upon us with musketry. A charge was ordered, and we pushed forward over a formidable abatis and entered one of the forts, and at the same moment the colors of the Thirty-first Wisconsin were planted upon the other; the enemy escaped with his artillery. I had one man severely wounded in the engagement. December 10, advanced and took position before Savannah. December 11, moved to the rear and took position near the railroad, seven miles from Savannah, for the protection of the wagon trains, where we remained until the capture of the city.

During the campaign my command captured 10 horses and 30 mules, and drew forage from the country equal to twenty days' subsistence. A large quantity of cotton was destroyed, but as much of it was not in bales it is impossible to state the exact amount.

Respectfully, your obedient servant,

JOHN GARRETT,
Captain, Comdg. Sixty-first Ohio Veteran Volunteer Infantry.

Capt. A. E. LEE,
Actg. Asst. Adjt. Gen., 3d Brig., 1st Div., 20th Army Corps.

No. 96.

Report of Lieut. Col. David Thomson, Eighty-second Ohio Infantry.

HDQRS. EIGHTY-SECOND REGT. OHIO VET. VOL. INFTY.,
Near Savannah, Ga., December 27, 1864.

CAPTAIN:*

On the 15th day of November the regiment left its camp in Atlanta and entered upon the campaign which ended with the capture and occupation of Savannah by our forces. During the campaign the troops were principally subsisted off the country through which we passed. On the 16th we reached and commenced destroying the railroad near Stone Mountain. My regiment here destroyed about two miles

*For portion of report (here omitted) relating to operations about Atlanta, see Vol. XXXIX, Part I, p. 662.

of the road. But small forces of the enemy were met, and until our arrival before Savannah it was necessary for the regiment to take a position in line of battle but twice. The first time was near Sandersville, on November 25. We met the enemy late in the afternoon. The fighting (which was nothing more than skirmishing) was principally done by our advance cavalry. The Third Brigade was in advance and formed in line of battle. We encamped in line, and the next morning the Second Brigade took the advance, the Third Brigade following. The enemy made but very little opposition, and we had no difficulty in occupying Sandersville. From this place we moved to Tennille Station, No. 13, and destroyed about half a mile of the railroad. On the 27th we reached Davisborough Station, on the Georgia Central Railroad, and early on the morning of the 28th commenced destroying the railroad. We destroyed about three miles of the road and at night went into camp at Station No. 11. The Third Brigade at this point was detached from the corps for the purpose of guarding the corps train. On the 30th we crossed the Little Ogeechee several miles above the railroad, in consequence of the destruction of the bridge, and encamped near the east bank of the river.

We marched and crossed the Augusta branch railroad on the 3d day of December, leaving Millen to our right. On the 5th our regiment was sent two miles from camp, with orders to destroy two mills. I destroyed the mills and returned to camp. From this time until the 9th nothing worthy of note occurred. On the 9th we found the enemy in considerable force in our front. They were in a strong position, had fortifications with two pieces of artillery, and their front and right was protected by a swamp. The Thirty-first Wisconsin and Sixty-first Ohio were thrown forward, and succeeded in passing through this swamp and attacked the enemy from the rear and right. The Eighty-second Ohio was thrown forward as a support, but before my regiment succeeded in passing through this swamp the Thirty-first Wisconsin and Sixty-first Ohio had attacked and routed the enemy. On the 10th, having reached Monteith, a station on the Savannah and Charleston Railroad, the Third Brigade was ordered to commence and effectually destroy as much of this road as possible. The Eighty-second Ohio Regiment destroyed about 300 yards of the road and also the station-house. The same day, having reached the enemy's lines in front of Savannah, the brigade took up a position, with three regiments in line of battle, with the Second Brigade on the right. My regiment was on the front line, connecting with the Thirty-first Wisconsin on the right and the One hundred and forty-third New York on the left. On the 11th the brigade was moved a short distance to the left, the regiments occupying the same positions in line. On the 13th the brigade was moved about three miles to the rear, where a second or rear line was formed for the purpose of protecting the rear. The Eighty-second occupied the right of this line, my pickets connecting with those of the One hundred and forty-third New York on my left. My command occupied this position until the surrender of Savannah and its occupation by our forces. The regiment entered its present encampment on the 23d of December, connecting on the right with the One hundred and forty-third New York and on the left with the Thirty-first Wisconsin.

During the campaign my command has captured 13 head of horses, 25 head of mules, 30 head of cattle, 150 head of hogs, 35 head of sheep, 200 pounds sugar, 4 tons fodder, 200 bushels of corn, 200 bushels of potatoes, 125 bushels of corn meal, 1,000 pounds of flour, 160 gallons of molasses, and chickens and turkeys innumerable.

My command also captured 30 negroes and destroyed in all six miles of railroad and 150 bales of cotton and burned two cotton gins.

I am, captain, very respectfully,

D. THOMSON,
Lieutenant-Colonel, Commanding Regiment.

Capt. A. E. LEE,
Acting Assistant Adjutant-General.

No. 97.

Report of Col. Francis H. West, Thirty-first Wisconsin Infantry.

HEADQUARTERS THIRTY-FIRST WISCONSIN VOLUNTEERS,
Savannah, Ga., December 25, 1864.

CAPTAIN: I have the honor to make the following report of operations of this regiment from the time of the occupation of Atlanta to this date:

During the occupation of Atlanta nothing of especial interest occurred in the regiment. It was engaged in the ordinary guard duty and in drilling and preparing for a new campaign, and also furnishing heavy details to work on fortifications. It twice during the time accompanied foraging expeditions to the vicinity of Stone Mountain and Yellow River; once, under command of Colonel Robinson, commanding Third Brigade, and once, under command of General Geary, commanding Second Division, Twentieth Corps. On each of these occasions some 800 wagon-loads of forage were obtained.

Of the campaign from Atlanta to Savannah the history of the regiment is so inseparably connected with that of the brigade to which it belongs, that it is difficult to make a special report of its operations. Leaving Atlanta at 7 a. m. November 15, with — effective enlisted men and — officers, our march was continuous, triumphant, and almost uninterrupted, through the rich and well-settled districts of Georgia, by the way of Decatur, Social Circle, Madison, Milledgeville, Eatonton, Sandersville, Millen, Louisville, and Springfield, to within five miles of Savannah, where we arrived on the 10th instant, followed by a large number of negroes, which had been gradually accumulating as we advanced through the country, but as none of them were especial followers of my regiment, I cannot claim to have brought in any certain number. It was noticeable that they were all very much delighted at the approach of the army, although but few of them had ever seen a "Yank" before. There was much appearance of wealth among nearly all the inhabitants living on the line of our march and we found great abundance of corn, beef, mutton, sweet potatoes, poultry, molasses, and honey along the whole route, upon which the regiment subsisted entirely, with the exception of about ten days' rations of hard bread and full rations of sugar, coffee, and salt, which were issued immediately previous to and during the march. We also captured 10 very large, fine mules and about 30 inferior mules and horses, which were used in packing supplies, and were subsisted, as were our private and public animals, from forage we obtained from the inhabitants. During the march we, in company with the balance of the brigade, assisted in destroying a large amount of the Georgia Central Railroad in the vicinity of Stone Mountain, Spiers Station, and Jonesborough, and also of the Charleston railroad at and near Monteith. The amount destroyed by my regiment I am unable to give.

Great attempts were made by the enemy to impede our progress by destroying bridges, felling timber in the road, &c., but this caused but little delay, as our efficient pioneer corps soon cleared away all obstructions and rebuilt the bridges. We met with no resistance in force until we arrived at Turkey Roost [or Monteith] Swamp, fifteen miles from Savannah. This is an almost impenetrable morass, many miles in extent, densely covered with brush and vines, interspersed with deep sloughs. Across this the road has been built. On a little elevation on the opposite side, at a place known as Harrison's field, and immediately commanding the road across the morass, which is about 500 yards wide, and which had been very heavily obstructed, the enemy had built two strong redoubts, which were defended by artillery and about 500 infantry, with which they resolutely disputed our farther progress. The First and Second Brigades of our division had been sent around to the right (which seemed the most feasible way of crossing the morass), with instructions if possible to flank the enemy and dislodge or capture them. Finding that they were not likely to be immediately successful, I was directed by Colonel Robinson, commanding brigade, to take my regiment, numbering 500 present (the immediate command of which devolved upon Lieutenant-Colonel Rogers), and the Sixty-First Ohio, numbering about 100 men, under command of Captain Garrett, and make a similar attempt by way of the left. Quickly moving around about half a mile to the left and on to the border of the morass, the line was formed for attack by placing the Sixty-first Ohio on the right and the Thirty-first Wisconsin on the left, with instructions to dash through the swamp by the right of companies, coming into line the moment they emerged on the open ground in vicinity of the fort. This the men did with great spirit and determination, struggling through to within about 300 yards of the forts where an open swamp extended down to within fifty yards of the forts, the last fifty yards being heavily covered with abatis. Emerging into this opening they formed instantly under a heavy fire from the enemy, and, delivering a steady volley upon the enemy, they dashed upon the works with such impetuosity that the enemy, becoming panic-stricken, fled in great confusion, abandoning much of their camp and garrison equipage and clothing. The colors of the Thirty-first Wisconsin were almost instantly flying from the parapets of the fort. Shortly after the brigades that had gone to the right succeeded in passing the morass and came up; also the balance of our brigade, which Colonel Robinson promptly sent to my support on hearing the firing. The loss of my regiment in this affair was 1 killed and 3 wounded. We escaped with so small a loss on account of the enemy firing too high. Loss of the enemy unknown—said to have been 14.

Through me the regiment, together with the Sixty-first Ohio, received the public thanks of Major-General Slocum, commanding Left Wing, Army of Georgia, General Williams, commanding Twentieth Army Corps, and of Colonel Robinson, commanding brigade, for the handsome manner in which they executed the affair.

As all in the command behaved equally well I can mention no names. I, however, here wish to make mention of the gallant conduct and efficient service rendered on this occasion by Captains Wallace and Hearrick, of Colonel Robinson's staff, who were detailed to assist me in the enterprise.

During the siege of Savannah, from the 10th to the 21st of December, at which time the enemy evacuated Savannah, the regiment was engaged in the ordinary siege duties, building works,

&c., without any engagement with the enemy or casualties therefrom. On the 23d we moved in and took position on the bank of the Savannah River about two miles above the city, and are now engaged in preparing for future operations. Since arriving near Savannah we have had but very limited supplies of rations or forage, and we are now suffering much for subsistence, the men receiving little else than small rations of rice, and our public and private animals almost nothing at all. It is probable that this is owing to the difficulty of landing supplies from the fleet.

The health and spirits of the men were never better than during the past campaign, the average daily number requiring medical attendance being about ten.

The casualties during the campaign were 1 man severely injured while destroying railroad, 1 killed, and 3 wounded by the enemy, and 3 captured while foraging, 2 of whom have since escaped and returned to the regiment. No sick were left on the road.

Very respectfully, your obedient servant,

F. H. WEST,
Colonel, Commanding Regiment.

Capt. A. E. LEE,
Actg. Asst. Adjt. Gen., Hdqrs. 3d Brig., 1st Div., 20th Corps.

No. 98.

Report of Brig. Gen. John W. Geary, U. S. Army, commanding Second Division.

HEADQUARTERS SECOND DIVISION, TWENTIETH CORPS,
January 6, 1865.

COLONEL:*

November 15, in accordance with orders received on the previous night, my division, with the exception of one regiment, the One hundred and eleventh Pennsylvania Veteran Volunteers, broke camp at an early hour in the morning, and at 7 o'clock moved out upon the Decatur road, following the First Division. Shortly after passing beyond the old line of rebel works I was obliged to halt, on account of the detention of the troops and trains in my front, and several hours elapsed before the road was sufficiently clear to allow of my advance. Resuming the march I moved on, keeping well closed upon the rear of the First Division, and halting for dinner near Decatur. After passing through the village I took advantage of every field to move the head of my column parallel to the train of the preceding division. The head of my column went into camp near Stone Mountain about 11 p. m. The march during the day was continually delayed by halts and detentions, caused by the miserable character of the animals in our train. The roads traveled were bad; the weather was beautiful. The distance marched during the day was fifteen miles. November 16, I broke camp at 8 a. m. and moved out in advance of the corps. Crossed Yellow River, at Rock Bridge, about 3 p. m., and went into camp three miles beyond, having marched during the day ten miles. The marching to-day was necessarily slow, owing to the bad character of the roads and bad condition of our animals. The country through which I passed

---

*For portion of report (here omitted) relating to operations about Atlanta, see Vol. XXXIX, Part I, p. 667.

was for the most part poor and undulating, and east of Yellow River the road crosses a number of swampy streams and steep ridges. November 17, moved from camp again at 5 o'clock, in advance of the corps. Encamped for the night on the west bank of the Ulcofauhachee River, having marched seventeen miles. The roads traveled were very good and the country traversed was fine. November 18, moved at 5 a. m., my division still in the advance. Crossed the Ulcofauhachee River, struck the Georgia railroad at Social Circle, east of which place we destroyed considerable of the track, and passed through Rutledge Station at noon, near which place we halted for dinner. At this place destroyed the depot, water-tank, and other railroad buildings, and tore up and burned the track. Encamped for the night within two miles of Madison, having marched eighteen miles. The roads from Social Circle to Madison were excellent, and the country was much superior to that previously passed through. Forage was abundant on every side, and during the day we made captures of horses and mules.

November 19, in accordance with orders from the general commanding the corps, my command was detached and moved at 5 a. m., unencumbered with wagons, leaving my whole train to be brought on with those of the other divisions. I passed through Madison before daylight, and moved along the road parallel to the Georgia railroad, halting for dinner at Buck Head Station, where I destroyed the water-tank, stationary engine, and all the railroad buildings. After marching one mile beyond the station I again halted and destroyed a portion of the railroad, also a large quantity of cord wood, and other railroad material. At Buck Head Station my advance exchanged shots with the enemy's scouts. I sent on a detachment in advance of the main body to drive these scouts and whatever there might be of the enemy's cavalry in the vicinity across the Oconee, and to burn the railroad bridge across the river; also another detachment several miles above to destroy a large mill and the ferry-boats across the Appalachee. Both of these parties were successful. The railroad bridge, which was a fine structure, about 400 yards long and 60 feet high from the water, and was approached by several hundred yards of trestle-work at each end, was thoroughly destroyed. At Blue Spring I halted and set my troops to work destroying railroad. Here at night encamped on the plantation of Col. Lee Jordan, on which I found 280 bales of cotton and 50,000 bushels of corn stored for the rebel Government. All the cotton and most of the corn was destroyed. In addition to this my command destroyed elsewhere during the day 250 bales of cotton and several cotton gins and mills. I also destroyed in all to-day about five miles of railroad and a large quantity of railroad ties and string timbers.

November 20, moved at 7 a. m.; the weather rainy, the roads very deep and swampy. Leaving the railroad I moved toward the Oconee, which was reached two miles below the railroad bridge, and then moved down parallel to the river to Parks' Mill, which was burned. The bridge across the river at this place had been previously washed away, and ferry-boats were used at the crossing; these I destroyed. Some annoyance was experienced as we moved along the river-bank from squads of rebel cavalry on the opposite shore. They were, however, soon driven off. A small party sent out from my command crossed the river near the burnt bridge and went on foot seven miles to Greensborough, driving a small force of cavalry through the town and taking possession of it. After remaining in undisturbed possession of the town for several hours, and having convinced the inhabitants that the most of General Sherman's army was close by with designs upon

Augusta, this little party returned safely, recrossing the river in canoes. I learned the next day that the enemy were tearing up the Georgia railroad at Union Point, seven miles east of Greensborough, apparently being possessed with the idea that General Sherman's army was moving on Augusta and using the railroad as it came. From all I could learn, then and since, it is my opinion that my small command could, at that time, have penetrated to Augusta without serious opposition. Leaving Parks' Mill and having crossed Sugar Creek I came to Glade's Cross-Roads, where I took the one leading to the left. Moving one mile and a half on this road I again turned to the left, on a smaller one, and encamped at dark near the large tannery and shoe factory and store owned by James Denham, one of the most extensive establishments of the kind in the South. Most of the leather stock and goods had been carried off; a few boxes of shoes and leather were found hidden in a barn and were turned over to the quartermaster's department for issue. My skirmishers and foraging parties during this day's march spread through all the country between the Oconee and the route of march taken by the rest of the corps. A large number of splendid mules and beef-cattle and some horses were captured, and the troops lived well on the produce of the country. Distance to-day, ten miles.

November 21, a heavy rain fell all last night and continued throughout to-day, rendering the roads very deep and the streams much swollen. After entirely destroying Denham's tannery and factory, I moved at 8 a. m. on the road to Philadelphia Church, reaching which I took the Milledgeville road, crossed Crooked Creek, and encamped at the forks of the road, one leading to Dennis' Mill and station, the other to Waller's Ferry, at the mouth of Little River. A very heavy, cold rain fell all day, and marching was quite difficult. The country passed through was a rich one and supplies were abundant. Distance marched, eight miles. The rain ceased toward night and the air became very cold. Among our captures to-day was Colonel White, of the Thirty-seventh Tennessee Regiment. He had been in command of the post at Eatonton, and in attempting to escape from the other column of our troops fell into my hands.

November 22, the weather was extremely cold. Moved at 6 a. m., taking the road to Dennis Station, having previously ascertained that it would be impossible for my command to cross Little River below the crossing of the railroad, there being no bridge and the ferry-boats having been destroyed by the inhabitants. Crossed Rooly Creek at Dennis' Mill. The stream here was quite large, and over it I constructed a foot bridge for the infantry, fording it with horses, artillery, and ambulances. Burned the mill and a cotton gin and press in vicinity, destroying a large amount of grain and cotton. Moved on to the railroad, which I reached at Dennis Station, and where I found the rear of the train of the other divisions just passing. Moved on in rear of the train to Little River, where I received orders to advance immediately to Milledgeville. Accordingly crossed the river on the pontoon bridge, passing the trains with much difficulty, and reached Milledgeville at dark, the other divisions having already encamped. Having passed through the town I crossed the Oconee on the large bridge and went into camp on the left of the First Division, with my left resting near the river. Marched during the day twenty miles. Weather to-night intensely cold.

November 23, remained in camp. In the afternoon sent out my Third Brigade to the Gordon and Milledgeville Railroad, where it remained until dark, destroying track.

November 24, in accordance with orders, moved at 7 a. m., but, finding the road completely blockaded with trains, I did not get my column fairly in motion until 10 o'clock. Just before dark crossed Town Creek, the bridge over which was very bad, and went into camp near Gum Creek, the First Division being encamped about three-quarters of a mile in advance, the Third Division about the same distance in my rear. The road traveled, although rather hilly, was in the main good. Marched during the day fourteen miles.

November 25, moved at 6.30 a. m., and marched about half a mile, when I came upon the trains preceding me not yet drawn out of park, and was obliged to halt until 9 o'clock, when I moved steadily forward until reaching Buffalo Creek, where I found the troops and trains of the First Division halted. This creek is an extensive, heavily timbered, swampy stream, being nearly half a mile wide where the road passes through it. The stream or swamp is here divided into eight channels, which are spanned by as many bridges, varying in length from 30 to 100 feet each. Between these earthen causeways are thrown up. These bridges had been destroyed by the enemy, and were reconstructed by 2 p. m., under the superintendence of Captain Poe, chief engineer on the staff of Major-General Sherman. By dark the road in my front was clear, and I crossed my command, encamping for the night one mile and a half east of the creek. The crossing in the extreme darkness of the night and through the swampy roads east of the creek was a very laborious one. During the night shots were exchanged between my pickets and some of Wheeler's cavalry. Distance marched, nine miles.

November 26, moved at 6 a. m. After marching about two miles came up with the trains preceding me, which had not yet left park. Here I parked my trains, being detained for two hours. Marching two miles farther, again found the trains in park, and the troops of the First Division skirmishing with Wheeler's cavalry and driving them through Sandersville. Moved on to Sandersville, where I parked my trains, and having left them under charge of Third Division, proceeded to Tennille (Station No. 13 on the Central railroad). Upon reaching the railroad I moved eastward, destroying two miles of the road, and went into camp near a school-house four miles east of Tennille. One battalion of Michigan Engineers, under Major Yates, reported to me for duty, assisted in the destruction of the rails, and encamped with my troops at night. Distance marched, thirteen miles.

November 27, in accordance with orders, moved this morning at 7 o'clock, destroying the railroad for four miles, to a point indicated, where a road crosses the railroad seven miles from Station No. 13. From here, in pursuance of my orders, I marched to Davisborough by the most direct road, and there encamped about 9 p. m. Distance marched, twelve miles.

November 28, the work of destroying the railroad west of Davisborough from the point indicated above, which was assigned by orders to the First Division, had not been performed, that division having missed the route and reached Davisborough without striking the railroad. Early this morning I received orders to detach Jones' brigade to guard the headquarters trains to Station No. 11, and with my two other brigades and a battalion of Michigan Engineers to destroy the part of the road specified from Davisborough westward. My orders were executed, and the remaining five miles of road, with a number of bridges, trestle-work and water-tanks, were effectually destroyed. While my troops were engaged in this work they were attacked by a portion of Ferguson's brigade of rebel cavalry, who kept up a desultory fire upon us for an hour and a half, and were driven off by my skirmishers. They wounded one of my men and captured four others who were out foraging. The fire of my skirmishers upon them was more effective, killing three and wounding a number. The country through which the railroad passes from No. 13 to No. 11 requires description. It is a continuous morass, known as Williamson's Creek, or Swamp. The stream is quite a large one, running in general direction parallel to the railroad and crossing it many times. The land in the vicinity of both sides is soft and swampy, with dense thickets of underbrush and vines. Through this swamp the railroad is constructed on an embankment of borrowed earth thrown up from the sides, averaging from six to ten feet in height. The superstructure consisted of cross-ties bedded in the earth, with string timbers pinned to them upon which the iron rails were spiked. The mode of destruction was to tear up, pile, and burn the ties and string timbers, with the rails across, which, when heated, were destroyed by twisting. Shortly after dark I returned to Davisborough and encamped there for the night. Distance traveled by a portion of my command to-day, fifteen miles.

November 29, moved at 6.30 a. m., following the main Louisville road for seven miles to Fleming's house; there turning square to the right by a small road, moved eight miles to Spiers Station (No. 11), which I reached at 1 o'clock. After a short halt for dinner moved on, following the road toward Station No. 10, and encamped about 7 p. m. on the east side of a small creek which crossed the road six miles from Station No. 11, the camp of the First Division being about one mile and a half in advance of mine. The roads traveled to-day were generally good and quite dry and hard west of Spiers Station. East of that place there was considerable swamp and marshy ground. The country through which we passed on the Louisville road was excellent, the plantations being large and the buildings fine. After leaving that road the country is poorer and appears to be newly settled. Distance traveled was twenty-one miles.

November 30, marched at 6 a. m., and reaching the encampment of the First Division found the troops had not yet left. At 10.30 we followed that division north toward Louisville, leaving Jones' brigade, which was then about three miles and a half distant, at the railroad bridge across the Ogeechee, to destroy that and the wagon bridge across the river, and then to follow to Louisville. After halting a few hours for dinner and to repair the bridge over the Ogeechee, which had been partly burned by the rebel cavalry, we crossed the river and encamped at dark two miles beyond, on the east side of Big Creek, on a high hill overlooking miles of the country, and two miles and a half south of Louisville. The country on both sides of the Ogeechee is an extensive swamp, with thick, tangled growths. These swamps, however, have good sandy bottoms, and it was not difficult to pass through them. The distance marched was ten miles.

December 1, moved at 7 a. m., my division leading, following the road toward Millen. My advance was preceded by the Ninth Illinois Mounted Infantry. Crossed Big, Dry, Spring, and Baker's Creeks, passing through the camp of Carlin's division, of the Fourteenth Corps, west of Baker's Creek, and encamped one mile and a half from Bark Camp Creek. The country passed through on this day's march was very swampy, although the roads in the main were very good. The facilities for forage were not as ample as on the previous days, the plantations being comparatively few, and although these few bore marks of having been well cultivated, the stock and provisions had been mostly removed. The distance traveled was thirteen miles.

December 2, my division, still retaining the advance, moved at 6 a. m., and crossing Bark Camp Creek moved easterly in the direction of Buck Head Creek, which I reached about noon. The roads traveled were excellent, following the course of a low dividing ridge. Passed but few plantations; among these was that of Doctor Jones, about five miles west of Buck Head Creek, one of the finest in this part of Georgia. Upon approaching the creek I found a number of rail defenses, which had been erected a few days previous during a fight between the cavalry of Kilpatrick and Wheeler. The bridge was destroyed and the enemy's pickets fired upon us from the eastern bank. These were soon driven away by a regiment of my command, and the bridge was reconstructed by the Michigan Engineers. I crossed it with my advance at 3 p. m., and encamped on the east side of the creek in the vicinity of Buck Head Church.

December 3, my division having been assigned the rear of the corps did not leave camp until 11 a. m., when I moved, following closely the rear of the Third Division. Colonel Dustin's brigade, of that division, having been directed to report to me, was assigned the charge of the train of Kilpatrick's cavalry, which was given me to guard. Lieutenant Newkirk's battery was also under my orders, and was placed in rear of my Third Brigade, which followed the trains. About five miles north of Millen, and not far from the railroad, there is a prison-pen or stockade in which had until recently been confined some 3,000 of our soldiers. The stockade was about 800 feet square, and inclosed nearly fifteen acres. It was made of heavy pine logs, rising from twelve to fifteen feet above the ground; on the top of these logs, at intervals of some eighty yards were placed sentry boxes. Inside of the stockade, running parallel to it at a distance from it of thirty feet, was a fence of light scantling, supported on short posts. This was the "dead line." About one-third of the area, on the western side, was occupied with a crowd of irregular earthen huts, evidently made by the prisoners. In these were lying unburied three of our dead soldiers, who were buried by us. Through the eastern part of the pen ran a ravine with a stream of good water. The atmosphere in the inclosure was foul and fetid. A short distance outside the stockade was a long trench, at the head of which was a board, bearing the inscription, "650 buried here." On rising ground a short distance southeast of the prison were two forts not yet completed; southwest of this stockade was a smaller one in process of construction. This prison, if indeed it can be designated as such, afforded convincing proofs that the worst accounts of the sufferings of our prisoners at Andersonville, at Americus, and Millen were by no means exaggerated. I crossed the railroad about three miles north of Millen. The track at the crossing had been destroyed, and the ties were burning, this work having been performed by the troops preceding. A short distance beyond the creek my column and trains became involved in a long and almost impassable swamp. To add to the difficulty night closed in before my advance had crossed, and it was with the utmost labor and only by the united efforts of myself, officers, and troops that I succeeded in bringing the wagons through. Encamped for the night within three miles of Big Horse Creek, the advance division of the corps being camped on the creek. The rear of my column did not reach camp until 6.30 a. m. of the 4th. The distance marched during the day was ten miles.

December 4, moved at 7.30 a. m., still in rear of the corps, and about noon came up with the Third Division trains in park on the western side of Crooked Run. The eastern side of this stream presents an extensive, level, swampy tract of land, across which trains could not pass until the roads were corduroyed. I found the Michigan Engineers engaged at this work. The last of the Third Division train crossed at dark. I then crossed my command, and by 11.30 p. m. had encamped them about one mile east of the creek, leaving Jones' brigade in camp on the other side. The weather continued fine, country poor, roads good, excepting through the large swamps at Big Horse Creek and Crooked Run. Distance to-day, four miles.

December 5, moved at 6.30 a. m. Crossed during the day Little Horse Creek, south fork of Little Ogeechee, and Little Ogeechee, destroying all the bridges after crossing. Much of the route to-day was through swamps, which had to be corduroyed for my trains. At the south fork of the Little Ogeechee I destroyed a large saw-mill. Here we heard what the inhabitants stated to be cannon in Charleston Harbor, about 100 miles distant. Weather pleasant; country poor. Distance to-day, twelve miles.

December 6, moved at 8 a. m., being the second division in line of march; was obliged to halt twice during the forenoon for the trains preceding to move out of my way. After having moved my command, advanced a mile and found all the trains of the Third Division parked and waiting for a long swamp to be corduroyed. I found but a few men working on the road, and immediately set a portion of my command at work, giving my personal superintendence until it was finished at dark. The Third Division trains then crossed, followed by my entire command. Crossed another smaller swamp a short distance beyond, and encamped my division on good, dry ground. The country was better than usual along the route to-day, and foraging parties were quite successful. Weather warm and pleasant. Distance, seven miles.

December 7, the forenoon was rainy. Moved at 7 a. m. and passed through a succession of terrible swamps, the surface crust of which in many places would not bear up either man or horse. I distributed my entire division along the trains, so that each brigade, regiment, and company had its specified number of teams to bring through. With this arrangement, under the personal superintendence and efforts of myself, my brigade commanders, and my staff, but little delay was allowed to occur, although so bad were the roads that at one time I counted twenty-four loaded wagons sunk to the wagon-beds. Mules in some places went in nearly out of sight. But the trains were kept quite well closed up through all these difficulties. Twice during the forenoon I halted and massed my troops and trains until those preceding me moved on. As we approached Turkey Creek the road improved. About 1 p. m. the rain ceased and the sun shone out warm and pleasant. At 2 p. m. reached Turkey Creek, quite a wide, fordable stream, with good bottom. Across this creek the corps pioneers had constructed a bridge for the troops, after cutting away a quantity of timber which had been felled to hinder our progress. By 5 p. m. the divisions preceding had finished crossing. I then crossed my command, moved three miles forward on an excellent road, and encamped within half a mile of Springfield. Distance, fifteen miles.

December 8, received orders to march in advance of the corps toward Monteith, leaving my trains under guard of the Third Division. Moved at 6 a. m. on a road running south by east from Springfield. After following this road six miles was ordered to take a small road branching off to the right, with a view of finding some middle road to Monteith. Followed this road, general direction west by south, for seven miles, and encamped in the woods about one mile and a half from the Louisville road, on which the Seventeenth Corps was then moving. The looked-for middle road was not found to-day. The roads were generally fair, although we crossed several small swamps. In them we found timber felled across the road. This was removed by our pioneers, without delaying the march more than thirty minutes at any one time. Most of our route to-day was through pine forests. We passed a number of plantation houses in these forests, and quite a large supply of potatoes, sugar cane, fodder, mutton, and poultry was obtained. It is worthy of note that the swamp water through this region is excellent for drinking purposes, being much superior to the well water. Weather to-day pleasant. Distance, thirteen miles.

December 9, moved at 8.30 a. m., following the First Division. At Zion Church we struck the Louisville road, and there turned to the left on the main road running due east to Monteith Station. At Monteith Swamp, five miles west of the station, we found the most extensive obstructions yet met with. The swamp is a very large one, about two miles wide where the road crosses it. Throughout this two miles of crossing the enemy had felled great quantities of timber, and at the eastern side of the swamp had erected two small redoubts with flanking rifle-pits. In these works they had two pieces of light artillery, supported by a small force of infantry. The artillery was so posted as to rake the road running through the swamp. While the division preceding me was engaged in movements for the dispersion or capture of the force opposing us, my command was halted and massed at the western side of the swamp. Receiving orders to that effect, I sent Jones' brigade rapidly forward to support Carman's brigade, of the First Division, which was working its way through to our right of the enemy's position. The services of this brigade were afterward found not to be required. At dusk my command was encamped on good, dry ground between the two portions of Monteith Swamp. Weather to-day was fine; roads were excellent. Distance, six miles.

SIEGE OF SAVANNAH.

December 10, order of march in the corps to-day: First, Third, and Second Divisions, the trains of the entire corps being guarded by my troops. My command moved at 10 a. m. on the direct road to Monteith Station. This road is broad, solid, and perfectly level. We passed the two redoubts captured last evening, and reached Monteith Station, on the Charleston railroad, ten miles from Savannah, at noon. Here the troops preceding me had destroyed considerable of the track. Having nooned, I moved toward Savannah on the Augusta road, the advance of the Fourteenth Corps coming in on that road and reaching Monteith as I left it. The advance of our corps having found the enemy behind their fortifications about three miles from Savannah, I received orders to encamp for the night near the Five-Mile Post. The trains came forward and parked in the woods in the vicinity of the troops. Distance to-day, ten miles.

December 11, at 7 a. m. Barnum's brigade was sent to reconnoiter between the Augusta road and Savannah River, to ascertain exactly the enemy's position in that direction. The duty was quickly performed, and their entire line was developed to the river, where my skirmishers drove the enemy from an advanced work into their main line, capturing a few prisoners. At 10 a. m. my other brigades were brought up and my line was established along an old rice-field dike—my left (Barnum's brigade) resting on the river-bank, my right (Pardee's brigade) extending toward the Augusta road, while Jones' brigade was massed in reserve in rear of Barnum's. Toward night the left of the First Division moved forward and connected with my right. Sloan's battery reported to me during the afternoon and took position on the river-bank near Jones' brigade. My front line was concealed by the woods, with the exception of my left, which lay in open ground within 250 yards of a large work on the river-bank in which the enemy had seven heavy guns. In front of my entire line were open fields, affording a full view of the intrenchments held by the enemy. Immediately in front of these intrenchments were extensive rice fields flooded with water, and between the fields in my front and these flooded rice fields was a canal twenty-five feet wide and five or six feet deep, which also was filled with water. The sluice gates to these fields were all under control of the enemy, as was also the mouth of the canal, between which and my position was the large advanced work before mentioned as being in front of my left. Besides this one the enemy had in my front three other works, mounted with heavy guns, in their main line across the flooded rice fields. These guns all opened upon us, keeping up a steady fire throughout the day, but causing very few casualties. No reply was made by my artillery, but my skirmishers were advanced as far as possible and annoyed the enemy considerably. Opposite my left, in the Savannah River, was the upper end of Hutchinson's Island, which extends from there down opposite the lower part of the city of Savannah. This island contains about 900 acres in rice fields, and on the upper end of it is a large rice mill. A great number of negroes had been left there. On discovering our troops a few of them crossed in canoes. Captain Veale, aide-de-camp of my staff, taking one of these canoes, went alone to the island, and, guided by a negro, walked nearly its entire length, reconnoitered the enemy's position along the river, and returned safely, bringing valuable information.

December 12, my troops strengthened their breast-works during the night so as to resist the enemy's heavy shot. A steady artillery fire was kept up by the enemy all day, causing a few casualties. I had Hutchinson's Island reconnoitered again, but found only a few of the enemy's scouts there.

December 13, the usual constant artillery fire was kept up by the enemy, their gunners improving in practice. They had posted some sharpshooters in the upper story of a house near their advanced fort on the river-bank. These sharpshooters annoyed the left of our line considerably. Among the casualties to-day was Lieutenant Ahreets, adjutant of the One hundred and thirty-fourth New York Volunteers, and acting assistant inspector-general, Twentieth Corps, who was killed instantly by a shot from that house while engaged in reconnoitering our lines. Last night the enemy landed some troops on Hutchinson's Island and captured a few of our men who had gone there for forage and supplies. To prevent such a recurrence Major Hoyt, One hundred and thirty-fourth New York Volunteers, was sent to the island to-day with a detachment of forty-seven men to hold the upper part of it. This evening he was re-enforced with 100 men, and the whole were placed under the command of Lieutenant-Colonel Jackson, of the One hundred and thirty-fourth New York Volunteers. A sunken battery was made to-day on the bank of the river near Jones' position, and was occupied by the four 3-inch rifled guns of Sloan's battery. These guns commanded the approaches up and down the river; also ranging across Hutchinson's Island toward the South Carolina shore. The supplies of food and forage in our trains being mostly exhausted, our troops were now subsisting upon fresh beef, coffee, and rice. Large quantities of the latter had been obtained upon the plantations in this vicinity, and a large rice mill on the Coleraine plantation, three miles up the river from my line, was kept constantly at work. Forage for our animals was obtained from rice straw and from the canebrakes. There was also tolerable grazing in the woods. An advanced line of pits for my skirmishers and sharpshooters was constructed to-night in the open field, within plain sight of all parts of the enemy's line and within good musket-range of it.

December 14, heavy and persistent artillery firing kept up all day from the enemy's batteries. The majority of their guns were 32-pounders; one was a 64-pounder, and there were a few light field pieces. Received to-day the official orders announcing the capture of Fort McAllister and our communication with the fleet. A small wagon train from my command was sent for supplies. At 10 a. m. one of the enemy's gun-boats came up on the high tide in Back River, the other side of Hutchinson's Island, fired several shots into Jones' camp, and withdrew. The practice was good, causing three or four casualties.

December 15, the usual artillery firing from the enemy. They expended an immense amount of ammunition in my front, averaging over 300 shots per day. No reply was made except by my sharpshooters, who were very active and accurate in their fire, causing much greater losses to the enemy than were produced among my troops by their artillery fire. My troops were kept well concealed, and it was impossible for the enemy to make any correct estimate of my force. Received to-day New York papers of the 10th, being our first Northern news since leaving Atlanta.

December 16, no change in position to-day. The usual sharpshooting from our side and artillery firing from the enemy was kept up. It having been decided to place some heavy guns in position on my line, a working party of 100 men from my Second Brigade was employed throughout the night constructing a strong lunette near the left of Barnum's line. The work was under the superintendence of Captain Schilling, topographical engineer on my staff. I had now two regiments of Jones' brigade, the Seventy-third Pennsylvania and One hundred and thirty-fourth New York Volunteers, both under command of Lieutenant-Colonel Jackson, encamped on Hutchinson's Island, and so intrenched as to hold the upper part of it against any force the enemy might bring. At high tide daily the enemy's gun-boats moved up in Back River and shelled these regiments. The enemy's land batteries also turned their fire in that direction frequently. Very few casualties occurred.

December 17, the work on Fort No. 1 (that in the left of Barnum's line) progressed so far last night that my details were working inside of it to-day, being protected by the heavy parapet. This work was but 250 yards distant from the advance fort on the enemy's right and could be plainly seen by them. They expended both artillery and musketry fire on it all day, but without effect. At 11 a. m. a large mail arrived for us and caused universal rejoicing, being our first during nearly six weeks. To-night working details from my First Brigade commenced constructing Fort No. 2, to be a large lunette for heavy guns in the open field in front of Pardee's left. This position being exposed to fire from all the batteries in my front, the work upon it had to be done quietly and at night.

December 18, the working detail on Fort No. 2 continued until 9 a. m., at which time the heavy fog lifted; that on Fort No. 1 worked all day inside the parapets. All the roads within my lines and to the rear were corduroyed to-day. The usual artillery firing continued by the enemy during the day and also throughout the night, their principal aim being to prevent our men from working on the forts, in which they did not succeed. To-night a working detail from my First Brigade began the construction of Fort No. 3 in the open field to the right and in advance of No. 2. Details from the Third Brigade continued working on the latter while Fort No. 1 was being finished by details from the Second Brigade.

December 19, a conference of the division and brigade commanders with the general commanding the corps was held at 10 a. m. to-day, with view to the adoption of a plan for storming the enemy's works as soon as the heavy guns should be in readiness to open fire. Fort No. 1 was finished this evening. The details from First and Third Brigades continued work on the other forts during the night under a heavy artillery fire from the enemy. Several casualties occurred, among them Major Wright, a most valuable officer, commanding the Twenty-ninth Ohio Volunteers, who was severely wounded by a shell. Sloan's battery of 3-inch rifled guns had already taken position in a work thrown up to the right of Fort No. 3 and in the open field.

December 20, the usual artillery firing and sharpshooting to-day. By this evening we had constructed and in readiness for use in the contemplated assault 200 large straw fascines to fill up ditches in front of the enemy's works, also a large number of fascines made of bamboo cane. The latter were to be used for bridging the canal by laying them across balks, which were furnished from the pontoon train for that purpose. The work on Forts 2 and 3 was well advanced to-day, and would probably be completed to-night. Three siege guns (30-pounder Parrotts) were brought down this evening and mounted in Fort No. 1. I ascertained this morning that the enemy had completed a pontoon bridge from Savannah across to the South Carolina shore, and notified the general commanding corps of the discovery. This bridge was about two miles and a half from my left. The usual artillery firing was kept up by the enemy during the day and night. During the night I heard the movement of troops and wagons across the pontoon bridge before mentioned, and sent a report of the fact to the general commanding corps. Leaving one of my staff to watch the sounds in that direction, I notified my officer of the day and brigade commanders to keep a vigilant watch upon the enemy, as they were probably evacuating. The details on Forts 2 and 3 continued working through the night, the enemy shelling them heavily.

December 21, after 3 o'clock this morning the firing ceased, and my pickets advancing to the enemy's line found them hastily retreating. Having possession of their line of works, with all their cannon in front of my own and the other divisions of the corps, I immediately sent a staff officer to notify the general commanding, and at the same time pushed forward rapidly in the direction of Savannah, hoping to overtake and capture a part of the enemy's forces. My skirmishers deployed, and swept over all the ground between the evacuated works and the Ogeechee Canal from the river to the Augusta road, while my main body of troops marched rapidly by the flank through McAlpin's plantation to the Augusta road and on into the city. Just outside of the city limits, near the junction of the Louisville and Augusta roads, I met the mayor of Savannah and a delegation from the board of aldermen, bearing a flag of truce. From them I received, in the name of my commanding general, the surrender of the city. This was at 4.30 a. m., and I sent immediately another staff officer to announce the surrender to the general commanding the corps. He had considerable difficulty in passing the line of another division of this corps on the Augusta road, but finally convinced them that he belonged to the Twentieth Corps and not to the enemy. In the meantime my entire division entered the city of Savannah at early dawn, and before the sun first gilded the morning clouds our National colors, side by side with those of my own division, were unfurled from the dome of the Exchange and over the U. S. custom-house. Barnum's brigade, which led in entering the city, was at once ordered to patrol it, reduce it to order and quiet, and prevent any pillaging or lawlessness on the part either of soldiers or citizens. My orders on the subject were very strict, and within a few hours this city, in which I had found a lawless mob of low whites and negroes pillaging and setting fire to property, was reduced to order; many millions of dollars' worth of cotton, ordnance, and commissary stores, &c., which would otherwise have been destroyed, were saved to the United States Government, and the citizens once more enjoyed security under the protection of that flag which again waved over them, exactly four years since the passage by the State of South Carolina of the secession act. Two regiments from Pardee's brigade, the Twenty-eighth Pennsylvania and Twenty-ninth Ohio Veteran Volunteers, were sent down to Fort Jackson, and early in the morning had possession of it and all the intermediate and surrounding works. The iron-plated ram Savannah, which lay in the river below the city, threw a few shells at these two regiments as they flung the Stars and Stripes to the breeze from the walls of Fort Jackson. All the other gun-boats of the enemy had been fired by them and burned to the water's edge. On the arrival of the major-general commanding the Left Wing, I was by his order placed in command of the city. Until nearly 10 a. m. continued firing was heard in the direction of Beaulieu, and supposing that a portion of the enemy might still be south of us I kept one brigade under arms during the forenoon. Three rebel flags were captured by my command, which will be duly forwarded.

The following table will exhibit as near as possible the amount of public property taken possession of by my command on the morning of the 21st of December:

	In enemy's front line.	In city of Savannah.	In forts below the city, including Fort Jackson.	Total.
Steam-boats		3		3
Schooner, unfinished		1		1
Locomotives		13		13
Cars		230		230
Cotton ... bales		25,000		25,000
Rice ... tierces		4,000		4,000
Corn ... bushels		2,000		2,000
Lumber ... feet		55,000		55,000
Heavy artillery ... pieces	6	1	88	95
Light artillery ... do	5	1	3	9
Muskets		479		479

	In enemy's front line.	In city of Savannah.	In forts below the city, including Fort Jackson.	Total.
Fixed ammunition—				
Artillery ... rounds		2,524	402	2,926
Infantry ... do		44,000		44,000
Shot and shell		7,600	4,483	11,543
Powder ... pounds		1,600	50	1,650
Other ordnance and ordnance stores—				
Artillery harness ... boxes		31		31
Gun slings		781		781
Copper ... boxes		6		6
Plate tin ... do		10		10
Fuse plugs		14,456		14,456
Sabots		5,619		5,619
Chocks		44		44
Saber knots		360		360
Vent covers		126		126
Tampions (artillery)		100		100
Saddle-bags		257		257
Cartridge-boxes—				
Infantry		440		440
Artillery		200		200
Bayonet scabbards		2,000		2,000
Waist belts		940		940
Saber belts		600		600
Leg guards		125		125
Rifle boots		168		168
Shoulder belts		447		447
Port fires		1,350		1,350
Glass ... boxes		3½		3½
Machine oil ... kegs		1		1
Lamp oil ... cans		1		1
Parrot oil ... barrels		1		1
Tar ... cans		1		1
Rope ... coils		2		2
Soft solder ... pounds		100		100
Cotton twine ... do		35		35
Lanterns		110		110
Equipments (artillery) *a*				
Matting *b*				
White twilled flannel ... bales		1		1
Zinc ... cases		1		1
Gun stocks in rough *c*				
Nails ... kegs		38		38
Flints ... boxes		½		½
Sabers (artillery)		500		500
Roller buckles ... gross		4		4
White cartridge-paper ... quires		50		50
Brown cartridge-paper ... reams		7		7
Horse brushes		1,400		1,400
Curry combs		850		850
Rolls		100		100
Friction tubes		7,500		7,500
Priming tubes		1,010		1,010
Appendages, small-arms *b*				
Powder flasks		100		100
Slow match ... feet		5,400		5,400
Slow match ... coils		123		123
Sensitive tubes		1,000		1,000
Horseshoe nails ... pounds		16		16
Friction primers		342		342
Bullet molds		500		500
Appendages, artillery *a*				
Tarred links		1,500		1,500
Oil ... bottles		1,200		1,200
Fuse, artillery ammunition		2,060		2,060
Wrapping paper ... bales		1		1
Ax helves		50		50
Spades		15		15
Picks		10		10
Buckles, rings, &c. *b*				
Hemp twine ... bags		1		1
Bayonets		140		140
Signal rockets		580		580
Hand spikes, artillery		700		700

a Number and names unknown.
b Large quantities.
c Several hundred.

I submit the following estimate of property and supplies appropriated or destroyed by my command during the march from Atlanta to Savannah:

Taken for use:		Taken for use:	
Horses	84	Potatoes ... bushels..	2,000
Mules	267	Meal ... sacks..	250
Corn ... pounds..	299,421	Salt ... barrels..	10
Corn fodder ... do....	262,000	Destroyed:	
Rice fodder ... do....	88,000	Cotton bales	2,700
Beef-cattle ... head..	700	Cotton gins and mills	50
Bacon ... pounds..	3,700	Flour mills	11
Sugar ... do....	1,000	Saw-mills	14
Molasses ... gallons..	1,000	Factories	3

The amounts of articles of forage and subsistence given above are those given in the returns of my quartermaster and commissary. In addition to these amounts, there was doubtless as much more of all such articles taken by the division for use of the men and animals, who subsisted bounteously on the country passed through.

Railroad destroyed.

	Miles.
On East Point Railroad	7
Between Atlanta and Chattahoochee	2½
Between Social Circle and Madison	1
Between Madison and Oconee	5
Between Milledgeville and Gordon	2
Between Tennille and Davisborough	9
Total	26½

Railroad bridges across the Oconee and Ocmulgee, besides a large number of small bridges, trestle, water-tanks, &c.; also large quantities of new ties, railroad timbers, cord wood, &c.

The following table will show the casualties and losses in my command during the entire campaign:

	During the march.		During siege of Savannah.	
	Officers.	Men.	Officers.	Men.
Killed	....	....	1	8
Wounded	....	1	5	53
Missing	....	37	....	9
Total	....	38	6	70

In concluding this report, I must express my high appreciation of the officers and men whom I have so long commanded, and whose conduct and general discipline on this campaign were worthy of their past well-earned reputation.

I desire to return my thanks to the gentlemen composing my staff, departmental and personal. Some deserve special mention for their efficiency and uniform attention to duty. To Capt. W. T. Forbes, assistant adjutant-general, I am especially indebted for the faithful performance of every duty devolving upon him. I must also commend Capt. Eugene Schilling, my topographical engineer, for his general industry and ability, and especially for his energy and faithfulness while laying out and superintending the erection of forts under the enemy's guns during the siege of Savannah.

I am, colonel, very respectfully, your obedient servant,

JNO. W. GEARY,
Brigadier-General, Commanding.

Lieut. Col. H. W. PERKINS,
Assistant Adjutant-General, Twentieth Army Corps.

No. 99.

Report of Col. Ario Pardee, jr., One hundred and forty-seventh Pennsylvania Infantry, commanding First Brigade.

HDQRS. FIRST BRIG., SECOND DIV., TWENTIETH CORPS,
Savannah, Ga., December 25, 1864.

CAPTAIN:*

Tuesday, November 15, at 7 a. m. the camp of the brigade was vacated and the command marched to near Stone Mountain, Ga., and bivouacked for the night. The road taken was that leading through Decatur; distance marched, thirteen miles. Early on the morning of November 16 the march was resumed. The position of the brigade was the third in line, the division being in the advance, and having the trains of the division and the supply and headquarters teams of the corps and wing in charge, was distributed among the wagons, each regiment having a certain number to guard and assist in the passage of obstacles. Yellow River was crossed at Rock Bridge. From this place the road leading through Sheffield was taken, near which place we encamped for the night; distance marched, twelve miles. November 17, this day we marched through Sheffield and camped near Social Circle, a distance of about eighteen miles. November 18, marched at 5 a. m., the brigade being in advance, and passed through Social Circle and Rutledge. At the last-named place the Twenty-eighth Pennsylvania Volunteers, Col. John Flynn, was temporarily detached from the column to destroy the depot and warehouses belonging to the railroad company, as well as to tear up the track and bend the rails near these buildings, all of which was effectually accomplished. This night we camped near Madison, having marched about eighteen miles.

November 19, the command moved at 5 a. m. All the trains were left behind, with a sufficient guard of men unable to make a rapid march, to proceed with the remainder of the corps. We marched to Blue Spring, near the railroad bridge over the Oconee River, at which point a considerable distance of the railroad was destroyed by burning the ties and bending and twisting the rails; distance marched, fifteen miles. November 20, from Blue Spring we moved in a direction parallel to the Oconee River to Parks' Ferry, and from thence to Philadelphia Church. November 20 and 21, to near Dennis Station, at which point we struck the railroad leading from Milledgeville to Eatonton. From this point we marched (November 22) along the railroad to Little River, and from there to Milledgeville, through which we passed and went into camp on the east side of the Oconee River. November 23, the brigade remained in camp this day. November 24, the command moved at 7 a. m.

---

*For portion of report (here omitted) relating to operations about Atlanta, see Vol. XXXIX, Part I, p. 670.

in a southeasterly direction, on the road leading to Hebron, and went into camp near Gum Creek for the night; distance marched, fourteen miles. November 25, we crossed Gum Creek at 7 a. m., and passed through Hebron, taking the road to Sandersville. On reaching Buffalo Creek Swamp the bridges were found to be destroyed. The construction of these detained the column until 5 p. m., when it went into camp on the east side of the creek. November 26, the brigade moved at daylight and marched to Sandersville, and from there to Tennille, a station on the Central railroad. Near this place we commenced tearing up the track and destroying it by burning the ties and bending, breaking, and twisting the rails; distance marched, fifteen miles. November 27, this day the brigade, in company with the balance of the division, were engaged in destroying the railroad. Two trestle bridges, each about seventy-five feet long, were burned, and the ties and rails for a mile and a half effectually destroyed. The camp for the night was at Davisborough. November 28, this day was spent in destroying the railroad between Davisborough and Tennille; two miles and a half of track and 500 feet of trestle-work were burned. November 29, marched from Davisborough to Spiers Station, and from thence parallel with the railroad to near New Bethel, making in all a distance of twenty-one miles. November 30, marched to near Louisville, ten miles.

December 1, marched at 7 a. m., taking the direct road to Millen, and camped for the night at Bark Camp Creek; distance marched, fourteen miles. December 2, the march was resumed at daylight, and was uninterrupted until Buck Head Creek was reached. The bridge over this place was partially destroyed, and a few of the enemy's cavalry were on the opposite side of the swamp. Major Wright, commanding Twenty-ninth Ohio Volunteers, was ordered to cross the creek with his regiment and drive and keep away this force, which was accomplished without loss. The command encamped for the night near Buck Head Church; distance marched, eight miles. December 3, the troops of the brigade were to-day in rear of the wagon trains of the division, in which were included the trains of General Kilpatrick's cavalry command, and did not march from the camp of the preceding night until 1 p. m. The roads were in a horrible condition, passing as they did through numerous swamps and across many unbridged streams. The progress of the trains was exceedingly slow in consequence. The brigade reached the camp of the division, three miles and a half from Horse Creek, at 6.30 a. m. December 4; distance marched, fourteen miles. December 4, marched at 9 a. m.; during the day Horse Creek and Crooked Creek were crossed; distance marched, ten miles. December 5, the distance marched this day was fifteen miles. The roads, as had been the case for several days past, were over plains of a sandy soil, well timbered (pine), and crossed numerous small streams and marshes. The Little Ogeechee River was crossed this day. December 6, nothing of any special importance transpired to-day. December 7, owing to the exceedingly bad condition of the roads, the troops of the brigade were distributed along the train, and rendered material assistance in pushing them along. The camp for the night was near Springfield, and the distance marched about twelve miles. December 8, the command moved at daylight, crossing Jack's Creek, and passing through Springfield, in the direction of Monteith. December 9 and 10, these two days were occupied in marching to a point on the Augusta road, five miles from Savannah, Ga. December 11, at 9 a. m. the brigade marched to the bank of Savannah River, opposite

Hutchinson's Island, and went into position in rear of the Third Brigade, Second Division, there skirmishing slightly with the enemy. In this position it remained until 3 p. m., when, in compliance with orders from the general commanding division, it was placed in position on the right of the Third Brigade, and relieved the troops of the Second Brigade, Second Division, Twentieth Corps. At 1 a. m. December 12, in obedience to orders, the brigade was placed under arms, and afterward formed in line in rear of the Third Brigade, to await the movement. The orders from the general commanding division were for me to occupy the position of the Third Brigade when it moved out, it being understood that these troops were to assault the works of the enemy at 2.30 a.m., and then report to him for further instructions. At 4.30 a. m. I received, through Captain Lambert, orders from the general commanding division to withdraw my command and march it to its original position, the assault having been postponed. December 12 to December 20, inclusive, the command remained in the position previously mentioned. A substantial line of works was thrown up for the protection of the command from the artillery of the enemy, and, in addition to this, two forts, with thirteen embrasures in the aggregate, were constructed by the command. The working parties on Fort No. 2 were under the command of Captain Kreider, One hundred and forty-seventh Pennsylvania Volunteers, and those on Fort No. 3 under command of Capt. E. B. Woodbury, Twenty-ninth Ohio Volunteers. Both these officers and the men under their command are deserving of praise for the energy and perseverance manifested in the prosecution of the duty assigned them. December 21, the enemy having evacuated their position the night previous, their works were occupied at an early hour by the skirmishers of the division, and by sunrise the city of Savannah was entered and occupied, this brigade being the second in line in the advance into the city. Soon after reaching the city the Twenty-eighth Pennsylvania and Twenty-ninth Ohio Volunteers, under the command of Col. John Flynn, Twenty-eighth Pennsylvania Volunteers, were, by order of the general commanding division, through Captain Veale, aide-de-camp, dispatched to occupy Fort Jackson and the smaller forts and batteries near it. The possession of the fort and other works was gained without resistance. The Fifth Ohio Volunteers, Lieutenant-Colonel Kirkup commanding, was placed in charge of the arsenal on President street. With the remainder of the command I took possession of the U. S. barracks. Attached to this report please find inventories of ordnance, and ordnance stores found at each of those places.*

I have the honor to call your attention also to the statements of the brigade quartermaster and brigade commissary, and would respectfully state that the forage and subsistence taken by the troops at halts and camps do not enter into these estimates.† The supply trains are in much better condition than they were on leaving Atlanta, notwithstanding the long and tedious march over roads which at times seemed almost impassable. The rations, owing to judgment exercised by Lieut. Samuel D. Conner in their issue, lasted until the night of the 15th instant. He is deserving of especial credit for the systematic manner in which he secured supplies, and for their equitable distribution to the troops of the command.

---

* Embodied in Geary's report, p. 280.

† These statements show 250 head beef cattle, 65 head sheep, 2,000 pounds bacon, 600 bushels sweet potatoes, 3 barrels salt, 2 barrels molasses, 250 sacks corn meal, 4 horses, 30 mules, 58,425 pounds corn, and 84,000 pounds fodder.

The pioneer corps, under command of Captain Hedges, rendered valuable service in the construction of bridges and the repair of roads, and especial thanks are due them for the part taken in the construction of the forts to which allusion has been made.

To the regimental commanders I tender my thanks for the strict obedience to orders, and the enforcement of the regulations prescribed in regard to the conduct of the march, and especially are they due to Maj. M. T. Wright, Twenty-ninth Ohio Volunteers, who was seriously wounded while supervising the working parties on the forts, for the promptitude exhibited by him in the execution of all orders, and his strict attention to the duties incumbent on him throughout the entire campaign.

To Lieut. A. H. W. Creigh, acting assistant adjutant-general; to Capt. J. W. Watkins, acting assistant inspector-general; to Surg. William R. Longshore, chief surgeon of brigade; and to Lieut. C. W. Kellogg, acting aide-de-camp, my especial thanks are due for their devotion to their duty, and for the creditable manner in which their several departments were conducted.

Accompanying this please find the reports of the regimental commanders, to which your attention is respectfully called, as well as to the list of casualties, which is hereunto annexed.*

Respectfully submitted.

ARIO PARDEE, JR.,
Colonel 147th Pennsylvania Vols., Commanding Brigade.

Capt. W. T. FORBES,
Assistant Adjutant-General.

No. 100.

Report of Lieut. Col. Robert Kirkup, Fifth Ohio Infantry.

HEADQUARTERS FIFTH OHIO VOLUNTEER INFANTRY,
Savannah, Ga., December 26, 1864.

SIR: I have the honor to forward the official report of operations of the Fifth Ohio Volunteer Infantry from September 2, 1864, to December 21, 1864:

The regiment entered the city of Atlanta, Ga., on the 4th day of September, 1864, and went into camp. The months of September and October were occupied in building defenses around the city and doing garrison duty.

On the 9th day of November the regiment was ordered into the works to assist in repulsing an attack made by the enemy's cavalry. On the 13th day of November the regiment was ordered to report at brigade headquarters, and then marched out to assist in destroying the Atlanta and Chattanooga Railroad. On the 15th day of November the regiment broke camp and marched out on the road leading to Decatur, Ga. Nothing of importance took place until the 18th instant, when the regiment halted and stacked arms and assisted in destroying the railroad near Rutledge, Ga., and on the 19th, when near Parks' Ferry, went into camp and destroyed the railroad. On the 22d we crossed the Oconee River and passed through Milledgeville, Ga., the capital of the State of Georgia, and camped outside the city, where we remained

---

* Nominal list (here omitted) shows 3 enlisted men killed; 1 commissioned officer and 8 enlisted men wounded.

until the 24th, when we again resumed the march, and entered Sandersville, Ga., on the 26th instant, and marched to Tennille Station, on Central railroad; there we assisted in destroying the railroad and camped for the night. On the 27th instant we continued the destruction of the road until 3 p. m., when we marched to Waynesborough and camped for the night. On the 28th instant we marched back toward Tennille and destroyed the railroad as we went, and then marched back to Waynesborough and camped for the night.

On the 1st of December we crossed the Ogeechee River, and continued our march without interruption until the 10th, when we arrived in camp near Savannah, Ga. On the 11th we moved into line, left in front, and near the Savannah River. At 3 p. m. we moved out and took position on a road leading to the Savannah River, where we remained, doing skirmish duty and erecting field-works, until the morning of the 21st, when we were ordered to fall in and moved into the city of Savannah, Ga., the enemy having evacuated. We were then put on guard over the ordnance and ordnance stores in park and arsenal which were left by the enemy, and an inventory taken.

Sir, respectfully submitted.

ROBERT KIRKUP,
Lieutenant-Colonel, Comdg. Fifth Ohio Volunteer Infantry.

Lieut. A. H. W. CREIGH,
Actg. Asst. Adjt. Gen., 1st Brig., 2d Div., 20th Army Corps.

No. 101.

Report of Maj. Myron T. Wright, Twenty-ninth Ohio Infantry, of operations November 15–December 19.

HDQRS. TWENTY-NINTH REGT. OHIO VET. VOL. INFTY.,
Savannah, Ga., December 28, 1864.

LIEUTENANT:*

15th [November], broke up camp at 6.30; marched slowly; stopped at Decatur for dinner, then marched in the direction of Stone Mountain; reached the base of Stone Mountain at 11 p. m. and encamped for the night; Twenty-ninth in the rear of the First Brigade. 16th, marched at 9 a. m. in between portions of the train; crossed Yellow River, and encamped for the night at 8 p. m. 17th, marched at 5 a. m.; camped near Social Circle at 5 p. m. for the night. 18th, marched about nine miles in forenoon, stopping often to tear up the railroad track; went into camp near Madison at 5 p. m. 19th, broke camp at 5 a. m; Twenty-ninth, rear guard of division; marched until 4 p. m. and camped for the night near Parks' Mill. 20th, marched about seven miles; camped near Dunham's. 21st, marched at 6.30 a. m.; halted at 4.30 p. m. for the night. 22d, moved at 7.30 a. m. and arrived at Milledgeville, Ga., at 9 p. m., and camped about three miles south of town. 23d, remained in camp; Twenty-ninth went on picket at 4 p. m. 24th, moved at 7 a. m.; Twenty-ninth (first battalion of First Brigade) marched fifteen miles and camped for the night. 25th, marched at 8 a. m.; Twenty-ninth train guard; arrived at Buffalo Creek; found the bridge destroyed; parked

---

*For portion of report (here omitted) relating to operations about Atlanta, see Vol. XXXIX, Part I, p. 671.

the train and stacked arms for dinner; remained here until the bridge was repaired, then crossed and went into camp for the night. 26th, moved at 8 a. m. in rear of the train; marched slowly until 1 p. m.; arrived in Sandersville; halted for dinner, then moved to Station 13; took the railroad to the east, tore up about one mile and a half of track, then went into camp for the night at 6 p. m.; marched thirteen miles. 27th, was called up at 1.30 a. m. by alarm; remained in line two hours, then lay down again; marched at 8 a. m.; commenced tearing up track; worked until noon; took dinner and lay quiet until 3 p. m., then marched rapidly; arrived in Davisborough at 9.30 p. m.; marched about thirteen miles. 28th, moved out on the railroad and tore up track until 5 p. m.; marched back to Davisborough and camped near our old camp. 29th, moved at 7.30; moved in a southeasterly direction until 7 p. m., and encamped for the night near Bostwick. 30th, marched at 7; crossed the Ogeechee River; marched about six miles and camped for the night.

December 1, moved at 8 a. m.; marched until dark and camped; marched about nineteen miles. 2d, marched at 6 a. m.; moved briskly until 12 m.; halted at ——— Creek for dinner; found the bridge destroyed and enemy on the other side. Twenty-ninth received orders to drive the enemy out of reach of the bridge and hold the ground; fell in, loaded, and moved across; moved about half a mile; came in contact with the enemy in small force; deployed three companies to the left of the road; deployed a line of skirmishers 500 yards to left of woods, the right resting in woods on right of road; also sent four companies, under command of Capt. Jonas Schoonover, to cover two roads leading from main road; commenced firing and drove the enemy from their position; advanced steadily to a ridge in open field about one mile from the bridge; threw up some works and extended the line to connect with Captain Schoonover; here waited until the bridge was finished, then joined the brigade in the field and camped for the night. 3d, moved at 10 a. m. and marched all day and night; made a distance of ten miles; camped near Millen, Ga. 4th, moved at 9 a. m.; marched about three miles; halted for repairing of a bridge; moved again at 2.30 p. m.; arrived at Big Horse Creek, and halted for trains to pass; crossed at 8 and camped for the night. 5th, moved at 7 a. m.; Twenty-ninth in charge of First and Third Brigade trains; moved fifteen miles and went into camp at 5 p. m. 6th, moved at 9; halted for supper at 6 p. m.; then crossed a big swamp and camped for the night. 7th, marched at 7 a. m.; Twenty-ninth assisted the trains; crossed Turkey Creek at dark; camped near Springfield. 8th, moved at 7 a. m.; marched twelve miles and camped for the night. 9th, marched at 9 a. m; took dinner near Eden; went into camp for the night at Walthour [Monteith] Swamp. 10th, received orders to report to Colonel Jones, Second Brigade; joined Second Brigade and marched back to the train; Twenty-ninth took position on the same grounds where we got dinner on the 9th; sent a company forward about 600 yards for picket; moved at 12 m.; Twenty-ninth took position in front of last 100 wagons; marched very briskly until 6 p. m.; joined First Brigade and went into camp for the night. 11th, moved at 10 a. m.; Twenty-ninth on right of First Brigade; moved to the Savannah River, with instructions to deploy a line connecting with Third Brigade on the right and extending to the river, with a heavy reserve at the river; found Colonel Barnum's line rested on it, and took position in supporting distance of his left; followed his skirmishers in line of battle to a fence about 700 yards from the enemy's works; remained here until 4 p. m.; joined the brigade, and moved to the right about half a mile; went into position on a road perpendicular to the river, about four miles and a half from the city of Savannah, Ga. 12th, in line of battle before Savannah; Twenty-ninth moved to the left in support of Third Brigade, which was to charge a fort in their front, but found a canal that they could not cross; they came back to their works; Twenty-ninth returned to our old position; nothing of interest occurred during the day. 13th, in line before Savannah; at 10 a. m. moved the Twenty-ninth to the rear about 300 yards; prepared timber for rifle-pits; at 4 p. m. took the four right companies on to the picket-line and placed them on duty; at 9 advanced the line 150 yards into an open field and put up pits. 14th, on skirmish line; considerable firing on both sides; Twenty-ninth pickets relieved by Fifth Ohio. 15th to 18th, nothing worthy of note transpired. 19th, received instructions to take charge of the fortifications in front of the First Brigade; commenced work at dark. While laying out a connection between Forts 2 and 3 I received a severe wound in my left foot. I then turned the command of the Twenty-ninth Ohio Veteran Volunteer Infantry over to Capt. Jonas Schoonover.

I am, with much respect, your obedient servant,

MYRON T. WRIGHT,
Major Twenty-ninth Ohio Veteran Volunteer Infantry.

Lieut. A. H. W. CREIGH,
Actg. Asst. Adjt. Gen., First Brig., Second Div., Twentieth Corps.

No. 102.

Report of Capt. Jonas Schoonover, Twenty-ninth Ohio Infantry, of operations December 20–24.

HDQRS. TWENTY-NINTH REGT. OHIO VET. VOL. INFTY.,
Savannah, Ga., December 28, 1864.

LIEUTENANT: In compliance with circular from headquarters First Brigade, Second Division, Twentieth Corps, dated Savannah, Ga., December 23, 1864, I have the honor most respectfully to make the following report:

I took command of the Twenty-ninth Ohio in front of Savannah, Ga., December 20, 1864. Nothing worthy of note occurred during this day. At 4 a. m. of the 21st the Twenty-ninth, in advance of First Brigade, took up a line of march to the city of Savannah, and from there to Fort Jackson, Ga., where I reported to Colonel Flynn, of the Twenty-eighth Pennsylvania Volunteers, for duty, and performed garrison duty until December 24, when the Twenty-ninth was ordered to march at 9.30 a. m., Twenty-ninth in rear of Twenty-eighth Pennsylvania Volunteers, and marched to and through the city where we are now encamped.

I am, very respectfully, your obedient servant,

JONAS SCHOONOVER,
Captain, Comdg. Twenty-ninth Ohio Veteran Vol. Infantry.

First Lieut. A. H. W. CREIGH,
Actg. Asst. Adjt. Gen., First Brig., Second Div., Twentieth Corps.

No. 103.

Report of Lieut. Col. Eugene Powell, Sixty-sixth Ohio Infantry, of operations September 4–December 21.

HDQRS. SIXTY-SIXTH REGT. OHIO VET. VOL. INFANTRY,
Savannah, Ga., December 26, 1864.

LIEUTENANT: In compliance with circular from headquarters First Brigade, Second Division, Twentieth Army Corps, I have the honor to make the following report of the part taken by this regiment in the campaign ending on the 21st instant:

This regiment broke camp on the 4th of September, 1864, on the Chattahoochee River, and moved to the city of Atlanta same day and went into camp in the enemy's outer line of works, with right resting near Marietta railroad. The 5th of September received orders to report to Colonel Beckwith, commissary of subsistence, Military Division of the Mississippi, for duty as supply guard, where we remained until the morning of the 15th of November, 1864, when, with the First Brigade, Second Division, Twentieth Army Corps, we started on the campaign just ended. Nothing transpired of note during the campaign until the 11th of December, 1864, when we reached the enemy's line of works, three miles and a half northeast of the city. Here we went into line, this regiment on the right of brigade. Have no casualties to report until the night of 19th, when I had 3 men killed and 3 wounded. We remained in line until the 21st, when we entered the city and are now encamped in Chippewa Square.

Casualties: Killed—Privates S. G. Johnson, Company A; Joseph Powell, Company B; John H. Atkinson, Company D. Wounded—Corpl. E. Kyle and Private I. Wood, Company E, and Private S. Keltner, Company I.

I have the honor to be, lieutenant, very respectfully, your obedient servant,

EUGENE POWELL,
Lieut. Col. Sixty-sixth Ohio Vet. Vol. Infty., Comdg. Regiment.

Lieut. A. H. W. CREIGH,
Actg. Asst. Adjt. Gen., 1st Brig., 2d Div., 20th Army Corps.

No. 104.

Report of Col. John Flynn, Twenty-eighth Pennsylvania Infantry, of operations September 2–December 21.

HDQRS. TWENTY-EIGHTH PENNSYLVANIA VET. VOL. INFTY.,
Savannah, Ga., December 28, 1864.

LIEUTENANT: In compliance with circular dated headquarters First Brigade, Second Division, Twentieth Army Corps, December 23, 1864, I have the honor to report the following as the part taken by the Twenty-eighth Regiment Pennsylvania Veteran Volunteer Infantry in the campaign which closed on the 21st instant by the occupation of the city of Savannah, Ga.:

This campaign is, throughout its entire extent, void of interest to the soldier, as we had such unparalleled success that a great part of the army has not had occasion to form for battle; few bloody fields have been lost or won; no sieges have been commenced and ended, as the enemy has not in one instance made a stand of sufficient length to require the necessity of such measures.

From the 2d of September to the 9th of November, 1864, nothing more than the regular routine of camp duties occurred. On the morning of November 9 we were unceremoniously awakened by the rattling of artillery and musketry by a small force of the enemy attempting to enter our lines, but in this they were defeated and repulsed, leaving two killed and taking several wounded with them; the Twenty-eighth Pennsylvania Volunteer Infantry sustained no loss. On the next morning we were prepared to leave Atlanta, which move commenced on the morning of November 15. We started from camp at 6.30 a. m. and marched seven miles in the direction of Decatur, Ga.; halted for dinner at 1 p. m.; started again at 3 p. m., and, after marching slowly, we halted at 12 p. m. for the night; distance marched, fifteen miles. November 16, started at 9 a. m. and marched fast for a distance of twelve miles; halted for dinner at 2 p. m. one mile from Rock Bridge. We crossed Yellow River and encamped for the night, after marching twelve miles without interest. November 17, started at 6 a. m.; marched until 12.15 p. m.; halted for dinner; started at 2 p. m. and marched to within six miles of Social Circle, on the Georgia Central Railroad; we halted and encamped here for the night, after a tedious march of fourteen miles. November 18, started at 5 a. m.; passed through Social Circle, where we found the railroad depot destroyed; moved on and halted at Rutledge for dinner at 11.30 a. m. We here burned the depot and store-house containing some rebel stores and started again at 2 p. m. and marched to within a distance of two miles of Madison, where we encamped for the night; distance marched, nineteen miles. November 19, started at 5 a. m.; passed through Madison at daylight; halted at 12 m. at Buck Head for dinner; started again at 1 p. m. and at 5 p. m. we halted at Jordan's plantation. The Twenty-eighth Pennsylvania Veteran Volunteer Infantry here assisted to tear up the railroad and destroyed 3,000 bushels of corn and 600 bales of cotton. We marched this day sixteen miles. November 20, started at 7 a. m. and marched eight miles without incident; halted for dinner at 12 m.; at 2 p. m. we started, and, after marching seven miles, encamped for the night at 6 p. m.; distance marched, fifteen miles. November 21, started at 7 a. m., the Twenty-eighth Pennsylvania Veteran Volunteer Infantry in advance of the division; halted for dinner at 1.30 p. m., and moved out again without incident at 2.30 p. m. and marched to Doctor Nesbit's plantation, where we were posted as picket guard for the division; this was a very cold day and night; distance marched nine miles. November 22, started at 7 a. m. as rear guard for the division; after marching for four miles we crossed the Central railroad at Dennis Station. Here we rejoined the corps, which had been separated since we came from Madison on the 18th. We traveled slow in the direction of Milledgeville and halted for dinner at 1 p. m. We passed through Milledgeville after a very tedious march and encamped at 11 p. m., having marched twenty miles. November 23, we remained in camp until 12 m., when we moved half a mile into the woods, where we remained all day. November 24, we got under way at 9 a. m., marching through swamps and mud to within five miles of Hebron, where we encamped for the night; marched this day a distance of twelve miles. November 25, started at 7.30 a. m., march slow and tedious; passed through

Hebron and came to Buffalo Creek. Here we found eight bridges burnt, which took considerable time to rebuild, but at 6 p. m. we moved across the creek and encamped half a mile from it for the night, after marching only six miles. November 26, started at 8 a. m. as guard for the division quartermaster's train; halted at 9.15 a. m. to reorganize the train; started again at 11 a. m; marched to within half a mile of Sandersville; we here halted for dinner, and at 2 p. m. we marched through the town of Sandersville and down to the Central railroad, which we struck at Tennille Station. We here commenced tearing up the track, burning the cross-ties, and totally destroying the railroad for a distance of two miles, when we encamped for the night. At about 1 p. m. we were aroused and the command put under arms, but nothing occurred; distance marched, sixteen miles. November 27, commenced tearing up the track at 8 a. m. and worked until 1 p. m., when we rested for dinner, and at 4 p. m. we started for Davisborough, and after a tedious march we arrived there at 9 p. m., marching to-day a distance of ten miles. November 28, went to work again on the railroad, about five miles west of Davisborough, at 7.30 a. m., and halted at 1 p. m. for dinner; at 3 p. m. commenced again and worked until 5 p. m.; the rebels made a dash upon the Third Brigade, and the Twenty-eighth Pennsylvania Veteran Volunteer Infantry, in company with the First Brigade, started to re-enforce them, but they had already been dispersed. We started at 6 p. m. on our return to Davisborough, which place we reached at 7.30 p. m., after working all day and marching a distance of nine miles. November 29, started at 7.20 a. m., and marched to Spiers Station, when we halted for dinner at 1 p. m.; left Spiers Station at 4 p. m. and marched fast and without incident to within two miles of Bostwick Station, where we halted at 7 p. m. for the night; distance marched, eighteen miles. November 30, started on the march again at 6.45 a. m.; marched quick and through swampy ground until 2 p. m., when we halted for dinner at the plantation of Doctor Blake, a great slaveholder, having at this time some 300 slaves on his plantation, mostly women. We left here at 4 p. m. and marched to join the corps at Miller's plantation, where we arrived at 6.30 p. m.; distance marched, ten miles.

December 1, this day's march was without incident. We left Miller's plantation at 7.25 a. m. and marched until 2 p. m., when we halted for dinner; started again at 4 p. m. and marched until 7 p. m., when we halted for the night, after marching twelve miles. December 2, left camp at 6.45 a. m. and marched until 12 m., when we halted for dinner; started at 1 p. m. and marched past Jones' plantation; we crossed Buck Head Creek and camped at 3.30 p. m.; the Twenty-eighth Pennsylvania, with 200 of the Fifth Ohio Volunteer Infantry, picketed for the division; posted pickets and passed the night without incident; distance marched, ten miles. December 3, started again at 2 p. m., and after tedious marching through swamps and in the rain, halting about every 100 steps, we stopped at 6.30 a. m. of the 4th; distance marched, twelve miles in direction east-southeast and northeast of Millen, crossing Little Buck Head Creek, having marched all night; a distance of twelve miles. December 4, started at 9.30 a. m. and marched until 11 a. m.; halted for dinner and were off again at 3 p. m., marching across a large swamp, and halted one mile from Horse Creek at 8 p. m., after marching eight miles without incident. December 5, this day we marched with the wagons, assisting them over the many muddy places in the road, and halting for the night at 6 p. m.; distance marched, fifteen miles. December 6, like yesterday, we spent this one with the teams and without halting for any length of time; we encamped at 6.30 p. m.; marched ten miles. December 7, again with the wagons, raining nearly all day and very bad roads; we marched ten miles in the direction of Springfield and encamped at 8 p. m. December 8, started at 8 a. m.; passed through Springfield, a small village; marching rather fast; halted for the night at 4 p. m., having marched thirteen miles. December 9, this was the first day that we heard artillery firing in our front. We started at 7 a. m., and having marched two miles halted to issue rations; started again at 1 p. m. and halted at 8 p. m.; distance marched, eight miles. December 10, we moved off this day at 12.30 p. m.; marched steady on a splendid road with the wagons until we came to about five miles of Savannah, where we halted at 5 p. m. and encamped for the night, after marching eleven miles. This day we came up to the rebel intrenchments.

December 11, at 10 a. m. we left camp and moved off in the direction of the Savannah River, which we struck at 2 p. m. From this point we had a fine view of the rebel fortifications about one mile off. Left here at 4.30 p. m. and moved on a road running at right angles about half a mile. We here relieved the Second Brigade and were posted in line, the Sixty-sixth Ohio Volunteer Infantry on our right, and the Twenty-ninth Ohio Volunteer Infantry on our left. Here we found a dike or drain for a rice plantation, which formed a very good rifle-work. December 12, at 1 a. m. we moved about half a mile to the left, without knapsacks, and lay here until 4 a. m. in support of the Third Brigade, which were to charge the enemy's works. The order being countermanded we returned to our original position at 4.15 a. m. Remained here all day without incident. Heard occasional shots of artillery all night. December 13, still in the same position. We to-day improved the breast-work and put the camp in order. Heavy firing on our right. No incident of note occurred to-day. December 14, the rebels opened their fire on the skirmish pits, which the Twenty-ninth Ohio Volunteer Infantry had constructed yesterday early; a few shots went over camp, but none doing any damage. Received official notice of the capture of Fort McAllister by the Second Division, Fifteenth Army Corps, thus allowing General Sherman to communicate with the fleet and army of General Foster. December 15 and 16, still in the same position. The rebels shell our camp continually, but do no damage. No incidents of note occurred during these days. December 17, still in the same position. Received our first mail to-day since leaving Atlanta. Nothing occurred beyond the regular routine of camp life. Heavy detail from the regiment to-night for fatigue duty. Building lunettes calculated for some heavy pieces. December 18, very hot weather; nothing of importance occurred; do not think the enemy has seen the lunettes built last night, which accounts for their not shelling them. December 19, the enemy shelled our works vigorously to-night, killing and wounding several of the brigade, but none of the Twenty-eighth Pennsylvania Volunteer Infantry; nothing of importance occurred. December 20, still in the same position; the rebels were rather quiet until about 4 p. m., when they shelled our works, wounding some more of the brigade; they continued shelling until 1 a. m. of the 21st, when we received notice that they were evacuating the city. To confirm this we marched into the city at daylight, and the Twenty-eighth Pennsylvania Volunteer Infantry and the Twenty-ninth Ohio Volunteer Infantry passed on to Fort Jackson, four miles down the river; here we arrived at 7 a. m.;

we entered the fort and immediately flung our colors to the breeze; we found the enemy had retreated, leaving the fort on fire and one of the magazines blown up; we captured in the fort and vicinity:*

Of the 91 guns captured, 14 only were found to have been spiked and shotted. The gun carriages were broken and temporarily disabled, and all the implements were broken and destroyed.

Thus has closed probably one of the most tedious, and yet one of the most successful campaigns on record in the world, and is a striking example of what can be accomplished when the soldiers of a country work with their general and he with them. We have been some thirty-six days on the march, and traveled a distance of 320 miles. We are now holding the defenses of our capture, but probably before long we may be on another move, and it is hoped that General Sherman and his army may be as successful as they have been in accomplishing the downfall of Savannah, Ga., December 21, 1864.

Respectfully submitted.

JOHN FLYNN,
Colonel, Commanding.

Lieut. A. H. W. CREIGH,
Acting Assistant Adjutant-General, First Brigade.

No. 105.

Report of Lieut. Col. John Craig, One hundred and forty-seventh Pennsylvania Infantry, of operations September 2–December 21.

HDQRS. 147TH REGT. PENNSYLVANIA VOL. INFANTRY,
Savannah, Ga., December 26, 1864.

SIR: In compliance with circular dated headquarters First Brigade, Second Division, Twentieth Army Corps, December 23, 1864, I have the honor to submit the following report:

On the 2d day of September we lay in line of works built by us a few days previous along the Chattahoochee River, and remained until September 4, when orders were received to strike tents as the brigade was ordered to Atlanta. We took up the line of march at 9.30 a. m., reaching the city at 1 p. m. Here we were put into line of works built by the enemy on the west side of the city, where we remained until November 15. We were, on account of the movement of the troops, obliged to change camp several times. We assisted in building the fortifications around the city. November 9, the enemy, with a strong force of cavalry and four pieces of artillery, made an attack at 7 a. m. on my immediate front, driving in the picket-line, advancing to within 200 yards of the main line. At the first firing I immediately ordered one company across the railroad into the fort on my right, where they opened fire on the enemy, repulsing them almost instantly. My skirmishers advanced immediately and took possession of the picket-line, finding 2 killed, 2 wounded, and 1 prisoner of the enemy inside of the picket-line; there was no loss out of my regiment. While encamped at Atlanta, Ga., repeated orders were received to make preparations for a fifty days' campaign. November 15, we took up the line of march, moving principally in an eastern direction nearly parallel with the Augusta and Atlanta Railroad until where it crosses the Oconee River,

---

* List of captures embodied in Geary's report, p. 280.

from whence we struck south toward Milledgeville, Ga., reaching it on the night of the 22d. On the morning of the 24th we again took up the line of march, moving principally southeast until December 11, which brought us within four miles of the city of Savannah, Ga. Here the enemy was found in force and well fortified. On the evening of this day we were placed in line, my right connecting with the Fifth Regiment Ohio Volunteer Infantry, and my left with the Sixtieth Regiment New York Volunteers, Third Brigade, Second Division, Twentieth Army Corps. Here we put up a line of works, where we remained until the morning of the 21st. The shelling of the enemy's guns was rather annoying, scattering in all directions through the camp. I had 3 men wounded, 2 of whom have since died. On the morning of the 21st, finding the enemy's works evacuated, we immediately followed up their retreat into the city of Savannah, Ga.

In conclusion I beg leave to thank the officers and men for their uniformity and willingness in discharging their duties. Our marches were long and tedious, marching over 300 miles in twenty-six days.

Accompanying please find report of casualties.*

JOHN CRAIG,

Lieut. Col. 147th Regt. Pennsylvania Volunteers, Commanding.

Lieut. A. H. W. CREIGH,

Acting Assistant Adjutant-General.

No. 106.

Report of Col. Patrick H. Jones, One hundred and fifty-fourth New York Infantry, commanding Second Brigade, of operations September 18–December 21.

HDQRS. SECOND BRIG., SECOND DIV., TWENTIETH CORPS,
Savannah, Ga., December 31, 1864.

CAPTAIN: I have the honor to state that on the 18th of September, 1864, I assumed command of this brigade, which was then lying in camp about 200 yards north of the McDonough road and southwest of Atlanta nearly three-quarters of a mile, where it remained until 3 p. m. November 5, 1864, when orders were received to be in readiness to march at an hour's notice. At 4 p. m. on the same day broke camp and marched about one mile in a southerly direction, and encamped for the night on or near the McDonough road. On the following day orders were received to return, when we marched back and reoccupied our camp. My brigade furnished all required details for fatigue and foraging expeditions during the occupation of Atlanta, Ga. On the morning of November 15, 1864, at 7 o'clock, we again broke camp, in accordance with orders received the previous evening, with thirty days' rations and sixty rounds of ammunition (in cartridge-boxes and knapsacks) per man. The course from Atlanta was southeasterly, along the Decatur pike, passing several small villages, of which the following in their order are the most prominent: Decatur, Stone Mountain, Social Circle, Madison, and on the 22d of November, 1864, reached Milledgeville, Ga., where we remained one day. On the 24th instant resumed the march in an easterly direction to Sandersville, from which place our course was due south to a point on the Macon and Savannah Railroad called Tennille, or Station No. 13. The brigade assisted in destroy-

*Nominal list (omitted) shows 2 enlisted men killed, 1 wounded, and 1 missing.

ing the railroad track until noon, when the march was resumed in the direction of Davisborough, where I arrived at 10 p. m. November 27, 1864. On the following morning the brigade was detached for the purpose of escorting the headquarters train Twentieth Corps to Spiers Station, where I encamped for the night. On the morning of November 29, 1864, I received orders to march the brigade to Station No. 10½, on the Macon and Savannah Railroad, with instructions to destroy one mile of railroad track to the west of said station, and to the east as far as the Ogeechee River, and also the bridge crossing it, which I did in a very effectual manner. The advance of the brigade marched as far as Station No. 10, destroying some cotton and cotton gins, and rejoined the brigade at the river before the destruction of the bridge and trestle-work was completed. During the afternoon of the 30th I was ordered to rejoin the division, and a guide was sent to conduct the brigade. After a tedious night march of about fifteen miles I reported the brigade to the division commander about three miles north of Louisville, Ga.

On the following morning the march was resumed, but, until the 9th of December, nothing of importance occurred. On that day the First Division, having the advance of the corps, encountered a force of the enemy intrenched behind a swamp about thirteen miles north of Savannah, when this brigade was ordered to the support of Colonel Carman's brigade, of the First Division, then preparing to attack the enemy. I reported with the brigade at the place indicated, but the enemy in the meantime abandoned the position, and I was directed to return and rejoin the division, which I did at night-fall of that day. On the following morning, December 10, I was ordered to march about two miles to the rear, where the train of the corps was parked and cover the approaches leading to it, and when it moved, follow at a proper distance as rear guard, for which purpose a section of Winegar's (New York) battery reported to me, together with one regiment of the First Brigade (the Twenty-ninth Ohio Veteran Volunteers). The train moved forward at 1 p. m. and went into camp about midnight on the line of the Charleston and Savannah Railroad, about five miles from the city. On the morning of December 11 the Third Brigade of this division, under command of Colonel Barnum, having reconnoitered the position of the enemy with a view to selecting ground for future operations, I was, about 10 a. m., ordered to move the brigade to the front and the left of our position on the Charleston and Savannah Railroad, and subsequently, at 3 p. m., assigned position, the left resting on the Savannah River and about three miles distant from the city, the brigade in the reserve of the division and about 500 yards behind the first line, composed of the Third and First Brigades. Under the instructions of the division commander I made disposition to protect the artillery in position on the river-bank and to picket the west bank of the river. On the 13th I was ordered to send a small force to the north of Hutchinson's Island, in the Savannah River, to observe the movements of the enemy and secure a rice mill on that part of the island which was to be used as a post of observation for our artillery and staff officers. Maj. William H. Hoyt, One hundred and thirty-fourth New York Volunteers, with sixty men, was sent for this purpose, and his force being insufficient I was further ordered by General Geary, commanding division, to send a small regiment for the purpose. Lieut. Col. A. H. Jackson, One hundred and thirty-fourth New York Volunteers, was accordingly sent, and subsequently the Seventy-third Pennsylvania Veteran Volunteers, Maj. (now Lieut-Col.) C. C. Cresson commanding. These regiments remained there until the morning of the 21st instant. The enemy having evacuated the city of Savannah on the night previous, on the morning of the 21st, about 4 o'clock, I was ordered to withdraw the regiments upon the island and march the brigade forward to the line of works formerly occupied by the enemy, and upon arriving there the general commanding division sent me orders to march to the city. Arriving in the city I was assigned the city parade-grounds, or Forsyth Place, as a ground for encampment, and the brigade assigned to the duty of guarding and patrolling a district of the city.

The casualties of the brigade during the operations embraced in this report were slight. A tabular statement accompanies this report. The officers and men of the command behaved with much consideration and propriety of conduct during the march, and but few instances of wanton destruction of property or pillage occurred.

To the officers of the staff I am under obligations for the faithful and diligent discharge of the duties devolving upon them.

All of which is respectfully submitted.

P. H. JONES,
Colonel 154th New York Volunteers, Commanding Brigade.

Capt. W. T. FORBES,
Asst. Adjt. Gen., Second Division, Twentieth Corps.

Numerical return of casualties of the Second Brigade, Second Division, Twentieth Corps, from the 15th day of November, 1864, until the 21st day of December, 1864.

Command.	Killed.		Wounded.		Missing.		Total.		Aggregate.
	Officers.	Men.	Officers.	Men.	Officers.	Men.	Officers.	Men.	
73d Pennsylvania Veteran Volunteers	......	......	......	1	......	......	......	1	1
109th Pennsylvania Veteran Volunteers	......	......	......	......	......	......	......	......	......
119th New York Volunteers	......	......	......	......	......	......	......	......	......
134th New York Volunteers	1	1	......	7	......	8	1	16	17
154th New York Volunteers	......	1	......	3	......	3	......	7	7
33d New Jersey Volunteers	......	......	......	1	......	......	......	1	1
Total	1	2	......	12	......	11	1	25	26

P. H. JONES,
Colonel 154th New York Volunteers, Commanding Brigade.

No. 107.

Report of Col. George W. Mindil, Thirty-third New Jersey Infantry, of operations September 2–December 21.

HDQRS. THIRTY-THIRD NEW JERSEY VOLUNTEERS,
Savannah, Ga., December 26, 1864.

CAPTAIN: I have the honor to submit the following official report of the movements of my regiment from the 2d of September to the 21st of December, 1864:

Upon entering the city of Atlanta the regiment was assigned a permanent camp to the right of the McDonough road, about one mile and a half from the court-house. In this camp it remained, devoting its time to drill and parades, and receiving complete outfits of clothing and camp and garrison equipage. On the 5th of November camp was broken and the regiment moved with the brigade at 3 p. m. out upon the McDonough road, camping two miles and a half from the city. On the 6th of November we returned to our old quarters. November 15, broke camp at 7 a. m., moved out upon the Decatur road and camped at 12 p. m. near Stone Mountain. November 16, moved at 8 a. m. and led the corps; marched fifteen miles, crossing Yellow River at Rock Bridge, and halting for the night five miles beyond it on the Sheffield road. November 17, moved at 6.30 a. m., marching through Sheffield over the Ulcofauhachee, and camped two miles from Social Circle. November 18, moved at 5.30 a. m., passing Rutledge, and camped at 5.30 p. m. one mile from Madison. November 19, moved at 5 a. m., passing through Madison; halted for dinner at Buck Head Station, and continued the march to within one mile and a half of Oconee River on Georgia railroad; tore up track afternoon and evening. November 20, moved at 7 a. m. toward Eatonton, passing Parks' Bridge and Glade's Cross-Roads; camped near Denham's Tannery at 6 p. m. November 21, moved at 6 a. m. toward Eatonton. November 22, struck Eatonton Branch Railroad, and passing through Milledgeville and over the Oconee River, camped two miles beyond it. November 23, in camp. November 24, moved at 10 a. m. on road to Hebron. November 25, passed through Hebron. November 26, entered Sandersville, and passed on to Tennille, on railroad, and camped three miles beyond it. November 27, moved at 7 a. m. and tore up seven miles of railroad and marched to Davisborough. November 28, brigade detached to guard the corps headquarters train; marched to Spiers Station on railroad. November 29, brigade again detached; moved by by-road to Station 10½; tore up railroad to bridge over the Ogeechee River. November 30, burned the bridge and then marched to Louisville, via Watkins' Bridge, reaching camp of division at 12 p. m.

December 1, moved at 8 a. m. and camped beyond Birdville. December 2, moved at 6 a. m. toward Millen and camped at Buck Head Creek. December 3, moved at 10 a. m.; crossed Augusta and Millen Railroad; camped six miles beyond it on the Sylvania road. December 4, moved at 7.30 a. m.; camped at Horse Creek. December 5, marched fourteen miles and camped, leaving Sylvania to our left. December 6, continued the march toward Springfield; roads very soft and marshy; camped after a tedious march of six miles. December 7, still continued the march toward Springfield and camped for the night near it. December 8, passed Springfield and marched twelve miles and camped near Zion Church. December 9, moved at 10 a. m. and struck Savannah road. First Division, Twentieth Army Corps, on our front; skirmished with the enemy, who had a battery in position covering the road; camped for the night sixteen miles from Savannah. December 10, pushing on, passed Harrison's plantation and Fourteenth Army Corps, struck Savannah and Charleston Railroad nine miles and a half from the city, and camped five miles and a half from it that night. December 11, placed in position as reserves on banks of Savannah River, opposite Hutchinson's Island and confronting the enemy's right flank, being in rear of the Third Brigade. December 12 to 20, we remained in the same position. December 21, entered the city of Savannah at 8 a. m. and were assigned a camp on the parade of the city.

During the entire campaign the troops have subsisted upon the country, and found food of all kinds in abundance, never suffering from scarcity of provisions. In front of Savannah we were unprotected by breast-works, being in the reserve line, and subject to a heavy fire of shrapnel and shell from the opposing batteries of the enemy in our front, and to a heavy and provoking fire from a Confederate gun-boat in the far channel round Hutchinson's Island.

I am happy to state but one casualty occurred, viz, the slight wounding of Private Terrence Sweeney, Company D.

Those soldiers reported as deserters in the accompanying schedule were all troublesome characters, and, despite repeated remonstrance and punishment and the constant vigilance of officers, succeeded in straggling and were captured by the enemy. Their absence being willful, I have marked them as deserters to the enemy, so that after exchange they are to be tried for this heinous offense. Before leaving Atlanta I received 136 substitutes, nearly all being raw recruits, many of them foreigners and unable either to write or speak the English language, and owing to physical disability caused by the exhaustion attendant upon so severe a campaign to new soldiers, many were compelled to leave the ranks at times, and by becoming separated from the regiment during its night marches, and being unable to intelligibly define their wants and ask the location of their regiment, have as yet failed to return, and are reported absent without leave. The larger part of these, it is to be hoped, are with some of the other corps, and will soon find their way into camp.

The command needs a complete outfit of clothing, shoes, &c., and will then be ready for a new campaign, as both health and esprit are excellent.

Subjoined is a list of casualties and desertions:

Name and company.	Date.	Remarks
Private Terrence Sweeney, Company D	Dec. 14, 1864	Wounded by shell from enemy's battery.
Corpl. James F. Dooley, Company C	Dec. 13, 1864	Deserted to the enemy.
Private —— Bennerman, Company C	....do	Do.
Private John Gardner, Company D	....do	Do.
Private Charles H. Chapman, Company I	....do	Do.
Private Adam Wetzel, Company K	Dec. 12, 1864	Do.
Private Francis McCarty, Company K	....do	Do.
Private John Smith, Company K	....do	Do.
Private Charles Wagner, Company K	....do	Do.

G. W. MINDIL,
Colonel, Commanding Thirty-third New Jersey Volunteers.

Capt. N. K. BRAY,
Acting Assistant Adjutant-General, Second Brigade.

No. 108.

Report of Col. John T. Lockman, One hundred and nineteenth New York Infantry, of operations September 1–December 21.

HDQRS. 119TH REGT. NEW YORK STATE VOLUNTEERS,
Savannah, Ga., December 23, 1864.

SIR: In compliance with circular order I have the honor to submit the following résumé of events since September 1, 1864, and report of the part taken by my regiment in the campaign just closed by the fall of Savannah, Ga.:

September 1, regiment engaged in building works near Pace's Ferry. September 2, still at Pace's Ferry; 1 p. m. our brigade received orders to move, and at 8 p. m. we halted at Atlanta. September 3, moved out and occupied rebel works on easterly side of the city. September 4, assigned position on westerly side of McDonough road. September 5 to November 5, inclusive, regiment occupied same position. On the afternoon of November 5 regiment was ordered to be ready to move, and at 3 p. m. marched out on McDonough road about one mile and a half and bivouacked for the night, and on 6th of November returned to our camp, where regiment remained until the morning of November 15, when regiment moved from camp and marched to the vicinity of Stone Mountain. On the 16th of November march resumed; bivouacked at night near Sheffield. November 17, marched to vicinity of Social Circle, destroying railroad track. November 18, moved at 5 a. m.; passed through Social Circle and bivouacked near Madison; portions of railroad track destroyed. November 19, moved at 5 a. m.; passed through Madison, the division being on special duty; several miles of railroad track destroyed, also depot at Buck Head; cavalry burned railroad bridge over Oconee River. November 20, moved at 7 a. m.; bivouacked at Denham's Mill. November 21, moved at 8 a. m. and marched toward the Oconee River; bivouacked about six miles from Eatonton. November 22, moved at 6.30 a. m. and crossed the Oconee River, and reached Milledgeville at 5 p. m.; passed through and bivouacked on the south side of the Oconee River. November 23, resting at Milledgeville. November 24, moved about eleven miles and bivouacked near Gum Creek. November 25, moved at 7 a. m. and bivouacked at Buffalo Creek. November 26, moved at 6 a. m., reaching Sandersville at 1 p. m.; at 4 p. m. moved to Tennille. November 27, moved at 6 a. m.; engaged all day in destroying railroad track and bridges; bivouacked at Davisborough. November 28, moved at 11 a. m. and reached Spiers at 6 p. m. and bivouacked. November 29, moved at 8 a. m. and marched to Bostwick; regiment engaged in tearing up and destroying railroad track. November 30, burned bridge over Ogeechee River, and trestlework over Williamson's Swamp. At 4 p. m. moved to rejoin division and reached Louisville at 9 p. m., where we bivouacked.

December 1, moved at 11 a. m. in the direction of Millen and bivouacked at night about twelve miles northeast from Millen. December 2, moved at 6 a. m. and bivouacked near Buck Head Creek. December 3, moved at 11 a. m. and bivouacked near ——— Creek; division as rear guard. December 4, moved at 10.30 a. m. and bivouacked near Horse Creek. December 5, moved at daylight and crossed Horse Creek; division still rear guard. December 6, regiment detailed to forage for brigade. December 7, regiment still on duty foraging for brigade; rejoined same near Springfield. December 8, moved at 7 a. m. and crossed Ebenezer Creek, and bivouacked for the night near Eden. December 9, moved at 8 a. m., First Division leading; at 2 p. m. rebels opened with artillery on the advance; the enemy was soon driven; our brigade sent to support Colonel Carman's brigade, of the First Division; the enemy retreated and we were not needed; bivouacked for the night fourteen miles from Savannah. December 10, moved at 2.30 p. m. and bivouacked four miles from Savannah. December 11 to 20, in reserve in rear of first line. December 21, moved at 5 a. m. and entered Savannah at 6.30 a. m.

There are no casualties to report.

Very respectfully, your obedient servant,

JOHN T. LOCKMAN,

Colonel, Commanding 119th New York Volunteers.

Capt. N. K. BRAY,

Actg. Asst. Adjt. Gen., Second Brig., Second Div., 20th Corps.

No. 109.

Report of Maj. William H. Hoyt, One hundred and thirty-fourth New York Infantry, of operations September 2–December 21.

Report of the One hundred and thirty-fourth New York Volunteers, from the capture of Atlanta, Ga., September 2, 1864, to the 21st of December, 1864, when the regiment entered the city of Savannah, Ga.:

September 2, the regiment, commanded by Capt. Otis Guffin, Company F, was ordered to march at 12 m.; advanced with the brigade into the city of Atlanta, Ga. September 3, took position with the brigade in the outer works of the city. September 4, was ordered to take a new position farther to the right and bivouacked for the night. September 5, went into camp in rear of the works and did its regular picket duty and fatigue. September 11, Maj. William H. Hoyt took command of the regiment and relieved Capt. Otis Guffin. September 13, changed camp; the regiment took a new position in the works, where it remained, under command of Maj. William H. Hoyt, doing its regular picket and fatigue duty and participating in the foraging expeditions until November 5, when it was ordered to move with the corps out of the works on the Macon road and encamp. November 6, the regiment returned to its old camp and remained until November 15, when it moved out of the city of Atlanta, Ga., with the army in the Savannah campaign; marched to near Stone Mountain and encamped at midnight. November 16, marched at 8 a. m.; Lieut. Col. Allan H. Jackson relieved Maj. William H. Hoyt, and took command of the regiment. November 17, broke camp at 5 a. m. and marched first in line, guarding the train; passed through Sheffield; crossed Gum Creek; halted for the night four miles from Social Circle. November 18, marched at 5 a. m., passed through Social Circle, and advanced to within two miles of Madison. November 19, moved out with the Second Division on a separate expedition; no fighting occurred; joined the corps in company with the brigade and division November 22, and entered the city of Milledgeville, Ga.; went into camp late at night. November 23, regiment lay still. November 24, marched until late at night. November 25, crossed a large swamp and encamped for the night. November 26, advanced into Sandersville; One hundred and thirty-fourth New York Volunteers formed part of the grand guard of the division. November 27, the regiment assisted in destroying a part of the Georgia Central Railroad. November 28, assisted the brigade in guarding the corps headquarters train to the Station No. 11. November 29, marched about seven miles, and destroyed railroad track the remainder of the day. November 30, assisted in destroying a railroad bridge across the Ogeechee River; marched fifteen miles at night to join the division.

December 1, regiment marched in advance of the ordnance train of the division. December 2, marched to Buck Head Creek and encamped for the night. December 3, guarded the train. December 4, marched with the brigade and went into camp 7 p. m. December 5, marched steadily all day. December 6, marched through a marshy country. December 7, had difficulty crossing swamps. December 8, advanced with division toward Savannah; did not encounter the enemy. December 9, advanced, with skirmishing in front; First Division met the enemy; One hundred and thirty-fourth New York Volunteers, leading the Second Brigade, were ordered to support the First Division; advanced splendidly on the double-quick; the enemy retreated; regiment went on picket. December 10, regiment remained on picket until 1 p. m.; advanced to within six miles of Savannah. December 11, moved at 8 a. m. slowly toward the left; took a position in range of the enemy's guns; were relieved and took a position on the left, on the river-bank in range of the enemy's guns. December 12, regiment lay still. December 13, had 1 commissioned officer killed and 1 man wounded; at night regiment crossed the river and fortified on Hutchinson's Island. December 14, advanced and took possession of rice mill and settlement, and fortified our position; held our position under a severe artillery fire from the enemy (where we had 6 men wounded and 1 killed) until December 21, when the enemy had evacuated the night before and the regiment advanced into the city of Savannah.

WM. H. HOYT,
Major, Commanding Regiment.

No. 110.

Report of Maj. Lewis D. Warner, One hundred and fifty-fourth New York Infantry.

HDQRS. 154TH REGIMENT NEW YORK VOLUNTEERS,
Savannah, Ga., December 26, 1864.

COLONEL: In obedience to the requirements of circular of the 23d instant, I have the honor to make the following report of the part taken by the One hundred and fifty-fourth Regiment New York Volunteers, under my command, in the various movements of the Army of Georgia from the 15th day of November to the 21st day of December, 1864, inclusive:

November 15, marched at 8 a. m. toward Decatur, the regiment leading the brigade; passed through Decatur and encamped within three miles of Stone Mountain. November 16, marched at 8 a. m., Second Brigade leading the corps; course, easterly along the line of the Georgia railroad. November 17, marched at 5 a. m.; course, the same as yesterday. November 18, marched at 5 a. m.; passed through the village of Social Circle, and encamped within two miles of Madison. November 19, marched at 5 a. m.; passed through Madison at daybreak; followed the line of the railroad, a considerable portion of which we tore up and burned, and encamped within two miles of the Oconee River. November 20, marched at 7 a. m.; course, down the right bank of the river toward Milledgeville. November 21, marched at 7.30 a. m. in a southerly direction, passing about six miles to the left of Eatonton. November 22, marched at 6 a. m., the regiment leading the division; crossed Little River on pontoon bridge; entered Milledgeville at dark; crossed to left bank of the river and encamped at 10 p. m.; entire regiment on picket. November 23, regiment on picket until near night, and was then relieved by troops of Third Brigade; did not march to-day. November 24, marched at 7 a. m. toward Sandersville. November 25, marched at 6.30 a. m.; passed through Hebron; halted near Buffalo Creek, while the bridge was being rebuilt; crossed after dark and encamped on the left bank. November 26, marched at 6 a. m.; regiment guard to brigade train; reached Sandersville about noon; halted until nearly night and then marched to the Georgia Central Railroad, which we struck at Tennille Station;

moved easterly along the road about two miles and encamped. November 27, roused up about 1 a. m. by a false alarm; moved the regiment to a new position; at 7 a. m. moved out upon the railroad, halting to tear up and burn the track as we advanced; followed the railroad about five miles, and then marched to Davisborough, where we encamped at 10 p. m. November 28, brigade detailed to accompany the corps train to Spiers Station, to march at 10 a. m., the One hundred and fifty-fourth New York leading the brigade; reached the station at sunset; regiment on picket. November 29, marched at 7 a. m. toward Station No. 10; reached here at 12 m. and passed the remainder of the day tearing up and burning the track from one mile west of the station to the Ogeechee River. November 30, passed nearly the whole day destroying the railroad bridge over the Ogeechee River; at 4 p. m. marched to join the division, which was encamped near Louisville; crossed the river here and encamped at 9 p. m.

December 1, marched at 8 a. m.; regiment guard to headquarters Left Wing; course, southeast toward Millen. December 2, marched at 6 a. m.; course, same as yesterday; crossed Buck Head Creek and encamped near its eastern bank. December 3, marched at 10 a. m.; regiment guard to division train; crossed the Augusta railroad about three miles north of Millen just at dark; moved slowly on and encamped at 10.30 p. m. December 4, marched at 10 a. m. in rear of corps and cavalry train; course, toward Springfield. December 5, marched at 7 a. m.; course, same as yesterday. December 6, marched at 8 a. m.; same course. December 7, marched at 7 a. m. and encamped at 8 p. m. within one mile of Springfield. December 8, marched at 6.30 a. m., passing through Springfield. December 9, marched at 7.30 a. m.; course, toward Savannah; some skirmishing in our front; regiment not engaged. December 10, Second Brigade marched back about two miles and took position in rear of the train, which we were to guard this day; moved forward at 12 m.; struck the Charleston railroad just before night and ten miles from Savannah; encamped at 8 p. m. within five miles of the city. December 11, moved at 10 a. m. toward the river; took position in front of the enemy's lines, which were covered by a canal and rice marsh; threw forward skirmishers and remained here for three hours, when we were relieved by the First Brigade, and moved to the left and rear, and encamped on the bank of the river in rear of the lines of the Third Brigade, where we remained, furnishing pickets for the river-bank and also heavy fatigue details for the fortifications in our front until the morning of December 21, when, the enemy having evacuated during the preceding night, we moved forward into the city, and encamped just outside, at the terminus of Bull street.

The casualties during the time covered by the above report were as follows.*

Several others received slight injuries from contusion by shells, which burst in camp at various times between the 11th and 21st, but the injuries were not sufficiently serious to call for a report.

All of which is respectfully submitted.

I am, colonel, very respectfully, your obedient servant,

L. D. WARNER,
Major, Commanding Regiment

Col. P. H. JONES,
Comdg. Second Brig., Second Div., Twentieth Army Corps.

---

* Nominal list (omitted) shows 1 killed, 3 wounded, and 4 missing.

No. 111.

Report of Lieut. Col. Charles C. Cresson, Seventy-third Pennsylvania Infantry.

HDQRS. SEVENTY-THIRD PENNSYLVANIA VETERAN VOLS.,
*Savannah, Ga., December 26, 1864.**

When [November 15] we again broke camp and resumed the line of march, having an uninterrupted march, with little variety, subsisting chiefly on the country through which we passed, losing no men by straggling or capture, arriving in front of Savannah, Ga., on the evening of December 10, and took up position the day following on the bank of the river directly opposite the center of Hutchinson's Island, where we remained until the 14th instant, when I received orders from Colonel Jones, commanding brigade, to cross my regiment to Hutchinson's Island and report to Lieutenant-Colonel Jackson, commanding forces on the island. I crossed my men in small boats about dusk and reported according to orders. We remained in this location, throwing up earthworks during the night to protect the men from the shelling of the enemy, who, from a gun-boat and a river shore battery, poured a constant fire at the mill around which we were posted. Owing to our exposed position we were unable to work during the day. The place being held as a point of observation, every exertion was made by me to obtain by personal attention as much of the movements of the enemy as possible. On the evening of the 20th instant a noise was detected in the direction of the city directly after dark, sounding much like the laying of a pontoon bridge. Especial attention was paid to the noise for about two hours, when, feeling confident that the enemy were throwing a body of troops from the Georgia to the Carolina shore, my adjutant, by order of Lieutenant-Colonel Jackson, crossed the river about 10 p. m. and reported the fact of the noise and the opinion of those on the island concerning the cause of it to Col. P. H. Jones, commanding Second Brigade, Second Division, Twentieth Army Corps. The morning following—December 21, instant—I was ordered to rejoin the brigade, which was then marching toward the city. Owing to the limited number of boats, my regiment was not all crossed until nearly noon, when we marched in the city and joined it at about 3 p. m. December 21, 1864.

Very respectfully, your obedient servant,

CHAS. C. CRESSON,
Lieut. Col., Comdg. Seventy-third Pennsylvania Vet. Vols.

Capt. N. K. BRAY,
Acting Assistant Adjutant-General.

No. 112.

Report of Capt. Walter G. Dunn, One hundred and ninth Pennsylvania Infantry.

History of the command of the One hundred and ninth Regiment Pennsylvania Veteran Volunteers from November 15, 1864, to December 21, 1864:

November 15, 1864, left Atlanta, Ga., at 7 a. m. and encamped near Stone Mountain, Ga., at 2.30 a. m. on the Rock Bridge road. November

* For portion of report (here omitted) relating to operations about Atlanta, see Vol. XXXIX, Part I, p. 672.

16, on the march from 8.30 a. m. until night. November 17, on the march. November 18, left camp at 7.30 a. m. and encamped at night near Madison, Ga. November 19, 1864, passed through Madison, Ga., at daylight, regiment in advance of the division destroying railroad. November 20, on the march destroying railroad at night and encamped. November 21, on the march. November 22, on the march; reached Milledgeville, Ga., at 6 p. m. November 23, lay in camp near Milledgeville, Ga. November 24, left camp at 7 a. m. third regiment in line as train guard; encamped at 11 p. m. near Gum Creek. November 25, on the march at 7 a. m. until noon; then halted; at night-fall crossed swamp and Big Buffalo Creek and encamped. November 26, on the march; advance guard of the division passed through Sandersville, Ga., and encamped at night near the railroad. November 27, command was engaged in destroying railroad; encamped at 11 p. m. near Davisborough, Ga.; rear guard of division. November 28, on the march; guard on corps headquarters train; encamped at night at Spiers Turnout. November 29, on the march at daylight, destroying railroad. November 30, still destroying railroad; also railroad bridge; then crossed the river and encamped at 11 p. m.

December 1, on the march. December 2, on the march all day; encamped at 4 p. m. near Buck Head Creek. December 3, on the march; train guard; swampy country. December 4, 5, and 6, on the march, making slow progress on account of swamps and poor roads. December 7, on the march at 8 a. m.; encamped at 8.30 p. m. near Springfield, Ga. December 8, passed Springfield, Ga., and encamped at 3.30 p. m. December 9, arms and accouterments inspected; then on the march and encamped at dark. December 10, left camp at daylight; rear guard on wagon train; marched till dark and encamped about five miles and a half from Savannah, Ga. December 11, took position on river. December 12 to 20, still lying near the river doing picket duty and giving details for foraging expeditions; also engaged in erecting fortifications. Casualties were none. December 21, left our position and entered Savannah, Ga., at 8 a. m.

WALTER G. DUNN,

Captain Company C, Comdg. 109th Regt. Pennsylvania Vols.

No. 113.

Report of Col. Henry A. Barnum, One hundred and forty-ninth New York Infantry, commanding Third Brigade.

HDQRS. THIRD BRIG., SECOND DIV., 20TH ARMY CORPS,
Savannah, Ga., December 26, 1864.

CAPTAIN:*

November 15, the brigade with the division broke camp at 7 a. m. and marched out on Decatur street, and at 9 a. m. took up the march. This command, being the rear of the Second Division in line, passed through Decatur and encamped at 4 a. m. of the 16th on the Rock Bridge road, fifteen miles from Atlanta. The One hundred and eleventh Pennsylvania Veteran Volunteers did not march with the brigade, but

* For portion of report (here omitted) relating to operations about Atlanta, see Vol. XXXIX, Part I, p. 673.

remained in the city until the 16th to assist in the destruction of railroads and public buildings, and then joined the column of the Fourteenth Corps. November 16, marched at 8 a. m., passed Mountain Creek at 10 a. m. and Yellow River at 12 m., and encamped at 6 p. m. on Henry's farm. During the most of the afternoon the brigade was engaged in assisting the trains up steep and difficult hills. Made eight miles this day. November 17, marched at 5 a. m., this brigade in advance of corps. Crossed Big and Little Haynes Creeks, also Gum Creek. Marched through Sheffield at 10 a. m. and encamped at 5 p. m. near Ulcofauhachee River. Day's travel, sixteen miles. November 18, marched at 5 a. m., the brigade being distributed as train guard. Passed Social Circle at 9 a. m., and encamped near Madison at 6 p. m. Day's travel, fifteen miles. November 19, marched at 5 a. m., division being detached from main column; passed through Madison and along the Augusta railroad, and bivouacked at Blue Spring, near the Oconee River, at 4 p. m. Detachment destroyed the bridge over the Oconee River, and the balance of the command destroyed the railroad in the vicinity. Day's travel, fifteen miles. November 20, marched at 7 a. m. and reached the Oconee River at 8 a. m. at Parks' Planing Mills, which were destroyed, and encamped at Denham's Factory. Day's travel, fifteen miles. November 21, marched at 7 a. m. Burned Denham's Factory, tannery, and adjacent buildings, except dwelling houses. Marched fifteen miles and encamped on Nesbit's plantation at 6 p. m. November 22, marched at 6 a. m. and joined the main column at 12 m. Passed through the city of Milledgeville unopposed at about 7 p. m. Crossed the Oconee and encamped about one mile east of the city at 9 p. m. Day's travel, fifteen miles. November 23, the One hundred and eleventh Pennsylvania Veteran Volunteers rejoined the brigade. The brigade marched to Midway, destroyed the station-house and railroad to the city, including a large trestle bridge over ——— Creek, and returned to camp at 6 p. m. Distance marched, six miles. November 24, marched at 6 a. m. and encamped at dark near Gum Creek, thirteen miles from Milledgeville. November 25, marched at 6.30 and reached Buffalo Creek at 12 m. Detained by destruction of bridges till 9 p. m. Crossed the creek and encamped. Day's travel, eight miles. November 26, marched at 6 a. m. Reached Sandersville at 12 m. Skirmish by the advance. Formed line south of town, and at 1 p. m. marched to Tennille Station with the division and destroyed railroad toward Davisborough till 6 p. m., and encamped for the night. Day's travel, twelve miles. November 27, renewed destruction of railroad at 7 a. m., and at 12 m. marched toward Davisborough, crossing Williamson's Swamp Creek, and encamping at Davisborough at 9.30 p. m. Day's travel, fifteen miles. November 28, marched at 7 a. m. with division and returned to a point about eight miles from Davisborough, and commenced the destruction of the railroad where we left off the day before. At about 2 p. m. this brigade was attacked by a force of cavalry, which was quickly repulsed and driven off with some loss. Had 1 man wounded and 4 men captured. At 5 p. m. marched back to Davisborough and encamped at 7 p. m. Day's travel, sixteen miles. November 29, marched at 6 a. m. to Spiers Station, thence to Bostwick, and encamped at 7 p. m. Day's travel, nineteen miles. November 30, marched at 7 a. m. Crossed the Ogeechee River at 4 p. m., and encamped at 7 p. m. Day's travel, ten miles.

December 1, marched at 7 a. m., this brigade leading the corps, and bivouacked at 6 p. m. near Bark Camp Creek. Day's travel, thirteen miles. December 2, marched at 6 a. m., crossed Buck Head Creek and encamped near Buck Head Church. Day's travel, eleven miles. December 3, marched at 12 m., passing near the prisoners' stockade north of Millen; crossed the Augusta railroad at 7 p. m.; engaged the rest of the night in assisting the trains over the almost impassable roads, and bivouacked at 4 a. m. December 4. Day's travel, fifteen miles. December 4, marched at 8 a. m. and passed over a very bad road and bivouacked at 7 p. m. Day's travel, fifteen miles. December 5, marched at 6 a. m.; crossed Crooked Creek at dark and bivouacked on east bank. Day's travel, sixteen miles. December 6, marched at 7 a. m.; progress slow; bivouacked at 7 p. m. Day's travel, nine miles. December 7, marched at 7 a. m.; 100 wagons assigned to this brigade to assist forward; bivouacked near Springfield at 8 p. m. Day's travel, ten miles. December 8, marched at 6.30, division being unencumbered with wheels; somewhat detained by the roads being blockaded; bivouacked at 5 p. m. near Wadley's Mills. Day's travel, ten miles. December 9, marched at 7.30; at 4 p. m. the brigade was massed in support of First Division, which was confronted by the enemy in works across the road; the enemy was soon routed and the command encamped at about 5 p. m. Day's travel, nine miles. December 10, marched at 10 a. m., this command guarding train; crossed the Charleston railroad at 12 m.; moved down the Augusta road to within six miles of Savannah and encamped at 3 p. m. Day's travel, ten miles.

December 11, ordered to penetrate to the Savannah River and develop the enemy's line between the Augusta road and the river; marched at 7 a. m.; moved down the Augusta road to within about 1,200 yards of a battery of the enemy covering the road; filed left and marched toward the river and parallel to the enemy's line, the One hundred and thirty-seventh New York Volunteers in advance as skirmishers, who engaged those of the enemy's at 10 a. m. The skirmish line was extended to the left by the deployment of the One hundred and second New York Veteran Volunteers, until they reached the river. The skirmish line then closed in on the enemy, but found him strongly posted in the thick woods and in a strong line of pits. The skirmish line was strengthened and ordered to charge the enemy's line, which, with loud cheers, was gallantly done. His line was routed and ran back in great disorder, our men following at a rapid run until they were opened upon with canister from a strong fort, which had been concealed from our view by the woods. Our men had reached to within seventy-five yards of this work before it was thus discovered to them. They were ordered back to the enemy's line of pits, which was strengthened and held until night, when the command threw up a strong breast-work with pits in advance, and the brigade occupied the line, which was only 150 yards from the fort, as has since been determined by actual measurement (for position of brigade see accompanying map).* December 12, the fort in front of the left of the brigade proved to be an advanced work, covering a canal connecting with the river, and through which the extensive swamps and rice-fields in front of the enemy's entire line was flooded. The brigade was subjected to a severe fire of artillery and musketry from this advanced work, and of artillery from his main line. Our works were, however, considerably strengthened and the position maintained. December 13 was a repetition of the experience of the 12th. December 14, at 12 a. m., with Captain Hobart and eight men of his company from the Sixtieth New York Veteran Volunteers, and Capt. L. S. Willson, acting assistant inspector-general of brigade, the commanding officer of brigade, made a close examination

* For map see p. 308.

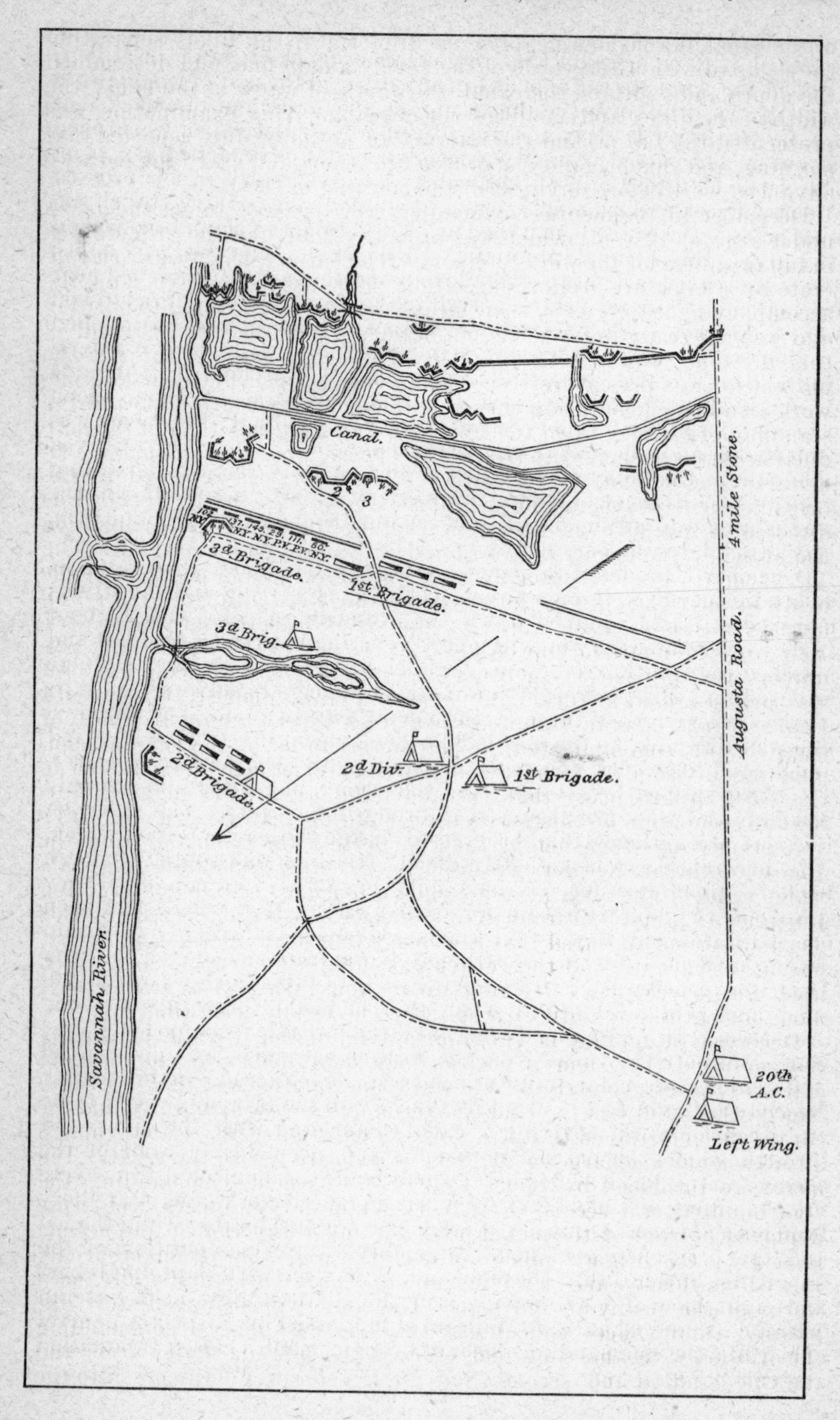
Canal.
2
3
3d Brigade.
1st Brigade.
3d Brig.
2d Div.
1st Brigade.
2d Brigade.
4 mile Stone.
Augusta Road.
20th A.C.
Left Wing.
Savannah River.

of the canal and flooded fields in our front; also the dikes separating the fields to within 150 yards of the enemy's main line, and determined the depth and width of the canal, the depth of water in the fields, the width of the dikes and facilities for crossing. This examination was prosecuted till 3 a. m. and the information obtained duly reported that morning, and this brigade was ordered to attack and carry the enemy's advanced work before daylight of the morning of the 15th.

December 15, regimental commanders were ordered to get their men under arms at 12 a. m., which was promptly done, and the brigade was in full readiness for the work by 1 a. m. The battery which was to co-operate by a flank fire from the position, noted as Battery No. 2 on the accompanying map, was by some means delayed in getting into position and was not ready until 3.30 a. m., besides which the First Brigade of this division, which with the Second Brigade was to support the movement, was prematurely marched along the immediate rear of our works, and much confusion ensued. It was a very cold night, and the stamping of the men upon the frozen ground and rekindling of the subdued fires was sufficient to alarm the enemy, who gave palpable evidence of being ready to receive us. This fact was reported to the brigadier-general commanding division, and the undersigned was directed to use his own discretion whether to proceed or to abandon the attack. The troops were ordered into position for assault. The Twenty-ninth Pennsylvania Veteran Volunteers was in position on the beach of the river, the One hundred and thirty-seventh New York Volunteers in the left of our works as reserve, and the Sixtieth New York Veteran Volunteers and One hundred and second New York Veteran Volunteers were in position in front of our works, and the One hundred and forty-ninth New York Volunteers and One hundred and eleventh Pennsylvania Veteran Volunteers nearly so, when Captain Lambert, of division staff, communicated the peremptory order of the general commanding division to withdraw, which was reluctantly done at 4.15 a. m. December 20, other than the above the brigade was engaged, during the occupation of this position, in building traverses in our works and otherwise strengthening them to protect the command from the almost continuous artillery fire from the enemy's works and gun-boats which came up the river so as to enfilade our line; also in constructing Batteries 1, 2, and 3 in front of this division. Toward evening of this day indications appeared that the enemy was either evacuating or preparing to evacuate, and the picket was ordered to keep a close watch upon his movements. He kept up an unusually severe artillery fire along his entire line until 11 p. m., when he totally ceased his fire.

December 21, at 12 a. m. the commandant of the brigade personally reconnoitered the enemy's position and consulted with the brigade officer of the day, Capt. S. B. Wheelock, One hundred and thirty-seventh New York Volunteers. At 2.30 the reconnaissance was repeated and the conviction entertained that the works in our front were vacated, though an occasional discharge of artillery was heard far to the right. Ten men were furnished by Lieut. Col. H. S. Chatfield, commanding the One hundred and second New York Veteran Volunteers, who were deployed in front of the picket-pits and, under direction of and accompanied by the brigade officer of the day and the commander, advanced cautiously, and receiving no opposition entered the advanced works of the enemy at 3.20 a. m. The undersigned immediately dispatched a staff officer to acquaint the brigadier-general commanding the division with this fact, and ordered the brigade under arms and the One hundred and second New York Veteran Volunteers into the works, and with the ten men advanced on the main line, crossing the flooded fields on the river-bank and the two dikes separating the fields and entering the enemy's main works at 3.40 a. m. Another staff officer was immediately dispatched to communicate this fact to the general commanding division, and the brigade was put into the main line, and a strong skirmish line advanced 500 yards. The undersigned also placed guards on all the guns found in the enemy's works from the Augusta road to the river, eleven in number, seven of which were in the advanced work nearest our line. The general commanding division having arrived further operations were conducted under his direction. After waiting some time for the First and Second Brigades of this division to arrive this brigade was put in motion and marched through Axley's plantation to the Augusta road, the brigade moving in the following order: One hundred and second New York Veteran Volunteers, One hundred and forty-ninth New York Volunteers, One hundred and thirty-seventh New York Volunteers, Twenty-ninth Pennsylvania Veteran Volunteers, One hundred and eleventh Pennsylvania Veteran Volunteers, and Sixtieth New York Veteran Volunteers, with a strong skirmish line from the One hundred and forty-ninth New York Volunteers extending from the river to the Augusta road. The column then moved down the Augusta road, and at about half a mile from the junction of the Augusta road with the Charleston railroad was met by the mayor and a delegation of aldermen of the city with a flag of truce, who formally surrendered the city of Savannah. With lusty cheers at every step the column pressed forward and entered the city on West Broad street from the Augusta road, marched down West Broad to Bay street, and down Bay street to the Exchange or City Hall, from the balcony of which was displayed the national colors of the regiments of this brigade and the division flag at 6 a. m. By order of the general commanding division the Sixtieth New York Veteran Volunteers was left at the entrance of the city at the canal crossing as guard, with instructions to prevent any other troops from entering the city until quiet and order could be established, and the undersigned was also directed to disperse the riotous crowds of poor whites and negroes, who were sacking the stores and store-houses. This brigade was immediately deployed throughout the city as patrols through the streets and guards over the various kinds of public property, ordnance, and stores, and two companies of the One hundred and thirty-seventh New York Volunteers were sent to Fort Jackson, citizens were sent to their houses, and crowds dispersed and order and quiet soon established. At 8.30 a. m., the First and Second Brigades having arrived, this brigade was assembled and put by regiments in sub-districts of that portion of the city bounded by Bull and Jones streets and the canal and Savannah River, constituting about one-third of the city. December 24, by order of General Geary, commanding division and post, the undersigned was appointed provost-marshal of the west half of the city from Bull street, and the troops of this command continued as provost guard, at which duty they are still employed.

In justice to the officers and men of this brigade it is here recorded that they were the first to discover the evacuation by the enemy of his works, the first to occupy them, the first to enter the city (the skirmishers of the One hundred and forty-ninth New York Volunteers having entered the city half an hour in advance of the brigade), the first to take possession of and guard all the captured ordnance and stores of every kind in and below the city and in the enemy's works from the Augusta road to the river; that they captured the greater part of the prisoners taken, and until 8.30 a. m. of the 21st were the only organized body of our troops in the city. Casualties have been heretofore reported in detail, a summary of which is hereto attached; also a comparative statement of the effective force at the commencement and close of the campaign.

Too much cannot be said in praise of the soldierly conduct of the men of this command generally throughout the campaign, and particularly since the occupation of this city; and the officers, with few exceptions, were worthy leaders of the men. Those who constitute the exceptions will not accompany us on the next campaign. My personal and departmental staff are hereby mentioned as exceedingly competent and faithful. The distance marched by this command from the time of leaving Atlanta until the occupation of Savannah was 325 miles.

Respectfully, your obedient servant,

H. A. BARNUM,
Colonel 149th New York Volunteers, Commanding Brigade.

Capt. W. T. FORBES,
Assistant Adjutant-General.

Summary of casualties in Third Brigade, Second Division, Twentieth Army Corps, for the campaign ending December 21, 1864.

Regiments.	Killed.		Wounded.				Missing.		Aggregate.
			Severely.		Slightly.				
	Officers.	Men.	Officers.	Men.	Officers.	Men.	Officers.	Men.	
60th New York Veteran Volunteers	......	......	1	2	1	2	......	......	6
102d New York Veteran Volunteers	......	......	......	6	1	8	......	1	16
137th New York Volunteers	......	1	......	7	......	1	......	4	13
149th New York Volunteers	......	......	......	2	......	......	......	1	3
29th Pennsylvania Veteran Volunteers	......	2	1	5	......	1	......	......	9
111th Pennsylvania Veteran Volunteers	......	......	......	......	......	1	......	......	1
Total	......	3	2	22	2	13	......	6	48

Comparative report of effective force.

Effective force September 2, 1864	1,199
Recruits received during campaign	128
	1,327
Effective force December 21, 1864	1,435
Increase in effective force	236

No. 114.

*Report of Maj. Thomas Elliott, Sixtieth New York Infantry.**

The regiment left Atlanta on the 15th of November, and on the 22d were among the first troops that entered the capital of Georgia. During the march to Milledgeville all public property and matter available to the enemy was either destroyed or appropriated; among the rest the

* For portion of report (here omitted) relating to operations about Atlanta, see Vol. XXXIX, Part I, p. 674.

noted and extensive Denham's tannery and shoe manufactory, near Eatonton, in which duty the regiment participated. On the 23d the command was engaged and assisted in destroying the railroad from Milledgeville in the direction of Gordon Junction, returning the same night and leaving Milledgeville on the 24th. On the 26th the Georgia Central Railroad was struck and the work of destruction commenced, which duty was repeated at times throughout the remainder of the campaign. On the 28th of November, while engaged in this duty near Davisborough, the regiment was attacked by and became engaged with about 200 cavalry of the enemy, who were driven from position and were among the first of the enemy seen since the campaign began. On the 30th, after crossing the Ogeechee River, the regiment was assigned to guard and destroy the bridge, which duty was thoroughly performed on the morning of December 1. The regiment rejoined the brigade the same day.

On the morning of the 11th the regiment was assigned to the right of the brigade, and before the day closed were in line confronting the enemy in front of Savannah. From the 1st to the 11th of December the duty of the regiment had been the usual destruction of public property and the laborious work of crossing Georgia swamps with heavy trains. The position taken by the regiment on the 11th was retained till the morning of the 21st, resulting in the following casualties: 2 officers and 4 enlisted men wounded. At 3.30 o'clock on the morning of the 21st the regiment was in line, constituting a portion of the command that entered Savannah at sunrise. The regiment was assigned the duty of guarding the approaches to the city near the canal. In performing this duty a body of the enemy was soon discovered, consisting of two commissioned officers and thirty-four enlisted men, who were guarding an extensive arsenal, which was duly surrendered with its guard to a detachment sent out for the purpose. Besides these, a number were captured on the occupation of the city.

With the capture of Savannah closes the campaign. History will record the results as a monumental record to the master mind conceiving it; a grateful nation awaits with a hearty greeting for the "willing hearts and strong arms that have executed."

Respectfully, your obedient servant,

THOMAS ELLIOTT,
Major, Commanding Sixtieth Regiment New York Veteran Vols.

No. 115.

Report of Lieut. Col. Harvey S. Chatfield, One hundred and second New York Infantry.

HDQRS. 102D REGIMENT NEW YORK VETERAN VOLS.,
Savannah, Ga., December 26, 1864.

CAPTAIN:*

November 15, pursuant to orders received from brigade headquarters, broke camp at 6 a. m. and started upon the campaign through Georgia. Marched on the Decatur road along the line of the Augusta railroad, starting at 7 a. m. Owing to the wagon trains, our progress was necessarily slow and tedious. Marched throughout the day. November 16, continued our march until 4 a. m., when the regiment

*For portion of report (here omitted) relating to operations about Atlanta, see Vol. XXXIX, Part I, p. 675.

bivouacked near Stone Mountain, having marched since the morning previous about fifteen miles. At 8 a. m. again moved forward about ten miles and bivouacked about 5 p. m. at Littlefield. November 17, started about 5 a. m.; marched about fifteen miles and bivouacked near Gum Creek at 5 p. m. November 18, started at 5.30 a. m.; marched about twenty miles and bivouacked near Madison, Ga., at 5.30 p. m. November 19, started about 5 a. m.; marched about ten miles and bivouacked just beyond Buck Head and near the Appalachee River at 4 p. m. During the afternoon the regiment destroyed about 800 yards of railroad track on the Augusta railroad by tearing up the track and burning the ties. November 20, started at 7 a. m.; left the line of the Augusta railroad; marched about fifteen miles and bivouacked at Denham's Factory at 5.15 p. m. November 21, started at 7 a. m.; marched about ten miles through a drenching rain-storm and bivouacked at Doctor Nesbit's plantation at 5.30 p. m. November 22, started at 6 a. m.; about noon crossed the Oconee River, joined the main column, and entered Milledgeville a little after dark; marched across the river at Milledgeville and bivouacked about one mile beyond the city at 9 p. m., having made about fifteen miles during the day. November 23, the regiment went with the rest of the brigade in the afternoon for the purpose of destroying the railroad running to Gordon on the Macon railroad; worked until dark and returned to the camp, this regiment having thoroughly destroyed about three-quarters of a mile of the track. November 24, started at 7 a. m.; marched about ten miles and bivouacked at 6 p. m. near Town Creek. November 25, started at 6.30 a. m.; marched about six miles and bivouacked at 9 p. m. just beyond Buffalo Creek. November 26, started at 5 a. m.; passed through Sandersville, Ga., and reached Station 13, on the Macon and Savannah Railroad, about 4 p. m., having marched fifteen miles in all. The regiment was ordered to go into position in advance of the brigade, so as to guard against any attack which might be made by the enemy's cavalry upon the troops who were at work destroying the railroad. This order was obeyed, and the regiment remained in line until after dark, when it bivouacked with the rest of the brigade near Station 13. November 27, broke camp at 6.30 a. m.; continued the destruction of the railroad until about 2 p. m., when our march was continued. Arrived at Davisborough about 10 p. m., having marched about twelve miles during the day. Placed the regiment on picket pursuant to instructions received from the division field officer of the day. November 28, moved at 7 a. m. back to point on the railroad distant some seven miles to continue the destruction of the railroad. Commenced tearing up the track about noon; after working a short time a portion of the troops so engaged were fired upon by a small party of the enemy. I ordered the flank companies to cease work and deploy as skirmishers on both sides of the railroad, to guard the remainder of the regiment against any attack and allow them to continue the destruction of the road. In a short time thereafter, pursuant to orders received from Col. H. A. Barnum, commanding, I ceased work upon the railroad and marched back to join the main body of troops. This order I obeyed with much reluctance, as the destruction of the track was incomplete and many of the bridges, which were numerous along this portion of the railroad, were left undestroyed. As soon as the troops were drawn in we marched back to division and bivouacked at 8 p. m. November 29, started at 6 a. m.; marched twenty miles and bivouacked at 6 p. m. November 30, started at 6 a. m.; marched about eight miles and bivouacked at 6 p. m. near Louisville.

December 1, started at 7 a. m.; marched, as advance guard, about twelve miles and bivouacked at 5 p. m. at Blazed Tree Church. December 2, started at 8 a. m.; marched about eleven miles and bivouacked about 6 p. m. near Buck Head Creek. December 3, started at 12.30 p. m.; marched until midnight with numerous halts and over a difficult road about eight miles. December 4, continued the march until 4 a. m., having made about three miles, when the regiment bivouacked. At 7.30 a. m. again started; marched about six miles; the regiment was placed on picket duty for the night, with the One hundred and thirty-seventh New York Volunteers. December 5, at 7 a. m. drew in the picket guard, and at 9 a. m. moved forward with the column; marched about fifteen miles and bivouacked at 9 p. m. December 6, moved at 8 a. m.; marched about twelve miles over very marshy roads and bivouacked at 6 p. m. December 7, started at 7 a. m.; marched about ten miles over very difficult roads and bivouacked at 6 p. m. near Springfield. December 8, started at 6.30 a. m.; marched about nine miles and bivouacked about 4 p. m. at Wadley's Mill. December 9, started at 7 a. m.; marched about six miles and bivouacked about 6 p. m. near Monteith. December 10, started at 9.30 a. m.; shortly after starting the regiment was placed in rear of the first 200 wagons of the corps train as guard for the 100 wagons immediately preceding it; marched about nine miles and bivouacked about 4 p. m. five miles and a half from Savannah, Ga. December 11, at 7 a. m. moved out upon the main road to Savannah with the rest of the brigade; moved forward about three-quarters of a mile thereon and turned off to the left toward the Savannah River. In a short time thereafter the command was halted, having come up with the enemy's pickets. In about an hour I was ordered by Colonel Barnum, commanding the brigade, to move forward the regiment and deploy it as skirmishers, connecting with the left of the One hundred and thirty-seventh New York Volunteers, which was already deployed and skirmishing with the enemy, and to continue my line until it reached the river, if possible. When but three companies upon the right had been deployed the river was reached. With the remainder of the regiment as a reserve I ordered the skirmishers forward. They had moved but about twenty-five yards when farther advance was prevented by a deep swamp, and the line had become so shortened as to render two companies sufficient to cover the space between the One hundred and thirty-seventh New York Veteran Volunteers and the river. I therefore ordered Company I to join the reserve. Moved the reserve forward nearly to the skirmish line and went forward with Colonel Barnum to reconnoiter the position. To get over the swamp with any force it was found necessary to cross a narrow dike or road, which was commanded by the enemy's sharpshooters. At this time Captain Maguire had succeeded in crossing with a few skirmishers, and he meeting with but little resistance, I ordered Company K, Capt. O. J. Spaulding, to cross the road, to quickly deploy, and with those already across advance toward the enemy's works. This was gallantly done, and the enemy driven into his main line of works. I immediately ordered the reserve forward, when the enemy opened upon the column with artillery, and the force being insufficient to carry the works by assault and unsupported, I ordered the regiment to form in line behind a natural dike, which had been previously occupied by the enemy and which was but 150 yards from their main line. During this attack the regiment had two wounded, Captain Spaulding and one private, both slight. The regiment remained in this position and improved and strengthened the earth-work in their front sufficiently to protect it from the enemy's fire. At 11.30 p. m. it was announced to regimental commanders by Colonel Barnum that a night attack was ordered and the plan detailed.

December 12, at 12.30 a. m. the regiment was called up and preparations made to assault the enemy's lines at 1 a. m. At that hour the regiment was in readiness, but the attack was delayed and the regiment did not commence to move outside our line of works to get into position until about 4 a. m. This regiment was to form the left of the second line of the assaulting column, and the left wing had filed over and in front of our works, when the order for attack was countermanded, and I received orders to take my original position within our line of works, which I did. Remained here during the day, nothing occurring except being annoyed by the enemy's sharpshooters and a few shells. December 13, early in the morning I ordered the construction of some rifle-pits in advance of our line about ten rods and four in number. The enemy's sharpshooters kept up an annoying fire, and occasionally their artillery opened, with no other effect than the wounding of one man slightly. December 14, our rifle-pits having been finished, my skirmishers or pickets were enabled to silence the enemy's sharpshooters to a considerable extent. During the day the gun-boat made its appearance in the river, nearly in a line with the left of my regiment, and opened fire upon the line with shot and shell from 6½ and 9 inch guns, from the effects of which I had five men slightly wounded. From this time until December 20 nothing occurred beyond the usual picket-firing and occasional shelling by the enemy. About 9 p. m. my pickets on the left of the regiment reported that the men in the enemy's works in our front could be seen apparently moving to the right (their left), and soon thereafter the enemy could be heard crossing a pontoon bridge, apparently opposite the city. A strict watch was instituted, and at about 10.30 p. m., becoming satisfied that they were leaving, went in person and reported these facts to the brigade commander. During this time the enemy kept up a vigorous fire from his artillery in our front. At 11 p. m. this ceased. From this until 12 o'clock the sounds of the enemy crossing the pontoon bridge could be heard continually.

December 21, from 1 a. m. to 3 a. m. the sounds made by crossing could be so distinctly [heard], and every indication of the evacuation of the city becoming so apparent, an advance was ordered by Colonel Barnum, who had come up in person to my position, to be made by ten men from my regiment, to reconnoiter the position in our front and discover whether or no the enemy was there. In a short time they reported the line evacuated, and at 3.20 a. m. I entered the first line of the enemy's works with the regiment, finding seven guns in position and a large quantity of ammunition, &c., destroyed. In a short time the men sent forward reported the enemy's second line across the canal also evacuated. In obedience to orders from the brigade commander, I detached one company to guard the guns captured, and with the remainder of the regiment crossed the canal and entered the second line, where we halted and awaited the coming up of the remainder of the brigade. Detached two companies to take possession of and guard the guns in this line from the Augusta road to the river. At 4.15 a. m. an advance toward the city was ordered. My regiment leading, marched rapidly forward until we reached the Augusta road, when I ordered one company in advance of the column as skirmishers; moved forward very rapidly and with no opposition except a few shots fired upon the advance guard from the bridge crossing the canal, and entered the city at daylight, capturing some few stragglers from the enemy and a large amount of stores of all kinds.

During the whole of the campaign both the officers and men of my command have behaved well, and it is sufficient to say have done their whole duty as becomes veterans. It is difficult, where all have so well performed their part, to make any distinction, yet I would especially mention Capt. O. J. Spaulding, commanding Company K; Capt. H. M. Maguire, Company C, and First Lieut. T. W. Root, acting adjutant, as deserving special mention for their bravery and vigilance throughout the campaign.

Respectfully submitted.

H. S. CHATFIELD,
Lieutenant-Colonel, Commanding Regiment.

Capt. O. T. MAY,
Actg. Asst. Adjt. Gen., 3d Brig., 2d Div., 20th Army Corps.

No. 116.

Report of Lieut. Col. Koert S. Van Voorhis, One hundred and thirty-seventh New York Infantry.

HEADQUARTERS 137TH NEW YORK VOLUNTEERS,
Savannah, Ga., December 24, 1864.

CAPTAIN:*

II.

Tuesday, November 15, when, in pursuance to orders received previously, we formed line at 7 a. m. Starting at 7.30 a. m., moved out of the city on the Decatur road. At 2 p. m. halted near Decatur for dinner. After dinner resumed the march, which was continued until 4.30 a. m. on Wednesday, November 16, when we halted, rested, and breakfasted, resuming the march at 7.15 a. m. Camped for the night at 7.15 p. m., marching distance from Atlanta being about twenty-seven miles. Thursday, November 17, left camp at 5.15 a. m., marching in a northeasterly direction, the Third Brigade in advance and this regiment as advance guard. Encamped at 5 p. m. within three miles of Social Circle, marching this day about twenty miles. Friday, November 18, took up line of march at 5.30 a. m., halting soon after in the road to allow wagon train to pass. Started again at 7.30 a. m., halting in the village of Rutledge for dinner. Encamped within a mile of Madison at 6.30 p. m., having marched about eighteen miles. Saturday, November 19, left camp at 5 a. m.; marched through Madison at daybreak in a moderate rain, which ceased about 7 o'clock. Halted near Buck Head for dinner. At 4 p. m. encamped for the night. After stacking arms proceeded to tear up track on the Augusta railroad, working with the division about two hours and a half. Distance marched this day, about fifteen miles.

Sunday, November 20, fell in at 7.30 a. m. and marched south from the railroad on the west bank of the Oconee River; encamped at 5 p. m., after having marched about fifteen miles. Monday, November 21, left our encampment at 8 a. m., marching in a southerly direction; raining hard the greater part of the day; halted for the night at 5 p. m.; marched about twelve miles. Tuesday, November 22, we left camp at 6.45 a. m., and about noon crossed Little River on a pontoon bridge. About 4.30 p. m. came in sight of Milledgeville. After numer-

---

* For portion of report (here omitted) relating to operations about Atlanta, see Vol. XXXIX, Part I, p. 676.

ous halts we at last entered the city, and passing through the city crossed the Oconee River on a toll bridge, and encamped about a mile from the river, going into camp at 8.10 p. m., having marched about twenty miles. Wednesday, November 23, remained in camp until 2 p. m., when we fell in and marched to the Gordon railroad depot, and soon after commenced the destruction of the road, burning the ties and bending the rails; also burned a trestle bridge and the depot. Our work being completed, at 7 p. m. we returned to our former camp. Thursday, November 24, left camp near Milledgeville at 7.30 a. m. Halted near the road until 10 a. m., when we moved on, marching in a southeasterly direction. At 6.15 p. m. bivouacked for the night, having marched about ten miles. Friday, November 25, started this morning at 8.30, marching in rear of wagon train. Halted at 1 p. m. for dinner. Did not move until 8.30 p. m. on account of the destruction by the enemy of bridges (nine in number), over Buffalo Creek. After crossing we camped for the night, having marched only five miles. Saturday, November 26, marched at 7.30 a. m., arriving at Sandersville soon after noon. At 2 p. m. we passed through the town and struck the Georgia Central Railroad about 4 p. m., when we immediately began tearing up the road, and continued it till dark, and camped near the road; marched fifteen miles.

Sunday, November 27, moved at 7.45 a. m., and resumed the destruction of the railroad track, working until noon. After dinner we joined the wagon train and marched with it about two miles, when we were ordered to "about face," and were marched back to the railway, and taking another road to Davisborough, arrived there at 9.30 p. m., and went on picket; marched about twelve miles. Monday, November 28, leaving the picket-line at 8.30 a. m. we struck for the railroad and marched on it back to the place where we had left off work the day before, the remainder of the brigade having marched around by the turnpike. Commenced work about noon, and at 3 p. m. the Sixtieth New York Veteran Volunteers on our right were fired upon by a squad of rebel cavalry, who dashed out of the woods near by, but after firing a few shots they fled. Our men immediately fell in, and, taking arms, were ordered to load, the first time since leaving Atlanta. Four men of this regiment were missing here, and were, it is supposed, captured by the enemy. At dark we returned to Davisborough and camped for the night. Distance marched, fifteen miles. Tuesday, November 29, left camp at 6.30 a. m.; halted for dinner at Spiers Station. Marched at 3.30, encamping for the night at 6.15 p. m. Marched about twenty miles. Wednesday, November 30, leaving camp at 6.45 a. m., marched almost directly north, crossing the Ogeechee River at 5.30 p. m. Bivouacked for the night at 6.15 p. m., having marched nine miles. Thursday, December 1, left camp at 7.15 a. m., our brigade in advance, marching nearly southeast, crossing numerous swamps and creeks. Went into camp at 5.15 p. m. Distance marched, about sixteen miles. Friday, December 2, marched this morning at 8 o'clock, our brigade in rear of the corps. Weather uncomfortably warm. Encamped for the night at 5.30 p. m.; marched about ten miles. Saturday, December 3, did not leave camp until 12.45 p. m. Were in rear to-day, and consequently marched very slow. Passed near the rebel stockade in which were confined Union prisoners but a few days before. Crossed the Augusta railroad after dark, leaving Millen on our right.

Sunday, December 4, continued the march of yesterday till 3.40 a. m.; then halted, resuming the march at 8 a. m. During the forenoon heard artillery firing to our right and rear. Halted at 2 p. m. for dinner.

Started again at 4.30, and at 6 p. m. halted for the night, and this regiment went on picket. Marched yesterday and to-day about seventeen miles. Monday, December 5, leaving camp at 9.15 a. m., marched steadily until 8.45 p. m. Distance marched, fifteen miles. Tuesday, December 6, started at 9 a. m., marching in rear of brigade wagon train. Were delayed much during the day by obstructions placed in the roads by the enemy. Went into camp at 8.45 p. m., having marched about nine miles. Wednesday, December 7, moved at 7 a. m., marching through swamps nearly all day. At 5 p. m. crossed Turkey Branch, and encamped at 6.30 p. m. Marched nine miles. Thursday, December 8, marched at 7.15 a. m. in advance of the train. Roads better to-day than usual. Encamped at 4.45 p. m., after having marched about twelve miles. Friday, December 9, left camp at 8.15 a. m. Cannonading heard on our right, apparently in the direction of Savannah. Troops of First Division had a slight skirmish with the enemy, driving them from two small forts. Marched about six miles. Saturday, December 10, left camp at 9.40 a. m., First and Third Divisions in advance. Marched on an excellent turnpike road leading directly to Savannah. Artillery firing heard more or less all day. After having marched about nine miles, at 3.45 p. m. brigade was formed in two lines of battle, and we encamped for the night.

Sunday, December 11, were in line at 7.30 a. m., and after marching about a mile on the main road, filed left on a cross-road, and again filing left from the cross-road the regiment was deployed as skirmishers. The extreme right and left of the line were well advanced, and the regiment was then advanced with extreme caution toward some negro houses, about a dozen in number, when the line was straightened, and we then found we were in close proximity to the enemy's skirmishers, and shots were exchanged lively. It was not deemed prudent to advance the line farther, owing to its exposing the left flank, and on communicating with Colonel Barnum, commanding brigade, he promptly sent the One hundred and second New York Veteran Volunteers, which deployed and connected on my left. About 2 p. m. it was deemed advisable to charge and drive them, if possible, from the ruins of some buildings, which afforded them a desirable shelter. One company of the One hundred and second started with a yell which this regiment took up, and advancing rapidly soon drove them inside their works. Our line was established within about 200 yards of their works. This regiment lost 1 sergeant killed; 2 privates wounded. Monday, December 12, at 1 a. m. we were ordered to "fall in," as our brigade were to charge the works in our front. The arrangements were completed at about 4 a. m., when the order was countermanded. The enemy shelled us at different times during the day. Weather very cold. Tuesday, December 13, skirmish and artillery firing was quite brisk by the enemy all day. We were very busy in strengthening our works, and at night established skirmish pits in our front. Wednesday, December 14, remained in same position all day. Order received from Major-General Sherman announcing the capture of Fort McAllister by the Second Division, Fifteeenth Corps, thereby opening communications with the fleet and General Foster. Thursday, December 15, nothing unusual occurred this day. Friday, December 16, a rebel gun-boat came up the river to-day and fired several shots very near us. At night a fort was laid out near the bank of the river on our left. Saturday, December 17, received first mail from the North since leaving Atlanta.

Monday, December 19, fresh hard bread was issued to-day, causing a feeling of general satisfaction among the men. A mail left the brigade. Tuesday, December 20, at dark the regiment was detailed to work on a fort in front of the right of our brigade, called Fort No. 3, where we worked until 1.30 a. m., on Wednesday, December 21, when, it being completed, we returned to camp, and soon after noticed signs of the enemy's evacuation of the city, which was ascertained, by Colonel Barnum sending a detail of ten men from the One hundred and second New York Veteran Volunteers across to their works, under command of Capt. Samuel B. Wheelock, of this regiment, to be true, when the brigade moved forward immediately, occupying their works, and from thence moved directly into the city, arriving at the City Hall at 6.15 a. m., when the brigade was formed in column by regiments, and Brig. Gen. John W. Geary, commanding division, took formal possession of the city, complimenting our brave brigade and its courteous and thorough commander in a fine speech, and soon after Col. H. A. Barnum addressed the brigade in a neat and appropriate speech. We were soon after assigned to duty as provost-guard.

Thus closed one of the most gigantic and successful campaigns ever projected and most certainly ever participated in by this regiment.

The casualties of this regiment during the campaign are as follows: Enlisted men—killed, 1; wounded, 8; missing, 4; total, 13.

Respectfully submitted.

K. S. VAN VOORHIS,
Lieutenant-Colonel, Commanding Regiment.

[Capt. O. T. MAY,
Acting Assistant Adjutant-General.]

No. 117.

Report of Maj. Nicholas Grumbach, One hundred and forty-ninth New York Infantry.

HEADQUARTERS 149TH NEW YORK VOLUNTEERS,
Savannah, Ga., December 26, 1864.

CAPTAIN:*

November 15, the regiment left their camp at Atlanta at 7 a. m. with 16 officers, 244 musket-bearing men, 46 daily duty men, musicians, and non-commissioned staff, being an aggregate of 306 men, and marched to near Stone Mountain, and bivouacked at 4 a. m. of the 16th. November 16, marched at 7 a. m, crossed Yellow River at 12.30 p. m., and bivouacked at 5.30 p. m. at Littlefield. November 17, marched at 5 a. m.; bivouacked at 4.30 p. m. near Ulcofauhachee River on Circle road. November 18, marched at 5.30 a. m. and crossed Ulcofauhachee River at 7 a. m; passed through Social Circle and halted for dinner at Ridgeway, fifty-seven miles from Atlanta; regiment and brigade guarding train; bivouacked at 6 p. m. one mile from Madison. November 19, marched at 5 a. m. Regiment, brigade, and division left the corps and went on an expedition by themselves. Our brigade was second in line and halted at 2 p.m. until the Second Brigade, which was in the advance, destroyed a large section of the Augusta railroad. Bivouacked at 3.30 p. m. on a large plantation at Blue Spring. Destroyed about 80 rods

* For portion of report (here omitted) relating to operations about Atlanta, see Vol. XXXIX, Part I, p. 678.

of the railroad. November 20, marched at 8 a. m., One hundred and forty-ninth in advance of division. Reached Oconee River at 9 a. m; halted for the night at Denham's Mills, and regiment went on picket. The regimental headquarters were at the house of Mr. Denham, owner of the mills and plantation. He had previously left with his family for Secessia. November 21, marched at 9 a. m; regiment rear guard. As we passed the mills of Mr. Denham they were burning splendidly. Bivouacked at dark till November 22. Marched at 7 a. m. and rejoined the corps at 12 m; sighted Milledgeville at 4 p. m. and passed through the capital city at 8 p. m., and crossed the Oconee River and bivouacked one mile east of the river at 11 p. m.

November 23, remained in camp till 1 p. m., when regiment and brigade, with one brigade of the First Division, went out three miles toward Gordon and destroyed railroad track. Returned to camp at 7 p. m. November 24, 7 a. m. marched into the main road and halted until the Fourteenth Corps passed. Resumed march and bivouacked at dark one mile southeast of Town Creek. November 25, marched at 9 a. m. as far as Buffalo Creek Swamp; remained until nine bridges destroyed by rebels were rebuilt across the swamp. At 8 p. m. moved across and bivouacked at 9.30 p. m. November 26, marched at 7 a. m., the regiment guarding ammunition train; passed through Sandersville at 1.30 p. m.; marched to Tennille Station, on the Macon and Savannah Railroad, reaching that point at 3.30 p. m. Our division, with the First, destroyed the depot and about two miles of railroad track. Bivouacked at 7 p. m. in a field beside the railroad. November 27, our regiment moved onto the railroad again at 8 a. m. in advance of the division and deployed Companies B and F as skirmishers. The balance of the regiment was the advance guard. The rest of the division engaged in destroying the track. Left the railroad at 3 p. m. and marched to Davisborough, and bivouacked at 9 p. m. November 28, the regiment marched at 8 a. m. back onto the railroad to the point at which they left it on the 27th, and tore up and destroyed the track to the wagon road leading to Davisborough. About 4 p. m. a small body of rebel cavalry made a dash at the Third Brigade, where they were at work, but seeing our strength skedaddled on double-quick, only wounding one man in the brigade. Returned to Davisborough and bivouacked at 8 p. m. November 29, marched at 6 a. m. Bivouacked at 7 p. m. six miles east of Spiers Station. Regiment went on picket. November 30, marched at 6.30 a. m. and crossed the Ogeechee River at 5 p. m.; bivouacked at 6.30 p. m. two miles east of the river, one mile from Louisville, and near the plantation of Herschel V. Johnson.

December 1, marched at 6.30 a. m.; brigade in advance; passed the Fourteenth Corps at 4 p. m. and bivouacked at 5 p. m. at Stone Cross-Roads. December 2, marched at 7 a. m.; regiment and brigade guarding division train. Crossed Buck Head Creek and bivouacked at Buck Head Church, four miles from Millen, the junction of the railroads from Augusta and from Macon for Savannah. December 3, marched at 12.30 p. m.; passed near the stockades, where thousands of our men, prisoners, had been confined. Crossed the Augusta railroad and continued our march until 4 a. m. of the 4th. December 4, marched at 8 a. m.; crossed Horse Creek at 12 m., and halted until dark for a bridge to be built across a swamp. Resumed march, crossed the swamp, and bivouacked at 7 p. m. December 5, marched at 9 a. m.; regiment rear guard; crossed Little Horse Creek; marched until 9 p. m. and bivouacked in the field. December 6, marched at 8.30 a. m; found the roads much obstructed by trees fallen across them—the work of rebels. Bivouacked in the field at 8 p. m. December 7, marched at 7 a. m., our brigade in advance of division; went into camp for the night near Springfield; regiment on picket. December 8, pickets recalled at 7 a. m. and regiment in rear of division. Marched to near Middleton's Mills and bivouacked at 4.30 p. m. December 9, marched at 7.30 a. m. Cannonading heard most of the day. At 3 p. m. our regiment, brigade, and division were formed in line of battle on the west side of a swamp, four miles from Monteith. The road through the swamp was blockaded by the rebels and was commanded also by a fort. The rebel force was flanked by two regiments crossing the swamp, one on each side of the road, and the rebels were thereby forced to retreat. At 4 p. m. we advanced and bivouacked in the swamp until December 10; marched at 8.30 a. m., regiment and brigade guarding wagon train. Passed the fort and obstructions in the road, crossed the Charleston and Savannah Railroad, and moved down on the main road between the railroad and Savannah River to within five miles of Savannah and bivouacked.

December 11, at 8 a. m. advanced toward the city and drove the enemy into their works. The siege of Savannah commenced. Our regiment occupied a ditch and formed breast-works of it. Were ordered out at 1 o'clock in the night to charge the enemy's works, but the order was countermanded and the troops returned to our own works. Regiment remained in the works until the 15th without any casualties. On the 15th Ezra Hall, of Company H, was wounded by a piece of shell. This was the first and only man wounded during the campaign. Regiment remained in our works, picketing our own front and under an almost incessant fire of shell from the rebel batteries, until the morning of December 21. At 2 a. m. it was discovered that the rebels had evacuated their works and were retreating. Our division advanced at 3 a. m. toward the city, our regiment the advance guard. Companies B and F were sent forward as skirmishers and entered the city at 5 a. m., closely followed by the rest of the division, and the city was surrendered and at once taken possession of by our forces. In the haste of the regiment to leave their works and enter the city the men left everything behind except arms and accouterments, and the One hundred and forty-ninth had the proud honor of first entering the city of Savannah.

Casualties: Wounded, 1; left on the march sick, 2; sent to hospital sick, 4; died from disease on march, 1; fell out on march, whereabouts unknown, 2; total, 10.

The regiment left Atlanta in excellent spirits and health and full of confidence of the successful termination of the campaign, and their conduct throughout the march and while in the trenches before the city was worthy of the cause for which we are fighting, and was such as commanded admiration from their commanders, and demonstrated that the utmost confidence exists between our generals and the Union soldiers.

Respectfully, your obedient servant,

NICHOLAS GRUMBACH,
Major, Commanding Regiment.

Capt. O. T. MAY,
Acting Assistant Adjutant-General.

No. 118.

Report of Lieut. Col. Samuel M. Zulich, Twenty-ninth Pennsylvania Infantry.

HDQRS. TWENTY-NINTH PENNSYLVANIA VETERAN VOLS.,
Savannah, Ga., December 24, 1864.

CAPTAIN: I have the honor to submit the following report, in compliance with orders from brigade headquarters received December 23, 1864:

November 15, 1864, broke camp at 7 a. m.; took the Decatur road and marched, in connection with the brigade, as rear guard to division train and reached camp at 4 a. m. 16th, beyond and to the right of Stone Mountain, some fifteen miles from Atlanta. 16th, received orders and took up line of march at 6 a. m., still acting as guard to division train; crossed the Yellow and Stone Rivers and Haynes Creek; marched about fourteen miles and bivouacked for the night. 17th, took up line of march, the division and brigade having the advance, and made a march of eighteen miles and bivouacked within two miles of Social Circle. 18th, broke camp at 6 a. m.; this regiment on the left of the brigade; the division still the advancing column; crossed the Little Haynes Creek, passed through the post villages of Social Circle and Rutledge; bivouacked near the town of Madison, having marched some seventeen miles. 19th, took up the line of march before the break of day; passed through the town of Madison; halted for dinner at Buck Head Station; the division having separated from the corps and train, taking a different but converging road, halted for the night at Blue Spring, on the plantation of General Jordan. At this point the command was turned out to destroy the Augusta railroad, which was effectually accomplished for several miles. A large amount of cotton (150 bales) and corn ready for shipment, on the plantation of General Jordan, was destroyed by fire by order of General Geary, commanding the division. 20th, broke camp at 7 a. m., this regiment being the advance guard of the column. After striking the Oconee River the column marched down this stream upon the west bank, passing through the village of Oconee; bivouacked at Denham's, a large and extensive Government boot, shoe, and tannery establishment; the regiment, in connection with the One hundred and forty-ninth New York Volunteers, being on picket; marched about fourteen miles. 21st, took up line of march at 8 a. m.; the brigade destroyed, by General Geary's orders, the tannery and workshops at Denham's; the roads heavy and incessant rain during the entire day; marched twelve miles and bivouacked on Doctor Wesley's plantation. 22d, marched at 7 a. m.; crossed the Little River on pontoons and joined the corps at Milledgeville, the capital of Georgia; marched about fifteen miles, crossed the Oconee, and reached camp about 9 p. m. and bivouacked for the night. 23d, remained in camp until 2 p. m., when the brigade and regiment, in connection with Third [First] Brigade (Col. Selfridge), First Division, were ordered to destroy several miles of the Gordon railroad, which was successfully accomplished; reached camp at 5 p. m. 24th, broke camp at 7 a. m.; crossed Town Creek and encamped for the night near Gum Creek, having marched twelve miles. 25th, moved at 9 a. m.; passed through the town of Hebron; halted while nine bridges were repaired over the swamps at this point, which had been destroyed by a citizen by the name of Tucker. The bridges having been repaired, took up line of march about 8 p. m.; crossed the swamps and bivouacked for the night, having marched about eight miles. 26th, moved at 7 a. m.;

reached Sandersville at noon; halted one hour for dinner; marched to Tennille, some three miles distant, at Station No. 13, on the Georgia Central Railroad; destroyed several miles of road toward Davisborough; encamped for the night in close proximity to the railroad. 27th, at 7 a. m. recommenced the destruction of the railroad and took up line of march at 2 p. m. for Davisborough, some twelve miles distant, which place we reached at 9 p. m. 28th, resumed the destruction of the railroad in vicinity of Davisborough, in conjunction with First Brigade of Second Division. While at work an assault was made upon the working parties by a detachment of Wheeler's cavalry, in which Private William Grouse, of Company H of this regiment, was wounded in the foot. Reached Davisborough about 8 p. m.; bivouacked for the night. 29th, moved at 7 a. m.; halted for dinner at Bartow Station, some thirteen miles from Davisborough; passed through Bethany, and bivouacked near the Ogeechee River, after a march of twenty-two miles. 30th, took up line of march at 9 a. m. in direction of Louisville; crossed the Ogeechee River about dusk; bivouacked near Louisville; marched about ten miles.

December 1, moved at 7 a. m., taking the advance; marched fifteen miles and bivouacked near Burke Camp-Ground. 2d, moved at 7 a. m.; marched some fifteen miles; crossed Buck Head Creek and bivouacked for the night. 3d, took up line of march at 12 m.; crossed the Augusta and Waynesborough Railroad three miles north of Millen; marched some ten miles and bivouacked at 4 a. m. 4th, broke camp at 7 a. m., being the advance guard of the division. Marched but six miles, owing to the destruction of a dam by the enemy, which flooded the road. 5th, started at 10 a. m.; Companies K and F were detailed as a rear guard. After crossing the north branch of the Little Ogeechee these two companies were ordered to destroy, by fire, the saw-mill and bridge and break the dam. After the same had been opened and the road flooded, three foraging teams came in sight on the other side of the road. The men were ordered to cross the burning bridge, which they did, and succeeded in backing the flames and brought the teams and horses across in safety. Halted for dinner at the Little Ogeechee; passed the First Division, and bivouacked for the night, after a march of fifteen miles. 6th, broke camp at 8 a. m.; marched this day but eight miles, owing to the obstructions placed across the road by the enemy. 7th, moved at 7 a. m.; marched to Springfield, fourteen miles. Regiment on picket, in connection with the One hundred and forty-ninth New York Volunteers. 8th, took up line of march at 7 a. m.; passed through Springfield; encamped at 4 p. m., having marched fourteen miles. 9th, marched at 8 a. m.; halted at Monteith Swamp for dinner. At this point a brigade of the First Division encountered the enemy. After handsomely repulsing them the Second Division was ordered to encamp about 5 p. m. 10th, moved at 9 a. m.; crossed the Savannah and Charleston Railroad, which had been destroyed by the First Division; bivouacked on the main road to and within five miles of Savannah. 11th, the brigade was ordered to break camp at 8 a. m., and move on a road to the left and toward the Savannah River to feel the enemy's lines; passed the Forty-sixth Pennsylvania Veteran Volunteers, First Division, Second [First] Brigade, doing picket duty and in close proximity to the enemy's lines. After a slight skirmish with the enemy by the One hundred and thirty-seventh and One hundred and second New York Regiments, in which they drove the enemy into their works, we took our position in a ditch made to drain the road and which served as good earth-works for the men, the Twenty-ninth being the fourth in line from the left of the brigade and within 300 yards of the enemy's works.

12th, the enemy kept up a brisk artillery fire, which was only responded to by the skirmish line on our front. At 11 p. m. received orders to prepare to charge the enemy's works. The positions of the regiments were changed, and the Twenty-ninth ordered to take the extreme left and charge the enemy's works on the river beach. The regiment took up its assigned position at 2 a. m., and at 4 a. m. was ordered into the intrenchments, the assault having been abandoned. 13th, heavy firing all day from the enemy with shot and shell. 14th, firing all day from the enemy. Received news of the capture of Fort McAllister. 15th, things unusually quiet. 16th, heavy firing from the enemy; 2 men wounded, both seriously. 17th, firing from the enemy unusually heavy; 2 enlisted men killed, 4 wounded (1 mortally), and 1 commissioned officer, Captain Beaumont, wounded in left leg. 18th, 19th, and 20th, nothing worthy of note. 21st, received notice to fall in at 2 a. m.; that the enemy had abandoned their works. Took up line of march, crossed to the enemy's lines, and pressed at once for the city, which we entered at 6 a. m., the Third Brigade, Second Division, Twentieth Corps, being in advance of all other troops belonging to the Federal army.

I take this opportunity of expressing my thanks to Capt. Sykes Beaumont, of Company E, a brave and efficient officer, who through the entire campaign has rendered me valuable assistance, the wound he received on Saturday, December 17, having resulted in the loss of his left leg, and will probably prove fatal to life.

I also inclose the following report of casualties.*

Respectfully, your obedient servant,

SAMUEL M. ZULICH,

Lieut. Col., Comdg. Twenty-ninth Pennsylvania Veteran Vols.

Capt. O. T. MAY,

Acting Assistant Adjutant-General.

No. 119.

Report of Lieut. Col. Thomas M. Walker, One hundred and eleventh Pennsylvania Infantry, of operations September 3–December 21.

HDQRS. 111TH REGIMENT PENNSYLVANIA VET. VOLS.,

Savannah, Ga., December 24, 1864.

CAPTAIN: I have the honor to report, in obedience to Special Orders, No. 97, the operations of my regiment from the capture of Atlanta to the occupation of Savannah.

September 3, 1864, by direction of the general commanding the corps, the One hundred and eleventh was detailed as one of the regiments of provost guard, and ordered to report to the commander of the post at Atlanta. We remained on this duty until the afternoon of November 16, when the regiments of provost guard, under command of Col. William Cogswell, took up their march as rear guard to the Fourteenth Corps. Everything having been moved through Atlanta, we marched via Decatur, and encamped ten miles from Atlanta. November 17, moved at 7 a. m. via Lithonia, and camped at Conyers Station 8.30 p. m.; distance, sixteen miles. November 18, moved at 9 a. m. in rear of Fourteenth Corps; crossed Yellow River and encamped for the night on the east bank; distance marched, eight miles. November 19, moved at 7 a m. via Covington; crossed the Ulcofauhachee River and encamped for the night at 5.30 p. m.; distance, ten miles. November 20, moved at 7 a. m. via New-

---

*Nominal list (omitted) shows 2 killed, 7 wounded.

born and Shady Dale; encamped for the night at 5.30 p. m.; distance marched, eighteen miles. November 21, moved at 7 a. m. via Eatonton Factory; crossed Little River and encamped for the night on the south bank at 5 p. m.; distance marched, ten miles. November 22, moved at 7 a. m. via Eatonton; encamped for the night near Meriweather at 6 p. m.; distance marched, seventeen miles. November 23, moved at 7 a. m.; passed through Milledgeville at 11 a. m.; crossed the Oconee River and rejoined our brigade about a mile from Milledgeville; distance marched, eight miles. November 24, moved at 7 a. m. via the Hebron road; encamped for the night three miles west of Hebron at 6 p. m.; distance marched, twelve miles. November 25, moved at 10 a. m.; crossed Buffalo Creek and encamped on the east bank for the night at 5 p. m.; distance marched, six miles. November 26, marched at 6.30 a. m. via Sandersville to Tennille Station, and destroyed railroad track until 6 p. m., and then encamped on the railroad one mile east of Tennille Station; distance marched, twelve miles. November 27, resumed work destroying railroad at 7.30 a. m.; continued until 2.30 p. m., when we marched for Davisborough, where we arrived at 9. 30 p. m. and encamped for the night; distance marched, ten miles. November 28, moved at 8 a. m. back on the railroad toward Tennille to complete the destruction of the road; returned to Davisborough at 8 p. m. and encamped for the night; distance marched, eighteen miles. November 29, moved at 6 a. m. via Spiers Station; encamped for the night two miles west of Bostwick; distance marched, nineteen miles. November 30, moved at 7 a. m. via the Louisville road; crossed the Ogeechee River about two miles south of Louisville, and encamped for the night at 6 p. m.; distance marched, ten miles.

December 1, marched at 7 a. m.; encamped for the night at 5 p. m.; distance marched, fifteen miles. December 2, moved at 7 a. m.; encamped for the night near Buck Head Church at 5 p. m.; distance marched, twelve miles. December 3, moved at 1 p. m., the regiment being part of the rear guard of the corps; marched all night and until 4 o'clock next morning; distance marched, eleven miles. December 4, moved at 7.30 a. m.; encamped for the night at 5.30 p. m. near Crooked Creek; distance marched, five miles. December 5, moved at 9 a. m.; crossed Little Horse Creek and Little Ogeechee River; encamped for the night at 8.30 p. m.; distance marched, sixteen miles. December 6, moved at 8 a. m.; encamped for the night at 6 p. m.; distance marched, eleven miles. December 7, moved at 7 a. m.; encamped near Springfield at 7 p. m.; distance marched, fifteen miles. December 8, moved at 6.30 a. m.; encamped for the night near Eden at 3.30 p. m.; distance marched, fourteen miles. December 9, marched at 7 a. m.; encamped for the night at 6 p. m.; distance marched, eight miles. December 10, moved at 9 a. m. via Savannah road; encamped for the night near the Five-Mile Post; distance marched, ten miles. December 11, went into position in line about four miles from Savannah, where we remained until December 21. At 4 a. m. moved toward Savannah and entered the city just at daylight.

Annexed I have the honor to forward list of casualties for the period herein mentioned.*

Very respectfully, your obedient servant,

THOS. M. WALKER,

Lieut. Col., Comdg. 111th Regiment Pennsylvania Veteran Vols.

Capt. OLIVER T. MAY,

Actg. Asst. Adjt. Gen., 3d Brig., 2d Div., 20th Army Corps.

---

*Shows 1 man wounded.

No. 120.

Report of Brig. Gen. William T. Ward, U. S. Army, commanding Third Division.

HDQRS. THIRD DIVISION, TWENTIETH ARMY CORPS,
Cheves' House, S. C., January 4, 1865.

COLONEL: *

On the 15th day of November I was ordered to march on the Decatur road at 9 a. m., following the troops and trains of the First and Second Divisions. Started about 11.30 o'clock; moved very rapidly to Decatur; made a dinner halt of an hour and a half, and started on toward Stone Mountain; column ahead moved haltingly. We would march half a mile and then halt for an hour. On the road all night; stopped for breakfast near Stone Mountain, and then pushed by First Division to take my place as second in line. Moved pretty well all day; crossed Yellow River toward night; camped near its banks at Rock Bridge Post-Office. November 17, moved at 5 a. m.; Second Division still leading us; passed Sheffield and Summers' Mills; camped four miles from Social Circle; rear of column came in very early in morning. November 18, moved on to Social Circle; detached Third Brigade to destroy railroad (Augusta and Atlanta); Colonel Ross tore up track to Rutledge (seven miles). The First and Second Brigades were several times halted to pile rails on the track and set them on fire. In this way the road was effectually destroyed for about twelve miles. Camped six miles from Madison, Ga. November 19, Second and Third Brigades moved at 5 a. m. to destroy railroad. First Brigade, with trains, moved at 7 a. m. to and through Madison to a camp four miles east of that place on the Eatonton road. Second and Third Brigades joined the First at Madison. November 20, marched in advance to within two miles of Eatonton; went into camp for the night in good season. November 21, raining; moved at 5 a. m. through Eatonton to within ten miles of Milledgeville; camped in pine woods on the Little River. November 22, First and Second Divisions, with trains, passed to our front; the crossing of the river was very slow, the hill being very bad. By order of General Williams moved two brigades (First and Third) into town (Milledgeville), passing trains and leaving the train of my division in charge of Second Brigade, Colonel Dustin; it came in about 3 a. m. November 23, all day in Milledgeville resting. November 24, moved at 6 a. m. across Oconee River; halted until 3 p. m., allowing Fourteenth Army Corps to pass; still in rear of corps; marched on Hebron road. November 25, passed Hebron to Buffalo Creek; division still in rear; bridge burned; went into camp in good season. November 26, moved at 6 a. m.; division in rear of corps; took up pontoons over Buffalo Creek; reached Sandersville at 2 p. m.; went into camp. November 27, division in charge of corps trains and artillery; marched to Davisborough, fourteen miles; went into camp early, getting everything in at an early hour. November 28, marched on Louisville road; still in charge of trains; bridge over Ogeechee destroyed; pontoniers and pioneers at work all afternoon. The Fourteenth Corps train passed us here. November 29, moved at 2 p. m.; crossed Rocky Comfort; passed through Louisville; went into camp on

* For portion of report (here omitted) relating to operations about Atlanta, see Vol. XXXIX, Part I, p. 678.

Big Creek, where the enemy had destroyed bridge; Second Brigade left at the Ogeechee to guard the pontoon train. November 30, remained in camp all day. By order of Major-General Slocum, commanding Left Wing, moved up Second Brigade and pontoon train; heavy fog settled at night; almost impossible to see five feet ahead. The brigade and trains came into camp at 12 o'clock (midnight).

December 1, marched at 1 p. m., division in rear of corps, in charge of cavalry train and General Carlin's train of Fourteenth Corps, Colonel Selfridge's brigade, of First Division, assisting this division to guard the increased train. Marched eight miles; rear in about 3 a. m. December 2, still in rear and in charge of same trains. Marched toward Buck Head Creek; camped within one mile of that stream about dark; ordered to cross that night; order countermanded at 9 p. m. December 3, crossed Buck Head Creek to move ahead of Second in rear of First Division. General Carlin's train ordered to report to its own division. Cavalry train and my Second Brigade ordered to report to General Geary. Moved across Millen and Augusta Railroad, leaving stockade to left; detached First Brigade to destroy railroad; effectually destroyed about four miles by piling fence rails on the track and setting them on fire. Moved into camp near Big Horse Creek; the First Brigade coming in about 11 p. m. December 4, moved, second division in line; went into camp at cross-roads, six miles from Sylvania. December 5, marched at 7 a. m.; passed First Division. Marched eight miles on Springfield road; went into camp at 1 p. m. Second Brigade joined the division about 7 p. m., having marched fifteen miles. December 6, marched in advance of corps fourteen miles; camped at 3 p. m. ten miles northwest of Springfield. December 7, marched again in advance. First Brigade, in advance, went into Springfield; balance of division camped one mile west of the town. Pioneers cleared the road of trees felled by enemy and built foot bridge across Jack's Branch. December 8, division in charge of corps trains; ordered to cross the branch, mass troops, and park trains around the town; 2 p. m., ordered to move at once; roads terrible. Head of column went into camp at forks of road, only six miles, but the rear of column did not come in until 8.45 o'clock the next morning. December 9, detailed Eighty-fifth Indiana, Lieutenant-Colonel Crane commanding, to repair roads ahead of trains. Had orders, if possible, to overtake troops of First and Second Divisions. Moved by Mount Zion Church; marched fifteen miles. Camped in rear of corps, fifteen miles and a half from Savannah. December 10, broke camp at 6.30 a. m. to march in rear of First Division. Moved on main road to Monteith (Ten-mile station, Savannah and Charleston Railroad). Here the General Jackson command was busily employed destroying the track. My division was ordered forward to protect the working party; threw First Brigade in line of battle near Cherokee Hill; received orders to move forward until I came to opposition; was not checked until within four miles and a half of Savannah. Here we ran upon the enemy's works; halted; ordered to form two brigades on right of Jonesville road and to hold one in reserve; this was done: First and Third Brigades in first line; Second Brigade in camp in rear. My left connected with right of First Division; my right with left of Fourteenth Army Corps. The enemy made no demonstration worthy of notice. He fired heavy guns freely, but they did little or no damage.

December 11, order from General Williams, commanding Twentieth Corps, to send a regiment over to Savannah River. Colonel Dustin, commanding Second Brigade, sent Twenty-second Wisconsin, Lieutenant-Colonel Bloodgood commanding. This regiment supported Captain Winegar's battery which, on the 13th [12th] instant, disabled the rebel transport Resolute to such a degree that she fell into our hands. A crew from the Twenty-second Wisconsin was put aboard of her and ran her up to within the week just past. On the 14th instant two regiments were detailed from Second Brigade as escort to a train sent into the country from corps headquarters; they returned same night. December 15, received orders to relieve Carman's brigade, of General Jackson's division. December 16, Colonel Dustin, commanding Second Brigade, relieved Colonel Carman on left of Louisville road at daybreak; the line very long, about 700 yards, and only three regiments to hold it. Colonel Dustin was ordered to complete the works and place his command in as strong position as possible. The brigades at this time were stationed as follows: Third Brigade on the right, First in center, Second on the left, covering a front of about one mile and a half. They retained this position until the evacuation of Savannah. By order of the corps commander the front of this position was frequently and thoroughly investigated. Every avenue of approach to the enemy's lines was ascertained, and reports of these investigations were promptly forwarded to Lieutenant-Colonel Perkins, assistant adjutant-general of the corps. On the morning of December 21, before day, I was notified that the enemy had left his works, that General Geary was in them; I was ordered to push my skirmish line forward to the city and to occupy the rebel pits with my line of battle; this was done. At 11 a. m. I received orders to put my command in camp west of the canal; the troops went in at once, Third Brigade on right, Second in center, First on left, wagon trains parked in rear of troops.

During the march from Atlanta to Savannah my command was subsisted almost entirely from the country. The report of my commissary, and those of my brigade commanders, will show how little we depended on the Government. The subsistence procured was of the best quality, greatly preferable to the army rations. Vegetables, especially sweet potatoes, were abundant, and at no former period has my command been so healthy as it was on reaching Savannah. The quartermaster's reports will show the number of mules and horses taken, and the comparative condition of transportation on leaving Atlanta and on reaching Savannah. Had it not been for the numbers of animals seized, more than half the train must have been abandoned; as it was, the class of animals is not only improved, but they are in fine condition, and with proper feeding are ready for another campaign at any time. As to the amount of cotton destroyed, I think that 5,000 bales would not be an overestimate. Of course, I allow a margin for the unauthorized burning by foraging parties. The amount may have been more than that given, as we kept no record of the amount burned. One thing I am sure of, there was not much left behind us.

Inclosed I transmit brigade, regimental, quartermaster, and commissary of subsistence reports. The report of the Seventy-ninth Ohio is not yet in, that regiment having been detailed since December 19, 1864.

Very respectfully, &c.,

W. T. WARD,

Brigadier-General, Comdg. Third Div., Twentieth Army Corps.

Lieut. Col. H. W. PERKINS,

Assistant Adjutant-General, Twentieth Army Corps.

No. 121.

Report of Col. Franklin C. Smith, One hundred and second Illinois Infantry, commanding First Brigade, of operations September 23–December 21.

HDQRS. FIRST BRIG., THIRD DIV., 20TH ARMY CORPS,
Savannah, Ga., December 26, 1864.

SIR: In obedience to your order of December 24, I have the honor to submit the following report:

The brigade which I have the honor to command was stationed at the railroad bridge across the Chattahoochee River during the interval between September 23 and the commencement of the campaign just ended.

On the 15th of October last I received permission from Major-General Slocum, commanding U. S. troops at Atlanta, to send out foraging parties on the north side of the Chattahoochee River. I subsisted the animals belonging to the post and also those belonging to myself and staff, up to the time of marching, entirely from the country.

November 13, at 4 p. m. I received orders to destroy the railroad from the Chattahoochee River toward Atlanta, and to continue till I met the working party sent out from that city, and then to join the division at Atlanta. November 14, at 9 a. m. I had completely destroyed three miles and a half of the road when we met the party sent from the city. I then moved with my command to Atlanta and reported to Brigadier-General Ward, commanding division, at 5 p. m. November 15, at 1 p. m. I moved my command as rear guard of the column in the direction of Decatur. Nothing worthy of particular mention occurred during the march, except that my entire command subsisted exclusively upon the country until my arrival before this city.

December 10, at this time I had in my train the same amount of subsistence for my brigade that I had at the beginning of the march, though not of the same kind. At the commencement of the campaign all of the animals belonging to the command, public and private, were much reduced, and many of them unfit for service. On the march I kept out foraging parties on the flanks, with instructions to seize all serviceable horses and mules they might find. In this way I replaced the unserviceable animals of the brigade train of twenty-three teams, putting in 120 fresh mules. I replaced the horses of the ambulances, six in number, with good mules. I also put into the ordnance train, which for the time being was assigned to the train of my brigade, thirty fresh animals. I also supplied the regiments with the proper number of pack-mules, sixty in number. Officers who were entitled to horses have been supplied with good ones in all cases where their own had become worn out and useless. I turned over to Lieutenant Thompson, provost-marshal of the division, at various times, seventy-eight horses, most of which were unserviceable, making an aggregate of seizures and captures as follows: Number of mules, 222; number of horses, 75; number of beef-cattle, 280.

On the 10th of December my brigade was in the advance of the column. After crossing the Charleston and Savannah Railroad I deployed the One hundred and second Illinois Infantry, in command of Captain Clay, as skirmishers, and advanced till we were within four miles and a half of this city, where the enemy's works were discovered one mile in advance of the head of the column. The brigade was then deployed in line of battle, the left resting on the road leading into

Savannah and connecting on the right with the Third Brigade near the Charleston and Savannah Railroad. The rebel works on our front were a continuous line of breast-works, strongly built, with heavy head logs, and extended at right angles with the road. In the road was a strong bastion with two embrasures, in which were two long 32-pounder cannon (old style). After dark I reconnoitered the works, and advanced to within 300 yards of the works and found them weakly manned, which I reported to the division commander. By direction of the division commander on the night of the 11th instant I established a squad of sharpshooters on the Savannah road, covering the guns in the bastion. On the night of the 12th these guns were removed from the embrasures and did not appear again during the investment. In obedience to orders received I reconnoitered the position of the enemy in my front during the night time from the 15th to the 19th, and found a swamp or pond of water extending its entire length, varying in depth from two to three feet and a half, and the enemy weak, which I also reported to the division commander, and in which report I also expressed the opinion that I could easily carry this position by assault. At daybreak on the 21st instant I received orders to advance my command, under the supposition that the enemy had evacuated his position. I immediately ordered my picket-line forward to his line of works in my front and found that the enemy had retired, leaving the guns above mentioned in our possession. When informed of this I immediately ordered a guard over the guns and a small quantity of ammunition designed for their use, which guard was relieved by the division picket on the evening of the same day. We moved forward at 8 a. m. from the enemy's works to our present encampment on the north side of the Charleston and Savannah Railroad.

I here beg leave to state that on the 3d day of December I was ordered to proceed north of Millen for the purpose of destroying a part of the Augusta railroad, and was so employed with my entire command for five hours, and burned and destroyed four miles of that road. At other different times during the march my brigade destroyed about two miles of railroad, making in all about nine miles and a half of railroad destroyed by my command.

I am gratified to be able to speak of the general good conduct of my men and their uniform cheerfulness to perform all labor and duty required of them.

Respectfully submitted.

F. C. SMITH,
Colonel, Commanding.

Brigadier-General WARD,
Commanding Third Division, Twentieth Army Corps.

No. 122.

Report of Maj. Hiland H. Clay, One hundred and second Illinois Infantry.

HEADQUARTERS 102D ILLINOIS VOLUNTEERS,
December 24, 1864.

SIR:*

On the following day [November 15] marched with the corps on the great raid through Georgia. During the campaign the regiment ob-

*For portion of report (here omitted) relating to operations about Atlanta, see Vol. XXXIX, Part I, p. 684.

tained its full share of subsistence from the country, consisting of flour, meal, molasses, yams, pork, chickens, turkeys, butter, honey, wine, whisky, and a variety of other articles too numerous to mention here. I think the regiment obtained from the country twice the amount of subsistence that would have been necessary to supply the men during the march. Vast quantities of provisions were unavoidably abandoned on the way, as the men could not well carry more than what their haversacks would hold.

During the raid the regiment captured horses, mules, and cattle as follows: Horses, 78; mules, 68; cattle, 88.

The loss sustained by the regiment in men was 3 captured, 1 severely wounded.

All of which is respectfully submitted.

H. H. CLAY,
Major, Commanding.

Lieut. A. H. TREGO,
Acting Assistant Adjutant-General, First Brigade.

No. 123.

Report of Maj. Henry D. Brown, One hundred and fifth Illinois Infantry.

HEADQUARTERS 105TH ILLINOIS INFANTRY VOLUNTEERS,
Savannah, Ga., December 24, 1864.

SIR:*

At noon on the 15th of November left Atlanta, marching out in the direction of Decatur on the Decatur pike. On the march my command passed through the towns of Decatur and Lithonia on the 15th and 16th of November, crossing a branch of the Ocmulgee River near the latter place, Social Circle and Rutledge Station on the Augusta branch of Georgia Central Railroad on the 18th, Madison on the 19th, leaving the railroad at Madison and passing through Eatonton, a point at the terminus of a branch of the railroad running from Milledgeville. Entered Milledgeville on the 22d and laid over until the morning of the 24th. On the 26th arrived at Sandersville, on the left of the Georgia Central Railroad. Camped at Davisborough on the railroad on the night of the 27th. Passed Louisville on the 29th, a point on the left of the Georgia Central Railroad. On the 30th laid over.

On the 7th of December arrived at Springfield. On the 8th laid over until dark at Springfield. On the 10th moved up within four miles and a half of Savannah, and, meeting the enemy's pickets, a line was formed on the right of the road; my regiment, with the exception of portion of the One hundred and second [Illinois], was on the right of the line. The march was concluded on the twenty-sixth day out from Atlanta. On the 11th and 12th of December my battalion changed its position in the establishment of the lines.

During the march forage was abundant and regular details were made to secure it. The men and officers subsisted almost entirely from the country. At Milledgeville my command was detailed and assisted in the destruction of rebel property. Several thousand stand of arms were destroyed, together with a quantity of ammunition; also

---

*For portion of report (here omitted) relating to operations about Atlanta, see Vol. XXXIX, Part I, p. 685.

twenty casks of salt, which were thrown into the river. While before Savannah my command threw up two lines of breast-works on the 17th and 20th instant.

Captain Forsyth, of Company H, was sent out in charge of ten men on a reconnaissance, on the night of the 18th instant, in front of the One hundred and fifth Regiment and on the right of the brigade. He proceeded to within twenty yards of the enemy's line, encountering a deep swamp in front of their works. He observed their fires and heard them talk. After drawing their fire, he returned with his men, having accomplished all that was practicable in the darkness of the night. The entire distance marched by my regiment cannot exactly be arrived at, but it will not fall far short of 400 miles.

The general good conduct of officers and men I am pleased to commend to your favorable consideration, especially on account of the manner in which they bore the fatigue and privations of a long march.

Hoping that the above may prove satisfactory, I have the honor to be,

Very respectfully, your obedient servant,

H. D. BROWN,
Major, Commanding Regiment.

Lieut. A. H. TREGO,
Actg. Asst. Adjt. Gen., 1st Brig., 3d Div., 20th Army Corps.

No. 124.

Report of Col. Henry Case, One hundred and twenty-ninth Illinois Infantry.

HEADQUARTERS 129TH ILLINOIS VOLUNTEER INFANTRY,
Savannah, Ga., December 25, 1864.

LIEUTENANT: In response to the order requiring me to make a report of the recent campaign, with approximate estimates of forage, horses, mules, &c., captured, so far as my regiment is concerned, I submit the following:

While our brigade was in camp at Chattahoochee bridge I was in charge of only one forage expedition. The amount of corn obtained on that expedition was about 4,500 bushels.

During the afternoon of the 13th of November my regiment completely destroyed about half a mile of the railroad lying between the Chattahoochee River and Atlanta. Our brigade broke camp the next morning and proceeded to Atlanta, and marched thence, on the recent campaign, on the 15th of November. Proceeding easterly we arrived at Madison on the 18th; thence we moved in a southeasterly direction and reached Milledgeville on the 22d. We marched thence on the 24th, and passed through Sandersville on the 25th, Louisville on the 29th; rested the 30th.

Passed Buck Head Church December 3 in the morning, and on the same day our brigade destroyed about one mile and a half of the railroad leading from Millen to Augusta; reached Turkey Creek about 4 p. m. December 6, and arrived within shelling distance of the works of the enemy, four miles from Savannah, about 10 a. m. on the 10th instant. Here the head of the column halted, and my regiment was sent forward, deployed as skirmishers, to reconnoiter the works of the enemy. I advanced to within eighty rods, when coming within full view of their works and encountering a heavy abatis on my left and wide and deep swamp on my right, I halted my skirmish line; was relieved at 9 p. m. same day, and went into camp with the brigade that night about one mile and a quarter behind the skirmish line previously held by my regiment. Our forces remained here in camp until the 21st instant, when, the enemy having evacuated Savannah, we came into the city and encamped in our present position.

The distance marched by us, from the Chattahoochee to Savannah, was 280 miles.

No casualties in my regiment, except Private Davis, Company A, was accidentally shot by some one foraging near the road November 18, and died that night; also a private of Company F was accidentally shot in camp, but not mortally.

It will be very difficult for me to give estimates of horses, mules, forage, &c., captured by my command during the march, but the following will at least approximate the actual results: Corn seized, 100 bushels; blade fodder, 1,500 pounds; rice, 1,000 pounds; fresh pork, 8,000 pounds; sweet potatoes, 50 bushels; molasses, 100 gallons; horses, 8; mules (quartermaster's department), 12; mules and horses for companies, 15. Of this number many were turned into brigade headquarters by orders, and afterward some were killed, as I understand, but the exact number I cannot now state.

Very respectfully,

H. CASE,
Colonel, Commanding Regiment.

Lieut. A. H. TREGO,
Actg. Asst. Adjt. Gen., 1st Brig., 3d Div., 20th Army Corps.

No. 125.

Report of Lieut. Col. Samuel Merrill, Seventieth Indiana Infantry.

HDQRS. SEVENTIETH INDIANA VOLUNTEER INFANTRY,
Savannah, Ga., December 24, 1864.

SIR: I have the honor to report that on the 1st day of November I resumed the command of the Seventieth Indiana, which, for six weeks previous, had been in charge of Maj. Z. S. Ragan. At that date the aggregate present of the regiment was 413, which was increased to 532 on the 5th by an addition caused by a consolidation with the Twenty-seventh Indiana. On the 14th we left the Chattahoochee River, reaching Atlanta the same day. On the 15th, the time of moving from Atlanta, there were nine animals in my possession, for which, in the fifteen days previous, there had been drawn only three days' rations, as the twelve days' rations were foraged from the neighboring regions. Thirteen animals were added to the above number, making in all twenty-two, for which the Government has furnished no rations, but forage was collected from the country to supply their wants.

The number of rations issued to the men of the command I have no means of ascertaining. Since the organization of the regiment the supply of food has never been so abundant as during the recent campaign.

The health of the command has been excellent, the average number unfit for duty being less than 1 in 100.

The daily report of the regiment has been no casualties.

Very respectfully, your obedient servant,

S. MERRILL,
Lieutenant-Colonel, Comdg. Seventieth Indiana Volunteers.

Lieut. A. H. TREGO,
Acting Assistant Adjutant-General.

No. 126.

Report of Col. Daniel Dustin, One hundred and fifth Illinois Infantry, commanding Second Brigade.

HDQRS. SECOND BRIG., THIRD DIV., 20TH ARMY CORPS,
Savannah, Ga., December 27, 1864.

SIR:*

November 15, pursuant to orders of the day before, the brigade moved out from Atlanta at 9 a. m., taking the Decatur road, the Third Division in the rear, and the Second Brigade in the center of the division. The march was seriously embarrassed by the trains, and with frequent and tedious delays was continued until 8 a. m. of November 16, when, after halting two hours for breakfast, the march was resumed, the Third Division in the center, the Second Brigade in advance. The roads were bad, and the progress of the column still seriously impeded by the trains. The brigade encamped at 8 p. m. near Rock Bridge, on Yellow River, having made twenty-five miles from Atlanta in the two days' march. November 17 moved at 6 a. m., passing through Sheffield and Summers' Mill, crossing Big Haynes Creek shortly after noon. March continued through the night until 3 o'clock in the morning of November 18. After halting for a short rest and breakfast, the brigade moved forward at 6 a. m., striking the Augusta and Atlanta Railroad at Social Circle at an early hour in the morning. Passing on toward Rutledge the brigade was halted near that town and destroyed, by tearing up and burning, nearly two miles of railroad track, then again moving forward and going into camp in good season about six miles west of Madison. November 19, broke camp at 5 a. m., and after marching a short distance were halted and commenced destroying railroad track. This destruction was very complete and extended to within half a mile of the railroad depot at Madison. Passing through Madison the brigade went into camp on the Milledgeville road four miles from Madison. November 20, marched at 6 a. m., Third Division in advance, Second Brigade in rear of division deployed in the trains. Encamped two miles north of Eatonton at dark, having marched fourteen miles. November 21, moved at 5 a. m., a heavy rain falling seriously affecting the roads; Third Division in advance, Second Brigade in advance of division. Eatonton is the terminus of a branch railroad intersecting the Central railroad at Gordon, and —— miles distant from the latter place. Encamped at 3 p. m. on the Little River, ten miles from Milledgeville, November 22. Here the brigade was detained by the crossing of the trains on the pontoon until 4 p. m., when it moved forward on Milledgeville road, Third Division in rear, Second Brigade in rear of division deployed on trains. The march was continued through the night with frequent detentions on account of the trains, the advance regiment of the brigade reaching Milledgeville about 10 p. m., the rear regiment arriving at 7 o'clock in the morning. The night was severely cold, and there was much suffering among the men.

November 23, remained in camp during the day; weather very cold. November 24, the brigade moved at 6 a. m., crossing the Oconee River, and then halting to allow the Fourteenth Corps to pass, until 3 p. m., when it moved forward slowly, greatly impeded by the trains on the

---

* For portion of report (here omitted) relating to operations about Atlanta, see Vol. XXXIX, Part I, p. 687.

Hebron road; Third Division in rear, Second Brigade in center; roads generally fair; marched until 3 next morning, making but twelve miles. November 25, rested three hours, moving again at 6 a. m., Third Division in advance, Second Brigade in advance of division; moved through Hebron to Buffalo Creek, where our advance exchanged a few shots with the enemy; went into camp, all the trains having crossed the creek except those of the Third Division, Twentieth Army Corps. November 26, broke camp at 6 a. m., crossing the creek at 10 a. m. and halting for the pontoon bridge to be taken up; moved forward to Sandersville, Third Division in rear, Second Brigade in rear, reaching Sandersville at 4.30 p. m. At this place our column was joined by the Fourteenth Corps from the left. November 27, broke camp at 7 a. m., the Third Division taking charge of the trains of the whole corps, the First and Second Divisions being detached destroying railroad track, Second Brigade in center of the division; made fourteen miles over a good road, crossing to the south side of the Central railroad, arriving at Davisborough at 7 p. m. November 28, marched at 6 a. m. on Louisville road, Second Brigade in advance, First and Second Divisions still at work upon the railroad; arrived at the Ogeechee River at 12 m.; the bridge having been destroyed by the enemy, the column was halted, and the brigade went into camp in good season with orders to be ready to move at 8 next morning. November 29, detained by crossing of trains until 10 p. m., when the brigade crossed, and, under orders, went into camp, remaining to guard rear of train and pontoon bridge and train. November 30, remained in camp until 7 p. m., when the brigade moved forward, taking pontoon train; crossed Rocky Comfort Creek, passed through Louisville at 9 p. m, and encamped about 12 m. near Dry Creek, three miles east of Louisville.

December 1, remained in camp, waiting for the passage of the trains, until 3 p. m. Brought up trains of Twentieth Corps, one division Fourteenth Corps, and General Kilpatrick's cavalry; Third Division in rear, Second Brigade in center. Crossed Big Creek and went into camp at midnight about one mile east of the crossing, having made eight miles during the day. December 2, moved at daylight, crossing Baker's Creek and passing through the most difficult swamp yet found; Third Division in rear, Second Brigade in advance of division; roads good, except the swamp just mentioned. Went into camp at dark near Jones' Creek, about one mile west of Buck Head Creek, having marched fifteen miles. December 3, moved at 7 a. m., the brigade having been ordered to report to General Geary, commanding Second Division. By his orders took charge of cavalry train of 240 wagons, crossed Buck Head Creek; passed Millen prison camp about noon, leaving Millen to the south; crossed the Augusta and Millen Railroad about dark, taking the Sylvania road, and going into camp about midnight four miles east of Millen. December 4, broke camp at 6.30 a. m., crossed Big Horn and Little Horn Creeks, still guarding cavalry train; marched eight miles. December 5, moved at 6.30 a. m. in the same order as for the past two days; rejoined the division and went into camp at 7 p. m., having marched fifteen miles. December 6, broke camp at 6 a. m., Third Division in advance, Second Brigade in advance of division; moved about thirteen miles, going into camp at 3 p. m. in a pine forest ten miles northwest of Springfield. December 7, broke camp at 8 a. m., Third Division in advance, Second Brigade in rear; crossed Turkey Creek, marched ten miles, and went into camp near Springfield at 4 p. m. December 8, remained in camp until noon for the First and Second

Divisions to pass; moved six miles, Second Brigade in center of division; went into camp about 11 p. m. December 9, broke camp at daylight, Second Brigade in advance; Eighty-fifth Indiana was detached and sent forward to repair the roads for the trains. The work was severe and constant, and the faithful manner in which it was performed was very creditable to the officers and men of the regiment. Moved fourteen miles, and went into camp at dark sixteen miles from Savannah. December 10, broke camp at 7 a. m., and marched to within five miles of Savannah on the Savannah and Augusta dirt road, crossing the Charleston and Savannah Railroad ten miles from the latter place. Here our advance, coming upon the enemy's troops, went into position. The Second Brigade being in reserve, went into camp in good season in rear of the line of the First and Third Brigades of our division.

December 11, remained in position until dark. In obedience to orders from corps headquarters the Twenty-second Wisconsin was detached and sent to Gibbon's plantation, on the Savannah River, to support a battery and blockade the river. At dark the brigade moved forward into the first line connecting the right of the First Brigade with the left of the Third Brigade, midway between the dirt and rail road, the general direction of the line of battle being nearly north and south. December 12, remained in position. December 13 [12], the battery supported by the Twenty-second Wisconsin attacked three boats attempting to pass the blockade—one being a gun-boat, the other two side-wheels, one armed. The unarmed boat was soon disabled by the battery, and the other two abandoned her, our forces immediately taking possession of her and her crew. The Twenty-second Wisconsin at the river took possession of rice mills on the river, and by details from the regiment commenced operating them, contributing very materially toward relieving the embarrassment of the subsistence department on account of the scarcity of supplies. This work was energetically prosecuted under direction of Lieutenant Harbert, acting commissary of subsistence of the Second Brigade, by details from the brigade. Line of battle corrected and advanced, Second Brigade again in reserve. December 14, by direction from corps headquarters two regiments, Eighty-fifth Indiana and Nineteenth Michigan, Colonel Crane commanding, made an expedition eight miles and a half into the country with twenty-four wagons, returning in eight hours with the wagons loaded with staves. December 15, remained in position. December 16, at 7 a. m. brigade moved to the left of the Augusta dirt road, occupying partially completed works just then evacuated by the Second Brigade, First Division, Twentieth Army Corps (Colonel Carman), connecting on the right with the First Brigade of our division and on the left with the First Brigade, First Division, Twentieth Army Corps. Picket-line 500 yards in advance of line of battle, and within 500 yards of the enemy's line of battle. December 17, remained in position. Details from the regiments were set to work, and the unfinished breastworks in front of the brigade put in good condition for defense. December 18, received the following order from division headquarters:

CIRCULAR.] HEADQUARTERS THIRD DIVISION, TWENTIETH ARMY CORPS,
Near Savannah, Ga., December 18, 1864.

To-night each brigade commander will send out to his front a reconnoitering party to ascertain every avenue to the enemy's position. A written report of the investigation will be sent to these headquarters by 9 a. m. to-morrow.

By command of Brig. Gen. W. T. Ward:

JOHN SPEED,
Captain and Assistant Adjutant-General.

In pursuance of which, after a careful personal examination of the ground by the colonel commanding, the following report was made:

HDQRS. SECOND BRIGADE, THIRD DIVISION, TWENTIETH ARMY CORPS,
Near Savannah, Ga., December 20, 1864.

CAPTAIN: I have the honor to submit the following report for the information of the general commanding:

This brigade (Second) has three regiments in line, the Twenty-second Wisconsin being detached and upon duty at Gibbon's plantation, on the Savannah River. The right of our line rests upon the Savannah and Augusta dirt road, connecting with the left of the First Brigade of this division (Colonel Smith), the left connecting with the right of the First Brigade, First Division, of this corps (Colonel Selfridge), with a front of 740 yards. The general direction of our line of battle is a little east of north, and is very well fortified. Our front is covered by a picket-line of 2 commissioned officers and 170 men, connecting on right and left as indicated above, and is 400 yards in advance of the line of battle, the intermediate ground being covered with pine. The ground is dry, with no serious obstacles to an advance in line of battle. In front of the entire length of our picket-line is an open space, probably 800 yards in width on our right and gradually widening toward the left. The enemy's line of battle (fortified) is just in the edge of the woods upon the opposite side of the open space just referred to, and continues (toward the left) along the edge of the woods, about half our brigade front. From this point toward the left their line is plainly visible in this open space. In front of the right of our picket-line there is an almost impenetrable slashing of timber 100 yards in width, and extends toward the left nearly half the front of our brigade. Between this slashing and the rebel skirmish line, there is a basin of water from 75 to 100 yards in width, the depth of which has not been ascertained. This basin of water widens and evidently deepens toward the left, where three flood-gates are plainly visible, indicating that this basin of water has been used for the purposes of irrigation.

On the 19th instant I made a careful personal examination of the ground. The same has been done by other officers of my staff and command. The ground to within a short distance of the enemy's picket-line has, I think, been very thoroughly explored. I have reason to believe that between the rebel skirmish line and their line of battle there is a ditch or canal, extending from the bridge on the main road toward the river. In my judgment an advance in our front for the purpose of assaulting the enemy's works would be extremely difficult and its success doubtful.

This report was very fully confirmed by facts transpiring with the evacuation, excepting perhaps the distance between the picket-line of this brigade and the enemy's line of battle. December 19, upon application of the colonel commanding permission was granted to build a new line of works 500 yards in advance of the old and the line laid out. From this new line our musketry, together with the artillery assigned to that part of the line, would have greatly controlled, if not rendered quite untenable, the enemy's lines in our front. December 20, work on new line commenced by details from the regiments, and energetically prosecuted through the day and night. December 21, early in the morning it having been discovered on the left that during the night the enemy's works in their front had been evacuated our skirmish line was advanced under direction of Lieutenant-Colonel Crane, Eighty-fifth Indiana, division officer of the day. Finding the works in our front empty the brigade was immediately moved forward, being the first to occupy the enemy's works in front of our division. Their artillery along the whole line in our front was abandoned and left standing in the embrasures. After halting in the works two hours the brigade was moved forward and went into its present position one mile northwest from the city, the brigade being in the center of the division. The picket-line of the brigade occupies the line of rebel works spoken of above, and consists of one commissioned officer and eighty-five men. December 25, the Twenty-second Wisconsin was relieved from duty on the river and rejoined the brigade.

During the march the brigade destroyed about ten miles of railroad track. Being without the usual facilities for this work, it was done under considerable disadvantage and much hard labor; it, however, was accomplished most effectually, and reflected great credit upon officers and men for their energy and zeal. I have the honor herewith to forward the reports of Major Hobbs, surgeon in chief of the brigade, Lieutenant Wing, acting assistant quartermaster, and Lieutenant Harbert, acting commissary of subsistence. From Lieutenant Wing's report it will be seen that the whole number of horses and mules and the amount of forage procured on the march is as follows: Horses, 36; mules, 32; corn, 99,312 pounds; fodder, 66,720 pounds. Lieutenant Harbert's report shows the following subsistence stores taken from the country: 150 head beef-cattle, 475 sheep, 8,000 pounds fresh pork, 2,000 pounds bacon, 10,000 pounds poultry, 6,600 bushels sweet potatoes, 5,000 pounds honey, 33 barrels sorghum sirup, 3,000 pounds corn meal, 2,300 pounds flour.

To the constant energy and systematic industry of Lieutenants Wing and Harbert the brigade is under especial obligations, which I take pleasure in here acknowledging. Lieutenant Harbert so managed his department that when the supplies of the other brigades of the division were exhausted, he still had on hand two days' rations of hard bread, having in the meantime satisfactorily supplied the troops with daily issues of sweet potatoes.

I have to express my gratification with the faithful, efficient, and gentlemanly manner in which I have been assisted by my staff officers. For more particular remarks in regard to the execution of the duties of the different staff departments, I desire to refer to the letter of advice by the brigade inspector, a copy of which is herewith transmitted.

In closing this report I desire to say that while my position has been somewhat embarrassing by being separated from my regiment and placed in command where I was comparatively a stranger, I am exceedingly well pleased with the brigade, and do not hesitate to pronounce it one of which any brigade commander may well be proud. The Twenty-second Wisconsin, Nineteenth Michigan, and the Eighty-fifth Indiana must be reckoned among the best troops in the service. For the well-known bravery in face of the enemy of the Thirty-third Indiana Veteran Volunteers, it will always be entitled to honorable mention. For its laxity in discipline, the present officers are by no means wholly responsible. The evil is of long standing, and therefore difficult to eradicate. The men are generally possessed of noble impulses, with pride and ambition to secure a good reputation in all that pertains to the true soldier; but to accomplish this they stand in great need of the proper direction and control from competent officers. Whether Lieutenant-Colonel Burton will inaugurate and prosecute this work to a successful issue remains to be seen.

Respectfully, your obedient servant,

DANL. DUSTIN,
Colonel, Commanding Brigade.

Capt. JOHN SPEED,
Asst. Adjt. Gen., Third Division, Twentieth Army Corps

No. 127.

Report of Lieut. Col. James E. Burton, Thirty-third Indiana Infantry.

HDQRS. THIRTY-THIRD INDIANA VETERAN VOLUNTEERS,
Savannah, Ga., December 26, 1864.

SIR:*

This date [November 15], under command of Colonel Dustin, commanding Second Brigade, Third Division, Twentieth Army Corps, we struck tents early and prepared for the march, which began at 9 a. m. We moved out on the Decatur road. The march was very slow, as the movement of the train was not yet regulated. Halted at 3.30 p. m. on the right of the road for dinner. At about 5 o'clock moved out again, passing through Decatur about dusk. After the corps had passed through many of the buildings were wrapped in flames. November 16, 1864, our march continued all night. Went into camp about eight miles east of Stone Mountain. Forage was nearly all taken by the forage forces of previous expeditions. Company A was detailed as foragers November 16, 1864. November 17, 1864, there was but little system in the management of the immense wagon train and troops, as we marched all day without stopping for dinner or supper. November 18, 1864, marched till 3.30 p. m., halted, and bivouacked for the night, having passed through Social Circle at noon, halting one hour for dinner. Here we found plenty of forage for both soldier and stock. After dinner moved out again. Reached the railroad at Rutledge Station, where the duty of destroying the road was assigned to the Second Brigade. The brigade destroyed about one mile of the road by making large rail fires; went into camp as above stated. November 19, 1864, the Thirty-third Indiana, with Second Brigade, was detailed to destroy the railroad. The day was wet and disagreeable; still the brigade destroyed the road as far as Madison, a distance of four miles. Passed Madison about 2 p. m. and camped for the night four miles from the town. November 20, 1864, the Second Brigade was deployed out along the train, four men to each wagon. The road was rough, and the movement of the train was very slow. The regiment did not halt till after dark; marched in a southerly direction. November 21, 1864, moved at 5 a. m., the brigade in advance of the division and the Thirty-third in advance of brigade. Passed through Eatonton about 9 a. m. Rained all day. November 22, 1864, we lay in camp till late in the evening, when we took up our line of march for Milledgeville. The regiment was deployed along the wagon train. November 23, 1864, entered Milledgeville, the capital, 3.40 a. m. Lay in camp at this place all day. November 24, 1864, marched at 6 a. m. this morning, crossed the Oconee River, and halted until 3 p. m., when we again moved forward. The march was very much delayed by bad roads through swamps. The weather was very cold, and the fences were set on fire to make the halts more comfortable. Marched till 3.30 a. m; then went into camp. November 25, 1864, at 7 a. m. we again moved out. Seven companies were deployed along the train of wagons, and two companies remained in rear of train as guards. The Thirty-third Indiana, in rear of brigade, marched about five miles and halted from 12 p. m. until 4 p. m., when we again moved to Buffalo Creek, a distance of about one mile, and went into camp for the night. The citizens had burned the bridge, and the army was delayed on that account.

---

*For portion of report (here omitted) relating to operations about Atlanta, see Vol. XXXIX, Part I, p. 688.

November 26, 1864 (the bridge was finished 25th, night), the brigade crossed the bridge, the Thirty-third on left center of the brigade. After crossing the creek, halted till after dinner; moved on again, reaching Sandersville about dark. November 27, 1864, this morning moved from Sandersville in solid column about three miles, and halted on the right of the road till afternoon, when we again deployed along the train. Reached Davisborough Station, on the Macon and Savannah Railroad, about 8 p. m., and went into camp for the night. November 28, 1864, moved out before daylight, Thirty-third Indiana in advance of the brigade; Companies F, D, I, and C were advanced guards, under command of Major Niederauer. As the advance approached the Ogeechee River they were fired into by the enemy from the opposite side of the river, who succeeded in burning the river bridge. The brigade was immediately moved out on the left of the road in an open field, the Thirty-third Indiana in the advance line. The brigade stacked arms, and remained in line of battle until near dark, when they moved to the rear about a quarter of a mile and went into camp in a single line of battle, Thirty-third Indiana on the right. November 29, 1864, the brigade lay in camp until about 5 p. m., when we moved out, the Thirty-third in rear of the brigade. We halted in line of battle on left of road, facing to the rear to guard against surprise. Company H was sent out as flankers on our right; we here waited until about 10 p. m., when all the brigade, except the Thirty-third, crossed the river. The Thirty-third was left on the west side as guards for the pontoon bridge. The pickets were soon posted and the regiment lay down to rest 11 p. m. November 30, 1864, we remained in camp until about 6 p. m., and were ordered to cross the river. After crossing, the bridge was taken up without interruption. We had to pass through a swamp about half a mile in width. During the day we had to pass through several severe swamps. We passed through Louisville, Jefferson County, in the evening. Later in the night a dense fog made the march very slow, and it was with much difficulty that we could keep together. Went into camp 1 a. m.

December 1, 1864, a foraging party was sent out from the Thirty-third, which was successful in getting subsistence for the whole brigade. Still we have swamps to pass on the road. Went into camp about 12 m. at night. December 2, 1864, moved out about day, the brigade in advance of corps and the Thirty-third in advance of brigade; the roads were better than usual; went into camp about 9 p. m. December 3, 1864, the brigade deployed along the wagon train. The Thirty-third Indiana, in rear of the brigade, halted a short time about 1 p. m., moved on till 2 a. m., then bivouacked for the night. December 4, 1864, the brigade was deployed through the train. We were delayed about an hour, waiting the completion of a bridge across the swamp. We crossed late in the evening and went into camp. December 5, 1864, during the forepart of the day the regiment was deployed along the train, but in the afternoon we marched in solid column. December 6, 1864, moved out early, the brigade in advance of corps and the Thirty-third in advance of the brigade. Received orders to carry four days' forage. We passed through large swamps, where forage is very scarce. The enemy blockaded the road, which delayed our movements but little, as the obstructions were easily removed. December 7, 1864, our march was more rapid to-day than usual; marched about fifteen miles and went into camp at dark. December 8, 1864, we lay in camp until afternoon. The regiment was again deployed. The Third Division detailed to guard the whole corps train. Marched in single file. We passed through Springfield, county seat of Effingham County; the road runs through very bad swamps, and it was with much difficulty that we got the train along; went into camp about 10.30 p. m. December 9, started on the march early; the road was almost impassable. The Eighty-fifth Indiana, the advance-regiment, was detailed to repair roads. The Thirty-third Indiana was pushed forward on double-quick to a cross-road about one mile in advance to guard against any surprise or attack by the enemy. We came up as the rear of the Seventeenth Corps passed. Company F was stationed on the road leading in from the right about 100 yards from the crossing, and Companies G and B, under Major Niederauer, were advanced across the main road leading to Savannah about 150 yards. We were soon relieved by the Nineteenth Michigan, of the Second Brigade. We moved on the Savannah road about one mile and halted for dinner. After dinner we moved about eight miles, and went into camp for the night, camping in line of battle. The road was blockaded to-day most of the way; the enemy planted artillery on commanding points. They kept up heavy firing during the day. December 10, 1864, moved out early, Thirty-third in advance. After the brigade was on the move Companies D and I were sent out as flankers on the right and left of the road. We halted on the right of the road at noon, and lay here till 3 p. m. Moved to the right on the Savannah and Charleston Railroad. December 11, 1864, seventy-five men, under command of Capt. J. T. Fleming, were detailed as foragers. About 4 p. m. the regiment moved to an advanced position. The line of battle was finally established, the left of the Thirty-third resting on the First Brigade and the right resting on the Eighty-fifth Indiana. December 12, 13, 14, and 15, we did not build any works in our front. Scarcely any picket-firing in our front. December 16, the brigade shifted to the left and went into camp in line of battle, the Thirty-third on the right, the right resting on the direct road leading to Savannah. December 17, 18, 19, and 20, during this time a straggling skirmish firing was kept up in our front. The enemy kept up almost a constant fire with artillery with but little effect. December 21, 1864, this morning about 5 we received word that the enemy were gone from our front and had evacuated Savannah. We were ordered to get ready to march immediately. We were soon on the march, the Thirty-third in the advance. The brigade halted at the first line of works in line of battle. About 10 a. m. moved out again, and by noon went into camp half a mile from the city, since which time the regiment has been engaged in building quarters, &c.

Very respectfully, your obedient servant,

JAS. E. BURTON,

Lieut. Col. Thirty-third Indiana Volunteers, Comdg. Regiment.

Capt. A. G. KELLAM,

Actg. Asst. Adjt. Gen., 2d Brig., 3d Div., 20th Army Corps.

No. 128.

Report of Lieut. Col. Alexander B. Crane, Eighty-fifth Indiana Infantry.

HDQRS. EIGHTY-FIFTH REGIMENT INDIANA INFANTRY,

Savannah, Ga., December 23, 1864.

I have the honor to report to you, pursuant to order, the proceedings of my regiment from the occupation of Atlanta to the 21st day of December, 1864, so much of said time as the regiment was under my command, it having been under the command of Maj. J. E. Brant, of the Eighty-fifth Regiment Indiana Infantry, from the time required by report to that date:

I assumed command of the regiment November 11, 1864; it was then encamped within the lines at Atlanta, doing only picket and fatigue duty. The regiment remained there preparing for a campaign until November 15, 1864, when, pursuant to orders, it moved, with the brigade, upon the Decatur road at 9 a. m. The march was hindered by wagon trains, and without making many miles were upon the march until 8 a. m. November 16, when stopped for breakfast, and was again upon the march, with the brigade, at 10 a. m., and camped about 8 p. m. that night. November 17, the regiment marched, with the brigade, at 5 a. m., the march impeded by the movements of the train, and moved on slowly, with long delays, until 3 a. m. December 18, 1864, when encamped under orders to move at 6 a. m. At that hour the regiment moved, with the brigade, through Social Circle nearly into Rutledge, when it stopped and destroyed a portion of the railroad, which it did also after passing Rutledge; then going into camp about five miles west of Madison. November 19, moved, with the brigade, at 5 a. m. about two miles, when the brigade stopped and destroyed railroad very expeditiously and effectively, so far as my regiment was concerned, to within a short distance of Madison, and then moved out upon the Milledgeville road four miles and encamped at 4.30 p. m. November 20, marched, with the brigade, at 6 a. m., guarding wagon train, and camped about two miles north of Eatonton at dark. November 21, marched at 5 a. m. and encamped at 3 p. m. ten miles from Milledgeville. November 22, remained in camp until 4.30 p. m., then moved with the brigade, guarding wagon train; delayed on the road until 3 a. m. November 23, when camped in Milledgeville. The regiment moved from its camp there November 24, at 6 a. m., with the brigade, across the Oconee, where it remained until 3 p. m., and then moved on slowly, impeded by the trains ahead, until 4.30 a. m. November 25, when we stopped, and again marched at 7 a. m. with the brigade, marching to Buffalo Creek, where encamped at 3 p. m. November 26, marched at 8 a. m. with the brigade, and camped at Sandersville at 3 p. m. November 27, marched fourteen miles with the brigade, and camped at dark. November 28, marched with the brigade at 6 a. m., and camped in the afternoon at the Ogeechee River, where the brigade remained until 8 p. m., November 29, when the regiment crossed the Ogeechee one mile and encamped, remaining there guarding the rear of wagon trains until, at 8 p. m., it marched with the brigade through Louisville four miles, and encamped at 1 a. m. December 1.

December 1, marched with the brigade from camp at 3 p. m., guarding rear of train; moving about eight miles, when encamped at midnight. December 2, marched some fifteen miles with the brigade and camped at dark. December 3, moved with brigade about noon, guarding cavalry train, and went into camp at 1 a. m. December 4. December 4, marched with the brigade eight miles, guarding cavalry train. December 5, marched about fifteen miles with the regiment deployed upon the train, guarding it, and camped about dark. December 6, marched with the brigade at 6 a. m., moving thirteen miles, and camped at 4.30 p. m. eleven miles west of Springfield. December 7, marched at 8 a. m. and camped near Springfield at 4 p. m. December 8, moved with brigade, guarding trains, about noon, and made five miles at 10 p. m., when encamped. December 9, marched in advance of brigade and division at 8.30 a. m., and employed my men all day in repairing roads for trains; moved until dark, when encamped about sixteen miles from Savannah. December 10, marched with the brigade at 7 a. m. to within about five miles of Savannah, when went into camp in second line before dark. December 11, remained in camp until 4 p. m., when the regiment moved forward to the first line, and encamped in line of battle. Remained in the same position until December 14, when, by orders, I reported at 8 a. m. with the Eighty-fifth Regiment Indiana Infantry and the Nineteenth Regiment Michigan Infantry at corps headquarters for special duty. At 9 a. m. took charge of twenty-four wagons, and pursuant to order went eight miles and a half and beyond the lines; loaded the wagons with staves and rails; reported back to the brigade at 5 p. m., having made a march of seventeen miles with those regiments in less than eight hours. Remained in original position until December 16, when, at 7 a. m. with other regiments of the brigade, moved to left of the Savannah road and camped in line in some earth-works. The regiment remained in this position until December 21, when it moved to its present camp, one mile northwest of Savannah. The regiment left Atlanta with 22 officers and 313 men, and arrived at its present camp without any casualty, and with the same number in good health, excepting three recently sent to the hospital.

The regiment destroyed three-quarters of a mile of railroad during the campaign.

The men endured the hardships of the campaign and its extra labors with cheerfulness—always punctual and well behaved. I feel a compliment due them for their soldierly conduct, when day by day, with inducements to forage all about them, and the example of large numbers of stragglers often within sight obtaining forage, they did not straggle; always present at roll-call before the regiment was dismissed to camp. In only three instances were there exceptions, which were cases of men who, during the laborious night marches, fell asleep by the roadside. The regiment has been in no engagement, and, as a regiment, only under artillery fire the few days we were before Savannah.

I am under obligations to my officers, field, line, and staff, for their uniform courtesy and the satisfactory manner in which they have filled their places and performed their duties. Both officers and men have endured all, confident of success, never imagining a reverse possible.

Respectfully submitted.

A. B. CRANE,

Lieutenant-Colonel Eighty-fifth Regt. Indiana Infty., Comdg. Regt.

Capt. KELLAM,

Actg. Asst. Adjt. Gen., 2d Brig., 3d Div., 20th Army Corps.

No. 129.

Report of Lieut. Col. John J. Baker, Nineteenth Michigan Infantry, of operations September 4–December 21.

HEADQUARTERS NINETEENTH MICHIGAN VOLUNTEERS,
Near Savannah, Ga., December 25, 1864.

CAPTAIN: I have the honor to submit the following report of this regiment from the occupation of Atlanta to December 21:

The day after its entry in Atlanta, September 4, it was temporarily detached from the brigade and ordered to report to Colonel Beckwith, chief commissary Military Division of the Mississippi. By him it was assigned to guard and fatigue duty in the quartermaster and commissary departments, under command of Colonel Crane, One hundred and seventh New York Volunteers, commanding Provisional Brigade. One company (B) was detailed for duty at Soldiers' Home. With this exception, the regiment continued upon this duty until November 14, when it was relieved by Major-General Slocum, and ordered to report to the brigade. It joined the brigade November 15, as it moved from Atlanta, and from that time until December 10 participated in all the marches of the brigade, performing the usual duties of picket and train guard incident to a march.

Captain Baldwin, with his company (D), was detailed for foraging November 18; a portion of his men returned December 19, the captain, with the balance of his company, being then engaged in running a rice mill.

The regiment was not any time in action, and lost no men except one, who was left on guard at a private house November 18, since which time he has not been heard from; it is probable he is captured.

From December 10 until the 21st the regiment, with the brigade, has been camped in line about four miles from Savannah, doing the usual picket duty in front of the enemy's line. At daylight on the 21st the regiment was ordered to move toward the city, the enemy having evacuated. We marched within the rebel works and lay in line a few hours, when we again moved forward, and came to our present camp, one mile from the city.

I am, captain, very respectfully, your obedient servant,

JOHN J. BAKER,
Lieutenant-Colonel, Commanding.

Capt. A. G. KELLAM,
Actg. Asst. Adjt. Gen., 2d Brig., 3d Div., 20th Army Corps.

No. 130.

Report of Lieut. Col. Edward Bloodgood, Twenty-second Wisconsin Infantry.

HDQRS. TWENTY-SECOND WISCONSIN INFANTRY VOLS.,
Savannah, Ga., December 25, 1864.

CAPTAIN:*

Early on the morning of November 15 the entire corps took the Decatur dirt road, and after getting beyond the fortifications stopped for dinner, being delayed by the trains of other divisions; crossed the Atlanta and Savannah railroad about half way between Atlanta and Decatur, and marched all night, only stopping about two hours on the morning of the 16th instant for breakfast. On this day the regiment was in the advance of brigade; marched all day, crossing the railroad again a little south of Stone Mountain and camping for night a mile east of Yellow River at Rock Bridge. 17th instant, broke camp at 3.30 a. m., marching till dark, in an easterly direction, crossing Big Haynes Creek shortly after dinner. 18th instant, marched all day and night with train, reaching Social Circle just after sunrise. Passing through Rutledge, we tore up and burned about a mile of railroad, and camped

---

*For portion of report (here omitted) relating to operations about Atlanta, see Vol. XXXIX, Part I, p. 691.

within eight miles of Madison. 19th instant, broke camp, and after marching a short distance commenced tearing up railroad, which we destroyed clear to Madison, and, passing through this town, went into camp three miles beyond at an early hour. 20th instant, broke camp at 8 a. m., marched all day in a southeast direction, reached camp after a hard day's march about dark, stopping near Eatonton. 21st instant, moved out through rain and mud, marching through Eatonton; traveled ten miles; reached camp at 2.30 p. m. 22d instant, cold and windy; lay in camp until nearly night, when we moved out, crossing Little River (a branch of the Oconee), on pontoons, guarding train. 23d instant, reached Milledgeville, the State capital, just at daybreak; remained here in camp during the day; weather still quite cold. 24th instant, broke camp at 8 a. m., but did not get fairly started until 3 p. m.; crossed the Oconee River on bridge. 25th instant, marched six miles and camped on west side of Buffalo Creek. 26th instant, breaking camp at 8 a. m., reached Sandersville at an early hour, and camped for night. 27th instant, marched at 7.30 a. m., reaching Davisborough, on the railroad, shortly after dark. 28th instant, marched at 6.30, our brigade in advance of the corps. On reaching the Ogeechee, some twelve miles from Davisborough, found the bridges burned by the rebels, and went into camp for night; engineers and pontoniers were at once put to work, and, 29th instant, the troops and trains commenced crossing. The rear of the train did not pass until nearly dark. Just at dark our brigade crossed, camping a short distance beyond the stream at 10 p. m. November 30, remained in camp all day, waiting for trains to pass, and starting at 9 in the evening, passing through Louisville, going very slowly, and camped at nearly morning, having accomplished but five miles.

December 1, remained in camp, waiting for passage of trains, until 3 p. m., and got over five miles of miserable country at midnight. December 2, broke camp at daylight; marched fifteen miles, camping at dark in corn-field west of Jones Creek. December 3, leaving camp at an early hour, and passing near Millen and the prison pen, where our prisoners were confined, keeping north of the Savannah railroad until dark when we crossed it, and, crossing some half dozen swamps, went into camp at midnight. December 4, after a rainy night broke encampment at 7.30 a. m. Our brigade marched as train guard; accomplished six miles over horrible roads. Cannonading can be heard in the direction of the coast. December 5, marched fifteen miles through a dead-level country, heavily timbered with pine; swamps numerous. December 6, broke camp at 5 a. m., our brigade in advance of corps; camped after going but a few miles. December 7, leaving camp at 8 a. m., marched ten miles, camping near Springfield, an unimportant town. December 8, our division in the rear lay in camp until noon, crossed a small creek, and remaining there until sundown, reached camp at 11 p. m. December 9, broke camp at daylight; marched fourteen miles; are getting within striking distance of Savannah. December 10, marching at daylight on an excellent road, we crossed the Charleston and Savannah road ten miles from the latter place. About four miles out our advance struck the enemy's outposts, and skirmishing continued throughout the day. Troops went into position, and our brigade, being in reserve, went into camp in good season. December 11, on the morning of this day, pursuant to orders from corps headquarters, the regiment moved back on the main road, and, accompanied by Battery I, First New York Artillery, which it was to support, took a cross-road leading to the bank of the Savannah River at a point about six miles from the city in a direct line. The object of this movement was to plant the battery in a position commanding the main channel of the river and prevent the enemy's gun-boats that were known to be up the river from getting to the city. The battery went into position and the regiment also, one wing being placed on the right, the other on the left of the guns. A strong earth-work was constructed, and parties were at once sent out to secure all small boats and rice barges (a species of scow) that were in the river, it being rightly foreseen that they would be of use in future. Opposite to us lay an island, several miles in length and from one to two in width. The island (called Argyle) was one grand rice swamp, and was thickly traversed by ditches, dikes, and canals. A large rice mill, just opposite to our position and on the farther or eastern side of the island, was guarded by Company F, Capt. R. T. Pugh. At dark the Third Regiment Wisconsin Infantry, Colonel Hawley, belonging to First Division, Twentieth Army Corps, commenced crossing over to the island, using all the boats collected by the regiment during the day. The Third Wisconsin relieved the guard over rice mills, and they returned to the regiment during the night.

December 12, the forenoon was occupied in strengthening works and collecting boats; guards were also sent to rice mills one and two miles above us on the river-bank. At about 3 p. m. a smoke was discovered some miles up the river, but rapidly nearing. At last they were made out to be three boats, two side-wheel wooden boats and one having the long, low hull and rakish build of a modern gun-boat. As they came within range our battery opened fire and was quickly responded to by the gun-boat, which was behind, and soon after by the second boat in the line. The battery worked rapidly, and by the time the boats had arrived within half a mile two of them had been struck. As they came to a turn in the channel that gave us a raking fire at them there appeared to be some hesitation, which ended in the two rear boats heading up stream, and, putting on full steam, rapidly leaving the boat on the lead to shift for herself, but she was both disabled and aground. This being observed word was at once sent to Colonel Hawley, proposing that he move his men up from the mill on the island and take possession of the boat, as she had gone ashore on Argyle Island, and as there were no boats that were available for that purpose at the regiment. This was done. The boat, Resolute, C. S. Navy, ran up the white flag and was boarded by our men. Her crew consisted of 7 officers and 22 men; she had no armament. The other two boats carried each several guns. A crew was selected from the regiment, who brought her off the bar and moored her just below the battery. Repairs were at once commenced. It was found that two shots had passed through her, and that she was also seriously damaged by colliding with the other boats as they turned round. No further attempt was made by the boats that escaped to get to the city. From this time nothing of importance occurred for some days. A party of the regiment, under the charge of myself, explored Argyle Island to the head, finding canals extending from one channel into the other. December 21, Savannah was occupied by the U. S. forces. The rebel gun-boats below the island were burned before the occupation. The enemy still hover about the South Carolina shore, and there is some skirmishing across the channel that separates Argyle Island from the shore. December 22, 23, and 24, remained in camp, sending guard of 100 men to first rice mill on river. December 25, broke camp at 10 a. m. and joined brigade in outskirts of the city.

During the past campaign there have been no casualties in this regiment. It numbers 315 men present. There is but little sickness and no deaths.

Appended is a table of distances from point to point, gathered from the most reliable sources within reach, and extending from Atlanta to Savannah:

	Miles.
Atlanta to Decatur	7
Decatur to Rock Bridge	14
Rock Bridge to Sheffield	13
Sheffield to Social Circle	14
Social Circle to Rutledge	7
Rutledge to Madison	9
Madison to Eatonton	20
Eatonton to Milledgeville	21
Milledgeville to Hebron	18
Hebron to Sandersville	10
Sandersville to Davisborough	10
Davisborough to Louisville	12
Louisville to Millen	30
Millen to Springfield	40
Springfield to Savannah	30
Atlanta to Savannah	255

Hoping the above will meet your approval,

Most respectfully, your obedient servant,

E. BLOODGOOD,
Lieutenant-Colonel, Commanding.

Capt. A. G. KELLAM,
Acting Assistant Adjutant-General.

No. 131.

Report of Col. Samuel Ross, Twentieth Connecticut Infantry, commanding Third Brigade.

HDQRS. THIRD BRIG., THIRD DIV., 20TH ARMY CORPS,
Savannah, Ga., December 27, 1864.

CAPTAIN:*

On the 15th of November this brigade, with the division and corps, left Atlanta on the campaign which terminated on the 21st of December in the capture of Savannah. We marched east through Decatur, passed Stone Mountain, crossed the Yellow River, through Rock Bridge to Social Circle, from Social Circle to Rutledge, a distance of seven miles. This command destroyed the Georgia State Railroad with short intervals. The destruction was thorough and complete. The ties were taken up and burned in piles, the rails laid on the piles, and bent so as to make them useless. The railroad buildings at Rutledge and Social Circle were also destroyed. The next day we destroyed about a mile of railroad with side track, at Madison; also some railroad buildings and 100 bales of cotton; marched thence southeast through Eatonton across Little River to Milledgeville, where we halted one day, crossed the Oconee River, passed Hebron, Sandersville, and Davisborough; crossed the Ogeechee River, thence through Louisville, and crossed the Augusta and Millen Railroad about three miles north of the latter place, thence to Springfield, and thence southeast toward Savannah, before which we arrived on the 10th of December, and formed line of battle on the right of the division, connecting with the Fourteenth Corps, facing east, with our right on the Georgia Central Railroad. Our picket-line was advanced to within 300 yards of the enemy's works. A strong line of works was constructed, and we lay under

*For portion of report (here omitted) relating to operations about Atlanta, see Vol. XXXIX, Part I, p. 69'

fire of the enemy's batteries until the morning of the 21st of December. At sunrise of that day I received orders from General Ward to advance my picket-line. The advance found that the enemy had evacuated their works during the night. We captured 36 prisoners (among whom were 2 officers), 5 large guns, and 1 brass piece, with ammunition. My men removed six torpedoes, two on the railroad track and four on the turnpike road leading into the city. I shortly after received orders to move my brigade toward the city and encamp it, which I did.

The casualties during the campaign are as follows:*

Since my command left Atlanta it has subsisted mainly from the country. Up to the time of the capture of Savannah ten days' rations only had been issued by the commissaries. On the march foraging parties were sent out daily from each regiment and found ample supplies, subsistence stores of all kinds, and forage. But four days' rations of forage were brought from Atlanta, and up to the date of this report all the forage that has been used has been taken from the country. I have estimated that the troops of my command have procured from the country 62,000 rations and 13,000 days' forage. It is proper to state that the supplies thus obtained were equal in quantity to double rations.

My command captured from the country 21 serviceable horses and 65 mules; besides these a number of animals were taken, which were used on the march and abandoned; also 150 head of cattle and 50 sheep.

Recapitulation.—Captured from the enemy and the country:

Artillery: Number of guns	6
Prisoners	36
Rations of subsistence	62,000
Days' forage	13,000
Horses	21
Mules	65
Cattle	150
Sheep	50

Casualties: Officers—wounded (since dead), 1. Enlisted men—wounded, 2; missing, 18. Total, 21.

I have the honor to be, captain, very respectfully, your obedient servant,

SAML. ROSS,
Colonel Twentieth Connecticut Infantry, Comdg. Brigade.

Capt. JOHN SPEED,
Assistant Adjutant-General.

No. 132.

Report of Lieut. Col. Philo B. Buckingham, Twentieth Connecticut Infantry.

HDQRS. TWENTIETH REGT. CONNECTICUT VOL. INFANTRY,
Savannah, Ga., December 24, 1864.†

At 7.30 a. m. [November 15] it moved out on the Decatur road with the Left Wing, Army of Georgia, to take part in the campaign which has just terminated in the capture of Savannah. The march was continued the first twenty-four hours, with only a halt for dinner at Decatur.

*Nominal list (here omitted) shows 1 commissioned officer mortally wounded, 2 enlisted men wounded, and 18 enlisted men missing.

†For portion of report (here omitted) relating to operations about Atlanta, see Vol. XXXIX, Part I, p. 692.

On the third day we reached Social Circle, where the brigade was directed to destroy the railroad, and the regiment assisted in destroying it for some six miles, working from 10 a. m. till dark, and then rejoined the division, ten miles in the advance. On the fourth day we reached Madison, where the regiment destroyed the switch track and some two miles of the main road, working from 9 a. m. till noon. The fifth day we reached Eatonton, and the seventh day Milledgeville, where we remained in camp, resting one day. On the 26th of November we reached Sandersville, and the following day arrived at Davisborough. The 29th we passed through Louisville, and on the 2d of December encamped at night near Birdville.

December 3, crossed railroad near Millen, and on the 8th passed through Springfield. On the 10th we encamped in line of battle within four miles of Savannah. The 11th we moved forward nearly a mile, immediately in front of the works of the enemy, and built rifle-pits, where we remained under the fire of the artillery of the enemy till the morning of the 21st, when, in conjunction with the corps, we entered the city of Savannah without opposition, the enemy having evacuated it on the previous night.

Only one casualty occurred in the regiment while in front of the city; Lieut. Henry Lewis, of Company K, was severely wounded in the leg. Eight enlisted men fell out on the march on the first night and have not since joined the regiment.

When we left Atlanta Company F of this regiment, under command of Captain Tarr, was detailed to report to Captain Sackett, acting commissary of subsistence of this brigade, and was engaged in foraging under his directions till we reached the works in front of Savannah, when it was relieved and rejoined the regiment. Parties were detailed daily, under the charge of a commissioned officer, to forage for the regiment, and in this way the officers and men obtained nearly all the supplies required.

Including the rations in the hands of the men when leaving Atlanta, the regiment has drawn during the campaign as follows, viz, six days' rations of salt meat, twelve of bread, twenty-one and a half of coffee, eleven of sugar, and eleven of salt.

Thirty-five horses and mules were captured and turned over to the brigade quartermaster during the march.

The following is a list of casualties since the date of last report: Commission officers wounded, 1; enlisted men missing, 9; aggregate, 10.

I am, sir, very respectfully, your obedient servant,

PHILO B. BUCKINGHAM,

Lieut. Col. Twentieth Connecticut Vol. Infty., Comdg. Regiment.

Capt. C. H. YOUNG,

Acting Assistant Adjutant-General.

No. 133.

Report of Lieut. Col. Elisha Doane, Thirty-third Massachusetts Infantry, of operations September 5–December 21.

HDQRS. THIRTY-THIRD MASSACHUSETTS VOLUNTEERS,

Savannah, Ga., December 24, 1864.

SIR: In accordance with circular received at these headquarters, I have the honor to submit the following report:

This regiment entered Atlanta Monday, September 5, and was immediately assigned to duty as guard at the military prison upon Peach

Tree street. Monday, September 12, it was relieved from this duty and ordered to report to Col. W. Cogswell, Second Massachusetts Volunteers, post commandant, for duty as provost guard. The regiment was continued upon this duty during the occupation of the city by our forces. During this period no foraging parties were sent out, but a small detail accompanied two general foraging expeditions and brought in each time a wagon load of corn fodder.

November 16, the regiment broke camp and started upon the march with the other regiments of the provost guard in the rear of the Fourteenth Corps. It moved on the line of the Augusta railroad as far as Covington; thence south, through Eatonton to Milledgeville, reaching the latter place November 23. At this point the regiment joined the brigade and has since remained with it.

Daily foraging expeditions were sent out from November 18 to December 10, inclusive. During the march the regiment was supplied almost entirely from the country. The following is as accurate a statement as I am able to give of the supplies so obtained: 330 bushels potatoes, 2,800 pounds fresh pork, 10 bushels corn meal, 5 barrels sorghum, 3 barrels beans, 375 chickens and other poultry, 8,250 pounds corn; also 3,200 pounds fresh beef received from brigade commissary.

The number of horses, &c., captured was as follows: 3 horses, 3 mules, 19 head of cattle.

I have no destruction of railroad to report, not having been detailed for that purpose during the march.

The report of the regiment since leaving Milledgeville is simply that of the brigade.

I have to report no casualties or skirmishes during the march or since arriving before this place.

Respectfully, yours,

ELISHA DOANE,
Lieutenant-Colonel, Commanding.

Lieut. P. E. WATSON,
Aide-de-Camp.

No. 134.

Report of Lieut. Col. Lester B. Faulkner, One hundred and thirty-sixth New York Infantry.

HEADQUARTERS 136TH NEW YORK VOLUNTEERS,
December 27, 1864.

CAPTAIN: I have the honor to submit the following as my report of the operations of my command since leaving Atlanta:

We left that place on the 15th of November, and, without incident worthy of special notice, marched about sixteen miles per diem until we reached Milledgeville, which occurred on the 22d of November. Having remained there until the 24th in the p. m. of that day, the march was resumed, but more moderately. We struck the Savannah and Charleston Railroad on the 11th of December, and on the same day took up position in rear of Savannah, where, subject to some annoyance from the enemy's shells, we remained until the 21st, when, the enemy having evacuated the city, we marched in, and afterward camped on the northwest side of the city, where my command now remains. With the exception of six and a half days' hard bread, ten days' coffee, eight days' sugar, seven days' bacon, and eight days' salt, my command subsisted during the march upon provisions taken from the country.

I am, captain, yours, respectfully, &c.,

LESTER B. FAULKNER,
Lieutenant-Colonel, Commanding.

Capt. C. H. YOUNG,
Actg. Asst. Adjt. Gen., 3d Brig., 3d Div., 20th Corps.

No. 135.

Report of Lieut. Col. Edwin H. Powers, Fifty-fifth Ohio Infantry.

HDQRS. FIFTY-FIFTH REGIMENT OHIO VOL. INFTY.,
Savannah, Ga., December 24, 1864.

CAPTAIN:*

On the 15th day of November, 1864, this regiment started (with the brigade to which it is attached) on the campaign through Georgia. Arrived at Social Circle on the 18th, where it destroyed about a quarter of a mile of railroad track. On the following day arrived at Madison, where it destroyed about ten rods of track and burned a building containing about fifty bales of cotton. Arrived at Milledgeville, Ga., November 22, where it remained until November 24; then marched in the direction of Savannah via Louisville and Millen. Arrived outside the defenses of Savannah on the 10th day of December, 1864, where it remained building and occupying breast-works until December 21, when (the city having been evacuated) it went into camp about three-quarters of a mile northwest of the city of Savannah, Ga.

During the recent march this regiment obtained from the country, upon estimation, as follows: Meat (of various kinds), 11,900 pounds; flour, 1,000 pounds; sweet potatoes, 300 bushels; corn meal, 500 pounds, besides other vegetables of various kinds of which I have no data upon which to estimate the amounts. The regiment (aside from two companies which were detached with the train) captured—mules, 8; cattle, 10. From the companies detached at the train were detailed men whose special duties were to make captures of horses and mules, and the result of their labors in that direction will probably be obtained from Lieutenant Tabor, brigade acting assistant quartermaster, under whose direction they operated.

The casualties in the regiment during the march from Atlanta were three men missing.

Very respectfully, your obedient servant,

E. H. POWERS,
Lieut. Col. Fifty-fifth Ohio Vol. Infantry, Commanding.

Capt. C. H. YOUNG,
Acting Assistant Adjutant-General, Third Brigade.

---

* For portion of report (here omitted) relating to operations about Atlanta, see Vol. XXXIX, Part I, p. 693.

No. 136.

Report of Lieut. Col. Samuel H. Hurst, Seventy-third Ohio Infantry, of operations September 2–December 21.

HDQRS. SEVENTY-THIRD REGT. OHIO VET. VOL. INFTY.,
Savannah, Ga., December 24, 1864.

CAPTAIN: In obedience to orders I have the honor to submit the following report of the operations of my command from the time of the occupation of Atlanta to the present date:

This command marched into and occupied a position in the defenses of Atlanta on the 2d day of September, 1864. From that time to the 21st of October the regiment performed picket-duty and worked upon the new line of fortifications projected for the defense of the city. On the 21st of October the regiment joined in an expedition commanded by Col. Daniel Dustin. The expedition went about twenty miles due east, collected over 800 wagon loads of forage, and returned to camp at Atlanta in four days without loss to this command. On the 15th day of November, 1864, this regiment moved from its camp in the defenses of Atlanta and began the march across the State of Georgia, occupying its position in the brigade in the line of march until it reached the defenses of Savannah without a single casualty in the command. The regiment assisted in destroying the railroad at Social Circle and at Madison.

My command subsisted for thirty days almost wholly upon the products of the country through which we passed.

I have to submit the following estimate of animals captured by my command: 10 horses, 20 mules, 6 head beef-cattle.

I have also to submit an estimate of commissaries and forage captured and used by the men and animals of my command: 200 hogs and pigs, 40 sheep, 2,000 chickens and turkeys, 100 bushels meal, 100 gallons molasses, 1,000 pounds honey, 300 bushels sweet potatoes, 2,000 pounds flour, 1,000 pounds sugar, 300 bushels corn, and 1 ton of rough forage.

The expedition was in nowise severe on this command. The health of the men was excellent throughout the campaign.

I have the honor, captain, to subscribe myself your obedient servant,

SAML. H. HURST,
Lieut. Col., Comdg. Seventy-third Ohio Vet. Vol. Infantry.

Capt. C. H. YOUNG,
Actg. Asst. Adjt. Gen., 3d Brig., 3d Div., 20th Army Corps.

No. 137.

Report of Lieut. Col. Frederick C. Winkler, Twenty-sixth Wisconsin Infantry, of operations September 4–December 21.

HDQRS. TWENTY-SIXTH WISCONSIN VOLUNTEER INFANTRY,
Savannah, Ga., December 24, 1864.

SIR: I have the honor to submit the following report of operations, required by circular of 23d instant:

Having pitched camp in Atlanta the 4th of September, my regiment remained there in peace and quiet till October 8, when, pursuant to orders received the night before, I marched it to the Chattahoochee railroad bridge, there reporting to Col. F. C. Smith, commanding post. Here we remained as part of the garrison until November 14, when, having the day previous contributed our quarter of a mile of destruction to the railroad between the bridge and that city, we marched to Atlanta with Colonel Smith, and were there ordered to join our own [brigade] again, which we did. November 15, we started from Atlanta about 10 a. m., and that day and ensuing night wended our way in rear of a laboring wagon train to Stone Mountain. November 16, marched to Rock Bridge and crossed Yellow River. About 10 a. m. November 18 arrived at Social Circle, and there commenced destroying railroad. We worked in different places; destroyed in all about half a mile's length. November 19, arrived at Madison and again destroyed a short piece of road immediately adjacent to the town, perhaps 250 or 300 yards. November 22, we arrived at Milledgeville. November 26, at Sandersville. November 27, at Davisborough. November 29, crossed the Ogeechee and marched through Louisville.

December 6, arrived at Springfield, and on the 10th in front of Savannah, where we took position. The next day the brigade was advanced and my regiment placed on the extreme left of the line. December 12, I was ordered to take my regiment to the right of the brigade and there take position between the Savannah and Charleston and Central Railroads, relieving the troops of the Fourteenth Corps then there. This I did, and there remained somewhat exposed to rebel shot and shell, but without sustaining a casualty, till December 21, when we entered the city of Savannah without opposition.

We captured on the march about one dozen mules and three horses.

As to the amount of provisions foraged, it is impossible to make an estimate; but I can safely say that from the time that we left Rock Bridge until we arrived in the vicinity of Springfield, two men and a pack-mule from each company, sent out daily, brought in sufficient to subsist the command wholly.

The regiment enjoyed the best health throughout the campaign. The ambulance with the regiment was but little used. Two men were with the division hospital ambulances a portion of the time, but there are none of those present with this army in hospital now.

I have the honor to be, very respectfully, your obedient servant,

FRED. C. WINKLER,

Lieut. Col., Commanding Twenty-sixth Wisconsin Volunteers.

Capt. C. H. YOUNG,

Actg. Asst. Adjt. Gen., 3d Brig., 3d Div., 20th Army Corps.

No. 138.

Report of Maj. John A. Reynolds, First New York Light Artillery, commanding Artillery Brigade, of operations September 2–December 21.

HDQRS. ARTILLERY BRIGADE, TWENTIETH CORPS,
Savannah, Ga., December 26, 1864.

COLONEL: I have the honor to submit the following report of the operations of the Artillery Brigade of this corps since the occupation of Atlanta:

With the rest of the corps the batteries entered the city of Atlanta on the 2d day of September, and were placed in the vacated works of the enemy on the east and south sides of the town, where they remained until about the 12th instant, when they were withdrawn and camped together in the northwestern part of the city. Soon afterward the artillery, being in excess of the proportion to infantry, the batteries were reduced from six to four guns each, leaving but twenty-four guns in the brigade instead of thirty-six. This was, however, increased to twenty-eight by the assignment of Battery K, Fifth U. S. Artillery, Captain Bainbridge, with four 20-pounder Parrott guns, to the corps. During the occupation several expeditions were sent out in the country for forage, a battery accompanying each, but meeting with but slight opposition, they were at neither time engaged. Previous to these expeditions being sent, and while our supplies were cut off, the horses of the batteries suffered terribly, many actually dying from starvation, and others being so reduced as to render them utterly unserviceable. Almost an entire new supply of horses had to be obtained. A short time before leaving Atlanta a still further reduction of the artillery was made. Battery K, Fifth U. S. Artillery, Captain Bainbridge; Battery I, First Michigan Artillery, Captain Smith, and Thirteenth New York Independent Battery, Captain Bundy, were relieved from duty with the corps and sent to Chattanooga, leaving but four batteries, two 12-pounders and two 3-inch Rodman, of four guns each.

On the 15th day of November the corps left Atlanta, the batteries being distributed through the column, marching in this manner until reaching the enemy's lines near Savannah, meeting with but slight resistance on the march. The batteries did not fire a gun; but twice only a section was placed in position, the infantry then driving back the enemy until we reached their lines about four miles from town, on the 10th of the present month.

On the 11th the two rifle batteries were placed in position, Battery E, Independent Pennsylvania Artillery, Captain Sloan, near the left of our line on the Savannah River, opposite the upper end of Hutchinson's Island; and Battery I, First New York Artillery, Captain Winegar, opposite Argyle Island, about two miles above. At 7 o'clock on the morning of the 12th instant two gun-boats and a steam transport made their appearance above Captain Winegar's position, coming down the river. Captain Winegar opened fire on them when about 2,500 yards distant, to which the gun-boats replied, using guns of heavy caliber. Captain Winegar succeeded in disabling the transport steamer Resolute, compelling her to surrender; he then directed his fire to the others, which soon turned back, and although several shots were seen to strike the lower one, they continued up the river and out of sight. On the same day Captain Sloan fired a few shots at a steamer crossing the river below him, and also a few shots into the city. On the 16th one section of Battery I, First New York Artillery, crossed the river to Argyle Island and exchanged a few shots with a section of the enemy on the Carolina shore. During the night of the 19th this section crossed to the Carolina shore with a brigade of infantry under command of Colonel Carman. A few rounds were fired at small bodies of the enemy during the 20th. About 3 p. m. a gun-boat came up from the city and opened on the rear of this force on the Carolina shore. Captain Sloan was directed to open on her from his position, and soon compelled her to withdraw. During the nights of the 18th, 19th, and 20th three field-works were constructed for heavy guns, one near the river and two in front of the center of General Geary's line. The last two were on the skirmish line, and being within so short range of the enemy's musketry and artillery the work could only be done during the night. Quite a number of casualties occurred among the working parties, the enemy having correct range with their artillery and using it freely at all times of the night. Works were also made for the light batteries, it being the intention to place them all on the line, and open simultaneously, previous to an assault. Four of the six 30-pounder Parrott guns were placed in the works during the night of the 20th and the other two were being put in, when it was found that the enemy had evacuated in our front, much to the chagrin of some of the artillery officers, who desired to test the accuracy and efficiency of these guns. On reaching the city, the 21st instant, about 10 a. m., the ram Savannah was discovered near the Carolina shore. Captain Sloan's battery, being in advance, took position on the lower end of Bay street and opened fire on her. Some excellent shots were made, though with guns of that caliber (3-inch) it is not probable much damage was done to an iron-clad, as she was reported to be. About 4.30 p. m. Captain De Gress' battery of 20-pounder Parrott guns took position and opened on her, firing with great accuracy. The 30-pounder Parrott guns arriving about sunset also opened on her, but, being so late in the day, with what effect could not be ascertained. It was intended that if she remained in sight to open again on her early the next morning, but during the night she was blown up. Owing to the little use required of the artillery there were no casualties in engagements. Captain Gary and two men of Battery C, First Ohio Artillery, were captured on the 12th instant on Hutchinson's Island, where they had gone to seek forage. One enlisted man of Battery E, Pennsylvania Artillery, died of disease on the march near Madison. The admirable policy of having eight horses on a carriage for a long march over bad roads was clearly demonstrated on this campaign.

The batteries subsisted mainly on the country during the march, securing principally their own supplies and forage. An exact account of the supplies and forage obtained cannot be given, but as near as can be ascertained is as follows: Amount obtained from expeditions sent out from Atlanta: 46,000 pounds corn; 3,000 pounds fresh meat; 50 bushels sweet potatoes. Amount obtained on the march from Atlanta to Savannah: 130,000 pounds corn; 20,000 pounds rice fodder; 10,000 pounds fresh meat; 500 pounds flour; 500 bushels sweet potatoes. Making in the aggregate, 176,000 pounds corn; 20,000 pounds rice fodder; 13,000 pounds fresh meat; 500 pounds flour; 550 bushels sweet potatoes. Animals captured: 40 horses, 100 mules; also 100,000 pounds of cotton destroyed.

The following amount of ordnance stores were destroyed at Milledgeville by Lieutenant Shepherd, ordnance officer Artillery Brigade, Twentieth Corps: 3,500 rounds fixed ammunition for 6-pounder and 12-pounder guns; 20,000 rounds infantry ammunition; 2 boxes Sharps primers; 2,000 pounds powder.

The number of guns found abandoned by the enemy in their works in front of the Twentieth Corps line, extending from the Savannah River to the railroad and from Fort Brown to Fort Jackson and Lawton Battery on the Carolina side, besides those on the gun-boats and ram destroyed, is 89, a list of which I send herewith. Besides these a large number of light and heavy gun carriages, caissons, battery wagons, forges, also a large amount of ammunition, was left here by the enemy.

Respectfully submitted.

J. A. REYNOLDS,
Major and Chief of Artillery, Twentieth Corps.

Lieut. Col. H. W. PERKINS,
Assistant Adjutant-General, Twentieth Corps.

[Inclosure.]

List of guns captured from the enemy at Savannah, Ga., in their works immediately in front of the Twentieth Army Corps about that part of the city occupied by said corps and in the fortifications east of Savannah on the river, including Forts Brown, Boggs, Barton, and Jackson, Lawton Battery opposite Fort Jackson:

* * * * * * *

Recapitulation.—Six 6-pounder rifled guns; four 6-pounder smooth-bore guns, brass; two 6-pounder smooth-bore guns, iron; two 12-pounder Blakely guns; four 24-pounder howitzer guns; three 24-pounder smooth-bore guns; nineteen 32-pounder smooth-bore guns; twenty-one 32-pounder rifled guns; one 32-pounder Blakely gun; three 24-pounder carronades; three 10-inch mortars; thirteen 8-inch columbiads; seven 10-inch columbiads; one 12-pounder smooth-bore gun. Serviceable, seventy-six; unserviceable, thirteen—eighty-nine.

Respectfully submitted.

J. A. REYNOLDS,
Major and Chief of Artillery, Twentieth Corps.

No. 139.

Reports of Capt. Charles E. Winegar, Battery I, First New York Light Artillery, of operations September 2–December 21.

HDQRS. BATTERY I, FIRST NEW YORK LIGHT ARTILLERY,
Savannah, Ga., December 24, 1864.

LIEUTENANT: In compliance to circular from headquarters chief of artillery Twentieth Corps, dated December 23, 1864, I have the honor to submit the following:

On the 2d day of September, 1864, the battery entered Atlanta, Ga., and took position in the abandoned works of the enemy, remaining there until about the 10th day of September, when we moved in the south-eastern part of the city and went into camp, together with the artillery of the corps, where we remained until the morning of October 21, when I was ordered to accompany a foraging expedition under Colonel Dustin, commanding Third Division, Twentieth Corps. Starting at daylight of the same day and moving in the direction of Lithonia, a small station on the Georgia Railroad, passing through the town of Decatur at sundown, we went into camp on a large plantation formerly owned by Clark and known as Clark's plantation, about fifteen miles from Atlanta. Remaining here until the evening of the 23d we succeeded in loading about 900 wagons with forage and provisions within a radius of five miles. About dark the train was put in motion, leading to Atlanta, by Colonel Dustin, my battery acting as rear guard as far as Decatur, where we arrived about 4 a. m. On the morning of the 24th, about 7 a. m., we again started for Atlanta, acting as advance guard, where we arrived about 10 a. m.; went into camp on our old camping-ground, where we remained until the morning of November 13, when we were ordered by Maj. J. A. Reynolds to report to Brigadier-General Geary, commanding Second Division, Twentieth Corps, as the enemy were making demonstrations, both with artillery and dismounted cavalry, on our lines around Atlanta, but in both of the above expeditions there was no expenditure of ammunition or any casualties in my command.

On the morning of the 15th day of November Atlanta was evacuated by the Federal forces, my battery moving with the troops of the Twentieth Corps in the direction of Savannah. When within about twelve miles from Savannah, on the afternoon of December 9, we encountered two small redoubts on the Augusta dirt road, occupied both by the enemy's artillery and infantry. One section of my battery, under Lieutenant Scott, was immediately thrown forward and put in position with a range of about 1,200 yards; the troops of the First Division, Twentieth Corps, were immediately deployed, and scattered the enemy without the use of artillery.

On the morning of the 11th day of December Maj. J. A. Reynolds again directed me to move my battery on the Savannah River, with the Twenty-second Wisconsin Infantry as a support, it being reported that the enemy's gun-boats had made their appearance. On the morning of the 12th day of December, about 8 o'clock, the enemy's gun-boats made their appearance, which afterward proved to be the Macon, armed with four 64-pounder rifle guns and two 32-pounder howitzers; also, the gun-boat Sampson, armed with two 32-pounder howitzers, with their tender Resolute, a small steamer. After an engagement of about three-quarters of an hour, from 2,400 to 2,700 yards, they were forced to retire up the river, leaving their tender behind disabled, together with her officers and crew, numbering about 30, our expenditure of ammunition being 138 rounds. On the morning of December 16 one section, under Lieutenant Scott, was thrown over the river, on Argyle Island, and immediately intrenched themselves. On the morning of the 18th engaged a section of rebel artillery on South Carolina shore. After firing thirteen rounds, silenced their guns at a distance of 1,500 yards, with no casualties. On the morning of the 19th a regiment of rebel cavalry made their appearance about 2,200 yards distance on the South Carolina shore; after firing three rounds case-shot they withdrew out of range. During the day Lieutenant Scott was relieved by Lieutenant Freeman, who I gave command of the four 3-inch guns, having received from Lieutenant Shepherd a battery of six 30-pounder Parrott guns, needing him to see that works were built preparatory to moving the light battery in front of the enemy's works on Augusta road. During the night Lieutenant Freeman was ordered by Colonel Carman, commanding brigade First Division, Twentieth Army Corps, to cross the river to the South Carolina shore and report to Colonel Cogswell, commanding Second Massachusetts Infantry. Went into position; built works, which were completed late in the morning of the 20th. During the day the section was ordered by Colonel Cogswell to fire at different objects, using thirty-two rounds of ammunition with no casualties. One section of the 30-pounder battery, under Lieutenant Adle, was placed in position in Fort No. 1 to reply to one of the rebel gun-boats, which had been reported advancing up the river from Savannah. During the night of the 20th the remaining four guns of heavy battery were placed in position in Forts No. 2 and 3.

Early in the morning of the 21st it was discovered that the enemy had evacuated the night before, when one section of light battery was ordered forward under Lieutenant Scott, who entered the town about 10 o'clock. Also the section under Lieutenant Freeman was directed to cross the river to the Georgia shore and join me at Savannah, but owing to high wind and tide he was unable to cross. During the day the heavy battery was ordered forward and arrived about sundown and was put into position at the foot of Bay street, bearing on the rebel ram Savannah, firing thirteen rounds with good effect with no casualties.

On the morning of the 22d found the ram had been blown up during the night; the heavy battery was taken out of position and brought up at the head of Huntington street, and parked with Lieutenant Scott's section. About 7 p. m. the section under Lieutenant Freeman arrived and parked with the rest of the battery, where we now remain.

Statement showing the expenditure of ammunition and casualties during the recent campaign just closed.a

10-POUNDER.

Date.	Case-shot.	Fuse-shell.	Percussion-shell.	Total.
December 12, 1864	29	47	62	138
December 18, 1864	13			13
December 19, 1864	3			3
December 20, 1864	10	12	10	32

a Casualties, none.

30-POUNDER.

Date.	Case-shot.	Fuse-shell.	Percussion-shell.	Total.
December 21, 1864		9	4	13

All of which is respectfully submitted.

CHAS. E. WINEGAR,
Captain, First New York Artillery.

Lieut. W. H. MICKLE,
Actg. Asst. Adjt. Gen., Arty. Brig., Twentieth Army Corps.

HDQRS. BATTERY I, FIRST NEW YORK ARTILLERY,
Savannah, Ga., December 25, 1864.

LIEUTENANT: I have the honor to report the following list of captures of animals and forage from the enemy during the recent campaign just closed: 15 horses, 15 mules, 500 bushels corn, 2 tons corn fodder, 8 tons rice in sheaf, 50 bushels sweet potatoes, 400 pounds flour, 10 horses and 15 mules turned over to quartermaster's department, 5 horses abandoned.

CHAS. E. WINEGAR,
Captain, First New York Artillery, Commanding Battery I.

Lieut. W. H. MICKLE,
Actg. Asst. Adjt. Gen., Arty. Brig., Twentieth Army Corps.

No. 140.

Report of Lieut. Edward P. Newkirk, Battery M, First New York Light Artillery, of operations September 2-December 21.

HDQRS. BATTERY M, FIRST NEW YORK ARTILLERY,
Savannah, Ga., December 23, 1864.

LIEUTENANT: I have the honor to state that on the 2d day of September, 1864, the battery entered Atlanta, taking position in a fort on Decatur street near rolling-mills, from which place it moved on the 15th of September into park on north side of city.

On the 16th of October marched with troops of the Second Division, General Geary commanding, on forage expedition, also on the 26th of October with troops of First Division, Colonel Robinson commanding, capturing for use of command, in both expeditions, 60 bushels corn and a quantity of corn fodder. The battery remained in park until November 15, expending no ammunition and meeting with no casualties.

On the 15th of November the battery moved from Atlanta with troops of the Left Wing, Army of Georgia, marching with it until the occupation of Savannah, expending no ammunition and meeting with no casualties.

With the exception of dry rations (sugar, coffee, &c.) the command subsisted entirely on the country. During the march the animals were fed 2,000 bushels of corn, besides corn fodder, &c. There were some twenty-five mules turned in through the chief of artillery, Twentieth Army Corps, to Captain Schoeninger, acting quartermaster, for which a less number were received.

The following is a recapitulation of forage and animals captured on march: Corn captured, 2,000 bushels; horses captured, 1; mules captured, 1.

All of which is respectfully submitted.

E. P. NEWKIRK,
First Lieut., Comdg. Battery M, First New York Artillery.

Lieut. W. H. MICKLE,
Actg. Asst. Adjt. Gen., Artillery, Twentieth Army Corps.

No. 141.

Report of Lieut. Jerome B. Stephens, Battery C, First Ohio Light Artillery, of operations September 2–December 24.

HDQRS. BATTERY C, FIRST OHIO LIGHT ARTILLERY,
Savannah, Ga., December 24, 1864.

LIEUTENANT: I have the honor of submitting the following report of operations of Battery C, First Ohio Light Artillery, during the time from the occupation of Atlanta to the present date:

On the 2d day of September, 1864, the battery moved into the city of Atlanta and took position in a fort to the south and west of the city. On the 12th of the month left this position and went into camp with the other batteries of the brigade to the west of the city, where it lay until the 21st day of October, when it formed part of the guard of the foraging expedition which went out that day under command of Colonel Dustin, commanding Third Division, Twentieth Army Corps, and was absent four days, returning to camp on the 24th. During the expedition I procured two large loads of corn and about 1,000 pounds pork, 300 pounds mutton, and 15 bushels potatoes. Previous to this two wagons were sent at two different times, and once after, three wagons, procuring during the several expeditions sent out about 270 bushels corn, 2,500 pounds meat, and 30 bushels potatoes. During the time that the battery lay in camp it was put in good order; carriages painted, harness oiled, and by the 15th of October was in every way ready for the field with the exception of horses and mules, which, on account of scarcity of forage, became very much reduced in flesh, and a majority of them died from starvation. On the 2d day of November

I received a new lot of horses and mules, and on the morning of the 15th moved out of the city on the Decatur road with the Twentieth Army Corps, with which we marched during the Savannah campaign, and arrived in front of the enemy's works around the city on the 10th day of December. On the 12th, by order of Major Reynolds, the battery was moved on to the river-bank opposite the head of Hutchinson's Island. From the commencement of the campaign to this date the battery was commanded by Capt. M. B. Gary, who was captured on Hutchinson's Island the 12th with two enlisted men. The battery then fell to my command. On the 14th instant, by command of Major Reynolds, I sent Lieutenant King with a section to report to Colonel Robinson, commanding Third Brigade, First Division, at Cherokee Hill. The balance of battery kept its position on the river until 11 a. m. on the 20th instant, when I received orders to move my battery, except the section at Cherokee Hill, to the city of Savannah, where I arrived at 3 p. m. and went into camp on the west end of Roberts street, where the battery now lies.

During the campaign the command has consumed about the following amount of forage and supplies: 90,000 pounds corn, 30,000 pounds fodder, 300 bushels sweet potatoes, 7,000 pounds fresh meat, and has captured 15 horses, 28 mules, picked up 7 negroes, and destroyed 35,000 pounds cotton. On leaving Atlanta there were 84 horses and 34 mules in the command. There have been 10 horses and 18 mules turned over to Captain Schoeninger and 8 mules to Captain McKell, ordnance officer Third Division, Twentieth Army Corps, and 1 horse died, leaving with the command at this present date 88 horses and 36 mules.

I am, very respectfully, your obedient servant,

J. B. STEPHENS,
First Lieutenant, Comdg. Battery C, First Ohio Light Artillery.

Lieut. WILLIAM H. MICKLE,
Actg. Asst. Adjt. Gen., Artillery, Twentieth Army Corps.

No. 142.

Report of Capt. Thomas S. Sloan, Battery E, Pennsylvania Light Artillery, of operations September 2–December 26.

HDQRS. INDPT. BATTERY E, PENNSYLVANIA ARTILLERY,
Savannah, Ga., December 26, 1864.

LIEUTENANT: I have the honor to submit the following report of operations of this battery from the occupation of Atlanta, September 2, 1864, until the present time:

From the occupation of the city until November 15 the battery was parked with other batteries of the corps in the northeastern part of the city, with the exception of two weeks immediately succeeding its capture, when we were stationed in the works on East Point Railroad. Battery took part in foraging expedition under Colonel Robinson, Eighty-second Ohio Volunteer Infantry, October 16, going as far as Flat Rock Shoals on South River. In the expedition were probably 600 wagons, which were all filled with corn and fodder. One section of battery accompanied another expedition, under General Geary, October 26, proceeding in direction of Lithonia, on Georgia railroad. From these and other expeditions from Atlanta, we received in all about 7,000 pounds of corn for the animals of the battery. We moved from Atlanta November 15, taking the Augusta road. One man died of disease November 18 near Madison. From this date until arriving in front of Savannah December 10 nothing worthy of note in a report transpired. December 13, nineteen rounds of ammunition were expended, mostly thrown into the city. Twenty rounds were fired on the 20th at a boat which had moved up from the city and was annoying our troops on Hutchinson's Island. Battery moved into Savannah December 21. One hundred and twenty rounds were expended on morning of 21st in endeavoring to drive off the enemy from a boat on the river, from which they were unloading supplies. On afternoon of same day battery was moved to West Broad street, where it is now parked.

On the march from Atlanta there were picked up by my command about 8 horses and 15 mules, in all 23 animals. The stock worn out on the march was turned into quartermaster's department.

On the march the animals were subsisted entirely off the country, as were also the men to a great extent. The amount of forage used by my command would foot up about 50,000 pounds. This, with what we secured from expeditions sent out from Atlanta, would make a total of 57,000 pounds corn taken from the country.

All of which is respectfully submitted.

THOS. S. SLOAN,
Captain Independent Battery E, Pennsylvania Artillery.

Lieut. W. H. MICKLE,
Actg. Asst. Adjt. Gen., Arty. Brig., Twentieth Army Corps.

Recapitulation.—Died of disease, enlisted men, 1. Animals picked up, horses, 8; mules, 15. Amount of forage captured, 57,000 pounds. Ammunition (rounds) expended, 154.

No. 143.

Report of Brig. Gen. Judson Kilpatrick, U. S. Army, commanding Third Cavalry Division.

HEADQUARTERS THIRD DIVISION, CAVALRY CORPS,
MILITARY DIVISION OF THE MISSISSIPPI,
Near Savannah, Ga., January 3, 1865.

Capt. E. B. BEAUMONT,
Assistant Adjutant-General, Cavalry Corps:

CAPTAIN: I have the honor herewith to transmit my official report, together with the reports of my brigade and regimental commanders, of the part taken by my command in the recent operations of the Army of Georgia, since leaving Atlanta, up to the occupation of Savannah. I would respectfully call the attention of the major-general commanding corps to the fact that no arms of any kind are to be had at this point, as I expected there would be. The Joslyn carbine, with which the Ninth Pennsylvania is armed, and the majority of my Sharps carbines, are utterly worthless. I earnestly request that 300 Spencer carbines be sent to this point, with as little delay as possible. My troops are worse armed at present than Wheeler's irregular, lawless cavalry. Hoping that the general will be pleased with my report and the operations in it described,

I am, captain, very respectfully, your obedient servant,

J. KILPATRICK,
Brigadier-General, U. S. Volunteers, Commanding Division.

HEADQUARTERS THIRD CAVALRY DIVISION,
MILITARY DIVISION OF THE MISSISSIPPI,
Near Savannah, Ga., December 27, 1864.

CAPTAIN: I have the honor to submit the following report of the part taken by my command in the recent movement of our army from Atlanta up to the occupation of Savannah:

On the 30th of October, in obedience to instructions from headquarters Military Division of the Mississippi, I concentrated my division at Marietta, and commenced at once to fit out a cavalry command for a long and rapid march through the enemy's country. But a few days were given for this important work. Horses, arms, and clothing had to be obtained, and regiments and detachments, widely scattered, ordered in. But by hard work and perseverance, in less than nine days the command ordered was ready for the field. Several regiments had been added to the old regiments and organized into two brigades, each numbering upward of 2,500 men. The First Brigade, Col. E. H. Murray, Third Kentucky Cavalry, commanding, was composed of the following regiments, viz: Ninth Pennsylvania Cavalry, Colonel Jordan; Fifth Kentucky Cavalry, Colonel Baldwin; Third Kentucky Cavalry, Lieutenant-Colonel King; Second Kentucky Cavalry, Captain Forman, and Tenth Wisconsin Light Artillery, Captain Beebe, commanding, amounting to 2,800 men. The Second Brigade, Colonel Atkins, Ninety-second Illinois Mounted Infantry, commanding, was composed of the following regiments, viz: Ninety-second Illinois Mounted Infantry, Lieutenant-Colonel Van Buskirk; Tenth Ohio Cavalry, Lieutenant-Colonel Sanderson; Ninth Ohio Cavalry, Colonel Hamilton; Fifth Ohio Cavalry, Colonel Heath; Squadron First Ohio Cavalry, Captain Dalzell, and Ninth Michigan Cavalry, Colonel Acker, amounting to 2,700 men.

I left my encampment at Marietta on the morning of November 14, with 5,500 men and six pieces of artillery; reached Atlanta same day and bivouacked for the night. Was informed by the general-in-chief that Milledgeville was our first objective point; that my command would move on the right of the Army of the Tennessee (the Right Wing); that I was to feint strongly toward Forsyth, cross the Ocmulgee, move on Macon as if to attack it, strike the Georgia Central Railroad and as near Macon as possible, then fall back toward Gordon, destroying track till the arrival of the infantry, when I was to report to the general-in-chief at Milledgeville. Seven days had been given to make the march and diversion indicated. We left Atlanta on the morning of November 15; crossed Flint River and occupied Jonesborough. A portion of General Wheeler's cavalry, and the Georgia militia under General Cobb, was reported to be at Lovejoy's Station. I met and drove back Wheeler's advance next morning and found him in position, occupying the old rebel earth-works constructed by Hood's army on its recent retreat from Jonesborough. Colonel Murray, First Brigade, charged and carried their works, capturing two 3-inch rifled guns (taken from General Stoneman), and killed and wounded a large number of the enemy. Wheeler now retreated in great confusion to Bear Creek Station, where he attempted to halt and make a stand, but Colonel Atkins (Second Brigade), being now in advance, charged him with the Tenth Ohio Cavalry, when he again broke and rapidly retreated with the Georgia militia to Griffin, a distance of fourteen miles.

Wheeler being disposed of for a time, I separated my command, marching on two roads, that the greater amount of cotton, cotton gins, and other valuable property might be destroyed. After pushing well in on Forsyth and being convinced that the impression had been made upon the enemy that our forces were moving directly on that point, I rapidly marched to Planters' Factory, crossed the Ocmulgee, and reached Clinton November 19. Learning that a portion of Wheeler's cavalry had also crossed the river near Macon, and was now in my immediate front, I moved on the road toward the city, forced back Wheeler's cavalry across Walnut Creek; charged and carried a portion of their works about East Macon. The Tenth Ohio Cavalry and Ninety-second Illinois Mounted Infantry, having the advance, did all the fighting and behaved most gallantly. Colonel Atkins, commanding Second Brigade, deserves great praise for the energy and skill displayed on this occasion. The command encamped that night on the railroad and road leading from Macon to Milledgeville, picketing Walnut Creek, one-third of the entire force being employed all night in destroying track. A detachment of Ninth Michigan Cavalry, Captain Ladd commanding, had already struck the railroad at Griswold Station, capturing a train of thirteen cars, loaded with engine driving wheels and springs for same. The station was destroyed; pistol, soap and candle factories burned. The following day occurred the battle at Griswold Station, my command repulsing every attack made by the enemy, both of infantry and cavalry. November 22, Wheeler advanced with his entire corps of cavalry and three brigades of infantry; drove in my pickets and skirmish line, but was finally checked and driven back by the Ninth Pennsylvania Cavalry (Colonel Jordan) and Fifth Kentucky Cavalry (Colonel Baldwin), the saber being principally used. General Walcutt, with his infantry, now came up, and the enemy was driven back beyond Griswold Station. The same day Colonel Atkins, Second Brigade, had some severe fighting on the Macon and Milledgeville road, and effectually prevented any attack on our trains that were this day moving from Clinton to Gordon. November 24, my command marched to Milledgeville and crossed the Oconee. Having met the general-in-chief the day previous at Milledgeville and received instructions from him to move rapidly in direction of Millen, and if possible rescue our prisoners reported to be at or near that point, I moved rapidly in direction of Augusta, crossed the Ogeechee at the shoals, and struck the railroad, November 27, at Waynesborough, the advance, under Captain Estes (my assistant adjutant-general), having destroyed a portion of the track and partly burned the railroad bridge over Brier Creek the day previous. During this march my flanks and rear had been attacked again and again by Wheeler's cavalry, but without serious results, and did not prevent the column from steadily marching on.

We passed through Waynesborough and encamped in line of battle on the railroad three miles south of the town. Several attacks were made during the night upon Colonel Murray's line, but they were repulsed, and did not prevent my people from destroying the track, one battalion of each regiment being detailed for that purpose. Here, to my great regret, I learned that our prisoners had been removed two days previous. It is needless to say that had this not been the case I should have rescued them; the Confederate Government could not have prevented me. After destroying sufficient track to prevent transportation on the road for a few days, I deemed it prudent to retire to our infantry. Accordingly, Colonel Atkins (Second Brigade) was ordered to move out to the intersection of the Waynesborough and Louisville road and there take up position. Colonel Murray was directed to move past Colonel Atkins and take up position in his rear, and so on, in succession, retire from any force that might be sent in pursuit. By some misunderstanding Colonel Atkins moved on without halting, as directed, and the consequence was that two regiments, the Eighth Indiana, Lieutenant-Colonel Jones, and Ninth Michigan Cavalry, Colonel Acker, together with myself and staff, were cut off and partly surrounded. But the brave officers and men of these two regiments by their splendid fighting broke through the rebel lines and slowly fell back, repulsing every attack of the enemy until the main column was reached We moved on, crossed Buck Head Creek, burning the bridge, and halted to feed two miles from the creek. Information soon reached me that Wheeler was crossing with his entire force. Parties were sent out and ascertained this report to be true. I now determined to give him a severe repulse before marching farther, and accordingly took up a strong position and constructed a long line of barricades, with my flanks thrown well to the rear. These dispositions were scarce completed ere the enemy came in sight, and in a few minutes made one of the most desperate cavalry charges I have ever witnessed, but he was most handsomely repulsed at all points, and with but slight loss to my command. This closed the fighting for the day. We moved a few miles farther on and encamped at the first place where forage could be obtained. The enemy made no further attempt to follow. My losses during the incessant fighting for three days and nights were not large. From information gained from scouts, prisoners, and deserters the loss of the enemy is estimated at 600 killed and wounded.

The following day we joined the Left Wing of our army at Louisville. Here we remained in camp several days, resting the men and horses for the first time during the march.

December 2 [1], the command moved on the Waynesborough road, in advance of a division of infantry under General Baird, the object being to cover the movements of our troops, marching in several columns on Millen. A small force of the enemy was encountered and dispersed by the Fifth Kentucky Cavalry, Colonel Baldwin, and Eighth Indiana Cavalry, Lieutenant-Colonel Jones, nine miles from Waynesborough, not, however, without a severe skirmish. On reaching Rocky Creek [December 2] the enemy was found in considerable force on the opposite side. General Baird's infantry came up, and a force of both cavalry and infantry crossed the creek, and simultaneously charged the enemy, who rapidly retreated toward Waynesborough and Augusta, being closely pursued for some distance by the cavalry. December 3, marched to Thomas' Station and encamped for the night, having made such disposition of my forces as to protect General Baird's infantry, deployed for miles along the track and busily engaged with its destruction. Wheeler, who had been encamped between Waynesborough and Brier Creek, moved in the early part of the evening to Waynesborough, and with a portion of his command made a vigorous attack upon one of Colonel Atkins' regiments, encamped upon the railroad three miles south of the town. This attack was easily repulsed, as were several others made during the night. As I had received orders that day from the general-in-chief to make a strong reconnaissance in the direction of Waynesborough, and to engage Wheeler wherever we met him, I directed brigade commanders to send surplus animals and all non-combatants to the wagon train; that in the morning the command would move to engage, defeat, and rout the rebel cavalry encamped at Waynesborough. Accordingly at daylight the following morning we moved out of camp, the Second Brigade, Colonel Atkins, having the advance. The enemy's skirmish line was met, quickly driven in, and finally retired upon his main line, which consisted of dismounted cavalry strongly posted behind long lines of barricades, with their flanks well secured. Colonel Atkins was directed to move forward and take the barricade, but the enemy was found to be more strongly posted than was anticipated, and the first attack was a failure. The Ninety-second Illinois Mounted Infantry was dismounted, the Tenth Ohio and Ninth Michigan Cavalry, in columns of four by battalions, were sent in on the right, and the Ninth Ohio Cavalry was placed in the same order on the left. The Tenth Wisconsin Battery (Captain Beebe) was brought up to within less than 600 yards, and opened on the barricades, and the enemy's artillery, in all five pieces, were forced to withdraw. At this moment, all being ready, the charge was sounded, the whole line moved forward in splendid order, and never halted for one moment until the barricades were gained and the enemy routed. A few hundred yards beyond he made several counter-charges to save his dismounted men and check our rapid advance. At one time he had nearly succeeded, when the Fifth Ohio Cavalry, Colonel Heath, who had been sent out on our right, charged the enemy in flank and rear, when he gave way at all points and rapidly fell back to the town of Waynesborough. Here he was found occupying a second line of barricades, with artillery, as before, and his flanks so far extended that it was useless to attempt to turn them. I therefore determined to break his center. Colonel Murray, having the advance, was directed to make a disposition accordingly. The Eighth Indiana (Lieutenant-Colonel Jones) was dismounted and pushed forward as skirmishers. The Ninth Pennsylvania (Colonel Jordan), in columns of fours by battalion, had the left; the Third Kentucky (Lieutenant-Colonel King) the center; the Fifth Kentucky (Colonel Baldwin) and Second Kentucky (Captain Forman) the right. The advance was sounded, and in less than twenty minutes the enemy was driven from his position, the town gained, and Wheeler's entire force completely routed. The Fifth Ohio, Fifth Kentucky, and a portion of the Ninth Pennsylvania Cavalry followed in close pursuit to Brier Creek, a distance of eight miles from the point where the first attack was made. After burning the bridges above and below the railroad bridge, as well as the latter, the command marched to Alexander and encamped for the night. In this engagement Wheeler's cavalry corps, consisting of four divisions and two independent brigades, as has since been ascertained, was not only defeated and driven a distance of eight miles, but completely routed. The men of my command fought most bravely throughout the day, and it is impossible to single out from among the officers individual cases of gallantry when all did so well. My casualties on this day, as well as on all others, will be found in a separate report accompanying this. Judging from the enemy's killed and wounded left on the field, his loss must have been severe; upward of 200 left in our hands were wounded by the saber alone.

December 5, we marched from Alexander to Jacksonborough, covering the rear of the Fourteenth Army Corps. December 6, Colonel Murray (First Brigade) marched to Springfield, moving in rear of the Twentieth Army Corps. The Second Brigade (Colonel Atkins) moved to Hudson's Ferry. December 7, when near Sister's Ferry, the Ninth Michigan Cavalry (Colonel Acker), acting as rear guard to the Second Brigade, received and repulsed an attack made by Ferguson's cavalry. December 8, Second Brigade crossed Ebenezer Creek, and the whole command united on the Monteith road, ten miles south of Springfield. From this point the command moved in rear of Seventeenth Army

Corps, detachments covering the rear of several army corps, till the army reached the rebel lines and commenced the investment of Savannah. December 13, my command crossed the Ogeechee and Cannouchee Rivers, and marched to attack and capture Fort McAllister. Striking distance had already been reached, a reconnaissance made, and all requisite information gained, when, in accordance with the expressed wish of the general-in-chief, I abandoned my designs of attack, and with my command moved to reconnoiter Saint Catherine's Sound and open up communication with our fleet. This was accomplished before 10 o'clock the same day on which Fort McAllister fell. December 16, the command returned to the vicinity of King's Bridge and went into camp, picketing the Cannouchee and country in direction of the Altamaha. December 17, Colonel Atkins, with upward of 2,000 men of my command, moved, in conjunction with a division of infantry under General Mower, to destroy a portion of the Gulf railroad, and, if possible, the railroad bridge over the Altamaha. Difficult approaches, and a strong force of the enemy which could not be dislodged, prevented the accomplishment of the latter. The railroad, however, was very thoroughly destroyed and the command returned to camp. December 21, the enemy evacuated Savannah, the army occupied the city, and the operations of the cavalry closed.

In carrying out the orders of the commander in chief, and in making the diversions in them indicated, some mistakes may have been made; yet I believe that the principal operations and diversions required of the cavalry have been, throughout the march, successfully accomplished. Certainly it is a fact, that not once has the enemy's cavalry been able to reach the train or flank of one of our many infantry columns. We have three times crossed from left to right, and right to left, in front of our army, and have marched upward of 541 miles since the 14th of November; have destroyed 14,007 bales of cotton, 271 cotton gins, and much other valuable property; have captured two 3-inch rifled guns, and have them now in use; captured and destroyed 865 stand of small-arms; have taken upward of 500 prisoners, and killed, wounded, and disabled not less than 1,500 of the enemy. We have lost 4 officers killed, 6 wounded, and 2 missing; 34 men killed, 153 wounded, and 166 missing.

Before closing my remarks I desire to make favorable mention of my brigade commanders, Colonels Murray and Atkins. Both have at all times faithfully performed the responsible duties that have devolved upon them. Always on duty, attentive to orders, energetic, skillful, and brave; both are educated gentlemen and accomplished cavalry soldiers; both merit promotion.

Lieutenant-Colonel Sanderson and his regiment, Tenth Ohio Cavalry, at East Macon; Colonel Acker and his regiment, Ninth Michigan, and Colonel Jones, Eighth Indiana, when cut off and surrounded near Waynesborough; Colonel Heath and his regiment, the Fifth Ohio, at Buck Head Creek; the Ninety-second Illinois Mounted Infantry, Lieutenant-Colonel Van Buskirk; the Ninth Pennsylvania, Colonel Jordan; the Third Kentucky, Lieutenant-Colonel King; Tenth Ohio, Ninth Ohio, and Ninth Michigan Cavalry, at Waynesborough, December 4, have all, at the various places mentioned, behaved most handsomely, and attracted my special attention. The Second Kentucky Cavalry, Captain Forman, although but a detachment, at Buck Head Creek and at Waynesborough, did the duty of a regiment, and deserves the highest praise.

Captain Beebe, commanding the artillery, and his lieutenants, Stetson, Fowler, and Clark, have performed their duty well and to the satisfaction of their immediate commanders.

I cannot speak too highly of the conduct of my staff. Through the exertions of Captains Dunbar (assistant quartermaster) and Brookfield (commissary of subsistence) my command has always been well supplied. Doctor Wise (surgeon-in-chief of division), Captains Brink (inspector-general), Day (provost-marshal), and my aides, Captain Hayes and Lieutenants Hollingsworth, Oliver, Fuller, and Griffin, have each, in their respective places, more than fulfilled my expectations. Captain Estes, my assistant adjutant-general, deserves special notice, not only for the faithful discharge of his eminent duties but for his reckless daring and invaluable assistance in every skirmish and engagement. This officer deserves and I earnestly hope that he may be promoted.

Accompanying this report will be found a nominal list of killed, wounded, and missing,* also provost-marshal's statement of captures and property destroyed. I also inclose the reports of my brigade and regimental commanders, which I respectfully request may be taken as part of this my official report.

Respectfully submitted.

J. KILPATRICK,
Brigadier-General, Commanding Cavalry.

E. B. BEAUMONT,
Assistant Adjutant-General, Cavalry Corps.

(Duplicate to Capt. L. M. Dayton, aide-de-camp to General Sherman.)

Report of prisoners of war captured and property captured and destroyed by Third Cavalry Division during the campaign terminating with the occupation of Savannah.

November 14–December 14.—233 prisoners of war (1 colonel, 1 major, 4 captains, 7 lieutenants, 220 enlisted men).

November 16.—2 cannon, Rodman, with carriages, and 100 rounds ammunition.

November 16.—3 caissons, captured at Jonesborough and burned.

November 15.—140 stand small-arms, captured from pickets.

November 16.—175 stand small-arms, captured at Lovejoy's, Ga.

December 4.—550 stand small-arms, captured at Waynesborough, Ga.

November 16.—4 boxes fixed ammunition for 3-inch regulation gun, destroyed.

November 28.—1 battle-flag of Fourth Georgia Cavalry, captured at Waynesborough, Ga.

November 21.—4 miles Macon and Savannah Railroad destroyed at, above, and below Griswold, Ga.

November 26.—3 miles Millen and Augusta Railroad destroyed at, above, and below Waynesborough, Ga.

November 21.—1 water-tank, 13 railroad cars, 3 sets engine drivers, 12 car wheels, 20 tons wrought iron destroyed at Griswold, Ga.

November 26.—8 railroad cars and 1 engine destroyed at Waynesborough, Ga.

November 14–December 14.—14,070 bales cotton, 12,900 bushels corn, 80 tons fodder, 36 grist-mills, 27 saw-mills, 271 cotton gins, 160 hides, burned during the campaign.

November 16.—500 bushels corn meal and 50 barrels molasses, rebel commissary stores, destroyed at Jonesborough, Ga.

---

* Nominal list (omitted) shows 3 officers and 12 men killed and 3 officers and 143 men wounded; total 165.

November 21.—1 pistol factory, 1 soap factory, 1 candle factory, 1 foundry, in employ of rebel Government, 400 boxes soap, destroyed at Griswold, Ga.; 12 wagons and carts, and 1 wagon load carpenters' tools, Government property, destroyed at Griswold, Ga.; 1 shoe-blacking factory destroyed at Griswold, Ga.

November 26.—1 wagon shop destroyed at Waynesborough, Ga.; 1 railroad bridge over Brier Creek destroyed, 1 bridge over Big Ogeechee at Flat Shoals destroyed.

November 21.—1 station-house destroyed at Griswoldville, Ga.

November 24.—25 barrels salt destroyed at Waynesborough, Ga.

November 2.—1 bridge over Little Ogeechee destroyed.

I certify that the above report is correct.

W. H. DAY,
Captain and Provost-Marshal, Third Cavalry Division.

ADDENDA:

HDQRS. MILITARY DIVISION OF THE MISSISSIPPI,
In the Field, Savannah, December 29, 1864.

Brig. Gen. JUDSON KILPATRICK,
Commanding Cavalry Division, Army of Georgia:

GENERAL: I have read with pleasure your report just received, as well as those of your brigade commanders. I beg to assure you that the operations of the cavalry under your command have been skillful and eminently successful. As you correctly state in your report, you handsomely feigned on Forsyth and Macon; afterward did all that was possible toward the rescue of our prisoners at Millen, which failed simply because the prisoners were not there; and I will here state, that you may have it over my signature, that you acted wisely and well in drawing back from Wheeler to Louisville, as I had instructed you not to risk your cavalry command; and subsequently at Thomas' Station, Waynesborough, and Brier Creek, you whipped a superior cavalry force, and took from Wheeler all chance of boasting over you. But the fact that to you, in a great measure, we owe the march of four strong infantry columns, with heavy trains and wagons, over 300 miles, through an enemy's country, without the loss of a single wagon and without the annoyance of cavalry dashes on our flanks, is honor enough for any cavalry commander.

I will retain your report for a few days, that I may in my report use some of your statistics, and then will forward it to the War Department, when I will indorse your recommendations and make such others as I may consider necessary and proper.

I am, truly, your friend.

W. T. SHERMAN,
Major-General, Commanding.

No. 144.

Report of Col. Eli H. Murray, Third Kentucky Cavalry, commanding First Brigade.

HDQRS. FIRST BRIGADE, THIRD CAVALRY DIVISION,
Near Savannah, Ga., December 25, 1864.

CAPTAIN: I have the honor to report that the First Brigade, Third Cavalry Division, Military Division of the Mississippi, composed of

Ninth Pennsylvania, Fifth Kentucky, Eighth Indiana, and Third and Second Kentucky Cavalry, left Marietta at 8 a. m. November 14, to follow our indomitable leaders through the Confederacy to the ocean; camped four miles southwest of Atlanta. November 15, moved at 9 a. m.; attacked and drove the enemy from Jonesborough, capturing three caissons filled with ammunition; this was accomplished by the Eighth Indiana and Fifth Kentucky Cavalry. November 16, marched at 8.30 a. m.; struck the enemy two miles from Lovejoy's Station, in force, behind intrenchments with artillery. The Eighth Indiana and Third Kentucky, dismounted, moved upon the works, which were taken possession of by the Eighth Indiana. The Third Kentucky, mounting, made a most brilliant and successful saber charge, resulting in a total demoralization of the enemy, and the capture of two pieces of artillery. The engagement also furnished us with 42 prisoners. The Second Kentucky, Captain Forman, coming up after the charge, pushed on, but only to find the enemy straggling. November 17, marched at 8 o'clock; encamped four miles southwest of Jackson. November 18, marched at 8 a. m.; camped near Cork; the Fifth Kentucky crossing the Ocmulgee River, succeeded in capturing 125 horses and mules. November 19, marched at midnight; crossed the Ocmulgee on pontoons at Planters' Factory; the Second Kentucky was left to protect the division supply train; camped fourteen miles from Clinton; the Ninth Pennsylvania, Colonel Jordan, making a detour to the right, obtained valuable information in regard to the movements of the enemy about Macon. November 20, marched to Clinton, participating in the demonstration that day made by our command on Macon; Captain Hancock, of the Ninth Pennsylvania, with 100 men, making a demonstration, attacking and gallantly combating two rebel regiments, to the right of our line of march on Macon; withdrawing from before Macon, camped near Griswoldville. November 21, took position at Griswoldville; skirmished mildly all day, being in position, tearing up track, destroying a pistol and soap factory of much value to the enemy; encamped three miles from Griswoldville. November 22, the pickets of the Ninth Pennsylvania at early morn were attacked and finally driven back to the encampment of the brigade, where this regiment for some time was earnestly engaged; the regiment fought well an enemy greatly superior in numbers. Their gallantry, stern resistance, and well-timed charge, baffled the enemy in what he supposed would prove to them a successful attack. Making preparations to attack with my whole force, received orders to withhold in order to allow the infantry column of General Walcutt to show themselves, moving in the direction of Griswoldville and Macon. The Fifth Kentucky, with General Kilpatrick, made a demonstration to the rear of the enemy's line of battle. This was the day of magnificent behavior and splendid fighting of General Walcutt's brigade, of General Woods' division, of the Fifteenth Army Corps. During the day, when the enemy, with greatly superior numbers, made such repeated and determined attacks upon General Walcutt, I took the responsibility of moving from camp with two regiments, placing them, one on each flank of our force then engaged, which, at that time, was in imminent danger of being turned.

November 23, marched to Gordon and encamped. November 24, marched to Milledgeville; received rations; thence across the Oconee eight miles, beginning our movement to strike the Augusta and Savannah Railroad. November 25, marched at 8 a. m., reaching the factory at Ogeechee Shoals. The Second Kentucky, which had rejoined us, in advance captured a picket-post of the enemy here. Traveled this day thirty miles. November 26, marched at 8 a. m.; traveled twenty-eight miles, camping two miles and a half south of Sylvan Grove. Here the enemy in force, under Wheeler, attacked the camp of the Eighth Indiana and Second Kentucky. These regiments, under Colonel Jones, of the Eighth Indiana, spent the most of the night in engaging the enemy, which was splendidly and successfully done. Convinced that the enemy in force had attacked me, took up position with barricades for my entire command. At the approach of day received direct orders to commence the march. The withdrawal of the Eighth Indiana and Second Kentucky was effected under heavy fire from the enemy. The enemy, attempting to follow, were effectually checked by the barricades of the Fifth Kentucky and Lieutenant Stetson with his artillery. At that time the enemy, covering my entire front, with two brigades on my left flank, dared not attack. I took up the line of march without the least difficulty or annoyance from them, moving in the direction of Waynesborough, at which point we struck the railroad, and at nightfall camped upon it, a mile and a half in the direction of Millen. The enemy having followed the rear of the Second Brigade all day, we had every reason to expect an attack here; therefore took up a strong position of two barricaded lines; the Third Kentucky, Eighth Indiana, and the Fifth Kentucky in the first line; the Ninth Pennsylvania and Second Kentucky holding the second one, my flanks being well protected by the railroad on the right and a large pond on the left. Not long after we were prepared did we wait; before 11 o'clock the pickets and our entire skirmish line were driven in, and before midnight they had completely enveloped our line and made a charge upon our works. From that until dawn six different and distinct charges were made upon our lines; six different times did they meet with bloody repulses. This was the second night that my command had been engaged, and for several days had been making long marches. The enemy, by reason of the darkness of the night, were unable to ascertain our position only by volleys they received from our Spencer rifles and carbines. At times they rushed within thirty yards of our barricades, with loud huzzahs of "Hunt their damned barricades," "Go for them," "We'll show you how to desolate our homes and burn our towns." I have every reason to believe that this fight was one of immense disaster to them in killed and wounded. Lieutenant Stetson, with his artillery at short range, used four guns; he never fires but what he makes an impression upon the enemy. Part of the Ninth Pennsylvania Cavalry, notwithstanding our constant work with the enemy, was engaged in tearing up the railroad. In accordance with orders from the general commanding, I, at daylight, withdrew, marching in the direction of Louisville.

This was a day of unusual activity. The charge made by that most excellent officer, Capt. John A. P. Glore, with his battalion of the Fifth Kentucky, and the engagements of the Eighth Indiana and Ninth Michigan that morning, was under the direct supervision of the general commanding and reflects great credit upon those engaged. My command formed the rear. This day the enemy seemed determined to do something. The greater portion of our command having crossed Buck Head Creek, they conceived the plan of cutting off and entirely destroying that portion, which, as yet, had not crossed. In this, however, they were sadly mistaken. Gaining a flitting advantage by reason of their heavy flanking columns, the next moment found them disappointed, discomfited, and retiring. The Second and Third Kentucky, our rear, bore the brunt of this attack. The Fifth Kentucky, quickly into line, the Ninth Pennsylvania and artillery into position, the enemy did not see proper to make farther advances, when we marched across the bridge. Here we found Colonel Heath, with his Fifth Ohio, and two howitzers in splendid position, covering the bridge, ready to give the enemy a warm reception and burn the bridge, both of which they afterward did. Moving on some three miles, by direction of the general commanding we halted, went into position, built barricades, and in every way prepared to whip the enemy, who had for two days been annoying our rear battalions, and for two nights had called my entire command from their blankets to give them repulses. The enemy, only delayed by the burning of the bridge, soon effected a crossing at another point and were before us. They made a most handsome attack, first on our center, then on our extreme right, and afterward on our left, each one of which was beautifully repulsed. Having accomplished that for which we halted, by direction of the general commanding we remounted and resumed the march. Hoping to take some prisoners, by my direction Captain Beggs, my acting assistant adjutant-general, directed Colonel Baldwin, commanding Fifth Kentucky, to move into the woods to our left, whence a portion of the rebels who charged our left had fled. This, however, Colonel Baldwin failed to do. Marched and encamped within ten miles of Louisville, the enemy no longer showing themselves. November 29, marched at 6 a. m. to Big Creek, near Louisville; camped near Louisville. November 30, remained in camp.

December 1, marched at 10.30 a. m. in the direction of Waynesborough. Found the enemy, two brigades strong, within four miles. After a stubborn fight. routed him. The action was brought on by Maj. C. T. Cheek, Fifth Kentucky Cavalry, a gallant and experienced officer. Colonel Baldwin, with the rest of his regiment, the Fifth Kentucky, moving forward to the fight, was soon engaged. Colonel Jones, with his Eighth Indiana, pushed forward, with one battalion on each flank of the Fifth and the third one up to their line. They went up in handsome style, met and engaged the enemy with the Fifth, who at that time was being heavy pressed. Moving forward, we encamped three miles beyond. December 2, marched at 7 o'clock. Found the enemy at Rocky Creek Church. He was charged and driven across the creek by Major Breathitt, with his battalion of the Third Kentucky Cavalry, Captain Thomas, with his battalion of the Third Kentucky, crossing the creek, charging the enemy behind barricades, and, together with a battalion of the Fifth Ohio, put the enemy to flight. Traveled fifteen miles and encamped. December 3, marched to Tompkins' [Thomas'] Station. December 4, Wheeler with his entire force being at Waynesborough, five miles distant, by direction of the general commanding, my command stripped for battle, and with our division moved to attack and rout him. The Second Brigade, in advance, my command in a second line within supporting distance, attacked and drove him to the town. Receiving orders from General Kilpatrick to take the town, the Second Brigade, having had their share, wheeled out of the road, and I moved forward to do so. The enemy held splendid positions. The approaches to the town were difficult, by reason of a stream almost impassable, save by the main road or railroad. The Third Kentucky pushing across, went into position on the right, under a heavy fire, the Ninth Pennsylvania forming on the left. In the meantime the Eighth Indiana (dismounted) moved across the stream, through the swamp; Lieutenant Stetson, with his artillery, and Colonel Baldwin, with the Fifth Kentucky, in position on the south side of the stream. The Second Kentucky ordered to follow within supporting distance of the first line. The Third Kentucky, charging on the right, found the enemy in barricades, and were subjected to a fire from front and flank. The Ninth Pennsylvania, pushing on the left, struck the enemy, relieving the Third Kentucky from the flank fire. These two regiments pushed forward in magnificent style. The Eighth Indiana and Second Kentucky moving up inch by inch, the enemy were driven through the town, the Ninth Pennsylvania and Third Kentucky pressing the enemy heavily. The appearance of the Eighth Indiana (dismounted), and the charge of the Second Kentucky, sent the enemy, panic-stricken, from the field. His loss in killed, wounded, and prisoners was heavy, and saved themselves from still more serious slaughter by fleeing to the woods. Having taken full possession of the town and from one to two miles in all directions, the Fifth Kentucky was ordered up, and pushed on the Augusta road, which the majority of the command of Wheeler had taken, following him closely until he had crossed Brier Creek. This was a most magnificent fight. Each regiment did nobly its part, conclusively showing by the manner in which they fought that nothing less than a complete rout to the enemy would be the result of the day's battle. The Third Kentucky lost heavily in the engagement by reason of the barricades, which they most determinedly attacked and carried. Aside from the good resulting from the victory itself, the enemy seemed to be convinced that the destination of the army of General Sherman was Augusta, whence they continued to flee. Taking the Alexander road encamped a distance of five miles.

December 5, marched at 7 o'clock, traveling twenty-two miles; encamped at Jacksonborough. December 6, marched through Sylvania to the Middle Ground road; covered the rear of the Twentieth Army Corps, moving on Springfield; encamped, having traveled twenty-four miles. During the day a scouting party from the Ninth Pennsylvania attacked in the rear, and entirely dispersing it, a small advance guard of the rebel General Ferguson, whose column was moving on this road. Changing his course, however, he attacked the Second Brigade, which was moving in the rear of the Fourteenth Corps. December 7, marched at 9 a. m., traveling eleven miles. December 8, marched at 10 a. m. through Springfield; camped at 12 m. The marches of December 6, 7, and 8 in the rear were hard ones, by reason of the swamps, rendered almost impassable by the march of an army corps over them. December 9, marched at 9 a. m.; passed to the rear of Seventeenth Army Corps; camped eleven miles northwest of Savannah, having traveled twenty-two miles. December 10, marched at 9 a. m. in the direction of Savannah; traveled four miles and encamped. December 11, marched at 7 o'clock.; passed along the canal and to the right of the Fifteenth Army Corps; traveled twenty miles and encamped ten miles southwest of Savannah. December 12, marched at 7 a. m. in the direction of Fort McAllister; camped at McAllister's plantation. December 13, marched at 7 a. m. to Midway. The rebel Colonel Hood, commanding the district composed of the counties of McIntosh, Liberty, and Screven, was greatly discomfited by our presence. His men, stationed at Sunbery, Dorchester, and Riceborough, and Station No. 3, were totally demoralized and fled, reckless of organization, to the Altamaha bridge, whenever attacked. This gave us free access to the ocean. Capt. E. A. Hancock, Ninth Pennsylvania, with 120 men from the brigade, pushed his way to the Altamaha bridge, and, although not able to destroy the bridge itself, burned effectually a long trestle, three-quarters of a mile, and other parts of the track, just this side, rendering by this the bridge useless to the enemy. Returned, bringing with him to camp 17 prisoners. December 14, remained in camp. December 15, marched in the direction of King's Bridge. December 16, marched and went into camp, two miles southwest of King's Bridge.

From Sunbery, our fleet, to be seen in the distance, brings to an end this meager outline of the operations of the brigade it was my honor to command in its passage through the Confederacy and its many engagements from Atlanta to the ocean.

It would be impossible to render unto all, individually, that praise which is due them. All so well have done their part, so nobly fought, a nation's gratitude is due them.

In regimental commanders the brigade has been extremely fortunate. I would beg before closing to call your attention to the following list, especially mentioned, of officers and non-commissioned officers, whose gallantry has come under my special notice, and who have rendered distinguished services throughout the campaign, namely: Col. Thomas J. Jordan, Ninth Pennsylvania, and Lieut. Col. F. A. Jones, Eighth Indiana, for their ability and skill as cavalry commanders and their ready anticipations of orders; Capt. A. G. Sloo and Lieutenant Kelly, Third Kentucky Cavalry, for their gallant conduct in the charge at Lovejoy's, which resulted in the capture of two pieces of artillery. I also take pleasure in commending the gallantry of Capt. E. V. Brookfield, commissary of subsistence, Third Cavalry Division, in this charge; Captain Crowell, of the Eighth Indiana, for gallantry on two different occasions in charging the enemy; Capt. E. A. Hancock, Ninth Pennsylvania, for gallant and meritorious conduct throughout the campaign; Lieut. McJ. Davis, of the Third Kentucky Cavalry, and Lieutenant Bryan, Fifth Kentucky, for their gallantry in charging the enemy at Buck Head Creek; Sergeant Emery, Company H, Sergeant Pepper, Company L, Second Kentucky Cavalry, and Sergt. James H. Taylor, commissary sergeant, Second Kentucky Cavalry, for their gallant behavior on different occasions.

To the efficient, energetic, and brave officers composing my staff, whose duties throughout the whole campaign have been most arduous, who have been exposed to fire in every engagement, I would tender my heartfelt thanks. Therefore, to you I commend Capt. James Beggs, Third Kentucky Cavalry, acting assistant adjutant general; Capt. Samuel Lyon, Second Kentucky Cavalry, acting assistant inspector-general; Lieut. H. D. Gorham, Fifth Kentucky Cavalry, aide-de-camp; Lieut. P. S. Bruner, Third Kentucky Cavalry, aide-de-camp; Lieut. William Waters, Third Kentucky Cavalry, provost-marshal; Captain Baker, Eighth Indiana, acting commissary of subsistence, and Lieutenant Winters, Eighth Indiana, acting ordnance officer, were ever assiduously at work, aside from their regular duties, in almost every engagement.

To Maj. R. M. Fairleigh, chief surgeon of the brigade, for his energy and efficiency displayed in the care of our wounded, I tender my thanks.

To Captain Offutt, Fifth Kentucky Cavalry, commanding pioneer corps, for his promptness, energy, and bravery, I am much indebted.

To Lieutenant Stetson, Tenth Wisconsin Battery, commanding his own section and my two pieces captured from the enemy, I cannot thank too much; throughout every engagement he has shown himself a superior artillerist and a brave soldier. Most heartily would I recommend him for promotion.

Remembering those brave captains, we deeply mourn the loss of Captains Forrester, Fifth Kentucky Cavalry, and White, Third Kentucky Cavalry, who so gallantly fought, so bravely died—the former at Buck Head Creek, the latter at Waynesborough—falling in defense of their country and her honor. Sacred will be their remembrance in the hearts of their comrades and many friends.

In conclusion I would tender to Col. Thomas J. Jordan, Ninth Pennsylvania; Colonel Baldwin, Fifth Kentucky; Lieutenant-Colonel Jones, Eighth Indiana, and Lieutenant-Colonel King, Third Kentucky Cavalry, and Captains Forman and Gilmore, Second Kentucky Cavalry, my heartfelt thanks for the hearty co-operation they have ever given me, and to return through them to the brave officers and men of their different regiments I am proud to command that heartfelt gratitude due them. Feeling assured that never will the hour come when dishonor will be breathed in connection with the First Brigade, but that each day and every battle will but serve to win them new laurels and brighten their fame, I again return to them thanks for their gallantry and soldierly bearing.

For list of casualties, number of prisoners taken, artillery captured, &c., see accompanying report.*

Respectfully submitted.

E. H. MURRAY,
Col. Third Kentucky Cav., Comdg. 1st Brig., 3d Cav. Div., Military Division of the Mississippi.

[Capt. L. G. ESTES,
Assistant Adjutant-General.]

No. 145.

Report of Lieut. Col. Fielder A. Jones, Eighth Indiana Cavalry.

HEADQUARTERS EIGHTH INDIANA CAVALRY,
December 21, 1864.

I have the honor to report that the Eighth Indiana Cavalry left Marietta, Ga., November 14, 1864, with 36 officers and 566 enlisted men. The horse equipments were in poor condition, as also were many of the horses, having been drawn at second-hand and nearly worn out by long and hard service.

On the evening of the 15th of November met the enemy in pretty strong force with artillery behind intrenchments at Jonesborough. After some pretty severe skirmishing, with the co-operation of the Fifth Kentucky, which came in on another road, the enemy was driven from the works and out of town, we picketing for the night. Lieutenant Snyder and one enlisted man were wounded. On the 16th, being in the advance of the division, we struck the enemy a few miles north of Lovejoy's; drove them into the old rebel works at that place. One battalion of the Eighth, dismounted, under Major Gordon, charged and quickly carried the works. This was followed by a charge of the entire brigade. Our route was blockaded by fallen trees and other obstructions, causing us to fail to be "in at the death," yet we captured some prisoners. Thence marched south by easy marches, capturing a few horses and mules, destroying cotton and other public property. Took no part in the attack on Macon; skirmished lightly with the enemy at Griswold. Marched to the capital of Georgia; thence to Sylvan Grove. At the last-named place, at 2 a. m. of the 27th of November, this regi-

* Not found.

ment, being isolated from the division, was attacked by Wheeler's entire force. Three heavy charges of the enemy were handsomely repulsed. Heavy skirmishing was kept up until daylight, when we were withdrawn by order of Colonel Murray. Marched to Waynesborough and was attacked again at night by Wheeler. Skirmished all night. The consequence was my men were sadly in need of rest and sleep.

On the 28th was detailed to cover the rear; marched quietly about three miles, when the rear guard, under Major Herring, was attacked by a strong force. I quickly disposed the balance of my command to cover the withdrawal of Major Herring. This had scarcely been done when the enemy charged our flanks in several columns, and had succeeded in throwing a heavy force on the road between my command and the division. At one time our position was perilous in the extreme. The regiment was separated by the flanking columns of the enemy into four detachments, and the fog was so dense we could not distinguish friend from foe at the distance of twenty paces. Almost every officer in the regiment was thrown upon his own resources, and each gallantly discharged his duties. Each detachment charged the enemy wherever [met] and soon cleared the road and flanks and extricated the regiment from its dangerous position with very little loss, while the enemy, by his own showing, lost in killed and wounded nearly 100 men, including 2 captains, 1 colonel, and General Robertson wounded. The regiment was relieved by Ninth Michigan, but Companies E and G, under Major Graham, detached accidentally from the regiment, remained with the rear all day, and at the church near Buck Head Bridge made a gallant charge, driving the enemy several hundred yards, and materially aided the column in crossing the bridge. My command were spectators only of the fight at Reynolds' plantation, being in reserve. After the battle again took the rear, and I must say that that night's march was the most severe on men and horses I ever experienced, and there was no earthly cause for it, except carelessness of company commanders. At no time that night did the rear march over 300 yards without a halt, and yet the road was good. Got into camp at 1.30 o'clock, having marched eight miles in eight hours and a half.

December 1, skirmished with the enemy; lost 1 man killed, 2 severely wounded. December 4, took part in the battle in Waynesborough. Charged, dismounted, through the town, and with the infantry pursued the routed foe to near Brier Creek. Marched with division in direction of Savannah. Pickets were attacked at Springfield. Captains Crowell and Stanley promptly charged and routed the enemy, killing 3 men, 2 horses, and capturing 5 horses. Near Jacksonborough Lieutenant McManaman, with a small foraging party, charged a detachment of rebels, causing them to throw down their arms and abandon their horses and seek safety in the swamps. The lieutenant destroyed 12 stand of arms and captured 12 horses. Arrived in camp near King's Bridge, December 17, 1864.

Have no complaints to make of officers. They did their duty and have my thanks. As to the brave enlisted men of Eighth Indiana, they have spoken for themselves by heroic action on many a bloody field and need no eulogy from me.

With a tear for our noble dead, a prayer for the speedy recovery of our wounded and the safe return of our captives, I am, captain, very respectfully,

F. A. JONES,

Lieutenant-Colonel, Commanding Eighth Indiana Cavalry.

Capt. J. BEGGS,
Actg. Asst. Adjt. Gen., First Brig., Third Cavalry Div.

No. 146.

Reports of Capts. Joseph T. Forman and Robert M. Gilmore, Second Kentucky Cavalry.

HEADQUARTERS SECOND KENTUCKY CAVALRY,
King's Bridge, Ga., December 21, 1864.

SIR: I have the honor to submit the following report of the movements and actions of my regiment from the 14th of November to December 6:

November 14, moved with the brigade from Marietta, Ga., in the direction of Atlanta, my regiment moving in rear of the brigade. November 15, the brigade moved in the direction of Jonesborough, my command being left with the Ninth Pennsylvania in rear to protect the train. November 16, the First Brigade, having the advance, came in contact with a body of rebel cavalry at Lovejoy's Station on the West Point railroad. Here my regiment was ordered to support a section of artillery. Afterward I was ordered with my command to move forward at double-quick to support the Third Kentucky, which in the meantime had charged the rebels, capturing their artillery and chasing them some four or five miles. My regiment then took the advance, skirmishing with the rebels as far as Bear Creek Station, where it was ordered to halt, rest our horses, and let the Second Brigade take the advance. November 17, moved on the Jackson road without meeting with any resistance. November 18, moved in advance of the brigade with my command in the direction of Ocmulgee River. November 19, crossed Ocmulgee River at Ocmulgee Mills, where I received orders to take my regiment and guard the division train through to Milledgeville. Arriving there on the 24th received orders to join the brigade, which moved in the direction of Sparta, camping some eight miles from Milledgeville. November 25, my regiment moved in the advance on the road to Ogeechee Shoals on Ogeechee River, at which place my advance guard surprised a party of rebels, capturing eight of them, also twelve valuable horses, which were acceptable about that time. We remained at that place during the night.

November 26, my regiment was left in the rear of the command for the purpose of burning the bridge over the river, also a large factory and mill. We then moved on the road to Augusta, meeting no enemy. That night my command, with the Eighth Indiana, was left at the forks of the road for picket, and to hold that position during the night. At 12 o'clock we were attacked by a large body of cavalry, surprising our pickets and moving directly upon our camp. After being repulsed some four or five times they concluded to wait until daylight before making another advance. At that time they attacked and were again repulsed. Finding that they could not move us from our position by attacking in front, they threw a heavy column on our flanks. While they were making this movement Colonel Jones, who was in command, received orders to retire behind the barricades, which were built near brigade headquarters. He gave me orders to mount my regiment and form it across the road; after his command passed to bring up the rear. Before we got fully mounted and moved out the enemy advanced, firing upon our led horses, causing some little confusion. I formed my command (after the Eighth Indiana had passed), moved back by alternate platoons, at the same time checking the rebel advance until we arrived at the barricades, where they were handsomely repulsed and driven off. During this engagement my loss was 1 man captured, 1 mortally and 2 slightly wounded, losing also several horses and equipments. November 27, we moved on the road to Waynesborough, leaving the

Second Brigade to hold the enemy in check. Nothing transpired through the day, and we went into camp about two miles from Waynesborough, having passed through town. In accordance with orders we built barricades for the purpose of holding the enemy in check during the night. They made several attempts through the night to drive us from our position, but were each time driven back.

November 28, at daylight we took up our line of march on the road leading from Waynesborough to Louisville, the enemy following closely and persistently upon our rear, at the same time throwing heavy columns upon our flanks. After we had moved about five miles my regiment was ordered to build barricades, and remain there until the column could pass and bring up the rear, at the same time being supported by the Third Kentucky Cavalry. After the column had passed, the enemy came up in front of the barricade. I opened a heavy fire upon them, driving them back in the road. They then commenced a heavy flank movement upon both flanks entirely secreted from us by a thick woods. Not being aware of this movement, I remained too long at the barricades. I then moved back across an open field, forming behind different barricades that were built in my rear, at the same time checking the rebel column, which was advancing in the road. Directly the enemy made their appearance upon both flanks and front, cutting off my rear from the command, and creating some confusion by firing upon us from every direction. It was impossible for me to get through without scattering my command, as there was a large swamp, and miserable road to move on. There was no place in the road for a mile where we could find open ground enough to form a line to check the enemy's advance. After we had cut through and came to where we could form, the men were easily rallied, formed, and the enemy driven back. In this engagement my loss was 2 commissioned officers and 14 enlisted men. Lieutenant Little was wounded and captured while gallantly doing his duty. I can also speak very highly of the conduct of Lieutenant Adams during the engagement, who was also captured. As far as I can learn, out of the 14 enlisted men lost, 3 were killed and 1 wounded. After moving some little distance farther upon the road, our whole column was halted and formed in order of battle, and an immense barricade built. Here the enemy made a bold front, throwing his whole column forward upon us, when they were suddenly repulsed with heavy loss by our artillery and dismounted cavalry. They were thrown into confusion and driven entirely off. We camped that night about twelve miles from Louisville, the enemy concluding it would be bad policy in following any farther. November 29, my command moved with the brigade, and encamped near Louisville. There we joined the infantry. November 30, remained in camp.

December 1, moved off on the road leading from Louisville to Waynesborough; we soon again met the enemy in force on that road; they charged with heavy column upon our advance, but were repulsed. My regiment was not engaged during the day. December 2, we moved in the direction of Waynesborough, driving the enemy before us. December 3, I was too unwell to remain in the saddle any longer, leaving the regiment in charge of Captain Gilmore. The command moved along the railroad and went into camp four miles from Waynesborough.

In conclusion it is necessary, and but just, that I should say something concerning the conduct of my regiment. Much praise is due the officers and men of my command for the manner in which they have conducted themselves on this weary and tedious campaign. I am not aware of a single man, either officer or private soldier, who deserves any censure on my part, but they have at all times inspired me with a great deal of confidence by their readiness and willingness to obey my commands. Capt. R. M. Gilmore has proven himself to be a gallant and efficient officer, being ever present where duty called him.

I regret exceedingly the loss of Lieut. W. C. Adams and Louis W. Little, lieutenant and adjutant of the regiment, who were beneficial to me on every occasion where true bravery and good counsel were required.

Sergeants Foley, Emery, Pepper, and Gilmore are worthy the praise due good soldiers, and I would recommend them for promotion. They have each been in command of a company since leaving Marietta.

Yours, very respectfully, &c.,

J. T. FORMAN,
Captain, Commanding Regiment.

December 4, I took command of the regiment, as Captain Forman was unable longer to do duty. We moved in the rear of the ambulance train toward Waynesborough. We had not gone very far, however, when the Second Brigade became engaged with Wheeler's forces. Our men, under the command of Colonel Atkins, drove them from one position to another, until we reached a point on the railroad about one mile from town, when the First Brigade relieved the Second Brigade and took the advance. The rebels fought with determination, and it was difficult to drive them from the position they had here taken. After the Third Kentucky had driven them from behind their barricades I was ordered to report to Colonel Murray, commanding the brigade, who was at the time on the skirmish line. He ordered me to charge through town, which order I obeyed as near as I could. While charging, some officer without my knowledge halted two companies, which was half of my command, and sent them to the right. This left me with fifty or sixty men, which I did not discover until I came upon the enemy beyond town, where I halted and formed a line. We remained here for a few hours, and marched on the road to Savannah some six or seven miles, and went into camp. My loss in this engagement was 2 men wounded and 5 horses killed. December 5, moved with the brigade in a southeastern direction and encamped. December 6, the division separated; our brigade taking the right-hand road and passing through the town of Sylvania, we came up with the Twentieth Army Corps. December 7 and 8, moved with the brigade in the rear of Twentieth Army Corps. December 9, I took the regiment on a forage expedition and got lost from the brigade. December 10, I came up with the brigade on the road to Savannah and went into camp with it. December 11, moved with the brigade toward the extreme right of the army. December 12, we moved on as usual, nothing transpiring, and camped four or five miles from King's Bridge. December 13, I moved in the advance of the brigade and marched to Midway Church and encamped. December 14, remained in camp. December 15, remained still in camp until 6 p. m., and we again marched a few miles, and went into camp. December 16, marched with the brigade to camp, where we now remain.

Attached to this you will find a report of casualties.*

Hoping this report will be satisfactory,

I remain, very respectfully, yours,

R. M. GILMORE,
Captain Company E, Second Kentucky.

Capt. JAMES BEGGS,
Acting Assistant Adjutant-General.

---

* Statement (here omitted) shows 6 enlisted men wounded, 2 commissioned officers and 24 enlisted men missing, and 1 enlisted man died of disease.

No. 147.

Report of Lieut. Col. Robert H. King, Third Kentucky Cavalry.

HEADQUARTERS THIRD KENTUCKY CAVALRY,
Near Savannah, Ga., December 16, 1864.

CAPTAIN: I have the honor to submit the following report of the operations of the Third Kentucky Cavalry during the march of the division from Marietta to this point:

The regiment broke camp at Marietta November 14, moving to the right of Atlanta, and encamped four miles from that point on the Macon railroad. The next day we moved to Anthony's Bridge, on Flint River. On the 16th we passed through Jonesborough, following the railroad. About three miles from Lovejoy's Station the advance encountered the enemy. My command was immediately deployed in line on the left of the road, and moved on the enemy for a short distance, when I received an order from General Kilpatrick to advance rapidly and drive the rebels from the station, the general supposing, from a dense smoke arising in front, that they were destroying their stores. I immediately ordered two battalions forward at a trot (Major Wolfley, with his battalion, having been sent in another direction to destroy a bridge over Flint River), and a moment afterward ordered a charge. Never did men obey an order with more alacrity or enthusiasm. They rushed upon the rebels with drawn sabers and a shout that scattered them in the wildest disorder. They fled in every direction of escape, leaving in our hands two splendid Rodman guns and a number of prisoners. The rout of the enemy was complete, and they have since acknowledged it to be disgraceful. Lieutenant Griffin, of the Fifth Kentucky Cavalry, and his brave scouts, were with my command in the charge, and rendered gallant and valuable service in routing the enemy and securing the trophies of the chase. After a short halt we moved forward. Passing Bear Creek Station, we left the railroad to our right, and for several days traversed the country in the neighborhood of Griffin, Forsyth, Jackson, Planters' Factory, and Clinton. On the 20th we moved toward Macon (from Clinton). Late in the evening we participated in a demonstration on Macon, which resulted in driving the enemy and destroying a portion of the Savannah railroad. After night-fall we moved toward Griswoldville and encamped. The next morning we moved to that point and commenced, with other portions of the command, the destruction of the railroad. Several miles of track were torn up, the ties burned, and the rails bent. The depot, several manufacturing establishments, and a large amount of machinery were also destroyed. During our stay some skirmishing (in which we were not engaged) occurred. In the evening moved toward Gordon, camping four miles from that place.

The next evening we were called out to guard the right of General Woods' infantry line, one brigade of which was then engaged with a heavy force of rebels. We were withdrawn at dark (the enemy having been repulsed and severely punished), when we moved out and encamped near Gordon. Remained in camp at Gordon most of the next day. On the 24th we arrived at Milledgeville, and, after remaining a few hours to draw rations, crossed the Oconee River and encamped seven miles from the city. In continuing our march we crossed Ogeechee Shoals, passing through Glascock County, leaving Sparta to the left and Sandersville to the right. We reached Waynesborough on the evening of the 27th, built a barricade near the railroad, and occupied it with my regiment. During the night the enemy made several desperate attacks upon our lines, but were each time handsomely repulsed without loss to us. The Eighth Indiana on our left were several times charged, but the enemy were in every instance driven back promptly. At 5 o'clock next morning we moved in direction of Louisville. During the march (my command, with the Second Kentucky Cavalry, having been left to protect the rear) we were charged in the rear and on both flanks whilst crossing a swamp. Recovering from a momentary disorder, Lieutenant Davis with a small force charged the enemy, driving them back, whilst the balance of the regiment formed on a line with the Fifth Kentucky, then in position. In this charge we lost nine men, one of whom was killed. Moving forward about four miles we went into position on the right of the division. In a short time the enemy attacked the division in front. We were deployed in line, with skirmishers in front, on the extreme right of Colonel Atkins' brigade, but were not engaged. Late in the evening, the enemy having been driven back, we moved out four or six miles and encamped.

The next day moved to Big Creek bridge, near Louisville, where we remained until the morning of December 1, when we moved out in rear of the Eighth Indiana on the Waynesborough road. During the day the enemy were encountered in force by the Fifth Kentucky and Eighth Indiana and driven from the field. The next day (December 2) we moved in the direction of Millen, my command being in advance of the brigade on the left of the infantry. Finding the enemy posted behind barricades at Rocky Creek Church, Major Breathitt, with the First Battalion of the regiment, charged them in gallant style, driving them from their cover and across Rocky Creek. Here the whole command halted until the infantry came up and were posted, when Captain Thomas, with the Third Battalion, took the advance, charged across the creek, and drove the enemy for two miles, dislodging them from three heavy barricades. In this charge we had one man wounded. Moved in the evening a short distance and encamped. The next day we struck the railroad at Thomas' Station, six miles from Waynesborough, where we remained during the night. Sunday morning, December 4, we moved with the division toward Waynesborough "to attack and rout the command of Wheeler," as the general commanding had informed us the evening previous. Leaving every incumbrance behind, we marched on the enemy with the full determination to give him a thrashing which would be a valuable lesson to the mounted chivalry of the South. After the Second Brigade (Colonel Atkins) had encountered General Wheeler's whole force in the morning and driven him from every part of the field, the enemy leaving many of his men (killed, wounded, and prisoners) in the hands of that brigade, the First Brigade moved forward to attack and drive the rebels from the "last ditch." My regiment took the advance, followed by the Ninth Pennsylvania Cavalry. Moving forward rapidly, we deployed to the right, the Ninth Pennsylvania to the left. After my command was formed, ready to charge in column of battalions, I received an order from General Kilpatrick to halt. I did so for a few moments, during which time we were exposed to a most galling fire from barricades in front and from our right and left. No body of men ever stood fire any more resolutely; not a man faltered. At length, the enemy's fire becoming fiercer and many of their comrades falling around them, they disregarded the restraints of discipline and rushed, with wild shouts, upon the enemy in their front. At first we were compelled to fall back; recovering immediately, they again charged and drove the rebels from their position and followed them for some distance and until the presence of several thousand of the enemy in our front warned us that a farther advance would be extremely hazardous. In this engagement I lost 1 commissioned officer and 21 enlisted men wounded; 10 of the men were severely wounded, some perhaps mortally.

The brave and gallant Capt. Charles L. White, of Company A, who was mortally wounded, and fell from his horse while leading his company in this action, died on the march, on the morning of December 7, and was buried at Springfield, Ga. The march of the regiment from Waynesborough to this point (King's Bridge) is devoid of special interest, and I do not deem it necessary to give a detailed account of it.

The conduct of the officers and men of this regiment from Atlanta to Savannah, their unflinching courage, their patient endurance of hardships necessarily attending such a march, their ready obedience to every order, deserve the thanks of every officer and soldier of this great army, and of every patriot of the land. I am proud of them and grateful for an opportunity of awarding them praise for their indomitable valor and of extolling their soldierly virtues. Many of them having served faithfully their term of enlistment will shortly return to their homes and firesides. The patriotic people of Kentucky will welcome them with warm hearts and open hands.

Respectfully,

R. H. KING,
Lieutenant-Colonel, Commanding Third Kentucky Cavalry.

Capt. JAMES BEGGS,
Actg. Asst. Adjt. Gen., First Brig., Third Cavalry Div.

No. 148.

Report of Col. Oliver L. Baldwin, Fifth Kentucky Cavalry.

HEADQUARTERS FIFTH KENTUCKY CAVALRY,
Camp near King's Bridge, Ga., December 17, 1864.

SIR: In compliance with circular of this date from brigade headquarters, I have the honor to submit the following report of the operations of my regiment from the 14th of November to present date:

November 14, marched from Mitchell's Cross-Roads to join the division at Turner's Ferry, on the Chattahoochee River, and from thence marched to a point four miles from Atlanta, on the East Point road, where we encamped. November 15, marched to Flint River and encamped near Jonesborough. During the afternoon I crossed the river, with one battalion of my regiment, having been ordered to open communication with Colonel Jones, who crossed the river above me. Pushing on toward the town my advance came upon a column moving out on the McDonough road. Lieutenant Baker, with Company E, immediately charged the enemy, and drove them hastily through the town. In the meantime another regiment of the enemy had taken position in rear of the town with artillery, sweeping the road before them. Hearing nothing of Colonel Jones, I deemed it best to retire, when I was met by an order to recross the river and encamp. The enemy lost one killed and two wounded in this affair. November 16, moved in the rear of the brigade to near Lovejoy's Station. The regiment was here placed in position to participate in an engagement then going on with Hanna's rebel brigade. Before we could join in the fight, however, the enemy was routed; marched to camp at Bear Creek on Jackson road.

November 17, moved out at 8 a. m. and proceeded with the column three miles, when I was met by Captain Beggs, acting assistant adjutant-general of the brigade, who gave me orders to move on a road diverging to the right to attack Lewis' brigade, then supposed to be encamped on the Towaliga River. The order was obeyed, and the result was that I charged my command two miles and a half after a force of not more than twenty men. Arriving at the bridge I found it burnt and the rebel camp evacuated. Had Lewis' brigade been at that bridge or in their former camp, with four pieces of artillery, as stated, and offered ordinary resistance, I have no hesitancy in saying there is not a regiment in the service which could have driven it from its position, and a charge such as I was ordered to make could have only resulted in a useless loss of life. Rejoined the command in the afternoon and encamped at crossing of Forsyth and Macon roads. November 18, crossed the Ocmulgee at Wetherby's Ferry, and encamped on Jenkins' plantation. Sent out scouting parties and gathered all the horses and mules which could be found. November 19, rejoined the brigade; marched and camped with it at night. November 20, marched within two miles of Macon and commenced destroying the railroad. Moved as rear guard of the brigade on leaving the railroad. Camped five miles from Macon on the road to Milledgeville. November 21, moved down the railroad to Griswoldville. Assisted in burning the town and railroad. Was ordered to move in advance of the brigade and encamped at a point three miles distant on the railroad. On reaching my camp I sent out a detail and destroyed one-quarter of a mile of road.

November 22, at quite an early hour the pickets of the Ninth Pennsylvania, which was encamped on my left and front, were attacked and quite a spirited engagement ensued. I immediately formed my regiment for battle, and being assured by Major Appel, commanding the Ninth Pennsylvania in the temporary absence of Colonel Jordan, that he could and would hold his position, I placed my regiment in position of battalions in echelon, one of the battalions being placed in a barricade. Hearing considerable yelling and firing near the camp I rode over to the Ninth and found they were driving the enemy. An orderly from Major Appel told me that a body of rebels were cut off and were in the woods on his right. I immediately dispatched Captain Glore with his battalion to drive them out or capture them. Scarcely had the battalion gone when fugitives came dashing down the road, and word was brought me that the Ninth was being driven. Major Cheek's battalion was instantly formed across the road, for the double purpose of reassuring the men of the Ninth and of charging the enemy should he again cross the ravine. Captain Glore found the rebels both on his right and left, but as soon as he formed they broke and fled; the captain did not pursue them, as there was a heavy swamp immediately in his front. I held my position until the infantry arrived, when the regiment was massed with the division. At 10.30 a. m. I was ordered to report with my command to General Kilpatrick, and proceeded with him to look for a wagon train of the enemy reported to be passing near us with a small infantry guard. We moved to the left and after marching near a mile came in sight of the wagon train, but instead of a small infantry guard Wheeler's whole command was moving on the road. I formed my regiment in an open field within full view of Wheeler's entire column and within 400 yards of it, and remained there for at least five minutes. The general commanding division ordered me to retire, and I most gladly left what I thought a very close place. In this affair I lost three men wounded and four horses. Adjutant Mitchell had his horse shot under him. Late in the afternoon my command was ordered to take position on the right of the infantry, then engaged in battle near Griswoldville, which position I occupied till dark, not becoming engaged, however. Moved three miles down the railroad and encamped for the night. November 23, marched down the railroad to within two miles of Gordon Station and encamped. November 24, marched to Milledgeville and drew rations. Rested till near dark, when we crossed the Oconee River and marched to camp seven miles and a half east on the Augusta road. November 25, marched to the Ogeechee Shoals, crossed the river, and camped. November 26, marched to a point near ten miles distant from Louisville and camped on the Waynesborough road.

November 27, the enemy sounded the reveille for us this morning, having attacked our pickets at quite an early hour. My command was in position at 3 a. m. I caused my front to be barricaded. Near daylight the Eighth Indiana and Second Kentucky Cavalry were withdrawn from my front, the enemy following them closely and advancing, evidently with the intention of making an attack upon our line. If such were their intentions, they failed, as they were easily checked by a spirited fire from my command, aided by a few shots from our artillery. The colonel commanding the brigade was present and witnessed this skirmish. At daylight I withdrew my command and took the advance of the brigade, marching on the road to Waynesborough. Passed through the town and camped three miles on the Millen road. Barricaded my front, and the men slept on their arms. My entire front was covered by a line of vedettes and skirmishers. My position was on the left of the line. The enemy attacked the brigade near midnight and were repulsed. My regiment did but little firing, as the men had been cautioned to save their ammunition.

Daylight of the 28th found us on the march, one battalion of my regiment being in rear of the artillery, the other battalion being detailed to assist the rear guard. After marching near three miles I met the general commanding division, who ordered me to leave a battalion to charge the enemy, who persistently and energetically hung upon our rear. The Second Battalion, Captain Glore commanding, was detailed. I did not see the charge made by his command, but understood it was gallant and well managed. As the charge was made under the eye of the general and by his order, it is for him to say whether it was well done or not. After passing the general, I continued with the column until it had probably marched two miles from the point where the general had ordered the charge, when a report reached me that the rear guard was cut off. Almost at the same time I received an order to form my command and barricade my front. This was done promptly, not, however, before fugitives from the rear guard began to pass through my lines. Major Cheek's battalion was now alone, the remainder of the brigade being fully a mile in front as we were marching, yet the men worked with a will, and looked calmly on while squad after squad passed through. The extreme rear, however, came up in good order and passed through my lines to the front. Here the Second Battalion rejoined me, and my regiment again became the rear guard of the division. The enemy was bold and persistent, and I was obliged to fall back slowly, causing repeated formations of squadrons to be made. The column was moving over a miserable road, and could not march rapidly, nor could it have formed in the swamps near them had the enemy broken my lines. This he failed to do, however, and after passing through as ugly a swamp as I ever saw, my regiment passed through the lines of the Second and Third Kentucky, who relieved me as rear guard. The column still moved slowly, and we had scarcely marched a mile and were just in the act of crossing a swamp when I heard firing almost immediately in my rear. I cast my eyes to the right and rear and saw the rebels and our men mixed up, and all dashing on my rear. No time was to be lost. Sending men forward to a cross fence to throw the fences, I moved my command rapidly to the right, forming on right by file, and gave the command to commence firing. Never did men do better than the gallant men of my regiment that day. Rapidly and steadily they came into line, each one seeming anxious to join in the fray.

In the meantime a column of the enemy commenced passing my left flank. Captain Forrester, of Company K, anticipating the order, wheeled his company and ordered a charge which drove the rebels back, but the gallant captain never lived to receive the praise due his noble action. He was shot at the head of his company while leading the charge. He was a noble officer, true to his profession, honorable in all things, and was equally beloved by his comrades as an officer and a gentleman. After the repulse of the enemy at this point I was ordered to move my command in column in rear of the artillery. This order of march was continued until we passed through the lines of the Second Brigade, halting and going into bivouac near Rocky Creek. Here I was assigned a position on the extreme left of the line, and in accordance with orders strong barricades were thrown up in our front. We had scarcely an hour of quiet when the enemy attacked us again, his first attack being on our front. Here he was repulsed. A small regiment charged my front but was easily repulsed, and I think severely punished for its temerity. Unexpectedly I received the order to mount my men, and I was greatly surprised when I found the whole command in retreat; still I formed my command, took the place assigned my regiment in column, and moved with it to camp. We camped at 11 p. m. that evening. November 29, moved out an hour before daylight and marched to Big Creek, and encamped after building a barricade at the cross-roads, near the creek. November 30, remained in camp.

December 1, marched at 10 a. m. in advance of the brigade, having the First Battalion, under Major Cheek, thrown forward as an advance guard. Advanced about four miles, when Major Cheek reported the enemy advancing to meet him. I immediately moved forward with the Second Battalion, Captain Glore commanding, and received orders as I passed the general to press forward rapidly, not to give the enemy time to form. I moved rapidly down the road, but on arriving at Major Cheek's position I found him heavily engaged with the enemy, and the nature of the country was such that a charge could only result in disaster. I therefore ordered Captain Glore to form his battalion as rapidly as possible while I rode forward to encourage, and if possible, to press my First Battalion forward. My lines were pressed forward to within thirty yards of the enemy's position in front, but as the enemy had the longest line he enveloped my flanks and caused some confusion. This confusion was greatly augmented by some one giving the command "Fours right" or "Left about," and quite a number of officers and men left the field acting, as I have since learned, upon the supposition that they had been ordered to retire. The majority of my men, regardless of company organizations, rallied, reformed, and held the enemy at bay until a battalion of the Eighth Indiana relieved my left flank and enabled me again to advance upon the enemy, which I continued to do until I was ordered to halt. This affair occurred at Millen's Grove and certainly was a very warm and spirited little fight, as my regiment attacked and fought single-handed for twenty minutes a brigade of rebels in their chosen position where it was impossible to use the saber and where nothing save bulldog fighting could do any good. The enemy lost between 30 and 40 men in killed and wounded. My command fought mounted simply because I had no time to have them dismounted, having been ordered to press forward and to charge. A charge was impossible, and in starting to make one I lost the opportunity of dismounting my command. I lost 1 killed, 7 wounded, and 20 horses. December 2 and 3, marched in column with the brigade; were not engaged. December 4, the command attacked Wheeler; my regiment moved with the command, but was not engaged in the fight; after the enemy had been driven from Waynesborough my regiment moved with the Fifth Ohio, of the Second Brigade, to a ford on Brier Creek and held the ford while the Fifth Ohio destroyed the railroad bridge over Brier Creek; retired near dusk and camped near Beaver Dam Creek. December 5 to 12, my regiment moved with the brigade, sharing in all its marches by day and by night. December 13, marched to Midway, at which place I was ordered to proceed with my regiment to Sunbery, on Sunbery River, also to send a battalion through Dorchester. A short distance from Midway my command came upon a few rebels. These were driven back upon another party; the whole numbering probably forty men. I ordered Lieutenant Jones, commanding Company D, to charge them, ordering Lieutenant Baker, with Company E, to support the charge. The rebels broke in all directions, leaving their guns, hats, blankets, and in fact everything which could impede them in their progress, behind them. On reaching the forks of the road Captain Glore's battalion pressed rapidly on to Dorchester, scattering, as he went, the remainder of Company B, Twenty-ninth Georgia Battalion; camped at Sunbery that night. December 14, remained in camp. December 15, rejoined the brigade and accompanied it to its present camp.

In recalling the scenes of the past campaign I can but feel that the officers and men of my command have had their full share of the dangers and hardships of the campaign, and are justly entitled to a full participation in whatever honor or glory may be awarded to those who rode down all opposition in the march from Atlanta to the Atlantic. To mention by name each officer who distinguished himself in battle would be to give a roll of all my officers with perhaps one single exception, for those who erred in Millen's Grove fought well and gallantly before that fight, in which I am willing that a misconstruction of orders should be their shield. However, I feel constrained to bear testimony to the good conduct and gallantry of Adjutant Mitchell, and of Lieutenants Jones, Baker, and Bryan; also to the gallantry of Sergeants Jackson, of Company B, and Holland, of Company H, and Private Pierce, of Company A, who when surrounded by rebels refused to surrender but fought his way out like a man.

To my battalion commanders, Maj. C. T. Cheek and Capt. John A. P. Glore, my heartfelt thanks are due. On all occasions when I needed brave men and true counsel I found them ready to support me, and I would especially recommend them to those who have the good of the country at heart as young and gallant soldiers worthy and deserving of promotion.

A tribute to the gallant dead all hearts must offer, and yet few can tell how deeply and sincerely we feel the loss of Capt. John W. Forrester, of Company K. He was a true soldier. In the camp and in the field he was always at his post. His business was always attended to promptly, while no danger deterred him from the performance of his duty.

Appended you will please find report of casualties, captures, &c.*

I am, sir, your most obedient servant,

O. L. BALDWIN,
Colonel, Commanding Fifth Kentucky Cavalry.

Capt. JAMES BEGGS,
Actg. Asst. Adjt. Gen., First Brig., Third Div., Cavalry Corps.

No. 149.

Reports of Col. Thomas J. Jordan, Ninth Pennsylvania Cavalry.

HEADQUARTERS NINTH PENNSYLVANIA CAVALRY,
Near Griswold, Ga., November 22, 1864.

CAPTAIN: I respectfully report that agreeably to orders I encamped on the right of the Fifth Kentucky Cavalry at a late hour last night, placing my pickets (two companies) at crossing of the creek, half a mile west of my camp. Soon after going into camp several attempts were made by the enemy to force back my pickets, and about 9 p. m. they charged heavily, but were repulsed. At daylight this morning the enemy again appeared in my front, and after skirmishing for some time, succeeded in charging over my picket and crossing the creek. They were met by Major Kimmel, who had four companies under his command, and charged back to the original position on the opposite bank of the creek. Here my line was met by a heavy force of cavalry under Wheeler, and again driven back to our original position. The infantry coming up, the contest with my regiment ceased, they taking up my skirmish line. My loss in this action is 5 killed, 21 wounded, and 42 missing, all of whom I believe to be captured. I also lost 49 horses, 14 of which were killed, the remainder captured.

Respectfully reported.

THOS. J. JORDAN,
Colonel Ninth Pennsylvania Cavalry.

[Capt. JAMES BEGGS,
Acting Assistant Adjutant-General.]

HEADQUARTERS NINTH PENNSYLVANIA CAVALRY,
Near King's Bridge, Ga., December 17, 1864.

CAPTAIN: I would respectfully report that the Ninth Pennsylvania Cavalry marched from Marietta, Ga., on the 14th day of November, 1864, with the First Brigade, Third Cavalry Division, attached to the army of Major-General Sherman, and on the 16th participated in the action against Wheeler at Lovejoy's Station, on the Macon and Atlanta Railroad. Marching toward Macon, it participated in the skirmishes before

* Statement (here omitted) shows 14 prisoners, 128 horses, and 52 mules captured.

that place on the 20th, and on the 21st at Griswold, covering the rear on withdrawing toward Gordon. On the morning of the 22d, shortly after daylight, the picket of the regiment on the Griswold road was attacked by the enemy under Wheeler. Major Kimmel at once re-enforced it by two companies, under Maj. Charles A. Appel. The enemy, being in strong force, succeeded in flanking the pickets, who did not fall back until nearly surrounded and had 18 captured, 1 killed, and 2 wounded, and upon the enemy appearing on the open ground Major Kimmel charged them with four companies, driving them three-quarters of a mile to and over a creek, where their main line was posted in order of battle. After receiving their fire and being charged by a largely superior force, he fell back toward our main line and again drew up his men in order of battle. The artillery now opened upon the enemy, and a brigade of infantry coming up, under Brigadier-General Woods, of the Fifteenth Corps, took up the fighting and drove the enemy from the ground. The loss of the regiment on this occasion was 5 killed, 21 wounded (2 of whom have since died), and 43 missing, supposed to be captured. In this action Maj. D. H. Kimmel particularly distinguished himself for his bravery, coolness under fire, and ability to command.

On the 20th of November, by order of Brigadier-General Kilpatrick, through Col. E. H. Murray, commanding First Brigade, Capt. E. A. Hancock was detached with 100 men of the Ninth Pennsylvania Cavalry, at Clinton, with orders to take a road leading to Macon to the right of the main column, and to engage any enemy he might meet. In obedience to this order he marched on the road indicated and engaged two regiments of the enemy, holding them in check for two days, when he again rejoined the regiment. His loss was two men wounded. For his bravery and good management he deserves much praise. From Griswold we marched through Gordon to Milledgeville, and thence toward Waynesborough. On the morning of the 27th the enemy again made demonstrations against our picket, and attacked the Eighth Indiana and Fifth Kentucky Regiments and my picket on the left heavily, but were repulsed, and we moved forward and that night encamped south of Waynesborough, on the railroad, which my regiment destroyed for half a mile, when the enemy again, November 28, attacked the position of the brigade, in which all the regiments participated, but without loss to my regiment. During the march of the 29th the enemy made several attacks upon our rear guard, and about 2 p. m. the division was drawn up on the Louisville and Millen road to give battle to Wheeler. The Ninth Pennsylvania Cavalry defended the center of the position, having barricaded their front. The enemy soon charged that position and our whole line, but were most disastrously beaten after three attempts, and we retired toward Louisville, the Eighth Indiana and Ninth Pennsylvania Cavalry acting as rear guard. But one man of my regiment was wounded in this action.

In the battle of Sunday, the 4th day of December, my regiment was brought into action about 10 o'clock, forming on the left of the Third Kentucky, and with it driving the cavalry of Wheeler and Williams (more than three times their number) from their barricades and the houses of Waynesborough. Major Kimmel, commanding First Battalion, and Capt. John M. Porter, since promoted major, commanding a portion of the Third Battalion, assaulted the barricades on the main street, and Major Appel, with the Second Battalion, drove in the right of the enemy, posted in the woods, from their position, exposing their flank to so hot a fire that the whole line gave way and victory was secured. My loss on that occasion was 1 killed, 2 mortally wounded (since died), and 11 wounded. From Waynesborough we marched on Savannah, passing to the south as far as Midway, and from thence to this place, occasionally skirmishing with Colonel Hood's battalion of rebel cavalry, but without any loss. On the morning of the 13th Capt. E. A. Hancock, with detachments from the brigade (120 men), marched on an expedition to Altamaha bridge, but found the enemy (two regiments of infantry and artillery) too strongly posted to attack them. He destroyed, however, several small bridges and a large trestle-work, and captured 16 of the enemy, returning to camp at Midway on the 15th.

Since this movement commenced my command has destroyed 49 cotton gins and presses, containing 731 bales of cotton, and a large amount of cotton unginned. My men for the most part have subsisted on the country, and though it was absolutely necessary for them to be often from under the eyes of their officers in their foraging excursions, yet have I not heard of a single act committed by them derogatory to their character as soldiers.

My officers have all done their duty with most commendable alacrity, and my men have borne the hardships of the campaign without a murmur, rendering prompt obedience to the orders of their officers and displaying a patience and bravery truly commendable.

Herewith I forward a report of casualties and a list of articles destroyed and captured by my regiment during the expedition.

Respectfully submitted.

THOS. J. JORDAN,
Colonel Ninth Pennsylvania Cavalry.

[Capt. JAMES BEGGS,
Acting Assistant Adjutant-General.]

[Inclosure No. 1.]

Report of casualties incident to the Ninth Pennsylvania Cavalry, First Brigade, Third Cavalry Division, Military Division of the Mississippi, since November 14, 1864.

Date.		Location, &c.	Killed.	Wounded.	Prisoners.	Missing.
Nov.	21	In action near Macon, Ga				1
	22	In action near Griswold	5	21	42	
Dec.	2	Foragers				4
	3	Foragers near Thomas' Station				8
	4	In action near Waynesborough	1	12		
		Foragers missing during the campaign				12
		Total	6	33	42	25

THOS. J. JORDAN,
Colonel Ninth Pennsylvania Cavalry.

NEAR KING'S BRIDGE, GA., *December 18, 1864.*

[Inclosure No. 2.]

HEADQUARTERS NINTH PENNSYLVANIA CAVALRY,
Near King's Bridge, December 18, 1864.

CAPTAIN: I respectfully submit the following report of articles captured and destroyed by my command during the recent campaign:

	Captured.	Abandoned.	Lost in action.
Horses	288	441	91
Mules	152	13	....
Carbines	2	13	95
Sabers	....	17	77
Colt revolvers	....	....	11
Horse equipments ......sets	....	57	97

I am, captain, respectfully, yours,

THOS. J. JORDAN,
Colonel Ninth Pennsylvania Cavalry.

Capt. JAMES BEGGS,
Acting Assistant Adjutant-General.

No. 150.

Report of Col. Smith D. Atkins, Ninety-second Illinois Mounted Infantry, commanding Second Brigade.

HDQRS. SECOND BRIGADE, THIRD CAVALRY DIVISION,
Near King's Bridge, Ga., December 24, 1864.

CAPTAIN: In compliance with orders I beg to report:

November 14, my brigade left Marietta, Ga., at 7 a. m.; crossed the Chattahoochee and encamped on railread near East Point. November 15, marched at 8 a. m., Ninth Michigan Cavalry in advance; drove rebel picket all day, and encamped four miles west of Jonesborough. The Tenth Ohio Volunteer Cavalry drove the enemy out of their camp, capturing eight prisoners. Lieutenant Cockley, acting aide-de-camp on my staff, while examining the roads in our front, attended by an orderly, encountered four rebels, and, armed only with a saber, himself captured the four, and brought them into camp. November 16, marched at 7 a. m. At noon my brigade took the advance and encountered Wheeler's cavalry at Bear Creek Station. The Tenth Ohio Volunteer Cavalry, Lieutenant-Colonel Sanderson commanding, made a gallant saber charge against the enemy posted behind rail barricades; dismounted they drove them in confusion, killing and wounding many with the saber, and captured 20 prisoners, including 3 commissioned officers. I saw the charge myself, and take great pleasure in assuring the commanding general that the Tenth did its whole duty. Our loss was 4 killed, 7 wounded, and 4 captured. We encamped that night near Bear Creek Station. November 18, marched eighteen miles, and encamped on the Ocmulgee River. November 19, marched at 12 p. m.; crossed the Ocmulgee on pontoons, and marched thirty miles to Clinton, Ga.

November 20, moved from Clinton at 12 m., my brigade in the advance. The Ninety-second Illinois Mounted Infantry Volunteers, Lieutenant-Colonel Van Buskirk commanding, encountered Crews' brigade about four miles out behind barricades. A part of the Ninety-second was dismounted and attacked the enemy on foot, when the enemy charged them on horseback. The charge was received and repulsed and the enemy charged in turn, when the entire brigade of the enemy cowardly ran off, scattering through the woods. We did not follow them, but pushed on toward Macon. At Walnut Creek, two miles from Macon, we found the enemy again, when the Ninety-second Illinois was deployed on foot and pushed forward to take possession of the creek. Our artillery opened and the enemy replied, when the Tenth Ohio Volunteer Cavalry was ordered to charge their battery. They crossed the creek in a most difficult place, and charged in column of fours up the road, and were successful in gaining momentary possession of the enemy's outer works and several pieces of artillery, which, however, could not be brought off, and the regiment retired. The charge was made under the fire of nine pieces of artillery, and was gallantly and well done. The Ninety-second Illinois Mounted Infantry Volunteers held the creek and road dismounted. The Fifth Ohio Volunteer Cavalry was held in readiness to support the Tenth Ohio Volunteer Cavalry. The Ninth Ohio Volunteer Cavalry, with portions of the Fifth and Tenth, tore up the railroad track and telegraph wire for about two miles. After night-fall my brigade was withdrawn, the Ninety-second Illinois Mounted Infantry Volunteers covering the rear. In the forenoon of this day, by order of General Kilpatrick, I sent 100 picked men of the Ninth Michigan Volunteer Cavalry, under Captain Ladd, of that regiment, to Griswoldville, with orders to burn public buildings and destroy the railroad. Starting from Clinton he found the enemy picketing the roads. Avoiding them he kept on through the woods, reached Griswoldville, and charged into the town, driving the enemy out, and under their fire captured and burned a locomotive and train of cars; burned the public buildings, and destroyed the railroad. After this work was accomplished he captured one of the enemy, and compelled him to lead his little party out of the town on a route to avoid the enemy, who had all the roads in their possession. The gallant conduct of Captain Ladd and his brave troopers is a fine example of what a few men can accomplish when daringly and persistently led.

November 21, moved back to junction of the Clinton and Macon, and Macon and Milledgeville roads, and went into position, barricading. The Ninety-second [Illinois] Mounted Infantry Volunteers was left in rear six miles from Macon, and was furiously attacked at 9 a. m. while in position behind rail barricades. The enemy charged them with one regiment dismounted and two columns mounted, at the signal of the bugle. They came on desperately close to the barricades, but the cool, steady fire of the Spencer rifles broke the charge, and doubled them back with great loss. A prisoner captured afterward reports the enemy's loss in the charge at 65 killed and wounded. The Ninety-second Illinois Mounted Infantry Volunteers was withdrawn and joined the brigade in position, where we remained during the night. November 22, marched at 9 a. m. and camped six miles from Gordon. November 23, moved three miles nearer Gordon and encamped, the Fifth Ohio Volunteer Cavalry picketing Jones' Cross-Roads. November 24, marched at 7 a. m.; passed through Milledgeville and encamped eight miles beyond on the Augusta road. November 25, marched at 8 a. m. and encamped within one mile and a half of the shoals of Ogeechee. November 26, marched at 7 a. m.; crossed the Ogeechee, marched thirty-five miles, and encamped. November 27, Wheeler attacked the First Brigade during the night. At 7 a. m. First Brigade moved through mine and took the advance. The Ninety-second Illinois Mounted

Infantry Volunteers, Lieutenant-Colonel Van Buskirk commanding, covered the rear of my brigade with one piece of artillery, assisted by the Ninth Michigan Volunteer Cavalry. We marched that day through Waynesborough, and encamped three miles south of the town. During the entire day Wheeler, with dogged persistence, continued to attack our rear. Colonel Van Buskirk, with his regiment of Spencer rifles, and occasionally using his rifled gun as opportunity occurred, continually held him at bay, and on several occasions administered severe punishment to the enemy, when the nature of the ground would admit of the concealment of his men. Colonel Van Buskirk handled his regiment splendidly, skillfully revolving his companies around one another, and covering successively their retreat.

November 28, moved at 4 a. m. in advance of the First Brigade, except Col. George S. Acker, with his regiment, the Ninth Michigan Volunteer Cavalry, which remained in rear of the division by order of General Kilpatrick, Colonel Acker reporting to the general of division. I presume the conduct of Colonel Acker and his regiment during that day will be more especially noticed by General Kilpatrick. After crossing Buck Head Creek I took up position and awaited the other brigade, covering the crossing with the Fifth Ohio Volunteer Cavalry, who did it well and destroyed the bridge after our troops were over. General Kilpatrick moved with the First Brigade to Reynolds' plantation, and took up position and barricaded, where I was ordered to join him with my brigade, and did so, going into position on the right of the road, and behind the barricade I found already built. I held in reserve, by order of the division general, two regiments, the Ninth Michigan and Tenth Ohio Volunteer Cavalry, with one battalion of my other three regiments; two battalions of the Ninth Ohio Volunteer Cavalry, Fifth Ohio Volunteer Cavalry, and Ninety-second Illinois Mounted Infantry Volunteers were dismounted to fight on foot, with skirmish line dismounted in front. One battalion of the Fifth Ohio Volunteer Cavalry was left as rear guard, which was soon attacked and fell back fighting handsomely. The rebels charged in splendid style, coming up in close range, when six pieces of artillery, double-shotted, and our dismounted troops, opened upon them, and repulsed them handsomely, with little loss to us. The loss of the enemy in this charge was very severe. As the enemy pushed around my right flank I threw in the Ninth Michigan Volunteer Cavalry, dismounted, and Tenth Ohio Volunteer Cavalry, mounted. After the enemy was handsomely repulsed, by order of General Kilpatrick I withdrew my brigade and marched six miles and encamped. November 29, marched at 5 a. m. to near Louisville, and encamped and remained until December 1; marched eight miles on the Waynesborough road, moving through the fields on the right flank of General Baird's division of infantry.

December 2, continued march same as yesterday. Col. T. T. Heath, with one battalion of his regiment, the Fifth Ohio Volunteer Cavalry, made a gallant little saber charge, successfully driving the enemy. December 3, marched fourteen miles and encamped at Thomas' Station. The Ninety-second Illinois Mounted Infantry Volunteers was placed on picket to cover the infantry of General Baird in tearing up track and skirmished with the enemy nearly all night. The enemy shelled the regiment with artillery, killing two and wounding one. December 4, moved at 7 a. m., my brigade in advance, to attack and rout Wheeler. We found him in strong position near Waynesborough, dismounted behind heavy rail barricades, and attacked him vigorously. The Ninety-second Illinois Mounted Infantry Volunteers (dismounted) moved in line in the center; the Ninth Ohio Volunteer Cavalry (mounted) in column on the left, and the Tenth Ohio Volunteer Cavalry in column in the road on the right of the Ninety-second Illinois Mounted Infantry Volunteers. Colonel Van Buskirk, with his regiment, the Ninety-second Illinois Mounted Infantry Volunteers (dismounted), moved steadily up in front of the barricades, keeping the enemy in constant fear of his Spencer rifles, and his regiment moved over the barricades of the enemy while many of them lay behind them with loaded guns in dumb-stricken fear, and as they attempted to leave the barricades poured in volley after volley with his repeating rifles. The Ninth Ohio Volunteer Cavalry, Colonel Hamilton commanding, held the left flank, skirmishing with rebels in the woods beyond. The Tenth Ohio Volunteer Cavalry charged in gallant style down the road. The Ninth Michigan Volunteer Cavalry, after passing the first barricade, charged by squadron to meet a counter-charge by the enemy, and did it finely, driving him back. Three successive lines of barricades were taken in the single charge, the enemy stubbornly resisting, but compelled to yield to our charging columns. Wheeler had chosen his position cautiously in the roughest, most inaccessible locality, and feeling himself safe against a saber charge hung to it tenaciously, but he was handsomely routed and rode over. The fruits of our victory were 50 of the enemy killed, thrice that number wounded, and 87 prisoners captured. My brigade was now withdrawn by command of General Kilpatrick, and Colonel Murray's brigade pushed the enemy through the town. All of my men and officers behaved with noticeable gallantry, but I am impelled to mention especially Captain Norton, of the Tenth Ohio Volunteer Cavalry, who was mortally wounded in this charge while nobly doing his duty at the head of his men. "Now for a name for our regiment," said he, as with gleaming saber he went forward into the fight. Generous soldier! the honor of his regiment was his uppermost thought. Corporal David Scott, the bearer of my brigade flag, was instantly killed in the thickest of the fight while waving the flag as high as he could reach and cheering on the men. The Fifth Ohio Volunteer Cavalry, Col. T. T. Heath, followed the enemy to Brier Creek, on the Augusta road, and completely destroyed the large railroad bridge over that creek. My brigade moved that night to Alexander and encamped. December 5, marched twenty-two miles and encamped at Jacksonborough. December 6, marched fourteen miles, covering rear of the Fourteenth Army Corps, and encamped at Buck Creek. December 7, marched at 8 a. m., the enemy attacking our rear as we left camp; the Ninth Michigan Volunteer Cavalry as rear guard. About 5 p. m. the enemy in strong force made a vigorous attack and were repulsed by the Ninth Ohio and Ninth Michigan Volunteer Cavalry. The attack was a most persistent one, and was met and returned as persistently by these two regiments. December 8, moved in rear of General Baird's division of infantry, Ninth Ohio Volunteer Cavalry as rear guard, the enemy following and fighting. About noon the infantry halted, the enemy still pressing, and we went into position on the right of the road, General Baird deploying a brigade of infantry on the left. We repulsed an attack of the enemy on the road, and again in attempting to turn our right flank the infantry repulsed an attack on the left. We remained in position until 12 p. m., when the infantry having withdrawn we did so, General Baird's second line remaining until we had crossed Ebenezer Creek, when we again took the rear, barricaded the road, and destroyed the bridge, the enemy shelling us with artillery while withdrawing, but without injuring us. December 9, moved to report to the division general, and encamped six miles south of Springfield. December 10, marched at 7 a. m. to Station No.

1, Georgia Central Railroad. Ninth Ohio Volunteer Cavalry sent to cover rear of the Twentieth Army Corps. December 11, moved to within six miles of Savannah, the Fifth Ohio Volunteer Cavalry sent to cover rear of Fifteenth Army Corps, and remained in camp on the 12th. December 13, marched at 9 a. m. and encamped three miles south of King's Bridge. December 14, marched to Midway and encamped. December 15 and 16, moved to King's Bridge and encamped, where this report was called for.

During the campaign my brigade has marched 520 miles, been frequently in action, and always successful. Have captured 104 prisoners, 1,159 mules and horses, have subsisted ourselves principally upon the country, and have burned 5,840 bales of cotton, 129 cotton gins and screws, and 11 flouring mills.

My brigade has lost 20 killed in action, 70 wounded in action, and 51 captured by the enemy.

My brigade was organized just before leaving Marietta. The regimental organizations were unaccustomed to act together, and officers and men were strangers. In this month's campaign, in bivouac and battle, they have become acquainted, have always acted in harmony and mutual support of each other, and I trust have not failed to win, as a brigade, the confidence and approval of their commanding general.

To officers and men I return my sincerest thanks for their soldierly conduct on all occasions, and their cheerful and prompt obedience to all of my commands. As brigade commander I am proud of my brigade. I feel confidence in it, and its soldierly conduct in this campaign is a sure augury of what it will always be ready to do.

To my personal staff I return my warmest thanks for their cheerful and ready assistance at all times. Major Helm, acting brigade surgeon (now division surgeon), was faithful to sick and wounded, attending to his duties under the enemy's fire. Lieutenant Spear, acting commissary of subsistence, acted as aide-de-camp, and carried my orders while the battle raged hardest. Captain Cornevin, aide-de-camp, Lieutenant Dawson, aide-de-camp, Lieutenant Swing, aide-de-camp, Lieutenant Cowan, provost-marshal, and Lieutenant Skinner, acting assistant inspector-general, were always faithful and efficient. Lieutenant Cockley, acting aide-de-camp, deserves especial mention. At Waynesborough he thrice requested to go with his regiment, the Tenth Ohio Volunteer Cavalry, in its charge, and when permission was granted, dashed forward and fought bravely at its head. To Captain Smith, my acting assistant adjutant-general, courteous, attentive, intelligent, cool, and brave under fire, I am greatly indebted for the harmonious working of my brigade. Lieutenant Bowles, my acting assistant quartermaster, was at all times faithfully attending to his duties.

I inclose herewith the reports of my regimental commanders, which I beg may be taken as a part of this my report.

In conclusion I take great pleasure in stating that nearly always, when my brigade has been engaged with the enemy, Brigadier-General Kilpatrick, commanding the division, has personally superintended the disposition of the troops, riding on the skirmish line in full view of the enemy, and cheering on the men by his presence and example.

I am, captain, most respectfully, your obedient servant,

SMITH D. ATKINS,

Colonel Ninety-second Illinois Infantry, Mounted, Comdg. Brigade.

Capt. L. G. ESTES,

Assistant Adjutant-General.

No. 151.

Report of Lieut. Col. Matthew Van Buskirk, Ninety-second Illinois Mounted Infantry.

HDQRS. NINETY-SECOND ILLINOIS VOL. MOUNTED INFTY.,
Near Savannah, Ga., December 20, 1864.

CAPTAIN: I have the honor to make the following report of the part which my regiment took during the campaign from Atlanta, Ga., through the center of the State to a point near Savannah, Ga.:

We left Atlanta, Ga., on the 15th day of November, but have nothing to record more than the usual duties of picketing and scouting until the 20th instant, when, near Macon, Ga., we encountered the enemy, my regiment acting as advance guard of the division. We drove them before us, charging them from behind several strong barricades, killing and wounding several and taking a few prisoners. When near Walnut Creek Company H, Capt. John F. Nelson commanding, was detached and ordered to proceed to the railroad between Macon and Griswoldville, for the purpose of tearing up the track and cutting the telegraph, all of which was successfully accomplished. After driving the enemy across Walnut Creek my regiment was dismounted. One squadron, Captain Hawk commanding, on the right, and one, Captain Becker commanding, on the left, were ordered to cross the creek to support the Tenth Ohio Volunteer Cavalry in a saber charge. The enemy were driven into their fortifications. The object for which the charge was made having been accomplished, we were ordered to withdraw and recross the creek, where we remained, holding the enemy in check, until after dark. Our casualties were two men wounded. After dark whole command withdrew, my regiment acting as rear guard. We were stationed on picket during the night.

On the morning of the 21st instant, my regiment being still on picket, the enemy attacked the outpost at daylight. Skirmishing continued until about 9 a. m., when they charged the outpost in front and on the flanks with not less than a brigade, driving them back to the reserve. Still on they came in their furious charge until within easy range of our guns, when we opened upon them a fire that sent them flying backward in great confusion, leaving their killed and wounded upon the field, the punishment inflicted upon them being so severe they did not again trouble us. A prisoner, since captured, reports their loss to have been 65 men killed and wounded. Our loss was 2 men captured. From the 21st to the 26th instant, nothing worthy of record occurred save the incidents usual to a march. On the 27th instant my regiment was detailed as rear guard. We fought the enemy all day, losing but one man wounded. In our action with Wheeler on the 28th instant my regiment formed the right center of the brigade, supporting a battery. The enemy charged but were beautifully repulsed. We lost one man wounded.

Our usual routine of march and picketing was uninterrupted until December 3, when my regiment was placed on picket on the railroad at Thomas' Station to protect the infantry while tearing up the track. We skirmished with the enemy, driving them back sufficiently to take position. Skirmishing continued until 8 p. m. About 11 p. m. they got a battery in position and shelled us. Our casualties were 2 men killed and 1 man wounded. At daybreak of the 4th instant the enemy advanced their skirmishers. Skirmishing continued until about 8 a. m., when the division came up, and my regiment was ordered forward in line, dismounted. We soon found the enemy strongly posted behind barricades in greatly superior numbers. We at once charged them, driving them from their successive lines of barricades, routing them in wildest confusion, they throwing away their arms and whatever else would impede their flight, many seeking safety behind trees and under houses, leaving their killed and wounded in our hands. My regiment captured some 40 prisoners, among whom was a major and a lieutenant. We lost in this action 3 men killed and 6 men wounded. Until the 8th instant nothing of moment occurred. On the 8th we had a skirmish with the enemy without casualty. We remained in line of battle nearly all night. On the morning of the 9th we crossed Ebenezer Creek, leaving one battalion, under command of Captain Becker, at the bridge to guard the pioneers while they destroyed the bridge and blockaded the road. While thus employed they were fired upon by the enemy's sharpshooters, wounding one man. From the 10th to the 20th instant nothing worthy of report occurred.

I have destroyed during the campaign 29 gin houses and gins, containing about 1,460 bales of cotton, and 1 flouring mill and 1 saw-mill. We captured 106 horses and 94 mules.

The casualties of my regiment are 5 killed, 12 wounded, and 12 missing, making a total of 29 men.

The conduct of both my officers and men on all occasions is worthy of the highest praise.

Respectfully submitted.

MATTHEW VAN BUSKIRK,
Lieut. Col., Comdg. Ninety-second Illinois Mounted Infantry.

Capt. H. J. SMITH,
Actg. Asst. Adjt. Gen., Second Brig., Third Cav. Div.

List of property captured and destroyed by the Ninety-second Illinois Volunteer Mounted Infantry, from November 14, 1864, to December 19, 1864.

	Captured.				Destroyed.		
	Horses.	Mules.	Small-arms.	Enfield ammunition.	Cotton gins.	Cotton.	Saw-mill.
				Rounds.		*Bales.*	
A	8	4	3	....	....	....	....
B	3	13	2	....	2	400	....
C	6	20	6	....	10	350	....
D	14	....	4	....	4	260	....
E	2	8	4	....	....	....	....
F	8	4	5	....	....	....	....
G	17	13	3	....	....	....	....
H	9	8	8	100	....	....	....
I	6	6	7	....	....	....	....
K	23	16	9	....	2	200	....
Third Indiana	9	3	5	....	11	250	1
Total	105	95	56	100	29	1,460	1

MATTHEW VAN BUSKIRK,
Lieutenant-Colonel, Commanding.

NEAR KING'S BRIDGE, GA., *December 23, 1864.*

List of property lost, destroyed, and abandoned by and captured from the Ninety-second Illinois Volunteer Mounted Infantry from the 14th day of November, 1864, to the 19th day of December, 1864.

	Abandoned.				Captured by the enemy.					
	Horses.	Mules.	Saddles and equipments.	Spencer rifles (broken).	Horses.	Mules.	Horse equipments.	Spencer rifles.	Spencer rifle ammunition.	Lost or stolen—Spencer rifles.
							Sets.		*Rounds.*	
A	5	3								
B	20		4							2
C	13	22		2	1		1	3		
D	11			2						2
E	8	6			2		2	2		
F	8	4	4		2			3		
G	33		8	4	1					
H	15		1		8		8	6	420	
I	11	3	2	3				1		
K	39		5	4		1	1			
Third Indiana	11	3								
Total	174	41	24	15	14	1	12	15	420	4

MATTHEW VAN BUSKIRK,
Lieutenant-Colonel, Commanding.

NEAR KING'S BRIDGE, GA., *December 23, 1864.*

No. 152.

Report of Col. George S. Acker, Ninth Michigan Cavalry.

HEADQUARTERS NINTH MICHIGAN VOLUNTEER CAVALRY,
December 19, 1864.

Herewith find a report of this campaign from November 14, 1864, to December 17, 1864:

Ninth Michigan Cavalry left camp near Atlanta on the 14th day of November, 1864, and moved on the Fairburn road, five miles in advance of the Second Brigade, Cavalry Division, where we encamped for the night. November 15, left camp and moved to within five miles of Jonesborough, Third Battalion being in the advance; drove in the enemy's picket. November 16, passing through Jonesborough, Lovejoy's, and Bear Creek Stations, moved three miles on the McDonough road and encamped for the night. November 17, left camp and marched about twenty-two miles and encamped for the night. 18th, marched fifteen miles. 19th, crossing the Ocmulgee, passed through Hillsborough and on to Clinton; arrived at 3 p. m. and encamped. During that day we marched thirty-nine miles and took six prisoners. 20th, Companies B, C, and D, being detached for a scout to Griswold Station in charge of Captain Ladd, meeting the enemy, but keeping them at bay, burned the town, destroying the railroad, cutting the telegraph wire, burned a train of cars. Fighting their way back, they returned to the regiment on the 23d of November, with the loss of 1 wounded and 3 captured. The remainder of the regiment left Clinton and marched to within three miles of Macon and moved back five miles on the Milledgeville road, and encamped. 21st, were drawn up in line of battle, and remained all day. Went on picket four miles from Macon, and remained during the night. 22d, marched about ten miles. 23d, marched about three miles and encamped; First Battalion on picket. 24th, marched to Milledgeville; went into camp, and drew five days' rations, and moved out five miles and encamped for the night. 25th, marched to Buffalo Creek. The bridge being burnt, forded the stream, and went into camp. On the night of the 25th Companies A and M were detailed to accompany a scout to Waynesborough. They tore up the railroad, burned the depot and burned the bridge, and joined the command near Waynesborough without losing a man, capturing 1 colonel, 1 major, 1 captain, and 10 enlisted men. 26th, marched through Gibson and went to within eight miles of Louisville, and encamped for the night. 27th, marched thirty-five miles, and encamped for the night near Waynesborough. 28th, received orders to report to Brigadier-General Kilpatrick for duty, this duty being to cover the rear of the division, skirmishing with the enemy the greater part of the day, losing 3 men killed and 1 wounded. 29th, left camp at 3 a. m., and marched to within three miles of Louisville and encamped. 30th, part of the regiment on a scout; nothing of importance occurred, and returned to camp.

December 1, marched about twenty-five miles. 2d, crossed Rocky Creek and went into camp. 3d, marched all day and went into camp at Thomas' Station. 4th, marched to Waynesborough; the First and Third Battalions made a saber charge on the enemy; took quite a number of prisoners. In our front there were 15 of the enemy dead. Our loss was 2 killed and 5 wounded. Adjt. William C. Cook, who in the charge dashed upon the enemy's banner and attempted to carry it off, was knocked from his horse, and had his horse shot, and still remains in the enemy's hands. We then moved from Waynesborough to Alexander and encamped. 5th, marched all day and went into camp at Brier Creek. 6th, marched to within three miles of the Savannah River and encamped. 7th, marched all day, the rebels in our rear; about 4 p. m. they attempted to cut us off at Cypress Swamp. One battalion, under Capt. J. G. McBride, charged and drove the enemy about two miles, then fell back, the enemy following them, when the whole regiment became engaged. After skirmishing about one hour we received orders to fall back across the swamp. Our loss was, Capt. F. S. Ladd and Lieut. William Bateman supposed to be killed, 5 missing, and 2 wounded. We moved back about two miles and encamped. 8th, received orders to report to Brigadier-General Kilpatrick at 4 a. m. We then proceeded to Ebenezer Creek, when we went into camp and fed. The bridge being finished, we crossed over and went to within three miles of Springfield and encamped for the night. 9th, moved to General Sherman's headquarters, within four miles of Savannah, and encamped. 10th, moved to within four miles of the Ogeechee River and encamped. 11th, moved across the Ogeechee River, marching toward Fort McAllister; captured one prisoner, and encamped at White Hall for the night. 12th, marched to Saint Catherine's Sound. 13th and 14th, in camp. 15th, marched to within two miles of King's Bridge. 16th and 17th, in camp, building fortifications.

During the thirty-one days' campaign we have destroyed 100 cotton gins and 10 grist-mills.

GEO. S. ACKER,
Colonel, Commanding Regiment.

ACTG. ASST. ADJT. GEN., SECOND BRIG., CAVALRY DIV.

HEADQUARTERS NINTH MICHIGAN VOLUNTEER CAVALRY,
December 18, 1864.

Report of casualties in the Ninth Michigan Cavalry from November 14, 1864, to December 17, 1864.*

GEO. S. ACKER,
Colonel, Commanding Regiment.

No. 153.

Report of Col. Thomas T. Heath, Fifth Ohio Cavalry.

HEADQUARTERS FIFTH OHIO VOLUNTEER CAVALRY,
Near King's Bridge, Ga., December 23, 1864.

CAPTAIN: I have the honor to report that the Fifth Ohio Cavalry (with the First Squadron Ohio Cavalry temporarily attached), with an aggregate of 563 men, marched with the Second Brigade, Col. S. D. Atkins commanding, from Marietta, Ga., on the 14th of November, 1864, on the expedition ending with the occupation of Savannah by our forces.

Just previous to marching 440 men of my regiment, and 9 officers, whose terms of service had expired, were ordered to Ohio to be mustered out of service. Myself and 11 other officers were retained on the order of Major-General Howard, commanding Army and Department of the Tennessee, though entitled to be ordered to Ohio for muster out of service on the 14th of November, 1864. During this most arduous campaign both officers and men have done their whole duty, never discontented at nor flagging in the routine of day and night marches, building breast-works, destroying railroads, picket, skirmish, and battle, through thirty-eight days and nights in an enemy's country. I am proud to say, that for intelligent and ready execution of all orders received, as well as for valorous action on the battle-field, my officers and men deserve the highest commendation, have my thanks, and promptly received acknowledgment in general orders from brigade and division commanders. Dogged by a persistent and relentless enemy from East Point to the walls of Savannah, through woods and swamps hitherto considered impracticable, the Fifth Ohio Cavalry has done its full share of every work, participated in every engagement, and never faltered. At Macon it supported the gallant Tenth Ohio in its charge, while one battalion tore up the railroad. On the 28th of November the First Brigade was hardly pressed in the swamp at Buck Head Creek. This regiment was ordered by Colonel Atkins to go to the rear and cover the crossing of the brigade. Moving rapidly to the rear, it took position, dismounted, threw up barricades of rails, planted its section of howitzers to cover the bridge, enabled the whole brigade to cross in safety, and checked the advance of Wheeler's whole force, which was exultingly pressing the rear. When the smoke of our discharge of canister had cleared away the rebels who were crowded on the causeways to the bridge were not seen, and Capt. William Jessup, Company D, with twenty of his men, under the fire of their riflemen daringly burned and completely destroyed the bridge, while shells from the howitzers compelled the enemy to ploy and seek crossing above and below. After two hours, finding the enemy was crossing at

---

* Nominal list (omitted) shows 3 enlisted men killed, 3 commissioned officers and 12 enlisted men wounded, and 2 commissioned officers and 12 enlisted men missing.

other points and gaining our flanks and rear, we steadily retired on the brigade, which had taken position two miles and a half to our front. We had not marched far before the enemy closed from either flank on the road we were marching and began skirmishing. Capt. Alexander C. Rossman, Company E, commanding Third Battalion, Fifth Ohio, as rear guard, skillfully and gallantly kept them in check until the advance battalion had been assigned position with the brigade at Reynolds' plantation. At this moment the enemy charged in two columns with vigor. Captain Rossman, with his battalion re-enforced by Company C and a line of dismounted skirmishers, fought in front of the barricade; the remainder of the regiment, with the howitzers, from behind the work. The enemy were quickly and easily repulsed with loss.

On the 2d of December, at Rocky Creek Church, the regiment reported to General Kilpatrick, and I was ordered to clear the left flank of rebels. Deploying the First Battalion, Capt. John Pummill commanding, I charged, and with a single battalion drove a force of full 1,000 rebels from behind rail barricades a distance of nearly two miles. After this charge was made six companies of the Third Kentucky came up and rendered valuable assistance. On the 4th of December, at the battle of Waynesborough, the regiment was not so heavily engaged as some others, though it charged twice and would have made a good list of prisoners, had not our own artillery, through mistake, fired on us, which caused a deflection of my columns to prevent unnecessary slaughter. Later we opened effective fire with carbines. In the afternoon of this day we were ordered five miles beyond Waynesborough to burn the railroad bridge over Brier Creek, which we accomplished in a thorough manner, firing seventy-nine bents of heavy trestle bridging. On the 8th of December the regiment was under arms and on picket for fifteen hours, covering the army in crossing a difficult swamp near Ebenezer Chapel. At midnight the enemy shelled furiously and the infantry picket fell back in confusion, while the Fifth Ohio and Ninety-second Illinois Mounted Infantry held their line firmly, and when ordered retired in perfect order. On December 11 I was ordered by Colonel Atkins to cover the rear of Major-General Howard's army. I took up position near Silk Hope and received orders from General Kilpatrick to accompany him on expedition to open communications with the fleet. Crossing the Ogeechee and Cannouchee Rivers on pontoons, we camped on the 12th near Fort McAllister, and on the 13th at 10 o'clock struck the coast on Saint Catherine's Sound. Captain Estes, assistant adjutant-general, a staff officer of Major-General Howard, in a small canoe; myself, Captain Day, provost-marshal, and Lieutenant Messenger, aide-de-camp, Third Division, Cavalry Corps, were ordered, in a second gum-tree canoe, to pull out to a vessel whose masthead was discerned in the offing. After a row of twelve or fifteen miles we spoke the bark Fernandina, U. S. Navy, Captain West commanding; were courteously received, and furnished a boat's crew and cutter, and with an officer of the vessel reported to General Kilpatrick, who immediately forwarded dispatches to the flag-ship. Having reported again to my brigade the regiment moved on the 17th of December with the expedition which destroyed Morgan Lake and river swamp trestle, near the Altamaha River, on the Gulf railroad.

During the campaign the regiment lost 1 man killed in action, 12 men wounded, 11 men captured by the enemy (7 of whom were captured near Shoals of Ogeechee while foraging for horses), and 9 horses killed.

My report would be incomplete did I not mention Maj. D. V. Rannels, surgeon, who, with remarkable assiduity and great skill, made the condition of our sick and wounded more than ordinarily comfortable on a wearisome march. No labor wearied him; no tax exhausted his patience.

Lieutenant Heath, regimental quartermaster, had charge of the train, which marched mostly with infantry columns, and brought it through without loss of a mule, wagon, or a cent's worth of Government property.

Lieut. Lee S. Haldeman, acting adjutant, on all occasions rendered me valuable assistance, exhibiting coolness and judgment which marked him as a young officer of superior talent and worthy of promotion.

Capt. William Jessup and Capt. Alexander C. Rossman were both entitled to muster-out on the 14th of November last, yet displayed the most admirable gallantry during the campaign, but more especially at Buck Head and Reynolds' plantation. The service is not ornamented by more worthy captains.

Captain Dalzell and Lieutenant Coates, of the First Ohio Independent Squadron, have a soldierly body of men, and have proven faithful and efficient during the whole campaign. Lieut. Joseph E. Overturf, commanding Company H, displayed great personal gallantry at Reynolds' plantation, and commanded his company in such splendid manner that I am happy to recommend his promotion to captain in acknowledgment of his services.

The regiment is now in camp near King's Bridge, Ga.

The various reports in detail required by the department will be forwarded as early as the exigencies of the service will allow.

I have the honor to be, your obedient servant,

THOMAS T. HEATH,
Colonel Fifth Regiment Ohio Volunteer Cavalry.

Capt. H. J. SMITH,
Actg. Asst. Adjt. Gen., Second Brig. Third Div., Cav. Corps.

No. 154.

Report of Col. William D. Hamilton, Ninth Ohio Cavalry.

KING'S BRIDGE, GA., *December 23, 1864.*

COLONEL: In compliance with your order, I have the honor to submit the following report of the participation of the Ninth Ohio Volunteer Cavalry in the events which transpired during the recent advance of the army, under Major-General Sherman, through Georgia, ending in the fall of Savannah:

On the 9th day of November, while stationed at Tunnel Hill, Ga., with part of my regiment, I received a telegram from Brigadier-General Kilpatrick that my command had been assigned to his cavalry division, which was being organized at Marietta, Ga.; that a portion of my regiment, consisting of 300 men, under command of Major Bowlus, was already with him, and ordering me to report at that point at once with all the effective men of my command. I was at the time illy prepared to comply with the order, as I had been informed by Major-General Wilson, chief of cavalry, that my regiment had been ordered to report to him at Nashville, and to make my arrangements accordingly. Part of my men were, consequently, lying at Chattanooga, partly dismounted and imperfectly clothed. After clothing them, I shipped the dismounted men, by General Kilpatrick's order, to Marietta; brought up the mounted men to Tunnel Hill, and on the 12th of November started from there with 350 mounted men for Marietta, leaving sixty dismounted men under Lieutenant Cochran, for whom no transportation could be procured. Upon reaching Calhoun I found the railroad destroyed and communication with the front cut off. We pushed forward, however, and when five miles south of that place were fired into by a party of the enemy, seriously wounding one man. Upon arriving at the Etowah River I found the bridge had been destroyed by the rear of our troops who had crossed twenty-four hours previously. I, however, cleared out an old ford which had been blockaded, and effected a crossing with my men and wagons and pressed forward until I overtook the rear of the army on the banks of the Chattahoochee, having traveled the last eighty miles in thirty-six hours. I overtook and reported to General Kilpatrick a few miles beyond Lovejoy's Station, November 17, and joined that portion of the regiment under Major Bowlus, in the Second Brigade, Colonel Atkins commanding. We proceeded south without opposition until arriving before Macon. In the demonstration upon that place I sent one battalion, under command of Major Bowlus, to burn the railroad bridge across the Ocmulgee River, and to tear up the road. The bridge was found, however, to be strongly defended by the enemy's artillery, which opened a heavy fire, thus preventing the destruction of the bridge. Major Bowlus, however, destroyed the road until within about 100 yards of the bridge. I, with the balance of the regiment, occupied our left flank, destroying the railroad, until ordered to withdraw and go into camp. In this affair the regiment met with no loss.

From Macon our march was harassed by the enemy's cavalry, under General Wheeler, with whom we had occasional skirmishing, and on November 28 General Kilpatrick made a stand, building a strong line of breast-works at a place known as the White House, and awaited the approach of the enemy. Here my command was posted, one battalion (mounted) as a reserve under Major Bowlus, and two battalions (dismounted) in the center, supporting the artillery. The enemy charged in column along the road on our front and left, and in line in our front and right, but were repulsed twice by our line of skirmishers, thrown out 400 yards in our advance, commanded by Sergeant (now Lieutenant) Briner. I beg leave to say that this line behaved admirably, standing firmly in an open field and holding the enemy in check after the line on the right and left had been withdrawn, firmly falling back as the enemy advanced, who, when within 150 yards of our works, were met by a heavy fire from our main force, which drove them in disorder from the field, leaving a number of killed and wounded in front of my command. Our loss was three wounded. My command next encountered the enemy on the morning of December 4, before Waynesborough. Our brigade being in the advance, I was ordered to deploy my regiment in three lines on the left flank. We moved forward in this form for more than a mile, driving the enemy before, when, by order of General Kilpatrick, I sent forward the First Battalion, under Major Bowlus, to charge the enemy drawn up in line of battle in a field upon our extreme left. This Major Bowlus did in a most gallant manner, driving them from their position through a swamp into the woods toward Waynesborough. In the meanwhile the enemy had formed his line across the railroad upon a stream near the town, and prepared to make a vigorous resistance to our advance. Here I was directed by you to charge his right. I at once formed the two battalions into one line, giving Lieutenant-Colonel Stough command of the left, with directions to prevent a counter movement on their part on their extreme right, which the presence of a thicket could enable them to do under cover, and with the right I charged upon their front, driving them through a swamp and across the stream, killing and wounding quite a number, most of whom they were compelled to leave upon the field. They also lost quite a number of horses in their flight. Lieutenant-Colonel Stough brought up the left and gallantly assisted in driving the enemy. We crossed the stream and were forming for a second charge when I received orders to return and give place to the First Brigade, which had come up to relieve us. In this engagement I lost four wounded.

Our next encounter with the enemy was on the 7th of December, while the column was crossing through a swamp near Ebenezer Creek. The enemy, who had not made his appearance since the engagement at Waynesborough, came upon our rear, consisting of the Ninth Michigan Cavalry. While the rear of the column was waiting for the advance to cross, I, being next in advance of the Ninth Michigan Cavalry, took two companies, A and B of my regiment, and went back to assist Colonel Acker, Ninth Michigan Cavalry, taking a position and deploying upon his extreme left in front of a road running off from the main road in that direction. The ground was covered with thick underbrush, which prevented us from seeing the movements of the enemy. After remaining here a few minutes we discovered a strong force moving immediately in our front, who from their uniform I supposed to be Colonel Acker's men. The enemy, however, evidently aware of the road above mentioned, had made a flank movement under cover of the thicket, and were approaching with a view of cutting off the rear guard. Discovering their true character I opened a heavy fire upon them, checking them for an instant, but, gathering, they rushed forward, part of their extended line gaining the road in our rear near a point touched by the extreme of a swamp, and would thus have cut us off had they not been held back by the fire of another company which I had fortunately left to guard that point, thereby enabling us to get round and form in the open ground between the swamps and main road upon which our column was moving. The enemy seemed determined to produce confusion in our column, pressed forward vigorously in heavy force, to check which I found it necessary to send for company after company until two battalions were deployed in different lines, holding him back until Colonel Acker brought up his regiment and passed all but the rear guard across the swamp. I, in the meantime, had my Third Battalion and part of his command formed on foot in front of the swamp, thus holding back the enemy until the entire mounted force had effected a crossing. In this affair our timely assistance and support, I am assured, saved the rear guard of our column on that occasion. Our loss was, wounded, 2; missing, 2.

Next day, December 8, my regiment being rear guard, was attacked by the enemy about noon, but held him in check until our column was massed in rear of the Fourteenth Corps, at Ebenezer Bridge, at which point he was held in check by our cavalry and infantry combined until the road was cleared and our whole force passed safely over and the bridge destroyed. My loss on this day was one missing.

Company G during the march was on detached service with the Tenth Wisconsin Battery.

No casualties at Altamaha bridge.

Casualties during the campaign, wounded, 10; missing, 3.

I have the honor to be, colonel, very respectfully, your obedient servant,

W. D. HAMILTON,
Colonel Ninth Ohio Volunteer Cavalry.

[Col. SMITH D. ATKINS.]

ADDENDA.

HEADQUARTERS NINTH OHIO CAVALRY VOLUNTEERS,
Near Savannah, Ga., December 28, 1864.

SIR: I have the honor to furnish the following report of casualties and deaths in this regiment, occurring between the time of leaving Tunnel Hill, Ga., and reaching Savannah, Ga.*

W. McMILLAN,
Assistant Surgeon, Ninth Ohio Cavalry.

Col. W. D. HAMILTON,
Ninth Ohio Volunteer Cavalry.

No. 155.

Report of Lieut. Col. Thomas W. Sanderson, Tenth Ohio Cavalry.

HEADQUARTERS TENTH OHIO VOLUNTEER CAVALRY,
King's Bridge, near Savannah, Ga., December 22, 1864.

SIR: I have the honor to submit the following report of the operations of the Tenth Regiment Ohio Volunteer Cavalry, under my command, from the time of leaving Marietta, Ga., until the arrival of the Third Cavalry Division at this place:

On the 16th day of November, Wheeler's command having been encountered at Bear Creek Station, the Tenth Ohio was ordered to the advance, and directed to drive the enemy two miles upon a road leading to the right. In attempting to do so two brigades of rebel cavalry were encountered strongly posted on a ridge behind barricades. Two squadrons of the regiment were dismounted on the enemy's left flank to engage their attention while his right was being turned by a saber charge, which was done in gallant style, under the command of Major Filkins, in command of one battalion of the regiment. The enemy were driven at all points from their barricades and closely pursued for more than a mile. No other troops assisted in this action. Twenty prisoners, including 3 commissioned officers, were captured. The loss of the enemy was not ascertained. The regiment lost 4 killed, 7 wounded, and 4 captured. It is but just that I should call attention to the heroic conduct of Sergt. Harry Shrieves, of Company C, who led his company, being several rods in front of them, in the saber charge, inciting the men by his example to deeds of valor until he fell wounded by a ball through the thigh. The complete success of the charge, against more than four times the number of those who made it, the assailed at the same time protected by barricades, was in a great measure attributable to his gallantry.

---

*Nominal list (omitted) shows 10 wounded and 5 missing.

The regiment was not engaged again until the arrival of the command at Macon on the 20th day of November, when, during the progress of the demonstration made by General Kilpatrick upon that place, the regiment was ordered to make a saber charge along the Clinton and Macon road, from which the enemy were then firing. The distance to reach the guns was something over half a mile along a road through deep woods which concealed the enemy's guns and their works. The regiment (except one battalion, detached), in pursuance of orders, charged along the road, reached the enemy's guns, which were in a redoubt, completely blocking the road, there being only room for two horses to enter the works abreast. In rear of and also extending from both flanks of the redoubt were long lines of breast-works and rifle-pits filled with infantry. On the left of the road there was also a battery commanding the road and the point where the road crossed a small but deep creek, being the point from which the regiment started on the charge. Notwithstanding all these obstacles the regiment charged into the redoubt and for a moment had complete possession of it, and could, if the men had possessed the means, have spiked the guns. As the head of the column entered the redoubt the first line of the enemy's infantry (apparently militia) seemed to be stampeded and panic-stricken and were rapidly falling back. The second line, however, were seen advancing to gain a position behind the works abandoned by the militia. An infantry line was also seen advancing from the woods on the left of the road, and seeing that the guns could not be removed, and that there was barely time to withdraw the regiment before the rebel infantry would be upon us, I ordered the column to retire. This was done in good order, under fire from the enemy's guns. The loss of the regiment in this charge was seven wounded. It is with pleasure I call the attention of the colonel commanding to the heroic conduct and bearing of Capt. J. H. Hafford, of Company M, commanding Companies C and M. His squadron was in the advance and its head. He was the first man to enter the fort, where his horse was shot under him, and falling upon him he could not extricate himself in time to prevent his capture. He is now in the hands of the enemy.

In the next action of note in which the division was engaged, at Reynolds, on the 28th of November, the Tenth being sent to the right flank of the line, which the enemy did not attack, was not specially engaged, and nothing more of note occurred until the engagement at Waynesborough, on the 4th of December. On the morning of that day, when the command moved from bivouac at Thomas' Station to attack Wheeler's command near Waynesborough, the Tenth Ohio Volunteer Cavalry moved in the advance, under orders from the colonel commanding brigade, that as soon as an opportunity occurred, to charge with the saber. A skirmish line was thrown out from the regiment, which drove the skirmish line of the enemy for more than a mile back in the direction of Waynesborough, upon their main line, strongly posted behind barricades, dismounted. As soon as this line was developed the regiment was arranged for a charge by battalions. The First Battalion, commanded by Capt. S. E. Norton, was directed to move down the railroad on the enemy's left flank; the Second, Major Platt, to move to the left so as to turn the barricades on the enemy's right; and the Third, Major Filkins, was ordered to move straight on to the barricades; all to charge with the saber at a given signal. At the same time the Ninety-second Illinois (dismounted) moved in line of battle toward the rebel line. As soon as that regiment got within range, I ordered the charge, which was made in splendid style, the barricades carried, and the whole rebel line stampeded. The regiment captured over 70 prisoners. I have not been able to learn their loss in killed and wounded. In this action the regiment lost 4 killed and 7 wounded. Among the wounded was Capt. S. E. Norton, commanding the First Battalion, whose wound proved mortal. His loss to the regiment is irreparable. For faithfulness in the discharge of all his duties as an officer, and bravery upon the battle-field, exhibited on every occasion when an opportunity presented, could not be surpassed. The brilliant victory of the day was dearly purchased in his loss to the army and the country.

The total loss of the regiment since leaving Marietta, Ga., November 14, 1864, is as follows: Officers—wounded, 4 (1 mortally); captured, 2. Enlisted men—killed, 7; wounded, 22; missing, 13.

During the campaign the regiment captured 229 horses and mules. There were 180 of these killed in action and abandoned.

The undersigned, as commanding officer of the regiment, is fully satisfied with the bravery and gallantry of the officers and men of his command during the campaign, and only hopes that they have met the expectations of the colonel commanding brigade in the faithful discharge of their duties of officers and soldiers, and in their conduct upon the battle-field in one of the most successful and glorious campaigns of the war.

I have the honor to be, most respectfully, your obedient servant,

THOS. W. SANDERSON,

Lieutenant-Colonel, Comdg. Tenth Ohio Volunteer Cavalry.

Capt. H. J. SMITH,

Actg. Asst. Adjt. Gen., Second Brig., Third Cavalry Div.

No. 156.

Report of Capt. Yates V. Beebe, Tenth Wisconsin Battery.

HEADQUARTERS TENTH WISCONSIN BATTERY,

December 18, 1864.

CAPTAIN: In compliance with a circular from your headquarters, dated December 17, 1864, I have the honor to report that the Tenth Wisconsin Battery left Marietta, Ga., on the 14th day of November, 1864. On the 16th day of November the battery was in action at Lovejoy's Station and at Bear Creek Station. At Lovejoy's Station the battery silenced the enemy's guns and took possession of two of them after the cavalry had run them down. On the 19th the battery crossed the Ocmulgee and marched thirty-two miles to Clinton. This day's march killed ten horses. On the 20th the battery was in action near Macon; had one wagon broken and destroyed. On the 23d, near Gordon, broke an axle and destroyed a caisson. On the 24th, 25th, 26th, and 27th the company marched 123 miles, to Waynesborough; had 30 horses killed and abandoned. On the 28th the battery was in action at Jones' plantation near Buck Head Church, and on the 29th arrived at Louisville, Ga.

December 1, 2, and 3, the battery marched with General Baird's division to Thomas' Station, seven miles south of Waynesborough. On the 4th the battery was in action at Waynesborough. On the 5th, 6th, 7th, and 8th the battery marched seventy-three miles, to Ebenezer. On the 11th the battery went into camp within five miles of Savannah, on the Macon and Savannah Railroad. On the 13th and 14th the battery marched thirty miles to Midway Church. On the 16th the battery went into camp at King's Bridge, where it remains yet.

During this campaign the company has been in action seven times and marched 520 miles. They have lost 1 wagon, 50 horses, and 1 caisson. They have captured 2 horses, 10 mules, and 2 guns.

In a report of this kind there cannot be much said to dazzle the imagination; but if cheerful fighting, tedious marching, and tireless vigilance does lack excitement, it cannot fail to command the admiration of friends and foes.

I am, captain, very respectfully, your obedient servant,

Y. V. BEEBE,
Captain Tenth Battery Wisconsin Volunteer Artillery.

Capt. H. J. SMITH,
Acting Assistant Adjutant-General.

No. 157.

Report of Maj. Gen. Joseph Wheeler, C. S. Army, commanding Cavalry Corps.

HEADQUARTERS CAVALRY CORPS,
Near Savannah, Ga., December 24, 1864.

COLONEL: I have the honor to submit the following report of the operations of my command from November 19, 1864, the date General Hardee assumed command:

For several days previous to that date I had been resisting the enemy's advance from Atlanta toward Macon, reporting daily to Generals Bragg, Hood, Hardee, and Taylor, and also to Governor Brown, almost the exact movements and intentions of the enemy. Anderson's brigade had been ordered to report to Maj. Gen. Howell Cobb, at Macon, in order that he might place him in position to observe the enemy approaching Macon on the east side of the Ocmulgee River. This brigade was placed in position by General Cobb on the Clinton road.

On the 19th I sent Crews' (Georgia) brigade with orders also to report to General Cobb. This brigade, Colonel Crews reports, was placed in position on the Milledgeville road, with instructions, as I afterward learned, to follow and engage any raiding party of the enemy which might move toward the railroad. Toward evening on the 19th I ascertained from my scouts that the main forces of the enemy had crossed the Ocmulgee River above the mouth of the Towaliga, which induced me to move to Macon in person, directing all my command, except Ferguson's and Breckinridge's brigades, to follow me.

On arriving at Macon, about 11 p. m., I found Lieutenant-General Hardee, who had assumed command of the department. He directed me to move at daylight with all my available force, except Crews' brigade, out on the Clinton road and ascertain the enemy's force and location. In obeying this order, and before marching toward Clinton, both my flanks were menaced by small parties of the enemy, which I was obliged to drive off, causing some delay. I then moved on rapidly with my advance guard to Clinton, and found Osterhaus' corps moving through the town. This was not observed until very near the column, owing to a dense fog. Six men dashed into the town and captured General Osterhaus' servant (an enlisted man) within twenty feet of General Osterhaus' headquarters. A regiment of the enemy's cavalry charged us, making the retreat of my small escort necessary. A squad of the enemy's cavalry had pressed in upon my line of retreat between my position and the body of my command. These, however, were soon cleared away by the approach of two of my regiments, which came up rapidly to my assistance. I immediately charged the advancing column of the enemy and drove it back upon their infantry. They then rallied and charged me again. We met this charge, checked and returned it with success, driving them back toward Clinton.

I now learned from my scouts that the enemy in considerable force were pressing down the road toward Griswoldville. I started promptly with a portion of my command in that direction, and soon met a courier from Colonel Crews with a note from him stating that the enemy's cavalry had moved toward the railroad, and that, pursuant to General Hardee's orders, he was going in pursuit. This left the Milledgeville road open, and fearing some difficulty I moved rapidly to that point. On arriving I found our artillery engaging the enemy's advance and our infantry in the redoubts ready to receive an attack. The enemy had already charged up the road, and four of them had attempted to capture a gun, but had been driven back, leaving an officer (whose horse was killed) in the hands of our infantry. Finding large unprotected intervals between redoubts, I placed Harrison's and Hagan's brigades in line, making the connection complete. After slight skirmishing the enemy retreated a short distance.

Pursuant to orders from General Hardee I moved out during the night, and the next day drove the enemy from Griswoldville, capturing a few prisoners. The next morning I again attacked and drove the enemy for some distance, capturing sixty prisoners, besides killing and wounding a large number.

It now being evident that the enemy were not intending to make any further demonstration upon Macon, I moved on toward the Oconee, which river I reached on November 24 and completed crossing the next day by swimming. A brigade under Lieutenant-Colonel Gaines was immediately sent to hold in check a portion of the enemy who were menacing the river near Ball's Ferry, and with the remainder of my command I moved during the night to Station No. 13, on the Central railroad. Scouts and pickets were sent upon all roads by which the enemy could reach the railroad or march in an easterly direction. The following day, pursuant to General Hardee's orders, I moved to Sandersville. The Fourteenth and Twentieth Corps of the enemy had marched from Milledgeville, crossed Buffalo Creek, and were marching upon the town, preceded by cavalry, which had dispersed the local troops, who had attempted to oppose them. I moved out on the lower road and sent a force out on the upper road. After moving three miles we were charged by the enemy, whom we met and checked, and then in turn charged and drove them back for a mile, capturing, killing, and wounding about thirty of the enemy, besides capturing several horses, mules, and one loaded wagon. I immediately sent word to the citizens of Sandersville that the enemy would enter the town the next morning, and I advised them to send off all movable property of value. At dark we established our pickets close to the enemy, and next morning were slowly driven back toward and finally through the town.

At evening I was informed by my pickets near Ogeechee Shoals that General Kilpatrick, with a large force of cavalry, had crossed the river on his way to Augusta. Leaving General Iverson to observe the enemy,

I started immediately with my command, overtaking him about midnight. I immediately attacked and captured his picket, and pushed on to his camp and drove him back from the main Augusta road and out of his camps, capturing 1 stand of colors, some prisoners, some 50 horses, clothing, blankets, camp equipage, &c., in considerable quantities. The enemy immediately started toward Augusta on the lower Augusta road. On reaching the house where General Kilpatrick had staid I learned that he and his officers had been overheard talking a great deal in private about Augusta. It was the opinion of citizens that this move was intended as a raid upon that place. Being mindful of the great damage that could be done by the enemy's burning the valuable mills and property which were not protected by fortifications, including the factories in the vicinity, the large portion of the city outside of the fortifications, the arsenal and sand hills, I hoped by pressing him hard he might be turned from his purpose. I also learned that the night previous he had sent a party of some 500 men to Waynesborough to destroy the railroad bridge, which convinced me that Augusta and not Waynesborough was Kilpatrick's destination, as had the latter place been the point he designed striking he would not have sent a small party there on the preceding day. Notwithstanding the jaded condition of my command, I therefore pushed on rapidly, engaging and defeating his rear guards, whom I found fortified at every favorable point, frequently separated by but 200 or 300 yards. Horses, arms, and prisoners were captured in nearly every engagement.

On reaching Brier Creek Swamp we pressed the enemy so warmly that he turned off toward Waynesborough. During the chase the enemy set fire to all corn cribs, cotton gins, and large number of barns and houses. We succeeded in driving him off in nearly half the instances in time to extinguish the flames, and frequently pressed him so rapidly as to prevent his firing a number of houses, thus saving a large amount of property.

I entered the town of Waynesborough with my staff just after dark, and just as the enemy were leaving it. The town was in flames, but with the assistance of my staff and escort we succeeded in staying the flames and in extinguishing the fire in all but one dwelling, which was so far burned that it was impossible to save it. I immediately moved on and attacked the enemy, who were engaged in tearing up the railroad. The attack had the effect to stop their work upon the railroad and to keep them in line of battle all night.

About 3 a. m. I sent Humes' division to gain the enemy's rear by turning his left flank, and sent a regiment to gain his rear by moving around his right. Unfortunately the commands failed to get into position. At daylight the enemy withdrew for a short distance unobserved, in consequence of a dense fog. As we advanced upon them they charged our line, which charge we met and easily repulsed. I charged the enemy's flank with Humes' and Anderson's commands, and attacked the front with the balance of my command, driving the enemy from his fortified position, capturing a number of prisoners, arms, and horses, and killing a great many who refused to surrender, and who were shot in the pursuit which ensued. The rout was complete, and General Kilpatrick was himself very nearly captured. We continued the charge until reaching a swamp, where the enemy had so constructed barricades as to make a very strong resistance. The enemy was soon driven from this position by a flank movement, after which I again charged and routed their entire force, capturing, killing, and wounding nearly 200, and completely stampeding the whole force. His destruction was only prevented by an intervening swamp at Buck Head Creek, which made it almost impossible to approach, and by the failure of the Fourth Tennessee Regiment to gain the enemy's rear, for which purpose it had been detached some two hours previous. The bridge over Buck Head Creek had been carefully prepared for burning by Kilpatrick's advance guard, and on our reaching it the torch had been applied and the bridge was in flames, while a terrific fire from the enemy on the other side prevented me from immediately extinguishing the flames. I dismounted the advance brigade and advanced it through the creek bottom to the bank, and finally drove the enemy sufficiently far from the opposite bank to enable a few brave men to work their way across and drive the enemy beyond range. By great energy and hard labor on the part of my men the fire was soon extinguished, and in little more than an hour the bridge was reconstructed and our troops passing over. The passage, however, was very slow, on account of the rude and frail construction of the bridge. After advancing a mile I discovered the enemy's position, and ordered General Dibrell to turn their right flank by moving through a wood which screened the movement.

As night was fast approaching it became important to strike the enemy immediately, although only about 1,200 of my command had crossed the creek. I moved upon the enemy and drove in his pickets. On discovering his line I observed that General Dibrell, in attempting to turn his flank (although he had moved nearly a mile to our left), had, nevertheless, encountered the enemy's line of battle, which extended still beyond his position. Having parts of Harrison's and Ashby's brigades with me, the former being in advance, I placed the Third Arkansas Regiment in line, and the Eighth and Eleventh Texas Regiments in column and charged the enemy's position. Nothing could have exceeded the gallantry with which these troops responded to the bugle's call, and hurled themselves upon the enemy, driving his cavalry in confusion and finally encountering the breast-works. This so terrified the enemy as to cause him to flee in uncontrollable confusion. Unfortunately the open ground did not continue, and we finally encountered a line so positioned that it could not be approached by cavalry. I ordered Ashby's brigade to turn the enemy's left flank and take possession of the Louisville road, upon which the enemy was retreating. Owing to approaching dusk, Colonel Ashby, by accident, got on a road to the left of the one indicated by my order, and notified me that he held possession of the Louisville road. This error enabled the enemy to move off, by scattering through fields and wood without order or organization.

During the night Kilpatrick sought the protection of his infantry, which he did not venture to forsake again during the campaign, no doubt being too much demoralized to again meet our cavalry. Fearing the enemy might make another attempt to raid or march upon Augusta, I placed pickets at all the crossings of Brier Creek, and located my main force at Rocky Springs Church.

On the morning of December 2, the Fourteenth Army Corps and Kilpatrick's cavalry marched upon Waynesborough by the Louisville road. I met and checked them at Rocky Creek. After a warm engagement they moved off to my left and crossed a short distance below on a temporarily constructed bridge, and, by moving through the fields, turned off toward Thomas' Station. This necessitated my falling back.

The following day I moved down and attacked the enemy, driving in their pickets and stopping their destruction of the railroad. Perceiving after night-fall that they had recommenced their work, I again attacked them about midnight, shelling their camp with good effect. At daylight the enemy in strong force marched upon Waynesborough. Most of my command had necessarily been sent some three miles after forage. We quickly concentrated and hastily threw up barricades, while a single regiment held the entire column in check. This rough screen was hardly completed when a general charge was made upon our lines, which was repulsed, with considerable loss to the enemy. A second, third, and fourth charge were made by the enemy, each of which was repulsed or met and driven back by counter-charges. Finally their long lines of infantry advanced, and, after warm fighting, their cavalry having turned our flanks, we were compelled to fall back, which was done by taking successive positions till we reached the town of Waynesborough. Here we were so warmly pressed that it was with difficulty we succeeded in withdrawing from our position. The moment our lines left our works I directed the Eighth Texas (Colonel Cook) and the Ninth Tennessee [Battalion] (Captain Bromley) to charge the enemy, which was gallantly done, meeting and driving back a charge of the enemy, and so staggering him that no further demonstration was made upon us until we were prepared to receive the enemy at our new position north of the town. During all the enemy's charges the loss of men and horses must have been severe. According to his own account his loss in men numbered 50 killed and 147 wounded. The enemy remained in town about three hours and then moved down the Savannah road. During all the engagements the enemy's cavalry were at least double my own numbers, and were, besides, re-enforced by one or more divisions of infantry.

Having been notified by the lieutenant-general commanding that the roads toward Savannah had been blockaded by his order, and having sent Lewis' brigade (re-enforced by the Fourth Tennessee Regiment) to fall back before the enemy, I, with the remainder of my command, remained to protect Augusta and to strike his flanks and rear.

On the first day I attacked his rear several times, driving him from his several positions, killing and wounding a great number and capturing about 100 prisoners. During his movement toward Savannah so warmly was he pressed that he blockaded the roads in his rear, frequently building fortifications two or three miles in length, and destroyed all bridges on his line of march. He occasionally attacked us by charging with his cavalry, which was invariably met by counter-charges and driven back in confusion with heavy loss. In every fight we captured horses, arms, and prisoners.

On the night of December 8 we shelled the camp of the Fourteenth Corps with good effect, throwing the corps into confusion and causing it to leave camp at midnight, abandoning clothing, arms, &c. By breaking up the camp during the extreme darkness a great many negroes were left in our hands, whom we sent back to their owners. We also captured three wagons and teams, and caused the enemy to burn several more wagons. The whole number of negroes captured from the enemy during the movement was nearly 2,000.

On the 8th we captured a dispatch (see Appendix A) from General Slocum to General Davis, giving the proposed location of Sherman's army before Savannah, which afterward proved to be correct. This paper was forwarded to General Hardee. On reaching a point within ten miles of the city, and finding it impossible to do any further harm to the enemy in that position, I moved back and crossed the Savannah River, leaving General Iverson's command to watch the enemy should he move in the direction of Augusta or Western Georgia. On reaching the South Carolina side, I moved down, and was placed by Lieutenant-General Hardee in command of the defenses of New River and adjacent landings, and charged with the duty of holding the line of communication from Huger's Landing to Hardeeville. This we succeeded in doing, although the enemy held the South Carolina side of the river with a division of infantry.

After the evacuation of the city, December 20, I removed all the guns and ammunition from Tunbridge and Mongan's Landings and New River bridge; also, the heavy guns, weighing 9,000 pounds each, from Red Bluff, together with the ammunition.

I omitted to state that during the entire movement of the enemy through Georgia I kept all my superiors fully informed of the strength and of all the movements of the enemy. At the same time I kept my cavalry in his front, rear, and on both flanks, preventing his cavalry from spreading over the country, retarding the enemy by fighting him on all sides and felling trees in his advance. This duty was fully done, and I thank my officers and men for their devotion, gallantry, and the self-sacrificing spirit they have ever exhibited. Every engagement was a success, and the utter defeat and discomfiture of the enemy's cavalry was most signal and complete, notwithstanding his force of cavalry was always superior to mine.

My force never exceeded 3,500 men, and was so distributed in front, rear, and on both flanks that I seldom had more than 2,000 under my immediate command, which 2,000 frequently charged and routed more than double their numbers. The enemy had been falsely informed by their officers that we took no prisoners, which caused him to fight with desperation and to run very dangerous gauntlets to escape capture, which frequently accounts for the large proportion of killed. In every rout of their cavalry, and in the many fights which ensued, they continued to flee, refusing to surrender, notwithstanding the demands of my men in close pursuit. Consequently, no alternative was left but to shoot or saber them to prevent escape.

During the trip I had parties to move a day or more in advance of the enemy, informing citizens where to run their negroes and stock in order to insure the safety of their property, offering them every assistance in so doing; but, generally, the citizens were so frightened as to be perfectly helpless. On the enemy's approach, pursuant to orders, I drove off such horses and mules as were exposed to the enemy's view, and have since taken every pains to restore said stock to its owners, generally with success. My command captured about 500 horses, many of which had been taken from citizens by the enemy, and have been returned to their owners when it was possible to do so.

I desire to tender my thanks for the devoted gallantry of my division and brigade commanders. Those whose conduct came especially under my notice were Generals Allen, Humes, Anderson, and Dibrell, and Colonels Ashby, Hagan, Crews, and Lieutenant-Colonel Anderson. General Allen was slightly wounded and had two horses shot under him at Waynesborough; Generals Humes and Dibrell also had their horses shot while gallantly engaging the enemy.

I also tender my thanks to General Robertson, who, while acting as my chief of staff in the temporary absence of his command, was severely wounded while gallantly charging the enemy.

Capt. S. W. Steele and Lieut. M. G. Hudson, aides-de-camp of my staff, were highly distinguished for gallantry and zeal. Lieuts. R. B. Ryan, J. M. Stewart, and Henry Chapman, acting upon my staff, were gallant and efficient.

In closing this report I will state that during the last five months my command has been without wagons or cooking utensils, with orders to subsist upon the country. Its food has been limited to bread baked upon boards and stones and meat broiled upon sticks. It has not been paid in twelve months, and has not had the regular issues of clothing which have been made to the infantry. During this time it has averaged in direct marching sixteen miles a day, and, being without wagons, has been obliged to pack all the forage and rations to camp on horseback, which, together with scouting and other duties, would make the average traveling of each soldier at least twenty miles each day. During these five months my troops have been continuously in the immediate presence of the enemy, fighting nearly every day, and with brilliant success, except in a few instances, when small detachments sent off from my command met vastly superior forces.

During these five months my command has captured, killed, and wounded more than its own effective strength. It has captured from the enemy in action and carried off the field 4 pieces of artillery, with caissons and battery wagons, 1,200 mules, over 200 wagons, 2,000 head of beef-cattle, 3,000 cavalry horses with equipments, and over 4,000 stand of arms. It has also captured a great number of the enemy's posts, with large amounts of stores, and has destroyed more railroad used by the enemy—stopping his communications for a longer time and with less loss—than any other cavalry command, although expeditions double its strength have been sent out on that duty. It has also captured and destroyed over a dozen trains of cars, generally loaded with supplies.

As we were continually fighting the enemy, our camps could not be designated before night-fall. Details had then to be sent out to procure forage and rations, frequently making it midnight before supper could be prepared for my men, and then they were often compelled to be in the saddle before daylight. No men in the Confederate States have marched more, fought more, suffered more, or had so little opportunities for discipline; yet they are to-day as orderly and as well disciplined as any cavalry in the Confederate service.

In our line of march officers and men were met who, in their anxiety to increase their commands, used every exertion to induce my men to desert, frequently offering them promotion and furloughs as a reward for dishonor. Notwithstanding this my command is to-day stronger and more efficient than it was at the beginning of a continuous campaign of eight months hard, constant, and successful fighting.

I must particularly commend my Tennessee and Kentucky troops, whom, though they saw their homes thrown open by the advance of General Hood's army, I brought from the Coosa River to Savannah without a single desertion. Afterward I had the mortification to see a body desert who had been informed they were to be punished without trial for crimes they had never committed.

Respectfully, colonel, your obedient servant,

J. WHEELER,
Major-General.

Lieut. Col. T. B. ROY,
Asst. Adjt. Gen., Headquarters Department, &c.

Appendix A.

HEADQUARTERS LEFT WING, ARMY OF GEORGIA,
Springfield, December 8, 1864—7 a. m.

GENERAL: General Sherman has information that the line of defense around Savannah is about four miles from the city. He desires to take the road extending from Cherokee Hill through Silk Hope to Litchfield as our first position. Your corps should be at or near Cherokee Hill. The Twentieth will be to the left of Pooler, Seventeenth on the right of Twentieth, and Fifteenth near Litchfield. The Twentieth Corps will be at Monteith to-night.

Yours, very respectfully,

H. W. SLOCUM,
Major-General.

This dispatch was directed on the envelope to General Jeff. C. Davis.

No. 158.

Report of Maj. Gen. Gustavus W. Smith, C. S. Army, commanding First Division, Georgia Militia, of operations October 12–November 30, including engagement at Honey Hill, S. C.

HEADQUARTERS FIRST DIVISION, GEORGIA MILITIA,
Savannah, December 6, 1864.

GENERAL: On the 12th of October last I received at Macon a telegram from General Hood directing me to assemble as rapidly as possible all our available forces in that vicinity and make a demonstration on Atlanta so soon as the necessary transportation could be procured. Under this order, I in a short time had at Lovejoy's Station a force numbering about 2,800 effective muskets, three batteries of Confederate artillery, and between 200 and 300 local reserve cavalry. The whole force was under my command, much the larger portion of infantry belonging to the First Division of Georgia Militia. Finding this force inadequate to make a direct assault upon Atlanta, garrisoned as it then was, General Hood suggested that I should, if practicable, cross the Chattahoochee and destroy the line of railroad between that river and the Etowah. For various reasons, which were submitted to Generals Beauregard and Hood (and by them approved), it was deemed neither practicable nor expedient to make a direct attack upon Atlanta, or upon the railroad line, as suggested; so my command continued in observation near Atlanta, preventing the enemy from foraging and keeping them in their line of works, supporting Brigadier-General Iverson, who had just in advance of us two brigades of cavalry.

On the night of the 12th of November Major-General Wheeler, of the cavalry, reached my headquarters, and soon after the advance of his forces from Alabama began to arrive. On the 15th of November the enemy moved out from Atlanta and advanced upon us with his whole force, viz, the Fifteenth, Seventeenth, and Twentieth Corps, with artillery and cavalry, which was soon after joined by the Fourteenth. Our cavalry were driven that afternoon from Jonesborough to Lovejoy's, and at dark I moved my force back to Griffin, at which place we had fortifications, and I felt we could there check the enemy should he advance directly upon us.

On the afternoon of the 16th it was ascertained the great mass of the enemy's forces had moved through McDonough, on the direct road from Atlanta to Macon, at which latter place there was at that time no garrison. At dark on the same day I left Griffin and marched my command to Forsyth, a distance of thirty-five miles in twenty-four hours. Learning that the enemy were crossing to the east bank of the

Ocmulgee River I moved the command to Macon, and about that time received orders from General Beauregard to report by letter to Lieutenant-General Taylor. A copy of that letter is herewith transmitted.*

All of my command except the Georgia militia and two regiments of State Line troops, which reported to me just before leaving Lovejoy's, were at this time turned over to Major-General Cobb. The defense of a portion of the line around Macon, on the west bank of the Ocmulgee, was assigned to the force still left in my command. Before the troops were fairly in position orders were received to cross the river and occupy a position covering East Macon. This movement occupied the whole night. Soon after daylight next morning my five brigades were in the respective positions assigned them, no two being in the same part of the field.

During the morning of Monday, the 21st, the First Brigade, under your own personal instructions, given direct to the colonel commanding, were sent along the line of the Central railroad, with orders to move as rapidly as possible, either by rail or otherwise, to the city of Augusta. In the afternoon of the same day Anderson's battery of artillery was assigned to the militia, and you directed me to move as soon as possible, with this battery, the Second, Third, and Fourth Brigades of militia, and the two regiments of the State Line, to Augusta. They moved Tuesday morning in the direction of Griswoldville, with orders to halt there and await further instructions from me. You also informed me that you had ordered Major Cook, with the Athens and Augusta battalions, to proceed to Augusta, and directed me to take them in my command if I came up with them on the route. Arrangements for transportation of ammunition and supplies detained me a few hours in Macon, which place you had left on the evening previous. Lieutenant-General Taylor arrived there on the morning of the 22d. Information having been received showing very clearly that a much larger force of the enemy was near the city than was supposed when you gave the orders for my troops to move, he authorized me to direct them to return. My order reached them on the eve of an engagement with what was supposed to be a small force of the enemy. Notwithstanding my order to avoid an engagement at that place and time, a collision occurred, we being the attacking party; and though the officers and men behaved with great gallantry, they failed to carry the works of the enemy, but held a position within 150 yards of their line until after dark, when they were withdrawn to Macon by my order. The First Brigade of militia were not engaged, having passed that point in the execution of orders given by yourself. Major Cook, commanding the Athens and Augusta battalions, moving under orders direct from yourself, was upon the ground and engaged in this action.

Our loss was a little over 600, being more than one-fourth of the effective muskets we had in the engagement. Several of the best field officers of the command were killed or wounded.

It is evident now that our men were opposed by the larger portion of one corps of the enemy, while another was marching from Clinton in their rear; and I consider the troops were very fortunate in being withdrawn without disaster. Lieutenant-General Taylor, having become satisfied that the enemy were leaving the vicinity of Macon, directed me to move my command on Friday morning by rail to Albany; thence march to Thomasville; thence by rail to Savannah.

---

*Not found.

We arrived in Thomasville by noon Monday, having marched from Albany, a distance between fifty-five and sixty miles, in fifty-four hours. At Thomasville instead of finding five trains, the number I had requested to be sent, there were but two, and these could not be started until after dark, and did not arrive here until 2 o'clock Wednesday morning, occupying twice the time necessary between Thomasville and Savannah, and leaving the Second, Third, and Fourth Brigades at the former place. Upon arriving here, almost broken down by fatigue and want of rest, with officers and men similarly situated, I received before leaving the cars a peremptory order from yourself requiring me to take the militia of Georgia beyond the limits of the State, which was in direct violation of the statute organizing and calling them into service. Considering the jaded condition of both officers and men, I determined not to move the militia or the State Line beyond the limits of Georgia until satisfied in my own mind that absolute necessity demanded it.

In a personal interview with yourself you informed me that the enemy had moved out from Broad River; were encamped within a few miles of the Savannah and Charleston Railroad, threatening Grahamville and Coosawhatchie, and unless vigorously opposed would undoubtedly break the road at one or both of these points soon after daylight; and that the only force you had in your whole command which could by any possibility be brought upon the ground in time was two regular Confederate regiments from Charleston, and you believed these would be there too late; and that if I could hold the enemy in check until 2 p. m. and prevent their cutting the road before that time, several thousand re-enforcements from North and South Carolina, intended for Savannah, would arrive.

In this interview I showed you my qualified authority from the Governor to withdraw the Georgia State forces under my command from Confederate service in case they were ordered beyond the limits of the State. After a full conference with yourself I was perfectly satisfied that for the purposes intended it was right and proper the movement should be made, and I gave orders accordingly. Notwithstanding some objections made by a portion of officers and men, the order was willingly obeyed.

The leading brigade arrived at Grahamville about 8 o'clock Wednesday morning, the 30th of November. You kindly tendered me the services of your chief of artillery (Colonel Gonzales), who, upon our arrival at Grahamville, introduced me to Colonel Colcock, commander of the military district; Major Jenkins, the commander of the immediate vicinity, and Captain De Saussure, Colonel Colcock's adjutant-general. To these four gentlemen particularly, and other officers acquainted with the locality, I am indebted for the information upon which I based the directions of the whole operation for the day.

Colonel Colcock reported the enemy rapidly advancing, skirmishing with some companies of his cavalry and a few pieces of artillery. He was just starting to the front, and I requested him to select a position for my leading brigade so soon as I could dispatch it to him. I awaited the arrival of the second train of my own troops and the Forty-seventh Georgia, which was momentarily expected from Charleston.

Having given the necessary orders to these forces, I joined Colonel Colcock a few minutes after 10 o'clock some four miles from the Grahamville depot and about one-half mile beyond the position we finally assumed. Colonel C. informed me the enemy had already occupied the position selected by him as the best for defense before my troops arrived. This made it necessary, in my judgment, that the leading brigade should be countermarched at once and placed in position on a line with our main battery. The troops in rear were hurried up and placed upon the same line, to the right and left of the road. The enemy in the meanwhile steadily advanced along the main road upon our position. After a proper disposition of our forces had been made and a skirmish line ordered forward, Colonel Colcock, the commander of the district and next officer in rank upon the field to myself, was assigned to the immediate executive command of the main line; Colonel Gonzales was placed in charge of the artillery, and Major Jenkins of all the cavalry; Captain De Saussure, who was thoroughly acquainted with the whole country, remained near me. The Forty-seventh Georgia had not yet reached the field. Within five or ten minutes after these dispositions had been made the battle began by an advance piece of our artillery firing upon the enemy. Their line of battle was soon formed, and from that time until near dark made continuous efforts to carry our position. We had actually engaged five pieces of artillery, and it is due to the South Carolina artillerists that I should say I have never seen pieces more skillfully employed and gallantly served upon a difficult field of battle.

In an hour the enemy had so extended and developed their attack that it became absolutely necessary for me to place in the front line of battle my last troops (the Forty-seventh Georgia Regiment), making in all about 1,400 effective muskets on the field, and all engaged. From time to time alterations had to be made in our lines, by changing the positions of regiments and companies, extending intervals, &c., to prevent being flanked; and while we could not from the dense wood accurately estimate the number of the enemy, it was very clear their force largely exceeded ours, and I awaited with some anxiety the arrival of the Thirty-second Georgia and the forces expected from North and South Carolina.

Too much credit cannot be given to Colonel Colcock and Colonel Gonzales, Major Jenkins, and Captain De Saussure; to all the officers of my own staff; to Colonel Willis, commanding First Brigade of Georgia Militia; Colonel Wilson, commanding State Line Brigade; Major Cook, commanding the Athens and Augusta battalions of reserves; Lieutenant-Colonel Edwards, commanding the Forty-seventh Georgia Confederate Regiment; and to all the officers and men of every arm engaged upon that field. In short, I have never seen or known of a battle-field upon which there was so little confusion, and where every order was so cheerfully and promptly obeyed, and where a small number of men for so long a time successfully resisted the determined and oft-repeated efforts of largely superior attacking forces. The flight of the enemy during the night and the number of their dead left upon the field is evidence of the nature of the attack as well as the defense.

About 4.30 p. m. Brigadier-General Robertson arrived with a portion of the Thirty-second Georgia from Charleston, a battery of artillery, and a company of cavalry. These constituted an effective reserve, but came up too late to be used in the action. During the night the enemy retired rapidly in the direction of their gun-boats.

Our loss in every arm of service was 8 men killed and 42 wounded. The enemy left over 200 of their dead upon the field, and their whole loss in killed and wounded is believed to be upward of 1,000.

At midnight Brigadier-General Chesnut arrived at Grahamville Station with about 350 effective muskets of South Carolina reserves, and a little before daylight upon the morning of the 1st of December Brigadier-General Baker came up with 860 of his brigade from North Carolina; the remainder of his command (about 1,100) reached Coosawhatchie at 9 o'clock. Lieutenant-General Hardee arrived at Grahamville Station between 8 and 9 o'clock of morning of the 1st of December.

The enemy having been beaten back on the 30th of November, and the Confederate forces having now arrived, there was, in my judgment, no longer any necessity for retaining the State troops of Georgia beyond their legal jurisdiction. I therefore asked and obtained permission to bring these exhausted troops back to their own State. They arrived here, by Lieutenant-General Hardee's order, about 10 o'clock that night.

For full particulars of the engagement near Grahamville, S. C., I refer you to the reports of subordinate commanders, which will be forwarded as soon as furnished.

G. W. SMITH,
Major-General.

Lieut. Gen. W. J. HARDEE,
Commanding Department.

The above copy is transmitted to General J. B. Hood because most of the operations referred to were by his direction while the militia formed part of his command.

G. W. S.

[Inclosure.]

MACON, *November 19, 1864.*

Lieut. Gen. RICHARD TAYLOR,
Commanding, &c., Selma, Ala.:

GENERAL: General Beauregard has informed me by telegraph that you will take the immediate command of the forces in Georgia, and directed me to report to you by letter. My own proper command consists of one division of militia, four brigades of infantry, numbering in all 1,900 effective muskets when we left Lovejoy's. I have not yet received the return since their arrival here yesterday afternoon. Besides the militia, there was temporarily assigned to me by General Cobb one regiment and two battalions of reserve infantry, numbering about 900, some 300 reserves and local cavalry, and one battalion of Confederate artillery. The forces other than the militia proper will, I take for granted, be now placed under some other commander. The enemy moved their strongest column through McDonough, and when I was at Griffin they had passed through McDonough, and were nearer Macon than I was. When I reached Forsyth, having made fifty miles in forty-eight hours, they were reported crossing the Ocmulgee, and could, by a rapid march, reach Macon by the left bank of the Ocmulgee without opposition. General Cobb ordered the cars to Forsyth for the infantry, and directed me to move the whole command to this place without delay. General Wheeler was the senior officer on this theater of operations, and without giving direct orders to the infantry and artillery, strongly advised, so soon as he developed the strength of the enemy, that I should move to Macon at once. I fully concurred in opinion with both General Wheeler and General Cobb. General Wheeler is confident that Sherman has with him in this movement at least 35,000 effective men, and informs me that the Fourteenth Army

Corps is moving in addition to join Sherman. Since I commenced this letter Lieutenant-General Hardee has come in. I will show him this letter before mailing it to your address.

I remain, general, very respectfully and truly, yours,

G. W. SMITH,
Major-General, First Division, Georgia Militia.

P. S.—General Hardee has just shown me his orders from Richmond, dated 17th instant, stating that he commands all Georgia south of the Chattahoochee, and directing him to gather convalescents, local troops, &c., to garrison this place.

G. W. S.

In the above I omitted the two regiments of State Line troops; they joined us the day before we left Lovejoy's. The two together number about 400 muskets.

G. W. S.

NOVEMBER 16-17, 1864.—Expedition from Barrancas to Pine Barren Bridge, Fla.

Report of Lieut. Col. Andrew B. Spurling, Second Maine Cavalry, commanding expedition.

CAMP SECOND MAINE VETERAN CAVALRY,
Barrancas, Fla., November 18, 1864.

GENERAL: I have the honor respectfully to report that, pursuant to orders from headquarters District of West Florida, I left camp at Barrancas, at 12 m. November 17 [16], in charge of all the then available force of the Second Maine Veteran and First Florida Cavalry, amounting in the aggregate to 450 men. After fording the bayou at Gun-boat Point, I marched the force fifteen miles in a northerly direction, and bivouacked a little after dark four miles from the Fifteen-Mile House, a point on the railroad leading from Pensacola to Montgomery and distant from Pensacola eleven miles. At 3 o'clock on the following morning the march was resumed on the road running parallel with the railroad. After a march of about three hours, and at sunrise, the advance guard, commanded by Lieutenant Sanders, Company F, First Florida, came upon a rebel picket of three men, surprising and capturing them; at a distance of a mile another picket of four was surprised and captured; and a mile farther on six men, constituting the reserve, were made prisoners, from whom it being ascertained that at 10 o'clock they were to be relieved, the column halted for an hour, and the advance guard was sent forward to intercept and capture the men who were anticipated as the relief. In a short time the men who were coming out to relieve the picket were captured and brought in. The column then moved forward and reached the bridge at Pine Barren Creek. I succeeded without difficulty in capturing the rebel picket on the bridge, not a single shot being exchanged, and without alarming their camp, although it was close by, within twenty rods. The bridge was in a very bad condition, having been partly swept away by the river, much swollen by recent rains. I succeeded, however, in crossing my advance guard mounted, and several squadrons dismounted, without being discovered by the enemy. A sudden dash was made upon the camp; nearly every man was captured, all their equipments, arms, horses, &c. The whole number of prisoners taken was 38; 47 horses, 3 mules, and 75 stand of arms, were captured. Nearly every effective man, including the lieutenant commanding, of Captain Leed's [Leigh's] company, Colonel Maury's Fifteenth Confederate Cavalry, was made a prisoner. Two companies had been ordered away the day before to some point on the railroad in the direction of Pollard, or undoubtedly they would have shared the same fate. All the barracks, stables, shelters, &c., sufficiently extensive for a regiment, were burned, together with what commissary and quartermaster's stores were found.

Having accomplished all that was intended I recrossed the bridge, destroyed what of it remained, and in accordance with my orders started for Barrancas. I arrived in camp with my command a little after midnight, bringing with me all the prisoners, captured mules, horses, &c.

There were no casualties among our troops; not a man was injured. The conduct of both officers and men was at all times good and all that could be desired.

It would hardly be doing justice did I not make special mention of Lieut. Joseph G. Sanders, Company F, First Florida Cavalry. He is a worthy officer, and deserves high praise for his meritorious conduct. He was at all times in command of the advance guard, and much of the success is due to the prompt and faithful manner in which all orders were executed. Among those under his command who did excellent service may be mentioned Sergeants Hollinger, Company E, Woodham, Company F, and Morgan, Company C, First Florida; Sergeants Butler, Company B, and Baker, Company F, Second Maine. These sergeants were at all times brave, active, and zealous in performing their duties. Major Hutchinson, commanding the Second Maine, and Major Ruttkay, commanding the First Florida Cavalry, were prompt and energetic.

I have the honor to be, general, very respectfully, your obedient servant,

A. B. SPURLING,

Lieutenant-Colonel Second Maine Cavalry, Comdg. Expedition.

Bvt. Brig. Gen. J. BAILEY,

Commanding District of West Florida.

NOVEMBER 30, 1864.—Engagement at Honey Hill, near Grahamville, S. C.

REPORTS.*

No. 1.—Maj. Gen. John G. Foster, U. S. Army, commanding Department of the South, including operations November 28–December 7.

No. 2.—Brig. Gen. John P. Hatch, U. S. Army, commanding Coast Division.

No. 3.—Brig. Gen. Edward E. Potter, U. S. Army, commanding First Brigade.

No. 4.—Col. William Gurney, One hundred and twenty-seventh New York Infantry.

No. 5.—Lieut. Col. Nathaniel Haughton, Twenty-fifth Ohio Infantry.

No. 6.—Col. Alfred S. Hartwell, Fifty-fifth Massachusetts Infantry, commanding Second Brigade.

No. 7.—Col. Henry L. Chipman, One hundred and second U. S. Colored Troops, commanding Second Brigade.

No. 8.—Lieut. Col. William Ames, Third Rhode Island Artillery, commanding Artillery Brigade.

No. 9.—Commander George H. Preble, U. S. Navy, commanding Marine Brigade.

---

* See also report of Maj. Gen. Gustavus W. Smith, p. 413; and f r reports of naval co-operating forces, see Annual Report of the Secretary of the Navy, December 4, 1865.

No. 1.

Report of Maj. Gen. John G. Foster, U. S. Army, commanding Department of the South, including operations November 28–December 7.

HEADQUARTERS DEPARTMENT OF THE SOUTH,
STEAMER NEMAHA,
Tullifinny River, December 7, 1864.

GENERAL: I have the honor to report that I left Hilton Head on the night of November 28 for Boyd's Neck, on the south side of Broad River, with all the disposable troops in this department, amounting to 5,000 infantry, cavalry, and artillery, with 500 sailors and marines. Owing to a thick fog and the incapacity of our pilots many of the boats lost their way and others grounded, so that the troops did not get ashore until late in the afternoon of the 29th. I then placed Brigadier-General Hatch in command of the force with orders to push forward and cut the railroad. He marched at once, but the maps and guides proved totally worthless, and after being twice misguided the troops reached the right road by morning. Thence, after daylight, they advanced toward Grahamville through a densely wooded country, driving back the enemy's artillery and infantry to a rise of ground called Honey Hill, a short distance this side of Grahamville, where they met a battery across the road, with seven guns. The enemy's infantry, rather over 4,000 and nearly equal to our own in number, was posted behind intrenchments in the woods on each side of the road. This position was immediately attacked with vigor and determination, but from the unfavorable nature of the ground, which admitted the employment of only one section of our artillery, we were unable to drive off the enemy, who did not, however, venture to advance beyond his intrenchments. After an obstinate fight of several hours, General Hatch, finding that the enemy's line could be neither successfully assaulted nor outflanked, retired after dark to a strong position about two miles and a half from Boyd's Neck. The rebels made no attempt to follow. Our loss was 88 killed, 623 wounded (140 of whom so slightly as not to be sent to the hospital), and 43 missing.

From November 30 to December 5, while keeping the greater part of the force at Boyd's Neck, I made at different points, with the assistance of the navy, several demonstrations—in one of which the Twenty-fifth Regiment Ohio Volunteer Infantry marched six miles into the interior toward Pocotaligo and captured two pieces of artillery at Church Bridge, near Gardner's Corners, one of which the men dragged off by hand. On the night of December 5 I embarked a force under command of Brigadier-General Potter. From Boyd's Neck proceeded, at daylight, to Tullifinny Creek, and landed the men at James Gregory's plantation, on the right bank, in pontoons and launches. General Potter pushed immediately forward, and about one mile and a half out met the enemy, whom he forced rapidly back to the spot where the road up the peninsula between the Coosawhatchie and Tullifinny meets the road running across from one river to the other. Here the rebels, being re-enforced from the south side of the Coosawhatchie, made a stand and attacked our left vigorously, but our men repulsed them handsomely, capturing a battle-flag and some prisoners, and got possession of the crossing, which we now firmly hold. A detachment sent to the right destroyed the road bridge over the Tullifinny. Our loss in the whole affair was about 5 killed and 50 wounded. The railroad is less than three-quarters of a mile from our front, separated by a dense wood, through which is only a bridle path, and in the skirt of which are our pickets. I have ordered nearly all the force from Boyd's Neck to this position, and also some 30-pounder Parrotts, with which we can reach the railroad, even should our men not succeed in gaining it, as I hope they may, as also the road bridge over the Coosawhatchie. Our position is strong, the spirit of the troops excellent, and the landings and means of communication good. The naval force, under orders from Admiral Dahlgren, have co-operated cordially and efficiently both by water and land. The reports received from prisoners and deserters relative to General Sherman's movements are very conflicting. A lieutenant who deserted on the 4th reports that General Sherman was in sight of Savannah. There can be no doubt that he is nearing Savannah, as all the deserters and prisoners who have recently come in agree that troops are leaving Charleston and Augusta for Savannah.

Very respectfully, your obedient servant,

J. G. FOSTER,
Major-General, Commanding.

Maj. Gen. H. W. HALLECK, U. S. Army,
Chief of Staff, Armies of United States, Washington, D. C.

No. 2.

Report of Brig. Gen. John P. Hatch, U. S. Army, commanding Coast Division.

HDQRS. COAST DIVISION, DEPARTMENT OF THE SOUTH,
Deveaux's Neck, S. C., December —, 1864.

CAPTAIN: I have the honor to make the following report of the movements of this division from the date of its embarkation at Hilton Head to the close of the action at Honey Hill:

The force collected from different points in the Department of the South, with the addition of a small brigade from the navy, numbered, including all arms, about 5,500 men, organized as follows: Two brigades of infantry, commanded by Brig. Gen. E. E. Potter and Col. A. S. Hartwell, Fifty-fifth Massachusetts Volunteers; Naval Brigade, Commander George H. Preble, U. S. Navy, commanding; portions of three batteries light artillery, Lieut. Col. William Ames, Third Rhode Island Artillery, commanding. It was embarked on the evening of the 28th November, with the intention of landing at Boyd's Neck at daylight the following morning. My command of the force was to commence after landing. At 2.30 a. m., the hour previously designated, the signal for sailing was given from the flag-ship of the department commander. The transports immediately got under way; but soon after, a dense fog covering the river, some came to anchor, others continuing the advance grounded, whilst others, by a mistake of the pilots, were taken up the Chechesse instead of the Broad River. The pilot of my own steamer advising me to wait daylight, I did so, and consequently it was from that transport the first troops commenced landing, at about 11 a. m. The steamer Canonicus, containing engineer troops and material, was unfortunately one of the transports that had gone up the Chechesse by mistake, and did not arrive at Boyd's Neck until about 2 p. m. This caused a delay in building the necessary landing to enable the artillery and means of transportation to be disembarked. The Naval Brigade was the first organized body landed. It was immediately pushed to the front to occupy a cross-roads two miles in advance of the landing. Attached to this brigade was a battery of eight light guns, drawn by sailors. The brigade met and drove toward Bee's Creek a small force of the enemy. The Thirty-second U. S. Colored Troops, as soon as landed, was sent to the support of the brigade. At 4 p. m. the detachment of cavalry and a large portion of Potter's brigade having landed, I determined to push forward immediately and attempt to seize the railroad at Grahamville, without waiting the landing of the artillery and the remainder of the infantry. The debarkation of the remainder of the troops continued through the night and following day as the transports arrived. Unfortunately the maps and guides proved equally worthless. The Naval Brigade had pushed back the enemy, who, retreating toward Bee's Creek, were followed two miles from the cross-roads in a direction opposite to the route we were to march, supposing it the direct road to Grahamville. Potter's brigade followed, and it was not until the latter had overtaken the Naval Brigade that the error was discovered. The troops countermarched and returned to the cross-roads. The sailors dragging the artillery were found to be worn out, and the Naval Brigade was left at that point, with orders to come up in the morning. We then pushed on with Potter's brigade and the cavalry. Two miles from the cross-roads was found a fork in the road near a church. The guide, pretending to recognize the point, led the column on the left-hand road. Four miles beyond the church it became evident that the guide had mistaken the road, and I returned to the church, where we bivouacked at 2 a. m. The men had then marched fifteen miles, had been up most of the previous night, had worked hard during the day, and were unable to march farther. The distance marched, if upon the right road, would have carried us to the railroad, and I have since learned we would have met, at that time, little or no opposition.

On the morning of the 30th the Artillery and Naval Brigades having come up, it was reported to me that horses had been furnished the naval battery, except for two mountain howitzers. These I directed to return to and hold the cross-roads, supported by four companies of the Fifty-fourth Massachusetts Volunteers. They were attacked, and repulsed a body of the enemy from the direction of Bee's Creek battery. I then marched on the direct road toward Grahamville in the following order: Cavalry; Potter's brigade, with Mesereau's battery, Third New York Artillery; Naval Brigade; Titus' battery, Third New York Artillery; and all of Hartwell's brigade that had arrived at the point, consisting of one regiment and two companies of a second. At 9.15 a. m. met the advance of the enemy, consisting of two pieces of artillery with an infantry support. Our column was marching in a narrow road with dense woods on both sides. The action was opened by General Potter, who advanced the One hundred and twenty-seventh New York Volunteers as skirmishers, supported by the Twenty-fifth Ohio and the One hundred and forty-fourth and One hundred and fifty-seventh New York Volunteers. The supports were deployed on the sides of the road when the country opened sufficiently to allow it. Hartwell's brigade was also brought forward as soon as it could find open ground on the right side of the road. We advanced gradually, driving the enemy about three miles and a half, their artillery being silenced at every opening of the section with our advance. Our casualties were not severe during this advance, but a valuable and gallant officer, First Lieut. Edward A. Wildt, Third New York Artillery, fell mortally wounded whilst sighting one of his guns. At 11 a. m. the head of the column came unexpectedly on the main body of the enemy in position. At this point the road bends to the left. The advance following it found themselves in front of an inclosed work pierced for four guns. The redoubt, situated on the crest of a small ridge, was the center of the enemy's line. It is said to have been built two years since, although until now unknown to us. Following the crest of the hill on either side the redoubt, the enemy had thrown up a line of rifle-pits, and within these waited with seven pieces of artillery our attack. In front of the enemy's line ran a small creek, bounded by a marsh covered with dense undergrowth. This was not impassable, but presented a serious obstacle to our advance, being completely commanded by the enemy's fire. Potter's brigade was quickly formed in line of battle parallel to that of the enemy. One section of Mesereau's artillery, placed in position in the road, opened fire upon the redoubt. The left of Potter's brigade—re-enforced by two companies of the Fifty-fourth Massachusetts Volunteers and part of the Fifty-fifth Massachusetts Volunteers, which had by mistake taken position on the left of the road—made two desperate attacks on the main work of the enemy, led by Col. A. S. Hartwell, commanding Second Brigade. They were repulsed with severe loss. The Fifty-fifth Massachusetts Volunteers were rallied, and, with the Marine Battalion, sent to the support of the right wing of the line of battle, with orders to turn the left flank of the enemy. They advanced gallantly, but were unable to carry the intrenchments. This wing finally fell back a short distance to take advantage of an inequality of the ground, which gave them a position from which they repulsed several attacks made by the enemy. Charges made on our left flank were repulsed with ease. Between 1 and 2 p. m. the One hundred and second U. S. Colored Troops reached the field, having arrived at the landing at 11 a. m.

The ammunition of the troops engaged being nearly expended, and none arriving from the rear, this regiment was necessarily held in reserve, as I received information from deserters and prisoners that large re-enforcements were being received by the enemy by railroad. One section of Mesereau's artillery, having been placed in battery in a position completely commanded by the artillery and sharpshooters of the enemy, lost two of its officers wounded, and most of its horses and cannoneers; two of the ammunition-chests on the limbers were blown up. A detail of a company from the One hundred and second U. S. Colored Troops was ordered to bring off the guns. Capt. A. E. Lindsay, commanding the company, was killed, and Lieut. H. H. Alvord was severely wounded. The command of the company devolved upon a sergeant, who did not understand the object of the advance, and failed to accomplish it. First Lieut. O. W. Bennett, One hundred and second U. S. Colored Troops, with thirty men was detached for the same purpose, and executed it in the coolest and most gallant manner. Mesereau's artillery was then sent to the rear, and Titus' battery brought into action. The artillery fire was directed to be continued slowly, as the ammunition was being expended and none received from the rear. The caissons as fast as emptied were ordered to the landing to refill. About 3 p. m. 6,000 rounds of musket ammunition was received and issued to those regiments entirely out. It was, however, now certain that the enemy's position could not be carried; and whilst a moderate fire was kept up, arrangements were commenced for retiring as soon as it became dark. The ammunition of Titus' battery, except twenty rounds each for two guns, being expended, the naval guns under Lieutenant

Commander Matthews were brought into action, one section at a time. The ambulances having been landed commenced reaching the front. One section of Titus' battery, supported by two regiments of infantry, took post half a mile in the rear. Two regiments of infantry were then drawn from the flanks and posted one mile farther to the rear, where the road crossed a ravine. Two regiments of infantry were detailed to carry the wounded. At dusk the retreat commenced. The Naval Brigade, with the exception of its two pieces of artillery, then engaged, was ordered to occupy the cross-roads; the One hundred and twenty-seventh New York Volunteers and One hundred and second U. S. Colored Troops, with one section naval artillery, remained at the front, keeping up a slow fire with artillery until 7.30 p. m., when, the main body of the command being well on its march, they withdrew, and were in their turn covered by the Fifty-sixth and One hundred and forty-fourth Regiments New York Volunteers; these were again covered by the Twenty-fifth Ohio and One hundred and fifty-seventh New York Volunteers, posted as before mentioned. The whole retrograde movement was executed without loss or confusion; there was no pursuit by the enemy or alarm of any kind; not a wounded man was left on the field, except those who fell at the foot of the enemy's works in the charges in which we were repulsed; no stores or equipments fell into the hands of the enemy, except some thrown away by the men on the advance, to enable them the better to follow the enemy in his retreat.

In closing this report I must give the gallant men the credit due them. The list of killed and wounded, none of whom fell in retreat, attest their good conduct. The affair was a repulse owing entirely to the strong position held by the enemy and our want of ammunition. A few instances of individual gallantry that have come particularly to my knowledge I will mention: Col. A. S. Hartwell, Fifty-fifth Massachusetts Volunteers, commanding brigade, received his third wound during the engagement at the foot of the enemy's intrenchments; Col. James C. Beecher, Thirty-fifth U. S. Colored Troops, twice wounded, refused to go to the rear until the close of the action; Lieut. George H. Crocker, Third New York Artillery, continued to serve his guns, after losing an eye, until they were withdrawn by order.

Lieut. Cols. W. T. Bennett and James F. Hall, of my staff; S. L. Woodford, One hundred and twenty-seventh New York Volunteers; N. Haughton, Twenty-fifth Ohio; James C. Carmichael, One hundred and fifty-seventh New York Volunteers; A. J. Willard, Thirty-fifth U. S. Colored Troops; Lieut. Commanders A. F. Crosman and E. O. Matthews, U. S. Navy; Capt. T. J. Mesereau, Third New York Artillery; Lieut. G. G. Stoddard, U. S. Marines; Lieuts. E. H. Titus and George C. Breck, Third New York Artillery, deserve particular mention. The brigade commanders—Brig. Gen. E. E. Potter, Commander G. H. Preble, U. S. Navy, and Lieut. Col. William Ames, Third Rhode Island Artillery—gave me a hearty support. General Potter, who commanded the advance, handled his troops handsomely, and personally superintended the withdrawal of the rear of the command on the retreat. To my own staff I am indebted for their energy and activity. Col. G. A. Pierce, quartermaster, volunteer aide, was wounded whilst making a reconnaissance. Capt. G. E. Gouraud, of General Foster's staff, won the praise of all, and is particularly commended for gallantry.* Capts. W. W. Sampson, acting aide-de-camp, and T. L. Appleton, assistant provost-marshal; Lieuts. L. B. Perry, acting assistant adjutant-general; E. B. Van Winkle, aide-de-camp; D. G. McMartin,

---

* Gouraud was awarded a Medal of Honor.

aide-de-camp, and T. C. Vidal, signal officer, did their duty nobly, and assisted in rallying at the front and leading forward those troops who, unable to stand the terrible fire of the enemy, were repulsed in the assault.

In the reports of brigade commanders, herewith inclosed, you will find personal mention of other officers. The medical department, under direction of Surg. George S. Burton, Third Rhode Island Artillery, proved itself highly efficient, and the corps of stretcher-bearers visited thoroughly all parts of the field where the troops were engaged. A list of the casualties accompanies this report. The total killed, wounded, and missing is 746. Of the 28 missing, I have been indirectly informed that 13 unwounded and 5 wounded men are in the hands of the enemy.

I am, captain, very respectfully, your obedient servant,

JNO. P. HATCH,
Brigadier-General, Commanding.

Capt. W. L. M. BURGER,
Assistant Adjutant-General, Hdqrs. Dept. of the South.

Recapitulation of the killed, wounded, and missing in the Coast Division, Department of the South, during the action at Honey Hill, S. C., November 30, 1864.

Coast Division.	Officers.				Men.				Aggregate
	Killed.		Missing.	Total.	Killed.	Wounded.	Missing.	Total.	
First Brigade	2	28	1	31	54	409	14	477	508
Second Brigade	3	10	1	14	28	160	8	196	210
Naval Brigade	......	......	......	......	1	7	4	12	12
Artillery Brigade	1	2	......	3	......	12	......	12	15
Cavalry	......	......	......	......	......	1	......	1	1
Total	6	40	2	48	83	589	26	698	746

JNO. P. HATCH,
Brigadier-General, Commanding.

No. 3.

Report of Brig. Gen. Edward E. Potter, U. S. Army, commanding First Brigade.

HEADQUARTERS FIRST BRIGADE, FIELD DIVISION,
Deveaux's Neck, December 11, 1864.

SIR: I have the honor to submit the following report of the part taken by the First Brigade in the affair of the 30th ultimo, at Honey Hill, near Grahamville, S. C.:

The brigade moved at 8 a. m., on the Grahamville road, from the church at the intersection of that road with the one leading from Boyd's Landing to Tenny's Landing. The One hundred and twenty-seventh New York were in advance, followed by the Twenty-fifth Ohio, and in its rear a section of Battery F, Third New York Artillery. After marching about half a mile the enemy was encountered. He had one piece of artillery in position on the road on slightly rising ground at the end of a swampy defile. The One hundred and twenty-seventh were deployed as skirmishers to the right and left of the road, and the Twenty-fifth Ohio, One hundred and fifty-seventh New York, and One hundred and forty-fourth New York, advanced to their support. On the left of the road was a thick jungle, almost impassable for infantry; on the right were occasional openings, but here the enemy had set fire to the tall grass and weeds, and this seriously impeded the advance of the troops. I was consequently obliged to order the regiments in the rear to advance by the flank along the road at double-quick, in order to expose them for as short a time as possible to the enemy's fire, which enfiladed the road. The section of Battery F, Third New York Artillery, also advanced and came into battery on the road. The enemy now fell back and the brigade marched a short distance by the flank on the road, with the One hundred and twenty-seventh deployed as skirmishers. The enemy took up a new position, from which he was soon driven, and the command moved forward without opposition until Honey Hill was reached. At this point the road to Grahamville takes a sharp turn to the left, and another road comes in from the right, probably connecting with the Coosawhatchie road. Along the last road and to the right of the Grahamville road the enemy was found intrenched; a vigorous charge of the Twenty-fifth Ohio drove them from these intrenchments, which connected with the main work placed on a hill thirty feet in height and mounting five guns. On the left of the Grahamville road the One hundred and twenty-seventh New York drove the enemy and got within 200 yards of their works. Our line was now formed, with the One hundred and forty-fourth New York, Twenty-fifth Ohio, Thirty-second U. S. Colored Troops, and marines on the right of the road, and the One hundred and twenty-seventh New York, Fifty-sixth New York, and One hundred and fifty-seventh New York upon the left. The section of Battery F, Third New York Artillery, went in battery on the road about the center of the line and opened a rapid and steady fire. I ordered the right of the line to press forward, swinging round to the left, and if possible to take the enemy's works in flank and rear; but after advancing a short distance, the dense undergrowth and deep swamps prevented their farther progress. The Thirty-fifth U. S. Colored Troops, which had come up about this time, was pushed out on our right center; but the heavy fire of the enemy and the difficulties of the ground compelled them to withdraw. Colonel Beecher was severely wounded, but kept the field. The regiment was reformed and held in reserve in rear of the section of Battery F, Third New York Artillery. On our extreme left the enemy pressed rather heavily, and the left wing of the Fifty-sixth New York was ordered to take position on the left, and in support of the One hundred and fifty-seventh New York. Here also the deep swamp and abatis in front of the enemy's works prevented the advance of our troops. We maintained our position thus taken until dark, keeping up and receiving a heavy fire, and suffering considerable loss from our exposed situation. At dusk, in accordance with instructions received from the brigadier-general commanding the Field Division, I commenced to withdraw the troops. A position was taken up about half a mile in our rear, and the One hundred and forty-fourth and Fifty-sixth New York formed a line on either side of the road to cover the retrograde movement. The One hundred and twenty-seventh New York and the One hundred and second U. S. Colored Troops, of the Second Brigade, were left as supports for a section of the Naval Battery, which kept up a fire against the enemy's works. The regiments on the left were first withdrawn, and then the regiments on the right. A second position was taken up about a mile in rear of the first, and the Twenty-fifth Ohio and One hundred and fifty-seventh New York ordered to hold it. The section of the Naval Battery and its supports were then withdrawn, and after they had passed the first line was held for two hours. At the expiration of this time the One hundred and forty-fourth and Fifty-sixth New York took up their march for the church. The second line was held for half an hour after the last-mentioned regiments had passed. I remained at the church until 3 a. m. of the 1st instant, with the One hundred and forty-fourth New York and Thirty-second U. S. Colored Troops and a section of Battery F, Third New York Artillery. These regiments then moved down to the cross-roads and bivouacked. The whole movement was conducted without confusion and in perfect order.

I cannot close this report without making honorable mention of the good conduct and steadiness displayed by the officers and men under the most trying circumstances. Exposed to a heavy fire from a concealed enemy who was strongly intrenched, and laboring under every disadvantage of ground, they maintained their position with the greatest tenacity and endurance. Nothing but the formidable character of the obstacles which they had to encounter prevented them from achieving success. Where all behaved so well it is difficult to specify marked instances of good conduct, but special mention may be made of the One hundred and twenty-seventh New York, Colonel Gurney, which had the advance, and the One hundred and fifty-seventh New York, Lieutenant-Colonel Carmichael, and Twenty-fifth Ohio, Lieutenant-Colonel Haughton, on the right and left of the line. These last two regiments met and resisted several charges of the enemy. The Thirty-second U. S. Colored Troops, Colonel Baird, and Thirty-fifth U. S. Colored Troops, Colonel Beecher, are also deserving of great credit. The former regiment lost Lieutenant-Colonel Geary, wounded. Colonel Beecher, of the latter regiment, was severly wounded early in the action, but kept the field until the close of the day. The One hundred and forty-fourth New York, Colonel Lewis, and Fifty-sixth New York, Lieutenant-Colonel Tyler, although not so warmly engaged as the other regiments, conducted themselves with great steadiness and courage.

My own staff—consisting of Captain Manning, acting assistant adjutant-general; Captain Silva, acting aide-de-camp; Captain Jewett, inspector of the District of Hilton Head, and Lieutenant Davis, Fourth Massachusetts Cavalry—were active and efficient in the discharge of their duties, displaying coolness and gallantry under fire, and great intelligence in the transmission of orders.

I forward herewith a report of casualties in the brigade.*

I am, very respectfully, your obedient servant,

EDWARD E. POTTER,
Brigadier-General, Commanding.

Lieut. L. B. PERRY,
Acting Assistant Adjutant-General.

No. 4.

Report of Col. William Gurney, One hundred and twenty-seventh New York Infantry.

HDQRS. 127TH REGIMENT NEW YORK VOLUNTEERS,
In the Field, near Boyd's Neck, S. C., December 3, 1864.

CAPTAIN: In obedience to circular order of this date, I have the honor to report that the regiment moved up the Grahamville road

---

* Embodied in statement, p. 425.

from the cross-road church at 8 a. m. of the 30th ultimo, having the advance of the line. After advancing some 250 yards the cavalry reported the rebels in our front with artillery. By order of General Potter the regiment was deployed on the right and left of the road as skirmishers. The rebel pickets were met at about 400 yards and firing began. The Thirty-second Colored and One hundred and forty-fourth New York Volunteers reported to me as supports to our skirmish line. The right wing of the Twenty-fifth Ohio Volunteers had already deployed as skirmishers on our right. I turned the command of the regiment over to Lieut. Col. Stewart L. Woodford and took charge of the skirmishers and supports as above. The latter were on the right of the road. The rebels fired the woods and dry grass in front of their artillery, and our line had to advance through and around the flames. Our artillery now coming into position on the road shelled the rebels' gun or guns back, and my command came into the road. I went forward to the new skirmish line, which was immediately thrown out. This line advanced with part of the Fifty-sixth New York Volunteers at the front, and the One hundred and forty-fourth New York Volunteers on the right of the road, and the One hundred and twenty-seventh New York Volunteers at the left. The rebel artillery had taken up a new position, and was shortly encountered again. Our artillery again shelled them back and our infantry moved up. The skirmish line on the left of the road met the rebel line, and fell back upon the One hundred and twenty-seventh New York Volunteers as a support. The action now opened on the left. The One hundred and forty-fourth New York Volunteers encountered the rebels on the right of the road, and the fight began there at the same moment. The heads of these two regiments pressed on to the cross-roads that turned into the rebel fort, and then other regiments moved up, as did the artillery, and the fighting became general. The One hundred and twenty-seventh held the left center in front of the fort, the right of the regiment resting on the road. It was immediately formed into line of battle facing the fort and forced the rebel line back some 200 yards, when it halted and held its ground. I still exercised my provisional command at the center of the front until the new and general disposition of the troops was made by General Potter, who was immediately at the front. Part of the Thirty-fifth U. S. Colored Troops came over to the left of the road, in front of the One hundred and twenty-seventh New York Volunteers, but were immediately moved back on the road to the right of our regiment. Lieutenant-Colonel Woodford reported to General Potter that he would charge the front of the works with our regiment, if a simultaneous charge could be made on the road to his right. The Fifty-fifth Massachusetts Volunteers immediately came up and charged. Colonel Hartwell was wounded just at the head of the cross roads as he formed his men for the charge. Captain Gouraud, aide-de-camp, brought the order for the charge. Colonel Hartwell and Captain Gouraud told me to take the Fifty-fifth in, but the terrible fire held the regiment in check, and this attempt was unsuccessful. Colonel Hartwell, although wounded, took the head of his regiment again and led them in. They met a heavy fire both in front and flank, and Colonel Hartwell was again wounded in two places. We got around the corner of the road, but the troops were then forced back.

Colonel Woodford reports that the One hundred and twenty-seventh New York Volunteers charged forward at nearly a right angle with the advance of the Fifty-fifth Massachusetts, crossing a creek and advancing into the marsh at the front of the fort until they came within 70 yards on the left of the regimental line and within 100 yards on the right. The ground here comparatively open, with isolated large trees and low brush; the soil was boggy, with standing water about ten to eighteen inches deep. The men got their foothold at the roots of the brushwood. The regiment remained here some ten minutes, firing from the shelter which the men took, until the infantry on the right center had been forced back, and their fire enfiladed our line. Then the One hundred and twenty-seventh fell back some fifty yards, formed a new line, and laid down, supporting the artillery on the road, which fired over them. Two companies of the One hundred and twenty-seventh were here formed across the road with fixed bayonets, to prevent straggling from the right center and the right. I then relinquished my temporary command in the road and rejoined my regiment. The artillery soon fell back a few yards, and the One hundred and twenty-seventh fell back to a new position in front of the artillery, and still under the guns, where it remained for an hour, when it was ordered back some twenty yards, and formed line with the same front but at the left of and in line with the advanced guns, where it remained until the action closed. The regiment was the last to leave the field, being ordered to act as rear guard. After it had fallen back as such in the rear for a quarter of a mile, it was relieved by another regiment, which took its place, under orders from General Potter. After reaching the cross-road church, it moved on to the cross-road leading to Boyd's Neck, and bivouacked for the night about 500 yards down this road.

I have the honor to submit herewith a report of casualties, as required, numbering 7 killed, 44 wounded, and 2 missing; total, 53.

Very respectfully, your obedient servant,

WM. GURNEY,
Colonel, Commanding 127th New York Volunteers.

Capt. W. C. MANNING,
Acting Assistant Adjutant-General.

No. 5.

Report of Lieut. Col. Nathaniel Haughton, Twenty-fifth Ohio Infantry.

HDQRS. TWENTY-FIFTH REGT. OHIO VET. VOL. INFTY.,
Boyd's Landing, S. C., December 3, 1864.

CAPTAIN: I have the honor to make the following report of the part taken by my regiment in the action of November 30, 1864:

About 9 a. m. we left the White Church, the One hundred and twenty-seventh New York in advance, taking the road toward Grahamville; had moved but a short distance when the enemy opened with a battery in front. I formed my regiment on the right and left of the road in line of battle, to support the advance of the One hundred and twenty-seventh New York. Moved forward until the advance was checked and the long grass in front [fired] by the enemy. My regiment then moved forward—the right wing farther to the right and the left wing farther to the left to avoid the burning grass—and met a division of the enemy on our right; the rebels soon fell back. I then moved to the road and advanced by the flank until their batteries opened from a second position; I then formed the right of a second line on the right of the road. Moved steadily forward by the right of companies until the first line—composed of the Thirty-second U. S. Colored Troops and a part or all of the One hundred and forty-fourth New York—was fired upon with musketry. This caused the first line to waver, and the Thirty-second fell back in considerable confusion. I immediately formed line of battle, and charging through the Thirty-second and a portion of the right of the One hundred and forty-fourth New York, we drove the enemy from the cross-road in confusion, without, however, doing him much damage, as the wood and brush were so thick that we could not see him when within fifteen or twenty yards, and I did not venture to fire for fear some of our men might be in front. Unexpectedly we came out on the cross-roads, where I rapidly formed my men, the Thirty-second arriving and forming on our right, and a portion of the One hundred and forty-fourth New York on our left; there was no firing in our front, but I could still hear firing to the left. Thinking I had gained an advantage over the enemy, was anxious to profit by it. I immediately sent an officer with some men to learn his position and see if his flank could be pressed. Receiving a favorable answer, I at once made a half change of front on my left company and moved forward into the woods about 80 or 100 yards, where we met a strong line of rebels; here a severe fight took place. We held our line till our ammunition was completely exhausted, even stripping our dead and wounded of the contents of their cartridge-boxes and borrowing of the Thirty-second U. S. Colored Troops, which rather tardily came up on our right, but did not swing far enough to support me sufficiently to warrant my making another charge, as the fire was far more severe on my left and center than on my right. Even had I been supplied with ammunition, I consider that it would have been imprudent to remain longer, as I found during the engagement that my immediate left was entirely unsupported. Under these circumstances, I thought it best to retire; and notifying Colonel Baird of my intention, I about-faced my regiment and moved slowly back to the cross-road, there receiving ammunition. The enemy showed little disposition to advance, and made no attack on our line while there. Soon after dark I received orders to fall back.

I hereby append a list of the casualties in my regiment during the whole action, all of which, with one exception, occurred in making the charge and in our advanced position; those marked wounded and missing are known to have been wounded.

I am, captain, very respectfully, your obedient servant,

N. HAUGHTON,
Lieutenant-Colonel, Commanding Regiment.

Capt. W. C. MANNING,
Acting Assistant Adjutant-General, First Brigade.

NOTE.—The list of casualties was lost, and cannot be replaced by reason of loss of company books.

No. 6.

Report of Col. Alfred S. Hartwell, Fifty-fifth Massachusetts Infantry, commanding Second Brigade.

GENERAL HOSPITAL,
Beaufort, S. C., December 6, 1864.

ADJUTANT: I have the honor to report that, pursuant to the instructions of Brig. Gen. J. P. Hatch, commanding expedition, I assumed command of the Second Brigade on Monday, the 28th ultimo, having for my staff officers, Lieut. G. F. McKay, Fifty-fifth Massachusetts, acting assistant adjutant-general; Capt. W. D. Crane, Fifty-fifth Massachusetts, acting aide; Lieut. E. R. Hill, Fifty-fifth Massachusetts, acting aide; Lieutenant Wilcoxson, Third Rhode Island Artillery, quartermaster. Having transmitted to the regimental commanders the printed orders and directions of the commanding general, and having caused some intrenchment tools to be sent to the Fifty-fourth Massachusetts, I went on board the steamer Golden Gate before midnight of the 28th and got under way at the signal as ordered. In passing around the bow of a small steamer, the small boats attached to the steamer Golden Gate were cut off. I put back in search of these, but in the dense fog three (or two) small boats could not be found. Ran aground and lost our way during the night. In the morning landed in small boat at what seemed to be the shore opposite Hall's Island. About noon succeeded in landing at Boyd's Neck with four companies Fifty-fourth Massachusetts. Found two companies Fifty-fourth Massachusetts already landed. Remained at Boyd's Neck during the day and night of the 29th, by verbal orders of the commanding general, throwing out pickets at dusk and putting the troops into position as soon as disembarked, with orders to be ready to march at daylight of the 30th. By verbal orders from the commanding general, sent out to the cross-roads two companies Fifty-sixth New York for picket. Having sent on a little before day of the 30th ultimo the Thirty-fifth U. S. Colored Troops, Fifty-sixth New York, and some of the Thirty-second U. S. Colored Troops to join their (First) brigade, and leaving the Thirty-fourth U. S. Colored Troops at the Neck for further orders, marched at daylight with eight companies Fifty-fourth Massachusetts, eight companies Fifty-fifth Massachusetts, and Mesereau's and Titus' batteries, under Lieutenant-Colonel Ames, Third Rhode Island Artillery. When half way between cross-roads and church received orders from commanding general to leave four companies as guard at cross-roads, to intrench, and left there four companies Fifty-fourth Massachusetts, with two small boat howitzers and detail of marines, who reported to me on the road for this purpose. On arriving near the church orders were received from the commanding general to forward the artillery, which was done; also orders to advance as the troops in front advanced, leaving two companies as guard at church. Left two companies at church with instructions to throw out vedettes to observe. About half a mile from the church, by orders from commanding general, went into line in a corn-field on our left as we advanced. Next advanced in the road by the flank, filed into a field on our right as we advanced, and formed column by company, putting out with the pioneers a fire in the grass. Advancing to the brow of the hill, received orders to halt and hold my command compact and ready. Next, by successive orders from the commanding general, advanced over and part way down the hill slowly and keeping the formation in column on the right of the road. Received here a verbal order from General Potter to send one regiment in support of the One hundred and twenty-seventh New York, I think, but am not positive, as another order was at the same moment brought from the commanding general for me to advance by the flank down the road in support of the Thirty-fifth U. S. Colored Troops. As I passed the commanding general he gave me verbal orders to support the Thirty-fifth U. S. Colored Troops, and not to go into action, if I could help it, until further orders, adding that a staff officer would show me the position. On reaching the base of the hill, a staff officer directed me to file to the right. I sent one of my aides to halt and front the Fifty-fifth Massachusetts as soon as its left should rest upon the road, which was done. An officer, I think Colonel Gurney, of the One hundred and twenty-seventh New York, informing [me] that our left was hard pressed, I directed the two remaining companies of the Fifty-fourth Massachusetts to file to our left and go on the right by file into line in support of the One hundred and twenty-seventh New York. My line now extended across the road. The musketry from the enemy was severe at this point; the men whom we had in front of my line along and near the road had come to the rear in confusion, and as I could not well remain where I was, and had no orders to fall back, I gave the order to advance. This was done in line for only two or three rods, when the strong fire from the enemy's artillery and musketry, aided by the obstructions of the thicket and swamp, forced me back. I was here hit in the hand by a musket-ball. Forming column of companies as well as possible in the road from the Fifty-fifth Massachusetts, I advanced until the guns from the enemy's fort threw canister so severely into the head of the column that I was obliged to fall back again. At this time Captain Gouraud assisted me in rallying my men, my own voice having nearly given out.

I must here give my testimony, that of the men of the Fifty-fifth Massachusetts who were near all cheerfully seemed to follow me to advance a second time toward the fort, under severe fire. On turning the last angle in the road in front of the fort, the grape and canister became insupportable. Captain Crane, acting aide, was killed, with his horse; Lieutenant Hill, second acting aide, was knocked off his horse by concussion; and my own horse was killed and fell on me. The road seemed to be swept of everything. I was pulled from under my horse and back by an officer and a man of the Fifty-fifth Massachusetts, and during the time was hit in the boot heel by a shot that burned my ankle, and in the side by a spent grape shot that knocked me down and partially stunned me, and lodged in the coat; also, by a spent musket-ball in the back, that lodged in the shirt; in consequence of which, I regret extremely to say, I was unable to give further orders or superintendence, and was taken to the rear.

Knowing the quality of the fine body of men assigned to my command, I am deeply pained to have been prevented from fighting them longer and showing myself deserving of the honor and responsibility placed upon me. Among many who did well, I beg to mention with great praise the following names for the consideration of the commanding general, these men having attracted my notice for particular coolness and efficiency under fire, viz: Major Nutt, Captains Woodward, Thurber, and Torrey, all of Fifty-fourth [Fifty-fifth] Massachusetts; Lieutenant McKay, Fifty-fifth Massachusetts, acting assistant adjutant-general, and Lieutenant Hill, Fifty-fifth Massachusetts, acting aide.

I am, sir, very respectfully, your obedient servant,

A. S. HARTWELL,

Colonel Fifty-fifth Massachusetts, Formerly Comdg. Second Brigade.

Lieut. L. B. PERRY,

Actg. Asst. Adjt. Gen. to Brigadier-General Commanding.

No. 7.

Report of Col. Henry L. Chipman, One hundred and second U. S. Colored Troops, commanding Second Brigade.

HEADQUARTERS 102D U. S. COLORED TROOPS,

December 4, 1864.

I have the honor to submit the following report of the part taken by the different regiments of the Second Brigade, Coast Division, in the action of Honey Hill, November 30, 1864:

I arrived at the front at 1 p. m. with my regiment, and was not informed that Colonel Hartwell had been wounded and taken from the field and that I was in command of the brigade till 3 p. m., at which time the regiments of the brigade were in line of battle on the right of the road, but separated. Soon after dark the Fifty-fourth Massachusetts Volunteers were withdrawn by the direct order of General Potter, without coming through me. I received orders to withdraw my own regiment at 7.30 p. m. The remainder of the night the regiments of the brigade acted independently. Eight companies of the Fifty-fourth Massachusetts Volunteers, under Lieutenant-Colonel Hooper, left the landing; six were in the engagement. Four companies (C, D, G, and K) were left at the cross-roads, under Captain Pope, and two (A and I) at the church. The two remaining companies, under Lieutenant-Colonel Hooper, moved forward and first entered the action on the left of the guns. The four companies under Captain Pope, having engaged and repulsed some 200 of the enemy's cavalry at the cross-roads, were relieved by four companies of the Thirty-fourth U. S. Colored Troops, and started immediately for the front, and went into action on the right of the road. The two companies under Lieutenant-Colonel Hooper, having been sent to the rear at about 5 p. m. with surplus ammunition, Lieutenant-Colonel Hooper learned the position of the four companies under Captain Pope, and rejoined him just as the latter had received orders from General Potter to retire. Soon after these six companies were ordered to assist in carrying wounded to the rear, and rendered most efficient service; the two companies left at the church had been already so employed. The following is a list of the killed, wounded, and missing in that regiment.*

The Fifty-fifth Massachusetts Volunteers, under command of Lieutenant-Colonel Fox, came first into action at about noon. Marching up the main road until it reached the section of artillery then in action there, it filed right into the woods until the left of the regiment rested on the road, then marching by the left flank in line of battle. At this point the right and left wings of the regiment became separated—the left, under Colonel Hartwell, charging the battery up the road, the right pressing forward into the woods. About 3 p. m. Lieutenant-Colonel Fox, finding that he had but three companies and a part of a fourth with him, left them in command of Major Nutt and went in search of the remnant of his regiment. Finding a portion of the left wing, under Captains Thurber and Torrey, he returned with them to the position occupied by Major Nutt in the old rifle-pits to the right of our battery, which Major Nutt had held against every attempt of the enemy to dislodge him. This regiment remained at the front till after dark, and then withdrew and assisted in carrying wounded to the rear. The casualties in this regiment are as follows.†

Three hundred men of the One hundred and second U. S. Colored Troops were all of that regiment who were engaged on the 30th. This portion of the One hundred and second U. S. Colored Troops under my command reached the landing at Boyd's Point at about 11 a. m. of the 30th and started immediately for the front, which it reached at 1 p. m. The two left companies were at once deployed across the road as guards, to stop and return to their regiments all stragglers from the front. Lieutenant-Colonel Ames, chief of artillery, having called for a detail to haul off some guns belonging to Battery B, Third New York Artil-

* Nominal list (omitted) shows 1 enlisted man killed, 3 commissioned officers and 36 enlisted men wounded, and 1 commissioned officer and 4 enlisted men missing.

† Nominal list (omitted) shows 2 commissioned officers and 25 enlisted men killed, 6 commissioned officers and 109 enlisted men wounded, and 2 enlisted men missing.

lery, which had been stripped of both men and horses, Capt. A. E. Lindsay was sent with his company to do this work, but before he reached the pieces he was killed, and his only officer, Lieut. H. H. Alvord, severely wounded in two places. The command now devolved upon the first sergeant, who knowing nothing of the object for which his company had been advanced, filed it right into the woods and formed line toward the enemy. Afterward, when the rest of the regiment was formed in line of battle, Sergeant Madry brought his company and formed it in its proper place in the battalion. The first attempt having thus failed a second was made, and First Lieut. O. W. Bennett was sent with his company to endeavor, if possible, to save the guns. Lieutenant Bennett, with thirty men, went forward fully 100 yards in advance of our first line, and succeeded in bringing away the three guns. Too high praise cannot be awarded to Lieutenant Bennett for the gallant manner in which he led his men in that perilous enterprise, nor to his men who so faithfully followed their leader.* At this time the regiment left the road and was posted in line of battle on the road, its left resting on the road, supporting the battery then in action at that point. At 3 p. m. I was informed of the wounding of Colonel Hartwell, and that I was in command of the brigade. From that time the command of the regiment devolved upon Capt. C. S. Montague. The regiment remained in line till 7.30 p. m., when it withdrew. After reaching the church it was also employed in carrying wounded to the rear. The following are the names of officers and enlisted men killed, wounded, and missing in that regiment.†

Major Nutt, Fifty-fifth Massachusetts Volunteers, is specially mentioned in regimental report for gallantry on the field.

I am, with respect, your obedient servant,

HENRY L. CHIPMAN,
Colonel 102d Regiment, U. S. Colored Troops,
Late in command of Second Brigade, Coast Division.

Lieut. L. B. PERRY,
Acting Assistant Adjutant-General.

No. 8.

Report of Lieut. Col. William Ames, Third Rhode Island Artillery, commanding Artillery Brigade.

HEADQUARTERS ARTILLERY BRIGADE,
Cross-Roads, December 5, 1864.

SIR: I have the honor to report that in pursuance of General Orders, No. 1, from headquarters Coast Division, I assumed command of this Artillery Brigade upon its arrival at Boyd's Landing, November 29. This brigade consisted of one section of Capt. W. H. Hamner's company (A, Third Rhode Island Artillery—3-inch Parrotts), four light 12-pounder guns of Capt. T. J. Mesereau's battery (B, Third New York Artillery), and four 12-pounder light guns of F Company, Third New York Artillery, commanded by First Lieut. E. H. Titus. The section of Parrotts did not arrive until the afternoon of November 30.

---

*Lieutenant Bennett was awarded a Medal of Honor for this service.

†Nominal list (omitted) shows 1 commissioned officer and 2 enlisted men killed, 1 commissioned officer and 15 enlisted men wounded, and 2 enlisted men missing.

November 30, at daylight I proceeded with the New York batteries, in rear of Second Brigade, to the church at forks of road, joining the main force at this point. One section of Mesereau's battery (B, Third New York Artillery), under First Lieut. E. A. Wildt, was placed in rear of the advance regiment of First Brigade, the remaining three sections followed in rear of the brigade. At 9 a. m. the First Brigade moved up the Honey Hill road. After advancing about one mile and a half fire was opened upon our advancing troops from a section of the enemy's guns in position at a point where the road turns to the right. The section of Battery B, Third New York Artillery, under Lieutenant Wildt, was put in position in the road, 600 yards from the enemy's guns, and, after firing seventy-five rounds, caused them to retreat. The approach to this point was by a narrow road bordered by dense woods, and the battery was brought into position under a sharp fire from the enemy's guns. The troops advanced from this point about three-quarters of a mile, when the enemy's guns were again encountered at a turn in the road. The section of artillery under Lieutenant Wildt was brought into battery in the road at a distance of 800 yards from the enemy; after firing twenty rounds the rebel artillery retreated. Whilst coming into battery at this point Lieutenant Wildt was mortally wounded, also one private of his command. The troops advanced from this point half a mile, when the Honey Hill battery was engaged. This battery is situated at the left and 600 yards from the road up which the advance was made, on slightly elevated ground. Four pieces of Mesereau's battery were placed in position to command the enemy's work and rifle-pits on its flanks. One section only could be placed in position within sight of the enemy's work, the left section being masked by the woods, which at this point were very dense and the road so narrow that great difficulty was experienced in bringing the two sections into battery. Fire was kept up upon the enemy from 11 a. m. until 3 p. m. At this time two ammunition-chests of the right section were exploded by the enemy's shells. First Lieut. George C. Breck, of Company B, Third New York Artillery, was much scorched in the face and hands by this explosion, also three privates of his section, which, being disabled, was relieved by one section of Lieutenant Titus' battery (F, Third New York Artillery), under Second Lieut. E. C. Clark. Lieut. George H. Crocker, in command of the left section of Mesereau's battery (B, Third New York Artillery), was shot in the right eye at this time (3 p. m.); also 8 horses and 7 cannoneers of Mesereau's battery. The disabled section of Battery B, Third New York Artillery, was drawn to the rear by a detachment of the One hundred and second U. S. Colored Troops. The pieces were afterward attached to the empty caissons going to the rear and drawn off. At 4 p. m., the ammunition in both batteries having been nearly expended, the guns of the New York batteries were relieved by four howitzers from the Naval Battery, under Lieutenant-Commander Matthews, who continued the fire until dark. When the troops retired to their position at the cross-roads one section of Titus' battery was left with rear guard, with which I remained until it arrived at the cross-roads at daylight on the morning of December 1. The section of Hamner's battery (A, Third Rhode Island Artillery) came up at about dark, but was not placed in position, as the troops were about retiring.

I take great pleasure in mentioning the gallant conduct of the officers under my command during the battle of Honey Hill. Captain Mesereau, Lieutenants Titus, Clark, Wildt, Breck, and Crocker were constantly at their posts; the two latter remained with their sections, although they were wounded, until relieved by my order. First Lieut. E. A. Wildt, Company B, Third New York Artillery, was killed while pointing a gun, and proved himself a brave and efficient officer.

The following casualties occurred in my command on the 30th of November.*

Very respectfully, your obedient servant,

WM. AMES,

Lieut. Col. Third Rhode Island Arty., Comdg. Artillery Brig.

Lieut. L. B. PERRY,

Actg. Asst. Adjt. Gen., Headquarters Coast Division.

No. 9.

Report of Commander George H. Preble, U. S. Navy, commanding Marine Brigade.

HEADQUARTERS MARINE BRIGADE,

In Camp on Grahamville Road, S. C., December 4, 1864.

GENERAL: In obedience to your order of yesterday, I have the honor to report the part taken by the naval force under my command in the action at Honey Hill, S. C., on the 30th of November, ultimo:

After landing the artillery battalion on the morning of the 29th, at 9 a. m., it was advanced, under command of Lieut. Commander E. O. Matthews, U. S. Navy, about two miles along the road, supported on the right by the sailor battalion of infantry, under command of Lieut. James O'Kane, U. S. Navy, and on the left by the battalion of marines, under command of First Lieut. of Marines G. G. Stoddard, thrown out in advance as skirmishers. At the forks of the road I halted the command and brought our artillery into a defensive position. Having no guide or map to refer to, and not satisfied that the crossing was the one designated as our halting place, from the road not continuing beyond, as shown me on your map at the landing, Lieut. Commander A. F. Crosman, acting adjutant of the brigade, with myself and fifteen of the sailor infantry, went out along the road to the right and disclosed the enemy's cavalry and infantry pickets watching our movements. A few rifle-shots were exchanged, when we fell back to the main command, and at 4 p. m. I moved it to the right or north about two miles, where we were intrenching our camp, when Brigadier-General Potter rode up and informed me that we were on the wrong road. I returned with the command to the forks of the road and encamped for the night, by his order, to refresh our men, who had been dragging the field pieces all day, General Potter continuing with his forces on his route to the left.

At 7 a. m. on the 30th we were on the march again along the southern road. At 7.45 a. m., on receipt of your order, the two lightest 12-pounder howitzers were sent back to the forks of the road we had left, to defend that point until the arrival of a battery from Beaufort. Actg. Ensign J. A. Edgren was detailed to take charge of these pieces. Their arrival was timely, and repulsed a party of cavalry and infantry who were advancing on our right. At 9 a. m. I reported to you in person at your headquarters, at the church. At 9.30 a. m. my brigade was formed in the rear of the First Brigade as the reserve, and was kept in

*Nominal list (omitted) shows 1 commissioned officer killed, and 2 commissioned officers and 12 enlisted men wounded.

the rear during the whole advance. About 11.30 a. m. the firing in front became quite heavy and continuous. At 3.30 p. m. Lieut. Commander E. O. Matthews was ordered to take a section of heavy 12-pounder howitzers to the front and relieve a section of New York artillery as soon as their ammunition was out. At 3 p. m. these pieces opened fire and continued firing until 6.30 p. m., when the troops were withdrawn. Lieutenant-Commander Matthews covered their withdrawal until relieved by a section of horse artillery, under command of Lieutenant-Colonel Ames. The remainder of the artillery battalion returned next in advance of the heavy artillery with the retiring column, as ordered, to the forks, where it had previously encamped and where it was joined by the section under Lieut. Commander E. O. Matthews, when the whole battery was placed in a defensive position to guard the roads until morning. I was much indebted to you for furnishing horses for the artillery, as the long march had greatly fatigued the men. Two companies of sailor infantry did good service in assisting at the drag ropes of the artillery, which could not have been brought up without such assistance. The remaining companies assisted in turning back stragglers from the front. Otherwise, much to the reluctance of its commanding officer, the sailor infantry was compelled to remain inactive in reserve, waiting your orders to move to the front. About noon the battalion of marines was ordered to advance, which they did by the right flank, led by Actg. Adjt. A. F. Crosman and commanded by First Lieut. George G. Stoddard, U. S. Marine Corps, to the road where a battery was in action; there filed to the right about 500 yards, then to the left, coming on to the line of battle in the rear of the Twenty-fifth Ohio Volunteers. They then filed to the right and came by the left flank in line of battle, taking position to the right a little in advance of the line previously formed and in a position pointed out by yourself on the field. The last mile and the coming into line was done on the double-quick. As soon as formed in line fire was opened on the enemy, who seemed to be in force on the left. At 2 p. m. Acting Ensign Carter, acting as major of the battalion, was sent with twenty men to deploy and advance on the right flank. He proceeded for 200 yards without finding the enemy. At 3.30 p. m. the line having fallen back on the left compelled the marine battalion to retire as the enemy advanced, which was done in good order, and a new position taken on the cross-road but still on the right of the line. This place was held by the marine battalion until about 6 p. m., when, in obedience to orders, it was marched to the rear, and took up its position at the forks on the left of the Naval Battery.

Lieutenant Stoddard calls attention to the gallant conduct of Sergeant Cogly in bringing up ammunition to the front under heavy fire, and thus enabling the battalion to hold its position.

With the exception of one man wounded in the battery, all the casualties in my command were among the marines. Considering that the marines were drawn from the vessels of the squadron scattered on the blockade, and had been formed into a battalion only two days previous, and that all the company officers were sergeants, I think their conduct creditable to the corps.

Asst. Surg. W. J. Bowdle, of U. S. Navy, my senior medical officer, at the request of Surg. George S. Burton, U. S. Army, chief medical officer of the military force, was detailed to the church hospital in the rear, and from 9 a. m. the 30th until 2 p. m. December 1 was constantly employed in attending to the wounded brought from the front, and has since been and is still employed at Boyd's Landing in that service.

Asst. Surg. E. M. Corson and Actg. Asst. Surg. H. L. Gibbs were at the front and rendered constant and efficient service to our own and the wounded of the army.

As the casualties in my brigade were fortunately slight, the service of all these surgeons was principally given to the military.

The medical supplies of the army not having arrived, those intended for this command, and happily at hand, were consumed for the wounded of the army.

Herewith I transmit Assistant Surgeon Bowdle's report of killed, wounded, and missing by name, as required by your order.* Henry Kittering, seaman, reported as missing, has since returned to the command.

In conclusion I congratulate you, general, on the brave troops you command. I am sure a more cheerful and reliant spirit or greater bravery could not have been displayed by any body of men, and it was only that the enemy was in too strong force and position for the limited force at your control that we did not carry his works.

I take this occasion to express my grateful appreciation of the many kind attentions received by myself and officers from our military brethren in arms. It has been, and shall be, my endeavor to cordially co-operate with the military forces.

I have the honor to be, very respectfully, your obedient servant,

GEO. HENRY PREBLE,
Commander, U. S. Navy, Commanding Naval Brigade, South Atlantic Blockading Squadron.

Brig. Gen. J. P. HATCH, U. S. Army,
Commanding Coast Division, U. S. Army.

DECEMBER 6-9, 1864.—Demonstrations against the Charleston and Savannah Railroad, S. C.

REPORTS.

No. 1.—Lieut. Col. Stewart L. Woodford, One hundred and twenty-seventh New York Infantry.

No. 2.—Maj. Gen. Samuel Jones, C. S. Army, commanding District of South Carolina, including operations December 5-31.

No. 3.—Brig. Gen. Beverly H. Robertson, C. S. Army.

No. 4.—Col. Aaron C. Edwards, Forty-seventh Georgia Infantry.

No. 1.

Reports of Lieut. Col. Stewart L. Woodford, One hundred and twenty-seventh New York Infantry.

HDQRS. 127TH REGIMENT NEW YORK VOLUNTEERS,
In the Field, Coosawhatchie and Beaufort Turnpike, S. C.,
December 8, 1864.

SIR: I have the honor to submit the following report of the part taken by the One hundred and twenty-seventh New York Volunteers in the fight at the Coosawhatchie and Beaufort turnpike on Tuesday, the 6th instant:

The regiment left Boyd's Neck at about 7 o'clock that morning on the steamer Charles Houghton, and landed between 9 and 11 a. m. at the upper landing of Gregory's plantation. Companies D, C, F, and H

---

* Shows 1 man killed, 6 men wounded, and 4 men missing.

were the first of the regiment ashore. These, with part of the One hundred and fifty-seventh New York Volunteers, Fifty-sixth New York Volunteers, Twenty-fifth Ohio, and the naval infantry immediately moved out on the dirt road, moving north to the Coosawhatchie and Beaufort turnpike. Colonel Gurney and myself were with this part of the regiment. The rebel pickets were soon met and driven back. Their skirmishers were encountered at about a quarter of a mile south of the turnpike. The center of our line of battle was on the dirt road; the right wing extended into an open field at right angles to this road and parallel to the turnpike; the left wing was refused and lay about forty-five degrees from northeast to southwest. The four companies of the One hundred and twenty-seventh New York Volunteers held the right center of the line; Company I soon came up, and was ordered in on the left; the remaining five companies came promptly up as soon as we landed, and were also subsequently sent in upon the left of the line of battle. The severe fighting was nearly over when these latter got into position. Soon after the firing became general, the rebels advanced the left of their line—which lay upon the turnpike, sheltered by the forest on the north and a heavy skirting of trees and hedge on the south—into the field, and endeavored to charge and break our right. The naval infantry, which lay immediately to the right of our regiment, were forced back about 100 or 150 yards, leaving our right uncovered. At this moment Colonel Gurney, commanding our regiment, was shot through the arm, and compelled to leave the field. With the four companies of my command which were with me I immediately charged the rebel line, but before we reached them they broke and retired. Part of them fell back into the woods north of the turnpike, and part moved west on the turnpike, under cover of their artillery, to their intrenchments near the railroad. Just before we charged we fired by rank, and under this discharge the flag of the regiment in our front—the Fifth Georgia Reserves—fell. They were driven back so rapidly as not to be able to rescue it. We passed over it, and it was picked up by some person connected with another regiment and sent to General Potter, who commanded our forces in the engagement. It was afterward turned over to our regiment. Having seized the turnpike, we subsequently moved up on it a quarter of a mile to the west, when we fell back and bivouacked for the night on the left of the line.

The losses in the four companies immediately under my command were 4 killed and 19 wounded. Capt. Frank K. Smith, of Company D, our senior captain, was shot in the left arm, in the early part of the fight, but remained upon the field with me until all was over. Officers and men alike behaved coolly and well. First Assistant Surgeon Dayton was shot through the right hand while attending to our wounded. Our entire loss was 5 killed and 22 wounded; total, 27. I submit herewith a list of our casualties in detail.

I cannot close this report without calling the attention of the commanding general to Sergt. Benjamin K. Conklin, of Company E, who, when General Potter asked for volunteers to endeavor to go up through the forest to the railroad, offered to go; Privates Joseph I. Kampe, of Company E, and Oscar L. Jagger, of Company K, also volunteered. I respectfully recommend Sergeant Conklin for a lieutenantcy in the colored troops,

And am, with great respect, your obedient servant,

STEWART L. WOODFORD,

Lieutenant-Colonel, Commanding Regiment.

Capt. W. C. MANNING,

A. A. A. G., Potter's Brigade, Coast Division, Dept. of the South.

HDQRS. 127TH REGIMENT NEW YORK VOLUNTEERS,
In the Field, near Coosawhatchie and Beaufort Turnpike,
Gregory's Neck, S. C., December 10, 1864.

SIR: I have the honor to present the following report of the part taken by the One hundred and twenty-seventh Regiment New York Volunteers in the operations and fight on Friday, December 9, near the Tullifinny Station, on the Charleston and Savannah Railroad:

We left our place of bivouac at the left of the intrenchments at daybreak and moved to the right of the advanced battery in the open field. At 9.10 a. m. the brigade of skirmishers, under command of Colonel Silliman, Twenty-sixth U. S. Colored Troops, advanced across the country road, or turnpike, moving due north to a point near the railroad. This regiment had the left and left center of the line. We encountered no fire until within about 350 yards of the rebel works, when we met their picket-line. After a sharp skirmish these were driven back until our line rested within about 200 yards of the rebel battery and the railroad. Colonel Silliman was severely wounded almost as soon as fire opened, and forced to leave the field. The command of the brigade then devolved upon me. This regiment lay upon the advance line from near 10 a. m. until 2.30 p. m., when we were ordered to retire and cover the withdrawal of the reserves. The latter were attacked upon their left when about three-quarters of a mile from our intrenchments, and a sharp fight ensued, lasting from about 2.45 until dark. During this action our skirmish line formed into a line of battle in one rank and covered the right of the general line. The rebels felt of us but once, when they advanced a small skirmish line against our center. We waited until they came fairly in view, when a few well-directed shots caused them to retire. After the troops withdrew from the field, we came in, covering their march. The One hundred and fifty-seventh New York Volunteers formed the rear skirmish line on this last movement.

The loss of the One hundred and twenty-seventh Regiment was 8 killed and 51 wounded; total, 59.

I submit herewith a detailed list of our casualties. The left of my regiment suffered most severely, as it was in and near a pine thicket, which furnished a complete cover to the rebel pickets and sharpshooters.

Capt. H. J. Long, who was in command of the left company but one, distinguished himself by his coolness and bravery. Although shot through his arm early in the fight he remained with us during the day, and suffered no one to know of his wound until we had returned to our place of bivouac at night.

This regiment has now, since the 30th ultimo, been in three engagements, and I feel it is due to the lieutenants who have acted as staff officers during that time to put upon record my acknowledgments of their valuable services. Lieut. William L. Conant, acting adjutant, and Lieut. William H. Dodge, regimental quartermaster, have been at the front under fire upon each occasion. They have carried orders with coolness and precision, and have evidenced sound judgment and high personal courage in an equal degree.

I am, very respectfully, your obedient servant,

STEWART L. WOODFORD,
Lieutenant-Colonel, Commanding Regiment.

Capt. W. C. MANNING,
A. A. A. G., Potter's Brigade, Coast Division, Dept. of the South.

HDQRS. 127TH REGIMENT NEW YORK VOLUNTEERS,
Deveaux's Neck, S. C., December 15, 1864.

LIEUTENANT: In obedience to a verbal order given me last evening by General Hatch, I have the honor to submit the following report of the operations of the "skirmish brigade" on Friday, the 9th instant:

The command consisted of the marine battalion, the One hundred and fifty-seventh New York Volunteers, and the One hundred and twenty-seventh New York Volunteers, and was under Colonel Silliman, of the Twenty-sixth U. S. Colored Troops, who was temporarily detached from his regiment for this purpose. We formed in front of the rifle-pits in the open field, at 9.10 a. m., in one rank—the marines having the right, the One hundred and fifty-seventh New York Volunteers the center, and the One hundred and twenty-seventh New York Volunteers the left. The men were deployed at a distance of two paces from each other, and one company of the One hundred and twenty-seventh was formed as flankers on the left. The line covered a front of near three-quarters of a mile, reaching from a point 100 yards to the left of the dirt road that runs into the Coosawhatchie turnpike. We advanced under cover of a heavy artillery fire, moving almost due north. The line was maintained with great regularity, and struck the rebel pickets about 350 yards from the railroad. These, after a few shots, fell rapidly back upon their reserves. These reserves, opposite our center and right, retired upon their main line, which immediately opened a heavy fire, both with musketry, grape, and canister. The rebel pickets upon our left appeared to rally upon their reserves, which were near their line, and these being sheltered by a heavy growth of young pines, maintained for some time a sharp and well-directed fire, which enfiladed our left. Colonel Silliman was shot in the leg soon after fire opened; his wound was very serious and he was forced to leave the field. Lieutenant Hill, of the Fifty-fifth Massachusetts, who was serving upon his staff, was killed. The command of the skirmish line thus devolved upon the undersigned as senior officer present. The skirmish line pushed steadily forward, pressing the place occupied by the rebel pickets, and took up position within about 200 yards of the railroad. The marines upon the right, under command of First Lieutenant Stoddard, U. S. Marine Corps, approached quite close to the rebel battery and made a gallant attempt to flank and charge it. They were exposed to a very severe fire; became entangled in a dense thicket between the forks of a creek upon the right, and were compelled to fall back. They retired upon the reserves, where they reformed and again moved to the front. Before they could be again deployed upon the skirmish line, they were detached from my command, by order of General Potter, and placed upon the left among the reserves. Their loss was 1 killed, 7 wounded, and 3 missing. Lieut. Commander A. F. Crosman, who accompanied Lieutenant Stoddard as adjutant of the Naval Brigade, and Lieutenant Stoddard alike behaved with great courage. The detachment of the One hundred and fifty-seventh New York Volunteers, under command of Captain Van Slyke, formed our extreme right after the marines had retired. They moved steadily in position until ordered back later in the day. They were cool, brave, and under remarkably good discipline. Captain Van Slyke and Lieutenant Baldwin, the regimental adjutant, deserve honorable mention for good conduct. This regiment lost 11 wounded. The One hundred and twenty-seventh New York Volunteers lay in its position to the left of the One hundred and fifty-seventh at about the same distance from the railroad. The left of this regiment, consisting of Companies G, K, and B, were exposed to the hot enfilading fire before mentioned, and suffered severely, especially Companies G and K. Captain Henry, of Company G, the senior captain present with us, was shot in the foot and so severely wounded as to be forced to leave the field. Capt. H. J. Long was shot through the arm, but remained with his company. These two companies were at length pushed into the pines on their left under a most galling fire, and after about an hour the enemy's fire upon this flank was almost silenced. These two companies alone lost 5 killed and 28 wounded. Too much credit can hardly be awarded to the men for their steadiness, and Captain Long, of Company K, and Lieutenant Abercrombie, of Company G, who commanded his company after Captain Henry was wounded, for their courage and good judgment in handling their men. Captain Long concealed the fact of his having been wounded from me until we had returned to our place of bivouac at night. The right wing of this regiment was under the charge of Captain Weston, of Company F, and the regiment was commanded by Captain Little, of Company A, after the charge of the brigade devolved upon me. Both these officers deserve especial mention for their good conduct. Lieutenant Sammis, commanding Company E, was wounded severely in the face while on the line.

The entire loss of the One hundred and twenty-seventh was 8 killed and 51 wounded; total, 59.

The skirmish brigade remained in its advanced position until the reserves fell back, when, at about 2.30 p. m., we were ordered to retire, and buried our dead before we began falling back. When about three-quarters of a mile from our intrenchments the rebels attacked the reserves upon our left flank, and a fight ensued, lasting until dark. During this fight our skirmish line was formed into line of battle in one rank, and formed the right of the general line. The rebels felt of us but once, when they advanced a small skirmishing party against our center. We waited until they came fairly in view, when a few well-directed shots caused them to retire. After the troops withdrew from the field, we came in, covering their march. The One hundred and fifty-seventh New York Volunteers formed the rear guard on this movement.

In closing this report I wish to recognize the valuable services of Lieutenant Man, of the Twenty-sixth U. S. Colored Troops, acting aide-de-camp to Colonel Silliman, who brought me the tidings of the colonel's wound and remained with me until we had returned to the intrenchments; also, the services of Lieut. W. L. Conant, of Company F, One hundred and twenty-seventh New York Volunteers, and Lieut. W. H. Dodge, our regimental quartermaster. These three officers acted as my aides-de-camp after I assumed command of the brigade. They carried orders with coolness and precision, and evidenced sound judgment and high personal courage in an equal degree.

I am, very respectfully, your obedient servant,

STEWART L. WOODFORD,
Lieutenant-Colonel 127th New York Volunteers.

Lieutenant PERRY,
Actg. Asst. Adjt. Gen., Coast Division, Department of the South.

No. 2.

Report of Maj. Gen. Samuel Jones, C. S. Army, commanding District of South Carolina, including operations December 5–31.

CHARLESTON, *January 11, 1865.*

COLONEL: The report of operations of the troops under my command in the late campaign ending in the evacuation of Savannah, called for by the lieutenant-general commanding on the 2d instant, has been delayed because of my absence from my headquarters on other duty and the failure of some of the subordinate commanders to forward to me their reports. They have not all yet been received, but as I have been ordered to another and distant command, I respectfully submit, without longer delay, the following report:

The dispatch from the lieutenant-general commanding, then in Savannah, directing me to establish my headquarters at or near Pocotaligo, was received in this city about sunset on the 4th ultimo. I started by the first train, but owing to detentions on the road did not reach Pocotaligo until nearly sunset on the 5th. I was not informed as to the number, description, or location of the troops in that vicinity, and immediately endeavored to obtain information on those points. I ascertained that the troops, with the exception of the Fifth and Forty-seventh Georgia Regiments, a battalion of the Thirty-second Georgia Regiment, the artillery, a part of the Third South Carolina Cavalry, and Kirk's squadron, were composed of Georgia and South Carolina reserves and South Carolina militia, and occupied positions extending from Pocotaligo to Savannah River, and up that river beyond Sister's Ferry. Those at and near Grahamville were commanded by Brigadier-General Chesnut; those at and near Coosawhatchie, by Brigadier-General Gartrell. They had arrived but a few days previously, and until my arrival were under the immediate orders of the lieutenant-general commanding, or other officer under him. The reserves were very imperfectly organized, and the militia without organization, and many of the men were without arms. Having obtained as accurate information as I could of their numbers and position, and the position and movements of the enemy, I ordered Brigadier-General Chesnut to send the Forty-seventh Georgia Regiment and a section of artillery by railroad, to be thrown thence to any point that might be threatened, the train to remain at Coosawhatchie and be held in readiness to move the troops at any moment. This order, I regret to say, was not promptly obeyed. Dispatches received during the night indicated that the enemy was threatening Coosawhatchie by way of Bee's Creek and the Coosawhatchie River.

At 10 o'clock the morning of the 6th General Gartrell telegraphed me, that the enemy was landing from twelve barges at Gregory's Point, on Tullifinny River; that he had moved forward a part of his force to meet them. The battalion of South Carolina cadets, having arrived at Pocotaligo, were ordered to guard the Tullifinny trestle and aid in checking any advance on Coosawhatchie. A section of artillery, supported by the battalion of the Thirty-second Georgia Regiment, was ordered to a point on the left of the Tullifinny, from which it was thought it could drive off or annoy the enemy's transports and barges, and I started myself to ride to Coosawhatchie; but before reaching Tullifinny bridge, the enemy, having landed in much larger force than was at first supposed, had pressed forward up Gregory's Neck to the Coosawhatchie or State road, and having driven back a battalion of the Fifth Georgia Regiment (about 150 men), interposed between me and Coosawhatchie.

Brigadier-General Gartrell has not submitted a report, but I ascertained from a conversation with him and his subordinate commanders that on first receiving information of the advance of the enemy he sent forward only a small battalion (150 men) of the Fifth Georgia, which encountered the enemy on the Gregory's Point road, about a mile from its junction with the State road, and drove back the advance guard.

But the enemy, discovering that the handful of men in their front was not the twentieth part of their own number, pressed forward and nearly enveloped the Fifth Georgia, forcing it back. The Georgia reserves and a section of artillery were then sent by Gartrell to the support of the Fifth Georgia, but it was too late. The entire line soon gave way, fell back in confusion, crossed the Coosawhatchie River, and partially destroyed the bridge immediately under the guns and within easy and effective musket-range of our works at Coosawhatchie.

Maj. John Jenkins, whom I had sent forward to ascertain the position of the enemy, was conducting the battalion of cadets under Major White into action—and that gallant body of youths was moving at double-quick, manifesting an eagerness to encounter the enemy, which they subsequently so handsomely sustained in action, and would in ten minutes have opened fire on the enemy's right—when our line gave way, as above stated, and the cadets were withdrawn to the railroad. The enemy having secured a footing at the junction of the Gregory's Point and State roads, immediately commenced intrenching, and I had no troops at hand with which to attack them that evening.

During the night of the 6th I concentrated on the railroad near the Tullifinny trestle all the available troops I could collect—being Forty-seventh Georgia and a battalion of the Thirty-second Georgia Regiment, a company of the First South Carolina Artillery, the battalion of cadets, and one of North Carolina reserves that had just arrived, and Bachman's battery of artillery—and ordered Colonel Edwards, the senior colonel, to attack the enemy with that force at daydawn the next morning. General Gartrell was ordered to make a spirited demonstration of attack from Coosawhatchie as soon as he should hear Colonel Edwards' guns, and if Edwards' attack proved successful, to press forward the attack from Coosawhatchie with all vigor. Colonel Edwards attacked as directed, with the result shown by his report, herewith forwarded.* The demonstration from Coosawhatchie was not made with any spirit, and their effort to dislodge the enemy failed. Not having a sufficient number of reliable troops to renew the attack, I endeavored, by defensive works, to hold the railroad, and the enemy was thus unavoidably allowed time, of which they availed themselves, to strengthen their position on Gregory's Neck.

In the meantime I had ordered Brig. Gen. B. H. Robertson from his subdivision to the immediate command of the troops from Bee's Creek to Pocotaligo.

On the morning of the 9th the enemy, endeavoring to get possession of the railroad, vigorously assailed our left near Tullifinny trestle, and were repulsed. Later in the day they concentrated and attacked our line near Coosawhatchie, and were again repulsed. Failing in this attack, they never renewed it, but strengthened their position within less than a mile of the railroad, and established several batteries, with which they endeavored, but unsuccessfully, to prevent us from using it.

On the 11th, under instructions from the lieutenant-general commanding, Brigadier-General Taliaferro was assigned to the immediate command of the troops from Bee's Creek to Pocotaligo.

I have stated thus minutely the operations of very small bodies of troops during the 6th, 7th, and 9th, because the result of those operations decided my subsequent action. If the Forty-seventh Georgia Regiment and the section of artillery which I ordered up from Grahamville within an hour after my arrival at Pocotaligo had been sent to

---

* See p. 447.

Coosawhatchie as I directed, or if, instead of sending forward only a battalion, General Gartrell had employed all of his available force to engage the enemy on the Gregory's Neck road, leaving a small support for the guns in the fort at Coosawhatchie, I think the enemy would not have succeeded in establishing themselves on Gregory's Neck. The position they succeeded in securing was strong, being on a peninsula, not more than a mile and a half in width, between the Coosawhatchie and Tullifinny, with both flanks protected by those rivers and swamps, some of them thickly wooded. They also occupied Mackay's Point, making it necessary that I should employ a part of my small force to watch the enemy on Graham's Neck to guard against a movement on the railroad from that quarter. I was convinced that I could not, with the force at my command, dislodge the enemy from his position by a direct attack in front, and therefore directed my attention to their rear. The only plan offering any prospect of success was an attack in the rear from the Tullifinny side. To do this it was necessary to bridge that stream and concentrate a column of reliable troops to attack the enemy in his intrenchments. The means of bridging the stream were procured, and I selected the most suitable point of passage; but at no time was I able to concentrate for the attack more than a thousand troops reliable for such service, for, by the concurrent testimony [of] the subordinate commanders, the reserves and militia could not be relied on to attack the enemy in their intrenchments. The number of the enemy on Gregory's Neck I estimate at between 4,000 and 5.000.

Under instructions from the lieutenant-general commanding, directing me if I could not dislodge the enemy from his position to strengthen my own, so as to hold the railroad and send him all the troops I could spare, I sent him the part of General Young's brigade that had arrived, and a few other troops to operate in the immediate vicinity of Savannah, and directed my attention to holding the road to Savannah River, watching and obstructing the crossings on that stream, and making preparations for dislodging the enemy on Gregory's Neck whenever I could collect the necessary force. While these operations were in progress near Coosawhatchie, Brigadier-General Chesnut guarded the road from Bee's Creek to Hardeeville, and Colonel Colcock guarded the line of the Savannah River to Hudson's Ferry until the arrival in that vicinity of Major-General Wheeler and Brigadier-General Young. I regarded it as my especial duty to hold the Charleston and Savannah Railroad and keep open communication to Savannah River. This was done; for though the enemy succeeded in establishing batteries within easy range of the railroad, and used their artillery very freely, we held that road, the passage of trains was never interrupted, and only one locomotive and one box-car damaged and two rails broken, until after Savannah had been evacuated and the troops and material brought from that city secured. Trains were passing over the road up to the 27th of December, when, under instructions from the lieutenant-general commanding, I turned over the immediate command of the troops in that vicinity to Major-General McLaws.

While these operations were going on from Pocotaligo to the Savannah River, the other troops under my command held securely Charleston and its harbor and all of the coast of South Carolina in our possession.

The artillery and other veteran troops behaved throughout with their accustomed steadiness and gallantry, and the South Carolina cadets, Major White commanding, who for the first time felt the fire of the enemy, so bore themselves as to win the admiration of the veterans who observed and served with them.

For the casualties—which, considering the heavy fire to which the troops were exposed for many days, were very few—and for other details, I respectfully refer to the reports of subordinate commanders.

I am, very respectfully, your obedient servant,

SAM. JONES,
Major-General.

Col. T. B. ROY,
Asst. Adjt. Gen., Dept. S. C., Ga., and Fla., Charleston, S. C.

No. 3.

Report of Brig. Gen. Beverly H. Robertson, C. S. Army.

HEADQUARTERS,
Adams' Run, S. C., January 5, 1865.

MAJOR: I have the honor to report that, in obedience to instructions from Major-General Jones, I assumed command of all the troops between Bee's Creek and Tullifinny trestle on the 8th of December, ultimo:

About 9 o'clock on the morning of the 9th the enemy opened on the left of my line a very rapid and continuous fire from some eight guns. His line of skirmishers advanced about 10 o'clock, and immediately after the entire left became hotly engaged, our men fighting behind temporary breast-works. Several attempts were made to carry our lines, but all were handsomely repulsed. The troops fought with great spirit. Foiled in his undertaking, the enemy moved to his left in the direction of Coosawhatchie. The engagement was renewed most vigorously on our right at 3 p. m., and after an obstinate resistance by the enemy, lasting some two hours, he was driven 800 yards from his original line. The Thirty-second and Forty-seventh Georgia Regiments, the Seventh North Carolina Battalion, and the battalion of South Carolina cadets, all under the immediate command of Colonel Edwards, occupied the left; the Fifth Georgia Regiment, the First and Third Georgia Reserves, under Colonel Daniel, the right. It was reported that General Gartrell was slightly wounded by a fragment of a shell before he reached the field.

The German Artillery, Captain Bachman, rendered very efficient service on the left, as was proved by the number of dead found in their front. Major Jenkins, commanding the cadets, was particularly conspicuous during the morning fight. Colonel Edwards deserves especial credit for the admirable disposition of his troops.

The enemy's loss, though not accurately ascertained, must have been heavy, as quite a number of his dead were left on the field. Our casualties during the day were 52 killed and wounded. A tabulated list is herewith inclosed.

Both the officers and men of my command behaved well. Captains Haxall and Worthington and Lieutenants Johnston and Stoney rendered most valuable assistance in the execution of orders while the fight was progressing.

I am, major, most respectfully, your obedient servant,

B. H. ROBERTSON,
Brigadier-General.

Maj. CHARLES S. STRINGFELLOW,
Assistant Adjutant-General, Charleston, S. C.

[Inclosure.]

Casualties.

Command.	Killed.		Wounded.		Total.		Aggregate.
	Officers.	Men.	Officers.	Men.	Officers.	Men.	
32d Georgia Volunteers	......	......	......	3	......	3	3
47th Georgia Volunteers	......	2	......	6	......	8	8
5th Georgia Volunteers	......	2	......	......	......	2	2
1st Georgia Reserves	......	1	1	5	1	6	7
3d Georgia Reserves	......	3	1	27	1	30	31
7th North Carolina Reserves	......	......	......	1	......	1	1
Total	......	8	2	42	2	50	52

PHILIP HAXALL,
Captain and Assistant Adjutant-General.

COOSAWHATCHIE, *December 9, 1864.*

ADDENDA.

POCOTALIGO, *December 9, 1864—7 p. m.*

Brig. Gen. B. H. ROBERTSON,
Coosawhatchie:

Congratulate you and your men on your good day's work. Keep on the alert; the attack may be renewed to-night or early to-morrow morning. I have ordered 500 of Chesnut's men and Young's dismounted men to you. They ought to be there now. Some other troops are on their way from Charleston, and shall go to you.

SAM. JONES,
Major-General.

No. 4.

Report of Col. Aaron C. Edwards, Forty-seventh Georgia Infantry.

HEADQUARTERS,
Tullifinny Works, S. C., December 19, 1864.

MAJOR: In obedience to instructions from Major-General Jones, dated Pocotaligo, December 6, 1864, directing me to attack the enemy early on the 7th in his position near this point, I made the following disposition of the force under my command—consisting of about 200 men of the Forty-seventh Regiment Georgia Volunteers, commanded by Capt. J. C. Thompson, two companies of the Thirty-second Georgia, with the Augusta battalion (local troops), one company of the First South Carolina Infantry [Regulars], (Captain King), and 130 South Carolina militia, commanded by Lieutenant-Colonel Bacon, of the Thirty-second Georgia, and the battalion of South Carolina cadets, commanded by Maj. J. B. White, making in all 700 or 800 men. Early in the morning four companies were thrown forward as skirmishers, under command of Major White. The line—composed of the Forty-seventh Georgia, on the right, and the troops under command of Lieutenant-Colonel Bacon, on the left—moved just in rear of the skirmishers. In a thick wood near a bend in the old Pocotaligo road the right of my skirmish line struck the enemy. The front was then changed gradually to the right until the line crossed the said road at nearly right angles, when it confronted the enemy, and became engaged throughout its entire length. At this stage of the action the command of Lieutenant-Colonel Nesbett arrived, and was posted on the left of my line of battle. Our skirmishers drove the enemy vigorously until the right of the line became engaged with the enemy's line of battle, our left at the same time overlapping his right. This position was maintained until after Colonel Daniel's demonstration on my right, when the enemy made new dispositions on and extending beyond my left. It becoming apparent that the enemy's force considerably outnumbered mine, which consisted largely of raw troops, it was deemed impracticable to attack him in force, without which it was impossible to drive him from his position. I therefore withdrew in good order, unpursued by the enemy, to my present position. The troops engaged, which were my skirmishers only, behaved with great gallantry.

By permission of the major-general commanding, we began on the morning of the 8th to fortify our position. The work was continued uninterruptedly until the morning of the 9th, when the enemy drove in our pickets and advanced in force to within 250 yards of our position. We opened upon him with artillery and musketry, and in a very short time drove him back, with considerable loss. On the afternoon of the same day, in the attempt to re-establish our picket-line, the enemy was found in the wood on our right within 100 yards of the railroad. After severe fighting for about two hours, he was driven off and our line re-established.

On the next morning it was ascertained that he had fallen back to his original position, and our picket-line was advanced 400 or 500 yards beyond its former position.

The casualties amounted in all to 4 killed, 1 commissioned officer and 31 men wounded, many of them very slightly. Judging from the unburied dead, the graves, and other evidences found upon the field, the enemy must have suffered a loss of not less than 250 in the fighting of the 9th, and not less than 50 in that of the 7th, making in all a loss of not less than 300.

Respectfully submitted.

A. C. EDWARDS,
Colonel, Commanding.

Maj. CHARLES S. STRINGFELLOW,
Assistant Adjutant-General, Charleston, S. C.

P. S.—I omitted to mention, in enumerating the force under my command on the 7th instant, the three pieces of Captain Bachman's battery, which, owing to the character of the country, it was found impracticable to use in the action.

Respectfully,

A. C. EDWARDS,
Colonel, Commanding.

DECEMBER 13-19, 1864.—Expedition from Barrancas, Fla., to Pollard, Ala., and skirmishes.

REPORTS.

No. 1.

Report of Brig. Gen. Thomas J. McKean, U. S. Army, commanding District of West Florida.

HEADQUARTERS DISTRICT OF WEST FLORIDA,
Barrancas, Fla., December 19, 1864.

COLONEL: I have the honor to report that an expedition sent out from here under Colonel Robinson, Ninety-seventh U. S. Colored Infantry, reached Pollard on the 16th; destroyed the depot and other public buildings, and a large amount of public property, consisting of forage, clothing, camp and garrison equipage, &c.; also, the railroad for miles, including several bridges, one very important one over the Little Escambia River. On their return our troops encountered a force of the enemy from Mobile, and considerable severe fighting took place at all the streams from the Little Escambia to Pine Barren Creek, when the enemy was finally handsomely repulsed, and did not show himself again. The expedition returned here to-day, bringing some 30 prisoners.

Our loss is 1 officer and 16 men killed and 3 officers and 61 men wounded. Colonel Robinson, commanding the expedition, severely, though not dangerously, wounded.

Very respectfully, your obedient servant,

THO. J. McKEAN,
Brigadier-General, U. S. Volunteers, Commanding District.

Lieut. Col. C. T. CHRISTENSEN,
Asst. Adjt. Gen., Mil. Div. of West Miss., New Orleans, La.

No. 2.

Report of General G. T. Beauregard.

CHARLESTON, *December 22, 1864.*
(Received 23d.)

On the 16th instant enemy, 800 strong, occupied Pollard. After burning Government and railroad buildings, retreated in the direction they came. They were pursued thirty miles, losing a portion of their transportation, baggage, and supplies, leaving many dead negro troops on the road. Our forces, commanded by General Liddell, acted with spirit and gallantry.

G. T. BEAUREGARD,
General.

General COOPER.

(Same to President, Secretary of War, and General Bragg.)

DECEMBER 20, 1864.—Skirmish near the Pocotaligo Road, S. C.

REPORTS.

No. 1.—Col. Edward N. Hallowell, Fifty-fourth Massachusetts Infantry, commanding Second Brigade, Coast Division.
No. 2.—Lieut. Col. Charles T. Trowbridge, Thirty-third U. S. Colored Troops.

No. 1.

Report of Col. Edward N. Hallowell, Fifty-fourth Massachusetts Infantry, commanding Second Brigade, Coast Division.

HEADQUARTERS SECOND BRIGADE, COAST DIVISION,
December 21, 1864.

I have the honor to report that the Thirty-third U. S. Colored Infantry, Lieut. Col. C. T. Trowbridge commanding, returned last night at 7 o'clock from their reconnaissance. Leaving camp at 3.30 p. m. they proceeded northward and took the direction of the Tullifinny Creek. When about two miles and a half from our lines, the column changed direction to the right, and proceeded in an easterly course till they found an outpost of the enemy. Two companies were detached with a view to capturing the post, but were discovered and the alarm given. The enemy, 300 strong, formed line of battle and made a stand in the skirts of the woods, near the Pocotaligo road, when Lieutenant-Colonel Trowbridge charged them and drove them back into the woods on the right. We here captured some of their blankets, overcoats, haversacks, canteens, &c., and then moved down the Pocotaligo road to camp.

Our casualties in this action are 7 wounded, 1 mortally; no prisoners were captured, and the loss of the enemy is not known.

Inclosed is Lieutenant-Colonel Trowbridge's report, including a nominal list of casualties.

First Lieut. C. H. Robbins, Twenty-sixth U. S. Colored Troops, accompanied Lieutenant-Colonel Trowbridge, and rendered very valuable services as guide.

I am, sir, respectfully, your obedient servant,

E. N. HALLOWELL,
Colonel, Commanding Second Brigade.

Lieut. L. B. PERRY,
Acting Assistant Adjutant-General.

No. 2.

Report of Lieut. Col. Charles T. Trowbridge, Thirty-third U. S. Colored Troops.

HEADQUARTERS THIRTY-THIRD U. S. COLORED TROOPS,
In the Field, December 21, 1864.

LIEUTENANT: I have the honor to report that, in accordance with instructions received from the colonel commanding brigade, I proceeded at 3.30 p. m. yesterday, the 20th, with 300 men of my command, along the right bank of the Tullifinny to a point two miles beyond our picket-line; then turned to the right and endeavored to strike the Pocotaligo road, a mile beyond the plantation house known as the Thomas Stewart place. When within three-quarters of a mile of the Pocotaligo road I encountered a strong cavalry picket-line of the enemy, apparently so posted that his left rested on the Pocotaligo River, his right reaching around to a swamp on the west side of the road and nearly a mile from it. As soon as I encountered the picket I ordered a halt and sent two companies, under the command of Major Whitney, who were ordered to get between the enemy's pickets and the swamp and capture them if possible; but in so doing they were discovered and fired upon by the enemy. They returned the fire, gave the alarm, and immediately the enemy's picket-line retired to their reserves, dismounted, formed line of battle, apparently 300 strong, under cover of the woods in my front, and opened a brisk fire on my men. I then sent forward a company of skirmishers to engage the enemy until the two companies under Major Whitney had rejoined the main column. I then formed line of battle and charged across the open field into the woods and routed the enemy, who broke and fled in the direction of the railroad. The number of the enemy killed or wounded is not known, but one killed was found on the field; but from the number of haversacks, blankets, and forage (all of which was destroyed on the field or brought away), their loss must have been considerable. The enemy had no artillery, but their cavalry horses are apparently very fine and the men armed with good carbines. My casualties were 7 enlisted men wounded, 4 seriously and 3 slightly.

My observations yesterday have convinced me that the only way to reach the railroad with a force from our present position is by the way of the Pocotaligo road, as the country on our left is full of swamps, which are impassable for anything except light troops. The Pocotaligo road between our intrenchments and the Stewart plantation I found obstructed in three places by felled trees.

My thanks are due to Lieutenant Robbins, of the Twenty-sixth U. S. Colored Troops, who proved himself to be a brave and efficient officer.

I am, sir, very respectfully, your obedient servant,

C. T. TROWBRIDGE,
Lieutenant-Colonel, Commanding Regiment.

Lieut. GEORGE F. MCKAY,
Acting Assistant Adjutant-General.

CORRESPONDENCE, ORDERS, AND RETURNS RELATING TO OPERATIONS IN SOUTH CAROLINA, GEORGIA, AND FLORIDA, FROM NOVEMBER 14 TO DECEMBER 31, 1864.

UNION CORRESPONDENCE, ETC.

SPECIAL FIELD ORDERS, No. 124. } HDQRS. MIL. DIV. OF THE MISS., *In the Field, Atlanta, Ga., Nov. 14, 1864.*

The armies will begin the movement on Milledgeville and Gordon to-morrow, the 15th of November, as follows:

I. The Right Wing will move, via McDonough and Monticello, to Gordon.

II. The Left Wing, General Slocum, will move, via Covington, Social Circle, and Madison, to Milledgeville, destroying the railroad in a most thorough manner from Yellow River to Madison.

III. The cavalry, General Kilpatrick commanding, will move in concert with the Right Wing, feigning strong in the direction of Forsyth and Macon, but will cross the Ocmulgee on the pontoon bridge of General Howard.

IV. Each column will aim to reach its destination—viz, Gordon and Milledgeville—on the seventh day's march, and each army commander will on arrival communicate with the other wing and the commanding general, who will accompany the Left Wing.

By order of Maj. Gen. W. T. Sherman:

L. M. DAYTON,
Aide-de-Camp.

SPECIAL ORDERS, No. 167. } HDQRS. DEPT. AND ARMY OF THE TENN., *White Hall, Ga., November 14, 1864.*

* * * * * * *

II. Corps commanders will direct a careful inspection to be made this p. m., to ascertain that every infantry soldier has his forty rounds of ammunition and that the batteries have their ammunition-chests well filled. Every commissioned officer in this army is reminded that our supply of ammunition is limited to that we have on hand, and that therefore the greatest possible economy must be observed in its use. The attention of corps and division commanders is called to the manner in which outpost duty is performed. Each division commander will select a permanent picket officer, one who is intelligent and indefatigable. It has been noticed several times that the pickets have come in in a disorderly manner, often singly and without orders. This practice must be corrected. Attention is again called to straggling. To prevent it great care will be taken in the detail of foragers. A provost guard to each brigade will be thoroughly organized and march in rear of the brigade. Commissioned officers will be arrested and punished for allowing straggling. All quartermasters will be held strictly responsible for the men in their charge. Corps commanders will regulate, in orders, foraging parties for their trains as well as for the infantry and artillery. Special attention is called to the Field Orders, Nos. 119 and 120, of Major-General Sherman, copies of which will be multiplied, so that every commissioned officer may have one in his possession.*

III. Capt. Christian Riebsame, One hundred and sixteenth Illinois Infantry Volunteers, is relieved from duty as acting assistant inspector-general First Brigade, Second Division, Fifteenth Army Corps, and will report without delay to his regimental commander.

IV. Capt. W. S. Bunn, Company A, One hundred and twenty-seventh Illinois Infantry Volunteers, is detached from his command and assigned to special duty as acting assistant inspector-general First Brigade, Second Division, Fifteenth Army Corps. He will report without delay to Col. Theodore Jones, commanding.

* * * * * * *

VI. This command will be in readiness to move forward to-morrow morning. Corps commanders will see that all their preparations for the contemplated march are perfected without delay. The precise time of starting and the route to be taken will be hereafter indicated. Corps commanders will, in their order of march, give the hour for each division to march, allowing time for the trains to get into position, in accordance with the orders of General Sherman.

* * * * * * *

VIII. Maj. A. C. Waterhouse, First Illinois Light Artillery, is assigned to duty as chief of artillery Seventeenth Army Corps, and will report for duty to Maj. Gen. F. P. Blair, commanding.

---

* See Vol. XXXIX, Part III, pp. 701, 713.

IX. Maj. C. Landgraeber, First [Second] Missouri Light Artillery, will report for duty to Maj. A. C. Waterhouse, chief of artillery Seventeenth Army Corps.

* * * * * * *

XI. This army will move forward toward McDonough, Ga., making twenty miles, if practicable, as follows:

1. The First Alabama Cavalry, Colonel Spencer commanding, will take the advance at 5.30 a. m., on the direct Atlanta and McDonough road.

2. Maj. Gen. F. P. Blair, commanding Seventeenth Army Corps, will move his command at 6.30 a. m., following the First Alabama Cavalry, on the Atlanta and McDonough road.

3. Maj. Gen. P. J. Osterhaus, commanding Fifteenth Army Corps, will move out his command at daylight, taking the road to McDonough via Rough and Ready.

4. The train of these headquarters will follow the ordnance train of the leading division of the Fifteenth Corps. The engineer regiment with the bridge train and the supply trains of this headquarters, in charge of Colonel Conklin, chief quartermaster, will move in advance of the rear division of the Seventeenth Corps. The supply train of General Kilpatrick's cavalry in the rear of that corps for rear guard. The cattle in charge of Lieutenant Todd, acting commissary of subsistence, will move on the Atlanta and McDonough road, pushing forward when practicable through the fields. The position of the several trains will be in accordance with the instructions of Major-General Sherman, as contained in Special Field Orders, No. 120.

XII. The Fourth Independent Company Ohio Cavalry, escort at these headquarters, having been recruited to the maximum, is restored to its company organization; and Capt. John L. King, commanding, having been duly appointed and commissioned, will be mustered in, to date September 7, 1864, at which time he had the complement of men to entitle him to be mustered.

By order of Maj. Gen. O. O. Howard:

SAML. L. TAGGART,
Assistant Adjutant-General.

CIRCULAR.] HEADQUARTERS FIFTEENTH APMY CORPS,
White Hall, Ga., November 14, 1864.

As the Fifteenth Corps will probably be the right of the army in its advance, division commanders will have a chain of flankers out on all sides, covering not only the troops but principally the train. It is imperative that the column should remain well closed up during the march. To gain this end the leading division will moderate its gait, and not move over two miles an hour, allowing a rest of five or ten minutes every hour. The regiments in themselves must preserve their compactness. After having started about one hour the commander of the leading division will halt his column for about twenty or thirty minutes, to give every person who may be delayed in camp time to join his company and take his place.

By order of Maj. Gen. P. Joseph Osterhaus:

FREDK. WHITEHEAD,
Assistant Adjutant-General.

SPECIAL ORDERS, No. 171. } HDQRS. FIFTEENTH ARMY CORPS, *White Hall, Ga., November 14, 1864.*

I. The habitual order of march whenever the corps moves in one column will be as follows: Advance guard—first, advance guard, composed of one brigade of infantry of the leading division, one light battery of artillery (without caissons, battery wagons, forge, &c.), to be supported by one regiment of the advance guard; column—second, the remaining troops of the leading division; third, division of infantry; fourth, batteries of Artillery Brigade, to be supported by one regiment of infantry detailed from the division second in column; fifth, division of infantry; sixth, one or two brigades of the rear division; rear—seventh, the remaining brigade of the last division, with one section of light artillery (without caissons, &c.), to take its place in column near the center of brigade. The caissons and other carriages of the artillery with the advance and rear guard will march with the Artillery Brigade. The ordnance train will be so distributed that each regiment of infantry will be followed by one wagon of ammunition, except the regiments of the advance and rear guards, whose reserve ammunition will be disposed of by respective division commanders. The reserve artillery ordnance will fall in behind the brigade of artillery preceding the division third in column. One ambulance will follow each regiment and brigade. The remaining ambulances will be distributed equally for and will follow their respective divisions. The supply train of each division will be apportioned to the brigades, and will follow in rear of same. The advance and rear guards must, however, remain unencumbered with their trains, and respective division commanders will assign them to suitable positions in column. The regimental wagons will follow their respective regiments in rear of ambulance. Headquarters train Fifteenth Army Corps will follow the leading division and in front of its headquarters train. Under these orders the column will necessarily be very long, and it becomes an imperative necessity that all commanding officers take such steps as will secure the most rapid progress. The favorite practice of halting to repair damages in case of accident by wagon-masters and teamsters (thus delaying the column) must be discontinued. Any wagons stopping for the purpose indicated must be drawn one side, necessarily losing their right of place, and will therefore fall in in rear of the column. All officers and employés of the quartermaster's department will be constantly with their trains unless otherwise detailed. Division commanders will detail sufficient guards to protect and assist the trains on the march. These guards must be controlled permanently by their officers, and march soldier-like on either side of the column or in squads, as circumstances require. Officers permitting their men to lay away their arms or straggle will be reported for summary punishment. It will be the particular province of the respective division officers of the day, with the assistance of brigade officers of the day, to give their untiring energies to the preservation of order and progress of the column. Division commanders are requested to make their orders of march with a view to rapid and sudden deployments whenever such may become necessary.

* * * * * * *

III. The command will move to-morrow from its present camp toward Rough and Ready as follows: First Division at 6.30 a. m., Second Division at 8 a. m., Artillery Brigade at 9.15 a. m., Third Division at 9.30 a. m., Fourth Division at 11 a. m.

The column will be formed according to Special Orders, No. 171, paragraph 1, from these headquarters.

The Fourth Division having not yet reported, General Smith, of Third Division, will detail two regiments of infantry as rear guard behind his train.

The department headquarters trains follow in rear of ordnance train First Division.

IV. Each division will be preceded by a strong provost guard, under a conscientious and reliable commander, who will see that no willful vandalism is perpetrated by worthless characters leaving their command. He will place one or more guards to all dwellings occupied by citizens, to be relieved by the division following.

Forage parties will on no pretense be permitted to enter houses except by written authority from their division commanders. Foraging parties not ordered in accordance with Special Orders, No. 164, paragraph III, are strictly forbidden and must be arrested by the provost guards and turned over to their respective commanders.

By order of Maj. Gen. P. Joseph Osterhaus:

FREDK. WHITEHEAD,
Assistant Adjutant-General.

SPECIAL ORDERS, No. 238. } HDQRS. FIRST DIV., 15TH ARMY CORPS,
White Hall, Ga., November 14, 1864.

* * * * * * *

II. The attention of the general commanding having been called to the irregular manner in which picket duty was heretofore being carried on, and the gross negligence of both officers and men being brought to his notice, it is required that from this time and during the coming campaign strict attention must be paid by officers and men to the performance of this most important duty. When the pickets are relieved they must all be assembled by the picket officer in charge, and marched from the picket-line in a body, and not be permitted, as has heretofore frequently been the case, to wander into camp at their leisure. The officer in command will himself be held responsible that the men under his charge do not discharge their fire-arms upon being relieved, and any violation of this order will be brought against the officer as disobedience of orders on his part.

III. The transportation of the command having been so materially reduced, the attention of regimental commanders is called to the propriety of dispensing with many extra duty men that heretofore may have been necessary. Regimental blacksmiths, wagon-masters, and men of that class, are no longer required, and should be forthwith placed in the ranks.

* * * * * * *

X. This division will move from its present camp toward Rough and Ready at 6.30 o'clock, promptly, to-morrow a. m., in the following order: First, Second Brigade, each regiment to be followed by one ambulance. Second, battery of artillery, without caissons or battery wagon, followed by one regiment of the Second Brigade. Third, pioneers. Fourth, the brigade tool wagon and regimental trains. Fifth, First Brigade, each regiment of which will be followed by one ambulance, the regimental wagon, and one wagon infantry ammunition. Sixth, one-half of the division supply train, followed by five wagons infantry ammunition. This train will be guarded by one regiment from the First Brigade, to be distributed by companies along the train. Seventh, Third Brigade, each regiment to be followed by one ambulance, the regimental wagon, and one wagon infantry ammunition. Eighth, headquarters trains department, Fifteenth Army Corps, of First Division, and of brigades, followed by the ambulance train and medical wagons, and the remaining half of the division supply train and the balance of the ordnance train, the above train to be guarded by one regiment of the Third Brigade, which will march by companies distributed along the column. Ninth, rear guard of one regiment from the Third Brigade; two companies of this, however, will be sent forward at the head of the column as guard for the houses.

By order of Brig. Gen. Charles R. Woods:

FRED. H. WILSON,
Acting Assistant Adjutant-General.

GENERAL ORDERS, No. 64. } HDQRS. SECOND DIV., 15TH ARMY CORPS, *White Hall, Ga., November 14, 1864.*

I. In order to carry out the directions of higher commanders, the supply, ordnance, and ambulance trains will be divided into three equal parts, and each assigned to the charge of a brigade quartermaster, who will assign one wagon of ammunition and an ambulance to each regiment of his brigade, and will march the remainder in the rear of the troops of the brigade. Regimental wagons will go in rear of their respective regiments, and all other brigade wagons in rear of their respective brigades, and all division wagons not included above in rear of the division.

II. Whenever a brigade performs the duty of advance or rear guard to the corps, its wagons will move in rear of the division.

III. Wagons and ambulances assigned to brigades will form permanent sections and will be parked separately. Brigade commanders will furnish proper guards to them when marching and when in park. Quartermasters and wagon-masters will at all times on the march remain with their trains, and will at once turn out broken wagons, or turn the column past them; will, when locking, cause the wagons to double, so as to lose no time; will cause the trains to pull out of the road and park whenever troops halt; and in every way exercise such authority and attention as will prevent any delay of the column in rear.

By order of Brig. Gen. W. B. Hazen:

G. LOFLAND,
Captain and Assistant Adjutant-General.

SPECIAL ORDERS, No. 181. } HDQRS. SECOND DIV., 15TH ARMY CORPS, *Near Atlanta, Ga., November 14, 1864.*

* * * * * * *

III. This division will move toward Rough and Ready to-morrow morning at 8 a. m., in the following order: First, Third Brigade, Col. Oliver commanding; second, Second Brigade, Col. W. S. Jones commanding; third, First Brigade, Col. Theodore Jones commanding. Reveille will be sounded at 5 a. m. Brigade commanders will see that their buglers repeat the calls sounded at these headquarters.

* * * * * * *

By order of Brig. Gen. W. B. Hazen:

G. LOFLAND,
Captain and Assistant Adjutant-General.

GENERAL ORDERS, No. 92. } HDQRS. THIRD DIV., 15TH ARMY CORPS,
White Hall, Ga., November 14, 1864.

Brigade and detachment commanders will hold their respective commands in readiness to move promptly at 9.30 a. m. to-morrow, the 15th instant, with three days' rations in haversacks.

Order of march: First, one regiment Second Brigade in advance, followed by one regimental wagon and one ambulance; second, pioneer corps, tool wagons, and one wagon; third, remainder of Second Brigade, each regiment to be followed by one wagon and one ambulance; fourth, two regiments First Brigade, each regiment followed by one wagon and one ambulance; fifth, ammunition train; sixth, division headquarters train and provost guard; seventh, Second Brigade train; eighth, First Brigade wagons; ninth, quartermaster's train; tenth, supply train; eleventh, remainder of ambulance corps not otherwise assigned; twelfth, two regiments First Brigade, each regiment followed by one wagon and one ambulance; thirteenth, one regiment First Brigade, which will be divided upon each flank of the trains, well deployed; and when the country is open, will move parallel with the trains at a distance of 200 yards from the same; when the country will not admit of this, it will close into the trains, and the commanding officer will be held strictly responsible that the men march in an orderly and soldierly manner and that they carry their arms and accouterments at all times.

No foraging will be permitted without authority from these headquarters, and, when necessary, directions will be given in what manner it shall be done. Officers and men are again reminded of the danger of straggling when marching in the enemy's country. All orders heretofore issued for discipline while on the march or in camp must be rigidly enforced, and officers will be held responsible for the manner in which their duties are performed.

By order of Brig. Gen. John E. Smith:

S. M. BUDLONG,
Assistant Adjutant-General.

SPECIAL FIELD ORDERS, No. 4. } HEADQUARTERS FOURTH DIVISION,
FIFTEENTH ARMY CORPS,
In the Field, Turner's Ferry, November 14, 1864.

I. This command will move to-morrow, the 15th instant, as follows: Captain Benjamin, acting assistant quartermaster of this division, will move his supply train at 4 a. m. sharp to Atlanta and load the train with supplies, and again join the command at once. The Second Brigade will act as escort, and take their brigade train with them. The remainder of the command will move at 7 a. m. in the following order: One regiment of the First Brigade, next the pioneer corps, and then the battery; all wagons will close on the battery—first, the First Brigade train; second, the Third Brigade train; third, the ordnance train; fourth, the ambulance corps. The First Brigade will march its other regiments on either side of the train. The Third Brigade will follow in the same manner, but will have one regiment act as rear guard.

By order of Brig. Gen. John M. Corse:

L. CARPER,
Captain and Assistant Adjutant-General.

SPECIAL ORDERS, No. 281. } HDQRS. SEVENTEENTH ARMY CORPS, *White Hall, Ga., November 14, 1864.*

* * * * * * *

III. Division commanders will prepare their commands for moving to-morrow morning. The hour and route will be hereafter indicated.

IV. If there are any men in the command for whom arms cannot be obtained, they will be required to carry either an ax, pick, or shovel.

V. During the campaign about to commence the flanks of the army will be infested to a greater or less extent with bands of guerrillas, whose principal object will be to pick up stragglers. The most rigid measures therefore will be taken to prevent straggling. There will be a rear guard to each regiment, brigade, and division, who will be instructed to arrest every soldier found out of his place without authority, and men so arrested will be reported to their division commander for punishment. To a great extent straggling is the fault of the company commanders and can by them be prevented. In order to bring officers who neglect their duty in this respect to an account, division provost-marshals will ascertain the name of the company commander of each man arrested, and where it shall appear that any officer is in the habit of allowing his men to straggle his name will be reported to these headquarters.

* * * * * * *

2. Division commanders will organize foraging parties by brigades, placing them under charge of competent and discreet officers. Commanders of forage parties must not permit their men to separate, but must keep them well in hand. Firing will not be permitted, except when in the presence of an enemy. Foraging will be conducted in accordance with General Sherman's Special Orders, Nos. 119 and 120.*

VI. Capt. Patterson Sharp, Company D, Thirtieth Illinois Infantry Volunteers, is detached from his regiment and assigned to duty as corps ambulance officer, and will forthwith report to Surg. J. H. Boucher, medical director Seventeenth Army Corps.

VII. The following are the orders for the movements to-morrow:

1. Brig. Gen. M. D. Leggett, commanding Third Division, will have the advance, moving promptly at 6.30 o'clock.

2. Brig. Gen. G. A. Smith, commanding Fourth Division, will follow the Third Division, moving at 7.30 o'clock.

3. Maj. Gen. J. A. Mower, commanding First Division, will follow the Fourth Division, moving at 8.30 o'clock.

4. Maj. A. C. Waterhouse, commanding Artillery Brigade, will assign a battery to each division, to move with it as the division commander may direct.

5. Lieut. Col. E. M. Joel, chief quartermaster, will divide the corps supply trains among the divisions for the movement.

---

* See Vol. XXXIX, Part III, pp. 701, 713.

6. Division commanders will arrange the order of the ambulance, ordnance, and supply trains in their commands in accordance with Special Field Orders, No. 120, military division headquarters.

7. Maj. Gen. J. A. Mower, commanding First Division, will detail from his command two regiments to act as rear guard to General Kilpatrick's train.

8. The train of these headquarters will follow the ordnance train of Third Division.

VIII. The Ninth Illinois Mounted Infantry, Lieutenant-Colonel Hughes commanding, having been assigned to the Seventeenth Army Corps, will report to Lieut. Col. D. T. Kirby, picket officer Seventeenth Army Corps, for instructions until further orders.

By command of Maj. Gen. F. P. Blair:

C. CADLE, JR.,
Assistant Adjutant-General.

GENERAL ORDERS, No. 64. } HDQRS. FIRST DIV., 17TH ARMY CORPS, *White Hall, Ga., November 14, 1864.*

I. Capt. William Hemstreet, Eighteenth Missouri Infantry, is hereby announced as judge-advocate of this division. He will be obeyed and respected accordingly.

II. This command will be prepared to march to-morrow at 8.30 a. m. promptly.

Order of march: First, pioneer corps. Second, Second Brigade. Third, Third Brigade. One battery will follow the leading regiment of the Third Brigade. Colonel Tillson will march one of his regiments on the flank of the supply train. Fourth, ambulance corps. Fifth, ordnance train. Sixth, supply train. Seventh, First Brigade. Brig. Gen. J. W. Fuller will march two of his regiments in rear of General Kilpatrick's train, which will follow immediately in rear of this division. The division headquarters wagons will follow in rear of the leading brigade. Hereafter, unless otherwise specially ordered, one ambulance and one regimental wagon will follow behind each regiment, and two ambulances and one ordnance wagon to a regiment behind each brigade.

III. Each brigade commander will immediately organize a foraging party, which should consist of at least thirty enlisted men and two competent and discreet commissioned officers, who will be held to a strict responsibility for the conduct of their men. No raw drafted men will be detailed as foragers. Foraging will be conducted in accordance with Special Orders, Nos. 119 and 120, headquarters Military Division of the Mississippi.

IV. There will be a rear guard to each regiment and brigade, who will arrest any soldier found straggling or out of his place without proper authority. In order to prevent straggling, company commanders will habitually march in rear of their companies, and any officer found guilty of allowing his men to straggle will be arrested and reported to these headquarters. The attention of all officers in this command is called to Special Orders, Nos. 119 and 120, headquarters Military Division of the Mississippi, and Special Orders, No. 281, headquarters Seventeenth Army Corps, and a strict compliance with their requirements is enjoined.

By order of Maj. Gen. Joseph A. Mower:

CHAS. CHRISTENSEN,
Lieutenant, Aide-de-Camp and Acting Assistant Adjutant-General.

SPECIAL FIELD ORDERS, No. 149.

HEADQUARTERS THIRD DIVISION, SEVENTEENTH ARMY CORPS, *In the Field, Ga., November 14, 1864.*

* * * * * * *

VI. The troops of this command will move at 6.30 a. m. to-morrow, i the following order: First, Second Brigade; second, artillery; third ordnance train, ten teams; fourth, headquarters train; fifth, suppl train, twenty-six teams; sixth, First Brigade, five regiments; seventh ordnance train, ten teams; eighth, supply train, twenty-seven teams ninth, one regiment First Brigade. Regimental wagons and one ambu lance will accompany each regiment; surplus ambulances in rear of eac brigade; brigade trains in rear of ordnance train after each brigade.

VII. The Seventeenth Wisconsin Veteran Volunteer Infantry i transferred from the First to the Second Brigade, this command, an will report accordingly.

By order of Brig. Gen. M. D. Leggett:

J. C. DOUGLASS,
Assistant Adjutant-General.

ORDERS.] HEADQUARTERS LEFT WING, ARMY OF GEORGIA, *Atlanta, Ga., November 14, 1864.*

The Twentieth Corps will move on the Decatur road to-morrow at a. m., except the provost guard, under Colonel Cogswell, which wil remain in Atlanta until all the troops have passed through the city when it will join the Fourteenth Corps. Colonel Cogswell will repor to Maj. Gen. J. C. Davis, commanding Fourteenth Corps, on his arriva at this place. The regiments detailed for duty in the quartermaster' and commissary departments are hereby relieved, and will report a once to their respective brigades. Guards for public property no under charge of these regiments will be furnished by Colonel Cogs well. Colonel Buell, commanding pontoon train, will report to Major General Davis, commanding Fourteenth Corps, and will accompan his corps on the march. Colonel Acker, commanding cavalry, will re port this evening in person to Brig. Gen. A. S. Williams, commandin Twentieth Corps, for instructions.

By order of Maj. Gen. H. W. Slocum:

H. C. RODGERS,
Assistant Adjutant-General.

HEADQUARTERS MILITARY DIVISION OF THE MISSISSIPPI, *In the Field, Atlanta, November 14, 1864.*

General DAVIS,
Commanding Fourteenth Corps:

GENERAL: Your aide, Litchfield, has reported all right and the gen eral is much pleased with your progress. All is working well here General Howard is all up and will move out toward McDonough earl in the morning, and the Twentieth Corps also moves. General Howar will destroy at once the bridge at Turner's, and General Sherman de sires you to effectually destroy the bridge by which your corps crosse the Chattahoochee. Your march to-morrow will be easy, about tw miles beyond the city.

I am, general, respectfully, your obedient servant,

L. M. DAYTON,
Aide-de-Camp.

HEADQUARTERS LEFT WING, ARMY OF GEORGIA,
Atlanta, Ga., November 14, 1864.

Maj. Gen. J. C. DAVIS,
Commanding Fourteenth Corps:

On the march from this point to Madison I shall accompany the Twentieth Corps. I shall endeavor to have this corps encamp Tuesday night near Stone Mountain, Wednesday night near Sheffield, Thursday night near Social Circle, and Friday night at Madison. You will move your corps on roads to the right of the one taken by the Twentieth Corps. I would advise you to move direct to Flat Rock, thence, via Snapping [Snapfinger?] Shoals, to Covington, thence to Madison via Brick Store. You will order the command under Colonel Cogswell to join the Twentieth Corps on your arrival at Madison or whenever the two corps may be in the same vicinity.

Very respectfully, your obedient servant,

H. W. SLOCUM,
Major-General, Commanding.

SPECIAL FIELD ORDERS, No. 19. } HDQRS. FOURTEENTH ARMY CORPS,
Chattahoochee River, November 14, 1864.

The troops will move to-morrow in the following order:

General Baird will move his division at daylight through Atlanta, and camp on the McDonough road beyond the town.

General Carlin will follow General Baird and camp in the same vicinity. He will leave either the Thirteenth or the Twenty-first Michigan camped on this side of the bridge, with directions to guard it until further orders.

General Morgan on arriving at the river will follow General Carlin.

The trains of General Baird and his artillery will move in advance of the corps supply train and those of the other divisions in its rear. The trains will move at daylight, and the infantry will march beside them so as not to interfere with them.

By order of Bvt. Maj. Gen. J. C. Davis:

A. C. McCLURG,
Assistant Adjutant-General and Chief of Staff.

HEADQUARTERS LEFT WING, ARMY OF GEORGIA,
Atlanta, Ga., November 14, 1864.

Brig. Gen. A. S. WILLIAMS,
Commanding Twentieth Corps:

The major-general commanding directs that should the Fourteenth Corps reach the Chattahoochee to-night, you will have all of the troops of the Twentieth Corps moved into Atlanta at once.

Very respectfully, your obedient servant,

E. W. GUINDON,
Major and Aide-de-Camp.

GENERAL ORDERS, No. 20. } HEADQUARTERS TWENTIETH CORPS,
Atlanta, Ga., November 14, 1864.

During the campaign about to commence the organization of the pioneers of this corps will be as follows:

At the headquarters of the corps, a battalion, to consist of six companies; at headquarters of each division, one company. The battalion will be organized from the pioneer companies now with the brigades. Each division commander will detail two of his present brigade pioneer companies, which will report at these headquarters with all their arms, equipments, and tools, to Capt. George E. Johnson, commanding pioneer battalion. The company belonging to the other brigade will be retained for duty with the division.

The battalion will always march at the head of the column, and be prepared to do such work as may be needed. The men will always carry their tools and arms.

The quartermaster's department will furnish a wagon for the use of the battalion, in which the knapsacks, &c., may be carried.

One wagon-load of tools will also be sent from each division, to report to Captain Johnson, for use by the battalion.

By command of Brigadier-General Williams:

H. W. PERKINS,
Assistant Adjutant-General.

GENERAL ORDERS, } HEADQUARTERS TWENTIETH CORPS,
No. 21. } *Atlanta, Ga., November 14, 1864.*

During the campaign about to commence this corps will generally march on one road.

The following general orders will govern, in the absence of others:

On the first day the order of march will be—First Division, Second Division, Third Division. On the succeeding day's march the division leading on the previous day will march in the rear, and the center division of the previous day will take the advance, thus alternating on each succeeding day's march. The leading brigade of the leading division and the rear brigade of the rear division will be entirely unencumbered with wagons or ambulances, and will be at all times ready for action.

The artillery will habitually march—one battery with the leading division, one with the rear division, and two with the center division. Each regiment, except those in the two brigades before mentioned, will be followed by its regimental wagon and one ambulance; each brigade, by its brigade ambulances, the wagons attached to the brigade, and its proportion of the division supply and ammunition trains. The wagons attached to the artillery will follow their respective batteries; those belonging to the headquarters of the corps, the chief commissary, and the chief quartermaster, will march immediately in rear of the leading division, unless otherwise ordered. The leading brigade will be followed by, and the rear brigade preceded by, its regimental and brigade supply and ammunition wagons.

Each brigade commander will detail a foraging party, to be sent out daily, under directions from the division commander. Each brigade quartermaster will furnish the wagons to forage for his brigade, and the brigade commander will furnish a strong guard to accompany them, under the command of a commissioned officer.

The picket duty for the corps will be done by the second brigade (in line) of the leading division, and the commanding officer of that brigade will be the general officer of the day.

The attention of all commanding officers is called to the necessity of economizing ammunition, and supplies generally; the practice of wasteful picket-firing, at night especially, must be checked by officers of the guard and of the day, who will be held strictly accountable in this particular.

Straggling and pillaging must be stopped by the most prompt measures; the safety of the corps depends upon this. To this end staff officers of divisions and brigades will be kept along their respective commands, who will report frequently. If any considerable break in the march is made it will be reported at once to the corps commander, who will habitually be found near the head of the leading division.

This order and Special Field Orders, No. 120, Military Division of the Mississippi,* will be communicated to all officers and men in the line and in the staff departments.

By command of Brig. Gen. A. S. Williams:

H. W. PERKINS,
Assistant Adjutant-General.

ORDERS.] HEADQUARTERS TWENTIETH CORPS,
Atlanta, Ga., November 14, 1864.

This corps will march to-morrow (under the orders already published) as follows: The First Division at 7 a. m.; the Second Division at 8 a. m.; the Third Division at 9 a. m. All detachments and guards in or about the city, except those from the Second Massachusetts Volunteers, the Thirty-third Massachusetts Volunteers, or the One hundred and eleventh Pennsylvania Volunteers, will be called in at daylight in the morning and rejoin their respective commands. These three regiments will remain on duty in the city until its complete evacuation, when they (under the command of Colonel Cogswell) will join the Fourteenth Corps, marching with it until such time as they can rejoin their proper commands. The ammunition train of the Artillery Brigade will march in rear of the center division.

By command of Brigadier-General Williams:

H. W. PERKINS,
Assistant Adjutant-General.

ORDERS.] HDQRS. FIRST DIVISION, TWENTIETH CORPS,
Atlanta, Ga., November 14, 1864.

This division will march to-morrow at 7 a. m. (under the orders already published), in the following order: First Brigade in advance, the Second Brigade following, and the Third Brigade in the rear. This order of march will be followed for three consecutive days, unless otherwise ordered. All detachments and guards in or about the city belonging to this command, except those from the Second Massachusetts Volunteers, will be called in at daylight to-morrow and rejoin their respective commands. Brigade commanders and officers in command of trains are referred for further instructions to General Orders, No. 21, headquarters Twentieth Corps, current series.†

By command of Brig. Gen. N. J. Jackson:

GEO. ROBINSON,
First Lieutenant and Acting Assistant Adjutant-General.

---

*See Vol. XXXIX, Part III, p. 713.
†See p. 462.

HEADQUARTERS TWENTIETH CORPS, ARMY OF GEORGIA,
Atlanta, Ga., November 14, 1864.

Col. WILLIAM COGSWELL,
Commanding Post:

COLONEL: The general commanding directs me to inform you that he has ordered the different regiments of Colonel Powell's command to report at once to their respective brigades. You will relieve by troops from your command all guards now furnished by Colonel Powell.

Very respectfully, your obedient servant,

H. W. PERKINS,
Lieutenant-Colonel and Assistant Adjutant-General.

HDQRS. FIRST BRIG., SECOND DIV., 20TH ARMY CORPS,
Atlanta, Ga., November 14, 1864.

Capt. W. T. FORBES,
Acting Assistant Adjutant-General:

CAPTAIN: I have the honor to report that, in compliance with instructions received yesterday, I destroyed the railroad from the city of Atlanta to a point 250 yards beyond the fourth mile post, in all about two miles and three-fourths of tracks. The ties have been burned and the rails bent and twisted so as to render them useless.

Very respectfully,

ARIO PARDEE, JR.,
Col. 147th Regiment Pennsylvania Volunteers, Commanding.

CIRCULAR.] HDQRS. THIRD DIV., TWENTIETH ARMY CORPS,
Atlanta, Ga., November 14, 1864.

The division will move at 9 o'clock to-morrow morning on Decatur road, in the following order: First, Third Brigade, Colonel Ross; second, Second Brigade, Colonel Dustin; third, First Brigade, Colonel Smith. Trains following brigades; provost brigade to remain in city until further orders. Regiments on duty in quartermaster's and commissary of subsistence departments are relieved, and will march with their respective commands.

By command of Brig. Gen. W. T. Ward:

JOHN SPEED,
Captain and Assistant Adjutant-General.

HEADQUARTERS DEPARTMENT OF THE SOUTH,
Hilton Head, S. C., November 14, 1864.

Maj. Gen. H. W. HALLECK, U. S. Army:

GENERAL: I have the honor to inclose to you a Savannah paper of the 12th instant, brought in by the flag-of-truce boat. The exchange is progressing favorably, I believe, under Colonel Mulford's direction. Reports from Morris Island represent that there are appearances of commotion among the rebels in Charleston and on James Island. I shall go up there to-night to see what is the matter. I hope and trust that it may be caused by the approach of General Sherman in the rear. Such a movement would be the finest of the war, and would capture Charleston and Savannah with all their stores of cannon, ammunition, and material, and open bases of supplies from which with his army he could utterly destroy and devastate the whole State of South Carolina. The health of the department is good, and with the precautions taken, and the lateness of the season, I apprehend no cases of yellow fever, even with the intercourse by flags of truce. Eight officers of the U. S. Army, escaped prisoners from Columbia, arrived here to-day.

Very respectfully, your obedient servant,

J. G. FOSTER,
Major-General, Commanding.

SPECIAL FIELD ORDERS, No. 125 } HDQRS. MIL. DIV. OF THE MISSISSIPPI,
In the Field, Atlanta, Ga.,
November 15, 1864.

I. Surg. John Moore, U. S. Volunteers, is hereby announced as chief medical director of this army; and will be obeyed and respected accordingly

* * * * * * *

By order of Maj. Gen. W. T. Sherman:

L. M. DAYTON,
Aide-de-Camp.

SPECIAL FIELD ORDERS, No. 168. } HEADQUARTERS DEPARTMENT AND ARMY OF THE TENNESSEE,
Near Stockbridge, Ga., November 15, 1864.

The army will resume its march to-morrow as follows: First, the First and Second Divisions of the Fifteenth Corps, on the road to McDonough via Stockbridge, moving out at 6 a. m., followed by the Seventeenth Corps at 8 o'clock; second, the Third and Fourth Divisions of the Fifteenth Corps will move on a road to the right leading into the Jonesborough and McDonough road, on which they will proceed to McDonough; third, the trains will move as in march of to-day with respective brigades and divisions; fourth, the engineer regiment with the bridge train and the supply trains of this headquarters will move in advance of the rear division of the Seventeenth Corps; fifth, the supply train of General Kilpatrick's cavalry will follow the Seventeenth Corps, with two regiments from that corps as rear guard; sixth, the cattle, in charge of Lieutenant Todd, acting commissary of subsistence, will follow the Seventeenth Corps. The trains not having been well closed up to-day, nearly double the space was occupied that should have been. Corps commanders will see that this is corrected hereafter.

By order of Maj. Gen. O. O. Howard:

SAML. L. TAGGART,
Assistant Adjutant-General.

NASHVILLE, TENN., *November 15, 1864.*

Maj. Gen. J. A. LOGAN,
Carbondale, Ill.:

It is not possible to overtake your command. Remain at home until you recover.

By order of Maj. Gen. W. T. Sherman:

R. M. SAWYER,
Assistant Adjutant-General.

HDQRS. DEPARTMENT AND ARMY OF THE TENNESSEE,
Near Stockbridge, Ga., November 15, 1864.

Maj. Gen. P. JOS. OSTERHAUS,
Commanding Fifteenth Army Corps:

GENERAL: The major-general commanding directs me to say, in sending inclosed order of march,* that although your proposed route is good, he does not deem it necessary to alter the order of march from that marked out. You can move your First Division as indicated in the order, and General Hazen's division by the way of Lee's Mill, on a road leading out near his present camp. Generals Smith's and Corse's divisions are so far behind that they can take the road through Jonesborough. The general directs me also to say that the trains from some cause were not to-day properly closed up, and he fears not as well guarded as they should have been, considering the proximity of the enemy's cavalry. He wishes them more carefully attended to and kept up. Flankers should be put out and every preparation made to repel any dash of the enemy's cavalry.

Very respectfully, your obedient servant,

SAML. L. TAGGART,
Assistant Adjutant-General.

SPECIAL ORDERS, No. 172. } HDQRS. FIFTEENTH ARMY CORPS,
In the Field, Ga., November 15, 1864.

* * * * * * *

II. In accordance with orders the corps will resume its march to-morrow as follows: The Second Division, Brigadier-General Hazen commanding, will have the advance and will leave camp at 6 a. m. and march for the Jonesborough and McDonough road, following the same to the latter place. The supply trains of the First and Second Divisions will fall in in rear of their respective commands, with only one regiment as rear guard for each train. Major Stolbrand, commanding Artillery Brigade, will detail one light battery to report to Brigadier-General Hazen for assignment to position with the advance brigade. The two remaining batteries will report to Brigadier-General Woods, who will place them in rear of the leading brigade of his division. The train guards of to-day were not considered sufficiently strong. Division commanders will therefore re-enforce them. There should be at least two or three regiments on the flank of each division train. The attention of Generals Smith and Corse is particularly called to the security of their trains; they being exposed to cavalry dashes, strong flanking and rear guards are very necessary,

By order of Maj. Gen. P. Joseph Osterhaus:

FREDK. WHITEHEAD,
Assistant Adjutant-General.

SPECIAL ORDERS.] HDQRS. FIRST. DIV., 15TH ARMY CORPS,
In the Field, Ga., November 15, 1864.

This division will march at 7 a. m. to-morrow in the direction of McDonough, following that of Brigadier-General Hazen, in the following order: First, First Brigade, each regiment to be followed by one ambu-

---

*See Special Field Orders, No. 168, p. 465.

lance, regimental team, and one wagon infantry ammunition. Second, pioneers. Third, headquarter's train First Division, half of the supply train, and the ordnance train of the division; one regiment of the First Brigade will escort this train, marching by companies along the column. Fourth, Third Brigade, one ambulance, regimental team, and one wagon infantry ammunition following each regiment. Fifth, the remaining half of the supply train, followed by the ambulance corps and medical wagons; one regiment of the Third Brigade will escort this train, marching by companies along the column. Sixth, Second Brigade, each regiment followed by one ambulance, regimental wagon, and one wagon infantry ammunition. Each brigade will be immediately followed by the headquarters teams of that brigade. The commanding officer of the Second Brigade will detail two companies from his rear regiment to march at the head of the column as provost guards for dwellings. The Seventeenth Army Corps follows the First Division on the same road.

By order of Brig. Gen. C. R. Woods:

FRED. H. WILSON,
Acting Assistant Adjutant-General.

GENERAL ORDERS, } HDQRS. FIRST DIV., 15TH ARMY CORPS,
No. 80. } *White Hall, Ga., November 15, 1864.*

I. George F. French, surgeon U. S. Volunteers, having reported for duty at these headquarters by order of major-general commanding the department, is hereby announced as medical director of the division. Surg. B. N. Bond, Twenty-seventh Missouri Infantry, surgeon-in-chief of this division, is relieved from such duty, and will report to the commanding officer of his regiment.

By order of Brig. Gen. C. R. Woods:

FRED. H. WILSON,
Acting Assistant Adjutant-General.

GENERAL ORDERS, } HDQRS. THIRD DIV., 15TH ARMY CORPS,
No. 93. } *In the Field, Ga., November 15, 1864.*

This division will march at 6 a. m. to-morrow, the 16th instant.

Order of march: First, one regiment First Brigade in advance, followed by one wagon and one ambulance; second, pioneer corps, tool wagons, one wagon (baggage), and one ambulance; third, remainder of First Brigade, each regiment to be followed by one wagon and one ambulance; fourth, ammunition train; fifth, division headquarters train and provost guard; sixth, First Brigade train; seventh, Second Brigade train; eighth, quartermaster's train; ninth, supply train; tenth, remainder of ambulance corps not otherwise assigned; eleventh, two regiments Second Brigade, well deployed, one upon each flank of the entire train; twelfth, remainder of Second Brigade as rear guard—their wagons and ambulances will be placed between the regiments.

The attention of General Raum is particularly directed to the security of the trains, and he will, when on the march, take such steps as he may think necessary for their protection.

By order of Brig. Gen John E. Smith:

S. M. BUDLONG,
Assistant Adjutant-General.

SPECIAL FIELD ORDERS, No. 5. } HEADQUARTERS FOURTH DIVISION, FIFTEENTH ARMY CORPS, *In the Field, near East Point, November 15, 1864.*

* * * * * * *

III. This command will be ready to move to-morrow, the 16th instant, at 6.30 a. m., in the following order: The infantry will move on either side of the trains, with the exception that the First Brigade will have one regiment in advance and the Second Brigade will have one regiment act as rear guard. After the advance regiment follows the pioneer corps, and then the battery. All wagons will close on the battery—first, the pioneer corps train; second, the First Brigade train; third, the Third Brigade train; fourth, the Second Brigade train; fifth, the ordnance train; sixth, the supply train; seventh, the ambulance train. The Third Brigade will move in the center. The column will not move until orders are given from these headquarters and it is ascertained the road is clear ahead of us.

By order of Brig. Gen. J. M. Corse:

L. CARPER,
Assistant Adjutant-General.

HDQRS. DEPARTMENT AND ARMY OF THE TENNESSEE,
Near Stockbridge, Ga., November 15, 1864.

Maj. Gen. F. P. BLAIR,
Commanding Seventeenth Army Corps:

GENERAL: The major-general commanding directs me to say, in sending you inclosed order* of march for to-morrow, that you will find it to advantage to cut a road parallel to the main road, and which will enter the main road a little east of these headquarters. The general suggests that you set the pioneers at work as early as 6.30 o'clock. Lieutenant-Colonel Strong will indicate the point where such road will enter the main road. The general wishes me to call your attention to the necessity of keeping the trains well closed up and properly guarded. Flankers should be kept out, and every preparation made to repel any attack of the enemy's cavalry.

I am, general, very respectfully, your obedient servant,

SAML. L. TAGGART,
Assistant Adjutant-General.

SPECIAL ORDERS, No. 282. } HDQRS. SEVENTEENTH ARMY CORPS, *Mitchell's House, Ga., November 15, 1864.*

* * * * * * *

II. The orders for the movement to-morrow are as follows:

1. Brig. Gen. G. A. Smith, commanding Fourth Division, will move out at 8 a. m.

2. Maj. Gen. J. A. Mower, commanding First Division, will follow the Fourth Division, moving at 9 o'clock.

3. Brig. Gen. M. D. Leggett, commanding Third Division, will follow the First Division, moving at 10 o'clock.

4. Maj. A. C. Waterhouse, commanding Artillery Brigade, will assign a battery to each division, to move as the division commander may direct.

5. The trains will move as in the march to-day.

---

* See Special Field Orders, No. 168, p. 465.

6. Brig. Gen. M. D. Leggett, commanding Third Division, will detail from his command two regiments to act as rear guard to the cavalry train.

7. The train of these headquarters will follow that portion of the ordnance train of the Fourth Division which follows the advance brigade.

8. Division commanders will take the necessary measures to protect their trains from the enemy's cavalry, and will see that their train guards carry their guns and accouterments, and do not place them in the wagons. The utmost endeavors will be used to keep the trains well closed up. The pioneer corps of the Third and Fourth Divisions will report at these headquarters to Captain Kossak, chief engineer, at 6 a. m.

* * * * * * *

By command of Maj. Gen. F. P. Blair:

C. CADLE, JR.,
Assistant Adjutant-General.

SPECIAL FIELD ORDERS, No. 150.

HEADQUARTERS THIRD DIVISION,
SEVENTEENTH ARMY CORPS,
In the Field, Ga., November 15, 1864.

* * * * * * *

III. This command will move to-morrow at — o'clock. Brig. Gen. M. F. Force, commanding First Brigade, will have the advance, moving with his command the artillery ordnance train (ten teams), headquarters train Third Division, and supply train (twenty-six teams), disposing his troops so as to protect same and insure its prompt movement. Col. R. K. Scott, commanding Second Brigade, will follow the First, moving with his command the ordnance train (ten teams) and supply train (twenty-seven teams), disposing his troops so as to protect the same and insure its prompt movement. Being in the rear, he will keep a strong rear guard. Ambulances, regimental and brigade teams will move as heretofore.

By order of Brig. Gen. M. D. Leggett:

J. C. DOUGLASS,
Assistant Adjutant-General.

SPECIAL ORDERS, No. 147.

HDQRS. FOURTH DIV., 17TH ARMY CORPS,
In the Field, November 15, 1864.

In accordance with orders from corps headquarters, this division will move to-morrow morning promptly at 8 o'clock.

The Third Brigade, Brig. Gen. W. W. Belknap commanding, will move in advance.

By order of Brig. Gen. Giles A. Smith:

CHAS. H. BRUSH,
Acting Assistant Adjutant-General.

HEADQUARTERS MILITARY DIVISION OF THE MISSISSIPPI,
In the Field, Atlanta, Ga., November 15, 1864.

Major General SLOCUM,
Commanding Left Wing, &c.:

GENERAL: The general-in-chief directs me to say that upon your arrival at Madison he desires that you will, if it can be done without too much delay, send eastward to the Oconee River, and destroy the railroad bridge, and also the wagon-road bridge. By looking at the map, you will see a force sufficient to do this work can be sent from Madison, and afterward join you farther on. It is important they should be destroyed.

I am, general, respectfully, your obedient servant,

L. M. DAYTON,
Aide-de-Camp.

SPECIAL FIELD ORDERS, No. 20. } HDQRS. FOURTEENTH ARMY CORPS, *Atlanta, Ga., November 15, 1864.*

Orders for to-morrow, November 16, 1864: General Carlin will march, accompanied with all his trains (including his supply train) and his artillery, at 7 a. m. upon the direct road toward Decatur. General Baird, accompanied by all his trains and his artillery, will follow General Carlin at 9 a. m. Colonel Buell, with his command and the pontoon train, will follow General Baird, and will be followed by corps headquarters trains and the reserve artillery. General Morgan will march, accompanied by all his trains and artillery, in the rear of corps headquarters. Colonel Cogswell, post commander, will move his command in the rear of General Morgan and will form the rear guard of the corps. Camping-grounds for the different divisions will be designated by the corps commander, and division commanders will habitually, until further orders, arrange for the security of their own divisions by posting the necessary pickets. The pickets will be posted with the countersign and parole furnished from headquarters Military Division of the Mississippi.

By order of Bvt. Maj. Gen. J. C. Davis:

A. C. McCLURG,
Assistant Adjutant-General and Chief of Staff.

SPECIAL ORDERS, No. 16. } HDQRS. FIRST DIV., 14TH ARMY CORPS, *Atlanta, November 15, 1864.*

* * * * * * *

V. Lieut. Col. J. H. Brigham, Sixty-ninth Ohio Veteran Infantry, will assume command of the Second Brigade, composed of the Sixty-ninth Ohio and Thirteenth and Twenty-first Michigan Volunteers.

By order of Brig. Gen. W. P. Carlin:

G. W. SMITH,
Captain and Acting Assistant Adjutant-General.

HEADQUARTERS FOURTEENTH ARMY CORPS,
Atlanta, Ga., November 15, 1864.

Lieutenant-Colonel PALMER,
Commanding Thirteenth Michigan Volunteers:

You will remain in your present position until dark, at which time, having collected all stragglers and having ascertained that all soldiers belonging to this army, as far as practicable, are across the river, you will destroy the bridge across the Chattahoochee River and march to this place, reporting to your division commander near the Decatur railroad, about a mile east of town. Send to-night a written report to these headquarters.

By order of Bvt. Maj. Gen. J. C. Davis:

A. C. McCLURG,
Assistant Adjutant-General and Chief of Staff.

CIRCULAR.] HDQRS. SECOND DIV., TWENTIETH ARMY CORPS,
November 15, 1864.

Each brigade commander will see that his troops and trains are kept well closed up at all times on the march with those preceding. If the train preceding him does not keep well closed, he will use his authority and make it move on out of the way. While on the march each command will conform to the movements of that preceding it, unless otherwise ordered. This will be done without awaiting orders.

By command of Brig. Gen. John W. Geary:

W. T. FORBES,
Acting Assistant Adjutant-General.

SPECIAL FIELD ORDERS, No. 169. } HEADQUARTERS DEPARTMENT AND ARMY OF THE TENNESSEE,
McDonough, Ga., November 16, 1864.

The army will move forward to-morrow morning as follows:

1. One division of the Seventeenth Corps and the engineer regiment with the bridge train will move on the Keys Ferry road, via Henderson, to Planters' (sometimes called Nutting's) Factory. Captain Reese, chief engineer, will accompany and guide the column.

2. The other divisions of the Seventeenth Corps will move on direct Jackson road, through Jackson, to Planters' Factory.

3. The Fifteenth Corps will move to Planters' Factory via Locust Grove, avoiding Jackson, if practicable.

4. All the columns will start at 6 a. m., and will be doubled on every road—the wagons, artillery, and ambulances forming one, and the troops the other, the road being sufficiently [wide] to admit of it.

5. The trains will move with their brigades and divisions as heretofore.

6. The train of General Kilpatrick's cavalry will follow the division of the Seventeenth Corps, via Jackson, with the rear guard from the Seventeenth Corps as heretofore.

7. The cattle in charge of Lieutenant Todd, acting commissary of subsistence, will follow the Seventeenth Corps, moving through the fields whenever practicable.

8. The Ninth Ohio Cavalry will form the rear guard to the column on the direct Jackson road.

9. The train of these headquarters will follow the leading division of the Seventeenth Corps.

10. The supply trains of these headquarters will move in advance of rear division of the Seventeenth Army Corps.

By order of Maj. Gen. O. O. Howard:

SAML. L. TAGGART,
Assistant Adjutant-General.

SPECIAL ORDERS, No. 173. } HDQRS. FIFTEENTH ARMY CORPS, *Near McDonough, Ga., November 16, 1864.*

I. The Fifteenth Corps will resume its march to-morrow, via Locust Grove, in the following order: The Third Division, Brigadier-General Smith commanding, will leave its present camp at 5.30 a. m., followed by the Fourth Division, Brigadier-General Corse commanding; Artillery Brigade, Major Stolbrand commanding, supported by two regiments Fourth Division; First Division, Brigadier-General Woods commanding; Second Division, Brigadier-General Hazen commanding.

Major Stolbrand, commanding Artillery Brigade, will detail one light battery to report to General Smith, and one section of artillery to report to Brigadier-General Hazen, to be assigned to positions, respectively, in the advance and rear brigade of the column. The very loose order of a portion of the trains during to-day's march renders it necessary to again call the attention of division commanders to this constant cause of annoyance, that it may be corrected. Quartermasters must be required to remain with their trains and oversee their movements in person. They will be held strictly responsible for all irregularities hereafter. It is perfectly preposterous to think that the troops should be delayed successively for hours, and thus lose the necessary amount of rest, because a worthless wagon-master or teamster sees fit to disregard his duties.

All train animals must be watered before leaving camp, as it must not be done after the trains are once strung out. Whenever practicable division commanders will push their troops alongside of their respective trains and artillery.

* * * * * * *

By order of Maj. Gen. P. Joseph Osterhaus:

FREDK. WHITEHEAD,
Assistant Adjutant-General.

GENERAL ORDERS, No. 94. } HDQRS. THIRD DIV., 15TH ARMY CORPS, *McDonough, Ga., November 16, 1864.*

This division will march at 5.30 a. m. to-morrow, the 17th instant. The troops will, until further orders, be supplied with three days' rations in haversacks.

Order of march: First, Second Brigade as advance guard, each regiment followed by one ambulance and one wagon; second, pioneer corps, tool wagons, one ambulance, and one wagon (baggage); third, artillery (one battery); fourth, one regiment First Brigade, followed by one ambulance and one wagon; fifth, ammunition train; sixth, division headquarters train and provost guard; seventh, Second Brigade train; eighth, First Brigade train; ninth, quartermaster's train; tenth, supply train; eleventh, remainder of ambulance corps not otherwise assigned; twelfth, two regiments First Brigade, well deployed, one upon each flank of the entire train; thirteenth, two regiments First Brigade, rear guard—one ambulance and one wagon for each of the flanking and rear-guard regiments will be placed between the last two regiments.

The attention of Colonel McCown is particularly directed to the security of the trains, and he will, while on the march, take such steps as he may think necessary for their protection.

By order of Brig. Gen. John E. Smith:

S. M. BUDLONG,
Assistant Adjutant-General.

SPECIAL FIELD ORDERS, No. 6. } HDQRS. FOURTH DIV., 15TH ARMY CORPS, *In the Field, near Cotton River, Ga., November 16, 1864.*

* * * * * * *

II. This command will move to-morrow, the 17th instant, at 6 a. m. The infantry, until otherwise ordered, will, whenever practicable, move on either side of the train. The order of march will be as follows: The Third Brigade will have the advance, and will have one regiment act as advance guard, and will be followed by the pioneer corps; next, the battery. The Second Brigade will have the center. All wagons will close on the battery as follows: first, the pioneers corps train; second, the Third Brigade train; third, the Second Brigade train; fourth, the First Brigade train; fifth, the ordnance train; sixth, the supply train; seventh, the ambulance train. The First Brigade will be in the rear, and have one regiment act as rear guard.

By order of Brig. Gen. John M. Corse:

L. CARPER,
Assistant Adjutant-General.

SPECIAL ORDERS, No. 283. } HDQRS. SEVENTEENTH ARMY CORPS, *Near McDonough, Ga., November 16, 1864.*

The orders for the movement to-morrow are as follows:

1. Maj. Gen. J. A. Mower, commanding First Division, will have the advance, moving out on the direct road to McDonough at 7 a. m.

2. Brig. Gen. M. D. Leggett, commanding Third Division, will follow the First Division, moving at 8 o'clock.

3. Brig. Gen. G. A. Smith, commanding Fourth Division, will move his command at 5 a. m. on a road to be pointed out by Captain Reese, chief engineer Department and Army of the Tennessee, taking charge of the bridge train.

4. Maj. A. C. Waterhouse, commanding Artillery Brigade, will assign a battery to each division, to move as the division commander may direct.

5. The column will be doubled when the road is wide enough, the troops moving on one side and the trains and artillery on the other.

6. Brig. Gen. M. D. Leggett, commanding Third Division, will detail two regiments to act as guard to the cavalry train.

7. The corps headquarters train will follow that part of the ordnance train which moves directly in rear of the advance brigade of the First Division.

By command of Maj. Gen. F. P. Blair:

C. CADLE, JR.,
Assistant Adjutant-General.

SPECIAL FIELD ORDERS, No. 151. } HEADQUARTERS THIRD DIVISION, SEVENTEENTH ARMY CORPS, *In the Field, Ga., November 16, 1864.*

I. The troops of this command will move at — o'clock to morrow morning. Col. R. K. Scott, commanding Second Brigade, will have the advance, disposing of his troops so as to afford assistance and protection to the artillery, ordnance train, division headquarters train, and supply train to follow his command. Brig. Gen. M. F. Force, commanding First Brigade, will follow the Second, disposing his command so as to afford protection and assistance to the ordnance train and supply train to follow his command. Ambulances, regimental and brigade trains will march as heretofore.

By order of Brig. Gen. M. D. Leggett:

J. C. DOUGLASS,
Assistant Adjutant-General.

SPECIAL ORDERS, No. 148. } HDQRS. FOURTH DIV., 17TH ARMY CORPS,
In the Field, near McDonough,
November 16, 1864.

This division will move to-morrow morning promptly at 6 o'clock The First Brigade will move in advance.

By order of Brig. Gen. Giles A. Smith:

CHAS. H. BRUSH,
Acting Assistant Adjutant-General.

SPECIAL FIELD ORDERS, No. 21. } HDQRS. 14TH ARMY CORPS,
Brandley's House, Ga., November 16, 1864.

Orders for to-morrow, November 17, 1864: The different commands of this column will march in the same order they have marched to-day and will start at daylight from their respective bivouacs.

By order of Bvt. Maj. Gen. J. C. Davis:

A. C. McCLURG,
Assistant Adjutant-General and Chief of Staff.

GENERAL ORDERS, No. 1. } HDQRS. 2D BRIG., 1ST. DIV., 14TH A. C.,
Atlanta, Ga., November 16, 1864.

I. In pursuance of Special Orders, No. 16, paragraph V, dated headquarters First Division, Fourteenth Army Corps, November 15, 1864, I hereby assume command of the Second Brigade of this division, composed of the Sixty-ninth Ohio, Thirteenth Michigan, and Twenty-first Michigan Volunteer Infantry.

J. H. BRIGHAM,
Lieutenant-Colonel, Commanding Second Brigade, First Division.

GENERAL ORDERS, No. 17. } HDQRS. SECOND DIV., 14TH ARMY CORPS,
Atlanta, Ga., November 16, 1864.

This division moves at 11 this a. m., in the following order: Second Brigade, battery, First Brigade, Third Brigade, ambulances, division headquarters wagons, brigade headquarters wagons in the order of march, hospital train, ordnance train, commissary and quartermaster trains. Each regimental commander will have his own wagon immediately in rear of his regiment. Only ambulances sufficient to carry the sick and broken-down men will follow in rear of the brigades, the remainder as indicated above. Cattle in rear of all the trains. All wagons, ambulances, and cattle will move in the above order daily till further orders. The brigades will change daily from right to rear as heretofore. The brigade last in the order of march will furnish two regiments as rear guard and guard for the train—fifteen companies to be distributed along the train and five companies as rear guard, whose duty it will be to bring up all stragglers. The troops marching with the train will assist the wagons over bad places, hills, &c. The officer in command of the rear and train guard will report, after he receives his detail from brigade headquarters, to Captain Stinson, provost-marshal of the division, for orders.

By order of Brig. Gen. James D. Morgan:

T. WISEMAN,
Captain and Assistant Adjutant-General.

HEADQUARTERS LEFT WING, ARMY OF GEORGIA,
Near Rock Bridge, November 16, 1864.

Brig. Gen. A. S. WILLIAMS,
Commanding Corps:

The major-general commanding directs that you move General Geary's division at 5 o'clock to-morrow morning, General Ward's division at the same hour, and General Jackson at 6 o'clock. The animals must all be fed and watered at 4 o'clock, and all quartermasters must give this matter their personal attention. General Ward and General Jackson will each detail eight regiments to assist their respective trains up the hills between here and General Geary's present camp, and at such other points as may be necessary on the march. All staff officers of the entire command will be distributed through the column to see that troops and trains are closed up and pushed forward as rapidly as possible. When a halt is ordered the troops and trains will always double up, and when possible the trains will park in the fields. General Geary will march as far as Sheffield and there await orders. Brigade inspectors will attend personally to the feeding of the animals in the morning, and certify whether or not the quartermasters are present, and whether the animals are fed as ordered.

Very respectfully, &c.,

H. C. RODGERS,
Assistant Adjutant-General.

ORDERS.] HEADQUARTERS TWENTIETH CORPS,
Near Yellow River, November 16, 1864.

In compliance with orders from headquarters Left Wing, this corps will march to-morrow toward Social Circle. The Second Division will start at 5 a. m.; the Third Division at 5 a. m.; First Division at 6. Generals Ward and Geary will be in readiness to start promptly at the hour named. In order to facilitate the march the following regulations are hereby established and will remain in force until further orders: All regimental quartermasters will report to the brigade quartermasters for assignment to duty with the trains. All officers of the quartermaster's department will remain constantly on duty with the wagon trains. Each division commander will detail a sufficient number of men to accompany the trains, that each wagon will have one man to lock and unlock the wheels. These men must not in any case be permitted to stray from the wagon to which they have been assigned. Brigadier-General Ward will detail 100 men to accompany and assist the trains of Captain Schoeninger and Captain Bickford. Each division commander will keep staff officers distributed with the train to keep it closed up and to urge it forward. Quartermasters are directed to put out of the trains all unauthorized vehicles that retard in the least the march.

By command of Brig. Gen. A. S. Williams:

ROBT. P. DECHERT,
Captain and Acting Assistant Adjutant-General.

HEADQUARTERS TWENTIETH CORPS,
Near Stone Mountain, Ga., November 16, 1864.

Brig. Gen. N. J. JACKSON,
Commanding First Division:

GENERAL: The time of marching to-day is changed as follows: The Second Division will march at 8 a. m., Third Division at 9 a. m., First Division at 10 a. m. Commanders of divisions will instruct their subordinate commanders to have their troops give all necessary assistance to the trains while on the road to enable them to keep closed up.

By command of Brigadier-General Williams:

ROBT. P. DECHERT,
Acting Assistant Adjutant-General.

(Same to Generals Geary and Ward.)

ORDERS.] HDQRS. FIRST DIVISION, TWENTIETH CORPS,
Near Yellow River, Ga., November 16, 1864.

In compliance with orders from headquarters of the corps, this division will move to-morrow at 6 a. m. in the direction of Social Circle. The animals will be fed and watered by 4 a. m., and all quartermasters will give their personal attention to this matter. The regulations for the march will be the same as those given verbally for to-day, viz: The two leading brigades and three regiments of the rear brigade will march by the side of the trains, and will give all necessary assistance to the wagons going up or down hill, or over bad places. The three remaining regiments of this rear brigade will form the rear guard. The staff officers of the brigades will be distributed through the column to see that the troops and trains are closed up and pushed forward as rapidly as possible. When a halt is ordered troops and trains will double up as much as possible. Brigade inspectors will attend personally to the feeding of the animals in the morning, and certify whether or not the quartermasters are present, and whether the animals are fed as ordered. Brigade commanders will hold regimental commanders responsible that there be no straggling either to the front or to the rear. Quartermasters are directed to put out of the train all unauthorized vehicles that retard in the least the march.

By command of Brig. Gen. N. J. Jackson:

GEO. ROBINSON,
First Lieutenant and Acting Assistant Adjutant-General.

HEADQUARTERS TWENTIETH CORPS, ARMY OF GEORGIA,
Near Stone Mountain, Ga., November 16, 1864.

Brig. Gen. J. W. GEARY,
Commanding Second Division:

GENERAL: I am directed by the brigadier-general commanding to say that the pontoon train will move to-day in rear of the leading brigade of your division until we reach Yellow River. The headquarters train of the corps and the corps supply train will move in rear of the troops of the rear brigade of your division.

Very respectfully, your obedient servant,

ROBT. P. DECHERT,
Captain and Acting Assistant Adjutant-General.

HDQRS. NORTHERN DISTRICT, DEPT. OF THE SOUTH,
FIRST SEPARATE BRIGADE,
Morris Island, November 16, 1864.

Capt. J. F. GREEN, U. S. Navy,
Commanding Blockading Squadron, off Charleston:

SIR: Colonel Kozlay, commanding the post of Folly Island, reports that the senior naval officer at Stono has received instructions to be on the watch for four cotton-clad barges which the rebels have ready to send down. I have the honor to inquire whether you have any information as to the direction from which these barges may be expected, and as to the nature of the apprehended attack. The officer commanding Battery No. 2, on the left of Cole's Island, has been ordered to exercise especial vigilance. This battery is directly on the bank of the Stono and nearly opposite the obstruction in that river.

Very respectfully, your obedient servant,

EDWARD E. POTTER,
Brigadier-General, Commanding.

HDQRS. NORTHERN DISTRICT, DEPT. OF THE SOUTH,
FIRST SEPARATE BRIGADE,
Morris Island, S. C., November 16, 1864.

Maj. Gen. J. G. FOSTER,
Commanding Department of the South:

GENERAL: I have had the Union refugees sounded, with the view of learning whether any of them are willing to return for the purpose of opening communication between us and those of our men who have enlisted in the rebel service. Neither of the three enlisted men is willing to undertake it. Captain Epeneter, Sixth [Seventh] U. S. Colored Heavy Artillery, says that he is ready to return for the purpose referred to, but wishes in the first place to visit his home. Captain E[peneter] says he could make his way into Charleston, either directly from here or in a blockade-runner via Nassau. He knows the city well and has German friends residing there. All these escaped prisoners will go to the Head to-night, their term of quarantine having expired, and you can yourself see Captain Epeneter, if you think fit. I send herewith the statement of these men, taken yesterday, and of which you desired a copy.

Very respectfully,

EDWARD E. POTTER,
Brigadier-General, Commanding.

SPECIAL FIELD ORDERS, No. 170. } HEADQUARTERS DEPARTMENT AND ARMY OF THE TENNESSEE, *Jackson, Ga., November 17, 1864.*

The army will continue its march to-morrow, as follows:

1. Lieutenant-Colonel Tweeddale, commanding engineer regiment, will push the bridge train to Planters' Factory, starting at 5 a. m.

2. Brig. Gen. G. A. Smith, commanding Fourth Division, Seventeenth Army Corps, will follow the bridge train at 7 a. m.

3. Major-General Blair, commanding Seventeenth Army Corps, will move his other two divisions, starting at 7.30 a. m., on the direct road to Planters' Factory.

4. Major-General Osterhaus, commanding Fifteenth Army Corps, will move his command as follows: The Third Division will move at 6.30 a. m., park his train near the river with a small guard, and cross the rest as fast as he can by the ferry. The remaining three divisions will be marched during the day to the vicinity of the river and take position covering all trains.

5. The entire crossing will be effected in the following order, viz: First, Kilpatrick's cavalry; second, Third Division, Fifteenth Corps; third, Fourth Division, Seventeenth Corps; fourth, remaining two divisions, Seventeenth Corps; fifth, Fourth Division, Fifteenth Corps; sixth, Second Division, Fifteenth Corps; seventh, First Division, Fifteenth Corps.

6. After having commenced crossing the bridge will be kept full night and day until the entire army is over.

7. At least a brigade of infantry from the First Division, Fifteenth Corps, will be retained on the bank till everything is crossed, and will act as rear guard to all trains during the first day's march after the bridge is taken up.

8. The troops will be posted on the other bank somewhat in the form of a bridge-head, the Seventeenth Corps on the left and Fifteenth on the right, leaving plenty of room for the trains.

9. The train of these headquarters will follow the ammunition train of the leading division of the Seventeenth Corps on the direct road.

By order of Maj. Gen. O. O. Howard:

SAML. L. TAGGART,
Assistant Adjutant-General.

SPECIAL ORDERS, No. 257. } HDQRS. DEPT. AND ARMY OF THE TENN., *Louisville, Ky., November 17, 1864.*

* * * * * * *

II. By direction of Major-General Sherman, commanding Military Division of the Mississippi, it is ordered that all officers and detachments of the Army of the Tennessee prevented from joining their proper commands by reason of the present movement of this army will proceed forthwith to Chattanooga, Tenn., and report to Major-General Steedman for assignment to duty.

* * * * * * *

IV. Maj. Gen. G. M. Dodge and staff will proceed to Saint Louis, Mo., and there establish his headquarters for the purpose of making out his reports of the campaign in Georgia and completing the records of the Left Wing of the Sixteenth Army Corps. He will then await further orders from headquarters of the department in the field.

Major Barnes, assistant adjutant-general, will accompany General Dodge to Saint Louis, Mo., or other points, for the purpose of assisting him in making his report. The quartermaster's department will furnish transportation for servants, horses, public and private property.

* * * * * * *

By order of Maj. Gen. O. O. Howard:

WM. T. CLARK,
Assistant Adjutant-General.

SPECIAL ORDERS, No. 174. } HDQRS. FIFTEENTH ARMY CORPS,
Jackson, Ga., November 17, 1864.

I. The movement of the corps to-morrow will be as follows: Brigadier-General Smith, commanding Third Division, will move his command at 5 a. m. to Planters' Factory, and will commence at once to cross his troops on the flat-boat now there, leaving, however, the train and artillery on this side of the river until the pontoon train is laid down. The corps will take up a defensive position as soon as they arrive on the east side of the Ocmulgee River and will throw up light works. Brigadier-General Corse, commanding Fourth Division, and Major Stolbrand, commanding Artillery Brigade, will remain in their present position until further orders. Brigadier-Generals Hazen and Woods, commanding Second and First Divisions, will march their commands at 5 a. m. to Indian Springs, where they will encamp, taking a strong position facing south and east, and await further orders.

II. Commissaries will, until further orders, issue only three-quarter rations of breadstuffs and sugar. Full rations of all other articles will be issued as heretofore.

By order of Maj. Gen. P. Joseph Osterhaus:

FREDK. WHITEHEAD,
Assistant Adjutant-General.

GENERAL ORDERS, No. 95. } HDQRS. 3D DIV., 15TH ARMY CORPS,
In the Field, four miles southeast of Jackson, Ga., November 17, 1864.

This command will move at 5 a. m. to-morrow, the 18th instant.

Order of march: First, one regiment First Brigade as advance guard, followed by one ambulance and one wagon; second, pioneer corps, tool wagons, one ambulance, and one wagon (baggage); third, three regiments First Brigade, each regiment followed by one ambulance and one wagon; fourth, artillery (Captain Arndt's battery); fifth, one regiment First Brigade; sixth, ammunition train; seventh, division headquarters train and provost guard; eighth, First Brigade train; ninth, Second Brigade train; tenth, quartermaster's train; eleventh, supply train; twelfth, remainder of ambulance corps not otherwise assigned; thirteenth, two regiments Second Brigade, well deployed, one upon each flank of all the trains; fourteenth, two regiments Second Brigade, rear guard; one ambulance and one wagon for each regiment of the Second Brigade will be placed between the last two regiments.

By order of Brig. Gen. John E. Smith:

S. M. BUDLONG,
Assistant Adjutant-General.

CIRCULAR.] HDQRS. FOURTH DIV., FIFTEENTH ARMY CORPS,
In the Field, near Jackson, Ga., November 17, 1864.

In order to secure to the soldier an equal share of stores gathered from the country, each brigade commander will send out daily, until further orders, foraging parties, composed of fifty privates and an adequate number of commissioned and non-commissioned officers, whose duty it will be to gather forage and meat rations. These parties will in no case go beyond supporting distance from the main column. The supplies collected must be brought to the roadside and there loaded in their respective brigade wagons and turned over to brigade quartermasters. Cattle and sheep are to be driven on the hoof whenever practicable. The officers in charge of these parties should enforce the strictest discipline and order. Foraging parties will on no pretense be permitted to enter houses except by written authority from the division commander. The assistant provost-marshal will see this last clause strictly enforced, and will arrest all soldiers found in houses without competent authority.

By order of Brig. Gen. John M. Corse:

L. CARPER,
Assistant Adjutant-General.

SPECIAL FIELD ORDERS, No. 7. } HEADQUARTERS FOURTH DIVISION, FIFTEENTH ARMY CORPS,
In the Field, near Jackson, Ga., November 17, 1864.

I. The Fourth Division will resume its march to-morrow, the 18th instant, at 6 a. m., in the following order: The Second Brigade will have the advance; the First Brigade will move in the center; the Third Brigade will bring up the rear. The brigade in the advance and the brigade in the rear will have one regiment, respectively, as advance and rear guard. From the regiment acting as advance guard one large company will be furnished to Capt. H. L. Burnham, assistant provost-marshal of this division, to act as provost guard. The pioneer corps will follow the advance regiment. The trains will follow well closed up—first, the pioneer corps train; second, the Second Brigade train; third, the First Brigade train; fourth, the Third Brigade train; fifth, the ordnance train; sixth, the supply train; seventh, the ambulance train.

By order of Brig. Gen. John M. Corse:

L. CARPER,
Assistant Adjutant-General.

SPECIAL ORDERS, No. 284. } HDQRS. SEVENTEENTH ARMY CORPS,
Jackson, Ga., November 17, 1864.

The order for to-morrow's movements are as follows:

1. Maj. Gen. J. A. Mower, commanding First Division, will have the advance, and will move his command at 7.30 a. m. to-morrow, on the direct road to Planters' Factory.

2. The Third Division, Brig. Gen. M. D. Leggett commanding, will follow the First Division at 8.30 a. m.

3. Maj. A. C. Waterhouse, commanding Artillery Brigade, will assign a battery to each division, to move therewith as the division commander may direct.

4. The column will be doubled when the road is wide enough, the troops moving on the right of the artillery and trains.

5. Brig. Gen. M. D. Leggett will cause two regiments to be detailed from his command to act as rear guard to the cavalry train.

6. The corps headquarters train will follow that part of the ordnance train which moves directly in rear of the advance brigade of the First Division.

7. The crossing of the river will be in the following order: First, Fourth Division; second, First Division; third, Third Division.

By command of Maj. Gen. F. P. Blair:

C. CADLE, JR.,
Assistant Adjutant-General.

SPECIAL FIELD ORDERS, No. 152.

HEADQUARTERS THIRD DIVISION, SEVENTEENTH ARMY CORPS,
In the Field, Ga., November 17, 1864.

I. The troops of this command will march at 8 a. m., the Second Brigade having the advance. The particulars of the march will be given before starting.

II. The hour of marching to-morrow is 8.30 a. m. The First Brigade, Brig. Gen. M. F. Force commanding, will have the advance; artillery trains and ambulances as heretofore.

By order of Brig. Gen. M. D. Leggett:

J. C. DOUGLASS,
Assistant Adjutant-General.

GENERAL ORDERS, No. 25.

HDQRS. FOURTH DIV., 17TH ARMY CORPS,
In the Field, Ga., November 17, 1864.

The following orders are published for the government of troops on this campaign:

I. Rear guards and foraging parties will be immediately established as prescribed in orders from superior headquarters. All surgeons and majors will remain constantly in rear of their respective regiments, permitting no one to fall behind except such as are unable to march, and providing them with transportation in ambulances. Rear guards will arrest all stragglers, no matter to what command they may belong, forwarding them at night to the headquarters to which they are attached for final disposition. If mounted their horses will be taken for the disabled and sore-footed soldiers, but will be sent with them to headquarters.

II. Every means possible will be taken to facilitate the movement of trains. To this end, when a halt occurs, either for a rest or on account of the road being blockaded in front, brigade commanders and officers in charge of trains will mass them whenever the ground will permit, leaving the road clear when practicable. In moving, when the road will permit, the wagons will move two abreast. Every wagon will be provided with two men beside the driver, with a non-commissioned officer for every five wagons, whose duty it will be to act as guard, to lock the wheels when necessary, and to use their utmost endeavor to assist in getting the wagons through muddy places or up steep hills. A staff officer from these headquarters will accompany the train each day, who, in connection with the quartermaster, commissary, ordnance officer, and one officer detailed from each brigade in charge of the men with the wagons, and one officer and thirty men from the pioneer corps, will see that no delay occurs with the trains.

III. Company commanders will be held responsible that no straggling is allowed from their commands, and their names, as well as officers in charge of foraging parties who permit men to leave the ranks, will be reported to these headquarters.

IV. It is hoped and believed that both officers and men of this command will keep constantly in mind that we are not warring upon women and children. Foraging parties will take such articles as are needed for the health or subsistence of the men, but no houses will be entered by them, and all officers, guards, or soldiers are ordered to shoot on the spot any person caught firing a building, or any other property, without orders.

V. Brigade, regimental, and company commanders will see that no firing of guns either on the march or in camp is permitted. This unsoldierly and unmilitary practice must be stopped.

VI. In marching heavy columns on the same road fatiguing and late marches are unavoidable. Soldiers will find a great relief, if not a certain preventative, for sore feet in nightly bathing them in cold water; and every care possible should be taken for their cleanliness, which is a great promoter of health.

VII. Our limited amount of rations render it necessary to prevent the increase of mouths to feed. Officers must do with their present number of servants until the end of this campaign; but all foraging parties or other officers will send such able-bodied negroes as desire it to the pioneer corps until 150 are obtained; no others will be taken. All captured horses and mules will be turned over to Captain Wilson, assistant quartermaster, to replace such as are run down in the trains.

VIII. The practice of marching regiments stretched out to two or three times their natural length is so unsoldierlike and unnecessary that all commanding officers who take any pride in their regiments will, I am sure, take measures to prevent it. Commanding officers of companies can and must march their men in good order.

IX. This order will be read to every regiment and detachment within twenty-four hours after its reception, and assistant inspectors-general and provost-marshals are charged with its execution.

By order of Brig. Gen. Giles A Smith:

CHAS. H. BRUSH,
First Lieutenant and Acting Assistant Adjutant-General.

ULCOFAUHACHEE BRIDGE, *November 17, 1864—5 p. m.*

Major-General SHERMAN:

I have just arrived at this point and shall move my command to near Madison to-morrow. If I meet with no opposition I shall push one division Saturday morning, unencumbered by wagons, to destroy the railroad and wagon bridges over the Oconee River, with instructions to join me at Eatonton on Sunday. I shall push a brigade into Madison to destroy all public property and such private property as can be of use to the enemy, and shall move my main command toward Eatonton while this is being done. I hope to be in Eatonton Sunday evening. I have seen no enemy and everything is working well.

H. W. SLOCUM,
Major-General.

HEADQUARTERS FOURTEENTH ARMY CORPS,
Near Yellow River, November 17, 1864.

Brig. Gen. W. P. CARLIN,
Commanding First Division, Fourteenth Army Corps:

The general commanding directs that you move at sunrise, cross a pontoon bridge over the Yellow River (which Colonel Buell will have laid by that time), and march to Covington, where further orders will reach you.

I have the honor to be, general, very respectfully, your obedient servant,

A. C. McCLURG,
Assistant Adjutant-General and Chief of Staff.

HEADQUARTERS FOURTEENTH ARMY CORPS,
Brandley's House, November 17, 1864.

Brig. Gen. W. P. CARLIN,
Commanding First Division, Fourteenth Army Corps:

The general commanding directs that marching at daylight you push direct for the river this side of Covington. You will destroy five miles of the railroad this side of the river, secure the crossings of Yellow River, and go into camp on the bank of the river. The general thinks you will be able to secure some forage and provisions on to-morrow's march.

By order of Bvt. Maj. Gen. J. C. Davis:

A. C. McCLURG,
Assistant Adjutant-General and Chief of Staff.

SPECIAL ORDERS, No. 17. } HEADQUARTERS FIRST DIVISION,
FOURTEENTH ARMY CORPS,
Camp on Yellow River, November 17, 1864.

I. Capt. Isaac Brinkworth, Thirty-eighth Indiana Volunteer Infantry, is hereby announced as aide-de-camp on the staff of the general commanding.

By order of Brig. Gen. W. P. Carlin:

G. W. SMITH,
Captain and Acting Assistant Adjutant-General.

SPECIAL FIELD ORDERS, No. 12. } HEADQUARTERS FIRST DIVISION,
FOURTEENTH ARMY CORPS,
Camp on Yellow River, November 17, 1864.

I. The use of cartridges in killing of sheep, hogs, cattle, &c., foraged in the country is positively forbidden. Ammunition is too scarce to be wasted for such purposes.

II. No houses, mills, or any buildings of any kind will be set on fire unless by order of the division commander, and care must be taken not to kindle or burn fires in the vicinity of forests, where they would be likely to spread over the country. This order will be read at the earliest practicable moment to every regiment in this division.

By order of Brig. Gen. W. P. Carlin:

G. W. SMITH,
Captain and Acting Assistant Adjutant-General.

ORDERS.] HEADQUARTERS TWENTIETH CORPS,
Near Flat Creek, Ga., November 17, 1864.

This corps will march to-morrow as follows: The Second Division at 5 a. m., Third Division at 6 a. m., First Division at 8 a. m., taking the road through Social Circle to Madison. The trains of Captain Schoeninger and Captain Bickford will march between the Third and First Divisions. General Ward will detail 100 men to report to Captain Schoeninger to assist his and the commissary train. The pontoon train will march immediately in rear of the advance brigade of General Geary's division. Commanders of divisions will instruct their brigade commanders to march their troops as much as possible on the side of the road, along the trains. Brigade commanders should give their personal attention to the movement of the trains in their charge; see that in case of necessity prompt assistance is rendered. They will also take measures to stop the straggling from the column and the unauthorized firing so noticeable to-day. If necessary they will deploy flankers and keep their men together. If it is necessary to kill animals for subsistence it must be done by other means than shooting, and only by persons properly authorized.

By command of Brigadier-General Williams:

ROBT. P. DECHERT,
Captain and Acting Assistant Adjutant-General.

ORDERS.] HDQRS. FIRST DIV., TWENTIETH ARMY CORPS,
Near Flat Creek, Ga., November 17, 1864.

This division will march to-morrow at 7 a. m., in the following order: Second Brigade in advance, Third Brigade following, and the First Brigade in rear. The two leading brigades, with the exception of one regiment of leading brigade for advanced guard and two regiments of the rear brigade, will march on the side of the road along the trains. Brigade commanders should give their prompt attention to the movements of the trains in their charge; see that, in case of necessity, prompt assistance is rendered. They will also take measures to stop the straggling from the column and the unauthorized firing so noticeable to-day, and of which complaints have been made by superior headquarters. If necessary they will deploy flankers to keep their men together. If it is necessary to kill animals for subsistence it must be done by other means than shooting, and only by persons properly authorized.

By command of Brig. Gen. N. J. Jackson:

GEO. ROBINSON,
First Lieutenant and Acting Assistant Adjutant-General.

NEAR STOCKBRIDGE, GA., *November 17, 1864.*

Brig. Gen. J. KILPATRICK,
Commanding Cavalry Division:

I am highly gratified at your dash and sweep, and to your brave officers and men. You must employ wagons of indifferent materials if you have not ambulances enough. Your aide will explain my march. If you can find a bridge below you had better take it, but I think there is none. My headquarters at Jackson to-night; to-morrow night at the river. I want you to make G. W. think we are making for Macon, via Forsyth. I think he will concentrate everything but his cavalry at Macon as soon as possible, but he may hope to head us off and create delay, particularly if he has as many old soldiers as you say. Please communicate to-morrow night.

Very respectfully, your obedient servant,

O. O. HOWARD,
Major-General.

CIRCULAR.] HDQRS. THIRD DIVISION, CAVALRY CORPS,
MILITARY DIVISION OF THE MISSISSIPPI,
November 17, 1864.

The general commanding desires to impress upon the minds of all officers and men the great importance of carefully saving their ammunition and properly caring for their horses. Regimental commanders will be held responsible for any unnecessary skirmishing and every round fired away without sufficient reason. The firing last evening in both brigades (Colonels Atkins and Murray), and throughout the entire command on the march from Bear Creek Station, and in the vicinity of regimental camps, for the purpose of killing hogs, was most unmilitary, and a willful waste of ammunition. This must cease at once.

The general commanding calls upon brigade, regimental, and company commanders to enforce this order. Let the men catch and kill their hogs with their sabers, a weapon that can be used equally as well to kill hogs as rebels.

No trotting of horses will hereafter be allowed. All marching and formations must be made at a walk. All company officers who allow the men of their companies to trot their horses, without orders having been properly received to that effect, and by the bugle from the head of the column, will be dismounted, placed under arrest, and sent to march with the division train till such point is reached where a court-martial can be convened for their trial and dismissal.

Each regimental commander must be furnished with a copy of this order, and will cause it to be read to his regiment, paraded for that purpose, twice each day until further orders.

The general commanding division gives fair warning that this order must be obeyed to the letter.

By command of Brigadier-General Kilpatrick:

L. G. ESTES,
Captain and Assistant Adjutant-General.

SPECIAL FIELD ORDERS, No. 171. } HEADQUARTERS DEPARTMENT AND ARMY OF THE TENNESSEE,
Planters' Factory, Ga., November 18, 1864.

* * * * * * *

II. The army will move to-morrow as follows: First, the Seventeenth Corps, Major-General Blair commanding, via Monticello, toward Hillsborough, starting at 7 a. m. Second, Major-General Osterhaus will commence his movement at 6 a. m. General J. E. Smith's division will proceed on the Hillsborough road toward Clinton and will encamp to-morrow night, if practicable, about three miles beyond Hillsborough. The other three divisions will be marched toward Hillsborough by both routes, at the option of General Osterhaus. Third, Brigadier-General

Kilpatrick will cross in rear of the Seventeenth Corps at 4 a. m. to-morrow, take the Hillsborough road and any road to the right he may choose between the Clinton road and the river. He will make for the Macon and Augusta Railroad as rapidly as possible and fulfill the instructions already received from General Sherman. His supply train will follow that part of the Fifteenth Corps that passes through Monticello. The cavalry regiment at Towaliga Creek will be moved up to the bridge as early as 12 m. to-morrow and will act as guard for the supply train. Fourth, the brigade of infantry heretofore ordered as rear guard will carefully guard the bridge train till it reaches Hillsborough, via Monticello. Fifth, Captain Reese, chief engineer, will direct the taking up of the bridge after the army has crossed. Sixth, the cattle, in charge of Lieutenant Todd, acting commissary of subsistence, will cross at Roach's Ferry and move, via Monticello, to Hillsborough. Seventh, the trains of these headquarters will move with the leading division of the Fifteenth Corps, on the direct Hillsborough road. Eighth, the commander of the rear guard before crossing will destroy the cotton factory and all cotton found in large quantities, but will not destroy the flouring mill at this place. Attention is again called to Special Field Orders, No. 120, of General Sherman.* Headquarters will be at Hillsborough to-morrow night.

* * * * * * *

By command of Maj. Gen. O. O. Howard:

SAML. L. TAGGART,
Assistant Adjutant-General.

SPECIAL ORDERS, No. 175. } HDQRS. FIFTEENTH ARMY CORPS, *In the Field, Ga., November 18, 1864.*

* * * * * * *

II. Brigadier-General Hazen, commanding Second Division, will leave his present camp at 4 a. m. to-morrow and march on the direct road to Roach's Ferry. There he will at once commence crossing his troops by the flat-boat. All headquarters and regimental wagons may be crossed by the same means; the supply and ordnance trains must, however, be sent to the pontoon bridge at Ocmulgee Mills, under an escort of two regiments of infantry. As soon as General Hazen's command is over, he will march in rear of the Seventeenth Army Corps to Monticello, and thence by the most direct road to Hillsborough.

III. Brig. Gen. John E. Smith, commanding Third Division, will move his command at 6 a. m. to-morrow, on the most direct road to Hillsborough, leaving the Monticello and Clinton road to his left. The battery of artillery now with the Third Division will report to Brigadier General Smith for assignment in his column.

IV. Brig. Gen. J. M. Corse will take possession of the pontoon bridge at Ocmulgee at 6 o'clock to-morrow, and cross his command with all possible expedition. When across he will march to Hillsborough, following General Smith's division.

V. As soon as Brigadier-General Hazen's command has fairly marched out of Indian Springs, Brig. Gen. C. R. Woods, commanding First Division, will move his command on the direct road to Ocmulgee Mills (or Planters' Factory), and cross the river on the pontoon bridge in rear of general ammunition and supply train, following the division of Brigadier-General Corse to Hillsborough.

---

*See Vol. XXXIX, Part III, p. 713.

VI. The section of artillery now at Indian Springs will report to General C. R. Woods, commanding First Division, for assignment in his column.

VII. Whenever it is practicable the troops must be marched alongside the trains, with the exception of the leading and rear brigades, which must remain unencumbered and ready for any emergency. Most of the roads can, with the assistance of the pioneer corps, easily be widened out for a double column. The practice of marching troops by single file must be discontinued; they always must move by fours and well closed up.

By command of Maj. Gen. P. Joseph Osterhaus:

FREDK. WHITEHEAD,
Assistant Adjutant-General.

GENERAL ORDERS, No. 96.

HDQRS. THIRD DIV., 15TH ARMY CORPS,
In the Field, two miles south of Planters' Mills, Ga., November 18, 1864.

This command will move at 6 a. m. to-morrow, the 19th instant.

Order of march: First, one regiment Second Brigade as advance guard, followed by one ambulance and one wagon; second, pioneer corps, tool wagons, one ambulance, and one wagon (baggage); third, remainder of Second Brigade, each regiment followed by one ambulance and one wagon; fourth, Battery B, First Michigan Light Artillery; fifth, one regiment First Brigade, followed by one ambulance and one wagon; sixth, ammunition train; seventh, division headquarters train and provost guard; eighth, Second Brigade train; ninth, First Brigade train; tenth, quartermaster's train; eleventh, supply train; twelfth, ambulance corps, except those assigned to regiments and detachments; thirteenth, two regiments First Brigade, well deployed, one upon each flank of all the trains; fourteenth, two regiments First Brigade, rear guard—one ambulance and one wagon for each of the flanking and rear-guard regiments will be placed between the last two regiments.

By order of Brig. Gen. John E. Smith:

S. M. BUDLONG,
Assistant Adjutant-General.

SPECIAL FIELD ORDERS, No. 8.

HEADQUARTERS FOURTH DIVISION,
FIFTEENTH ARMY CORPS,
In the Field, near Jackson, Ga., November 18, 1864.

I. The regiment acting as rear guard will furnish one commissioned officer, three non-commissioned officers, and twenty men, to follow in rear of the column when on the march, to destroy by burning all cotton found. The commanding officer of the guard will make a report daily to the division provost-marshal, who will send to corps headquarters an estimate of the number of bales so destroyed. The brigade commanders will furnish the commissioned officer so detailed written instructions.

II. This command will move at once in the order prescribed in Special Field Orders, No. 7, from these headquarters.

III. This command will move to-morrow, the 19th instant, at 5 a. m. sharp, as follows: The First Brigade will have the advance; the Third

Brigade will move in the center; the Second Brigade will bring up the rear. The brigade in the advance and the brigade in the rear will have one regiment, respectively, as advance and rear guard. The provost guard will be furnished as heretofore from the advance regiment. The pioneer corps will follow the advance regiment. The trains will follow it, well closed up—first, the pioneer corps train; second, the First Brigade train; third, the Third Brigade train; fourth, the Second Brigade train; fifth, the ordnance train; sixth, the supply train; seventh, the ambulance corps. Reveille to be sounded at 3.30 a. m.

By order of Brig. Gen. J. M. Corse:

L. CARPER,
Assistant Adjutant-General.

SPECIAL ORDERS, No. 285. } HDQRS. SEVENTEENTH ARMY CORPS,
In the Field, Ga., November 18, 1864.

I. The orders for the movement to-morrow are as follows:

1. Brig. Gen. M. D. Leggett, commanding Third Division, will have the advance, and will move at 7 o'clock, on the road to Monticello.

2. Maj. Gen. J. A. Mower, commanding First Division, will follow the Third Division, moving at 8 o'clock.

3. Brig. Gen. G. A. Smith, commanding Fourth Division, will follow the First Division, moving at 9 o'clock.

4. Maj. A. C. Waterhouse, commanding Artillery Brigade, will assign a battery to each division, to move as the division commander may direct.

5. The train of these headquarters will follow that portion of the ordnance train which moves in rear of the advance brigade of the Third Division.

II. Each division commander in this corps will at once cause to be detailed from his command ten good men who have had experience as teamsters, for driving in pontoon train, to report forthwith to Captain Buzard in charge.

By command of Maj. Gen. F. P. Blair:

C. CADLE, JR.,
Assistant Adjutant-General.

SPECIAL FIELD ORDERS, No. 153. } HEADQUARTERS THIRD DIVISION,
SEVENTEENTH ARMY CORPS,
In the Field, Ga., November 18, 1864.

I. The troops of this command will march at 7 a. m. to-morrow. The Second Brigade, Col. R. K. Scott commanding, will have the advance. Artillery trains and ambulances as heretofore.

By order of Brig. Gen. M. D. Leggett:

J. C. DOUGLASS,
Assistant Adjutant-General.

HEADQUARTERS MILITARY DIVISION OF THE MISSISSIPPI,
In the Field, near Yellow River, Ga., November 18, 1864.

Major-General SLOCUM,
Commanding Left Wing, &c.:

Dispatch received. All is well with this column, which will be to-night on the east side of the Ulcofauhachee, and to-morrow will take the Milledgeville road, leaving you the Eatonton road. Don't be in a hurry, but break up that railroad as far as the Oconee in the most thorough manner, so that every rail will be disabled; better do that work well now when there is no opposition, and you will have to give it personal attention else it will be slighted by your officers. Impress on them its great importance, and that, if done well now, it will not have to be gone over at some future time under less favorable circumstances. I had every man of Davis' command at work yesterday all day and into the night, and yet they slighted some of their work, but I will set them at work again to-day between the Yellow and Alcovy Rivers about Covington. Our own experience shows how easily roads may be relaid if we have iron; therefore, I want each bar of iron actually twisted, either around a tree, or with one of the hooks.

One division will be amply sufficient to go down to the bridges on Oconee. If you reach Eatonton by Monday, it will be early enough. Keep your men fresh, and devour large quantities of the potatoes and corn along the route.

W. T. SHERMAN,
Major-General.

GENERAL ORDERS, No. 21. } HDQRS. FOURTEENTH ARMY CORPS,
Ulcofauhachee River, November 18, 1864.

Until further orders the Artillery Brigade of the corps will be distributed as follows: The Nineteenth Indiana Battery will constitute the reserve artillery of the corps, and, together with the artillery ammunition train, will be under the immediate control of Major Houghtaling, chief of artillery; Battery C of the First Illinois is assigned to the First Division; Battery I, Second Illinois, is assigned to the First [Second] Division; and the Fifth Wisconsin Battery, to the Third Division. These batteries will report directly to the division commanders, will be taken up on the returns and reports of the divisions, and will be rationed by the division commissaries.

By order of Bvt. Maj. Gen. J. C. Davis:

A. C. McCLURG,
Assistant Adjutant-General and Chief of Staff.

CIRCULAR.] HEADQUARTERS FOURTEENTH ARMY CORPS,
Ulcofauhachee River, November 18, 1864.

The corps commander has observed within the last two days a great increase of straggling and marauding, which must be checked, not only for the reputation of the corps, but for the safety of the men. Men must be taught that, even in the midst of an enemy's country, the dictates of humanity must at least be observed, and that no good can result to the cause of their country from indiscriminate destruction of property or burning of the homes of women and children. Division commanders will take immediate steps to prevent these disorders among their own men, and, as the most effective method, should hold the intermediate commanders directly responsible for the enforcement of orders on the subject, not forgetting that the general commanding the Military Division of the Mississippi has forbidden men entering houses on any pretense. Frequent roll-calls should be prescribed and enforced. In gross cases of offense, not only the offender himself (the enlisted man), but his immediate commanding officer, should be punished. Especially stringent measures should be taken to force officers intrusted with foraging parties to keep their men together and control them. The safety of the men demands this. In particular, quartermasters and other officers in charge of trains and detailed men must be taught (what they seemed never to have learned) that they are just as responsible for the whereabouts and conduct of their men as the captain of a company is for his, and not only for the conduct of their own men, but for all men about their trains. Let it be instilled into all that the true soldier is chivalrous as well as brave.

By order of Bvt. Maj. Gen. J. C. Davis:

A. C. McCLURG,
Assistant Adjutant-General and Chief of Staff.

SPECIAL FIELD ORDERS, No. 22. } HDQRS. FOURTEENTH ARMY CORPS, *In the Field, Ga., November 18, 1864.*

Orders for to-morrow, November 19, 1864: General Morgan will move at daylight on the road leading to Shady Dale, and will be followed by, successively, the headquarters trains of the Military Division and the corps, the reserve artillery, the artillery ammunition trains, and the First Michigan Engineers and Mechanics, with their trains. General Baird will march on the same road immediately in the rear of these trains; General Carlin immediately in rear of General Baird; Colonel Buell's command, with the pontoon train, in the rear of General Carlin; Colonel Cogswell's brigade will bring up the rear, and constitute the rear guard.

By order of Bvt. Maj. Gen. J. C. Davis:

A. C. McCLURG,
Assistant Adjutant-General and Chief of Staff.

HEADQUARTERS FOURTEENTH ARMY CORPS,
Ulcofauhachee River, November 18, 1864.

Brig. Gen. A. BAIRD,
Commanding Third Division, Fourteenth Army Corps:

The general commanding directs that you send forward at the earliest dawn to the bridge over the Ulcofauhachee River two companies of infantry, with instructions to repair the flooring for the passage of your trains and remain as guards until the arrival of Colonel Cogswell's column.

I have the honor to be, general, very respectfully, your obedient servant,

A. C. McCLURG,
Assistant Adjutant-General and Chief of Staff.

HEADQUARTERS TWENTIETH CORPS,
Doctor Jones' House, four miles from Madison,
November 18, 1864—5.30 p. m.

Lieut. Col. H. C. RODGERS,
Assistant Adjutant-General:

COLONEL: I have encamped Ward's division at this place, four miles from Madison. I have ordered General Jackson's division to encamp at Brown's house, one mile and a half in the rear.

Very respectfully, your obedient servant,

A. S. WILLIAMS,
Brigadier-General, Commanding.

P. S.—From information received I think the trains of both divisions are well closed up. Unless otherwise ordered I shall march at 5 o'clock in the morning.

HEADQUARTERS LEFT WING, ARMY OF GEORGIA,
Near Madison Grove, November 18, 1864. (Received 7.15 p. m.)

Brig. Gen. A. S. WILLIAMS,
Commanding Twentieth Corps:

The major-general commanding directs that General Geary, with his division and Knap's battery, move at 5 a. m. to-morrow to the Oconee River, destroy the bridges, both railroad and wagon, and rejoin the main column by Sunday evening near Eatonton. General Geary will move without transportation, except wagons for pioneer corps and ambulances. You will send two brigades to report at these headquarters at 6 o'clock to-morrow morning, without transportation (except wagons for pioneers). The remainder of your corps will move to-morrow morning at an early hour, taking charge of all the transportation of the corps, through Madison, and encamp to-morrow night about twelve miles from the latter place on the road to Eatonton. The two brigades ordered to report here will rejoin you to-morrow night.

Very respectfully, your obedient servant,

H. C. RODGERS,
Assistant Adjutant-General.

ORDERS.]

HEADQUARTERS TWENTIETH CORPS,
Jones' House, Ga., November 18, 1864.

The movement of this corps to-morrow will be as follows:

General Geary and his division, with Captain Sloan's battery, will move at 5 a. m. to the Oconee River, to destroy the bridges there, and will rejoin the main column by next Sunday night, near Eatonton. General Geary will report to Major-General Slocum for detailed instructions. His ambulances and pioneer tool wagons only will accompany his troops; all other transportation of his division will march with the main column, the quartermasters, &c., remaining with them.

General Ward, with the Second and Third Brigades of his division, will report for a special duty at 6 a. m. to Major-General Slocum. In order to do so they will leave their present camp at 5 a. m. The main column will move as follows: One brigade of General Jackson's division, as an advance guard, at 6 a. m.; next, the pontoon train; next, the train of the First Division; next, the train of the Second Division, at 7 a. m.; next, the train of the Third Division, at 7.30 a. m.; lastly, the First Brigade of the Third Division, as rear guard. Two brigades of the First Division will be distributed on the flanks of the entire train, as a guard, and to give all necessary assistance. For the day's march the commanding officer of the First Brigade, Third Division, will report to General Jackson.

By command of Brig. Gen. A. S. Williams:

ROBT. P. DECHERT,
Captain and Acting Assistant Adjutant-General.

ORDERS.] HDQRS. FIRST DIVISION, TWENTIETH CORPS,
Brown's Plantation, Ga., November 18, 1864.

This division will move to-morrow at 6 a. m., in the following order: The Third Brigade as an advance guard; the Second Brigade to follow, to be distributed on the flanks of the pontoon train, the train of the First Division, which follows the pontoon train, and part of the Second Division train; the First Brigade next, as a guard to the remainder of the Second Division train and the train of the Third Division; the First Brigade of the Third Division, which reports to General Jackson, will form the rear guard. Captain Hard will report to the commanding officers of the First and Second Brigades such ambulances as will be necessary for the use of the brigades, to be disposed of by those commanding officers as they see fit.

By command of Brig. Gen. N. J. Jackson:

GEO. ROBINSON,
First Lieutenant and Acting Assistant Adjutant-General.

HEADQUARTERS DEPARTMENT OF THE SOUTH,
Hilton Head, S. C., November 18, 1864.

Col. P. P. BROWN, Jr.,
One hundred and fifty-seventh New York Volunteers,
Comdg. District of Hilton Head, &c., Hilton Head, S. C.:

COLONEL: The major-general commanding directs that 200 of the prisoners of war now confined at Fort Pulaski, Ga., be at once removed to Fort Sherman, Hilton Head, and placed under the immediate charge of the One hundred and forty-fourth New York Volunteers. No change in their diet will be allowed. You are further directed to provide common tents for them, to put up in the fort (Sherman).

Very respectfully, your obedient servant,

W. L. M. BURGER,
Assistant Adjutant-General.

SPECIAL ORDERS, No. 259. } HDQRS. DEPT. AND ARMY OF THE TENN.,
Louisville, Ky., November 19, 1864.

* * * * * * *

III. Capt. P. A. Taylor, chief signal officer, having reported to these headquarters in compliance with Special Orders, No. 343, of date October 12, 1864, from the War Department, Adjutant-General's Office, Washington, D. C., and being unable to join the army in the field, will remain at this place until further orders.

* * * * * * *

By order of Maj. Gen. O. O. Howard:

WM. T. CLARK,
Assistant Adjutant-General.

SPECIAL FIELD ORDERS, No. 172.

HEADQUARTERS DEPARTMENT AND ARMY OF THE TENNESSEE,
Hillsborough, Ga., November 19, 1864.

I. The movements of the army to-morrow will be—first, Major-General Osterhaus, starting his column at 6.30 a. m., will move his command on the Macon road to Clinton, so that three divisions shall be at Clinton and the remaining one in the immediate vicinity to-morrow night; second, Major-General Blair, starting his column at 6.30 a. m., will move his command via Tranquilla and Fortville as far toward Gordon as practicable; third, the First Alabama Cavalry will continue with the column of Major-General Blair, moving in the advance; fourth, in passing through Hillsborough, the artillery and trains of both corps will move over the road at the same time, the Fifteenth Corps having the right and the Seventeenth Corps the left of the road, with the infantry on the right and left through fields; fifth, the bridge train, engineer regiment, the train of General Kilpatrick's cavalry, and the cattle, in charge of Lieutenant Todd, acting commissary of subsistence, will follow the Fifteenth Corps, on the Macon road; sixth, the train of these headquarters will move with the leading division of the Fifteenth Corps; seventh, headquarters to-morrow night will be at Clinton.

II. Corps commanders will prohibit their soldiers from entering houses, and enforce the order by severe penalties. More care must be taken in the selection of foragers. Many have been drunk and disorderly. Foraging for the different headquarters must be regulated. Division and brigade commanders will be required to be with their commands during the march.

By command of Maj. Gen. O. O. Howard:

SAML. L. TAGGART,
Assistant Adjutant-General.

HILLSBOROUGH, GA., *November 19, 1864.*

Maj. Gen. P. JOS. OSTERHAUS,
Commanding Fifteenth Army Corps:

General Hazen's division is so far to the rear that I prefer that you move General John E. Smith's division at 6.30 a. m. to-morrow at the head of your column. Please be careful that he moves in double column except his leading brigade.

Very respectfully, your obedient servant,

O. O. HOWARD,
Major-General.

SPECIAL ORDERS, No. 176. } HDQRS. FIFTEENTH ARMY CORPS, *Hillsborough, Ga., November 19, 1864.*

* * * * * * *

III. General Smith will move his command at 5 a. m. to-morrow to Planters' Factory, and commence at once to cross the troops on the flat-boat there, leaving, however, the train and artillery on this side until the pontoon bridge is laid down. This corps will take a defensive position as soon as they arrive on the east side of the Ocmulgee and throw up some light works. General Corse and artillery will remain in his present position until further orders. Generals Woods and Hazen will march to Indian Springs and remain there until further orders, taking strong position fronting south and east.

* * * * * * *

By order of Maj. Gen. P. Joseph Osterhaus:

FREDK. WHITEHEAD,
Assistant Adjutant-General.

GENERAL ORDERS, No. 97. } HDQRS. THIRD DIV., 15TH ARMY CORPS, *Near Hillsborough, Ga., November 19, 1864.*

This command will move at 6.30 a. m. to-morrow, the 20th instant.

Order of march: First, one regiment First Brigade as advance guard, followed by one ambulance and one wagon; second, pioneer corps, tool wagons, one ambulance, and one wagon (baggage); third, three regiments First Brigade, each followed by one ambulance and one wagon; fourth, Battery B, First Michigan Light Artillery; fifth, one regiment First Brigade, followed by one ambulance and one wagon; sixth, ammunition train; seventh, division headquarters train and provost guard; eighth, First Brigade train; ninth, Second Brigade train; tenth, quartermaster's train; eleventh, Fifteenth Army Corps headquarters train; twelfth, supply train; thirteenth, ambulance corps, except ambulances assigned to regiments and detachments; fourteenth, two regiments Second Brigade, well deployed, one upon each flank of all the trains; fifteenth, two regiments Second Brigade, rear guard—one ambulance and one wagon for the flanking and rear guard regiments will be placed between the last two regiments.

By order of Brig. Gen. John E. Smith:

S. M. BUDLONG,
Assistant Adjutant-General.

SPECIAL FIELD ORDERS, No. 9. } HDQRS. FOURTH DIV., 15TH ARMY CORPS, *In the Field, Ocmulgee Mills, Ga., November 19, 1864.*

* * * * * * *

IV. This command will move to-morrow, the 20th instant, as follows: The Third Brigade will have the advance; the Second Brigade will move in the center; the First Brigade will bring up the rear. The brigade in advance and the brigade in the rear will have one regiment, respectively, as advance and rear guard. The provost guard will be furnished from the advance regiment. The pioneer corps will follow the advance regiment. The supply train will cross the river to-night—

first, the pioneer train will commence crossing at 4.30 a. m.; second, the Third Brigade train; third, the Second Brigade train; fourth, the First Brigade train; fifth, the ambulance train. The wagons will keep well closed up and cross as rapidly as possible. The troops will move in the order indicated after the trains have crossed the river. The provost guard required by Special Field Orders, No. 8, paragraph II, to be detailed daily from the rear guard, will be continued until further orders.

By order of Brig. Gen. John M. Corse:

L. CARPER,
Assistant Adjutant-General.

SPECIAL ORDERS, No. 286. } HDQRS. SEVENTEENTH ARMY CORPS, *Near Hillsborough, Ga., November 19, 1864.*

I. The orders for the movement to-morrow are as follows:

1. Maj. Gen. J. A. Mower, commanding First Division, will have the advance, moving out on the Hillsborough road at 6.30 o'clock.

2. Brig. Gen. G. A. Smith, commanding Fourth Division, will move at 6.30 o'clock, on the direct Hillsborough road, and, on reaching the rear of the First Division, will follow it.

3. Brig. Gen. M. D. Leggett, commanding Third Division, will follow the Fourth Division, moving at 7 o'clock.

4. Maj. A. C. Waterhouse, commanding Artillery Brigade, will assign a battery to each division, to move as the division commander may direct.

5. The train of these headquarters will move after the ordnance train that follows the advance brigade of the First Division.

6. The pioneer corps of each division will report to Captain Kossak, chief engineer, at 5.30 a. m. to-morrow at these headquarters.

* * * * * * *

IV. The Twenty-fifth Wisconsin Volunteer Infantry, now on duty as train guard, is relieved from such duty, and will report forthwith to its brigade commander.

By command of Maj. Gen. F. P. Blair:

C. CADLE, JR.,
Assistant Adjutant-General.

SPECIAL FIELD ORDERS, No. 154. } HEADQUARTERS THIRD DIVISION, SEVENTEENTH ARMY CORPS, *Near Hillsborough, Ga., November 19, 1864.*

* * * * * * *

IV. This command will march to-morrow morning at — o'clock. The First Brigade, Brig. Gen. M. F. Force commanding, will have the advance. Ambulances, trains, and artillery as usual. Until further orders, Lieutenant Tiffany, acting assistant quartermaster, will superintend the formation, marching, and parking of the trains.

By order of Brig. Gen. M. D. Leggett:

J. C. DOUGLASS,
Assistant Adjutant-General.

HEADQUARTERS SEVENTEENTH ARMY CORPS,
Near Hillsborough, Ga., November 19, 1864.

Brig. Gen. GILES A. SMITH,
Commanding Fourth Division:

GENERAL: In accordance with instructions from department headquarters, the Third Iowa Infantry will report to the commanding officer Second Iowa Infantry (Fourth Division, Fifteenth Army Corps), as directed by Special Field Orders, No. 159, extract I, the first time we are encamped near the Fifteenth Army Corps.

By command of Maj. Gen. F. P. Blair:

C. CADLE, JR.,
Assistant Adjutant-General.

HEADQUARTERS FOURTEENTH ARMY CORPS,
Mrs. Shy's House, November 19, 1864.

Brig. Gen. J. D. MORGAN,
Commanding Second Division, Fourteenth Army Corps:

The general commanding directs that you move your command at sunrise and push on toward Eatonton Factory; this will lead you toward the right of Eatonton. The objective point is Milledgeville, and it is desired that the road through Eatonton be left for the Twentieth Corps. A staff officer from these headquarters will reach you before you arrive at Eatonton Factory.

Very respectfully, your obedient servant,

A. C. McCLURG,
Assistant Adjutant-General and Chief of Staff.

HEADQUARTERS LEFT WING, ARMY OF GEORGIA,
November 19, 1864.

Brig. Gen. A. S. WILLIAMS,
Commanding Corps:

The major-general commanding desires you to move the corps at 5 a. m. to-morrow, and go as far as Eatonton, if possible.

Very respectfully, your obedient servant,

H. C. RODGERS,
Assistant Adjutant-General.

ORDERS.] HEADQUARTERS TWENTIETH CORPS,
Harris' House, near Madison, Ga., November 19, 1864.

The corps will move to-morrow toward Eatonton, as follows: Third Division at 5 a. m.; Second Division train at 6 a. m.; First Division at 7 a. m. General Ward will march one unencumbered brigade in front. The balance of his command will march alongside the train, and will cover half of the train of the Second Division. General Jackson will march one brigade in rear of the entire train, the balance of his command being distributed along the train so as to cover half of General Geary's trains. The pontoon train will march in rear of the Second Division train, starting at 7 a. m. Major Reynolds, chief of artillery, will assign one battery to march immediately in rear of the advanced brigade, one in the center of the column, and one to immediately precede the rear brigade. The trains of Captain Schoeninger and Captain Bickford will march in rear of the Third Division train. The Ninth Illinois Mounted Infantry will precede the column.

By command of Brig. Gen. A. S. Williams:

ROBT. P. DECHERT,
Captain and Acting Assistant Adjutant-General.

ORDERS.] HDQRS. FIRST DIVISION, TWENTIETH CORPS,
Near Madison, Ga., November 19, 1864.

This division will move to-morrow at 7 a. m., in the following order: The Third Brigade in advance, to guard the rear half of Second Division train, pontoon train, and fifty wagons of First Division train; the Second Brigade to follow, to guard the remainder of First Division train; the First Brigade will form the rear guard of the corps, preceded by a battery. Pursuant to orders from corps headquarters, all regimental quartermasters will report to the brigade quartermasters for assignment to duty with the trains.

By command of Brig. Gen. N. J. Jackson:

GEO. ROBINSON,
First Lieutenant and Acting Assistant Adjutant-General.

HILLSBOROUGH, GA., *November 19, 1864.*

Brig. Gen. J. KILPATRICK,
Commanding Cavalry Division:

Your dispatch of 7 p. m. all right. I will give you no new orders. I send you my order of march, and will expect to hear from you at Clinton. I have heard of some State troops that have been concentrated at Eatonton by Governor Brown.

Very respectfully, your obedient servant,

O. O. HOWARD,
Major-General.

SPECIAL FIELD ORDERS, No. 173. } HEADQUARTERS DEPARTMENT AND ARMY OF THE TENNESSEE,
Clinton, Ga., November 20, 1864.

I. The army will move forward to-morrow as follows: First, the Fifteenth Corps, in two columns—the right column, consisting of two divisions (First and Second), with small trains, on the Clinton and Irwinton road as far as the railroad, starting at 7 a. m.; the other two divisions, with the remaining trains, &c., of the right column, the engineer regiment, bridge train, and train of General Kilpatrick's cavalry, cattle, &c., forming the left column, on the Clinton and Gordon road, to Gordon, starting at 7 a. m. Second, the Seventeenth Corps will continue the march toward Gordon, reaching that point as soon as practicable. The train of these headquarters will move with the Third Division, Fifteenth Army Corps, on the Clinton and Gordon road.

* * * * * * *

By order of Maj. Gen. O. O. Howard:

SAML. L. TAGGART,
Assistant Adjutant-General.

HDQRS. THIRD CAVALRY DIVISION, CAVALRY CORPS,
MILITARY DIVISION OF THE MISSISSIPPI,
On Clinton and Macon Road, November 20, 1864—9 p. m.

Major-General HOWARD:

GENERAL: I met the enemy's cavalry five miles from Clinton, and after considerable skirmishing and charging, in which the enemy lost seven killed, he was driven to Walnut Creek, one mile from East Macon. We finally forced him from the railroad and the creek to the fortified hills about East Macon; these we charged, and, although my men gallantly rode over and into a strong earth-work, we were unable to drive the enemy from and hold the position. I have torn up the track from the creek back toward Gordon for one mile and a half. My command is encamped to-night on and from the railroad over across to the lower Clinton road and at a point four miles from Macon. At an early hour to-morrow morning I will move down to Griswold on the railroad and down to the Milledgeville road, where the Clinton road leaves it, and hold these roads until the trains are well out of the way.

Very respectfully, your obedient servant,

J. KILPATRICK,
Brigadier-General, U. S. Volunteers.

SPECIAL FIELD ORDERS, No. 177.

HDQRS. FIFTEENTH ARMY CORPS,
In the Field, Clinton, Ga.,
November 20, 1864.

I. In publishing paragraph II, Special Field Orders, No. 172, from department headquarters,* the attention of all officers commanding foraging parties is again called to the importance of enforcing the very strictest discipline while on such duties. These parties must absolutely be conducted in obedience and in conformity to existing orders; when found guilty of violating the restrictions laid down in that order must be punished by their commanding officer. The fine imposed should not be less than the deduction of one month's pay. Officers in charge of foraging parties who permit their men to straggle or commit unwarrantable acts must be reported to these headquarters, and their names will be sent forward for summary dismissal from service for incompetence, for failing to enforce discipline, and for disobedience of orders.

II. The corps will continue its advance to-morrow in the following order: The First Division will leave camp at 7 a. m., and after passing through Clinton will advance on the Irwinton road to the railroad crossing. The Second Division, Brigadier-General Hazen commanding, will follow the First. Each division will be accompanied by one light battery, to be detailed by the chief of artillery. Five wagons only infantry ammunition, a part of the ambulance train, and the respective headquarters and regimental wagons, will accompany these divisions. The Third Division, together with the remaining batteries of artillery, will also leave at 7 a. m., marching on the direct road to Gordon. All the reserve ammunition wagons, supply and ambulance trains of both divisions will also march with the Third Division and in front of its rear guard. The reserve trains of the First and Second Divisions will each be guarded by one regiment, to be detailed from the respective divisions. The Fourth Division, Brigadier-General Corse commanding, will follow on the road assigned to the Third Division, but is not

* See November 19, p. 493.

expected to get beyond Clinton with the large trains moving with it; but in order to secure proper communication with the corps, General Corse will push one brigade to the point on the Gordon road where it crosses the Milledgeville and Macon road.

Notwithstanding the fact that General Kilpatrick's cavalry will remain before Macon to-morrow, it is necessary that the utmost vigilance be shown by the several commands, to insure them against any attack of the large rebel force in the vicinity. In camping the troops good defensive positions will be chosen fronting toward the south generally. The rear is to be well guarded, and all the trains must be inside the lines and properly corralled. The Twenty-ninth Missouri Mounted Infantry marches with the right column.

III. When the corps is not together in one camp or column, and the artillery apportioned to the several divisions, the officers commanding the artillery must consider themselves under the orders of the general commanding the division to which he is ordered to report. The general commanding division will in such cases assign the artillery their position in the column, and in camp give it the necessary escorts and supports.

By order of Maj. Gen. P. Joseph Osterhaus:

FREDK. WHITEHEAD,
Assistant Adjutant-General.

GENERAL ORDERS, No. 98. } HDQRS. THIRD DIV., 15TH ARMY CORPS, *In the Field, near Clinton, Ga., November 20, 1864.*

This division will continue its march at 7 a. m. to-morrow, the 21st instant:

Order of march: First, one regiment Second Brigade as advance guard, followed by one ambulance and one wagon; second, pioneer corps, tool wagons, one ambulance, and one wagon (baggage); third, remainder of Second Brigade, each regiment followed by one ambulance and one wagon; fourth, artillery; fifth, one regiment First Brigade, followed by one ambulance and one wagon; sixth, ammunition train; seventh, division headquarters train and provost guard; eighth, Second Brigade train; ninth, First Brigade train; tenth, quartermaster's train; eleventh, commissary of subsistence train; twelfth, ambulance corps, except ambulances assigned to regiments and detachments; thirteenth, two regiments First Brigade, well deployed, one upon each flank of all the division trains; fourteenth, reserve ammunition wagons, supply and ambulance trains of the First and Second Divisions, those of each division to be guarded by one regiment from its respective division; fifteenth, two regiments First Brigade, rear guard—one ambulance and one wagon for each of the flanking and rear guard regiments will be placed between the last two regiments.

By order of Brig. Gen. John E. Smith:

S. M. BUDLONG,
Assistant Adjutant-General.

SPECIAL FIELD ORDERS, No. 10. } HEADQUARTERS FOURTH DIVISION, FIFTEENTH ARMY CORPS, *In the Field, Monticello, Ga., November 20, 1864.*

* * * * * * *

II. This command will move to-morrow, the 21st instant, at 5 a. m., and take the Hillsborough road—the Second Brigade will have the advance; the First Brigade will march in the center; the Third Brigade will bring up the rear. The pioneer corps will follow the advance regiment, and repair the roads and bridges. Trains will move in the following order: pioneer corps train; then the brigade trains in their respective order of march; followed by the ordnance train, supply train, and ambulance corps train.

By order of Brig. Gen. John M. Corse:

L. CARPER,
Assistant Adjutant-General.

HDQRS. DEPARTMENT AND ARMY OF THE TENNESSEE,
Clinton, Ga., November 20, 1864—7.30 p. m.

[Maj. Gen. F. P. BLAIR,
Commanding Seventeenth Army Corps:]

DEAR GENERAL: I am sorry you found so bad a road; I think you will have a better to-morrow. Our road, too, is spoilt by the rain. If you can get within three miles of Gordon to-morrow night, it will answer. Kilpatrick has had some firing this p. m., but with what result I have not heard. I will go with the column that moves directly on Gordon, and will encamp to-morrow night somewhere in that vicinity.

Respectfully,

O. O. HOWARD,
Major-General.

SPECIAL ORDERS, No. 287.

HDQRS. SEVENTEENTH ARMY CORPS,
In the Field, Ga., November 20, 1864.

I. The following additional rules are published for the regulation of foraging parties:

1. The forage parties of any division of the corps may forage along the whole length of the corps, not going farther to the front than the head of the infantry column.

2. Commanding officers of forage parties must keep their men together, except when they are left along the road to bring forward or guard forage, in which cases they will not be molested.

3. Foragers from the different headquarters not under a commissioned officer must be provided with passes, approved by a division or superior commander.

II. The orders for the movements to-morrow are as follows:

1. Brig. Gen. G. A. Smith, commanding Fourth Division, will take the advance, and will move his command on the Fortville road, at 6.30 a. m.

2. Brig. Gen. M. D. Leggett, commanding Third Division, will start from Blountsville at 6.30 o'clock and move forward to the rear of the Fourth Division, which he will follow.

3. Maj. Gen. J. A. Mower, commanding First Division, will follow the Third Division, moving at 8.30 o'clock.

4. Maj. A. C. Waterhouse, commanding Artillery Brigade, will assign a battery to each division, to move as the division commander may direct.

5. The train of these headquarters will move as heretofore.

III. Hereafter, until further orders, three days' issue of rations will be made to last five days.

IV. The order of march for to-morrow is changed, the Fourth and Third Divisions starting at 7 a. m. and the First Division at 9 a. m.

By command of Maj. Gen. F. P. Blair:

C. CADLE, JR.,
Assistant Adjutant-General.

HEADQUARTERS MILITARY DIVISION OF THE MISSISSIPPI,
In the Field, Eatonton Factory, November 20, 1864.

Major-General SLOCUM,
Commanding Left Wing:

GENERAL: I am directed by the general-in-chief to give you the general news, &c. Last night this portion of the command camped just north of Shady Dale, and to-night the Fourteenth Corps has one division near Little River, with a picket at the bridge, and the other divisions are camped in good support. Thus far forage has been good and men and animals thrive. To-morrow morning General Davis will cross Murder Creek, take the Monticello road, and aim to reach Milledgeville Tuesday; he will also send you the brigade of the Twentieth Corps left in Atlanta as a rear guard, and one regiment to communicate and bring back a report from you to the general-in-chief, who will remain near here until he hears from you in Eatonton. No enemy has been found on our march, save a picket of some twenty-five men at the Eatonton Factory bridge. The bridge, however, was saved and the factory burned. You will move so as to reach Milledgeville in conjunction with General Davis, and on the route will destroy any railroad bridge or trestle on the Eatonton branch, but need not delay your march to destroy track. Fill up well with forage, sweet potatoes, and chickens, and such rations, preparatory to a couple or more days' stay in Milledgeville.

Since writing the above the general has such authentic information as to feel sure portions of your command have been or are in Eatonton, and therefore will not send the regiment to you, but dispatch a staff officer, expecting to hear in return, and will remain hereabout until about noon for that purpose. In moving to Milledgeville, keep your force on the east of the railroad, and General Davis will keep his west.

I am, general, respectfully, yours, &c.,

L. M. DAYTON,
Aide-de-Camp.

HEADQUARTERS MILITARY DIVISION OF THE MISSISSIPPI,
In the Field, Eatonton Factory, Ga., November 20, 1864.

Bvt. Maj. Gen. J. C. DAVIS,
Commanding Fourteenth Army Corps:

GENERAL: The general-in-chief directs that you put your command in motion to-morrow morning by any road crossing Murder Creek and leading into the Monticello or Hillsborough and Milledgeville road, on which you will move to within about twelve miles of Milledgeville and camp to-morrow night. The brigade belonging to the Twentieth Corps he wishes you to send to report to General Slocum at Eatonton. You will also direct one regiment to feel for General Slocum at Eatonton to-morrow morning and bring back a report to himself. He hears that General Slocum's cavalry were in Eatonton to-day. The general-in-chief will remain here until he hears from General Slocum, who is to be in Eatonton to-morrow. He wishes you also to give the necessary directions that your command on the march to-morrow may be well closed and in hand, to guard against any enemy that may be in the vicinity.

I am, general, respectfully, yours, &c.,

L. M. DAYTON,
Aide-de-Camp.

GENERAL ORDERS, No. 22. } HDQRS. FOURTEENTH ARMY CORPS,
Eatonton Factory, Ga., November 20, 1864.

I. The discharge of fire-arms by foragers and others has become an evil which must be stopped. Many men have already been wounded and a waste of ammunition incurred which we cannot now afford. Hereafter no firing will be permitted under any circumstances. Animals and fowls must be caught, not shot.

II. Useless negroes are being accumulated to an extent which would be suicide to a column which must be constantly stripped for battle and prepared for the utmost celerity of movement. We cannot expect that the present unobstructed march will continue much longer. Our wagons are too much overladen to allow of their being filled with negro women and children or their baggage, and every additional mouth consumes food, which it requires risk to obtain. No negroes, therefore, or their baggage, will be allowed in wagons and none but the servants of mounted officers on horses or mules.

III. One pack-animal may be allowed to each company and so many to brigade and division headquarters as division commanders may think proper. All animals taken from the country are the property of the Government, and must be turned over to the quartermasters. All surplus draft animals must be used to strengthen the wagon trains. Indiscriminate mounting of unauthorized men cannot be allowed. Every commanding officer is responsible that no unauthorized man under him is mounted.

IV. Attention is again called to the circular from these headquarters dated November 14. Division commanders will see that it, or orders based upon it, are at once read to every company and detachment and to all teamsters and detailed men. Orders are useless unless promulgated and enforced.

By order of Bvt. Maj. Gen. J. C. Davis:

A. C. McCLURG,
Lieutenant-Colonel and Chief of Staff.

HEADQUARTERS FOURTEENTH ARMY CORPS,
Near Eatonton Factory, November 20, 1864.

Brig. Gen. J. D. MORGAN,
Commanding Second Division, Fourteenth Army Corps:

The general commanding the corps directs that you put your command in motion, on the road leading to Stanfordville, at daylight to-morrow. A staff officer from these headquarters will join you soon after with further instructions.

I have the honor to be, general, very respectfully, your obedient servant,

A. C. McCLURG,
Assistant Adjutant-General and Chief of Staff.

HEADQUARTERS TWENTIETH CORPS. ARMY OF GEORGIA,
November 20, 1864.

Lieut. Col. H. C. RODGERS,
Assistant Adjutant-General:

COLONEL: My corps is encamped to-night—the Third Division and the trains of the Second Division, with the pontoon train, at the point directed by the major-general commanding Left Wing; the First Division at this point, two miles back. In the march of to-morrow the Third Division will lead, starting at 5 a. m. as ordered.

Very respectfully, your obedient servant,

A. S. WILLIAMS,
Brigadier-General, Commanding.

HEADQUARTERS LEFT WING, ARMY OF GEORGIA,
November 20, 1864.

Brig. Gen. A. S. WILLIAMS,
Commanding Twentieth Corps:

The major-general commanding desires you to move the corps at 5 a. m. to-morrow toward Milledgeville, via Eatonton. Let the command march through the latter place with ranks well closed and bands playing. If the First Division is well closed up to-night, there will be no objection to its having the advance to-morrow; but if it is far behind to-night it will be well to keep the Third Division in advance, as it is essential to make as much progress on the march as possible. Please send word which division is to have the advance. The general desires you to issue an order forbidding the destruction of property except by your order or his own, and also to take some effective measures to stop this firing on our flanks and around the camps. The captured animals should all be turned over to the corps quartermaster, and distributed through the trains. It would perhaps be well to send out parties from each brigade to-night to collect in animals.

Very respectfully, your obedient servant,

H. C. RODGERS,
Assistant Adjutant-General.

ORDERS.] HEADQUARTERS TWENTIETH CORPS,
Near Eatonton, Ga., November 20, 1864.

The most stringent measures will be adopted to stop the waste of ammunition occasioned by the indiscriminate firing by foraging parties.

Such animals as are necessary for the subsistence of the troops must be killed by other means than shooting.

Although this order has been given before, there is good reason to think that it has not been published to the troops, particularly in the Third Division. This must be done at once, and all offenders summarily punished.

Hereafter no buildings will be burned or destroyed, except upon the order of the corps commander, which will be given only to the commander of the rear division.

Division commanders will be held responsible that this order is strictly complied with in their commands.

By command of Brig. Gen. A. S. Williams:

ROBT. P. DECHERT,
Captain and Acting Assistant Adjutant-General.

ORDERS. HEADQUARTERS TWENTIETH CORPS,
Near Eatonton, Ga., November 20, 1864.

This corps will march to-morrow toward Milledgeville, through Eatonton, as follows: Colonel Hughes' mounted infantry at 4.30 a. m.; Third Division at 5 a. m.; Second Division train at 6 a. m.; First Division at 7 a. m.

General Ward will march one unencumbered brigade in advance. The balance of his command will be distributed along his train and that of the Second Division, covering half of the latter.

General Jackson will march one brigade in rear of the entire train, the balance of his command being distributed along his train and the latter half of the train of the Second Division.

The pontoon train will march in rear of the Second Division train, starting at 6.30 a. m. The trains of Captain Schoeninger and Captain Bickford will march in rear of the Third Division train, starting at 5.30 a. m. The artillery will be distributed in the column the same as in the order for the march of to-day.

By command of Brig. Gen. A. S. Williams:

ROBT. P. DECHERT,
Captain and Acting Assistant Adjutant-General.

ORDERS.] HDQRS. FIRST DIVISION, TWENTIETH CORPS,
Near Eatonton, Ga., November 20, 1864.

This division will march to-morrow at 7 a. m., in the following order: The Second Brigade in advance, to be distributed along the rear half of Second Division train, the pontoon train, and twenty-five wagons of First Division train; the First Brigade to follow, to be distributed along the remainder of First Division train. The commanding officers of these brigades will require their commands to give all necessary assistance to the wagons. The Third Brigade will form the rear guard, preceded by a battery. The report of effective force will be required to-morrow.

By command of Brig. Gen. N. J. Jackson:

GEO. ROBINSON,
First Lieutenant and Acting Assistant Adjutant-General.

HEADQUARTERS TWENTIETH CORPS,
November 20, 1864—1.30 p. m.

Lieutenant-Colonel HUGHES,
Commanding Ninth Illinois Mounted Infantry:

COLONEL: Brigadier-General Williams, commanding, directs that you remain with your command in Eatonton till about 3.30 o'clock, then return, joining the column, camping near the head of it.

Very respectfully, your obedient servant,

H. W. PERKINS,
Lieutenant-Colonel and Assistant Adjutant-General.

HEADQUARTERS SEVENTEENTH ARMY CORPS,
In the Field, Ga., November 20, 1864.

Col. GEORGE E. SPENCER,
Commanding First Alabama Cavalry:

COLONEL: The major-general commanding directs me to say to you that the outrages committed by your command during the march are becoming so common, and are of such an aggravated nature, that they call for some severe and instant mode of correction. Unless the pillaging of houses and wanton destruction of property by your regiment ceases at once, he will place every officer in it under arrest, and recommend them to the department commander for dishonorable dismissal from the service.

Very respectfully, your obedient servant,

C. CADLE, JR.,
Assistant Adjutant-General.

HDQRS. NORTHERN DISTRICT, DEPT. OF THE SOUTH,
Morris Island, November 20, 1864.

Maj. Gen. J. G. FOSTER,
Commanding Department of the South:

GENERAL: Escaped prisoners, four of whom came in yesterday, agree in saying that it is believed in Charleston that Sherman is marching east. I think myself that he will move first on Charleston; that in his possession, Savannah would not be defended. The rebels are reported strengthening the works in rear of Charleston, but I do not believe they can do much in the little time and with the small force they have. Your instructions will be complied with, and such arrangements made as will enable this district to send at a moment's notice the regiments you mention. Sherman will, however, himself cut the railroad with his cavalry. If any movement is made for that purpose I would recommend that it be made up Broad River. That would enable you to use the whole of the force at Hilton Head and Beaufort, which, with the force to be drawn from other points, would enable you to fortify on the line of the road and keep up a line of communication with your base at Hilton Head. I do not know anything about the nature of the country there, but suppose it as good for operations as any in this section of the country. It has a very decided advantage over the John's Island route, in being so far from Charleston that they will not be willing to detach a force from the garrison of the city to attack it. Guns were heard yesterday up Ashley River, supposed to be artillery practice with heavy guns. An intercepted dispatch to-day asks for 230 suits of clothes for the three companies First South Carolina stationed at Beach Inlet.

Very respectfully, your obedient servant,

JNO. P. HATCH,
Brigadier-General, Commanding.

P. S.—The point at which I recommend striking the road would also be a convenient point for Sherman to communicate with you, no matter for which point he was striking.

HDQRS. NORTHERN DISTRICT, DEPT. OF THE SOUTH,
Morris Island, November 20, 1864.

Capt. W. L. M. BURGER,
Assistant Adjutant-General:

CAPTAIN: Nothing of material importance has occurred since my arrival here. Escaped prisoners report that the enemy are engaged in fortifying the rear of the city, and that it is reported that Sherman is marching east with five corps. The naval battery is not yet completed, but soon will be. I do not, however, think that its fire will be of any effect. The battering of Sumter is, in my opinion, an idle waste of material, and the guns would be useless in an attack on Charleston. The stockade at the pen will be used to strengthen the works on the front. Guns (probably practice) are heard in the rear of Charleston.

Very respectfully, your obedient servant,

JNO. P. HATCH,
Brigadier-General, Commanding.

HEADQUARTERS DEPARTMENT OF THE SOUTH,
Hilton Head, S. C., November 20, 1864.

Maj. Gen. H. W. HALLECK, U. S. Army,
Chief of Staff, Armies of the United States, Washington, D. C.:

GENERAL: I have the honor to state that, in consequence of the great want of horses for the use of the quartermasters of this department, I have been obliged, as a military necessity, to dismount the Seventy-fifth Ohio Mounted Infantry, doing duty in Florida. We have now only one battalion of the Fourth Massachusetts Cavalry. This has been so reduced by captures and losses in battle as to number only 100 men for duty, which is entirely inadequate for the service to be performed. I would therefore respectfully, but urgently, request that a cavalry regiment may be sent to this department for duty. I would not ask for this, since I have been directed to remain strictly on the defensive, were it not absolutely necessary for defensive operations, particularly in Florida, where it is imperatively necessary to keep a large mounted force constantly on duty as pickets and scouts. In case a cavalry regiment cannot be sent here, I request that the two battalions of the Fourth Massachusetts Cavalry, taken with the Tenth Army Corps, may be returned to this department.

Very respectfully, your obedient servant,

J. G. FOSTER,
Major-General, Commanding.

CITY POINT, *November 21, 1864—4 p. m.*

Lieutenant-General GRANT:

File of Richmond papers of to-day just received.

From the Dispatch:

From Sherman's army we have the intelligence that it is moving in two columns, one upon Augusta and the other upon Macon. It is not likely that he is about to separate his columns for any length of time, and his march will probably be as follows: The column marching on the Georgia State road for Augusta will go as far as Madison, sixty miles, and there turning to the right march on Milledgeville, the capital of Georgia. The column marching on Macon will probably go to Crawford's, within fifteen miles of the town, and then turn off to Milledgeville and form a junction with the other body. By the movement Macon falls, and the enemy are at liberty to move on Augusta by following the Georgia Central Railroad to Brownsville, and then marching north; or on Savannah, by following the railroad to its terminus there. We shall soon hear of their cavalry around Macon, and very near possibly to Augusta. Sherman is moving rapidly, and is not much troubled with transportation. He has burned several stations at the depots he passed, and is destroying the country generally in foraging.

From the Examiner:

Our information from Georgia in regard to Sherman is meager. All that we know certainly is that he left Atlanta about one week ago with a force generally estimated at 30,000 men of all arms, and that he was moving in the direction of Macon. Some official accounts state that he had advanced as far as Griffin, a town of some 2,000 inhabitants, situated on the Macon and Western Railroad, forty-three miles south of Atlanta and fifty-eight miles northwest of Macon. It is believed that he was in the vicinity of Griffin as late as Thursday last. He moves slowly, and ere he reaches Macon he will find that the execution of a plan is quite a different thing from its projection.

LATER.—We hear that Sherman has divided his army. He has sent nearly all his mounted force in the direction of Augusta; with his main body of troops, he himself marches on to Macon.

From the Whig:

MACON, *November 18.*

The excitement in the city has somewhat subsided. No definite information of the whereabouts of the enemy has yet been received. They are supposed to be still in the neighborhood of Griffin, burning everything in their rear. They will get a warm reception if they attempt to come here.

MACON, *November 19.*

The military authorities are active and vigilant, and every man is under arms. Confidence is being restored. The enemy is believed to be on our right, distant about thirty miles. The city will be defended to the last.

From the Sentinel:

We have nothing additional from Georgia that it would be prudent to publish while certain military operations are taking place which it is believed will bring Mr. Sherman up with a short turn. The enemy is without information as to his movements, and we have no intention of enlightening him on the subject.

The Enquirer says the Senate has passed a bill suspending for sixty days the section of the law which requires the State reserve force not to go beyond their respective States, and hopes that the House may concur. It urges the people to burn everything in the way of supplies on the route of Sherman's advance; and lest they should fail to do so, urges it as the duty of the military authorities to take the matter of destroying provisions in their hands.

JNO. A. RAWLINS,
Brigadier-General and Chief of Staff.

(Same to Secretary of War.)

CITY POINT, VA., *November 21, 1864.*

Lieutenant-General GRANT,
General-in-Chief:

Perhaps it would be well not to take official notice of this summary of news from the Richmond papers, lest the rebel authorities prohibit the publication of news from Sherman altogether.

JNO. A. RAWLINS,
Chief of Staff.

HEADQUARTERS CAVALRY COMMAND,
Griswold, Ga., November 21, 1864.

Capt. L. M. DAYTON,
A. D. C. and A. A. A. G., Mil. Div. of the Mississippi:

CAPTAIN: This is the first time I have deemed it necessary to send you a communication since I left Atlanta. I first struck Wheeler's cavalry at Lovejoy's Station. After a few minutes' fighting, and with slight loss, he was routed and driven beyond Bear Creek Station, with a loss of many killed and wounded. We recaptured two 3-inch rifled guns taken from General Stoneman. Wheeler was supported by Georgia militia, under General Cobb. I crossed the Ocmulgee on the morning of the 19th, drove Wheeler's cavalry from the neighborhood of Clinton, forced him back within the enemy's works about East Macon. My people made a gallant charge, mounted and dismounted, crossed Walnut Creek, and actually rode over and into the enemy's works, but was finally forced to retire to the south side of Walnut Creek. My loss thus far has not been heavy. I am now firmly settled on the railroad, and thoroughly destroying the track as I retire. We have captured a train of cars loaded with locomotive driving wheels and springs for locomotives. We have destroyed at this point a pistol factory and a soap and candle factory, both large and valuable. I send you a Macon paper of the 21st, printed on the 20th, giving you all the news at that point. Beauregard and Hardee, you will see, are both at that point. Beauregard made a speech to the troops there yesterday. I will move to Gordon in the morning. My command is in good condition and spirits, and on reaching you hope to have something to do. General Howard is moving on Gordon to-day; I cover his rear.

I am, captain, very respectfully, your obedient servant,

J. KILPATRICK,
Brigadier-General, U. S. Volunteers.

P. S.—The enemy have made several feints this morning on different portions of my command. He is now moving, I am satisfied, to force me from the road; but I shall destroy every foot of the track until I reach General Howard's infantry. Do not be uneasy; I will be careful of my command.

J. K.

CLINTON, GA., *November 21, 1864.*

Brig. Gen. J. KILPATRICK,
Commanding Third Cavalry Division:

Your dispatch received. I approve of your move. Am sorry you could not have held on, but am much obliged for what you have done. Please hold your position strongly. Make them think you are going for them again, by demonstrations well to the front. Please send me your news of the strength of the enemy, and tear up as much track as you can.

Very respectfully, your obedient servant,

O. O. HOWARD,
Major-General.

PITTS' MILL, *Near Gordon, Ga., November 21, 1864.*

Brig. Gen. J. KILPATRICK,
Commanding Third Cavalry Division:

I hear you have difficulty in getting forage where you now are locating. I think you can send foraging parties out without any risk. I heard that a portion of the cavalry had appropriated silver plate, &c. I want you to take unusual pains to prevent pillage. It is so tempting in a hostile country for soldiers to load themselves with plunder that it is done almost before we think of it. I mean to take every opportunity to strip the infantry of useless trash. We occupy Gordon. General Sherman is probably near Milledgeville to-night. You had better try and communicate with him frequently.

Very respectfully, your obedient servant,

O. O. HOWARD,
Major-General.

HEADQUARTERS THIRD CAVALRY DIVISION,
Griswold, Ga., November 21, 1864—12 m.

Major-General HOWARD:

GENERAL: The enemy has made attacks on my people in position on Milledgeville road, but has each time been repulsed. He is now moving down the railroad. I am firmly settled and fastened upon it. Have effectually destroyed already over four miles of track, captured and burned a train of cars. I expect to be attacked all along my line in a few minutes; the enemy is now moving on the roads in my front, I think, for that purpose. Do not be alarmed; we can repulse any attack that may be made.

J. KILPATRICK,
Brigadier-General, Commanding.

Hardee and Beauregard are both in Macon. Beauregard made a speech to the soldiers yesterday.

PITTS' MILL, *near Gordon, Ga., November 21, 1864.*

Maj. Gen. W. T. SHERMAN,
Commanding Military Division of the Mississippi:

We have reached Gordon with the head of the column. Giles Smith's division is in camp there to-night; Woods' division is also on the railroad, about five miles nearer Macon, and Hazen's division within supporting distance; Mower's and Leggett's divisions are near the Macon and Milledgeville wagon roads; Corse, with the bridge train and the trains belonging to Kilpatrick, is yet between Clinton and Hillsborough. To-morrow I will have everything substantially at Gordon. Our marches at first, until we reached the Ocmulgee, were very pleasant, having good roads and good weather. Since then our roads have been very heavy, and the rain continuous. We have found the country full of provisions, and thus far have drawn very little upon our rations. We have destroyed a large amount of cotton, the Planters' Factory, a pistol factory and a mill at Griswold, the latter three by General Kilpatrick. I will inclose you General Kilpatrick's dispatches, so as to show you what he has been doing; also, dispatches captured at Gordon. His headquarters are to-night at Griswold, and he is covering the approaches from Macon. The mayor of Milledgeville surrendered the town formally to Captain Duncan and a few scouts. Afterward, a company of the First Alabama Cavalry entered the town with Captain Duncan and destroyed the depot and some 75 or 100 boxes of ammunition and telegraph office. We have found quite a number of mules and horses, and been able to replace our poor ones and those that were broken down; our herds, too, have increased rather than diminished.

My information yet as to the strength of the force at Macon is indefinite; there is, however, considerable cavalry on this side of the river (Ocmulgee), supported by infantry and some artillery. The arrival of some troops from Savannah, and the drawing back of some 2,000 or 3,000 militia from Griffin, has been reported. Beauregard, Hardee, and Johnston were reported in Macon. Beauregard assured the people in a speech yesterday that he had us now just where he wanted us. From all quarters he seems to have already collected from 10,000 to 15,000 men. Rebel rumors place you at Eatonton. I shall expect further orders from you at Gordon to-morrow.

Very respectfully, your obedient servant,

O. O. HOWARD,
Major-General.

SPECIAL ORDERS, No. 260. } HDQRS. DEPT. AND ARMY OF THE TENN., *Louisville, Ky., November 21, 1864.*

* * * * * * *

III. Lieut. Col. James Wilson, provost-marshal-general of this army, having reported from leave of absence to these headquarters November 13, 1864, and being unable to join the army in the field, will remain at these headquarters until further orders.

* * * * * * *

By order of Maj. Gen. O. O. Howard:

WM. T. CLARK,
Assistant Adjutant-General.

SPECIAL FIELD ORDERS, No. 174. } HEADQUARTERS DEPARTMENT AND ARMY OF THE TENNESSEE, *Pitts' Mill, Near Gordon, Ga., November 21, 1864.*

The following will be the movement of this army to-morrow: First, Major-General Blair, commanding Seventeenth Army Corps, will concentrate his command at Gordon, moving to that point at 7 a. m. Second, Major-General Osterhaus, commanding Fifteenth Army Corps, will, with the exception of his First Division, move his command to the vicinity of Gordon. He will direct Brigadier-General Woods, commanding First Division, to take up a strong position on the railroad and send one brigade to demonstrate toward Macon. Third, Brig. Gen. J. Kilpatrick, commanding Third Cavalry Division, will take position on the right of General Woods and send out a force on all the roads toward Macon. Fourth, Brig. Gen. John E. Smith, commanding Third Division, Fifteenth Corps, will cut and make a road parallel and near to that taken by the Seventeenth Corps. Fifth, the trains will be brought up as rapidly as possible, the right of way to be given, whenever practicable, to the bridge train, and parked to the east of Gordon. Sixth, the trains of these headquarters will move with the leading division of the Seventeenth Corps. Seventh, when possible, the troops will destroy the railroad in their immediate vicinity.

By command of Maj. Gen. O. O. Howard:

SAML. L. TAGGART,
Assistant Adjutant-General.

HEADQUARTERS FIFTEENTH ARMY CORPS,
Cross-Roads, November 21, 1864—4.30 p. m.

[Maj. Gen. O. O. HOWARD:]

GENERAL: Woods' division passed this point at 3 p. m., and will go in camp at the railroad crossing where I left my mounted infantry this a. m. Hazen's division will be at these cross-roads in about one hour, and I will let them camp there, in order to have them fresh to-morrow. The distance between the two camps is three miles and a half. The fact that General Kilpatrick sent me word that he would fall back before night is another reason to let the Second Division remain here, as the cavalry not only will now hold its present position, and General Smith and train is thus amply covered. Distance to Gordon from Woods, six miles and a half; from Hazen, ten miles. General Hazen will leave here to-morrow at 6.30 a. m.

Very respectfully,

OSTERHAUS.

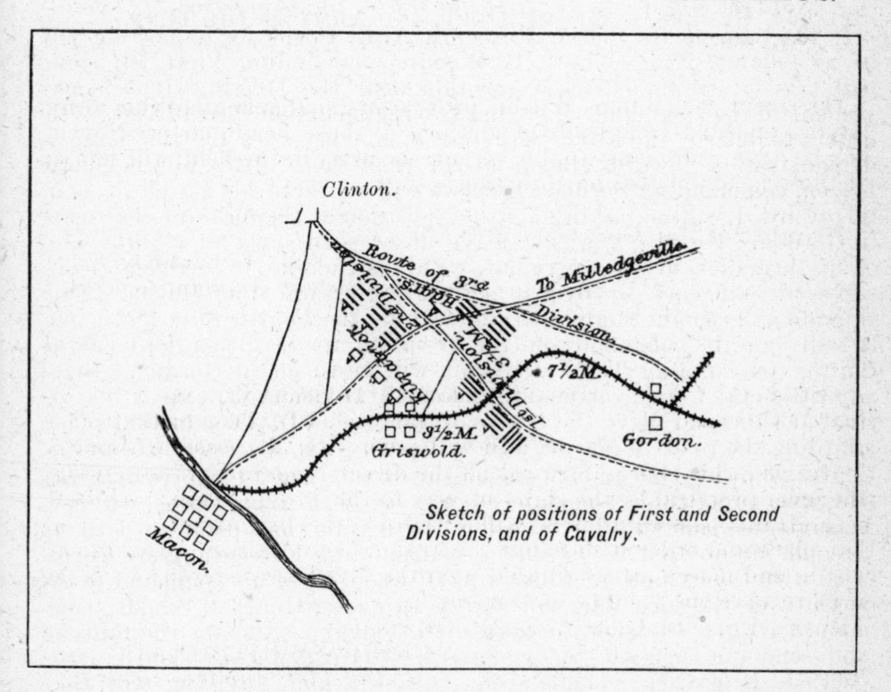

Sketch of positions of First and Second Divisions, and of Cavalry.

HEADQUARTERS FIFTEENTH ARMY CORPS,
Macon Cross-Roads, Ga., November 21, 1864—6.45 p. m.

Maj. Gen. O. O. HOWARD,
Commanding Army:

GENERAL: The First and Second Divisions are in camp as indicated in the sketch sent you this p. m., with the exception of one brigade of Second Division, which General Hazen took back to Clinton, that place having been threatened by rebel cavalry. I have not at this hour any information in regard to the condition of things there, but hope that everything is safe. Would it not be well to keep the place occupied until General Corse arrives and can bring by his very large trains? Some cavalry would be very desirable. The train of First Division was attacked by a rebel party when passing the fork of the road to Griswold, which I considered well guarded from the protestations of General Kilpatrick's adjutant-general to that effect. My train guard repulsed the rebels, of course, and so far all is right. I am with General Hazen's division; the troops are encamped in supporting distance of General Kilpatrick's line in a strong position.

Awaiting your kind orders for to-morrow's movement, I am, general, with great respect, your obedient servant,

P. JOS. OSTERHAUS,
Major-General of Volunteers.

P. S.—Information just received report Clinton all quiet. General Hazen put the regiments with him in camp four miles from town.

SPECIAL ORDERS, No. 178. } HDQRS. FIFTEENTH ARMY CORPS, *In the Field, Ga., November 21, 1864.*

I. The movements of the Fifteenth Army Corps for to-morrow will be as follows: Brig. Gen. C. R. Woods, commanding First Division, will take a strong defensive position near the Meeting-House, convenient to the command. Leaving two regiments on the railroad, with orders to destroy the same, with one of his brigades he will make a demonstration toward Macon at an early hour. Brigadier-General Hazen, commanding Second Division, will continue his march at 6 a. m. toward Irwinton, taking a strong position at the forks of the roads to Gordon. He will, however, leave at or send back to Clinton one of his brigades, or its equivalent, with instructions to intrench themselves at that place, to cover it against any assault from Macon. This brigade will remain there until relieved by the Fourth Division, when it will join its command on the Irwinton road. Brigadier-General Smith, commanding Third Division, will move on to Gordon. Brigadier-General Corse, commanding Fourth Division, will, upon his arrival at Clinton, relieve the troops of the Second Division at that place guarding the road to Macon, and will push with all possible rapidity the trains in his charge forward on the direct road to Gordon, giving, whenever practicable, the right of way to the bridge train. As soon as the trains pass Clinton he will withdraw the brigade on guard at that place and order it to follow the train. The Artillery Brigade will remain and march as distributed with the divisions yesterday until the corps reaches the vicinity of Gordon.

By order of Maj. Gen. P. Joseph Osterhaus:

FREDK. WHITEHEAD,
Assistant Adjutant-General.

GENERAL ORDERS, No. 99. } HEADQUARTERS THIRD DIVISION, FIFTEENTH ARMY CORPS, *In the Field, at ——— Mills, November 21, 1864.*

This command will move at 7 a. m. to-morrow, the 22d instant, in the following order: first, one regiment First Brigade as advance guard, followed by one ambulance and one wagon; second, pioneer corps, tool wagons, one ambulance, and one wagon (baggage); third, three regiments First Brigade, each regiment followed by one ambulance and one wagon; fourth, artillery; fifth, one regiment First Brigade, followed by one ambulance and one wagon; sixth, ammunition train; seventh, division headquarters train and provost guard; eighth, First Brigade train; ninth, Second Brigade train; tenth, quartermaster's train; eleventh, commissary of subsistence train; twelfth, ambulance corps, except ambulances assigned to regiments and detachments; thirteenth, two regiments Second Brigade, well deployed, one upon each flank of all of the division trains; fourteenth, reserve ammunition wagons, supply and ambulance trains of the First and Second Divisions; fifteenth, two regiments Second Brigade, rear guard—one ambulance and one wagon for each of the flanking and rear-guard regiments will be placed between the last two regiments.

By order of Brig. Gen. John E. Smith:

S. M. BUDLONG,
Assistant Adjutant-General.

SPECIAL FIELD ORDERS, No. 11.

HEADQUARTERS FOURTH DIVISION, FIFTEENTH ARMY CORPS,
In the Field, Hillsborough, Ga., November 21, 1864.

I. This command will move to-morrow, the 22d instant, as follows: The pontoon train will move at 6 a. m.; the First Brigade has the advance, and will move at 6.30 a. m.; the Third Brigade will march in the center, and move at 7 a. m.; the Second Brigade will bring up the rear, and will follow close on the Third Brigade. The pioneer corps will move in the rear of the advance regiment, and repair the roads and build bridges, that the trains may be delayed as little as possible. The trains will move closed up—first, the pioneer corps train; then the brigade trains in their respective order of march; followed by the ordnance, supply, and, last, the ambulance train. As we are near a large rebel cavalry force it is important that the utmost vigilance be shown by the different brigade commanders; men and trains should be kept well in hand. In case of an attack the general commanding should be at once informed. The practice of shooting without orders is forbidden, and brigade commanders will promulgate an order, to be read to their respective commands to-morrow morning before marching, that the firing of muskets without orders must cease, and will have the violators of such orders severely punished. Attention is also called to Special Orders, No. 172, paragraph II, from department headquarters, and to Special Orders, No. 177, paragraph I, corps headquarters.

By order of Brig. Gen. John M. Corse:

L. CARPER,
Assistant Adjutant-General.

SPECIAL ORDERS, No. 288.

HDQRS. SEVENTEENTH ARMY CORPS,
Pitts' Mill, near Gordon, Ga., November 21, 1864.

I. The following are the orders for to-morrow's movement:

1. The First Division, Maj. Gen. J. A. Mower commanding, will move forward to Gordon at 7 a. m.

2. The Third Division, Brigadier-General Leggett commanding, will move forward at 7 a. m., following the First Division.

3. The commanding officer Artillery Brigade will detail one battery to move with each division, as the division commander may direct.

4. The train of these headquarters will move in rear of the ordnance train with the advance brigade of the First Division.

By command of Maj. Gen. F. P. Blair:

C. CADLE, JR.,
Assistant Adjutant-General.

HEADQUARTERS SEVENTEENTH ARMY CORPS,
November 21, 1864.

Brig. Gen. M. D. LEGGETT, *Commanding Third Division:*

GENERAL: The major-general commanding directs that you move forward, taking the road to Fortville, at 10 o'clock, if possible. If you cannot move at that hour start as soon as you can.

Very respectfully, your obedient servant,

C. CADLE, JR.,
Assistant Adjutant-General.

HEADQUARTERS MILITARY DIVISION OF THE MISSISSIPPI,
In the Field, Vann's House, November 21, 1864.

General J. C. DAVIS, *Commanding Fourteenth Corps:*

GENERAL: I am directed by the general-in-chief to say that at Lawrence's, about three miles and a half from your quarters, the road forks—the one leading to the right, on which Morgan now is, is the longer but somewhat the better; by the left there is a ford to pass the Cedar Creek. He thinks you will do well to send two divisions, the engineers, and the pontoon train by the right-hand road, and one division by the left hand and ford. Inclosed is a small sketch* by Captain Poe. The distance by the left is about sixteen miles from the fork to Milledgeville, touching the railroad some five miles from it, but not intersecting the road by which the Twentieth Corps is marching. Both your columns will enter Milledgeville about the same point. The general wishes your columns kept pretty compact, regardless of the time it takes you to reach Milledgeville.

I am, general, respectfully, yours, &c.,

L. M. DAYTON,
Aide-de-Camp.

HEADQUARTERS FOURTEENTH ARMY CORPS,
Murder Creek, Ga., November 21, 1864.

Brig. Gen. J. D. MORGAN,
Commanding Second Division, Fourteenth Army Corps:

GENERAL: Your march has been a good one to-day, except perhaps a little remissness on the part of your train guards in not pushing up the trains. You will remain in your present camp until further orders. General Baird's division will take the advance to-morrow. This will give you the greater part of the day in which to rest, &c., secure the crossing at Cedar Creek, picket well, and give the Michigan Engineers any help they may desire to work the roads.

Yours, very respectfully,

JEF. C. DAVIS,
Brevet Major-General, Commanding.

HEADQUARTERS TWENTIETH CORPS,
Five miles back from Little River, November 21, 1864—1.30 p. m.

Lieut. Col. H. C. RODGERS, *Assistant Adjutant-General:*

COLONEL: I have just received a note from Lieutenant-Colonel Asmussen stating that the general commanding expects the whole corps to encamp to-night at Little River. I do not think the First

---

* Not found.

Division will be able to reach there. They are at least three miles back, and the road is almost impassable. I will do the best I can to get them up. The Second Division train has not all passed this point yet.

Very respectfully, your obedient servant,

A. S. WILLIAMS,
Brigadier-General, Commanding.

HEADQUARTERS TWENTIETH CORPS,
Garrard's House, November 21, 1864—5.30 p. m.

Lieut. Col. H. C. RODGERS,
Assistant Adjutant-General:

COLONEL: The First Division will encamp here to-night (the place where you dined). The head of their column is here, and parking. In the absence of other orders, I will have this division start at 5 a. m. to-morrow, and have it pass the other divisions near the river. The animals in the First Division's train are much exhausted, and should have the best road to-morrow.

Very respectfully. your obedient servant,

A. S. WILLIAMS,
Brigadier-General, Commanding.

ORDERS.] HEADQUARTERS TWENTIETH CORPS,
Near Dennis Station, Ga., November 21, 1864.

This corps will move to-morrow toward Milledgeville, as follows: First Division in advance, starting at 5 a. m.; Second Division train at 7 a. m.; Third Division at 8 a. m.

The corps supply and ordnance trains will march in front of the First Division to Little River, when they will fall in rear of it. General Jackson will detail one regiment to march with and assist them. Colonel Hughes' mounted infantry will start from their present camp at 5.30 a. m.

The pontoon bridge will be taken up as soon as the rear of the column has passed, the rear brigade of General Ward's division giving such assistance and protection to it as may be necessary.

All of the pontoon train not required for the bridge over Little River will march in rear of the First Division, starting at 7 a. m. The artillery will be distributed in the column the same as heretofore. General Jackson and General Ward will each distribute their troops, except the advance brigade of the First Division and the rear brigade of the Third Division, along the trains, so as to cover each a half of the train of the Second Division, and will give them all necessary assistance.

By command of Brigadier-General Williams:

H. W. PERKINS,
Assistant Adjutant-General.

HEADQUARTERS TWENTIETH CORPS,
On the Road, five miles from Little River, November 21, 1864.

Brig. Gen. N. J. JACKSON,
Commanding First Division:

GENERAL: The general commanding the corps directs me to say that he has been ordered by General Slocum to encamp the whole corps, if possible, to-night at Little River. He desires to have you push on as far as possible, but as soon as dark he directs that you turn the head of your column into park and camp. The pontoon train is needed to cross Little River, and they must be hurried up to that point to-night. Please give them all the assistance they require. Should your division not reach Little River, the general directs that you start, in the absence of further orders, at 5 o'clock to-morrow morning with the trains that have been in advance of yours to-day, still occupying the same place in the column. He also desires that in the march of to-morrow that you detail a regiment to assist the corps supply and ammunition trains.

Very respectfully, your obedient servant,

H. W. PERKINS,
Assistant Adjutant-General.

ORDERS.] HDQRS. FIRST DIVISION, TWENTIETH CORPS,
Near Dennis Station, Ga., November 21, 1864.

This division will march to-morrow at 5 a. m. toward Milledgeville, in the following order: The Second Brigade in advance, to guard and assist the corps supply and ordnance trains to Little River, after which it will march unencumbered as advance guard; the First Brigade next, to be distributed along the train of the First Division, excepting the last twenty-five wagons of the train; the Third Brigade in rear, to be distributed along the last twenty-five wagons of First Division train and the first half of the Second Division train; also, after passing the river, this brigade will guard and assist the corps supply and ordnance trains, which fall in rear of the First Division train at the river.

By command of Brig. Gen. N. J. Jackson:

GEO. ROBINSON,
First Lieutenant and Acting Assistant Adjutant-General.

HEADQUARTERS DEPARTMENT OF THE SOUTH,
Hilton Head, S. C., November 21, 1864.

Maj. Gen. H. W. HALLECK, U. S. Army,
Chief of Staff, Armies of the United States, Washington, D. C.:

GENERAL: I have the honor to report that the affairs of the department remain in a satisfactory state. The troops are kept constantly employed in drilling, policing, and in perfecting and strengthening the defenses.

In the Northern District, the addition to Fort Putnam of the new battery, composed of six 11-inch Dahlgren guns, is completed. It is furnished with excellent bomb-proofs and magazines. On account of our want of men, and especially of good artillery, the admiral has agreed to man this new battery, and to furnish, in addition to the guns, the ammunition. Fort Putnam is now in excellent order, and has been surrounded with a new and strong palisading outside of the parapet. The batteries on Cummings Point lying next to Fort Putnam, denominated Batteries Chatfield, Seymour, and Barton, have all been united into one fort, to be called Fort Chatfield, which is furnished with magazines and bomb-proof, with a strong stockade, with flanking arrangements in the rear, and in the front, outside of the parapet, a strong palisading in course of erection. Fort Strong is already furnished with a good palisading, and is in perfect order. As soon, therefore, as the palisading in front of Fort Chatfield is completed, these three strong forts will be perfectly secure from any attempts to carry them by surprise and escalade by any force landing from boats. They are also in a most effective condition, with the exception of some guns which have burst and are not yet replaced, no new ones being here on hand. The importance of having these advanced batteries in a perfectly secure and unassailable condition was felt more decidedly from the knowledge that the enemy is constantly building bateaux and launches at Charleston, having already 125 completed, capable of carrying from twenty-five to sixty men each, several of them being filled with howitzers. Our picket stations on Long Island, Black Island, and Cole's Island are also strengthened by intrenchments, which are furnished with light field pieces. These field-works are likewise surrounded with palisades and other obstacles, and are judged to be safe against any sudden attack of the enemy.

In the other districts similar preparations have been made continuously, until I am now in a condition, in case of need, to draw from each district one or two regiments to resist an attack in any other portion of the department, or to constitute a small force to attack the enemy. An opportunity of this kind may shortly occur, if, as appears from the late rebel papers, General Sherman really be upon the march from Atlanta to Savannah or Charleston. If such prove to be the case, I shall consider it my duty to aid him in every way I can. Although I am ordered to stand strictly on the defensive, and have received no instructions or information from the commanding general relating to this probable event, yet I take it for granted that I am expected to act effectively under such an emergency, should it arise.

The health of the department continues good. The exchange of prisoners is progressing under the charge of Lieutenant-Colonel Mulford. I understand that all the rebels have been delivered and most of our men received; also, that the condition of the latter received is fully as good as that of the rebels delivered. Information received from deserters, refugees, and escaped officers and soldiers, represent that great dejection is felt at the result of the re-election of President Lincoln; that a sharp discussion is going on about arming negroes; that the yellow fever is abating in Charleston, and has not been an epidemic in Savannah, from which it has now disappeared; that a considerable number of Union prisoners have enlisted with the rebel army, being driven to this step by privations and suffering; that the most of these have been sent to join Pat. Cleburne's division, of Hood's army, but that 400 of them are in Georgia regiments posted on James Island; that our prisoners are suffering for clothes and food; that the Union officers at Columbia have insufficient food and no shelter, except bough houses constructed by themselves; and that extraordinary exertions are now being made to get the militia and reserves into the field to meet the present emergency. In consequence of the deficient rations given to our officers, I have reduced the rations of the rebel officers in my hands accordingly.

Very respectfully, your obedient servant,

J. G. FOSTER,
Major-General, Commanding.

MORRIS ISLAND, S. C., *November 21, 1864.*

Maj. Gen. J. G. FOSTER,
Commanding Department of the South:

GENERAL: You were kind enough to ask me for my views relating to the cutting of the railroad between Savannah and Charleston. In my letter of yesterday I stated that I thought it would be best to strike the road from Broad River. The more I examine it the better satisfied I am that that is the true point of operations. By landing where the road from Grahamville strikes the river, opposite Whale Island, a march of less than twenty miles puts you on the road at Gopher Hill. One regiment, with a battery detached, should take the road to the right and throw up intrenchments on the bank of the creek where the road from the Coosawhatchie divides. The main force would throw up a strong fort at Gopher Hill, which is probably a commanding position; a detachment could then be sent to Ferebeeville, to fortify there. The line from Gopher Hill to Broad River would then be entirely free from molestation, and constant communication could be kept up with Hilton Head, and supplies furnished Sherman's army, if Lee, abandoning Richmond, should come down to protect Charleston. I would not injure the road, as Sherman may desire to use it. I would get up to Hilton Head the two locomotives from Jacksonville, and have them put in repair, if they need it; also, all the cars and extra pairs of wheels. Of these latter, there is quite a number at Jacksonville and some at Fernandina. There are also at Fernandina spare parts of locomotives that may be found useful. To make the movement the whole of the force at Hilton Head and three-quarters of that at Beaufort could be used without running any risk. Two regiments from Florida and three from here might be spared; certainly one could be sent from Florida and three from here. By garrisoning the forts here the force might be much reduced. It is as I thought about the Star Fort, on Folly Island; there was never a day's work done on it after you came in command; what work was done has nearly blown away. I will commence work on it immediately. It will make a difference of seven companies to defend that portion of the island; a regiment is now used when three companies with the fort is an ample force.

Very respectfully, your obedient servant,

JNO. P. HATCH,
Brigadier-General.

CITY POINT, *November 22, 1864--7 p. m.*

Lieutenant-General GRANT:

The Richmond papers of this date, just received, have but little news of Sherman. The Whig says:

> We are unable to obtain any later intelligence from Georgia this forenoon, except a report, seemingly reliable, that Sherman was only eighteen miles from Macon yesterday. We did not receive any exchanges to-day from points beyond Greensborough, the mail having failed to connect at that point.

The Sentinel says:

> If the rains which have been falling here for several days extend to Georgia, Sherman will have heavy traveling. It will operate greatly to his disadvantage and to our benefit; it will retard his movements and make foraging extremely difficult. Our concentration of troops to operate against him being by railroad, will not experience the like interruption. We trust that the Black Jack will hold him until our generals gather all around him for his destruction.

Other Richmond papers make no mention of Sherman whatever.

JNO. A. RAWLINS,
Brigadier-General and Chief of Staff.

(Same to the Secretary of War.)

HEADQUARTERS MILITARY DIVISION OF THE MISSISSIPPI,
In the Field, Cobb's Plantation, November 22, 1864.

General HOWARD,
Commanding Army of the Tennessee:

GENERAL: I am directed by the general-in-chief to write you as follows: The march of this wing has been, since leaving Atlanta, in two columns, and very successful up to this time. The Fourteenth Corps is now on the Hillsborough road, ten miles west of Milledgeville, and the Twentieth Corps must now be in the capital, having marched by the Eatonton road. The Georgia railroad, from and including the Oconee bridge, west to Lithonia, is well destroyed. Troops in fine condition, having fed high on sweet potatoes and poultry. Stock is also doing well, though the roads have been very heavy.

The general desires you will report to him at Milledgeville to-morrow (where he will go early), in detail, your operations since leaving Atlanta; also, the position of your command, in view of his making further orders. In the meantime you cannot do too much permanent damage to that railroad east of Macon or about Gordon. You will also notify General Kilpatrick a similar report is desired from him.

I am, general, respectfully, yours, &c.,

L. M. DAYTON,
Aide-de-Camp.

HDQRS. DEPARTMENT AND ARMY OF THE TENNESSEE,
Gordon, Ga., November 22, 1864—3 p. m.

Maj. Gen. W. T. SHERMAN,
Commanding, &c.:

I send you, by General Kilpatrick, dispatches just captured. My command will be pretty well closed up to-night. I have directed Major-General Blair to push Giles A. Smith's division, with a regiment of cavalry to try and save the railroad bridge over the Oconee. I shall move, as soon as the bridge can be gotten up, to the crossing six miles below that bridge. I hope, however, before starting, to hear from you. I sent dispatches to you this morning by Captain Duncan.

Respectfully, &c.,

O. O. HOWARD,
Major-General.

[Inclosure No. 1.]

MACON, *Thursday Morning, November 17, 1864.*

DEAR GOVERNOR: Things are very bad here. Sherman in person is leading, say, 30,000 men against us. We are retreating as rapidly as possible consistent with order and efficiency. The militia are retreating in admirable order and good discipline, as General Cobb reports. I will meet them between this and Forsyth this evening. I believe the Legislature will grant you large and liberal powers. Tell them the country is in danger. Let all of her sons come to the rescue.

Yours, faithfully,

R. TOOMBS.

P. S.—We have called for the troops in Wilmington, Charleston, and Savannah. If we do defend here they will be on us by Monday. Cavalry force said to be about 6,000. Send all the troops you can. If we do not get help we must abandon this place.

Yours,

R. TOOMBS.

[Inclosure No. 2.]

STATE OF GEORGIA,
ADJUTANT AND INSPECTOR GENERAL'S OFFICE,
Gordon, November 20, 1864.

Maj. Gen. HOWELL COBB, *Macon:*

I report here with 200 men. Send me 10,000 rounds of ammunition, .69 caliber, and a medical officer.

H. C. WAYNE,
Major-General.

[Inclosure No. 3.]

GORDON, *November 20, 1864.*

Major-General MCLAWS,
Savannah:

It is my opinion you had better send troops to guard Oconee bridge. Keep your telegraph office open.

H. C. WAYNE,
Major-General.

[Inclosure No. 4.]

GORDON, *November 21, 1864.*

Major-General MCLAWS,
Savannah:

I have been cut off from Macon for thirty hours. It is reported to me that Macon will be evacuated by our troops, the enemy being too strong. I have, therefore, in council, decided to fall back to the Oconee, the now important point in this neighborhood. My force is 450, including sixty cavalry and four pieces of artillery. I report to you for orders.

HENRY C. WAYNE,
Major-General.

[Inclosure No. 5.]

GORDON, *November 21, 1864.*

Maj. H. T. HALL:

Courier just in reports 40,000 men marching down Western and Atlantic Railroad on Macon, 20,000 marching down Georgia road on Augusta. I have nothing from Macon. The enemy left Griswold last night in direction for Milledgeville, as understood, passing to east of me.

HENRY C. WAYNE,
Major-General.

Keep the telegraph on the alert.

[Inclosure No. 6.]

GORDON, *November 21, 1864.*

Colonel RAINS, *Augusta:*

Send me 250 cartridge boxes and belts. The rain is ruining my powder.

H. C. WAYNE,
Major-General.

[Inclosure No. 7.]

GORDON, *Central Railroad, November 21, 1864.*

Capt. R. W. B. ELLIOTT,
Assistant Adjutant-General, Headquarters, Savannah:

Major-General Wayne proposes falling back from this place to the Oconee bridge. The enemy are reported 40,000 strong, moving on

Macon, and 20,000 on Augusta. A small force of the enemy were in Milledgeville yesterday evening. I await further orders. Telegraph me at No. 14.

A. L. HARTRIDGE,
Major, &c.

[Inclosure No. 8.]

AUGUSTA, [*November*] *21, 1864.*

General FRY,
Commanding, &c., Augusta:

Have you any news of importance from Macon? The wires are cut, but I will send a courier through. Cavalry force of the enemy moving on the east of me, as if for Milledgeville. Keep me advised.

HENRY C. WAYNE,
Major-General.

[Inclosure No. 9.]

HEADQUARTERS WILLIAMS' KENTUCKY BRIGADE,
November 21, 1864—3 p. m.

Major POOLE,
Assistant Adjutant-General for General Hardee:

I found the enemy about four miles from Clinton, about one regiment strong. I have driven them over a mile and am still driving them. Have not as yet learned anything of the force they have in their rear.

Very respectfully, &c.,

WM. C. P. BRECKINRIDGE,
Colonel, Commanding Brigade.

GENERAL FIELD ORDERS, No. 26.

HEADQUARTERS DEPARTMENT AND ARMY OF THE TENNESSEE,
Gordon, Ga., November 22, 1864.

It having come to the knowledge of the major-general commanding that the crime of arson and robbery have become frequent throughout this army, notwithstanding positive orders both from these and superior headquarters have been repeatedly issued, and with a view to the prompt punishment of offenses of this kind, it is hereby ordered: That hereafter any officer or man of this command discovered in pillaging a house or burning a building without proper authority will, upon sufficient proof thereof, be shot. Corps commanders are required to notify every member of their respective commands of all departments of this order.

By order of Maj. Gen. O. O. Howard:

W. BEDFORD,
Assistant Adjutant-General.

SPECIAL FIELD ORDERS, No. 175.

HEADQUARTERS DEPARTMENT AND ARMY OF THE TENNESSEE,
Gordon, Ga., November 22, 1864.

* * * * * * *

III. The following-named troops composing this army will move to-morrow, as follows: First, Major-General Osterhaus, commanding Fifteenth Corps, will move the Second Division of his command, with its trains, on the Irwinton road, starting at 7 a.m. He will cause the

First Division of his command to move on the same road to this vicinity. He will direct Brigadier-General Corse to move with his command on the direct road to this place, reaching here at as early an hour as practicable. The Third Division will remain at Gordon, and Brig. Gen. J. E. Smith, commanding, will be directed to send from headquarters teams, and those that have the lightest loads, fifty-five six-mule teams, to move up the boats in the bridge train to Gordon in the quickest possible time, the officers in charge reporting with teams to Captain Reese, chief engineer, at these headquarters, for instructions, at 6.30 a. m. to-morrow. Second, Major-General Blair, commanding Seventeenth Army Corps, will cause the Fourth Division of his command, Brig. Gen. G. A. Smith, commanding, to move toward the railroad bridge, fulfilling instructions already given. He will march the infantry of the other two divisions of his command along the railroad and detail men to destroy it en route—one division to commence eight miles from Gordon and destroy to some point opposite Irwinton, and there encamp, and the other from Gordon, and encamp eight miles out. The trains of the Seventeenth Corps will move along the Jackson Ferry wagon road, with small guard, and park with their divisions. Third, it is the intention for the Seventeenth Corps to cross the Oconee River at Jackson's Ferry, two miles and a half north of the railroad bridge, and the Fifteenth Corps at a point six miles south of the railroad bridge. The chief engineer will take measures to lay pontoons at these points as soon as practicable. Fourth, Lieut. W. B. Todd, in charge of cattle, will move on the upper road along Commissioner's Creek, toward Jackson's Ferry. In order to expedite the movement of the bridge train, all other trains will give up the right of way.

By order of Maj. Gen. O. O. Howard:

SAML. L. TAGGART,
Assistant Adjutant-General.

SPECIAL ORDERS, No. 179.

HDQRS. FIFTEENTH ARMY CORPS,
Gordon, Ga., November 22, 1864.

I. The movements of the Fifteenth Army Corps for to-morrow will be as follows: General Hazen, commanding Second Division, will at 7 a. m. continue his march toward Irwinton, and will proceed about eight miles beyond his present camp, selecting a strong defensive position for his command. As soon as such is established, he will order up his train now at Gordon. Brigadier-General Woods, commanding First Division, will follow with his command to the fork of the road to Gordon, some distance east of the position now occupied by Second Division. The Twenty-ninth Missouri Mounted Infantry will report to Brigadier-General Woods for duty during the movement. Brigadier-General Smith, commanding Third Division, will remain at Gordon, giving particular attention to the guarding of all avenues to the place by a well-established picket-line. In order to accelerate the arrival of the much-needed bridge train, General Smith will have selected and sent toward General Corse's column, on the direct road to Clinton, from the different headquarters trains of the Third Division, fifty-eight six-mule teams. The officer in charge of the same will report at 6.30 a. m. to-morrow to Captain Reese, chief engineer, department headquarters. The Fourth Division, Brigadier-General Corse commanding, is expected here at an early hour, and will encamp at this place. He will give to the bridge train the right of way. The batteries now with the First and Second Divisions will remain and march with them. The remaining batteries of Artillery Brigade will continue with General Smith's division at Gordon.

By order of Maj. Gen. P. Joseph Osterhaus:

FREDK. WHITEHEAD,
Assistant Adjutant-General.

SPECIAL FIELD ORDERS, No. 12. } HEADQUARTERS FOURTH DIVISION, FIFTEENTH ARMY CORPS, *In the Field, near Clinton, Ga., November 22, 1864.*

I. This command will move to-morrow, the 23d instant, as follows: The pioneer corps will leave camp at 5 a. m., and repair the roads and bridges toward Clinton; the Third Brigade will have the advance, and move into the road at 6.30 a. m.; the Second Brigade will move in the center, and close up on the Third Brigade; the First Brigade will bring up the rear. The advance and rear brigades will each have one regiment act as advance and rear guard, respectively. The trains will move in the following order: First, the pioneer corps train, followed by the ordnance, supply, and, last, the ambulance train.

By order of Brig. Gen. John M. Corse:

L. CARPER,
Assistant Adjutant-General.

SPECIAL ORDERS, No. 289. } HDQRS. SEVENTEENTH ARMY CORPS, *Gordon, Ga., November 22, 1864.*

* * * * * * *

II. 1. Maj. Gen. J. A. Mower, commanding First Division, will cause two miles of the Milledgeville railroad to be destroyed at once, commencing at the junction and working north.

2. Brig. Gen. M. D. Leggett, commanding Third Division, will cause two miles of the Milledgeville and Savannah railroad to be destroyed at once, commencing at the junction and working west.

* * * * * * *

IV. The following are the orders for the movement of this corps to-morrow:

1. The Third Division, Brig. Gen. M. D. Leggett commanding, will have the advance, moving at 7 a. m.

2. The First Division, Maj. Gen. J. A. Mower commanding, will follow the Third Division, moving at 8 o'clock.

3. The Artillery Brigade will move as heretofore.

4. The infantry will move along the railroad, destroying it as it moves, as follows: The Third Division will commence at a point eight miles from Gordon and destroy about four miles; the First Division will commence at the point where Brig. Gen. John E. Smith left off and destroy to where Brigadier-General Leggett commences.

5. The trains and batteries will move along the Jackson Ferry road, and each division commander will detail at least two regiments as guard to his train and the battery that marches with his command.

6. The road will be destroyed by firing the sleepers, and it will not be necessary to tear up the track, as the rails will be completely ruined, if the firing is properly done.

7. The train of these headquarters will move as heretofore.

By command of Maj. Gen. F. P. Blair:

C. CADLE, JR.,
Assistant Adjutant-General.

HEADQUARTERS TWENTIETH CORPS,
Two miles south of Oconee River, November 22, 1864.

Brigadier-General GEARY,
Commanding Second Division:

GENERAL: The general commanding directs that you push forward your infantry past the trains, following immediately in rear of the infantry of the Third Division. The wagon trains will park here while the infantry and artillery push on to the town. Leave one regiment to guard your train and assist them.

Very respectfully, your obedient servant,

H. W. PERKINS,
Assistant Adjutant-General.

HEADQUARTERS TWENTIETH CORPS,
Two miles south of Oconee River, November 22, 1864.

Brig. Gen. W. T. WARD,
Commanding Third Division:

GENERAL: The general commanding directs that you leave one of your brigades (the rear one) to bring up the trains to the place assigned for them to park near here, and push on through the train to the front with your infantry. The brigade that is left will assist all the trains up the hills on this side of the river. You will leave one regiment of this brigade to assist in taking up the pontoon bridge and bringing it to park. Direct them to destroy the ferry-boat. All of the infantry, except this brigade, are to push forward; it will remain to guard the wagons.

Very respectfully, your obedient servant,

H. W. PERKINS,
Lieutenant-Colonel and Assistant Adjutant-General.

HEADQUARTERS TWENTIETH CORPS,
Milledgeville, Ga., November 22, 1864.

Brig. Gen. W. T. WARD,
Commanding Third Division:

GENERAL: The general commanding directs that you detail one small regiment from your command for a picket at a bridge, a short distance from this place, on the Gordon road. The commanding officer of the regiment detailed will report to General Slocum for detailed instructions and to ascertain the exact location of the bridge. General Slocum's quarters are at the Milledgeville Hotel.

Very respectfully, your obedient servant,

H. W. PERKINS,
Lieutenant-Colonel and Assistant Adjutant-General.

CONFIDENTIAL.] HDQRS. DEPARTMENT OF THE SOUTH,
Hilton Head, S. C., November 22, 1864.

Maj. Gen. H. W. HALLECK,
Chief of Staff, Armies of the United States:

GENERAL: I have the honor to inform you that the information I have received leaves little doubt that General Sherman has captured

Gordon, situated sixty miles this side of Macon, and that he is rapidly marching in this direction. There is a panic in Charleston and Savannah. The rebel officers with the flag-of-truce boat refuse to give us their late papers. General Hardee has left Charleston, with his staff, to meet Sherman. He is collecting every man to defend the State. He has withdrawn considerably from the force guarding the Savannah and Charleston Railroad. I do not consider that my orders to stand strictly on the defensive were intended to prevent my taking advantage of such a favorable opportunity, and I shall therefore scrape together a small force of 3,000 men and attack and capture, if possible, some point on the railroad. Beyond this, if General Sherman really comes across, I shall consider it my duty to aid him to the utmost, and to obey his orders. The weather is now so cold as to remove all apprehension of yellow fever, which must by this time have disappeared from Charleston.

Very respectfully, your obedient servant,

J. G. FOSTER,
Major-General, Commanding.

HEADQUARTERS DEPARTMENT OF THE SOUTH,
Hilton Head, S. C., November 22, 1864.

Brig. Gen. JOHN P. HATCH,
Commanding Northern District, Morris Island, S. C.:

GENERAL: I have received your letter of the 20th instant, and fully concur with you in your views as to the point of attack. I write now to inform you that the time I shall require you, with the regiments you can spare, to leave Morris and Folly Islands, will be on the night of the 27th instant. I appoint the night of the 27th as I desire the movement to be entirely concealed from the enemy, which cannot be effected except under cover of darkness. As I mentioned before, I shall require three regiments. I would suggest that you select the three most available. You must endeavor, when there is a choice, to take the best and strongest regiments. It will not be necessary to disturb the camps; they can be left as they are. All the forts and batteries should be pretty well manned, and perhaps it would be better to move the most of the remaining men to the batteries, leaving only a few to guard the camps. It is judged that the regiments that remain, together with the convalescents and others, will be sufficient to guard the place. The pickets might remain undisturbed. Bring all the mounted force you possibly can; in addition, bring four pieces of a battery, provided that number can be properly armed, manned, and horsed. Five days' cooked rations will be brought with them. The rations of coffee, sugar, and salt must be put up in separate bags, which will have to be prepared for the purpose, and carried so as neither to be dissolved nor mixed with other provisions. Each man will carry his blanket, overcoat, rubber blanket or shelter-tent, and one extra pair of good socks. All the infantry must wear shoes. One hundred extra rounds of ammunition per man will be brought in boxes; twenty rounds to be distributed just previous to landing. What steamers can be spared for transportation will be sent by the 24th. Although I shall be near, and endeavor to aid you as much as possible, I shall not be able to go very far into the country. You, therefore, will have to command the force, which will consist of a small division, composed of two brigades, as follows: First Brigade, regiments from Morris Island; Second Brigade, under

General Potter, composed of parts of nine regiments, from here, Beaufort, and Florida; also, four pieces of Day's battery and fifty cavalry from Florida. If you desire the services of General Saxton in command of one of the brigades, I will order him to report; but otherwise, not. Let me know upon this last point at once.

Very respectfully, your obedient servant,

J. G. FOSTER,
Major-General, Commanding.

HEADQUARTERS DEPARTMENT OF THE SOUTH,
Hilton Head, S. C., November 22, 1864.

Brig. Gen. E. E. POTTER,
Commanding Hilton Head District:

I am instructed by the major-general commanding to state that the movement of which he spoke to you has been postponed until the 27th instant.

Very respectfully, your obedient servant,

W. B. DEAN,
Lieutenant and Acting Assistant Adjutant-General.

HEADQUARTERS DEPARTMENT OF THE SOUTH,
Hilton Head, S. C., November 22, 1864.

Brig. Gen. E. P. SCAMMON,
Commanding District of Florida, Jacksonville, Fla.:

GENERAL: The information received indicates that General Sherman is rapidly marching toward the eastern sea-ports. I am, therefore, getting ready to make an attack upon some point of the enemy's line, so as to aid him. For this purpose, I am getting together all the regiments that can be spared from all the districts. I shall require from your district two regiments and four pieces of artillery from Day's battery. These will have to be sent so as to leave the Saint John's River by the evening of the 26th instant, if possible. You will have to issue immediately orders to prepare them for the move. You had better select the regiments most disposable, and order them to bring five days' cooked rations. The rations of coffee, sugar, and salt must be put up in separate bags, which will have to be prepared for the purpose, and carried so as not to be dissolved nor mixed with other portions of the provisions. Each man will carry his blanket, overcoat, rubber blanket or shelter-tent, and one extra pair of good socks. All the men must wear shoes. Each man will likewise carry twenty extra rounds of ammunition. One hundred rounds will be brought with the troops in boxes, and twenty rounds to be distributed previous to landing. I expect these two regiments to number 1,000 effective men; if not, you must, if possible, add a company or more to make the number. Besides the infantry and artillery, you will also send fifty men of the Fourth Massachusetts Cavalry mounted, equipped, and prepared for active service. The Wyoming will bring the artillery to the best advantage; the Mary Benton and Delaware will carry the infantry and cavalry; with another steamer to be sent to guard against accidents.

Respectfully, yours,

J. G. FOSTER,
Major-General, Commanding.

SPECIAL FIELD ORDERS, No. 127. } HDQRS. MIL. DIV. OF THE MISSISSIPPI, *In the Field, Milledgeville, Ga., November 23, 1864.*

The first movement of this army having proved perfectly successful, and the weather now being fine, the following will constitute the second stage of the campaign, and the movement will commence to-morrow, November 24:

I. General Kilpatrick, with his cavalry command, unencumbered by wagons, will move via Milledgeville by the most practicable route eastward, break the railroad between Millen and Augusta, then turn and strike the railroad below Millen; after which he will use all possible effort to rescue our prisoners of war now confined near Millen. He will communicate back to the wings of the army, as often as it is safe, any information of roads and the enemy that may be of interest to them.

II. The Right Wing, General Howard, will move substantially along but south of the railroad to a point opposite Sandersville, breaking up and destroying in the most thorough manner the railroad and telegraph, at which point further orders will be issued.

III. The Left Wing, General Slocum, will move directly from Milledgeville to the railroad opposite Sandersville, and at once commence destroying the railroad forward to the Ogeechee.

IV. Great attention should be paid to the destruction of this road, as it is of vital importance to our cause. Besides burning bridges and trestles, the iron should be carefully twisted and warped, so that it will be impossible to ever use it again; to this end, the rate of travel will be reduced to ten miles a day.

V. Increased attention must be given to the care of trains, for it is known that the enemy intend to harass our march by means of cavalry, and we should aim to punish him severely for a first attempt, as it will deter him from repeating it. Also, more attention must be paid to the subject of foraging; none but the regular organized foraging parties should be allowed to depart from the right and left of the road, and the foraging parties themselves should, in addition to former instructions, be instructed to capture wagons to bring their plunder to camp, after which the wagons should be burned. All the useless wagons, ox-teams, &c., which encumber our trains should now be destroyed; and the commander of any brigade is hereby authorized to destroy any wagon that delays the march or opens a gap in the column, no matter to whom it belongs; and, generally, the troops should be distributed along the trains, as we have no large enemy to threaten and nothing but dashes of cavalry at our flanks. Advance guards should be strengthened, attended by a pioneer corps prepared to construct temporary bridges in case of their destruction by the enemy; and wherever any such obstruction occurs the commanding officer of the troops present on the spot will deal harshly with the inhabitants near by, to show them that it is to their interest not to impede our movements. Should the enemy burn forage and corn on our route houses, barns, and cotton-gins must also be burned to keep them company.

VI. The general-in-chief will accompany the Left Wing until it reaches Sandersville, when he will join the Army of the Tennessee.

By order of Maj. Gen. W. T. Sherman:

L. M. DAYTON,
Aide-de-Camp.

HEADQUARTERS MILITARY DIVISION OF THE MISSISSIPPI,
In the Field, Milledgeville, Ga., November 23, 1864.

Major-General HOWARD,
Commanding Army of the Tennessee:

By instructions of the general-in-chief, I give you the following directions: Continue to destroy the railroad eastward to the Oconee in the most complete and thorough manner, burning and twisting every rail, and the same for a distance to the west toward Macon; also, destroy the Oconee bridge. You may lay your pontoon over the Oconee, but do not cross any of your command until further orders. Hardee has probably swung around via Albany for Savannah, which the general says is all right, and he don't care particularly. Kilpatrick will be moved here, or in this vicinity, for the present. The probability is we will concentrate at or near Sandersville. Prosecute the railroad destruction in the most thorough manner, and communicate with the general-in-chief frequently.

I am, general, respectfully, yours, &c.,

L. M. DAYTON,
Aide-de-Camp.

HEADQUARTERS MILITARY DIVISION OF THE MISSISSIPPI,
In the Field, Milledgeville, November 23, 1864.

Major-General HOWARD,
Commanding Army of the Tennessee:

GENERAL: I am directed by the general-in-chief to acknowledge the receipt of your detailed and interesting report* of the operations of the Army of the Tennessee since its departure from Atlanta, and, further, to say he is well pleased with the promptness of its movements and efficiency of its service. Special Field Orders, No. 127, containing the instructions for the next movement, were dispatched you to-day, and, as promised, I inclose another copy in this. Major-General Slocum's column entered this city yesterday, and the Fourteenth Corps came in about noon to-day; everything with these two columns has been eminently successful. At this place quite extensive magazines and arsenals have been found, besides large quantities of arms in the State Capitol itself, which will be appropriated or destroyed. The enemy will be minus a large and valuable quantity of property by our possession of the place. The railroad also has been most thoroughly destroyed. This wing will move early in the morning by two columns, the Twentieth Corps now being east of the river. The general-in-chief would write you did not his arm trouble him so much as to prevent him.

I am, general, very respectfully, your obedient servant,

L. M. DAYTON,
Aide-de-Camp.

SPECIAL FIELD ORDERS, No. 176.

HEADQUARTERS DEPARTMENT AND ARMY OF THE TENNESSEE,
Gordon, Ga., November 23, 1864.

* * * * * * *

III. The following are the orders for to-morrow, the 24th instant, viz: First, Major-General Blair will move his corps along the railroad, on the north side, completely destroying it en route toward the Oconee

* See p. 65.

River, his First Division, Major-General Mower commanding, leaving its present position at 7 a. m. The pontoon train will probably reach this point to-night. Captain Reese, chief engineer, will divide the boats, &c., train guard, and engineer regiment, assigning a portion for each of the corps. Major-General Blair will lay his bridge at Jackson's Ferry, two miles and a half north of the railroad bridge, if such ferry exists, and, if not, he must select some practicable point north of Ball's Ferry, if possible. Second, Major-General Osterhaus, commanding Fifteenth Corps, will move his command, by easy marches, to the vicinity of Ball's Ferry, where he will lay his pontoons. He will, however, retain his Third Division (Smith's) at this point till day after to-morrow, and move his Fourth Division (Corse's) to the position now occupied by General Woods' (First) division, to encamp to-morrow night. He will direct Brig. Gen. John E. Smith, commanding Third Division, to send a sufficient number (at least 100) of men, with axes and implements, to destroy the trestle-work three miles and a half west of this point. Two regiments of infantry should accompany the detail as guard while the work is being done. The whole cavalry command of Brigadier-General Kilpatrick has been ordered to Milledgeville to-morrow, starting at 6 a. m. Department headquarters will remain at this point to-morrow.

IV. To facilitate the movements of their pontoon trains each corps commander will cause the number of mules to their empty and lightly laden wagons to be reduced to four, and assign the surplus number to that train, so that each team thereof shall consist of eight mules. This to be done without delay.

By order of Maj. Gen. O. O. Howard:

SAML. L. TAGGART,
Assistant Adjutant-General.

HEADQUARTERS FIFTEENTH ARMY CORPS,
Irwinton Road, November 23, 1864.

General O. O. HOWARD,
Commanding Army:

General Hazen's division is in camp about half way from his last camp and Irwinton, about eight miles west of the latter place; General Woods' division will be near these headquarters, two miles south of Gordon. I sent a small party toward Irwinton, and am waiting its report in regard to the forage General Smith spoke of, and of roads leading to the river. Anything of interest will be promptly forwarded.

Very respectfully,

P. JOS. OSTERHAUS,
Major-General of Volunteers.

SPECIAL ORDERS, No. 180. } HDQRS. FIFTEENTH ARMY CORPS,
Near Gordon, Ga., November 23, 1864.

The movements of the Fifteenth Army Corps for to-morrow will be as follows:

1. Brigadier-General Woods, commanding First Division, with his artillery, will move from present camp at 7 a. m. to Irwinton. The Twenty-ninth Missouri Mounted Infantry will report to him for duty during the movement. The Second Division, Brigadier-General Hazen commanding, with his artillery, will follow as soon as the trains of the

First Division pass its camp, making Irwinton his destination also. The Third Division, Brigadier-General Smith commanding, with Battery H, First Illinois Light Artillery, will remain at Gordon until further orders, and will send a sufficient number of men (at least 100), with axes and implements, to destroy the trestle-work three and a half miles west of Gordon, early in the day, if the work has not already been accomplished. Two regiments of infantry should accompany this detail as guard while the work is being done. Brigadier-General Corse, commanding Fourth Division, will move to Gordon, and encamp two miles south of that place, occupying the position vacated by the First Division, where he will await further orders. Major Stolbrand, commanding Artillery Brigade, will cause Battery H, First Illinois Light Artillery, to report to Brigadier-General Smith, Third Division, as indicated above, and the Missouri battery of 12-pounders to report to Brigadier-General Corse, Fourth Division, for position with his command to-morrow. The remaining batteries of Artillery Brigade will, until further orders, remain with the divisions to which they are now assigned.

By order of Maj. Gen. P. Joseph Osterhaus:

FREDK. WHITEHEAD,
Assistant Adjutant-General.

SPECIAL FIELD ORDERS, No. 13.

HEADQUARTERS FOURTH DIVISION, FIFTEENTH ARMY CORPS,
In the Field, near Gordon, Ga., November 23, 1864.

I. This command will move to-morrow, the 24th instant, as follows: The Second Brigade has the advance, and will move at 5.30 a. m.; the First Brigade will move in the center, and break camp at 6 a. m.; the Third Brigade will bring up the rear, and close upon the First Brigade. The pioneer corps will move in rear of the advance regiment, and repair the roads whenever it may be necessary. The trains will move as follows: First, the pioneer corps train; then the brigade trains in their respective order of march; followed by the ordnance, supply, and, last, the ambulance train.

By order of Brig. Gen. John M. Corse:

L. CARPER,
Assistant Adjutant-General.

SPECIAL FIELD ORDERS, No. 156.

HEADQUARTERS THIRD DIVISION, SEVENTEENTH ARMY CORPS,
Gordon, Ga., November 23, 1864.

I. The troops of this command will move at 7 a. m. The order of march will be indicated.

By order of Brig. Gen. M. D. Leggett:

J. C. DOUGLASS,
Assistant Adjutant-General.

HEADQUARTERS SEVENTEENTH ARMY CORPS,
Near No. 16, November 22 [23], 1864—10 p. m.

Captain TAGGART,
Asst. Adjt. Gen., Army and Dept. of the Tennessee:

CAPTAIN: General Blair directs me to forward the accompanying communication from General Smith, and to state that we have moved the troops across Commissioner's Creek and are now engaged in destroying the railroad. We have burned about five miles from Station No. 16 westwardly. The road from Gordon to this point is a very fair one, with the exception of the crossing at Commissioner's Creek, which is very bad. Notwithstanding General Smith's information that there is no road or crossing between the railroad bridge and Tucker's Ferry, the general is of the opinion that there is such a crossing, as we have positive information from citizens and one now at our headquarters that there is a road leading to and crossing at the intersection of Oconee River and Commissioner's Creek. The general has had a party out nearly all day looking up the road leading to Jackson's Ford on the north side of Commissioner's Creek, but they have not yet returned; when last heard from they were of the opinion that they could reach the ford by that route. The party sent out to discover a route south of Commissioner's Creek have reported a good road leading to Station No. 15, on the south side of the railroad, and from information are of the opinion that there is a road leading from No. 15 to Jackson's Ford. The general can pass his troops along the last-mentioned road without interfering with the lower or Irwinton road. He would suggest the propriety of moving his command up to No. 15, from which point he can send out a reconnaissance to determine the practicability of the upper or Jackson's Ford road and crossing, and if such a road and crossing does not exist, he will then be at the most convenient point for a movement toward Ball's Ferry.

Attention is called to General Smith's statement in reference to operations at Ball's Ferry. As General Smith's command is not within supporting distance, the general would suggest the propriety of sending a sufficient force from this division to secure the crossing, and, if possible, drive the enemy from the bridge.

Very respectfully, your obedient servant,

A. HICKENLOOPER,
Lieutenant-Colonel and Assistant Inspector-General.

[Inclosure.]

OCONEE BRIDGE, *November 23, 1864—5.30 p. m.*

[Maj. Gen. F. P. BLAIR:]

GENERAL: We left Station 15 about 12 o'clock, marched here, seven miles, and have driven the rebels out of two stockades. Spencer got the first one before we got up, and we now occupy this side of the river, and the enemy tolerably well intrenched close down to the bank on the other. Two guns is all we have developed so far, though they are said to have four. Their force we have no means of knowing, but they are estimated all the way from 600 to 1,500; probably the first is nearer the force. The railroad runs through a swamp about two miles; the ground is impassable, except occasionally a place that a skirmish line can wade through. The troops were mostly sent down on the railroad. We also got one gun down the track about half a mile and shelled them out of a stockade about one mile this side of the bridge. The balance of the road is trestle-work, and to get the artillery down will require a heavy job of bridging and corduroying, which I think is impracticable, as we are not laying siege to places on this trip. It would cost considerable ammunition then to shell them out. My opinion is that there is no crossing above this bridge except Tucker's Ferry, twenty-two miles from here. I directed Colonel Spencer to send 150 men from Station 15 to Ball's Ferry. The major in command has just sent a dispatch that he has the ferry; he had a sharp skirmish with a body of militia; the boat is on the opposite side, but he is constructing a raft to go over for it, and said he would have it in half an hour. I directed him to remain there until he was supported by you. If you do not want him to remain please send him orders. It is sixteen miles from here to Ball's Ferry by Station 15, which is the only route. It is also about the same distance to Irwinton. As this route for crossing the river is impracticable I suppose the next object is to destroy all the railroad we can. I am working on it now, but will not disturb the bridge until I hear from you. We could not do much toward bridging the swamp to-night, and I hope to hear from you by daylight. Please inform me where you are and any movement you contemplate, so I shall know where to communicate with you. It will take us a day to get to Ball's Ferry from here. The country here is very poor; nothing but corn to be had. My supply train is at Station 15; the remainder is four miles from the bridge; all well guarded.

Very respectfully, your obedient servant,

GILES A. SMITH,
Brigadier-General.

ORDERS.] HEADQUARTERS LEFT WING, ARMY OF GEORGIA,
Milledgeville, Ga., November 23, 1864.

This command will move to-morrow morning, as follows: The Twentieth Corps, Brig. Gen. A. S. Williams commanding, at 6 o'clock, toward Sandersville, via Hebron; the Fourteenth Corps, Maj. Gen. J. C. Davis commanding, at 7 o'clock, toward Sandersville, via Black Spring and Long Bridge. When not engaged in destroying railroads the command will endeavor to march about fifteen miles per day. Increased attention must be given to the care of trains, as it is known that the enemy intend to harass our march by means of cavalry. None but the regular organized foraging parties will be allowed to depart from the right and left of the road. The foraging parties will, when necessary, seize wagons to bring their plunder to camp, after which the wagons should be burned. All useless and surplus wagons, ox-teams, &c., which now encumber our trains will be destroyed; and the commander of any brigade is hereby authorized to destroy any wagon that delays the march or opens a gap in the column, no matter to whom it belongs; and, generally, the troops will be distributed along the trains. Advance guards should be strengthened, and attended by a pioneer corps prepared to construct temporary bridges in case of their destruction by the enemy; and wherever any such destruction occurs the commanding officer of the troops present on the spot will deal harshly with the inhabitants near by, to show them it is for their interest not to impede our movements. Should the enemy burn forage and corn on our route houses, barns, and cotton-gins must also be burned to keep them company.

The major-general commanding will for the present accompany the Twentieth Corps.

By command of Maj. Gen. H. W. Slocum:

H. C. RODGERS,
Assistant Adjutant-General.

SPECIAL FIELD ORDERS, No. 23. } HDQRS. 14TH ARMY CORPS,
Milledgeville, Ga., November 23, 1864.

Orders for to-morrow, November 24, 1864: General Carlin will march at 7 a. m., and will cross the bridge over the Oconee River. Further instructions will reach him in the morning. Colonel Buell will move his command and trains in the rear of General Carlin, followed by corps headquarters, the reserve artillery, and artillery ammunition trains, and the First Michigan Engineers. General Morgan will march at 10 a. m., and will follow the Michigan Engineers. General Baird will follow the rear of General Morgan when it shall have passed his camps.

By order of Bvt. Maj. Gen. J. C. Davis:

A. C. McCLURG,
Assistant Adjutant-General and Chief of Staff.

CIRCULAR.] HEADQUARTERS TWENTIETH CORPS,
Milledgeville, Ga., November 23, 1864.

In the future marches, two brigades, with a section of artillery and the pontoon train, will precede the column at least two miles. The corps pioneer battalion will accompany the advance, and take care that roads are properly repaired. In case of unbridged streams the pontoon will be laid with the least possible delay. These advanced brigades will furnish the pontoon trains with necessary guards and assistance. The rear guard will also consist of two brigades and a battery; it will habitually march about a mile in rear of the column. The remaining brigades will cover the trains, each regiment being kept together, but will always halt on hills and bad parts of the road to help forward the trains, until the following regiment comes up. Each division and brigade commander will attend personally to his part of the line, pass from the front to the rear of his command, as often as the nature of the road may require, to see that trains are properly cared for and that his command is doing its duty. There has been, on the part of brigade commanders especially, too great neglect in this particular; neglect hereafter will be taken notice of and reported. In all halts, regiments will be kept near their arms, and not permitted to straggle. We shall probably be attacked by small bodies of cavalry. A small body of infantry, in order, can always easily repulse them; but scattered troops are at the mercy of the enemy. The brigadier-general commanding expects of every officer a strict and constant attention to his duties, and a cheerful co-operation in whatever labor and exposure are in the future of this campaign. There is much labor ahead; but to those who do well, he will endeavor to see that there is an adequate recognition of their services.

By command of Brig. Gen. A. S. Williams:

ROBT. P. DECHERT,
Captain and Acting Assistant Adjutant-General.

ORDERS.] HEADQUARTERS TWENTIETH CORPS,
Milledgeville, Ga., November 23, 1864.

During our onward march a large force of the enemy's cavalry will undoubtedly hover on our line of march, ready to attack every weak point. Division commanders will make special precautions for these attacks. To this end orders heretofore issued will be strictly enforced, especially in reference to destroying unauthorized wagons and keeping the number of pack-mules within the prescribed limits. The purpose sought of shortening our train by the reduction of army wagons is wholly destroyed by the admission into the column of hundreds of other vehicles and pack-animals. Division commanders will at once, through their provost-marshals and inspectors, see that every serviceable animal is taken up for the use of the public wagons, supplying their ammunition trains first. Each division commander will also send twenty serviceable mules to the pontoon train. A report will be made to-day to the chief quartermaster of the corps of the number of serviceable animals found in each division not already in use in the Government wagons. The chief quartermaster will make a systematic distribution of the trains of each division, so that a certain number will always be in charge of an officer of his department. Officers of this department who neglect to report, and who do not faithfully attend to their duties, will be reported at the end of each day's march.

By command of Brig. Gen. A. S. Williams:

ROBT. P. DECHERT,
Captain and Acting Assistant Adjutant-General.

ORDERS.] HEADQUARTERS TWENTIETH CORPS,
Near Gum Creek, November 23, 1864.

This corps will march to-morrow toward Sandersville, as follows: First Division at 6 a. m.; Second Division at 6.30 a. m.; Third Division at 7 a. m. The cavalry will precede the column, starting at 5.30 a. m. All other trains and the artillery will march in the same order as to-day. The advanced and rear guards will be the same as in the march of to-day, the pontoon train accompanying the advance. Brigadier-General Geary will detail one regiment to accompany and assist the corps supply train; also, 100 men to assist the artillery ammunition train. The attention of all commanding officers is called to the orders already published prohibiting straggling from the column and the firing of buildings and unauthorized firing of muskets. General Ward will direct the commander of the rear brigade to destroy, after the passage of all the troops, all bridges on the road.

By command of Brigadier-General Williams:

ROBT. P. DECHERT,
Captain and Acting Assistant Adjutant-General.

ORDERS.] HDQRS. FIRST DIVISION, TWENTIETH CORPS,
Milledgeville, Ga., November 23, 1864.

This division will march to-morrow at 6 a. m. promptly, in the following order: The Third Brigade in advance, and the First Brigade to follow. These leading brigades will be accompanied by a battery and unencumbered by all trains except the pontoon train, which will be guarded by the First Brigade (the second in line of march), and will precede the main column about two miles. The remaining brigade (the Second) will cover the trains of the division, each regiment being kept together, but will halt on hills and bad parts of the road to give assistance to the wagons until the following regiment comes up. All of the troops and the wagons of the division will move to the east side of the Rock Spring road before 7 a. m., as that road will be occupied by the column of the Fourteenth Corps. The pioneer battalion will accompany the advance guard.

By command of Brig. Gen. N. J. Jackson:

GEO. ROBINSON,
First Lieutenant and Acting Assistant Adjutant-General.

HEADQUARTERS TWENTIETH CORPS,
Milledgeville, Ga., November 23, 1864.

Col. WILLIAM HAWLEY,
Commanding Third Wisconsin Volunteers:

COLONEL: The general commanding directs that you rejoin your brigade with your own regiment and the One hundred and seventh New York to-morrow morning by 6 o'clock, as the First Division will move at that hour.

Very respectfully, your obedient servant,

ROBT. P. DECHERT,
Captain and Acting Assistant Adjutant-General.

WASHINGTON, D. C., *November 23, 1864.*

Major-General FOSTER,
Hilton Head, S. C.:

GENERAL: Lieutenant-General Grant directs that the expenditure of ammunition upon Charleston and Fort Sumter be discontinued, except so far as may be necessary to prevent the enemy from establishing new batteries at the latter place. This is not intended to prohibit the throwing of occasional shell into Charleston, if circumstances should require. The object is to economize ordnance stores.

Very respectfully, your obedient servant,

H. W. HALLECK,
Major-General and Chief of Staff.

MORRIS ISLAND, S. C., *November 23, 1864.*

Major-General FOSTER,
Commanding Department of the South:

GENERAL: I send on the steamer Houghton the detachment of cavalry on duty in this district. I thought it better to get them as far as Hilton Head, where they can be consolidated with the remainder of the cavalry. They have no orders to prepare for any expedition, and do not know of any being in contemplation; they must, therefore, receive their orders at Hilton Head. The command will consist of Fifty-sixth New York, the Fifty-fourth and Fifty-fifth Massachusetts (colored). I will have two sections of artillery, in good order. There is no cotton here to make the coffee bags, but I think the men will be able to devise some means of carrying it. As it is important to have some means of communicating with General Sherman after occupying our position, I would like to recommend a man. He is named Smith; is employed as an expressman on the road from Jacksonville to Saint Augustine. He has been a scout for me in Southern Georgia, and can be relied upon. He should be sent for by first boat going to Florida. The provost-marshal at Jacksonville will know who I mean. A merchant here will send by this steamer for the cotton cloth.

Very respectfully, your obedient servant,

JNO. P. HATCH,
Brigadier-General.

HDQRS. DEPARTMENT AND ARMY OF THE TENNESSEE,
Gordon, Ga., November 24, 1864.

Maj. Gen. W. T. SHERMAN,
Commanding Military Division of the Mississippi:

GENERAL: As General Kilpatrick has a squadron of cavalry going from this place to join him, I send Colonel Howard to communicate with you and join me at Irwin's Cross-Roads. Everything is now past this point. Captains Roots and Douglass, with the general cattle herd, have arrived. I have divided the bridge into two sections, and sent them on. General Blair is at Station 15, with his advance at Oconee railroad bridge. General Giles A. Smith drove the enemy from his stockade on this side, and finds some small force, with two or four pieces of artillery. I have dispatches this moment received, which I inclose. You may have to threaten them from the north; the swamps are so difficult that an inferior force may hinder a crossing. I will be obliged to cross everything in the vicinity of Ball's Ferry. Osterhaus must have reached there to-day with his advance; Corse and John E. Smith follow to-morrow morning. My headquarters to-morrow night will be at that point.

Respectfully,

O. O. HOWARD,
Major-General.

[Inclosure.]

HEADQUARTERS SEVENTEENTH ARMY CORPS,
DEPARTMENT AND ARMY OF THE TENNESSEE,
Station 15, November 24, 1864—3.25.

Capt. S. L. TAGGART,
Assistant Adjutant-General:

CAPTAIN: There is no Jackson's Ferry, nor any practicable crossing between Milledgeville and Ball's Ferry. There is no doubt but that the enemy at the river are being re-enforced, and no time should be lost in obtaining possession of the crossing at Ball's Ferry. The Third Division will be here this evening, and I shall move it down to Ball's Ferry early to-morrow morning, and obtain possession of it, if it meets your views. I inclose General Smith's report of the situation at the railroad bridge. General Smith can move his troops along the bank of the river from the railroad bridge to Ball's Ferry.

Very respectfully,

FRANK P. BLAIR, JR.,
Major-General.

[Sub-inclosure.]

RAILROAD BRIDGE, *November 24, 1864—12 m.*

Colonel HICKENLOOPER:

Your communication of this morning is received. I suppose Kirby has joined you before this, and corrected the mistake of his orderly about our being or having troops at Jackson's Ferry. He joined us here, and I suppose his orderly thought it was Jackson's Ferry. The detachment of cavalry were driven from Ball's Ferry last night, with a loss of 10 or 12 killed and wounded; consequently the rebels now hold that point, and are probably intrenching; they had commenced works before Major Tramel drove them away yesterday morning. I am satisfied there is no Jackson's Ferry, nor any practical crossing for ten or fifteen miles above here. I think by a little work we can fix the bank so as to lay two bridges at Ball's Ferry. I have got two pieces of artillery nearly down, near enough the bridge to open. They have two trains on the track, and apparently considerable of a force. We may be able to shell them out; at any rate, we will clear out the trains. It is supposed they were re-enforced last night. A train came in which caused great rejoicing. Their works do not appear very formidable; but the ground this side is so bad we cannot get much down there to operate with. I suppose you will be at Station 15 by the time this reaches you. I would not lose much more time in hunting a crossing above the bridge; I am satisfied nothing will be gained by it. Department order says we will cross above, if practicable. I do not believe it is, though we may be able to do so a short distance above Ball's. There are swamps on the other side, and we must cross where there are roads, or we might find ourselves surrounded by swamps on the other side.

GILES A. SMITH,
Brigadier-General.

SPECIAL FIELD ORDERS, No. 177.

HEADQUARTERS DEPARTMENT AND ARMY OF THE TENNESSEE,
Gordon, Ga., November 24, 1864.

* * * * * * *

II. The mills along the route of this army must not and will not be damaged or destroyed, without positive orders from these headquarters; they are necessary to grind corn and wheat for the use of the army. Corps commanders will instruct their officers and men to this effect, and upon their advance reaching a mill will cause a guard to be immediately placed over it, that it may be preserved in order until taken possession of by a commissary of subsistence, who will run it day and night as long as practicable.

By order of Maj. Gen. O. O. Howard:

SAML. L. TAGGART,
Assistant Adjutant-General.

SPECIAL FIELD ORDERS, No. 178.

HEADQUARTERS DEPARTMENT AND ARMY OF THE TENNESSEE,
Ball's Ferry, Ga., November 24, 1864.

I. As soon as the bridges are laid at Ball's Ferry a double road will be constructed to the first fork beyond. The Fifteenth Corps will move to Irwin's Cross-Roads by direct road; the Seventeenth Corps will take the left fork, and move, via Oconee, to Irwin's Cross-Roads. The cattle belonging to divisions cross with respective divisions; all others will cross in advance of the rear guard of the Seventeenth Corps, and will follow by the right of the Fifteenth Corps, through fields. The train of these headquarters will move with the Fifteenth Corps, in such order as may be hereafter directed.

II. As soon as the crossing of the Oconee is effected Capt. C. B. Reese, chief engineer, will cause an equitable division of the boats, wagons, and appurtenances of the pontoon train, train guard, and engineer regiment to be made between the Fifteenth and Seventeenth Corps. Each corps commander will assume the responsibility of the conduct of his pontoon train, and will see that it is supplied with suitable animals to enable it to move promptly with his command. They are authorized, and are hereby ordered, to burn empty wagons, and use the animals in their pontoon or other teams.

III. The following are the orders for the movements of this army to-morrow: First, Major-General Blair will move his command, with the exception of a sufficient guard for his trains (which will be brought up near this point and parked west of the Augusta wagon road), to Oconee, and completely destroy the railroad from that point east to the point nearest Irwin's Cross-Roads; also, including, if not already done, the railroad bridge over the Oconee and trestle-work this side. Second, Major-General Osterhaus will send from his command a sufficient force to destroy the railroad from the point reached by General Blair to Station No. 13, leaving his trains parked and properly guarded near this point. These headquarters will remain here to-morrow.

By order of Maj. Gen. O. O. Howard:

SAML. L. TAGGART,
Assistant Adjutant-General.

SPECIAL ORDERS, No. 181. } HDQRS. FIFTEENTH ARMY CORPS,
Gordon, Ga., November 24, 1864.

I. General Corse, commanding Fourth Division, will continue his march to Oconee to-morrow morning at 7 a. m., and will encamp near Irwinton, taking position so as to cover the eastern and southern approaches to that place. General John E. Smith, commanding Third Division, will follow the Fourth Division, at 8.30 a. m., making Irwinton his destination also. Upon arriving at that place he will take position covering the western front. The trains must be corralled inside the lines and all measures taken to repel sudden dashes of rebel cavalry. During the march all roads leading south from the Irwinton road must be well guarded, especially while the trains are passing. In the line of march all trains must be in front of the rear brigade of the Third Division.

II. The movement of the corps for to-morrow will be as follows: The First Division, Brigadier-General Woods commanding, will march at 7 a. m., without supply trains, to Lightwood Knot Bridge, on Big Sandy. Upon his arrival there he will secure his position against any assault, and will destroy all means of crossing said creek. The Second Division, Brigadier-General Hazen commanding, will leave its present camp at 7 a. m., for Ball's Ferry, marching on the direct road. The first section pontoon train and engineer troops, in charge of Lieutenant-Colonel Tweeddale, will accompany General Hazen, who will assign them to a position in his column. The supply and reserve ammunition trains of the First Division, escorted by one strong or two small regiments, will follow the Second Division, and, on reaching its camp, will park within the lines of that command, remaining until the First Division arrives at Ball's Ferry. The Third Division, Brigadier-General Smith commanding, on reaching Irwinton to-morrow, will take a defensive position, guarding well all approaches to that place; and on the next day, November 26, will continue his march to Ball's Ferry, moving on the direct road. The Fourth Division, Brigadier-General Corse commanding, will not remain as indicated in paragraph I, Special Orders, No. 181, of date, but will continue its march, on the Ball's Ferry road, to Milton, where General Corse will encamp his command until further orders, guarding well all his approaches to that place. Corps headquarters will be established at Ball's Ferry.

III. It being probable, under late orders from General Sherman, that the corps will be expected to make but light marches during the next few days, and as the different divisions will likely be separated, it is proper to assign to each division a proportion of the artillery; and therefore the chief of artillery of the corps will order the batteries of his command to report as follows: Twelfth Wisconsin Battery to General C. R. Woods, commanding First Division; Battery H, First Illinois Artillery, to General W. B. Hazen, commanding Second Division; Battery B, First Michigan Artillery, to General John E. Smith, commanding Third Division; Battery H, First Missouri Artillery, to General John M. Corse, commanding Fourth Division. With each battery goes the proper share of the reserve ammunition; this distribution to be effected as soon as practicable. The headquarters of the artillery brigade will move with the corps headquarters.

Division commanders will give to the artillery and train assigned to them by this order all the necessary assistance to render that arm of the service as effective as possible. They will, for all logical and practical purposes, consider the batteries a part of their command until further orders.

* * * * * * *

By order of Maj. Gen. P. Joseph Osterhaus:

FREDK. WHITEHEAD,
Assistant Adjutant-General.

SPECIAL ORDERS, No. 236. } HDQRS. THIRD DIV., 15TH ARMY CORPS,
Gordon, Ga., November 24, 1864.

I. This command will move at 8.30 a. m. to-morrow, the 25th instant.

Order of march: First, one regiment Second Brigade as advance guard, followed by one ambulance and one wagon; second, pioneer corps, tool wagons, one ambulance, and one wagon (baggage); third, Battery H, First Illinois Artillery, followed by three wagons; fourth, one regiment Second Brigade, followed by one ambulance and one wagon; fifth, ammunition train; sixth, division headquarters train and provost guard; seventh, Second Brigade train; eighth, First Brigade train; ninth, quartermaster's train; tenth, commissary of subsistence train; eleventh, ambulance corps, except ambulances assigned to regiments and detachments; twelfth, two regiments Second Brigade and one regiment of First Brigade, well deployed, upon the right flank of the division trains; thirteenth, four regiments of First Brigade, rear guard. The wagons of the flanking and rear-guard regiments will go with their respective brigade trains.

By order of Brig. Gen. John E. Smith:

S. M. BUDLONG,
Assistant Adjutant-General.

SPECIAL FIELD ORDERS, No. 14. } HEADQUARTERS FOURTH DIVISION, FIFTEENTH ARMY CORPS,
In the Field, near Gordon, Ga., November 24, 1864.

* * * * * * *

II. In compliance with orders from corps headquarters, this command will move to Irwinton to-morrow, the 25th instant, at 5.30 a. m. The First Brigade has the advance, followed by the battery; the Third Brigade will move in the center; the Second Brigade will bring up the rear, and close on the Third Brigade; the pioneer corps train will follow the advance regiment. The trains will move as follows: First, the pioneer corps train; second, the First Brigade train; third, the Third Brigade train; fourth, the Second Brigade train; fifth, the ordnance train; sixth, the supply train; seventh, the ambulance train. At the forks of the road, the ordnance and other trains in the rear will wait until the brigades and their trains get on the Irwinton road.

By order of Brig. Gen. John M. Corse:

L. CARPER,
Assistant Adjutant-General.

HDQRS. DEPARTMENT AND ARMY OF THE TENNESSEE,
Gordon, Ga., November 24, 1864.

Maj. Gen. F. P. BLAIR, *Commanding Seventeenth Corps:*

GENERAL: Your dispatches received. I think the order of march of yesterday answers your suggestions. You can mass your rear division at Station 15, if you wish, till you secure a practicable point of crossing. If no use can be made of the railroad bridge, it must be destroyed; I will look out for the bridges across Commissioner's Creek in this vicinity, and have them destroyed. Please communicate with me at this point to-night, if possible, and let me know whether you can find any practicable point of crossing except at Ball's Ferry. If none other can be found within a reasonable distance from the railroad, your bridge will be sent there.

Respectfully,

O. O. HOWARD,
Major-General.

P. S.—The bridge train is now here. I want you to take your section and put it in shape as soon as you can. Painful cases of robbery have come to my knowledge, as money stealing, &c.

O. O. H.,
Major-General.

HDQRS. DEPARTMENT AND ARMY OF THE TENNESSEE,
Gordon, Ga., November 24, 1864—9 p. m.

Maj. Gen. F. P. BLAIR, *Commanding Seventeenth Corps:*

GENERAL: Your dispatch is just received. You may move to Ball's Ferry. I think Osterhaus' advance reached here this evening, so that there will be no haste needed. I prefer that you should threaten the Oconee railroad bridge until your bridge is down at some other point. I will join you to-morrow. Everything is up, cattle and all, and your bridge section sent on. The approach of Slocum's column to Sandersville will make the enemy uneasy; it will be near there to-morrow.

Respectfully,

O. O. HOWARD,
Major-General.

HEADQUARTERS SEVENTEENTH ARMY CORPS,
November 24, 1864.

Brig. Gen. M. D. LEGGETT, *Commanding Third Division:*

GENERAL: The major-general commanding directs that you cause two miles of road to be destroyed to-night, from the station toward the town.

Very respectfully, your obedient servant,

C. CADLE, JR.,
Assistant Adjutant-General.

HEADQUARTERS SEVENTEENTH ARMY CORPS,
Station 15, November 24, 1864.

Brig. Gen. M. D. LEGGETT, *Commanding Third Division:*

GENERAL: The major-general commanding directs that you move your command forward to Ball's Ferry at 7 a. m. to-morrow, and obtain possession of the crossing if practicable. If the Fifteenth Corps should strike your column to-morrow and cut your train off, you will have to cut a new road alongside of the present one.

Very respectfully, your obedient servant,

C. CADLE, JR.,
Assistant Adjutant-General.

CIRCULAR.] HDQRS. FOURTH DIVISION, 17TH ARMY CORPS,
In the Field, near Oconee Bridge, Ga., November 24, 1864.

This division will move to-morrow morning at 7 o'clock to Ball's Ferry, via Station 15, excepting the three regiments of the Third Brigade now at this place. General Belknap will relieve the regiments of Colonel Potts' brigade now on duty in front at 6 o'clock to-morrow morning. He will send his horses, mules, and all wheeled vehicles around with the division, and remain with nothing but his infantry. General Belknap will report at these headquarters by 7 o'clock in the morning for further instructions.

By order of Brig. Gen. Giles A. Smith:

CHAS. H. BRUSH,
First Lieutenant and Acting Assistant Adjutant-General.

SPECIAL FIELD ORDERS, } HDQRS. FOURTEENTH ARMY CORPS,
No. 24. } *Milledgeville, Ga., November 24, 1864.*

General Morgan will march out at daylight and push on toward Sandersville, via Long Bridge, passing the camps of General Carlin. Colonel Buell will move immediately in the rear of General Morgan, followed, successively, by the reserve artillery and ammunition train of the corps, under Major Houghtaling, and the First Michigan Engineers. General Carlin will remain in the position he shall occupy to-night until further orders. General Baird will move at daylight upon the road taken by the remainder of the corps, and will pass the camps of General Carlin. He will order Colonel Este's brigade to bring up the rear, with instructions to see first that the city and its suburbs are entirely clear of troops and stragglers, and then to cross and burn the bridge, reporting this to the corps commander, and then joining his division. General Carlin may cross his trains over the river this evening after the bridge is clear of General Kilpatrick's command.

By order of Bvt. Maj. Gen. J. C. Davis:

A. C. McCLURG,
Lieutenant-Colonel and Chief of Staff.

HEADQUARTERS FOURTEENTH ARMY CORPS,
Milledgeville, Ga., November 24, 1864.

Brig. Gen. A. BAIRD,
Commanding Third Division, Fourteenth Army Corps:

The general commanding directs that you remain in your present position to-night, in order to allow General Kilpatrick to move his cavalry and trains across the bridges. The road will be allowed to him at once. Colonel Este will remain in command of the post, and sufficient pickets will be established to insure the safety of your command and the city. Unless further orders should reach you, you will move your command at daylight in the morning, upon the road taken by the remainder of the corps.

I have the honor to be, general, very respectfully, your obedient servant,

A. C. McCLURG,
Assistant Adjutant-General and Chief of Staff.

HEADQUARTERS FOURTEENTH ARMY CORPS,
Milledgeville, Ga., November 24, 1864.

Col. GEORGE P. ESTE,
Comdg. Third Brig., Third Div., Fourteenth Army Corps:

The general commanding directs that you send two companies to picket in advance of the bridge over Fishing Creek, on road leading to Midway, in addition to the picket already there. Patrols should thoroughly secure the safety of the village of Midway. He would also call your attention to the necessity of keeping a close guard upon the bridge over the Oconee, in order to secure it against any attempts of incendiaries.

I have the honor to be, colonel, very respectfully, your obedient servant,

A. C. McCLURG,
Assistant Adjutant-General and Chief of Staff.

ORDERS.] HEADQUARTERS TWENTIETH CORPS,
Near Gum Creek, Ga., November 24, 1864.

This corps will march to-morrow toward Sandersville, as follows: First Division at 6 a. m.; Second Division at 6.30 a. m.; Third Division at 7 a. m. The cavalry will precede the column, starting at 5.30 a. m.

* * * * * * *

By command of Brig. Gen. A. S. Williams:

H. W. PERKINS,
Assistant Adjutant-General.

ORDERS.] HDQRS. FIRST DIVISION, TWENTIETH CORPS,
Near Gum Creek, Ga., November 24, 1864.

This division will march toward Sandersville to-morrow promptly at 6 a. m. (having the advance), in the same order as to-day, and will be governed by the same regulations. The attention of all commanding officers is called to the orders heretofore published prohibiting straggling from the column and the firing of buildings and unauthorized firing of muskets.

By command of Brigadier-General Jackson:

GEO. ROBINSON,
First Lieutenant and Acting Assistant Adjutant-General.

FLAG STEAMER PHILADELPHIA,
Port Royal Harbor, S. C., November 24, 1864.

Maj. Gen. J. G. FOSTER,
Comdg. Dept. of the South, Headquarters Hilton Head:

GENERAL: The following is extracted from a communication by the senior naval officer at Stono:

I have visited the water line in our front, and find the enemy are active. They are repairing the bridge leading on John's Island, and appear to be at work back in the woods on the island. Their pickets have been also strengthened along the water front. Last night one of our picket-boats discovered a large boat of the enemy near the mouth of the Kiawah River. They retreated as soon as discovered. I have pulled up the creek on the north side of Cole's Island to the fort and sounded the creek as I passed up at half tide. I found from five to two and a half fathoms of water all the way; at the mouth in Folly River, thirteen feet. I see nothing to prevent the enemy, with ordinary sagacity, using the creek. Our fort is mounted with small smooth-bore guns, so near a bend in the creek the enemy would be close on them before discovered on a dark night.

My force there now is much weaker than I like, but it is the best I can do, as the work off Charleston requires every steamer I can muster, and more, too. The wear and tear of incessant service keeps so many under repair. The vessels now in Stono are the McDonough (engine not usable, being under repair), a small steamer (Sweetbrier), and a mortar schooner. Another mortar schooner is on the way to Stono.

I am, general, very respectfully, your obedient servant,

J. A. DAHLGREN,
Rear-Admiral, Comdg. South Atlantic Blockading Squadron.

FLAG STEAMER PHILADELPHIA,
Port Royal, November 24, 1864.

General J. G. FOSTER:

GENERAL: I have your note of to-day, and shall certainly and gladly render all the aid in my power to General Sherman. I think I can muster twenty to thirty 12-pounder boat guns, on field carriages, smooth and rifled. Of vessels, I may say two iron-clads, not including those on blockade at Charleston and Wassaw, with a dozen steamers of light draft and moderate draft, but many of them with very light guns.

Very respectfully, your obedient servant,

J. A. DAHLGREN,
Rear-Admiral, Commanding, &c.

SPECIAL ORDERS, No. 182. } HDQRS. FIFTEENTH ARMY CORPS,
Ball's Ferry, November 25, 1864.

The Fourth Division, Brigadier-General Corse commanding, will march from its present camp at 7 a. m. to-morrow, taking the direct road to Ball's Ferry, making that place its destination.

* * * * * * *

By order of Maj. Gen. P. Joseph Osterhaus:

FREDK. WHITEHEAD,
Assistant Adjutant-General.

SPECIAL ORDERS, No. 237. } HDQRS. THIRD DIV., 15th ARMY CORPS,
Irwinton, Ga., November 25, 1864.

I. This command will march at 6.30 a. m. to-morrow, the 26th instant: Order of march: First, one regiment First Brigade as advance guard, followed by one ambulance and one wagon; second, pioneer corps, tool wagons, one ambulance, and one wagon; third, Battery H, First Illinois Light Artillery, followed by three wagons; fourth, one regiment First Brigade, followed by one ambulance and one wagon; fifth, ammunition train; sixth, divison headquarters train and provost guard; seventh, First Brigade train; eighth, Second Brigade train; ninth, quartermaster's train; tenth, commissary of subsistence train; eleventh, ambulance corps, except ambulances assigned to regiments and detachments; twelfth, three regiments First Brigade, well deployed, upon the right flank of the division trains; thirteenth, Second Brigade, rear guard. The regimental wagons of the Second Brigade will go with the brigade train.

By order of Brig. Gen. John E. Smith:

S. M. BUDLONG,
Assistant Adjutant-General.

SPECIAL FIELD ORDERS, No. 15. } HEADQUARTERS FOURTH DIVISION, FIFTEENTH ARMY CORPS,
Milton, Ga., November 25, 1864.

I. This command will move to-morrow, the 26th instant, on the Ball's Ferry road, as follows:

The Third Brigade has the advance, and will move out at 5.30 a. m., two regiments to act as advance guard, and the remainder of the brigade to march in rear of the artillery.

The pioneer corps will join the command at the Oconee River, and take its position in the rear of the second regiment of the Third Brigade. The battery will follow, well closed up.

The Second Brigade will move in the center, on either side of the trains.

The First Brigade will bring up the rear. The trains will move as follows: First, pioneer corps train; second, the Third Brigade train; third, the Second Brigade train; fourth, the First Brigade train; fifth, the ordnance train; sixth, the supply train; seventh, the ambulance train.

Brigade commanders will allow no details to be made for foraging parties until the river is crossed by the command, and they will also have rear guards to each regiment, to prevent straggling.

By order of Brig. Gen. John M. Corse:

L. CARPER,
Assistant Adjutant-General.

HEADQUARTERS FOURTEENTH ARMY CORPS,
Buffalo Creek, Ga., November 25, 1864—3.35 p. m.

Major YATES,
Commanding First Michigan Engineers:

The general commanding directs me to inform you that Colonel Buell, commanding pontoniers, is now bridging Buffalo Creek, and that you will send forward at once to this point a sufficient engineer force to corduroy the road leading over the marsh. The general is of opinion that the work can be easily accomplished this evening and early to-morrow morning.

By command of Bvt. Maj. Gen. J. C. Davis:

JOHN F. SQUIER,
Captain and Aide-de-Camp.

HEADQUARTERS FOURTEENTH ARMY CORPS,
Giles' House, November 25, 1864.

Brig. Gen. J. D. MORGAN,
Commanding Second Division, Fourteenth Army Corps:

The general commanding directs that you move your command at daylight in the morning toward Sandersville.

I have the honor to be, general, very respectfully, your obedient servant,

A. C. McCLURG,
Lieutenant-Colonel and Chief of Staff.

HEADQUARTERS FOURTEENTH ARMY CORPS,
Giles' House, November 25, 1864.

Brig. Gen. A. BAIRD,
Commanding Third Division, Fourteenth Army Corps:

The general commanding directs me to acknowledge the receipt of your note, and directs that you encamp your command for to-night upon the ground on this side of Buffalo Creek, and near this house, and march for Sandersville at daylight to-morrow.

I have the honor to be, very respectfully, your obedient servant,

A. C. McCLURG,
Assistant Adjutant-General and Chief of Staff.

ORDERS.] HEADQUARTERS TWENTIETH CORPS,
Near Sandersville, Ga., November 25, 1864.

This corps will move to-morrow morning to Sandersville, in the same order as in the march of to-day, each division starting at 6 a. m. General Jackson will send two brigades as an advanced guard. Major Reynolds will order a battery of artillery to accompany the advance. The cavalry will precede the column, starting at 5.30 a. m.

By command of Brigadier-General Williams:

H. W. PERKINS,
Assistant Adjutant-General.

ORDERS.] HDQRS. FIRST DIVISION, TWENTIETH CORPS,
Near Sandersville, Ga., November 25, 1864.

This division will move to-morrow morning toward Sandersville, starting at 6 a. m., in the following order: Second Brigade in advance, followed by a battery; Third Brigade to follow, both being advanced guard; the First Brigade in rear, to guard the wagon train of the division. This division will have the advance.

By command of Brig. Gen. N. J. Jackson:

GEO. ROBINSON,
First Lieutenant and Acting Assistant Adjutant-General.

HEADQUARTERS TWENTIETH CORPS,
Beyond Buffalo Creek, Ga., November 25, 1864—4.30 p. m.

Brig. Gen. J. W. GEARY,
Commanding Second Division:

GENERAL: The brigadier-general commanding directs that, in case you do not receive further orders, you will move your division to-morrow morning, at 5 o'clock, to Sandersville.

Very respectfully, your obedient servant,

ROBT. P. DECHERT,
Captain and Acting Assistant Adjutant-General.

HEADQUARTERS TWENTIETH CORPS,
Three miles beyond Buffalo Creek, Ga., November 25, 1864—5 p. m.

Brigadier-General GEARY,
Commanding Second Division:

GENERAL: I am directed by the general commanding to say that the First Division has met the enemy's cavalry at this point. He wishes to inform you that in your camp to-night you will have to extend your own picket-line, so as to protect your own division and trains.

Very respectfully, your obedient servant,

ROBT. P. DECHERT,
Captain and Acting Assistant Adjutant-General.

(Same to General Ward, commanding Third Division.)

Colonel CRAIG,
Division Officer of the Day:

The general commanding division wishes you to have your picketing most thoroughly and carefully performed—pickets thrown well out.

Very respectfully,

W. T. FORBES,
Acting Assistant Adjutant-General.

HEADQUARTERS TWENTIETH CORPS,
Buffalo Creek, Ga., November 25, 1864.

Brig. Gen. W. T. WARD,
Commanding Third Division:

GENERAL: The general commanding directs that you encamp your division to-night just on the east side of Buffalo Creek, covering the bridge. In the absence of further orders, he directs that you march, at an early hour in the morning, to Sandersville. He also directs that you give all needed assistance to the pontoon train, bringing it forward with your division to-morrow morning. The bridge can be taken up as soon as your rear has passed.

Very respectfully, your obedient servant,

H. W. PERKINS,
Lieutenant-Colonel and Assistant Adjutant-General.

CONFIDENTIAL.] HDQRS. DEPARTMENT OF THE SOUTH,
Hilton Head, S. C., November 25, 1864.

Maj. Gen. H. W. HALLECK, U. S. Army:

GENERAL: I have the honor to acknowledge the receipt of your confidential letter of the 13th,* which was received on the 22d, after the sailing of the Arago.

I am preparing to carry out your instructions. Although my disposable force is very small, I think I can do what is required. I shall move on the night of the 28th, and make my attack on the next day. I shall continue to attack whether I succeed in the first attempt or not, and do the enemy as much damage as I can until I see General Sherman.

Very respectfully, your obedient servant,

J. G. FOSTER,
Major-General, Commanding.

HDQRS. DISTRICT OF FLORIDA, DEPT. OF THE SOUTH,
FOURTH SEPARATE BRIGADE,
Jacksonville, Fla., November 25, 1864.

Col. J. C. BEECHER,
Commanding Thirty-fifth U. S. Colored Troops:

COLONEL: You will embark on board the Delaware to-morrow morning at 3 o'clock, with your regiment rationed and equipped, as ordered by verbal order from these headquarters. The companies at Batteries Foster and Hatch and at Yellow Bluff are to accompany you. Orders have been given to the companies at Yellow Bluff to be in readiness. Three companies of the Thirty-fourth U. S. Colored Troops will be placed on the Mary Benton, and the remainder of said regiment on the Delaware. Lieutentant-Colonel Marple will make his headquarters on the Mary Benton. The detachment of Fourth Massachusetts Cavalry will be on the Mary Benton, and the battery of Third New York Light Artillery on the Wyoming. All the troops have been notified in regard to their being in readiness, and you will assume command of such troops as soon as you get on board. Immediately on all being on board, of which you will be notified by a staff officer from these headquarters, you will proceed with all dispatch to the mouth of the river and take on board your steamer the two companies of your regiment at Yellow Bluff, cautioning the commanding officer left there, in the name of the general commanding, to be very vigilant. After receiving these companies on board you will proceed over the bar on the evening tide, and once outside you will keep as near the other steamers as possible, and proceed to Hilton Head, reporting on your arrival there to Maj. Gen. J. G. Foster. Your attention is called to Revised Army Regulations relative to troops on board transports; and in embarking and proceeding down the river you will be as quiet in transit as possible, not allowing any beating of drums or loud talking or huzzaing, keeping the men as much out of sight as possible.

By order of Brig. Gen. E. P. Scammon:

THOMAS J. ROBINSON,
Lieutenant and Acting Assistant Adjutant-General.

---

* See Vol. XXXV, Part II, p. 328.

SPECIAL ORDERS, No. 183. } HDQRS. FIFTEENTH ARMY CORPS, *Ball's Ferry, Ga., November 26, 1864.*

* * * * * * *

II. The corps will move forward this a. m. on the direct road to Irwin's Cross-Roads, as soon as the bridge is completed, in the following order: First, the Fourth Division, with artillery and train; second, the First Division, with artillery and train; third, the Second Division, with artillery and train; fourth, the Third Division, with artillery and train. The train of corps headquarters will move with the Fourth Division.

III. The following are the orders for the movements of the corps to-morrow: Commanding generals of the First and Fourth Divisions will each send two brigades of infantry to the railroad, and have it destroyed thoroughly, from about six miles west until they strike the Seventeenth Army Corps, the brigades of the First Division taking the west and those of the Fourth Division the east end of the task. The destruction of the railroad, particularly of the iron, must be as complete as possible. After having completed the work of destruction, it will not be necessary for the brigades to rejoin their respective divisions here, as they will receive orders to meet them at another point east. The men will carry two days' rations in haversacks. The remaining brigades of the First and Fourth Divisions will remain in their present camps at the cross-roads with the division trains, which must be closely parked and guarded, until further orders. Particular attention is called to the necessity of having all precautionary measures taken to secure the camps and working parties against sudden dashes of rebel cavalry forces in our vicinity. The Second and Third Divisions, Brigadier-Generals Hazen and Smith commanding, will march to this point early to-morrow morning, the Second Division having the advance.

By order of Maj. Gen. P. Joseph Osterhaus:

F. F. WHITEHEAD,
Assistant Adjutant-General.

SPECIAL ORDERS, No. 185. } HDQRS. SECOND DIV., 15TH ARMY CORPS, *Near Ball's Ferry, Ga., November 26, 1864.*

All men of the Eighth Missouri Infantry now on detached service within the division, except those at division headquarters, are hereby relieved, and will report to these headquarters at once. All men of this regiment are, for convenience and efficiency, consolidated into a single company, and are for service attached to the Sixth Missouri Infantry. Capt. John W. White, of the Eighth Missouri Regiment, is assigned to command them. He will, without delay, arm and equip them, making the company as complete for service as possible.

By order of Brig. Gen. W. B. Hazen:

G. LOFLAND,
Captain and Assistant Adjutant-General.

SPECIAL ORDERS, No. 238. } HDQRS. THIRD DIV., 15TH ARMY CORPS, *In the Field, on Ball's Ferry Road, Ga., November 26, 1864.*

I. This command will move forward at 5.30 a. m. to-morrow, the 27th instant, in the following order: First, one regiment First Brigade as advance guard, followed by one ambulance and one wagon; second, pioneer corps, tool wagons, one ambulance, and one wagon (baggage); third, one section Battery B, First Michigan Artillery, followed by wagons belonging to the battery; fourth, ammunition train; fifth, division headquarters train and provost guard; sixth, First Brigade train; seventh, Second Brigade train; eighth, quartermaster's train; ninth, commissary of subsistence train; tenth, ambulance corps, except ambulances assigned to regiments and detachments; eleventh, one section Battery B, First Michigan Artillery; twelfth, two regiments First Brigade, well deployed, upon the right flank of the division trains; thirteenth, two regiments First Brigade, rear guard (the regimental wagons of the flanking and rear guard regiments will go with the brigade trains); fourteenth, the Second Brigade, Bvt. Brig. Gen. Green B. Raum commanding, will act as rear guard to the Fifteenth Army Corps. General Raum will remain with his command upon the west side of the Oconee River until everything belonging to the corps has passed over. He will then cross with his command to the opposite side of the river, where he will halt until the pontoon bridge belonging to the Fifteenth Army Corps has been taken up and the train has started for Irwin's Cross-Roads. He will then follow and rejoin the division. One ambulance will accompany each regiment of the Second Brigade; their regimental wagons will go with the brigade train.

* * * * * * *

By order of Brig. Gen. John E. Smith:

S. M. BUDLONG,
Assistant Adjutant-General.

SPECIAL FIELD ORDERS, No. 16.

HDQRS. FOURTH DIV., 15TH ARMY CORPS,
In the Field, Irwin's Cross-Roads,
November 26, 1864.

The following are the orders for the movements of this division to-morrow: The First and Third Brigades, General Rice and Lieutenant-Colonel Hurlbut commanding, will move at 7 a. m. to the railroad to destroy it. The men will carry two days' rations in haversacks. It will not be necessary for the brigades to rejoin the division here, as they will receive orders to meet them at another point. The Second Brigade, battery, pioneer corps, and all trains will remain in camp until further orders.

By order of Brig. Gen. J. M. Corse:

L. CARPER,
Assistant Adjutant-General.

HDQRS. DEPARTMENT AND ARMY OF THE TENNESSEE,
Irwin's Cross-Roads, November 26, 1864—5.30 p. m.

Maj. Gen. F. P. BLAIR,
Commanding Seventeenth Army Corps:

GENERAL: The major-general commanding directs me to instruct you to commence your march very early to-morrow morning for Oconee, and destroy the railroad to a point opposite Irwin's Cross-Roads. The teams can come down to Irwin's Cross-Roads by the parallel road you have been preparing. I will send a portion of the Fifteenth Corps to do the rest of the work to Station No. 13.

Very respectfully, your obedient servant,

SAML. L. TAGGART,
Assistant Adjutant-General.

SPECIAL ORDERS, No. 290. } HDQRS. SEVENTEENTH ARMY CORPS, *Near Ball's Ferry, Ga., November 26, 1864.*

I. The following are the orders for to-day's movement:

1. Col. G. E. Spencer, commanding First Alabama Cavalry, will immediately upon completion of the bridge cross the river, and, moving to Station No. 14, destroy the remainder of the railroad bridge and trestle-work at and near that point.

2. Brig. Gen. M. D. Leggett, commanding Third Division, will hold his command in readiness to move at 11 o'clock, crossing the river in rear of the First Alabama Cavalry.

3. The Fourth Division, Brig. Gen. Giles A. Smith commanding, will follow the Third Division.

4. The First Division, Maj. Gen. J. A. Mower commanding, will follow the Fourth Division, moving via the left fork through Oconee to Irwin's Cross-Roads.

5. Maj. A. C. Waterhouse will detach a battery to move with each division as heretofore.

II. Upon crossing the river, all unauthorized animals with this command will be seized and appropriated to legitimate purposes.

Capt. J. C. Marven, provost-marshal, is charged with the execution of this order.

III. The Twenty-fifth Wisconsin Volunteers, Lieutenant-Colonel Rusk commanding, is hereby assigned as guard to the section of the bridge train with this corps. Lieutenant-Colonel Rusk will have entire control of the train and the detachment of engineers serving with it, and will use every effort to push it forward as soon as the Seventeenth Corps is across. He will use the engineers in cutting and repairing the roads.

IV. The following are the orders for the movement to-morrow:

1. Maj. Gen. J. A. Mower, commanding First Division, will have the advance, and will move out at 6 a. m., on the road taken this afternoon by the division in advance of him.

2. The train of the Third Division will follow the First Division.

3. Brig. Gen. M. D. Leggett, commanding Third Division, will move out his command at 6 a. m., and, taking the first left-hand road after passing these headquarters, will proceed to Station No. 14, on the railroad, and destroy the road effectually from that point to a point opposite Irwin's Cross-Roads. His train will move as directed in the second section of this order.

4. Brig. Gen. G. A. Smith, commanding Fourth Division, will be prepared to move at 8 o'clock, and will follow the train of the Third Division.

5. Maj. A. C. Waterhouse, commanding Artillery Brigade, will move the artillery as heretofore, except the battery that moves with the Third Division, which will be assigned to the First Division for to-morrow's march.

6. Lieutenant-Colonel Rusk, commanding the Twenty-fifth Wisconsin Volunteers, will move out the bridge train at 7 o'clock a. m., and will follow the Fourth Division.

7. These headquarters will move as heretofore.

Each division commander in this corps will at once send to the pontoon train at the river twenty-six serviceable mules. They will be reported to Capt. B. F. Buzard, commanding pontoon train. If necessary empty wagons will be burned and the mules taken for this purpose. It is essential that the mules should be sent down to-night, in order that the train may move in the morning.

By command of Maj. Gen. F. P. Blair:

C. CADLE, JR.,
Assistant Adjutant-General.

HEADQUARTERS SEVENTEENTH ARMY CORPS,
DEPARTMENT OF THE TENNESSEE,
Near Ball's Ferry, Ga., November 26, 1864.

Brig. Gen. M. D. LEGGETT,
Commanding Third Division:

GENERAL: The major-general commanding directs me to say to you that he will send you orders to-morrow, by the time you reach Station No. 13, as to your camping-ground. The First Alabama Cavalry is encamped to-night near Station No. 14, and will move under your orders to-morrow. You will direct it to move on your left flank, so as to cover your working parties. It will be impossible for you to take any wheels with you to-morrow.

Very respectfully, your obedient servant,

C. CADLE, JR.,
Assistant Adjutant-General.

ORDERS.] HEADQUARTERS LEFT WING, ARMY OF GEORGIA,
Sandersville, Ga., November 26, 1864.

The following movements are ordered, and will commence at an early hour to-morrow morning:

Major-General Davis, commanding Fourteenth Corps, will send two divisions, unencumbered by wagons (except a pontoon train), to Louisville, via Fenn's Bridge, crossing both branches of the Ogeechee River and moving down the east bank of the east branch to Louisville. The divisions, having in charge the trains of the corps, will move to Louisville, via Davisborough.

Brigadier-General Williams, commanding Twentieth Corps, with two divisions, will continue the destruction of the railroad, and send the other division in charge of the trains of the corps to Davisborough as soon as the road is cleared by the Fourteenth Corps.

By command of Major-General Slocum:

H. C. RODGERS,
Assistant Adjutant-General.

SPECIAL FIELD ORDERS, No. 25. } HDQRS. 14TH ARMY CORPS,
Sandersville, Ga., November 26, 1864.

The troops of the corps will move upon Louisville, Ga., to-morrow in the following order: The Second and Third Divisions, under command of Brigadier-General Baird, leaving their general supply and ammunition trains and all other surplus wagons, will march light at daylight, by way of Fenn's Bridge, and thence by such road as General Baird may deem best, with a view of turning Louisville and obtaining possession of that place. The trains of the corps will be under the charge of Brigadier-General Carlin, and will be escorted and guarded by his division by way of Davisborough, for which point they will move at daylight, in the following order: One brigade of the division as advance guard, followed, successively, by the First Division trains; a second brigade of the division; corps headquarters train; reserve artillery and ammunition trains; trains of Third Division; trains of Second Division; and the remaining brigade as rear guard. General Carlin will make such further dispositions as he may deem necessary for the safety of his column. The quartermasters of the Second and Third Divisions will report their trains to-night to Captain Remington, who will have general supervision of all the trains. Colonel Buell will divide his pontoon train, reporting such portion as may be required to General Baird, and moving the remainder in the rear of the ammunition train of the corps and immediately in front of the trains of Third Division. The corps commander will remain with the First Division.

By order of Bvt. Maj. Gen. J. C. Davis:

A. C. McCLURG,
Assistant Adjutant-General and Chief of Staff.

HEADQUARTERS TWENTIETH CORPS,
Station No. 13, Macon and Savannah Railroad,
November 26, 1864—2.45 p. m.

Lieut. Col. H. C. RODGERS,
Assistant Adjutant-General:

COLONEL: The head of my column has reached the railroad without molestation, and are at work destroying it. A small body of the enemy's cavalry left here about half an hour before its occupation by my advance. My headquarters will be here to-night.

Very respectfully, your obedient servant,

A. S. WILLIAMS,
Brigadier-General, Commanding.

ORDERS.] HEADQUARTERS TWENTIETH CORPS,
Tennille Station, Ga., November 26, 1864.

To-morrow the Second Division will continue the destruction of the railroad toward Davisborough, commencing at an early hour. Brigadier-General Jackson, with the First Division, starting at 6 a. m., will proceed by the road on the south side of the railroad to the point where that road crosses the railroad, about seven miles from this point, where he will commence destroying the railroad toward Davisborough. The two batteries now here, with all other vehicles, will accompany the First Division. The pioneer battalion will march with the First Division. The Michigan Engineers will remain with the Second Division and assist in destroying the railroad.

Brigadier-General Ward will take charge of the train, and as soon as the road is opened by the Fourteenth Corps, will march it to Davisborough. He will use his division and the two batteries now with the train as a guard for this purpose.

Major Reynolds, chief of artillery, will direct Captain Winegar and Lieutenant Newkirk, with their batteries, to report to General Ward. The cavalry of Colonel Hughes will precede the column of General Jackson, starting at 5.30 a. m.

By command of Brig. Gen. A. S. Williams:

ROBT. P. DECHERT,
Captain and Acting Assistant Adjutant-General.

ORDERS.] HDQRS. FIRST DIVISION, TWENTIETH ARMY CORPS,
Tennille Station, Ga., November 26, 1864.

The division will move to-morrow at 6 a. m., by the road on the south side of the railroad, to a point where that road crosses the railroad about seven miles from this place, and commence destroying the railroad toward Davisborough. The following will be the order of the march: First, First Brigade; second, a battery; third, Third Brigade; fourth, a battery and the wagons; fifth, Second Brigade.

By order of Brig. Gen. N. J. Jackson:

GEO. ROBINSON,
First Lieutenant and Acting Assistant Adjutant-General.

HDQRS. SECOND DIVISION, TWENTIETH CORPS,
Two miles and a half East of Station No. 13,
November 26, 1864—7 p. m.

Lieut. Col. H. W. PERKINS,
Assistant Adjutant-General, Twentieth Corps:

COLONEL: I have the honor to report that I have encamped my division at this point, having destroyed the railroad one mile and a half east of here.

Very respectfully, your obedient servant,

JNO. W. GEARY,
Brigadier-General, Commanding.

CIRCULAR.] HDQRS. SECOND DIVISION, 20TH ARMY CORPS,
In the Field, Ga., November 26, 1864.

Unless otherwise ordered, the troops will be in readiness to march at 6.30 in the morning. Order of brigades: Third, First, Second.

By command of Brig. Gen. John W. Geary:

W. T. FORBES,
Acting Assistant Adjutant-General.

FLAG STEAMER PHILADELPHIA,
Port Royal Harbor, S. C., November 26, 1864.

Maj. Gen. J. G. FOSTER,
Comdg. Department of the South, Headquarters Hilton Head:

GENERAL: In order to man the howitzers properly for service, I have been obliged to detach the men from the naval battery on Morris Island and supply their places by other men, fewer in number and less experienced. As I have no intimation that you propose to open fire from the island, I suppose this will not be of consequence. If, however, you consider the battery on Morris Island as of more consequence, please to let me know. The squadron is short handed, and a large number of the men entirely inexperienced, so that it is difficult to get up a detached force and organize it decently. I shall, however, be ready at the time named.

I am, general, very respectfully, your obedient servant,

J. A. DAHLGREN,

Rear-Admiral, Commanding South Atlantic Blockading Squadron.

SPECIAL ORDERS, No. 238.

HDQRS. NORTHERN DISTRICT, DEPARTMENT OF THE SOUTH, *Morris Island, S. C., November 26, 1864.*

* * * * * * *

V. The following troops will embark on the night of the 27th instant, for special service, from Folly Island: The Fifty-sixth New York Volunteers, eight companies of the Fifty-fifth Massachusetts Volunteers, five companies of the Fifty-fourth Massachusetts Volunteers, and one section of Battery B, Mesereau's New York artillery; from Morris Island, four companies of the Fifty-fourth Massachusetts Volunteers and one section of Battery B, Mesereau's light battery.

By order of Brig. Gen. J. P. Hatch:

LEONARD B. PERRY,

First Lieut., 55th Massachusetts Vols., and Actg. Asst. Adjt. Gen.

FORT MONROE, VA., *November 26, 1864.*

Maj. T. T. ECKERT:

Steamer Hermann Livingstone arrived at 6 p. m., with 753 exchanged prisoners; lost two on passage; the rest are reported doing well, and improving very fast.

Savannah Daily Morning News of the 23d has following telegraph news:

AUGUSTA, *November 22.*

The Central train, from Davisborough, reports that Milledgeville and Gordon were captured yesterday. The State House, Governor's mansion, and penitentiary were burned. General Wayne holds the Oconee bridge. Nothing from Macon. Passengers from Georgia road report that the train went to Greensborough to-day. The enemy appears to have all gone in the direction of Milledgeville and Macon, but nothing certain is known.

The Augusta Constitutionalist of Monday evening says:

The passengers by the Georgia road train last evening report the Oconee bridge, five miles above Gordon, was burned about noon yesterday by a small party of the enemy's cavalry, who retired, after burning the bridge, to their camp, on the north side of the river. The force of the enemy on the line of this road is estimated at 15,000, advancing slowly and cautiously. Governor of South Carolina has ordered the Reserve Militia of that State to assemble at Hamburg. Governor Brown has issued a proclamation, making a levy en masse of all citizens between the ages of sixteen and fifty-five, to serve for forty days.

Captain Baker, of the Hermann Livingstone, says it was reported, before he left, that Sherman occupied Macon; that there were 2,500 Union prisoners at Macon, on the way to Savannah to be exchanged, but the road being interrupted, they could not be brought through; otherwise, the exchange was going on well.

GEO. D. SHELDON,

Cipher Operator, U. S. Military Telegraph.

WASHINGTON, D. C., *November 27, 1864.*

CHIEFS OF QUARTERMASTER'S,
COMMISSARY, AND ORDNANCE DEPARTMENTS:

Advices just received state that General Sherman had crossed the Oconee River. It is therefore quite certain that he will come out on the Atlantic coast. But as it would not be safe to withdraw stores from Pensacola yet, additional supplies should be immediately prepared for shipment to Hilton Head.

Very respectfully, your obedient servant,

H. W. HALLECK,
Major-General and Chief of Staff.

HDQRS. MILITARY DIVISION OF THE MISSISSIPPI,
In the Field, Tennille Station, Ga., November 27, 1864—10.15 a. m.

Maj. Gen. O. O. HOWARD,
Commanding Army of the Tennessee:

GENERAL: The general commanding is now at this point, and has put in motion two divisions of the Fourteenth Corps, without wagons, from Sandersville, by Fenn's Bridge, to Louisville. The Twentieth Corps, with all the trains of the Left Wing, will move to Louisville by the road passing through Davisborough. He wishes you to move your two corps eastward on the two roads, starting from Irwin's Cross-Roads, as follows: The right column, crossing Ohoopee River, straight for Johnson; thence along the main Savannah road to the point where it intersects the road from Swainsborough, through Canoochee, Bark Camp, and Rocky Creek Church, to Waynesborough. At that point the commanding officer should have instructions to turn toward Station No. 9, in the absence of other orders. The left column to take the road from Irwin's Cross-Roads direct toward Louisville until it intersects the road from Sandersville next south of the railroad, and south of Williamson's Swamp Creek, until abreast of Station No. 10 (or Sebastopol), where it is probable we will cross the Ogeechee. The general proposes to attend this latter column himself.

Please renew your instructions to the detail breaking up the railroad from Oconee to Tennille not to be in too great a hurry, but to do their work well. From this point it can join its proper corps on either of the above-named routes. The general finds it difficult to get information of roads, but those described exist on all our maps.

Very respectfully, your obedient servant,

HENRY HITCHCOCK,
Major and Assistant Adjutant-General.

HDQRS. DEPARTMENT AND ARMY OF THE TENNESSEE,
Irwin's Cross-Roads, Ga., November 27, 1864.

Maj. Gen. W. T. SHERMAN,
Commanding Military Division of the Mississippi:

Your dispatch of this date just received. I suppose the route named would be taken, except that the places of crossing the Ogeechee are different. General Blair will take the Louisville road to the intersection described; General Corse will join his reserve brigade and wagon train at the intersection of Louisville and Jackson roads, after he has destroyed the railroad as far as Station 13; General Osterhaus will meet Corse at Johnson, having found a settlement road leading directly from this place to that point. I will accompany the south column, and communicate with you constantly.

Very respectfully, your obedient servant,

O. O. HOWARD,
Major-General.

HEADQUARTERS MILITARY DIVISION OF THE MISSISSIPPI,
In the Field, Tennille Station, Ga., November 27, 1864—1 p. m.

Major-General HOWARD,
Commanding Army of the Tennessee:

GENERAL: General Corse is now here, and from conversation with him the general-in-chief is in doubt about the destruction of the Oconee and Buffalo Creek railroad bridges, and he wishes to be sure beyond any question that they are destroyed. To this end, you will give the necessary orders that will insure the complete destruction of both, unless they are already destroyed.

I am, general, respectfully, yours, &c.,

L. M. DAYTON,
Aide-de-Camp.

HDQRS. DEPARTMENT AND ARMY OF THE TENNESSEE,
Irwin's Cross-Roads, Ga., November 27, 1864.

Maj. Gen. W. T. SHERMAN,
Commanding Military Division of the Mississippi:

General Blair crossed his cavalry yesterday the first thing, with orders to destroy those bridges. He has not yet been officially informed about it, but has renewed his order to completely destroy them. I think from the fires yesterday seen in that direction there is little doubt that they are consumed. The railroad on the other side is burned from Gordon up to the railroad bridge, but I fear that a part is not as well done as usual, owing to the great difficulty of getting the rail off the longitudinal pieces; but these and the cross-pieces are so much burned that all will have to be gotten up and replaced. In some places, on account of the water, the trestle-work could not be burned. There it was effectually cut down. You may be sure it will cost some labor to repair damages between the Ocmulgee and the Oconee.

Very respectfully, your obedient servant,

O. O. HOWARD,
Major-General.

P. S.—I renewed my order as to the completeness of the work.

SPECIAL FIELD ORDERS, No. 179.

HEADQUARTERS DEPARTMENT AND ARMY OF THE TENNESSEE,
Irwin's Cross-Roads, Ga., November 27, 1864.

* * * * * * *

V. The army will move forward, substantially, as follows: First, Major-General Osterhaus will move his left column of two divisions by the Louisville road and to the intersection of the Johnson road, and thence to Johnson this evening, being careful to clear that intersection at an early hour to-morrow morning. His right column will move by a settlement road directly to Johnson, starting at 7 a. m. to-morrow. Second, Major-General Blair will move on the Louisville road (starting his column at 7 a. m. to-morrow, or earlier at his option) till he reaches the nearest parallel road to the railroad on the south side, south of Williamson's Swamp Creek. He will follow this road till abreast of Station No. 10 (or Sebastopol), where it is probable he will cross the Ogeechee. Major-General Sherman proposes to accompany this column in person. Headquarters will be at Johnson to-morrow night, the train moving with the leading division of the right column. The herds of cattle (other than those belonging to divisions) will follow the right column to Johnson, a regiment from the rear division of which will remain at this point till everything is passed, and will then follow on to Johnson, carefully guarding all roads leading south.

* * * * * * *

By order of Maj. Gen. O. O. Howard:

SAML. L. TAGGART,
Assistant Adjutant-General.

HDQRS. DEPARTMENT AND ARMY OF THE TENNESSEE,
Irwin's Cross-Roads, Ga., November 27, 1864.

Maj. Gen. P. JOS. OSTERHAUS,
Commanding Fifteenth Army Corps:

Major-General Howard directs me to say that General Sherman now requires that as long marches as possible be made each day, to effect which he would advise early starts and as steady marching as the trains and troops can stand and the state of the roads will admit, halting, however, the head of column of each division in time to allow the division train to get up and into park before a late hour in the evening. As there is no enemy to speak of to encounter, it is not essential that the command should be massed each night, but the troops and trains of each division should be concentrated. The divisions should not, however, be allowed to get more than three miles apart.

I am, general, very respectfully, your obedient servant,

SAML. L. TAGGART,
Assistant Adjutant-General.

(Same to Major-General Blair.)

SPECIAL ORDERS, No. 184. } HDQRS. FIFTEENTH ARMY CORPS,
Irwin's Cross-Roads, Ga., November 27, 1864.

* * * * * * *

III. The following are the movements of the corps for this p. m.: The two brigades of the First Division, Brigadier-General Woods commanding, in camp at this place, will, at 1 o'clock, march, with the entire division train, on the Augusta road, to the intersection of the Sandersville and Johnson roads. Brig. Gen. John M. Corse, commanding Fourth Division, will order his train, escorted by the brigade in camp here, to follow the First Division, with a view to the same destination. On arriving at the cross-roads, the troops and trains are to encamp on the south side of the Augusta road, which must be entirely clear for the Seventeenth Corps to-morrow morning. The Third Brigade, First Division, now at work on railroad, will rejoin its division at Irwin's Cross-Roads, the commanding officer of which will report at these headquarters for further instructions. The two brigades of the Fourth Division now at work on railroad will rejoin their division via railroad station No. 13, from whence they will march along the direct Johnson road to the intersection of the Augusta road. These brigades must also be south of the latter road by to-morrow morning.

* * * * * * *

V. The corps will move forward to Johnson at 7 a. m. to-morrow, in the following order: The Fourth Division, Brigadier-General Corse commanding, with trains, will move on the direct road, followed by the First Division, Brigadier-General Woods commanding, with trains, &c. The right column will also move on the direct road from their present camp, the Third Division, Brigadier-General Smith commanding, in advance, accompanied by the pontoon train and trains of department and corps headquarters, to be followed by the Second Division, Brigadier-General Hazen commanding. General Hazen will detail from his command one regiment, which will remain at this point until everything has passed, and will then follow on to Johnson, carefully guarding all roads leading south.

By order of Maj. Gen. P. Joseph Osterhaus:

F. F. WHITEHEAD,
Assistant Adjutant-General.

SPECIAL ORDERS, No. 245. } HDQRS. FIRST DIV., 15TH ARMY CORPS, *Irwin's Cross-Roads, Ga., November 27, 1864.*

The commanding officers of the First and Third Brigades of this division will at once have their commands in readiness to move, the men supplied with two days' rations in their haversacks, and also carrying such tools as are requisite in the destruction of railroads. The teams belonging to these brigades will immediately be driven near the supply train of the division, and there neatly parked, as they will not accompany the brigades. Colonels Williamson and Smith, of the Third and First Brigades, respectively, will report here with their commands forthwith for instructions.

By order of Brig. Gen. C. R. Woods:

FRED. H. WILSON,
Acting Assistant Adjutant-General.

SPECIAL ORDERS, No. 239. } HDQRS. THIRD DIV., 15TH ARMY CORPS, *Near Irwin's Cross-Roads, Ga., November 27, 1864.*

I. This command will move at 7 a. m. to-morrow, the 28th instant, in the following order: First, one regiment Second Brigade, followed by one ambulance and one wagon; second, pioneer corps, tool wagons, one ambulance, and one wagon (baggage); third, Battery B, First Michigan Artillery, followed by the wagons belonging to the battery; fourth, remainder of Second Brigade, each regiment followed by one ambulance and one wagon; fifth, ammunition train; five and a half, Fifteenth Army Corps headquarters train; sixth, division headquarters train and provost guard; seventh, Second Brigade train; eighth, First Brigade train; ninth, quartermaster's train; tenth, commissary of subsistence train; eleventh, ambulance corps, except ambulances assigned to the regiments and detachments; twelfth, three regiments First Brigade, well deployed, upon the right flank of the division trains; thirteenth, two regiments First Brigade, rear guard. The regimental wagons of the flanking and rear-guard regiments will be placed in advance of the rear guard.

By order of Brig. Gen. John E. Smith:

S. M. BUDLONG,
Assistant Adjutant-General.

SPECIAL FIELD ORDERS, No. 17. } HDQRS. FOURTH DIV., 15TH ARMY CORPS,
In the Field, Irwin's Cross-Roads,
November 27, 1864.

The Second Brigade, Col. R. N. Adams commanding, will move on the Augusta road to-day at 2 p. m., in the rear of the First Division, in the following order: One regiment in advance, followed by the battery; one regiment on either side of the trains; and one regiment in the rear. The trains will move as follows: First, the Second Brigade train; second, the First Brigade train; third, the Third Brigade train; fourth, the pioneer corps train; fifth, the ordnance train; sixth, the supply train; seventh, the ambulance corps train. The train should be kept well closed up, to make it as short as possible.

By order of Brig. Gen. John M. Corse:

LEO CARPER,
Assistant Adjutant-General.

SPECIAL FIELD ORDERS, No. 18. } HDQRS. FOURTH DIV., 15TH ARMY CORPS,
In the Field, Widow Peacock's, Ga.,
November 27, 1864.

I. The Second Brigade, Col. R. N. Adams commanding, will move on the Sandersville and Johnson road to-morrow, the 28th instant, at 5.30 a. m., in rear of the First Division, in the following order: One regiment in the advance, followed by the battery; one regiment on either side of the trains; and one regiment in the rear. The trains will move as follows: First, the Second Brigade train; second, the First Brigade train; third, the Third Brigade train; fourth, the pioneer corps train; fifth, the ordnance train; sixth, the supply train; seventh, the ambulance train. The train should be kept well closed up, to make it as short as possible.

By order of Brig. Gen. John M. Corse:

LEO CARPER,
Assistant Adjutant-General.

HEADQUARTERS SEVENTEENTH ARMY CORPS,
November 27, 1864.

Capt. SAMUEL L. TAGGART,
Assistant Adjutant-General, Dept. and Army of the Tennessee:

CAPTAIN: I received notice from General Howard on the morning of the 24th instant that my section of the bridge train was at Gordon, and that he wished me to "put it in shape" as soon as I could. I at once called on my division commanders for animals, and the next morning sent down my provost-marshal with 152 mules, with which he put the train in order, and brought it forward to the river, the number of mules to each wagon having been increased to eight. I received notice last night that another division of the train had been made, which left my section short eighty mules. I would respectfully state that an equitable division of the pontoon train could not possibly leave ten of my wagons without mules or harness, when I had just placed the whole section in an efficient condition. The mules were sent to the bridge at once, and the officer in charge of the bridge directed that as soon as the cattle of the army had crossed he would take up the bridge and move forward to the command. This morning the Fifteenth Army Corps section was taken up, and my section used to cross General John E. Smith's division. My bridge train is still at the river, together with a regiment of this corps as guard, and will probably not be up to the command before to-morrow morning.

Very respectfully, your obedient servant,

FRANK P. BLAIR, JR.,
Major-General.

P. S.—I make this statement because I was informed this morning by one of General Howard's staff that my bridge was taken up before the cattle crossed.

[First indorsement.]

HDQRS. DEPARTMENT AND ARMY OF THE TENNESSEE,
Irwin's Cross-Roads, Ga., November 27, 1864.

Respectfully referred to Capt. C. B. Reese, chief engineer, for investigation and report.

By order of Maj. Gen. O. O. Howard:

SAML. L. TAGGART,
Assistant Adjutant-General.

[Second indorsement.]

HDQRS. DEPARTMENT AND ARMY OF THE TENNESSEE,
OFFICE OF CHIEF ENGINEER,
Irwin's Cross-Roads, Ga., November 27, 1864.

Respectfully referred to Lieut. Col. William Tweeddale, who will report, showing with as much detail as possible, how the division of the transportation, including wagons, mules, and harness, has been made.

C. B. REESE,
Capt. of Engineers, Chief Engineer Dept. and Army of the Tenn.

[Third indorsement.]

HDQRS. FIRST REGIMENT ENGINEERS, MISSOURI VOLS.,
Clifton Crossing, Ga., December 3, 1864.

Respectfully returned with the following report:

The pontoon train previous to its division at Gordon consisted of 330 mules and harness, 28 boat wagons, 12 chess wagons, 2 tool wagons, 1 battery wagon, 1 abutment wagon, 1 forge wagon, 10 army wagons—total, 55—of which there were turned over at Gordon to form the first section, 14 road wagons, 6 chess wagons, 1 tool wagon, 46 mules and harness. At the Oconee River there were turned over to Lieutenant

Lyle, acting assistant quartermaster, by Lieutenant Morton, 80 mules and harness complete; making in first section, 126 mules and harness, 21 wagons and saddles; in second section, 204 mules and harness, 24 pontoon wagons and saddles, 10 army wagons.

W. TWEEDDALE,
Lieut. Col., Comdg. First Regt. Engineers, Missouri Volunteers.

[Fourth indorsement.]

HDQRS. DEPARTMENT AND ARMY OF THE TENNESSEE,
Near Mill Ray, Ga., December 5, 1864.

Respectfully returned to the adjutant-general Department of the Tennessee.

C. B. REESE,
Capt. of Engineers, Chief Engineer Dept. and Army of the Tenn.

[Fifth indorsement.]

HDQRS. DEPARTMENT AND ARMY OF THE TENNESSEE,
Wright's Bridge, Ga., December 6, 1864.

Respectfully returned to Maj. Gen. F. P. Blair, commanding Seventeenth Army Corps, and attention invited to indorsements.

By order of Maj. Gen. O. O. Howard:

SAML. L. TAGGART,
Assistant Adjutant-General.

SPECIAL ORDERS, No. 291. } HDQRS. SEVENTEENTH ARMY CORPS,
Irwin's Cross-Roads, Ga., November 27, 1864.

I. The orders for the movement to-morrow are:

1. Maj. Gen. J. A. Mower, commanding First Division, will have the advance, and will move out on the Louisville road at 6 a. m.

2. Brig. Gen. G. A. Smith, commanding Fourth Division, will be prepared to move at 7 o'clock, and will follow the First Division.

3. Brig. Gen. M. D. Leggett, commanding Third Division, will move at 6 a. m., on the Sandersville road, one mile and a quarter, then turning to the right will move on a road parallel to the one taken by the First and Fourth Divisions.

4. The trains of the First Alabama Cavalry and Ninth Illinois Mounted Infantry will follow the train of the First Division.

5. The pontoon train and its guard, Lieutenant-Colonel Rusk commanding, will move in advance of the Fourth Division.

6. These headquarters will move as heretofore.

* * * * * * *

III. The following assignment of the artillery of this corps is hereby made, and the battery commanders will forthwith report accordingly: Company C, [First] Michigan Artillery, to the First Division; Fifteenth Ohio Battery, to the Third Division; First Minnessota Battery, to the Fourth Division. Division commanders will have perfect military control of the battery assigned to them.

The subsistence and ordnance stores and train of the artillery will be divided among the divisions. Lieut. Col. E. M. Joel, chief quartermaster, will apportion the subsistence train, and Lieut. S. J. Smith, acting ordnance officer, the ordnance train. Maj. A. C. Waterhouse, commanding Artillery Brigade, will relieve all details for guard duty serving with him, and order them to report to their respective commanders.

* * * * * * *

By command of Maj. Gen. F. P. Blair:

C. CADLE, JR.,
Assistant Adjutant-General.

HEADQUARTERS SEVENTEENTH ARMY CORPS,
Irwin's Cross-Roads, Ga., November 27, 1864.

Brig. Gen. M. D. LEGGETT, *Commanding Third Division:*

GENERAL: The major-general commanding directs me to say to you that you may make as long a march to-morrow as you can with comfort to your command, moving parallel to the route of the other divisions and keeping within communicating distance of the general. You may go into camp at such time as will enable your whole command to be in at a reasonable hour in the evening.

Very respectfully, your obedient servant,

C. CADLE, JR.,
Assistant Adjutant-General.

CIRCULAR.] HDQRS. FOURTH DIV., 17TH ARMY CORPS,
Near Irwin's Cross-Roads, Ga., November 27, 1864.

The troops of this division will move to-morrow morning promptly at 7 o'clock. The Third Brigade will have the advance; the artillery and trains in regular order.

By order of Brig. Gen. Giles A. Smith:

CHAS. H. BRUSH,
First Lieutenant and Acting Assistant Adjutant-General.

SPECIAL ORDERS, No. 202. } HDQRS. FOURTEENTH ARMY CORPS,
LEFT WING, ARMY OF GEORGIA,
Sandersville, Ga., November 27, 1864.

I. Surg. W. C. Daniels, U. S. Volunteers, chief surgeon Second Division, Fourteenth Army Corps, is hereby relieved from duty with that division, and will at once report for duty at these headquarters as medical director of the Fourteenth Army Corps.

* * * * * * *

By order of Bvt. Maj. Gen. J. C. Davis:

A. C. McCLURG,
Assistant Adjutant-General and Chief of Staff.

HEADQUARTERS LEFT WING, ARMY OF GEORGIA,
Davisborough, Ga., November 27, 1864.

Brig. Gen. A. S. WILLIAMS, *Commanding Twentieth Corps:*

The major-general commanding directs that you move your wagon train at 6 o'clock to-morrow morning, in charge of one division, on the direct road to Louisville. The two other divisions will continue the destruction of the railroad. The ties must all be taken up and placed in piles in the center of the road, the rails placed thereon, and the whole burned, after which the rails will be twisted. Each brigade will be assigned two miles of the road, which it is expected they will thoroughly destroy. Two companies of the First Michigan Engineers will accompany each brigade, to twist the rails. As soon as each brigade has accomplished its work to the satisfaction of the engineer officer, and in accordance with the orders on that subject, it will move along the road to Spiers Station, or near there. The next day these same divisions will continue the destruction of the road up to the Ogeechee River, and then join the main command on the road to Louisville (east of the river), near Old Town, on Spring Creek.

Very respectfully, &c.,

H. C. RODGERS,
Assistant Adjutant-General.

ORDERS.] HEADQUARTERS TWENTIETH CORPS,
Davisborough, Ga., November 27, 1864.

The entire wagon train of this corps and all of the artillery and cavalry will break camp to-morrow morning and march on the dirt road to Louisville. The Third Division will accompany the trains as escort, General Ward taking charge of the column, and will start it at 6 a. m.

The First and Second Divisions, with the Michigan Engineers and the pioneer battalion, will continue the destruction of the railroad. General Geary will thoroughly destroy the track from where he left off to-day to this point, commencing work at daylight. The First Division, commencing at the same time, will begin at the railroad station and destroy the track eastward. The bridge will not be destroyed until all of the troops have passed there. It is expected that these two divisions will reach Spiers Station to-morrow night. Division commanders will assign the work to their different brigades. It is expected that each brigade will thoroughly destroy two miles of road per day. The iron must be thoroughly destroyed by heating and twisting.

Major Yates, commanding First Michigan Engineers, will direct half of his regiment to accompany and work with the First Division, and the other half with the Second Division—two companies to work with each brigade of infantry.

The route to be traversed by these two divisions being entirely impracticable for wagons all vehicles must accompany the train, which we will probably reach the second night out. All tools, baggage, provisions, &c., must be carried on pack-animals, and but as few of these as possible should be taken.

General Geary, after destroying the track up to this point, will pass the First Division and commence work beyond them.

By command of Brig. Gen. A. S. Williams:

ROBT. P. DECHERT,
Captain and Acting Assistant Adjutant-General.

ORDERS.] HDQRS. FIRST DIVISION, TWENTIETH CORPS,
Davisborough, Ga., November 27, 1864.

The entire wagon train of this division will break camp to-morrow at 6 a. m. and march toward Louisville. The Third Division will accompany and guard the train of the whole corps. This division will commence at daylight to tear up the railroad. The First Brigade will commence at the station, and work eastward; the Second Brigade will commence one mile east of the station, and the Third Brigade two miles east of the station, each working eastward. It is expected that each brigade will thoroughly destroy two miles of the track per day. The rails must be thoroughly destroyed by heating and twisting. Two companies of the Michigan Engineers will work with each brigade. Brigade commanders will throw out sufficient guard to protect themselves while working. No vehicles can be taken with the division, the road being entirely impracticable for wagons. All tools, baggage, and provisions must be carried on pack-animals, and as few of these as possible should be allowed.

By command of Brig. Gen. N. J. Jackson:

GEO. ROBINSON,
First Lieutenant and Acting Assistant Adjutant-General.

FLAG STEAMER PHILADELPHIA,
Port Royal Harbor, November 27, 1864.

Maj. Gen. J. G. FOSTER,
Comdg. Department of the South, Headquarters Hilton Head:

SIR: The horses you are so good as to offer will be very acceptable. The trouble will be for forage, unless an order is given to that effect from the army supplies. I would also ask for drivers or teamsters, having no persons aboard familiar with the care of horses. When the seamen are landed with the howitzers it will be impossible for the vessels to ration them. Can an order be given to your commissariat for rations while ashore?

I am, general, very respectfully, your obedient servant,

J. A. DAHLGREN,
Rear-Admiral, Commanding South Atlantic Blockading Squadron.

HEADQUARTERS DEPARTMENT OF THE SOUTH,
Hilton Head, S. C., November 27, 1864.

Brig. Gen. R. SAXTON, *Commanding District of Beaufort:*

GENERAL: The major-general commanding directs that you have the One hundred and twenty-seventh [New York] Regiment entire, one section of artillery, and all of the Twenty-sixth U. S. Colored Troops that can be spared, prepared to march at an hour's notice. The men will be provided with five days' cooked rations. The rations of coffee, sugar, and salt must be put up in separate bags, which will have to be prepared for the purpose, and carried so as not to be dissolved nor mixed with other provisions. Each man will carry an overcoat, rubber blanket, and one extra pair of socks. All the men must wear shoes. One hundred rounds of ammunition per man will be brought in boxes, of which twenty extra rounds per man will be distributed previous to landing. You will embark the troops on board the steamers John Adams and Philadelphia. After the above-mentioned troops are embarked, transportation will be sent for one-half of the One hundred and second U. S. Colored Troops, which will be in readiness, the men being equipped as directed above.

Very respectfully, your obedient servant,

W. L. M. BURGER,
Assistant Adjutant-General.

SPECIAL ORDERS, No. 239.

HDQRS. NORTHERN DISTRICT, DEPARTMENT OF THE SOUTH,
Morris Island, S. C., November 27, 1864.

I. Capt. A. W. Colwell, Third Rhode Island Artillery, is hereby detailed as chief of artillery during the temporary absence of Capt. J. Lanahan.

By order of Brig. Gen. J. P. Hatch:

LEONARD B. PERRY,
First Lieut., 55th Massachusetts Vols., and Actg. Asst. Adjt. Gen.

HDQRS. DEPARTMENT AND ARMY OF THE TENNESSEE,
Cross-Roads, Opposite Station 11, Ga., November 28, 1864.

Maj. Gen. W. T. SHERMAN,
Commanding Military Division of the Mississippi:

I have the honor to report the Fifteenth Corps, of my command, with the exception of one brigade of General Corse's division (which is at Wrightsville, having gotten off the road and mistaken that place for Johnson), at or near this point. General Woods' division is at the intersection of the roads shown on the map as Johnson, while the other divisions are camped along the road on which they marched. The brigade of General Corse's division at Wrightsville will be brought up, and the corps will move toward No. 9 to-morrow. The roads traveled by the Fifteenth Corps to-day were tolerably good, with a few bad places. Information is received from prisoners taken to-day to the effect that Early's corps has been, or is to be, moved to Millen, and that corps, with Wheeler's cavalry and the militia, will give us a fight at that point.

Very respectfully, your obedient servant,

O. O. HOWARD,
Major General.

HDQRS. DEPARTMENT AND ARMY OF THE TENNESSEE,
Cross-Roads, Opposite Station 11, Ga., November 28, 1864.

Maj. Gen. P. J. OSTERHAUS,
Commanding Fifteenth Army Corps:

Your order already given covers everything. Please so regulate your marches as to effect a crossing of the Ogeechee near Station 9. Department and army cattle will follow your column. Department headquarters will follow your leading division to-morrow.

Very respectfully, your obedient servant,

O. O. HOWARD,
Major-General.

(Copy to Colonel Remick.)

SPECIAL ORDERS, No. 185.

HDQRS. FIFTEENTH ARMY CORPS,
In the Field, Ga., November 28, 1864.

I. The following are the orders for the movement of the corps to-morrow: The brigades of the Fourth Division encamped near this place will march at 5 a. m., following the road taken by the First Division, Brigadier-General Woods commanding. They must clear the cross-roads by 8 a. m. The Third Division, Brigadier-General Smith commanding, will march, accompanied by the pontoon train and train of these headquarters, at 7 a. m., on the Savannah or any other road, to a point south of Sebastopol (railroad depot No. 10), avoiding all roads occupied by the Seventeenth Corps. The Second Division, Brigadier-General Hazen commanding, will leave its present camp at 7.30 a. m., following Third Division. The First Division, Brigadier-General Woods commanding, will move as already instructed. Division commanders will cause their pioneer corps to repair thoroughly and substantially all bad places in the roads traveled, and whenever practicable, will leave a pioneer detail, under an efficient officer, at all such places until their respective trains have passed. Whenever possible, the column will be doubled.

By order of Maj. Gen. P. Joseph Osterhaus:

F. F. WHITEHEAD,
Assistant Adjutant-General.

SPECIAL ORDERS, No. 240. } HDQRS. THIRD DIV., 15TH ARMY CORPS,
Savannah Cross-Roads, Ga., November 28, 1864.

I. This command will move at 7 a. m. to-morrow, the 29th instant, in the following order: First, one regiment First Brigade as advance guard, followed by one ambulance and one wagon; second, pioneer corps, tool wagons, one ambulance, and one wagon (baggage); third, Battery B, First Michigan Artillery, followed by wagons belonging to the battery; fourth, three regiments First Brigade, each followed by one ambulance and one wagon; fifth, ammunition train; sixth, Fifteenth Army Corps headquarters train; seventh, division headquarters train; eighth, First Brigade train; ninth, Second Brigade train; tenth, quartermaster's train; eleventh, commissary of subsistence train; twelfth, ambulance corps, except ambulances assigned to regiments and detachments; thirteenth, pontoon train; fourteenth, one regiment First Brigade and two regiments of Second Brigade, well deployed, upon the right flank of the division trains; fifteenth, two regiments Second Brigade, rear guard. The regimental wagons of the flanking and rear-guard regiments will be placed in advance of the rear guard.

By order of Brig. Gen. John E. Smith:

S. M. BUDLONG,
Assistant Adjutant-General.

HEADQUARTERS FIRST ALABAMA CAVALRY,
November 28, 1864.

Maj. Gen. F. P. BLAIR,
Commanding Seventeenth Army Corps:

GENERAL: I have the honor to report that the headquarters of the Twentieth Corps is to-night at Station No. 11, two miles and a half from my camp, and that the Fifteenth Corps is camped about the same distance on my right. One of my flanking companies to-night found about 10,000 bushels of corn, cribbed and partly shelled, about a mile in front of your headquarters and a mile to the left of the road. I also have the honor, general, to send you herewith Savannah papers of the 23d and 24th instant.

I have the honor to be, your obedient servant,

GEO. E. SPENCER,
Colonel, Commanding.

[Indorsement.]

HEADQUARTERS SEVENTEENTH ARMY CORPS,
New Hope Church, Ga., November 28, 1864.

Respectfully forwarded for the information of the general-in-chief.

I would forward the newspapers but for the fact that I am aware of the general's having seen them.

FRANK P. BLAIR, JR.,
Major-General.

SPECIAL ORDERS, No. 292. } HDQRS. SEVENTEENTH ARMY CORPS,
New Hope Church, Ga., November 28, 1864.

The following are the orders for the movement to-morrow:

1. Brig. Gen. G. A. Smith, commanding Fourth Division, will have the advance, and will move forward, on the road marched on to-day, at 6 a. m.

2. Brig.Gen. M. D. Leggett, commanding Third Division, will move at 6.30 a. m., following the Fourth Division.

3. Maj. Gen. J. A. Mower, commanding First Division, will be prepared to move at 8 a. m., and will follow the Third Division.

4. The pontoon train and its guard, Lieutenant-Colonel Rusk commanding, will move in rear of the Third Division.

5. The trains of the First Alabama Cavalry and Ninth Illinois Mounted Infantry will follow the train of the First Division.

6. The train of the headquarters Military Division of the Mississippi and of these headquarters will follow the advance brigade of the Fourth Division.

* * * * * * *

By command of Maj. Gen. F. P. Blair:

C. CADLE, JR.,
Assistant Adjutant-General.

SPECIAL FIELD ORDERS, No. 160. } HEADQUARTERS THIRD DIVISION,
SEVENTEENTH ARMY CORPS,
In the Field, Ga., November 28, 1864.

I. This command will move at 6.30 a. m. to-morrow. The Second Brigade, Col. R. K. Scott commanding, will have the advance. Artillery and trains as heretofore.

By order of Brig. Gen. M. D. Leggett:

J. C. DOUGLASS,
Assistant Adjutant-General.

GENERAL ORDERS, No. 26. } HDQRS. 4TH DIV., 17TH ARMY CORPS,
In the Field, near Irwin's Cross-Roads,
November 28, 1864.

Hereafter, until further orders, unless otherwise specially directed, the following will be the order of march for the troops and trains of this division: First, pioneer corps; second, one brigade, except its last regiment; third, First Minnesota Light Artillery; fourth, last regiment of advance brigade; Fifth, teams of advance brigade; sixth, Fourth Division headquarters train and teams of pioneer corps;

seventh, ordnance train; eighth, the remaining brigade, except its last regiment; ninth, teams of the rear brigade; tenth, remaining regiment of rear brigade, as rear guard to the train; its commanding officers will in all cases assist the train over all bad places. The ambulance and one team to each regiment will follow their respective regiments as heretofore.

By order of Brig. Gen. Giles A. Smith:

CHAS. H. BRUSH,
Acting Assistant Adjutant-General.

NOVEMBER 28, 1864.

General GEARY,
Commanding, &c.:

GENERAL: The general commanding directs that, as soon as you have completed the destruction of the railroad to Davisborough, you march your division to Spiers Station, camping there to-night.

Very respectfully, your obedient servant,

H. W. PERKINS,
Assistant Adjutant-General.

CONFIDENTIAL.] QUARTERMASTER-GENERAL'S OFFICE,
Washington, D. C., November 28, 1864.

Bvt. Brig. Gen. STEWART VAN VLIET,
Quartermaster, New York:

GENERAL: You will send to Hilton Head 150 barrels of salt for use of the animals of General Sherman's army, unless you have good reasons to know that there is already a sufficient supply at that depot. General Sherman appears to be heading for the Atlantic coast, and orders have been given to send more supplies to Hilton Head. I direct Col. S. L. Brown to-day to commence shipping, in light-draught vessels, to Hilton Head 30,000 rations of grain and the same of hay daily until further orders, or until the receipt of certain intelligence of the point which will be made his new base of operations. The stores sent to Pensacola will not be withdrawn until such information is received. I inclose an unsealed letter to General Foster, commanding Department of the South, and also one for Maj. C. W. Thomas, chief quartermaster of that department, which, after reading, you will forward to their destination by first steamer.

I am, respectfully, your obedient servant,

M. C. MEIGS,
Quartermaster-General, Brevet Major-General.

[Inclosure No. 1.]

CONFIDENTIAL.] QUARTERMASTER-GENERAL'S OFFICE,
Washington City, November 28, 1864.

Major-General FOSTER,
Commanding Department of the South, Hilton Head:

(Through General Van Vliet, Quartermaster's Department, New York.)

GENERAL: Supplies of clothing and of quartermaster's stores of forage, grain, and hay have been shipped to Hilton Head and also to

Pensacola to meet General Sherman, as, according to the best information received, he appears now to have crossed the Oconee and to be heading toward the Atlantic coast. Orders are to-day issued to the forage officer in New York to ship daily until further orders, or definite information shows a change to be necessary, 30,000 rations of grain and the same of hay. All this is ordered to the chief quartermaster of Department of the South, Maj. C. W. Thomas, who is instructed to take charge of it, and, subject to your instructions, forward it to such point on the coast as may ultimately prove most convenient for General Sherman. The supplies at Pensacola are intended for him; and if he should arrive at any point within your department and open communication with you, he should be informed that they are at that place, and that such orders as he may send there will be obeyed. Captain Whittemore, assistant quartermaster, has gone to Pensacola in charge of the supplies sent to that place. Among the first shipments, which were equally divided between Pensacola and Hilton Head, were clothing to refit 30,000 men and a supply of harness, wagons, ambulances, portable barges, &c. The Subsistence and Ordnance Departments will doubtless inform you of the supplies which they have sent forward. I have ordered to-day some salt sent to Hilton Head for the horses and mules, which, after a long interior march, will feel the want of it.

I am, respectfully, your obedient servant,

M. C. MEIGS,
Quartermaster-General, Brevet Major-General.

[Inclosure No. 2.]

CONFIDENTIAL.] QUARTERMASTER-GENERAL'S OFFICE,
Washington, D. C., November 28, 1864.

Maj. C. W. THOMAS,
Chief Quartermaster Department of the South, Hilton Head:
(Through General Van Vliet, Quartermaster's Department, New York.)

MAJOR: Supplies of clothing, forage, subsistence, ammunition, and quartermaster's stores have been shipped to Hilton Head, as a rendezvous, to wait the movements of General Sherman's army, for some weeks past. To-day orders for daily shipment of 30,000 rations each of hay and grain have gone forward. I have also ordered 150 barrels of salt for the animals to be shipped to you. You will take charge of all these stores, and hold them in readiness for transportation to whatever point General Sherman may make his base. You will take the instructions of General Foster on this subject. I have written to him fully this day. Supplies of clothing, forage, and quartermaster's stores have gone to Pensacola. The quantity heretofore shipped to each post—Port Royal and Pensacola—was estimated to be sufficient for the immediate wants of an army 15,000 strong at each place. Should General Sherman establish his base on the Atlantic within the Department of the South, the fact that supplies are at Pensacola waiting his orders should be made known to him, and, if he directs, a fast-sailing steamer should go to Pensacola to order them to such post as he may designate. Captain Whittemore, assistant quartermaster, has sailed for Pensacola, and will remain there in charge of the supplies specially intended for General Sherman until he receives other orders.

I am, respectfully, your obedient servant,

M. C. MEIGS,
Quartermaster-General, Brevet Major-General.

CONFIDENTIAL.] QUARTERMASTER-GENERAL'S OFFICE,
Washington City, November 28, 1864.

Col. S. L. BROWN,
Forage Division, No. 66 Cedar Street, New York:

COLONEL: General Sherman appears to be heading toward the Atlantic. If he strikes that coast, Hilton Head will be the rendezvous for all supply vessels until he establishes his base of operations. In addition to former orders, you will ship daily until further orders, or until definite information of General Sherman's route makes a change evidently necessary, 30,000 rations of grain and 30,000 rations of hay (30,000 each) for the use of his army. These should be shipped in as light-draught vessels as possible, and ordered to the chief quartermaster of the Department of the South, who will direct their future movements upon such official information as he may receive.

I am, very respectfully, your obedient servant,

M. C. MEIGS,
Quartermaster-General, Brevet Major-General.

HEADQUARTERS DEPARTMENT OF THE SOUTH,
Hilton Head, S. C., November 28, 1864.

Rear-Admiral J. A. DAHLGREN,
Commanding South Atlantic Blockading Squadron:

ADMIRAL: I have just received your favor of the 27th instant. Horses will be supplied for the naval howitzers from the quartermaster's department, with a proper amount of forage. Teamsters will also be furnished by the quartermaster of the department. The chief commissary will issue rations to the detachment from the navy while they are on shore, and, if necessary, receipts can be passed at some future time.

Very respectfully, your obedient servant,

J. G. FOSTER,
Major-General, Commanding.

GENERAL SLOCUM'S HEADQUARTERS,
Near Louisville, Ga., November 29, 1864.

Major-General SHERMAN,
Commanding Military Division of the Mississippi:

GENERAL: I have the honor to report the safe arrival of General Kilpatrick with his command on Big Creek, three miles from Louisville, at 10 a. m. to-day. The particulars of the expedition I will give you more fully in person some time to-morrow.

We burned the bridge, about 120 feet long, over Brier Creek, four miles north of Waynesborough, during Saturday night. Captured at Waynesborough a train of 8 box and 3 platform cars and a locomotive, all of which were burned, the cargo, hogs for Augusta, turned loose.

We encamped Sunday night on the railroad, toward Millen, building fires for nearly two miles. The prisoners had been moved to a point 100 miles south of Savannah, on the Gulf railroad, so reported by one of our escaped prisoners who joined us. Augusta papers of 25th report Bragg at that place (people say Longstreet also) and Hardee at Millen. Wheeler met us at Sylvan Grove at 11 p. m. on Saturday, and kept up a most persistent attack from that time until last evening, when we handsomely repulsed his charge. We lost yesterday over 100.

The enemy having no artillery, and charging our barricades mounted, and being repulsed with artillery and Spencer rifles, could not have gone unhurt. The Augusta papers say you, not being able to whip Hood, were compelled to retreat in this way. Our route was across Long Bridge, Factory Gibson, Sylvan Grove, Woodburn, Waynesborough, back across Rocky Creek, Rocky Creek Church, Buck Head Creek, and Louisville. Country generally very open; forage in abundance.

Very respectfully,

JOS. C. AUDENRIED,
Captain, U. S. Army, and Aide-de-Camp.

HDQRS. DEPARTMENT AND ARMY OF THE TENNESSEE,
Cross-Roads, opposite Station 10, November 29, 1864.

Maj. Gen. W. T. SHERMAN,
Commanding Military Division of the Mississippi:

GENERAL: I have the honor to report my command in camp to-night, as follows, viz: The Seventeenth Corps on Rocky Creek, ten or twelve miles from the river; the First Division, Fifteenth Corps, at Summerville, where the road from 95 intersects the Savannah road; my headquarters are at cross-roads, opposite Station 10, some five miles west of General Woods; the remainder of the Fifteenth Corps is at Sutherland's Mill, on Battle Creek, on Savannah road. I inclose copy of order for the movement to-morrow. I have directed General Blair to cross the river either at Station No. 10 or 95, as may be most practicable, and, unless orders are received to the contrary, to concentrate with the Fifteenth Corps near Herndon (or Station 9), not knowing but that you may have other directions.

Respectfully,

O. O. HOWARD,
Major-General.

[Inclosure.]

SPECIAL FIELD ORDERS, No. 180.

HDQRS. DEPT. AND ARMY OF THE TENN.,
Cross-Roads, opposite Station 10, Ga., November 29, 1864.

1. Major-General Blair, commanding Seventeenth Army Corps, will cross his command over the Ogeechee at Station No. 10 or Station No. 95, as may be most practicable, and, after crossing, will, unless otherwise directed, concentrate with the Fifteenth Corps near Herndon.

2. Major-General Osterhaus, commanding Fifteenth Army Corps, will concentrate his command at Station No. 9 (as indicated on the map) as rapidly as possible.

The train proper of these headquarters will move with General Woods' division (First Division, Fifteenth Army Corps), and the supply train of same, in charge of Colonel Conklin, chief quartermaster, will be placed at the head of the supply train of General John E. Smith's division (Third Division, Fifteenth Army Corps).

The herds of cattle will continue to move with the Fifteenth Corps.

By order of Maj. Gen. O. O. Howard:

SAML. L. TAGGART,
Assistant Adjutant-General.

HEADQUARTERS MILITARY DIVISION OF THE MISSISSIPPI,
In the Field, November 29, 1864.

Maj. Gen. O. O. HOWARD,
Commanding Right Wing, Army of Georgia:

GENERAL: The general commanding directs me to acknowledge receipt of your dispatch of this evening, and to say that your order of movement for to-morrow is all right, except that he does not wish the Fifteenth Corps to cross the Ogeechee until he learns positively where the enemy propose to resist us. We find her that a brigade of the Twentieth Corps is in possession of the Ogeechee railroad bridge, having broken the railroad all the way up from Station 15. He has also learned that Kilpatrick was engaged in fighting the enemy yesterday north and east of Louisville, and rumors of intention to offer us battle about Millen reach us. To-morrow the Seventeenth Corps will cross at 95; and as soon as the commanding general can learn definitely the state of affairs north and east of the Ogeechee, he will give more definite orders concerning the Fifteenth Corps. In the meantime, he wishes that corps to be kept well in hand, ready to move rapidly to turn the position at Millen by crossing at Paramore's Hill.

Should you fail to receive orders, always move toward Savannah, keeping abreast or ahead of the Seventeenth Corps, crossing the Ogeechee only when necessary to meet an enemy. There is a rumor of Longstreet and his corps coming to Augusta; but the general thinks Longstreet is there in person with fragments of troops collected from Charleston and North Carolina, but that the corps remains still in Virginia. The probabilities are that the Seventeenth Corps will move substantially along the railroad, whilst the Left Wing, with Kilpatrick's cavalry, will move about eight or ten miles to the north of Millen, keeping up the feint toward Augusta as long as we deem it necessary.

Respectfully, your obedient servant,

H. HITCHCOCK,
Major and Assistant Adjutant-General.

SPECIAL FIELD ORDERS, No. —.

HEADQUARTERS FIRST DIVISION,
FIFTEENTH ARMY CORPS,
Near Summertown, Ga., November 29, 1864.

At 8 o'clock to-morrow morning this division will resume its march in the direction of Summertown, as follows: First Brigade; pioneers; Twelfth Wisconsin Battery; headquarters train First Division; ambulance train; ten wagons infantry ammunition; train of the First, Second, and Third Brigades; supply train; ordnance train; Third Brigade; the Second Brigade will march by regiments on the right flank of the train, covering the ambulance and ordnance trains inclusive. Two companies of the rear regiment of the Third Brigade will be sent forward at the head of column before starting, for provost duty. Colonel Smith, commanding First Brigade, will send forward his advance regiment at 7 a. m., supplied with axes and instructed to corduroy the road, beginning at the first swampy crossing in front of the camp.

By order of Brig. Gen. Charles R. Woods:

FRED. H. WILSON,
Acting Assistant Adjutant-General.

HEADQUARTERS LEFT WING, ARMY OF GEORGIA,
Near Big Creek, November 29, 1864.

Maj. Gen. J. C. DAVIS,
Commanding Fourteenth Corps:

GENERAL: The major-general commanding desires me to say that General Williams with two divisions has been ordered up here, and will cross on the bridges we now have. The approaches below are very bad. He cannot possibly reach here until to-morrow evening. The general desires you to send one division (unencumbered with wagons) and one battery to Sebastopol, to communicate with General Sherman and uncover the crossing for the Army of the Tennessee, the command to start at daylight to-morrow. The general thinks Kilpatrick should send a brigade of cavalry with this division, and desires you to communicate with him on the subject. A pontoon bridge has [been] thrown over Big Creek, and the other streams are reported as fordable.

Very respectfully, your obedient servant,

H. C. RODGERS,
Assistant Adjutant-General.

HEADQUARTERS FOURTEENTH ARMY CORPS,
Louisville, Ga., November 29, 1864.

Brig. Gen. W. P. CARLIN,
Commanding First Division, Fourteenth Army Corps:

Inclosed you will find an official copy of a note* of this date just received from Major-General Slocum. The general commanding directs that, in accordance with its instructions, you march at daylight to-morrow with your division upon Sebastopol, leaving your general supply and ammunition trains. General Kilpatrick has been requested to order a brigade of cavalry to report to you.

I have the honor to be, general, very respectfully, your obedient servant,

A. C. McCLURG,
Assistant Adjutant-General and Chief of Staff.

HEADQUARTERS FOURTEENTH ARMY CORPS,
Louisville, Ga., November 29, 1864.

Brig. Gen. W. P. CARLIN,
Commanding First Division, Fourteenth Army Corps:

The general commanding desires me to inform you that the brigade of cavalry will not be sent to accompany you as intended; but an attempt will probably be made in the morning to engage Wheeler in our front.

I have the honor to be, general, very respectfully, your obedient servant,

A. C. McCLURG,
Assistant Adjutant-General and Chief of Staff.

---

* See next, *ante*.

SPECIAL ORDERS, } HDQRS. SECOND DIV., 14TH ARMY CORPS,
No. 113. } *Louisville, Ga., November 29, 1864.*

I. Surg. Louis Watson, Sixteenth Illinois Infantry, is hereby detailed as surgeon-in-chief of this division. He will report to Surgeon Daniels, U. S. Volunteers, chief medical director Fourteenth Army Corps, for orders, forthwith.

By order of Brig. Gen. James D. Morgan:

T. WISEMAN,
Captain and Assistant Adjutant-General.

HEADQUARTERS FOURTEENTH ARMY CORPS,
Louisville, Ga., November 29, 1864.

Brig. Gen. A. BAIRD,
Commanding Third Division, Fourteenth Army Corps:

The general commanding directs that you send a brigade, with the least possible delay, to the bridge over Deep Creek, on the Waynesborough road, to relieve and support General Kilpatrick. They will have instructions to repair the bridge at once.

Very respectfully, your obedient servant,

A. C. McCLURG,
Lieutenant-Colonel and Chief of Staff.

HEADQUARTERS TWENTIETH CORPS,
Bethany Camp-Ground, five miles west of Ogeechee River,
November 29, 1864—2 p. m.

Lieut. Col. H. C. RODGERS,
Assistant Adjutant-General:

COLONEL: I have destroyed the railroad to within three miles of the river and [am] still at work at it; will have it finished to-night. All of the road and railroad bridges over the Ogeechee have been destroyed by the enemy, so there is no way of crossing without the pontoons. I will encamp these two divisions on the west side of the river to-night, and await orders from you. There is no road up the river which crosses the railroad nearer the river than this point, the intermediate country being impassable. My camps to-night will be at the Ragford Bridge, the first one above the railroad. The road forks at this point—one leading to Old Town, and the other to the Ragford Bridge. The citizens report Ragford's crossing as the best place to lay the pontoon bridge, the crossing on the Old Town road being very swampy on each side of the river, requiring trestle approaches.

Very respectfully, your obedient servant,

A. S. WILLIAMS,
Brigadier-General, Commanding.

HEADQUARTERS LEFT WING, ARMY OF GEORGIA,
Camp on Big Creek, near Louisville, Ga.,
November 29, 1864—6 p. m.

Brig. Gen. A. S. WILLIAMS,
Commanding Twentieth Corps:

GENERAL: I am directed by the major-general commanding to say that you will have to move your two divisions up the west side of the

Ogeechee to Louisville, and join us at this point. For this purpose, our bridges over the Ogeechee and Rocky Comfort Creek will be left standing to-morrow, and we shall await here until you arrive. The general desires you to take an early start and get here as soon as possible.

Very respectfully, your obedient servant,

H. C. RODGERS,
Assistant Adjutant-General.

P. S.—Please send the inclosed dispatch* to General Sherman, who must be near you in the direction of Sebastopol.

Very respectfully,

H. C. RODGERS.

HEADQUARTERS TWENTIETH CORPS,
Spiers Station, Ga., November 29, 1864.

Brig. Gen. J. W. GEARY,
Commanding Second Division:

GENERAL: The general commanding directs that you follow with your troops on the road along the railroad towards the Ogeechee River, bringing the Michigan Engineers with you.

Very respectfully, your obedient servant,

H. W. PERKINS,
Lieutenant-Colonel and Assistant Adjutant-General.

HDQRS. SECOND DIVISION, TWENTIETH ARMY CORPS,
Six miles east of Station No. 11, November 29, 1864—7 p. m.

Lieut. Col. H. W. PERKINS,
Assistant Adjutant-General, Twentieth Army Corps:

COLONEL: I have the honor to report that I have reached this point, and am encamping my troops on the east side of a creek which crosses the road. I have marched twenty-one miles to-day, from Davisborough, and my troops are much wearied. I learn that the troops with you are encamped two or three miles ahead. I will move forward early in the morning. Yesterday my two brigades, with the Michigan Engineers, thoroughly destroyed a little more than five miles of railroad west of Davisborough, to effect which part of my command marched in all during the day fifteen miles. We returned to Davisborough, and encamped there after 8 p. m., finding it out of the question to march to Spiers Station. During the afternoon my troops, in addition to the work on the railroad, had considerable skirmishing with a force of rebel cavalry, part of Ferguson's brigade, which, moving down from Sandersville to annoy the flank of the Seventeenth Corps, attempted to cross the railroad at a point where I had but few men. The only casualties in my command were one man slightly wounded and five or six captured.

I am, colonel, very respectfully, your obedient servant,

JNO. W. GEARY,
Brigadier-General, Commanding.

---

*See 7 p. m., p. 574.

HEADQUARTERS TWENTIETH CORPS,
Near Ogeechee River, Ga., November 29, 1864.

Brigadier-General GEARY,
Commanding Second Division:

GENERAL: The general commanding directs me to say that he wishes you to start with your command to-morrow morning as soon as possible after daylight. He wishes the Michigan Engineers marched at the head of your column, so as to reach here as soon as possible.

Very respectfully, your obedient servant,

ROBT. P. DECHERT,
Captain and Acting Assistant Adjutant-General.

HEADQUARTERS FOURTEENTH ARMY CORPS,
Louisville, Ga., November 29, 1864.

Brigadier-General KILPATRICK,
Commanding Cavalry:

Inclosed you will find a copy of a note just received from Major-General Slocum. General Carlin's division has been ordered out, in accordance with it,* at daylight to-morrow. General Davis directs me to request you to order a brigade of cavalry to report to General Carlin at his headquarters, about a mile from town, on the direct road to your camp.

I have the honor to be, general, very respectfully, your obedient servant,

A. C. McCLURG,
Assistant Adjutant-General and Chief of Staff.

HDQRS. DEPARTMENT AND ARMY OF THE TENNESSEE,
Opposite No. 9½, Ga., November 30, 1864.

Maj. HENRY HITCHCOCK,
Assistant Adjutant-General, Mil. Div. of the Mississippi:

MAJOR: General Howard directs me to say, for the information of the general-in-chief, that Captain Duncan, commanding scouts, has just returned to camp, and reports he was to-day within three miles of Millen, on this side of the river, and found no enemy. He sent a sergeant and three men across the river into Millen, and expects to hear from them to-morrow morning. He captured a lieutenant on General Humes' staff, who says he left General Wheeler to-day, about six miles north of Station No. 9. Not much information could be got from him. Says his intention was to visit Southern Alabama on important private business, but lives in Northern Alabama. Was told by General Wheeler that he would find no enemy on this side of the river; that they had all crossed. Speaks quite confidently, and says he presumes we will not meet with any very great opposition before reaching the coast, where he says it is supposed we are going, but there they will have a large force to oppose us. Thinks their policy is to evacuate Richmond for the purpose of capturing Sherman; believes that when they fight us Lee will in person command the army. The general thinks he is a bearer of dispatches to Hood, but none have yet been found on him.

Very respectfully, your obedient servant,

SAML. L. TAGGART,
Assistant Adjutant-General.

---

* See Rodgers to Davis, p. 575.

SPECIAL FIELD ORDERS, No. 181.

HEADQUARTERS DEPARTMENT AND ARMY OF THE TENNESSEE,
Opposite Station No. 9½, Ga., November 30, 1864.

I. The following are the orders for the movements of this army to-morrow: First, Major-General Blair will move his command toward Millen, effectually destroying the railroad en route from Station 9½ or 95, communicating frequently with the column south of the Ogeechee. Second, Major-General Osterhaus will move his command at 7 o'clock, two columns of two divisions each—one column following the Savannah road near the river, reaching to-morrow night a point opposite Station 8 (intersection of Jones' Ferry and Savannah road), and the other pursuing any parallel route south, keeping as near as possible to the contiguous column, and will halt to-morrow night as nearly due south of Station No. 9 as possible. To facilitate communication the heads of the columns should be on the Jones' [Ferry] road. The train proper of these headquarters will follow the ammunition train of the leading division of the left column, and the supply train will move in advance of the supply train of the same division. Headquarters to-morrow night will be at or near the intersection of Savannah and Jones' Ferry road, nearly opposite and south of Station No. 8.

II. The attention of corps commanders and commanders of unattached regiments and detachments is called to the irregularities existing in foraging, and the manner in which this privilege is often abused. It is noticed that many men not belonging to proper foraging parties are allowed to straggle from the ranks and forage for themselves without any authority whatever. It is by such men the greater part of the pillaging is done and depredations committed, of which there is so much complaint. Officers in charge of foraging parties must be continually instructed to keep their men well in hand, never allowing them to precede the advance guard of the column, and to use more discretion in taking from the poor, being careful to leave them sufficient for their immediate subsistence. It is also noticed that the number of mounted men is very largely increasing, and that the ranks are correspondingly diminished. Means will be at once taken to check this growing evil. The number of mounted foragers to each brigade should be limited and regulated in orders, which, if not done, mounted foragers will be no longer allowed. We are now nearing the enemy, and foraging parties should be cautioned against preceding the advance from the column.

By order of Maj. Gen. O. O. Howard:

SAML. L. TAGGART,
Assistant Adjutant-General.

SPECIAL ORDERS, No. 186.

HDQRS. FIFTEENTH ARMY CORPS,
Pine Lodge, Ga., November 30, 1864.

I. The movements of the corps for to-morrow will be as follows: The First Division, Brigadier-General Woods commanding, will leave its present camp, accompanied by train of these headquarters, at 7 a. m., being the advance of the left column, continuing his march on the Savannah road to the intersection of the Jones' Ferry road leading to railroad station No. 8, where he will encamp. Lieutenant-Colonel Fort, chief quartermaster Fifteenth Army Corps, will cause the pontoon train to be brought forward, and will close the same on First Division train. The Fourth Division, Brigadier-General Corse commanding, will follow the route of the First Division, with a view to the same destination.

II. The Second Division, Brigadier-General Hazen commanding, having the advance of the right column, will leave his present camp at Summerville at 7 a. m., taking the old Savannah road and marching on it to the intersection of the Jones' Ferry road leading to Station No. 8, about six miles southwest of the cross-roads, to which the left column is ordered. The Third Division, Brigadier-General Smith commanding, will follow the Second Division to same destination. If the conformation of the roads is such as to admit of two columns marching abreast, Generals Corse and Smith may take a parallel route to the divisions in advance, leaving, however, the right of the roads to Generals Woods and Hazen, respectively.

By order of Maj. Gen. P. Joseph Osterhaus:

F. F. WHITEHEAD,
Assistant Adjutant-General.

SPECIAL ORDERS, No. 242. } HDQRS. THIRD DIV., 15TH ARMY CORPS,
Summerville, Ga., November 30, 1864.

I. This command will move at 8 a. m. to-morrow, December 1, in the following order: First, pioneer corps and tool wagons in advance; second, Battery B, First Michigan Artillery, followed by the wagons of the battery; third, ambulances (one for each regiment) of First Brigade and pioneer corps (one); fourth, ammunition train; fifth, division headquarters train; sixth, First Brigade train and pioneer corps wagons (baggage); seventh, Second Brigade train; eighth, quartermaster's train; ninth, commissary of subsistence train; tenth, ambulance corps, except ambulances assigned to the regiments and detachments; eleventh, regimental wagons Second Brigade. The infantry will march, the First Brigade in advance, upon the right flank of the artillery and trains, except two regiments of Second Brigade, which will march in rear of the trains as rear guard.

By order of Brig. Gen. John E. Smith:

S. M. BUDLONG,
Assistant Adjutant-General.

SPECIAL FIELD ORDERS, No. 20. } HDQRS. FOURTH DIV., 15TH ARMY CORPS,
In the Field, Wells' Plantation, Ga.,
November 30, 1864.

* * * * * * *

III. This command will move to-morrow, the 1st day of December, at 6 a. m. The Second Brigade will have the advance, followed by the battery; the First Brigade will move in the center, on either side of the trains; the Third Brigade will move in the rear. The pioneer corps will leave camp at 5.30 a. m., and repair the roads thoroughly whenever necessary, in advance of the arrival of the column, if possible. The trains will move as follows: First, pioneer corps train; second, Second Brigade train; third, First Brigade train; fourth, Third Brigade train; fifth, ordnance train; sixth, supply train; seventh, ambulance corps train.

By order of Brig. Gen. John M. Corse:

L. CARPER,
Assistant Adjutant-General.

SPECIAL ORDERS, No. 294. } HDQRS. SEVENTEENTH ARMY CORPS,
Station 95, Ga., November 30, 1864.

The orders for the movement to-morrow are as follows:

1. Brig. Gen. G. A. Smith, commanding Fourth Division, will move his infantry across the river at as early an hour as practicable, and will proceed to destroy the railroad for a distance of four miles west from the depot.

2. Maj. Gen. J. A. Mower, commanding First Division, will destroy the railroad for a distance of four miles east from the depot, commencing at 7 a. m.

3. When the work assigned is completed, the First and Fourth Divisions will proceed to camp, which will be on the direct Millen road, about seven miles from Station 95. The division which first completes its work will take the advance.

4. Brig. Gen. M. D. Leggett, commanding Third Division, will take charge of the entire train and artillery of the corps, moving them in the same order as to-day, and will move forward on the Millen road at 8 a. m.

5. The train of the Military Division of the Mississippi and of these headquarters will move in advance of the train of the corps.

6. Brigadier-General Smith will direct his rear guard to completely destroy the bridge over the swamp on the opposite side of the river and the bridge across the river.

7. In destroying the road every tie and sleeper must be burned and every rail heated and warped.

* * * * * * *

By command of Maj. Gen. F. P. Blair:

C. CADLE, JR.,
Assistant Adjutant-General.

HEADQUARTERS MILITARY DIVISION OF THE MISSISSIPPI,
In the Field, Ga., Station No. 9½, November 30, 1864—3 p. m.

Major-General SLOCUM,
Commanding Left Wing, &c.:

Your dispatch of 7 p. m. 29th instant just received, and the general-in-chief directs that you move your whole command by all practicable roads in the direction of Millen, keeping well to the north, in the neighborhood of Bark Camp, Birdville, and Buck Head Church, making a lodgment on the railroad north of Millen, destroying a section of track in the direction of Augusta, and turning on Millen in case you hear the sound of battle. We are at Station 9½—marked Barton on our map—and will finish the railroad up to Millen. As we are a day ahead you will have to march pretty briskly.

L. M. DAYTON,
Aide-de-Camp.

HEADQUARTERS MILITARY DIVISION OF THE MISSISSIPPI,
In the Field, Station 9½, Ga., November 30, 1864.

Major-General SLOCUM,
Commanding Left Wing, &c.:

Your dispatch of last night has been received. By direction of the general-in-chief, you will move your entire command and Kilpatrick's cavalry by practicable roads, via Birdville, on Millen. Instructions of the same character as these have been sent you by the couriers bringing your dispatches, also including the destruction of railroad toward Augusta.

I am, &c.,

L. M. DAYTON,
Aide-de-Camp.

HEADQUARTERS FOURTEENTH ARMY CORPS,
Louisville, Ga., November 30, 1864.

Col. H. C. RODGERS,
Chief of Staff, Left Wing:

COLONEL: Carlin's division marched early this morning to Sebastopol, as ordered. I gave General Carlin a copy of your instructions for his guidance. I have heard nothing from this command since it left. The enemy's cavalry have made repeated demonstrations against my pickets on different roads to-day, but have been repulsed in every instance. Morgan's pickets killed three of the enemy in repulsing one of their dashes this afternoon. Our foragers are circumscribed to the limits of the picket-lines; so the general commanding will see the necessity of our getting out of this soon. An officer from Williams informs me that his troops are crossing about two miles below this place.

The above items sum up the news of the day from this corps.

I am, very respectfully, your obedient servant,

JEF. C. DAVIS,
Brevet Major-General, Commanding.

HEADQUARTERS LEFT WING, ARMY OF GEORGIA,
November 30, 1864.

[General DAVIS,
Commanding Fourteenth Corps:]

GENERAL: Your note has been received. General Williams informs me that the Army of the Tennessee was crossing at Sebastopol to-day. As yet, I have heard nothing from General Sherman. I hope to get orders to night, as we must move to-morrow on account of lack of forage. In the absence of further orders you will advance your corps on the Waynesborough road from three to five miles. The Twentieth Corps will advance about the same distance on the road to Birdville.

Yours, respectfully,

H. W. SLOCUM,
Major-General.

HEADQUARTERS FOURTEENTH ARMY CORPS,
Louisville, Ga., November 30, 1864—12 p. m.

Brig. Gen. W. P. CARLIN,
Commanding First Division, Fourteenth Army Corps:

The general commanding directs that you move your command, immediately on receipt of this order, upon the road leading from Station No. 10 to Waynesborough; cross the main road leading from Louisville to Birdville (leaving it free for the Twentieth Corps); take position just north of the latter road, and there await orders from General Slocum.

I have the honor to be, general, very respectfully, your obedient servant,

A. C. McCLURG,
Assistant Adjutant-General and Chief of Staff.

HEADQUARTERS FOURTEENTH ARMY CORPS,
Louisville, Ga., November 30, 1864.

Brig. Gens. J. D. MORGAN and A. BAIRD,
Comdg. Second and Third Divisions, 14th Army Corps:

The general commanding directs that you hold your commands in readiness to move at 8 o'clock to-morrow morning.

I have the honor to be, very respectfully, your obedient servant,

A. C. McCLURG,
Lieutenant-Colonel and Chief of Staff.

HEADQUARTERS LEFT WING, ARMY OF GEORGIA,
November 30, 1864.

Brig. Gen. A. S. WILLIAMS,
Commanding Twentieth Corps:

The major-general commanding directs that you move your command on the road to Birdville at 7 o'clock to-morrow morning.

Very respectfully, your obedient servant,

H. C. RODGERS,
Assistant Adjutant-General.

HEADQUARTERS TWENTIETH CORPS,
Ogeechee River. November 30, 1864.

Brigadier-General GEARY,
Commanding, &c.:

GENERAL: The general commanding desires that you have Colonel Jones encamp his brigade on the east side of the river, at this bridge, for the night, with instructions to leave the bridge untouched till morning, then destroy it, and bring forward his brigade to join the division.

Very respectfully, your obedient servant,

H. W. PERKINS,
Assistant Adjutant-General.

[First indorsement.]

HEADQUARTERS SECOND DIVISION, TWENTIETH CORPS,
November 30, 1864.

Respectfully referred to Colonel Jones, commanding Second Brigade, who will carry out the order. The Second Brigade will encamp not far from this bridge.

By command of Brigadier-General Geary:

W. T. FORBES,
Acting Assistant Adjutant-General.

[Second indorsement.]

Colonel Jones will take the right-hand road at the first fork of the road on the east side of the river, when he marches to join the command in the morning.

Respectfully,

W. C. ARMOR,
Lieutenant and Aide-de-Camp.

HDQRS. SECOND DIVISION, TWENTIETH ARMY CORPS,
November 30, 1864.

Col. H. A. BARNUM,
Commanding Third Brigade:

COLONEL: The general commanding division directs that the detachment from your brigade sent to the bridge, destroy it as nearly as possible in the morning, and then rejoin their brigade without further delay. To enable them to do this it will be necessary for you to send them axes to-night. The bridge should be destroyed early in the morning. This change of order results from the coming in of the Sixtieth New York Veteran Volunteers before the arrival of Colonel Jones' brigade, which is now here. The general directs that you send, in addition to the 100 men already sent, one regiment, to reach the bridge before daylight, to assist in destroying it, and then return with the detachment and overtake the main body, which will probably be on the march.

I am. colonel, very respectfully, your obedient servant,

W. T. FORBES,
Acting Assistant Adjutant-General.

HDQRS. THIRD BRIG., SECOND DIV., 20TH ARMY CORPS,
Near Louisville, Ga., November 30, 1864.

Maj. THOMAS ELLIOTT,
Commanding Sixtieth New York Veteran Volunteers:

MAJOR: The colonel commanding directs that you take your regiment and destroy the bridge over the Ogeechee River that you were left to guard to-day. You will thoroughly destroy the bridge by cutting and burning, and then rejoin the brigade as soon as possible, without further orders.

I am, major, respectfully, your obedient servant,

O. T. MAY,
Captain and Acting Assistant Adjutant-General.

HDQRS. THIRD CAVALRY DIVISION, CAVALRY CORPS,
MILITARY DIVISION OF THE MISSISSIPPI,
Near Louisville, Ga., November 30, 1864—12 m.

Major-General SHERMAN:

GENERAL: Captain Audenried no doubt has reached you by this time and furnished you with a detail of account of my operations since leaving Milledgeville. I am now encamped five miles from Louisville, on the road to Millen. General Wheeler, with about 6,000 cavalry, including several bands of from 50 to 200 each, commanded by partisan leaders, such as Lyllie, Jewett, Slie, and others of lesser note. I encamped upon the enemy's road between Augusta and Millen during the night of the 27th, employing one-third of my entire force in tearing up track, the enemy keeping the majority of my troops constantly on the alert in repulsing determined and persistent attacks. Learning positively that our prisoners had been removed from Millen, and hearing that a considerable force had been concentrated at that point under General Hardee, I deemed it prudent to return within supporting distance of the infantry. I fell back to this point under the most difficult circumstances, but successfully, and, with slight loss, repulsed the repeated and reckless attacks upon my rear and flanks. From the enemy's first attack at Sylvan Grove, on the evening of the 26th, up to his final attack and repulse near Buck Head Creek, just above the mouth of Rocky Creek, on the evening of the 28th, the enemy is known to have suffered severely. From reports of deserters, negroes, and prisoners, his loss could not have been less than 600 killed and wounded. I regret, general, that our prisoners had been removed before I could reach them. Every man of them had been taken away two days before I struck the railroad. I left Milledgeville at 6 o'clock on Thursday evening, and reached the railroad, with my advance at Waynesborough, at 11 p. m. Saturday evening, having marched upward of ninety miles in fifty-three hours, and this in the face of much opposition on the part of the enemy. I passed within five miles of the stockade above Millen in which our prisoners had been confined, and would have rescued them, as I promised, had they not been removed. My ambulances are now full of our wounded; wagons, however, will be emptied, so that none will be left behind. My command is in good condition, and as ready as ever for any enterprise. In the absence of any orders from your headquarters I will move upon the left and in advance of the Fourteenth Army Corps.

Hoping, general, that our efforts this far to carry out your orders and fulfill your expectations have won your approbation,

I am, with great respect, your obedient servant,

J. KILPATRICK,
Brigadier-General, Commanding.

P. S.—I learn that a considerable force of the enemy, which has been concentrated for the last few days at Augusta, has been ordered to Millen, and that an effort will be made at that point to check our further advance. The Tenth and Twentieth North Carolina Regiments reached Augusta day before yesterday. Convalescent soldiers, soldiers home on furlough, the old and young, all are rapidly being concentrated at the country towns, and from these points are hurried to Augusta and Millen. With all their efforts, however, I do not think they can concentrate a very considerable force; yet I do not hesitate in saying, from my own experience within the last few days, that every effort will be made to check our farther advance. The enemy will boldly and recklessly attack whenever the opportunity offers.

Very respectfully, your obedient servant,

J. K.

[Inclosure.]

General Kilpatrick wishes to know what he shall do with prisoners. I have several officers of rank that I wish to retain as hostages. Several of my men have been killed after [being] taken prisoners; others have been found with their bodies mutilated, throats cut, &c. I wish permission to send communication to General Wheeler, who is now in my immediate front, informing him of these facts, that I have prisoners of rank who I intend to retain as hostages, and will retaliate.

STEAMER NEMAHA, *Port Royal, November 30, 1864.*

Maj. Gen. H. W. HALLECK,
Chief of Staff, U. S. Armies:

GENERAL: I have the honor to report that I landed General Hatch, with a small force, yesterday at Boyd's Neck, opposite Whale Island, Broad River, with orders to push on and destroy the railroad near Grahamville. When I left the landing, at 4 p. m., he was four miles out at the intersection of the roads. Had it not been for the ignorance and inefficiency of our pilots, we should have reached the landing at daylight and been enabled to destroy the road yesterday. After making a lodgment at Gopher Hill, General Hatch is ordered to destroy the bridge to the southwest, and thus to march with his whole force and attack the work guarding the Coosawhatchie bridge. Admiral Dahlgren has contributed to our force quite a regiment of sailors and marines, with six pieces of artillery.

Very respectfully, yours,

J. G. FOSTER,
Major-General.

HEADQUARTERS DEPARTMENT OF THE SOUTH,
Hilton Head, S. C., November 30, 1864.

Major-General FOSTER,
Commanding Department:

GENERAL: In accordance with instructions contained in your letter to me of this date, directions were again sent to the pickets to look out for the escaped prisoners; also, to all boats on picket duty around the island. Not knowing where to communicate with the naval picket-boat (which your letter informed me the admiral was to send), I proceeded to the New Hampshire (the admiral being absent), and was told by Captain Reynolds that no picket-boats had been sent out by the admiral. The telegraph cable to Fort Pulaski was not mended; there was no operator to establish a station at the end of the island, and no one of the signal corps at Fort Pulaski to receive a message by signals. I therefore sent a letter to Colonel Brown, commanding at the fort, through Major Thomas, by the steamer Eliza Hancox. Three of the escaped rebels have been recaptured and brought in; all efforts are being made to secure the others.

Very respectfully, your obedient servant,

W. B. DEAN,
Lieutenant and Acting Assistant Adjutant-General.

HEADQUARTERS DEPARTMENT OF THE SOUTH,
Hilton Head, S. C., November 30, 1864.

Captain PRATT,
Provost-Marshal:

CAPTAIN: I am not satisfied with the performance of duty by the guards at the time the six rebel officers escaped. The derelict parties must be punished. If the outside guards were not asleep or bribed it would be impossible to escape. In detecting other prisoners in the attempt to escape they must be shot down at once. Great efforts must continue to be made to rearrest the escaped officers.

Respectfully, yours,

J. G. FOSTER,
Major-General, Commanding.

HEADQUARTERS DEPARTMENT OF THE SOUTH,
Hilton Head, S. C., November 30, 1864.

Lieutenant BERRYMAN,
32d U. S. Colored Troops, in charge of Pickets, &c., Seabrook:

The general commanding directs that you use every precaution, both with the pickets on land and with the picket-boats, to prevent the escaped rebel prisoners from leaving the island. If there are any naval boats near you notify them. Acknowledge receipt by telegraph.

W. B. DEAN,
Lieutenant and Actg. Asst. Adjt. Gen., Department of the South.

HEADQUARTERS DEPARTMENT OF THE SOUTH,
Hilton Head, S. C., November 30, 1864.

Col. P. P. BROWN,
Commanding at Fort Pulaski:

I am instructed by the major-general commanding to notify you that some of the rebel prisoners of war have escaped from the guard-house here, and three of them are still at large and believed to be on this island. The commanding general directs that you use the utmost vigilance in regard to the prisoners under your charge.

W. B. DEAN,
Lieutenant and Acting Assistant Adjutant-General.

HEADQUARTERS COAST DIVISION,
November 30, 1864.

Maj. Gen. J. G. FOSTER,
Commanding Department of the South:

GENERAL: The naval brigade yesterday, while skirmishing, took the wrong road, going toward Coosawhatchie. The mistake was not discovered until we overtook them last night. After countermarching and going about three miles from the forks of the road we made a similar mistake, getting off three miles to the left on the wrong road. We countermarched, and arrived between 12 and 1 o'clock last night at the point where the last error was made. Move again this morning with the whole force.

Very respectfully, your obedient servant,

JNO. P. HATCH,
Brigadier-General, Commanding.

Please send both forage and rations with the first wagons. The navy are short of rations.

FORT MONROE, VA., *November 30, 1864.*

Major ECKERT:

Have just received Savannah Daily Morning News of November 26. Came to me through the post-office from Major Mulford. Following is news:

SITUATION AND PROSPECT.

We take the following from the Augusta Chronicle of the 24th:

"The grand prize, which was to be obtained in case Augusta was captured, has been removed. The powder-works, arsenal, armories, and machine shops, located at this place, have been completely dismantled, and the valuable portion of their machinery has been removed to a location of safety not threatened. The last car-load, we understand, left to-day. The machinery was sent away merely as a matter of precaution.

"RE-ENFORCEMENTS FROM AN UNEXPECTED QUARTER.

"It will be seen from a dispatch in another column that General Bragg has left Wilmington with re-enforcements for this place. These, we are told, number about 10,000. These, in addition to those who started for Augusta from another section, on Saturday, will make quite a formidable array.

"MAYOR'S OFFICE, *Augusta, Ga., November 23.*

"TO THE PEOPLE OF AUGUSTA:

"I have received a telegram from General Bragg informing me that he is on his way to Augusta with re-enforcements. Other re-enforcements are expected within a few hours. I exhort the people to be calm, to resolve on the defense of their homes and their property, and to rely upon their own and the valor of those who are hastening to our relief. A few days, perhaps hours, may find us redeemed from the proximity of the foe.

"ROBT. H. MAY,
"*Mayor.*"

The following is the dispatch referred to:

WILMINGTON, *November 22.*

"Hon. R. H. MAY,
"*Mayor of Augusta:*

"I leave here to-day with re-enforcements for Augusta. Exhort your people to be confident and resolute.

"BRAXTON BRAGG."

Re-enforcements are constantly arriving in our city. The air resounds with the shriek of the engine-whistle day and night. The soldiers appear to enjoy the prospect of a fight ahead. The gloom which overspread our city a short time since has disappeared entirely. Everything wears a cheerful aspect.

FROM HOOD'S ARMY.

Intelligence received from a highly responsible source states that Hood's army is in fine spirits and several thousand stronger than when they left Georgia. They are in excellent condition, with abundance of supplies, under marching orders, with Nashville almost in sight.

The same paper, of 22d, has the following:

"FROM THE CENTRAL RAILROAD.

"A gentleman who arrived last night from Savannah reports that the bridge over the Oconee River, on that road, was not burned yesterday morning, but was being stoutly defended by General Wayne. The position held by General Wayne is considered a very strong one. Milledgeville is in the hands of the Federals, and Atlanta in the possession of the Confederates.

"FROM UP THE GEORGIA ROAD.

"We conversed with an intelligent gentleman, who arrived last night by the passenger train up the Georgia Railroad. He informs us that on Monday the Federals left the line of the Georgia road, going directly to Eatonton. The only Yankees who came to Greensborough were a few stragglers, who were captured. The trains ran up to Greensborough and Athens yesterday. A portion of Major Graham's command reached this city last night. They report that they visited Atlanta several days since, and found it completely evacuated and burned. They stated that the Federals took all the cattle and forage in their route, but did not molest those who remained at home. They captured 2,000 or 3,000 stragglers, who will probably reach here to-day. They also corroborate the statement of the Federals leaving the Georgia Railroad and going in the direction of Eatonton."

The Constitutionalist of the 25th contains the following:

"FROM THE FRONT—6. a. m.

"A large number of refugees passed through from Putnam last night, bringing intelligence of the occupation of Eatonton yesterday morning by the Yankees. Several scouts went out to reconnoiter, and were fired upon. Young Dennis' horse returned without the rider; supposed to be killed. As our informant left, the advance guard of twenty-five raiders entered the town, and several cattle drivers for the Government arrived, who stated that our scouts saw 1,500 Yankees passing at 10 o'clock yesterday on the road from Greensborough to Eatonton, probably those reported to have been in Greensborough by the down train yesterday morning. If so, the raiders have turned their course from this region, perhaps for Milledgeville or Macon. Heavy cannonading was heard all yesterday afternoon, in the direction of Macon, believed to be a battle between Sherman and our forces.

"OBSERVER."

THE SITUATION.

The latest reliable intelligence from the direction of Macon comes from our scouts sent out from Sparta. These scouts, who came in last evening, report that a body of from 600 to 1,000 cavalry had crossed the Oconee, and were moving slowly and nervously toward Sparta. Beyond some burning and stealing, this small band of troopers has no special significance. We have reason to believe they will be seriously bushwhacked, and, we trust, cut to pieces. One of the most encouraging features of this invasion is the fact, which we have from the most undoubted testimony, that hundreds of the enemy are straggling from their main bodies and searching for somebody to take them into custody. They are sprawling all about the country, and those who are not willing to surrender can be beautifully bushwhacked. Let all the old and young folks turn out and give the rascals a taste of Georgia State sovereignty. This demoralization of our enemy is most providential for us, and ought to stiffen the backbone of the most timid among us. Three hundred prisoners arrived last night from up the Georgia road, and 400 more are to arrive to-day. These prisoners report that a division of 3,000 of our cavalry has followed them all the way, dashing upon them, constantly picking up stragglers and capturing wagons. Hampton's invincible cavalry will be with us in a day or so, and hang upon their eastern flank. General Wayne has whipped Kilpatrick's cavalry division at the Oconee bridge, driving them headlong and in confusion. He telegraphs that he is perfectly able to take care of himself. Wheeler, with many thousand men, has intercepted the enemy at a point at present unmentionable, and is giving them no rest, night or day. The main body of the enemy is moving down the western side of the Oconee, and has shown no disposition thus far to attempt its passage.

The skies are brightening. Everything looks glorious, and, ere long, Mr. Sherman will get a lashing that he little dreamed of when he made his "On to the Gulf." The gulf of perdition be upon him.

HEADQUARTERS HAMPTON'S CAVALRY,
November 24.

COMMANDING OFFICER,
Augusta:

Please insert this dispatch in all newspapers in Augusta:

"All men of my command now in Georgia will rendezvous forthwith at Augusta, and those in South Carolina at Columbia, and await orders.

"WADE HAMPTON,
"*Major-General.*"

General Joseph E. Johnston has arrived in Columbia from Augusta. He intends for the present to make Columbia his home.

SAVANNAH, *Saturday Morning, 26th.*

We have no reliable information from the front to-day of any movements that are going on. We learn that the opinion prevails to some extent in military circles that Sherman intends yet to fall upon Macon, and not press on toward the coast at present. Our own forces are gathering and going to the proper place. We are informed that over 3,000 rations were issued in this city this morning to newly arrived veteran troops, and we are also officially informed that 4,000 or 5,000 will pass through here in two or three days.

GEO. D. SHELDON.

Abstract from returns of the Union Forces in the Savannah Campaign, Maj. Gen. William T. Sherman commanding, for November 30, 1864.

Command.	Present for duty.		Aggregate present.	Aggregate present and absent.	Pieces of field artillery.
	Officers.	Men.			
Army of the Tennessee:					
Fifteenth Army Corps (Osterhaus)	774	15,685	18,942	29,110	18
Seventeenth Army Corps (Blair)	416	11,911	13,905	23,916	14
Total Right Wing (Howard)	1,190	27,596	32,847	53,026	32
Army of Georgia:					
General headquarters	6	......	6	6	......
Fourteenth Army Corps (Davis)	607	13,922	16,346	27,658	16
Twentieth Army Corps (Williams)	676	14,024	16,634	29,126	16
Total Left Wing (Slocum)	1,289	27,946	32,986	56,790	32
Cavalry (Kilpatrick)	249	5,075	6,210	10,229	4
Grand total	2,728	60,617	72,043	120,045	68

[NOVEMBER 30, 1864.—For organization of Sherman's army during the Savannah Campaign, see p. 19, and for the "effective strength," see p. 16.]

Abstract from return of the Department of the South, Maj. Gen. John G. Foster, U. S. Army, commanding, for November 30, 1864.

Command.	Present for duty.		Aggregate present.	Aggregate present and absent.	Pieces of artillery.	
	Officers.	Men.			Heavy.	Field.
General headquarters	50	81	132	134	......	......
1st New York Engineers (battalion, Place)	8	576	616	684	......	......
Northern District (Hatch)	156	4,648	5,560	6,616	......	6
District of Beaufort (Saxton)	35	1,011	1,594	2,851	......	7
District of Hilton Head *a* (Brown)	69	2,024	2,711	3,285	66	11
District of Florida (Scammon)	93	2,571	3,285	4,265	......	......
Total	411	10,911	13,898	17,835	66	24

a NOTE ON RETURN.—All the regiments of the Third Separate Brigade [Hilton Head] are at the front. On account of the November return not having been received from said brigade, its October return has been used in making up this return, deducting the Engineers therefrom, which are accounted for in a body separately on this return.

Organization of troops in the Department of the South, Maj. Gen. John G. Foster, U. S. Army, commanding, November 30, 1864.

NORTHERN DISTRICT.*

Brig. Gen. JOHN P. HATCH.

MORRIS ISLAND.

Col. EDWARD N. HALLOWELL.

54th Massachusetts (colored),† Lieut. Col. Henry N. Hooper.
56th New York,† Lieut. Col. Rockwell Tyler.
52d Pennsylvania, Maj. Thomas B. Jayne.
21st U. S. Colored Troops, Lieut. Col. Augustus G. Bennett.
3d New York Light Artillery, Battery B,† Capt. Thomas J. Mesereau.
3d Rhode Island Heavy Artillery, 1st Battalion, Capt. Jeremiah Lanahan.

FOLLY ISLAND.

Col. EUGENE A. KOZLAY.

55th Massachusetts (colored),† Lieut. Col. Charles B. Fox.
54th New York, Maj. Stephen Kovacs.
33d U. S. Colored Troops, Maj. Charles T. Trowbridge.

DISTRICT OF BEAUFORT.‡

Brig. Gen. RUFUS SAXTON.

127th New York,† Col. William Gurney.
26th U. S. Colored Troops, Col. William Silliman.
102d U. S. Colored Troops,† Col. Henry L. Chipman.
3d Rhode Island Heavy Artillery, Company A,† Capt. William H. Hamner.
2d U. S. Colored Light Artillery, Battery G, Capt. Jeremiah S. Clark.

DISTRICT OF HILTON HEAD.§

Col. PHILIP P. BROWN, Jr.

144th New York,† Col. James Lewis.
157th New York,† Lieut. Col. James C. Carmichael.
25th Ohio,† Lieut. Col. Nathaniel Haughton.
32d U. S. Colored Troops,† Col. George W. Baird.

DISTRICT OF FLORIDA.‖

Brig. Gen. ELIAKIM P. SCAMMON.

17th Connecticut, Col. William H. Noble.
75th Ohio, Col. Andrew L. Harris.
107th Ohio, Capt. Edward S. Meyer.
3d U. S. Colored Troops, Col. Benjamin C. Tilghman.
34th U. S. Colored Troops,† Lieut. Col. William W. Marple.
35th U. S. Colored Troops,† Col. James C. Beecher.
4th Massachusetts Cavalry,† 2d Battalion, Capt. George R. Hurlbut.
3d New York Light Artillery, Battery F,† Lieut. Edgar H. Titus.

UNATTACHED.

1st New York Engineers (battalion), Maj. James E. Place.

---

* Or First Separate Brigade.

† Constituted the Coast Division, commanded by Brig. Gen. John P. Hatch, and engaged in expedition against the Charleston and Savannah Railroad. The First Brigade of this division was commanded by Brig. Gen. Edward E. Potter, and the Second Brigade by Col. Alfred S. Hartwell, Fifty-fifth Massachusetts Infantry (colored).

‡ Or Second Separate Brigade.

§ Or Third Separate Brigade.

‖ Or Fourth Separate Brigade.

*Abstract from return of the District of West Florida, Col. George D. Robinson, Ninety-seventh U. S. Colored Troops, commanding, for November 30, 1864.**

Command.	Present for duty.		Aggregate present.	Aggregate present and absent.	Pieces of artillery.	
	Officers.	Men.			Heavy.	Field.
Headquarters	2	....	2	2	......	......
First Brigade (Robinson)	49	1,473	1,902	1,983	2	5
Second Brigade (Woodman)	46	865	1,149	1,459	......	......
Nineteenth Iowa (Bruce)	23	375	551	684	......	......
Fort Pickens (Reisinger)	8	158	222	231	90	......
Fort Barrancas (Hitchcock)	12	252	334	388	32	......
Total	140	3,123	4,160	4,747	124	5

HEADQUARTERS MILITARY DIVISION OF THE MISSISSIPPI,
In the Field, Station No. 9½, December 1, 1864—8 a. m.

Major-General HOWARD,
Commanding Army of the Tennessee:

GENERAL: Yours of date November 30 just received. To the information conveyed about Lee, Hood, &c., obtained from Hardee's officer, the general-in-chief says, "All right." The army is moving and destroying railroad; the Left Wing is also moving.

I am, general, respectfully, &c.,

L. M. DAYTON,
Aide-de-Camp.

HDQRS. DEPARTMENT AND ARMY OF THE TENNESSEE,
Kent's Farm, opposite Station 8, December 1, 1864.

Maj. Gen. W. T. SHERMAN,
Commanding Military Division of the Mississippi:

GENERAL: I have just returned to camp from Station 13. We have here a good plank road from our Savannah road to the river. About twenty-four feet of planking and stringers were removed from the bridge. We now have a good foot bridge, and will soon have repairs made so as to throw over cavalry and artillery, as well as infantry, if there should be need.

On the arrival of a company of the Twenty-seventh Missouri about forty mounted rebels departed in haste. I had the depot, a large quantity of lumber, ties, &c., and portions of the railroad track destroyed. I have directed General Blair to continue along the railroad, destroying it as he goes, and directed General Osterhaus to move opposite No. 7 to-morrow. I am a little in the dark as to your intention. Please inform me as far as you can consistently, that I may conform to your wishes as to the length of march, &c.

Very respectfully, your obedient servant,

O. O. HOWARD,
Major-General.

---

* Bvt. Brig. Gen. Joseph Bailey, temporarily absent with cavalry expedition under General Davidson.

HEADQUARTERS MILITARY DIVISION OF THE MISSISSIPPI,
In the Field, No. 9, Ga., December 1, 1864.

Major-General HOWARD, *Commanding Army of the Tennessee:*

GENERAL: Yours of this date from opposite No. 8 is to hand, which I acknowledge by direction of the general-in-chief. He has read your orders to General Blair, and says all right; he does not wish you to move to-morrow further than abreast of No. 7. General Slocum is now about abreast of us here, and to-morrow all will reach the vicinity of Buck Head Church, where there will be some delay to us while Slocum is swinging around, and you may calculate on staying at No. 7 a day or two for us to get up even. At present Wheeler is very active, and Kilpatrick is operating in connection with General Slocum. You will make disposition to cross at No. 7, but whether it will be necessary to to do so will depend on the dispositions of the enemy.

I am, general, yours, &c.,

L. M. DAYTON,
Aide-de-Camp.

HDQRS. DEPARTMENT AND ARMY OF THE TENNESSEE,
Kent's Farm, opp. Station 8, Ga., December 1, 1864—10.30 p. m.

Maj. Gen. W. T. SHERMAN, *Comdg. Military Div. of the Mississippi:*

GENERAL: Two of my scouts just returned from Millen; find no force there except a small number of the enemy's cavalry. From depot to Millen just four miles; considerable trestle-work along the road. A plank road runs parallel with and near the railroad a part of the way, and then bends off a mile and a half. Scouts heard that some of the planking had been taken up, and the gap defended by rebel cavalry. A train of cars came into Millen from direction of Savannah while the scouts were near by, apparently with great caution, and soon returned in the direction from which it came.

Respectfully,

O. O. HOWARD,
Major-General.

SPECIAL FIELD ORDERS, No. 182.

HEADQUARTERS DEPARTMENT AND ARMY OF THE TENNESSEE,
Kent's Farm, opp. Station 8, Ga., December 1, 1864.

I. This army will continue its movements to-morrow, as follows: First, Major-General Blair, commanding Seventeenth Corps, will continue his march along the Savannah railroad, making complete destruction of that road as he goes. Second, Major-General Osterhaus, commanding Fifteenth Army Corps, will move his command in two columns of two divisions each—the right column moving toward Statesborough as far as Scull's Creek (main branch), and the left column pursuing the main Savannah road to a point opposite Station No. 7. The herds of cattle will follow the left column. The train of these headquarters proper will follow the ammunition wagons of the leading division of the left column, and the supply train of same will move in advance of supply train of same division.

* * * * * * *

By order of Maj. Gen. O. O. Howard:

SAML. L. TAGGART,
Assistant Adjutant-General.

SPECIAL ORDERS, } HEADQUARTERS 15TH ARMY CORPS,
No. 187. } *Near Millen, Ga., December 1, 1864.*

I. The attention of division commanders and commanding officers of detachments is called to the irregularities existing in foraging and the manner in which this privilege is often abused. It is noticed that many men not belonging to proper foraging parties are allowed to straggle from the ranks and forage for themselves, without any authority whatever. It is by such men that the greater part of the pillaging is done and depredations committed, of which there is so much complaint. Officers in charge of foraging parties must be continually instructed to keep their men well in hand, never allowing them to precede the advance guard of the column; and to use more discretion in taking from the poor, being careful to leave them sufficient for their immediate subsistence. It is also noticed that the number of mounted men is very largely increasing, and that the ranks are correspondingly diminished. Measures will be at once taken to check this growing evil. The number of mounted foragers to each brigade should be limited and regulated in orders, which, if not done, mounted foragers will be no longer allowed. We are now nearing the enemy, and foraging parties should be cautioned against preceding the advance or extending their operations to too great a distance from the column.

II. The movements of the corps for to-morrow will be as follows: The right column, composed of Second and Third Divisions, will move from their present camps at 7 a. m., the Third Division, Brigadier-General Smith commanding, in advance, followed by the Second Division, Brigadier-General Hazen commanding, marching on the Statesborough road to the main branch of Scull's Creek. If practicable General Hazen will move his division parallel with the Third Division, either on the right or left, giving, however, the right of way to that division. The left column, composed of First and Fourth Divisions, will move from its present camp at 7 a. m., the Fourth Division, Brigadier-General Corse commanding, in advance, accompanied by pontoon train and engineer regiment, followed by First Division, Brigadier-General Woods commanding. This column will march on the main Savannah road to a point opposite No. 7 where it will encamp. The herds of cattle will follow the left column. The trains of department and corps headquarters with the ammunition wagons of the Fourth Division. The department supply train will move in advance of the Fourth Division supply train. Corps headquarters will be established with the left column.

By order of Maj. Gen. P. Joseph Osterhaus:

F. F. WHITEHEAD,
Assistant Adjutant-General.

SPECIAL ORDERS, } HDQRS. THIRD DIV., 15TH ARMY CORPS,
No. 243. } *Near Canoochee, Ga., December 1, 1864.*

I. This command will move at 6 a. m. to-morrow, the 2d instant, in the following order: First, pioneer corps and tool wagons; second, Battery B, First Michigan Artillery, followed by the wagons of the battery; third, ambulances of Second Brigade (one for each regiment) and pioneer corps (one); fourth, ammunition train; fifth, division headquarters train and provost guard; sixth, Second Brigade train and pioneer corps wagon (baggage); seventh, First Brigade train; eighth, quartermaster's train; ninth, commissary of subsistence train; tenth, ambulance corps, except ambulances assigned to regiments and detachments; eleventh, regimental wagons First Brigade.

The infantry will march, the Second Brigade in advance, upon the right flank of the artillery and trains, except two regiments of the First Brigade, which will march in rear of the trains as rear guard.

By order of Brig. Gen. John E. Smith:

S. M. BUDLONG,
Assistant Adjutant-General.

SPECIAL FIELD ORDERS, No. 21.

HEADQUARTERS FOURTH DIVISION, FIFTEENTH ARMY CORPS,
In the Field, near Millen, Ga., December 1, 1864.

I. The movement of the division for to-morrow will be as follows: The First Brigade, Brigadier-General Rice commanding, has the advance, and will move at 5.30 a. m., on the main Savannah road, to a point opposite Station No. 7. The battery will follow the First Brigade. The pontoon train and engineer regiment will close up on the battery. The Third Brigade, Lieutenant-Colonel Hurlbut commanding, will move in the center, on either side of the trains. The pioneer corps will march with the advance, to make all necessary repairs on the road. The trains of the division will move in the following order: First, the pioneer corps train; second, the First Brigade train; third, the Third Brigade train; fourth, the Second Brigade train; fifth, the ordnance train; sixth, the supply train; seventh, the ambulance corps train.

By order of Brig. Gen. John M. Corse:

L. CARPER,
Assistant Adjutant-General.

HDQRS. DEPARTMENT AND ARMY OF THE TENNESSEE,
Kent's Farm, opposite Station No. 83, December 1, 1864.

Maj. Gen. F. P. BLAIR, Jr.,
Commanding Seventeenth Corps:

GENERAL: My headquarters are about two miles from and opposite Station No. 83. We saved the most of the bridge, driving away some forty rebel cavalry. Please move up a picket, at least to this station, that we may communicate without hindrance. I have directed you to continue along the Savannah railroad. If you receive any direct orders from General Sherman do not fail to inform me.

Respectfully,

O. O. HOWARD,
Major-General.

HEADQUARTERS SEVENTEENTH ARMY CORPS,
Near Station 9, Georgia Central Railroad, December 1, 1864.

Capt. SAMUEL L. TAGGART,
Asst. Adjt. Gen., Department and Army of the Tennessee:

CAPTAIN: This command is encamped at Jones' plantation, one mile west of Station 9. From all that I can learn I think there is no force in Millen. There is a brigade of rebel cavalry some distance on our left. A division of the Twentieth Corps is encamped about seven miles from us, on our left. I shall move forward and cross the creek this side of Millen to-morrow, camping at Millen, if practicable.

Very respectfully, your obedient servant,

F. P. BLAIR, JR.,
Major-General.

HEADQUARTERS SEVENTEENTH ARMY CORPS,
Near Station 9, Ga., December 1, 1864.

Col. GEORGE E. SPENCER,
Commanding First Alabama Cavalry:

COLONEL: The major-general commanding desires you to move a battalion of your command to Station 8 at once, to picket the approaches to the bridge near there and keep open communication with General Howard. The orderly who delivers this communication will conduct the battalion to that point.

Very respectfully, your obedient servant,

C. CADLE, JR.,
Assistant Adjutant-General.

SPECIAL ORDERS, No. 295. HDQRS. SEVENTEENTH ARMY CORPS,
Near Station 9, Ga., December 1, 1864.

I. The orders for the movements to-morrow are:

1. Maj. Gen. J. A. Mower, commanding First Division, will have the advance, and will move at 7 a. m., on the Millen road.

2. Brig. Gen. G. A. Smith, commanding Fourth Division, will be prepared to move at 8 o'clock, and will follow the First Division.

3. Brig. Gen. M. D. Leggett, commanding Third Division, will be prepared to move at 9 o'clock, and will follow the Fourth Division.

4. Brig. Gen. M. D. Leggett will move one brigade of his command on the railroad, with orders to destroy the bridge and trestle-work up to Station 8.

5. The pontoon train and guard, Lieutenant-Colonel Rusk commanding, will move [in] advance of the supply train of the First Division.

6. The trains of headquarters Military Division of the Mississippi and these headquarters will move as heretofore.

II. The practice of indiscriminate firing must be stopped. Our supply of ammunition is limited and cannot be renewed until we reach a new base of supplies. Before that time all that we have may be needed. Commanding officers must impress on the minds of their men the necessity of being careful of their ammunition. An alarm is, or should be, given by the discharge of firearms, but the indiscriminate firing renders this mode useless, so that the safety of the army is endangered. The most of the firing is done by forage parties. Commanding officers of forage parties will be held to a strict responsibility for the conduct of their men in this respect. The cartridge-boxes of forage parties will be inspected on their return from duty each day, and the men will be charged 50 cents for each cartridge missing that cannot be satisfactorily accounted for. The charge will be stopped against them on the next muster and pay roll.

This order will be read at once to each company and detachment in the corps.

By command of Maj. Gen. F. P. Blair:

C. CADLE, JR.,
Assistant Adjutant-General.

ORDERS.] HDQRS. FIRST DIVISION, 17TH ARMY CORPS,
In the Field, Ga., December 1, 1864.

The troops of this command will be prepared to march to-morrow at 7 a. m. Order of march: First, pioneer corps; second, Second Brigade;

third, First Michigan Battery;* fourth, Third Brigade; fifth, First Brigade; sixth, ambulance corps; seventh, ordnance train; eighth, pontoon train; ninth, supply train.

By order of Maj. Gen. J. A. Mower:

CHAS. CHRISTENSEN,
Lieutenant and Acting Assistant Adjutant-General.

HEADQUARTERS SEVENTEENTH ARMY CORPS,
Near Station 9, Ga., December 1, 1864.

Brig. Gen. M. D. LEGGETT,
Commanding Third Division:

GENERAL: The major-general commanding directs me to say to you that the commanding officer of the brigade sent from your division on the railroad will be instructed to use the whole day on the road, if necessary. He will tear up a section the length of his brigade on each mile of the road, burning the ties and sleepers and bending the rails. He will burn all the culverts and trestle-work, depots or store-houses, piles of wood, ties, and lumber belonging to the road, and any mills or cotton on or near the road. He will work up to the railroad bridge across Buck Head Creek, but will not destroy that, as it may be needed to cross the infantry. He will forward a report of the day's work to these headquarters.

Very respectfully, your obedient servant,

C. CADLE, JR.,
Assistant Adjutant-General.

SPECIAL FIELD ORDERS, No. 163. } HEADQUARTERS THIRD DIVISION, SEVENTEENTH ARMY CORPS,
In the Field, Ga., December 1, 1864.

* * * * * * *

II. This command will march at 7 a. m. to-morrow. Brig. Gen. M. F. Force, commanding First Brigade, will have the advance. Artillery and trains as heretofore.

III. The number (twelve) of pack-animals allowed to each regiment will still be permitted, provided neither enlisted man nor negro be allowed to ride the same; they are for packing purposes, and must not be used for any other. No enlisted man will be permitted to ride, except those already mounted under existing orders. "Bummers" are entitled to a position in the ranks, and must be provided with it. No foragers will leave camp mounted, excepting the officers in charge. Brigade commanders will see that this order is strictly enforced.

By order of Brig. Gen. M. D. Leggett:

J. C. DOUGLASS,
Assistant Adjutant-General.

SPECIAL FIELD ORDERS, No. 26. } HDQRS. FOURTEENTH ARMY CORPS,
Louisville, Ga., December 1, 1864.

The Fourteenth Corps will move upon Birdville, in the following order: General Baird, unincumbered with wagons and supported by

* Battery C, First Michigan Light Artillery.

Kilpatrick's cavalry will march at once upon the direct road to Waynesborough until they shall have crossed Buck Head Creek. From thence he will take the best practicable road toward Birdville, scouring the country well, so as to secure complete protection to the entire trains of the corps, which will move on a road leading to the right of the Waynesborough road toward the mouth of Mill Creek. General Morgan will be charged with the care of the trains of the corps, which will move at once upon the road above indicated, in the following order: Second Division trains, corps headquarters trains, reserve artillery and ammunition trains, Colonel Buell's command, and Third Division trains. General Carlin will move from his present position, in the vicinity of Old Town, upon the road leading to Waynesborough, cross the road leading direct from Louisville to Birdville, and upon the north side of that road (leaving it free for the Twentieth Corps) will await further orders from General Slocum.

By order of Bvt. Maj. Gen. J. C. Davis:

A. C. MCCLURG,
Lieutenant-Colonel and Chief of Staff.

HDQRS. THIRD DIVISION, FOURTEENTH ARMY CORPS,
December 1, 1864.

Major-General DAVIS,
Commanding Fourteenth Corps:

GENERAL: I am in camp on the east side of Buck Head Creek, which is a trifling brook at this place. General Kilpatrick left his camp at 12.15 and I followed at 1.30. He halted and formed line. He was then skirmishing, and reported four brigades of rebel cavalry in his front. Immediately after he asked me to move to the front, and I did so, he moving a column of cavalry on each side of me. We then moved rapidly. The cavalry which passed us came from toward Millen and moved toward Augusta. I can only hear of 300 between here and Waynesborough. I have found no road leading to Millen, and can hear of none this side of Rocky Creek; just beyond a road leads off, intersecting the railroad five miles south of Waynesborough; and if I find no other, and am not strongly opposed, I propose to take that road and begin to destroy the railroad as soon as I reach it. I ought to reach within ten miles of Millen to-morrow night and clear the way for your advance. I want Kilpatrick to destroy Brier Creek bridge, but perhaps may have to move my infantry there to get him to do it properly. Rely upon it that I will do the best I can, according to circumstances.

Most respectfully, your obedient servant,

A. BAIRD,
Brigadier-General, Commanding.

HEADQUARTERS LEFT WING, ARMY OF GEORGIA,
Camp on Buck Head Creek, December 1, 1864.

Maj. Gen. J. C. DAVIS,
Commanding Fourteenth Corps:

The major-general commanding desires you to continue the march on the road you are now on, making as many miles per day as you can conveniently. On reaching the railroad he desires you to destroy a short section toward Augusta and then push on in the direction of Jacksonborough. We shall try to reach a point on the railroad a little north of Millen to-morrow night; and when convenient the general would like you to communicate with him.

Very respectfully, your obedient servant,

H. C. RODGERS,
Assistant Adjutant-General.

ORDERS.] HEADQUARTERS TWENTIETH CORPS,
Near Birdville, Ga., December 1, 1864.

This corps will march this morning through Birdville, as follows: Second Division at 7 a. m.; First Division at 8 a. m.; Third Division at 9 a. m. The cavalry will precede the column, starting at 6.30 a. m. General Geary will march two unincumbered brigades and a battery of artillery as an advanced guard, and General Ward two unincumbered brigades and a battery of artillery as a rear guard. The Michigan Engineers will march in rear of the advanced guard, starting at 7 a. m. Their tool wagons will accompany them; the balance of their train will march immediately in rear of the train of the leading division. The pontoon train will precede the train of the leading division. The other trains and the artillery will march as heretofore ordered.

By command of Brig. Gen. A. S. Williams:

ROBT. P. DECHERT,
Captain and Acting Assistant Adjutant-General.

ORDERS.] HEADQUARTERS TWENTIETH CORPS,
Bark Camp Creek, Ga., December 1, 1864.

The march will be continued to-morrow in the same order as to-day, toward Millen. Each division will start at 6 a. m. The Michigan Engineers, the pontoon train and all other trains, and the artillery, will occupy the same places in the column as to-day, and will be ready to start at 6 a. m. The cavalry will march at 5.30 a. m. The brigadier-general commanding desires to have the whole corps reach Buck Head Creek to-morrow night. During the march to-morrow each brigade commander will send out a foraging party of fifty men, to fill, as far as possible, all the forage and subsistence wagons, gathering all the sweet potatoes and other vegetables that can be found. These parties can be sent out on the flanks of the column for a distance of two miles, within which limit an abundance of all required stores can be found. Under no circumstances will any party be allowed to forage in advance of the column, and any party so found will be arrested. All foragers must be provided with a pass and authority, as required by existing orders. Colonel Hughes, commanding cavalry, will arrest and send to the rear all unauthorized persons found straggling in front of the column. Attention is again called to the existing orders prohibiting unauthorized firing by foragers.

By command of Brig. Gen. A. S. Williams:

ROBT. P. DECHERT,
Captain and Acting Assistant Adjutant-General.

ORDERS.] HDQRS. FIRST DIVISION, TWENTIETH CORPS,
Near Birdville, Ga., December 1, 1864.

This division will march at 8 a. m. this morning through Birdville, in the following order: Second Brigade in advance, Third to follow, and First Brigade in rear. The brigades will be so disposed as to guard the train of the division in the manner heretofore ordered, each brigade taking one-third of the wagons, viz, about seventy-five wagons. The division will be preceded by the Second Division and followed by the Third Division.

By command of Brig. Gen. N. J. Jackson:

GEO. ROBINSON,
First Lieutenant and Acting Assistant Adjutant-General.

ORDERS.] HDQRS. FIRST DIVISION, TWENTIETH CORPS,
Near Bark Camp Creek, December 1, 1864.

This division will march to-morrow toward Millen, starting at 6 a. m., in the following order: The Third Brigade in advance, four regiments of which will march in advance of the train and the remaining two regiments to guard fifty of the leading wagons of the division; the Second Brigade to follow, to guard the remainder of the train, with one regiment in rear of the wagons. Pursuant to orders from corps headquarters, each brigade commander will send out to-morrow a foraging party of fifty men, to fill, as far as possible, all the forage and subsistence wagons, gathering all the sweet potatoes and other vegetables that can be found. These parties can be sent out on the flanks of the column for a distance of two miles, within which limit an abundance of stores can be found. Under no circumstances will any party be allowed to forage in advance of the column, Colonel Hughes, commanding cavalry, having authority to arrest all such. All foraging parties must be provided with a pass, properly approved, as required by existing orders. Attention is again called to the existing orders prohibiting unauthorized firing by foragers.

By command of Brig. Gen. N. J. Jackson:

GEO. ROBINSON,
First Lieutenant and Acting Assistant Adjutant-General.

HEADQUARTERS TWENTIETH CORPS,
Near Spring Creek, Ga. (on the road), December 1, 1864.

Brig. Gen. W. T. WARD,
Commanding Third Division:

GENERAL: The general commanding directs that at 5 o'clock this evening, wherever the head of your column may be, that you encamp for the night. The brigade of Colonel Selfridge, of the First Division, will encamp with you. He directs that you move at daylight to-morrow morning toward Birdville, unless you receive further orders.

Very respectfully, your obedient servant,

ROBT. P. DECHERT,
Captain and Acting Assistant Adjutant-General.

HEADQUARTERS TWENTIETH CORPS,
Bark Camp Creek, Ga., December 1, 1864.

Brig. Gen. W. T. WARD,
Commanding Third Division:

GENERAL: The general commanding directs that you march toward Birdville at 6 a. m. to-morrow. He further directs that in case any of the wagons in your train are unable to keep closed up that you turn them out and burn them, either your own or the wagons belonging to the cavalry. He desires that you will keep a strong rear guard with artillery. Keep General Kilpatrick's wagons in rear all the time, and detail a field officer to keep them closed up; if they do [not] burn them.

Very respectfully, your obedient servant,

H. W. PERKINS,
Lieutenant-Colonel and Assistant Adjutant-General.

HEADQUARTERS MILITARY DIVISION OF THE MISSISSIPPI,
In the Field, Station No. 9, December 1, 1864.

Brig. Gen. J. KILPATRICK,
Commanding Cavalry Division:

GENERAL: Your dispatch of 12 m. yesterday just received, and Captain Audenried has also returned. Your operations have been entirely satisfactory to the general-in-chief. He wishes you to move on the flank of the Right [Left] Wing, holding your command well in hand for further work, but always giving the enemy all he wants when he offers you battle. As regards retaliation, you must be very careful as to the correctness of any information you may receive about the enemy murdering or mutilating our men. You may keep the prisoners you have, or turn any portion of them over to General Slocum's infantry to guard, and keep such as you may wish to retain for your object. You may communicate with Wheeler by flag of truce, and notify him of the conduct of his command toward our men, and that you will retaliate, which you may do until you feel satisfied. When our men are found, and you are fully convinced the enemy have killed them after surrender in fair battle, or have mutilated their bodies after being killed in fair battle, you may hang and mutilate man for man without regard to rank.

I am, general, respectfully, yours, &c.,

L. M. DAYTON,
Aide-de-Camp.

HEADQUARTERS DEPARTMENT OF THE SOUTH,
OFFICE PROVOST-MARSHAL-GENERAL,
Hilton Head, S. C., December 1, 1864—12 m.

[Lieut. Col. J. F. HALL:]

DEAR COLONEL: Three rebel deserters have just arrived—one lieutenant and two enlisted men—from Savannah. They report General Sherman's forces advancing in three columns—one column is crossing at Sister's Ferry, about seventy miles above Savannah; one column is moving from Millen, seventy-nine miles from Savannah; one column marching between Oconee and Ocmulgee Rivers. It is supposed that one column is striking for Pocotaligo. It was reported at Savannah that General Grant was to land a portion of his forces at Pocotaligo to form a junction with Sherman. The utmost excitement prevails in

Savannah. They are moving all their quartermaster's stores from that place. They are busily engaged in fortifying Savannah in the rear. There are only about one brigade of infantry at Savannah. No troops at Savannah to spare against the expedition at present going on by General Foster. These deserters left Savannah on the 29th ultimo, and the citizens there expected Sherman to arrive at Savannah on Saturday next. Our prisoners are being sent through Savannah to No. 9, on the Gulf and Atlantic Railroad; 15,000 have passed through Savannah.

More deserters just arrived, and as a boat is now leaving I send you a summary in haste. Will try and send you more complete information by next opportunity.

In haste,

FRANK GEISE,
Lieutenant and Assistant Provost-Marshal-General.

HEADQUARTERS MILITARY DIVISION OF THE MISSISSIPPI,
In the Field, Millen, Ga., December 2, 1864.

Maj. Gen. O. O. HOWARD,
Commanding Army of the Tennessee:

GENERAL: The next movement will be on Savannah, your two corps moving along down the Ogeechee—General Blair to destroy the railroad as far as Ogeechee Church, and the Fifteenth Corps keeping on the south and west bank, ready to cross over in case of opposition to General Blair, otherwise it will not cross until near Eden (No. 2). General Slocum will take the two roads north of the railroad, and between it and the Savannah River. As he will have to make a wide detour we must allow him until the fourth day to reach the road from Mill Ray to Halley's Ferry, on the Savannah River. This will make slow marching for you, but, as a general rule, the rear of the Fifteenth Corps should be about abreast of General Blair's head of column. The general has a Savannah paper of yesterday, from which he notices the enemy still remain in doubt as to his intention, being divided between Macon, Augusta, and Savannah, and also that an expedition of gun-boats has passed up the Broad River toward the Coosawhatchie. If at any time during your progress you judge it feasible, you might dispatch a small and bold party of scouts down toward Hinesville, to burn some culverts and tear up some track and cut the telegraph wire in several places on the Savannah and Gulf Railroad, over which the city of Savannah is now chiefly supplied. The fewer the men and the sooner such a party starts the better. The country is very sparsely settled, and very favorable for such an expedition.

I am, general, &c.,

L. M. DAYTON,
Aide-de-Camp.

HDQRS. DEPARTMENT AND ARMY OF THE TENNESSEE,
Clifton Ferry, Ga., December 2, 1864.

Maj. Gen. W. T. SHERMAN,
Commanding Military Division of the Mississippi:

GENERAL: The Fifteenth Corps marched in two columns as ordered. The left column reached Scull's Creek between 10 and 11 a. m.; the ford was too deep for wagons and ammunition, yet the pontoon bridge was crossed by it. General Corse built a log bridge across it; meanwhile the engineer regiment threw a bridge across at Clifton Ferry, and before 2 p. m. a brigade of General Corse's was sent to destroy as much of the railroad as possible; one mile was completely burned. A scouting party went three miles below, to Scarborough, and captured a mail and procured some information, which I inclose. The right column is now on Statesborough road, near the intersection of Clifton Ferry road. To-morrow the Fifteenth Corps will assist the Seventeenth to destroy the railroad as far as Scarborough, but will not advance unless you so direct.

I am now in readiness to cross at Clifton Ferry, or to move on and cross wherever you may wish.

Respectfully,

O. O. HOWARD,
Major-General.

[Inclosure.]

FORAGE DEPARTMENT, QUARTERMASTER'S OFFICE,
Savannah, November 22, 1864.

Mr. WILLIAM B. FARR,
Screven County:

DEAR SIR: It is of the utmost importance that grain be forwarded from Screven County immediately, and I hereby direct you to work, if necessary, night and day to accomplish this end. On the Central road the agents who are not agents for collection of tax in kind, I direct you to employ as my agents for the time. On Savannah River, if necessary, I hereby empower you to use my name in employing such agents, for the time being, as may be necessary to forward these supplies. I expect from 6,000 to 10,000 bushels corn from you in next ten days, as tax in kind. I have empowered Colonel Lawton to impress all surplus forage. Upon the prompt receipt of forage from Screven County may depend the defeat of Sherman, as this city is evidently his objective point.

Sacks have been sent to you at Nos. 5, 6, and 7, Charleston railroad.

BENJ. E. CRANE,
Major and Quartermaster.

PROVOST-MARSHAL-GENERAL'S OFFICE,
DEPARTMENT AND ARMY OF THE TENNESSEE,
Near Clifton Ferry, Ga., December 2, 1864.

Maj. Gen. O. O. HOWARD,
Commanding Army of the Tennessee.

GENERAL: I have the honor to report that, after the laying of the pontoon bridge this a. m., I crossed with your escort company, and, in accordance with instructions received from you, advanced four miles southeast from the bridge and entered Scarborough, or Station No. 7, about 3 o'clock. A train, consisting of an engine and four box-cars, had been there two hours previous, having come up from Savannah and immediately returned. I found in the post-office a file of late papers which I inclose. Citizens report that nineteen car-loads of troops passed south on Monday last. No other troops have gone south during the past two weeks. They have seen nothing of Wheeler's forces, except two or three small scouting parties of eight or ten men each. One of the citizens had come up from Savannah the day previous, and stated that the forces there numbered about 3,000 men, under command of General Dick Taylor. Bragg was expected from Wilmington, via Charleston, with from 10,000 to 15,000 men. General Wayne was at Waynesborough, or Station 4½, with 2,000 militia. No other troops were on the road between No. 7 and Savannah. Troops were sent up from Savannah to aid in repulsing an attack by the Federal forces from Port Royal, on the Charleston railroad. He represents the fighting as having been severe, resulting in the repulse of the Federals. Attention is called to the report of Mr. Lonergan, telegraph operator, who accompanied me.

Very respectfully, your obedient servant,

D. W. WHITTLE,
Captain and Assistant Provost-Marshal-General.

[Inclosure.]

HDQRS. DEPARTMENT AND ARMY OF THE TENNESSEE,
Near Clifton Ferry, Ga., December 2, 1864.

Maj. Gen. O. O. HOWARD,
Commanding:

GENERAL: I have the honor to report that I tapped the Confederate telegraph line at Station No. 7, communicating with Savannah. I listened for about fifteen minutes to the rebel telegraph operators asking each other questions, none of which are important enough to quote. Hearing the signal "9" given repeatedly, I ventured to answer to that call, and succeeded well in deceiving the operator at Savannah, he thinking that I was the proper person. He asked, "What is the news? What is going on?" (These questions satisfied me that I answered properly.) To which I replied, "The Yankees have not yet crossed the river, and all is quiet." I then asked, "What is the news from the East? How are things looking in Savannah?" He then asked for my name. (In the meantime Captain Taggart, assistant adjutant-general, ascertained the operator's name, who had left an hour and a half previous to the capture of the station.) To which I replied promptly. The operator whose name I assumed had just arrived at the next office south of Station No. 7, and at once disclosed as to who I was. Knowing that I was discovered, and, at the suggestion of Captain Taggart, sent a message to the commanding officer at Savannah giving the compliments of General Howard and staff, signing Capt. S. L. Taggart's name; also, the compliments of General Howard to the mayor of Savannah, hoping to meet him soon, &c. Having been informed by a citizen who had left Savannah this day that Bragg was expected there with 10,000 men, I asked if he had arrived; to which the rebel operator replied, "Yes, and will soon give you all the information you desire;" to which I replied, "We will be happy to see him and ascertain, as we did at Missionary Ridge." Darkness approaching and camp being some distance off, the conversation ended.

Respectfully, yours,

JNO. LONERGAN,
Operator.

SPECIAL FIELD ORDERS, No. 183.

HEADQUARTERS DEPARTMENT AND ARMY OF THE TENNESSEE,
Clifton Ferry, Ga., December 2, 1864.

The following are the orders for this army to-morrow, the 3d instant: First, Major-General Blair will continue his march along the railroad, which he will thoroughly destroy en route to No. 7, where he will encamp his command to-morrow night. Second, no general movement of the Fifteenth Corps will take place. Major-General Osterhaus, commanding, will send out his mounted infantry on both sides of the river toward Station No. 5, to reconnoiter and gather information, &c., and secure any bridges or fords on the river between this point and that station. He will also send two brigades across the river at Clifton Ferry, which, with the brigade already over, will assist the Seventeenth Corps in destroying the railroad—one brigade to work from present break toward Millen, until met by the Seventeenth Corps; one to destroy toward No. 7, and the third to act as a reserve and guard. Division commanders will employ their pioneer corps in repairing and corduroying bad places in the main Savannah roads, as far in advance as practicable.

By order of Maj. Gen. O. O. Howard:

SAML. L. TAGGART,
Assistant Adjutant-General.

SPECIAL ORDERS, No. 188.

HDQRS. FIFTEENTH ARMY CORPS,
Scull's Creek, Ga., December 2, 1864.

I. As the command will remain at its present camp to-morrow division commanders will cause an inspection to be made of the arms, accouterments, and ammunition in the hands of the men; also, of the stock and transportation of the command. Regimental commanders will not permit more than thirty of their command to be mounted for foraging and other purposes, and men thus authorized to be mounted must be furnished with a written certificate, stating the nature of duty, regiment to which he belongs, &c.

II. Brigadier-General Woods, commanding First Division, will detail one brigade of infantry from his command, and will cause the same to cross the river at the pontoon bridge and assist in destroying the railroad, commencing at the present break and working toward Millen until it strikes the Seventeenth Army Corps. Brigadier-General Corse, commanding the Fourth Division, will detail one brigade of infantry to assist in destroying the railroad, commencing at the present break and ending at Station No. 7; also one brigade to act as a reserve guard for the troops while working. The brigades to march at 6.30 a. m. to-morrow.

* * * * * * *

By order of Maj. Gen. P. Jos. Osterhaus:

F. F. WHITEHEAD,
Assistant Adjutant-General.

SPECIAL FIELD ORDERS, No. 22.

HEADQUARTERS FOURTH DIVISION, FIFTEENTH ARMY CORPS,
In the Field, Scull's Creek, Ga., December 2, 1864.

In compliance with instructions received from corps headquarters, the First Brigade, Brig. Gen. E. W. Rice commanding, will assist to-morrow in destroying the railroad, commencing at the present break and ending at Station No. 7. Col. R. N. Adams, commanding Second Brigade, will act as a reserve guard for the troops while working. The troops to march at 6.30 a. m.

By order of Brig. Gen. John M. Corse:

L. CARPER,
Assistant Adjutant-General.

HEADQUARTERS SEVENTEENTH ARMY CORPS,
Millen, Ga., December 2, 1864.

Capt. L. M. DAYTON,
Aide-de-Camp:

CAPTAIN: I send you a copy of another dispatch. The operator at Augusta called this office this afternoon before any dispatches were taken off, and said that he knew there was a Yankee operator on the line, and that he might as well let the cat out of the bag and acknowledge that he was there, and they would have a talk. Our operator has done nothing to excite his suspicions more than answering his call for a new office that has been put on the line to-day, and not far from here. Since this last dispatch was taken off they have been talking, as operators often do, about various subjects, our man assuming to be at the new station mentioned above. Among other things, the Augusta man said he never saw so many troops passing through the town as there were to-night. Upon being asked what troops they were, he said they were from Virginia. Our operator thinks now that they know what's up, and are trying to stuff him; and I think he is right in his opinion. They are very communicative, and answer anything that is asked. The chief operator at Augusta is the one working the line.

Very respectfully,

C. CADLE, JR.,
Assistant Adjutant-General.

HEADQUARTERS MILITARY DIVISION OF THE MISSISSIPPI,
In the Field, near Millen, December 2, 1864.

Maj. Gen. F. P. BLAIR,
Commanding Seventeenth Corps:

GENERAL: The general-in-chief has made his camp on the west side of Buck Head Creek. He wishes you to camp a brigade near it and let the pontoon bridge remain until further orders.

I am, general, very respectfully, &c.,

L. M. DAYTON,
Aide-de-Camp.

HEADQUARTERS MILITARY DIVISION OF THE MISSISSIPPI,
In the Field, December 2, 1864.

Maj. Gen. F. P. BLAIR,
Commanding Seventeenth Corps:

GENERAL: The general-in-chief does not expect you to move more than five miles to-morrow, to the vicinity of Paramore's Hill; but wishes you to make the most complete and perfect possible break of the railroad about Millen. Let it be more devilish than can be dreamed of.

I am, general, very respectfully, yours,

L. M. DAYTON,
Aide-de-Camp.

HEADQUARTERS SEVENTEENTH ARMY CORPS,
Millen, Ga., December 2, 1864.

Capt. SAMUEL L. TAGGART,
Asst. Adjt. Gen., Department and Army of the Tennessee:

CAPTAIN: My command will be in camp at this place before dark. The road has been completely destroyed along my route. We were obliged to use the pontoons in crossing Buck Head Creek. There were a few of the enemy at the depot early this morning, but they did not oppose us. I forward copy of General Sherman's directions for my movement to-morrow.*

Very respectfully, your obedient servant,

FRANK P. BLAIR, JR.,
Major-General.

SPECIAL ORDERS, No. 296. } HDQRS. SEVENTEENTH ARMY CORPS,
Millen, Ga., December 2, 1864.

This command will move about five miles to-morrow. The main object will be to destroy the railroad. To effect this each division will detach a brigade to work on the road, as follows:

The brigade from Brig. Gen. M. D. Leggett's division will destroy from and including the railroad bridge to the end of the double track east of the depot. The depot will not be burned until all trains have passed it. The brigade from Maj. Gen. J. A. Mower's division will destroy from the end of the double track two miles and a half east. The brigade from Brig. Gen. G. A. Smith's division will destroy two miles and a half, commencing at the east end of the work assigned to General Mower's brigade.

The work on the railroad will commence at 7 a. m. The destruction of the railroad must be complete; nothing must be left but old iron and the roadbed.

Brig. Gen. G. A. Smith, commanding Fourth Division, will move his command at 8 a. m. on the road on the south side of the railroad.

Brig. Gen. M. D. Leggett, commanding Third Division, will be prepared to move at 9 a. m., and will follow the Fourth Division.

Maj. Gen. J. A. Mower, commanding First Division, will move at 10 a. m. on the road north of the railroad. Should the road taken by Major-General Mower intersect the road taken by the other two divisions, he will wait until they pass and follow the Third Division.

The pontoon train, Lieutenant-Colonel Rusk commanding, will follow the train of the Third Division.

By command of Maj. Gen. F. P. Blair:

C. CADLE, JR.,
Assistant Adjutant-General.

ORDERS.] HDQRS. FIRST DIVISION, 17TH ARMY CORPS,
Near Millen, Ga., December 2, 1864.

The troops of this command will march to-morrow at 10 a. m. Order of march: First, pioneer corps; second, Third Brigade; third, First Michigan Battery;† fourth, First Brigade; fifth, Second Brigade; sixth, ambulance corps; seventh, ordnance train; eighth, supply train.

---

* See next, *ante.*

†Battery C, First Michigan Light Artillery.

The Second Brigade, Brigadier-General Sprague commanding, will destroy two miles and a half of railroad, commencing at the end of the double track east of the station house, at 7 a. m., and will work eastward. The road must be destroyed thoroughly; nothing must be left but the old iron and the roadbed.

By order of Maj. Gen. J. A. Mower:

CHAS. CHRISTENSEN,
Lieutenant and Acting Assistant Adjutant-General.

HDQRS. FIRST BRIG., THIRD DIV., 17TH ARMY CORPS,
In the Field, Ga., December 2, 1864.

Capt. C. CADLE, Jr.,
Assistant Adjutant-General:

CAPTAIN: I have the honor to report that I struck the railroad at Station 9 at the beginning of dawn this morning, and worked thence to Buck Head Creek, destroying in each mile a section the length of the brigade, all trestles and culverts, burning the depot and tanks, a considerable amount of new ties and prepared lumber, and a flat-boat loaded with cord wood. In the section destroyed the ties and stringers were burned and the rails bent. A pile of rails near the road was also bent by fire. A small section of quadruple track west of Station 9 was also destroyed. No cotton was found. The road was extremely intersected with culverts and small trestles; some of them were banked up and the track partly excavated, in the hope that rising water might destroy it. I regret to say that the trestle nearest Buck Head Creek may not be thoroughly destroyed; it was reached at the close of the afternoon, and was thought at first to be needed for the crossing of troops. I never saw men work more honestly; they toiled zealously on the track ten hours, with one short respite for coffee.

I am, captain, very respectfully, your obedient servant,

M. F. FORCE,
Brigadier-General, U. S. Volunteers.

SPECIAL ORDERS, } HDQRS. FOURTH DIV., 17TH ARMY CORPS,
No. 153. } *Millen, Ga., December 2, 1864.*

I. This command will move about five miles to-morrow. Brig. Gen. W. W. Belknap will move his brigade at 7 a. m., by any practicable route, to an intermediate point on the railroad between mile posts 76 and 77, and completely destroy the railroad from that point to mile post 74, so that nothing will be left but old iron and the roadbed. The First Brigade, battery, trains, &c., of this division will move at 8 a. m. to-morrow on the road on the south side of the railroad. The train of the Third Brigade will follow the train of these headquarters. After having destroyed the road Brig. Gen. W. W. Belknap's brigade will go into camp near the First Brigade, in the vicinity of mile post 74.

II. Capt. J. H. Davis, commanding pioneer corps, will issue to the contrabands belonging to his corps such articles of military clothing as are absolutely necessary for their comfort until other clothing can be procured.

By order of Brig. Gen. Giles A. Smith:

CHAS. H. BRUSH,
First Lieutenant and Acting Assistant Adjutant-General.

HEADQUARTERS MILITARY DIVISION OF THE MISSISSIPPI,
In the Field, near Millen, Ga., December 2, 1864.

Maj. Gen. H. W. SLOCUM,
Commanding Left Wing, &c.:

GENERAL: The general-in-chief has made camp near the mouth of Buck Head Creek, and the troops are passing over into Millen. He wishes you to-morrow to make a good break of the railroad from Millen to Augusta, to the right and left of the points crossed by the Fourteenth and Twentieth Corps, after which to move out and continue to march toward Savannah by two roads, leaving the one along the railroad for General Blair. The two roads indicated on our maps—the one passing near Millen and near Hunter's Mills, and the other sweeping around by Sharp's and Buck Creek Post-Office—will answer; but if one can be found leading from the upper road, through Sylvania, toward Halley's Ferry, on the Savannah River, it would answer our purpose better for your left corps. General Kilpatrick will be instructed to confer with you and cover your rear. Dress to the right on the Seventeenth Corps, whose progress you can rate by the smokes. General Blair will continue to burn the railroad as he marches as far as Ogeechee Church. The general wishes all the heads of columns to be on the road leading from Mill Ray to Halley's Ferry on the fourth day, including to-morrow. Communicate as often as possible with him, but failing to hear from him always act in concert with General Blair's column, which alone is expected to meet opposition. General Howard, with the Fifteenth Corps, will continue on the south bank of the Ogeechee, ready to turn any position of the enemy in case he offers opposition to our progress.

I am, general, very respectfully, &c.,

L. M. DAYTON,
Aide-de-Camp.

HEADQUARTERS FOURTEENTH ARMY CORPS,
Hodges' House, December 2, 1864.

Brig. Gen. A. BAIRD,
Commanding Third Division, Fourteenth Army Corps:

The general commanding directs me to acknowledge the receipt of your note of yesterday to him. He desires you to cross Rocky Creek, and thence follow one of the roads indicated on the maps toward Reynolds' and between Rocky Creek and the railroad. He desires General Kilpatrick to take care of the bridge over Brier Creek (which he already reports destroyed), and does not wish you to venture so far with your infantry. He will move from this point (ten miles east of Louisville) with Morgan and the trains, and camp at Buck Head bridge to-night. We have met no opposition on this road, and can hear of none this side of Buck Head, where report places Wheeler. The general desires you to advance as far to-day in the general direction indicated as you can do with safety.

I have the honor to be, general, very respectfully, your obedient servant,

A. C. McCLURG,
Assistant Adjutant-General and Chief of Staff.

ORDERS.] HEADQUARTERS TWENTIETH CORPS,
Buck Head Church, Ga., December 2, 1864.

This corps will march to-morrow toward Sylvania, as follows: First Division at 6.30 a. m.; Third Division at 7 a. m.; Second Division at 10 a. m. The cavalry will start at 6 a. m. The advance will consist of two brigades of infantry, the Michigan Engineers, and a battery of artillery. The Michigan Engineers will march between the two advanced brigades. On arriving at the railroad, the column will halt, and the leading brigade and the engineers be set to work destroying it, halting for that purpose about two hours. The cavalry wagons for the march will be considered as a part of the train of the rear division, and will be taken care of by General Geary; for this purpose General Ward will detach one brigade to assist him. The pontoon train will precede the train of the First Division; and the train of Captain Schoeninger and the artillery ammunition train, with the wagons of the Michigan Engineers for the march, will be considered as part of the train of the leading division, marching in rear of it. General Jackson will give them all necessary care and assistance; one of his regiments will march in rear of them. The wagons of the cavalry will march in the extreme rear.

By command of Brig. Gen. A. S. Williams:

ROBT. P. DECHERT,
Captain and Acting Assistant Adjutant-General.

ORDERS.] HDQRS. FIRST DIVISION, TWENTIETH CORPS,
Buck Head Church, Ga., December 2, 1864.

This division will march to-morrow (having the advance), at 6.30 a. m., toward Sylvania, in the following order: First Brigade in advance and Third Brigade to follow, both to be unencumbered with wagons. The Michigan Engineers and a battery of artillery will march between these two brigades. The Second Brigade will be so disposed as to guard the pontoon train (which precedes the division train), the wagon train of the division, the corps supply train, the artillery ammunition train, and the wagons of the Michigan Engineers, one of the regiments being placed in rear of all these trains. On arriving at the railroad the column will halt and the leading brigade be set to work, with the Michigan Engineers, destroying the track, halting for that purpose two hours. Captain Hard will assign a sufficient number of the empty ambulances for the temporary use of each brigade to the brigade commanders, who will inform the chief quartermaster of the division what position they wish them to have in the train.

By command of Brig. Gen. N. J. Jackson:

GEO. ROBINSON,
First Lieutenant and Acting Assistant Adjutant-General.

HDQRS. THIRD DIVISION, TWENTIETH ARMY CORPS,
Three Miles and a Half East of Birdville, December 2, 1864—12 m.

Lieut. Col. H. W. PERKINS,
Assistant Adjutant-General, Twentieth Army Corps:

COLONEL: Close up on rear of First (General Jackson's) Division. Have halted for dinner. Will start again at 1.30 p. m.

Very respectfully, your obedient servant,

W. T. WARD,
Brigadier-General, Commanding Division.

HEADQUARTERS TWENTIETH CORPS,
Buck Head, Ga., December 2, 1864.

Brig. Gen. W. T. WARD,
Commanding Third Division:

GENERAL: The general commanding directs me to say that you may encamp your command on the east side of Buck Head Creek to-night, and move early in the morning. If the trains of the First Division should not have pulled out on the road to-morrow morning, he wishes you to cross your train, and park it on this side until it is on the road.

Very respectfully, your obedient servant,

ROBT. P. DECHERT,
Captain and Acting Assistant Adjutant-General.

HEADQUARTERS MILITARY DIVISION OF THE MISSISSIPPI,
In the Field, near Millen, Ga., December 2, 1864.

General J. KILPATRICK,
Commanding Cavalry Division:

GENERAL: The army will move on Savannah, delaying only to continue the destruction of the railroad from Millen as far as Ogeechee Church. General Howard will continue to move along the south bank of the Ogeechee, General Blair along the railroad, and General Slocum by the two roads lying north of the railroad, between it and the Savannah River. The general wishes you to confer with General Slocum, to make a strong feint up in the direction of Waynesborough, and then to cover his rear from molestation by dashes of cavalry. I send you copies of two letters from members of Wheeler's staff which will interest you. After reading, please return, for file in this office.

I am, general, respectfully, yours, &c.,

L. M. DAYTON,
Aide-de-Camp.

CITY POINT, VA., *December 3, 1864.*

Maj. Gen. W. T. SHERMAN,
Commanding Armies, near Savannah, Ga.:

The little information gleaned from the Southern press indicating no great obstacle to your progress, I have directed your mails, which had been previously collected in Baltimore by Colonel Markland, special agent of the Post-Office Department, to be sent as far as the blockading squadron off Savannah, to be forwarded to you as soon as heard from on the coast. Not liking to rejoice before the victory is assured I abstain from congratulating you and those under your command until bottom has been struck. I have never had a fear of the result. Since you left Atlanta no very great progress has been made here. The enemy has been closely watched though, and prevented from detaching against you. I think not one man has gone from here except some 1,200 or 1,500 dismounted cavalry. Bragg has gone from Wilmington. I am trying to take advantage of his absence to get possession of that place. Owing to some preparations Admiral Porter and General Butler are making to blow up Fort Fisher, and which, while I hope for the best, do not believe a particle in, there is a delay in getting the expedition off. I hope they will be ready to start by the 7th, and that Bragg will not have started back by that time. In this letter I do not intend to give you anything like directions for future action, but will state a general idea I have, and will get your views after you have established yourself on the sea-coast. With your veteran army I hope to get control of the only two through routes from east to west possessed by the enemy before the fall of Atlanta. This condition will be filled by holding Savannah and Augusta, or by holding any other port to the east of Savannah and Branchville. If Wilmington falls a force from there can co-operate with you. Thomas has got back into the defenses of Nashville, with Hood close upon him. Decatur has been abandoned, and so have all the roads, except the main one leading to Chattanooga. Part of the falling back was undoubtedly necessary, and all of it may have been; it did not look so, however, to me. In my opinion Thomas far outnumbers Hood in infantry, in cavalry Hood has the advantage in morale and numbers. I hope yet Hood will be badly crippled, if not destroyed. The general news you will learn from the papers better than I could give it. After all becomes quiet, and roads up here so bad that there is likely to be a week or two that nothing can be done, I will run down the coast and see you. If you desire it, I will ask Mrs. Sherman to go with me.

U. S. GRANT,
Lieutenant-General.

HEADQUARTERS MILITARY DIVISION OF THE MISSISSIPPI,
In the Field, near Millen, Ga., December 3, 1864—2.30 a. m.

Major-General HOWARD,
Commanding Right Wing, &c.:

Your dispatch of the 2d, with papers, &c., are at hand. The general-in-chief has sent you instructions in a cipher dispatch, and further directs you to remain as at present, for him to hear from General Slocum. He has no objection to your sending expeditions out to break small portions of the railroad, which might be done by small parties going down in boats and landing. This will prevent the enemy getting supplies into Savannah, which is very desirable. In tapping the wire here we learned that Bragg was to leave Augusta in this direction to-night, 2d, with 10,000 men, to be followed by part of Wade Hampton's cavalry. Bragg will be likely to attack in rear if he can.

I am, general, very respectfully, &c.,

L. M. DAYTON,
Aide-de-Camp.

SPECIAL FIELD ORDERS, No. 184.

HEADQUARTERS DEPARTMENT AND ARMY OF THE TENNESSEE,
Clifton Ferry, Ga., December 3, 1864.

I. This army will move forward to-morrow, the 4th instant, as follows: First, Major-General Blair, commanding Seventeenth Army Corps, will move his command, starting at 6.30 a. m., along the railroad, which he will continue to destroy en route to Cameron (or No. $5\frac{1}{2}$). Second, Major-General Osterhaus, commanding Fifteenth Corps, will continue to move his command in two columns, on the west side of the river, the right column continuing its march toward Statesborough, making to-morrow a distance of fifteen miles. He will recall the portion of his command now on the east side of the river this p. m., except a sufficient force for a bridge guard, which will recross at an early hour to-morrow, and the bridge then be taken up. Third, his left column will move forward at 6.30 a. m., on the upper Savannah (or River) road, to a point opposite No. 5½ (or Cameron). Fourth, the train proper of these headquarters will follow the ammunition wagons of the leading division of the left column, and the supply train will move in advance of the supply train of such division. The cattle will continue to follow the column with which they have heretofore moved.

* * * * * * *

By order of Maj. Gen. O. O. Howard:

SAML. L. TAGGART,
Assistant Adjutant-General.

SPECIAL ORDERS, No. 189. } HDQRS. FIFTEENTH ARMY CORPS,
Scull's Creek, Ga., December 3, 1864.

I. When the corps is marching against the enemy in two columns and the major-general commanding is marching with the left column, the right column, composed of Second and Third Divisions, whenever circumstances demand the co-operation of the same, will be under the immediate command of Brig. Gen. W. B. Hazen, by virtue of seniority of rank.

II. The corps will continue its march to-morrow in the following order: First, the right column will march to Statesborough. The Second Division, Brigadier-General Hazen commanding, having the advance, will march from its present camp at 6.30 a. m. The Third Division, Brigadier-General Smith commanding, will follow the Second Division, making its destination the same. The proximity of the enemy makes it necessary that the two divisions forming the right column encamp within supporting distance. Therefore, if Statesborough cannot be reached by the divisions forming that column, any camp west of that place affording a strong defensive position will be chosen. Second, the left column will also leave its present camp at 6.30 a. m. for Cameron, opposite 5½, the First Division, Brigadier-General Woods commanding, having the advance, to be followed by the Fourth Division, Brigadier-General Corse commanding. Lieutenant-Colonel Tweeddale, commanding engineer troops, will cause the bridge at Clifton Crossing to be taken up at 6.30 a. m., and will follow the left column with his train of the same. The brigade of Fourth Division now stationed at the bridge will escort the train until it rejoins the column, which, if arriving in time and circumstances will admit of it, the entire pontoon train, together with engineer troops, will fall in column and march in rear of First Division train, otherwise they will follow the train of Fourth Division. Division commanders will be very careful and encamp their commands with a view to defense, as the expected approach of a large force of the enemy renders a sudden attack very probable. The exposed wings should be very strong, and, if possible, rest on a natural point of security, such as creeks, swamps, &c. The picket and outpost duties, which have been neglected for some time, must be enforced with the utmost strictness, and officers intrusted with this very important service will act with all circumspection and attention demanded by the duties of the occasion.

* * * * * * *

By order of Maj. Gen. P. Joseph Osterhaus:

F. F. WHITEHEAD,
Assistant Adjutant-General.

SPECIAL FIELD ORDERS, No. 23. } HEADQUARTERS FOURTH DIVISION, FIFTEENTH ARMY CORPS, *In the Field, Scull's Creek, Ga., December 3, 1864.*

* * * * * * *

IV. This command will move to-morrow, the 4th instant, at 6.30 a. m. The pioneer corps will make, as near as practicable, a parallel road to the one used by the First Division. The Third Brigade will have the advance, followed by the battery; the Second Brigade will move in the center, on either side of the trains; the First Brigade will bring up the rear. Ambulances loaded with sick and wounded will hereafter, and until further orders, move in the rear of the brigade trains. The trains will move in the following order: First, the pioneer corps train; second, the Third Brigade train; third, the Second Brigade train; fourth, the First Brigade train; fifth, the ordnance train; sixth, the supply train.

By order of Brig. Gen. John M. Corse:

L. CARPER,
Assistant Adjutant-General.

HDQRS. FIRST BRIG., FOURTH DIV., 15TH ARMY CORPS,
In the Field, Ogeechee River, Ga., December 3, 1864.

Capt. LEO CARPER,
Asst. Adjt. Gen., Fourth Division, Fifteenth Army Corps:

CAPTAIN: To-day, as I was finishing the work of destroying the railroad assigned to me, I received direct an order from General Howard directing me to withdraw my working parties across the river, also directing that the regiments then occupying the tête-de-pont which I constructed to cover the pontoon bridge should remain there during the night. This last order I gave to Colonel Adams, commanding Second Brigade, whose regiments were then occupying the works. After my brigade was encamped about three-quarters of a mile from the bridge, Colonel Adams withdrew his command from the tête-de-pont, thus leaving the bridge uncovered. My command worked hard yesterday, a portion of it until 11 o'clock at night, besides working hard to-day, or I would order two regiments back without troubling you. Under the circumstances I think Colonel Adams should order two regiments back to the tête-de-pont.

E. W. RICE,
Brigadier-General, Commanding.

SPECIAL ORDERS, No. 297. } HDQRS. SEVENTEENTH ARMY CORPS, *Station 7, Ga., December 3, 1864.*

I. Each division will detach a brigade to-morrow for the destruction of the railroad. The brigade from the Fourth Division will destroy from Station 7 three miles east. The brigade from the First Division will destroy from the end of the work assigned to the Fourth Division three miles east. The brigade from the Third Division will destroy from the end of the work assigned to the Fourth Division three miles east. The work will commence at 6 a. m., and will be complete.

The command will move as follows:

Brig. Gen. M. D. Leggett, commanding Third Division, will move out his command on the Savannah road at 7 a. m.

Maj. Gen. J. A. Mower, commanding First Division, will be prepared to move at 8 o'clock, and will follow the Third Division.

Brig. Gen. G. A. Smith, commanding Fourth Division, will be prepared to move at 9 o'clock, and will follow the First Division.

The pontoon train, Lieut. Col. J. M. Rusk commanding, will follow the train of the Third Division.

The trains of the headquarters Military Division of the Mississippi and of these headquarters will follow the advance brigade.

II. Forage parties will not be permitted to move in advance of the column; they must keep on the flank of the command. Hereafter all stragglers and foragers found in advance of the column of infantry will be arrested and held for punishment. The pickets will be instructed not to permit foragers or stragglers to pass the lines before the column starts.

The commanding officer of the First Alabama Cavalry is instructed to arrest all stragglers moving with or in advance of his command, and report them to the corps provost-marshal.

Commanding officers of forage parties must keep their men together, and will only permit those men to separate from their commands who are left to guard or bring along forage.

This order must be strictly complied with, and violations of it will subject the offender to punishment.

* * * * * * *

By command of Maj. Gen. F. P. Blair:

C. CADLE, JR.,
Assistant Adjutant-General.

ORDERS.] HDQRS. FIRST DIVISION, 17TH ARMY CORPS,
In the Field, Ga., December 3, 1864.

The troops of this command will be prepared to march to-morrow morning at 8 a. m. Order of march: First, pioneer corps; second, First Brigade; third, battery; fourth, Second Brigade; fifth, ambulance train; sixth, ordnance train; seventh, supply train.

Col. John Tillson, commanding Third Brigade, will move his command out to-morrow morning at 6 o'clock to a point on the railroad three miles east of Station No. 7, where he will commence the destruction of the railroad, and will break it for a distance of three miles east. After having thoroughly completed the work of destruction he will join the column by the most practicable route.

By order of Maj. Gen. Joseph A. Mower:

CHAS. CHRISTENSEN,
Lieut., Aide-de-Camp and Acting Assistant Adjutant-General.

SPECIAL FIELD ORDERS, No. 164. } HEADQUARTERS THIRD DIVISION, SEVENTEENTH ARMY CORPS,
In the Field, Ga., December 3, 1864.

I. This command will be in readiness to move at 9 a. m. Brig. Gen. M. F. Force, commanding First Brigade, will have the advance. Artillery and trains will move as heretofore.

II. This command will move at 7 a. m. to-morrow. The Second Brigade, Col. R. K. Scott commanding, will have the advance. Artillery and trains will move as heretofore.

III. Capt. Alexander McIntosh, assistant quartermaster, Third Division, will cause one empty wagon to report to each regiment of this command one hour before marching to-morrow morning. These wagons will be used by the regiments for transporting their supplies—rations of flour, meal, potatoes, and bacon—and nothing else. They will accompany the regimental wagons, and will not be taken from the direct line of march.

By order of Brig. Gen. M. D. Leggett:

J. C. DOUGLASS,
Assistant Adjutant-General.

CIRCULAR.] HDQRS. FOURTH DIVISION, 17TH ARMY CORPS,
Scarborough, Ga., December 3, 1864.

The First Brigade of this command will destroy the railroad from Station 7 to a point three miles east, commencing at 6 a. m. to-morrow. The remainder of the division will be prepared to move at 9 a. m. to-morrow, on the Savannah road. An officer of the staff will assign the different commands their respective places in order of march.

By order of Brig. Gen. Giles A. Smith:

CHAS. H. BRUSH,
First Lieutenant and Acting Assistant Adjutant-General.

HEADQUARTERS MILITARY DIVISION OF THE MISSISSIPPI,
In the Field, Millen, Ga., December 3, 1864.

Major-General SLOCUM,
Commanding Left Wing, &c.:

GENERAL: Concentrate your command at or near Buck Head Church, prepared to move toward Savannah by two or more roads, dressing to the right on General Blair, who will move by the railroad. Look to your rear toward Augusta. Kilpatrick will be with you. I await your coming at Millen.

Respectfully, &c.,

W. T. SHERMAN,
Major-General.

HEADQUARTERS MILITARY DIVISION OF THE MISSISSIPPI,
In the Field, Millen, Ga., December 3, 1864.

Major-General SLOCUM,
Commanding Left Wing, &c.:

GENERAL: The general-in-chief wishes to know if you have received the cipher instructions, indicating the roads you are to move on to-day and following. General Blair is moving along the railroad, destroying it, and will be near Paramore's Hill to-night. No communications have been received from you for two or more days, and the general is not advised of your progress. He wishes you to inform him of your present position, viz, of the Fourteenth and Twentieth Corps, and also of General Kilpatrick, and any other information or news you may have that will be of interest or service to him.

Yours, &c.,

L. M. DAYTON,
Aide-de-Camp.

HEADQUARTERS LEFT WING, ARMY OF GEORGIA,
Four Miles from Millen, on the Augusta Railroad,
December 3, 1864—10 a. m.

Maj. Gen. W. T. SHERMAN,
General-in-Chief:

Your cipher dispatches of 3 p. m. and 12 midnight yesterday were received at Buck Head Church during last night. The Twentieth Corps and two divisions of the Fourteenth Corps camped last night near Buck Head Church. The Twentieth Corps marched at 6 a. m., and are moving on the old Savannah road, which passes just north of Hunter's Mills. The corps will probably encamp on Horse Creek to-night. The two divisions of the Fourteenth Corps that were camped with the Twentieth last night will march to-day on a road north of this, leading through Sylvania to Halley's Ferry. One division of the Fourteenth Corps and Kilpatrick's cavalry took the road from Louisville to Waynesborough, with instructions to strike across from where that road crosses Rocky Creek to Alexander, and move on the road to Jacksonborough; that is the only column that has met with any opposition from the enemy, and the opposition with them has been but slight. I shall entirely destroy four or five miles of the Augusta railroad. We have found forage and subsistence abundant, and the command is in fine condition and spirits.

Very respectfully, your obedient servant,

H. W. SLOCUM,
Major-General.

HEADQUARTERS FOURTEENTH ARMY CORPS,
Lumpkin's Station, Ga., December 3, 1864.

Brig. Gen. W. P. CARLIN,
Commanding First Division, Fourteenth Army Corps:

General Morgan will take the advance in the morning, in charge of all the trains except your own, which will be moved with your own division in the rear. You will begin at 7 o'clock in the morning to tear up the railroad, and will keep your men at work until all the other troops and trains have passed, after which you will form your column and follow General Morgan.

By order of Bvt. Maj. Gen. J. C. Davis:

A. C. McCLURG,
Assistant Adjutant-General and Chief of Staff.

HEADQUARTERS FOURTEENTH ARMY CORPS,
Lumpkin's Station, Ga., December 3, 1864.

Brigadier-General MORGAN:

GENERAL: Carlin's division will go into camp at this place, and be prepared to destroy the track early to-morrow morning. You can put your division and train in camp a mile or two back of this, and move out in the same order as to-day, at 6.30 in the morning. Let Colonel Buell's command and my headquarters wagons come on to this place as soon as you let them pass. My headquarters will be here.

Very respectfully,

JEF. C. DAVIS,
Brevet Major-General, Commanding.

HEADQUARTERS FOURTEENTH ARMY CORPS,
Lumpkin's Station, Ga., December 3, 1864.

Brig. Gen. A. BAIRD,
Commanding Third Division, Fourteenth Army Corps:

The corps is going into camp at this point, and will move for Jacksonborough at an early hour to-morrow morning. Will reach that place some time the next day. You will move from Thomas' Station to Alexander, and thence, via Sardis Church, toward Jacksonborough. You will direct Kilpatrick to protect your left flank and rear, and to destroy all the bridges on Brier Creek, beginning at the railroad crossing, if you think advisable.

By order of Bvt. Maj. Gen. J. C. Davis:

A. C. McCLURG,
Assistant Adjutant-General and Chief of Staff.

HDQRS. THIRD DIVISION, FOURTEENTH ARMY CORPS,
Thomas' Station, Ga., December 3, 1864.

Brevet Major-General DAVIS:

GENERAL: After a tedious march about the country to-day I reached this point about 4 p. m. On the way I encountered a small body of rebel cavalry, which I drove toward Waynesborough. The cavalry will not move one inch toward the enemy in advance of my column, and I have to go with it in order to accomplish what is necessary to be done. Kilpatrick will go into Waynesborough to-morrow morning, starting from here at 7 o'clock; but to induce him to do so I have promised to wait here till 8.30 o'clock, so that if he finds Wheeler there I can go up and help to whip him. If he finds him there I can well spend a day or two in trying to thrash him; if he does not find him I will move at the hour named, via Alexander, for Sardis, where I expect to be to-morrow night. I will communicate to General Kilpatrick your wishes with regard to the destruction of the railroad bridge; and it is my intention to reach Brier Creek myself from the vicinity of Alexander downward. If the cavalry understood itself to be completely under my orders I could work it to advantage; as it is we can get along well together, and I think do some good. I have thoroughly destroyed three miles of railroad to-night.

Most respectfully,

A. BAIRD,
Brigadier-General, Commanding Division.

HEADQUARTERS TWENTIETH CORPS,
Near Horse Creek, Ga., December 3, 1864.

Lieutenant-Colonel HUGHES,
Commanding Ninth Illinois Mounted Infantry:

COLONEL: I am directed by the general commanding to say that the order of march to-morrow will be the same as to-day. The column will start at 6 a. m.

Very respectfully, your obedient servant,

ROBT. P. DECHERT,
Captain and Acting Assistant Adjutant-General.

(Copies to Lieutenant-Colonel Moore, commanding pontoon train, and Major Yates, commanding Michigan Engineers.)

HEADQUARTERS TWENTIETH CORPS,
Near Horse Creek, Ga., December 3, 1864.

Brig. Gen. N. J. JACKSON,
Commanding First Division:

GENERAL: The general commanding directs me to say that you need not wait to-morrow morning for the Michigan Engineers to precede you, as they have been ordered to remain at the crossing of the creek until further orders.

Very respectfully, your obedient servant,

ROBT. P. DECHERT,
Captain and Acting Assistant Adjutant-General.

ORDERS.] HDQRS. FIRST DIVISION, TWENTIETH CORPS,
Big Horse Creek, Ga., December 3, 1864.

This division will march to-morrow (having the advance) at 6 a. m., in the following order: Second Brigade in advance, First Brigade to follow, both to be unencumbered with wagons. The Michigan Engineers, followed by four tool wagons and a battery of artillery, will have a place in the column between these two brigades. The Third Brigade will be so disposed as to guard the following trains, viz: The pontoon train, the division train, the corps supply train, the artillery ammunition train, and the wagons of the Michigan Engineers, with one regiment in rear of all these trains. The same arrangement of ambulances will be made as ordered for to-day. The leading brigade will be on the road with the head of column near the creek in our front promptly at 6 o'clock.

By command of Brig. Gen. N. J. Jackson:

GEO. ROBINSON,
First Lieutenant and Acting Assistant Adjutant-General.

HEADQUARTERS TWENTIETH CORPS,
Big Horse Creek, Ga., December 3, 1864.

Brigadier-General GEARY,
Commanding Second Division:

GENERAL: The First Division is encamped at this point. The general commanding directs that you get as far forward with your troops and trains as practicable, and go into camp. There is no camping-ground near here except in the woods. In the absence of further orders the general directs that you resume the march at 6 a. m. to morrow, under the same regulations as to-day.

Very respectfully, your obedient servant,

H. W. PERKINS,
Assistant Adjutant-General.

P. S.—Please report your location to-night.

(Same to Brigadier-General Ward.)

HDQRS. SECOND DIVISION, TWENTIETH ARMY CORPS,
In the Field, Ga., December 3, 1864.

Lieut. Col. H. W. PERKINS,
Assistant Adjutant-General, Twentieth Corps:

COLONEL: I have the honor to report that I have selected camping-ground at a point on the road which your orderly states is about one mile and a half in rear of the Third Division camp. My trains will not probably be in before 10 o'clock.

I am, colonel, very respectfully, your obedient servant,

JNO. W. GEARY,
Brigadier-General, Commanding.

HEADQUARTERS TWENTIETH CORPS,
Railroad Crossing, December 3, 1864.

Brig. Gen. W. T. WARD,
Commanding Third Division:

GENERAL: The general commanding directs that you detach one of your brigades, to follow the road that branches from the one on which you are marching, at the place where the house of Mrs. Jones was burned this morning (near the stockade), to destroy the railroad. They will work from where they strike the road this way till they meet the working party sent from here. They can, after their work is completed, follow along the railroad and join their division at this point.

Very respectfully, your obedient servant,

H. W. PERKINS,
Lieutenant-Colonel and Assistant Adjutant-General.

HDQRS. DEPARTMENT AND ARMY OF THE TENNESSEE,
Wiley's Farm, Ga., December 4, 1864.

Maj. Gen. W. T. SHERMAN,
Commanding Military Division of the Mississippi:

GENERAL: The right column reaches Statesborough, or near it, to-day. General Woods is going into camp near Wilson's Creek (the one next to Nevil's, and not named on the map). The two columns will come together opposite Guyton (or No. 3) to-morrow. I don't suppose General Blair can quite make that point, but he can come within five miles of it. The bridges across the Ogeechee at 6 and 5 are burned. What was the firing to-day? Are you meeting with resistance on the left?

Respectfully,

O. O. HOWARD,
Major-General.

SPECIAL ORDERS, } HDQRS. DEPT. AND ARMY OF THE TENN.,
No. 273. } *Louisville, Ky., December 4, 1864.*

I. Maj. Gen. John A. Logan, commanding Fifteenth Army Corps, having reported to these headquarters on expiration of his leave of absence, and being unable to join his command on account of the present movement of the army, has permission, at his own request, to visit City Point, Va.

By order of Maj. Gen. O. O. Howard:

WM. T. CLARK,
Assistant Adjutant-General.

SPECIAL FIELD ORDERS, No. 185. } HEADQUARTERS DEPARTMENT AND ARMY OF THE TENNESSEE, *Wiley's Farm, Ga., December 4, 1864.*

The movements of this army to-morrow, the 5th instant, will be: First, the Seventeenth Corps, Major-General Blair commanding, will continue its march along the railroad, destroying the same as far as Ogeechee Church, and will then push as far forward toward No. 3 (or Guyton) as possible. Second, the Fifteenth Corps, Major-General Osterhaus commanding, will concentrate at the junction of the upper and lower Savannah roads, opposite Guyton (or No. 3), the left column moving at 6.30 a. m. Third, the train proper of these headquarters will follow the ammunition wagons of the leading division of the left column, and the supply train will move in advance of the supply train of same division. The cattle will continue to move with the right column.

By order of Maj. Gen. O. O. Howard:

SAML. L. TAGGART,
Assistant Adjutant-General.

HEADQUARTERS FIFTEENTH ARMY CORPS,
Opposite 5½, December 4, 1864.

Capt. S. L. TAGGART,
Assistant Adjutant-General, Army of the Tennessee:

CAPTAIN: The officer of my staff just returning from the right column reports that General Hazen had a skirmish with some rebel cavalry on entering Statesborough. It lasted about thirty minutes, when the rebs ran away in confusion, leaving some killed, wounded, and prisoners in our hands. General Hazen's loss will not exceed 4 or 5 wounded. The enemy's force is estimated at about 300 men.

Very respectfully,

P. JOS. OSTERHAUS,
Major-General of Volunteers.

SPECIAL ORDERS, No. 190. } HDQRS. FIFTEENTH ARMY CORPS, *Wilson's Farm, Ga., December 4, 1864.*

The movements of the corps for to-morrow will be as follows: The right column (Second and Third Divisions) will leave its present camp at 6.30 a. m., and march to the junction of the upper and lower Savannah roads, opposite Guyton (or No. 3), near Branhan's Store, the Third Division, Brigadier-General Smith commanding, having the advance, if closed up on General Hazen's division. Should General Smith's command, however, not be close on to General Hazen's division the latter will continue in advance. The left column (First and Fourth Divisions) will leave its present camp at 6.30 a. m. and also move to the junction mentioned above, the Fourth Division, Brigadier-General Corse, in advance. Brigadier-General Woods, commanding First Division, if practicable, will move his command parallel with General Corse's command; if impracticable, in rear of Lieutenant-Colonel Tweeddale's command and pontoon train, which will follow the Fourth Division. The trains of department and corps headquarters will follow the ammunition wagons of the leading division (the Fourth), and in advance of the supply train of same division.

By order of Maj. Gen. P. Joseph Osterhaus:

F. F. WHITEHEAD,
Assistant Adjutant-General.

SPECIAL ORDERS, No. 244. } HDQRS. THIRD DIV., 15TH ARMY CORPS, *Near Scull's Creek, Ga., December 4, 1864.*

I. This command will move at 6.30 a. m. this day. The order of march will be the same as on the 1st instant.

By order of Brig. Gen. John E. Smith:

S. M. BUDLONG,
Assistant Adjutant-General.

SPECIAL FIELD ORDERS, No. 24. } HDQRS. FOURTH DIV., 15TH ARMY CORPS, *In the Field, Hodges' Plantation, Ga., December 4, 1864.*

I. This command will move to-morrow, the 5th instant, at 5 a. m., and march to the junction of the upper and lower Savannah roads, opposite Guyton (or No. 3), near Branhan's Store. The pioneer corps will move at the head of the column, to repair roads; the Second Brigade has the advance, followed by the battery; the First Brigade will move in the center, on either side of the trains; the Third Brigade will bring up the rear. The trains will move as follows: First, the pioneer corps train; second, the Second Brigade train; third, the First Brigade train; fourth, the Third Brigade train; fifth, the ambulances; sixth, ordnance train; seventh, the supply train.

By order of Brig. Gen. John M. Corse:

L. CARPER,
Assistant Adjutant-General.

HEADQUARTERS SEVENTEENTH ARMY CORPS,
Near Station 5½, Ga., December 4, 1864.

Capt. S. L. TAGGART,
Assistant Adjutant-General, Dept. and Army of the Tennessee:

CAPTAIN: We have marched sixteen miles to-day, and we encamped opposite Station 5½. Have destroyed nine miles of railroad. My cavalry have been to near 4½, and skirmished with the enemy from this point all the way, the last part very heavy. The enemy are on the other side of the Little Ogeechee River, reported to be fortifying. They are estimated at from 2,000 to 5,000 strong, and have artillery. They have burned the railroad bridge over the Little Ogeechee River. I shall have to use my pontoons there to-morrow. One of my staff and another officer who was with him in the advance with the cavalry report to me that Captain Duncan, commanding scouts from your headquarters, and the two of his men who were shot were disgustingly drunk to-day, and that had they been sober his men would probably not have been wounded.

Very respectfully, your obedient servant,

FRANK P. BLAIR, JR.,
Major-General.

SPECIAL ORDERS, No. 298. } HDQRS. SEVENTEENTH ARMY CORPS, *Station 5½, Ga., December 4, 1864.*

I. The Forty-first Illinois Battalion, Major McFadden commanding, is hereby temporarily detached from the Fourth Division, and assigned to duty at these headquarters as provost guard, and will forthwith report accordingly.

II. Capt. John Berry, Thirty-second Illinois Volunteers, commanding provost guard, is hereby relieved from duty at these headquarters, and will at once report with his command to his division commander.

III. This command will move forward about ten miles to-morrow, as follows:

1. Maj. Gen. J. A. Mower, commanding First Division, will have the advance, and will move forward on the Savannah road at 8 a. m.

2. Brig. Gen. Giles A. Smith, commanding Fourth Division, will be prepared to move at 9 a. m., and will follow the First Division.

3. Brig. Gen. M. D. Leggett, commanding Third Division, will be prepared to move at 10 o'clock, and will follow the Fourth Division.

4. The pontoon train, Lieut. Col. J. M. Rusk commanding, will follow the advance brigade of the First Division.

5. The trains of the headquarters Military Division of the Mississippi and these headquarters will move as heretofore.

6. Each division will detach a brigade to destroy two miles of railroad—the Third Division commencing at a point opposite their camp and working east, the Fourth Division destroying the next two miles east, the First Division the next two miles east of the Fourth Division.

IV. Lieut. Col. D. T. Kirby, picket officer Seventeenth Army Corps, will proceed, at 8.30 o'clock to-morrow morning, with the First Alabama Cavalry on the left flank of the corps, covering it. On reaching the Little Ogeechee River he will cross it at some bridge or ford above the main road. If on crossing the river the enemy are retreating he will attack them whenever practicable, according to the instructions already received by him.

By command of Maj. Gen. F. P. Blair:

C. CADLE, JR.,
Assistant Adjutant-General.

HDQRS. FIRST DIVISION, SEVENTEENTH ARMY CORPS,
In the Field, Ga., December 4, 1864.

Capt. C. CADLE, Jr.,
Assistant Adjutant-General, Seventeenth Army Corps:

My headquarters are on the right of the road going east, near Major-General Sherman's headquarters.

Respectfully,

JOS. A. MOWER,
Major-General, Commanding Division.

ORDERS.] HDQRS. FIRST DIVISION, 17TH ARMY CORPS,
In the Field, Ga., December 4, 1864.

The troops of this command will march to-morrow at 8 a. m. Order of march: First, pioneer corps; second, Second Brigade; third, battery; fourth, pontoon train; fifth, headquarters train Military Division of the Mississippi and headquarters Seventeenth Army Corps; sixth, Third Brigade; seventh, ambulance train; eighth, ordnance train; ninth, supply train.

By order of Maj. Gen. Joseph A. Mower:

CHAS. CHRISTENSEN,
Lieut., Aide-de-Camp and Acting Assistant Adjutant-General.

SPECIAL ORDERS, } HDQRS. FOURTH DIV., 17TH ARMY CORPS,
No. —. } *Near Station No. 5½, Ga., December 4, 1864.*

In accordance with Special Orders, No. 298, army corps headquarters, this division will be prepared to move at 9 a. m. to-morrow.

The First Brigade will have the advance. The artillery and trains will move relatively in the same order as to-day.

Brig. Gen. W. W. Belknap, commanding Third Brigade, will commence the destruction of the railroad (leaving camp at 6 a. m. to-morrow), commencing at a point two miles east of the present camp of the Third Division, and destroy two miles east from that point.

By order of Brig. Gen. Giles A. Smith:

CHAS. H. BRUSH,
First Lieutenant and Acting Assistant Adjutant-General.

HDQRS. MILITARY DIVISION OF THE MISSISSIPPI,
In the Field, Station No. 5½, Central Railroad,
December 4, 1864—3.15 p. m.

Major-General SLOCUM,
Commanding Left Wing, &c.:

GENERAL: Your note of 10 a. m. has been received. The day has been so good that General Blair has got to the point on our map indicated by the intersection of the main road with that leading through Sylvania, Hunter's Mills, and Paris Academy, viz, four miles west of Halcyondale. He keeps three brigades breaking railroad abreast of him. His advance on arrival here was fired on, but by parties who took good care to fire at long range and take to their heels. My judgment is that if any opposition is made to us this side of Savannah it will occur near Ogeechee Church, but Howard's movement south of Ogeechee, by Mill Ray, will turn that position. You have nothing to apprehend on your front, but should look to your rear, especially on General Davis' flank, until you get in the neck between Ogeechee Church and Halley's Ferry. I want you to report to me frequently, but in the absence of orders to move your entire wing, with Kilpatrick's cavalry, in the direction of Springfield and Monteith, getting your left flank on the Savannah and Charleston Railroad, about Saint Augustine Creek. General Blair will continue to move along the railroad, and the Fifteenth Corps will continue on the west side of the Ogeechee until abreast of Eden (No. 2). We continue to find abundance of forage, and all our animals are in first-rate condition. Nevertheless, I want to impress upon all the importance of filling all empty wagons, as it may be to our interest to act rapidly, without waiting to draw supplies from our new base. If our marching on this flank is too fast for you please notify me, and I will check it, as I am aware you are moving on a large circle. We heard the firing to-day which you report, which, from its rate of fire, I inferred to be from Kilpatrick, who is fond of using artillery. I do not know that I reported to you that at Millen we got a dispatch that Bragg proposed to follow us, with 10,000 men, from Augusta. If we can draw him down toward Savannah we can turn on him and send him off at a tangent.

I am, general, &c.,

W. T. SHERMAN,
Major-General.

HEADQUARTERS MILITARY DIVISION OF THE MISSISSIPPI,
In the Field, near No. 5½, Ga., December 4, 1864.

Maj. Gen. H. W. SLOCUM,
Commanding Right Wing:

GENERAL: Your dispatch of 10 a. m. was received as the general's answer at 3.15 p. m. will show. Since it was written a reconnoitering party sent to No. 4½ has reported the enemy was found there in force from 2,000 to 5,000. The general-in-chief wishes you to swing around on the enemy's rear, if possible, but keeping in communication with General Davis, and see he gets in no trouble. General Howard also, with the Fifteenth Corps, moves down the Ogeechee, and will turn the enemy where he now opposes us. Please make an answer by my couriers, who will return here, giving any information you may have; or if nothing worth note drop a line that we may know all is well.

I am, general, very respectfully, &c.,

L. M. DAYTON,
Aide-de-Camp.

HEADQUARTERS FOURTEENTH ARMY CORPS,
December 4, 1864.

Brig. Gen. J. D. MORGAN,
Commanding Second Division, Fourteenth Army Corps:

The general commanding directs that you move to-morrow morning at 6.30 a. m., and make as much distance as you think can be accomplished by the trains. The order of march will be the same as to-day.

Very respectfully, your obedient servant,

A. C. McCLURG,
Assistant Adjutant-General and Chief of Staff.

HDQRS. THIRD DIVISION, FOURTEENTH ARMY CORPS,
Thomas' Station, December 4, 1864.

Brevet Major-General DAVIS,
Commanding Fourteenth Corps:

GENERAL: Last night about 11.30 o'clock the enemy opened with artillery on the regiment picketing the extremity of my line, on the railroad, toward Waynesborough, about one mile and a half from here. The shots seemed to come from Napoleon guns; afterward he seemed to be intrenching during the night. Kilpatrick thinks that the fight of the campaign will take place here to-day. I do not see it in that light, but will support him; and as I have only forty rounds of ammunition it might be well for you to keep a lookout, and in case you hear firing to any extent have more ready to send me, and, perhaps, also a division to move in this direction. I will communicate with you during the day.

Respectfully,

A. BAIRD,
Brigadier-General.

HEADQUARTERS FOURTEENTH ARMY CORPS,
Lumpkin's Station, Ga., December 4, 1864.

Brig. Gen. A. BAIRD,
Commanding Third Division, Fourteenth Army Corps:

Your note is just received. The firing last night was heard by us, and supposed to be what you report it. A demonstration in the direction of Waynesborough will keep the enemy in the belief that we are advancing on Augusta; do not delay, however, long, as the troops on our right are ahead of us and are pushing. The Twentieth Corps reached Horse Creek last night. Morgan is now on the march across the railroad; he has all the trains in charge. Carlin is destroying the road, and will be on it until 10 or 11 o'clock.

Yours, truly,

JEF. C. DAVIS,
Brevet Major-General, Commanding.

HEADQUARTERS TWENTIETH CORPS,
Two Miles and a Half from Little Ogeechee River,
December 4, 1864—11 a. m.

Brig. Gen. A. S. WILLIAMS,
Commanding Twentieth Corps.

GENERAL: I halted the cavalry here until the infantry comes up, when I shall push for the bridge; the citizens report it unharmed. I think another hour's march will bring us to and across the river. Shall, therefore, not halt for dinner, unless ordered to do so; please send instructions by bearer. The cannonading on our left, or north of us, ceased about an hour ago, only occasional shots being heard. I heard about forty or fifty shots, and the cavalry reports that they heard it since daylight. Shall report as soon as my scouts return from the bridge.

Respectfully,

CHAS. W. ASMUSSEN,
Assistant Inspector-General.

HEADQUARTERS TWENTIETH CORPS,
Near Little Ogeechee Creek, Ga., December 4, 1864—6.30 p. m.

Brigadier-General GEARY,
Commanding Second Division:

GENERAL: I am directed by the general commanding to say that he has encamped at this place. The march to-morrow will be but six miles from this point, and you may exercise your discretion whether you get up here to-night or encamp farther back. In case you do not get up he directs that you resume the march to-morrow morning.

Very respectfully, your obedient servant,

ROBT. P. DECHERT,
Captain and Acting Assistant Adjutant-General.

HEADQUARTERS SECOND DIVISION, TWENTIETH CORPS,
Crooked Run, Ga., December 4, 1864.

Lieut. Col. H. W. PERKINS,
Assistant Adjutant-General, Twentieth Corps:

COLONEL: I have the honor to report that I am encamping my troops on the east side of this creek, leaving Jones' brigade on the other side to cover the crossing. My trains commenced crossing the stream at dark, at which time the last of the Third Division trains crossed. It will probably occupy nearly all night to get my trains over. In the absence of other orders I will move forward as early as possible in the morning.

I am, colonel, very respectfully, your obedient servant,

JNO. W. GEARY,
Brigadier-General, Commanding.

HEADQUARTERS CAVALRY COMMAND,
December 4, 1864.

Major-General WHEELER,
Commanding Confederate Cavalry:

GENERAL: For the memory of old associations, please let Corpl. M. D. Lacey, Tenth Ohio Cavalry, remain to attend a wounded soldier, one for whom you should have every respect, for he is very brave and a true gentleman. Captain Norton was wounded to-day charging your barricades. Please show him such attention as is in your power, and at some future day you shall have the thanks of your old friend,

J. KILPATRICK,
U. S. Army.

WASHINGTON, D. C., *December 5, 1864.*

SURGEON-GENERAL U. S. ARMY, *Washington:*

The Secretary of War directs that all supplies, stores, and material for General Sherman's army be immediately sent to Hilton Head, S. C., to be landed at such place, or places, as may be there ordered. Competent officers of each department should be at that place to forward and issue stores without delay.

Very respectfully, your obedient servant,

H. W. HALLECK,
Major-General and Chief of Staff.

(Copies to the Chief of Commissary Department, Chief Engineer, Chief of Ordnance, and the Quartermaster-General, Washington.)

CONFIDENTIAL.] DECEMBER 5, 1864.

Col. S. L. BROWN,
Q. M., Chief of Forage Division, No. 66 Cedar street, New York:

COLONEL: There should be no failure in the shipment of the daily supply of forage ordered for the army on the Potomac, the James, and those expected at Port Royal. The present indications are that somewhere within reach of Port Royal General Sherman will establish his base of supplies. I estimate the number of animals with which he will reach the coast at about 32,000. Your shipments should be sufficient for these, in addition to those already in the Department of the South. I am directed by the Secretary of War to instruct you to resort, if necessary, to the seizure of hay, rather than allow any failure to fill your orders. Such an instruction will be mailed to you with this. I need not say that this extreme measure is to be avoided if possible; but it is necessary to the safety of the country that the army trains and cavalry horses be kept in efficient condition, and, rather than let them suffer, the seizure of hay will be resorted to. Probably, if you knew of any great stock held for speculations, on intimation that if necessary this extreme measure will be employed, it will induce the owners to accept a reasonable price. For hay purchased the Department will pay as promptly as possible; hay seized will only be paid for after our debts for such as is purchased are discharged.

I am, very respectfully, your obedient servant,

M. C. MEIGS,
Quartermaster-General, Brevet Major-General.

HEADQUARTERS MILITARY DIVISION OF THE MISSISSIPPI,
In the Field, Ogeechee Church, Ga., December 5, 1864.

Major-General HOWARD,
Commanding Army of the Tennessee:

DEAR GENERAL: Since sending the messenger to you this morning General Blair has entered this place almost unopposed. Some field works are fresh, and, so far as I have examined, would be such as would be thrown up by 5,000 inexperienced hands. General Slocum reports he will be to-night at the point where his road next north of this intersects the one from here to Poor Robin, but he has not heard from Generals Davis and Kilpatrick since he heard their firing yesterday morning. Davis has orders to move from the point where he separated from Slocum, viz, Buck Head Church, to Halley's Ferry, abreast of this on the Savannah, via Sylvania. I have sent a courier to General Slocum, to communicate with General Davis at once and report to me at what moment he will be ready to move on. You will observe that, with Davis at Halley's, we threaten South Carolina, and to that extent will confuse our enemy; but I will not lose a moment, only we must move in concert, or else will get lost. You may make all the dispositions to cross at 3, but the point 2 is the true one, unless modified by local geography. I will disturb the railroad but little south of this, as we may have use for it out this far. Still, Blair can burn the bridges and culverts, and also enough cotton-gins and barns to mark the progress of his head of column. I don't want him to start till I know Davis is abreast.

Yours, &c.,

W. T. SHERMAN,
Major-General, Commanding.

SPECIAL FIELD ORDERS, No. 186.

HEADQUARTERS DEPARTMENT AND ARMY OF THE TENNESSEE,
Lane's Farm, Ga., December 5, 1864.

* * * * * * *

III. First, the command will remain substantially to-morrow as in camp this evening. Second, General Osterhaus will make a demonstration toward No. 2, and with his cavalry and a brigade of infantry secure, if possible, the bridge eight miles below this place. He will to-night send forward parties to break the railroad in two or three different places. The landing near here will be prepared and a small guard retained on either bank of the Ogeechee River during to-morrow.

By order of Maj. Gen. O. O. Howard:

SAML. L. TAGGART,
Assistant Adjutant-General.

HEADQUARTERS FIFTEENTH ARMY CORPS,
Opposite No. 3, Ga., December 5, 1864.

Brigadier-General WOODS,
Commanding First Division:

GENERAL: You will please order one of your brigades, equipped in the lightest marching order but with plenty of ammunition, to report at these headquarters at 5 a. m. to-morrow. They are destined to support the Twenty-ninth Missouri Mounted Infantry on an expedition to take Wright's Bridge or crossing, eight miles below here. A section of artillery would be desirable; also a good detail of pioneers.

By order of Maj. Gen. P. Joseph Osterhaus:

F. F. WHITEHEAD,
Assistant Adjutant-General.

SPECIAL ORDERS, No. 250. } HDQRS. FIRST DIV., 15TH ARMY CORPS,
In the Field, Ga., December 5, 1864.

I. Brigade commanders will at once have the troops of their commands supplied with three days' rations in haversacks and forty rounds of ammunition in cartridge-boxes. This division will be in readiness to move at 7 a. m. to-morrow, or at an earlier hour if called on, toward the river crossing.

* * * * * * *

By order of Brig. Gen. C. R. Woods:

FRED. H. WILSON,
Acting Assistant Adjutant-General.

HEADQUARTERS FIFTEENTH ARMY CORPS,
Opposite No. 3, December 5, 1864.

Brigadier-General HAZEN,
Commanding Second Division:

GENERAL: The slow progress of the Left Wing of the army will necessarily detain the corps at this place for a day. It is desirable, however, that your column should move toward the Savannah road in the vicinity of these headquarters. There is a road leading from this place to your camp which can easily be repaired. I am authorized by Major-General Howard to make an attempt to get possession of Wright's Bridge, about eight miles below this place, which is supposed to be guarded by the rebels. To assist this movement you will please push one brigade of your command, or more if you deem it necessary, forward to Eden (No. 2), in order to make the cavalry in your front believe that we intend to force the bridge there. Only a demonstration is intended, but if the Eden bridge can be brought under the control of our guns it would be a great success. I intend to start from here with another column by 4 a. m., and you will make your arrangements accordingly. Delay the march of your main column and trains to this place until you know the result of the expedition to Eden. If successful your main column may move directly to that station, and probably be the first to enter Savannah. The troops designated for the expedition should move as light as possible.

I am, general, very respectfully,

P. JOS. OSTERHAUS,
Major-General.

SPECIAL ORDERS, No. 245. } HDQRS. THIRD DIV., 15TH ARMY CORPS,
Statesborough, Ga., December 5, 1864.

I. This command will move promptly at 6.30 a. m. this day. The order of march will be the same as on the 2d instant, except that one regiment instead of two will march in rear of trains as rear guard.

By order of Brig. Gen. John E. Smith:

S. M. BUDLONG,
Assistant Adjutant-General.

HEADQUARTERS SEVENTEENTH ARMY CORPS,
Ogeechee Church, Ga., December 5, 1864.

Capt. S. L. TAGGART,
Assistant Adjutant-General:

CAPTAIN: My command is encamped at this point. I would have moved to the point designated in your orders, but General Sherman ordered me to remain at this place, he not knowing how far the other column on the left had advanced. The enemy, numbering about 5,000 infantry, left here early this a. m., except a few cavalry, with whom I had some skirmishing. Generals Hardee, Wayne, McLaws, and Baker were here. I have not yet received orders from General Sherman as to my movements to-morrow.

Very respectfully,

FRANK P. BLAIR, JR.,
Major-General.

SPECIAL ORDERS, No. 300. } HDQRS. SEVENTEENTH ARMY CORPS,
Station 4½, Ga., December 5, 1864.

* * * * * * *

V. The movement to-morrow will be as follows:

1. Brig. Gen. G. A. Smith, commanding Fourth Division, will have the advance, and will move forward at 7 a. m.

2. Brig. Gen. M. D. Leggett, commanding Third Division, will be prepared to move at 8 o'clock, and will follow the Fourth Division.

3. Maj. Gen. J. A. Mower, commanding First Division, will be prepared to move at 9 o'clock, and will follow the Third Division.

4. The First Michigan Engineer Regiment and train will move in advance of the supply train of the Fourth Division.

5. The pontoon train and guard, Lieut. Col. J. M. Rusk commanding, will follow the train of the Third Division.

6. The trains of Military Division headquarters and of these headquarters will move as heretofore.

7. Brig. Gen. G. A. Smith, commanding Fourth Division, will detach from his command one regiment to move on the railroad, keeping abreast of the corps, with orders to destroy bridges and culverts, without tearing up the track.

By command of Maj. Gen. F. P. Blair:

C. CADLE, JR.,
Assistant Adjutant-General.

HEADQUARTERS SEVENTEENTH ARMY CORPS,
DEPARTMENT OF THE TENNESSEE,
Station 4½, Ga., December 5, 1864.

Brig. Gen. M. D. LEGGETT,
Commanding Third Division, Seventeenth Army Corps:

GENERAL: The major-general commanding directs me to inform you that probably there will be no movement to-morrow.

I am, general, very respectfully, your obedient servant,

C. CADLE, JR.,
Assistant Adjutant-General.

HEADQUARTERS LEFT WING, ARMY OF GEORGIA,
On River, near Hunter's Mills, December 5, 1864—1 a. m.

Capt. L. M. DAYTON,
Aide-de-Camp:

Your dispatch of last evening is received. The one you allude to, written at 3.15 p. m., has not come to hand yet. Soon after my dispatch of 10 a. m. yesterday the enemy cut a mill-dam on Little Horse Creek, flooding the road to such an extent as to entirely stop that portion of the column on the other side. Being in the advance I did not hear of this until I had nearly reached this point. All of Geary's and part of Ward's division is still back of Little Horse Creek (ten miles from here), unable to cross. I cannot move from here until they close up, which will probably be nearly night. I have learned that the Fourth Tennessee Cavalry passed from Sylvania to No. 5, about 10 a. m. yesterday, and it is reported that a regiment of militia had gone in the same direction. I have not heard from Davis, but think he is some distance in rear. I think the two orderlies I sent to you at 10 a. m. yesterday must have been captured, as there have been small squads of cavalry between this column and the Seventeenth Corps.

Very respectfully, your obedient servant,

H. W. SLOCUM,
Major-General.

HEADQUARTERS LEFT WING, ARMY OF GEORGIA,
Near Hunter's Mills, December 5, 1864—9 a. m.

Capt. L. M. DAYTON,
Aide-de-Camp:

I have the honor to inform you that the general's note of 3.15 p. m. yesterday, which I supposed was captured, has just come to hand. I have sent a staff officer, with what cavalry I have got, to open communication with General Davis and General Kilpatrick, and hope to hear from them during the day. This column is moving to-day, and the advance will probably encamp at the intersection of the road from Poor Robin to Ogeechee Church.

Very respectfully, your obedient servant,

H. W. SLOCUM,
Major-General.

HEADQUARTERS MILITARY DIVISION OF THE MISSISSIPPI,
In the Field, Little Ogeechee, No. 4½, December 5, 1864.

Major-General SLOCUM, *Commanding, &c.:*

GENERAL: General Blair is now crossing Ogeechee (Little) at No. 4½. It is no longer necessary to demonstrate on its flank, but look to collecting your entire command, including General Kilpatrick's, and getting it on the road heretofore described, which runs from Ogeechee Church to Halley's Ferry. Report at the earliest practicable moment the time you will be able to move from that road to Savannah. It may be our interest to push matters, until, at all events, we get on the Charleston road. Your note of 9 this a. m. is received, and do not know whether the rear of the Twentieth Corps is closed up. If not, you had better wait until it is well closed up, and also until you hear from General Davis. The two couriers who brought your dispatch of 10 a. m. 4th played possum, and instead of going back with answer at 3.15 p. m., as ordered, put away their horses, kept out of my sight, and sloped off this morning after daylight. They should certainly be punished.

I am, general, yours, &c.,

L. M. DAYTON,
Aide-de-Camp.

HEADQUARTERS MILITARY DIVISION OF THE MISSISSIPPI,
In the Field, No. 4½, Central Railroad, December 5, 1864.

Maj. Gen. H. W. SLOCUM,
Commanding Left Wing:

GENERAL: General Blair's troops secured this place early to-day, with a very little skirmishing, the movement of General Howard having had the desired effect. Field-works of a poor character were found. The general-in-chief is desirous of hearing from you, giving the position of your command and intelligence from General Kilpatrick, if any. He also wishes to know when you will be up on and prepared to move beyond the Halley's Ferry road. General Howard is to-night opposite No. 3. Both of these columns will remain as now until your command is up and ready to advance. There is no general news. Yours of 9 a. m. to-day is the last received.

Yours, respectfully,

L. M. DAYTON,
Aide-de-Camp.

SPECIAL FIELD ORDERS, } HDQRS. FOURTEENTH ARMY CORPS,
No. 27. } *Lawton's House, Ga., December 5, 1864.*

General Morgan, with the advance and in charge of the trains of his own and the trains of the First Division, reserve artillery, and corps ammunition trains, will move at 6.30 a. m., on the main river road, toward Savannah, and will camp to-morrow night as far in advance as the roads will permit. General Carlin will march (with Colonel Buell's command in advance of him) upon the road taken by General Morgan, starting at 6.30 a. m. and making as much distance as possible. General Baird will commence crossing Beaver Dam Creek at 8 a. m., and will march in such order as to effectually cover in the rear the two divisions in advance, with their trains. General Kilpatrick will cross Beaver Dam Creek in rear of General Baird, after which he will destroy the bridge. He will then march in the rear of the column, disposing his forces in such manner as to secure its rear and right flank from any sudden dashes of cavalry. Until further orders the column will move daily in this order, each command starting at 6.30 a. m. and endeavoring to march at least fifteen miles per day.

By order of Bvt. Maj. Gen. J. C. Davis:

A. C. McCLURG,
Lieutenant-Colonel and Chief of Staff.

ORDERS.] HEADQUARTERS TWENTIETH CORPS,
Near Little Ogeechee Creek, Ga., December 5, 1864.

This corps will march to-morrow, toward Springfield, as follows: Third Division at 6 a. m.; Second Division at 8 a. m.; First Division at 9 a. m. The cavalry will start at 5.30 a. m. The pontoon train will precede the wagon train of the leading division, and will start from their camp at 5 a. m. The wagon train of General Kilpatrick's cavalry division will be subdivided, under the superintendence of Capt. H. M. Whittelsey, acting chief quartermaster Twentieth Corps, into three sections, each section hereafter to march with and constitute part of the train of each division, and will be taken care of by the division commander and treated as a brigade train. All other trains and the artillery will occupy the same position in the column as heretofore ordered.

The order heretofore issued in reference to burning buildings, &c., is hereby reiterated, and commanders of divisions will be held responsible that it is obeyed. Great care must be taken that the grass and woods are not fired by the troops, as such fires occasion great delay, especially to the ammunition train. The advanced guard is hereby authorized and directed to arrest all soldiers found straggling to the front, and to seize all animals and stores they may have in their possession, and turn them over to the provost-marshal of the corps for confiscation. It is distinctly understood that no officer is authorized to give permits or passes to foraging parties to go in advance of the head of the column. All foraging must hereafter be done by the parties regularly authorized by the brigade commanders, and these parties must be kept well together. All foraging by individuals is especially prohibited. Officers who desire to send out their servants to forage for their messes must send them with the party regularly detailed from the brigades. Foraging parties hereafter will not be less than 100 men.

By command of Brig. Gen. A. S. Williams:

ROBT. P. DECHERT,
Captain and Acting Assistant Adjutant-General.

ORDERS.] HDQRS. FIRST DIVISION, TWENTIETH CORPS,
Near Little Ogeechee Creek, Ga., December 5, 1864.

This division will move to-morrow toward Springfield, at 9 a. m. (having the rear), in the following order: First Brigade in advance, two regiments to be unencumbered with wagons, and two regiments to guard fifty of the leading wagons; Second Brigade to follow, to be so disposed as to guard the remainder of the division train, including a portion of the cavalry train; the Third Brigade to be rear guard, to be preceded by a battery, and to be unencumbered with wagons.

By command of Brig. Gen. N. J. Jackson:

GEO. ROBINSON,
First Lieutenant and Acting Assistant Adjutant-General.

HDQRS. SECOND DIVISION, TWENTIETH ARMY CORPS,
December 5, 1864.

Colonel DUSTIN,
Commanding Second Brigade, Third Division:

COLONEL: Pursuant to orders from corps headquarters, the general commanding division directs that you move forward with your entire brigade and report to General Ward, commanding your division.

I am, colonel, very respectfully, your obedient servant,

W. T. FORBES,
Acting Assistant Adjutant-General.

HEADQUARTERS THIRD CAVALRY DIVISION,
Alexander, Ga., December 5, 1864.

Captain DAYTON,
Aide-de-Camp to the General-in-Chief:

I have the pleasure of reporting that I attacked Wheeler yesterday morning in position behind long lines of barricades, one mile and a half from Thomas' Station and three and a half from Waynesborough, on the railroad. Wheeler had five pieces of artillery, and, as far as can be ascertained from prisoners, about 6,000 men. I drove in his pickets and skirmish line at 7.30 a. m., and rode over his barricades in less than thirty minutes. He left 23 dead and 41 wounded on the field. I then drove him from one position to another, till he made a final stand in and about the town of Waynesborough. Here his lines were too long to be flanked, so we boldly charged and broke his center. He fought stubbornly for a time, but finally gave way before our flashing sabers, and in twenty minutes was retreating in great confusion through the woods, fields, and on every available road leading toward Augusta. I continued the pursuit upward of four miles; rushed him across and beyond Brier Creek. It was now 3 p. m., and being so far from the main army I deemed it best to halt. After burning various bridges on Brier Creek above and below the railroad bridge, including the latter, which I found had been imperfectly burned before, and, in fact, had been nearly repaired, I retired to Alexander and went into camp. The railroad bridge destroyed is certainly a very important one, reported by Colonel Heath, Fifth Ohio Cavalry, to be upward of 500 feet long. I have to thank General Baird for kindly tendering me a brigade of infantry to support my attack. The infantry, however, was not engaged. My loss has been quite severe, particularly in horses, having lost upward of 200 in killed and wounded. As I am now marching in the rear of the army it is impossible to supply myself with fresh animals. I most respectfully suggest that captured horses now with the different army corps, and not needed by them, be sent to me, or left at some convenient point along my line of march. The enemy's loss is not known; certainly could not be less than 500 killed and wounded, judging from his dead left upon the field, a large percentage being officers. My command is somewhat jaded, but I will make every effort to bring it up. All I need is some few hundred horses to supply the place of those broken down. These I could supply myself, were I marching upon the flank or in front. It is impossible, however, to find a single horse or mule in rear of the infantry; and would again most respectfully urge that a few hundred horses be turned over to me from one or more of the army corps marching on roads parallel or near to my line of march.

Very respectfully, your obedient servant,

J. KILPATRICK,
Brigadier-General, Commanding Cavalry.

HEADQUARTERS CAVALRY CORPS,
Waynesborough, December 5, 1864.

General J. KILPATRICK,
Commanding Cavalry, U. S. Army:

GENERAL: Your letter of yesterday was received to-day. I assure you Captain Norton has and will receive every attention which can be bestowed upon a wounded soldier. I am pleased to inform you that he was doing well and out of pain at last accounts. Since the commencement of this sad war I have used untiring exertions to maintain in my soldiers principles of chivalry and true soldierly honor. They have been taught to despise and spurn the cowardly instincts which induce low men to frighten, abuse, and rob defenseless women and children. You allude to old associations, and promise to return any kindness to Captain Norton. I have only to ask, for the sake of these old associations, for your own sake, and for the sake of the institution where military honor was taught, that you will offer some protection to the families necessarily left defenseless, and not to leave them at the mercy of a brutal soldiery. By so doing, not only will other advantages be gained, but your name will stand before the world in a much more enviable light. It is useless for me to recount the atrocities committed; suffice it to say, that the history of no war, however barbarous, can tell of atrocities equal to those daily and hourly committed by your command.

Respectfully, general, your obedient servant,

J. WHEELER,
Major-General, C. S. Army.

HILTON HEAD, S. C., *December 5, 1864.*

Maj. Gen. J. G. FOSTER,
Commanding Department of the South:

GENERAL: The telegraph operator here has just received a dispatch from Port Royal Ferry, stating that a rebel officer who has deserted brings information that General Sherman is within sight of Savannah, and that all of the women and children were sent out of the city last night. I send you by the Charles Houghton some letters handed me by Captain Burger, and also a package from Mrs. Foster. Colonel Mulford has just returned from Charleston, but brings no news.

I am, very respectfully, your obedient servant,

C. W. THOMAS,
Major and Chief Quartermaster.

HEADQUARTERS DEPARTMENT OF THE SOUTH,
U. S. Steamer Nemaha, December 5, 1864.

Brig. Gen. J. P. HATCH,
Commanding Field Division:

GENERAL: You will have all the white regiments of Brigadier-General Potter's command prepare at once two days' rations (cooked, if time permits), and twenty extra rounds of ammunition in pockets, and move to the landing to-night as early as possible, for embarkation on transports. The naval brigade will be relieved immediately and report to the admiral, the horses, carts, &c., to remain as at present, in charge of the naval brigade. You will have Day's battery also, with two days' rations, report at the dock at daylight to-morrow, to embark to follow and join Potter's brigade. The remaining regiments of your command you will dispose of to the best advantage, to hold your present position as long as possible. One of the batteries, with a regiment in reserve, may, if you prefer, be placed on the interior line of defense. Have this movement made as silently as possible, so as not to betray it to the enemy.

By order of Maj. Gen. J. G. Foster:

W. B. DEAN,
Lieut., 127th New York Vols.. Acting Assistant Adjutant-General.

CITY POINT, VA., *December 6, 1864.*
(Received 15th.)

Maj. Gen. W. T. SHERMAN,
Commanding Military Division of the Mississippi:

On reflection since sending my letter by the hands of Lieutenant Dunn I have concluded that the most important operation toward closing the rebellion will be to close out Lee and his army. You have now destroyed the roads of the South, so that it will probably take three months, without interruption, to re-establish a through line from east to west. In that time I think the job here will be effectually completed. My idea now, then, is that you establish a base on the sea-coast, fortify, and leave in it all your artillery and cavalry, and enough infantry to protect them, and, at the same time, so threaten the interior that the militia of the South will have to be kept at home. With the balance of your command come here by water with all dispatch. Select yourself the officer to leave in command, but you I want in person. Unless you see objections to this plan, which I cannot see, use every vessel going to you for purposes of transportation. Hood has Thomas close in Nashville. I have said all I could to force him to attack, without giving the positive order until to-day. To-day, however, I could stand it no longer, and gave the order without any reserve. I think the battle will take place to-morrow. The result will probably be known in New York before Colonel Babcock, the bearer of this, leaves New York. Colonel Babcock will give you information of all operations now in progress.

U. S. GRANT,
Lieutenant-General.

CONFIDENTIAL.] DECEMBER 6, 1864.

Bvt. Brig. Gen. S. VAN VLIET,
Quartermaster, New York:

GENERAL: General Sherman appears to be approaching the Atlantic coast, and it is determined to send supplies to meet him at Port Royal, or rather to await there until he establishes his base of supplies. In the letter of this office dated November 3 last an estimate of supplies was sent to you for a force of 30,000 men. It is believed that the force with General Sherman will reach 60,000 men, of which 10,000 will be cavalry, and that he will have with him from sixty to eighty pieces of artillery and about 30,000 horses and mules. The supplies ordered on 3d of November were divided, one-half to Pensacola, one-half to Port Royal. Col. S. L. Brown, chief of the forage division, has been ordered to send daily to Port Royal forage for 30,000 animals. I notice that in the letter of 3d of November last no blankets were ordered. I presume, however, that under the general order to send clothing to refit 30,000 men, General Vinton turned over to you a proper proportion of blankets. You will call upon General Vinton for the following clothing and equipage, which you will send to Port Royal as soon as possible, there to await news from General Sherman, which will determine the ultimate destination of the supplies. They will be subject to the orders of General Foster, through the chief quartermaster of the Department of the South, Maj. C. W. Thomas:

Clothing.—30,000 sack coats; 30,000 trowsers; 60,000 shirts; 60,000 pairs drawers; 60,000 pairs socks; 100,000 pairs shoes and boots; 20,000 forage caps; 10,000 greatcoats; 20,000 blankets, unless this number has already been shipped; 10,000 waterproof blankets.

Equipage.—10,000 shelter-tents; 100 hospital tents; 10,000 knapsacks; 20,000 haversacks; 10,000 canteens; 2,000 camp kettles; 5,000 mess pans; 5,000 felling axes, two handles each; 1,000 hatchets, handled; 2,000 spades; 2,000 picks.

You will also send the following quartermaster's stores:

Transportation.—Wheel harness for 400 mules; lead harness for 800 mules; 10,000 pounds bar-iron, assorted; 5,000 pounds steel; 1,000 pounds harness leather; 40 sets shoeing tools and 40 extra hammers; thread, wax, needles, awls, &c., for repairing harness; 500 pounds wrought nails; 20 buttresses; 200 horse rasps; 100 large files, assorted; 50 shoeing knives, extra; 4,000 pounds manilla rope, assorted; 15,000 bushels smith's coal (this coal will be ordered from Washington); 200 extra wagon wheels; 50 extra ambulance wheels; 100,000 pounds horse and mule shoes; 10,000 pounds horse and mule shoe-nails.

All this should be done in such manner as to attract as little attention as possible, and it is desirable to give the enemy no clue to the preparations making for reception of General Sherman.

I am, respectfully, your obedient servant,

M. C. MEIGS,
Quartermaster-General, Brevet Major-General.

CONFIDENTIAL.] QUARTERMASTER-GENERAL'S OFFICE,
Washington, D. C., December 6, 1864.

Col. HERMAN BIGGS,
Quartermaster, Philadelphia:

COLONEL: You will send to Port Royal, to Maj. C. W. Thomas, the following quartermaster's stores (probably they can be taken on board one of the light-draught steamers built by Messrs. Cramp & Sons, which I suppose to be ready to sail): 50 extra king bolts; 500 linch pins; 200 wagon tongues; 400 extra whippletrees; 50 double trees, ironed ready for use; 100 coupling poles; 200 front hounds for wagons; 100 hind hounds for wagons; 200 mule hames, ironed ready for use; 200 mule collars; 500 wagon bows; 100 wagon whips; 1,000 open links, for repairing trace chains; 500 open rings; 100 water buckets.

I am, respectfully, your obedient servant,

M. C. MEIGS,
Quartermaster-General, Brevet Major-General.

SPECIAL FIELD ORDERS, No. 128. } HDQRS. MIL. DIV. OF THE MISSISSIPPI,
In the Field, Ogeechee Church, Ga.,
December 6, 1864.

I. Each army corps commander will, on the receipt of this order, collect from his command 100 horses, the best adapted to cavalry uses, together with a sufficient number of mounted negroes to lead them, and dispatch them to General Slocum's headquarters, for delivery to the cavalry command of General Kilpatrick. General Slocum's command is at this moment near the intersection of the road running through Statesborough and Armenia to Halley's Ferry, on the Savannah River, about six miles north of Ogeechee Church, and will march by the middle road toward Springfield.

II. The officer charged with these horses will be instructed to deliver them to any officer whom General Kilpatrick may appoint to receive them.

By order of Maj. Gen. W. T. Sherman:

L. M. DAYTON,
Aide-de-Camp.

HDQRS. DEPARTMENT AND ARMY OF THE TENNESSEE,
Lane's Farm, Ga., December 6, 1864.

Maj. Gen. W. T. SHERMAN,
Commanding Military Division of the Mississippi:

Two divisions of the Fifteenth Corps (First and Fourth) are nearly opposite Station No. 3, and the other two divisions are about four or five miles distant and abreast of us, on the direct road from Statesborough to Eden Station. Reconnaissances are being made to-day toward Wright's Bridge and the bridge to Eden Station, and both of them will be secured, if possible. Preparations were being made last night to cross the river near Station No. 3, but when I learned that they, the enemy, had left Ogeechee Church, I did not deem it necessary to lay the pontoon bridge. I shall be ready to move forward with this command when General Blair leaves Ogeechee Church. I agree with you that Eden Station is the point to be made now, and it may be necessary to cross still lower down, as I learn the enemy intends to make a stand at that place. Lieutenant Harvey, who was sent over last night with a select party to strike the Gulf railroad, found the bridges across the Cannouchee all burned and the approaches strongly guarded by rebel cavalry, and was compelled to return without accomplishing his object. Another party has been sent out to strike for a point still higher up, but I am fearful that they will find all the approaches well guarded, and that they will not succeed in crossing the river. As soon as I reach Eden Station, I will make a strong demonstration of infantry toward the Cannouchee, sufficient to enable me to cross a party and strike the road.

Very respectfully, your obedient servant,

O. O. HOWARD,
Major-General.

HEADQUARTERS MILITARY DIVISION OF THE MISSISSIPPI,
In the Field, Ogeechee Church, December 6, 1864—3.45 p. m.

Major-General HOWARD,
Commanding Army of the Tennessee:

GENERAL: Your dispatch of to-day is just received. Reports from General Slocum and General Kilpatrick have also been received. The former will camp to-night on Turkey Creek, in advance of this column, with his command well closed up. The latter attacked Wheeler near Thomas' Station, and drove him through Waynesborough and across Brier Creek in confusion, killing and wounding a number and capturing 100 of his men; he also burned all the bridges on Brier Creek, including (for good) the railroad bridge. To-morrow the entire army will move, General Slocum's left reaching Ebenezer; himself, Springfield; and the Seventeenth Corps, Guyton. The general-in-chief desires you, in conjunction, to reach Eden, opposite No. 2, and while General Blair threatens No. 2 by moving on No. 3 (Guyton), to effect a crossing at or below No. 2.

I am, general, yours, with regard,

L. M. DAYTON,
Aide-de-Camp.

SPECIAL FIELD ORDERS, No. 187.

HEADQUARTERS DEPARTMENT AND ARMY OF THE TENNESSEE,
Lane's Farm, Ga., December 6, 1864.

* * * * * * *

II. The following movements will be made by this army to-morrow, the 7th instant: First, Major-General Osterhaus, commanding Fifteenth Army Corps, will move forward his command, leaving one division to make a demonstration at Wright's Bridge, concentrating the balance opposite Eden (No. 2), from which place he will push one division at least two or three miles below, and thence make a demonstration with one brigade on the Cannouchee River, crossing a party at some point to strike and break the Savannah and Gulf Railroad. He will push his pontoon trains well in advance. Second, Major-General Blair, commanding Seventeenth Army Corps, will move his command toward Eden (No. 2), as heretofore ordered, opposite which point the Fifteenth Corps will await his arrival. Third, the cattle, in charge of Captain Roots and Lieutenant Todd, will follow the Fifteenth Corps toward Eden Station. These headquarters will be at or near Wright's Bridge to-night.

III After crossing the river mounted foragers from the infantry will not be allowed; the foraging must be done on foot. The horses and mules used by unauthorized persons will be taken up at the bridge and turned in to the quartermaster's department. They will be collected by the division quartermaster, who will consult with the chief quartermaster of the army as to their further disposition.

By order of Maj. Gen. O. O. Howard:

SAML. L. TAGGART,
Assistant Adjutant-General.

SPECIAL ORDERS, No. 191. } HDQRS. FIFTEENTH ARMY CORPS, *Opposite No. 3, Ga., December 6, 1864.*

I. Division commanders will proceed at once to collect all milk cows in vicinity of their respective commands, and will retain possession of the same until the army arrives at its destination, when they will be turned over to the medical department for the benefit of the sick and wounded.

II. The following are the orders for the movements of the corps tomorrow, the 7th instant: The right column (Second and Third Divisions) will march from its present camp at daybreak, on the direct road toward railroad station No. 2 (Eden), the Second Division, Brigadier-General Hazen commanding, having the advance. On arriving opposite the said station this division will be pushed forward in a southern direction, taking a position near or at Black Creek, and there General Hazen will order one brigade to make a demonstration on the Cannouchee River. A select party from this brigade will cross the river at a convenient point and attempt to cut the Savannah and Gulf Railroad. Some very reliable and energetic officer should have charge of this party, as the success of the enterprise will have great bearing on our future movements. If the brigade sent to-day by General Hazen to demonstrate against Eden encamped in the vicinity of that railroad station, it would be expedient to push to the Cannouchee River in the morning. Brigadier-General Smith, commanding Third Division, will mass his command and corral his teams opposite No. 2. The Fourth Division, Brigadier-General Corse commanding, will march from its present camp, at 7 a. m., to the Eden Crossing also, where it will encamp. The First Division, Brigadier-General Woods commanding, will, until further orders, remain at Wright's Bridge. The bridge train must be started to Eden in advance of the Fourth Division, for which Lieutenant-Colonel Fort, chief quartermaster, will make due preparations, and will have the same on the road by 5 a. m. to-morrow. Corps headquarters will accompany the Fourth Division and will be established at Eden to-morrow.

By order of Maj. Gen. P. Joseph Osterhaus:

F. F. WHITEHEAD,
Assistant Adjutant-General.

SPECIAL ORDERS, } HDQRS. THIRD DIV., 15TH ARMY CORPS,
No. 246. } *In the Field, Ga., December 6, 1864.*

I. This command will move at 8 a. m. to-morrow, the 7th instant, in the following order: First, Battery B, First Michigan Artillery, followed by the wagons and ambulances of the battery; second, ambulances of First Brigade (one for each regiment) and pioneer corps (one); third, ammunition train; fourth, division headquarters train; fifth, First Brigade train, including regimental wagons; sixth, Second Brigade train; seventh, quartermaster's train; eighth, commissary of subsistence train; ninth, ambulance corps, except ambulances assigned to regiments and detachments; tenth, regimental wagons Second Brigade.

The infantry will march, the First Brigade in advance, upon the right flank of the artillery and trains, except two regiments of Second Brigade, which will march in rear of the trains as rear guard.

By order of Brig. Gen. John E. Smith:

S. M. BUDLONG,
Assistant Adjutant-General.

SPECIAL FIELD ORDERS, } HEADQUARTERS FOURTH DIVISION,
No. 25. } FIFTEENTH ARMY CORPS,
In the Field, Ogeechee River, Ga., December 6, 1864.

I. Paragraph I, Special Field Orders, No. 8, from these headquarters, of date November 18, 1864, is hereby revoked.

II. This command will move to-morrow, the 7th instant, at 6.30 a. m., to the Eden Crossing. The First Brigade will have the advance, followed by the battery; the Third Brigade will move in the center, on either side of the trains; the Second Brigade will bring up the rear; the pioneer corps will move in rear of the advance guard, and repair roads and construct bridges whenever necessary. The trains will move as follows: First, pioneer corps train; second, First Brigade train; third, Third Brigade train; fourth, Second Brigade train; fifth, ambulance train; sixth, ordnance train; seventh, supply train.

By order of Brig. Gen. John M. Corse:

L. CARPER,
Assistant Adjutant-General.

CIRCULAR.] HDQRS. FOURTH DIV., FIFTEENTH ARMY CORPS,
In the Field, Ogeechee River, Ga., December 6, 1864.

The attention of brigade commanders is again directed to the looseness of discipline in the command and the want of interest manifested by regimental and company officers in the proper control of their men. The indiscriminate firing that has so disgraced the division is owing, in an eminent degree, to the fact that officers do not hold to a prompt responsibility their next in rank. While the general commanding is desirous of assisting his subalterns in every way practicable by his power and rank, he declines peremptorily interfering with their legitimate duties, and will not punish their men for violation of orders, but hold the officers themselves to a strict responsibility that the men are properly punished Brigade commanders will at once acquaint the regimental officers that they must require their company officers to keep their men in camp, and not allow them to remove their arms from the stacks without proper authority after once being placed there. Brigade commanders must further stimulate their subalterns to use every endeavor to maintain an esprit de corps, and in various ways strive to restore discipline and order to their respective commands.

By order of Brig. Gen. John M. Corse:

L. CARPER,
Assistant Adjutant-General.

HDQRS. DEPARTMENT AND ARMY OF THE TENNESSEE,
Lane's Farm, Ga., December 6, 1864.

Maj. Gen. F. P. BLAIR,
Commanding Seventeenth Army Corps:

GENERAL: I am directed by the major-general commanding to say to you that two divisions of Fifteenth Corps (First and Fourth) are nearly opposite Station No. 3, and the other two are about four or five miles distant and abreast of us, on the direct road from Statesborough to Eden Station. Preparations were being made last night to cross the river above Station No. 3, but when the general learned that the enemy had left your front at Ogeechee Church, and fallen back, he did not deem it necessary to lay the pontoon bridge. He, however, caused the road leading to the ferry, on this side, to be repaired by the pioneers, so that he could lay the bridge and cross a force quickly to assist you in case it was needed. A small force was thrown over the river, by means of row-boats, to guard the crossing, and will remain there to-day. Reconnaissances are being made to-day toward Wright's Bridge and the bridge at Eden Station, and both of them will be secured if possible. The general is confident that No. 2 is the point to be made now, as he learns the enemy propose to make a stand there, and it may be necessary to cross the river still lower down, in order to turn the position. Lieutenant Harvey was sent last night, with a select party, to strike the Gulf road, but he was compelled to return without accomplishing anything. He found the bridges across the Cannouchee burned, and the approaches strongly guarded by rebel cavalry. Another party has been sent to strike for a point higher up, but the general thinks it barely possible that they will be successful. As soon as this command reaches Eden Station, the general intends to make a strong demonstration of infantry toward the Cannouchee, sufficient to enable him to cross a party and reach the road. The general desires that you will notify him when you move from Ogeechee Church.

I have the honor to be, very respectfully, your obedient servant,

WILLIAM E. STRONG,
Assistant Inspector-General and Chief of Staff.

HEADQUARTERS MILITARY DIVISION OF THE MISSISSIPPI,
In the Field, Ogeechee Church, Ga., December 6, 1864.

Major-General BLAIR,
Commanding Seventeenth Corps:

GENERAL: The army being now in position ready for farther movements, the general-in-chief directs that you move your command to-morrow morning, on the Savannah road, via Guyton, and leaving Eden

(No. 2) to your right, as rapidly as you may wish to march. He will accompany your column, and if occasion requires will modify these orders.

I am, general, yours, respectfully,

L. M. DAYTON,
Aide-de-Camp.

You will keep a small force moving abreast of your column on the railroad, with orders to burn all bridges and culverts, but need not tear up or burn track.

L. M. DAYTON
Aide-de-Camp.

ORDERS.] HDQRS. FIRST DIVISION, 17TH ARMY CORPS,
In the Field, Ga., December 6, 1864.

The troops of this command will be prepared to march to-morrow at 9 a. m. Order of march: First, pioneer corps; second, Third Brigade; third, Company C, First Michigan [Artillery]; fourth, First Brigade; fifth, Second Brigade; sixth, ambulance train; seventh, ordnance train; eighth, supply train. Brigadier-General Sprague will designate one regiment to march in rear of the train.

By order of Maj. Gen. Joseph A. Mower:

CHAS. CHRISTENSEN,
Lieut., Aide-de-Camp and Acting Assistant Adjutant-General.

SPECIAL FIELD ORDERS, No. 167. } HEADQUARTERS THIRD DIVISION, SEVENTEENTH ARMY CORPS,
Station No. 4½, Ga., December 6, 1864.

* * * * * * *

III. This command will be held in readiness to move at 8 o'clock to-morrow. The Second Brigade, Col. R. K. Scott commanding, will have the advance. Artillery and trains as heretofore.

By order of Brig. Gen. M. D. Leggett:

J. C. DOUGLASS,
Assistant Adjutant-General.

HEADQUARTERS LEFT WING, ARMY OF GEORGIA,
Near intersection Mill Ray and Halley's Ferry Road,
December 6, 1864—7 a. m.

Capt. L. M. DAYTON,
Aide-de-Camp:

Your note of yesterday is received. The officer I sent to open communication with General Davis returned last night. Kilpatrick's fight with Wheeler (the 4th) commenced near Thomas' Station, from which point Kilpatrick drove the enemy through Waynesborough and across Brier Creek. He burned the railroad bridge over that stream and all the road bridges between there and Jacksonborough. Kilpatrick lost in killed and wounded about 200 men, and brought in 100 prisoners. Two divisions of the Fourteenth Corps, with the entire corps train, encamped last night at Buck Creek Post-Office; the other division, with Kilpatrick's cavalry, was at Jacksonborough. The Twentieth Corps is well closed up at this point, and moving this morning. In the absence of further orders, I shall push both columns forward as rapidly as possible, encamping the Twentieth Corps to-night near Turkey Creek, and to-morrow night at Springfield. Both columns are in good condition, and can be pushed forward as rapidly as you think proper.

Very respectfully, your obedient servant,

H. W. SLOCUM,
Major-General.

HEADQUARTERS MILITARY DIVISION OF THE MISSISSIPPI,
In the Field, No. 4½, Ogeechee Church, December 6, 1864.

Major-General SLOCUM,
Commanding Left Wing:

GENERAL: Your dispatch of 7 a. m. is received; General Kilpatrick has also reported his operations. The general-in-chief desires you to rather decrease your rate of movement of the Twentieth Corps than to push it, in order to let Davis get up abreast of it. He will put the Seventeenth Corps in motion to-morrow, and it will reach to the vicinity of Guyton (No. 3); you will be able to follow its progress by the smokes. General Howard will move by the road south of the river to Eden (No. 2), and probably cross there. The general will move with General Blair. There is no news worth reporting, save the general feels convinced that the Charleston road is broken. Citizens report our fleet off Savannah, sending up rockets nightly, so it is on the watch for us.

I am, general, yours, respectfully,

L. M. DAYTON,
Aide-de-Camp.

HEADQUARTERS LEFT WING, ARMY OF GEORGIA,
December 6, 1864—1.30 p. m.

Capt. L. M. DAYTON,
Aide-de-Camp:

I have the honor to inform you that the Twentieth Corps is on the march, and getting on finely. The head of the column is now thirteen miles from Springfield. We shall camp to-night near Turkey Creek and to-morrow beyond Springfield as far as possible. Generals Davis and Kilpatrick are well up on our left. Please indicate what road I shall take after reaching Springfield. I sent you a communication at 8 a. m. to-day, giving particulars of Kilpatrick's fight and positions of all of this wing. Kilpatrick was successful; and everything is moving on finely.

Very respectfully, your obedient servant,

H. W. SLOCUM,
Major-General.

HEADQUARTERS MILITARY DIVISION OF THE MISSISSIPPI,
In the Field, Ogeechee Church, December 6, 1864—3.30 p. m.

Major-General SLOCUM,
Commanding Left Wing:

GENERAL: Your dispatch of 1.30 p. m. is just received, as also yours of 7 a. m., which was answered. The general is pleased at the progress of General Davis, but not knowing where he was, it compelled the halting of this column here to close up. To-morrow the general-in-chief expects General Howard to be at Eden (No. 2), General Blair at

Guyton, and if General Davis' head of column reaches Ebenezer, and can lay a bridge over that creek, it will answer. He wishes you not to pass Springfield, but from there to communicate with him at Guyton; but in the absence of orders, the movement for the day following should be such as to place General Davis at or in advance of Saint Augustine Creek, and the column you are with at or near Monteith. General Blair will be at Eden (No. 2), and Howard will cross the river.

I am, general, yours, respectfully,

L. M. DAYTON,
Aide-de-Camp.

THREE MILES FROM ROAD LEADING FROM
OGEECHEE CHURCH TO HALLEY'S,
December 6, 1864.

[General J. C. DAVIS:]

GENERAL: The Fifteenth Corps is on the west side of the Ogeechee at No. 3. The Seventeenth is on this side at No. 4½. The Twentieth Corps will encamp to-night on Turkey Creek, and to-morrow at Springfield. Your corps must follow the road you are now on, and reach the Charleston and Savannah Railroad, at Saint Augustine Creek, as soon as practicable. Fill your wagons with corn if possible. Communicate with me as often as once a day if you can, as General Sherman makes very frequent inquiry.

Yours, &c.,

H. W. SLOCUM,
Major-General.

ORDERS.] HEADQUARTERS TWENTIETH CORPS,
Near Turkey Creek, Ga., December 6, 1864.

This corps will continue the march to-morrow in the same order as to-day, each division starting at 7.30 a. m. Generals Geary and Jackson will start all their pioneers, at daybreak, to repair the road they are to pass over. The pioneer battalion of the corps, with all the pioneers of the Third Division and the pioneer detail of the Fifty-eighth Indiana Volunteers, will start at daybreak, escorted by the cavalry of Colonel Hughes, and repair the roads toward Springfield. Division commanders will afford all assistance that may be needed by the pioneers. All bad places in the road must be corduroyed, as it is ascertained that no other method of repairing them is durable enough to pass the whole train over. It is desired that the whole corps reach Springfield to-morrow. The tool wagons of the center and rear divisions will move at the head of the division trains, and those of the leading division in advance of the pontoon train.

By command of Brig. Gen. A. S. Williams:

ROBT. P. DECHERT,
Captain and Acting Assistant Adjutant-General.

HEADQUARTERS TWENTIETH CORPS,
Near Turkey Creek, Ga., December 6, 1864.

Brig. Gen. N. J. JACKSON,
Commanding First Division:

GENERAL: The general commanding wishes you to get the head of your column up as far as possible to-day, and at dark halt and encamp wherever you may be. He wishes you to advise him at once upon encamping where you are. In the absence of further orders he wishes you to move early in the morning.

Very respectfully, your obedient servant,

ROBT. P. DECHERT,
Captain and Acting Assistant Adjutant-General.

ORDERS.] HDQRS. FIRST DIVISION, TWENTIETH CORPS,
Smoke's House, Ga., December 6, 1864.

This division will move to-morrow at 6 a. m. (being in the rear), in the following order: Second Brigade in advance, to be unencumbered with wagons, except one regiment, which will guard thirty of the leading wagons; Third Brigade next, to guard the remainder of the trains, including cavalry train; the First Brigade in rear, to be preceded by a battery of artillery, and to be unencumbered with wagons.

By command of Brig. Gen. N. J. Jackson:

GEO. ROBINSON,
First Lieutenant and Acting Assistant Adjutant-General.

HEADQUARTERS TWENTIETH CORPS,
Near Turkey Creek, Ga., December 6, 1864.

Brigadier-General GEARY,
Commanding Second Division:

GENERAL: I am directed to inform you that the Third Division has encamped on the east side of Turkey Creek, as laid down on the map. The general commanding wishes your division to encamp at the cross-roads about one mile west of this place if possible. In the absence of further orders your command will move early to-morrow morning.

Very respectfully, your obedient servant,

ROBT. P. DECHERT,
Captain and Acting Assistant Adjutant-General.

HEADQUARTERS MILITARY DIVISION OF THE MISSISSIPPI,
In the Field, No. 4½, Ogeechee Church, December 6, 1864.

General KILPATRICK,
Commanding Cavalry:

GENERAL: Your report of December 5 has been received, and gives the general-in-chief great satisfaction. He begs you to convey to your command his thanks for their gallant and valuable services in driving the enemy in confusion from beyond Brier Creek, and in destroying those bridges, so useful to the enemy. At your suggestion, he has ordered each army corps commander to select from his command 100 cavalry horses, with a sufficient number of negroes to lead them, and to conduct them for your use to General Slocum's column, which is now on the middle Savannah road, where it crosses the Statesborough and Halley's Ferry road. A copy of that order is inclosed,* and you can

---

* See p. 638.

adopt your own course to secure them. You may always rely upon the general for cavalry horses, as, in order to keep you well mounted, he will dismount every person connected with the infantry not necessary for its efficient service, and take team horses, even if the wagons and contents have to be burned. On this flank matters have moved smoothly, and as we are a good distance in advance are lying by for General Davis and yourself to get up abreast. General Howard is now near Branhan's Store, west of the Ogeechee, abreast of Springfield. General Blair is here at Ogeechee Church, where McLaws with about 5,000 men had prepared quite an extensive line of intrenchments, but Howard's movement outflanked him, and he quit without a fight, and is now supposed to be at Eden (No. 2). General Slocum is about six miles north of Ogeechee Church, waiting for General Davis to get up abreast on the Halley's Ferry road. As soon as all are up we will move on Savannah by the four main roads from Branhan's Store, Ogeechee Church, Springfield, and the Savannah River road. As Wheeler is disposed of you might, for the sake of forage, divide your command, coming together, say, about Monteith. We find a great deal of forage, but presume our infantry trains consume it all; still, they do not seem to know that rice in the straw, fed in moderation, is a most excellent forage; and you can take advantage of it, as you will find an abundance along the Savannah and Ogeechee Rivers. As you come down make a good deal of smoke and fuss about Halley's (now Hutchinson's) Ferry and Sister's Ferry, as though threatening to cross into South Carolina, and should Ebenezer Creek be up, send word to General Davis to leave his bridge down until you are across. No news from the outside world of any interest; but the fleet is known to be watching for us, as the citizens report it sending up rockets every night.

I am, general, with much regard,

L. M. DAYTON,
Aide-de-Camp.

CIRCULAR.] HDQRS. THIRD DIVISION, CAVALRY CORPS,
MILITARY DIVISION OF THE MISSISSIPPI,
December 6, 1864.

I take great pleasure in tendering the thanks of the general-in-chief, expressed in official communication* of to-day, to the gallant officers and men of my command for the brilliant cavalry action and victory at Waynesborough. He desires me to thank you for this victory over superior numbers, and for the invaluable service rendered, assuring you that he will see that the command is well mounted, if he has to take horses from the infantry teams and burn the wagons and contents. Soldiers! you have won the admiration of the united Army of the Union, now sweeping onward to victory, and the respect and thanks of the great Sherman. Soldiers! I congratulate; I am proud to command you.

By order of Brigadier-General Kilpatrick:

L. G. ESTES,
Captain and Assistant Adjutant-General.

---

* See next, *ante*.

HDQRS. NORTHERN DISTRICT, DEPT. OF THE SOUTH,
Morris Island, December 6, 1864.

Lieutenant-Colonel MULFORD,
U. S. Agent for Exchange of Prisoners:

COLONEL: For your information, I have the honor to communicate the following facts relative to the flag of truce commenced in Charleston Harbor on Sunday, the 4th instant:

In accordance with the mutual understanding, our own and the enemy's batteries ceased firing. Early on the morning of the 5th instant the enemy opened fire with sharpshooters from Fort Sumter upon our batteries on the north end of Morris Island. After this had continued for an hour, I ordered our guns and mortars to open on Sumter and James Island, which was kept up for about another hour. At this time, a small boat, displaying a white flag, appeared off Fort Sumter; a boat from the picket monitor went to meet it, and received the following communication to me from the officer commanding at Fort Sumter:

FORT SUMTER, S. C., *December 5, 1864.*

OFFICER COMMANDING U. S. FORCES ON MORRIS ISLAND:

SIR: Having just been informed by the proper authorities of the continuance of the truce which commenced yesterday, I beg leave to offer an apology for having fired upon the batteries on the northern end of Morris Island this morning with sharpshooters.

I have the honor to be, very respectfully, your obedient servant,

T. A. HUGUENIN,
Captain, Commanding.

To this communication I forwarded the following reply:

HEADQUARTERS U. S. FORCES,
Morris Island, S. C., December 5, 1864.

Capt. T. A. HUGUENIN,
Commanding Confederate Forces in Fort Sumter:

SIR: Your communication of this a. m., in explanation of the firing from Fort Sumter, is received. The explanation is satisfactory. The firing from the batteries on this island will be discontinued.

I have the honor to be, very respectfully, your obedient servant,

E. N. HALLOWELL,
Colonel, Commanding.

Since the above correspondence there has been an entire cessation of firing on both sides. In case of any probable discussion of the matter between yourself and the Confederate agent, I deemed it advisable to apprise you of the circumstances of the affair.

Very respectfully, your obedient servant,

E. N. HALLOWELL,
Colonel Fifty-fourth Massachusetts Vols., Commanding District.

HDQRS. DEPARTMENT AND ARMY OF THE TENNESSEE,
Jenks' Bridge, Ga., December 7, 1864.

Maj. Gen. W. T. SHERMAN,
Commanding Military Division of the Mississippi:

On the arrival of the bridge at this point, Captain Reese, finding the enemy on the other shore, threw over a regiment of Hazen's division in boats and cleared the way. The bridge was immediately laid, and a brigade of General Corse's division, General Rice commanding, pushed over, met the enemy's skirmishers about 500 yards beyond, drove them, and routed a battalion of rebels, behind rail piles, in a very handsome manner, capturing 17 prisoners, and killing and wounding several. He lost 2 killed and 2 or 3 wounded. He then pushed on to Twenty-Mile Station. General Woods' brigade from Wright's Bridge formed a junction with General Rice near that point. These troops are all I have now near Station No. 2; the rest of the Fifteenth Corps is still on this side of the Ogeechee. I propose while General Blair is coming up to-morrow to reconnoiter down both banks of the Ogeechee, break the Gulf railroad, and secure, if possible, the wagon road bridges. It is again reported by General Hazen that our prisoners are on the Gulf road, but only seventy miles out, at a place called Doctor Town. Prisoners and negroes report breast-works in progress of construction about twelve miles from Savannah. They claim to have 17,000 men with which to man them. We shall soon see. I send yesterday's papers. Schofield victory is not quite satisfactory.

Very respectfully, your obedient servant,

O. O. HOWARD,
Major-General.

SPECIAL FIELD ORDERS, No. 188.

HEADQUARTERS DEPARTMENT AND ARMY OF THE TENNESSEE,
Jenks' Bridge, Ga., December 7, 1864.

* * * * * * *

III. This army will move to-morrow as follows: First, Major-General Osterhaus, commanding Fifteenth Army Corps, will move his Fourth Division, Brigadier-General Corse commanding, toward Station No. 1, on the Gulf railroad, and between the Ogeechee and Little Ogeechee Rivers, reaching, if possible, the Savannah Canal, and reconnoitering thence to ascertain the position of the enemy's forces, and securing, if possible, the bridge across the Ogeechee just below the mouth of the Cannouchee. Second, the First and Second Divisions of the Fifteenth Corps will leave the principal part of their trains at Jenks' Bridge, and be moved to, or near to, the Cannouchee River; thence it will reconnoiter for the purpose of breaking the Gulf railroad, and, if possible, securing the Ogeechee bridge, near the mouth of the Cannouchee. Third, the Third Division, Brigadier-General Smith commanding, will remain near Jenks' Bridge, and guard his own trains and those of the other divisions left there. Fourth, the spare boats of the pontoon bridge will be sent forward to General Hazen, under an efficient officer, with a detachment of pontoniers, leaving camp to-morrow at 5 a. m.; this is to facilitate the crossing of troops at the Cannouchee. Fifth, the Seventeenth Corps will continue to pursue the direct Savannah road, and pass at least three miles south of Station No. 2. Sixth, the cattle, in charge of Captains Roots and Douglass and Lieutenant Todd, will remain in this vicinity to-morrow. Seventh, these headquarters will move at 9 a. m. to some point in the vicinity of No. 2, following the Fourth Division, Fifteenth Army Corps. General Woods will cause the brigade of his division now at Station No. 2 to remain there until relieved by the arrival of the Seventeenth Army Corps.

By order of Maj. Gen. O. O. Howard:

SAML. L. TAGGART,
Assistant Adjutant-General.

SPECIAL ORDERS, No. 192. } HDQRS. FIFTEENTH ARMY CORPS, *Jenks' Bridge, Ga., December 7, 1864.*

I. The movements of the corps to-morrow will be as follows: First, the First and Second Divisions will, after leaving the principal part of their trains at Jenks' Bridge, move from their present camps, at 7 a. m., to a point near the mouth of the Cannouchee River, with a view to crossing that stream and breaking the Gulf railroad, and, if possible, securing the Ogeechee bridge. Brigadier-General Woods will cause the brigade of his division now at Station No. 2 to remain there until relieved by the arrival of the Seventeenth Army Corps. Second, the Fourth Division, Brigadier-General Corse commanding, will, at 7 a. m., move from its present camp toward Station No. 1 of the Gulf railroad, and between the Ogeechee and Little Ogeechee Rivers, reaching, if possible, the Savannah Canal, and reconnoitering thence to ascertain the position of the enemy's forces, and to secure, if possible, the bridge across the Ogeechee just below the mouth of the Cannouchee River. Third, the Third Division, Brigadier-General Smith commanding, will remain near Jenks' Bridge, and guard its own trains and those of the other divisions left there. Lieutenant-Colonel Tweeddale, commanding engineer troops, will cause the extra pontoons and chess wagons, with necessary detail, to accompany the Third Division. Corps headquarters will move with the Second Division.

By order of Maj. Gen. P. Joseph Osterhaus:

F. F. WHITEHEAD,
Assistant Adjutant-General.

SPECIAL FIELD ORDERS, No. 26. } HEADQUARTERS FOURTH DIVISION, FIFTEENTH ARMY CORPS, *Ogeechee River, Ga., December 7, 1864.*

* * * * * * *

II. This command will move to-morrow, the 8th instant, at 5.30 a. m., with two days' rations in haversacks, as follows:

The Third Brigade will have the advance, followed by the pioneer corps, and then the battery; the Second Brigade will move in the center, followed by the trains hereafter designated; the First Brigade will bring up the rear. The battery will take three wagons loaded with canister, two wagons loaded with shell, and one wagon loaded with shot. Each brigade will take five ordnance wagons loaded with caliber .58, and for each regiment armed with Henry rifles one wagon-load of that kind of ammunition will be taken. The pioneer corps will be accompanied by its tool wagons, and two ambulances will be taken for each regiment. The command will cross to the east side of the Ogeechee River, and take the first right-hand road leading to the canal and to the Station No. 1 on the Gulf railroad. The First Brigade, which is now occupying the east side of the river, will join the command and bring up the rear. The remainder of the trains will move, under the direction of Capt. H. R. Benjamin, acting assistant quartermaster of this division, to the position now occupied by the First Brigade, go in park there, and remain until further orders. Brigade commanders will keep their men well in hand, and will allow no foraging.

By order of Brig. Gen. John M. Corse:

L. CARPER,
Assistant Adjutant-General.

SPECIAL ORDERS, No. 301. } HDQRS. SEVENTEENTH ARMY CORPS,
Station 3, Ga., December 7, 1864.

* * * * * * *

II. Mounted foragers from the infantry will not hereafter be permitted; foraging must be done on foot by the infantry details. All animals now used by infantry foragers must be turned in at once to the division quartermasters, to be disposed of by them as the chief quartermaster of the corps may direct.

III. This command will move forward to-morrow as follows:

1. Brig. Gen. M. D. Leggett, commanding Third Division, will have the advance, and will move forward at 7 a. m.

2. Maj. Gen. J. A. Mower, commanding First Division, will follow the Third Division, being prepared to move at 8 o'clock.

3. Brig. Gen. G. A. Smith, commanding Fourth Division, will follow the First Division, being prepared to move at 9 o'clock.

4. The First Regiment Michigan Engineers will be prepared to move at 7.30 a. m., and the regiment will move at the head of the column, with a sufficient number of tools for clearing or repairing the road. Their train will move in rear of the train of the Third Division.

5. The pontoon train, Lieut. Col. J. M. Rusk commanding, will move in rear of the First Division train. The train of headquarters Military Division of the Mississippi and of these headquarters will move as heretofore.

By command of Maj. Gen. F. P. Blair:

C. CADLE, JR.,
Assistant Adjutant-General.

ORDERS.] HDQRS. FIRST DIVISION, 17TH ARMY CORPS,
Near Station No. 3, Ga., December 7, 1864.

The troops of this command will be prepared to march to-morrow at 7 a. m. Order of march: First, pioneer corps; second, First Brigade; third, battery; fourth, Second Brigade; fifth, Third Brigade; sixth, ambulance train; seventh, ordnance train; eighth, supply train.

By order of Maj. Gen. Joseph A. Mower:

CHAS. CHRISTENSEN,
Lieut., Aide-de-Camp and Acting Assistant Adjutant-General.

SPECIAL FIELD ORDERS, No. 168. } HEADQUARTERS THIRD DIVISION,
SEVENTEENTH ARMY CORPS,
Near Station No. 3, Ga., December 7, 1864.

I. This command will move at 7 a. m. to-morrow. The First Brigade, Brig. Gen. M. F. Force commanding, will have the advance. Artillery and trains as heretofore.

By order of Brig. Gen. M. D. Leggett:

J. C. DOUGLASS,
Assistant Adjutant-General.

HDQRS. MILITARY DIVISION OF THE MISSISSIPPI,
In the Field, Two Miles and a Half from No. 3,
December 7, 1864.

Major-General SLOCUM, *Commanding Left Wing:*

GENERAL: Owing to the rain, General Blair did not reach Guyton to-day, but is at this point, about two miles and a half northwest of Guyton. The bridge over the small stream without name is burned, and some obstructions there are now being removed, so that early in the morning his column will move right forward on the road which passes about two miles west of Guyton and about the same distance east of Eden, where your road and ours come together. It will be well if you can find a road passing from Springfield to Monteith and Pooler, and General Davis should be instructed to reach Saint Augustine and the vicinity of Cherokee Hill. He must first secure the road indicated from Cherokee Hill to Silk Hope and Litchfield. We hear that the enemy is fortifying in a semi-circle around and about four miles from Savannah.

I am, general, respectfully, yours,

W. T. SHERMAN,
Major-General, Commanding.

HEADQUARTERS,
Springfield, December 7, 1864—3 p. m.

Capt. L. M. DAYTON,
Aide-de-Camp:

CAPTAIN: The Twentieth Army Corps will be well closed at this point to-night. Morgan's division, of the Fourteenth, encamped last night nine miles south of Halley's Ferry; the other two, at the ferry; cavalry, four miles in rear. Davis wrote me he should make twenty miles to-day, which will bring him well up with this corps. I shall await orders at this point.

Yours, very respectfully,

H. W. SLOCUM,
Major-General.

HDQRS. MILITARY DIVISION OF THE MISSISSIPPI,
In the Field, Two Miles and a Half from Guyton,
December 7, 1864—5 p. m.

Maj. Gen. H. W. SLOCUM,
Commanding Left Wing:

GENERAL: Your dispatch of 3 p. m. just received. All very well. The general wrote you an hour since describing the march of to-day and giving orders. He now wishes you to move on Savannah, with your command well in hand, General Davis to reach the railroad about Saint Augustine Creek, and your column to be in communication with General Blair about Pooler. He will not expect your Twentieth Corps to reach to-morrow further than the vicinity where the road you are on comes into the road General Blair moves on; but if you can find a road to the left leading to Pooler, it is desirable General Davis should be abreast. A Savannah paper, 5th, says Hood attacked Thomas at Franklin, and was defeated, with loss of 6,000, and 1,000 prisoners; Yankee loss, 500. Copied from New York papers.

I am, general, respectfully, yours,

L. M. DAYTON,
Aide-de-Camp.

HEADQUARTERS LEFT WING, ARMY OF GEORGIA,
Four Miles from Springfield, December 7, 1864—11 a. m.

Maj. Gen. J. C. DAVIS,
Commanding Fourteenth Corps:

The major-general commanding desires me to say that this column will probably reach Springfield to-night. We find the roads badly obstructed, and the rain is constantly making them worse. The Seventeenth Corps will be at Guyton (No. 3, Central railroad) to-night and the Fifteenth Corps at or near Eden (No. 2); they are crossing to-day. The general is of the opinion that the enemy will not give up the Charleston and Savannah road without a fight, and thinks you may be attacked at any time before you reach that road. He desires me to suggest that you strengthen your advance guard, keep your column well closed up, and let Kilpatrick take care of your rear. Please indicate where you will probably encamp to-night, and, if possible, communicate with us to-morrow. We shall not move beyond Springfield until further orders and until we know where your column is.

Very respectfully, your obedient servant,

H. C. RODGERS,
Assistant Adjutant-General.

HEADQUARTERS FOURTEENTH ARMY CORPS,
Five Miles North of Sister's Ferry, December 7, 1864—3.10 p. m.

Col. H. C. RODGERS,
Chief of Staff, Left Wing:

COLONEL: Your dispatch by Corporal Cureton and party is just received. My advance division took dinner at Sister's Ferry; my rear will reach there to-night. My headquarters will be about five miles from that place. The enemy shows himself at all the ferries on the opposite bank of the river. A little skirmishing has been reported in my rear this morning. We find fallen timber across all the creeks and swamps. I sent a messenger to you at daylight this morning. Our roads are bad, but I will make nearly twenty miles to-day by dint of hard work and rapid marching. I had already made arrangements to place more troops in my front.

Yours, respectfully,

JEF. C. DAVIS,
Brevet Major-General, Commanding.

HEADQUARTERS TWENTIETH CORPS,
December 7, 1864—12 m.

[Brig. Gen. A. S. WILLIAMS,
Commanding Twentieth Corps:]

GENERAL: There is a small stream ahead of the Turkey Creek which does not amount to more than eight or ten inches of water. The water in Turkey Creek is nearly three to three and a quarter feet deep. It will take the pioneers and pontoniers at least two hours to fix a good corduroy to cross it. As soon as the infantry comes across Turkey Creek I shall proceed to keep you further advised.

Respectfully,

CHAS. W. ASMUSSEN,
Assistant Inspector-General.

HEADQUARTERS TWENTIETH CORPS,
Two Miles and a Half from Springfield, December 7, 1864—1 p. m.

[Brig. Gen. A. S. WILLIAMS:]

GENERAL: The road is in excellent condition, with the exception of one bad place, which twenty pioneers can fix in half an hour. The orderly knows the place. Good camping-ground all along here. The citizens say there is only one bad place to cross between here and near Springfield. Shall report from there.

Respectfully,

CHAS. W. ASMUSSEN,
Assistant Inspector-General.

ORDERS.] HEADQUARTERS TWENTIETH CORPS,
Near Springfield, Ga., December 7, 1864.

The movements of this corps to-morrow will be as follows: General Geary, with the troops of the Second Division, will break camp at 6.30 a. m., and march on the direct road through Springfield. His division pioneers and the pioneer battalion will accompany him. He will clear the road, toward Monteith, of all obstructions and make it passable for infantry and artillery.

The First Division will break camp at daylight, and march, with their trains, to Springfield, where the trains will be parked, and the troops move on to join the Second Division, when these two divisions, with two batteries of artillery, will push on toward Monteith.

The trains of the Second Division will cross Jack's Creek first, the trains of the First Division next, those of the Third Division last; the pontoon train preceding the train of the Second Division, and the corps and artillery supply and ammunition trains following it.

The Third Division will remain with the trains, and protect them. The troops will be so disposed about the park on the east side of Jack's Creek as to afford sufficient protection in case an attack on them should be made.

The cavalry of Colonel Hughes will accompany the advance, starting at 6.30 a. m.

Major Reynolds, chief of artillery, will detail two batteries of artillery, one to accompany each division.

By command of Brig. Gen. A. S. Williams:

ROBT. P. DECHERT,
Captain and Acting Assistant Adjutant-General.

HEADQUARTERS TWENTIETH CORPS,
Four Miles from Springfield, Ga., December 7, 1864.

Brig. Gen. N. J. JACKSON,
Commanding First Division:

GENERAL: Major-General Slocum has ordered that this corps be concentrated to-night at Springfield. In accordance therewith, the general commanding the corps directs that you continue the march to-day to that point, unless you receive further orders. This same order has been sent to General Geary. We are having the roads repaired as far as possible so as to make an easy passage for your trains.

Very respectfully, your obedient servant,

H. W. PERKINS,
Assistant Adjutant-General.

ORDERS.] HDQRS. FIRST DIVISION, 20TH ARMY CORPS,
Near Springfield, Ga., December 7, 1864.

This division will move to-morrow, at 7 a. m., toward Monteith, in the following order: Third Brigade in advance; First, next; and Second in rear. The trains of the division will move with the division, following the Second Division, across Jack's Creek, and be parked in the vicinity of Springfield, and will be guarded by the Third Division. A battery of artillery will accompany the division, moving in rear of the leading brigade.

By command of Brig. Gen. N. J. Jackson:

GEO. ROBINSON,
First Lieutenant and Acting Assistant Adjutant-General.

HEADQUARTERS TWENTIETH CORPS,
Four Miles from Springfield, December 7, 1864.

Brigadier-General GEARY,
Commanding Second Division:

GENERAL: Major-General Slocum has directed that this corps concentrate at Springfield to-night. In accordance therewith the general commanding the corps directs that you continue the march until you reach that point, unless you receive further orders.

Very respectfully, your obedient servant,

H. W. PERKINS,
Assistant Adjutant-General.

HEADQUARTERS DEPARTMENT OF THE SOUTH,
Steamer Nemaha, Tullifinny River, December 7, 1864.

Maj. Gen. H. W. HALLECK, U. S. Army,
Chief of Staff, Armies of United States, Washington, D. C.:

GENERAL: I have the honor to report that to put into the field the force of 5,000 men, with which I am now acting against the enemy, I have been obliged to strip the Beaufort and Hilton Head Districts, placing the citizens on guard and garrison duty, and also to take from the Northern and Florida Districts more men than I think consistent with entire safety. My loss in killed and wounded is not far from 1,000, and I would respectfully suggest that if any troops are disposable, they be sent to me.

Very respectfully, your obedient servant,

J. G. FOSTER,
Major-General, Commanding.

STEAMER NEMAHA,
Mouth of Tullifinny Creek, December 7, 1864.

Capt. W. L. M. BURGER,
Assistant Adjutant-General:

CAPTAIN: The major-general commanding desires me to inform you that the principal base is changed to Tullifinny Point, where a landing has been established. Only one regiment and a section of artillery will be left at Boyd's Neck. Six 20-pounder or 30-pounder Parrotts are to be sent here immediately; also eight or ten wagons, and horses for the wagons and also to drag the guns. If there is not a sufficient number of horses that can be spared from Hilton Head, take quartermaster's horses from Morris Island. General Halleck has ordered the firing at Morris Island on Fort Sumter and the city to cease temporarily, and consequently the horses will not be needed there to drag ammunition. Send here twenty or thirty recruits for Day's battery, who are now at Hilton Head, and any other artillery or ordnance men unassigned to duty let them report to the ordnance officer at Hilton Head, to come up with the heavy guns. Order the remainder of the battery at Beaufort, one section to Mackay's Point (horsed, if possible), and one section to Boyd's Neck, which may be without horses. Lieutenant Arnold goes to Hilton Head about the ordnance, but the general desires you to issue the necessary orders, and to see that they are promptly complied with. Please show this letter, or a copy of it, to Colonel Thomas.

Very respectfully, your obedient servant,

JOHN C. GRAY, JR.,
Major, Judge-Advocate and Acting Aide-de-Camp.

HDQRS. NORTHERN DISTRICT, DEPT. OF THE SOUTH,
FIRST SEPARATE BRIGADE,
Morris Island, S. C., December 7, 1864.

Lieut. W. B. DEAN,
Acting Assistant Adjutant-General:

SIR: I have the honor to acknowledge the receipt of your letter of the 3d, directing, by command of Maj. Gen. J. G. Foster, that all firing should cease from the batteries in this district bearing upon the city and harbor of Charleston till such time as Lieutenant-Colonel Mulford, U. S. agent of exchange, should notify me that the truce was over. In compliance with which I caused all work of a military nature on the batteries at Cummings' Point and all firing from said batteries to cease. Early on the morning of the 5th the enemy opened fire with sharpshooters from Fort Sumter. Thinking this was done through mistake, and not with the intention of violating the truce, I did not open fire upon the city, but did order the batteries on Cummings' Point to open fire upon Fort Sumter and the batteries on James Island. At about noon the enemy sent a small boat from Fort Sumter bearing a white flag. This boat was met by a navy picket-boat, and a communication, of which the inclosed (marked A), is a true copy (see preceding letter to Lieutenant-Colonel Mulford), was, by the navy picket-boat, brought ashore to me, upon receipt of which I ordered the batteries to cease firing, and sent a communication, of which the inclosed (marked B) is a true copy, to the commanding officer of Fort Sumter, by the navy picket-boat.

The troops of this command are in good health and spirits. Nothing worthy of mention has transpired since the departure of Brig. Gen. J. P. Hatch, with the exception of the above.

I have the honor to be, very respectfully, your obedient servant,

E. N. HALLOWELL,
Colonel Fifty-fourth Massachusetts Volunteers,
Commanding Northern District, Department of the South.

[Inclosures.]

A.

FORT SUMTER, S. C., *December 5, 1864.*

OFFICER COMMANDING U. S. FORCES ON MORRIS ISLAND:

SIR: Having just been informed by the proper authorities of the continuance of the truce which commenced yesterday, I beg leave to offer an apology for having fired upon the batteries on the northern end of Morris Island this morning with sharpshooters.

I have the honor to be, very respectfully, your obedient servant,

T. A. HUGUENIN,
Captain, Commanding.

B.

HEADQUARTERS U. S. FORCES,
Morris Island, S. C., December 5, 1864.

Capt. T. A. HUGUENIN,
Commanding Confederate Forces in Fort Sumter:

SIR: Your communication of this a. m., in explanation of the firing from Fort Sumter, is received. The explanation is satisfactory. The firing from the batteries on this island will be discontinued.

I have the honor to be, very respectfully, your obedient servant,

E. N. HALLOWELL,
Colonel, Commanding.

HEADQUARTERS DEPARTMENT OF THE SOUTH,
Hilton Head, S. C., December 7, 1864.

Brigadier-General SCHIMMELFENNIG:

The major-general directs that you proceed at once to Morris Island and assume command of the Northern District. The Delaware leaves this evening. The major-general commanding also directs that Colonel Hallowell, of the Fifty-fourth Massachusetts Volunteers, be ordered to report at once to Brigadier-General Hatch, at Tullifinny Point, to take command of the brigade lately commanded by Colonel Hartwell; 500 troops also to be sent from the Northern District, to report to Brigadier-General Hatch for duty at the front, without delay. Lieutenant-General Grant has ordered that the firing cease from Morris Island until further orders. You will therefore fire no guns unless absolutely necessary. The major-general has ascertained that there are 150 small boats in Charleston which the enemy intend to use in an assault on Morris Island. You are therefore requested to keep a sharp lookout for them, and use all your available force to keep the batteries in perfect order for action.

Very respectfully, your obedient servant,

W. L. M. BURGER,
Assistant Adjutant-General.

HEADQUARTERS DEPARTMENT OF THE SOUTH,
Hilton Head, S. C., December 7, 1864.

Brigadier-General SCAMMON,
Commanding District of Florida:

The major-general commanding directs that 500 troops be sent from your command at once to this place for duty at the front. The base of operations has been changed to Tullifinny Point, where a landing has been established, and it is necessary to have every man that can possibly be spared.

Very respectfully, your obedient servant,

W. L. M. BURGER,
Assistant Adjutant-General.

HEADQUARTERS MILITARY DIVISION OF THE MISSISSIPPI,
In the Field, December 8, 1864—10.30 a. m.

Major-General HOWARD,
Commanding Army of the Tennessee:

GENERAL: Your dispatch of 7th, with copies of your orders 6th, is just received all right. General Blair is moving on that road which will intersect the road from No. 2 to Savannah, southeast of No. 2, on the east side of the Little Ogeechee. General Davis is still behind, and it will be to-morrow before he can reach the Charleston road about Morton Hall. The best route for the Fifteenth Corps appears, from the map, to be via Litchfield and the plank road; but I will make more specific orders when I see how far General Blair will reach to-night. I expect to meet General Slocum at the intersection of roads east of Eden some time to-day.

I am, with respect,

W. T. SHERMAN,
Major-General, Commanding.

HEADQUARTERS MILITARY DIVISION OF THE MISSISSIPPI,
In the Field, December 8, 1864—7 p. m.

Major-General HOWARD,
Commanding Army of the Tennessee:

GENERAL: We are at a point on the road from Millen to Savannah, about two miles north of No. 2, called Mount Zion Church. General Slocum is but a short distance from us, and will move to-morrow on a road which branches off from this road and comes into the Augusta road ten miles north of Savannah, where he will effect a junction with General Davis, destroy that railroad, drive the enemy within his intrenchments, and then work to the right and form a junction with us, on this road, as near Savannah as we may get. General Blair will move on this road by Pooler, and so on until we drive the enemy within the intrenchments of Savannah, wherever they may be. The general wishes you to get down in the neighborhood of Beverly, Silk Hope, or Litchfield, so as to advance in the direction of the plank road until we come together, or communicate by the road which leads from Silk Hope to Cherokee Hill. He aims to push the enemy far enough into Savannah to have the use of the Shell road as a route of supply. If you can possibly do so, he wishes you to send a note by a canoe down the Ogeechee, pass the railroad bridge in the night, and inform the naval commander that we have arrived in fine condition and are moving directly against Savannah, but, for the present, do not risk giving any details.

I am, general, with respect, &c.,

L. M. DAYTON,
Aide-de-Camp.

SPECIAL FIELD ORDERS, No. 189.

HEADQUARTERS DEPARTMENT AND ARMY OF THE TENNESSEE,
Eden (No. 2), Ga., December 8, 1864.

The following will be the movements of this army to-morrow, the 9th instant: First, Major-General Osterhaus, after having broken the Gulf railroad, will cross his First and Second Divisions and the cattle, in charge of Captains Roots and Douglass and Lieutenant Todd, over the Ogeechee, laying his pontoons near the mouth of the canal, at an old ferry, about one mile north of Dillon's Bridge, near Fort Argyle. In case King's Bridge can be saved there will be no objection to crossing at that point. Second, Brig. Gen. J. E. Smith's division will cross the Ogeechee at Jenks' Bridge, and follow the Fourth Division, General Corse commanding, leaving camp at 6 a. m. Third, the Third Brigade, First Division, Fifteenth Corps, Colonel Williamson commanding, will recross the river at Jenks' Bridge at 5 a. m., making all possible haste to clear the bridge for General Smith's division. He will guard the trains of the First and Second Divisions until they reach their respective divisions. Fourth, as soon as the division of General Smith has passed, the bridge will be taken up, and the pontoon train will proceed with the trains of the First and Second Divisions. Fifth, Brigadier-General Corse, commanding Fourth Division, will, at 11 a. m., push forward his division to the intersection of the King's Bridge road with the road on which he is now moving, and there take up a strong position, sending out a force to break the Savannah and Gulf Railroad. Sixth, the Seventeenth Corps, Major-General Blair commanding, will follow the Third Division, Fifteenth Corps, Brigadier-General Smith commanding, keeping on the west bank of the Little Ogeechee, moving at 7 a. m. After reaching the canal, Major-General Blair will reconnoiter, with a view to moving toward Savannah along the tow-path. Seventh, each division commander in the column moving on the east side of the road will be careful to move his troops on the left of his trains, giving the trains the road to facilitate this movement.

By order of Maj. Gen. O. O. Howard:

SAML. L. TAGGART,
Assistant Adjutant-General.

HEADQUARTERS FIFTEENTH ARMY CORPS,
Bryan Court-House, December 8, 1864.

[General O. O. HOWARD:]

GENERAL: I arrived here by 1 p. m. The direct road to Dillon's Bridge (near Fort Argyle) was represented to be exceedingly bad and practicable only for horsemen, and consequently I marched via Court-House (Eden). Both divisions will be here, notwithstanding there are two or three places which will delay the trains some time. Colonel Oliver's brigade is at the river about two miles from here. The bridge was burned when his troops arrived yesterday night. The enemy is in some force on the south bank, and opened to-day with artillery. My cavalry is looking up and down the river for a practicable place to cross. As soon as the parties return I will report again. The pontoons will be up before night, when I will try to cross some men here. The description which I received of the road beyond the Cannouchee is anything but inviting; the only good road seems to be the one from King's

Bridge (above the mouth of Cannouchee), seven miles of which are planked. King's Bridge is burned, and so is every other bridge across the two streams.

Very respectfully,

P. JOS. OSTERHAUS,
Major-General.

HDQRS. DEPARTMENT AND ARMY OF THE TENNESSEE,
Eden (No. 2), Ga., December 8, 1864.

Maj. Gen. P. JOS. OSTERHAUS,
Commanding Fifteenth Army Corps:

I accompanied General Corse to-day. He met no opposition except obstructed roads. He has bridged the canal, and probably made a foot bridge across the Ogeechee where Dillon's Bridge was partially burned. Just one mile above Dillon's Bridge is a ferry, and a first-rate place for pontoons. I will try and get General Blair down there at an early hour to-morrow. If, however, I should fail in this, you will still have your own bridge that you can put down at that point. I think the Ogeechee will be too wide to bridge below Fort Argyle. I have sent your trains, cattle, &c., down on the west bank, because there is not a particle of forage on this. My headquarters will be to-morrow with General Corse. If you saved King's Bridge that will be the best place to cross.

Very respectfully, your obedient servant,

O. O. HOWARD,
Major-General.

SPECIAL ORDERS, No. 247. } HDQRS. THIRD DIV., 15TH ARMY CORPS,
Near Eden (No. 2), Ga., December 8, 1864.

I. This command will move at 6 a. m. to-morrow, the 9th instant, in the following order: First, one regiment Second Brigade as advance guard; second, pioneer corps and tool wagons; third, Battery B, First Michigan Artillery, followed by wagons of the battery and one ambulance; fourth, Battery H, First Illinois Artillery, followed by wagons of the battery and one ambulance; fifth, ambulances of Second Brigade (one for each regiment) and pioneer corps (one); sixth, ammunition train; seventh, division headquarters train and provost guard; eighth, Second Brigade train, including regimental wagons and pioneer corps wagon (baggage); ninth, First Brigade train; tenth, quartermaster's train; eleventh, commissary of subsistence train; twelfth, ambulance train, except ambulances assigned to regiments and detachments; thirteenth, regimental wagons First Brigade; fourteenth, two regiments First Brigade, rear guard; fifteenth, the infantry, with the exception of the advance and rear guard, will march, the Second Brigade in advance, upon the left flank of the artillery and trains, giving where possible the artillery and trains the road, to facilitate the movement.

By order of Brig. Gen. John E. Smith:

S. M. BUDLONG,
Assistant Adjutant-General.

HDQRS. DEPARTMENT AND ARMY OF THE TENNESSEE,
Eden Station, Ga., December 8, 1864.

Brig. Gen. J. M. CORSE,
Commanding Fourth Division, Fifteenth Army Corps:

GENERAL: Since making the order for the movements of the army to-morrow, General Howard has returned from a visit over at General Sherman's headquarters, and has modified the order so far as to put the Seventeenth Corps on the next road to the left. The Third Division will follow on by your road. We have communicated with General Osterhaus to-night, and have sent him the orders by Colonel Strong. The general desires that you make a foot bridge across the river, even if it takes all the old houses in the neighborhood to do it. General Blair's pontoons will move out on your road with the Third Division, and will be pushed forward as rapidly as possible. The general will leave here at 6 o'clock in the morning, and join you before you move.

Respectfully, &c.,

SAML. L. TAGGART,
Assistant Adjutant-General.

HDQRS. FOURTH DIVISION, FIFTEENTH ARMY CORPS,
Dillon's Bridge, December 8, 1864.

Major-General HOWARD:

Captain Kirlin, of your staff, came to the opposite bank this evening, and reported that General O. was at Eden; that the road east of Eden, crossing the Cannouchee near where it flows into the Ogeechee, is a myth; that General Osterhaus has met a force intrenched on the south side of the Cannouchee, estimated from 1,000 to 5,000. The cannonading heard late to-day was from the rebels. General Osterhaus will try to effect a crossing west of where the Eden road crosses the Cannouchee. Our fleet came into Ossabaw Sound and signaled for Sherman's forces on Saturday, landed forces and signaled again Monday. The foot bridge we found impracticable, but have a boat, by means of which we communicate with the western bank of the Ogeechee. My mounted force went out three miles and struck a rebel force on the main Savannah road, intrenched and with artillery. They developed the position and force of the enemy, but were so hotly pressed as to be compelled to leave one wounded man in the enemy's possession. I am prepared to advance in the morning, either toward Savannah or the Gulf railroad, as you may be pleased to direct. There are six couriers on the other bank of the Ogeechee. In case you want orders to go to General O. this will prove your speediest route.

I am, very respectfully, your obedient servant,

JOHN M. CORSE,
Brigadier-General, Commanding.

HEADQUARTERS MILITARY DIVISION OF THE MISSISSIPPI,
In the Field, Mount Zion Church, December 8, 1864.

Maj. Gen. F. P. BLAIR, *Commanding Seventeenth Corps:*

GENERAL: The general-in-chief directs that you move your command to-morrow by the direct Savannah road, as usual, pushing any enemy that may be found into his intrenchments.

I am, general, with respect, &c.,

L. M. DAYTON,
Aide-de-Camp.

HDQRS. DEPARTMENT AND ARMY OF THE TENNESSEE,
Near Savannah, Ga., December 8, 1864.

Maj. Gen. F. P. BLAIR, Jr., *Comdg. Seventeenth Army Corps:*

GENERAL: The major-general commanding instructs me to direct you to cause parties to be at once employed in the construction of fascines, for the purpose of corduroying at different points from the mainland to the east branch of the Little Ogeechee. They should be made of some light material, and he suggests rice straw as the most practicable and convenient.

Very respectfully, your obedient servant,

SAML. L. TAGGART,
Assistant Adjutant-General.

SPECIAL ORDERS, No. 302. } HDQRS. SEVENTEENTH ARMY CORPS,
Station 2, Ga., December 8, 1864.

The orders for the movement to-morrow are as follows:

1. Maj. Gen. J. A. Mower, commanding First Division, will have the advance, and will move forward at 7 a. m.

2. Brig. Gen. G. A. Smith, commanding Fourth Division, will be prepared to move at 8 o'clock, and will follow the First Division.

3. Brig. Gen. M. D. Leggett, commanding Third Division, will be prepared to move at 9 o'clock, and will follow the Fourth Division.

4. The First Michigan Engineers and train will follow the First Division train.

5. The pontoon train, Lieutenant-Colonel Rusk commanding, will move in rear of the train of the Fourth Division.

6. The trains of the headquarters Military Division of the Mississippi and these headquarters will move as heretofore.

By command of Maj. Gen. F. P. Blair:

C. CADLE, JR.,
Assistant Adjutant-General.

ORDERS.] HDQRS. FIRST DIVISION, 17TH ARMY CORPS,
In the Field, Ga., December 8, 1864.

The troops of this command will be prepared to march to-morrow at 7 a. m. Order of march: First, pioneer corps; second, Second Brigade; third, battery; fourth, headquarters train Military Division and Seventeenth Army Corps train; fifth, Third Brigade; sixth, First Brigade; seventh, ambulance corps; eighth, ordnance train; ninth, supply train; tenth, First Michigan Engineers and train.

By order of Maj. Gen. Joseph A. Mower:

CHAS. CHRISTENSEN,
Lieut., Aide-de-Camp, and Acting Assistant Adjutant-General.

HEADQUARTERS LEFT WING, ARMY OF GEORGIA,
Springfield, December 8, 1864—7 a. m.

Capt. L. M. DAYTON:

This column is now moving. I shall try to find a road to the left of the one you are on. I fear Davis is not as far advanced as I hoped last night. He wrote me at 2 p. m. that his roads were badly obstructed.

Yours, very respectfully,

H. W. SLOCUM,
Major-General.

HEADQUARTERS LEFT WING, ARMY OF GEORGIA,
Springfield, December 8, 1864—7 a. m.

[General DAVIS]:

GENERAL: General Sherman has information that the line of defense around Savannah is about four miles from the city. He desires to take the road extending from Cherokee Hill, through Silk Hope, to Litchfield, as our first position. Your corps should be at or near Cherokee Hill; the Twentieth will be to the left of Pooler; Seventeenth on right of Twentieth; and Fifteenth near Litchfield. The Twentieth Corps will be at Monteith to-night.*

Yours, very respectfully,

H. W. SLOCUM,
Major-General.

HEADQUARTERS FOURTEENTH ARMY CORPS,
Ebenezer Creek, Ga., December 8, 1864—8 a. m.

Lieut. Col. H. C. RODGERS,
Chief of Staff, Left Wing:

I have the honor to report my arrival at this point last night. Ebenezer is a large stream and requires bridging, and considerable to be cut out of the road. Our road was obstructed by timber at many points yesterday; notwithstanding, we made twenty miles. Kilpatrick reports his rear attacked yesterday afternoon; number of force not reported. We heard some artillery and small-arms yesterday evening in rear of the Twentieth Corps. The bridge in my front will be done by 10 a. m.; I will then commence crossing. It will take all day to get on the other side of Ebenezer. I sent you a messenger yesterday morning, who has not returned.

JEF. C. DAVIS,
Brevet Major-General, Commanding.

HEADQUARTERS FOURTEENTH ARMY CORPS,
Near Ebenezer Creek, Ga., December 8, 1864.

Brig. Gen. A. BAIRD,
Commanding Third Division, Fourteenth Army Corps:

General Carlin has just begun to advance toward the crossing. The general commanding directs you to take charge of the cavalry, dispose it as you may deem best to cover your crossing, and cross your division over the creek to-night. He desires that you give orders to the commanders of the cavalry to hold possession of the causeway on this side of the bridge until to-morrow noon at least. Having crossed his animals, he will thoroughly obstruct the road with fallen timber and will destroy the bridge as completely as possible.

Very respectfully, your obedient servant,

A. C. McCLURG,
Assistant Adjutant-General and Chief of Staff.

---

* This dispatch was captured by General Joseph Wheeler.

DECEMBER 8, 1864—11 a. m.

General WILLIAMS:

GENERAL: General Slocum wants to have all the trains and the Third Division started on this road as soon as possible, and have them get as far forward to-night as they can.

Very respectfully, your obedient servant,

H. W. PERKINS,
Assistant Adjutant-General.

HEADQUARTERS TWENTIETH CORPS,
Near Heim's Mills, Ga., December 8, 1864.

Brigadier-General GEARY,
Commanding Second Division:

GENERAL: The general commanding directs that your command be in readiness to move at 7 o'clock to-morrow morning. He directs that all the pioneers of your division report at daybreak to-morrow to Lieutenant Ludlow, at General Slocum's headquarters.

Very respectfully, your obedient servant,

ROBT. P. DECHERT,
Captain and Acting Assistant Adjutant-General.

HEADQUARTERS TWENTIETH CORPS,
On the March, December 8, 1864—12 m.

Brig. Gen. W. T. WARD,
Commanding Third Division:

GENERAL: The general commanding directs that you move all the trains of the corps at once on the road the troops have taken to-day. He wishes you to push forward as far as possible to-day, and to report your position this evening.

Very respectfully, your obedient servant,

ROBT. P. DECHERT,
Captain and Acting Assistant Adjutant-General.

HDQRS. THIRD DIVISION, TWENTIETH ARMY CORPS,
Forks of the Road, December 8, 1864.

Capt. R. P. DECHERT,
Acting Assistant Adjutant-General, Twentieth Army Corps:

CAPTAIN: I am using every effort to get the trains forward. The roads have all given out, and need repair. My train will not get in until after midnight, maybe not until morning. Wagons are scattered from here to Springfield. The train started from there after dark.

Very respectfully,

W. T. WARD,
Brigadier-General.
Per SPEED,
Assistant Adjutant-General.

HEADQUARTERS TWENTIETH CORPS,
Near Heim's Mills, Ga., December 8, 1864—5.30 p. m.

Brig. Gen. W. T. WARD,
Commanding Third Division:

GENERAL: The general commanding directs that you have a strong guard (at least two or three regiments) at the house where you turn to the right to reach this point, to remain there until the rear of the wagon train shall have passed. He directs that the roads at that point be blockaded sufficiently to prevent a sudden attack by a cavalry force. He wishes to know whether you need any further assistance, and he directs that you report to him frequently.

Very respectfully, your obedient servant,

ROBT. P. DECHERT,
Captain and Acting Assistant Adjutant-General.

HDQRS. THIRD DIVISION, TWENTIETH ARMY CORPS,
Mrs. Jadaun's House, December 8, 1864—6 p. m.

Lieut. Col. H. W. PERKINS,
Assistant Adjutant-General, Twentieth Army Corps:

COLONEL: My command is encamping at this point (forks of road). The road has been extremely bad, wheels cutting through to the hub. Nearly two miles and a half to work; have large details at it, and hope to get the rear in by 12 o'clock. Pontoon train is just in.

Very respectfully, your obedient servant,

W. T. WARD,
Brigadier-General, Commanding Division.

HEADQUARTERS TWENTIETH CORPS,
Near Eden, Ga., December 8, 1864.

Brig. Gen. W. T. WARD,
Commanding Third Division:

GENERAL: The general commanding the corps desires to have you push on at daybreak to-morrow to this point with your train. The corps pioneers will be sent from here early in the morning to repair the roads that you will have to pass over. The major-general commanding the Left Wing is anxious to have the trains hurried up as fast as possible. Please do the best with them that you can.

Very respectfully, your obedient servant,

H. W. PERKINS,
Lieutenant-Colonel and Assistant Adjutant-General.

HEADQUARTERS DEPARTMENT OF THE SOUTH,
Hilton Head, S. C., December 8, 1864.
(Received 8.15 p. m. 12th.)

Maj. Gen. H. W. HALLECK, U. S. Army,
Chief of Staff, Armies of the United States, Washington, D. C.:

GENERAL: Have been demonstrating strongly against the Charlestown and Savannah road. Had obstinate fight near Grahamville on the 30th; result, a drawn battle. Have kept a large force of the enemy sharply employed. Now hold a position within three-quarters of a mile of the railroad between the Coosawhatchie and Tullifinny Rivers. Deserters' reports are conflicting, but agree that Sherman is nearing Savannah.

Very respectfully, your obedient servant,

J. G. FOSTER,
Major-General, Commanding.

HEADQUARTERS DEPARTMENT OF THE SOUTH,
Hilton Head, S. C., December 8, 1864.

Maj. Gen. H. W. HALLECK, U. S. Army,
Chief of Staff, Armies of the United States, Washington, D. C.:

GENERAL: I have the honor to acknowledge the receipt of your confidential letter of the 13th ultimo.* The instructions contained therein will be carried out in every particular. I had already commenced a demonstration against the enemy, the particulars of which I have sent in another communication.

Very respectfully, your obedient servant,

J. G. FOSTER,
Major-General, Commanding.

HEADQUARTERS DEPARTMENT OF THE SOUTH,
Hilton Head, S. C., December 8, 1864.

Maj. Gen. H. W. HALLECK, U. S. Army,
Chief of Staff, Armies of the United States, Washington, D. C.:

GENERAL: I have the honor to acknowledge the receipt of your communication of the 23d ultimo, in which Lieutenant-General Grant directs that the expenditure of ammunition upon Fort Sumter and Charleston be discontinued, except so far as may be necessary. I have accordingly sent the necessary instructions to the commanding officer of the Northern District of this department.

Very respectfully, your obedient servant,

J. G. FOSTER,
Major-General, Commanding.

HEADQUARTERS DEPARTMENT OF THE SOUTH,
Hilton Head, S. C., December 8, 1864.

Maj. Gen. M. C. MEIGS,
Chief Quartermaster U. S. Army, Washington, D. C.:

GENERAL: I have the honor to acknowledge the receipt of your confidential communication of the 28th ultimo in regard to supplies sent to this department for General Sherman's army should he make for this coast.

Very respectfully, your obedient servant,

J. G. FOSTER,
Major-General, Commanding.

---

* See Vol. XXXV, Part II, p. 328.

HDQRS. NORTHERN DISTRICT, DEPT. OF THE SOUTH,
Morris Island, S. C., December 8, 1864.

Lieut. W. B. DEAN,
Acting Assistant Adjutant-General:

LIEUTENANT: I have the honor to report, for the information of the major-general commanding, that I have not been able to comply fully with his instructions regarding the immediate shipment of 500 troops from this district, owing to the fact of my not finding here available transportation for more than 400 men. The remaining 100 are here in readiness, awaiting the first means of transportation which shall present. I have also the honor to report that I find here some 400 men of the Twenty-first U. S. Colored Troops, who are wholly unarmed, with the exception of a few who are doing provost-guard duty. They are consequently entirely ineffective for defensive purposes. I am informed that the requisite arms have been already drawn for these men upon the proper requisitions, and that they are now at the arsenal awaiting transportation. I have, therefore, ordered Ordnance Sergeant Scherer to that post, for the purpose of taking charge of their shipment, and I request that they may be placed under his care at the earliest opportunity, and that every facility may be rendered him for their immediate transshipment.

I have the honor to be, lieutenant, very respectfully, your obedient servant,

A. SCHIMMELFENNIG,
Brigadier-General, Commanding.

ONE MILE AND A HALF FROM NO. 1,
December 9, 1864.

Major-General SHERMAN,
Commanding, &c.:

GENERAL: The dirt road runs to the left of the railroad. The troops continue to advance. General Blair thinks there is only cavalry in front. You can safely come to this point. The train has been ordered to follow the Fourth Division, which is second in advance.

Respectfully,

JOS. C. AUDENRIED,
Captain and Aide-de-Camp.

SPECIAL FIELD ORDERS, No. 129.

HDQRS. MIL. DIV. OF THE MISSISSIPPI,
In the Field, Pooler Station, Ga.,
December 9, 1864.

I. Especial attention is called to paragraph V, Special Field Orders, No. 17,* and all persons unauthorized riding horses should at once be dismounted and the animals turned over for cavalry use.

II. Brigadier-General Kilpatrick is authorized to organize a patrol to seize all horses and mules ridden by any persons without authority of law, or who may be away from their proper command, appropriating such animals for the use of his cavalry command.

By order of Maj. Gen. W. T. Sherman:

L. M. DAYTON,
Aide-de-Camp.

---

* See Vol. XXXVIII, Part IV, p. 406.

HDQRS. DEPARTMENT AND ARMY OF THE TENNESSEE,
Savannah Canal Bridge, Ga., December 9, 1864.

Maj. Gen. W. T. SHERMAN,
Commanding Military Division of the Mississippi:

On my arrival at the canal General Corse pushed out his reconnaissance. He encountered about 600 rebel infantry, with two pieces of artillery, near the cross-roads. His advance brigade quickly dislodged them, capturing one piece of artillery and some prisoners. He followed them up across the Little Ogeechee, seven miles from Savannah. I went to the railroad with some mounted infantry, and saw the road broken at that point. King's Bridge was burned by the rebels, and all that were on the west side of the Ogeechee withdrew this morning. The bridge for General Blair, near Fort Argyle, is now (5.25 p. m.) finished. In all probability General Osterhaus has burned the railroad bridge before this time, as two brigades of his had crossed the Ogeechee at last accounts. General Corse has taken up a strong position, by my direction, about twelve miles out of Savannah on this road. General Smith with his division is encamped near this place. I have not heard from General Blair, except from his guns. General Smith will send one brigade about two miles up the tow-path, and General Blair can communicate that way, if he gets ahead far enough. Please let him read this note.

Very respectfully, your obedient servant,

O. O. HOWARD,
Major-General.

P. S.—I met Mr. King to-day, and find him the possessor of King's Bridge. I mean your Marietta friend. He will be pleased to see you when you come this way. Since writing the above, Captains Duncan and King and Lieutenant McQueen report that they captured a locomotive, with a train of seven cars loaded with plunder, which was being run out of Savannah, which they destroyed.

HEADQUARTERS MILITARY DIVISION OF THE MISSISSIPPI,
In the Field, Pooler (No. 1), December 9, 1864—8 p. m.

Major-General HOWARD,
Commanding Army of the Tennessee:

GENERAL: Your dispatch from Canal bridge just received. The Seventeenth Corps moved at the usual hour to-day, and found the enemy defending the position covered by the swamp, about fifteen miles from Savannah. There was some skirmish fighting and use of artillery on both sides, but General Mower, who was in the advance, handsomely drove the enemy from his positions and works, and we reached this point and encamped in good season. The Seventeenth Corps will move as usual to-morrow morning, and will proceed until it reaches the main line of the enemy's works, supposed to be about four miles from Savannah, when it will work to the right and connect with you. The general-in-chief desires you to move on the direct road on Savannah as usual, making progress until the enemy's main line is developed; he also wishes you to communicate with the fleet if possible. General Kilpatrick's command is divided, covering this and General Davis' column, and reports positively that Wheeler is on the east side of the Savannah River. If the Cuyler you have as a prisoner be R. R. Cuyler, brother of Surgeon Cuyler of the old Army, or his son George, the general wishes you to send him to us when practicable, and in the meantime treat him as well as possible. Present the general's best wishes to Mr. King, and say he regrets Brown had not the good sense to follow his advice. The general thinks best for you to leave a brigade at the bridge at Fort Argyle, to hold and guard it, as we may need it. We have not heard from General Slocum direct, but the sound of his guns would place him at Cherokee Hill or near there—we heard them about sundown.

I am, general, yours, &c.,

L. M. DAYTON,
Aide-de-Camp.

SIGNAL CORPS, U. S. ARMY,
HEADQUARTERS ARMY OF THE TENNESSEE,
December 9, 1864—7 p. m.

CHIEF SIGNAL OFFICER OF FLEET:

SIR: It is the wish of the general commanding to open communication with the fleet as early as possible, and as we may be in calling distance ere long you will please have a strict watch kept for a flag or torch. At present we will use the old code. If communication should be opened we can arrange the numbers for the remainder of the month.

Yours, respectfully,

JAS. M. McCLINTOCK.

SPECIAL FIELD ORDERS, No. 190. } HDQRS. DEPT. AND ARMY OF THE TENN.,
Savannah Canal, near Dillon's Bridge, Ga.,
December 9, 1864.

The operations of this army to-morrow will be as follows: First, Major-General Osterhaus, commanding Fifteenth Army Corps, will direct Brig. Gen. J. E. Smith, commanding Third Division, to push his division forward toward a point marked on the map as Beverly, reconnoitering and feeling for the enemy by the plank and other roads leading into Savannah. Second, he will direct Brigadier-General Corse, commanding Fourth Division, to continue his reconnaissance toward a point marked Hermitage, carefully feeling toward Savannah by all the roads in his front leading thereto. Third, the two divisions of the Fifteenth Corps on the west side of the Ogeechee will leave their trains, with small guards, to follow them, and, crossing the river as heretofore directed, will move the leading division to the support of General Smith and the other to the support of General Corse. Fourth, Major-General Osterhaus will take charge of the right column, and the general commanding will in person take command of the left column. Fifth, Major-General Blair, commanding Seventeenth Army Corps, will move his command forward by the Pooler and Savannah road, feeling toward the Silk Hope and Cherokee Heights road, so as to communicate with General Smith. Sixth, each corps commander will locate his train as will be most convenient, and with the view of obtaining forage for it from the other as well as from this side of the Ogeechee.

By order of Maj. Gen. O. O. Howard:

SAML. L. TAGGART,
Assistant Adjutant-General.

HEADQUARTERS FIFTEENTH ARMY CORPS,
Cannouchee River, December 9, 1864.

General O. O. HOWARD:

GENERAL: The enemy evacuated his position opposite me this morning, probably impelled by some movement on his flank. I have put one brigade of Second Division across, and am making preparations to cross the entire Second Division, when I will push toward King's Bridge and to the nearest point on the railroad. There is a great deal of traffic over the Gulf road, trains passing almost continually. I will report again as soon as I have anything new to report.

I am, very respectfully, your obedient servant,

P. JOS. OSTERHAUS,
Major-General.

HDQRS. DEPARTMENT AND ARMY OF THE TENNESSEE,
Savannah Canal Bridge, Ga., December 9, 1864.

Maj. Gen. P. JOSEPH OSTERHAUS,
Commanding Fifteenth Army Corps:

I have just returned from Corse's front. He encountered the rebels at the cross-roads, drove them back, and pursued them across the Little Ogeechee. He captured about a dozen prisoners, a piece of artillery, a cart loaded with hogs, and several mules and wagons and negroes; burned a portion of the railroad at 1 p. m., about eleven miles from Savannah, and then took up a strong position about opposite Twelve-Mile Station. The bridge is completed across the Ogeechee at Fort Argyle. General Smith is here with his division, encamping one brigade south of the canal, and the other and train north of the canal. Please have the roads put in order, and move everything over to-morrow. My headquarters are just south of the canal. Further instructions will be sent you this evening. I have heard General Blair's guns, but nothing further. General Corse's advance is about seven miles from Savannah.

Very respectfully, your obedient servant,

O. O. HOWARD,
Major-General.

HEADQUARTERS FIFTEENTH ARMY CORPS,
Cannouchee Bridge, December 9, 1864.

Maj. Gen. O. O. HOWARD,
Commanding Army of the Tennessee:

GENERAL: Please accept my thanks for your very interesting account of the successful movement of General Corse's division. We pushed things here as fast as possible; by 11.30 the bridge across the river was completed, and by 1.30 p. m. the Gulf road was cut simultaneously at Way's and Fleming's Stations; bridges, culverts, and the trestle-works in the Ogeechee swamps are burning. The two expeditions sent out to Way's and Fleming's will return this evening, and early to-morrow morning the First and Second Divisions will march to the pontoon bridge near Dillon's Ferry. The supply trains of the above divisions will have a hard time to reach General Woods on account of the miserable roads; from Woods' camp to the pontoon bridge the road is well repaired. We made a small number of prisoners, and my cavalry is driving now the enemy's pickets from the railroad stations. I will move my headquarters to the Fourth Division very early to-morrow.

Very respectfully, your obedient servant,

P. JOS. OSTERHAUS,
Major-General of Volunteers.

[Indorsement.]

HDQRS. DEPARTMENT AND ARMY OF THE TENNESSEE,
Savannah Canal, near Dillon's Bridge, Ga.,
December 9, 1864.—7 p. m.

Respectfully forwarded.

We have captured here to-day probably 50 prisoners. Fort McAllister is said to be occupied by the enemy entirely independent of any other force. I have to-night sent Captain Duncan and two scouts in a canoe down the river to attempt to communicate with the fleet. Two empty trains left Savannah on the Gulf road, and are cut off; two attempted to leave this evening, one of which I reported as burned.

Respectfully,

O. O. HOWARD,
Major-General.

SPECIAL ORDERS, } HEADQUARTERS FIFTEENTH ARMY CORPS,
No. 194. } *Cannouchee Bridge, December 9, 1864.*

* * * * * * *

II. The corps will continue its march to-morrow, in the following order: First, First Division, Brigadier-General Woods commanding, will march from its present camp early to-morrow morning to the pontoon bridge near Dillon's Ferry. On arriving there General Woods will cross his division and trains, turning over the trains of Second Division to General Hazen. The brigade of the First Division stationed at Eden Court-House will leave camp at 5 a. m., and march on the direct road from Eden to Dillon, the commanding officer of which will take measures to pass the old camp of Second Division by 7 a. m. Major Stolbrand will cause the commanding officer of the Twelfth Wisconsin Battery to join the brigade of the First Division marching from Eden Court-House when en route. Second, the Second Division, Brigadier-General Hazen commanding, will march from its present camp at 7 a. m., by the direct road from Cannouchee bridge, to Dillon's Ferry. As soon as his troops and trains have re-crossed the Cannouchee River the commanding officer of the First Missouri Engineers will cause the pontoon bridge to be taken up, and will follow the Second Division. The rear guard of the Second Division will escort the pontoon train, and to that end will remain here until the same is well on the road. As soon as the First Division is over the Ogeechee River Brigadier-General Hazen will proceed to cross his command.

III. The Third Division, Brigadier-General Smith commanding, will leave its present camp at 7 a. m. to-morrow for the place laid down on the maps as Beverly. It will follow substantially the tow-path, on the south side of the canal, but will at the same time patrol and reconnoiter the plank and country roads into Savannah. The Fourth Division, Brigadier-General Corse commanding, will, at 8 a. m., continue its reconnaissance toward the point indicated as Hermitage, scouring all the approaches to Savannah in his front, with a view of obtaining the most perfect information of the enemy's position and works. The First and Second Divisions, after having executed the movements as ordered in paragraph II, Special Orders, No. 194, of date, will continue to close on the leading divisions, as follows: The First Division, Brigadier-General Woods commanding, will follow the Third Division, while Brigadier-General Hazen with the Second Division will march to the support of the Fourth Division, Brigadier-General Corse commanding. In order to join as fast as possible their respective columns Generals Hazen and Woods will, on their arrival at the Ogeechee River, leave their respective trains in charge of one regiment each, with instructions to guard and corral them east of the Ogeechee and on the south side of the canal until further orders. Department headquarters will march with the left column (First and Third Divisions), while the corps commander will accompany the right column (Second and Fourth Divisions).

By order of Maj. Gen. P. Joseph Osterhaus:

F. F. WHITEHEAD,
Assistant Adjutant-General.

SPECIAL ORDERS, No. 248. } HDQRS. THIRD DIV., 15TH ARMY CORPS,
Savannah Canal, near Dillon's Bridge, Ga., December 9, 1864.

I. This command will move at 7 a. m. to-morrow, the 10th instant, in the following order: First, one regiment First Brigade as advance guard, followed by regimental wagons and one ambulance; second, pioneer corps, tool wagons, baggage wagon, and one ambulance; third, Battery B, First Michigan Artillery, followed by wagons of the battery and one ambulance; fourth, Battery H, First Illinois Artillery, followed by wagons of the battery and one ambulance; fifth, four wagons of ammunition (musket); sixth, remainder of First Brigade, each regiment followed by regimental wagons and one ambulance; seventh, three regiments Second Brigade, each regiment followed by regimental wagons and one ambulance; eighth, the trains, except such portions as are mentioned above, will remain in their present camp, guarded by one regiment of Second Brigade.

By order of Brig. Gen. John E. Smith:

S. M. BUDLONG,
Assistant Adjutant-General.

SPECIAL FIELD ORDERS, No. 27. } HEADQUARTERS FOURTH DIVISION, FIFTEENTH ARMY CORPS,
Near Savannah Canal, December 9, 1864.

I. This command will move to-day at 11 a. m., in the following order: The Second Brigade will move in the advance, followed by the battery; the First Brigade will move in the center; the Third Brigade will bring up the rear. The pioneer corps will follow the advance guard, and remove all obstructions that may have been placed in the road by the enemy. The trains will move as follows: First, the pioneer corps train; second, the Second Brigade train; third, the First Brigade train; fourth, the Third Brigade train; fifth, the ambulance corps train; sixth, the ordnance train; seventh, the supply train.

By order:

LEO CARPER,
Assistant Adjutant-General.

HDQRS. THIRD BRIG., FOURTH DIV., 15TH ARMY CORPS,
Near Gulf Railroad, Ga., December 9, 1864.

Maj. E. S. JOHNSON,
Commanding Detachment Seventh Illinois Mounted Infantry:

MAJOR: By direction of Brig. Gen. John M. Corse, commanding Fourth Division, Fifteenth Army Corps, you will, at early daylight to-morrow morning, December 10, move with your command across the bridge you are now guarding, and, if possible, take possession of the ridge on the other side, sending word to these headquarters immediately on gaining the ridge, or sooner, if possible, if you develop the enemy in force.

By order of Lieut. Col. F. J. Hurlbut, Fifty-seventh Illinois Infantry, commanding:

N. FLANSBURG,
Lieutenant and Acting Assistant Adjutant-General.

SPECIAL ORDERS, No. 303. } HDQRS. SEVENTEENTH ARMY CORPS,
Station 1, Ga., December 9, 1864.

The following are the orders for the movement to-morrow:

1. Brig. Gen. G. A. Smith, commanding Fourth Division, will have the advance, and will move forward at 7 a. m.

2. Brig. Gen. M. D. Leggett, commanding Third Division, will follow the Fourth Division.

3. Maj. Gen. J. A. Mower, commanding First Division, will follow the Third Division.

4. The First Michigan Regiment of Engineers, with a sufficient number of tools to repair the road, in wagons, will follow the Fourth Division.

5. The division trains, except the ordnance train and ambulances, which will follow their respective divisions, will move in rear of the troops in the same order of march as the command to which they belong, and each division commander will leave with his train a light guard to protect the flanks. The rear will be protected by a brigade from General Kilpatrick's cavalry. When practicable the wagons will move two abreast.

6. The train of the headquarters Military Division of the Mississippi and of these headquarters will move at the head of general train.

By command of Maj. Gen. F. P. Blair:

C. CADLE, JR.,
Assistant Adjutant-General.

SPECIAL FIELD ORDERS, No. 169. } HEADQUARTERS THIRD DIVISION,
SEVENTEENTH ARMY CORPS,
Near Station No. 2, Ga., December 9, 1864.

I. This command will be in readiness to move at 9 a. m. The Second Brigade, Col. R. K. Scott commanding, will have the advance. Artillery and trains as heretofore.

II. The following are the orders for the movement to-morrow: First, Brig. Gen. M. F. Force, commanding First Brigade, will move forward at 7 a. m., following the First Regiment of Michigan Engineers; second, artillery, Fifteenth Ohio Battery; third, Col. R. K. Scott, commanding Second Brigade, will follow the artillery; fourth, ambulances and ordnance train, all the wagons will follow in rear of the corps in same order of march as their respective commands; fifth, each brigade commander will detail one company for train guard, to report at wagon corral, at 7 a. m. to-morrow, to Lieut. George W. Porter, aide-de-camp, for further instructions.

By order of Brig. Gen. M. D. Leggett:

J. C. DOUGLASS,
Assistant Adjutant-General.

HEADQUARTERS MILITARY DIVISION OF THE MISSISSIPPI,
In the Field, Pooler (No. 1), December 9, 1864.

Major-General SLOCUM,
Commanding Left Wing:

GENERAL: As yet we have heard nothing from you to-day except your guns, nearly due north, from 3 to 5 p. m. General Howard has reported, and is in possession of the Gulf railroad; captured one piece of artillery, some prisoners, and a train of cars; both corps have met opposition, but have overcome it; and Howard will move the Fifteenth via the plank road, and the Seventeenth via this the main road, on Savannah, in the morning.

The general wishes you to continue along the Savannah River in your movement on the city, making as much progress as you can until the enemy's main line is developed.

I am, general, respectfully, yours, &c.,

L. M. DAYTON,
Aide-de-Camp.

HEADQUARTERS FOURTEENTH ARMY CORPS,
Two Miles South of Ebenezer Creek, December 9, 1864—9 a. m.

Col. H. C. RODGERS,
Chief of Staff, Left Wing:

COLONEL: My rear only completed the crossing of the creek at daylight. I am now moving for Saint Augustine Creek, and if the obstructions or opposition is not too great will reach there to-day. One of the enemy's gun-boats made several demonstrations against our bridge yesterday, but a few shells satisfied them they could accomplish nothing, and it gave up the project. My troops skirmished all day. Fewer attacks in rear. I have destroyed the bridge behind me, and do not think I shall be troubled from the rear to-day. I can hear nothing of the Twentieth Corps. Heavy cannonading is now progressing in the direction of Savannah or Coosawhatchie.

I am, very respectfully,

JEF. C. DAVIS,
Brevet Major-General, Commanding.

ORDERS.] HEADQUARTERS TWENTIETH CORPS,
Near Monteith, Ga., December 9, 1864.

The movements of this corps to-morrow will be as follows: The First Division will break camp at 6.30 a. m., and push forward toward the Savannah and Charleston Railroad. The cavalry of Colonel Hughes will precede the infantry, starting at 6 a. m. The Third Division will follow the First Division, starting from their present camp at 6 a. m. The Second Division will remain in charge of the trains. General Geary will send one of his brigades to guard the rear of the train, and hold his other two brigades in their present camps, but be in readiness to move at short notice. The train will remain in its present park until further orders. All pack-animals of the First and Third Divisions, except the animals that carry the pioneers' tools, will be left with the trains. Fifteen wagons from the ammunition train of the First Division and five from the ammunition train of the Third Division will accompany the advanced forces. These wagons, with the headquarters wagons and ambulances, will march in rear of the center brigade of the Third Division.

By command of Brig. Gen. A. S. Williams:

ROBT. P. DECHERT,
Captain and Acting Assistant Adjutant-General.

ORDERS.] HDQRS. FIRST DIVISION, TWENTIETH CORPS,
Near Monteith, Ga., December 9, 1864.

This division will move to-morrow at 6.30 a. m., in the following order: Second Brigade in advance, followed by a battery; Third brigade next, and First in rear. The trains will remain in their present park, under General Geary, until further orders. All pack-animals, except those that carry pioneer tools, will be left with the trains. Captain Augustine, ordnance officer, will send fifteen wagons of ammunition, which will have a position in the column with the different headquarters wagons and ambulances, in rear of the center brigade of the Third Division, which immediately follows the First Division.

By command of Brig. Gen. N. J. Jackson:

GEO. ROBINSON,
First Lieutenant and Acting Assistant Adjutant-General.

HDQRS. THIRD DIVISION, TWENTIETH ARMY CORPS,
December 9, 1864—6 a. m.

Lieut. Col. H. W. PERKINS,
Assistant Adjutant-General, Twentieth Army Corps:

COLONEL: The Third Division train (rear) is not nearly all in. The ground will not even hold corduroy. I will push on as soon as possible, but my movements will necessarily be very slow, as I hear that most of the road ahead has to be worked.

Very respectfully, your obedient servant,

W. T. WARD,
Brigadier-General, Commanding Division.

HEADQUARTERS TWENTIETH CORPS,
Near Zion Church, Ga., December 9, 1864.

Brig. Gen. W. T. WARD,
Commanding Third Division:

GENERAL: The general commanding directs me to inform you that one mile from where he encamped last night, at Zion Church, you take the road to the left; it is a road not laid down on the map. He directs that you place two regiments to hold the road leading to the right, at this church.

Very respectfully, your obedient servant,

ROBT. P. DECHERT,
Captain and Acting Assistant Adjutant-General.

HEADQUARTERS TWENTIETH CORPS,
Near Mount Zion Church, Ga., December 9, 1864—10.15 a. m.

Brig. Gen. W. T. WARD,
Commanding Third Division:

GENERAL: The First and Third Divisions are halted here awaiting the train. The enemy are in front of us, and the general deems it imprudent to push the troops farther until the arrival of the train, as it would be too much exposed. The general commanding the corps desires to have you report every two hours the location and state of affairs along the train, where your rear is, &c. In dating your notes, please state the hour and place.

Very respectfully, your obedient servant,

H. W. PERKINS,
Lieutenant-Colonel and Assistant Adjutant-General.

HEADQUARTERS ARMY OF THE TENNESSEE,
Near Savannah Canal, Ga., December 9, 1864.

COMMANDING OFFICER U. S. NAVAL FORCE,
IN THE VICINITY OF SAVANNAH, GA.:

SIR: We have met with perfect success thus far. Troops in fine spirits, and near by.

Respectfully,

O. O. HOWARD,
Major-General, Commanding Right Wing of Army.

SPECIAL FIELD ORDERS, No. 130. } HDQRS. MIL. DIV. OF THE MISSISSIPPI,
In the Field, near Savannah, Ga.,
December 10, 1864.

The army having arrived before Savannah, will proceed to invest the place, and to open up communication with our fleet in Ossabaw and Wassaw Sounds.

I. The Left Wing, Major-General Slocum, will make a left flank near the Savannah River above the city, and extend round to a point near the plank road. He is also charged with the utter destruction of the Savannah and Charleston Railroad back to and including the Savannah River bridge, as also the Central Georgia road from his line back to Pooler (No. 1). One battalion of the First Regiment Michigan Engineers and Mechanics will be ordered to report to General Slocum, to twist the rails.

II. The Right Wing, Major-General Howard, will extend from General Slocum's right to the Savannah River below the city, or to the Shell road. General Howard is also charged with opening communication with the fleet and the destruction of the Gulf railroad back to and including the Ogeechee River bridge.

III. Capt. O. M. Poe, chief engineer, will forthwith cause thorough reconnaissances to be made, so as to compile an approximate map for the use of army commanders, and will also cause roads to be examined and opened, to facilitate communication with the different parts of it.

IV. Brigadier-General Kilpatrick, commanding cavalry, will watch all roads to the rear, and also assist General Howard in opening communication with the fleet; and army and corps commanders will at once overhaul their trains, and be prepared, on short notice, to send to the fleet everything not absolutely required for our success.

By order of Maj. Gen. W. T. Sherman:

L. M. DAYTON,
Aide-de-Camp.

HDQRS. DEPARTMENT AND ARMY OF THE TENNESSEE,
Little Ogeechee, near Savannah, December 10, 1864.

Maj. Gen. W. T. SHERMAN,
Commanding Military Division of the Mississippi:

I have directed that to-morrow Major-General Blair so place his command that his right flank will rest on King's Bridge and Savannah road; that General Osterhaus will push his corps to the right, his left flank resting on the same road. I find that on this side of the Ogeechee every inlet to the sea to which access can be had is commanded either by a fort or battery. I think, however, that on the other side of the river access can be had to Ossabaw Sound; and, with a view to this, I have directed Captain Reese, of my staff, to repair King's Bridge, and shall throw over a reconnaissance for the purpose of ascertaining whether it is practicable to communicate with the west side of the river. The party I sent last night down the river for that purpose has not yet returned. I have not yet received any further orders from you than what you gave me verbally to-day.

Very respectfully, your obedient servant,

O. O. HOWARD,
Major-General.

SPECIAL FIELD ORDERS, No. 191. } HDQRS. DEPT. AND ARMY OF THE TENN.,
Savannah Canal, near Dillon's Bridge, Ga.,
December 10, 1864.

Major-General Osterhaus, commanding Fifteenth Army Corps, will not at present take up his pontoon bridge over the Ogeechee, but leave the same, with one strong regiment well disposed for guard, until further orders.

LITTLE OGEECHEE, NEAR SAVANNAH, GA.,
December 10, 1864.

The following are the orders for the operations of this army to-morrow: First, Major-General Osterhaus, commanding Fifteenth Army Corps, will move his entire corps around to the right of the King's Bridge and Savannah road, placing one division in reserve on that road, from which will be furnished the pioneer corps, and such other details of men, teams, &c., as may be required by Captain Reese, chief engineer, in the reconstruction of King's Bridge. Second, Major-General Blair, commanding Seventeenth Army Corps, will move his command by the Darien road around to the right, until his right rests on the King's Bridge and Savannah road. Third, all the trains, cattle, &c., on the west side of the Ogeechee will be crossed over to the east side, the trains, with small guards, to be parked, as nearly as practicable, in rear of their respective divisions, and the cattle occupying such places in the rear of the army as may be most convenient for forage, &c. Fourth, the portion of the engineer regiment with the Fifteenth Corps, and as many officers and men of same as can be spared from the Seventeenth Army Corps (leaving enough to take care of the bridge at Dillon's Ferry), will report, with tools, &c., without delay, to Capt. C. B. Reese, chief engineer, at King's Bridge. Fifth, the pontoon bridge at Dillon's will not be taken up until King's Bridge is repaired, or until further orders. Sixth, corps commanders will direct an equitable division of the rations on hand to be made to their divisions.

By order of Maj. Gen. O. O. Howard:

SAML. L. TAGGART,
Assistant Adjutant-General.

HDQRS. DEPARTMENT AND ARMY OF THE TENNESSEE,
Little Ogeechee, near Savannah, Ga., December 10, 1864.

Brig. Gen. JOHN M. CORSE,
Commanding Fourth Division, Fifteenth Army Corps:

I have heard that you have discovered a way by which you think you can turn the flank of a portion of the enemy's force in your front. If such is the case every effort you make for that purpose will meet my hearty approbation.

Very respectfully, your obedient servant,

O. O. HOWARD,
Major-General.

HEADQUARTERS FIFTEENTH ARMY CORPS,
In the Field, Ga., December 10, 1864.

Brigadier-General CORSE,
Commanding Fourth Division:

GENERAL: The major-general commanding directs that you protect your front by throwing up earth-works opposite such places as will enable the enemy to move forward across the marshes and rice fields.

I am, general, very respectfully, your obedient servant,

F. F. WHITEHEAD,
Assistant Adjutant-General.

HDQRS. FOURTH DIVISION, FIFTEENTH ARMY CORPS,
In the Field, Ga., December 10, 1864.

Col. R. N. ADAMS,
Comdg. Second Brigade, Fourth Div., 15th Army Corps:

The general wishes you to make a crossing at some point below the railroad as early to-morrow as possible. It is very important that a crossing should be made. The general says the first to make the crossing shall have the honor. The general says he cannot spare the Eighty-first Ohio Volunteer Infantry. A staff officer will be there early to-morrow morning.

Respectfully,

H. L. BURNHAM,
Captain and Provost-Marshal.

SPECIAL ORDERS, No. 304. } HDQRS. SEVENTEENTH ARMY CORPS,
Near Savannah, Ga., December 10, 1864.

The command will be prepared at 7 a. m. to-morrow to draw out from its present position, upon being relieved by the Fourteenth Corps, and to move to the right. The necessary directions for the movement will be given in the morning. Unless otherwise directed, Brig. Gen. M. D. Leggett, commanding Third Division, will move out first, to be followed successively by Maj. Gen. J. A. Mower, commanding First Division, and Brig. Gen. G. A. Smith, commanding Fourth Division. The trains will move with their respective divisions. The First Michigan Engineers will follow the Third Division. The train of the headquarters Military Division of the Mississippi and of these headquarters will move at the head of the Third Division train.

By command of Maj. Gen. F. P. Blair:

C. CADLE, JR.,
Assistant Adjutant-General.

HEADQUARTERS SEVENTEENTH ARMY CORPS,
Near Savannah, Ga., December 10, 1864.

Maj. Gen. J. A. MOWER,
Commanding First Division:

GENERAL: The major-general commanding directs me to say to you that you will send out three or four men in your front, to creep up as far as possible toward the enemy's works, and ascertain the nature of the ground between you and the works. Should there be no swamps or creek in front of your left brigade, and the ground prove favorable for an advance, you will proceed to throw up to-night works for two batteries—one in front and to the right of where Generals Sherman and Blair and yourself were standing together to-day, the works to be placed so as to be masked by the bushes that are there; the other on the crest that is in front and a little to the left of the point mentioned where you were standing.

Very respectfully, your obedient servant,

C. CADLE, JR.,
Assistant Adjutant-General.

ORDERS.] HDQRS. FIRST DIVISION, 17TH ARMY CORPS,
Near Savannah, Ga., December 10, 1864.

The troops of this command will be prepared to march to-morrow at 7 a. m. Order of march: First, pioneer corps; second, First Brigade; third, battery; fourth, Second Brigade; fifth, Third Brigade; sixth, ambulance train; seventh, ordnance train; eighth, supply train.

By order of Maj. Gen. Joseph A. Mower:

CHAS. CHRISTENSEN,
Lieut., Aide-de-Camp, and Acting Assistant Adjutant-General.

HEADQUARTERS SEVENTEENTH ARMY CORPS,
December 10, 1864.

Brig. Gen. M. D. LEGGETT,
Commanding Third Division:

GENERAL: The major-general commanding directs me to say to you that you will move third in the order of march to-day, following the First Division, which follows the Fourth Division.

Respectfully, your obedient servant,

C. CADLE, JR.,
Assistant Adjutant-General.

SPECIAL FIELD ORDERS, No. 170.

HEADQUARTERS THIRD DIVISION, SEVENTEENTH ARMY CORPS,
Before Savannah, Ga., December 10, 1864.

I. This command will be held in readiness to move at 7 a. m. to-morrow, on being relieved by the Fourteenth Corps. The Second Brigade, Col. R. K. Scott commanding, will have the advance. Artillery and trains as heretofore.

By order of Brig. Gen. M. D. Leggett:

J. C. DOUGLASS,
Assistant Adjutant-General.

HEADQUARTERS LEFT WING, ARMY OF GEORGIA,
Four Miles from Savannah and Charleston Railroad,
December 10, 1864—4.30 a. m.

Capt. L. M. DAYTON,
Aide-de-Camp:

CAPTAIN: At this point my column found our road very badly obstructed and the enemy on opposite side with two small works. We drove him from the works, and have removed all obstructions, and I do not anticipate much difficulty between here and the railroad. We move at daylight. Davis is moving, but his road is a difficult one. I think I shall meet him near Cherokee Hill to-day.

Very respectfully, &c.,

H. W. SLOCUM,
Major-General.

HEADQUARTERS LEFT WING, ARMY OF GEORGIA,
Five Miles from Savannah, December 10, 1864—2 p. m.

Maj. Gen. J. C. DAVIS,
Commanding Fourteenth Corps:

The major-general commanding directs that you put your command in camp where you now are. He intends to develop the enemy's line with the Twentieth Corps this p. m., and as soon as we can find out something about the country here a position will be found for your corps. The Seventeenth Corps are well up on our right, and have been feeling of the enemy a little this forenoon. You had better send a staff officer forward to find a place to park your train near here.

Very respectfully, your obedient servant,

H. C. RODGERS,
Assistant Adjutant-General.

HEADQUARTERS LEFT WING, ARMY OF GEORGIA,
Five Miles from Savannah, December 10, 1864—7.30 p. m.

Maj. Gen. J. C. DAVIS,
Commanding Fourteenth Corps:

The major-general commanding directs that you move your corps to-morrow morning and occupy the line now held by the Seventeenth Corps on the right of the Twentieth Corps. Please send the division you intend to occupy the left of your line first, and have it leave camp at 7 a. m. The pioneers should accompany this division to repair the roads from here to the position you are to occupy. The other two divisions to follow with your entire train about 11 a. m., and on the way they are to burn thoroughly all the bridges and trestle-work on the railroad up to this point.

Very respectfully, your obedient servant,

H. C. RODGERS,
Assistant Adjutant-General.

HEADQUARTERS FOURTEENTH ARMY CORPS,
Ten Miles from Savannah, Ga., December 10, 1864—10.30 p. m.

Brig. Gen. A. BAIRD,
Commanding Third Division, Fourteenth Army Corps:

The general commanding has directed me to acknowledge the receipt of your note to him, and to say to you that you will not probably move from your present position before 11 a. m. to-morrow. He desires you, if possible, meanwhile, to reach and destroy the railroad bridge and to destroy the trestle-work as completely as practicable.

I have the honor to be, general, very respectfully, your obedient servant,

A. C. McCLURG,
Assistant Adjutant-General and Chief of Staff.

HEADQUARTERS TWENTIETH CORPS,
Five Miles from Savannah, Ga., December 10, 1864.

Brig. Gen. N. J. JACKSON,
Commanding First Division:

GENERAL: The general commanding directs that your command be in readiness to move to-morrow morning at about 9 o'clock.

Very respectfully, your obedient servant,

ROBT. P. DECHERT,
Captain and Acting Assistant Adjutant-General.

(Same to Brig. Gen. W. T. Ward, commanding Third Division.)

HEADQUARTERS TWENTIETH CORPS,
Five Miles from Savannah, Ga., December 10, 1864.

Brigadier-General GEARY,
Commanding Second Division:

GENERAL: The general commanding the corps directs that you send at 7 a. m. to-morrow one of your brigades to reconnoiter the country between this road and the Savannah River. He wishes to ascertain the nature of the country and the enemy's position. Captain McDowell, chief topographical engineer of the corps, will accompany the brigade; he has been over a portion of the road. The general desires that you will have the balance of your command in readiness to move at 9 a. m. to-morrow.

Very respectfully, your obedient servant,

H. W. PERKINS,
Assistant Adjutant-General.

HDQRS. SECOND DIVISION, TWENTIETH ARMY CORPS,
December 10, 1864.

Col. H. A. BARNUM,
Commanding Third Brigade:

COLONEL: The general commanding division directs that you take your brigade, at 7 a. m. to-morrow, and reconnoiter the country between Augusta road and the railroad to ascertain the nature of the country and the enemy's position. Captain McDowell, chief topographical engineer of the corps, and Captain Schilling, topographical engineer of division, will accompany you.

Very respectfully, your obedient servant,

W. T. FORBES,
Acting Assistant Adjutant-General.

GENERAL ORDERS, No. 8. } HDQRS. THIRD DIV., 20TH ARMY CORPS,
Near Savannah, Ga., December 10, 1864.

The following-named staff officers are hereby announced on the staff of the general commanding, and will be obeyed and respected accordingly: Capt. F. C. Crawford, Eighty-fifty Indiana Volunteers, aide-de-camp; Capt. E. W. Ward, Third Kentucky Volunteer Cavalry, aide-de-camp.

By command of Brig. Gen. W. T. Ward:

JOHN SPEED,
Captain and Assistant Adjutant-General.

SPECIAL ORDERS, No. 4. } HEADQUARTERS COAST DIVISION,
December 10, 1864.

I. The Thirty-fourth U. S. Colored Troops is hereby transferred from the First to the Second Brigade. The commanding officer will report to Col. E. N. Hallowell, commanding Second Brigade.

II. The Seventy-fifth and One hundred and seventh Regiments Ohio Volunteers are hereby assigned to the First Brigade. The commanding officers will report to Brig. Gen. E. E. Potter, commanding.

By order of Brig. Gen. J. P. Hatch:

LEONARD B. PERRY,
First Lieutenant, Fifty-fifth Massachusetts Volunteers, and Acting Assistant Adjutant-General.

HEADQUARTERS MILITARY DIVISION OF THE MISSISSIPPI,
In the Field, near Savannah, December 11, 1864—2 a. m.

Maj. Gen. O. O. HOWARD,
Commanding Army of the Tennessee:

GENERAL: Your dispatch of December 10, and also Special Field Orders, No. 191, are just received. The general-in-chief wishes you to secure the trains cut off on the Gulf road, and also describe to him what is the position of King's Bridge and Dillon's Ferry. Neither is on the map. I have had couriers looking for you since 5 p. m. 10th, with orders, but they are unable to find your headquarters. I send inclosed another copy.* The general understands the trains to be between Way's and Fleming's Stations.

I am, general,

L. M. DAYTON,
Aide-de-Camp.

HDQRS. DEPARTMENT AND ARMY OF THE TENNESSEE,
Little Ogeechee, Eleven Miles from Savannah, December 11, 1864.

Maj. Gen. W. T. SHERMAN,
Commanding Military Division of the Mississippi:

GENERAL: I inclose you a rough sketch† made by Captain Reese. He will have a better very soon. The King's Bridge road is the prolongation of the plank road. I have received your Field Orders, No. 130. My headquarters are now on the King's Bridge and Savannah road, three miles and a half in rear of Corse's advanced line. I shall move up this morning, and will send an officer to let you know where I shall be. I think the atmosphere is now clear enough to communicate with the fleet by signal from a point Captain McClintock, signal officer, has selected. The Darien road is an excellent one from the canal across to this road, and will give us easy communication.

Very respectfully,

O. O. HOWARD,
Major-General.

HDQRS. DEPARTMENT AND ARMY OF THE TENNESSEE,
Little Ogeechee, near Savannah, December 11, 1864.

Maj. Gen. W. T. SHERMAN,
Commanding Military Division of the Mississippi:

GENERAL: I have carefully reconnoitered this part of the rebel position. I find that there are at least five batteries, one of them mounting four guns and the others probably one each. The marsh extending along their whole front is impassable either to foot or horsemen, and the only way by which it can be crossed, leading from Doctor Cheves' plantation, has a battery planted at the other shore. Their line runs along the eastern branch of the Little Ogeechee, terminating near its mouth, where it cannot be approached owing to the swamps bordering the river. At Screven's there is a good landing, opposite which is Fort McAllister. The fort is well supplied with guns; some of the negroes saying that there are thirty-five mounted—others, less—and that there

---

* See No. 130, p. 676.

† Not found.

are but fifty men fit for duty. I have given General Kilpatrick four pontoons, and ordered him to cross the Cannouchee and take the fort if possible. If he is unsuccessful I shall march down a division. King's Bridge will be finished to-morrow night, and from there to Fort McAllister there is a good road, without obstructions. We have tried in every way to communicate with the fleet, but have thus far been unsuccessful. I hope that by to-night we shall be able to do so with signal rockets. I find that about 150 feet of the Ogeechee railroad bridge at each end had been destroyed at the first breaking of the road. We find no trains between Way's and Fleming's Stations.

Respectfully,

O. O. HOWARD,
Major-General.

SPECIAL FIELD ORDERS, No. 192.

HEADQUARTERS DEPARTMENT AND ARMY OF THE TENNESSEE,
Little Ogeechee, near Savannah, December 11, 1864.

I. The scarcity of forage, and the necessity of horses and mules for the cavalry service, necessitates the issuing of the following orders, viz: First, all general, staff, and other officers entitled to be mounted will be allowed only the number of horses prescribed by regulations and orders. Second, officers, officers' servants, clerks, foragers, and all other unauthorized persons riding Government horses and mules, will be at once dismounted, and the animals turned over to respective division quartermasters, the serviceable to be turned over, under the direction of the chief quartermaster, for the use of the cavalry, and the unserviceable and worthless to be shot and buried. Third, all horses and mules captured during the late march must now be properly taken up, branded, and accounted for as public property. Fourth, corps commanders will cause a rigid inspection to be made in their commands, in accordance with this order, and will be responsible that in spirit and intent it is fully carried out. Fifth, orderlies and other soldiers entitled to be mounted while on duty with their commands should be provided with passes, or orders to that effect, to prevent their horses being taken, as provided for in Special Field Orders, Nos. 17 and 129, Military Division of the Mississippi, current series.

II. Major-General Osterhaus, commanding Fifteenth Army Corps, will cause to be detailed from his command one section of Captain De Gress' battery and one small regiment of infantry, to report to Maj. T. W. Osborn, chief of artillery, at these headquarters to-morrow at 7 a. m., for duty at Cheves' Mill.

By order of Maj. Gen. O. O. Howard:

SAML. L. TAGGART,
Assistant Adjutant-General.

HDQRS. DEPARTMENT AND ARMY OF THE TENNESSEE,
Little Ogeechee, near Savannah, December 11, 1864.

Maj. Gen. P. JOSEPH OSTERHAUS,
Commanding Fifteenth Army Corps:

The major-general directs me to instruct you to place two of your divisions in position, facing the enemy, on the right of the King's Bridge and Savannah road, and place one division in reserve, as indicated in

Special Field Orders, No. 191, of yesterday. Your remaining division will, in accordance with General Sherman's Special Field Orders, No. 130, copy herewith inclosed,* encamp in convenient proximity to the Gulf railroad. To it will be intrusted the destruction of that road, as specified in General Sherman's order (Special Field Orders, No. 130). The Ogeechee bridge will not, however, be destroyed until a party has been sent across to secure the trains reported to be between Way's and Fleming's Stations.

Very respectfully, your obedient servant,

SAML. L. TAGGART,
Assistant Adjutant-General.

SPECIAL ORDERS, No. 195. } HDQRS. FIFTEENTH ARMY CORPS, *Anderson's Plantation, Ga., December 11, 1864.*

* * * * * * *

II. The following are the orders for the operations of the corps to-morrow: The First, Third, and Fourth Divisions will move, by the right flank, south of the King's Bridge and Savannah road, at 8 a. m., in the following order: Brigadier-General Corse, commanding Fourth Division, will move his entire command to the right, toward the railroad, as far as the conformation of the ground will permit, placing his brigades in double lines. He will cause, however, the regiments now on the railroad to remain in their present positions. Brigadier-Generals Woods and Smith will close up, by the right flank, on General Corse's lines, respectively, and will place their troops on an alignment, with General Smith resting his left on the King's Bridge and Savannah road. The entire movement must be well screened from the view of the enemy, and division commanders will be careful in selecting their roads to attain that end. The present pickets or skirmish-line of the Fourth Division will remain until the three divisions are in position, when division commanders will relieve those on the right of the Savannah road in their respective fronts; those on the left of said road will remain until relieved by the Seventeenth Army Corps. Brigadier-General Hazen, commanding Second Division, will take up a reserve position west of the Little Ogeechee, covering well his flank and rear by pickets. He will furnish to Captain Reese, chief engineer of the army, the pioneer corps of his command, and all such details of men, teams, &c., as may be necessary in the reconstruction of King's Bridge. All the teams and cattle will be ordered up to their respective divisions, and will be parked and corralled with a view to the convenience of forage. As the article will become very scarce during our stay, the greatest economy in the use of it is recommended, and the collecting and distributing of the same must be well systematized within the divisions to prevent waste. The regiments of General Woods' division now on guard at Dillon's Bridge will remain there and secure the said bridge by a tête-de-pont on the west side of the Ogeechee.

By order of Maj. Gen. P. Joseph Osterhaus:

F. F. WHITEHEAD,
Assistant Adjutant-General.

---

* See p. 676.

HEADQUARTERS FIFTEENTH ARMY CORPS,
Anderson's Plantation, Ga., December 11, 1864.

Brig. Gen. C. R. WOODS,
Commanding First Division:

GENERAL: You will cause to be detailed from your command one small regiment of infantry, to report to Maj. T. W. Osborn, chief of artillery, at department headquarters, to-morrow at 7 a. m., for duty at Cheves' Mill.

By order of Maj. Gen. P. Joseph Osterhaus:

F. F. WHITEHEAD,
Assistant Adjutant-General.

SPECIAL ORDERS, No. 249. } HDQRS. THIRD DIV., 15TH ARMY CORPS,
On Savannah Canal, Four Miles from Savannah, Ga., December 11, 1864.

I. This command will move at 8 a. m., in the following order: First, Second Brigade in advance; second, Battery B, First Michigan Artillery; third, pioneer corps and tool wagons; fourth, four regiments First Brigade; fifth, ammunition wagons; sixth, ambulance corps; seventh, division headquarters, regimental, and detachment wagons; eighth, one regiment First Brigade, rear guard.

By order of Brig. Gen. John E. Smith:

S. M. BUDLONG,
Assistant Adjutant-General.

HDQRS. DEPARTMENT AND ARMY OF THE TENNESSEE,
Little Ogeechee, near Savannah, Ga., December 11, 1864.

Maj. Gen. F. P. BLAIR,
Commanding Seventeenth Army Corps:

The major-general commanding directs me to say that, in accordance with General Sherman's Special Field Orders, No. 130 (of which you have a copy), you will, as fast as General Slocum gains ground to the right, vacate the position indicated for your command in Special Field Orders, No. 191, extract 2, from these headquarters, moving to the right of the plank road and to the rear of General Osterhaus' position.

Very respectfully, your obedient servant,

SAML. L. TAGGART,
Assistant Adjutant-General.

SPECIAL ORDERS, No. 305. } HDQRS. SEVENTEENTH ARMY CORPS,
Near Savannah, Ga., December 11, 1864.

The orders for to-morrow are as follows:

1. Brig. Gen. M. D. Leggett, commanding Third Division, will have the advance, and will move back on the main road, starting at 7 a. m.

2. Maj. Gen. J. A. Mower, commanding First Division, will follow the Third Division.

3. The division trains will move together after the First Division, in the same order as their divisions, except the ordnance and ambulance trains, which will follow their respective divisions.

4. Brig. Gen. G. A. Smith, commanding Fourth Division, will move after the general train.

5. Each division commander will move a detachment of their pioneer corps with their train, to keep the road in repair.

By command of Maj. Gen. F. P. Blair:

C. CADLE, JR.,
Assistant Adjutant-General.

HDQRS. FIRST DIVISION, SEVENTEENTH ARMY CORPS,
Near Savannah, Ga., December 11, 1864.

Capt. C. CADLE, Jr.,
Assistant Adjutant-General, Seventeenth Army Corps:

I have had the ground examined between my works and those of the enemy in front. The ground is reported wet, but hard. They could not get near enough [to see] whether or not there is a ditch in front of the work, as there were working parties of the enemy outside.

Respectfully, your obedient servant,

JOS. A. MOWER,
Major-General, Commanding.

CIRCULAR.] HDQRS. FIRST DIVISION, 17TH ARMY CORPS,
Near Savannah, Ga., December 11, 1864.

The troops of this command will be prepared to march to-morrow at 7.30 a. m. Order of march: First, pioneer corps; second, Second Brigade; third, battery; fourth, Third Brigade; fifth, First Brigade; sixth, ambulance corps; seventh, ordnance train; eighth, the train of this division will follow the train of the Third Division.

By order of Maj. Gen. Joseph A. Mower:

CHAS. CHRISTENSEN,
Lieut., Aide-de-Camp, and Acting Assistant Adjutant-General.

HEADQUARTERS SEVENTEENTH ARMY CORPS.
December 11, 1864.

Brig. Gen. M. D. LEGGETT,
Commanding Third Division:

GENERAL: I am directed by the major-general commanding to say to you that we move west on the main road about one mile from where you left it to-day to go into camp; we then take a left-hand road, crossing the canal, and go into position in rear of the Fifteenth Corps.

Very respectfully, your obedient servant,

C. CADLE, JR.,
Assistant Adjutant-General.

SPECIAL FIELD ORDERS, No. 171. } HEADQUARTERS THIRD DIVISION, SEVENTEENTH ARMY CORPS,
Before Savannah, Ga., December 11, 1864.

I. This command will move at 7 a. m. to-morrow: First, the First Brigade, Brig. Gen. M. F. Force commanding, will have the advance;

second, artillery, Fifteenth Ohio Battery; third, Col. R. K. Scott, commanding Second Brigade, will follow the artillery; fourth, ambulance and ordnance trains; all other wagons will follow in rear of First Division in same order of march as their respective commands.

By order of Brig. Gen. M. D. Leggett:

J. C. DOUGLASS,
Assistant Adjutant-General.

HEADQUARTERS LEFT WING, ARMY OF GEORGIA,
December 11, 1864—7 p. m.

Capt. L. M. DAYTON,
Aide-de-Camp:

Some of Wheeler's cavalry were at Monteith, the residence of General Harrison, when the party sent to arrest him (Harrison) arrived there. I have sent a brigade of infantry to cover my rear and protect trains. The left of my line is now established in very close proximity to the line of the enemy. I have sent a regiment across the river to scout the country, and am throwing up two redoubts on the river-bank.

Very respectfully, &c.,

H. W. SLOCUM,
Major-General.

HEADQUARTERS MILITARY DIVISION OF THE MISSISSIPPI,
In the Field, near Savannah, December 11, 1864.

Major-General SLOCUM,
Commanding, &c.:

GENERAL: It is reported to the general-in-chief by Colonel Atkins, commanding cavalry brigade, that his scouts saw a brigade of the enemy's cavalry to-day on Louisville and Savannah road, opposite Springfield, and that they were moving north to the Augusta road, and I am directed by the general to give you the information.

I am, general, yours, &c.,

L. M. DAYTON,
Aide-de-Camp.

HEADQUARTERS FOURTEENTH ARMY CORPS,
In Front of Savannah, Ga., December 11, 1864.

Brig. Gen. A. BAIRD,
Commanding Third Division, Fourteenth Army Corps:

The general commanding the corps has directed me to say to you that he wishes you to take position for to-night upon Saint Augustine Creek (the first creek this side of the Ten-Mile Station). He wishes you to destroy all the trestle-works on this side of the bridge toward this point, and desires a report of your operations this morning and of your success in destroying the railroad bridge. He also wishes to know if you deem it practicable to construct a boom above the bridge which will obstruct the passage of boats upon the river.

I have the honor to be, general, very respectfully, your obedient servant,

A. C. McCLURG,
Assistant Adjutant-General and Chief of Staff.

HEADQUARTERS FOURTEENTH ARMY CORPS,
December 11, 1864—6.15 p. m.

Colonel RODGERS, *Chief of Staff:*

COLONEL: I have the honor to report that by this time two divisions of my corps are in position, having relieved the Seventeenth Corps entirely. Baird's division is still at Saint Augustine Creek. The inclosed report of General Baird will show the general commanding the state of affairs at the railroad crossing. My trains are stuck in the mud for the balance of the night on the road Colonel Asmussen advised me to take; it will be corduroyed by morning. My headquarters are on the Georgia Central road, about a mile west of General Sherman's. The bearer can stay at the headquarters of the Left Wing and bring any communications desired.

Very respectfully,

JEF. C. DAVIS,
Brevet Major-General, Commanding.

[Inclosure.]

HDQRS. THIRD DIVISION, FOURTEENTH ARMY CORPS,
December 11, 1864—2 p. m.

Col. A. C. MCCLURG, *Assistant Adjutant-General:*

SIR: I have received your note directing me to encamp on Saint Augustine Creek, and asking a report of my operations this morning. I found the trestle-work about fifteen feet high, built upon piles and through a swamp not passable except upon bridges, which it would take days to build if we had the material. The farther end was occupied by the rebels with a battery, which was so remote that their shot barely reached us; our Napoleons would not have reached them. It was utterly impossible to get near the battery, as the only approach was along the railroad track, under fire of the battery. There was a locomotive and platform-car near the rebel battery, and perhaps it had a gun on it. The bridge over the river was not visible, and unless a way can be found through the swamp, which I am assured there is not, it is not possible to get near the river on this side at this point. A small train of cars was seen on the South Carolina side, not in motion. My men went out on the trestle-work and burned it for considerable distance from this end; they also tore up and destroyed about three-quarters of a mile of track. To use the railroad bridge for foot passengers they will have to build over the portion of the burned trestle-work on top of the piles, which can be done, but the track [can] not be repaired in some time. I find rebels now on my flank, on the Monteith road, I presume.

Respectfully, your obedient servant,

A. BAIRD,
Brigadier-General, Commanding.

HEADQUARTERS TWENTIETH CORPS,
Five miles from Savannah, Ga., December 11, 1864.

Brig. Gen. J. W. GEARY, *Commanding Second Division:*

GENERAL: The general commanding directs that if you can find any boats in the river you send fifty or sixty men to Hutchinson's Island to ascertain what they can.

Very respectfully, your obedient servant,

ROBT. P. DECHERT,
Captain and Acting Assistant Adjutant-General.

HEADQUARTERS 3D CAVALRY DIVISION, CAVALRY CORPS,
MILITARY DIVISION OF THE MISSISSIPPI,
December 11, 1864.

Capt. L. M. DAYTON,
Aide-de-Camp to Major-General Sherman:

CAPTAIN: My people have been all day making a road out of range of the rebel guns. I have thoroughly examined the entire country on the south of General Howard between the Ogeechee and the rebel lines. It is impossible to cross the Little Ogeechee at any point. I have been in sight of Fort McAllister; it has about 200 men and thirteen guns mounted. I have proposed to General Howard to cross the Ogeechee with my command and a force of infantry, and take the fort. I am certain from what I learn that I can take it, and once done the fleet can come up to within two miles of General Howard's right. Boats will then be at our disposal, and the Little Ogeechee can be crossed. I saw, I think, the fleet to-day behind Green's Island. Captain Hayes, of my staff, will make the attempt to-night to reach the fleet; a negro has volunteered to pilot him through in a boat. General Howard has accepted my proposition; will give me the infantry asked for, and I only now await your permission. I promise to take the fort—if it is as represented to me—and let in our fleet; at all events, will reach the Sound and communicate with the fleet.

Very respectfully, your obedient servant,

J. KILPATRICK,
Brigadier-General, U. S. Volunteers.

HEADQUARTERS CAVALRY CORPS,
Seventeen Miles from Savannah, December 11, 1864.

General J. KILPATRICK,
Commanding Cavalry, U. S. Army:

GENERAL: Since writing the letter herewith transmitted I have received the inclosed note from Doctor Byne, announcing the death of Captain Norton. I have directed that Corporal Lacey be sent to me, that he may be transmitted safely to your lines. I shall not consider him a prisoner of war, as he was not captured in action. I also send herewith a book containing writing by yourself, which I presume you must value, and which must have been left by accident at a house where you spent the night. While writing you I take the opportunity to suggest that we adopt a system for exchanging prisoners belonging to our respective commands. It certainly would aid us in reclaiming from prison our friends, and would enable us both to do a great deal toward alleviating the sufferings of our officers and soldiers who are now in prison, or who may hereafter become prisoners of war. Should you assent to this proposition I will obtain the release of such officers and men of your command as we have in prison, and will send you a list of the officers and men I desire released. I will also agree, upon the release of any of my officers and men, to release on similar parole a like number of officers and men of your command. Believing that you will think as I do, that every commanding officer's duty is to take advantage of every opportunity which presents itself to benefit the condition of his men, I trust to receive a favorable response.

Respectfully, general, your obedient servant,

J. WHEELER,
Major-General, C. S. Army.

[Inclosure.]

WAYNESBOROUGH, GA., *December 6, 1864.*

General WHEELER:

DEAR SIR: Captain Norton, of the Yankee cavalry, died last night at my house, and Mr. Michael D. Lacey, Company B, Tenth Ohio Cavalry, U. S. Volunteers, who was left as nurse, is still at my house awaiting orders from you.

Yours,

EDMUND BYNE.

HDQRS. SECOND BRIGADE, THIRD CAVALRY DIVISION,
MILITARY DIVISION OF THE MISSISSIPPI,
Near Savannah, Ga., December 11, 1864—2 p. m.

Captain DAYTON:

My scouting party sent out to Springfield this morning reports a brigade of rebel cavalry nineteen miles from Savannah, moving south on a road north of this (the Louisville road) and in the direction of the Augusta road. They saw one regiment pass, and a lady said there was a brigade with five ambulances and no artillery. I have notified Colonel Hamilton, Ninth Ohio Volunteer Cavalry, who is on the Augusta road.

I am, colonel, most respectfully, your obedient servant,

SMITH D. ATKINS,
Col. Ninety-second Illinois Mounted Infty. Vols., Comdg. Brigade.

HEADQUARTERS U. S. FORCES,
Fort Pulaski, Ga., December 11, 1864.

Capt. W. L. M. BURGER,
Assistant Adjutant-General:

CAPTAIN: I have the honor to report that three deserters (privates) from the First Georgia Regulars, Colonel Wayne commanding, stationed on Whitemarsh and Wilmington Islands, came to this post this morning. They were on picket on Wilmington, and left Thursday night. They report that their regiment was under orders to go to Ogeechee, on the Gulf railroad, to meet some of Sherman's forces, as an attack was daily expected. They also report that the day they left the adjutant of the regiment said a dispatch had been received from Savannah that Sherman was within twelve miles of the city. An irregular cannonading has been heard in the direction of Savannah since 2 o'clock this morning. At times it has been quite brisk, and other times more slow and irregular. As near as we have been able to judge the firing seemed to be of light and heavy artillery. The commanding officer of the Wissahickon reports that from his mast head the bursting of shells was occasionally seen.

I have the honor to be, captain, very respectfully, your obedient servant,

P. P. BROWN, JR.,
Colonel, Commanding Post.

HEADQUARTERS MILITARY DIVISION OF THE MISSISSIPPI,
In the Field, December 12, 1864—7 p. m.

Maj. Gen. W. T. SHERMAN,
Commanding, &c.:

DEAR GENERAL: I send you a couple of letters* from Wheeler to Kilpatrick, from which you may draw inferences as to the former's whereabouts. The officer who brought them was sent off again, and told if there was any answer we would find some way of communicating to General Wheeler. Some of his escort told our men he or they belonged to Ross. I will inform Generals Slocum and Davis—could have sent these earlier had I not expected you. Captain Audenried has just arrived, and yours to General Slocum has been sent. The firing we heard before you left this morning was by his battery on the river and the enemy's gun-boats—two of them and a transport (naval) tried to go down the river, but the battery disabled and captured the latter and drove the former back. He got some 25 Confederate naval men and officers, and some few stores. A few hours' work will repair the steamer.

I am, general, yours, &c.,

L. M. DAYTON,
Aide-de-Camp.

HDQRS. MILITARY DIVISION OF THE MISSISSIPPI,
In the Field, December 12, 1864.

Mr. R. R. Cuyler and brother, who were captured with a train on the Gulf railroad, having given their word of honor not to divulge anything they may have learned while in the hands of this army, are permitted to proceed to King's Bridge, on the Ogeechee, and thence to their residence at No. 2½ on the Gulf railroad, or to Macon, Ga.

By order of Maj. Gen. W. T. Sherman:

L. M. DAYTON,
Aide-de-Camp.

SPECIAL FIELD ORDERS, No. 193.
HEADQUARTERS DEPARTMENT AND ARMY OF THE TENNESSEE,
Little Ogeechee, near Savannah, December 12, 1864.

As soon as King's Bridge is completed Major-General Osterhaus, commanding Fifteenth Army Corps, will direct his Second Division, Brigadier-General Hazen commanding, to proceed against Fort McAllister and take it.

By order of Maj. Gen. O. O. Howard:

SAML. L. TAGGART,
Assistant Adjutant-General.

HDQRS. DEPARTMENT AND ARMY OF THE TENNESSEE,
Little Ogeechee, near Savannah, Ga., December 12, 1864.

Maj. Gen. P. JOS. OSTERHAUS,
Commanding Fifteenth Army Corps:

The major-general commanding directs me to say that he wishes you, if you have not already done so, to give instructions to such of your troops as are fronting the enemy to throw up a light work, even if it

---

* See pp. 690, 691.

be nothing more than a line of rails. It will indicate the line and serve as a rallying place in case of an attack. He also directs that, as we shall probably have to make considerable use of the King's Bridge and Savannah road, you cause it to be repaired to-morrow from the front line back to Little Ogeechee Church, bringing dry sand from convenient points to fill up small ruts and bad places, and corduroying the bad ones wherever needed to keep the road in good hauling order. General Blair will repair it from Little Ogeechee Church to King's Bridge.

Very respectfully, your obedient servant,

SAML. L. TAGGART,
Assistant Adjutant-General.

HEADQUARTERS FIFTEENTH ARMY CORPS,
Anderson's Plantation, Ga., December 12, 1864.

Brigadier-General HAZEN,
Commanding Second Division:

You will, as soon as King's Bridge is completed, proceed with your command against Fort McAllister and take it, reporting the fact to these headquarters as soon as accomplished.

By order of Maj. Gen. P. Joseph Osterhaus:

F. F. WHITEHEAD,
Assistant Adjutant-General.

SPECIAL ORDERS, No. 250. } HDQRS. THIRD DIV., 15TH ARMY CORPS,
Near Anderson's Plantation, Ga., December 12, 1864.

I. This command will move at 7 this a. m. in the following order: First, one regiment First Brigade in advance; second, pioneer corps and tool wagons; third, remainder of First Brigade; fourth, three regiments Second Brigade; fifth, ammunition wagons; sixth, ambulances; seventh, division headquarters, regimental, and detachment wagons; eighth, one regiment Second Brigade, rear-guard.

By order of Brig. Gen. John E. Smith:

S. M. BUDLONG,
Assistant Adjutant-General.

HDQRS. FOURTH DIVISION, FIFTEENTH ARMY CORPS,
Near Savannah, December 12, 1864.

Brig. Gen. E. W. RICE,
Commanding First Brigade:

GENERAL: Major-General Osterhaus is of the impression the enemy is gone and orders me to send a regiment to the Anderson house and make a feint of crossing. You will, therefore, send a regiment to the point designated at 4.30 p. m., push out skirmishers well through the swamp, and if they discover no signs of the enemy's presence move the regiment down till you develop whether they have a force on the other side or not. General Woods will move a regiment down on the main Savannah road at the same time and for the same purpose. Be cautious and do not get the command under fire in the swamp till you are satisfied the enemy is either very weak or gone.

Very respectfully,

JNO. M. CORSE,
Brigadier-General, Commanding.

HDQRS. DEPARTMENT AND ARMY OF THE TENNESSEE,
Little Ogeechee, near Savannah, Ga., December 12, 1864.

Maj. Gen. F. P. BLAIR,
Commanding Seventeenth Army Corps:

As we shall probably have occasion to make much use of King's Bridge and Savannah road, the major-general commanding directs that you cause it to be placed and kept in good condition from Little Ogeechee Church to King's Bridge. Bring dry sand from convenient points to fill up and smooth over the lesser ruts and bad places, and corduroying the worse ones. General Osterhaus has been directed to repair it also.

Very respectfully, your obedient servant,

SAML. L. TAGGART,
Assistant Adjutant-General.

KING'S BRIDGE, *December 12, 1864—4.30 p. m.*

General SLOCUM:

The Ogeechee here is a large navigable stream. Fort McAllister is six miles below, on the west bank, and to-morrow early I will send Hazen's division to attack it. Kilpatrick is over already, and will examine Saint Catherine's Sound and Sunbery; but if we can get Ossabaw we are all right. I want you to be active to-morrow, and to get two or more of your (largest range guns) batteries at the point south of the canal where Mower was and where Carlin went in last night. That is the only point I know of where guns will reach the heart of Savannah. Your line need not reach the plank road, but the causeway about two miles this side the canal, the point where the enemy has the range of the road; there Blair will connect with you. Keep rather thin lines, and your troops massed ready for action. I want to connect with the fleet before doing anything positive. Send me word of anything of interest on that flank to-morrow. The fleet can be seen, or is reported, but as yet has answered none of our signals, but I think to-morrow I will make them notice us.

Yours,

W. T. SHERMAN,
Major-General.

HEADQUARTERS LEFT WING, ARMY OF GEORGIA,
December 12, 1864—8 p. m.

Major-General SHERMAN,
General-in-Chief:

GENERAL: Your dispatch of 4[.30] p. m. has been received. I have carefully examined the left of our lines and the right of the rebel lines to-day. I fully believe I can turn their line and sweep them away. I have given my views to Captain Poe and asked him to present them to you. Your instructions for to-morrow shall be obeyed. We captured the steamer Resolute this morning, with seven naval officers and a crew of twenty men; she will be repaired to-morrow. We drove back two gun-boats that were with her. Commodore Lovell was on board one of them.

Yours, very respectfully,

H. W. SLOCUM,
Major-General.

HEADQUARTERS MILITARY DIVISION OF THE MISSISSIPPI,
In the Field, December 12, 1864.

General SLOCUM,
Commanding, &c.:

GENERAL: A flag of truce to-day brought in letters from Wheeler to Kilpatrick. One was headed Waynesborough, 6th, and the other seventeen miles from Savannah, 11th December. The officer bringing it said he belonged to Wheeler's staff. The men of his escort said they or he were from Ross. The flag came to our picket on Louisville and Savannah road, and I give you all I know, from which you may judge Wheeler's position. He may be concocting devilment for us, or it might be a blind to cover up. The general, you know, is at King's Bridge. I will send word to General Davis.

I am, general, yours, &c.,

L. M. DAYTON,
Aide-de-Camp.

GENERAL ORDERS, No. 2. } HDQRS. LEFT WING, ARMY OF GEORGIA,
Before Savannah, Ga., December 12, 1864.

While the army remains in its present position all regular foraging parties from either corps will be permitted to forage upon both banks of the Savannah River and upon the islands in the river. All guards will respect the passes of any corps or division commander for this purpose.

By command of Maj. Gen. H. W. Slocum:

H. C. RODGERS,
Assistant Adjutant-General.

HEADQUARTERS FOURTEENTH ARMY CORPS,
Before Savannah, Ga., December 12, 1864.

Lieut. Col. H. C. RODGERS,
Chief of Staff, Left Wing, Army of Georgia:

COLONEL: A number of different foraging parties sent from this command to-day report to me that they had attempted to cross to the island in the Savannah River opposite this point (the only region accessible where it is possible to obtain forage), and all unite in saying that they were prevented from crossing by guards from the Twentieth Corps. Guards also from the same command were found posted upon all the rice fodder upon this bank of the river, of which I am informed there is a very large quantity. The animals of my command are entirely out of food, and the men soon will be if this state of things continues. I would respectfully suggest that the major-general commanding will take such measures as will allow my men to forage in the region mentioned, and that they be permitted to procure a portion of the rice fodder upon this side of the river. I desire to send out parties in the morning

Very respectfully, your obedient servant, &c.,

JEF. C. DAVIS,
Brevet Major-General, Commanding.

HEADQUARTERS LEFT WING, ARMY OF GEORGIA,
December 12, 1864—10 p. m.

Maj. Gen. J. C. DAVIS,
Commanding Fourteenth Corps:

The following dispatch* has just been received from General Sherman, and the major-general commanding desires you to carry out the instructions so far as they relate to your portion of the line.

Very respectfully, your obedient servant,

H. C. RODGERS,
Assistant Adjutant-General.

Weekly effective force report of Fourteenth Army Corps for Monday, December 12, 1864.

Command.	Headquarters.			Infantry.			Artillery.			Total.				
	Officers.	Men.	Total.	Officers.	Men.	Total.	Officers.	Men.	Total.	Officers.	Men.	Aggregate.	Horses.	Guns.
Fourteenth Army Corps	25	766	791	....	......	......	....	....	....	25	766	791	....	....
First Division	9	61	70	....	......	......	....	....	....	9	61	70	....	....
First Brigade	5	27	32	68	1,427	1,495	....	....	....	73	1,454	1,527	....	....
Second Brigade	6	40	46	60	1,448	1,508	....	....	....	66	1,488	1,554	....	....
Third Brigade	7	75	82	45	922	967	....	....	....	52	997	1,049	....	....
Battery C, 1st Illinois	....	......	......	....	......	......	5	118	123	5	118	123	80	4
Total First Division	27	203	230	173	3,797	3,970	5	118	123	205	4,118	4,323	80	4
Second Division	15	76	91	....	......	......	....	....	....	15	76	91	....	....
First Brigade	7	71	78	85	1,947	2,032	....	....	....	92	2,018	2,110	....	....
Second Brigade	8	30	38	78	1,488	1,566	....	....	....	86	1,518	1,604	....	....
Third Brigade	7	9	16	78	1,603	1,681	....	....	....	85	1,612	1,697	....	....
Battery I, 2d Illinois	....	......	......	....	......	......	1	113	114	1	113	114	100	4
Total Second Division	37	186	223	241	5,038	5,279	1	113	114	279	5,337	5,616	100	4
Third Division	10	76	86	....	......	......	....	....	....	10	76	86	....	....
First Brigade	10	77	87	79	1,749	1,828	....	....	....	89	1,826	1,915	....	....
Second Brigade	4	34	38	87	1,615	1,702	....	....	....	91	1,649	1,740	....	....
Third Brigade	7	44	51	62	1,275	1,337	....	....	....	69	1,319	1,388	....	....
5th Wisconsin Battery	....	......	......	....	......	......	3	133	136	3	133	136	75	4
Total Third Division	31	231	262	228	4,639	4,867	3	133	136	262	5,003	5,265	75	4
19th Indiana Battery	....	......	......	....	......	......	3	119	122	3	119	122	90	4
Grand total	120	1,386	1,506	642	13,474	14,116	12	483	495	774	15,343	16,117	345	16

JEF. C. DAVIS,
Brevet Major-General, Commanding.

HEADQUARTERS FOURTEENTH ARMY CORPS,
Before Savannah, Ga., December 12, 1864.

Brig. Gen. A. BAIRD,
Commanding Third Division, Fourteenth Army Corps:

The general commanding the corps directs that you move the two remaining brigades of your division toward this point at an early hour

---

* See Sherman to Slocum, 4.30 p. m., p. 694.

to-morrow morning, pursuing the route taken by the wagon trains, and reporting your arrival when the head of your column has reached the crossing of the Georgia Central Railroad, when further instructions will be given you.

I have the honor to be, general, very respectfully, your obedient servant,

A. C. McCLURG,
Lieutenant-Colonel and Chief of Staff.

HEADQUARTERS LEFT WING, ARMY OF GEORGIA,
December 12, 1864.

Brig. Gen. A. S. WILLIAMS,
Commanding Twentieth Corps:

The major-general commanding desires you to have the steamer Resolute (captured this morning) turned over to Captain Whittelsey at once, and the commissary stores on board of her turned over to Colonel Balloch, chief commissary of subsistence.

Very respectfully, your obedient servant,

H. C. RODGERS,
Assistant Adjutant-General.

HEADQUARTERS TWENTIETH CORPS,
Five Miles from Savannah, Ga., December 12, 1864.

Capt. H. M. WHITTELSEY,
Acting Chief Quartermaster:

CAPTAIN: General Jackson has been directed to detail fifteen engineers and mechanics to repair the steamer Resolute. They will report to you to-morrow morning.

Very respectfully, your obedient servant,

ROBT. P. DECHERT,
Captain and Acting Assistant Adjutant-General.

HDQRS. SECOND BRIG., FIRST DIV., 20TH ARMY CORPS,
December 12, 1864.

Lieut. Col. H. W. PERKINS,
Assistant Adjutant-General, Twentieth Army Corps:

LIEUTENANT-COLONEL: In compliance with orders from headquarters First Division, I detailed last evening one regiment (Third Wisconsin Volunteers) to proceed across the river upon the island for duty. I ordered my acting commissary of subsistence to accompany the regiment and to take possession of whatever supplies he might find for the use of the brigade. He found upon the boat captured this p. m. a small quantity of flour, &c., which he took possession of. Colonel Hawley, commanding Third Wisconsin Volunteers, was ordered by General Williams to turn over the stores to the corps commissary. I would respectfully request that these stores be issued to my brigade.

I am, colonel, very respectfully, your obedient servant,

E. A. CARMAN,
Colonel, Commanding Brigade.

[First indorsement.]

HDQRS. FIRST DIVISION, TWENTIETH ARMY CORPS,
December 12, 1864.

Respectfully forwarded approved, as there is neither flour nor hard bread in this brigade.

N. J. JACKSON,
Brigadier-General, Commanding.

[Second indorsement.]

HEADQUARTERS TWENTIETH CORPS,
Five Miles from Savannah, Ga., December 13, 1864.

Respectfully returned.

Instructions have been given to the chief commissary of the corps as to the disposition of the stores.

By command of Brig. Gen. A. S. Williams:

ROBT. P. DECHERT,
Captain and Acting Assistant Adjutant-General.

HEADQUARTERS THIRD CAVALRY DIVISION,
MILITARY DIVISION OF THE MISSISSIPPI,
McAllister's Plantation, December 12, 1864.

Major-General SHERMAN:

GENERAL: Your dispatch* has just been received. I met the enemy's picket near the railroad, and chased Major Anderson, the commanding officer at Fort McAllister, back to his fort. From one of his escort captured, I learn that the fort is garrisoned by five companies, two of artillery and three militia; in all, about 200 men none of whom, however, have ever been under fire. There is a deep broad ditch to cross on entering the fort, and considerable opposition, no doubt, will be met with. There is a low swamp about one mile this side the fort; a battery of four guns covers the road leading through this swamp; by forcing this battery to retire, a charging party could follow it directly into the fort, and the affair would be over. I did not intend, general, to attempt the capture of the fort by a sudden dash, but I intended to deliberately storm the works. I have old infantry regiments, armed with Spencer rifles, who could work their way up to within easy range and force every man to keep his head beneath the parapet, and, finally, force my way into the fort—of course, I intended to maneuver my troops as infantry. I will march in the morning to accomplish the objects set forth in your communication. I cannot understand why our gun-boats do not move up, and make us aware of their presence by throwing a few shells into Fort McAllister. My headquarters are to-night four miles from the fort; my advance is within one mile and a half. A few hundred mounted men, under Colonel Ross, are guarding the country on this side the river; his is the only force I can hear of. I find over here many rich plantations, and can subsist my command for a month.

Very respectfully, your obedient servant,

J. KILPATRICK,
Brigadier-General, Commanding Cavalry.

---

*Not found.

HILTON HEAD, S. C., *December 12, 1864.*
(Via Fort Monroe 7 p. m. 14th.)

Maj. Gen. H. W. HALLECK,
Chief of Staff:

GENERAL: Captain Duncan, of General Howard's scouts, has just come in from Howard's, having descended the Ogeechee River in a small boat. He left the army on the evening of the 9th. General Sherman's whole army was then within ten miles of Savannah, advancing to attack it. The enemy's works, five miles from the city, were probably attacked yesterday, as heavy firing was heard in that direction. Captain Duncan represents the army to be in the best spirits possible and most excellent condition. Very little opposition had been met with on the march, as the enemy could not tell what routes were to be taken. The army has lived off the country, and has accumulated considerable number of horses, mules, and cattle; it was also well supplied. I am going to the Ogeechee River to open communication with General Sherman. My small force is now in position between the Coosawhatchie and Tullifinny Rivers, within 1,200 yards of the railroad, which our batteries command. Only one train has been able to steal past since our batteries were in position. I will send further dispatch as soon as I meet General Sherman.

The following is a copy of the dispatch brought by Captain Duncan:

HEADQUARTERS ARMY OF THE TENNESSEE,
Near Savannah Canal, Ga., December 9, 1864.

COMMANDING OFFICER U. S. NAVAL FORCE, IN VICINITY OF SAVANNAH, GA.:

SIR: We have met with perfect success thus far. Troops in fine spirits, and near by.

Respectfully,

O. O. HOWARD,
Major-General, Commanding Right Wing of Army.

Another dispatch was brought by Captain Duncan directed to the signal officer of the fleet, from General Howard's chief signal officer, requesting a good lookout to be kept for signals.*

I have the honor to be, very respectfully, your obedient servant,

J. G. FOSTER,
Major-General.

HDQRS. NORTHERN DISTRICT, DEPT. OF THE SOUTH,
Morris Island, S. C., December 12, 1864.

Lieut. Col. A. G. BENNETT,
Commanding Post, Morris Island, S. C.:

COLONEL: I am directed by the brigadier-general commanding to inform you that a movement of the enemy on the northern shore of Charleston Harbor has been reported to these headquarters. You will caution commanders of forts and outposts to be vigilant and watchful. In case of any attack the general's instructions are that artillery fire shall be opened at once. Lieutenant-Colonel Mulford will send ashore from the flag-of-truce boat to-morrow morning fifteen more dead bodies for burial. You will, therefore, cause coffins for that number to be made to-night; also, thirty additional ones to be sent to Colonel Mul-

* See p. 669.

ford in the morning. If your available force be not sufficient for that purpose, you will make use of all the civilians at this post, whether in the service of the Government or otherwise.

I have the honor to be, colonel, very respectfully, your obedient servant,

J. W. DICKINSON,
Capt., 21st U. S. Colored Troops, and Actg. Asst. Adjt. Gen., Northern District, Department of the South.

HEADQUARTERS DEPARTMENT OF THE SOUTH,
Hilton Head, S. C., December 12, 1864.

Col. P. P. BROWN, Jr.,
Commanding 157th New York Volunteers, Fort Pulaski, Ga.:

COLONEL: The attention of the major-general commanding has been called to the publication in the Charleston Courier of a complimentary letter to you, signed by a number of exchanged rebel prisoners of war that had been confined in Fort Pulaski under your charge. Praise from the enemy is the last thing that an officer should seek, or permit to be bestowed upon him. These officers were sent to this department for the purpose of retaliation, and your instructions were to treat them in precisely the same manner that our prisoners of war in the hands of the enemy are treated. If these instructions had been faithfully carried out on your part, as they should have been, very few compliments would have been extended to you by the prisoners. The major-general commanding regrets exceedingly to be obliged to censure an officer for such conduct.

Very respectfully, your obedient servant,

W. L. M. BURGER,
Assistant Adjutant-General.

HEADQUARTERS U. S. FORCES,
Fort Pulaski, Ga., December 12, 1864.

Capt. W. L. M. BURGER, *Assistant Adjutant-General:*

CAPTAIN: I have the honor to acknowledge the receipt of your communication of to-day censuring me for failing to carry out the instructions given me with reference to the treatment of the prisoners of war placed under my charge. The instructions mentioned in your communication have failed to reach me, and until the censure reached me today I was not aware of their existence. I would therefore respectfully request that another copy be sent me, that I may know in what particulars I have erred, and be able to make the necessary changes.

I have the honor to be, general, very respectfully, your obedient servant,

P. P. BROWN, JR.,
Colonel, Commanding Post.

ON BOARD DANDELION,
Ossabaw Sound, December 13, 1864—11.50 p. m.
(Received 15th.)

Hon. E. M. STANTON,
Secretary of War, Washington, D. C.:

To-day, at 5 p. m., General Hazen's division of the Fifteenth Corps carried Fort McAllister by assault, capturing its entire garrison and stores. This opened to us Ossabaw Sound, and I pushed down to this gun-boat to communicate with the fleet. Before opening communication we had completely destroyed all the railroads leading into Savannah and invested the city. The left of the army is on the Savannah River, three miles above the city, and the right on the Ogeechee, at King's Bridge. The army is in splendid order, and equal to anything. The weather has been fine, and supplies were abundant. Our march was most agreeable, and we were not at all molested by guerrillas. We reached Savannah three days ago, but owing to Fort McAllister could not communicate; but now that we have McAllister we can go ahead. We have already captured two boats on the Savannah River, and prevented their gun-boats from coming down. I estimate the population of Savannah at 25,000 and the garrison at 15,000; General Hardee commands. We have not lost a wagon on the trip, but have gathered a large supply of negroes, mules, horses, &c., and our teams are in far better condition than when we started. My first duty will be to clear the army of surplus negroes, mules, and horses. We have utterly destroyed over 200 miles of rails, and consumed stores and provisions that were essential to Lee's and Hood's armies. The quick work made with McAllister, the opening of communication with our fleet, and our consequent independence as to supplies, dissipate all their boasted threats to head us off and starve the army. I regard Savannah as already gained.

Yours, truly,

W. T. SHERMAN,
Major-General.

ON BOARD DANDELION,
Ossabaw Sound, December 13, 1864—11.50 p. m.
(Received 15th.)

General H. W. HALLECK, *Washington:*

To-day, at 5 p. m., General Hazen's division of the Fifteenth Corps carried Fort McAllister by assault, capturing its entire garrison and stores. This opened to us the Ossabaw Sound, and I pulled down to this gun-boat to communicate with the fleet. Before opening communication we had completely destroyed all the railroads leading into Savannah and invested the city. The left is on the Savannah River, three miles above the city, and right on the Ogeechee, at King's Bridge. Were it not for the swamps we could march into the city, but as it is I would have to assault at one or two places over narrow causeways, leading to much loss; whereas in a day or two, with my communications restored and the batteries in position within short range of the city, I will demand its surrender. The army is in splendid order, and equal to anything. Weather has been fine, and supplies abundant. Our march was most agreeable, and we were not at all molested by guerrillas. We reached Savannah three days ago, but owing to Fort McAllister we could not communicate; but now we have McAllister we can go ahead. We have already captured two boats in the Savannah River, and prevented their gun-boats from coming down, and, if General Foster will prevent the escape of the garrison of Savannah and its people by land across South Carolina, we will capture all. I estimate the population at 25,000 and the garrison at 15,000; General Hardee commands. We have on hand plenty of meat, salt, and potatoes; all we need is bread, and I have sent to Port Royal for that. We have not lost a wagon on the trip, but have gathered in a large supply of negroes, mules, horses, &c., and our teams are in far better condition than when we started. My first duty will be to clear the army of surplus negroes, mules, and horses, and suppose General Saxton can relieve me of these.

I am writing on board a dispatch-boat, down Ossabaw, at midnight, and have to go back to where I left my horse, eight miles up, in a row-boat, and thence fifteen miles over to our lines by daylight, so that I hope this will be accepted as an excuse for this informal letter; but I know you are anxious to hear of our safety and good condition. Full and detailed reports of the events of the past month will be prepared at a more leisure moment, and in the meantime I can only say that I hope by Christmas to be in possession of Savannah, and by the new year to be ready to resume our journey to Raleigh. The whole army is crazy to be turned loose in Carolina; and with the experience of the past thirty days I judge that a month's sojourn in South Carolina would make her less bellicose.

The editors in Georgia profess to be indignant at the horrible barbarities of Sherman's army, but I know the people don't want our visit repeated. We have utterly destroyed over 200 miles of railroad, and consumed stores and provisions that were essential to Lee's and Hood's armies. A similar destruction of roads and resources hence to Raleigh would compel General Lee to come out of his intrenched camp. I hope General Thomas has held Hood. My last accounts are of the fight at Franklin, but rebel papers state that Decatur, Ala., has been evacuated. This I regret, though it is not essential to the future. If Hood is making any real progress I would not hesitate to march hence, after taking Savannah, for Montgomery, which would bring him out of Tennessee; but it seems to me that winter is a bad time for him. I will try and see Admiral Dahlgren and General Foster before demanding the surrender of Savannah, which I do not propose to make till my batteries are able to open. The quick work made with McAllister, and the opening communication with our fleet, and consequent independence for supplies, dissipated all their boasted threats to head me off and starve the army. The efforts thus far have been puerile, and I regard Savannah as already gained.

Yours, truly,

W. T. SHERMAN,
Major-General.

SPECIAL ORDERS, No. 198. } HDQRS. FIFTEENTH ARMY CORPS, *Anderson's Plantation, Ga., December 13, 1864.*

I. Brigadier-General Woods, commanding First Division, will cause a rifle-pit to be thrown up along the ridge in the open field on the right and left of the Cemetery battery for at least three regiments of infantry. Brigadier-General Corse, commanding Fourth Division, will continue this line of works to the right for a similar number of troops, selecting for a position the edge of the belt of timber on the right of the buildings in front of his left wing. In case of an attack these works will be occupied at once by the troops of the above-mentioned divisions, the commanders of which will keep the troops necessary for this purpose under daily orders.

* * * * * * *

By order of Maj. Gen. P. Joseph Osterhaus:

F. F. WHITEHEAD,
Assistant Adjutant-General.

HEADQUARTERS FIFTEENTH ARMY CORPS,
Anderson's Plantation, Ga., December 13, 1864.

Brig. Gen. C. R. WOODS,
Commanding First Division:

GENERAL: In order to employ the enemy's attention in our front, and at the same time draw it from Fort McAllister, which Brigadier-General Hazen is about attacking, you will push your skirmishers, supported by some regiments, toward the enemy's line as soon as the tide commences to run out. The artillery will open a brisk fire at the same time. The demonstration will assume a menacing attitude during the day by brisk firing, &c.

By order of Maj. Gen. P. Joseph Osterhaus:

F. F. WHITEHEAD,
Assistant Adjutant-General.

(Same to General Corse, commanding Fourth Division.)

HDQRS. DEPARTMENT AND ARMY OF THE TENNESSEE,
Little Ogeechee, near Savannah, Ga., December 13, 1864.

Maj. Gen. F. P. BLAIR,
Commanding Seventeenth Army Corps:

The major-general commanding directs me to say that, at General Sherman's request, he has gone with him to-day down to Cheves' Mill, to witness the attack of General Hazen's division on Fort McAllister. He desires you to occupy the attention of the enemy as much as possible during the day.

Very respectfully, your obedient servant,

SAML. L. TAGGART,
Assistant Adjutant-General.

(Same to Major-General Osterhaus.)

HEADQUARTERS FOURTEENTH ARMY CORPS,
Before Savannah, Ga., December 13, 1864.

Brig. Gen. A. BAIRD,
Commanding Third Division, Fourteenth Army Corps:

The general commanding directs that you detail a brigade as guard and escort to a foraging train, which is ordered to start at 7 a. m. to-morrow, from a point on the Milledgeville road near your headquarters, for the purpose of procuring subsistence for the animals of the corps. The train will go out about eight miles, but it will not be necessary for the whole brigade to march more than four miles, a smaller guard being dispatched to guard the trains the whole distance, the remainder being held as a support.

I have the honor to be, general, very respectfully, your obedient servant,

A. C. McCLURG,
Assistant Adjutant-General and Chief of Staff.

KING'S BRIDGE, *December 13, 1864—8 a. m.*

General SLOCUM:

I have your report, or note, of last night 8 p. m., and think you can make good use of that boat. Don't attempt too much, for a failure of any kind will lead to a reaction; but if the people of Savannah discover us gaining little by little, but surely, it will have a strong effect. The bridge here is now done and is a considerable affair, and Hazen is passing over. I think Fort McAllister, too, will be found a strong work, and, therefore, I depend on another point which is being examined. Forage, &c., is more plentiful over here, but still it is limited. I cannot imagine what the fleet is about; they may be off on some special errand, or may be expecting us elsewhere. I will go to a point where I can see all the Ogeechee country and Ossabaw Sound. I will be home to-night, or in the course of the night.

Yours, truly,

W. T. SHERMAN,
Major-General.

HEADQUARTERS MILITARY DIVISION OF THE MISSISSIPPI,
In the Field, December 13, 1864.

Maj. Gen. H. W. SLOCUM,
Commanding, &c.:

DEAR GENERAL: Take a good big drink, a long breath, and then yell like the devil. The fort was carried at 4.30 p. m., the assault lasting but fifteen minutes. The general signaled from this side to the fleet and got answers, and vessels were seen coming up the sound when Colonel Ewing left.

I am, general, yours, &c.,

L. M. DAYTON,
Aide-de-Camp.

HEADQUARTERS TWENTIETH CORPS,
Near Savannah, Ga., December 13, 1864.

Col. WILLIAM HAWLEY,
Commanding Third Wisconsin:

COLONEL: The general commanding the corps directs that you have all the boats in your charge, or in that of Colonel Bloodgood, on this side of the river by 8 a. m. to-morrow, and in readiness to cross troops. The whole of Colonel Carman's brigade will cross. The general will be there in person.

Very respectfully, your obedient servant,

H. W. PERKINS,
Lieutenant-Colonel and Assistant Adjutant-General.

HEADQUARTERS TWENTIETH CORPS,
Near Savannah, Ga., December 13, 1864.

Brig. Gen. J. W. GEARY,
Commanding Second Division:

GENERAL: The general commanding directs that you seize all the boats in the river near your line, and not allow any persons to cross to the island except under your direction.

Very respectfully, your obedient servant,

ROBT. P. DECHERT,
Captain and Acting Assistant Adjutant-General.

CIRCULAR ORDERS, } HDQRS. SECOND DIV., 20TH ARMY CORPS,
No. 141. } *In the Field, Ga., December 13, 1864.*

Until further orders, no parties will be allowed to cross the river to the island, or to the other shore, except with passes approved at division headquarters, or by higher authority. Colonel Jones, commanding Second Brigade, will detail a guard, under an officer, to collect all boats, scows, &c., in the vicinity of our lines and keep them constantly under guard, allowing no one to use them except properly authorized parties.

By command of Brig. Gen. John W. Geary:

W. T. FORBES,
Acting Assistant Adjutant-General.

HDQRS. SECOND DIVISION, TWENTIETH ARMY CORPS,
In the Field, Ga., December 13, 1864.

Col. ARIO PARDEE, Jr.,
Commanding First Brigade:

COLONEL: The general commanding division desires you to organize for your brigade a company of sharpshooters, by selecting from your regiments twenty-five or thirty marksmen, and placing them under command of one of your best skirmish officers. During such operations as the present this company will not be subject to other detail than for sharpshooting.

I am, colonel, very respectfully, your obedient servant,

W. T. FORBES,
Acting Assistant Adjutant-General.

HEADQUARTERS TWENTIETH CORPS,
Near Savannah, Ga., December 13, 1864.

Brig. Gen. W. T. WARD,
Commanding Third Division:

GENERAL: The general commanding the corps directs that you detail from your command two regiments of infantry, to accompany an expedition to-morrow morning. They will report to these headquarters at 8 a. m. to-morrow. They are to accompany a wagon train, and will return to-morrow night.

Very respectfully, your obedient servant,

H. W. PERKINS,
Lieutenant-Colonel and Assistant Adjutant-General.

HEADQUARTERS THIRD DIVISION, CAVALRY CORPS,
MILITARY DIVISION OF THE MISSISSIPPI,
Kilkenny Bluff, Ga., December 13, 1864—1.30 p. m.

Major-General SHERMAN:

GENERAL: I am at Kilkenny. The Octorara, one of our gun-boats, is in sight. Captain Estes has gone out to communicate with her. I expect to see the officer at this place inside of three hours. I have directed my troops under Colonel Murray to encamp to-night at Midway, one regiment at Sunbery. With two regiments I have been examining the entire country below Fort McAllister around to a point opposite Sunbery. I understand that our fleet is near Wassaw Sound. Kilkenny is decidedly the point to which our fleet should come. We have here at all times between nine and twelve feet of water, never less than nine, besides, a good dock could easily be constructed, and but fifteen miles from King's Bridge, and certainly one of the best military roads I have ever seen. Lieutenant Hollis, from the gun-boat, was at this point last evening making inquiries regarding our army. The fleet is expecting us to cross the Little Ogeechee and push our right flank in around upon Thunderbolt. I have opened up communication with my people at Sunbery, and have directed Colonel Murray to send a determined officer with sufficient force to destroy the bridge (over the Altamaha), telegraph wire, &c.

Hoping, general, my success will please you, I am, with great respect, your obedient servant,

J. KILPATRICK,
Brigadier-General, Commanding Cavalry.

HEADQUARTERS THIRD DIVISION, CAVALRY CORPS,
MILITARY DIVISION OF THE MISSISSIPPI,
Kilkenny Bluff, Ga., December 13, 1864.

Major-General SHERMAN:

GENERAL: Inclosed please find answer to Major-General Wheeler's communication. If you are satisfied with the contents in it contained, I should like to have it forwarded by flag of truce. I should be pleased to make the exchange referred to in Wheeler's communication, and will await your decision on the subject. Is Wheeler upon this side of the Savannah? If so, at what point had I best concentrate my command? Captain Brink will bring back any instructions you may have.

Very respectfully, your obedient servant,

J. KILPATRICK,
Brigadier-General, Commanding.

[Inclosure.]

HEADQUARTERS CAVALRY COMMAND,
King's Bridge, Ga., Tuesday, December 13, 1864.

Major-General WHEELER,
Commanding Cavalry Corps, C. S. Army:

Your communications of December 5 [6] and 11 have just been received. In reference to the depredations committed by my command while marching through your country, I will simply say that the same complaints have been made by the citizens of Georgia against officers and men of your own command, and call your attention to Governor Brown's message on that subject. If you cannot control your men while they are among their friends, you cannot expect me to prevent my men from committing depredations upon their known enemies—a people who have betrayed them in the past, and for whom they have now no sympathy. Do not understand by this that I have allowed my men to commit depredations along my line of march; such has not been the case. An order has been issued to my command authorizing and instructing my officers to shoot upon the spot any soldier who shall be caught committing any outrage. War is terrible, and the people of Georgia are now being made to feel this in all its force. Had the people of the Confederate States, and especially those of South Carolina, ever known and felt what the people of Georgia know and feel now, no hostile shot would ever have struck the sacred walls of Sumter. I am willing and ready now, as I know my Government always has been, to enter at once into any fair exchange of prisoners. I will consult with Major-General Sherman on the subject, and give you his decision at the earliest possible moment.

Thanking you, general, for your kind attention to one of my officers, and for returning to me a book high prized,

I am, very respectfully, your obedient servant,

J. KILPATRICK,
Brigadier-General, U. S. Army.

HEADQUARTERS CAVALRY COMMAND,
December 13, 1864.

Major-General SHERMAN:

GENERAL: Lieut. B. H. Chadwick, of the ——, is with me. He says this is the best possible point to land our stores. We have here at all times twelve feet of water, and eighteen feet at most points. He will send any message to our fleet you may desire. Our gun-boats are all up with Foster. I can have a dispatch sent to Admiral Dahlgren by daylight to-morrow morning.

J. KILPATRICK,
Brigadier-General, Commanding Cavalry.

HDQRS. SECOND BRIGADE, THIRD CAVALRY DIVISION,
In the Field, December 13, 1864.

ASSISTANT ADJUTANT-GENERAL, 14TH ARMY CORPS:

By command of General Kilpatrick my brigade of cavalry will march at 9 a. m., to cross the Ogeechee River at King's Bridge.

Most respectfully, your obedient servant,

SMITH D. ATKINS,
Colonel, Commanding Brigade.

HEADQUARTERS DEPARTMENT OF THE SOUTH,
Steamer Nemaha, Savannah River, December 13, 1864.

Major-General SHERMAN:

GENERAL: I am rejoiced to hear from Captain Duncan of your successful march. I hope you will wipe out Savannah, which, I think, you can readily do. The enemy's force is about 15,000, about one-third veterans. Only a few scattering regiments have come from Virginia; none, I believe, from Lee's army. It has been gathered from Wilmington, Charleston, and Augusta. The enemy's forts on this coast are Fort Jackson, Batteries Lee, Savannah, Lamar, and Maine, guarding the Savannah River in the vicinity of Fort Jackson. The batteries are believed to be open at the gorge, with the exception of Fort Jackson. Fort Bartow, thirty guns, inclosed, is three miles east of Savannah, guarding both Saint Augustine Creek and Savannah River. Thunderbolt Battery, strong, nine guns, is situated near Wassaw, guarding the

Wilmington River. Turner's Rocks Battery is on the same river, opposite side, and two miles farther down. Some light batteries are at Isle of Hope. Beaulieu Battery, nine guns, open gorge, guards the Vernon River; shell road from it to Savannah. Rosedew Battery guards the Little Ogeechee River, open gorge, two guns; good road to Savannah. All these roads are well furnished with batteries at favorable points. Fort McAllister guards the Great Ogeechee River, fourteen guns, strong, inclosed. Communication with the fleet may be opened by taking Fort McAllister, or Batteries Rosedew or Beaulieu. I think the two latter are preferable, and easier taken, My own force is strongly posted between the Coosawhatchie and Tullifinny Rivers, and commands with its batteries the railroad, which is within 1,200 yards.

Ample supplies are here awaiting your orders. Communications may be sent to any river sound in this vicinity, and find a vessel of the fleet ready to receive them. I hold Boyd's Neck on the south side of Broad River, where couriers in that direction may come in better than at Coosawhatchie, where we are confronted by 5,000 men, veterans and militia. I inclose a traced map of this immediate coast.

Respectfully, yours,

J. G. FOSTER,
Major-General, Commanding.

P. S.—An officer of General Grant's staff has arrived with dispatches for you; also a mail for your army of nearly twenty tons weight.

J. G. F.

SAVANNAH RIVER, *December 13, 1864.*

[General SHERMAN:]

GENERAL: Captain Duncan reached me on the morning of the 12th at 8 a. m. I have two iron-clads at Wassaw and a force of gun-boats at Ossabaw and Savannah River; will await your movements to establish a communication; the best may be by the Ogeechee; this is guarded by Fort McAllister, which has always resisted attack by water, but would be easily reduced from the rear. The rebels have no force of consequence south of McAllister. The Vernon is guarded by Battery Beaulieu, the Little Ogeechee by Rosedew, both able to keep vessels from passing the narrow channels, but of no force landward. The island formed by the Coosawhatchie and Tullifinny (head of Broad River) is crossed by the railroad, and is now occupied by General Foster south of the railroad, whose batteries will reach it. I think you will find the rivers going into Ossabaw convenient for communication.

Very respectfully,

J. A. DAHLGREN,
Rear-Admiral, Comdg. South Atlantic Blockading Squadron.

U. S. STEAMER FLAG,
Ossabaw Sound, December 13, 1864—7 p. m.

Maj. Gen. J. G. FOSTER,
Commanding Department of the South:

GENERAL: I have succeeded in communicating by signals to the signal officer of General Sherman's army, stationed on a fort about three miles northwest of Fort McAllister, on the north side of the

Ogeechee River. I was unable to open full communication by flags with them, as it was most dark, but could see large numbers of troops arriving at that point. I shall return immediately to open communication by torch and rockets.

Very respectfully, your obedient servant,

GEO. A. FISHER,
First Lieutenant, Signal Corps, U. S. Army.

U. S. BARK FERNANDINA,
Saint Catherine's, Ga., December 13, 1864.

[General JOHN G. FOSTER:]

SIR: I have just communicated with our army at Kilkenny. General Kilpatrick and his staff are there. His forces hold the coast between here and Sapello. He wishes to make this place a base for supplies. One of my officers is now at Kilkenny waiting for dispatches from General Sherman, which I will forward as soon as received. I have only this moment received the above intelligence by one of my scouts.

Very respectfully,

LEWIS WESS.

General Sherman's headquarters are at Henry Munger's plantation, on the right hand of the Ogeechee, going up about northwest from Fort McAllister, distance three miles.

HEADQUARTERS DEPARTMENT OF THE SOUTH,
Hilton Head, S. C., December 13, 1864.

Brig. Gen. JOHN P. HATCH,
Commanding Coast Division, Tullifinny Point:

GENERAL: I am instructed by the major-general commanding to state that Admiral Dahlgren intends making a demonstration somewhere in the vicinity of Savannah, and will probably have to call upon you for the Naval Brigade. You are therefore directed, in case these men are sent for by the admiral, to send all excepting a sufficient number to man the navy guns. Nothing from Sherman since his scouts arrived yesterday morning.

Very respectfully, your obedient servant,

W. L. M. BURGER,
Assistant Adjutant-General.

HDQRS. NORTHERN DISTRICT, DEPT. OF THE SOUTH,
Morris Island, S. C., December 13, 1864.

Lieut. W. B. DEAN,
Acting Assistant Adjutant-General, Dept. of the South:

LIEUTENANT: I have the honor to report most respectfully that nothing of importance has occurred since I assumed command. No deserters or refugees have entered our lines. The camps and outposts of the enemy are the same as they have been for several months back. The only information which I have received with regard to the enemy's strength has been series of intercepted dispatches of which I have the honor to annex copies.* It gives the strength of the enemy in Charleston and to the northern part of the harbor. I am not of opinion that these dispatches were intended as a ruse to mislead us. The only method by which I can ascertain with any degree of certainty the strength of the enemy will be by attacking his outposts, which I consider myself sufficiently strong to do. Troops left Charleston yesterday, one light battery from Mount Pleasant, and 3 officers and 100 men from Sullivan's Island; further is not known. The flag of truce is still in operation.

I have the honor to be, lieutenant, very respectfully, your obedient servant,

A. SCHIMMELFENNIG,
Brigadier-General, Commanding District.

P. S.—At this moment the Hancox has arrived bringing dead bodies from the flag-of-truce boat. Her captain reports that prisoners exchanged to-day have informed him that it was reported in Charleston that Savannah surrendered to-day with 10,000 prisoners after a fight of eight hours. Nothing official from Colonel Mulford.

Respectfully,

A. SCHIMMELFENNIG,
Brigadier-General, Commanding.

GENERAL FIELD ORDERS, No. 33.

HEADQUARTERS DEPARTMENT AND ARMY OF THE TENNESSEE,
Near Savannah, Ga., December 14, 1864.

The major-general commanding the Army of the Tennessee publishes the following order of the general-in-chief with great satisfaction. The thanks of the army are due to Brigadier-General Hazen and his command for the distinguished service they have rendered.†

By order of Maj. Gen. O. O. Howard:

SAML. L. TAGGART,
Assistant Adjutant-General.

SPECIAL FIELD ORDERS, No. 194.

HEADQUARTERS DEPARTMENT AND ARMY OF THE TENNESSEE,
Little Ogeechee, near Savannah, Ga., Dec. 14, 1864.

First, corps commanders will hold their reserve troops, without artillery, in readiness to be moved around to the right by transports. Second, Major-General Osterhaus, commanding Fifteenth Army Corps, is charged with the holding of Fort McAllister and King's Bridge. The attention of corps commanders is again called to the necessity of keeping the road to King's Bridge in good hauling condition.

By order of Maj. Gen. O. O. Howard:

SAML. L. TAGGART,
Assistant Adjutant-General.

---

* Not found.

† See Special Field Orders, No. 131, p. 111.

HDQRS. DEPARTMENT AND ARMY OF THE TENNESSEE,
Little Ogeechee, near Savannah, Ga., December 14, 1864.

Maj. Gen. P. JOS. OSTERHAUS,
Commanding Fifteenth Army Corps:

In sending you inclosed order* (No. 194) the major-general commanding desires me to say that he deems one brigade of General Hazen's division sufficient to hold Fort McAllister and King's Bridge, leaving the balance with General Smith's division, to be moved around to the right by transports. General Blair, leaving Third Division in present position, and one brigade of General Mower's division on the canal, will have four brigades to move. The general also desires me to say that he considers it of the utmost importance to have the road to King's Bridge placed as soon as possible and kept in good hauling condition; and, to this end, suggests that each section of it be placed in charge of a good, competent officer, who will see that the work required is done with as little delay as possible.

Very respectfully, your obedient servant,

SAML. L. TAGGART,
Assistant Adjutant-General.

SPECIAL ORDERS, No. 194.
HEADQUARTERS SECOND DIVISION, FIFTEENTH ARMY CORPS,
Fort McAllister, Ga., December 14, 1864.

In consideration of the conspicuous part taken by the Seventieth Ohio Volunteer Infantry in the assault of Fort McAllister yesterday, that regiment is detailed to temporarily garrison that place, and will make its camp near the fort, with such force as the colonel may deem requisite on duty in it. He will take immediate steps to put the fort in order, cleansing it and adopting a proper system of policing.

By order of Brig. Gen. W. B. Hazen:

G. LOFLAND,
Captain and Assistant Adjutant-General.

HDQRS. DEPARTMENT AND ARMY OF THE TENNESSEE,
Little Ogeechee, near Savannah, Ga., December 14, 1864.

Maj. Gen. F. P. BLAIR,
Commanding Seventeenth Army Corps:

GENERAL: It is represented that there is no guard at King's Bridge, or that, at least, there was none last night. It was supposed that General Hazen would leave a guard for it, but it appears he did not. As you are intrusted with the repairing of that part of the road please see that the bridge is properly protected.

By order of Maj. Gen. O. O. Howard:

SAML. L. TAGGART,
Assistant Adjutant-General.

---

* See next, *ante*.

HDQRS. DEPARTMENT AND ARMY OF THE TENNESSEE,
Little Ogeechee, near Savannah, Ga., December 14, 1864.

Maj. Gen. F. P. BLAIR,
Commanding Seventeenth Army Corps:

In sending you inclosed order (No. 194)* the major-general commanding desires me to say that he wishes the brigade on the canal to be retained there for the present; this, leaving General Leggett's division in present position, will give you four brigades to move by transports to the right. General Osterhaus will have General Smith's and (with the exception of four brigades left to hold Fort McAllister and King's Bridge) General Hazen's divisions. The general also desires me to say that he considers it of the utmost importance to have the road to King's Bridge placed as soon as possible and kept in good hauling order. To this end he suggests that each section of it be placed in charge of a good, competent officer, who will see that the work required is done with as little delay as possible.

Very respectfully, your obedient servant,

SAML. L. TAGGART,
Assistant Adjutant-General.

SPECIAL ORDERS, No. 306. } HDQRS. SEVENTEENTH ARMY CORPS,
Near Savannah, Ga., December 14, 1864.

Brig. Gen. G. A. Smith, commanding Fourth Division, will detail from his command three companies of infantry for guard at King's Bridge. They will proceed to that point at once, and will protect the bridge until relieved.

By command of Maj. Gen. F. P. Blair:

C. CADLE, JR.,
Assistant Adjutant-General.

SPECIAL ORDERS, No. 157. } HDQRS. FOURTH DIV., 17TH ARMY CORPS,
Near Savannah, Ga., December 14, 1864.

Col. B. F. Potts, commanding First Brigade, Fourth Division. Seventeenth Army Corps, will, in accordance with Special Orders, No. 306, army corps headquarters, detail from his command three companies of infantry, properly officered, for guard at King's Bridge. They will proceed to that place forthwith, and will protect the bridge until relieved.

By order of Brig. Gen. Giles A. Smith:

CHAS. H. BRUSH,
First Lieutenant and Acting Assistant Adjutant-General.

SPECIAL ORDERS, No. 4. } HDQRS. LEFT WING, ARMY OF GEORGIA,
Before Savannah, Ga., December 14, 1864.

The detachments of the pontoon train now on duty with the Fourteenth and Twentieth Corps are relieved from such duty, and Colonel Buell will hereafter report direct to these headquarters.

By command of Maj. Gen. H. W. Slocum:

H. C. RODGERS,
Assistant Adjutant-General.

---

*See p. 710.

HDQRS. SECOND DIVISION, TWENTIETH ARMY CORPS,
Near Savannah, Ga., December 14, 1864.

Col. JOHN FLYNN, *Division Officer of the Day:*

COLONEL: I am directed by the general commanding division to say that there is some probability that the enemy will evacuate their position. The general desires you to direct the pickets to keep a special watch for any movement of the kind by throwing forward vedettes for close observation, and if any such movement takes place occupy their works at once and send notice to these headquarters.

I am, colonel, very respectfully, your obedient servant,

W. T. FORBES,
Acting Assistant Adjutant-General.

HEADQUARTERS DEPARTMENT OF THE SOUTH,
Hilton Head, S. C., December 14, 1864.

Lieut. Gen. U. S. GRANT, *Comdg. Armies of the United States:*

GENERAL: I have the honor to inform you that I have just returned from meeting General Sherman, whom I met at Fort McAllister at daylight this morning. Fort McAllister was taken by assault at 4.30 last evening by Hazen's division of the Fifteenth Corps. The garrison, numbering 250 men, were all made prisoners, and the armament of 21 guns, with stores, ammunition, &c., fell into our hands. This important capture opens the Great Ogeechee River to supplies of all kinds, which can be safely landed immediately in the rear of General Sherman's army. This army now holds Savannah closely besieged, having driven in the enemy from all his advanced positions until the left wing rests on the Savannah River three miles and a half above the city, and the right on the Ogeechee River. General Slocum, on the left wing, holds Argyle Island, and has a captured steamer in use on the river at that point. A second captured steamer was burned. The Central railroad is thoroughly destroyed; also the Savannah and Charleston Railroad from the Savannah River to within three miles and a half of the city. The Gulf road is also destroyed for a long distance, and the bridge over the Ogeechee burned. General Sherman is perfectly sure of capturing Savannah; and I am now forwarding a siege battery of 30-pounder Parrotts to be placed in position. In two days he will summon the city to surrender, and if not yielded will open his batteries. To prevent the escape of Hardee and the garrison, General Sherman intends to throw one division across the Savannah River at Argyle Island, to hold the river-bank opposite the city. I am also to hold the railroad and stage road in my present position between the Coosawhatchie and Tullifinny Rivers. Admiral Dahlgren is to demonstrate against the water defenses of Savannah to keep the garrisons in those works. Everything now seems extremely favorable to the entire success of General Sherman's expectations. His army is in splendid condition, having lived on its march on the turkeys, chickens, sweet potatoes, and other good things of the richest part of Georgia. The opposition to his march has been feeble. I am supplying everything needed and aiding in every way within my power.

I will send another dispatch as soon as Savannah falls.

I have the honor to be, very respectfully, your obedient servant,

J. G. FOSTER,
Major-General, Commanding.

(Same to General Halleck.)

HEADQUARTERS DEPARTMENT OF THE SOUTH,
Hilton Head, S. C., December 14, 1864.

Maj. Gen. H. W. HALLECK,
Chief of Staff of Armies of United States, Washington, D. C.:

GENERAL: I have the honor to report that I opened communication with General Sherman in the Ogeechee River at daylight this morning. Fort McAllister, with its garrison and armament of twenty-one guns, was taken by assault at 4.30 p. m. yesterday by Hazen's division of the Fifteenth Corps. This important capture opens the Ogeechee River to General Sherman as a base of supplies, which, with a siege train of 30-pounder Parrotts, are being rapidly forwarded. His army closely invests Savannah on the south side of the Savannah River, and a force which will take position on the north side of that river will prevent the escape of Hardee or the garrison. Argyle Island, in the Savannah River, is held by our troops, who have captured two steamers on the river at that point, one of which is in running order; the other was burnt. The Central railroad is completely destroyed; also the Charleston and Savannah Railroad to within three and a half miles of the city. A long distance on the Gulf road is also destroyed, together with the bridge over the Ogeechee. General Sherman will without doubt capture Savannah and all its garrison and armament. His army is in splendid condition and morale.

I am, general, very respectfully, your obedient servant,

J. G. FOSTER,
Major-General, Commanding.

HILTON HEAD, S. C., *December 14, 1864.*

Bvt. Maj. Gen. M. C. MEIGS,
Quartermaster-General:

General Sherman has arrived near here, and at least six large steamers, drawing not more than seven or eight feet, in addition to those already in the department, will be required to transport supplies to his army. The sailing vessels now here with supplies for him draw so much water that they cannot go up the Ogeechee River as far as required.

C. W. THOMAS,
Major and Chief Quartermaster Department of the South.

HEADQUARTERS ARMY OF THE JAMES,
December 14, 1864—2.50 p. m.

Lieutenant-General GRANT:

A Richmond paper of to-day says:

Up to yesterday morning no fighting had taken place between Sherman's army and the Confederate troops in the defense of Savannah. An official dispatch of yesterday mentioned that Sherman had developed his army near the town.

The Whig says:

So far as we can learn Sherman's army has invested Savannah; beyond the usual skirmishing no fight had taken place. A press telegram dated yesterday, 13th, from Augusta, says in the fight at Coosawhatchie, Friday, General Gartrell was badly wounded in the side by a shell. Notwithstanding his severe wound he remained on the field until the fight closed.

None of the papers contain particulars of the Coosawhatchie. No information of any conflict at that point since the 30th has been received at the War Department.

E. O. C. ORD,
Major-General.

(Copy to Secretary of War.)

WASHINGTON, *December 15, 1864—11.10 a. m.*

Lieutenant-General GRANT,
City Point, Va.:

You are aware that a large amount of supplies were collected at Pensacola for General Sherman, and that Canby held troops there and at Mobile, to open communication with him if necessary. Should not General Canby now be instructed to use these troops and supplies for other purposes? Will General Sherman, after taking Savannah, base himself on that place and operate against Charleston, Branchville, or Augusta? I do not know what instructions have been given him on this subject; but if he is to base himself on the coast, recruits, convalescents, &c., as well as future supplies, should be sent there for his army.

H. W. HALLECK,
Major-General and Chief of Staff.

WASHINGTON CITY, *December 15, 1864.*

Major-General HALLECK,
Chief of Staff of the Army:

GENERAL: Please communicate with Sherman, and direct him to send no troops from his army to Virginia until plan of campaign is fully agreed upon. My last instructions to Sherman contemplated his sending troops to operate against Richmond, retaining all his artillery, cavalry, and infantry sufficient to hold our base on the Atlantic secured by his campaign and to compel the enemy to retain there at least the force he now has against us. Also, that artillery can be sent from here to supply his wants.

U. S. GRANT,
Lieutenant-General.

WAR DEPARTMENT,
QUARTERMASTER-GENERAL'S OFFICE,
Washington, D. C., December 15, 1864. (Via Port Royal, S. C.)

Maj. Gen. W. T. SHERMAN:

MY DEAR GENERAL: We have to-day official advices of your position, and that you have communicated, or that General Howard has communicated, with General Foster. I congratulate you on your successful march. You have made the greatest and most remarkable marches of the war, and have demonstrated several times that an army can move more than twenty-five miles from a navigable river or railroad without perishing. We have been shipping supplies for you, and I hope that you will have abundance of all necessaries, though I have been somewhat uncertain as to your numbers. The first orders required

200,000 rations of grain and 500,000 of provisions and 100 rounds of ammunition to be shipped to meet you. They were at first ordered to rendezvous at Port Royal; subsequently, orders were given to send one-half of these supplies to Pensacola. I added a supply of clothing, some wagons, harness, and quartermaster's stores. These estimates and orders appear to have been based upon a column of 30,000 men. As soon as your movements, as reported by the rebel papers, showed that you would probably strike the Atlantic coast, orders were given to send further supplies to Hilton Head, and having ascertained that your force was probably much greater than that noted above, I ordered more clothing and quartermaster's stores, and directed forage, hay, and grain for 30,000 animals to be shipped daily. Of course I have sent forward all subsistence and ammunition turned over to the Quartermaster's Department for shipment.

I presume that you have more animals now than when you started, and I desire to call your attention to the difficulty, as well as the expense, of furnishing a large army with forage on the Atlantic coast. With all the exertions of the forage officer of this department, with a practically unlimited command of money, he has not been able to accumulate at Washington and at City Point enough long forage for the armies in Virginia to meet a few days' interruption by storm or ice. We can supply grain enough, but there is always a short supply of hay. He has agents in all the hay districts, and buys all that he can in the great markets. Still the armies complain of short allowance of hay. If you have more animals than you need for intended operations they should be sent off to some point where the country can subsist them, or else you will, I fear, lose many by the diseases resulting from constant feeding on grain without enough long forage. If you reduce the number of animals to the lowest point consistent with safety and efficiency the hay we can procure will subsist them in better condition. The expense and difficulty of maintaining a large army stationary is enormous. The wonderful resources of the Northern States have enabled us thus far to keep the Army of the Potomac fully supplied, except with hay, and of the want of that it complains bitterly. Should you rest upon the coast, as the Army of the Potomac has done, this hay question will be a great difficulty. I presume, however, that your army will be actively employed, and live, as it has heretofore, to some extent, upon the enemy. I hope so, and I believe that if there be a general officer in the service who can effect this, it is yourself.

Congratulating you again upon your brilliant and successful operation, I am, most sincerely, your friend and servant,

M. C. MEIGS,

Quartermaster-General, Brevet Major-General, U. S. Army.

SPECIAL FIELD ORDERS, No. 195.

HEADQUARTERS DEPARTMENT AND ARMY OF THE TENNESSEE,
Near Savannah, Ga., December 15, 1864.

* * * * * * *

IV. 1. The reserve troops of Major-General Blair's command, Seventeenth Corps, will not be moved to the right by transports, as intimated in Special Field Orders, No. 194.

2. Major-General Blair is charged with constructing a wharf, suitable for landing supplies for this army, at such point on the river near King's Bridge as General Easton, chief quartermaster Military Divis-

ion of the Mississippi, may select. General Blair will cause the work to be placed in charge of a competent, energetic officer, and the collecting of the material will be commenced immediately.

3. The Engineer Regiment, Lieutenant-Colonel Tweeddale commanding, will report to Major-General Blair for assignment to duty on this work.

4. General Blair will cause all further necessary details of men, teams, &c., to push this work forward to speedy completion, to be made from his command.

5. General Easton will be at King's Bridge to-morrow morning to select the most suitable point for the wharf.

6. A large mail will be at King's Bridge to-morrow; corps commanders will cause all necessary arrangements to be made to procure and properly distribute the same.

By order of Maj. Gen. O. O. Howard:

SAML. L. TAGGART,
Assistant Adjutant-General.

HEADQUARTERS FIFTEENTH ARMY CORPS,
Near Fort McAllister, Ga., December 15, 1864.

General W. B. HAZEN,
Commanding Second Division:

You will garrison Fort McAllister with a regiment of about 300 men, under an energetic officer, who will be charged with putting the land fronts of the fort, including ditches and abatis, in complete order again. It will be desirable to have all the heavy guns not in position on the river front put in toward the land. Please report the name of the commanding officer of the fort to these headquarters. For your division you may select a comfortable camp until further orders.

Very respectfully, your obedient servant,

P. JOS. OSTERHAUS,
Major-General.

HDQRS. DEPARTMENT AND ARMY OF THE TENNESSEE,
Near Savannah, Ga., December 15, 1864.

Brig. Gen. W. B. HAZEN,
Comdg. Second Div., 15th Army Corps, Fort McAllister:

Dismount two 32-pounder rifled guns, and have them placed on the bank ready for shipment by water to King's Bridge to-morrow.

By order of Maj. Gen. O. O. Howard:

SAML. L. TAGGART,
Assistant Adjutant-General.

HEADQUARTERS SEVENTEENTH ARMY CORPS,
Near Savannah, Ga., December 15, 1864.

Brig. Gen. M. D. LEGGETT,
Commanding Third Division:

GENERAL: The pioneer corps of the First and Fourth Divisions are at work on the road to King's Bridge. The major-general commanding directs that you make the necessary details from your command to assist your pioneer corps in throwing up the work for the siege guns. Captain Robinson, Company C, First Michigan Artillery, will superintend the work, and will be at your headquarters in a short time.

Very respectfully,

C. CADLE, JR.,
Assistant Adjutant-General.

HEADQUARTERS MILITARY DIVISION OF THE MISSISSIPPI,
In the Field, near Savannah, Ga.
(Major-General Howard's Headquarters), December 15, 1864—2 p. m.

Maj. Gen. H. W. SLOCUM, *Commanding Left Wing:*

GENERAL: The general has just returned from a visit to Ossabaw and Wassaw Sounds, and directs me to inform you in full terms of the result. After having opened communication by signal with the gun-boats and got possession of Fort McAllister, he went in person to the gun-boat below Fort McAllister, which proved to be a messenger-boat from the flag-ship lying at the mouth of Ossabaw Sound. After making communications to Washington, &c., he returned to Fort McAllister, and was overtaken by a messenger from General Foster, just from Port Royal. The general went on board General Foster's boat, and proceeded with him down the bay in hopes to meet the admiral, but did not find him till after running around to Wassaw Sound. General Foster then proceeded to Port Royal at 12 m. yesterday, to return with a fleet of transports loaded with 600,000 rations and ten days' forage for 40,000 animals, and promised to be here by to-night. He will also bring with him six 20-pounder Parrott guns and six 30-pounder Parrotts, with 300 rounds of ammunition per gun. The general then transferred to the admiral's vessel and returned to Fort McAllister, whence the admiral accompanied him as far up as the rice mill, where he had left his horse. He is now at General Howard's headquarters, and has sent for his camp to be transferred to a point near this, which is not far from the Seven-Mile Post on the main road leading west from Savannah to the Ogeechee, marked on our maps as a plank road. This point is about five miles from his present headquarters, on the Louisville road. General Foster has 5,000 men near the Charleston railroad, north of Broad River, and near enough to the railroad to command it, so that he feels sure that cars cannot pass either way; but he has been unable to reach the railroad itself with his men, on account of the enemy's force. The gun-boats and General Howard occupy all other avenues of approach to Savannah connecting with your right. Now, if you can close the Savannah River to navigation, and also get a force over the Savannah River to threaten in flank any dirt road leading out of Savannah, between the city and Coosawhatchie, the investment of the city will be complete and the enemy will have no escape.

The general wants to place the batteries expected from General Foster in position as near the heart of Savannah as possible, ready to bombard it as soon as possible. You may, therefore, send horses to the Ogeechee River, at King's Bridge, ready to haul those guns to your right front, and, as soon as they are well in position, ready to open on the city, he proposes to demand its surrender. In the meantime our stores of all kinds will come up Ossabaw Sound and the Ogeechee to King's Bridge, and thence be hauled to the camps. The canal is admirably adapted to your use, and the general suggests that you send some competent staff officer over to the Ogeechee, and, in concert with General Easton, chief quartermaster, collect as many boats as possible to transport your stores from King's Bridge, through the canal, up to your very camp. At Doctor Cheves' plantation, ten miles from King's Bridge, the general himself saw at least half a dozen fine, large flats, built expressly to transport rice through the canal to Savannah, the very things wanted, and he has no doubt on other plantations at least twenty or twenty-five boats could be collected, each capable of transporting twenty tons. In dry weather the wagons will be best, but in case of rainy weather these boats would be admirable. As soon as possible the general wants your batteries, which are nearest the city, prepared to execute the foregoing plans, and he wants you to write him in full to-night any ideas that may have been suggested by your closer observation of the ground in your immediate front; and you may at once give orders for hauling provisions and forage from King's Bridge, as Admiral Dahlgren assured him this morning that he would have all torpedoes and obstructions removed in the course of to-day. There is also a steam-boat load of mail for your army, Col. A. H. Markland in charge, which will be at King's Bridge the instant the torpedoes are removed. Captain Merritt brings this to you, and can satisfy all your inquiries, as he has been with the general.

I have the honor to be, general, very respectfully, your obedient servant,

HENRY HITCHCOCK,
Major and Assistant Adjutant-General.

HEADQUARTERS LEFT WING, ARMY OF GEORGIA,
December 15, 1864—5 p. m.

Maj. HENRY HITCHCOCK, *Assistant Adjutant-General:*

MAJOR: Your communication of 2 p. m. has just come to hand. The heavy guns can be used to advantage in my front. From my extreme left I can shell the city with the 3-inch gun. I think I can safely place a force on the Carolina side of the river and gradually work my way opposite the city. I shall send team for stores at once.

I will write fully to-morrow.

Very respectfully, &c.,

H. W. SLOCUM,
Major-General.

HEADQUARTERS LEFT WING, ARMY OF GEORGIA,
December 15, 1864—9 p. m.

[Major-General SHERMAN:]

GENERAL: I have two regiments on the Carolina shore north of Clydesdale Creek. To-morrow morning the remainder of the brigade, three additional regiments, will endeavor to take the line from Clydesdale Creek to a point on the Savannah River opposite to Cruger's Island, with orders to intrench on that line and feel forward toward the causeway road. With your consent I will try to place a division on the line marked 2 on the inclosed diagram. It will be necessary to move with some caution on that side; and, to render the position entirely safe, it may be necessary to throw an entire corps over, with instructions to intrench strongly. There are many points in front of our present position that can be guarded by a good picket-line. If a portion of the line now held by Davis can be held by General Howard, or by the troops under General Foster, the Twentieth Corps can be spared, and will seal up that side of the city and be in a position to shell every portion of it. I shall go no further than to send a brigade over to take the line marked 1 until I hear from you; but I have no fear of placing a corps on that side; and this done the fate of the city is sealed. I think Foster's command might be of use in the swamps on this side if placed behind the line already established. I think there are points on the left of my line from which the city can be shelled with those heavy guns to more advantage than on the right of the line. The point held by Carlin, where Mower was, is within three miles and a half of the city, but there are points nearer the river quite as close, and from which the city can be seen. Please give me your views as to the propriety of attempting to throw one entire corps over. We can send supplies via Argyle Island, which is held by us. The enemy hold the lower part of Hutchinson's Island, and command the whole island, with their batteries on this side. They also send a small gun-boat up to a point between Cruger's Island and Hutchinson's, at a point marked B. She has one heavy gun and gives us some annoyance. She is just out of range of our field guns.

Very respectfully, your obedient servant,

H. W. SLOCUM,
Major-General.

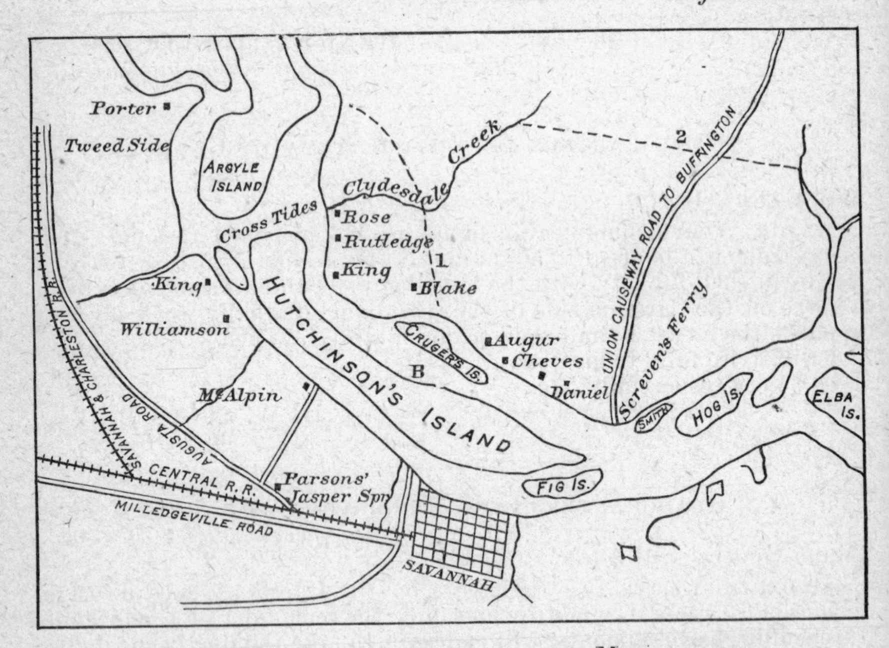

HDQRS. MILITARY DIVISION OF THE MISSISSIPPI,
In the Field, near Savannah, Ga.,
(Major-General Howard's Headquarters), Dec. 15, 1864—11.30 p. m.

Maj. Gen. H. W. SLOCUM, *Comdg. Left Wing, Army of Georgia:*

GENERAL: The general-in-chief directs me to write you as follows: "Your note of 9 p. m. is just received. For the present do not send more than one brigade, and instead of threatening south toward the Union Causeway, rather let it threaten eastward toward the road marked as running up toward Augusta on the east side of the Savannah River, seemingly threatening in flank the movement of troops attempting to escape from Savannah. There are some points which I will explain in person as soon as I can ride over to see you. A messenger is just arrived from General Grant with dispatches of importance. Prepare for the rifled guns and get them into position as soon as possible. Let the engineer regiment continue to destroy the railroad, and cover their work up as far as the bridge, including it if possible. After making some letters to-morrow I will come over to see you. Also get from the island in the river all the rice you can as forage for your horses."

I have the honor to be, &c.,

HENRY HITCHCOCK,
Major and Assistant Adjutant-General.

HEADQUARTERS FOURTEENTH ARMY CORPS,
Before Savannah, Ga., December 15, 1864.

Brig. Gens. W. P. CARLIN and J. D. MORGAN,
Comdg. First and Second Divisions, Fourteenth Army Corps:

A brigade from General Baird's division has been ordered to start from near General Baird's headquarters to-morrow, at 7 a. m., as guard and escort to foraging trains and parties from the different divisions. The expedition will proceed toward the Ogeechee River, and division commanders are authorized to make details of wagons and foragers to accompany it.

By order of Bvt. Maj. Gen. J. C. Davis:

A. C. McCLURG,
Assistant Adjutant-General and Chief of Staff.

HEADQUARTERS FOURTEENTH ARMY CORPS,
Before Savannah, Ga., December 15, 1864.

Brig. Gen. A. BAIRD,
Commanding Third Division, Fourteenth Army Corps:

The general commanding the corps directs that you detail one brigade to escort and guard foraging trains from the different divisions on a foraging expedition toward the Ogeechee River, the expedition to start from near your headquarters to-morrow at 7 a. m.

I have the honor to be, general, very respectfully, your obedient servant,

A. C. McCLURG,
Assistant Adjutant-General and Chief of Staff.

HEADQUARTERS TWENTIETH CORPS,
Near Savannah, Ga., December 15, 1864.

Brigadier-General JACKSON, *Commanding First Division:*

GENERAL: The general commanding the corps desires to have you watch well the enemy's batteries in your front, and report at once any movement of their artillery. It is possible that they may take away some of the pieces.

Very respectfully, your obedient servant,

H. W. PERKINS,
Assistant Adjutant-General.

(Same to General Geary, commanding Second Division.)

HEADQUARTERS TWENTIETH CORPS,
Near Savannah, Ga., December 15, 1864.

Brig. Gen. N. J. JACKSON,
Commanding First Division:

GENERAL: The brigadier-general commanding the corps directs that you send the Second Massachusetts Volunteers, Colonel Cogswell commanding, to report at once to Colonel Hawley, commanding on Argyle Island, for temporary duty. It is necessary that the regiment should start at once.

Very respectfully, your obedient servant,

H. W. PERKINS,
Lieutenant-Colonel and Assistant Adjutant-General.

HEADQUARTERS TWENTIETH CORPS,
Near Savannah, Ga., December 15, 1864.

Brigadier-General JACKSON,
Commanding First Division:

GENERAL: The general commanding the corps directs that you order the balance of Colonel Carman's brigade (now in the line) to march to-morrow morning to the landing where the captured steamboat is, starting from camp in time to reach there at 7 a. m. The interval that will be left in your line by taking out these troops will have to be filled by putting in the reserve regiments of the other brigades, and, if necessary, increase the intervals between the regiments. The general will go over the river in the morning and would like to have you accompany him. He will start from here about 8 a. m.

Very respectfully, your obedient servant,

H. W. PERKINS,
Assistant Adjutant-General.

HEADQUARTERS TWENTIETH CORPS,
Five Miles from Savannah, Ga., December 15, 1864.

Brig. Gen. N. J. JACKSON,
Commanding First Division:

GENERAL: I am directed by the general commanding to say that Colonel Carman's brigade, of your division, will start for the river as soon as relieved to-morrow morning. That brigade will be relieved at daybreak by a brigade of General Ward's division.

Very respectfully, your obedient servant,

ROBT. P. DECHERT,
Captain and Acting Assistant Adjutant-General.

HEADQUARTERS TWENTIETH CORPS,
Near Savannah, Ga., December 15, 1864.

Brigadier-General JACKSON,
Commanding First Division:

GENERAL: The general commanding directs that you have all the pioneers now with your division and the tool wagons of the whole division accompany Colonel Carman's brigade to-morrow morning.

Very respectfully, your obedient servant,

H. W. PERKINS,
Assistant Adjutant-General.

HEADQUARTERS TWENTIETH CORPS,
Near Savannah, Ga., December 15, 1864.

Brig. Gen. W. T. WARD,
Commanding Third Division:

GENERAL: The general commanding directs that the brigade of your division now in reserve relieve Colonel Carman's brigade, of the First Division, to-morrow morning at daybreak.

Very respectfully, your obedient servant,

ROBT. P. DECHERT,
Captain and Acting Assistant Adjutant-General.

HEADQUARTERS THIRD BRIGADE,
In the Field, December 15, 1864.

Colonel ASMUSSEN:

SIR: The officer that I sent this morning to see about the connection between the Fourteenth Corps and the left of the Thirty-first Wisconsin has just returned, and reports that the connection heretofore was not fully made, but the evil has been remedied and the connection is now complete. Lieutenant-Colonel Rogers, brigade officer of the day, reported to Captain Reynolds on yesterday that the connection had been made, and Captain Reynolds so reported to me yesterday. I gave positive instructions to the brigade officers of the day upon the subject. It seems that the Thirty-first picketed to the swamp, refusing their left, and the Fourteenth to the swamp on the other side, refusing their right. The officer has measured the distance, and reports that the Fourteenth Corps cover this portion of the ground. I shall increase the detail from my brigade to-day in order to strengthen the entire line; it will in the future be 250 men. I have built breast-works in front of the Thirty-first Wisconsin, Sixty-first Ohio, One hundred and first Illinois, and Eighty-second Illinois. The two pieces of artillery are also protected by works on railroad and main wagon road.

Very truly,

J. S. ROBINSON,
Colonel, &c.

HDQRS. COAST DIVISION, DEPARTMENT OF THE SOUTH,
Deveaux's Neck, S. C., December 15, 1864—4.30 p. m.

Major-General FOSTER,
Commanding Department of the South:

GENERAL: I have just received your letter.* We will be ready to move as soon as possible, but you are aware that we cannot get off this strip of land in less than two days with the transportation we have. I do not think the enemy intend sending more re-enforcements to Savannah. One train got down yesterday and one to-day; no train has gone north either yesterday or to-day. A train came from toward Savannah last night and discharged at Coosawhatchie; it then returned. Night before last we killed the engineer and one fireman and disabled a train. We keep up a slow fire on the road, and fire briskly when a train attempts to pass. The force in front of me is small, not over 2,000, if the stories told by deserters are true. I think the road might be cut toward Pocotaligo without any serious mishap. Major Thomas is sending for all the launches and scows; I have directed Colonel Ransom to

---

*Not found.

send them. The 30-pounder Parrotts have, I think, got the range of the road. Our battery that is to open at 800 yards on the railroad is, I find, commanded by a battery 400 yards from it. I dare not open until I get a slashing cut through the wood, to enable my batteries in camp to play on that of the enemy; I intend then to capture it. The whole command turned out and cheered General Sherman last night about 9 o'clock. One of our scouts heard one of the rebels say, "Uncle Abe must have issued a new proclamation." Not bad. We will shut up the railroad by day after to-morrow, if not earlier. Kind regards to the madam.

Very respectfully, your obedient servant,

JNO. P. HATCH,
Brigadier-General.

Our right battery, deserters tell me, cut the rails in three places. The scouts, who can hear talk on the railroad, assure me that the employees are dissatisfied at having to pass us. I shall send Lieutenant Harrold, New York Engineers, down in arrest. He is worse than useless, as he fills a place that a decent sergeant might occupy to advantage.

J. P. H.

HEADQUARTERS DEPARTMENT OF THE SOUTH,
Hilton Head, S. C., December 15, 1864.

Lieut. Col. JOHN E. MULFORD,
Assistant Agent of Exchange:

COLONEL: I am directed by the major-general commanding to acknowledge the receipt of your dispatches and rebel papers, and to return you his thanks for the same. General Foster desires me to state that he is ready at any time for you to declare the truce at an end, and requests that you will inform Brigadier-General Schimmelfennig, commanding the Northern District, of the fact that hostilities may recommence at once. General Sherman has arrived. He called on General Foster on board the steamer Nemaha in the Ogeechee River about daylight yesterday morning. Fort McAllister, on the Ogeechee River, was assaulted by Hazen's division, of the Fifteenth Corps, and captured, with about 250 prisoners and 21 guns, with ammunition and stores. The Ogeechee River is now open to supplies for General Sherman's army. The railroads leading to Savannah are cut and the city invested, excepting the north side. General Sherman's army is in fine condition and in excellent spirits. They have lived on the country almost entirely during their march from Atlanta.

Very respectfully, your obedient servant,

W. L. M. BURGER,
Assistant Adjutant-General.

HEADQUARTERS DEPARTMENT OF THE SOUTH,
Hilton Head, S. C., December 15, 1864.

Brig. Gen. A. SCHIMMELFENNIG,
Commanding Northern District, Morris Island, S. C.:

GENERAL: The major-general commanding directs that as soon as Lieut. Col. John E. Mulford, assistant agent of exchange, notifies you that the truce is declared at an end, you may recommence hostilities, in accordance with a letter of instructions delivered to you when you retook command of the district. Those instructions were to fire only occasionally, as the War Department wishes to economize ammunition as much as possible.

W. L. M. BURGER,
Captain and Assistant Adjutant-General.

HEADQUARTERS DEPARTMENT OF THE SOUTH,
Hilton Head, S. C., December 15, 1864.

Col. P. P. BROWN, Jr.,
Fort Pulaski, Ga.:

COLONEL: Escaped Union prisoners just arrived from Columbia, S. C., report the following as the ration issued to our prisoners by the rebel authorities: Six (one pint) cups unbolted corn-meal every five days, one-half pint molasses per day, one-half pint rice occasionally for five days, three tablespoonfuls salt every five days, and no meat or grease whatever. You are, therefore, directed by the major-general commanding to furnish the prisoners now in your custody with rations in accordance with the above, giving them half a pound of bread in lieu of the rice, and issuing to them no meat or grease. You will acknowledge the receipt of this letter immediately upon its being received.

Very respectfully, your obedient servant,

W. L. M. BURGER,
Assistant Adjutant-General.

(Same letter, excepting the last sentence, sent to Capt. Joseph T. Pratt, provost-marshal, Hilton Head District.)

HEADQUARTERS DEPARTMENT OF THE SOUTH,
Hilton Head, S. C., December 15, 1864.

Col. P. P. BROWN, Jr.,
Fort Pulaski, Ga.:

COLONEL: I have the honor to acknowledge the receipt of your communication of the 12th instant in answer to the letter of censure sent you by direction of the major-general commanding. You state that the instructions mentioned in the letter failed to reach you, and request a copy to be sent that you may know in what particular you have erred. It is perfectly well understood by every officer in this department that these prisoners were sent here for the purpose of retaliation, to be treated in precisely the same manner that our prisoners are treated that are in the hands of the enemy, and for no other reasons whatever. Full instructions were sent you on the 4th ultimo for the care and management of these prisoners, and a corrected copy of your General Order, No. 11, which you were directed to issue and strictly enforce in place of the one you published. This letter alone contained sufficient instructions for your guidance in their management, and was thought to cover all the points. Duplicate copies of the letter and order are herewith inclosed. Instructions have been sent to you repeatedly, through the commanding officer of the district, in regard to the ration to be issued, &c. The letter was sent you, not only because you did not treat those prisoners in accordance with your instructions, but because you permitted yourself to be complimented by our enemies for conduct that that same enemy would scorn to bestow on our prisoners in their hands. The major-general commanding directs that you immediately acknowledge the receipt of this letter, and state whether you received the letter of instructions of November 4, with the corrected copy of your General Order, No. 11.

Very respectfully, your obedient servant,

W. L. M. BURGER,
Assistant Adjutant-General.

HEADQUARTERS MILITARY DIVISION OF THE MISSISSIPPI,
In the Field, near Savannah, December 16, 1864.

Lieut. Gen. U. S. GRANT,
Commander-in-Chief, City Point, Va.

GENERAL: I received day before yesterday, at the hands of Lieutenant Dunn, your letter of December 3, and last night, at the hands of Colonel Babcock, that of December 6. I had previously made you a hasty scrawl from the tug-boat Dandelion, in Ogeechee River, advising you that the army had reached the sea-coast, destroying all railroads across the State of Georgia and investing closely the city of Savannah, and had made connection with the fleet. Since writing that note I have in person met and conferred with General Foster and Admiral Dahlgren, and made all the arrangements which I deemed essential to reducing the city of Savannah to our possession. But since the receipt of yours of the 6th I have initiated measures looking principally to coming to you with 50,000 or 60,000 infantry, and, incidentally, to take Savannah, if time will allow. At the time we carried Fort McAllister by assault so handsomely, with its 22 guns and entire garrison, I was hardly aware of its importance; but since passing down the river with General Foster and up with Admiral Dahlgren I realize how admirably adapted are Ossabaw Sound and Ogeechee River to supply an army operating against Savannah. Sea-going vessels can easily come to King's Bridge, a point on Ogeechee River fourteen and a half miles west of Savannah, from which point we have roads leading to all our camps. The country is low and sandy, and cut up with marshes, which, in wet weather, will be very bad; but we have been so favored with weather that they are all now comparatively good, and heavy details are constantly employed in double corduroying the marshes, so that I have no fears even of a bad spell of weather. Fortunately, also, by liberal and judicious foraging, we reached the sea-coast abundantly supplied with forage and provisions, needing nothing on arrival except bread; of this, we started from Atlanta provided with from eight to twenty days' supply per corps, and some of the troops only had one days' issue of bread during the trip of thirty days; and yet they did not want, for sweet potatoes were very abundant, as well as corn meal, and our soldiers took to them naturally.

We started with about 5,000 head of cattle and arrived with over 10,000; of course, consuming mostly turkeys, chickens, sheep, hogs, and the cattle of the country. As to our mules and horses, we left Atlanta with about 2,500 wagons, many of which were drawn by mules, which had not recovered from the Chattanooga starvation, all of which were replaced, the poor mules shot, and our transportation is now in superb condition. I have no doubt the State of Georgia has lost by our operations 15,000 first rate mules. As to horses, Kilpatrick collected all his remounts, and it looks to me, in riding along our columns, as though every officer had three or four led horses, and each regiment seems to be followed by at least fifty negroes and foot-sore soldiers riding on horses and mules. The custom was for each brigade to send out daily a foraging party of about fifty men, on foot, who invariably returned mounted, with several wagons loaded with poultry, potatoes, &c.; and as the army is composed of about forty brigades you can estimate approximately the quantity of horses collected. Great numbers of these were shot by my order, because of the disorganizing effect on our infantry of having too many idlers mounted. General Easton is now engaged in collecting statistics in this line; but I know the Government will never receive full accounts of our captures, although the result aimed at was fully attained, viz., to deprive our enemy of them. All these animals I will have sent to Port Royal, or collected behind Fort McAllister, to be used by General Saxton in his farming operations, or by the quartermaster's department, after they are systematically accounted for. Whilst General Easton is collecting transportation for my troops to James River I will throw to Port Royal Island all our means of transportation I can, and collect the balance near Fort McAllister, covered by the Ogeechee River and intrenchments to be erected, and for which Captain Poe, my chief engineer, is now reconnoitering the ground; but in the meantime will act as I have begun, as though Savannah City was my objective, namely: the troops will continue to invest Savannah closely, making attacks and feints wherever we have firm ground to stand upon; and I will place some 30-pounder Parrotts, which I have got from General Foster, in position near enough to reach the center of the city, and then will demand its surrender. If General Hardee is alarmed or fears starvation he may surrender; otherwise, I will bombard the city, but not risk the lives of my men by assaults across the narrow causeways by which alone I can now reach it. If I had time, Savannah, with all its dependent fortifications, is already in our possession, for we hold all its avenues of supply. The enemy has made two desperate efforts to get boats from above to the city, in both of which he has been foiled—General Slocum, whose left flank rests on the river, capturing and burning the first boat, and in the second instance driving back two gun-boats and capturing the steamer Resolute, with seven naval officers and a crew of twenty-five seamen.

General Slocum occupies Argyle Island and the upper end of Hutchinson's Island, and has a brigade on the South Carolina shore opposite, and he is very urgent to pass one of his corps over to that shore; but, in view of the change of plans made necessary by your order of the 6th, I will maintain things in statu quo till I have got all my transportation to the rear and out of the way, and until I have sea transportation for the troops you require at James River, which I will accompany and command in person. Of course I will leave Kilpatrick with his cavalry, say 5,300, and it may be a division of the Fifteenth Corps; but before determining this I must see General Foster, and may arrange to shift his force (now over above the Charleston railroad, at the head of Broad River) to the Ogeechee, where, in co-operation with Kilpatrick's cavalry, he can better threaten the State of Georgia than from the direction of Port Royal. Besides, I would much prefer not to detach from my regular corps any of its veteran divisions, and would even prefer that other less valuable troops should be sent to re-enforce Foster from some other quarter. My four corps, full of experience and full of ardor, coming to you en masse, equal to 60,000 fighting men, will be a re-enforcement that Lee cannot disregard. Indeed, with my present command, I had expected upon reducing Savannah instantly to march to Columbia, S. C., thence to Raleigh, and thence to report to you; but this would consume, it may be, six weeks time after the fall of Savannah, whereas by sea I can probably reach you with my men and arms before the middle of January.

I myself am somewhat astonished at the attitude of things in Tennessee. I purposely delayed at Kingston until General Thomas assured me that he was "all ready," and my last dispatch from him, of the 12th of November, was full of confidence, in which he promised me that he would "ruin Hood," if he dared to advance from Florence, urging me to go ahead and give myself no concern about Hood's army in Tennessee. Why he did not turn on Hood at Franklin, after checking and discomfiting him, surpasses my understanding. Indeed, I do not approve of his evacuating Decatur, but think he should have assumed the offensive against Hood from Pulaski in the direction of Waynesburg [Waynesborough]. I know full well that General Thomas is slow in mind and in action, but he is judicious and brave, and the troops feel great confidence in him. I still hope he will out-maneuver and destroy Hood.

As to matters in the Southeast, I think Hardee, in Savannah, has good artillerists, some 5,000 or 6,000 infantry, and it may be a mongrel mass of 8,000 to 10,000 militia and fragments. In all our marching through Georgia he has not forced me to use anything but a skirmish line, though at several points he had erected fortifications and tried to alarm us by bombastic threats. In Savannah he has taken refuge behind a line constructed behind swamps and overflowed rice fields, extending from a point on the Savannah River about three miles above the city around by a branch of the Little Ogeechee, which stream is impassable from its salt marshes and boggy swamps, crossed only by narrow causeways or common corduroy roads. There must be 25,000 citizens—men, women, and children—in Savannah that must also be fed, and how he is to feed them beyond a few days I cannot imagine, as I know that his requisitions for corn on the interior counties were not filled, and we are in possession of the rice fields and mills which could alone be of service to him in this neighborhood. He can draw nothing from South Carolina, save from a small corner down in the southeast, and that by a disused wagon road. I could easily get possession of this, but hardly deem it worth the risk of making a detachment, which would be in danger by its isolation from the main army.

Our whole army is in fine condition as to health, and the weather is splendid; for that reason alone, I feel a personal dislike to turning northward. I will keep Lieutenant Dunn here until I know the result of my demand for the surrender of Savannah; but, whether successful or not, shall not delay my execution of your order of the 6th, which will depend alone upon the time it will require to obtain transportation by sea.

I am, with respect, &c., your obedient servant,

W. T. SHERMAN,
Major-General, U. S. Army.

HEADQUARTERS OF THE ARMY,
Washington, December 16, 1864. (Via Hilton Head.)

Major-General SHERMAN:

GENERAL: Lieutenant-General Grant informs me that in his last dispatch sent to you he suggested the transfer of your infantry to Richmond. He now wishes me to say that you will retain your entire force, at least for the present, and with such assistance as may be given you by General Foster and Admiral Dahlgren, operate from such base as you may establish on the coast. General Foster will obey such instructions as may be given by you. Should you have captured Savannah, it is thought that by transferring the water batteries to the land side, that place may be made a good depot and base for operations on Augusta, Branchville, or Charleston. If Savannah should not be captured, or if captured and not deemed suitable for this purpose, perhaps Beaufort would serve as a depot. As the rebels have probably removed their most valuable property from Augusta, perhaps Branchville would be the most important point at which to strike, in order to sever all connection between Virginia and the Southwestern Railroad. General Grant's wishes, however, are that this whole matter of your future action should be entirely left to your discretion. We can send you from here a number of complete batteries of field artillery, with or without horses, as you may desire. Also, as soon as General Thomas can spare them, all the fragments, convalescents, and furloughed men of your army. It is reported that Thomas defeated Hood yesterday near Nashville, but we have no particulars nor official reports, telegraphic communication being interrupted by a heavy storm. Our last advices from you was General Howard's note announcing his approach to Savannah.

Yours, truly,

H. W. HALLECK,
Major-General and Chief of Staff.

HEADQUARTERS MILITARY DIVISION OF THE MISSISSIPPI,
King's Bridge, December 16, 1864.

Maj. Gen. W. T. SHERMAN:

GENERAL: The mail-boat and General Foster's steamer, neither capable of carrying any freight, are the only vessels that have arrived here as yet. These boats report only six feet water on the bars below this place at low tide. I fear the steamers and other vessels below, which contain our supplies, draw too much water to get up. I will go down the river in the morning and lighten up the transports, and do everything else that can be done to get supplies to this point.

Very respectfully, your obedient servant,

L. C. EASTON,
Chief Quartermaster.

SPECIAL FIELD ORDERS, No. 133.

HDQRS. MIL. DIV. OF THE MISSISSIPPI,
In the Field, near Savannah, Ga., December 16, 1864.

I. Capt. O. M. Poe, chief engineer, will cause all the railroads leading out of Savannah to be most thoroughly destroyed—the Charleston road as far as and, if possible, including the bridge over Savannah River; the Macon road as far as Station $1\frac{1}{2}$; and the Gulf road as far as and including the Ogeechee River bridge.

II. Major-General Howard will dispatch two divisions, without wagons, to destroy the Gulf road as far as the Altamaha River bridge, and exhaust the country in that direction of supplies. General Kilpatrick with his cavalry will cover this working force, and co-operate with it.

III. The depot of supplies is for the present at King's Bridge. General Easton, chief quartermaster, may use his discretion in landing supplies at Fort McAllister and the rice mill.

IV. Army commanders will forthwith send to General Easton, chief quartermaster, at King's Bridge, all negroes, horses, mules, and wagons rendered surplus by our change in operations, or to such points on the Ogeechee River as General Easton may indicate, in order that they may be sent to Port Royal Island, where they can be more easily supplied; they will also avail themselves of the present favorable weather to bring forward ten days' food, and will reserve for that purpose enough wagons to handle them; all other wagons must be sent to the Ogeechee River as soon as possible.

By order of Maj. Gen. W. T. Sherman:

L. M. DAYTON,
Aide-de-Camp.

SPECIAL FIELD ORDERS, No. 196.

HEADQUARTERS DEPARTMENT AND ARMY OF THE TENNESSEE,
Near Savannah, Ga., December 16, 1864.

I. In accordance with directions from Major-General Sherman, commanding Military Division of the Mississippi, the Gulf railroad from the Ogeechee to and including the bridge over the Altamaha will, in the most thorough and complete manner, be immediately destroyed. To this end Major-General Osterhaus will direct Brigadier-General Hazen, commanding Second Division, to place his command, except such portion thereof as is charged with the garrisoning of Fort McAllister, in convenient proximity to the railroad, and to him will be intrusted the destruction of the road for twenty miles out from the Ogeechee. Major-General Blair, commanding Seventeenth Army Corps, will send one division, without transportation and without artillery (except one section), to commence at a point twenty miles out from the Ogeechee, and, in concert with General Kilpatrick's cavalry, destroy the road to and including the bridge over the Altamaha. Five days' time is given to complete this destruction, which must be most thorough, every tie to be burned and every rail twisted.

* * * * * * *

By order of Maj. Gen. O. O. Howard:

SAML. L. TAGGART,
Assistant Adjutant-General.

SPECIAL ORDERS, No. 199.

HDQRS. FIFTEENTH ARMY CORPS,
Anderson's Plantation, Ga., December 16, 1864.

I. Brig. Gen. W. B. Hazen will place his command, except such portion thereof as is charged with the garrisoning of Fort McAllister and King's Bridge, in convenient proximity to the railroad. To this command will be assigned the duty of destroying the Gulf railroad to a point twenty miles out from the Ogeechee. The destruction must be most thorough, every tie to be burned and every rail twisted. The railroad, from a point twenty miles out to Altamaha bridge, will be destroyed by a division of the Seventeenth Corps, in concert with General Kilpatrick's cavalry. The troops will move as light as possible and without trains. The artillery at King's Bridge will be directed to report at these headquarters.

* * * * * * *

By order of Maj. Gen. P. Joseph Osterhaus:

F. F. WHITEHEAD,
Assistant Adjutant-General.

FORT MCALLISTER, GA., *December 16, 1864.*
(Received 12 m.)

General SHERMAN, or HOWARD:

Transports with rations have arrived below the fort. I have ordered one to be brought to the fort wharf. If any command is pressed they can send by land via King's Bridge.

HAZEN,
Brigadier-General.

HEADQUARTERS MILITARY DIVISION OF THE MISSISSIPPI,
In the Field, near Savannah, Ga., December 16, 1864.

General HAZEN,
Fort McAllister:

General Sherman directs that the vessels having supplies for this army be sent to King's Bridge. General Easton and Colonel Beckwith are there to receive them.

Very respectfully, your obedient servant,

L. M. DAYTON,
Aide-de-Camp.

GENERAL ORDERS, No. 70. } HDQRS. SECOND DIV., 15TH ARMY CORPS,
Fort McAllister, Ga., December 16, 1864.

In compliance with Special Orders, No. 199, from headquarters Fifteenth Army Corps, each brigade of this division, leaving one regiment in camp, will prepare to march, without wagons, to destroy the Gulf railroad, as follows: The Second Brigade from Walthourville east to a point two miles east of McIntosh; the Third Brigade from a point two miles east of McIntosh to the crossing of the railroad with the Medway or Saint Catherine River; the First Brigade from the Saint Catherine River to the Ogeechee.

It will be seen by the order referred to from corps headquarters that the work should be done in the most thorough manner, every tie burned and every rail twisted.

By order of Brig. Gen. W. B. Hazen:

G. LOFLAND,
Captain and Assistant Adjutant-General.

HEADQUARTERS SEVENTEENTH ARMY CORPS,
Near Savannah, Ga., December 16, 1864.

Capt. SAMUEL L. TAGGART,
Assistant Adjutant-General, Dept. and Army of the Tennessee:

CAPTAIN: I have the honor to report that, by orders received direct from Major-General Sherman, I have sent Major-General Mower's division to destroy the Gulf road from Station 3 to the Altamaha River, and one brigade of General Smith's division to King's Bridge to unload transports.

Very respectfully, your obedient servant,

FRANK P. BLAIR, JR.,
Major-General.

SPECIAL ORDERS, No. 308. } HDQRS. SEVENTEENTH ARMY CORPS,
Near Savannah, Ga., December 16, 1864.

I. Brig. Gen. G. A. Smith, commanding Fourth Division, will send the First Brigade of his command, Col. B. F. Potts commanding, to encamp at King's Bridge. They will proceed there forthwith, and report to General Easton, chief quartermaster Military Division of the Mississippi.

II. Lieut. Col. A. Hickenlooper, assistant inspector-general, Seventeenth Army Corps, is hereby placed in charge of the building of the wharf at King's Bridge. The First Missouri Engineers, Lieutenant-Colonel Tweeddale commanding, will report to him for orders.

III. In compliance with Special Field Orders, No. 196, department headquarters (copy inclosed),* Major-General Mower, commanding First Division, will move the two brigades of his command now in camp to a point twenty miles west of the Ogeechee River, on the Gulf road, and will, in concert with General Kilpatrick, destroy the road from there to and including the bridge over the Altamaha River. He will take with him one section of artillery, and will leave in camp his transportation, moving as lightly as possible. He will take three days' rations, and will live as far as possible off the country.

* * * * * * *

V. Col. George E. Spencer, commanding First Alabama Cavalry, will, at 7 a. m. to-morrow, move out on the road to Station 3, on the Gulf railroad, and on overtaking Maj. Gen. J. A. Mower, commanding First Division, will report to him, and be subject to his orders during the time General Mower is absent destroying the road.

* * * * * * *

By command of Maj. Gen. F. P. Blair:

C. CADLE, JR.,
Assistant Adjutant-General.

HEADQUARTERS SEVENTEENTH ARMY CORPS,
Near Savannah, Ga., December 16, 1864.

Maj. Gen. J. A. MOWER,
Commanding First Division:

GENERAL: The major-general commanding directs me to say to you that you will have to proceed without rations. You will be able to procure plenty in the section to which you are going. You may take six wagons of infantry ammunition. It will be necessary to return within the time limited, and to expedite the destruction of the road you can send the First Alabama Cavalry to the other end to do the work.

Very respectfully, your obedient servant,

C. CADLE, JR.,
Assistant Adjutant-General.

---

* See p. 730.

SPECIAL ORDERS, } HDQRS. FIRST DIV., 17TH ARMY CORPS,
No. 170. } *Near Savannah, Ga., December 16, 1864.*

I. In accordance with Special Orders, No. 308, headquarters Seventeenth Army Corps, of this date, the First Brigade, Brig. Gen. J. W. Fuller commanding, and the Third Brigade, Col. John Tillson commanding, and one section of Battery C, First Michigan Artillery, of this command, will be prepared to march immediately. The troops will move light. One ambulance and one wagon will be taken by each regiment. The artillery will take one wagon-load of ammunition. No other wagons allowed. Three days' rations will be drawn upon the arrival of the troops at the river.

* * * * * * *

III. Lieut. William E. Ells, acting commissary of subsistence of this division, will remain back in his present camp; but should supplies arrive here for the troops within five days from this date he will bring the necessary supplies forward to this command wherever it may be on the Gulf railroad.

By order of Maj. Gen. Joseph A. Mower:

CHAS. CHRISTENSEN,
Lieut., Aide-de-Camp, and Acting Assistant Adjutant-General.

HDQRS. DEPARTMENT AND ARMY OF THE TENNESSEE,
Near Savannah, Ga., December 16, 1864.

Col. THOMAS CURLY,
Commanding at Cheves' Mill:

The major-general commanding directs me to instruct you to cause to be procured from the Cheves' and all other plantations on the river between Fort McAllister and King's Bridge all the small boats of whatsoever description you can find, and send them to King's Bridge, to report to Lieutenant-Colonel Hickenlooper, of General Blair's staff, or officer in charge of construction of wharves at that point, with as little delay as possible. Should there be more boats at Fort McAllister than are necessary for use at that place you will take them also.

Very respectfully, your obedient servant,

SAML. L. TAGGART,
Assistant Adjutant-General.

HEADQUARTERS FOURTEENTH ARMY CORPS,
December 16, 1864.

Brigadier-General MORGAN,
Commanding Second Division, Fourteenth Army Corps:

GENERAL: General Carlin reports that the enemy is working to establish a battery within range of the right of your picket-line, and that your pickets report that they could dislodge the working party if they had not orders to hold their fire. Please give orders to your pickets to stop this work, if it prove true that the work being erected is within range.

Yours, very respectfully,

JEF. C. DAVIS,
Brevet Major-General, Commanding.

[Indorsement.]

HDQRS. SECOND BRIG., SECOND DIV., 14TH ARMY CORPS,
Near Savannah, Ga., December 16, 1864.

Respectfully returned to Brig. Gen. James D. Morgan, with the statement that the pickets of this brigade have at no time been ordered to hold their fire at all times, but, on the contrary, to fire upon the enemy whenever, in their judgment, their fire could be made effective and good accomplished.

I have the honor to be, general, very respectfully, your obedient servant,

JOHN S. PEARCE,
Lieutenant-Colonel, Commanding Brigade.

HEADQUARTERS TWENTIETH CORPS,
Near Savannah, Ga., December 16, 1864.

Col. E. A. CARMAN,
Commanding Brigade:

COLONEL: The brigadier-general commanding the corps directs that you cross your command to the South Carolina side of the Savannah River to-morrow morning. You will commence the movement before daylight. He directs that you use at first, until a sufficient number of troops have been crossed to drive away or silence the battery, only the small boats; as soon as it is safe to do so, you will use the flat-boats and barges. He further directs that you have the second piece of artillery crossed to-night and put in position near where the one is that was crossed to-day. He also directs that you have all the flat-boats, barges, &c., taken around to the north side of the island to-night, so that they may be in readiness to cross the troops. He also directs that, after you have crossed, you occupy and hold a position near the river, not attempting to advance far into the country.

Very respectfully, your obedient servant,

H. W. PERKINS,
Assistant Adjutant-General.

HEADQUARTERS TWENTIETH CORPS,
Near Savannah, Ga., December 16, 1864.

Brigadier-General JACKSON,
Commanding First Division:

GENERAL: In accordance with directions from the brigadier-general commanding the corps, the order for Colonel Carman to cross his brigade to the South Carolina side of the Savannah River to-morrow morning is hereby countermanded. The general commanding directs that you have him send over a force of 90 or 100 men, in small boats, to effect a lodgment, if possible, and feel the enemy's position. He wishes him to take only such force as can be readily brought back in case the enemy is too strong for them. He also desires that Colonel Carman will send reconnoitering parties up the island, to examine the country and channel, and see if a crossing can be effected farther up the river; it may, perhaps, be well to send a small boat or two with this party. The two pieces of artillery will be put in position near the mill, as directed in the former order. The general desires to have one-half of the flat-boats brought to this side of the island, the other half to be kept on the north side, in the vicinity of the mill, where they can be sheltered as much as possible.

I am, general, very respectfully, your obedient servant,

H. W. PERKINS,
Assistant Adjutant-General.

HDQRS. SECOND BRIG., FIRST DIV., TWENTIETH CORPS,
Argyle Island, Ga., December 16, 1864.

Lieut. GEORGE ROBINSON,
Acting Assistant Adjutant-General:

SIR: I have the honor to report, that I have made my arrangements to cross my brigade to the main South Carolina shore, if deemed advisable. General Jackson desired me to advance my skirmishers on the enemy at daybreak; and, I understood him to say, to support it with two or three regiments, if deemed advisable. I would respectfully ask, if I succeed in getting a lodgment with my skirmishers and two regiments, if I am to cross my whole brigade without further orders, or act on my judgment?

I am, very respectfully,

E. A. CARMAN,
Colonel, Commanding Brigade.

CIRCULAR.] HDQRS. 2D BRIG., 1ST DIV., 20TH ARMY CORPS,
Argyle Island, Ga., December 16, 1864.

This command will be in readiness to move at 4.30 a. m. to-morrow. Col. William Hawley, Third Wisconsin Volunteers, and Col. William Cogswell, Second Massachusetts Volunteers, will each detail one commissioned officer and fifty enlisted men, under command of a competent officer from the Third Wisconsin Volunteers who is acquainted with the country on the north side of the river, to cross in small boats at 5 a. m. precisely; they will act as skirmishers. The Third Wisconsin Volunteers, Second Massachusetts Volunteers, One hundred and fiftieth New York Volunteers, One hundred and seventh New York Volunteers, and Thirteenth New Jersey Volunteers will follow in barges in the order named. Each regiment will carry two axes and twenty shovels. Regiments that are not already supplied can procure the tools by sending to these headquarters early in the morning. Col. William Hawley, Third Wisconsin Volunteers, will report to the commanding officer of the brigade, at 5 a. m. to-morrow, as commanding officer of the advance.

By command of Col. E. A. Carman, commanding brigade:

J. R. LINDSAY,
Captain and Acting Assistant Adjutant-General.

HEADQUARTERS DEPARTMENT OF THE SOUTH,
Steamer Nemaha, Ogeechee River, Ga., December 16, 1864.

Major-General SHERMAN,
Commanding:

GENERAL: On my way up to-day I sounded the river, obtained two good pilots, one of whom is on the Island City, and removed a pier and the burnt rubbish of the railroad bridge so as to permit vessels to pass. Between that bridge and this point there is only seven feet of water at high water; up to the railroad bridge from the mouth of the river there is ten feet of water at low water. All the vessels with supplies may come to the railroad bridge, but from there to this point lighters must be used, except at high water, when the light-draught steamers may come up. The siege battery of 30-pounder Parrotts is in the river, three pieces on the steamer Sylph and three more on another steamer. Forage is also here on vessels, both steam and sailing. Two large steamers and one schooner with commissary stores are also in the river coming up. In going down I will endeavor to pick up on the plantations pilots enough to place one on each vessel, if possible, and hurry them up. All of them should arrive at the railroad bridge at noon to-morrow. The Sylph is of light-draught, and can come directly here and land the 30-pounder Parrotts at the landing. I shall leave as soon as the water rises sufficiently to proceed directly to Hilton Head, to send a steamer to Fortress Monroe with Lieutenant-Colonel Babcock. After that I shall return at once.

Respectfully, yours,

J. G. FOSTER,
Major-General, Commanding.

CITY POINT, VA., *December 17, 1864.*

Lieutenant-General GRANT:

The Richmond papers of to-day contain the following:

FROM GEORGIA—SHERMAN'S MOVEMENTS.

The Augusta Register, received this morning, says that it was stated in that city on the 13th that the Federals have possession of the Savannah, Albany and Gulf Railroad. It is also said that they captured a passenger train on the same. Among the persons taken was R. R. Cuyler, esq., the president of the road. It is also reported that the Yankees have possession of the Charleston and Savannah Railroad bridge over the Savannah River. The Charleston Mercury of the day before says that, meantime, Sherman has been pressing steadily toward the city; our forces had fallen back to the junction of the Georgia Central and Charleston and Savannah Railroad, about three miles from the city. At this important point, which commands both roads, General Hardee took his stand. It was confidently reported yesterday, and we think, that Sherman's forces were in Hardee's front, and that a demand for the surrender of the city having been refused, heavy fighting ensued, and was going on yesterday. Of the result, however, if any, no news whatever has reached us. We may hear something to-day. The community of Savannah seem firm and quiet. For the present, the trains will cease to run through between the two cities. General Gartrell states that for several days he observed frequent signals between the Federal forces toward Port Royal and Sherman's forces in the direction of Sister's Ferry, on the Savannah railroad. The impression of the South was that Sherman was crossing at the ferry, and would co-operate with Foster's forces in opening the way to Port Royal.

The Dispatch, speaking of the raid into Southwest Virginia, says that:

Information was received here yesterday that the main body had left the railroad at Glade's Spring and started toward the salt-works, six miles distant; and that the smaller party, previously mentioned, had passed Marion and were advancing on Wytheville, which is fifty-five miles this side of Abingdon. The object of this party is doubtless to break up the railroad, and thereby prevent re-enforcements from being sent from the east to our troops at the salt-works. They will, of course, destroy as much property as possible along their route.

JNO. A. RAWLINS,
Brigadier-General and Chief of Staff.

HEADQUARTERS MILITARY DIVISION OF THE MISSISSIPPI,
In the Field, near Savannah, Ga., December 17, 1864.

General WILLIAM J. HARDEE,
Commanding Confederate Forces in Savannah:

GENERAL: You have doubtless observed from your station at Rosedew that sea-going vessels now come through Ossabaw Sound and up Ogeechee to the rear of my army, giving me abundant supplies of all kinds, and more especially heavy ordnance necessary to the reduction of Savannah. I have already received guns that can cast heavy and destructive shot as far as the heart of your city; also, I have for some days held and controlled every avenue by which the people and garrison of Savannah can be supplied; and I am therefore justified in demanding the surrender of the city of Savannah and its dependent forts, and shall await a reasonable time your answer before opening with heavy ordnance. Should you entertain the preposition I am prepared to grant liberal terms to the inhabitants and garrison; but should I be forced to resort to assault, and the slower and surer process of starvation, I shall then feel justified in resorting to the harshest measures, and shall make little effort to restrain my army—burning to avenge a great national wrong they attach to Savannah and other large cities which have been so prominent in dragging our country into civil war. I inclose you a copy of General Hood's demand for the surrender of the town of Resaca, to be used by you for what it is worth.

I have the honor to be, your obedient servant,

W. T. SHERMAN,
Major-General.

[Inclosure.]

HEADQUARTERS ARMY OF TENNESSEE,
In the Field, October 12, 1864.

TO THE OFFICER COMMANDING U. S. FORCES AT RESACA, GA.:

SIR: I demand the immediate and unconditional surrender of the post and garrison under your command, and should this be acceded to, all white officers and soldiers will be paroled in a few days. If the place is carried by assault no prisoners will be taken.

Most respectfully, your obedient servant,

J. B. HOOD,
General.

HDQRS. DEPT. OF S. CAROLINA, GEORGIA, AND FLORIDA,
Savannah, Ga., December 17, 1864.

Maj. Gen. W. T. SHERMAN,
Commanding Federal Forces, near Savannah, Ga.:

GENERAL: I have to acknowledge receipt of a communication from you of this date, in which you demand "the surrender of Savannah and its dependent forts," on the ground that you have "received guns that can cast heavy and destructive shot into the heart of the city," and for the further reason that you "have for some days held and controlled every avenue by which the people and garrison can be supplied." You add that should you be "forced to resort to assault, or to the slower and surer process of starvation, you will then feel justified in resorting to the harshest measures, and will make little effort to restrain your army," &c. The position of your forces, a half a mile beyond the outer line for the land defenses of Savannah, is, at the nearest point, at least four miles from the heart of the city. That and the interior line are both intact. Your statement that you "have for some days held and controlled every avenue by which the people and garrison can be supplied" is incorrect. I am in free and constant communication with my department. Your demand for the surrender of Savannah and its dependent forts is refused. With respect to the threats conveyed in the closing paragraphs of your letter, of what may be expected in case your demand is not complied with, I have to say that I have hitherto conducted the military operations intrusted to my direction in strict accordance with the rules of civilized warfare, and I should deeply regret the adoption of any course by you that may force me to deviate from them in future.

I have the honor to be, very respectfully, your obedient servant,

W. J. HARDEE,
Lieutenant-General.

HEADQUARTERS FIFTEENTH ARMY CORPS,
Anderson's Plantation, Ga., December 17, 1864.

Brig. Gen. C. R. WOODS,
Commanding First Division, Fifteenth Army Corps:

GENERAL: You will cause a detail to be made from your command for the purpose of covering that portion of the Savannah road corduroyed by pioneer corps with at least six inches of sand, &c. The road being a double one, the task of the several divisions will be as follows: To the First Division will be assigned the north side of the road as far as the bridge; to the Fourth Division the south side to the bridge; and to the Third Division that portion of the road corduroyed beyond the bridge; and also an officer of pioneer corps to superintend the extra working detail.

By order of Maj. Gen. P. Joseph Osterhaus:

F. F. WHITEHEAD,
Assistant Adjutant-General.

HEADQUARTERS FOURTEENTH ARMY CORPS,
Before Savannah, Ga., December 17, 1864.

Brig. Gen. A. BAIRD,
Commanding Third Division, Fourteenth Army Corps:

The general commanding directs that you detail a large regiment from your command, with instructions to support and protect the First Michigan Engineers while engaged in tearing up the railroad above Station No. 1 (or Pooler), on the Georgia Central Railroad. Major Yates, the commanding officer of the First Michigan Engineers, will be found at or near Pooler. The commanding officer of the regiment detailed will see and consult with him in regard to position.

I have the honor to be, general, very respectfully, your obedient servant,

A. C. McCLURG,
Assistant Adjutant-General and Chief of Staff.

FORT MONROE, VA., *December 17, 1864—7.30 a. m.*
(Received 10.40 a. m.)

Maj. Gen. H. W. HALLECK,
Chief of Staff:

I have the honor to report my arrival here this morning at 5 o'clock, with dispatches from Sherman and Foster. I send you in cipher a telegram from Foster. I will be in Washington this p. m. with full and detailed dispatches from General Sherman.

JNO. F. ANDERSON,
Major and Additional Aide-de-Camp, Staff of General Foster.

HDQRS. COAST DIVISION, DEPARTMENT OF THE SOUTH,
Deveaux's Neck, S. C., December 17, 1864.

[Major-General FOSTER,
Commanding Department of the South:]

GENERAL: One train passed up yesterday morning; it consisted of two passenger and one freight car. We got a battery into position last night bearing on the bridge; have not opened with it, as we hope to catch a train crossing this morning. The enemy have but four regiments opposite me; they have also one at Pocotaligo. A train was lying all day yesterday below Coosawhatchie, but out of sight; it would move when we threw shells into the woods. No deserters this morning.

Very respectfully, your obedient servant,

JNO. P. HATCH,
Brigadier-General, Commanding.

HDQRS. NORTHERN DISTRICT, DEPT. OF THE SOUTH,
FIRST SEPARATE BRIGADE,
Morris Island, S. C., December 17, 1864.

Capt. W. L. M. BURGER,
Assistant Adjutant-General, Department of the South:

CAPTAIN: I have the honor to inform you that the truce existing in Charleston Harbor, for the purpose of exchange of prisoners, terminated to-day at 10 a. m. by mutual agreement. Instructions to that effect were furnished me by Lieutenant-Colonel Mulford, a copy of which I have the honor to annex. There is nothing further of importance to communicate. The enemy remain quiet, as well as myself, not a shot having been fired on either side since I assumed command. A small regiment returned on the 14th, passing from John's Island over the bridge to James Island. They are probably the Forty-seventh Georgia, as the men were heard conversing in loud tones during the following night in the camp of that regiment. The only quarter in which the enemy exhibits increased activity is in the vicinity of the batteries on John's Island, which have been erected for the purpose of covering the bridge which crosses to Fort Pringle. About 200 men, infantry, four heavy pieces of artillery, and a wagon train were observed yesterday crossing Stono River from James to John's Island, marching in a westerly direction. The guard at Charleston proper has been re-enforced by one company of infantry and one company of cavalry, which latter is doing outpost duty north of Charleston at the distance of several miles (intercepted dispatch). I have found the forts in good condition and the guns fully provided with ammunition, having from 100 to 200 rounds per gun on hand; but the position has been weakened to a certain extent, from the fact that all the booms in Light-House Inlet, as well as in Secessionville Creek, have been carried away, and have not been replaced. With regard to offensive operations, I have to state that the planking intended for the completion of the plankway across the marsh on Morris Island, and that which was provided for the flooring of the bridge to cross from Cole's to James Island, have been used for other purposes.

I have to acknowledge the receipt of your two communications dated December 14 and 15; the former with regard to the arrival of General Sherman, and the latter touching the commencement of hostilities at the expiration of the truce.

I have the honor to be, captain, very respectfully, your obedient servant,

A. SCHIMMELFENNIG,
Brigadier-General, Commanding District.

CONFIDENTIAL.] HDQRS. ARMIES OF THE UNITED STATES,
Washington, D. C., December 18, 1864.

Maj. Gen. WILLIAM T. SHERMAN,
Commanding Military Division of the Mississippi:

MY DEAR GENERAL: I have just received and read, I need not tell you with how much gratification, your letter to General Halleck. I congratulate you and the brave officers and men under your command on the successful termination of your most brilliant campaign. I never had a doubt of the result. When apprehensions for your safety were expressed by the President, I assured him, with the army you had, and you in command of it, there was no danger but you would strike bottom on salt water some place; that I would not feel the same security—in fact, would not have entrusted the expedition to any other living commander. It has been very hard work to get Thomas to attack Hood. I gave him the most peremptory order, and had started to go there myself before he got off. He has done magnificently, however, since he started. Up to last night 5,000 prisoners and 49 pieces of captured artillery, besides many wagons and innumerable small arms, had been received in Nashville. This is exclusive of the enemy's loss at Franklin, which amounted to 13 general officers killed, wounded, and captured. The enemy probably lost 5,000 men at Franklin, and 10,000 in the last three days' operations. Breckinridge is said to be making for Murfreesborough; if so, he is in a most excellent place. Stoneman has nearly wiped out John Morgan's old command, and five days ago entered Bristol. I did think the best thing to do was to bring the greater part of your army here and wipe out Lee. The turn affairs now seem to be taking has shaken me in that opinion. I doubt whether you may not accomplish more toward that result where you are than if brought here, especially as I am informed since my arrival in the city that it would take about two months to get you here, with all the other calls there are for ocean transportation. I want to get your views about what ought to be done and what can be done. If you capture the garrison of Savannah it certainly will compel Lee to detach from Richmond, or give us nearly the whole South. My own opinion is that Lee is averse to going out of Virginia, and if the cause of the South is lost he wants Richmond to be the last place surrendered. If he has such views it may be well to indulge him until everything else is in our hands.

Congratulating you and the army again upon the splendid result of your campaign, the like of which is not read of in past history, I subscribe myself, more than ever, if possible,

Your friend,

U. S. GRANT,
Lieutenant-General.

HEADQUARTERS OF THE ARMY,
Washington, December 18, 1864. (Via Hilton Head.)

Maj. Gen. W. T. SHERMAN,
Savannah:

MY DEAR GENERAL: Yours of the 13th, by Major Anderson, is just received. I congratulate you on your splendid success, and shall very soon expect to hear of the crowning work of your new campaign in the capture of Savannah. Your march will stand out prominently as the great one of this great war. When Savannah falls, then for another raid south through the center of the Confederacy. But I will not anticipate. General Grant is expected here this morning, and will probably write you his own views. I do not learn from your letter or from Major Anderson that you are in want of anything which we have not provided at Hilton Head. Thinking it possible that you might want more field artillery, I had prepared several batteries, but the great difficulty of foraging horses on the coast will prevent our sending any unless you actually need them. The hay crop this year is short, and the Quartermaster's Department has great difficulty in procuring a supply for our animals. General Thomas has defeated Hood near Nashville, and it is hoped that he will completely crush his army. Breckinridge, at last accounts, was trying to form a junction near Murfreesborough; but as Thomas is between them Breckinridge must either retreat or be defeated. General Rosecrans made very bad work of it in Missouri, allowing Price with a small force to overrun the State and destroy millions of property. Orders have been issued for all officers and detachments having three months or more to serve to rejoin your army via Savannah; those having less than three months to serve will be retained by General Thomas. Should you capture Charleston, I hope that by some accident the place may be destroyed, and if a little salt should be sown upon its site it may prevent the growth of future crops of nullification and secession.

Yours, truly,

H. W. HALLECK,
Major-General and Chief of Staff.

HEADQUARTERS MILITARY DIVISION OF THE MISSISSIPPI,
In the Field, near Savannah, Ga., December 18, 1864—8 p. m.

Lieut. Gen. U. S. GRANT,
City Point, Va.:

GENERAL: I wrote you at length by Colonel Babcock on the 16th instant. As I therein explained my purpose, yesterday I made a demand on General Hardee for the surrender of the city of Savannah, and to-day received his answer, refusing. Copies of both letters are herewith inclosed.* You will notice that I claim that my lines are within easy cannon range of the heart of Savannah, but General Hardee claims we are four miles and a half distant. But I, myself, have been to the intersection of the Charleston and Georgia Central railroads, and the three-mile post is but a few yards beyond, within the line of our pickets. The enemy has no pickets outside of his fortified line, which is a full quarter of a mile within the three-mile post, and I have the evidence of Mr. R. R. Cuyler, president of the Georgia Central Railroad, who was a prisoner in our hands, that the mile posts are measured from the Exchange, which is but two squares back from the river. But by to-morrow morning I will have six 30-pounder Parrotts in position, and General Hardee will learn whether I am right or not. From the left of our line, which is on the Savannah River, the spires can be plainly seen, but the country is so densely wooded with pine and live oak, and lies so flat, that we can see nothing from any other part of our lines. General Slocum feels confident that he can make a successful assault at one or two points in front of the Twentieth Corps, and one or two in front of General Davis' (Fourteenth) Corps. But all of General Howard's troops, the Right Wing, lie behind the Little Ogeechee, and I doubt if it can be passed by troops in the face of an enemy; still, we can make strong feints, and if I can get a sufficient number of boats I shall make a co-operative demonstration up Vernon River or Wassaw Sound. I should like very much indeed to take Savannah before coming to you; but, as I wrote to you before, I will do nothing rash or hasty, and will embark for the James River as soon as General Easton, who has gone to Port Royal for that purpose, reports to me that he has an approximate number of vessels for the transportation of the contemplated force. I fear even this will cost more delay than you anticipate, for already the movement of our transports and the gun-boats has required more time than I had expected. We have had dense fogs, and there are more mud banks in the Ogeechee than were reported, and there are no pilots whatever. Admiral Dahlgren promised to have the channel bouyed and staked, but it is not done yet. We find only six feet water up to King's Bridge at low tide, about ten up to the rice mill, and sixteen to Fort McAllister. All these points may be used by us, and we have a good strong bridge across Ogeechee at King's, by which our wagons can go to Fort McAllister, to which point I am sending the wagons not absolutely necessary for daily use, the negroes, prisoners of war, sick, &c., en route for Port Royal.

In relation to Savannah, you will remark that General Hardee refers to his still being in communication with his War Department. This language he thought would deceive me, but I am confirmed in the belief that the route to which he refers—namely, the Union plank road, on the South Carolina shore—is inadequate to feed his army and the people of Savannah; for General Foster assures me that he has his force on that very road near the head of Broad River, and that his guns command the railroad, so that cars no longer run between Charleston and Savannah. We hold this end of the Charleston railroad, and have destroyed it from the three-mile post back to the bridge—about twelve miles. In anticipation of leaving this country I am continuing the destruction of their railroads, and at this moment have two divisions and the cavalry at work breaking up the Gulf railroad from the Ogeechee to the Altahama; so that even if I do not take Savannah, I will leave it in a bad

---

* See p. 737.

way. But I still hope that events will give me time to take Savannah, even if I have to assault with some loss. I am satisfied that unless we take it the gun-boats never will, for they can make no impression upon the batteries which guard every approach from the sea; and I have a faint belief that when Colonel Babcock reaches you you will delay operations long enough to enable me to succeed. With Savannah in our possession at some future time, if not now, we can punish South Carolina as she deserves, and as thousands of people in Georgia hoped we would do. I do sincerely believe that the whole United States, North and South, would rejoice to have this army turned loose on South Carolina to devastate that State, in the manner we have done in Georgia, and it would have a direct and immediate bearing on your campaign in Virginia.

I have the honor to be, your obedient servant,

W. T. SHERMAN,
Major-General, Commanding.

HEADQUARTERS MILITARY DIVISION OF THE MISSISSIPPI,
In the Field, near Savannah, Ga., December 18, 1864.

Maj. Gen. O. O. HOWARD,
Commanding Army of the Tennessee:

GENERAL: The general-in-chief has just returned from General Slocum's, where he made a demand for the surrender of Savannah, &c., which was denied. He wishes you to make the necessary preparations at once for assaulting the place. He wishes to know if the crossing of the creek is practicable, and if you can make a diversion about Rosedew. General Slocum has received his orders, and General Davis and General Williams are ready, or nearly so.

I am, general, with respect, &c.,

L. M. DAYTON,
Aide-de-Camp.

HDQRS. DEPARTMENT AND ARMY OF THE TENNESSEE,
Near Savannah, Ga., December 18, 1864.

Maj. Gen. W. T. SHERMAN,
Commanding Military Division of the Mississippi:

GENERAL: Your letter of date just received. Major-General Blair thinks he can make a lodgment in his front, and has been directed to proceed as rapidly as possible with the preparations. In the other fronts I can at least make strong demonstrations. If I can get the water transportation from General Foster in time I believe the diversion just beyond Beaulieu to be practicable—that is, with one division.

Respectfully,

O. O. HOWARD,
Major-General.

SPECIAL FIELD ORDERS, No. 198.

HEADQUARTERS DEPARTMENT AND ARMY OF THE TENNESSEE,
Near Savannah, Ga., December 18, 1864.

I. The prisoners of war taken by this army, now in charge of the several provost-marshals, will immediately be turned over to Maj. F. C. Gillette, provost-marshal Fifteenth Army Corps, who, with a suitable guard, will proceed with them to Hilton Head, S. C., where they will be delivered to the proper authority. Major-General Osterhaus, commanding Fifteenth Army Corps, will furnish the necessary guard. Quartermaster's department will furnish the necessary transportation.

* * * * * * *

By order of Maj. Gen. O. O. Howard:

SAML. L. TAGGART,
Assistant Adjutant-General.

HDQRS. DEPARTMENT AND ARMY OF THE TENNESSEE,
Near Savannah, Ga., December 18, 1864.

Maj. Gen. P. JOS. OSTERHAUS,
Commanding Fifteenth Army Corps:

The major-general commanding directs me to send you inclosed copy of letter* from Major-General Sherman, and to say that he wishes you to confer with your division commanders as to the practicability of an assault from our lines, and to make preparations for at least a strong demonstration; also to hold General Smith's division in readiness to be thrown around to the right.

Very respectfully, your obedient servant,

SAML. L. TAGGART,
Assistant Adjutant-General.

GENERAL ORDERS, No. 56. } HDQRS. FIFTEENTH ARMY CORPS,
Anderson's Plantation, Ga., December 18, 1864.

I. Capt. John B. Foster, Forty-sixth Ohio Volunteer Infantry, is hereby relieved from duty as acting assistant inspector-general of the First Division. He will turn over all books and papers pertaining to the office to his successor.

II. Capt. A. B. Smith, Company K, One hundred and third Illinois Volunteer Infantry, is hereby appointed acting assistant inspector-general of the First Division, Fifteenth Army Corps, vice Captain Foster, relieved. He will be obeyed and respected accordingly.

By command of Maj. Gen. P. Joseph Osterhaus:

F. F. WHITEHEAD,
Assistant Adjutant-General.

SPECIAL ORDERS, No. 201. } HDQRS. FIFTEENTH ARMY CORPS,
Anderson's Plantation, Ga., December 18, 1864.

I. The Twelfth Regiment Illinois Volunteer Infantry is hereby detailed for special duty to escort prisoners of war to Hilton Head in compliance with paragraph I, Special Field Orders, No. 198, current series, from department headquarters, and will, without delay, report to Maj. Frank C. Gillette, provost-marshal Fifteenth Army Corps, for instructions. The regiment must be supplied, if possible, before leaving the place with five days' rations, which if not procured must be drawn at the nearest depot.

* * * * * * *

By order of Maj. Gen. P. Joseph Osterhaus:

F. F. WHITEHEAD,
Assistant Adjutant-General.

---

*See p. 743.

HEADQUARTERS FIFTEENTH ARMY CORPS,
Anderson's Plantation, Ga., December 18, 1864.

Brigadier-General WOODS,
Commanding First Division:

GENERAL: The major-general commanding desires that you report in person at these headquarters at once.

I am, general, very respectfully, your obedient servant,

F. F. WHITEHEAD,
Assistant Adjutant-General.

HDQRS. FOURTH DIVISION, FIFTEENTH ARMY CORPS,
Anderson's Plantation, December 18, 1864.

General E. W. RICE,
Commanding First Brigade, &c.:

In the execution of the crossing to-night be careful to caution the officer you place in charge of the enterprise to observe the utmost secrecy. Fascines and boat will be delivered at or near the reserve picket on the Lone Tree dike. Do not fail to commence as early after dark as practicable, and as soon as a lodgment is effected push over 100 or 200 men with intrenching tools sufficient to cover themselves at once. Notify me as soon as you are confident your party has succeeded.

Very respectfully,

JNO. M. CORSE,
Brigadier-General.

HDQRS. DEPARTMENT AND ARMY OF THE TENNESSEE,
Near Savannah, Ga., December 18, 1864.

Maj. Gen. F. P. BLAIR,
Commanding Seventeenth Army Corps:

GENERAL: The major-general commanding directs me to send you inclosed copy of letter* from Major-General Sherman, and to say that he depends on you to continue your preparations for an early assault. He will see you in person and confer further on the subject.

Very respectfully, your obedient servant,

SAML. L. TAGGART,
Assistant Adjutant-General.

HDQRS. DEPARTMENT AND ARMY OF THE TENNESSEE,
Near Savannah, Ga., December 18, 1864.

Maj. Gen. F. P. BLAIR, Jr.,
Commanding Seventeenth Army Corps:

GENERAL: The major-general commanding instructs me to direct you to cause parties to be at once employed in the construction of fascines, for the purpose of corduroying at different points from the mainland to the east branch of the Little Ogeechee. They should be made of some light material, and he suggests rice straw as the most practicable and convenient.

Very respectfully, your obedient servant,

SAML. L. TAGGART,
Assistant Adjutant-General.

(Same to Major-General Osterhaus).

---

* See p. 743.

SPECIAL ORDERS, No. 310. | HDQRS. SEVENTEENTH ARMY CORPS, *Near Savannah, Ga., December 18, 1864.*

* * * * * * *

VIII. Brig. Gen. J. W. Sprague, commanding Second Brigade, First Division, will cause the pontoon bridge now being protected by him to be taken up at once and sent, with the train belonging to it, to park in the fields in rear of these headquarters. He will leave in his present position the two smallest regiments of his command, and with the rest will proceed to King's Bridge at an early hour to-morrow morning, reporting to General Easton, chief quartermaster Military Division of the Mississippi, and relieving the First Brigade of the Fourth Division. He will cause the section of artillery now with him to report to Maj. A. C. Waterhouse, chief of artillery, Seventeenth Army Corps.

IX. Brig. Gen. J. W. Sprague, commanding Second Brigade, First Division, will detail from his command two commissioned officers experienced in working men and one good non-commissioned officer. They will report to Lieut. Col. A. Hickenlooper, assistant inspector-general, Seventeenth Army Corps, at King's Bridge, at 7 a. m. to-morrow, and will remain on duty with Lieutenant-Colonel Hickenlooper until the wharf is finished. He will detail each morning, to report to Lieutenant-Colonel Hickenlooper, at King's Bridge, at 7 o'clock, 150 axmen, properly officered, and six wagons with teams complete, but without beds, with two men to each team as assistants. First detail will report to-morrow morning.

X. Maj. J. C. Marven, Eleventh Iowa Volunteers, provost-marshal, Seventeenth Army Corps, and Capt. J. H. Davis, Forty-first Illinois Volunteers, commanding pioneer corps, Fourth Division, Seventeenth Army Corps, are hereby authorized, subject to the approval of the War Department, to raise a regiment of U. S. Colored Troops, to be employed in this corps as pioneers. Maj. J. C. Marven will at once select ten good men, upon recommendation of division commanders, and assign them to the duty of recruiting the regiment. As fast as companies are organized men will be assigned by orders from these headquarters as officers, and their names forwarded to the War Department for appointment.

XI. Col. B. F. Potts, commanding First Brigade, Fourth Division, will, on being relieved to-morrow morning, at King's Bridge, by the Second Brigade, First Division, report to Brig. Gen. G. A. Smith, commanding Fourth Division.

By command of Maj. Gen. F. P. Blair:

C. CADLE, JR.,
Assistant Adjutant-General.

HDQRS. THIRD DIVISION, SEVENTEENTH ARMY CORPS,
In the Field, before Savannah, December 18, 1864.

Captain CADLE,
Assistant Adjutant-General:

CAPTAIN: During the day I have carefully examined the front of my lines, and have made a rough sketch of the position. The distances, or rather relative distances, are only judged by the eye. The enemy's position is certainly a strong one, and whether we can carry his works by storm depends almost wholly upon the spirit the enemy may display in their defense. To give a reasonable hope of success Lawton's battery,

Pine Point battery, and the plank-road battery should all be charged simultaneously. The greatest obstacle to overcome prior to reaching the enemy's works is the canal, which is represented by the negroes as being about four feet deep in front of Lawton's battery, but from five to six feet deep in front of the other two.

Very respectfully,

M. D. LEGGETT,
Brigadier-General.

P. S.—Lieutenant Hasler, Twentieth Ohio, now on picket, represents just this moment that the enemy moved a considerable body of troops to the vicinity of the plank-road battery just before sundown. I have sent for him, and if I find his statements of account I will forward them. I have not seen him myself.

M. D. L.

HDQRS. THIRD DIVISION, SEVENTEENTH ARMY CORPS,
In the Field, December 18, 1864.

Captain CADLE,
Assistant Adjutant-General:

CAPTAIN: I have just had a talk with Lieutenant Hasler, Twentieth Ohio. He says that he distinctly saw a large column of rebel troops move down the big road and file into the rear of their works in this front and the front of General Woods. He thinks there was nearly or quite a division of them. He says he could see but one point in the road, and they were about one hour passing that point, and seemed well clothed, and all dressed in dark clothing, black or blue. This took place from 4 to 5 this p. m. He says that several soldiers who were at the rifle-pit with him saw the same. Lieutenant Hasler sustains the reputation of a good officer and reliable man. I can hardly think they intend a demonstration upon us, neither do I believe they can afford so many troops to garrison our front. I have just sent my picket officer out to put the pickets and reserves on the alert.

Respectfully, your obedient servant,

M. D. LEGGETT,
Brigadier-General.

P. S.—The same officer says there was considerable commotion in the rebel camp last night, and he thinks they moved away a portion of their artillery.

M D. L.

HEADQUARTERS LEFT WING, ARMY OF GEORGIA,
December 18, 1864.

Maj. Gen. J. C. DAVIS,
Commanding Fourteenth Army Corps:

GENERAL: I presume General Sherman called on you to-day, and informed you of his intention to attempt to carry the first line in our front as soon as our artillery can be placed in position. I think everything will be in readiness within two days. The assault will be made simultaneously at every accessible point on the line. There are several points in front of the Twentieth Corps which I think can be carried. We are making fascines of straw and canebrakes; also practicing with the pontoon bridge materials. Perhaps it would be well for you to send two or three officers over to examine these fascines, as they may be useful on your line. I hope every brigade-commander on your front will make a most careful examination of the lines in his front, and be prepared for the work. I shall order Williams to bring to the front all of the brigade now guarding our rear, except one regiment. About one-third of his command will be held in reserve at our present line. Works have already been constructed for all his artillery, and I intend he shall use all of it for fifteen or twenty minutes before he advances his infantry. I will try to see you to-morrow or next day.

Yours, &c.,

H. W. SLOCUM,
Major-General.

SPECIAL ORDERS, No. 208. } HDQRS. FOURTEENTH ARMY CORPS, LEFT WING, ARMY OF GEORGIA,
Before Savannah, Ga., December 18, 1864.

* * * * * * *

III. First Lieut. Stephen G. Grubb, Battery C, First Illinois Artillery, is hereby appointed ordnance officer of the corps (vice Capt. George Estep, who is about to be mustered out of the service), and will report to Maj. Charles Houghtaling, chief of artillery, Fourteenth Army Corps.

By command of Bvt. Maj. Gen. J. C. Davis:

A. C. McCLURG,
Assistant Adjutant-General and Chief of Staff.

ORDERS.] HDQRS. FIRST DIVISION, 14TH ARMY CORPS,
Near Savannah, Ga., December 18, 1864.

Col. D. Miles, commanding Third Brigade, will relieve Col. J. H. Brigham's (Second Brigade) quietly and without attracting the notice of the enemy at daylight to-morrow morning, the 19th instant.

Col. J. H. Brigham, upon being relieved by Colonel Miles' command, will encamp his brigade on the ground now occupied by Colonel Miles' command, withdrawing his troops cautiously.

By order of Brig. Gen. W. P. Carlin:

G. W. SMITH,
Captain and Acting Assistant Adjutant-General.

CIRCULAR.] HEADQUARTERS TWENTIETH CORPS,
Before Savannah, Ga., December 18, 1864.

Commanders of divisions will reconnoiter by day and night all roads and approaches to their lines from the enemy's position, using for this purpose general and field officers of the day and staff officers. The object of these examinations is to ascertain every avenue to the line of the enemy's defenses. They will send to these headquarters daily reports of their investigations.

By command of Brig. Gen. A. S. Williams:

ROBT. P. DECHERT,
Captain and Acting Assistant Adjutant-General.

CIRCULAR.] HDQRS. SECOND BRIG., FIRST DIV., 20TH CORPS,
Argyle Island, Ga., December 18, 1864.

This command will be in readiness to move at 5.30 a. m. to-morrow. The Third Wisconsin Volunteers and Second Massachusetts Volunteers will cross the river to the South Carolina shore at 6 a. m.; the Thirteenth New Jersey Volunteers will follow as support. Col. William Hawley, Third Wisconsin Volunteers, will take command of the three regiments above-named, and will receive detailed instructions from the brigadier-general commanding the division to-night. The above-named regiments will leave their knapsacks upon this side. They will carry the extra twenty rounds of ammunition upon their persons. The One hundred and seventh New York and One hundred and fiftieth New York Volunteers will relieve the three regiments above-named in their present work at 6 a. m. Lieutenant-Colonel Sill, One hundred and seventh New York Volunteers, will leave one company in his present camp.

By command of Col. E. A. Carman, commanding brigade:

J. R. LINDSAY,
Captain and Acting Assistant Adjutant-General.

HEADQUARTERS TWENTIETH CORPS,
Near Savannah, Ga., December 18, 1864.

Brig. Gen. J. W. GEARY,
Commanding Second Division:

GENERAL: The general commanding desires to meet yourself and your brigade commanders at these headquarters to-morrow morning at 10 o'clock.

Very respectfully, your obedient servant,

ROBT. P. DECHERT,
Captain and Acting Assistant Adjutant-General.

(Copy to Brig. Gen. W. T. Ward, commanding Third Division.)

CONFIDENTIAL.] HDQRS. MILITARY DIV. OF THE MISSISSIPPI,
In the Field, near Savannah, Ga., December 18, 1864—8 p. m.

Maj. Gen. J. G. FOSTER,
Commanding Department of the South:

GENERAL: In compliance with the plan I indicated to you some days since, I made a demand during yesterday on General Hardee for the surrender of the city of Savannah and its dependent forts, and to-day received his answer declining to accede. You are aware that I am ordered to carry this army to Virginia by sea, but I hope still to be able to get possession of Savannah before sufficient transportation can be had to enable me to comply with General Grant's orders. The 30-pounder Parrotts which you sent me are now being hauled to batteries prepared for them, and in about two days' time, if we can possibly get the ground to stand upon, we shall assault the enemy's lines at four or more points. It is all important that the railroad and telegraph wire should be broken between the Savannah River and Charleston, and the very best point is where your force is represented to be, near the Tullifinny. It seems to me that our operations here, especially along the Savannah River, must have drawn away every man from that quarter that they could possibly spare, and a bold rush on the railroad would probably develop a weaker force there than is supposed to be; or it may be that you could diminish that force and use the balance in a small, handy detachment east of the Tullifinny over about Old Pocotaligo. I merely throw out these ideas, and merely reiterate that it would aid us very much in this quarter if that force of yours be kept most active, more especially if you succeed in breaking the railroad and the telegraph wire—the farther toward Charleston the better. Even if nothing better can be done let them whale away with their 30-pounder Parrotts and break the road with cannon balls. It is possible, as a part of the general movement, that I may send a force, in co-operation with the navy, toward the Union plank-road, in the direction of Bluffton. I will go over and see the admiral again to-morrow, and it may be that I will see you, as in your last note you said that you would return again.

I have the honor to be, your obedient servant,

W. T. SHERMAN,
Major-General, Commanding.

HEADQUARTERS DEPARTMENT OF THE SOUTH,
Hilton Head, S. C., December 18, 1864.

Lieut. Col. JOHN E. MULFORD,
Assistant Agent of Exchange, Charleston Harbor:

COLONEL: General Sherman requires for immediate and pressing use all the vessels that he can possibly procure. He therefore requests me to require of you, as a military necessity, all the vessels of every description that you can possibly spare, and that you order them to report to General Easton, at Fort McAllister, in the Ogeechee River, as soon as possible.

Very respectfully, your obedient servant,

J. G. FOSTER,
Major-General, Commanding.

HEADQUARTERS DEPARTMENT OF THE SOUTH,
Hilton Head, S. C., December 18, 1864.

Brigadier-General HATCH,
Commanding Coast Division, Deveaux's Neck:

GENERAL: I received your letters, and am pleased that you have pushed up your batteries and, in a measure, stopped the running of the trains. I am not, however, fully satisfied with the damage we are doing them, and therefore want you to take the railroad, if you can, and destroy it; if you cannot do this, be sure and secure such an artillery fire as will destroy any train that attempts to pass. I think you can best destroy the road by crossing the Tullifinny with a portion of your force and striking the road near the Pocotaligo River.

Yours, in haste,

J. G. FOSTER,
Major-General, Commanding.

HDQRS. SIGNAL DETACHMENT, DEPT. OF THE SOUTH,
Hilton Head, S. C., December 18, 1864.

Capt. JESSE MERRILL,
Chief Signal Officer, Department of the South:

CAPTAIN: I have the honor to make the following special report of duty performed by me, which resulted in opening communication with General Sherman, in Ogeechee River:

On the morning of the 12th instant I was ordered by you to accompany you on board the U. S. revenue cutter Nemaha, to proceed with General Foster down the coast, to endeavor to open communication with General Sherman's army if it approached the coast. We left Hilton Head at 10.30 a. m., and proceeded through the inland passage to Fort Pulaski. Here I obtained twelve signal rockets from the ordnance officer of the fort by order of General Foster. Not being able to obtain any information here we proceeded through Lazaretto Creek into Wassaw Sound. I closely examined the shore as we passed along for some indications of General Sherman's approach to the coast. Arrived at Wassaw Sound at 3 p. m. and proceeded outside. We arrived at Ossabaw Sound, where the U. S. steamer Flag was doing blockading duty at mouths of Ogeechee, Vernon, and Little Ogeechee Rivers. Here I was ordered by you to go on the Flag, and received instructions from General Foster to use every means in my power to find General Sherman, and to reconnoiter those different rivers closely, and to go up on the picket-boat, if one was sent out. I then proceeded on board the Flag with Sergeant Hardy and Private Smedes, and was introduced to Captain Williamson, commanding, by Maj. J. F. Anderson, chief of staff to General Foster. Captain Williamson promised to render me every assistance in his power, but had no picket-boats to send out, but as soon as the tug Dandelion returned would let me have her to proceed up the Ogeechee and Vernon Rivers. Finding I could do nothing that night in reconnoitering, I induced the captain to fire his heavy guns six times in rapid succession, after which I threw up several rockets in rapid succession, and closely scanned the horizon inland for some answering signal. After waiting some time a faint shoot of light was seen to arise in the direction of the Ogeechee River, but not being satisfied, I threw up two more at once, and again saw the response, but at so great a distance as to be almost indiscernible. It was then about 3 a. m. of the 13th instant.

The tug having returned, I desired Captain Williamson to send me up, but as Admiral Dahlgren desired the pilot to go out over the bar, he wished me to wait until daylight. At 8 a. m. I went on board the tug Dandelion and proceeded up the Ogeechee River, looking closely in every direction with my glass for some signal or sign of General Sherman's army. We proceeded up the river to a point just out of range of the rebel fort McAllister and the batteries on the opposite side of the Little Ogeechee River. Here the captain was afraid to proceed any farther on account of the cross-fire which the different forts could bring upon him; but desiring to reconnoiter their position, I obtained the use of a small row-boat, and, accompanied by Sergeant Hardy and Private Smedes, and four men to row, I proceeded up along the shore until I arrived nearly opposite Fort McAllister's guns, and had passed the forts on the Little Ogeechee. Here I put the boat into a small creek, where we were concealed from the enemy by the high grass of the marsh. I then made a careful and close reconnaissance of the forts and the surrounding country. While so engaged I was very much surprised to find that we were not discovered by the enemy; but I soon heard musketry as of skirmishers advancing in the woods above Fort McAllister, and soon a few heavy guns were fired from the fort inland. I then looked about and saw, about three miles northwest of where I was lying in the marsh, a flag upon the top of an old rice mill, but there being no air stirring I was unable to make out of what nature it was. I could then indistinctly see persons through a broken part of the roof, one of whom, taking hold of the end of the flag, drew its folds out so that I could see our own glorious Stars and Stripes. I then immediately returned to the boat and rowed back as rapidly as possible to the tug-boat. I then gave orders for the tug to be moved up past an opening in the woods through which Fort McAllister had the range of the river. As soon as the anchor was got up the tug was put under full head of steam, and we ran the gauntlet of fire from Fort McAllister without any shot striking us. I could then distinctly see the rice mill, with the Stars and Stripes waving over it; and raising my white flag I had the general call made, and immediately an answering signal was made from the broken part of the roof. My first message was—

Who are you?

FISHER,
Lieutenant.

McClintock, General Howard's signal officer.

How can I get to you? What troops are at Fort McAllister?

FISHER,
Lieutenant.

We are now investing Fort McAllister with Hazen's division.

HOWARD,
General.

General HOWARD:

What can we do for you? We are ready to render you any assistance.

FOSTER,
General.
DAHLGREN,
Admiral.
FISHER,
Lieutenant.

General FOSTER:

Can you assist us with your heavy guns?

SHERMAN,
General.

General SHERMAN:

Being only a tug-boat, no heavy guns aboard.

FISHER,
Lieutenant.

This was about 5 p. m. During the time these communications were being sent the musketry about the fort became more distinct. I then saw the signal made from the station I had been communicating with to some station in the woods near Fort McAllister, to General Hazen:

It is absolutely necessary that the fort be taken immediately. The Stars and Stripes must wave over the battery at sundown.

SHERMAN,
General.

In a few moments I heard the rallying call of the bugle, and a moment after the bugle pealed out the charge, and in a very few moments the troops were swarming over the parapets, which were perfectly black with them, and loud cheers filled the air.

I then received the following message:

General FOSTER:

Fort McAllister is ours. Look for a boat. General Sherman will come down to-night.

HOWARD,
General.

It was then getting dark and too dark to see a flag, and not having any torches with me, and desiring to send dispatch to General Foster and Admiral Dahlgren, I turned about and returned with the tug to the Flag, where I wrote my dispatches, which were immediately sent. I then returned to the obstructions just below Fort McAllister and anchored, and in a short time a small boat was seen approaching, which was hailed. "What boat is that?" The answering response came back: "Sherman." And the boat came alongside, and Generals Sherman and Howard came on board and were welcomed with twice three cheers by those on board. I then told General Sherman of General Foster's efforts to open communication with him, and that I had sent dispatches to him. They remained on board until about midnight, General Sherman writing his dispatches to General Halleck, and also writing to General Foster and Admiral Dahlgren. I then accompanied them back to the fort, and proceeded around the fort with them. After spending half an hour at the fort I returned to the tug and started down the river with the dispatches for General Foster and Admiral Dahlgren. Had got down nearly to the mouth of the river when we met the U. S. revenue cutter Nemaha coming up. I then went aboard and reported to General Foster, and had my party transferred from the tug to the Nemaha, the general's flag-ship. We then proceeded up the river again until we arrived just below the obstructions, when I signaled to the fort:

MCCLINTOCK:

General Foster is here, and would like to see General Sherman.

FISHER,
Lieutenant.

I will send for him. He has gone to General Howard's headquarters at Gr's Creek.

MCCLINTOCK.

How far off?

FISHER,
Lieutenant.

Not more than a mile.

MCCLINTOCK.

O. K.

FISHER.

General FOSTER:

General Sherman will come to the fort as soon as he can.

MCCLINTOCK.

A boat was then sent to the fort, and returned with General Sherman to the Nemaha. We then started down the river again—it was about daybreak of the 14th instant—and proceeded out of Ossabaw

Sound into Wassaw Sound, where we arrived about 11 o'clock 14th instant, and found Admiral Dahlgren, who came aboard and remained for an hour or more; and then General Sherman went aboard the Harvest Moon, the admiral's flag-ship, and returned with him to Ossabaw Sound and to his army, while we returned to Hilton Head, where we arrived at about 6 p. m.

In concluding my report I take great pleasure in making honorable mention of the gallant conduct of both Sergeant Hardy and Private Smedes, who accompanied me upon the reconnaissance, and who I would recommend to your favorable consideration.

I have the honor to be, captain, very respectfully, your obedient servant,

GEORGE A. FISHER,
First Lieutenant, Signal Corps, U. S. Army.

CITY POINT, VA., *December 19, 1864—3.30 p. m.*

Hon. E. M. STANTON,
Secretary of War, Washington:

On reflection, I think it would have a good effect to allow Sherman's letter to General Halleck, except such facts as refer to future movements, to be published. It is refreshing to see a commander after a campaign of more than seven months' duration ready for still further operations, and without wanting any outfit or rest.

U. S. GRANT,
Lieutenant-General.

WASHINGTON, D. C., *December 19, 1864—3.50 p. m.*

Lieutenant-General GRANT,
Fort Monroe, or City Point:

The steamer Louise, about to leave here for Hilton Head, has orders to touch at Fort Monroe for dispatches. As this vessel will probably reach Sherman several days before Major Anderson from New York, I suggest the propriety of sending a copy of your dispatch of yesterday by her. Could you not telegraph it to Fort Monroe in cipher?

H. W. HALLECK,
Major-General and Chief of Staff.

CITY POINT, VA., *December 19, 1864.*

Maj. Gen. WILLIAM T. SHERMAN,
Commanding Military Division of the Mississippi:

While North I met a number of our officers who had just been paroled from Columbia, S. C. They informed me that they understood before leaving that our prisoners who were in the line of your march had generally been removed to Florida. If this is the case Foster might send an expedition to rescue them. Jeff. Davis is said to be very sick; in fact, deserters report his death. The people had a rumor that he took poison in a fit of despondency over the military situation. Of course I credit no part of this, except that Davis is very sick, and do not suppose his reflections on military matters soothe him any.

U. S. GRANT,
Lieutenant-General.

WASHINGTON, *December 19 1864—12 m.*

Lieutenant-General GRANT,
Commanding Armies of the United States:

GENERAL: Hilton Head some days since called for at least six light steamers to ply between the ocean fleet of steamers and supply vessels and Sherman's army, on the Ogeechee. I ordered the steamers to be selected from among those in the Chesapeake waters as the quickest way of supplying this necessity. I am told that yesterday verbal orders, by your authority, were given forbidding the detachment of the steamers. What shall be done? The forage and supply vessels rendezvoused at Port Royal cannot ascend the Ogeechee.

M. C. MEIGS,
Quartermaster-General.

CITY POINT, VA., *December 19, 1864—3.30 p. m.*
(Received 4 p. m.)

Bvt. Maj. Gen. M. C. MEIGS,
Quartermaster-General:

My order against sending vessels to Savannah was given with the understanding that vessels were being sent to move Sherman's army. I soon learned the facts, and directed General Ingalls to go on.

U. S. GRANT,
Lieutenant-General.

QUARTERMASTER-GENERAL'S OFFICE,
Washington City, December 19, 1864

Major-General SHERMAN,
Commanding, at Savannah:

GENERAL: I wrote you fully a day or two since in regard to supplies. As it is reported that you will not find light steamers enough on the coast to supply you up the Ogeechee, I have ordered six of the most suitable to be sent from the Chesapeake. The Louise, a very fine iron steamer, goes this morning, and I write by her unless my other dispatch may miscarry. I see you are aware of the importance of stripping your army of all useless mouths. The only supply about which I have any anxiety is hay; this we have not been able to procure in sufficient quantities. There is no difficulty, so long as the credit of the Government holds out, in sending on everything else in abundance. But I hope that you will get rid of every mule and horse not absolutely needed about Savannah.

Wishing you continued success, I am, very truly, your friend,

M. C. MEIGS,
Quartermaster-General, Brevet Major-General.

P. S.—Donaldson telegraphs that his organized quartermaster's volunteers were assigned an important position in the lines at Nashville, which they held until Hood was driven off, and that this enabled Thomas to put a considerable number of troops into the assault, who, but for the organization of these 7,000 quartermaster's employés, would have been required to hold the lines. They also defended Johnsonville, on the Tennessee, when attacked by Forrest last month.

HEADQUARTERS MILITARY DIVISION OF THE MISSISSIPPI,
In the Field, near Savannah, Ga., December 19, 1864.

Maj. Gen. O. O. HOWARD,
Commanding Army of the Tennessee:

GENERAL: The general-in-chief has gone to the Bay. He wishes you to push the preparations for attacking Savannah with all possible speed, but to await orders for the attack. He will see General Foster and the admiral before returning, and will get co-operation from both if possible. Should anything occur that you would like to communicate to the general I will forward for you.

I am, general, with respect,

L. M. DAYTON,
Aide-de-Camp.

HEADQUARTERS MILITARY DIVISION OF THE MISSISSIPPI,
In the Field, King's Bridge, Ga., December 19, 1864—12 m.

Major-General HOWARD,
Commanding Right Wing,
Major-General SLOCUM,
Commanding Left Wing:

GENERAL: The general-in-chief directs me to address you the following note for your joint information and direction:

On arrival at the bridge I found Colonel Potts' brigade relieved by two regiments of General Sprague's, containing less than 600 men. These are insufficient. I have ordered General Sprague back to his important post between Big and Little Ogeechee, and Colonel Potts' brigade to remain for the present. As a permanent working party at King's Bridge, the fairest way will be for each corps to send a regiment, of an average strength of 350 men, and each wing a working party of negroes, 100 each, to report to Colonel Beckwith, chief commissary. Please make your orders accordingly, and when they have arrived Colonel Potts' brigade will be returned to its proper division. I may be absent, say, one or two days. You had better let General Sprague have a battery of four guns.

I have the honor to be, respectfully, your obedient servant,

HENRY HITCHCOCK,
Major and Assistant Adjutant-General.

SPECIAL FIELD ORDERS, No. 199.

HEADQUARTERS DEPARTMENT AND ARMY OF THE TENNESSEE,
Near Savannah, Ga., December 19, 1864.

* * * * * * *

II. Lieutenant-Colonel Tweeddale, commanding First Regiment Missouri Engineers, will forthwith send one company to Fort McAllister, to report to Capt. C. B. Reese, chief engineer.

* * * * * * *

IV. The major-generals commanding Fifteenth and Seventeenth Corps will each cause to be immediately sent from their command one regiment, of an average strength of 350 men, and a working party of fifty negroes, to report to Colonel Beckwith, chief commissary, at the landing at King's Bridge. A similar detail from the Left Wing has been made, and when the whole shall report to Colonel Beckwith the brigade of the Fourth Division, Seventeenth Army Corps, now at King's Bridge, will return to its division.

* * * * * * *

By order of Maj. Gen. O. O. Howard:

SAML. L. TAGGART,
Assistant Adjutant-General.

HEADQUARTERS FIFTEENTH ARMY CORPS,
Cannouchee River, December 19, 1864.

[General HOWARD:]

GENERAL: The enemy evacuated his position opposite me this morning, probably impelled by some movement on his flank. I have put one brigade of Second Division across, and am making preparations to cross the entire Second Division, when I will push toward King's Bridge and to the nearest point on the railroad. There is a great deal of traffic over the Gulf road, trains passing almost continually. I will report again as soon as I have anything new to report.

I am, very respectfully, your obedient servant,

P. JOS. OSTERHAUS,
Major-General.

HEADQUARTERS SEVENTEENTH ARMY CORPS,
Near Savannah, Ga., December 19, 1864.

Capt. SAMUEL L. TAGGART,
Asst. Adjt. Gen., Department and Army of the Tennessee:

CAPTAIN: In accordance with orders from General Howard, I ordered General Sprague to proceed to King's Bridge (leaving two regiments in his present position) and relieve Colonel Potts' brigade, of the Fourth Division, which I ordered to the front. General Sherman has ordered General Sprague and his command back to its original position, and now there are no troops at the bridge to unload supplies.

Very respectfully, your obedient servant,

FRANK P. BLAIR, JR.,
Major-General.

SPECIAL ORDERS, No. 311. } HDQRS. SEVENTEENTH ARMY CORPS,
Near Savannah, Ga., December 19, 1864.

* * * * * * *

II. Brig. Gen. J. W. Sprague, commanding Second Brigade, First Division, will forthwith send two regiments of his command to King's Bridge for the purpose of unloading vessels. The senior officer will report to the officer in charge of the unloading of subsistence stores.

III. Special Orders, No. 311, extract II, from these headquarters, of this date, directing General Sprague to send two regiments from his command to King's Bridge, is hereby revoked.

IV. Brig. Gen. G. A. Smith, commanding Fourth Division, will direct Colonel Potts' brigade to remain at King's Bridge until relieved by a regiment from each corps, as ordered by General Sherman (copy inclosed). When the brigade is relieved General Smith will order one regiment (350 strong) and fifty negroes from his pioneer corps, under a commissioned officer, to report to Colonel Beckwith, chief commissary Military Division of the Mississippi.

V. The officer in charge of ordnance stores captured at Fort McAllister will deliver to Lieut. S. J. Smith, acting ordnance officer Seventeenth Army Corps, such ordnance and ordnance stores as he may require for the 32-pounder now being mounted by his corps.

VI. Brig. Gen. M. D. Leggett will cause a detail of 200 men from his command, properly officered, to report at 7 a. m. to-morrow to Maj. R. H. McFadden, Forty-first Illinois, at these headquarters for fatigue duty.

VII. Maj. R. H. McFadden, commanding Forty-first Illinois Veteran Battalion, will detail from his command 100 men, and will, with 200 men of the Third Division, report to Lieutenant-Colonel Hickenlooper at 7 a. m. to-morrow.

VIII. Division commanders will cause all negro women and children, and all negro men in their commands not fit for service, to be sent to-morrow morning to Colonel Beckwith, acting chief quartermaster Military Division of the Mississippi, at King's Bridge.

By command of Maj. Gen. F. P. Blair:

C. CADLE, JR.,
Assistant Adjutant-General.

HEADQUARTERS MILITARY DIVISION OF THE MISSISSIPPI,
In the Field, near Savannah, Ga., December 19, 1864—12 m.

Brigadier-General SPRAGUE,
Comdg. Second Brig., First Div., Seventeenth Corps, present:

GENERAL: You may return to the position assigned you in former orders, and hold securely the neck of land between the Great and Little Ogeechee, reporting, as heretofore, through your corps commander, to General Howard, commanding Right Wing.

By order of Major-General Sherman:

Respectfully, your obedient servant,

HENRY HITCHCOCK,
Assistant Adjutant-General.

KING'S BRIDGE, *December 19, 1864.*

Capt. C. CADLE, Jr.,
Assistant Adjutant-General:

CAPTAIN: I am here with two regiments as ordered. General Easton is absent. Colonel Beckwith claims to be in command. He says he wants the regiments to report to him and be entirely under his command. I cannot turn over my command to a quartermaster without an order. I am unable to see what I am here for, and desire light. Colonel Beckwith says he will order the First Brigade to remain in the name of General Sherman.

Respectfully, &c.,

J. W. SPRAGUE.

HEADQUARTERS SEVENTEENTH ARMY CORPS,
Near Savannah, Ga., December 19, 1864.

Brig. Gen. J. W. SPRAGUE,
Commanding Second Brigade, First Division:

GENERAL: I have referred your communication of this morning to the major-general commanding, and he directs me to say to you that your command was sent to King's Bridge to take the place of Colonel Potts' brigade in furnishing such details as General Easton, chief quartermaster, might call on you for to unload vessels. Colonel Beckwith cannot order the First Brigade, Fourth Division, to remain at the bridge, nor can he take command of your troops, or any others. The First Brigade, Fourth Division, is ordered to the front to take part with the rest of the Fourth Division in the assault on Savannah. Colonel Beckwith can have all the men necessary to perform the work he has in hand from your command, and he must not assume the responsibility of detaining troops from their part in the coming assault.

Very respectfully, your obedient servant,

C. CADLE, JR.,
Assistant Adjutant-General.

HDQRS. SECOND BRIG., FIRST DIV., 17TH ARMY CORPS,
King's Bridge, December 19, 1864.

Capt. C. CADLE, Jr.,
Assistant Adjutant-General:

CAPTAIN: Your dispatch just received. After sending my note this a. m. I met General Sherman, and he dictated in person the following order.*

I am consequently on the way to my former position with one regiment; the other is to escort supplies to Major-General Mower, and will leave the bridge to-morrow. After giving me the order copied herein General Sherman said he wanted a battery sent to report to me, and would send the order to General Howard. The boat was waiting for him, and he may have neglected to send the order.

Respectfully, your obedient servant,

J. W. SPRAGUE,
Brigadier-General.

HEADQUARTERS FIRST BRIGADE,
Before Savannah, December 19, 1864.

Capt. J. C. DOUGLASS,
Assistant Adjutant-General:

CAPTAIN: I have the honor to report that the firing on the left this morning is occasioned by General Belknap's brigade moving into position on the ground lately held by the Eighty-eighth Indiana. His skirmish line advanced into the open field in front of the rebel four-gun battery on Larkin's plantation, and took position on the crest of the hill. The rebel pickets fell back beyond the water. Musketry then ceased, and the rebels began shelling the woods.

I am, captain, very respectfully, your obedient servant,

M. F. FORCE,
Brigadier-General, Commanding First Brigade.

---

* See Hitchcock to Sprague, 12 m., p. 758.

SPECIAL ORDERS, } HDQRS. FOURTH DIV., 17TH ARMY CORPS,
No. 161. } *Near Savannah, Ga., December 19, 1864.*

I. In order to comply with Special Orders, No. 311, headquarters Seventeenth Army Corps, Col. B. F. Potts, commanding First Brigade, Fourth Division, Seventeenth Army Corps, will remain at King's Bridge until relieved by one regiment from each corps of the army. Colonel Potts will leave one regiment, 350 strong, at the bridge to Colonel Beckwith, and when relieved will move the other regiments of his command to this place, as heretofore directed.

* * * * * * *

By order of Brig. Gen. Giles A. Smith:

CHAS. H. BRUSH,
Acting Assistant Adjutant-General.

HDQRS. FIRST BRIG., FOURTH DIV., 17TH ARMY CORPS,
King's Bridge, Ga., December 19, 1864.

Capt. C. CADLE, Jr.,
Assistant Adjutant-General:

CAPTAIN: The brigade of General Sprague was sent back by General Sherman in person to his old camp. I am not relieved by him, nor any other command, but was ready to move, having everything loaded, and Colonel Beckwith said he would arrest me if I obeyed General Blair's order, and I returned to camp, and will await further orders, or until I am relieved. General Sherman went down to the fleet, and took 150 men to transfer supplies from one vessel to the other. I have unloaded about 200,000 rations to-day at this point, and other vessels are in sight. If I leave here there will be no organization of guards left to guard the supplies.

I am, your friend and obedient servant,

B. F. POTTS,
Colonel, &c.

HDQRS. 17TH ARMY CORPS, DEPT. OF THE TENNESSEE,
Near Savannah, Ga., December 19, 1864.

Col. B. F. POTTS,
Commanding First Brigade, Fourth Division:

COLONEL: The major-general commanding instructs me to say to you that you will start at 4 o'clock this p. m. to the front to report to Brig. Gen. G. A. Smith. The hour is fixed at 4 so that you will have the cover of the night to cross your troops over the causeway.

Very respectfully, your obedient servant,

C. CADLE, JR.,
Assistant Adjutant-General.

[Indorsement.]

KING'S BRIDGE, GA., *December 19, 1864.*

The major-general commanding the Military Division of the Mississippi was at King's Bridge this morning, and directed me to retain your command on its present duties, and communicated with the commander of the Army of the Right Wing in relation thereto. He further in person directed General Sprague, who had arrived here to relieve you, to return with his command. You will, therefore, adhere to the order of Major-General Sherman given you this morning in writing.

By command of Maj. Gen. W. T. Sherman:

A. BECKWITH,
Col., Aide-de-Camp and Actg. Chief Qrmr. Mil. Div. of the Miss.

HEADQUARTERS MILITARY DIVISION OF THE MISSISSIPPI,
In the Field, near Savannah, Ga., December 19, 1864.

Major-General SLOCUM,
Commanding Left Wing:

GENERAL: The general-in-chief has gone to the Bay. He directs me to further instruct you to push the preparations for the attack of the defenses of Savannah as rapidly as possible, and then await further directions before doing more. He will endeavor to get co-operation from Admiral Dahlgren and General Foster, with whom he will confer before returning. If, in the meantime, anything should occur that you would wish to communicate to him, please send to me and I will forward.

I am, general, with respect,

L. M. DAYTON,
Aide-de-Camp.

HEADQUARTERS LEFT WING, ARMY OF GEORGIA,
Before Savannah, Ga., December 19, 1864.

Maj. Gen. J. C. DAVIS,
Commanding Fourteenth Corps:

The major-general commanding desires you to detail one regiment, of at least 350 men, to report to Colonel Beckwith, chief commissary, at King's Bridge, for fatigue duty, and, if possible, send fifty negroes with them, the whole to constitute a permanent fatigue party. General Williams will furnish a like detail.

Very respectfully, your obedient servant,

H. C. RODGERS,
Assistant Adjutant-General.

CIRCULAR.] HEADQUARTERS FOURTEENTH ARMY CORPS,
Before Savannah, Ga., December 19, 1864.

In view of active operations against the city of Savannah which will probably be inaugurated, division commanders will at once prepare their commands and hold them in readiness for an attack. Generals Carlin and Morgan will make thorough reconnaissances of the grounds in their front; examine the approaches of the enemy's works which give the greatest promise of successful assault, and make full reports to these headquarters by 12 m. to-morrow. Fascines, planks, &c., and whatever may assist in the passage of swamps, ditches, and other intervening obstacles, will be immediately prepared.

By order of Bvt. Maj. Gen. J. C. Davis:

A. C. McCLURG,
Assistant Adjutant-General and Chief of Staff.

HEADQUARTERS TWENTIETH CORPS,
Before Savannah, Ga., December 19, 1864.

Col. E. A. CARMAN,
Commanding Second Brigade, First Division:

COLONEL: The general commanding directs me to say that the pioneer corps of your brigade, with their wagon, has been ordered to report to you at once. He directs that in your defense you may make use of the dikes wherever you can.

Very respectfully, your obedient servant,

ROBT. P. DECHERT,
Captain and Acting Assistant Adjutant-General.

HDQRS. SECOND BRIG., FIRST DIV., TWENTIETH CORPS,
December 19, 1864.

Lieut. GEORGE ROBINSON,
Acting Assistant Adjutant-General, First Division, 20th Corps:

LIEUTENANT: I have the honor to report that the enemy have again opened upon our force across the river with artillery; and Colonel Hawley reporting that it was impossible to hold his position without more troops, I have moved the remainder of my brigade over, with the exception of three companies of the One hundred and fiftieth New York Volunteers, and have established my headquarters upon the South Carolina shore. I would also say that I need some intrenching tools if I am to remain there.

Very respectfully,

E. A. CARMAN,
Colonel, Commanding Brigade.

[Indorsement.]

HDQRS. FIRST DIVISION, TWENTIETH ARMY CORPS,
December 19, 1864.

Respectfully forwarded for the information of the brigadier-general commanding the corps, with the request that a portion at least of the tools loaned to General Geary be returned to Colonel Carman, commanding Second Brigade, on Argyle Island.

N. J. JACKSON,
Brigadier-General, Commanding.

HEADQUARTERS 101ST ILLINOIS VOLUNTEER INFANTRY,
Near Savannah, Ga., December 19, 1864.

Capt. A. E. LEE,
Acting Assistant Adjutant-General, Third Brigade:

CAPTAIN: I have the honor to make the following report of the expedition under my command to-day, in accordance with the order issued yesterday from your headquarters:

The expedition, consisting of two companies from each regiment of the brigade, with one wagon from each regiment and one wagon from each brigade and division headquarters, numbering in all about 200 men, started from the camp of the One hundred and first Illinois Volunteers about 7 a. m. this morning, and proceeded to Monteith, where I detached a lieutenant and fifteen men to come back on the road with a wagon sent for that purpose and gather up telegraph wire. The expedition then proceeded toward Redoubt No. 1, on the route traveled by the Fourteenth Corps, and about 400 yards beyond the redoubt encountered a rebel outpost, who fired into the advance and retreated, and fired into them again as we advanced still farther. Making inquiries near mile post 16 I learned that the sweet potatoes had been carried away on the preceding Friday by the rebels, and learned that the rebels were encamped in considerable force between mile posts 17 and 18. I then turned off to the left, in the direction of the Middle Ground road, designing to strike the road formerly traveled by the Twentieth Corps, but was encountered by a rebel picket on the first road that I come to, at Mrs. Davis' plantation, and upon inquiring of her I learned that there was a body of 600 rebels within a mile of her house. I then turned to the left and reached the road we had gone out on, at Redoubt No. 1, where, finding no prospect of forage, I returned to camp without further molestation. I am glad to report that no one of the expedition was injured, and that one prisoner was captured, whom I have delivered to the provost-marshal.

Respectfully submitted.

JOHN B. LE SAGE,
Lieutenant-Colonel 101st Illinois Vols., Commanding Expedition.

HEADQUARTERS SECOND DIVISION, TWENTIETH CORPS,
Near Savannah, Ga., December 19, 1864.

Lieut. Col. H. W. PERKINS,
Assistant Adjutant-General, Twentieth Corps:

COLONEL: In accordance with orders received yesterday, I have the honor to report that after careful investigation, I do not discover anything not known before respecting the enemy's position in my front and the roads or avenues of approach leading from my line to theirs.

I have the honor to be, very respectfully, your obedient servant,

JNO. W. GEARY,
Brigadier-General, Commanding Division.

HDQRS. SECOND DIVISION, TWENTIETH ARMY CORPS,
Near Savannah, Ga., December 19, 1864.

Col. ARIO PARDEE, Jr.,
Commanding First Brigade:

COLONEL: The general commanding division directs that you take charge of the work on Fort No. 2, and push it if possible to completion by morning, keeping as many men as can be worked constantly busy. He wishes the working parties thoroughly organized in the most efficient manner before dark, and the officers in charge of them to be held responsible that they do not neglect their work, as was the case last night. The working detail he wishes to be under command of an energetic field officer who understands the work.

I am, colonel, very respectfully, your obedient servant,

W. T. FORBES,
Acting Assistant Adjutant-General.

HDQRS. SECOND DIVISION, TWENTIETH ARMY CORPS,
Near Savannah, Ga., December 19, 1864.

Col. H. A. BARNUM,
Commanding Third Brigade:

COLONEL: The general commanding division directs that you take charge of the construction of Fort No. 3, and push it as far toward completion to-night as possible. He wishes the working parties thoroughly organized in the most efficient manner before dark, the whole to be under command of an energetic field officer who understands how the work should be done. The officers in charge of them he wishes you to hold responsible for every man under their command, that they will not neglect their work, as was done last night.

I am, colonel, very respectfully, your obedient servant,

W. T. FORBES,
Acting Assistant Adjutant-General.

HEADQUARTERS DEPARTMENT OF THE SOUTH,
Hilton Head, S. C., December 19, 1864.

Capt. C. R. SUTER,
Chief Engineer Dept. of the South, Hilton Head, S. C.:

CAPTAIN: The major-general commanding directs that you proceed immediately to the front, and remain with the Coast Division during its operations.

Very respectfully, your obedient servant,

W. L. M. BURGER,
Assistant Adjutant-General.

DECEMBER 19, 1864.

[General JOHN G. FOSTER:]

GENERAL: The lady who makes the inclosed statement is the most observing person I have found, and I think that her statement is more likely to be true. It seems probable that the people of Savannah may be able to hold out for thirty days. I think this an outside calculation.

Respectfully,

JAMES F. HALL,
Lieut. Col. 1st New York Engrs., Pro. Mar. Gen., Dept. of the South.

[Inclosure.]

Mrs. Hodges states that there was a large quantity of provisions in Savannah when she left on the 3d of November. She knew of two Government stores on Broughton street, one over 150 feet and one 75 feet; the lower floor was filled with rice, hominy, meal, and bacon; there was a great quantity. There was another store on Bay street, where provisions were sold to the people. There were a number of private stores filled with provisions. She estimates that there is rice, hominy, and bacon enough to supply the present army and inhabitants at least two weeks. The people depended principally on the markets. The chief supply came from the Albany and Gulf Railroad. The citizens have mostly private supplies to a considerable amount. It might be that they could hold out for a month.

SPECIAL ORDERS, No. 11. } HDQRS. COAST DIV., DEPT. OF THE SOUTH, *Deveaux's Neck, S. C., December 19, 1864.*

* * * * * * *

II. Col. E. N. Hallowell, commanding Second Brigade, will dispatch the Fifty-fourth Massachusetts Volunteers and the Thirty-third U. S. Colored Troops to the lower landing, to embark to-night, and will himself report at these headquarters for instructions.

III. Brig. Gen. E. E. Potter will place a regiment of his command, to replace the Thirty-third U. S. Colored Troops, in the rifle-pit to the left of the right battery, and one, to replace the Fifty-fourth Massachusetts Volunteers, on the right of the same battery. This disposition will be made at once.

By order of Brigadier-General Hatch:

LEONARD B. PERRY,
Lieutenant and Acting Assistant Adjutant-General.

CITY POINT, VA., *December 20, 1864—2 p. m.*

Hon. E. M. STANTON, *Secretary of War:*

Colonel Babcock, of my staff, has just returned from bearing dispatches to Sherman. As he visited and saw all the army with Sherman I have thought it might prove interesting to you to see him. He will leave in the mail-boat in the morning with a copy of Sherman's letter.*

U. S. GRANT,
Lieutenant-General.

HEADQUARTERS ARMIES OF THE UNITED STATES,
City Point, Va., December 20, 1864.

Col. A. H. MARKLAND,
Special Agent Post-Office Department, Eutaw House, Baltimore, Md.:

I would be pleased to have you obtain the authority from the Postmaster-General to go to Savannah and arrange for the regular transmission and distribution of the mails for General Sherman's army. I understand Mrs. Markland desires to accompany you; if so, she has permission to go.

U. S. GRANT,
Lieutenant-General.

[DECEMBER 20, 1864.—For the "effective strength" of General Sherman's army, see p. 16.]

HDQRS. DEPARTMENT AND ARMY OF THE TENNESSEE,
Near Savannah, Ga., December 20, 1864.

Col. A. BECKWITH,
Military Division of the Mississippi:

General Giles A. Smith has but two brigades (Colonel Potts' included), and his division has been selected for making a lodgment on the enemy's works; therefore I wish to have Colonel Potts' brigade rejoin

---

* Of December 16, p. 726.

its division. General Sherman's order said as soon as the four regiments reported to you that brigade would be relieved. Have the kindness to relieve it and oblige,

Yours, respectfully,

O. O. HOWARD,
Major-General.

HDQRS. DEPARTMENT AND ARMY OF THE TENNESSEE,
Near Savannah, Ga., December 20, 1864.

Major-General OSTERHAUS;
Commanding Fifteenth Army Corps:

GENERAL: General Corse requested the privilege of raising a negro regiment for his division for the purpose of pioneer duty, details for work in the quartermaster's and commissary departments, &c. I will approve the raising of two negro regiments, one for each army corps, for the purposes above specified, and give the provisional appointments of such officers as the corps commanders may recommend, subject to the approval of the War Department. Each regiment must be denominated Pioneer Battalion, in conformity with Special Field Orders, No. 120, Military Division of the Mississippi, and must be paid as pioneers are now paid, should the War Department fail to approve my action.

Respectfully, &c.,

O. O. HOWARD,
Major-General.

(Same to Maj. Gen. F. P. Blair, commanding Seventeenth Army Corps.)

HEADQUARTERS FIFTEENTH ARMY CORPS,
Anderson's Plantation, Ga., December 20, 1864.

Major STOLBRAND,
Chief of Artillery, Fifteenth Army Corps:

MAJOR: You will please order the following distribution of the artillery to assist in the expected assault on the rebel lines: Savannah road battery, four 12-pounder guns; Cemetery battery, two 12-pounder guns; Lone Tree battery, four 20-pounder guns; Railroad battery, John E. Smith, two 3-inch guns; Barbette battery (to the right of), two 12-pounder guns. The remaining pieces, to wit, one section 12-pounder guns, one section 3-inch guns, will be kept in reserve, and for that purpose placed near the breast-works on General Corse's right near the causeway. They will be kept ready to be thrown to any point where they may be needed. Order the battery commanders to whom the different positions will be assigned to prepare substantial platforms and secure magazines, and to get everything ready to meet any emergency.

Very respectfully, yours, &c.,

P. JOS. OSTERHAUS,
Major-General.

HEADQUARTERS FIFTEENTH ARMY CORPS,
Near Savannah, Ga., December 20, 1864.

Brigadier-General HAZEN,
Commanding Second Division:

GENERAL: You will cause your strongest brigade to report at these headquarters to-morrow night (the 21st) to assist in the contemplated assault on the rebel lines. The men will be provided with three days' rations in haversacks and eighty rounds of ammunition.

By order of Major-General Osterhaus:

F. F. WHITEHEAD,
Assistant Adjutant-General.

SPECIAL ORDERS, No. 312.
HDQRS. SEVENTEENTH ARMY CORPS,
Near Savannah, Ga., December 20, 1864.

I. Brig. Gen. G. A. Smith, commanding Fourth Division, will detail from the First Minnesota Battery one gunner and three men to report to Maj. A. C. Waterhouse, chief of artillery, at the battery on the causeway immediately.

II. Brig. Gen. M. D. Leggett, commanding Third Division, will detail from the Fifteenth Ohio Battery one sergeant and three men to report to Maj. A. C. Waterhouse, chief of artillery, at the battery on the causeway immediately.

* * * * * * *

IV. As soon as a regiment from each corps in the Army of Georgia has reported, in accordance with orders from Major-General Sherman, to Colonel Beckwith, acting chief quartermaster, Military Division of the Mississippi, at King's Bridge, Col. B. F. Potts, commanding First Brigade, Fourth Division, Seventeenth Army Corps, will proceed to the front with his command and report to his division commander.

* * * * * * *

By command of Maj. Gen. F. P. Blair:

C. CADLE, JR.,
Assistant Adjutant-General.

HEADQUARTERS SEVENTEENTH ARMY CORPS,
Near Savannah, Ga., December 20, 1864.

Brig. Gen. G. A. SMITH,
Commanding Fourth Division:

GENERAL: I am directed by the major-general commanding to say to you that the order sent herewith* is to be considered imperative and to be obeyed by Colonel Potts without regard to any orders he may receive from Colonel Beckwith to the contrary. He wishes you to have your regiment (350 strong) and fifty negroes report to Colonel Beckwith, in accordance with Special Orders, No. 311, extract IV, from these headquarters, of yesterday's date, before the brigade is relieved.

Very respectfully, your obedient servant,

C. CADLE, JR.,
Assistant Adjutant-General.

---

* See next, *ante*.

HEADQUARTERS LEFT WING, ARMY OF GEORGIA,
December 20, 1864—8 a. m.

Capt. L. M. DAYTON,
Aide-de-Camp, Military Division of the Mississippi:

CAPTAIN: I am now fully prepared to execute any orders the general-in-chief may issue. All our batteries are finished, but the six 20-pounder guns have not yet come. As soon as they are received I think I can silence the enemy's guns and make a successful assault. If you have any information as to the 20-pounder guns I wish you would give it to me. I have teams waiting for them. I have a brigade on the South Carolina shore.

Very respectfully, your obedient servant,

H. W. SLOCUM,
Major-General.

HEADQUARTERS MILITARY DIVISION OF THE MISSISSIPPI,
In the Field, December 20, 1864—12 m.

Major-General SLOCUM,
Commanding, &c.:

GENERAL: Yours of 8 a. m. is just to hand. The general-in-chief has not yet returned from the Bay. I expect him this p. m., when yours shall be placed before him. Being five miles from the dock, and all the staff with the general, I am unable to give you any information as regards the 20-pounders, but will try to find out, and will write you promptly all I can learn. There is no news, and no later papers than you have seen.

I am, general, with respect, &c.,

L. M. DAYTON,
Aide-de-Camp.

HEADQUARTERS MILITARY DIVISION OF THE MISSISSIPPI,
In the Field, December 20, 1864—5 p. m.

Major-General SLOCUM,
Commanding, &c.:

GENERAL: General Howard reports being ready; but the general-in-chief has not returned, and has not, to my knowledge, authorized any orders. We are therefore in a respectable condition to remain quiet until he gives orders of execution. Word from King's Bridge says plenty of rations there; also oats, &c.

I am, general, with respect,

L. M. DAYTON,
Aide-de-Camp.

HEADQUARTERS FOURTEENTH ARMY CORPS,
Before Savannah, Ga., December 20, 1864.

Lieut. Col. H. C. RODGERS,
A. A. G. and Chief of Staff, Left Wing, Army of Georgia:

I have the honor to state for the information of the general commanding that the regiment required was ordered to report to Colonel Beckwith, at King's Bridge, for fatigue duty this morning. Efforts have been made to find fifty negroes in the corps who could be sent with the regiment, but without effect as all the unemployed negroes had already been sent, 544 in number, and a large proportion of them able-bodied men.

I have the honor to be, colonel, very respectfully, your obedient servant,

JEF. C. DAVIS,
Brevet Major-General, Commanding.

HDQRS. SECOND DIVISION, FOURTEENTH ARMY CORPS,
Near Savannah, Ga., December 20, 1864.

Lieutenant-Colonel MCCLURG,
Asst. Adjt. Gen. and Chief of Staff, 14th Army Corps:

SIR: In compliance with circular from corps headquarters, dated December 19, 1864, I have the honor to report that I made a personal examination of my lines with reference to finding some point from which an assault could be made upon the enemy's works. I am sorry to say that I have no place from which one could be made with any reasonable hope of success. Inclosed herewith please find map* of my position. Running diagonally across my entire front is a deep and, to an army, impenetrable swamp; on my left is the Milledgeville road, running nearly perpendicular to my front; the road is commanded by a well-constructed fort, with abatis and other obstructions in front, the water of the swamp over and across the road for some eighty yards, depth not known. To advance a column by the flank upon this road without any ground for deployment, under a heavy fire, would be a useless destruction of life, without a corresponding advantage. On my left is the canal; the only approach by this flank is the tow-path, with undoubled files, and advance under heavy fire from more than one battery. I have ordered a section of Lieutenant Rich's battery to be placed in position on Milledgeville road, about 300 yards from rebel battery. Fascines are being constructed as ordered, also foot bridges across the canal.

All of which is respectfully submitted.

I have the honor to be, colonel, your obedient servant,

JAMES D. MORGAN,
Brigadier-General.

HEADQUARTERS TWENTIETH CORPS,
Before Savannah, Ga., December 20, 1864.

Colonel BUELL,
Commanding Pontoon Train:

COLONEL: I am directed by the brigadier-general commanding the corps to request you to send two wagon-loads of balks to Brigadier-General Geary, commanding Second Division.

Very respectfully, your obedient servant,

ROBT. P. DECHERT,
Captain and Acting Assistant Adjutant-General.

---

*Not found.

HDQRS. THIRTY-THIRD MASSACHUSETTS VOL. INFANTRY,
Near Savannah, Ga., December 20, 1864.

Capt. C. H. YOUNG,
Acting Assistant Adjutant-General:

I have the honor to submit the following, which is a correct statement of two scouts sent out last night for the purpose of reconnoitering in front of the enemy's works:

STATEMENT OF CORPORAL BLACK.

After arriving at the picket-line he started to about forty paces to the left of the Savannah and Charleston Railroad; advanced some seventy paces on clear ground without discovering any obstructions and no impediments, after which encountered large pine trees felled, ground uneven and no water; with some difficulty climbed over the felled trees and came to swampy ground, and still further on came to a pond varying from six to twelve feet in width, tried the depth of the pond by means of a pole and judged it to be some five feet deep with soft spongy ground, after which moved further to the left by creeping under and climbing over the fallen trees and found tolerable good ground, no water, but fallen timber, and as far as he could see it was all fallen timber—not trimmed. To his judgment advanced to within some 200 yards of the enemy's main works, could distinctly hear the enemy talk and see them gathered around their camp-fires; owing to the reflection of their fires it was difficult to see very distinctly. On returning he kept still further to our left, thinking by avoiding the trees he could return much easier than going over the same ground he advanced over, encountering less obstructions.

STATEMENT BY PRIVATE M'GOWAN.

Started from picket-line about forty paces to the left of the point where Corporal Black started from, advanced nearly 100 paces without encountering any obstructions, then encountered small trees apparently carefully fallen to obstruct the advance of troops; here he was unable to advance any further, upon which he went further to the left encountering the same obstruction; ground uneven and sloping down to swampy ground, which appearance indicated there must be a stream of water running through and trees fallen clean to the enemy's works; could plainly hear the enemy talk and see them around their camp-fires; returned nearly on the same ground with about the same obstructions.

Very respectfully, yours,

ELISHA DOANE,
Lieutenant-Colonel, Commanding.

HEADQUARTERS DEPARTMENT OF THE SOUTH,
Hilton Head, S. C., December 20, 1864.

General W. T. SHERMAN:

GENERAL: Dispatch received. General Easton left for Fort McAllister yesterday morning on the steamer Mayflower. Please come on shore; I want to see you very much.

Yours, respectfully,

J. G. FOSTER,
Major-General Volunteers.

HDQRS. COAST DIVISION, DEPARTMENT OF THE SOUTH,
Deveaux's Neck, S. C., December 20, 1864.

Maj. Gen. J. G. FOSTER:
Commanding Department of the South:

GENERAL: Yesterday morning I put three rifled guns in the marsh, 900 yards from the small railroad bridge, and damaged it so much that no trains have passed since. The ground is so bad that I can not get the 30-pounders there. I have a platform laid down for one 30-pounder that will reach the railroad at a range of 1,300 yards. Am not firing now, as we are out of all kinds of ammunition, except that for our muskets; have sent to the Head for more, but no attention is paid to our requisitions, or no transportation is furnished to bring it up. Have put two more regiments on Mackay's Neck. Intend making a feint there, but hope to cross the main force over the Coosawhatchie and assault the fort in the rear. To-day the Thirty-third [U. S. Colored] had an affair two miles and a half from Jenkins' plantation. They dispersed a force of 300 of the enemy, capturing their camp and blankets, but getting no prisoners. They lost 2 killed and 9 wounded.

Very respectfully, your obedient servant,

JNO. P. HATCH,
Brigadier-General, Commanding.

I hope you will find time to make us a visit.

J. P. H.

HDQRS. NORTHERN DISTRICT, DEPT. OF THE SOUTH,
Morris Island, S. C., December 20, 1864.

Capt. W. L. M. BURGER,
Assistant Adjutant-General, Department of the South:

CAPTAIN: I have the honor to report that nothing of especial importance has occurred within the command since my last communication. The enemy on my front have remained exceedingly quiet, and no movement has been attempted on my part.

I have the honor to be, with the highest respect, your obedient servant,

A. SCHIMMELFENNIG,
Brigadier-General, Commanding.

HEADQUARTERS MILITARY DIVISION OF THE MISSISSIPPI,
In the Field, December 21, 1864—9 a. m.

[Gen. W. T. SHERMAN:]

DEAR GENERAL: I have sent you two dispatches via Fort McAllister in hopes of reaching you. General Slocum reports enemy gone from his front and he has got eight guns—this report at 4 a. m. He is also gone from this front and General Howard reports Leggett near the city, and no enemy. General Woods also got six guns. General Slocum is moving and General Howard the same and I have no doubt both are in Savannah now. I will ride with General Howard, at his request, and leave our camp until the matter is more definite and you make orders.

I am, general, &c.,

L. M. DAYTON,
Aide-de-Camp.

HEADQUARTERS MILITARY DIVISION OF THE MISSISSIPPI,
In the Field, Savannah, Ga., December 21, 1864.

Admiral DAHLGREN,
Commanding South Atlantic Squadron:

SIR: Savannah is ours, with upwards of sixty heavy guns and a large quantity of public property, cars, cotton, &c. In the absence of General Sherman, General Howard requests you to clear away the torpedoes and other obstructions in the Savannah River channel.

I am, sir, with respect,

L. M. DAYTON,
Aide-de-Camp.

KING'S BRIDGE, *December 21, 1864.*

Captain DAYTON,
Aide-de-Camp:

DEAR CAPTAIN: News has reached here by an orderly that Savannah was evacuated last night. It is highly important that we should know whether this news be correct or not. Please, therefore, give me the earliest information in regard to it.

Yours, in haste,

A. BECKWITH,
Colonel and Chief Commissary of Subsistence.

HEADQUARTERS MILITARY DIVISION OF THE MISSISSIPPI,
In the Field, December 21, 1864.

Colonel BECKWITH,
Chief Commissary of Subsistence:

I send a letter* for the general, giving the condition of things up to this time. Please see that he gets it soon as possible. The enemy has abandoned the outer works, and probably the city itself. We have now fourteen guns, and are near the city.

L. M. DAYTON,
Aide-de-Camp.

SAVANNAH, *December 21, 1864.*

Maj. Gen. W. T. SHERMAN,
Commanding U. S. Military Forces near Savannah:

SIR: The city of Savannah was last night evacuated by the Confederate military and is now entirely defenseless. As chief magistrate of the city I respectfully request your protection of the lives and private property of the citizens and of our women and children.

Trusting that this appeal to your generosity and humanity may favorably influence your action, I have the honor to be, your obedient servant,

R. D. ARNOLD,
Mayor of Savannah.

---

* See 9 a. m., p. 771.

HDQRS. DEPARTMENT AND ARMY OF THE TENNESSEE,
Near Savannah, Ga., December 21, 1864.

Capt. L. M. DAYTON,
Aide-de-Camp, Military Division of the Mississippi:

It was reported at sunrise by Brigadier-General Leggett that the enemy had evacuated his works; subsequently, by Brig. Gen. G. A. Smith, that the large fort was in his possession and that the enemy was reported to have gone to Hardeeville, S. C. I have directed an immediate pursuit.

Very respectfully,

O. O. HOWARD,
Major-General.

SPECIAL FIELD ORDERS, No. 201.

HEADQUARTERS DEPARTMENT AND ARMY OF THE TENNESSEE,
Savannah, Ga., December 21, 1864.

I. Colonel Woods, commanding Seventy-sixth Ohio Infantry, First Brigade, First Division, Fifteenth Army Corps, is appointed provost-marshal of that portion of the city of Savannah east of Bull street (a continuation of the White Bluff road), and will enter at once upon his duties as such, reporting without delay for further instructions to Brig. Gen. John W. Geary, Second Division, Twentieth Army Corps, commandant of the post of Savannah.

* * * * * * *

III. Maj. Gen. P. Joseph Osterhaus, commanding Fifteenth Army Corps, will picket all roads from the plank road around to his left (facing to the rear), former right. Major-General Blair, commanding Seventeenth Army Corps, will cause the brigade of Brigadier-General Sprague to remain in its present position on the canal until further orders, and will give instructions for it to picket all roads in its vicinity as far east as the Darien road.

By order of Maj. Gen. O. O. Howard:

SAML. L. TAGGART,
Assistant Adjutant-General.

HEADQUARTERS FIFTEENTH ARMY CORPS,
Savannah, Ga., December 21, 1864.

Capt. SAMUEL L. TAGGART,
Asst. Adjt. Gen., Department and Army of the Tennessee:

CAPTAIN: In reply to your communication of date, I have the honor to report the capture by my command of 13 pieces of artillery, 8 pieces in front of First Division and 5 pieces in front of Fourth Division. The troops are disposed of as follows: The First Division on the right of Savannah road, inside and parallel to works; the Third Division in prolongation of First Division line, reaching across Gulf railroad; the Fourth Division inside the lines of First and Third Divisions, with a brigade thrown across Gulf railroad at the crossing of Fort Jackson road, facing southeast; one brigade of Second Division in rear of First Division, and remainder of division garrisoning Fort McAllister and destroying Gulf railroad.

Very respectfully, your obedient servant,

P. JOS. OSTERHAUS,
Major-General.

HDQRS. SECOND DIVISION, FIFTEENTH ARMY CORPS,
Fort McAllister, Ga., December 21, 1864.

ASSISTANT ADJUTANT-GENERAL,
Headquarters Department of the Tennessee:

I have the honor to report the Gulf railroad, from a point near Walthourville, twenty-two miles from the Ogeechee River, to within two miles of that stream, thoroughly destroyed, and the remainder will be by sunset to-day. The rails are all twisted and the ties all burned. In obedience to orders from headquarters Fifteenth Corps one of the brigades will be sent direct from the railroad with extra ammunition and rations for service in front of the enemy's lines.

I am, respectfully, your obedient servant,

W. B. HAZEN,
Brigadier-General.

HEADQUARTERS FIFTEENTH ARMY CORPS,
Savannah, Ga., December 21, 1864.

Brig. Gen. W. B. HAZEN,
Commanding Second Division:

GENERAL: The major-general commanding directs me to say that Savannah was evacuated during last night and occupied by our forces this a. m. The enemy left quite a number of guns and a large quantity of military stores of all kinds. The general directs that you hold your command in its present position until further orders. The brigade ordered to be sent forward can remain with its division and encamp at any convenient place near King's Bridge.

I am, general, very respectfully, your obedient servant,

F. F. WHITEHEAD,
Assistant Adjutant-General.

SPECIAL ORDERS, No. 258. } HDQRS. 3D DIV., 15TH ARMY CORPS,
Station No. 1, Gulf Railroad, Ga.,
December 21, 1864.

I. This command will move at once in the following order: First, pioneer corps and tool wagons; second, Second Brigade; third, four regiments of First Brigade; fourth, ammunition train; fifth, division headquarters train and provost-guard; sixth, pioneer corps wagons; seventh, Second Brigade train, including regimental wagons; eighth, First Brigade train, including regimental wagons; ninth, quartermaster's train; tenth, commissary of subsistence train; eleventh, ambulance corps, except ambulances assigned to regiments and detachments; twelfth, one regiment First Brigade, rear guard. One ambulance will follow each regiment and pioneer corps.

By order of Brig. Gen. John E. Smith:

S. M. BUDLONG,
Assistant Adjutant-General.

HDQRS. FOURTH DIVISION, FIFTEENTH ARMY CORPS,
Near Savannah, December 21, 1864.

Col. R. N. ADAMS,
Commanding Second Brigade:

COLONEL: The enemy is gone. General Woods has a regiment across. The general directs that you push your brigade over, using the small boats, and move to the railroad, holding the same so as to cover the crossing of the Third Division. Make all haste possible.

I am, colonel, very respectfully, your obedient servant,

L. CARPER,
Assistant Adjutant-General.

HEADQUARTERS SEVENTEENTH ARMY CORPS,
Corner York and Abercorn Streets,
Savannah, Ga., December 21, 1864.

[Capt. S. L. TAGGART:]

CAPTAIN: I have the honor to report that General Leggett's division is encamped on the Ogeechee road, on the edge of the city. One brigade of General Smith's division is at the same place, and one brigade at King's Bridge. General Sprague's brigade, of the First Division, is at the mouth of the canal, and the other two brigades are still out on the Gulf road, but should be back to-night. One regiment from the Third Division is on the road to the rear of our headquarters. A report of the guns captured will be sent in as soon as ascertained.

Very respectfully,

FRANK P. BLAIR, JR.,
Major-General.

HEADQUARTERS SEVENTEENTH ARMY CORPS,
Corner York and Abercorn Streets,
Savannah, Ga., December 21, 1864.

Capt. S. L. TAGGART,
Asst. Adjt. Gen., Department and Army of the Tennessee:

CAPTAIN: I have the honor to report the following as the number of pieces of artillery captured by this corps to-day: smooth, nine 32-pounders, three 24-pounders, two 12-pounders, three 6-pounders; one 20-pounder Parrott, one 10-pounder Parrott—in all nineteen pieces. I also have the honor to report that Major-General Mower has reached camp.

Very respectfully, your obedient servant,

FRANK P. BLAIR, JR.,
Major-General.

HDQRS. THIRD DIVISION, SEVENTEENTH ARMY CORPS,
Near Savannah, December 21, 1864.

Capt. C. CADLE, Jr.,
Assistant Adjutant-General:

CAPTAIN: General Leggett desires me to inform you that he is near the city of Savannah with the First Brigade of this command; that he has taken some prisoners, and they state that the city is evacuated.

I am, captain, very truly, yours,

J. C. DOUGLASS,
Assistant Adjutant-General.

HDQRS. FOURTH DIVISION, SEVENTEENTH ARMY CORPS,
Savannah, Ga., December 21, 1864.

Lieut. Col. A. HICKENLOOPER,
Inspector-General, Seventeenth Army Corps:

SIR: I have the honor to report that the Fourth Division, Seventeenth Army Corps, captured in their front this morning two 32, one 12, and two 6-pounder smooth-bore guns. We are now encamped on the plank road, about one mile out on the right-hand side; our left joining the Third Division near the cemetery; our line running nearly parallel to the road. Please show this to the assistant adjutant-general, as that officer has just called for a similar report.

Very respectfully, your obedient servant,

R. H. ALLISON,
Major and Division Inspector-General.

HDQRS. DEPARTMENT AND ARMY OF THE TENNESSEE,
Near Savannah, Ga., December 21, 1864.

Maj. Gen. H. W. SLOCUM,
Commanding Left Wing, Army of Georgia:

GENERAL: The enemy evacuated my front between 12 m. and morning. General Sherman is not back. I presume you are by this time in possession of the city. If you are you had better place a division as guard and throw a bridge as soon as possible where Hardee had his. I will join you and co-operate. If Hardee makes a stand at the inner line we will close in on him as soon as possible.

Very respectfully,

O. O. HOWARD,
Major-General.

HEADQUARTERS LEFT WING, ARMY OF GEORGIA,
Savannah, Ga., December 21, 1864—7 a. m.

Capt. L. M. DAYTON,
Aide-de-Camp:

I have just arrived here. General Geary occupied the town at 5 o'clock this a. m. with his division. I have for the present placed guards over all public and private property, and await orders from the general-in-chief.

Very respectfully, your obedient servant,

H. W. SLOCUM,
Major-General.

HEADQUARTERS MILITARY DIVISION OF THE MISSISSIPPI,
In the Field, December 21, 1864—7 a. m.

General SLOCUM,
Commanding, &c.:

GENERAL: Yours 4 a. m. just received. The general-in-chief has not returned. I will notify General Howard at once of your progress, and if you wish to do anything more than what you propose General Howard will make orders for you.

I am, general, with respect,

L. M. DAYTON,
Aide-de-Camp.

HEADQUARTERS MILITARY DIVISION OF THE MISSISSIPPI,
December 21, 1864—7.15 a. m.

General SLOCUM,
Commanding, &c.:

GENERAL: Coming to General Howard, he informs me that about sunrise it was reported to him the enemy had left his front. He at once gave orders to push on and follow up, which is now being done. I will telegraph General Sherman, who may be coming up.

I am, with respect,

L. M. DAYTON,
Aide-de-Camp.

HEADQUARTERS MILITARY DIVISION OF THE MISSISSIPPI,
In the Field, Savannah, Ga., December 21, 1864.

Maj. Gen. H. W. SLOCUM,
Commanding Left Wing:

GENERAL: An officer of General Howard has been to Fort Beaulieu and communicated with the Sonoma from which he learned the general-in-chief has gone to Hilton Head, though it is not sure. However, the fleet is fully aware of our position here, and I will make dispatch to the admiral, requesting him to at once commence on the obstructions in the channel. To have a complete understanding about pickets and road guards it seems to be best that you should take charge of that section from the Savannah on the west around to the plank road, and General Howard from there around to the Savannah on the east. This is his suggestion. He will also guard the plank road back to King's Bridge. Some of his troops are now properly stationed about it and will obviate moving troops especially. The King's Bridge will be necessarily our base for several days, and should be well secured against cavalry from the west. General Howard will retain a division at the Ogeechee for that purpose. General Howard wishes you to reconnoiter and if practicable throw a bridge from Hutchinson's Island to the main land in South Carolina.

I am, general, very respectfully, &c.,

L. M. DAYTON,
Aide-de-Camp.

SPECIAL ORDERS, No. 7. } HDQRS. LEFT WING, ARMY OF GEORGIA,
Savannah, Ga., December 21, 1864.

I. Brig. Gen. John W. Geary, U. S. Volunteers, is hereby assigned to the command of the city of Savannah.

II. Corps commanders will furnish, upon the application of General Geary, the necessary details for guards, &c., for that portion of the city lying west of Bull street, being the prolongation of White Bluff road as laid down in the city map.

By command of Major-General Slocum:

H. C. RODGERS,
Assistant Adjutant-General.

HEADQUARTERS LEFT WING, ARMY OF GEORGIA,
December 21, 1864—4 a. m.

General J. C. DAVIS,
Commanding Fourteenth Army Corps:

GENERAL: The enemy has abandoned his exterior line in front of the Twentieth Corps, and has probably evacuated the city, as he left eight guns in one of the works in our front. Move your command forward and see if there is anything in your front.

Yours, very respectfully,

H. W. SLOCUM,
Major-General.

SPECIAL FIELD ORDERS, No. 28.

HDQRS. FOURTEENTH ARMY CORPS,
Before Savannah, Ga.,
December 21, 1864.

The corps will move to-morrow, to go into camp near Savannah, in the following order:

General Carlin will march at 7.30 a. m., move down the canal on the south bank until he reaches the road crossing the canal about three miles from Savannah; he will then take the right-hand road, move to the next crossing, and there take the road leading east, and will go into camp on the south of this road. A staff officer will be prepared to show him the position more definitely.

General Morgan will move at 7.30 a. m. upon the main Savannah road to the cross-road about three miles from Savannah; he will there take the right-hand road, cross the canal, and go into camp between General Carlin and the canal.

General Baird will march east upon the main Savannah road as soon as General Morgan's trains have cleared the road, and will go into camp in line with Generals Carlin and Morgan between the Savannah and Louisville road and the canal.

The corps will be arranged in as perfect order, in accordance with prescribed regulations, as the ground will admit of, and will be faced west and southwest. The picket-lines will be formed in the old rebel works under the supervision of the corps inspector, Lieutenant Litchfield.

The trains and artillery will be parked in the rear of their respective divisions as compactly as possible, and Generals Carlin and Morgan will thoroughly repair the roads upon which their respective divisions move.

By order of Bvt. Maj. Gen. J. C. Davis:

A. C. McCLURG,
Lieutenant-Colonel and Chief of Staff.

HDQRS. FIRST DIVISION, FOURTEENTH ARMY CORPS,
December 21, 1864.

Colonel MILES, *Commanding Third Brigade:*

COLONEL: Advance your skirmish line in the direction of the city of Savannah, going as far as it can, supported by a regiment of your brigade. Direct the commanding officer to send you reports of our own or the enemy's troops when necessary.

By order of General Carlin:

G. W. SMITH,
Captain and Acting Assistant Adjutant-General.

HEADQUARTERS FOURTEENTH ARMY CORPS,
Before Savannah, Ga., December 21, 1864—5.30 a. m.

Brig. Gen. J. D. MORGAN,
Commanding Second Division, Fourteenth Army Corps:

General Slocum reports the enemy gone from the front of the Twentieth Corps, or at least from the exterior works, leaving eight guns, and probably the city evacuated. The general commanding directs that you move your picket-line forward at once and hold your entire command in readiness.

I have the honor to be, general, very respectfully, your obedient servant,

A. C. McCLURG,
Assistant Adjutant-General and Chief of Staff.

HEADQUARTERS TWENTIETH CORPS,
Before Savannah, Ga., December 21, 1864—5 a. m.

Brig. Gen. N. J. JACKSON,
Commanding First Division:

GENERAL: I am directed by the general commanding to inform you that General Geary is in possession of the enemy's advance forts on the left, and that the enemy has evacuated. He directs that you move forward your pickets to the town and hold your command in readiness to move.

Very respectfully, your obedient servant,

ROBT. P. DECHERT,
Captain and Acting Assistant Adjutant-General.

(Same to Brig. Gen. W. T. Ward, commanding Third Division.)

HEADQUARTERS TWENTIETH CORPS,
Before Savannah, Ga., December 21, 1864—5.30 a. m.

Brig. Gen. N. J. JACKSON,
Commanding First Division:

GENERAL: The general commanding directs that you move forward your brigade now in the line of works and occupy the enemy's works.

Very respectfully, your obedient servant,

ROBT. P. DECHERT,
Captain and Acting Assistant Adjutant-General.

HEADQUARTERS TWENTIETH CORPS,
Before Savannah, Ga., December 21, 1864.

Brig. Gen. N. J. JACKSON,
Commanding First Division:

GENERAL: The general commanding directs that Colonel Carman's brigade be moved to this side of the river, leaving one regiment on the island for the present. He wishes the brigade encamped on this side so that they will protect the two rice mills.

Very respectfully, your obedient servant,

ROBT. P. DECHERT,
Captain and Acting Assistant Adjutant-General.

HEADQUARTERS TWENTIETH CORPS,
Savannah, Ga., December 21, 1864.

Brigadier-General GEARY,
Commanding Second Division:

GENERAL: By direction of Major-General Slocum, commanding Left Wing, Army of Georgia, you are hereby placed in temporary command of the city of Savannah. You will at once establish such regulations as are necessary to preserve order throughout the city.

Very respectfully, your obedient servant,

H. W. PERKINS,
Assistant Adjutant-General.

HDQRS. SECOND DIVISION, TWENTIETH ARMY CORPS,
Savannah, Ga., December 21, 1864.

Lieut. Col. H. W. PERKINS,
Assistant Adjutant-General, Twentieth Corps:

COLONEL: I have the honor to report that a detachment of my troops occupy Fort Jackson. It was found evacuated and is occupied by two regiments from my First Brigade. The captures there are fifteen heavy guns, and considerable ammunition and other material, the amounts of which have not yet been reported to me.

I am, colonel, very respectfully, your obedient servant,

JNO. W. GEARY,
Brigadier-General, U. S. Volunteers, Commanding Division.

HEADQUARTERS TWENTIETH CORPS,
Savannah, Ga., December 21, 1864.

Brig. Gen. J. W. GEARY,
Commanding Second Division:

GENERAL: The general commanding directs me to say that the troops of your command now at the rice mills on the river will be relieved to-morrow morning by other troops. The mill is still running.

Very respectfully, your obedient servant,

ROBT. P. DECHERT,
Captain and Acting Assistant Adjutant-General.

HEADQUARTERS U. S. FORCES,
Fort Jackson, Ga., December 21, 1864.

Capt. WILLIAM T. FORBES,
Actg. Asst. Adjt. Gen., Second Division, 20th Army Corps:

CAPTAIN: I have the honor to report that, in compliance with orders received from Col. Ario Pardee, commanding First Brigade, Second Division, Twentieth Army Corps, the Twenty-eighth Regiment Pennsylvania Veteran Volunteer Infantry and Twenty-ninth Regiment Ohio Volunteer Infantry, in all numbering 572 enlisted men and 16 commissioned officers, took possession of Fort Jackson at 7 a. m., this 21st of December, 1864. The fort was found to have been fired by the enemy, burning the quarters of the officers and men, and blowing up one of the magazines. A large amount of ordnance and ordnance stores were found, an inventory of which is herewith inclosed. There is now in the fort a magazine, the contents of which it is deemed advisable not to handle, as the doors are fastened in such a manner as indicate that an explosion would occur upon entering them. The fire in the fort was extinguished immediately upon my arrival.

Respectfully submitted,

JOHN FLYNN,
Colonel, Commanding Detachment.

[Inclosure.]

Inventory of ordnance and ordnance stores taken possession of by Col. John Flynn, commander detachment of First Brigade, Second Division, Twentieth Army Corps, at Fort Jackson and vicinity, December 21, 1864.

64-pounders	4
32-pounders	44
10-inch columbiads	2
8-inch columbiads	20
Rifled 32-pounders	2
24-pound howitzers	12
10-inch mortars	3
8-inch mortar	1
3-inch rifled field pieces	3
10-inch solid shot	400
8-inch solid shot	587
7-inch solid shot	149
6-inch solid shot	2,272
10-inch shell	411
8-inch shell	320
6-inch shell	120
8-inch grape	15
7-inch grape	27
6-inch grape	13
8-inch canister	32
7-inch canister	41
6-inch canister	60
6½-inch canister	32
6½-inch shell, fixed	224
8-inch shell, fixed	130
6½-inch conical shell, fixed	48
Rifled musket powder ... pounds	50

The principal implements of the guns were destroyed, the wheels of the gun carriages were broken, rendering them temporarily unserviceable. The powder, except 50 pounds, was all destroyed by being thrown into the water. The guns were found to be in good order, fourteen of the ninety-one only being spiked and shotted. For the want of lanterns and time I have been unable to examine all the magazines, therefore there must be a large amount of ammunition not included in this inventory.

JOHN FLYNN,
Colonel, Commanding Detachment.

SPECIAL FIELD ORDERS, No. 9. } HDQRS. THIRD BRIGADE, SECOND DIVISION, TWENTIETH ARMY CORPS,
Savannah, Ga., December 21, 1864.

I. That portion of the city of Savannah bounded as follows, viz, east by Bull street, south by Jones street, west by the canal, and north by the Savannah River, having been assigned to the command for quarters and government, it is hereby subdivided as follows: Sub-District No. 1, bounded east by Bull street, south by South Broad street, west by West Broad street, north by the Savannah River, is assigned to the One hundred and second New York Volunteers, Lieut. Col. H. S. Chatfield commanding; Sub-District No. 2, bounded east by Bull street, south by Jones street, west by West Broad street, north by South Broad street, is assigned to the One hundred and eleventh Pennsylvania Veteran Volunteers, Lieut. Col. Thomas M. Walker commanding; Sub-District No. 3, bounded east by West Broad street, south by Jones street, west by the canal and city limits, north by Margaret street, is assigned to the Sixtieth New York Volunteers, Maj. Thomas Elliott commanding; Sub-District No. 4, bounded east by West Broad street, south by Margaret street, west by the canal, north by Bryan street, is assigned to the One hundred and forty-ninth New York Volunteers, Maj. N. Grumbach commanding; Sub-District No. 5, bounded east by West Broad street, south by Bryan street, west by the canal, and north by the Savannah River, is assigned to the Twenty-ninth Pennsylvania Volunteers, Lieut. Col. S. M. Zulich commanding. Commanders of these sub-districts will at once place their commands within their prescribed limits and establish thorough patrols through all the principal streets and protect all peaceable persons and public and private property, quell all disturbances, arresting all disorderly persons and turning them over to the brigade provost guard. Unoccupied buildings may be taken as quarters for officers and men. Regimental commanders will quarter their different companies throughout their district and at the best and most convenient points for guarding and protecting the same buildings, as their company and regimental commanders will locate their headquarters as near the center of their district as practicable. Lieut. Col. K. S. Van Voorhis, commanding One hundred and thirty-seventh New York Volunteers, will receive separate instructions, for his existing orders in regard to passes will be rigidly enforced. Every officer of the command is enjoined to put forth the most strenuous efforts to establish and maintain perfect order and subordination. All breaches of discipline on the part of either officers or men will be punished to the severest extent. All men found within or prowling about the houses of citizens will be arrested and turned over to the provost guard.

By command of Col. H. A. Barnum:

O. T. MAY,
Captain and Acting Assistant Adjutant-General.

HEADQUARTERS TWENTIETH CORPS,
Savannah, Ga., December 21, 1864.

Brig. Gen. W. T. WARD,
Commanding Third Division:

GENERAL: The general commanding directs that the Twenty-second Wisconsin Volunteers relieve the guard of 100 men of General Geary's command at the rice mills on the river to-morrow morning.

Very respectfully, your obedient servant,

ROBT. P. DECHERT,
Captain and Acting Assistant Adjutant-General.

HEADQUARTERS DEPARTMENT OF THE SOUTH,
Hilton Head, S. C., December 21, 1864.

Maj. C. W. THOMAS,
Chief Quartermaster Dept. of the South, Hilton Head, S. C.:

MAJOR: The propellers Monterey and Ashland were sent from here on the 14th instant laden with subsistence stores, with instructions to proceed to the Ogeechee River with said stores for Major-General Sherman's army. Instead of obeying their instructions they dropped anchor at the mouth of the river, much to the detriment of the service and the annoyance of General Sherman's army, who were suffering for some of the provisions on board these vessels. These vessels remained at anchor until ordered up the river by Major-General Foster. For this dereliction of duty on the part of the captains of the above-named propellers, the major-general commanding directs that you deduct $1,000 from the charter party of each of these propellers unless the captains can show good cause for such neglect of duty.

Very respectfully, your obedient servant,

W. L. M. BURGER,
Assistant Adjutant-General.

VERNON RIVER, *December 21, 1864.*

Major-General FOSTER:

SIR: Savannah is ours. General Hardee has gone with his forces to Hardeeville. I heard General Sherman express some anxiety about your position on the Tullifinny, hence this note. Tatnall intends passing out of the Savannah River to-night with the iron-clad Savannah; at least this is reported by Generals Sherman and Howard. We will try and head him off. Please to notify Captain Reynolds and the senior naval officer off Charleston, in case the latter port should be the Savannah's destination. We have Beaulieu, Rosedew, &c.

I am, general, your obedient servant,

J. M. BRADFORD,
Fleet Captain, South Atlantic Blockading Squadron.

SAVANNAH, GA., *December 22, 1864.*
(Via Fort Monroe 6.45 p. m. 25th.)

His Excellency President LINCOLN:

I beg to present you, as a Christmas gift, the city of Savannah, with 150 heavy guns and plenty of ammunition, and also about 25,000 bales of cotton.

W. T. SHERMAN,
Major-General.

HDQRS. DEPARTMENT AND ARMY OF THE TENNESSEE,
Savannah, Ga., December 22, 1864.

Maj. Gen. P. JOS. OSTERHAUS, *Comdg. Fifteenth Army Corps:*

GENERAL: The major-general commanding directs me to notify you that General Sherman desires to review the Army of the Tennessee as soon as it may be ready therefor, and names Saturday, day after to-morrow, as the day on which he will review your command.

Very respectfully, your obedient servant,

SAML. L. TAGGART,
Assistant Adjutant-General.

[Indorsement.]

HEADQUARTERS FIFTEENTH ARMY CORPS,
Savannah, Ga., December 22, 1864.

In compliance with the within order each division commander will at once cause his command to be put in readiness, and will see that it is in a complete and thorough state for the expected review.

By order of Maj. Gen. P. Joseph Osterhaus:

F. F. WHITEHEAD,
Assistant Adjutant-General.

SPECIAL ORDERS, No. 204. } HDQRS. FIFTEENTH ARMY CORPS,
Savannah, Ga., December 22, 1864.

I. The Fourth Division, Brigadier-General Corse commanding, will move from its present camp and occupy the ground between Fort Brown on Shell road and Fort No. 25. Brigadier-General Smith, commanding Third Division, may, if he finds suitable ground, remove the camp of his command to a point between the Shell road and the Gulf railroad. The following will be the assignment of pickets, to take effect immediately: The Fourth Division will picket from the river to the Shell road; the Third Division from the Shell road (where they will connect with the Fourth Division pickets) to the Gulf railroad; the First Division will picket its own front, connecting on the left with pickets of the Third Division and stretching across the plank road to connect with the pickets on their right. Division commanders will immediately send to these headquarters a corrected report of guns captured near Little Ogeechee and around Savannah, giving caliber, &c. General Corse will include in his report all guns between the river and the Shell road; General Smith, those between the Shell road and Gulf railroad; General Woods, those from Gulf railroad to plank road.

By order of Maj. Gen. P. Joseph Osterhaus:

F. F. WHITEHEAD,
Assistant Adjutant-General.

HDQRS. DEPARTMENT AND ARMY OF THE TENNESSEE,
Savannah, Ga., December 22, 1864.

Maj. Gen. F. P. BLAIR,
Commanding Seventeenth Army Corps:

GENERAL: The major-general commanding directs me to say that General Sherman, by a new division, requires this army to picket along the canal from the Ogeechee River to and including the Darien road. He directs me to say that you are intrusted therewith, and will provide and keep on the canal a force sufficient for that purpose. He further tells me to notify you that General Sherman desires to review the Army of the Tennessee as soon as it may be ready therefor, and proposes to review the Fifteenth Corps on Saturday (day after to-morrow), the 24th instant.

I am, general, with respect, yours, &c.,

SAML. L. TAGGART,
Assistant Adjutant-General.

HEADQUARTERS MILITARY DIVISION OF THE MISSISSIPPI,
In the Field, near Savannah, Ga., December 22, 1864—5 a. m.

Brigadier-General KILPATRICK,
Commanding Cavalry Division, Army of Georgia:

GENERAL: The general-in-chief has just returned to his headquarters, having been somewhat delayed on his way back from Port Royal by high winds. You are no doubt already aware that the enemy has evacuated Savannah, and our troops are in full possession of the city. For the present, however, supplies will continue to be received via Ogeechee River and the King's Bridge road. The general directs me to say that he wishes you, until further orders, to continue to guard the depot of supplies at King's Bridge with your cavalry, on the west of the river, in connection with the brigade of infantry still remaining between Big and Little Ogeechee. He is anxious to hear as soon as possible from General Mower's force, sent down the Gulf railroad; also from your cavalry sent toward the Altamaha; and desires that you will at once send him all information you have or may obtain respecting them. He will himself go into Savannah this morning, and remove his headquarters thither, and will send you further orders after going there.

I am, general, respectfully, your obedient servant,

HENRY HITCHCOCK,
Major and Assistant Adjutant-General.

CIRCULAR.] HDQRS. THIRD DIVISION, CAVALRY CORPS,
MILITARY DIVISION OF THE MISSISSIPPI,
King's Bridge, Ga., December 22, 1864.

I. The First Brigade, Colonel Murray commanding, will move, at an early hour to-morrow morning, to the vicinity of a church on King's Bridge road, five miles from the bridge, and will there go into camp. Colonel Murray will examine the country, and establish a picket-line running from the Ogeechee River along the line of the canal, to some convenient and safe point, and thence across to the Savannah.

II. Colonel Atkins, commanding Second Brigade, will remain in his present camp, picketing the Cannouchee and the country in the direction of the Altamaha.

III. The headquarters of the division will be at or near the headquarters of the First Brigade. Colonel Murray will encamp one regiment near by, and protect the division train.

IV. After the camps are once established brigade commanders may detail one battalion each day of their respective commands, with their officers, to proceed (mounted) to the city of Savannah to see the city and enjoy themselves generally. It is to be hoped that these officers and men while in the city will so conduct themselves as to reflect no discredit upon the command.

By command of Brigadier-General Kilpatrick:

L. G. ESTES,
Captain and Assistant Adjutant-General.

STEAMER GOLDEN GATE,
Savannah River, December 22, 1864—7 p. m.
(Received 7 p. m. 25th.)

Lieutenant-General GRANT:

I have the honor to report that I have just returned from General Sherman's headquarters in Savannah. I send Major Gray, of my staff, as bearer of dispatches from General Sherman to you, and also a message to the President. The city of Savannah was occupied on the morning of the 21st. General Hardee, anticipating the contemplated assault, escaped with the main body of his infantry and light artillery on the afternoon and night of the 20th by crossing the river to the Union Causeway opposite the city. The rebel iron-clads were blown up and the navy-yard burned. All the rest of the city is intact and contains 20,000 citizens, quiet and well disposed. The captures include 800 prisoners, 150 guns, 13 locomotives in good order, 190 cars, a large supply of ammunition and material of war, 3 steamers, and 32,000 bales of cotton safely stored in warehouses. All these valuable fruits of an almost bloodless victory have been, like Atlanta, fairly won. I opened communication with the city with my steamers to-day, taking up what torpedoes we could see, and passing safely over others. Arrangements are made to clear the channel of all obstructions.

I have the honor to be, very respectfully, your obedient servant,

J. G. FOSTER,
Major-General, Commanding Department of the South.

HEADQUARTERS MILITARY DIVISION OF THE MISSISSIPPI,
In the Field, Savannah, Ga., December 22, 1864.

Major-General FOSTER,
Commanding Department of the South:

GENERAL: We are now in full possession of Savannah and all its dependencies. Hardee is supposed to be about Hardeeville, and General Sherman directs me to say that he suggest you take a strong defensive position about the head of Broad River, and if you need any help he will furnish you all assistance speedily. Hardee has from 15,000 to 20,000 men. As we are in possession, the proposed co-operation will not be required or necessary, but if you need help it will be at once sent you on notice. Please forward to the lieutenant-general the accompanying dispatch,* by request of General Sherman.

I am, general, with respect,

L. M. DAYTON,
Aide-de-Camp.

HDQRS. FIRST BRIG., COAST DIV., DEPT. OF THE SOUTH,
Talbird's, December 22, 1864.

General J. P. HATCH:

GENERAL: The officer in command of the guard at the marsh battery reports that the enemy's troops were marching on the railroad toward Charleston at 3 p. m. this day. He thought that three regiments passed; he saw that number of colors. He also reports that a train passed at 4 a. m. this morning; saw the light of the locomotive.

Very respectfully,

EDWARD E. POTTER,
Brigadier-General.

---

* See p. 6.

SPECIAL ORDERS, No. 13. } HEADQUARTERS COAST DIVISION, *Deveaux's Neck, S. C., December 22, 1864.*

* * * * * * *

II. The Seventy-fifth Regiment Ohio Volunteers is hereby ordered to proceed to Hilton Head, S. C., and report to department headquarters for orders. Transportation will be furnished by some boat returning to Hilton Head, S. C.

* * * * * * *

By order of Brig. Gen. J. P. Hatch:

LEONARD B. PERRY,
First Lieut., 55th Mass. Vols., and Actg. Asst. Adjt. Gen.

HEADQUARTERS U. S. FORCES, DISTRICT OF BEAUFORT,
Beaufort, S. C., December 22, 1864.

Maj. Gen. W. T. SHERMAN, U. S. Army,
Commanding Army of Occupation, Savannah, Ga.:

GENERAL: I would respectfully suggest that a large number of contrabands might be sent to Saint Simon's Island, Ga., and Edisto, S. C. There are a large number of vacant houses on each of these islands and a regiment of colored troops could hold them securely. These islands have both been occupied by our troops, but were vacated in 1863 by order of General Hunter, then commanding this department. I presume there are no rebels on either of them, and it would require but a small force to hold them securely. If one of the colored regiments now at our front in the vicinity of the railroad could be sent to occupy these islands, they perhaps might aid your operations as much as they are now doing. I very much regret, general, that my power to relieve you of the burden of these people is not equal to my inclination, but I have no means at all under my control. Even a small steamer sent to me by the War Department for special service, the control of which is absolutely essential to this service, has been taken from me by General Foster. I greatly fear that if these contrabands are sent to this post there will be much suffering among them, as I have neither men nor means at my command to provide them with shelter. With this statement of my situation and of facts as they exist at present, which I deem it my duty to make, I beg to assure you, general, that I am prepared to do all that you may desire me to do in this matter, and am ready to report to you at Savannah for the purpose, or anywhere else you may desire. Every cabin and house on these islands is filled to overflowing—I have some 15,000. It has occurred to me that I might render you more service by coming to Savannah. I shall be governed entirely by your wishes or orders in the case.

I am, very respectfully,

R. SAXTON,
Brigadier-General of Volunteers.

HEADQUARTERS MILITARY DIVISION OF THE MISSISSIPPI,
In the Field, Savannah, Ga., December 23, 1864.

General J. D. WEBSTER,
Nashville, Tenn.:

DEAR GENERAL: Major Dickson arrived last night, bringing your letter* of the 10th of December, for which I am very much obliged, as it

* Not found.

gives me a clear and distinct view of the situation of affairs at Nashville up to that date. I have also from the War Department a copy of General Thomas' dispatch, giving account of the attack on Hood on the 15th, which was successful, but not complete. I await further accounts with anxiety, as Thomas' complete success is necessary to vindicate my plans for this campaign; and I have no doubt that my calculations that Thomas had in hand (including A. J. Smith's troops) a force large enough to whip Hood in a fair fight was correct. I approve of Thomas' allowing Hood to come north far enough to enable him to concentrate his own men, though I would have preferred that Hood should have been checked about Columbia. Still, if Thomas followed up his success of the 15th and gave Hood a good whaling, and is at this moment following him closely, the whole campaign in my division, will be even more perfect than the Atlanta campaign; for at this end of the line I have realized all I had reason to hope for, except in the release of our prisoners, which was simply an impossibility. I know you all must await with deep anxiety the full details of the movements of my immediate command, and in time I will give them with full official minutia; and, in order that you may answer all inquiries, I will now endeavor to give you a brief outline.

On the 10th of November I was at Kingston, and, having sent to Thomas at Nashville the Fourth and Twenty-third Corps, learned that A. J. Smith had reached Paducah with his two divisions; and, having also learned from General Thomas that he felt perfectly able to contend with Hood, then lying about Florence and Tuscumbia, I gave the final signal to begin the work. Corse, at Rome, burned the bridges and all property that could be used by an enemy to our disadvantage and marched to Kingston.

On the 12th we moved to Allatoona, leaving the railroad north of the Etowah untouched, on the theory that in a very short while it would be to our interest to reoccupy the country as far as the Etowah. On the 13th, 14th, and 15th we broke up the railroad from the Etowah to Atlanta, and by the night of the 15th, the whole army was in or around Atlanta, ready for the forward movement. Marietta, Cassville, and Atlanta are destroyed in all respects, save mere dwelling houses, and cannot be used to our prejudice for three years. On the 16th all our columns were in motion. Howard, with the Fifteenth and Seventeenth Corps, moved southeast, by Jonesborough and McDonough, in the direction of Forsyth, crossing the Ocmulgee at Planters' Mills, or the Seven Islands; thence by Clinton to Gordon, the first objective point. He met with no opposition whatever, and reached it on the seventh day, the one appointed. In the meantime Kilpatrick, leaving Atlanta when Howard did, swept round by Griffin and Forsyth, and made a feint on Macon, at that point driving the rebels inside their works and recapturing two rifled guns, with equipments complete, taken by them from Stoneman last summer. He then came up with Howard at Gordon, covering his rear. Howard broke up the railroad a short distance west of Gordon (ten or fifteen miles); and while doing this posted Walcutt's brigade at Griswoldville, on the railroad, with a regiment of cavalry on either flank. The enemy sent out three brigades from Macon and attacked this force on the 22d of November, but were repulsed and severely punished. We buried 300 of their dead on the field, and the total rebel loss is stated at over 1,000, while our loss was less than 100 killed, wounded, and missing. The Left Wing, under Slocum, moved out from Atlanta to Decatur and along the Georgia railroad, destroying it as far as Madison, also destroying the important railroad bridge over Oconee River, east of that, and turned down to Milledgeville, the Twentieth Corps via Eatonton, the Fourteenth Corps via Shady Dale and Eatonton Factory, the two columns reaching Milledgeville by the 23d [22d], also the appointed time, without resistance or impediment. The penitentiary at Milledgeville was burned by convicts before our arrival. I burned the railroad buildings and the arsenal; the State House and Governor's mansion I left unharmed. On the 24th the Left Wing crossed the Oconee and burned the bridge at Milledgeville, moving thence to Sandersville, six or eight miles west of which the Twentieth Corps was delayed three or four hours to rebuild the bridges across Buffalo Creek, destroyed to impede us. Just outside of Sandersville, on the 26th, Wheeler, with 2,000 cavalry, attempted resistance; but a single line of infantry skirmishers drove him at double-quick into and through Sandersville. From this point the Fourteenth Corps went direct to Louisville, crossing the Ogeechee there, above their intended point of defense, without opposition; while the Twentieth Corps followed and destroyed the Central railroad from Tennille (or Station 13) to and across the Ogeechee at Station 10. Kilpatrick, with his division of cavalry, came up to Milledgeville from Gordon on the 24th, and at once started out on and around our left flank in the direction of Sparta, Gibson, and Sylvan Grove, with instructions to cut the railroad leading to Augusta at or near Waynesborough, and thence, if our prisoners were still at Millen, to make a dash to release them, and, returning, to join Davis at Louisville. He did cut the railroad at Waynesborough, partially burning the railroad bridge over Brier Creek (four miles north of that), but learned that our prisoners had already been removed from Millen, and returned to Louisville, joining the Fourteenth Corps there as ordered. During this march Wheeler hung around and attacked him in flank and rear, and gave him some trouble but no real injury. From Gordon Howard followed the Central railroad, crossing the river at Oconee bridge, thence to Irwin's Cross-Roads, destroying the railroad to Tennille (No. 13), including nearly three miles of trestle-work on both sides of and over the Oconee, some of it eighteen to twenty feet high. The attempt to resist at this crossing collapsed when the Left Wing reached Sandersville and amounted to nothing; hence Howard marched in two columns parallel to and south of the railroad, Blair's (Seventeenth) corps turning north and crossing the Oconee, without opposition, at Barton (or Station 9½). Hardee had announced at Tennille the day before I was there his purpose to dispute our passage at No. 10; but the movement on Louisville turned the line of the Ogeechee, and he at once fell back down the railroad and river. The next day, December 3, the Seventeenth Corps entered Millen without opposition. At this point, which was no town, but an important railroad center, the very handsome depot, railroad hotel, and three or four large storehouses were burned. From Louisville the Fourteenth Corps moved on an outer line eastward across the railroad between Millen and Augusta by Sharpe's, about where Brier Creek turns eastward to the Savannah River, and Buck Head Post-Office to the Savannah River, at Halley's Ferry; thence down along or near the right bank of the Savannah to the Charleston railroad opposite Monteith. The Twentieth Corps at the same time followed a nearly parallel route next west of this, through Birdville and Sylvania, down to Springfield and Monteith; the Seventeenth Corps worked down along the Central railroad all the way from Station 9½ to the outskirts of this city, while the Fifteenth Corps remained on and marched down the west bank of the Ogeechee until opposite Eden (or Station No. 2). The complete destruction of the Central railroad was continued by the Seventeenth Corps, with which I was, after leaving Sandersville, as far as Station 4½, but from that point to Savannah, so confident was I of taking the city, I allowed it to remain undisturbed, with the view of using it to that distance ourselves. Kilpatrick left Louisville with instructions to cover the rear of the columns moving down the peninsula, and also, if he got an opportunity, to attack and punish Wheeler, who had falsely claimed to have whipped and driven him back on his former expedition to Waynesborough. On the 4th of December Kilpatrick attacked Wheeler's whole force, amounting, as we know, to over 6,000 men, with five guns, at Thomas' Station, on the railroad, four miles south of Waynesborough, and whipped him completely and well, broke his center, and drove him back in confusion through and beyond Waynesborough and across Brier Creek, four miles north of it, again and completely burned the railroad bridge across Brier Creek, and then returned leisurely to Alexander, and down the peninsula, covering our rear. It was evident that the only point on the peninsula between Ogeechee and Savannah Rivers where the rebels could attempt to make a stand was at its narrowest point—from Ogeechee Church (or Station 4½) on the railroad to Sister's Ferry on the Savannah River, some twelve miles across. Here the railroad crosses the Little Ogeechee Creek, on whose east bank were thrown up some earthworks commanding the bridge over the creek, and they had also at considerable labor built more substantial works across the railroad. But, on the morning of December 5, when the skirmishers of the Seventeenth Corps advanced to cross the creek, they found the works deserted save by a few pickets, who fled at one volley. The movement of the Fifteenth Corps, down the west side of the Ogeechee, already below this point, had left the rebels at Ogeechee Church no alternative but to run or be cut off in rear. From this point there was no further opposition until within twelve or fourteen miles of Savannah, save ineffectual attempts to delay us by felling trees where our road crossed creeks or swamps; but in no case did the obstructions cause serious delay—the Seventeenth Corps losing but thirty minutes in all in waiting for their removal, and the Fourteenth Corps, having the most creeks, &c., to cross, and being most annoyed in this way, making, nevertheless, sixty miles in three days; the Fifteenth Corps, on the west side of Ogeechee, met no opposition or difficulty.

On the 7th of December our four heads of column were nearly on an east and west line—General Howard's headquarters being at Eden (or Station 2), nineteen miles from Savannah, on the railroad; the Seventeenth Corps two miles east of that; and the Twentieth and Fourteenth nearly as far down. At this point (Eden) Howard crossed part of the Fifteenth Corps to east bank of the Ogeechee, with which Corse pushed down along the river, crossed the canal, and had a smart little encounter at a cross-roads east of the mouth of the Cannouchee, capturing one piece of artillery and driving back the rebels to the Little Ogeechee River, northeast of Station 1, on the Gulf railroad, where he brought up against the outer defense of the city in that direction. Meanwhile the remainder of the Fifteenth Corps, still west of the Ogeechee River, moved down toward the Gulf railroad on two roads, feinted to cross the Cannouchee near its mouth, crossed it higher up, and cut the Gulf railroad at Way's Station and another point west of that. The Gulf road was also cut east of the Ogeechee, at or near Station 1, and a train of cars captured, on which was taken Mr. R. R. Cuyler, president of the Georgia Central Railroad, whom I treated kindly, and sent on his way to Macon; and between the several breaks of this railroad, as above, three locomotives and sundry cars were caught. The divisions of the Fifteenth Corps west of the Ogeechee River then crossed it at or near Fort Argyle (abandoned), and supported the other divisions already along the Little Ogeechee. The Seventeenth Corps on the 9th of December pushed on down the main (or Louisville dirt) road, on the upper (east) and north side of the Central railroad, and, driving back with a line of skirmishers some artillery stationed on the causeway, through a swamp between Station 2 and Station 1 (or Pooler), camped that night at the latter point. We lost two or three men, wounded by the explosion of two torpedoes buried in the road, before entering the swamp; seven were dug up by prisoners we held. On the 10th of December the Seventeenth Corps advanced to a point five miles from the city, and developed, in part, the rebel defenses in that quarter. On our left the Twentieth and Fourteenth Corps had continued to advance as rapidly as the swamps and narrow roads would permit; and by the 11th of December all the army corps were close up to the rebel outer line from the Savannah to the Little Ogeechee River—the Twentieth Corps on our extreme left, on the river-bank, and crossing the Charleston railroad three miles from the city; the Fourteenth Corps on its right, to the canal; the Seventeenth and Fifteenth forming our right; the whole an irregular line some fifteen miles long. The next day or two was occupied in tracing the rebel line, irregular and re-entrant in correspondence with the extensive swamps lying all round the rear of the city, crossed only by narrow causeways commanded by batteries of heavy guns. During this time a river boat was brought to on her way up, run aground, and burned by our infantry; and we captured a tender to two gun-boats which attempted to pass Winegar's battery (3-inch rifled guns) on the river-bank, but were driven back up the river, leaving their tender (a New York Harbor tug) in our hands almost uninjured. On Monday, 12th instant, I went over to our right and ordered for next day the assault by Hazen's division, of Fifteenth Corps, on Fort McAllister, the obstacle to our communication with the fleet in Ossabaw Sound. You will have already received, no doubt, through the papers [an account] of this very gallant and handsome affair, which lasted just fifteen minutes from the time the signal to charge was given till the old flag waved over the fort which has so long defied attack by sea. Our total loss was 11 killed, 80 wounded, largely caused by the torpedoes buried thickly around the line of abatis. I witnessed the assault from a rice mill on the river, about three miles distant across the salt marshes, though the troops marched ten miles around to reach the fort before attacking it, and immediately went down in a boat to the fort the same evening, thence on down to the fleet, where I met Admiral Dahlgren and General Foster. After arranging with them for bringing supplies from Hilton Head, especially bread and forage, which were beginning to be needed, and also for 30-pounder Parrotts to bombard the city, I returned on the 15th to my camp. That night Colonel Babcock arrived with dispatches of importance from General Grant bearing upon my plans here. The length of my lines (nearly fifteen miles) and the nature of the soil, even on the causeways made through the swamps, made necessary a large amount of corduroying to pass my trains to and from the depot of supplies which I directed General Easton to establish at King's Bridge (over the Ogeechee), which the continued development of the rebel lines occupied last week. On the 17th I sent in to General Hardee, by flag of truce, on our left, a summons to surrender, the 30-pounder Parrotts ordered from Hilton Head having arrived at King's Bridge, to which, on the 18th, he returned a refusal. I had now for some days held the three railroads leading out of Savannah, and all other avenues of approach west of the Savannah River, the only other avenue being the Union Causeway, an old wagon road running from the east bank of the Savannah River from the city up toward Hardeeville. To attempt to close this by extending our left across the river would have involved the risk of isolating the troops across a deep river too wide for my pontoon train, and upon which the rebels had two gun-boats (one iron-clad) at the city wharf, with boats to throw their whole force across against them. I determined rather to close this avenue from my right flank; and on the 19th again went down to the fleet and up with the admiral to Port Royal, where, on the 20th, I arranged with General Foster and the admiral for immediately bringing round a sufficient force from the Ogeechee to unite with General Foster's troops, then lying at the head of Broad River for this purpose. High winds and rough weather delayed my return from Port Royal, and before I had reached Fort McAllister, on the way back, a message met me from General Howard that Hardee had evacuated the city in haste, and our troops had marched in without resistance that morning, the 21st. Two days more and the garrison would have been hemmed in completely; as it is, the campaign ends with the capture of this important city and numerous dependent forts, including, as reported to me, 25,000 bales of cotton, at least 150 guns, many of them 10-inch, immense ordnance stores, 13 locomotives, 190 cars, a pontoon train (boats), &c., and a population of about 20,000, including any quantity of negroes. We have also captured three more boats, one of them a wooden gun-boat, the rebels having blown up their iron-clad Savannah, just below the city, on the night of the 21st.

The Savannah River, though obstructed for the present to large vessels, is open for those drawing six or seven feet, and will, as soon as possible, be cleared for large vessels, thus opening the way for our gun-boats almost, if not quite, to Augusta, and insuring the permanent subdivision of the Confederacy by this line, with a new base for operations against Lee's rear.

I forbore to destroy the Georgia Central Railroad below Station 4½ (say, forty-five miles from Savannah) on my way down, with a view to use the road ourselves that far after taking the city. After receiving General Grant's dispatches, however, it appeared not impossible that this army might be ordered to the James River by sea, without giving time to insure the fall of Savannah, and I therefore destroyed the railroad for fifteen miles back from the city. The whole number of miles of railroad I have destroyed is about 265—about 60 miles on the Georgia road, from Atlanta to Madison, and 140 miles on the Georgia Central Railroad, from a point, say, ten miles west of Gordon to Savannah, as above, and about 50 miles out from Savannah on the Gulf railroad, and about 15 miles on the Charleston railroad. It would be some time before Jeff. Davis could restore the communications so rudely interrupted, across the heart of his empire, even if we had no objections to make.

You may have shared the concern on our account which the newspapers and our friends on the coast tell us was felt in the States; you know by this time that any such anxieties were groundless. The weather through our march was perfect, only two days of rain from Atlanta to the outskirts of Savannah; the roads in fine order; forage, pigs, poultry, and sweet potatoes first rate, and abundant; and the men and animals in better order when they reached here than when they started.

As to the "lion" in our path, we never met him. The affair at Griswoldville, where one brigade of infantry was engaged, and Kilpatrick's punishment of Wheeler, were the only things on the march like a fight.

The city is perfectly quiet ever since we came in. The first thing our troops had to do was to stop the riots and plundering which the lower classes begun as soon as Hardee's rear crossed the river. The white people here are the worst whipped and subjugated you ever saw, and the negroes are having their "jubilee" and calling in crowds to see "Mr. Sherman."

December 24.—I have just received a letter from General Grant, giving a detail of General Thomas' operations up to the 18th, and I am gratified beyond measure at the result. Show this letter to General Thomas, and tell him to consider it addressed to him, as I have not time to write more now. I want General Thomas to follow Hood to and beyond the Tennessee, and not to hesitate to go on as far as Columbus, Miss., or Selma, Ala., as I know that he will have no trouble whatever in subsisting his army anywhere below Sand Mountain and along the Black Warrior. In the poorest part of Georgia I found no trouble in subsisting my army and animals, some of my corps not issuing but one day's bread from Atlanta to Savannah. Keep me fully advised by telegraph, via New York, of the situation of affairs in Tennessee. I will be here probably for ten days longer, and in communication for a longer time.

I am, very truly, yours,

W. T. SHERMAN,
Major-General.

SPECIAL FIELD ORDERS, No. 139.

HDQRS. MIL. DIV. OF THE MISSISSIPPI,
In the Field, Savannah, Ga., December 23, 1864.

Savannah, being now in our possession, and the river partially cleared out, and measures having been taken to remove all obstructions, will at once be made a grand depot for future operations.

I. The chief quartermaster, General Easton, will, after giving the necessary orders touching the transports in Ogeechee River and Ossabaw Sound, come in person to Savannah and take possession of all public buildings, all vacant store-rooms, warehouses, &c., that may be now or hereafter needed for any department of the army. No rents will be paid by the Government of the United States during the war, and all buildings must be distributed according to the accustomed rules of the quartermaster's department, as though they were public property.

II. The chief commissary of subsistence, Col. A. Beckwith, will transfer the grand depot of the army to the city of Savannah, secure possession of the needful buildings and offices, and give the necessary orders, to the end that the army may be supplied abundantly and well.

III. The chief engineer, Captain Poe, will at once direct which of the enemy's forts are to be retained for our use and which dismantled and destroyed; and the chief ordnance officer, Captain Baylor, will, in like manner, take possession of all property pertaining to his department captured from the enemy and cause the same to be collected and carried to points of security. All the heavy sea-coast guns will be dismounted and carried to Fort Pulaski.

IV. The troops, for the present, will be grouped about the city of Savannah, looking to the convenience of camps, General Slocum taking from the Savannah around to about the seven-mile post, on the canal, and General Howard thence to the sea. General Kilpatrick will hold King's Bridge until Fort McAllister is dismantled and the troops withdrawn from the south side of the Ogeechee, when he will take post about Anderson's plantation, on the plank road, and picket all the roads leading from the north and west.

V. General Howard will keep a small guard at Forts Rosedew, Beaulieu, Wimberly, Thunderbolt, and Bonaventure, and he will cause that shore and Skidaway Island to be examined very closely, with a view to finding many and convenient points for the embarkation of troops and wagons on sea-going vessels.

By order of Maj. Gen. W. T. Sherman:

L. M. DAYTON,
Aide-de-Camp.

SPECIAL FIELD ORDERS, No. 203.

HEADQUARTERS DEPARTMENT AND ARMY OF THE TENNESSEE,
Savannah, Ga., December 23, 1864.

* * * * * * *

V. In accordance with Special Field Orders, No. 139, Military Division of the Mississippi, Maj. Gen. P. Joseph Osterhaus, commanding Fifteenth Army Corps, will send and keep a small guard, in charge of a good officer, at Forts Rosedew, Beaulieu, Wimberly, Thunderbolt, and Bonaventure. Second, Col. J. T. Conklin, chief quartermaster, will closely examine the shores in the vicinity of these forts and Skidaway Island, with the view of finding many and convenient points for the embarkation of troops and wagons in sea-going vessels, and will as soon as possible report thereon in writing to these headquarters.

By order of Maj. Gen. O. O. Howard:

SAML. L. TAGGART,
Assistant Adjutant-General.

SPECIAL ORDERS, No. 205.

HDQRS. FIFTEENTH ARMY CORPS,
Savannah, Ga., December 23, 1864.

* * * * * * *

III. The commanding officer of Second Division will cause to be detailed one regiment of an average strength of 350 men, and a working party of fifty negroes, to report forthwith to Colonel Beckwith, chief commissary, at the landing, King's Bridge. The First, Third, and Fourth Divisions of the Fifteenth Army Corps will be ready for review to-morrow at 9.30 a. m., and drawn up in line in the following order: General Charles R. Woods, commanding First Division, will deploy his line, the right resting on the park, fronting north, and running west to the corner of West Broad street, and thence down that street. General John E. Smith, commanding Third Division, takes up the alignment of the First Division, extending his line down West Broad, and then at right angles into South Broad street. General John M. Corse deploys the Fourth Division in South Broad street, on the left, and on alignment with General Smith's division. The Artillery Brigade forms on the extreme left, under special instructions from these headquarters.

Officers and men are expected to appear as clean and neat as possible—officers with saber and sash; the men in light marching order, without knapsacks, blankets, or haversacks. The companies of each battalion must be equalized, regiments with less than 400 men in eight, with more, in ten companies; full regiments to be equalized in platoons. Field music and regimental bands will be collected by brigades and placed on the right of their respective brigades.

Division commanders will, on the approach of the reviewing officers, give the command to open ranks and present arms. Whenever the reviewing officers have passed a brigade, the brigade commander will order the shoulder arms, order arms, parade rest. Preparatory to the passing in review the division commanders will command to close order, break into column of companies (except full regiments which will be broken into platoons). The column will pass in quick step, and therefore only mounted officers will salute the reviewing officers. Commanding officers are cautioned to preserve, after having passed by the reviewing officers, the formation of their columns, and not to break the companies by the right flank and file left. Such changes interfere with the troops in the rear and create very annoying disturbances. The artillery will pass by sections.

By order of Maj. Gen. P. Joseph Osterhaus:

F. F. WHITEHEAD,
Assistant Adjutant-General.

GENERAL ORDERS, No. 74. } HDQRS. SECOND DIV., 15TH ARMY CORPS,
Fort McAllister, Ga., December 23, 1864.

The general commanding the division is pleased to announce that official dispatches have been received from Major-General Thomas saying that he had attacked Hood in front of Nashville; had driven his left and left center eight miles, capturing 16 guns, a large number of prisoners, flags, earth-works, and trains; that night closed the battle, but that he would fight or follow the next day, and expected to destroy the entire army. Our troops did all they were asked to do and all that could be expected.

The fall of Savannah, so soon following the splendid assault and capture of Fort McAllister by ourselves, is deemed a fitting occasion to congratulate the division upon its uniform good and brave conduct since he has had the honor of commanding it, and upon the brilliant close of the late campaign, of which it can justly claim so important a part.

By order of Brig. Gen. W. B. Hazen:

G. LOFLAND,
Captain and Assistant Adjutant-General.

GENERAL ORDERS, No. 69. } HDQRS. FIRST DIV., 17TH ARMY CORPS,
Near Savannah, Ga., December 23, 1864.

The troops of this command, except the Second Brigade, Brig. Gen. J. W. Sprague commanding, will move to the city to-morrow, and will start at 8 a. m. Order of march: First, First Brigade, Brigadier-General Fuller commanding; second, one section Battery C, First Michigan; third, Third Brigade, Col. John Tillson commanding;

fourth, ambulance corps; fifth, ordnance train; sixth, supply train. Col. John Tillson will detail five companies of his command to march in rear of the train.

By order of Maj. Gen. J. A. Mower:

CHAS. CHRISTENSEN,
Lieut., Aide-de-Camp, and Acting Assistant Adjutant-General.

CIRCULAR.] HEADQUARTERS FOURTEENTH ARMY CORPS,
Savannah, Ga., December 23, 1864.

The corps will be prepared for review by Major-General Sherman on Tuesday or Wednesday next in the streets of Savannah, the men without knapsacks and marching by platoons. Division commanders will, in the short time which intervenes, place their respective commands in the best possible state of drill, discipline, and soldierly appearance, and will see that every available man is under arms.

By order of Bvt. Maj. Gen. J. C. Davis:

A. C. McCLURG,
Lieutenant-Colonel and Chief of Staff.

GENERAL ORDERS, No. 1. HEADQUARTERS CITY OF SAVANNAH,
Savannah, Ga., December 23, 1864.

In accordance with orders received, the undersigned has assumed command of the city. The following staff officers are announced: Capt. W. T. Forbes, assistant adjutant-general and chief of staff; Capt. S. B. Wheelock, acting assistant adjutant-general; Lieut. Col. A. H. Jackson, inspector; Capt. Moses Veale, aide-de-camp; Capt. John J. Cantine, aide-de-camp; Lieut. William C. Armor, aide-de-camp; Capt. Ira B. Seymour, provost-marshal; Capt. G. L. Parker, assistant quartermaster, post quartermaster; Capt. James Gillette, commissary of subsistence, post commissary. They will be obeyed and respected accordingly. The offices of the general commanding and of the adjutant-general's and inspector's departments will be in the Central Railroad Bank Building, next to the U. S. Custom House. Office hours for ordinary business from 10 a. m. to 3 p. m. The offices of the other staff departments will be in the Exchange Building and vicinity.

JNO. W. GEARY,
Brigadier-General, U. S. Volunteers.

POST-OFFICE DEPARTMENT, APPOINTMENT OFFICE,
Washington, December 23, 1864.

Col. A. H. MARKLAND,
Special Agent Post-Office Department, Present:

SIR: You will proceed immediately to the headquarters of General Sherman, near Savannah, Ga., and report to him as the agent of this department, to arrange for the regular transmission and distribution of the mails for his army. You will have the entire and exclusive control of these mails, subject only to the orders and directions of General Sherman.

I am, respectfully, &c.,

ALEX. W. RANDALL,
Acting Postmaster-General.

HEADQUARTERS MILITARY DIVISION OF THE MISSISSIPPI,
Savannah, Ga., December 24, 1864.

Lieut. Gen. U. S. GRANT,
City Point, Va.:

GENERAL: Your letter of December 18 is just received. I feel very much gratified at receiving the handsome commendation you pay my army. I will, in general orders, convey to the officers and men the substance of your note. I am also gratified that you have modified your former orders, as I feared that the transportation by sea would very much disturb the unity and morale of my army, now so perfect. The occupation of Savannah, which I have heretofore reported, completes the first part of our game, and fulfills a great part of your instructions, and I am now engaged in dismantling the rebel forts which bear upon the sea channels, and transferring the heavy ordnance and ammunition to Fort Pulaski, where they can be more easily guarded than if left in the city. The rebel inner lines are well adapted to our purpose, and, with slight modifications, can be held by a comparatively small force, and in about ten days I expect to be ready to sally forth again. I feel no doubt whatever as to our future plans; I have thought them over so long and well that they appear as clear as daylight. I left Augusta untouched on purpose, because now the enemy will be in doubt as to my objective point after crossing the Savannah River, whether it be Augusta or Charleston, and will naturally divide his forces. I will then move either on Branchville or Columbia, on any curved line that gives me the best supplies, breaking up in my course as much railroad as possible; then, ignoring Charleston and Augusta both, occupy Columbia and Camden; pausing there long enough to observe the effect I would strike for the Charleston and Wilmington Railroad, somewhere between the Santee and the Cape Fear River, and, if possible, communicate with the fleet under Admiral Dahlgren (whom I find a most agreeable gentleman, in every way accommodating himself to our wishes and plans); then I would favor Wilmington, in the belief that Porter and Butler will fail in their present undertaking. Charleston is now a mere desolated wreck, and is hardly worthy the time it would take to starve it out; still, I am aware that, historically and politically, much importance is attached to the place, and it may be that, apart from its military importance, both you and the administration would prefer I should give it more attention, and it would be well for you to give me some general idea on that subject, as otherwise I would treat it as I have expressed, as a point of little importance after all its railroads leading into the interior are destroyed or occupied by us. But, on the hypothesis of ignoring Charleston and taking Wilmington, I would then favor a movement direct on Raleigh. The game is then up with Lee, unless he comes out of Richmond, avoids you, and fights me, in which event I should reckon on your being on his heels.

Now that Hood is used up by Thomas, I feel disposed to bring the matter to an issue just as quick as possible. I feel confident that I can break up the whole railroad system of South Carolina and North Carolina, and be on the Roanoke, either at Raleigh or Weldon, by the time the spring fairly opens. And if you feel confident that you can whip Lee outside of his intrenchments, I feel equally confident that I can handle him in the open country. One reason why I would ignore Charleston is this, that I believe they will reduce the garrison to a small force, with plenty of provisions, and I know that the neck back of Charleston can be made impregnable to assault, and we will hardly have time for siege operations. I will have to leave in Savannah a garrison, and, if

Thomas can spare them, I would like to have all detachments, convalescents, &c., belonging to these four corps sent forward at once. I don't want to cripple Thomas, because I regard his operations as all important, and I have ordered him to pursue Hood down into Alabama, trusting to the country for supplies. I reviewed one of my corps to-day, and shall continue to review the whole army. I don't like to boast, but I believe this army has a confidence in itself that makes it almost invincible. I wish you would run down and see us; it would have a good effect, and would show to both armies that they are acting on a common plan. The weather is now cool and pleasant, and the general health very good.

Your true friend,

W. T. SHERMAN,
Major-General.

HEADQUARTERS MILITARY DIVISION OF THE MISSISSIPPI,
In the Field, Savannah, Ga., December 24, 1864.

Maj. Gen. H. W. HALLECK,
Chief of Staff, Washington City, D. C.:

GENERAL: I had the pleasure to receive your two letters of the 16th and 18th instant to-day, and I feel more than usually flattered by the high encomiums you have passed on our recent campaign, which is now complete by the occupation of Savannah. I am also very glad that General Grant has changed his mind about embarking my troops for James River, leaving me free to make the broad swath you describe through South and North Carolina, and still more gratified at the news from Thomas in Tennessee, because it fulfills my plan, which contemplated his being fully able to dispose of Hood in case he ventured north of the Tennessee River; so I think, on the whole, I can chuckle over Jeff. Davis' disappointment in not turning my Atlanta campaign into a Moscow disaster. I have just finished a long letter to General Grant, and have explained to him that we are engaged in shifting our base from the Ogeechee over to the Savannah River, dismantling all the forts made by the enemy to bear upon the salt-water channels, and transferring the heavy ordnance, &c., to Fort Pulaski and Hilton Head, and in remodelling the enemy's interior lines to suit our future plans and purposes. I have also laid down the programme of a campaign which I can make this winter, and put me in the spring on the Roanoke, in direct communication with him on the James River. In general terms, my plan is to turn over to General Foster the city of Savannah, and to sally forth, with my army resupplied, cross the Savannah, feign on Charleston and Augusta, but strike between, breaking en route the Charleston and Augusta Railroad, also a large part of that from Branchville and Camden toward North Carolina, and then rapidly moving to some point of the railroad from Charleston to Wilmington, between the Santee and Cape Fear Rivers; then, communicating with the fleet in the neighborhood of Georgetown, I would turn upon Wilmington or Charleston according to the importance of either. I rather prefer Wilmington, as a live place, over Charleston, which is dead and unimportant when its railroad communications are broken. I take it for granted the present movement on Wilmington will fail, because I know that gun-boats cannot take a fort, and Butler has not the force or the ability to take it. If I should determine to take Charleston I would turn across the country, which I have hunted over many a time, from Santee to Mount Pleasant, throwing one wing on the peninsula between Ashley and Cooper. After accomplishing one or other of these ends I would make a bee-line for Raleigh, or Weldon, when Lee would be forced to come out of Richmond or acknowledge himself beaten. He would, I think, by the use of the Danville railroad, throw himself rapidly between me and Grant, leaving Richmond in the hands of the latter. This would not alarm me, for I have an army which I think can maneuver, and I would force him to attack me at a disadvantage, always under the supposition that Grant would be on his heels; and if the worst came to the worst I could fight my way down to Albemarle Sound or New Berne.

I think the time has come now when we should attempt the boldest moves, and my experience is that they are easier of execution than more timid ones, because the enemy is disconcerted by them—as for instance, my recent campaign. I also doubt the wisdom of concentration beyond a certain point, as the roads of this country limit the amount of men that can be brought to bear in any one battle; and I don't believe any one general can handle more than 60,000 men in battle. I think my campaign of the last month, as well as every step I take from this point northward, is as much a direct attack upon Lee's army as though I were operating within the sound of his artillery. I am very anxious that Thomas should follow up his successes to the very uttermost point. My orders to him before I left Kingston were, after beating Hood, to follow him as far as Columbus, Miss., or Selma, Ala., both of which lie in districts of country which I know to be rich in corn and meat. I attach more importance to these deep incisions into the enemy's country, because this war differs from European wars in this particular. We are not only fighting hostile armies, but a hostile people, and must make old and young, rich and poor, feel the hard hand of war, as well as their organized armies. I know that this recent movement of mine through Georgia has had a wonderful effect in this respect. Thousands who had been deceived by their lying papers into the belief that we were being whipped all the time, realized the truth, and have no appetite for a repetition of the same experience. To be sure, Jeff. Davis has his people under a pretty good state of discipline, but I think faith in him is much shaken in Georgia; and I think before we are done, South Carolina will not be quite so tempestuous. I will bear in mind your hint as to Charleston, and don't think salt will be necessary. When I move the Fifteenth Corps will be on the right of the Right Wing, and their position will bring them, naturally, into Charleston first; and if you have watched the history of that corps you will have remarked that they generally do their work up pretty well. The truth is the whole army is burning with an insatiable desire to wreak vengeance upon South Carolina. I almost tremble at her fate, but feel that she deserves all that seems in store for her. Many and many a person in Georgia asked me why we did not go to South Carolina, and when I answered that I was en route for that State the invariable reply was, "Well, if you will make those people feel the severities of war, we will pardon you for your desolation of Georgia." I look upon Columbia as quite as bad as Charleston, and I doubt if we shall spare the public buildings there, as we did at Milledgeville. I have been so busy lately that I have not yet made my official report, and think I had better wait until I get my subordinate reports before attempting it, as I am anxious to explain clearly, not only the reasons for every step, but the amount of execution done, and this I cannot do until I get the subordinate reports; for we marched the whole distance in four or more columns, and, of course, I could only be present with one, and generally that one engaged in destroying railroads. This work of destruction was performed better than usual, because I had an engineer regiment provided with claws to twist the bars after being heated. Such bars can never be used again, and the only way in which a railroad line can be reconstructed across Georgia will be to make a new road from Fairburn Station, twenty-four miles southwest of Atlanta, to Madison, a distance of 100 miles; and before that can be done I propose to be on the road from Augusta to Charleston, which is a continuation of the same. I felt somewhat disappointed at Hardee's escape from me, but really am not to blame. I moved as quick as possible to close up the "Union Causeway," but intervening obstacles were such that before I could get my troops on the road Hardee had slipped out. Still, I know that the men that were in Savannah will be lost, in a measure, to Jeff. Davis; for the Georgia troops, under G. W. Smith, declared they would not fight in South Carolina, and have gone north en route for Augusta, and I have reason to believe the North Carolina troops have gone to Wilmington—in other words, they are scattered. I have reason to believe that Beauregard was present in Savannah at the time of its evacuation, and I think he and Hardee are now in Charleston, doubtless making preparations for what they know will be my next step.

Please say to the President that I received his kind message through Colonel Markland, and feel thankful for his high favor. If I disappoint him in the future, it shall not be from want of zeal or love to the cause. Of you I expect a full and frank criticism of my plans for the future, which may enable me to correct errors before it is too late. I do not wish to be rash, but want to give my rebel friends no chance to accuse us of want of enterprise or courage.

Assuring you of my high personal respect, I remain, as ever, your friend,

W. T. SHERMAN,
Major-General.

[Indorsement.]

Maj. Gen. H. W. HALLECK,
Chief of Staff of the Army:

GENERAL: This letter was brought by Lieutenant Dunn, of my staff, with the request that I would open and read it, as it contained one or two points which his letter addressed to me does not contain.

Respectfully,

U. S. GRANT,
Lieutenant-General.

HEADQUARTERS MILITARY DIVISION OF THE MISSISSIPPI,
Savannah, Ga., December 24, 1864.

Major-General WHEELER, Confederate Army,
Screven's Ferry, South Carolina:

GENERAL: Yours of this date is received. I will let that lady land, but no more. No provision has been made for the families in Savannah, and many of them will suffer from want—and I will not undertake to feed them. I will give notice that all families who wish to leave can do so, and will provide the means of getting them to General Hardee's headquarters. You need not send in for small parties, and I will not permit any more flags of truce by subordinate commanders.

I am, your obedient servant,

W. T. SHERMAN,
Major-General, Commanding.

P. S.—If your pickets fire on our boats, I will clear Savannah and river of all unfriendly parties.

W. T. SHERMAN,
Major-General.

THUNDERBOLT BATTERY,
Saturday, December 24, 1864—12.30 p. m.

Maj. Gen. W. T. SHERMAN, U. S. Army,
Comdg. Army of the Military Division of the Mississippi:

GENERAL: Vessels drawing fifteen feet and under can come up to this place now, entering at Wassaw Sound. The river has been dragged for torpedoes, and none have yet been discovered. The monitor Sangamon, Captain Young, and the Passaic, Captain Fillebrown, are now close beside the work at Turner's Rocks, and will be at anchor at this place in a few hours. I have my vessel at work sounding and putting up marks for navigation, and will anchor here to-night. I respectfully recommend making this place your present depot for large vessels. A short wharf, 100 feet long, will suffice for vessels of deep draft, and materials for its construction are near at hand.

Respectfully,

CHAS. O. BOUTELLE,
Assistant, Coast Survey, Commanding U. S. Steamer Bibb.

SPECIAL FIELD ORDERS, No. 141.

HDQRS. MIL. DIV. OF THE MISSISSIPPI,
In the Field, Savannah, Ga., December 24, 1864.

I. General Easton, chief quartermaster, is charged with the general responsibility of public property in the city. He will take possession of all cotton and other quartermaster's stores. He will also assign quarters to officers and troops, and designate such buildings, lots, &c., for public use, and have full control thereof. Officers serving with troops will not be allowed to occupy buildings in the city unless the troops are also doing duty in the city, and corps, division, and brigade quartermasters and commissaries will not be allowed to establish themselves at any depot in the city or elsewhere except upon consultation with the chief quartermaster or chief commissary of subsistence. The occupation and use of buildings or rooms for amusement will be regulated by General Easton, and no private property will be removed from buildings, or made use of, by officers or troops except by consent of him.

II. The chief commissary of subsistence, Colonel Beckwith, will take possession of all subsistence stores and be charged with their distribution, as also the supplying of destitute families, conferring with the mayor of the city as regards the necessities, &c., and army commanders will not make issues directly.

III. Corps commanders will furnish the chief quartermaster 500 men each, in regiments, for guard and fatigue duty. They will also use all effort to supply him with a force of negroes for labor. Recruiting agents are forbid recruiting negroes for military service, as all are wanted for labor.

IV. The provost-marshal's department, under the direction of the commanding officer of the post, is charged with the maintenance of good order in the city and the guarding of prisoners, and has nothing to do with property. Passes within the city limits will not be required.

By order of Maj. Gen. W. T. Sherman:

L. M. DAYTON,
Aide-de-Camp.

HDQRS. DEPARTMENT AND ARMY OF THE TENNESSEE,
Savannah, December 24, 1864.

Major-General SHERMAN,
Commanding Military Division of the Mississippi:

GENERAL: The Fifteenth Corps will be ready to be reviewed by you at 11 o'clock this a. m. Forsyth Place is the point selected for the review to take place. I will join you at your headquarters and accompany you to the spot.

Respectfully, yours,

O. O. HOWARD,
Major-General.

HDQRS. DEPARTMENT AND ARMY OF THE TENNESSEE,
Savannah, Ga., December 24, 1864.

Maj. Gen. P. JOSEPH OSTERHAUS,
Commanding Fifteenth Army Corps:

I am directed by the major-general commanding to say that, in accordance with the instructions of Major-General Sherman, he desires you to direct Brigadier-General Hazen to at once proceed in the work of dismantling Fort McAllister, and have the guns in readiness to be removed by water. Major-General Foster has promised to send the boats to transport them. The general suggests that, in order to facilitate their loading, they be first got onto flat-boats, from which they can be more readily hoisted aboard a ship. As soon as this is done General Hazen's command will be withdrawn and assigned a position near the city.

Very respectfully, your obedient servant,

SAML. L. TAGGART,
Assistant Adjutant-General.

HDQRS. 17TH ARMY CORPS, DEPT. OF THE TENNESSEE,
Savannah, Ga., December 24, 1864.

Brig. Gen. M. D. LEGGETT,
Commanding Third Division:

GENERAL: The major-general commanding directs me to say to you that you will not move to your new camp until it is definitely ascertained that there is water there. At any rate, you will not move to-morrow.

Very respectfully, your obedient servant,

C. CADLE, JR.,
Assistant Adjutant-General.

HDQRS. THIRD DIVISION, SEVENTEENTH ARMY CORPS,
Savannah, Ga., December 24, 1864.

Capt. C. CADLE,
Assistant Adjutant-General, Seventeenth Army Corps:

CAPTAIN: I have the honor to request that Brig. Gen. M. F. Force, commanding First Brigade in my division, be recommended to the President for promotion to the brevet rank of major-general. General Force has proved one of our most gallant and efficient officers—brave and dashing, yet discreet and cool. He is a man of fine education, correct habits, and a perfect gentleman in his intercourse with both subordinates and superiors. His gallantry in leading the charge upon the enemy's works near Atlanta on the 21st of July last, and in the battle of the 22d of July, entitle him to the highest respect of military men. He has commanded a brigade in the division since the beginning of the siege of Vicksburg.

Very respectfully,

M. D. LEGGETT,
Brigadier-General.

HDQRS. THIRD DIVISION, SEVENTEENTH ARMY CORPS,
Savannah, Ga., December 24, 1864.

Capt. C. CADLE,
Assistant Adjutant-General, Seventeenth Army Corps:

CAPTAIN: I have the honor to recommend for promotion to the rank of brigadier-general Col. R. K. Scott, Sixty-eighth Regiment Ohio Veteran Volunteer Infantry. Colonel Scott is now commanding the Second Brigade of my division, and has commanded it since leaving Vicksburg last March. During the Atlanta campaign, and in our late campaign from Atlanta, Colonel Scott has shown himself a very capable and gallant officer. He is a man of correct habits, excellent health, great energy, and indomitable will. There is no braver man lives and few more worthy of promotion. His original term of service has about expired, and the number in his regiment will not admit of his remustering. He can only be retained in the service by promotion, and his loss to the service will be a serious loss to his brigade and this division. I earnestly hope he will be immediately promoted to the rank of brigadier-general.

Very respectfully,

M. D. LEGGETT,
Brigadier-General.

HDQRS. THIRD DIVISION, SEVENTEENTH ARMY CORPS,
Savannah, Ga., December 24, 1864.

Brig. Gen. L. THOMAS,
Adjutant-General U. S. Army:

GENERAL: I have the honor to recommend that Capt. John C. Douglass, assistant adjutant-general of this division, be promoted to the rank of major. Captain Douglass has been the adjutant-general of this division more than one year, and has discharged the duties of his office with distinguished faithfulness and exactness and ability. He has never been absent from his post of duty a day; has acted as aide as well as adjutant in all the engagements in which the division has participated, and has distinguished himself for his coolness and valor. He is a man of strictly temperate and correct habits, and I recommend that he be promoted to the rank of major and assistant adjutant-general.

Very respectfully,

M. D. LEGGETT,
Brigadier-General.

SPECIAL ORDERS, No. 164. } HDQRS. FOURTH DIV., 17TH ARMY CORPS, *Savannah, December 24, 1864.*

The Third Brigade, Brig. Gen. W. W. Belknap commanding, will move to a new camp near Bonaventure Cemetery promptly at 7 a. m. to-morrow morning. The column will move by these headquarters, from which point they will be conducted by Captain Gurley to their camp.

By order of Brig. Gen. Giles A. Smith:

CHAS. H. BRUSH,
Acting Assistant Adjutant-General.

GENERAL ORDERS, No. 2. } HDQRS. CITY OF SAVANNAH, GA., *December 24, 1864.*

I. For convenience in military government all that portion of the city lying east of Bull street is designated as the eastern district; that lying west of Bull street, as the western district. Col. William B. Woods, Seventy-sixth Ohio Volunteers, is announced as provost-marshal of the eastern district; his headquarters will be in the U. S. barracks on Bull street. Col. H. A. Barnum, One hundred and forty-ninth New York Volunteers, is announced as provost-marshal of the western district; his headquarters will be near the corner of Barnard and South Broad streets. All applications for protection of persons and private property, or for redress of grievances, will be made to the provost-marshal of the district or to the nearest officer of the guard.

II. Each regiment on provost duty will have assigned to it definite limits within which to perform guard and patrol duty, and the regimental commanders will be held responsible for the peace and good order of their respective sections. The provost-marshals of districts will number the sections assigned to these regiments.

III. All public and private property will be protected, and whenever necessary for such purpose special guards will be assigned. No private property will be taken or used against the consent of the owners, except upon an order from proper authority.

IV. Officers and others entitled to quarters for private or public use will make application to Brigadier-General Easton, chief quartermaster.

V. All persons within the city who have been in any way connected with the rebel army will report, without delay, to Capt. Ira B. Seymour, provost-marshal (office in Exchange Building), and there register their names.

VI. No citizen will be arrested except for misdemeanor, or upon written orders from these headquarters or from a provost-marshal.

VII. The fire department of this city has been represented by the civil authorities as highly efficient. Mr. Casey, acting chief of the fire department, is authorized to continue operations, and will be held responsible for the faithful performance of his duties. All members of the different fire companies will continue subject to his orders, and neglect of duty on their part will be duly punished. In case of fire, the provost-marshal of the district will send immediately strong detachments of guards to preserve order in the vicinity.

VIII. Those persons connected with the water-works and gas-works of the city will continue to perform their duties as usual. The manager of these works will apply to the provost-marshal of the district in which they are located for sufficient guards for the protection of the works, together with the fuel and other material pertaining to them.

IX. All soldiers found within the city limits, absent from their camps without passes from their respective commanders, will be arrested and sent to their commands.

X. Capt. Silas Spicer is announced as harbor master of this port, and is invested with full authority for the transaction of business in his department. Office, on Bay, opposite Dayton street.

XI. Citizens desirous of leaving the city to go within the rebel lines will make application at these headquarters. They will be transported to our exterior picket-line.

XII. Citizens destitute of provisions can make application at the city store, where they will be supplied upon the order of Doctor Arnold, mayor of the city.

XIII. Tattoo will be beaten throughout the city at 8 p. m.; taps at 9. After taps all enlisted men found on the streets who are not on duty, and who have not proper passes, will be arrested by the patrol. Suspicious or disorderly characters will also be arrested after that hour. Care must be taken in carrying out this order not to make improper arrests of citizens who may be attending to their lawful business in an orderly manner.

By command of Brig. Gen. John W. Geary, commanding:

W. T. FORBES,
Assistant Adjutant-General.

HDQRS. DEPARTMENT AND ARMY OF THE TENNESSEE,
Savannah, Ga., December 24, 1864.

Brig. Gen. J. KILPATRICK,
Commanding Cavalry Division:

GENERAL: I am very pleased to be able to certify to the eminent services you have performed as a cavalry commander during the present campaign, particularly when operating with my wing of the army. The assistance of deceiving the enemy as to my intention before and after crossing the Ocmulgee River; the bold engagements near Lovejoy's and Macon; the disposition of your forces so as to cover our trains and protect our flanks—in fact, all the duties appertaining to a cavalry officer have during the campaign been completely performed. My gratitude, or rather that of the Government, is due to yourself and your officers for their untiring energy and faithful service. Be pleased so to express it. You have my best wishes for your promotion and other personal interests, and must call upon me ever as a friend without stint.

Respectfully and truly, yours,

O. O. HOWARD,
Major-General.

SPECIAL ORDERS, No. 416. } HDQRS. DEPARTMENT OF THE SOUTH, *Hilton Head, S. C., December 24, 1864.*

I. Bvt. Brig. Gen. M. S. Littlefield, U. S. Volunteers, is hereby temporarily assigned to the command of the District of Hilton Head, Fort Pulaski, Saint Helena, and Tybee Islands, during the absence of Brig. Gen. E. E. Potter.

* * * * * * *

By command of Maj. Gen. J. G. Foster:

W. L. M. BURGER,
Captain and Assistant Adjutant-General.

HDQRS. NORTHERN DISTRICT, DEPT. OF THE SOUTH,
FIRST SEPARATE BRIGADE,
Morris Island, S. C., December 24, 1864.

Capt. W. L. M. BURGER,
Assistant Adjutant-General, Dept. of the South:

CAPTAIN: I have the honor most respectfully to report that nothing of importance has occurred in this district since my last communication. Troops have evidently returned to James Island, and to other parts of the enemy's lines. It is not known in what numbers, as no refugees or deserters have come to our outposts. The enemy has employed during the past week large fatigue parties in completing and repairing his fortifications in our front; he has been particularly busy on James and John's Islands at those points upon which we advanced against them in July last. They are to be seen at work clearing the space in front of their works of brush and undergrowth, and are also repairing the roads in their rear. The last official information which I have received in regard to the operations of our forces in other districts of the department is to the effect that Savannah was evacuated by the enemy on the 20th instant, and that the iron-clad Savannah intended to attempt to make her escape on the following night. I have given the necessary orders for her reception should she succeed in running out and attempt to enter Charleston Harbor.

I have the honor to be, captain, very respectfully, your obedient servant,

A. SCHIMMELFENNIG,
Brigadier-General, Commanding District.

CITY POINT, VA., *December 25, 1864—8 p. m.*

SECRETARY OF WAR,
Washington:

I have just received General Foster's dispatch announcing the capture of Savannah, with artillery, munitions of war, railroad cars, and cotton. I wish Hardee's 15,000 to 18,000 of a garrison could have been added to the other captures. It is a good thing the way it stands, and the country may well rejoice over it.

U. S. GRANT,
Lieutenant-General.

HEADQUARTERS MILITARY DIVISION OF THE MISSISSIPPI,
In the Field, Savannah, December 25, 1864.

Maj. Gen. M. C. MEIGS,
Quartermaster-General U. S. Army, Washington, D. C.:

GENERAL: In reply to your letter of the 16th [15th] instant I beg to inform you that I have referred the same to Brig. Gen. L. C. Easton, my chief quartermaster, who will report fully to you in respect to all matters within his department connected with our recent march. As you say, my marches have demonstrated the great truth that armies, even of vast magnitude, are not tied down to bases. In almost any quarter of the South armies of from 30,000 to 50,000 may safely march, sure to find near their route forage of some kind or other for their animals. It is a physical impossibility to supply an army with forage, and you do perfectly right in demanding that each army should provide itself with long forage and a large proportion of its grain. In the interior of Georgia we found an abundance of the best kind of corn and fodder, and even here on the sea-board we find an abundance of rice in the straw, which our animals eat with avidity and seem to like. It will not be long before I shall sally forth again, and I feel no uneasiness whatever on the score of forage. You may use my name in any circular addressed to the quartermasters of the army to the effect that every part of the southern country will support their animals by a judicious system of foraging. More animals are lost to your department whilst standing idle, hitched to their wagons, than during the long and seemingly hard marches into the interior. I beg to assure you that all my armies have been abundantly supplied by your department, and I am sometimes amazed at the magnitude of its operations. I think I have personally aided your department more than any general officer in the service, by drawing liberally from the enemy, thereby injuring him financially, and to the same extent helping ourselves, and you may always rely upon my cordially co-operating with any system you may establish. General Easton is now endeavoring to reduce to a system of accountability our captures; but so long as we keep our trains and animals well up, and prevent as far as possible the appropriation of public property to private use, I take it for granted you will pardon any mere departure from the established rules of accountability. I want nothing in the way of horses or transportation, and would merely ask from time to time some few artillery horses of a size and weight which cannot be found in this country; at present we need none, as I do not propose to increase my artillery arm; but as I have 400 or 500 miles more to march before spring, it might be prudent to reserve for us 400 or 500 good artillery horses. If my cavalry cannot remount itself in the country it may go afoot.

Thanking you for your many expressions of confidence and respect,

I am, as ever, your friend and servant,

W. T. SHERMAN,
Major-General.

SAVANNAH, GA., *December 25, 1864.*

Rev. Mr. WYNN, *Methodist Clergyman:*

SIR: Have the kindness to receive and aid your Christian brother George W. Pepper, chaplain Eightieth Ohio Infantry, giving him such facilities for services in your church as will not interrupt your own.

Respectfully, yours,

O. O. HOWARD,
Major-General.

SPECIAL ORDERS, No. 207. } HDQRS. FIFTEENTH ARMY CORPS, *Savannah, Ga., December 25, 1864.*

* * * * * * *

II. In accordance with Special Field Orders, No. 139, Military Division of the Mississippi, and 203, current series, from department headquarters, the Fifteenth Army Corps garrisons the forts at Rosedew, Beaulieu, Wimberly, Thunderbolt, and Bonaventure. Division commanders will therefore detach from their commands as follows: Brigadier-General Woods, 75 men to Rosedew and 100 men to Beaulieu; Brigadier-General Smith, 100 men to Wimberly; Brigadier-General Corse, 80 men to Thunderbolt and 80 men to Bonaventure. Great care is recommended in the selection of commanding officers for these detachments; they must be zealous and energetic. All assistance that can be rendered by these garrisons will be given to Colonel Conklin, chief quartermaster, who is ordered to explore the waters in the vicinity of the above forts, or to officers who may be authorized to dismantle the fortifications.

* * * * * * *

By order of Maj. Gen. P. Joseph Osterhaus:

F. F. WHITEHEAD,
Assistant Adjutant-General.

GENERAL ORDERS, No. 3. } HDQRS. LEFT WING, ARMY OF GEORGIA, *Savannah, Ga., December 25, 1864.*

I. Corps commanders will at once make all necessary preparations for another campaign. All officers who, by intemperance, inefficiency, or ignorance of their duties, have shown themselves unqualified for the positions they hold should at once be recommended for dismissal.

II. No leaves of absence or furloughs will be granted except upon the surgeon's certificate of disability.

III. The interest of the service at this time requires that at least one commissioned officer shall be present with each company, and one field officer with each regiment; and no officer will be mustered out of service in violation of this rule, until the completion of the ensuing campaign.

By command of Maj. Gen. H. W. Slocum:

H. C. RODGERS,
Assistant Adjutant-General.

U. S. STEAMER BIBB, THUNDERBOLT BATTERY,
Wilmington River, Ga., Sunday, December 25, 1864.

Maj. Gen. J. G. FOSTER, U. S. Army,
Commanding Department of the South, Hilton Head, S. C.:

MY DEAR SIR: I have marked this river up to this point, four miles and a half from Savannah, with a good road between the two places. There is a good passage through the obstructions between this place and the battery below here at Turner's Rocks. Vessels drawing fifteen feet can come directly here; least water at low water ten feet (near the obstructions); rise and fall of tide seven feet. All large vessels can come here without difficulty or danger, so far as we can discover. I have recommended to General Sherman to use this place as a transportation depot, and in an interview with him last night understood him to say that he would do so. What glorious news all round!

Yours, respectfully and truly,

CHAS. O. BOUTELLE.

EXECUTIVE MANSION,
Washington, December 26, 1864.

MY DEAR GENERAL SHERMAN: Many, many thanks for your Christmas gift, the capture of Savannah. When you were about leaving Atlanta for the Atlantic coast, I was anxious, if not fearful; but feeling that you were the better judge, and remembering that "nothing risked, nothing gained," I did not interfere. Now, the undertaking being a success, the honor is all yours; for I believe none of us went further than to acquiesce. And taking the work of General Thomas into the count, as it should be taken, it is indeed a great success. Not only does it afford the obvious and immediate military advantages, but, in showing to the world that your army could be divided, putting the stronger part to an important new service, and yet leaving enough to vanquish the old opposing force of the whole—Hood's army—it brings those who sat in darkness to see a great light. But what next? I suppose it will be safer if I leave General Grant and yourself to decide. Please make my grateful acknowledgments to your whole army, officers and men.*

Yours, very truly,

A. LINCOLN.

WAR DEPARTMENT,
December 26, 1864.

Lieutenant-General GRANT,
City Point:

I wish you a merry Christmas, if not too late, and thank you for the Savannah news. It is a sore disappointment that Hardee was able to get off his 15,000 from Sherman's 60,000. It looks like protracting the war while their armies continue to escape. I hope you will give immediate instructions to seize and hold the cotton. All sorts of schemes will be got up to hold it under sham titles of British and other private claimants; they should all be disregarded; and it ought not to be turned over to any Treasury agent, but held by military authority until a special order of the Department is given for the transfer. Sherman has been nominated for major-general.

EDWIN M. STANTON,
Secretary of War.

HEADQUARTERS ARMIES OF THE UNITED STATES,
City Point, Va., December 26, 1864.

Maj. Gen. W. T. SHERMAN,
Savannah, Ga.:

GENERAL: Your very interesting letter of the 22d instant, brought by the hands of Major Gray, of General Foster's staff, is just at hand.

---

* See Special Field Orders, No. 6, p. 16.

As the major starts back at once, I can do no more at present than simply acknowledge its receipt. The capture of Savannah, with all its immense stores, must tell upon the people of the South. All well here.

Yours, truly,

U. S. GRANT,
Lieutenant-General.

HEADQUARTERS MILITARY DIVISION OF THE MISSISSIPPI,
In the Field, Savannah, Ga., December 26, 1864.

Lieut. Gen. U. S. GRANT,
City Point:

GENERAL: Your letter of the 19th instant is received. I have already written you fully since arriving here, in answer to your previous letters. I am very glad to learn that Jeff. Davis is in the condition reported to you, and hope that before this time he is dead and out of the way. From my intercourse with the people of Georgia I think it would give great satisfaction to them generally to know that this was so. Still I shall, of course, go on with my preparations without reference to anything of the kind, and as though the Southern Confederacy possessed all the vitality which they boast of.

Very truly, your friend, and obedient servant,

W. T. SHERMAN,
Major-General.

HEADQUARTERS MILITARY DIVISION OF THE MISSISSIPPI,
In the Field, Savannah, Ga., December 26, 1864—1 p. m.

Lieutenant-General GRANT,
City Point:

GENERAL: In my letter to you of this morning I omitted to answer your inquiry in relation to our prisoners held by the rebels. I have reason to know that they were hurried down from Millen to Savannah, and from here, on our approach, were sent down the Gulf railroad to its termination at Thomasville, and have since been taken back to the old place at Andersonville. I have had my cavalry down to the Altamaha, some fifty miles down the Gulf road, and do not think this is the point from whence they could be reached; but if an expedition were sent up the Apalachicola River, and the Apalachicola Arsenal taken, I think they could be reached from that direction.

Very truly, your friend,

W. T. SHERMAN,
Major-General.

HEADQUARTERS MILITARY DIVISION OF THE MISSISSIPPI,
In the Field, Savannah, December 26, 1864.

Admiral JOHN A. DAHLGREN,
Commanding South Atlantic Squadron, near Savannah, Ga.:

ADMIRAL: Your note of this date is received. Captain Boutelle and Captain Fillebrown had already reported to me, night before last, to the same effect, that the Wilmington River was the best channel, and navigable up to Thunderbolt for vessels of fifteen feet draught; but I had not heard further from them. I will refer your letter to General Easton, who is instructed to arrange so as to get sea-going vessels up to the city wharves, which, if possible, I am very anxious to do, even at considerable expense of labor and money, as I desire to avoid lightering and trans-shipment if possible. I am informed by the Quartermaster-General, from Washington, that six light-draft steamers are now en route to us from the Chesapeake. We had a very pleasant Christmas; I trust you had the same.

Very truly, yours,

W. T. SHERMAN,
Major-General.

HEADQUARTERS MILITARY DIVISION OF THE MISSISSIPPI,
In the Field, Savannah, December 26, 1864.

Maj. Gen. M. C. MEIGS,
Quartermaster-General U. S. Army, Washington City, D. C.:

GENERAL: I have to acknowledge the receipt of your letter of the 19th instant, before receiving which, however, I had already written you fully. General Easton is busily engaged in reducing to order and system all matters pertaining to his department, and your letters are referred to him to act in accordance with them. You may rely upon my drawing from this country everything it affords for our wants, and adding as little as possible to the burdens of the Government. I am much pleased to hear of the efficient service rendered by the quartermaster's employés in Tennessee. I shall always favor their organization for such purposes, and furnish them with anything subject to my order.

Very truly, your friend and obedient servant,

W. T. SHERMAN,
Major-General.

HDQRS. MILITARY DIVISION OF THE MISSISSIPPI,
CHIEF ENGINEER'S OFFICE,
Savannah, Ga., December 26, 1864.

Maj. Gen. W. T. SHERMAN,
Commanding:

GENERAL: In accordance with your instructions, I have the honor to submit the accompanying rough sketch* of plan for the defense of this city. I have reduced the garrison to the lowest probable limit; a smaller one would render it difficult to use any part of it for such offensive operations as might be desirable. The proposed line will be so close to the city that some of the buildings will have to be torn down, and in case of attack all parts of the city will be under artillery fire. Still, the presence of the women and children of the enemy within our lines will render such a fire extremely improbable; and should it be decided by the enemy that they ought to bombard the city, all stores and other valuable property will be quite secure at or near the levee. It is proposed to hold Fort Jackson only because a temporary occupation of it by the enemy would cause us serious inconvenience; to destroy it would require much labor, and even then its site would remain, which would be as detrimental to our interests as the fort itself. Fort Boggs

---

* Not found.

should be dismantled, and so much of it as can give a fire upon the city should be destroyed, because, being an inclosed work, an enemy might effect a lodgment and hold it for a limited time, much to our annoyance. All the remainder of the enemy's old line, being open to the rear, can do us no injury, and can therefore stand as it is. It is a good line, but too extensive for any garrison that will probably be left in the city; it would require 15,000 men to man it completely. The accompanying sketch does not show the character of the works proposed, but merely the approximate position of the line. The line of works should consist of a system of detached redoubts, in defensive relations, which could be connected by infantry parapet at our leisure.

All of which is respectfully submitted.

O. M. POE,
Captain and Chief of Engineers.

SPECIAL FIELD ORDERS, No. 143.

HDQRS. MIL. DIV. OF THE MISSISSIPPI,
In the Field, Savannah, Ga., December 26, 1864.

The city of Savannah and surrounding country will be held as a military post and adapted to future military uses; but as it contains a population of some 20,000 people who must be provided for, and as other citizens may come, it is proper to lay down certain general principles that all within its military jurisdiction may understand their relative duties and obligations.

I. During war the military is superior to civil authority, and where interests clash the civil must give way, yet where there is no conflict every encouragement should be given to well-disposed and peaceful inhabitants to resume their usual pursuits; families should be disturbed as little as possible in their residences, and tradesmen allowed the free use of their shops, tools, &c.; churches, schools, and all places of amusement and recreation should be encouraged, and streets and roads made perfectly safe to persons in their pursuits. Passes should not be exacted within the line of outer pickets, but if any person shall abuse these privileges by communicating with the enemy, or doing any act of hostility to the Government of the United States, he or she will be punished with the utmost rigor of the law. Commerce with the outer world will be resumed to an extent commensurate with the interests of the citizens, governed by the restrictions and rules of the Treasury Department.

II. The chief quartermaster and commissary of the army may give suitable employment to the people, white and black, or transport them to such points as they may choose where employment can be had, and may extend temporary relief, in the way of provisions and vacant houses, to the worthy and needy, until such time as they can help themselves; they will select, first, the buildings for the necessary uses of the army, next, a sufficient number of stores to be turned over to the Treasury agent for trade stores; all vacant store-houses or dwellings and all buildings belonging to absent rebels will be construed and used as belonging to the United States until such times as their titles can be settled by the courts of the United States.

III. The mayor and city council of Savannah will continue, and exercise their functions as such, and will, in concert with the commanding officer of the post and the chief quartermaster, see that the fire companies are kept in organization, the streets cleaned and lighted, and keep up a good understanding between the citizens and soldiers; they will ascertain, and report to the chief commissary of subsistence as soon as possible, the names and number of worthy families that need assistance and support. The mayor will forthwith give public notice that the time has come when all must choose their course, viz., to remain within our lines and conduct themselves as good citizens, or depart in peace. He will ascertain the names of all who choose to leave Savannah, and report their names and residence to the chief quartermaster, that measures may be taken to transport them beyond the lines.

IV. Not more than two newspapers will be published in Savannah, and their editors and proprietors will be held to the strictest accountability, and will be punished severely in person and property for any libelous publications, mischievous matter, premature news, exaggerated statements, or any comments whatever upon the acts of the constituted authorities; they will be held accountable even for such articles though copied from other papers.

By order of Maj. Gen. W. T. Sherman:

L. M. DAYTON,
Aide-de-Camp.

SPECIAL FIELD ORDERS, No. 205.

HEADQUARTERS DEPARTMENT AND ARMY OF THE TENNESSEE,
Savannah, Ga., December 26, 1864.

* * * * * * *

V. Maj. T. W. Osborn, chief of artillery, Department and Army of the Tennessee, is intrusted with the dismantling of all the forts on the coast and river. He will consult with the engineer and ordnance departments in reference thereto, and make arrangements to remove the guns and material to Fort Pulaski or other points.

By order of Maj. Gen. O. O. Howard:

SAML. L. TAGGART,
Assistant Adjutant-General.

SPECIAL ORDERS, No. 208.

HDQRS. FIFTEENTH ARMY CORPS,
Savannah, Ga., December 26, 1864.

* * * * * * *

II. It is probable that our stay here will be of several weeks' duration, therefore immediate steps must be taken to put the command again in the most perfect condition. First, the troops must be thoroughly refitted in clothing and armament. All requisitions must be made out in full, and the officers having charge of these departments must see that every effort is made to procure the necessary stores. Not only the outfit of the men is to be looked to, but the discipline, bearing, and drill of the soldier must be improved. Division commanders will at once make the necessary regulations regarding drills and theoretical instruction (which must embrace all the different branches of garrison and field duties), the daily guard mounts, dress parade, and Sunday inspections. These regulations must be enforced rigidly, with a view to make every man familiar with his various duties, and at the same time rid the corps of a slovenness of appearance which is hardly becoming to a soldier. Second, a recitation course for, principally, commissioned officers and non-commissioned officers is absolutely necessary, and must be instituted in every regiment, battalion, and battery. Camp guards will be placed around the camp of this corps, and the men will not be permitted to go beyond these guards without authority from their company officers. Whenever allowed to visit the city or other camps, the men must be as neat in their appearance as possible, and always wear their waist-belts and side-arms. Third, division commanders alone have authority to grant passes to go beyond the pickets. They will also take measures to stop all foraging hereafter, as the Government is amply prepared to furnish full supplies. Fourth, only the regularly appointed officers of the respective administrative departments are authorized to collect horses, mules, or subsistence stores; all others are forbidden to indulge in such operations.

* * * * * * *

By order of Maj. Gen. P. Joseph Osterhaus:

F. F. WHITEHEAD,
Assistant Adjutant-General.

SPECIAL ORDERS, No. 50. } HDQRS. FOURTH DIV., 15TH ARMY CORPS,
Savannah, Ga., December 26, 1864.

I. Maj. E. S. Johnson, Seventh Illinois Infantry Volunteers, will immediately proceed with the dismounted portion of his regiment to Fort Bonaventure, and garrison the same. Such assistance as can be rendered will be given to officers who may be authorized to dismantle the fortifications.

II. In compliance with orders from corps headquarters, Brig. Gen. E. W. Rice, commanding First Brigade, will assign eighty men to garrison Fort Thunderbolt. Great care is recommended in selecting commanding officers for this detachment. They must be zealous and energetic. All assistance that can be rendered by this garrison will be given to Colonel Conklin, chief quartermaster, who is authorized to explore the waters in the vicinity of the above fort, or to officers who may be authorized to dismantle the fortifications.

* * * * * * *

By order of Brig. Gen. J. M. Corse:

A. W. EDWARDS,
Captain and Acting Assistant Adjutant-General.

HEADQUARTERS SEVENTEENTH ARMY CORPS,
Savannah, Ga., December 26, 1864.

Capt. S. L. TAGGART,
Assistant Adjutant-General, Dept. and Army of the Tennessee:

CAPTAIN: I have the honor to renew my recommendation, made at the close of the Atlanta campaign, for the promotion of Brig. Gen. Giles A. Smith, commanding Fourth Division of this corps, and Brig. Gen. M. D. Leggett, commanding Third Division, to the rank of major-general. They served with great gallantry and efficiency on the Atlanta campaign, and on the campaign just ended served equally well; they are justly entitled to promotion, and I earnestly recommend that they receive it at once. I desire to recommend Col. B. F. Potts, Thirty-second Ohio, commanding First Brigade, Fourth Division, and Col. R.

K. Scott, Sixty-eighth Ohio Volunteers, commanding Second Brigade, Third Division, for promotion to the rank of brigadier-general. These officers have commanded brigades for about one year, with credit to themselves and the country, and are justly entitled to promotion; they are brave and gallant officers. I cordially recommend Brig. Gen. M. F. Force, commanding First Brigade, Third Division, for promotion to the brevet rank of major-general. General Force was severely wounded on the 22d of July, before Atlanta, while gallantly defending his position against the assaults of the enemy.

Very respectfully, your obedient servant,

FRANK P. BLAIR, JR.,
Major-General.

SPECIAL ORDERS, No. 317. } HDQRS. SEVENTEENTH ARMY CORPS,
Savannah, Ga., December 26, 1864.

* * * * * * *

III. The review of this corps by General Sherman will take place tomorrow. The following are the orders for the movement:

1. The right of the command will rest on Gaston street, extending along Whitaker street to Hall, westwardly along Hall to West Broad street, northwardly along West Broad to Bay street, eastwardly along Bay to East Broad street, southwardly along East Broad to Liberty street, and westwardly along Liberty as far as necessary.

2. The First Alabama Cavalry will take up position on the right at 9 a. m.

3. Maj. Gen. J. A. Mower, commanding First Division, will take up his position at 9 a. m., with his right resting on the First Alabama Cavalry.

4. Brig. Gen. M. D. Leggett, commanding Third Division, will take his position at 9.30 o'clock, his right resting on the First Division.

5. Brig. Gen. G. A. Smith, commanding Fourth Division, will take his position at 10 a. m., his right resting on the Third Division.

6. Maj. A. C. Waterhouse will form the artillery of the corps on the left of the Fourth Division.

* * * * * * *

By command of Maj. Gen. F. P. Blair:

C. CADLE, JR.,
Assistant Adjutant-General.

HEADQUARTERS MILITARY DIVISION OF THE MISSISSIPPI,
In the Field, Savannah, December 26, 1864.

Maj. Gen. H. W. SLOCUM,
Commanding Left Wing, Army of Georgia:

GENERAL: The general-in-chief requests that you will, as early as practicable, detail some competent engineer officer of your command, with instructions to report to Brigadier-General Easton, chief quartermaster, with a party, for the purpose of examining and removing the obstructions in the Savannah River.

I have the honor to be, general, respectfully, your obedient servant,

HENRY HITCHCOCK,
Assistant Adjutant-General.

GENERAL ORDERS, No. 4. } HDQRS. LEFT WING, ARMY OF GEORGIA, *Savannah, Ga., December 26, 1864.*

The following officers are announced on the staff of the major-general commanding; they will be obeyed and respected accordingly: Lieut. Col. S. H. Sturdevant, chief commissary of subsistence; First Lieut. William Ludlow, chief engineer.

By command of Maj. Gen. H. W. Slocum:

H. C. RODGERS,
Assistant Adjutant-General.

SPECIAL FIELD ORDERS, No. 29. } HDQRS. 14TH ARMY CORPS, *Savannah, Ga., December 26, 1864.*

The order of review for to-morrow, December 27, will be as follows:

The different divisions will be drawn up in open order on the south side of three parallel streets, as follows, the right of each resting on Price street: The First Division, General Carlin, upon Jones or Taylor street; the Second Division, General Morgan, upon Liberty street; the Third Division, General Baird, upon South Broad street. After the reviewing officer has passed around the lines, the troops of the corps—in the following order: Third Division, Second Division, First Division—will march down Price street to Bay, and up Bay, passing in review before the reviewing officer, upon the latter street, in columns of companies; after which they will turn south upon West Broad and return to their respective camps. The reserve artillery will march in the rear of the First Division. The divisions will march into position as follows: General Baird down the Louisville road, General Morgan down the canal, and General Carlin by the nearest road south of the canal, to the position indicated.

By order of Bvt. Maj. Gen. J. C. Davis:

A. C. McCLURG,
Lieutenant-Colonel and Chief of Staff.

HEADQUARTERS DEPARTMENT OF THE SOUTH,
Hilton Head, S. C., December 26, 1864.

Lieut. Gen. U. S. GRANT,
Commanding Armies of the United States:

GENERAL: I have the honor to inclose a copy* of my usual report by each steamer to General Halleck, by the hands of Captain Dunn, of your staff. Captain Dunn bears full dispatches from General Sherman, and will be able to explain to you fully the highly encouraging character of the situation in this department. General Sherman is in excellent spirits, and his troops in splendid condition. His army, with its present morale and condition, is, in my humble opinion, more than a match for any army the rebels can concentrate against it on this continent. Should it please you to give this department a visit you will, it is needless to assure you, receive the most cordial welcome.

I am, general, very respectfully, your obedient servant,

J. G. FOSTER,
Major-General, Commanding.

---

* See next, *post*.

HEADQUARTERS DEPARTMENT OF THE SOUTH,
Hilton Head, S. C., December 26, 1864.

Maj. Gen. H. W. HALLECK, U. S. Army,
Chief of Staff, Armies of the United States, Washington, D. C.:

GENERAL: I have the honor to inform you that everything in this department and at Savannah is progressing favorably. General Sherman is clearing his army of incumbrances, and getting ready for another move, which, with his present army, actuated by its sanguine spirit, will be resistless by any force that the rebels can collect this side of Richmond. I am now having the guns at Fort McAllister dismounted and brought, with the carriages, &c., to Hilton Head; those in Forts Beaulieu and Rosedew, and perhaps one or two other batteries, will likewise be removed. General Sherman proposes to leave the city in my charge, with a division of his troops for present emergencies. As soon as possible I am to arrange the different works necessary to be held to secure Savannah, so as to be able to hold the city with my present force, with one or perhaps two brigades, the remainder of the division to rejoin his column as soon as arrangements to that effect can be completed. At the request of General Sherman I have notified the Treasury agent that he can take possession of the cotton and forward it to New York. The negroes are being removed—those that are not able-bodied—as also women and children, to Beaufort, to be put on the plantations in that district. Of the able-bodied men, all, except a few hundred absolutely necessary in the quartermaster's department, will be sent, agreeably to General Grant's order, to City Point. I do not, however, expect this transfer of able-bodied men can be made before General Sherman's army leaves, inasmuch as they are all now actively employed in loading and unloading steamers, and in other necessary work in Savannah.

The people of Savannah are, in a measure, destitute, and will have to be supported, to a certain extent, until such time as the ordinary course of labor and of supplies is resumed in the city. General Sherman has made excellent arrangements by which the mayor, receiving captured rice and other rebel stores, can so distribute them as to meet all the immediate demands of the destitute. In a very short time the supplies which I can allow to enter the city by the inland route will meet the wants of the people. Such products as they have may also be exported by the same route without any new change in the Treasury regulations. Having this supply and trade under my own control I can restrict it to proper and safe limits.

As far as can be judged the people feel a sense of relief in having their city occupied by the Union troops and being freed from rebel rule. As an evidence of this it is known that the mayor and council protested against General Hardee's attempting to defend the city. Most of the citizens remain, and show no alarm, but, on the contrary, the utmost confidence in General Sherman and his troops. Several general officers left their wives in the city, Mrs. General G. W. Smith and Mrs. General Robert H. Anderson among the number. Yesterday the different churches were opened and filled with people as usual. Ladies walk the streets without alarm.

As to the enemy and his movements, it is reported by deserters that the few regiments of old troops, only five or six in number, have gone toward Charleston or Wilmington. All the militia, which constituted the main body of General Hardee's force, have gone back into Georgia, and, it is reported, to concentrate at Augusta. The Georgia troops, on leaving Savannah, evinced a determined reluctance to fight for South Carolina, or to remain within the borders of that State. My force is still posted, controlling the railroad, but will shortly be moved, a portion being returned to their original stations and the balance to Savannah. I would respectfully suggest that if there are any new regiments or colored regiments disposable at the North I can make them effective by placing them in garrisons, and by that means be enabled to relieve all of General Sherman's veteran regiments.

The facilities in the way of transportation, &c., are now ample, and I apprehend no difficulty in supplying General Sherman's army up any of the rivers in South Carolina, should he, during the course of his march, require supplies of any kind.

The health of the troops here is good, and all the wounded are doing well.

I have the honor to be, general, very respectfully, your obedient servant,

J. G. FOSTER,
Major-General, Commanding.

HEADQUARTERS DEPARTMENT OF THE SOUTH,
Hilton Head, S. C., December 26, 1864.

ALBERT G. BROWNE, Esq.,
Supervising Special Agent of the Treasury, Beaufort, S. C.:

SIR: At General Sherman's request I have the honor to inform you that he will turn over to you the cotton recently captured by him in the city of Savannah.

Very respectfully, your obedient servant,

J. G. FOSTER,
Major-General, Commanding.

SPECIAL ORDERS, No. 417. } HDQRS. DEPARTMENT OF THE SOUTH,
Hilton Head, S. C., December 26, 1864.

* * * * * * *

III. Lieut. Col. S. L. Woodford, One hundred and twenty-seventh New York Volunteers, having been mentioned with commendation by his brigade and division commanders for gallant conduct during the recent operations upon November 30 and December 6 and 9, near the Charleston and Savannah Railroad, and having been recommended, on account of such service, by Brig. Gen. J. P. Hatch, commanding Coast Division, for promotion to the colonelcy of the Twenty-sixth U. S. Colored Troops (vice Colonel Silliman, deceased, from wounds received in action December 9, 1864), he is hereby appointed acting colonel of the Twenty-sixth U. S. Colored Troops, subject to the approval of His Excellency the President.

* * * * * * *

By command of Maj. Gen. J. G. Foster:

W. L. M. BURGER,
Captain and Assistant Adjutant-General.

Field report of Coast Division, Department of the South, December 26, 1864.

Troops.	Effective.		Present.		Aggregate.
	Officers.	Men.	Officers.	Men.	
First Brigade	122	2,447	130	2,973	3,103
Second Brigade	89	1,877	89	2,246	2,335
Artillery	8	235	8	235	243
Naval Brigade	19	405	21	457	478
Engineers	1	54	1	57	58
Cavalry	3	32	3	32	35
Total	242	5,050	252	6,000	6,252

HDQRS. NORTHERN DISTRICT, DEPT. OF THE SOUTH,
FIRST SEPARATE BRIGADE,
Morris Island, S. C., December 26, 1864.

Lieut. Col. A. G. BENNETT,
Commanding Post, Morris Island, S. C.:

COLONEL: The brigadier-general commanding directs that you cause dry brush to be piled in front of the forts and batteries on this island where the ground admits, at a distance of from 200 to 300 yards, and at those points where it might be supposed that the enemy would make an attack. This is intended, in the latter case, to be fired, so as to throw a strong light on the space in front, thus enabling the garrison of the works to see the enemy.

I have the honor to be, colonel, very respectfully, your obedient servant,

J. W. DICKINSON,
Captain, 21st U. S. Colored Troops, and Actg. Asst. Adjt. Gen.

HEADQUARTERS MILITARY DIVISION OF THE MISSISSIPPI,
In the Field, Savannah, December 26, 1864.

Brig. Gen. R. SAXTON,
Commanding District of Beaufort, S. C.:

GENERAL: I am directed by the general-in-chief to acknowledge your communication to him under date of 22d instant, and to express his appreciation of your readiness to aid him in respect to the disposition of the contrabands. He regards your suggestions as to the islands you mention as well worthy of consideration, especially with reference to the women and children. For the able-bodied men, General Easton, chief quartermaster, to whom the subject is referred, seems to think he can find employment for most, if not all, of them, and Lieutenant-General Grant has also signified his wish that a number shall be sent to him, including a due proportion of women and children. The general would be pleased to see you here to confer with himself and General Easton on the subject.

I am, general, respectfully, your obedient servant,

HENRY HITCHCOCK,
Major and Assistant Adjutant-General.

WAR DEPARTMENT,
December 27, 1864—1 p. m.

Lieutenant-General GRANT:

Is there any objection, on military grounds, to the President removing the blockade of Savannah by proclamation, and opening it to public trade, except contraband of war?

EDWIN M. STANTON,
Secretary of War.

CITY POINT, VA., *December 27, 1864—3.30 p. m.*

Hon. E. M. STANTON,
Secretary of War:

I think it would be better to defer the removal of the blockade of Savannah by proclamation until military operations in that quarter are ended.

U. S. GRANT,
Lieutenant-General.

HEADQUARTERS ARMIES OF THE UNITED STATES,
City Point, Va., December 27, 1864.

Maj. Gen. W. T. SHERMAN,
Commanding Military Division of the Mississippi:

GENERAL: Before writing you definite instructions for the next campaign, I wanted to receive your answer to my letter written from Washington. Your confidence in being able to march up and join this army pleases me, and I believe it can be done. The effect of such a campaign will be to disorganize the South, and prevent the organization of new armies from their broken fragments. Hood is now retreating, with his army broken and demoralized. His loss in men has probably not been far from 20,000, besides deserters. If time is given the fragments may be collected together and many of the deserters reassembled; if we can we should act to prevent this. Your spare army, as it were, moving as proposed, will do this. In addition to holding Savannah, it looks to me that an intrenched camp ought to be held on the railroad between Savannah and Charleston. Your movement toward Branchville will probably enable Foster to reach this with his own force. This will give us a position in the South from which we can threaten the interior, without marching over long narrow causeways easily defended, as we have heretofore been compelled to do. Could not such a camp be established about Pocotaligo, or Coosawhatchie? I have thought that Hood being so completely wiped out for present harm, I might bring A. J. Smith here with from 10,000 to 15,000 men. With this increase I could hold my lines and move out with a greater force than Lee has. It would compel Lee to retain all his present force in the defenses of Richmond, or abandon them entirely. This latter contingency is probably the only danger to the easy success of your expedition. In the event you should meet Lee's army, you would be compelled to beat it, or find the sea-coast. Of course I shall not let Lee's army escape if I can help it, and will not let it go without following to the best of my ability. Without waiting further directions, then, you may make preparations to start on your northern expedition without delay. Break up the railroads in South and North Carolina, and join the armies operating against Richmond as soon as you can. I will leave out all suggestions about the route you should take, knowing that your information, gained daily in the progress of events, will be better than any that can be obtained now. It may not be possible for you to march to the rear of Petersburg, but failing in this you could strike either of the sea-coast ports in North Carolina held by us; from there you could take shipping. It would be decidedly preferable, however, if you could march the whole distance. From the best information I have, you will find no difficulty in supplying your army until you cross the Roanoke. From there here is but a few days' march, and supplies could be collected south of the river to bring you through. I shall establish communication with you there by steam-boat and gun-boat. By this means your wants can be partially supplied. I shall hope to hear from you soon, and to hear your plan and about the time of starting. Please instruct Foster to hold on to all the property captured in Savannah, and especially the cotton. Do not turn it over to citizens or Treasury agents without orders of the War Department.

Very respectfully, your obedient servant,

U. S. GRANT,
Lieutenant-General.

HEADQUARTERS MILITARY DIVISION OF THE MISSISSIPPI,
In the Field, Savannah, Ga., December 27, 1864.

Captain BOUTELLE,
U. S. Coast Survey:

CAPTAIN: I have the honor to request that you will, at the earliest practicable moment, take the necessary steps to have the Tybee Light-House rebuilt, put in good order, and relighted; and also that the channels leading up to Savannah be buoyed and lighted as soon as possible.

I have the honor to be, your obedient servant,

W. T. SHERMAN,
Major-General.

SPECIAL ORDERS, No. 291. } HDQRS. DEPT. AND ARMY OF THE TENN.,
Louisville, Ky., December 27, 1864.

* * * * * * *

III. Col. M. C. Garber, senior chief quartermaster of this department, will at once proceed to New York City and procure transportation to Savannah, Ga., for the headquarters Department and Army of the Tennessee and the headquarters Fifteenth Army Corps, with the officers and men attached thereto.

* * * * * * *

By order of Maj. Gen. O. O. Howard:

WM. T. CLARK,
Assistant Adjutant-General.

SPECIAL FIELD ORDERS, No. 206. } HEADQUARTERS DEPARTMENT AND ARMY OF THE TENNESSEE,
Savannah, Ga., December 27, 1864.

* * * * * * *

V. The several pioneer corps of this army will report to Lieutenant Stickney, Corps of Engineers, U. S. Army, for work on the line of fortifications to be constructed about the city. Corps commanders will direct the commanding officers thereof to report forthwith to Lieutenant Stickney for assignment to camping-ground for their commands contiguous to its place of labor.

By order of Maj. Gen. O. O. Howard:

SAML. L. TAGGART,
Assistant Adjutant-General.

GENERAL FIELD ORDERS, No. 38.

HEADQUARTERS DEPARTMENT AND ARMY OF THE TENNESSEE,
Savannah, Ga., December 27, 1864.

The interests of the service demanding the presence of all efficient officers and men with their commands, in view of another short and decisive campaign, no leaves of absence or furloughs, except on surgeon's certificate of disability, or in extreme cases of family suffering and distress, will, for the present, be granted in this command.

By order of Maj. Gen. O. O. Howard:

SAML. L. TAGGART,
Assistant Adjutant-General.

GENERAL FIELD ORDERS, No. 39.

HEADQUARTERS DEPARTMENT AND ARMY OF THE TENNESSEE,
Savannah, Ga., December 27, 1864.

The attention of the major-general commanding has of late been frequently called to the violation of orders concerning gambling. This offense, so criminal and detrimental to the interests of the service, must be stopped, and hereafter all offenders in this regard, whether commissioned officers or enlisted men, must be arrested and charges preferred against them. Upon discovery the offender shall be dispossessed of the moneys staked, which will be turned over to the provost-marshal's department. All division commanders, and officers of the inspector-general and provost-marshal departments, are particularly enjoined to be vigilant in the execution of this order. It is expected that regimental commanders will at all times be careful to discourage this growing evil. This order will be read at the head of every regiment, battery, and detachment in this command at the three successive dress parades immediately following its receipt. Officers in the quartermaster and commissary departments will also cause it to be read to all the enlisted men in their employment.

By order of Maj. Gen. O. O. Howard:

SAML. L. TAGGART,
Assistant Adjutant-General.

SPECIAL ORDERS, No. 318.

HDQRS. SEVENTEENTH ARMY CORPS,
Savannah, Ga., December 27, 1864.

* * * * * * *

II. The formation of this corps for the review to-morrow will be as follows, instead of the manner designated in Special Orders, No. 317, extract III:

1. The First Alabama Cavalry will form on Price street, with its right resting on Bay street.

2. The First Division, Maj. Gen. J. A. Mower commanding, will form on South Broad street, with the right resting on Price street.
3. The Third Division will form on Liberty street, with its right resting on Price street.
4. The Fourth Division will form on Jones street, with its right resting on Price street.
5. Maj. A. C. Waterhouse, chief of artillery, will form the artillery on the open ground on the corner of Price and Liberty streets.
6. The position of the reviewing officer will be at the Exchange, on Bay street.
7. The hour for the formation will be the same as formerly designated.

* * * * * * *

By command of Maj. Gen. F. P. Blair:

C. CADLE, JR.,
Assistant Adjutant-General.

SPECIAL FIELD ORDERS, No. 184.

HEADQUARTERS THIRD DIVISION, SEVENTEENTH ARMY CORPS,
Savannah, Ga., December 27, 1864.

I. Col. R. K. Scott, Sixty-eighth Ohio Veteran Volunteer Infantry, having been ordered North, Col. G. F. Wiles, Seventy-eighth Ohio Veteran Volunteer Infantry, is hereby detached from his regiment and assigned to the command of the Second Brigade, this division.

* * * * * * *

By order of Brig. Gen. M. D. Leggett:

J. C. DOUGLASS,
Assistant Adjutant-General.

HEADQUARTERS TWENTIETH CORPS,
Savannah, Ga., December 27, 1864.

Brig. Gen. W. T. WARD,
Commanding Third Division:

GENERAL: The general commanding the corps directs that you hold your division in readiness to cross to-morrow morning to the north side of Savannah River. The movement will not be made, however, until you receive further orders.

Very respectfully, your obedient servant,

H. W. PERKINS,
Lieutenant-Colonel and Assistant Adjutant-General.

HDQRS. SIGNAL DETACHMENT, DEPT. OF THE SOUTH,
Hilton Head, S. C., December 27, 1864.

Capt. W. L. M. BURGER,
Assistant Adjutant-General, Department of the South:

CAPTAIN: I have the honor to report, for the information of the general commanding, that communication is now open from Hilton Head to Fort Pulaski.

Very respectfully, your obedient servant,

GEO. A. FISHER,
First Lieutenant, Signal Corps, U. S. Army.

HEADQUARTERS DEPARTMENT OF THE SOUTH,
Hilton Head, S. C., December 27, 1864.

General POTTER,
Deveaux's Neck:

GENERAL: Send the Twenty-sixth U. S. Colored Troops to Beaufort, and the One hundred and forty-fourth New York Volunteers to Hilton Head, as soon as convenient. I have given Mr. Lawrence, an honest man, permission to bring up to Tullifinny Point, for sale, a supply of tobacco, &c. He will only charge a fair profit, 25 per cent. Your command will probably be in its present position from five to seven days longer. I go to Savannah to-day, to be back in three days.

Yours, truly,

J. G. FOSTER,
Major-General, Commanding.

P. S.—One corps of General Sherman's army will, in a few days, cross the Savannah and commence the destruction of the railroad. You can co-operate in any way that you deem advisable at the time; only do not sacrifice men, as General Sherman will take care, in time, to destroy the railroad. You can, at least, cut off all that is below you when the army corps advances.

J. G. F.

P. S. S.—Send down Captain Suter to report to me at Savannah.

J. G. F.

DEVEAUX'S NECK, *December 27, 1864.*

Maj. Gen. J. G. FOSTER:

GENERAL: Your note of this date is received. I will send the One hundred and forty-fourth New York and Twenty-sixth Colored Troops by the first steamers. I suppose I shall receive information of the exact time of General Sherman's corps advancing, that the movements of this force may be guided thereby. The rebels have opened a battery in front of and within 500 yards of old "marsh battery." They have the range nicely. They yesterday killed 1 man and wounded 2 of the One hundred and seventh Ohio, and to-day killed 1 man of the Third New York [Light Artillery] and wounded another. Our own battery is rather weak in construction; I shall have it strengthened to-night. We had expected for some time that the enemy would bring guns down to this point. Please tell General Hatch that the Coosawhatchie does run between our battery and the point in question.

Very respectfully,

EDWARD E. POTTER,
Brigadier-General, Commanding.

HDQRS. DISTRICT OF FLORIDA, DEPT. OF THE SOUTH,
FOURTH SEPARATE BRIGADE,
Jacksonville, Fla., December 27, 1864.

Captain BURGER,
Assistant Adjutant-General, Department Headquarters:

CAPTAIN: I regret to inform you that on the 24th instant Colonel Noble, Seventeenth Connecticut, Captain Young, One hundred and seventh Ohio, and Lieutenant Rice, Thirty-fifth U. S. Colored Troops, were captured by three of the enemy's scouts while en route from this place to Saint Augustine. Colonel Noble was here as a witness before a general court-martial, and was to have returned before Monday 9 a. m. When I gave Colonel Noble permission to go to Saint Augustine I cautioned him especially in reference to the necessity of being always armed, of not traveling without escort, &c. As far as I can learn neither of the parties captured had arms with them. Captain Young was permitted to go at large on the ground of ill-health and retirement from service about to be consummated. Every practicable effort is being made to rescue these officers, but I have very little expectation, notwithstanding the hopes held out by scouts, &c., that they will be successful. I trust that the cavalry force destined for this district may be sent as soon as practicable, and that the infantry, temporarily withdrawn, may be also returned.

I have the honor to be, very respectfully, &c.,

E. P. SCAMMON,
Brigadier-General, Commanding.

CITY POINT, VA., *December 28, 1864.*

Hon. E. M. STANTON,
Secretary of War:

The Richmond papers contain the following items from Georgia:

The latest official advices from Georgia indicate that Sherman has already followed up the occupation of Savannah by sending a force of cavalry, artillery, and infantry upon an expedition, whose destination can only be guessed at from the direction in which it has moved. These troops are reported to have gone toward the Altamaha river, and we shall no doubt next hear that they have crossed that stream and are moving to Southwestern Georgia, in quest of the prisoners of war who were supposed to be at Andersonville. Sherman's programme for his grand campaign northward seems to be no secret. He will start from Port Royal and move straight on Branchville, the point of junction between the Georgian and Carolinian railroads; he then proposes to follow the main lines of railroad toward Virginia, stealing and murdering as much as he can by the way. All very fine; but if Sherman proposes, Lee disposes.

From Wilmington, the following official dispatch was received last night:

"WILMINGTON, *December 27, 3 p. m.*

"His Excellency the PRESIDENT OF THE CONFEDERATE STATES:

"The enemy has embarked under cover of his fleet. His movement is not developed. I have visited Fort Fisher and find the damage slight, except the buildings not necessary for defense; only two guns disabled. The marks remaining indicate that the bombardment was very heavy. Major-General Whiting, commanding the defenses at the mouth of the river, Colonel Lamb, commanding the fort, and the officers and men composing the garrison deserve especial commendation for the gallantry, efficiency, and fortitude displayed under very trying circumstances.

"BRAXTON BRAGG."

From Southwestern Virginia:

The Lynchburg Virginian has the following additional in relation to the capture of the salt-works, announced officially on yesterday:

We had been led to hope that these important works were safe, but the sources from which their reported capture comes leave us no room to doubt its correctness. They were occupied by the enemy on Tuesday the 20th, and held by them, as is stated, until Thursday, when they retreated towards Bristol. We learn that the place was held by about 200 reserves, under Colonel Preston, the most of whom escaped capture. The works are reported to be but little damaged, and we understand that persons who have visited them since the occupation by the enemy think they can be put in working order again by the first of February. A large quantity of salt, already gotten out, was destroyed, and all the buildings at the place were burned; several pieces of artillery were also captured by them, but they got but little else of any kind. General Breckinridge, at the last accounts, was at Saltville, preparing to follow the enemy on his retreat. Beyond continued skirmishing with their rear guard, no further fighting has taken place than that already reported. A gentleman who passed over the railroad from Bristol to Glade Spring after the enemy advanced says the bridges between these places are all burned, but that the track is uninjured.

U. S. GRANT,
Lieutenant-General.

HEADQUARTERS MILITARY DIVISION OF THE MISSISSIPPI,
In the Field, Savannah, December 28, 1864.

General J. D. WEBSTER,
Nashville, Tenn.:

GENERAL: Inclosed please find an order for removal of headquarters to this place; and I will further explain General Sherman's wishes, as he has given me the directions. The officers to be transferred are General Webster, Colonel Sawyer, Captain Rochester, Captain Coverdale, and Lieutenant Towner, of General Barry's staff; also Captain Jenney, with Captain Poe's office. All the other officers on duty at headquarters will be relieved and returned to their commands, as also all clerks, orderlies, and messengers not belonging to organizations in this part of the command. All public property at headquarters will be properly disposed of by orders, and left, and the office records, papers, &c., proper, be brought along. Your private horses will be disposed of as each of you may prefer, by sale, by taking quartermaster's receipts, or otherwise, but not be brought here, as transportation from New York cannot be obtained. The Regular Battalion Thirteenth Infantry will not come. Captain Poe sends instructions for Captain Jenney; and in the absence of General Barry I presume Lieutenant Towner must bring only his office proper. The general wishes his trunk, and also the effects or baggage for all the staff here should be brought along; all of us have more or less with Colonel Sawyer and yourself. You will come via New York, and thence by regular steamer. You can make the necessary orders covering these points and giving transportation. The clerks, messengers, and orderlies belonging to this part of the command will be brought along. This relieves from duty at headquarters Captain Rankin, Captain Stockdale, Lieutenant Newlin, and any others not enumerated as to come here.

I am aware the general has written you fully the news, &c., regarding the campaign just closed, and I can only add, all seems to be working well here.

I am, general, with respect, &c.,

L. M. DAYTON,
Aide-de-Camp.

[Inclosure.]

SPECIAL FIELD ORDERS, No. 144. } HDQRS. MIL. DIV. OF THE MISSISSIPPI,
In the Field, Savannah, Ga., December 27, 1864.

* * * * * * *

XI. The general and business headquarters of this military division will be moved from Nashville, Tenn., to Savannah, Ga., under direction of Brig. Gen. J. D. Webster.

By order of Maj. Gen. W. T. Sherman:

L. M. DAYTON,
Aide-de-Camp.

HEADQUARTERS MILITARY DIVISION OF THE MISSISSIPPI,
In the Field, Savannah, December 28, 1864.

Messrs. P. J. STANFIELD, A. J. PAGETT, and others,
Of Liberty and Tattnall Counties, Ga.:

GENTLEMEN: I have a copy of the resolutions adopted by you. They are surely strong enough and patriotic enough. I will aid you all possible, and do all in my power to encourage you and defend you in your course. I do think we have been at war long enough for truth to reveal itself. We are fellow-countrymen and bound by every principle of honor and honesty to maintain and defend the Union given us by Washington, and that is all I aim at, and the moment Georgia resumes her place in the Union and sends Representatives to Congress she is at once at peace, and all the laws both national and State are revived. If you will stay at home quietly, and call back your sons and neighbors to resume their peaceful pursuits, I will promise you ammunition to protect yourselves and property. If rebel soldiers do any of you violence I will retaliate, and if you will bring your produce to Savannah I will cause it to be protected in transitu, and allow it to be sold in market to the highest bidder, and our commissary will buy your cattle, hogs, sheep, &c. It would be well to form a league, and adopt some common certificate, so that our officers and soldiers may distinguish between you and open rebels. I will be glad to confer with any of your people, and will do all that is fair to encourage you to recover the peace and prosperity you enjoyed before the war.

I am, with respect, &c.,

W. T. SHERMAN,
Major-General.

ADDENDA.

When dominant political factions become so corrupt as to prefer the destruction of the General Government to their own overthrow as mere parties, and in support of such preference set at defiance the authority of such General Government, and finally actually inaugurate a war for the destruction of the same, we deem it the right and duty of all men living in the country where such parties are formed, who desire to continue loyal to their Government, to resist if possible all attempts to make them take up arms against the same; but if not able to make an open resistance, then we deem it not at all dishonorable to evade stealthily such unnatural, unlawful, and treasonable measures, nor do we deem it dishonorable to aid in the same or any other manner the open defenders of our cause.

Be it therefore resolved, That we, the undersigned citizens of Liberty and Tattnall Counties and the State of Georgia, either deserted from the army of the so-called Confederate States at home, in violation of the conscript law thereof, or by reason of our old age, will never aid in carrying on this wicked rebellion against our Government.

Resolved, That we will band together, under the leadership of some suitable person, in order that we may better defend our lives and our property against the execution of barbarous threats and orders uttered and issued against us by rebel leaders.

Resolved, That the occupation of Georgia by the Federal army is in accordance with our wishes, and that we will render any assistance in our power to said army that may [be] asked.

Resolved, That we are opposed to the principle of secession, and look upon all who support said principle as traitors to our Government.

Resolved, That hereafter, as heretofore, we will recognize the Constitution of the United States, and that alone, as the supreme law of our land, to which, though temporarily suspended here, we steadily look for that protection which, as American citizens, we are entitled to enjoy.

Resolved, That two members of this meeting be appointed to proceed as soon as practicable with a copy of these resolutions to the nearest Federal camp.

We do solemnly swear that we will not divulge to any one at all not present at this meeting anything connected therewith, or transpired thereat, without the full consent and approbation of the chairman thereof, so help me God.

Be it resolved, That the penalty will be death for any person who reveals any part of the above obligation or resolution or proceeding of this meeting that has been transacted, or may hereafter be transacted at any subsequent.

The following-named persons will act to form resolutions for this meeting to be governed by: P. J. Standfield, A. J. Pagett, Asa Barnett, J. E. Beasly, Jno. S. Long.

SPECIAL FIELD ORDERS, No. 145. } HDQRS. MIL. DIV. OF THE MISSISSIPPI,
In the Field, Savannah, Ga., December 28, 1864.

* * * * * * *

V. Capt. O. M. Poe, chief engineer, is hereby authorized, in the execution of instructions to build a line of defense for the city of Savannah, to remove or destroy buildings of any character, to give orders for the removal of any camp of troops or other obstacles in the way, and commanders of troops will assist Captain Poe as much as possible in the removal of camps that may interfere with his proposed line.

* * * * * * *

By order of Maj. Gen. W. T. Sherman:

L. M. DAYTON,
Aide-de-Camp.

HDQRS. DEPARTMENT AND ARMY OF THE TENNESSEE,
Savannah, Ga., December 28, 1864.

Maj. Gen. W. T. SHERMAN,
Commanding Military Division of the Mississippi:

GENERAL: In consequence of the rain I have postponed the review of Major-General Blair's command to 11 a. m. Friday, the 30th instant.

Very respectfully, yours, &c.,

O. O. HOWARD,
Major-General.

HDQRS. DEPARTMENT AND ARMY OF THE TENNESSEE,
Savannah, Ga., December 28, 1864.

Maj. Gen. W. T. SHERMAN,
Commanding Military Division of the Mississippi:

GENERAL: It is reported to me by my officers that the animals of this army are actually suffering for want of forage. It is reported to me by Major Thomas that there is a large quantity within six miles of this city, and that it can be landed without any trouble at Thunderbolt.

Very respectfully, your obedient servant,

O. O. HOWARD,
Major-General.

HEADQUARTERS MILITARY DIVISION OF THE MISSISSIPPI,
In the Field, Savannah, December 28, 1864.

Maj. Gen. O. O. HOWARD,
Commanding, &c.:

GENERAL: The chief quartermaster represents that paragraph III, Special Field Orders, No. 141,* has not been complied with as yet, and he desires it shall be as soon as possible, for the reason that for the absence of this guard and fatigue service, the public property cannot be protected nor the supplies arrived be furnished the army. Please give this your earliest attention, as General Easton is in pressing need of the detail of men.

I am, general, with respect,

L. M. DAYTON,
Aide-de-Camp.

HEADQUARTERS DEPARTMENT OF THE TENNESSEE,
ENGINEER OFFICE,
Savannah, Ga., December 28, 1864.

Capt. O. M. POE,
Chief Engineer Military Division of the Mississippi:

I have to report that I have examined the ground for the new line of fortifications about the city. The line will run so as to render it necessary to destroy some old buildings (some of them occupied by families) and to remove some of the camps of our troops. I have located the line to interfere with both of these as little as possible. I think it necessary to give me authority, in orders, to have all buildings or camps in the way of the line of works removed at once.

I am, very respectfully, your obedient servant,

C. B. REESE,
Capt. of Engineers, Chief Engineer Department of the Tennessee.

SPECIAL FIELD ORDERS, No. 207. } HEADQUARTERS DEPARTMENT AND ARMY OF THE TENNESSEE,
Savannah, Ga., December 28, 1864.

* * * * * * *

III. Permission to proceed to Hilton Head and Beaufort, S. C., to return as soon as practicable, is granted to Maj. Gen. P. Joseph Oster-

* See p. 802.

haus, commanding Fifteenth Army Corps, and Surgeon Niccolls, U. S. Volunteers, with one hospital steward. U. S. Government transports will furnish the necessary transportation.

* * * * * * *

By order of Maj. Gen. O. O. Howard:

SAML. L. TAGGART,
Assistant Adjutant-General.

GENERAL ORDERS, No. 81. } HDQRS. FIRST DIV., 15TH ARMY CORPS,
Savannah, Ga., December 28, 1864.

I. During the temporary absence of the general commanding, Col. James A. Williamson, Fourth Iowa Infantry, will assume command of this division.

By order of Brig. Gen. C. R. Woods:

FRED. H. WILSON,
Acting Assistant Adjutant-General.

GENERAL ORDERS, No. 8. } HDQRS. 3D BRIG., 1ST DIV., 15TH A. C.,
Savannah, Ga., December 28, 1864.

During the absence of Col. James A. Williamson, temporarily commanding the First Division, Fifteenth Army Corps, Col. George A. Stone, Twenty-fifth Iowa Infantry, will assume command of this brigade.

By order of Col. James A. Williamson:

CHARLES MACKENZIE,
Acting Assistant Adjutant-General.

HEADQUARTERS FIFTEENTH ARMY CORPS,
Savannah, Ga., December 28, 1864.

Colonel MARTIN,
Commanding Second Brigade, Second Division:

COLONEL: The major-general commanding directs that you move your command to a point within four or five miles of this place, suitable for a good camp, in order that you may more easily communicate with the city, your base for supplies.

I am, colonel, respectfully, your obedient servant,

F. F. WHITEHEAD,
Assistant Adjutant-General.

SPECIAL ORDERS, No. 178. } HDQRS. FIRST DIV., 17TH ARMY CORPS,
Near Savannah, Ga., December 28, 1864.

* * * * * * *

II. In accordance with Special Orders, No. 319, extract V, headquarters Seventeenth Army Corps, of date December 28, 1864, the Twenty-fifth Indiana Regiment Volunteer Infantry is detached from the Third Brigade of this command, and will report to General Easton, chief quartermaster Military Division of the Mississippi, for duty. The commanding officer of the regiment will at once report in person to General Easton for orders.

* * * * * * *

By order of Maj. Gen. J. A. Mower:

CHAS. CHRISTENSEN,
Lieut., Aide-de-Camp, and Acting Assistant Adjutant-General.

HDQRS. FIFTY-FIFTH REGT. OHIO VOLUNTEER INFANTRY,
Savannah, Ga., December 28, 1864.

Capt. C. H. YOUNG,
Acting Assistant Adjutant-General:

CAPTAIN: In reply to your communication of the 28th instant, I respectfully submit the following report:

At 6 a. m. of the 21st instant, being then on duty as officer of the day for the brigade, I was informed that General Geary reported that his pickets occupied the enemy's works. Hastening to the picket-line I ordered the officer in charge of the line of sentinels to send a few men forward to reconnoiter the enemy's works. Before these men, however, had started I saw a white flag passing up the railroad track, and ordered the whole line forward immediately. Before reaching the enemy's works, however, a serious obstruction was met. A dense slashing of small timber filled the depression in our front, which was so well constructed as to be nearly impassable. No great depth of water was found, but two or three ditches had been filled with water to the depth of three or four feet. It was nearly fifteen minutes before all the pickets succeeded in reaching the railroad, and while collecting them the division officer of the day appeared and ordered me to advance, keeping the right of my line on the railroad. Some six of the enemy now appeared and gave themselves up, pointing out at the same time three torpedoes which had been imbedded in the bed of the railroad. These prisoners were immediately sent with a guard to brigade headquarters, and the line moved into the enemy's works. These works were not minutely examined by me, as I was ordered to move rapidly along, but it is my impression that the number of guns in the works at this point was six, five of them being heavy iron guns mounted upon siege carriages and one brass piece mounted upon a field carriage. There was also quite a good supply of ammunition for these guns. I left a guard over the captured guns and ammunition consisting of one sergeant and eight men. This fact was reported to the brigade officer of the day who succeeded me. The line having been reformed was now moved toward the city. Troops could be seen in the distance passing over the railroad, but it could not be determined whether or not they were the enemy. Upon reaching a point about a mile from the enemy's works an officer of the Third Division having with him a few men called to me from a road leading to the right, and requested me to send some men with him to take possession of a magazine near by which was said to be guarded. One officer and about twenty-five men were detached for this purpose, who reported about half an hour later that the magazine, containing considerable ammunition, had been taken, and with it 1 captain and 32 men left as a guard. This was reported to the division officer of the day and received his approval. The troops passing over the railroad before us had by this time been discovered to be of our own forces, and the deployed line having been drawn in the column marched by the flank down the railroad. Upon reaching the railroad bridge near the city a guard forbade further advancing, and I reported to the division officer of the day, who ordered me to march to the present camp-ground of the division and await the arrival of the brigade. The brigade arrived about 11 a. m., at which time the pickets were dismissed and my successor reported for duty.

I have the honor to remain, captain, your obedient servant,

H. OSBORN,

Captain, Fifty-fifth Regiment Ohio Volunteer Infantry.

FLAG-SHIP MALVERN,

At Sea, off coast of North Carolina, December 29, 1864.

Maj. Gen. W. T. SHERMAN, U. S. Army,

Commanding Military Division of the Mississippi:

MY DEAR GENERAL: I send Captain Breese to communicate with you, and tell you about matters and things in this quarter. I congratulate you on your success, which I knew was sure when you started. I told the world you would be off Savannah on the 10th, and you were not far off on that day. I feel certain that you are in Savannah to-day, or will be there in a week. When you have captured that place I invite you to add to your brow the laurels thrown away by General Butler after they were laid at his feet by the navy, and which neither he nor those with him had the courage to gather up. I felt sure that it would be so when we started on the expedition. We attacked Fort Fisher, silenced it, blew it up, burned it out, and knocked it to pieces. An officer belonging to the small skirmishing party of twenty men sent out by the force that landed on the beach went on the parapet of Fort Fisher and brought away the flag that we had shot down. A sergeant went through the sally-port into the fort, and met there a rebel orderly ready to mount a horse for the purpose of carrying a letter. He killed the orderly, searched his body, found the dispatch, mounted the horse and rode out of the fort. Another soldier went in and brought out a mule that was stowed away in a bomb-proof; another fired his musket at a crowd of cowering wretches stowed away in the bomb-proof. Notwithstanding all this General Butler decided not to attack Fort Fisher, "as the navy fire has not injured it as a defensive work!" Great heavens! what are we coming to? Well, I think that Providence intended it to be so; and it rests with you to add new honors to your name, already famous, notwithstanding the newspaper reporters. This is merely on your way to Richmond. Take this place and you take the "crême de la crême" of the rebellion. I leave to Captain Breese to tell you all my views; and I do hope, my dear general, that you will second me here and let our people see the folly of employing such generals as Butler and Banks. I have tried them both, and God save me from further connection with such generals. With you I feel sure of success, and shall bless the day when I shall once more see your esteemed self in our midst. A host of old friends are here to welcome you, and show you the most magnificent naval fight you ever laid your eyes on. I hope soon to see you here. I have much to tell you that will astonish you.

Very truly and sincerely, yours,

DAVID D. PORTER,

Rear-Admiral.

HEADQUARTERS MILITARY DIVISION OF THE MISSISSIPPI,
In the Field, Savannah, December 29, 1864.

Brig. Gen. R. DELAFIELD,
Chief Engineer U. S. Army, Washington, D. C.:

GENERAL: I have the honor to acknowledge the receipt of your circular dated November 21, 1864, requesting me to furnish for your information the names of officers connected with my command of the Corps of Engineers who have been mentioned for distinguished and meritorious conduct during the present or previous campaigns against the rebellious States, with recommendations for brevet rank. In compliance therewith I have the honor to recommend for promotion by brevet, as below stated, the following officers of the Corps of Engineers connected with my command during the late and previous campaigns:

First. Capt. O. M. Poe, Corps of Engineers, chief engineer of the Military Division of the Mississippi, has been in constant daily service near my person since the beginning of the Atlanta campaign. His services have been of the very highest value throughout that and the campaign just ended, and have been rendered with a zeal, promptitude, and fidelity which have left nothing to desire. I consider that he has fairly earned the commission he formerly held as brigadier-general of volunteers, but I prefer that he should be brevet brigadier-general in the Regular Army, in order that I may retain him near my person as long as I have the honor to exercise an active command in the Army of the United States. I find him so thoroughly qualified that I would be lost without him.

Second. Capt. C. B. Reese, chief engineer of the Department and Army of the Tennessee, has proved himself a most earnest and efficient officer, to whom the highest praise is awarded by his immediate superiors for the valuable service he has rendered in all departments under his control. I respectfully recommend him for the brevet rank of colonel, U. S. Army.

Third. First Lieut. Amos Stickney, Corps of Engineers, assigned to duty with the Department and Army of the Tennessee, is recommended as a zealous and efficient officer, who has at all times satisfactorily performed the duties imposed upon him, and has fairly earned promotion by one grade.

Fourth. First Lieut. William Ludlow, Corps of Engineers, joined my command during the Atlanta campaign—afterward doing duty at Rome, Ga., under Brigadier-General Corse, participating in the heroic defense of Allatoona Pass, and serving during the recent campaign as chief engineer of the Left Wing of this army, under Major-General Slocum, commanding, who has expressed satisfaction with his discharge of the duties thus assigned him. For Lieutenant Ludlow's participation in the defense of Allatoona Pass, I respectfully recommend him for the brevet rank of captain, U. S. Army, and for that of major in consideration of his services during the last campaign.

I have the honor to be, general, respectfully, your obedient servant,

W. T. SHERMAN,
Major-General, Commanding.

P. S.—Please send a copy of your circular to Major-General Thomas, at Nashville, that he may report direct to you concerning the officers of the Engineer Corps serving in that branch of my command.

W. T. S.,
Major-General.

WAR DEPARTMENT,
OFFICE OF DIRECTOR AND GENERAL MANAGER OF
MILITARY RAILROADS U. S.,
Washington, December 29, 1864.

Maj. Gen. W. T. SHERMAN,
Savannah, Ga.:

GENERAL: I am instructed to send military railroad operatives to Savannah to put the captured rolling-stock in good order, and perform any service you may require of the railroad. Col. W. W. Wright, chief engineer, is ordered upon this duty, and will shortly leave for Savannah with a sufficient force.

Very respectfully, your obedient servant,

D. C. McCALLUM,
Bvt. Brig. Gen. and General Manager of Military Railroads U. S.

SPECIAL FIELD ORDERS, No. 208.
HEADQUARTERS DEPARTMENT AND ARMY OF THE TENNESSEE,
Savannah, Ga., December 29, 1864.

* * * * * * *

VI. At the special request of Maj. Gen. P. Joseph Osterhaus, commanding Fifteenth Army Corps, Maj. Max. Woodhull, assistant adjutant-general, U. S. Volunteers, is relieved from duty at these headquarters and temporarily assigned as assistant adjutant-general, Fifteenth Army Corps, and will report forthwith accordingly.

* * * * * * *

By order of Maj. Gen. O. O. Howard:

SAML. L. TAGGART,
Assistant Adjutant-General.

SPECIAL ORDERS, No. 210.
HDQRS. FIFTEENTH ARMY CORPS,
Savannah, Ga., December 29, 1864.

* * * * * * *

III. Brigadier-General Hazen, commanding Second Division, will move his command at once to the vicinity of this place, and have them ready for review by Major-General Sherman at 11 a. m. on Saturday next (December 31).

* * * * * * *

By order of Maj. Gen. P. Joseph Osterhaus:

H. N. WHEELER,
Assistant Adjutant-General.

GENERAL ORDERS, No. 10.
HDQRS. 3D BRIG., 4TH DIV., 17TH A. C.,
Savannah, Ga., December 29, 1864.

The brigade commander tenders his thanks to the officers and men of this command, and congratulates them on their excellent appearance at the review of this day. In their execution of the different movements, their steadiness and accuracy of march, and the general cleanliness and good condition of arms, accouterments, and clothing, they more than equaled his expectation, and the more so because a large portion of the brigade consists of recruits who have had but little opportunity for drill or exercise in the manual. General Sherman was much gratified, saying that the brigade was "a fine body of men." While thanking the command for having acquitted themselves thus well, the general would remind them it is only by improving every leisure opportunity, and especially the present one, in constant drill and the manual, that they can preserve to the brigade the reputation they have gained.

By order of Brig. Gen. W. W. Belknap:

O. D. KINSMAN,
Assistant Adjutant-General.

HEADQUARTERS TWENTIETH CORPS,
Savannah, Ga., December 29, 1864.

Brig. Gen. N. J. JACKSON,
Commanding First Division:

GENERAL: The Third Division is ordered to cross the river early to-morrow morning. The general commanding the corps directs that you take up, at daybreak to-morrow morning, in addition to the line you now hold, that now held by the Third Division.

Very respectfully, your obedient servant,

H. W. PERKINS,
Assistant Adjutant-General.

GENERAL ORDERS, No. 172. HDQRS. DEPARTMENT OF THE SOUTH,
Hilton Head, S. C., December 29, 1864.

Col. C. L. Kilburn, assistant commissary-general of subsistence, U. S. Army, having reported at these headquarters in compliance with Special Orders, No. 431, paragraph 47, current series, from the War Department, dated Adjutant-General's Office, Washington, D. C., December 5, 1864, is hereby announced as chief commissary of subsistence of this department, and will be obeyed and respected accordingly.

By command of Maj. Gen. J. G. Foster:

W. L. M. BURGER,
Assistant Adjutant-General.

HDQRS. NORTHERN DISTRICT, DEPT. OF THE SOUTH,
Morris Island, S. C., December 29, 1864.

Capt. W. L. M. BURGER,
Assistant Adjutant-General, Department of the South:

CAPTAIN: I have the honor to report that nothing of importance has occurred in this command since my last communication. Five deserters of the First South Carolina Infantry from Sullivan's Island and one of the Second South Carolina Artillery from James' Island have come into our lines. The general information brought by these men is the same as is already in our possession. They state that the details from the troops on Sullivan's Island that had been sent to Pocotaligo and Savannah (only about 150 men) returned last week. They represent a depressed, dispirited feeling as existing amongst officers and men, and give various rumors that are flying about camp which tend to corroborate this. The enemy continues fatigue work on some of his batteries on James Island, and especially on the new batteries near Stono River on John's Island. As regards sending Mrs. Thomas and her daughters across our lines by flag of truce, I endeavored to communicate with the enemy in the harbor on the first day of the ladies' arrival here, but my flag of truce was not accepted. Yesterday was too stormy to admit of meeting in the harbor, and to-day I propose to send a flag of truce over from Cole's Island and endeavor to effect the transfer there.

I have the honor to be, respectfully, your obedient servant,

A. SCHIMMELFENNIG,
Brigadier-General, Commanding District.

PRIVATE AND CONFIDENTIAL.]

HEADQUARTERS OF THE ARMY,
*Washington, D. C., December 30, 1864.**

Maj. Gen. W. T. SHERMAN,
Savannah:

MY DEAR GENERAL: I take the liberty of calling your attention, in this private and friendly way, to a matter which may possibly hereafter be of more importance to you than either of us may now anticipate. While almost every one is praising your great march through Georgia and the capture of Savannah, there is a certain class, having now great influence with the President, and very probably anticipating still more on a change of Cabinet, who are decidedly disposed to make a point against you—I mean in regard to "Inevitable Sambo." They say that you have manifested an almost *criminal* dislike to the negro, and that you are not willing to carry out the wishes of the Government in regard to him, but repulse him with contempt. They say you might have brought with you to Savannah more than 50,000, thus stripping Georgia of that number of laborers and opening a road by which as many more could have escaped from their masters; but that instead of this you drove them from your ranks, prevented them from following you by cutting the bridges in your rear, and thus caused the massacre of large numbers by Wheeler's cavalry.

To those who know you as I do such accusations will pass as the idle winds, for we presume that you discouraged the negroes from following you simply because you had not the means of supporting them and feared they might seriously embarrass your march. But there are others, and among them some in high authority, who think, or pretend to think, otherwise, and they are decidedly disposed to make a point against you.

I do not write this to induce you to conciliate this class of men by doing anything which you do not think right and proper and for the interest of the Government and the country, but simply to call your attention to certain things which are viewed here somewhat differently than from your standpoint. I will explain as briefly as possible: Some here think that, in view of the scarcity of labor in the South, and the probability that a part, at least, of the able-bodied slaves will be called into the military service of the rebels, it is of the greatest importance to open outlets by which the slaves can escape into our lines, and, they say, that the route you have passed over should be made the route of escape and Savannah the great place of refuge. These I know are the views of some of the leading men in the administration, and they now express dissatisfaction that you did not carry them out in your great raid.

---

* General Sherman's reply of January 12, 1865, refers to this letter as dated January 1st, but General Halleck's copy is dated as here given.

Now that you are in possession of Savannah, and there can be no further fears about supplies, would it not be possible for you to reopen these avenues of escape for the negroes without interfering with your military operations? Could not such escaped slaves find, at least, a partial supply of food in the rice fields about Savannah, and occupation in the rice and cotton plantations on the coast?

I merely throw out these suggestions; I know that such a course would be approved by the Government, and I believe that a manifestation on your part of a desire to bring the slaves within our lines will do much to silence your opponents.

You will appreciate my motives in writing this private letter.

Yours, truly,

H. W. HALLECK.

SAVANNAH, GA., *December 30, 1864.*

Maj. Gen. M. C. MEIGS,
Quartermaster-General U. S. Army, Washington, D. C.:

GENERAL: I am instructed by Major-General Sherman to say that he wishes to accumulate at this place as soon as possible sixty days' forage for 35,000 animals. We have to-day but one day's grain on hand and none in the sound or river. I understand there is a ship-load at Hilton Head. I sent a steamer last night to tow the ship to this place, and hope she will be at the bar before we are entirely out. The corps quartermasters are slow in getting in their estimates for supplies. I send you inclosed an estimate of clothing and camp equipage which I require in addition to what you have already sent to Hilton Head and Pensacola. I will be glad to get the clothing mentioned on this estimate as soon as possible. I have sent to Pensacola for the clothing you sent to that point. I will try and send you an estimate of quartermaster's stores by next mail. Supplies should be sent to this place, if possible, in vessels not drawing over thirteen feet water; if larger vessels are sent the freight will have to be trans-shipped to small steamers. We want here very much a light class of steamers and Schuylkill barges for the purpose of removing freight from heavy-draft vessels lying at the roadstead below this place, and communicating from here to Hilton Head, and through other inland passages. I will be glad if you will send me six steamers suitable for this purpose. The class of boats most needed are high-pressure, double-engine boats, of wide beam and very light draft. I desire, also, that you send me twenty Schuylkill barges, six of them to be double-deckers or pleasure barges. The steamers we now have here are not suitable for our purpose, as there is only four feet water at low tide on the bar in the south channel, which we are compelled to use owing to obstructions in the north channel. Admiral Dahlgren reports that these obstructions cannot be removed. I am preparing to give them a trial myself, and hope I will succeed.

I am, general, very respectfully, your obedient servant,

L. C. EASTON,
Brevet Brigadier-General, Chief Quartermaster.

By sending vessels around through Wassaw Sound we can get about thirteen feet water up to this place at high tide. Order forward the sixty days' grain as rapidly as possible.

L. C. EASTON,
Quartermaster.

GENERAL ORDERS, No. 60. } HDQRS. FIFTEENTH ARMY CORPS, *Savannah, Ga., December 30, 1864.*

Maj. Maxwell Woodhull, assistant adjutant-general, U. S. Volunteers, having reported in accordance with paragraph VI, Special Field Orders, No. 208, headquarters Department and Army of the Tennessee, is hereby assigned to duty as assistant adjutant-general at these headquarters, and will be obeyed and respected accordingly.

By command of Maj. Gen. P. Joseph Osterhaus:

H. N. WHEELER,
Assistant Adjutant-General.

GENERAL ORDERS, No. 61. } HDQRS. FIFTEENTH ARMY CORPS, *Savannah, Ga., December 30, 1864.*

In accordance with paragraph 3, General Orders, No. 59, headquarters Department and Army of the Tennessee, series of 1863, the following-named officers are relieved from duty with their respective commands and are hereby assigned as acting assistant inspectors-general, and will be obeyed and respected accordingly: Capt. Albert Head, Tenth Iowa Volunteers, for Second Brigade, Third Division, Fifteenth Army Corps; Lieut. A. D. Cameron, Seventh Iowa Veteran Volunteers, for Second Brigade, Fourth Division, Fifteenth Army Corps.

By command of Maj. Gen. P. Joseph Osterhaus:

MAX. WOODHULL,
Assistant Adjutant-General.

SPECIAL ORDERS, No. 211. } HDQRS. FIFTEENTH ARMY CORPS, *Savannah, Ga., December 30, 1864.*

I. Division commanders will take immediate steps to prevent the destruction of the railroad, telegraph lines, or buildings connected with the same, in the vicinity of their respective camps.

* * * * * * *

By order of Maj. Gen. P. Joseph Osterhaus:

MAX. WOODHULL,
Assistant Adjutant-General.

HEADQUARTERS TWENTIETH CORPS,
Savannah, Ga., December 30, 1864.

Brig. Gen. W. T. WARD,
Commanding Third Division:

GENERAL: The general commanding directs that your division move early to-morrow morning to Hutchinson's Island, where a pontoon bridge will be laid to the South Carolina shore.

Very respectfully, your obedient servant,

ROBT. P. DECHERT,
Captain and Acting Assistant Adjutant-General.

HEADQUARTERS DEPARTMENT OF THE SOUTH,
Hilton Head, S. C., December 30, 1864.

Maj. Gen. H. W. HALLECK, U. S. ARMY,
Chief of Staff, Armies of the United States, Washington, D. C.:

GENERAL: Availing myself of the opportunity afforded by the sailing of the steamer, I have the honor to inform you that everything in this department is progressing favorably. I have just returned from Savannah, where I left General Sherman with his whole army. Preparations are rapidly being made for offensive operations, and the different corps are being reviewed by General Sherman in person. Supplies are being landed at the city, and although General Easton has not been able to effect his arrangements, yet, by rapid transfer by lighters from the vessels having them on board to the wharves of Savannah, it is expected that this will soon be facilitated so as to meet all demands. The admiral having relinquished his efforts to remove the obstructions in the north channel at the upper end of Elba Island, so as to allow the vessels of sixteen feet draught to go to the city wharves, I have undertaken to do it, and expect to accomplish the work in about three weeks. At present the lighters have to carry the supplies three miles by way of the south channel, which has only five feet of water at low tide. I intend to-morrow to go through Wilmington River, via Thunderbolt and Saint Augustine Creeks, and expect to be able to find a passage that way for vessels drawing ten feet of water, certainly as far as Thunderbolt, and probably up to the wharves of the city. The supply of forage thus far received here is very inadequate to the wants of General Sherman's army. The commissary supplies have been thus far sufficient. Five or six steamers sent by General Meigs have just arrived and have made the water transportation ample. I have no news of importance to communicate from either of the districts of the department.

Very respectfully, your obedient servant,

J. G. FOSTER,
Major-General, Commanding.

HDQRS. NORTHERN DISTRICT, DEPT. OF THE SOUTH,
Morris Island, S. C., December 30, 1864.

Capt. W. L. M. BURGER,
Assistant Adjutant-General, Department of the South:

CAPTAIN: I have the honor to inform you that nothing of special interest has occurred in my command since my last report. The inclosed copy of an intercepted dispatch gives the news they had in Charleston this morning with regard to our forces at Wilmington. My outposts report that night before last (the 28th to the 29th) the cars were running frequently on the Charleston and Savannah Railroad to the city. Last night (the 29th–30th) trains seemed to be running to and from the city as often as about once in every forty-five minutes. At about 1 a. m. a band was heard playing on James Island, and also considerable cheering. These indications, of course, lead me to suppose that troops are arriving on or returning to my front. At the request of Admiral Dahlgren, I have given instructions for Fort Strong and Battery Chatfield to throw rifle and mortar shells at intervals during the night to those points in the harbor where the enemy might be supposed to be placing new obstructions. The naval battery will also open fire with the same object, and, in fact, do most of the firing. If this arrangement meets the approval of the major-general commanding, it will be continued for the present, not expending more than about twenty-five shots during the twenty-four hours. Arrangements have finally been completed for the transfer of Mrs. Thomas and daughters to the enemy's lines from the right of Cole's Island to-morrow, the 31st instant.

I have the honor to be, your obedient servant,

A. SCHIMMELFENNIG,
Brigadier-General, Commanding District.

[Inclosure.]

By signal from Fort Ripley to Castle Pinckney, December 30, 1864.

What is the news?

LAWRENCE.

Castle Pinckney to Fort Ripley.

No papers received this a. m. News last evening that the enemy's forces ashore were badly cut up by the guns of Fort Fisher. They are probably below the fort.

O.

HDQRS. NORTHERN DISTRICT, DEPT. OF THE SOUTH,
FIRST SEPARATE BRIGADE,
Morris Island, December 30, 1864.

Lieut. Col. A. G. BENNETT,
Commanding Post, Morris Island, S. C.:

COLONEL: Information having been officially received at these headquarters of the destruction of the iron-clads at Savannah, the brigadier-general commanding directs the precautions recently adopted for defense against the same may be relaxed, and citizens who have been detailed on guard duty in this district will be relieved therefrom.

I have the honor to be, colonel, very respectfully, your obedient servant,

J. W. DICKINSON,
Capt. 21st U. S. Colored Troops and Actg. Asst. Adjt. Gen.

WASHINGTON, D. C., *December 31, 1864.*

Lieutenant-General GRANT,
City Point:

I learn from a letter of General Foster that all able-bodied negroes brought in by Sherman are to be shipped to City Point. Permit me to suggest that they be armed, organized, and used in the Department of the South during the winter. Our experience is that negroes brought North during the cold weather, from a warm climate, are almost useless; moreover, they suffer much from cold. To send them North at the present time would create a panic among them, and prevent others from coming in from the interior of the country. Rebel papers are already harping on this point in order to frighten their slaves. The Secretary of War and General Meigs concur in these views.

H. W. HALLECK,
Major-General and Chief of Staff.

HEADQUARTERS MILITARY DIVISION OF THE MISSISSIPPI,
Savannah, Ga., December 31, 1864—3 p. m.

[General U. S. GRANT:]

DEAR GENERAL: A mail leaves at 5 p. m. for Hilton Head and New York. I have written a short official letter to General Halleck, amounting to nothing, simply because I suppose you want to hear from me at every opportunity. I have already reviewed my four corps, and wind up in a day or two with Kilpatrick's cavalry, which I keep out about nine miles. There is no doubt of it but this army is in fine condition and impatient to go ahead. I would like to have Foster re-enforced, if possible, so that I will not have to leave him a division to hold Savannah. I will have all the heavy work done, such as moving the captured artillery to Hilton Head, where it can be more safely guarded, and building the redoubts in the new line for the defense of Savannah. This will be close in, for we don't care if the enemy does shell the town. Five thousand men will be plenty, and white troops will be best, as the people are dreadfully alarmed lest we garrison the place with negroes. Now, no matter what the negro soldiers are, you know that people have prejudices which must be regarded. Prejudice, like religion, cannot be discussed. As soon as I can accumulate enough provisions and forage to fill my wagons, I will be ready for South Carolina, and if you want me to take Charleston I think I can do it, for I know the place well. I was stationed there from '42 to '46, and used to hunt a good deal all along the Cooper River. The direction to approach Charleston is from the northwest, down the peninsula between Ashley and Cooper, as also that ending on the bay at Mount Pleasant. You had better notify General Meigs to send at once enough provisions for 65,000 men and 40,000 horses and mules for sixty days, instead of the daily allowance, for you know I must work on the surplus and not on the daily receipts. We have pretty well eaten up all the rice and rice straw for fifty miles. By making a wide circuit by Barnwell, Orangeburg, Columbia, and Santee I can reach the neighborhood of Georgetown and get a resupply. I do not issue rations to the people, but order the mayor to look to the people, and have given him the rough rice to be sold and exchanged into flour and meat. Thus the expense will fall on the holders of this rough rice, which I treat as prize of war. Inasmuch as Hardee refused to surrender, and thereby escaped with his garrison, I take it for granted that we will have to fight in South Carolina, though I believe G. W. Smith, with his Georgia militia, has returned to Georgia, by way of Augusta, saying he would be damned if he would fight for South Carolina. The people here seem to be well content, as they have reason to be, for our troops have behaved magnificently; you would think it Sunday, so quiet is everything in the city day and night. All recognize my army a different body of men than they have ever seen before. I hope you will push Thomas up. Keep him going south anywhere. Let him make a track down into Alabama, or, if you think better, he can again come to Chattanooga and as far down as the Etowah, to which point I preserved the iron rails ready to be used again.

I am fully aware of your friendly feeling toward me, and you may always depend on me as your steadfast supporter. Your wish is law and gospel to me, and such is the feeling that pervades my army. I have an idea you will come to see me before I start.

Yours, in haste,

W. T. SHERMAN,
Major-General.

HEADQUARTERS MILITARY DIVISION OF THE MISSISSIPPI,
In the Field, Savannah, Ga., December 31, 1864.

Maj. Gen. H. W. HALLECK,
Chief of Staff, Washington, D. C.:

GENERAL: The steamer leaves with the mail this afternoon at 5 p. m. I write only to say that since my last to you there is nothing of importance to communicate. The city is perfectly quiet and orderly. The enemy appear to be making preparations to receive us over in South Carolina. As soon as I can accumulate a sufficient surplus of forage and provisions to load my wagons, I shall be ready to start. We find the Savannah River more obstructed than we expected. It is filled with crib-works loaded with paving stones, making mud islands, with narrow, tortuous, and difficult channels. All our stores have to be lightered up from the ship anchorage about Tybee. I have been engaged in reviewing my troops, and feel a just pride in their fine soldierly condition and perfect equipment. I propose at once to make lodgments in South Carolina, about Port Royal, opposite this city, and up about Sister's Ferry. When all is ready I can feign at one or more places and cross at the other, after which my movements will be governed by those of the enemy, and such instructions as I may receive from Lieutenant-General Grant before starting. I do not think I can employ better strategy than I have hitherto done, namely, make a good ready and then move rapidly to my objective, avoiding a battle at points where I would be encumbered by wounded, but striking boldly and quickly when my objective is reached. I will give due heed and encouragement to all peace movements, but conduct war as though it could only terminate with the destruction of the enemy and the occupation of all his strategic points. The weather is fine, the air cool and bracing, and my experience in this latitude convinces me that I may safely depend on two good months for field-work. I await your and General Grant's answers to my proposed plan of operations before taking any steps indicative of future movements. I should like to receive, before starting, the detachments left behind in Tennessee belonging to these four corps, and it would be eminently proper that General Foster should be re-enforced by about 5,000 men, to enable him to hold Savannah without calling upon me to leave him one of my old divisions, which is too valuable in the field to be left behind in garrison. I would also deem it wise, so far to respect the prejudices of the people of Savannah, as not to garrison the place with negro troops. It seems a perfect bugbear to them, and I know that all people are more influenced by prejudice than by reason. The army continues in the best of health and spirits, and, notwithstanding the habits begotten during our rather vandalic march, its behavior in Savannah has excited the wonder and admiration of all.

I am, with great respect, very truly, yours,

W. T. SHERMAN,
Major-General, Commanding, &c.

HEADQUARTERS MILITARY DIVISION OF THE MISSISSIPPI,
In the Field, Savannah, Ga., December 31, 1864.

Admiral D. D. PORTER,
Commanding North Atlantic Blockading Squadron:

DEAR ADMIRAL: Captain Breese has this moment arrived with your letter of December 29, and I assure you it does my heart good to feel that I am once more near you. I hope soon we will meet again in person. I have already submitted to Generals Halleck and Grant a plan for a campaign which will bring my whole army to Wilmington, which I know I can take as easily, if not more so, than Savannah. I do not think you can take those shore batteries with your gun-boats, or do more than drive the gunners to the cover of their bomb-proofs. I have examined carefully many of the forts about Savannah, and find them so well covered by traverses and bomb-proof shelters, that you might blaze away at them for a month from the direction of the sea channels without materially harming them. I have no doubt, however, from what you say, that Butler's men ought to have taken Fort Fisher in about three minutes, for its bomb-proofs cannot possibly shelter more than 200 men, who would be, as you say, crouching in a defenseless position as against an attacking force. But even after you have got Fisher, then comes Caswell, Fort Johnston, and, I suppose, a string of forts all the way back to Wilmington. Now, I propose to march my whole army through South Carolina, tearing up railroads and smashing things generally, feign on Charleston, and rapidly come down upon Wilmington from the rear, taking all their works in reverse. I submitted this plan to General Grant on the 24th, and shall expect his answer very soon, and will be ready to start the moment I can replenish my wagons with bread, sugar, coffee, &c.

At present the Savannah River is badly obstructed by heavy cribs filled with cobblestones, which have served to make islands of mud and sand, leaving narrow, difficult, and tortuous channels between. Through these channels all our stores have to be brought in launches and light-draught boats, of which we have an inadequate number, so that thus far we barely get enough for daily consumption. But all hands are hard at work, and I hope by the 10th of January to get enough ahead to load our wagons, and be ready to start. It will take some time for me to reach Wilmington, but I am certain that mine is the only mode by which the place can be taken effectually. My army is a good one, but not large enough to make detachments from. I had to leave with Thomas enough men to whip Hood, and have written to General Grant to send to Foster enough men to hold Savannah, whilst I move with my entire force. It is very important that I should have two or more points along the coast where I can communicate with you, and where I could have some spare ammunition and provisions in reserve—say, Bull's Bay, Georgetown, and Masonborough. Can't you arrange to get all these points in your jurisdiction? Admiral Dahlgren is very accommodating, but you and I understand each other better. I think when you come to consider my position, you will agree with me that my proposition is better than to undertake to reduce in detail the forts about Wilmington, and you can so maneuver as to hold a large portion of the enemy to the sea-coast, whilst I ravage the interior, and when I do make my appearance on the coast, we will make short work of them all. I have shown to Captain Breese my letters to Grant and Halleck, and will explain to him fully everything that will interest you, and as soon as I can hear from General Grant will send a steamer to you, advising you of the time of starting. I rather fear, however, that the President's anxiety to take Charleston may induce Grant to order me to operate against Charleston, rather than Wilmington, though I much prefer the latter—Charleston being a dead cock in the pit altogether.

I am, most truly, your friend,

W. T. SHERMAN,
Major-General.

QUARTERMASTER-GENERAL'S OFFICE,
Washington City, December 31, 1864.

Hon. E. M. STANTON,
Secretary of War, Washington, D. C.:

SIR: I am informed by Brevet Brigadier-General Easton, chief quartermaster of General Sherman's army, that the transportation of that army is now in better condition than he has ever seen it; "in fact, it is in first-rate order." The animals, of which there are about 35,000 with the army, of which 12,000 are horses, eat rice straw, and will not suffer for long forage. He asks that shipments of grain continue while the army remains at Savannah, and that a small shipment of hay be also continued. I have ordered the daily shipment of hay to be reduced one-half, *i. e.*, to 100 tons. I inclose a copy of a letter* from General Sherman, which is interesting as giving some results of his late experience, and which also bears testimony to the services of the Quartermaster Department, by which he says all his "armies have been admirably supplied." General Sherman states that his experience shows that every part of the Southern country will support the animals of an army moving through it, if a judicious system of foraging is adopted, and that more animals are lost while tied to wagons of the trains of armies at rest than in the long and seemingly hard marches into the interior. His own army is fully supplied with horses and mules, and he is of opinion that he can continue to supply it in the South with all the animals needed during contemplated operations. He may possibly, in the course of the spring, need some heavy artillery horses, but has a full supply at present.

I am, very respectfully, your obedient servant,

M. C. MEIGS,
Quartermaster-General U. S. Army, Brevet Major-General.

SPECIAL FIELD ORDERS, No. 148. } HDQRS. MIL. DIV. OF THE MISSISSIPPI,
In the Field, Savannah, Ga., December 31, 1864.

I. The work of constructing the fortifications of Savannah will commence at once, under the supervision of Captain Poe, chief engineer, and the line will be divided into two divisions, the Ogeechee road being the dividing line, and he is authorized to call upon army commanders for such details for labor as he may require.

II. Major-General Slocum, commanding Left Wing, will furnish details to Captain Poe for that part of the work north of and between the Ogeechee road and Savannah River, and Major-General Howard, commanding Right Wing, will furnish details for the work south of the Ogeechee road.

* * * * * * *

By order of Maj. Gen. W. T. Sherman:

L. M. DAYTON,
Aide-de-Camp.

---

* See Sherman to Meigs, December 25, p. 807.

GENERAL ORDERS, No. 83. } HDQRS. FIRST DIV., 15TH ARMY CORPS, *Savannah, Ga., December 31, 1864.*

I. The general commanding having returned to duty, Col. James A. Williamson, Fourth Iowa Infantry, will reassume command of the Third Brigade of this division.

By order of Brig. Gen. C. R. Woods:

FRED. H. WILSON,
Acting Assistant Adjutant-General.

GENERAL ORDERS, No. 77. } HDQRS. SECOND DIV., 15TH ARMY CORPS, *Fort McAllister, Ga., December 31, 1864.*

The troops of the United States being about to temporarily vacate the country west of the Ogeechee River, and the people south of the Gulf railroad, on what is known as Bryan Neck, being destitute of provisions, Mr. Maxwell, Doctor Johnson, and Mr. Cranston, residents, are hereby appointed a committee to ascertain the number and wants of the people on said Neck, both the black and white; also, to, without delay, take possession of the rice now in the Middleton Mills, guard the same, supplying from it the wants of said people. No more than two weeks' supply will be furnished any family at any one time. Frequent inspections by officers of the army appointed for that purpose will be made, to see that this order is complied with fairly and in good faith.

By order of Brig. Gen. W. B. Hazen:

G. LOFLAND,
Assistant Adjutant-General.

HDQRS. SECOND BRIG., SECOND DIV., 15TH ARMY CORPS,
OFFICE ACTING ASSISTANT INSPECTOR-GENERAL,
Near Savannah, Ga., December 31, 1864.

Capt. C. A. EARNEST,
Actg. Asst. Insp. Gen., Second Div., Fifteenth Army Corps:

SIR: I have the honor to submit the following record of events of the Second Brigade, Second Division, Fifteenth Army Corps, from the 15th to the 31st of December, 1864:

On the 17th instant the command left camp near Fort McAllister, for the purpose of destroying the Gulf railroad at and near McIntosh Station, Ga., as directed by General Orders, No. 70, headquarters Second Division, Fifteenth Army Corps. About 12 m. the 18th the command encamped at McIntosh Station, and commenced the destruction of the road, and by the evening of the 20th had effectually destroyed, by burning the ties and twisting the rails, nine miles of railroad.

Morning of the 21st broke camp at 6 a. m., and commenced the return march for Fort McAllister. On the road received orders to report to corps headquarters. Camped for the night one mile east of the Ogeechee River, having marched twenty miles.

On the morning of the 22d received orders to move three miles east of the Ogeechee River, and encamp until further orders; remained in camp until the 29th, when the command moved to present camp, four miles west of Savannah.

Total number of miles marched, forty-five.

Very respectfully, yours,

THOS. O. PEIRCE,
Captain and Acting Assistant Inspector-General.

HEADQUARTERS MILITARY DIVISION OF THE MISSISSIPPI,
In the Field, Savannah, Ga., December 31, 1864.

Maj. Gen. F. P. BLAIR,
Commanding Seventeenth Army Corps:

GENERAL: Your note inclosing Mr. Cohen's of this date is received, and I answer frankly, through you, his inquiries.

First. No one can practice law as an attorney in the United States without acknowledging the supremacy of our Government. If I am not in error an attorney is as much an officer of the court as the clerk, and it would be a novel thing in a government to have a court to administer law that denied the supremacy of the Government itself.

Second. No one will be allowed the privileges of a merchant, or rather to trade is a privilege which no one should seek of the Government, without, in like manner, acknowledging its supremacy.

Third. If Mr. Cohen remains in Savannah as a denizen, his property, real and personal, will not be disturbed, unless its temporary use be necessary for the military authorities of the city. The title to property will not be disturbed, in any event, until adjudicated by the courts of the United States.

Fourth. If Mr. Cohen leaves Savannah under my Special Orders, No. 143, it is a public acknowledgment that he "adheres to the enemies of the United States," and all his property becomes forfeited to the United States. But as a matter of favor he will be allowed to carry with him clothing and furniture for the use of himself, his family, and servants, and will be transported, at our cost, within the enemy's lines, but not by way of Fort Royal.

These rules will apply to all parties, and from them no exceptions will be made.

I have the honor to be, general, your obedient servant,

W. T. SHERMAN,
Major-General.

WASHINGTON, *December 31, 1864.*

Maj. Gen. J. G. FOSTER,
Savannah, Ga.:

GENERAL: Your letter of the 26th has been received and submitted to the Secretary of War, who directs that the families of all rebel officers in Savannah be placed outside our lines, so that they may enjoy the society and share the fortunes of their husbands and fathers. And no such persons will hereafter be permitted to remain or come within the lines of the Union armies. The Secretary also directs that you report the receipt of this order and the time of its execution. If General Sherman should still be in Savannah on its receipt, you will deliver it to him and so report. There are no troops available to be sent to your department at the present time, except the fragments of General Sherman's command on leave and with General Thomas. All have been ordered to New York for transportation to Savannah.

Very respectfully, your obedient servant,

H. W. HALLECK,
Major-General and Chief of Staff.

HEADQUARTERS OF THE ARMY,
Washington, December 31, 1864.

Major-General FOSTER,
Savannah, Ga.:

GENERAL: The Secretary of War directs that the order to send able-bodied or other negroes from your department to City Point be suspended, and that you organize all you can get for service there. You will give them the proper regimental and company organization, muster them into the service of the United States, and appoint their officers provisionally, reporting these appointments for confirmation. You will also arm and clothe them, and have them carefully drilled and exercised. They will soon be of service for the defense of your fortifications. It is presumed that you will find among your officers, non-commissioned officers, and privates men desirous of and competent for commands in colored regiments. If General Sherman has not left this will be submitted to him. It would be well to circulate a notice that you will receive, pay, clothe, and arm all able-bodied negroes who will join you.

Very respectfully, your obedient servant,

H. W. HALLECK,
Major-General and Chief of Staff.

HDQRS. SIGNAL DETACHMENT, DEPT. OF THE SOUTH,
Hilton Head, S. C., December 31, 1864.

Capt. W. L. M. BURGER,
Assistant Adjutant General:

CAPTAIN: I have the honor to state that I have just received a message from Captain Bachtell, chief signal officer with General Sherman, that the line is open to Savannah by telegraph from here to Braddock's Point and by signal from there to Savannah. The stations between Fort Pulaski and Savannah are over low, marshy ground, and the communication will, I fear, often be interrupted by mist and fog.

I am, captain, very respectfully, your obedient servant,

JESSE MERRILL,
Captain and Chief Signal Officer.

HEADQUARTERS DEPARTMENT OF THE SOUTH,
Hilton Head, S. C., December 31, 1864.

Lieut. Gen. W. J. HARDEE,
Comdg. Confederate Forces, Dept. of S. C., Ga., and Fla.:

GENERAL: I have the honor to request that you cause one of your staff officers to meet Lieutenant-Colonel Woodford, of my staff, at Port Royal Ferry, S. C., on Wednesday, January 4, proximo, at 2 p. m., for the purpose of receiving several communications and mails for prisoners of war. Unless I hear from you to the contrary, I shall consider that the time and place of meeting are agreeable to yourself.

Very respectfully, your obedient servant,

J. G. FOSTER,
Major-General, Commanding.

HDQRS. NORTHERN DISTRICT, DEPT. OF THE SOUTH,
FIRST SEPARATE BRIGADE,
Morris Island, December 31, 1864.

Lieut. Col. A. G. BENNETT,
Commanding Post, Morris Island, S. C.:

COLONEL: The brigadier-general commanding directs that hereafter the command of the northern point of this island will be designated otherwise than as the Northern District Morris Island, this term being liable to mislead when used in an abbreviated form. It will be hereafter known as the command of Forts Strong, Putnam, and the Batteries at Cummings' Point, which can be abbreviated, "Forts Strong, Putnam, &c.," if so desired.

I have the honor to be, colonel, very respectfully, your obedient servant,

J. W. DICKINSON,
Capt., 21st U. S. Colored Troops and Actg. Asst. Adjt. Gen.

Abstract from returns of the Union forces at Savannah, Ga., Maj. Gen. William T. Sherman, commanding, for December 31, 1864.

Command.	Present for duty.		Aggregate present.	Aggregate present and absent.	Pieces of field artillery.
	Officers.	Men.			
Army of the Tennessee:					
Fifteenth Army Corps (Osterhaus)	729	14,839	18,038	28,145	18
Seventeenth Army Corps (Blair)	437	11,803	13,681	24,219	14
Total Right Wing (Howard)	1,166	26,642	31,719	52,364	32
Army of Georgia:					
General headquarters	7	....	7	7	......
Fourteenth Army Corps (Davis)	598	13,722	15,917	27,757	16
Twentieth Army Corps (Williams)	654	13,464	16,184	28,788	16
Total Left Wing (Slocum)	1,259	27,186	32,108	56,552	32
Cavalry (Kilpatrick)	231	4,649	5,800	9,868	6
Grand total	2,656	58,477	69,627	118,784	70

Organization of the Union Forces at Savannah, Ga., commanded by Maj. Gen. William T. Sherman, December 31, 1864.

HEADQUARTERS GUARD.

7th Company Ohio Sharpshooters, Lieut. James Cox.

ENGINEERS.

1st Missouri (five companies), Lieut. Col. William Tweeddale.

RIGHT WING.

Maj. Gen. OLIVER O. HOWARD.

ESCORT.

15th Illinois Cavalry, Company K, Lieut. John A. McQueen.
4th Company Ohio Cavalry, Capt. John L. King.

FIFTEENTH ARMY CORPS.

Maj. Gen. PETER J. OSTERHAUS.

FIRST DIVISION.

Brig. Gen. CHARLES R. WOODS.

First Brigade.

Col. MILO SMITH.

12th Indiana, Maj. Elbert D. Baldwin.
26th Iowa, Maj. John Lubbers.
27th Missouri (seven companies), Col. Thomas Curly.
29th Missouri, Lieut. Col. Joseph S. Gage.
31st and 32d Missouri Battalion, Maj. Abraham J. Seay.
76th Ohio, Lieut. Col. Edward Briggs.

Second Brigade.

Col. ROBERT F. CATTERSON.

26th Illinois, Capt. George H. Reed.
40th Illinois, Lieut. Col. Hiram W. Hall.
103d Illinois, Lieut. Col. George W. Wright.
97th Indiana, Capt. George Elliott.
100th Indiana, Maj. Ruel M. Johnson.
6th Iowa, Maj. William H. Clune.
46th Ohio, Maj. Edward N. Upton.

Third Brigade.

Col. JAMES A. WILLIAMSON.

4th Iowa, Lieut. Col. Samuel D. Nichols.
9th Iowa, Capt. Paul McSweeney.
25th Iowa, Col. George A. Stone.
30th Iowa, Lieut. Col. Aurelius Roberts.
31st Iowa, Lieut. Col. Jeremiah W. Jenkins.

SECOND DIVISION.

Brig. Gen. WILLIAM B. HAZEN.

First Brigade.

Col. THEODORE JONES.

55th Illinois, Capt. Charles A. Andress.
116th Illinois, Lieut. Col. John E. Maddux.
127th Illinois, Capt. Charles Schryver.
6th Missouri, Lieut. Col. Delos Van Deusen.
30th Ohio, Capt. Emory W. Muenscher.
57th Ohio, Capt. Robert W. Smith.

Second Brigade.

Col. JAMES S. MARTIN.

111th Illinois, Maj. William M. Mabry.
83d Indiana, Lieut. Col. George H. Scott.
37th Ohio, Lieut. Col. Louis von Blessingh.
47th Ohio, Col. Augustus C. Parry.
53d Ohio, Capt. Robert Curren.
54th Ohio, Maj. George F. Kili.

Third Brigade.

Col. JOHN M. OLIVER.

48th Illinois, Maj. Edward Adams.
90th Illinois, Lieut. Col. Owen Stuart.
99th Indiana, Lieut. Col. John M. Berkey.
15th Michigan, Lieut. Col. Frederick S. Hutchinson.
70th Ohio, Lieut. Col. Henry L. Philips.

THIRD DIVISION.

Brig. Gen. JOHN E. SMITH.

First Brigade.

Col. JOSEPH B. MCCOWN.

63d Illinois, Lieut. Col. James Isaminger.
93d Illinois,* Lieut. Col. Nicholas C. Buswell.
48th Indiana, Lieut. Col. Edward J. Wood.
59th Indiana, Lieut. Col. Jefferson K. Scott.
4th Minnesota, Col. John E. Tourtellotte.

Second Brigade.

Bvt. Brig. Gen. GREEN B. RAUM.

56th Illinois, Capt. James P. Files.
10th Iowa, Capt. William H. Silsby.
17th Iowa,† Lieut. Col. Samson M. Archer.
26th Missouri (four companies),‡ Capt. Charles A. Meyers.
80th Ohio, Lieut. Col. Pren Metham.

---

*Non-veterans 18th Wisconsin attached.
†On veteran furlough.
‡Detachment 10th Missouri attached.

FOURTH DIVISION.

Brig. Gen. JOHN M. CORSE.

First Brigade.

Brig. Gen. ELLIOTT W. RICE.

52d Illinois, Lieut. Col. Jerome D. Davis.
66th Indiana, Lieut. Col. Roger Martin.
2d Iowa, Col. Noel B. Howard.
7th Iowa, Lieut. Col. James C. Parrott.

Second Brigade.

Col. ROBERT N. ADAMS.

12th Illinois, Maj. Wheelock S. Merriman.
66th Illinois, Capt. William S. Boyd.
81st Ohio, Maj. William C. Henry.

Third Brigade.

Lieut. Col. FREDERICK J. HURLBUT.

7th Illinois, Lieut. Col. Hector Perrin.
50th Illinois, Capt. Timothy D. McGillicuddy.
57th Illinois, Capt. Frederick A. Battey.
39th Iowa, Maj. Joseph M. Griffiths.

ARTILLERY.

Maj. CHARLES J. STOLBRAND.

1st Illinois Light, Battery H, Capt. Francis De Gress.
1st Michigan Light, Battery B, Capt. Albert F. R. Arndt.
1st Missouri Light, Battery H, Lieut. John F. Brunner.
Wisconsin Light, 12th Battery, Capt. William Zickerick.

SEVENTEENTH ARMY CORPS.

Maj. Gen. FRANK P. BLAIR, Jr.

ESCORT.

11th Illinois Cavalry, Company G, Capt. Stephen S. Tripp.

FIRST DIVISION.

Maj. Gen. JOSEPH A. MOWER.

First Brigade.

Col. CHARLES S. SHELDON.

64th Illinois, Capt. Joseph S. Reynolds.
18th Missouri, Lieut. Col. William H. Minter.
27th Ohio, Capt. James Morgan.
39th Ohio, Capt. John W. Orr.

Second Brigade.

Brig. Gen. JOHN W. SPRAGUE.

35th New Jersey, Col. John J. Cladek.
43d Ohio, Col. Wager Swayne.
63d Ohio, Maj. John W. Fouts.
25th Wisconsin, Lieut. Col. Jeremiah M. Rusk.

Third Brigade.

Col. JOHN TILLSON.

10th Illinois, Lieut. Col. McLain F. Wood.
25th Indiana, Maj. James S. Wright.
32d Wisconsin, Col. Charles H. De Groat.

THIRD DIVISION.

Brig. Gen. MORTIMER D. LEGGETT.

Provost Guard.

20th Illinois, Capt. Henry King.

First Brigade.

Brig. Gen. MANNING F. FORCE.

30th Illinois, Lieut. Col. William C. Rhoads.
31st Illinois, Lieut. Col. Robert N. Pearson.
45th Illinois, Maj. John O. Duer.
12th Wisconsin, Col. James K. Proudfit.
16th Wisconsin, Capt. Joseph Craig.

Second Brigade.

Col. GREENBERRY F. WILES.

20th Ohio, Capt. Harrison Wilson.
68th Ohio, Lieut. Col. George E. Welles.
78th Ohio, Capt. Israel C. Robinson.
17th Wisconsin, Maj. Patrick H. McCauley.

FOURTH DIVISION.

Brig. Gen. GILES A. SMITH.

First Brigade.

Col. BENJAMIN F. POTTS.

14th Illinois, } Lieut. Alonzo J. Gillespie.
15th Illinois, }
41st Illinois, Maj. Robert H. McFadden.
53d Illinois, Col. John W. McClanahan.
23d Indiana, Lieut. Col. George S. Babbitt.
53d Indiana, Capt. Henry Duncan.
32d Ohio, Lieut. Col. Jefferson J. Hibbets.

Third Brigade.

Brig. Gen. WILLIAM W. BELKNAP.

32d Illinois, Capt. John J. Rider.
11th Iowa, Lieut. Col. Benjamin Beach.
13th Iowa, Capt. Justin C. Kennedy.
15th Iowa, Maj. George Pomutz.
16th Iowa, Capt. Leo Schumacher.

ARTILLERY.

Maj. ALLEN C. WATERHOUSE.

1st Michigan Light, Battery C, Lieut. William W. Hyzer.
Minnesota Light, 1st Battery, Lieut. Henry Hurter.
Ohio Light, 15th Battery, Lieut. Lyman Bailey.

LEFT WING.

Maj. Gen. HENRY W. SLOCUM.

PONTONIERS.

58th Indiana, Col. George P. Buell.

ENGINEERS.

1st Michigan (detachment), Maj. John B. Yates.

FOURTEENTH ARMY CORPS.

Bvt. Maj. Gen. JEFFERSON C. DAVIS.

FIRST DIVISION.

Brig. Gen. WILLIAM P. CARLIN.

First Brigade.

Col. HARRISON C. HOBART.

104th Illinois, Lieut. Col. Douglas Hapeman.
42d Indiana, Capt. Gideon R. Kellams.
88th Indiana, Lieut. Col. Cyrus E. Briant.
33d Ohio, Capt. Joseph Hinson.
94th Ohio, Lieut. Col. Rue P. Hutchins.
21st Wisconsin, Lieut. Col. Michael H. Fitch.

Second Brigade.

Lieut. Col. JOSEPH H. BRIGHAM.

13th Michigan, Lieut. Col. Theodoric R. Palmer.
21st Michigan, Maj. Benton D. Fox.
69th Ohio, Capt. Jacob J. Rarick.

Third Brigade.

Lieut. Col. DAVID MILES.

38th Indiana, Capt. James H. Low.
21st Ohio, Lieut. Col. Arnold McMahan.
74th Ohio, Maj. Robert P. Findley.
79th Pennsylvania, Maj. Michael H. Locher.

SECOND DIVISION.

Brig. Gen. JAMES D. MORGAN.

First Brigade.

Col. ROBERT F. SMITH.

16th Illinois, Capt. John A. Chapman.
60th Illinois, Lieut. Col. George W. Evans.
10th Michigan, Col. Charles M. Lum.
14th Michigan, Maj. Thomas C. Fitzgibbon.
17th New York, Lieut. Col. Joel O. Martin.

Second Brigade.

Lieut. Col. JOHN S. PEARCE.

34th Illinois, Capt. Peter Ege.
78th Illinois, Lieut. Col. Maris R. Vernon.
98th Ohio, Capt. James R. McLaughlin.
108th Ohio, Maj. Frederick Beck.
113th Ohio, Capt. Toland Jones.
121st Ohio, Maj. Aaron B. Robinson.

Third Brigade.

Lieut. Col. JAMES W. LANGLEY.

85th Illinois, Capt. James R. Griffith.
86th Illinois, Lieut. Col. Allen L. Fahnestock.
110th Illinois (four companies), Lieut. Col. E. Hibbard Topping.
125th Illinois, Capt. George W. Cook.
22d Indiana, Capt. William H. Snodgrass.
52d Ohio, Lieut. Col. Charles W. Clancy.

THIRD DIVISION.

Brig. Gen. ABSALOM BAIRD.

First Brigade.

Col. MORTON C. HUNTER.

82d Indiana, Lieut. Col. John M. Matheny.
23d Missouri, Lieut. Col. Quin Morton.
17th Ohio, Lieut. Col. Benjamin H. Showers.
31st Ohio, Capt. Michael Stone.
89th Ohio, Lieut. Col. William H. Glenn.
92d Ohio, Col. Benjamin D. Fearing.

Second Brigade.

Col. NEWELL GLEASON.

75th Indiana, Maj. Cyrus J. McCole.
87th Indiana, Maj. Richard C. Sabin.
101st Indiana, Lieut. Col. Thomas Doan.
2d Minnesota, Lieut. Col. Judson W. Bishop.
105th Ohio, Lieut. Col. George T. Perkins.

Third Brigade.

Col. GEORGE P. ESTE.

74th Indiana, Lieut. Col. Thomas Morgan.
18th Kentucky, Lieut. Col. Hubbard K. Milward.
14th Ohio, Lieut. Col. Albert Moore.
38th Ohio, Capt. Charles M. Gilbert.

ARTILLERY.

Maj. CHARLES HOUGHTALING.

1st Illinois Light, Battery C, Lieut. Joseph R. Channel.
2d Illinois Light, Battery I, Lieut. Judson Rich.
Indiana Light, 19th Battery, Capt. William P. Stackhouse.
Wisconsin Light, 5th Battery, Capt. Joseph McKnight.

TWENTIETH ARMY CORPS.

Brig. Gen. ALPHEUS S. WILLIAMS.

FIRST DIVISION.

Brig. Gen. NATHANIEL J. JACKSON.

First Brigade.

Col. JAMES L. SELFRIDGE.

5th Connecticut, Lieut. Col. Henry W. Daboll.
123d New York, Lieut. Col. James C. Rogers.
141st New York, Capt. William Merrell.
46th Pennsylvania, Maj. Patrick Griffith.

Second Brigade.

Col. EZRA A. CARMAN.

2d Massachusetts, Col. William Cogswell.
13th New Jersey, Maj. Frederick H. Harris.
107th New York, Lieut. Col. Allen N. Sill.
150th New York, Maj. Alfred B. Smith.
3d Wisconsin, Col. William Hawley.

Third Brigade.

Col. JAMES S. ROBINSON.

82d Illinois, Maj. Ferdinand H. Rolshausen.
101st Illinois, Lieut. Col. John B. Le Sage.
143d New York, Lieut. Col. Hezekiah Watkins.
61st Ohio, Capt. John Garrett.
82d Ohio, Lieut. Col. David Thomson.
31st Wisconsin, Col. Francis H. West.

SECOND DIVISION.

Brig. Gen. JOHN W. GEARY.

First Brigade.

Col. ARIO PARDEE, Jr.

5th Ohio, Lieut. Col. Robert Kirkup.
29th Ohio, Capt. Jonas Schoonover.
66th Ohio, Lieut. Col. Eugene Powell.
28th Pennsylvania, Col. John Flynn.
147th Pennsylvania,* Lieut. Col. John Craig.

Second Brigade.

Col. PATRICK H. JONES.

33d New Jersey, Col. George W. Mindil.
119th New York, Col. John T. Lockman.
134th New York, Lieut. Col. Allan H. Jackson.
154th New York, Maj. Lewis D. Warner.
73d Pennsylvania, Lieut. Col. Charles C. Cresson.
109th Pennsylvania, Capt. Walter G. Dunn.

Third Brigade.

Col. HENRY A. BARNUM.

60th New York, Maj. Thomas Elliott.
102d New York, Lieut. Col. Harvey S. Chatfield.
137th New York, Lieut. Col. Koert S. Van Voorhis.
149th New York, Maj. Nicholas Grumbach.
29th Pennsylvania, Lieut. Col. Samuel M. Zulich.
111th Pennsylvania, Lieut. Col. Thomas M. Walker.

---

*Detachment Battery E, Pennsylvania Artillery, attached.

THIRD DIVISION.

Brig. Gen. WILLIAM T. WARD.

First Brigade.

Col. HENRY CASE.

102d Illinois, Maj. Hiland H. Clay.
105th Illinois, Lieut. Col. Everell F. Dutton.
129th Illinois, Lieut. Col. Thomas H. Flynn.
70th Indiana, Lieut. Col. Samuel Merrill.
79th Ohio, Lieut. Col. Azariah W. Doan.

Second Brigade.

Col. DANIEL DUSTIN.

33d Indiana, Lieut. Col. James E. Burton.
85th Indiana, Lieut. Col. Alexander B. Crane.
19th Michigan, Lieut. Col. John J. Baker.
22d Wisconsin, Lieut. Col. Edward Bloodgood.

Third Brigade.

Col. SAMUEL ROSS.

20th Connecticut, Lieut. Col. Philo B. Buckingham.
33d Massachusetts, Lieut. Col. Elisha Doane.
136th New York, Lieut. Col. Lester B. Faulkner.
55th Ohio, Lieut. Col. Edwin H. Powers.
73d Ohio, Lieut. Col. Samuel H. Hurst.
26th Wisconsin, Lieut. Col. Frederick C. Winkler.

ARTILLERY.

Maj. JOHN A. REYNOLDS.

1st New York Light, Battery I, Capt. Charles E. Winegar.
1st New York Light, Battery M, Lieut. Edward P. Newkirk.
1st Ohio Light, Battery C, Lieut. Jerome B. Stephens.
Pennsylvania Light, Battery E, Capt. Thomas S. Sloan.

CAVALRY.

THIRD DIVISION.

Brig. Gen. JUDSON KILPATRICK.

First Brigade.

Col. THOMAS J. JORDAN.

8th Indiana, Lieut. Col. Fielder A. Jones.
2d Kentucky, Capt. Joseph T. Forman.
3d Kentucky, Lieut. Col. Robert H. King.
5th Kentucky, Col. Oliver L. Baldwin.
9th Pennsylvania, Lieut. Col. David H. Kimmel.

Second Brigade.

Col. SMITH D. ATKINS.

92d Illinois (mounted infantry), Lieut. Col. Matthew Van Buskirk.
3d Indiana (two companies), Capt. Charles U. Patton.
9th Michigan, Col. George S. Acker.
5th Ohio, Maj. George H. Rader.
9th Ohio, Col. William D. Hamilton.
10th Ohio, Lieut. Col. Thomas W. Sanderson.
McLaughlin's (Ohio) Squadron, Capt. John Dalzell.

Unattached.

1st Alabama Cavalry, Col. George E. Spencer.
9th Illinois Mounted Infantry, Lieut. Col. Samuel T. Hughes.

Artillery.

Wisconsin Light, 10th Battery, Capt. Yates V. Beebe.

Abstract from return of the Department of the South, Maj. Gen. John G. Foster, U. S. Army, commanding, for December 31, 1864.

Command.	Present for duty.		Aggregate present.	Aggregate present and absent.	Pieces of artillery	
	Officers.	Men.			Heavy.	Field.
General headquarters	51	81	132	134	......	......
First New York Engineers (battalion, Place)	8	576	616	684	......	......
First Separate Brigade (Schimmelfennig)	66	2,474	3,241	6,754	......	6
Second Separate Brigade (Saxton)	27	756	1,073	2,912	......	2
Third Separate Brigade *a* (Brown)	69	2,024	2,711	3,285	66	11
Fourth Separate Brigade (Scammon)	50	1,337	1,766	4,195	......	......
Total*	271	7,242	9,539	17,964	66	19

a All the regiments composing the Third Separate Brigade are stationed at the front. The latest return received therefrom is for October, 1864, from which this return has been made.

Organization of troops in the Department of the South, Maj. Gen. John G. Foster, U. S. Army, commanding, December 31, 1864.

FIRST SEPARATE BRIGADE.†

Brig. Gen. ALEXANDER SCHIMMELFENNIG.

MORRIS ISLAND.

Lieut. Col. AUGUSTUS G. BENNETT.

54th Massachusetts (colored),‡ Col. Edward N. Hallowell.
56th New York,‡ Col. Charles H. Van Wyck.
52d Pennsylvania, Capt. John A. Hennessy.
21st U. S. Colored Troops, Maj. Richard H. Willoughby.
3d New York Light Artillery, Battery B,‡ Capt. Thomas J. Mesereau.
3d Rhode Island Heavy Artillery, First Battalion, Capt. Augustus W. Colwell.

FOLLY ISLAND.

Col. EUGENE A. KOZLAY.

55th Massachusetts (colored),‡ Lieut. Col. Charles B. Fox.
54th New York, Maj. Stephen Kovacs.
33d U. S. Colored Troops, Maj. Charles T. Trowbridge.

SECOND SEPARATE BRIGADE.§

Brig. Gen. RUFUS SAXTON.

127th New York,‡ Col. William Gurney.
26th U. S. Colored Troops,‡ Lieut. Col. William B. Guernsey.
102d U. S. Colored Troops,‡ Col. Henry L. Chipman.
3d Rhode Island Heavy Artillery, Company A,‡ Capt. William H. Hamner.
2d U. S. Colored Light Artillery, Battery G, Capt. Jeremiah S. Clark.

THIRD SEPARATE BRIGADE.‖

Bvt. Brig. Gen. MILTON S. LITTLEFIELD.

144th New York,‡ Col. James Lewis.
157th New York,‡ Col. Philip P. Brown, jr.
25th Ohio,‡ Lieut. Col. Nathaniel Haughton.
32d U. S. Colored Troops,‡ Col. George W. Baird.

---

* The Coast Division (composed of details from the brigades) was commanded by Brig. Gen. John P. Hatch. The department return shows this division to have had 230 officers and 4,588 men for duty.
† Or Northern District.
‡ Constituted the Coast Division, commanded by Brig. Gen. John P. Hatch, on expedition against Charleston and Savannah Railroad.
§ Or District of Beaufort.
‖ Or District of Hilton Head.

FOURTH SEPARATE BRIGADE.*

Brig. Gen. ELIAKIM P. SCAMMON.

17th Connecticut, Lieut. Col. Albert H. Wilcoxson.
75th Ohio, Col. Andrew L. Harris.
107th Ohio,† Capt. Edward S. Meyer.
3d U. S. Colored Troops, Col. Benjamin C. Tilghman.
34th U. S. Colored Troops,† Lieut. Col. William W. Marple.
35th U. S. Colored Troops,† Lieut. Col. Ammiel J. Willard.
4th Massachusetts Cavalry,† 2d Battalion, Capt. George R. Hurlbut.
3d New York Light Artillery, Battery F,† Capt. Samuel C. Day.

UNATTACHED.

1st New York Engineers (battalion), Maj. James E. Place.

Abstract from return of the District of West Florida, Brig. Gen. Thomas J. McKean, U. S. Army, commanding, for December 31, 1864.

Command.	Present for duty.		Aggregate present.	Aggregate present and absent.	Pieces of artillery.	
	Officers.	Men.			Heavy.	Field.
Headquarters	3	......	3	3	......	....
First Brigade (Yarrington)	42	1,414	1,870	1,961	2	4
Second Brigade (Woodman)	47	912	1,169	1,460	......	....
Fort Barrancas (Hitchcock)	13	266	331	386	32	....
Fort Pickens (Reisinger)	7	179	215	231	90	....
14th New York Cavalry, Company M (Schmidt)	2	26	60	70	......	....
Total	114	2,797	3,648	4,111	124	4

[December 31, 1864.—For organization of troops serving in the District of West Florida, see Vol. XLI, Part IV, p. 977.]

GENERAL ORDERS, No. 3. } WAR DEPT., ADJT. GENERAL'S OFFICE, *Washington, January 14, 1865.*

The following resolution of the Senate and House of Representatives is published to the Army:

PUBLIC RESOLUTION NO. 4.—Joint resolution tendering the thanks of the people and of Congress to Maj. Gen. William T. Sherman, and the officers and soldiers of his command, for their gallant conduct in their late brilliant movement through Georgia.

Be it resolved by the Senate and House of Representatives of the United States of America in Congress assembled, That the thanks of the people and of the Congress of the United States are due, and are hereby tendered, to Maj. Gen. William T. Sherman, and through him to the officers and men under his command, for their gallantry and good conduct in their late campaign from Chattanooga to Atlanta, and the triumphal march thence through Georgia to Savannah, terminating in the capture and occupation of that city; and that the President cause a copy of this joint resolution to be engrossed and forwarded to Major-General Sherman.

Approved, January 10, 1865.

By order of the Secretary of War:

W. A. NICHOLS,
Assistant Adjutant-General.

---

* Or District of Florida.
† Constituted the Coast Division, commanded by Brig. Gen. John P. Hatch, on expedition against Charleston and Savannah Railroad.

CONFEDERATE CORRESPONDENCE, ETC.

JONESBOROUGH, GA., *November 14, 1864—9.25 p. m.*

General BRAXTON BRAGG,
Richmond, Va.:

Prisoners taken yesterday report Sherman with three corps in and about Atlanta. Scouts and prisoners report enemy destroying railroad between Atlanta and Marietta. Yankee camp rumors say Sherman will move forward.

JOS. WHEELER,
Major-General.

(Same to General Hardee.)

JONESBOROUGH, *November 14, 1864.*

General JOHN B. HOOD,
Tuscumbia:

Scouts report Fifteenth and Seventeenth Corps marched into Atlanta yesterday. Large fires been seen in Atlanta for last three days. Prisoners say camp rumors are they intend marching to Augusta and Savannah; also, that Sherman is in Atlanta.

JOS. WHEELER,
Major-General.

JONESBOROUGH, GA., *November 14, 1864.*

General J. B. HOOD:

Sherman, with Fifteenth and Twentieth Corps and Kilpatrick's cavalry, is in Atlanta. Prisoners and citizens say camp rumors are that they will march to Augusta and Savannah. Scouts and prisoners report Sherman destroying railroad from Atlanta to Allatoona.

J. WHEELER,
Major-General.

(Same to General Bragg, Richmond; Lieutenant-General Hardee, Charleston; Lieutenant-General Taylor, Selma; Major-General Cobb, Macon; Maj. Gen. G. W. Smith, Lovejoy's; Governor Joseph E. Brown, Milledgeville, and Col. M. H. Wright, Columbus.)

JONESBOROUGH, *November 14, 1864.*

Lieut. Gen. R. TAYLOR,
Selma, Ala.:

Scouts and prisoners report enemy destroying railroad between Atlanta and Marietta. Prisoners report Sherman in Atlanta, and that camp rumors say he will move toward Mobile or Savannah. Prisoners also report Fifteenth, Seventeenth, and Twentieth Corps at Atlanta. Large fires observed in Atlanta for last three days.

JOS. WHEELER,
Major-General.

(Same to General Hood.)

NEAR ATLANTA, *November 14, 1864.*

General J. H. CLANTON,
Blue Mountain:

The enemy's cavalry may move through Carrollton toward West Point and Montgomery Railroad. Keep it well watched.

J. WHEELER,
Major-General.

GRIFFIN, *November 15, 1864.*

General S. COOPER:

The enemy has burned Atlanta and destroyed railroad to Allatoona, burning bridge over Chattahoochee. He moved out of Atlanta with very large force in direction of Macon by Jonesborough and McDonough. We have no force to hinder him and must fall back to Macon, where re-enforcements should be sent at once to meet him successfully.

HOWELL COBB,
Major-General, Commanding.

NEAR JONESBOROUGH, *November 15, 1864—2.30 p. m.*

General J. B. HOOD:

Enemy advanced with infantry, cavalry, and wagons early this morning. Have driven our cavalry back to this place. Strength not yet ascertained. Enemy have burned many houses in Rome, Marietta, and Atlanta; also destroyed railroad and burned bridge over Chattahoochee.

J. WHEELER,
Major-General.

(Same to General Braxton Bragg, Richmond; Lieutenant-General Hardee, Charleston; Lieut. Gen. R. Taylor, Selma; Maj. Gen. G. W. Smith, Lovejoy's; Governor Joseph E. Brown, Milledgeville; General G. T. Beauregard, Tuscumbia, and Col. M. H. Wright, Columbus.)

LOVEJOY'S, *November 15, 1864—3.45 p. m.*

Major-General WHEELER,
Commanding, &c.:

GENERAL: Yours of 2.30 p. m. is received. My trains are getting ready to start. The wagons came in just as your note was received notifying me that the pickets were driven in and the enemy at Morrow's Mills. If they come too close to me I will endeavor to give them a warm reception. If nothing occurs to prevent I will move to-night to the position spoken of yesterday afternoon.

Yours, truly,

G. W. SMITH,
Major-General.

CIRCULAR.] HEADQUARTERS WHEELER'S CORPS,
November 15, 1864.

I. All orders heretofore issued regarding destroying supplies and removing stock before the enemy are modified as follows:

II. All mills near the enemy's line of march will be rendered useless to the enemy by breaking the machinery, and, when practicable, by drawing off the water.

III. No mill building, corn-crib, or any other private property will be burned or destroyed by this command.

IV. All horses, mules, and other stock which citizens have left on the enemy's line of march will be driven off and proper receipts left for the same. When no owner can be found, accurate accounts will be kept, so that the stock can be reclaimed by the owner.

V. Commanders of troops in falling back before the enemy will send reliable officers and men at least one day in advance to instruct citizens in which direction to drive their stock.

By order of Major-General Wheeler:

M. G. HUDSON,
First Lieutenant, Aide-de-Camp, and Actg. Asst. Adjt. Gen.

TUSCUMBIA, *November 16, 1864—3 p. m.*

General S. COOPER,
Richmond:

Reports of General Wheeler indicate that Sherman is about to move with three corps from Atlanta to Augusta or Macon; thence probably to Charleston or Savannah, where a junction may be formed with enemy's fleet. The threatened attack on Wilmington in that event must be intended for Charleston. I would advise all available force which can be spared from North and South Carolina be held ready to move to defense of Augusta or crossing of Savannah River, in conjunction with forces in State of Georgia. Should Sherman take Charleston or reach Atlantic coast, he might then re-enforce Grant. General Taylor has been ordered to move with the available forces into Georgia, and assume command of all troops operating against Sherman should he move as reported.

G. T. BEAUREGARD.

LOVEJOY'S, [*November*] *16, 1864—11 a. m.*
(Via Barnesville.)

General BRAGG:

Scouts from enemy's rear report that Sherman left Atlanta yesterday morning with Fifteenth, Seventeenth, and Twentieth Corps in two columns—one on Jonesborough, and one on McDonough road; cavalry on his flanks. Many houses been burned in Rome, Marietta, and Atlanta, and railroad bridge over Chattahoochee destroyed by the enemy. Enemy advancing this morning.

JOS. WHEELER,
Major-General.

(Same to Generals Beauregard, Cobb, Hardee, Hood, Smith, and Taylor, and Governor Brown.)

GRIFFIN, *November 16, 1864—4 p. m.*
(Received Richmond 1.10 p. m. 17th.)

General BRAGG:

Enemy checked this evening near Bear Creek. Enemy evidently marching to Macon.

JOS. WHEELER,
Major-General.

(Same to Generals Beauregard, Cobb, Hardee, Hood, Smith, Taylor, and Governor Brown.)

NEAR JONESBOROUGH, GA., *November 16, 1864—Daylight.*

General J. B. HOOD,
Tuscumbia:

Fifteenth, Seventeenth, and Twentieth Corps, with Kilpatrick's cavalry, left Atlanta yesterday morning in two columns—one on Jonesborough, and the other on McDonough road. Fourteenth Corps has reached Atlanta, giving Sherman four corps, fully 60,000 men.

JOS. WHEELER,
Major-General.

(Same to General G. T. Beauregard, Tuscumbia; General Braxton Bragg, Richmond; Lieut. Gen. Hardee, Charleston; Lieut. Gen. R. Taylor, Selma; Major-General Cobb, Macon; Maj. Gen. G. W. Smith, Forsyth; Governor Joseph E. Brown, Milledgeville; Col. M. H. Wright, Columbus.)

NOVEMBER 16, 1864.

Major-General WHEELER,
Jonesborough, Ga.:

Telegraph me daily, whether you have news of importance or not. If Sherman advances to the south or east destroy all things in his front that might be useful to him, and keep a portion of your force constantly destroying his trains.

J. B. HOOD,
General.

CAMP STEPHENS, NEAR GRIFFIN, GA.,
November 16, 1864—9.30 a. m.

Major-General WHEELER,
Commanding, &c., near Lovejoy's:

GENERAL: The rear of my command arrived here at 3 o'clock this morning in very good condition, considering the night's march, for new troops. By 1 or 2 o'clock this afternoon they will, I think, be perfectly ready for anything that may turn up; in fact, are ready now if heavy work is necessary. My movements must, of course, depend in great degree upon the force and movements of the enemy and your ability to hold them in check. If too much engaged yourself please have one of your staff officers notify me of every change in the position of affairs. If the full force of the enemy is moving toward Macon my command should be well ahead of them to put the house in order for defense. If they move in full force toward Augusta it is still important for us to reach Macon soon to take the cars. The rolling-stock of this railroad is not adequate since their losses in Atlanta. If they are not in largely superior force it is best for us to fight them here. You, I know, will appreciate my anxiety to know the force and movements of the enemy. At General Cobb's request I inclose some papers which he wishes referred to you.

Yours, very truly,

G. W. SMITH,
Major-General.

GRIFFIN, *November 16, 1864—12 m.*

Major-General WHEELER,
Commanding, &c., near Lovejoy's:

GENERAL: Yours of 6 a. m. was received in my camp at 10.35, and was forwarded to me here in a few minutes. Last night yours of 10.30 was received at Bear Creek Station at 12 m. I call your attention to these delays; at this time they may be the cause of very serious evil. Mine of 9.30 a. m. would have been greatly modified had yours of 6 o'clock been previously received. I dislike to refer to these matters, but they are just now of great importance. The heavy column marching by McDonough makes it necessary, in my judgment, for this command to move promptly to Forsyth. I have sent for cars. If they come this afternoon will make arrangements for starting, leaving all commissary stores and forage not needed by my command for the use of yours. Colonel Dibrell has just come in. He says his instructions from you will justify his taking position near Griffin, toward McDonough, instead of six or seven miles southwest as now. He will report to you his exact position as soon as he selects it. General Cobb and myself both recommended this strongly to Colonel Dibrell, and have no doubt it will meet with your approval. It is very important that this heavy column by McDonough should be opposed by a strong cavalry force. They are on the direct road from Atlanta to Macon. If they turn toward Augusta we ought still to be in Macon as soon as practicable. Colonel Anderson, of my staff, will hand you this, and give you my views more fully.

Yours, very truly,

G. W. SMITH,
Major-General.

SELMA, ALA., *November 16, 1864.*

Major-General WHEELER:

Please keep me advised of enemy's movements. I have your dispatches of yesterday and day before. Should enemy move east better telegraph General Hardee and Richmond direct.

R. TAYLOR,
Lieutenant-General.

MACON, GA., [*November 17,*] *1864.*

President DAVIS,
Richmond, Va.:

Sherman's move upon this place is formidable, and the most dangerous of the war. His policy is universal destruction. If by concentration of all forces that can be brought together Sherman's army could be crushed, he having cut loose from his communications, it would be the greatest result of the war. The only mode I see for making defense and destroying Sherman is to order garrisons of Charleston, Savannah, and Wilmington here at once. If not beaten here he will either march to Charleston or Savannah.

HOWELL COBB,
Major-General.

MACON, *November 17, 1864.*

General COOPER,
Adjutant and Inspector General:

I left Griffin at 10.30 last night, and telegraphed the joint views of General Wheeler and myself. The enemy are advancing in two columns, by Griffin and McDonough, evidently moving on Macon. His forces estimated at 35,000, including Kilpatrick's cavalry. We are falling back rapidly to this place. The enemy will probably be here by Monday. We are too weak to resist them unless re-enforced promptly. The prisoners should be removed from this State.

HOWELL COBB,
Major-General.

MACON, *Thursday Morning, November 17, 1864.*

[Governor J. E. BROWN:]

DEAR GOVERNOR: Things are very bad here. Sherman in person is leading, say, 30,000 men against us. We are retreating as rapidly as possible, consistent with good order and efficiency. The militia are retreating in admirable order and good discipline, as General Cobb reports. I will meet them between this and Forsyth this evening. I believe the Legislature will grant you large and liberal powers. Tell them the country is in danger. Let all of her sons come to her rescue.

Yours, faithfully.

R. TOOMBS.

P. S.—We have called for the troops in Wilmington, Charleston, and Savannah. If we do defend here they will be on us by Monday. Cavalry force said to be below 6,000. Send all the troops you can. If we do not get help we must abandon this place.

Yours,

R. TOOMBS.

TUSCUMBIA, [*November 17, 1864*].

General S. COOPER,
Richmond:

General R. Taylor has been ordered to repair forthwith to Georgia and take command of all Confederate troops now operating against Sherman.

G. T. BEAUREGARD.

TUSCUMBIA, *November 17, 1864.*

General S. COOPER:

I leave for Corinth this morning, whence I will move according to circumstances. No news since report of yesterday.

G. T. BEAUREGARD.

TUSCUMBIA, [*November 17, 1864*].

General S. COOPER,
Adjutant and Inspector General, Richmond:

General Wheeler reports from Jonesborough, Ga., enemy advanced with infantry, artillery, cavalry, and wagons on morning of 15th instant, driving back our cavalry to Jonesborough.

G. T. BEAUREGARD.

RICHMOND, [*November 17, 1864*].

General BEAUREGARD,
Tuscumbia:

Generals Cobb and Wheeler report Sherman moving with three corps on Macon. This information has probably been communicated to you, if not anticipated by you, but we are not informed. Have you taken measures to meet it? You are aware that few, if any, troops out of your department can now be sent to its defense.

By direction of the President:

S. COOPER,
Adjutant and Inspector General.

RICHMOND, VA., *November 17, 1864.*

General BEAUREGARD,
Tuscumbia, Ala.:

Your dispatch of yesterday just received. You were dispatched this morning respecting Sherman's movements on Macon. At same time General Taylor was telegraped to call for the reserve forces of his department, and if possible to aid in resisting the army of Sherman. Your order to General Taylor to move with the available forces into Georgia is approved. General Hardee was telegraphed this morning that his command, for the present, was extended to embrace all that part of Georgia south of the Chattahoochee River, and directed to move promptly to the scene of operations, and endeavor to obtain an adequate force by concentrating detachments from garrisons, convalescents from hospitals, reserves, militia, and volunteers. Copy of your dispatch has been sent to the President, and I await his further directions.

S. COOPER,
Adjutant and Inspector General.

NEAR GRIFFIN, GA., *November 17, 1864—11 a. m.*

Lieutenant-General HARDEE,
Charleston:

Enemy are turning their columns on shortest road to Macon. Scouts from enemy's rear report Fourteenth Corps moving up to join Sherman.

JOS. WHEELER,
Major-General.

(Same to General Howell Cobb, Macon; Governor J. E. Brown, Milledgeville, and General R. Taylor, Selma.)

CHARLESTON, *November 17, 1864.*

Hon. J. A. SEDDON, *Secretary of War, Richmond:*

General Cobb has called on me for re-enforcements to defend Macon. I will send him the Fifth Georgia, now stationed at Florence, which is the only troops I can spare without stripping the coast and leaving it open to the enemy.

W. J. HARDEE,
Lieutenant-General.

RICHMOND, [*November 17, 1864*].

General HARDEE, *Charleston:*

It is reported that Sherman is moving rapidly upon Macon. Your command, for the present, is extended to embrace all that part of Georgia south of the Chattahoochee River. You will move promptly to the scene of active operations, and endeavor to obtain an adequate force by concentrating detachments from garrisons, convalescents from hospitals, reserves, militia, and volunteers.

By order of the President:

S. COOPER,
Adjutant and Inspector General.

NOVEMBER 17, 1864.

Major-General WHEELER, *Comdg. Cavalry, Lovejoy's Station:*

Call Clanton's command to you and give him such orders as you think best to assist you in retarding the advance of Sherman.

J. B. HOOD,
General.

GRIFFIN, *November 17, 1864—12 m.*

General JOHN B. HOOD, *Tuscumbia:*

Scouts from enemy's rear report that Fourteenth Corps crossed the Chattahoochee on 15th on way to join Sherman, giving him four corps.

JOS. WHEELER,
Major-General.

(Same to General Braxton Bragg, Richmond; Lieut. Gen. W. J. Hardee, Charleston; Lieut. Gen. R. Taylor, Selma; General Howell Cobb, Macon, and Governor J. E. Brown, Milledgeville.)

NEAR GRIFFIN, GA., *November 17, 1864—2.20 p. m.*

General J. B. HOOD, *Tuscumbia:*

Enemy are turning their columns on shortest road to Macon. Scouts from enemy's rear report Fourteenth Corps moving up to join Sherman. I have no orders regarding holding any city, should enemy besiege or assault. Please send orders to me or General Cobb.

JOS. WHEELER,
Major-General.

(Same to General Braxton Bragg, Richmond, and General Beauregard.)

TWELVE MILES NORTH OF FORSYTH,
November 17, 1864—6.40. (Via Macon.)
(Received 2.30 p. m. 18th.)

General BRAGG:

Enemy still moving toward Macon by shortest direct road. Scouts report a force of the enemy between Yellow and South Rivers.

JOS. WHEELER,
Major-General.

RICHMOND, [*November 17, 1864*].

Maj. H. C. GUERIN:

Sherman's movement may cut us off at any moment from Southwest Georgia. Urge the collection [of] corn with utmost activity, and push forward to Wellford. Telegraph your district officers to lose no time.

By order of Commissary-General:

J. C. ABRAMS,
Captain and Assistant Commissary of Subsistence.

RICHMOND, [*November 17, 1864*].

General TAYLOR,
Selma:

You are authorized to call for the reserves of your department, and requested, as far as practicable, to aid in resisting the army of Sherman, reported to be moving south from Atlanta.

S. COOPER,
Adjutant and Inspector General.

MILLEDGEVILLE, *November 18, 1864.*

President DAVIS:

A heavy force of the enemy is advancing on Macon, laying waste the country and burning the towns. We have not sufficient force. I hope you will send us troops as re-enforcements till the exigency is passed.

JOS. E. BROWN.

RICHMOND, VA., *November 18, 1864.*

General H. COBB,
Macon, Ga.:

In addition to the troops of all kinds you should endeavor to get out every man who can render any service, even for a short period, and employ negroes in obstructing roads by every practicable means. Colonel Rains, at Augusta, can furnish you with shells prepared to explode by pressure, and these will be effective to check an advance. General Hardee has, I hope, brought some re-enforcements, and General Taylor will probably join you with some further aid. You have a difficult task, but will realize the necessity for the greatest exertion.

JEFFN. DAVIS.

CORINTH, *November 18, 1864—7 a. m.*

HON. J. A. SEDDON:

I have just arrived here on my way to Georgia. Please order immediately to General Cobb, at Macon, a large supply of Rains' subterra shells, with competent person to employ them.

G. T. BEAUREGARD,
General.

[Indorsement.]

NOVEMBER 19, 1864.

ADJUTANT-GENERAL:

Instruct General Rains to give immediate attention to this.

J. A. S.,
Secretary.

CORINTH, *November 18, 1864—11 a. m.*
(Received 19th.)

General S. COOPER:

General Taylor telegraphs from Mobile that he may not, through accident on roads, reach Macon before Sherman's force. I am in same condition here. I therefore respectfully urge that General Hardee should be ordered to assume temporary command forthwith of the troops operating in Georgia.

G. T. BEAUREGARD,
General.

CORINTH, *November 18, 1864.*
(Received 19th.)

General S. COOPER:

General Cobb reports from Macon, November 17:

Enemy is advancing in two columns, by Griffin and McDonough, evidently moving on Macon. His force three corps, estimated at 30,000, including Kilpatrick's cavalry. We are falling back rapidly to this place. Enemy will probably be here Monday.

I have ordered Generals Hood and Taylor, and requested General Hardee, to send General Cobb all the re-enforcements they can spare. I have ordered General Taylor to Macon forthwith, and am going there in person rapidly as condition of roads will permit.

G. T. BEAUREGARD.

CORINTH, *November 18, 1864—4 p. m.*
(Received 19th.)

General S. COOPER,
Adjutant and Inspector General:

General Hood reports from Florence, 18th:

Jackson's cavalry division could not be spared from this army without seriously embarrassing Stewart's operations, while General Wheeler has with him some thirteen brigades of cavalry.

I have suggested to General Hood, if he could not spare troops for Georgia, to take the offensive immediately to relieve it.

G. T. BEAUREGARD.

RICHMOND, *November 18, 1864.*

TO THE PEOPLE OF GEORGIA:

You have now the best opportunity ever yet presented to destroy the enemy. Put everything at the disposal of our generals; remove all provisions from the path of the invader, and put all obstructions in his path. Every citizen with his gun, and every negro with his spade and axe, can do the work of a soldier. You can destroy the enemy by retarding his march. Georgians, be firm! Act promptly, and fear not!

B. H. HILL,
Senator.

I most cordially approve the above.

JAMES A. SEDDON,
Secretary of War.

CORINTH, *November 18, 1864.*

TO THE PEOPLE OF GEORGIA:

Arise for the defense of your native soil! Rally round your patriotic Governor and gallant soldiers! Obstruct and destroy all roads in Sherman's front, flank, and rear, and his army will soon starve in your midst! Be confident and resolute! Trust in an overruling Providence, and success will crown your efforts. I hasten to join you in defense of your homes and firesides.

G. T. BEAUREGARD.

CORINTH, *November 18, 1864.*

General J. B. HOOD,
Florence:

Batteries ordered from Macon cannot now be expected here. Send two soon as possible until others can be had.

G. T. BEAUREGARD.

CORINTH, *November 18, 1864—3 p. m.*

General J. B. HOOD,
Commanding, &c.:

General Wheeler reports from Griffin yesterday that scouts from enemy's rear report Fourteenth Corps crossed Chattahoochee on 15th to join Sherman, giving him four corps. Should that be true, could you not spare then, at once, some troops for Georgia, or take the offensive immediately? General Cobb is urgent in his calls for assistance.

G. T. BEAUREGARD,
General.

CORINTH, MISS., *November 18, 1864.*

Major-General WHEELER:

Employ your cavalry to best advantage, retarding advance of Sherman's army and destroying supplies in his front.

G. T. BEAUREGARD.

FORSYTH, *November 18, 1864—10 p. m.*
(Received 19th.)

General BRAGG:

Enemy pressing on rapidly.

JOS. WHEELER,
Major-General.

HEADQUARTERS,
Florence, Ala., November 18, 1864.

Major-General WHEELER,
Commanding Cavalry, Griffin, Ga.:

Your dispatches of 17th received. It is very important that you should not allow any portion of your mounted force to be shut up in a beseiged city, but keep them constantly harassing the enemy, destroying his trains, and cutting off his foraging parties.

J. B. HOOD,
General.

HEADQUARTERS,
Florence, Ala., November 18, 1864.

Major-General WHEELER,
Commanding Cavalry, Griffin, Ga.:

In returning the section of artillery to Roddey which is with Hannon, you need only send the men and horses, as other and better guns have been obtained.

A. P. MASON,
Assistant Adjutant-General.

FORSYTH, *November 18, 1864—9 p. m.*

Major-General WHEELER,
Commanding, &c.

GENERAL: About half of my infantry started for Macon by rail last night, and the trains have this moment returned. The rest of the infantry will be put upon the cars in a few minutes. I sent fourteen pieces of artillery, under Major Palmer, for Macon at 1 o'clock this morning. My wagon train has started, and as soon as the infantry are off I will start. General Beauregard telegraphs me that General Taylor has been ordered to take command of troops in Georgia. In meantime directs everything to be done to check Sherman's advance, which, in my opinion, can, under present circumstances, be best done by the infantry, by being in the fortifications at Macon, leaving the outside work to the cavalry. There is a large amount of stores here; I will endeavor to get cars sent up to remove them. In case you have to fall back suddenly to this place please notify the trains below. I received information this morning that a large force of the enemy were moving down the Georgia railroad. If this is so, and I am disposed to credit the man who sent the information, Sherman may stop on the Towaliga and move the mass of his forces east. In that case he will endeavor to break Central railroad to prevent our going by rail to Augusta. I shall always be glad to hear how you are getting on.

Yours, very truly,

G. W. SMITH,
Major-General.

COLUMBIA, *November 18, 1864.*

President DAVIS:

If the emergency warrants am I authorized to go into Georgia with such force as I can carry, and retain there my rank.

JAS. CHESNUT, JR.,
Brigadier-General, Commanding Reserves.

RICHMOND, *November 19, 1864.*

TO THE PEOPLE OF GEORGIA:

We have had a special conference with President Davis and the Secretary of War, and are able to assure you that they have done and are still doing all that can be done to meet the emergency that presses upon you. Let every man fly to arms! Remove your negroes, horses, cattle, and provisions from Sherman's army, and burn what you cannot carry. Burn all bridges and block up the roads in his route. Assail the invader in front, flank, and rear, by night and by day. Let him have no rest.

JULIAN HARTRIDGE, MARK H. BLANDFORD,
J. H. ECHOLS, GEO. N. LESTER,
JOHN T. SHEWMAKE, JAS. M. SMITH,
Members of Congress.

PETERSBURG, *November 19, 1864.*

His Excellency JEFFERSON DAVIS,
Richmond, Va.:

I have not received General Cooper's dispatch. I know of no troops within reach of Sherman except those in Georgia, nor do I know of a ———.* All roads, bridges, provisions, &c., within Sherman's reach should be destroyed. The population must turn out. Wheeler could do much. It would be extremely hazardous and ———.* Savannah will probably be Sherman's object. Troops that can be spared from Charleston, Savannah, &c., should take the field under Hardee.

R. E. LEE.

CORINTH, *November 19, 1864.* (Received 20th.)

General S. COOPER:

I leave this morning for Macon, via Mobile, the nearest route. Weather and roads are so bad that movements of Army of Tennessee are much retarded.

G. T. BEAUREGARD.

CORINTH, *November 19, 1864.* (Received 20th.)

General S. COOPER,
Adjutant and Inspector General:

General Wheeler telegraphs from Griffin, on 17th, that enemy are turning their columns on shortest route to Macon, and scouts from

---

* Cipher unintelligible.

enemy's rear report Fourteenth crossed Chattahoochee to join Sherman, giving him four corps. This information has been communicated to General Hood. It is left optional with him to divide and re-enforce Cobb, or take the offensive immediately to relieve him.

G. T. BEAUREGARD.

MACON, *November 19, 1864.*

Hon. JAMES A. SEDDON,
Secretary of War:

There is great scarcity of arms in Georgia and South Carolina to meet the enemy. It is necessary to have additional arms to put into the hands of the levy en masse ordered by the Legislature of Georgia, and the reserve militia of South Carolina now called out by Governor Bonham. Please have all spare arms sent to Charleston, S. C., subject to my orders.

W. J. HARDEE,
Lieutenant-General.

MACON, *November 19, 1864.*

General S. COOPER:

I reached here this morning. The enemy on both sides Ocmulgee River, about thirty miles from Macon. A column is reported near Social Circle marching on Augusta. My opinion, hastily formed from the information before me, is that the enemy will ultimately form junction and march upon Augusta; General Cobb concurs. The force of the enemy consists of the Fourteenth, Fifteenth, Sixteenth, Seventeenth, and Twentieth Army Corps; and the infantry under General Cobb is around Macon.

W. J. HARDEE,
Lieutenant-General.

MACON, *November 19, 1864—8 p. m.*

General S. COOPER,
Adjutant and Inspector General:

Enemy's cavalry entered Clinton to-day. Enemy reported seven miles this side Madison at 9 o'clock this morning; said to be Slocum's corps.

W. J. HARDEE,
Lieutenant-General.

MACON, *November 19, 1864.* (Received 20th.)

General S. COOPER,
Adjutant and Inspector General:

I have ordered Wheeler to make an attack on the enemy to-morrow at Clinton (20th), [so] as to ascertain definitely his movements and intentions.

W. J. HARDEE,
Lieutenant-General.

MACON, *November 19, 1864.*

Major-General MCLAWS:

Colonel Ould will declare paroled prisoners exchanged as soon as he can make Yankee delivery. Enemy's movements indicate an advance on Augusta. What defense have you to protect Savannah from land attack?

W. J. HARDEE,
Lieutenant-General.

SAVANNAH, GA., *November 19, 1864.*

General HARDEE,
Macon, Ga.:

Have no defenses but an inundation, which is not complete and does not cover the crossing of the Charleston railroad over Savannah River. I need the troops on the way to Oconee bridge. Can I recall them?

L. MCLAWS,
Major-General.

MACON, *November 19, 1864.*

Maj. Gen. L. MCLAWS:

The force at the Oconee bridge cannot be spared yet. General Wheeler says that prisoners report that Sherman is going to Savannah by way of Augusta. Be prepared to press negroes if you need them.

W. J. HARDEE,
Lieutenant-General.

TENNILLE, *November 19, 1864.*

General MCLAWS, or Colonel ANDERSON:

SIR: The Yankees are expected at Oconee bridge. We are determined to dispute their passage and defend the bridge. Please send us if possible one howitzer and caisson, with canister and grape, occupying an open car. We have some twenty old artillerists cut off from their commands who will man the piece.

WM. A. IRWIN,
Aide-de-Camp, Twentieth Military District.

TENNILLE, *November 19, 1864.*

General L. MCLAWS:

Men are mustering fast. I think I can start with 100 in an hour, and have 200 by noon. Shall I press an engine and train to carry men. I have rifles and ammunition.

H. T. HALL,
Major.

TENNILLE, *November 19, 1864.*

General MCLAWS:

No transportation here to move troops. Have sent over fifty cavalry to Oconee bridge. Will have over 100 infantry ready for afternoon train. Captain McKee, at 14, is mustering strong. I leave at once.

H. T. HALL,
Major and Commissary of Subsistence.

FORSYTH, *November 19, 1864—1.30 p. m.*

General BRAGG:

Scouts near Hillsborough report enemy moving toward Augusta.

JOS. WHEELER,
Major-General.

MACON, GA., *November 19, 1864.*

Major-General WHEELER:

General Taylor has been ordered here; left Mobile yesterday morning. General Hardee expected this morning. Re-enforcements are promised.

HOWELL COBB,
Major-General.

AUGUSTA, *November 19, 1864—11 a. m.*

General S. COOPER:

Enemy advancing toward Macon; also a strong column of all arms along the railroad from Atlanta to Augusta; were at Social Circle yesterday. General Hardee passed last evening on his way to Macon.

B. D. FRY,
Brigadier-General.

RICHMOND, *November 19, 1864.*

Brig. Gen. JAMES CHESNUT,
Columbia, S. C.:

You are authorized to go into Georgia with such voluntary force as you can take consistently with public necessity, and command there according to your rank.

JEFF'N DAVIS.

WEST POINT, *November 20, 1864—10 a. m.*

General J. B. HOOD:

Push on active offensive immediately. Colonel Brent informs me first order for movement one of Jackson's brigades to Wheeler has been suspended by you. It is indispensable; it should be sent by best and quickest route to Newnan, to cut off communications of enemy with Kingston, and to protect construction of telegraph lines and railroad to Augusta via Atlanta. I have appealed to people of Georgia to defend their homes.

G. T. BEAUREGARD,
General.

AUGUSTA, GA., *November 20, 1864.*

His Excellency President DAVIS:

General Hardee requested me to inform you that he passed through to Macon Friday. He could bring no troops but Fifth Georgia, about

200 muskets. Carolina reserves (1,700) all needed to guard prisoners at Columbia. We have to put in trenches here about 2,000 locals and convalescents. Rumors of enemy's advance on this place unreliable. I will do my utmost to aid General Fry in every contingency. I use "victory" key.

W. M. BROWNE.

GORDON, *November 20, 1864.*

Major-General MCLAWS,
Savannah:

It is my opinion you had better send troops to guard Oconee bridge. Keep your telegraph office open.

H. C. WAYNE,
Major-General.

OCONEE BRIDGE, *November 20, 1864.* (Via Tennille.)

Captain ELLIOTT,
Assistant Adjutant-General:

I arrived here safely this morning. Have no news at present to report. Could you not send up an operator and battery with the next train, as his presence here would save great inconvenience in dispatching. There is no operator here, and I have to send to Tennille for the purpose of dispatching. Answer.

A. L. HARTRIDGE,
Major, Commanding, &c.

GORDON, *November 20, 1864.*

Maj. Gen. HOWELL COBB,
Macon:

I report here with 200 men. Send me 10,000 rounds of ammunition, .69 caliber, and a medical officer.

H. C. WAYNE,
Major-General.

CHARLESTON, *November 20, 1864.*

Major-General MCLAWS:

General Fry telegraphs from Augusta that he wants 500 small arms; none here; and Major Huger has telegraphed to Savannah to have all sent on which you can spare. Would be well to inform Fry of what he can get.

R. S. RIPLEY,
Brigadier-General, Commanding.

AUGUSTA, *November 20, 1864—2 p. m.*

General S. COOPER:

Telegraph to Macon just broken. General Hardee was there this morning. Slocum's corps at Madison, on Georgia railroad, yesterday. Will make the best defense I can here.

B. D. FRY,
Brigadier-General.

AUGUSTA, *November 20, 1864—7 p. m.*

General S. COOPER:

This morning enemy had advanced on the line of Georgia railroad as far as Oconee River. I believe it to be Slocum's corps. Wires cut near Macon. I have no communication with General Hardee since morning. Fighting reported near Macon.

B. D. FRY,
Brigadier-General.

WEST POINT, MISS., *November 20, 1864.*

General WHEELER:

General Hardee will for the present give orders for the defense of Georgia east of the Chattahoochee. My views are that positions should be defended only so long as not to risk safety of troops and materials required for active operations in the field. Meanwhile remove to safe locality all Government property on line of enemy's march, and consume or destroy all supplies within his reach.

G. T. BEAUREGARD,
General.

Abstract from return of the Department of South Carolina, Georgia, and Florida, Lieut. Gen. W. J. Hardee commanding, for November 20, 1864.

Command.	Present for duty.		Effective total present.	Aggregate present.	Aggregate present and absent.	Pieces of field artillery.
	Officers.	Men.				
General staff	19	....	....	19	24	.....
McLaws' division	211	2,597	2,968	3,736	5,803	44
Ripley's brigade	86	1,657	1,951	2,152	2,854	4
Trapier's brigade	22	361	415	496	726	8
Robertson's brigade	39	853	899	1,013	1,443	26
Miller's brigade	96	1,224	1,314	1,578	2,973	10
Taliaferro's brigade	137	2,792	3,009	3,383	4,401	8
Post of Florence, S. C	90	1,209	1,279	1,567	2,492	......
Post of Columbia, S. C	46	616	631	736	962	......
Total	746	11,309	12,466	14,680	21,678	100

Organization of troops in the Department of South Carolina, Georgia, and Florida, commanded by Lieut. Gen. William J. Hardee, November 20, 1864.

McLAWS' DIVISION.

Maj. Gen. LAFAYETTE McLAWS.

1st Georgia Regulars, Col. Richard A. Wayne.
Barnwell's (Georgia) Light Artillery, Col. Richard A. Wayne.
22d Georgia Battalion (six companies), Maj. Thomas D. Bertody.
27th Georgia Battalion, Company D, Lieut. W. R. McLaws.
29th Georgia Battalion Cavalry (six companies), Capt. J. T. Wimberly.
3d South Carolina Cavalry (eight companies), Capt. A. M. Lowry.
Symons' Reserves (ten companies), Maj. John Cunningham.
Beaufort (South Carolina) Artillery, Lieut. John J. Rhodes.
Bonaud's (Georgia) Battalion (two companies), Capt. Malcolm T. McGregor.
Terrell (Georgia) Light Artillery, Capt. John W. Brooks.
Clinch's (Georgia) Light Artillery (two companies), Maj. George W. Anderson.
Cobb Guards (two companies), Maj. Alfred L. Hartridge.
Daniell's (Georgia) Light Battery,
Guerard's (Georgia) Light Battery, } Capt. J. A. Maxwell.
Maxwell's (Georgia) Light Battery,
German (South Carolina) Artillery, Company A, Capt. F. W. Wagener.
German (South Carolina) Artillery, Capt. William K. Bachman.
Hanleiter's (Georgia) Battery, Capt. Cornelius R. Hanleiter.
South Carolina Horse Artillery (section), Lieut. Richard Johnson.
Lafayette (South Carolina) Artillery, Capt. J. T. Kanapaux.
Mercer (Georgia) Artillery, Lieut. Col. William R. Pritchard.
2d Engineer Troops, Company D, Capt. James W. McAlpine.

RIPLEY'S BRIGADE.

Brig. Gen. ROSWELL S. RIPLEY.

32d Georgia Volunteers (seven companies and detachment), Capt. S. J. Heath.
1st South Carolina Regulars (ten companies), Col. William Butler.
1st South Carolina Cavalry, Company K, Capt. Angus P. Brown.
Keitt's (South Carolina) Mounted Rifles, Capt. Ellison S. Keitt.
Ripley (South Carolina) Rangers, Lieut. C. P. Bolton.
1st South Carolina Artillery (seven companies), Maj. Ormsby Blanding.
Gist Guards (South Carolina) Artillery, Lieut. Theodore G. Boag.

TRAPIER'S BRIGADE.

Brig. Gen. JAMES H. TRAPIER.

Kirk's Squadron (South Carolina) Cavalry (two companies), Capt. M. J. Kirk.
Steele's Company (South Carolina) Cavalry, Capt. J. J. Steele.
German (South Carolina) Artillery, Company B, Capt. F. Melchers.
Santee (South Carolina) Light Artillery, Capt. Christopher Gaillard.
Waccamaw (South Carolina) Light Artillery, Capt. Mayham Ward.

ROBERTSON'S BRIGADE.

Brig. Gen. BEVERLY H. ROBERTSON.

3d South Carolina Cavalry, Company B, Capt. Archibald L. Campbell.
Stono (South Carolina) Scouts, Capt. John B. L. Walpole.
2d South Carolina Artillery (two companies), Capt. Medicus Rickenbaker.
Marion (South Carolina) Artillery, Capt. Edward L. Parker.
Palmetto Battery Light Artillery (three companies), Capt. Charles E. Kanapaux.
Washington (South Carolina) Artillery, Capt. George H. Walter.
Mathewes' (South Carolina) Heavy Artillery, Capt. J. Raven Mathewes.
South Carolina Siege Train, Company A, Capt. Benjamin C. Webb.

TALIAFERRO'S BRIGADE.

Brig. Gen. WILLIAM B. TALIAFERRO.

47th Georgia (six companies), Col. Aaron C. Edwards.
1st South Carolina Cavalry (nine companies), Palmetto Light Artillery, Company E, South Carolina Siege Train (two companies), } Lieut. Col. William H. Campbell.
1st South Carolina Artillery (three companies), Bonaud's Battalion Georgia Volunteers, } Lieut. Col. Joseph A. Yates.
2d South Carolina Artillery (eight companies), Col. A. D. Frederick.
Lucas' (South Carolina) Battalion (three companies), Maj. J. Jonathan Lucas.
Chatham (Georgia) Artillery, Lieut. Samuel B. Palmer.
Orleans Guard Battery, Capt. G. Le Gardeur, jr.

MILLER'S BRIGADE.

Brig. Gen. WILLIAM MILLER.

Battalion Florida Reserves, Capt. Isaac B. Nichols.
2d Florida Cavalry (ten companies), Lieut. Col. Abner H. McCormick.
5th Florida Battalion (three companies), Capt. W. H. Milton.
29th Georgia Battalion (two companies), Capt. F. L. Pepper.
Independent (Florida) Cavalry Company, Capt. ——— Chisolm.
Florida Reserves (seven companies), Capt. ——— Gilchrist.
Abell's (Florida) Artillery, Capt. Henry F. Abell.
Kilcrease (Florida) Light Artillery, Capt. F. L. Villepigue.
Campbell's (Georgia) Siege Artillery, Capt. Charles G. Campbell.

POST OF FLORENCE, S. C.

Col. GEORGE P. HARRISON, Jr.

1st South Carolina Cavalry, Capt. J. S. Wilson.
3d Battalion South Carolina Reserves, Maj. William P. Gill.
4th Battalion South Carolina Reserves, Lieut. Col. James H. Williams.
5th Battalion South Carolina Reserves, Lieut. Col. Thomas R. Brown.
6th Battalion South Carolina Reserves, Maj. Robert Meriwether.
7th Battalion South Carolina Reserves, Maj. J. W. Ward.

POST OF COLUMBIA, S. C.

Lieut. Col. ROBERT S. MEANS.

South Carolina State Reserves (five companies), Capt. Edward Powell.
Williams' Battalion (South Carolina) State Reserves (two companies), Lieut. John McCarley.
Detachment of Artillery, Lieut. ——— Holyland.
Post Guard, Capt. Rufus D. Senn.
Provost Guard, Capt. D. H. Hamilton, jr.

WAR DEPARTMENT, C. S. A.,
Richmond, Va., November 21, 1864.

Governor JOSEPH E. BROWN:
(Care of General Fry, Augusta, Ga.)

Your telegram to the President has been referred to the Department for answer. The movements of the enemy in Georgia are viewed with interest and concern. Whatever re-enforcements of men and means the Department can command from its limited resources, in consistency with general safety, will be afforded.

J. A. SEDDON,
Secretary of War.

MACON, *November 21, 1864.*
(Received 22d.)

General S. COOPER,
Adjutant and Inspector General:

Believing the enemy has gone toward Augusta I have ordered all the disposable force from this place to that point. I shall leave myself to-night or early to-morrow. As far as I can learn the damage done the railroad is very slight; I am having it repaired. No injury to the railroads west or south of this place.

W. J. HARDEE,
Lieutenant-General.

SPECIAL ORDERS, No. 282. } HDQRS. DEPT. OF S. C., GA., AND FLA.,
Charleston, S. C., November 21, 1864.

I. Pursuant to paragraph XV, Special Orders, No. 264, Adjutant and Inspector General's Office, Maj. Gen. Robert Ransom is assigned to command of the Second Military Sub-District of South Carolina, formerly First District of South Carolina.

* * * * * * *

By command of Lieutenant-General Hardee:

H. W. FEILDEN,
Assistant Adjutant-General.

MACON, [*November*] *21, 1864,*
(Via Oconee 22d.)

Major-General McLAWS:

Believing the enemy is moving on Augusta, I have ordered all the disposable force from this place to that point. Send up cars to take away the troops. The damage done the railroad is believed to be inconsiderable; I am having it repaired. Hasten the cars forward. I shall leave to-morrow morning.

W. J. HARDEE,
Lieutenant-General, Commanding.

OCONEE, *November 21, 1864.*

Major-General McLAWS,
Savannah, Ga.:

Can you send me 1,000 men from Charleston or Savannah? The enemy are flanking me on the right. Send me a map of the State of Georgia.

H. C. WAYNE,
Major-General.

[Indorsement.]

NOVEMBER 21, 1864.

Send copy to headquarters, Charleston, and to Colonel Cuyler.

L. McLAWS,
Major-General, Commanding.

CENTRAL RAILROAD COMPANY,
Savannah, November 21, 1864.

Major-General McLAWS:

DEAR SIR: Every car at this time is engaged bringing prisoners from Camp Lawton. The very instant I can command cars I will place a train at No. 13 for Government stores, and I will give directions immediately thereafter to bring down the stores at Millen. Our road is not injured as yet from Gordon down. I received the following from Augusta, from our operator at Gordon, written yesterday:

The lumber train was captured at Griswoldville and burned to-day. Negroes all safe. Destroyed the machine shops and foundry and Georgia Chemical Works. Road burned at Griswoldville.

Very respectfully, your obedient servant,

R. R. CUYLER,
President.

GORDON, [*November*] *21, 1864.*

Major-General McLAWS,
Savannah:

I have been cut off from Macon for thirty hours. It is reported to me that Macon will be evacuated by our troops, the enemy being too strong. I have therefore, in council, decided to fall back to the Oconee, the now important point in this neighborhood. My force is 450, including 60 cavalry and 4 pieces of artillery. I report to you for orders.

HENRY C. WAYNE,
Major-General.

GORDON, *November 21, 1864.*

Colonel RAINS,
Augusta:

Send me 250 cartridge boxes and belts. The rain is ruining my powder.

H. C. WAYNE,
Major-General.

G[ORDON, *November*] *21, 1864.*

General FRY,
Commanding, &c., Augusta:

Have you any news of importance from Macon? The wires are cut, but I will send a courier through. Cavalry force of the enemy moving on the east of me as if for Milledgeville. Keep me advised.

HENRY C. WAYNE,
Major-General.

AUGUSTA, *November 21, 1864.*

General S. COOPER:

At least one corps of the enemy has advanced as far as Oconee River on railroad from Atlanta. Railroad and telegraph cut near Macon. I have had nothing from General Hardee since yesterday. After the enemy passes through I could be again at work here. The machinery is all important, and to save it I must have control of my workmen and also as much transportation as I may require. Unless such instructions are immediately given I cannot accomplish it.

GEO. W. RAINS.
Colonel, Commanding.

CENTRAL RAILROAD, *Gordon, November 21, 1864.*

Capt. R. W. B. ELLIOTT,
Assistant Adjutant-General, Headquarters Savannah:

Major-General Wayne proposes falling back from this place to the Oconee bridge. The enemy are reported 40,000 strong, moving on Macon, and 20,000 on Augusta. A small force of the enemy were in Milledgeville yesterday evening. I await further orders. Telegraph me at No. 14.

A. L. HARTRIDGE,
Major, &c.

OCONEE, *November 21, 1864.*

Captain ELLIOTT,
Assistant Adjutant-General:

If the enemy should attempt to go round for the purpose of destroying the Ogeechee railroad bridge, I will need a train to transport troops there for its defense. Can you not send a train here subject to my orders?

A. L. HARTRIDGE,
Major, &c.

OCONEE, *November 21, 1864.*

Capt. R. W. B. ELLIOTT:

Assistant Surgeon West has arrived, but without medicines. Captain Fremder's cavalry company not yet arrived. I have seized all the fords above and below the railroad bridge, and have ordered all boats to be kept on this side, and destroyed if necessary. I have received the major-general's dispatch allowing me to retain the Twenty-seventh Georgia Battalion. No citizens have reported yet.

A. L. HARTRIDGE,
Major, &c.

OCONEE, *November 21, 1864.*

Captain ELLIOTT,
Assistant Adjutant-General:

General Wayne and his command, between 400 and 500 men, left Gordon at 3.30 o'clock, and are now here. As we left Gordon the Yankees entered it, but no information could be gathered as to their strength. General Wayne has assumed command here. I await further orders.

A. L. HARTRIDGE,
Major, &c.

HEADQUARTERS,
Macon, Ga., November 21, 1864.

Major-General WHEELER,
Commanding Cavalry:

GENERAL: Lieutenant-General Hardee wishes you, when you reach the nearest point of your march to the Oconee bridge, on the Central railroad, to send a regiment there to aid in its defense. There are about 100 men there at present, but he does not think that force sufficient.

Respectfully, general, your obedient servant,

D. H. POOLE,
Assistant Adjutant-General.

HEADQUARTERS WILLIAMS' KENTUCKY BRIGADE,
November 21, 1864—3 p. m.

Major POOLE,
Assistant Adjutant-General for General Hardee:

I found the enemy about four miles from Clinton, about one regiment strong. I have driven them over a mile, and am still driving them. Have not as yet learned anything of the force they have in their rear.

Very respectfully, &c.,

WM. C. P. BRECKINRIDGE,
Colonel, Commanding Brigade.

HEADQUARTERS DISTRICT OF SOUTH CAROLINA,
Charleston, November 21, 1864.

J. R. TUCKER,
Flag Officer, Charleston, S. C.:

MY DEAR SIR: J. H. Toombs, chief engineer under your command, has suggested that from his knowledge of the use of torpedoes and the roads over which the enemy will probably pass in Georgia, that he may be able to delay their advance and inflict serious injury on them. If you can dispense with his services for a short time, and order him to report to me, I will detach him on that service.

Very respectfully, your obedient servant,

SAM. JONES,
Major-General.

RICHMOND, VA., *November 22, 1864.*

Col. WILLIAM M. BROWNE,
Aide-de-Camp, &c., Augusta, Ga.:

You will convey to generals commanding armies or posts in Southern Georgia my instructions that every effort will be made, by destroying bridges, felling trees, planting subterra shells, and otherwise, to obstruct the advance of the enemy. All supplies which are likely to fall into the enemy's hands will be destroyed. Communicate with General Hardee, commanding forces in Southern Georgia, or to General Beauregard, if he has arrived, to learn whether any force has been sent from the Army of Tennessee to co-operate in the defense of Southeastern Georgia. If it is not too late I wish that Forrest with his cavalry should be sent to impede the march of Sherman's army and prevent it from foraging on the country.

JEFF'N DAVIS.

RICHMOND, VA., *November 22, 1864.*

General B. BRAGG,
Wilmington, N. C.:

If the condition of affairs will permit I wish you to proceed via Columbia to Augusta to direct efforts to assemble and employ all available force against the enemy now advancing into Southeastern Georgia. General Hardee and perhaps Taylor and Beauregard are at Macon; Brigadier-General Fry, and perhaps Chesnut, at Augusta. General Lee will telegraph you.

JEFF'N DAVIS.

WILMINGTON, *November 22, 1864—9 p. m.*

His Excellency JEFFERSON DAVIS,
Richmond:

I will leave by first train but shall carry but few troops, most of these here being reserves which cannot be taken from the State.

B. BRAGG.

WILMINGTON, *November 22, 1864.*

Hon. R. H. MAY,
Mayor of Augusta:

I leave here to-day with re-enforcements for Augusta. Exhort your people to be confident and resolute.

BRAXTON BRAGG.

OCONEE, *November 22, 1864.*

General L. McLAWS:

The Fourth Kentucky Infantry (mounted) is on its way to my support, and will be here at about 1 o'clock to-night. Ordered here by General Wheeler. The cannonading heard this afternoon was Wheeler pressing the enemy in the rear down the railroad.

H. C. WAYNE.

OCONEE, *November 22, 1864.*

Major-General McLAWS:

Some of the militia are coming in. Can you not send me 100 arms and ammunition, say 40 rounds for each?

H. C. WAYNE,
Major-General.

TENNILLE, *November 22, 1864.*

Major-General MCLAWS:

Please send 5,000 rations (breadstuffs, meat, and salt) to Oconee bridge; 4,000 rounds .69 and 6,000 rounds .54.

H. C. WAYNE,
Major-General.

CHARLESTON, *November 22, 1864.*

Major-General MCLAWS:

Dispatch received. Telegraph communication with General Hardee, at Macon, is broken. It is suggested that General Wayne may be able to communicate with him and get his orders on the subject-matter of your telegram. Do you or General Wayne want a map of Georgia?

T. B. ROY,
Assistant Adjutant-General.

OCONEE, *November 22, 1864.*

Major-General MCLAWS:

One hundred and eighty-five enlisted men you sent up, 145 cadets, 200 militia—my cavalry and artillery horses have not yet come up—total, 530 men. No medical supplies or instruments.

H. C. WAYNE,
Major-General.

OCONEE, *November 22, 1864.*

General MCLAWS:

My cavalry and artillery horses just in; reported the force of the enemy at Gordon at 2,400; a portion went up the Milledgeville road, and the rest this way, tearing up both roads. Heavy cannonading now going on in the direction of Macon; firing rapid.

H. C. WAYNE,
Major-General.

OCONEE BRIDGE, *November 22, 1864.*

Major-General MCLAWS:

I have just received information that seems reliable that a heavy force of the enemy entered Gordon last evening after I left it, and this morning started for this bridge. Macon was to be attacked last evening or this morning. The enemy are moving, it seems, down the country on Macon or Augusta and down this road.

H. C. WAYNE,
Major-General.

OCONEE, *November 22, 1864.*

Capt. R. W. B. ELLIOTT:

In falling back from Gordon I have lost eighteen of my artillery horses, leaving me but six. I intend pressing eighteen from the farmers in the adjacent country. Can you supply me with artillery harness? Please answer at once.

H. C. WAYNE,
Major-General.

OCONEE BRIDGE, *November 22, 1864.*

Capt. R. W. B. ELLIOTT:

I do not think the enemy who entered Gordon yesterday were over 200 strong; they are probably the same party who entered Milledgeville the day before. I have sent Captain Brown down with a train this morning after supplies. Please have a train furnished him so he may return immediately.

A. L. HARTRIDGE,
Major, &c.

OCONEE BRIDGE, *November 22, 1864.*

Capt. R. W. B. ELLIOTT,
Assistant Adjutant-General:

I will hold the bridge until I get other orders from you.

A. L. HARTRIDGE,
Major, &c.

OCONEE, *November 22, 1864.*

Capt. R. W. B. ELLIOTT,
Assistant Adjutant-General:

Major Hall reports the enemy as having crossed at Blackshear Ferry, twenty miles from here.

A. L. HARTRIDGE,
Major, &c.

AUGUSTA, *November 22, 1864.*

Major-General MCLAWS:

Your telegram received. As president of the senate I have assumed command of the militia of the State east of the Oconee River, and have ordered all able-bodied men to report to me here. I will try and see General Wayne to-day, and conceive some measure with him to impede the enemy's progress. Am short of arms; can you furnish any? Date of my commission, June 3, 1862.

A. R. WRIGHT.

RICHMOND, VA., *November 22, 1864.*

General B. D. FRY,
Augusta, Ga.:

You will, to enable Colonel Rains to save the valuable machinery, allow him such of his workmen and such amount of transportation as may be necessary. The great and first wish being the repulse of the enemy in the event of an advance on Augusta, every other consideration will be regarded as subordinate to that.

JEFF'N DAVIS.

AUGUSTA, *November 22, 1864.*

General S. COOPER,
Adjutant and Inspector General:

On Sunday the Seventeenth and Twentieth Corps moved from Madison, on Georgia railroad, toward Milledgeville, which is now in hands of enemy, who have cut Central railroad from Oconee to Gordon.

General Hardee was at Macon on Sunday; have not heard from him since. Sherman seems to be moving on Augusta and Savannah, 45,000 strong. I can as yet count only 4,000 for defense here. Am gathering all. People show little spirit.

B. D. FRY,
Brigadier-General.

AUGUSTA, *November 22, 1864.*

General S. COOPER:

An intelligent lieutenant, with fifteen scouts, has just reported he followed enemy from Eaton Mountain to Morgan County, and came here by railroad, which we still use to Greensborough. Twentieth and Fourteenth Corps, under Slocum, form left of Sherman's army, and are moving down Oconee River; may move others on Augusta or Savannah. Have just heard from General Hardee, at Macon, date yesterday; says he will come here.

B. D. FRY,
Brigadier-General.

AUGUSTA, *November 22, 1864.*

President DAVIS:

Have not been able to see General Wayne to-day; hope to do so to-morrow. I have reliable authority that Milledgeville was not occupied by the enemy as late as 3 o'clock Sunday morning. A company of cavalry has just reached here, which left Macon late Saturday afternoon. They marched directly from there, passing through Milledgeville, and saw no enemy on their route.

A. R. WRIGHT.

MACON, *November 22, 1864.*

Major-General WHEELER,
In the Field:

GENERAL: I am directed by Lieutenant-General Taylor to instruct you to send a company, immediately on receipt of this, under a strictly reliable and competent officer, around to some safe point on the Georgia Central Railroad, and between the enemy and Savannah, with instructions to station his men at suitable distances, and apply by telegraph to the commanding officer at Savannah, in Lieutenant-General Taylor's name, for full information as to the condition of affairs eastward and toward Augusta, and report the same fully and promptly to this place.

Most respectfully, general, your obedient servant,

W. F. BULLOCK, JR.,
Assistant Adjutant-General.

FLORENCE, *November 22, 1864.*

Capt. W. F. NANCE:

Your dispatch received twenty-four hours after date. Merriwether's battalion was sent by General Hardee's orders to Augusta before your dispatch was written. I suppose from date, &c., it was for same purpose you ordered Williams. Who is in command of the department?

GEO. P. HARRISON, JR.,
Colonel, Commanding.

[Indorsement.]

It seems that Colonel Harrison had received a dispatch prior to the one from this office and sent another battalion in place of Williams'.

Respectfully,

NANCE,
Assistant Adjutant-General.

CHARLESTON, *November 22, 1864.*

General S. COOPER,
Adjutant and Inspector General:

It seems that General Sherman is marching to the coast; I believe to this place. You will see by last department returns that I have not the troops to make a defense by land. If troops are withdrawn from the harbor batteries, the enemy's fleet and troops are in sight and ready to enter. I earnestly ask for re-enforcements, and such instructions as may be thought necessary. Lieutenant-General Hardee is in Georgia, and communication with him cut off.

SAM. JONES,
Major-General.

HEADQUARTERS DISTRICT OF SOUTH CAROLINA, &C.,
Charleston, November 22, 1864.

[General HARDEE?:]

GENERAL: I have sent Mr. Toombs, chief engineer C. S. S. Chicora, of the Navy Department, with some torpedoes, which he thinks he can use to some advantage against the enemy in their advance through Georgia. I have directed him to call on you and explain the nature of the service on which he is sent, and I have to request that you will give him such aid as you can to enable him to carry out the object in view.

Very respectfully, your obedient servant,

SAM. JONES,
Major-General.

GENERAL ORDERS, No. 7. } HDQRS. SUB-DIST. SOUTH CAROLINA,
Charleston, November 22, 1864.

Pursuant to paragraph I, Special Orders, No. 282, Department of of South Carolina, Georgia, and Florida, the undersigned assumes command of the Second Sub-District of South Carolina. All existing orders will remain in force until otherwise ordered.

The officers of the present district staff will continue on duty with these headquarters.

First Lieut. B. F. Taylor and First Lieut. J. W. Jones are announced as aides-de-camp, and will be obeyed and respected accordingly.

R. RANSOM,
Major-General, Commanding.

AUGUSTA, *November 23, 1864.*

His Excellency President DAVIS:

Your dispatch received and orders obeyed. Nothing definite known of enemy's advance. I will keep you advised of all information I receive from military authorities here.

W. M. BROWNE.

AUGUSTA, *November 23, 1864—9.10 p. m.*

Dr. W. S. MORRIS:

Major Hartridge drove enemy back across river. General Wayne with militia and operator back again, and office reopened. Enemy have taken flat-boat; am building another.

J. A. BRENNER,
Superintendent.

[Indorsement.]

NOVEMBER 24, 1864.

Respectfully submitted for the information of the President.

JAMES A. SEDDON,
Secretary of War.

RICHMOND, VA., *November 23, 1864.*

General B. BRAGG,
Augusta, Ga.:

The law which restricts reserve troops to service within their State has been suspended for sixty days. I did not suppose those at Wilmington could be spared. You will exercise a large discretion in the disposition of the forces which may be made available.

JEFF'N DAVIS.

SAVANNAH, *November 23, 1864.*

General S. COOPER:
Adjutant and Inspector General:

I left Macon Monday night for this place, via Fort Valley, Albany, and Thomasville, and reached here to-night. When I left Macon I could hear of no enemy west of the Ocmulgee. The enemy had not been at Forsyth, Griffin, or Barnesville. It was believed that Sherman was moving with his main force on Augusta. I could, however, gain no definite or reliable information respecting the movement of the enemy's infantry. Wheeler attacked the enemy's cavalry at Clinton Sunday, but gained no advantage and got no information. The same day Colonel Crews drove the enemy from Griswold, but being re-enforced, Crews was in turn driven from the place. Monday Wheeler advanced on Griswold and drove Kilpatrick, who retreated on Milledgeville. Believing Macon would not be attacked, in which my principal officers concurred, I ordered General Smith's entire force, and a part of Cobb's, to move on Augusta via the Central railroad. This road was broken, but as far as heard from could be easily repaired. Lieutenant-General Taylor was in Columbus Monday, and was expected at Macon Tuesday following, and would assume command.

W. J. HARDEE,
Lieutenant-General.

OCONEE BRIDGE, *November 23, 1864.*

Major-General McLAWS:

Road not repaired as the enemy is still on it in my front making for the bridge. I am expecting an attack momentarily. Have not seen General Hardee. His courier followed the enemy and came in last evening, and will try to return this morning. The people in Macon, from my dispatches, know little of what has transpired on the road between that town and this place. Will send you word when the road shall be open for cars.

H. C. WAYNE,
Major-General.

OCONEE BRIDGE, [*November 23*], *1864—9 p. m.*

Major-General McLAWS:

Major Hartridge has driven the enemy back across this river, but they have the flat. Austin, with the cadets, has gallantly held the bridge The enemy are constructing a flat in the woods to try to cross below me to-night. Send me 5,000 .54 cartridges.

H. C. WAYNE,
Major-General.

TENNILLE, *November 23, 1864.*

Major-General McLAWS:

A courier just in from General Wayne reports, engaged the enemy at 12 m. at the bridge; about 200 crossed at Ball's Ferry, and were driven back by Major Hartridge. General Wayne says send him 5,000 rounds of .54 cartridges; and also says shall he hold his position if he is flanked. Train waits answer.

H. T. HALL,
Major, Commissary of Subsistence.

SAVANNAH, *November 23, 1864.*

Major-General WAYNE,
Tennille:

Bring off the stores with you from Tennille.
By order of Major-General McLaws:

R. W. B. ELLIOTT,
Assistant Adjutant-General.

The operator at the Bay office says the stores at Tennille have all been loaded and will leave to-night.

D. C. B.,
Operator.

OCONEE, *November 23, 1864.*

Capt. R. W. B. ELLIOTT,
Assistant Adjutant-General:

Enemy reported four miles on the other side of the river, advancing on bridge.

A. L. HARTRIDGE,
Major, &c.

OCONEE, *November 23, 1864.*

Capt. R. W. B. ELLIOTT:

The enemy reported fighting our pickets at Ball's Ferry, four miles below here. I am going there with part of my command.

A. L. HARTRIDGE,
Major, &c.

OCONEE BRIDGE, *November 23, 1864.*

Capt. R. W. B. ELLIOTT,
Assistant Adjutant-General:

I left one man killed and one wounded at Ball's Ferry. There will probably be fighting here to-morrow. If Captain Brown has reported send him back with supplies; also, 2,000 cartridges (.57) at once.

A. L. HARTRIDGE,
Major, &c.

OCONEE, *November 23, 1864.*

Capt. R. W. B. ELLIOTT:

Major Hartridge has gone to meet the enemy at Ball's Ferry. Our forces are fighting the enemy on the other side of the river, at the end of the trestle-works.

W. A. REID,
Lieutenant and Acting Adjutant.

OCONEE, *November 23, 1864.*

Capt. R. W. B. ELLIOTT,
Assistant Adjutant-General:

Lieutenant-Colonel Thompson has arrived here with the Fourth Kentucky Infantry (mounted), consisting of eighty men.

A. L. HARTRIDGE,
Major, &c.

HEADQUARTERS,
Macon, Ga., November 23, 1864—11 p. m.

Major-General WHEELER,
Commanding Cavalry Corps, in the Field:

GENERAL: The lieutenant-general commanding directs that you furnish him at the earliest practicable moment with any information you may have relative to the enemy's movement toward the Oconee—whether he is going directly toward the railroad bridge from this side, or is moving to cross the river below the railroad bridge, with the view of striking the railroad again at Davisborough or Tennille; and also such information as you may have from General Wayne, who, when last heard from, was proceeding to east side of the Oconee to take position at railroad bridge, with eleven pieces of artillery and about 500 or 600 men. If you possess any information on these points when this reaches you, you will communicate it at once to these headquarters. He further directs you to cross the Oconee without delay, place yourself in front of the enemy, and inform General Wayne relative to his movements. Should the enemy leave the railroad and strike toward Augusta you will get on his flank, annoy him as much as possible, and communicate promptly and constantly with Lieutenant-General Hardee at Savannah. The lieutenant-general commanding desires you on receipt of this to endeavor to learn the present whereabouts, if possible, of Carswell's brigade, Georgia militia, now commanded by Colonel Willis, which must be somewhere south of the railroad and this side of the Oconee. The enemy is reported to have left Clinton about sundown this evening, taking the direct Milledgeville road. Brigadier-General Ferguson and Colonel Breckinridge have been ordered to follow closely, harassing him as much as possible, and send scouts to the right for the purpose of getting in communication with and receiving orders from you.

I am, general, most respectfully, your obedient servant,

W. F. BULLOCK, JR.,
Assistant Adjutant-General.

RICHMOND, *November 23, 1864.*

Gen. A. R. WRIGHT,
Augusta, Ga.:

I deem it very fortunate that you are in position to exercise at the same time the authority of your Confederate and State commission. The Adjutant-General, C. S. A., will issue an order placing you on duty in Georgia. This telegram in the meantime will be sufficient for that purpose.

JEFF'N DAVIS.

AUGUSTA, *November 23, 1864.*

President DAVIS,
Richmond:

I am here with a portion of my command; more expected.

JAS. CHESNUT, JR.,
Brigadier-General.

AUGUSTA, *November 23, 1864.*

General MCLAWS:

Making every preparation for defense. General Bragg telegraphs that he will leave to-day with re-enforcements. Chesnut and Gartrell are here. People much more cheerful.

B. D. FRY,
Brigadier-General.

CHARLESTON, *November 23, 1864.*

General S. COOPER,
Adjutant and Inspector General:

If any troops are sent from Virginia I ask that Major Basinger's battalion be of the number. His officers and men are instructed in the use of heavy artillery. There is but one company here now to man the city batteries, and I am in daily expectation of an attack by water. Re-enforcements are absolutely essential here.

SAM. JONES,
Major-General.

HEADQUARTERS DISTRICT OF SOUTH CAROLINA, &c.,
Charleston, S. C., November 23, 1864.

Brig. Gen. J. H. TRAPIER,
Georgetown, S. C.:

GENERAL: Lieutenant-General Hardee directs me to prepare for a very heavy attack on this city.. It is necessary to have every available force at and near this place. You will, therefore, order Gaillard's battery from Santee, and Kirk's squadron from Georgetown, to repair without delay to Mount Pleasant and report for temporary duty to Maj. Gen. R. Ransom, commanding the Second Sub-District. The troops will bring with them as full supplies of subsistence and ammunition as practicable, and prepared for active service. Hold your remaining force, with the exception of Melchers' company, to move at the shortest notice to the same point--Mount Pleasant. I desire to see and confer with you, and will be glad if you will repair to this city as soon as you have given the necessary orders to carry out the foregoing instructions. Order Captain Melchers to use the utmost care and watchfulness, and, in the event of an attack during your absence, to defend his post to the last extremity, and if forced to retire to [save] his guns, or, if too hard pressed for that, to spike them and save his men, bringing them to Mount Pleasant. Instruct your staff officers, in the event of a threatened attack on Georgetown, to move the Government property in their charge to the Pee Dee bridge.

I am, very respectfully, general, your obedient servant,

SAM. JONES,
Major-General, Commanding.

MACON, *November 24, 1864.*
(Via Savannah 28th. Received 29th.)

President JEFFERSON DAVIS:

I arrived here this morning. Reports indicate enemy's advance to have reached a line extending from Davisborough to Warrenton, moving eastwardly, destroying Central and Georgia railroads. Probabilities are that the enemy will follow most direct route to Port Royal, intending to re-enforce Grant as soon as practicable. State militia and reserves leave in the morning, under General G. W. Smith, to re-enforce General Hardee. Have ordered General Hood to take active-offensive in Middle Tennessee to relieve General Lee.

G. T. BEAUREGARD.

MACON, GA., *November 24, 1864.*
(Via Mobile.)

General J. B. Hood:

Sherman's movement is progressing rapidly towards Atlantic coast, doubtless to re-enforce Grant. It is essential you should take offensive and crush enemy's force in Middle Tennessee soon as practicable, to relieve Lee.

G. T. BEAUREGARD,
General.

SAVANNAH, *November 24, 1864.*

General S. COOPER,
Adjutant and Inspector General:

I left Macon to go to Augusta, believing my presence there more necessary than at Macon. Since my arrival here I have learned with pleasure that General Bragg is ordered there. There was fighting to-day at Ball's Ferry, near the Oconee bridge; the enemy was repulsed. I have 600 or 700 men guarding the Oconee bridge and the river.

W. J. HARDEE,
Lieutenant-General.

RICHMOND, VA., *November 24, 1864.*

General W. J. HARDEE,
Savannah, Ga.:

When the purpose of the enemy shall be developed every effort must be made to obstruct the route on which he is moving, and all other available means must be employed to delay his march, as well as to enable our forces to concentrate, as to reduce him to want of the necessary supplies. Your attention is called to the prisoners of war who have been collected in Ware County. The position is, I suppose, only designed for temporary occupation. You will keep in constant communication with General Bragg, while you remain on the coast, so as to have entire unity of design and operation.

JEFF'N DAVIS.

SPECIAL ORDERS, No. 279. } ADJT. AND INSP. GENERAL'S OFFICE,
Richmond, Va., November 24, 1864.

* * * * * * *

XLI. Brig. Gen. A. R. Wright, Provisional Army, C. S., is assigned to duty with the forces operating against General Sherman, commanding United States forces in Georgia.

* * * * * * *

By command of Secretary of War:

JOHN W. RIELY,
Assistant Adjutant-General.

OCONEE, *November 24, 1864—1 a. m.*

General McLAWS:

You must get some one else to remove stores from Tennille, for it is questioned if we get out of this pickle. Am holding the bridge, and holding Ball's Ferry, eight miles below, but how long my men can hold out, with the movements I am compelled to make against Kilpatrick's 3,000 men, will be the question.

H. C. WAYNE,
Major-General.

OCONEE, *November 24, 1864.*

General McLAWS:

The enemy have planted a battery in front of the bridge and are trying to shell us out.

H. C. WAYNE,
Major-General.

OCONEE, *November 24, 1864.*

Major-General MCLAWS:

Enemy sent up a rocket last night and opened heavily again at daybreak this morning and still at it. Am nearly out of .54, only twenty-five rounds to the man left. Send me up ammunition, and, if possible, 1,000 men.

WAYNE,
Major-General.

OCONEE, *November 24, 1864.*

Major-General MCLAWS:

I am again attacked at Ball's Ferry in force. Do send me ammunition; I am nearly out.

H. C. WAYNE,
Major-General.

OCONEE, *November 24, 1864—8.55 p. m.*

Major-General MCLAWS:

I have held the bridge to the last extremity. The enemy have succeeded in setting fire to the trestle-work on the other end of the bridge; it is burning slowly. We still hold this side, and shall continue to hold it until driven back. The enemy are in heavy force on the other side. I believe I have more than Kilpatrick's division in front of me. Wheeler has not yet come up.

H. C. WAYNE,
Major-General.

OCONEE BRIDGE, *November 24, 1864.*

Major-General MCLAWS:

Major Hall reports to me that the enemy are on the Linton road to Tennille, fifteen miles off.

H. C. WAYNE,
Major-General.

OCONEE, *November 24, 1864.*

Capt. R. W. B. ELLIOTT,
Assistant Adjutant-General:

The force of the enemy is, in my opinion, exaggerated. I do not think there are more than 800 men. Major Hall, at No. 13, reports the enemy seen fifteen miles on the other side of Buffalo Creek, the bridges over which are all destroyed, but they may force a passage. Sharpshooters of the enemy on this side of the river, and ours on the other, firing on each other.

A. L. HARTRIDGE,
Major, &c.

OCONEE, [*November*] *24, 1864.*

Capt. R. W. B. ELLIOTT:

My men are in good spirits, but I cannot depend much on the militia. The enemy are attacking us in front. I will hold the bridge as long as possible. If forced to fall back I will retreat in direction of Ogeechee bridge. Please send me three days' cooked rations for 200 men.

A. L. HARTRIDGE,
Major, &c.

OCONEE, *November 24, 1864.*

Captain ELLIOTT,
Assistant Adjutant-General:

General Wheeler with 10,000 men is crossing Blackshear Ferry, twenty miles below here, and is coming to our assistance. We still hold our position at the bridge. The enemy have burned the long trestle on the other side. Our loss this morning, 2 killed and 5 wounded.

A. L. HARTRIDGE,
Major, Commanding.

OCONEE, *November 24, 1864.*
(Received 4 p. m.)

General MCLAWS:

They have opened a piece of artillery on us.

A. L. HARTRIDGE.

OCONEE, *November 24, 1864.*
(Received 4 p. m.)

General MCLAWS:

The enemy are still fighting us in front, and are moving slowly down the river with wagons, I think with the intention of throwing a pontoon bridge across the river.

A. L. HARTRIDGE,
Major, &c.

OCONEE, *November 24, 1864.*

General MCLAWS:

The enemy have turned their artillery in the opposite direction and are shelling. They must be attacked in the rear.

A. L. HARTRIDGE,
Major, &c.

HEADQUARTERS,
Oconee Bridge, November 24, 1864.

Major-General WHEELER,
Commanding, &c.:

GENERAL: Your dispatch of to-day by Hamilton Smith is just received at 2 p. m.; your dispatch of yesterday by Hodges has not been received. The enemy are now trying to shell me out. Force in front of me is from 3,000 to 4,000. They are trying to cross on pontoon a mile below me. Hurry a strong force to my assistance; also send a force below to No. 13, Central railroad, where a part of the enemy, estimated at 500, are marching on Sandersville.

Very respectfully, your obedient servant,

HENRY C. WAYNE,
Major-General.

2.10.

The enemy have this instant turned their guns to their rear. Did you send men up the river on the other side?

H. C. W.

AUGUSTA, *November 24, 1864.*

General HARDEE:

Captain Culver, who has been scouting since Sunday, reports main body of enemy moving down west side of Oconee; that a cavalry force of 600 to 1,000 has crossed, and was at Island Creek at 6 p. m. yesterday, moving slowly towards Shorte. Island Creek is sixteen miles west of Shorte. One hundred and sixty-three prisoners have been brought [in].

B. D. FRY,
Brigadier-General.

AUGUSTA, *November 24, 1864—12 o'clock.*

Dr. W. S. MORRIS:

General Wheeler with 10,000 men now crossing Oconee River, twenty miles below bridge, at Blackshear Ferry, and coming to assistance of General Wayne. Enemy have burned long trestle-work on other side of bridge.

J. A. BRENNER.

AUGUSTA, *November 24, 1864—12.30 o'clock.*

Dr. W. S. MORRIS:

General Wayne's courier reports main body of enemy moving through Linton on Sandersville. This is a point three miles from railroad station, Tennille, which station is twelve miles from Oconee.

J. A. BRENNER,
Superintendent.

HEADQUARTERS HAMPTON'S CAVALRY,
November 24, 1864.

COMMANDING OFFICER,
Augusta:

Please insert this dispatch in all newspapers in Augusta: All men of my command now in Georgia will rendezvous forthwith at Augusta, and those in South Carolina, at Columbia, and await orders.

WADE HAMPTON,
Major-General.

SAVANNAH, *November 24, 1864.*

Maj. Gen. S. JONES:

Recent information places the enemy between the Oconee and Ocmulgee Rivers. I confess, however, that my information is not definite or reliable. When I left Macon it was not believed that Macon would be attacked. Lieutenant-General Taylor is in command there. Give me the news in your district.

W. J. HARDEE,
Lieutenant-General.

AUGUSTA, *November 25, 1864.*

Col. JOHN B. SALE,
Military Secretary, Richmond:

Arrived last night late, and take command this morning. We learn from General Wayne, who holds the Oconee railroad bridge, that the enemy has not crossed the river in any force. He has concentrated at Milledgeville, and seems to be tending south. Our cavalry, under Wheeler, is in his front, and has been ordered to destroy every vestige of subsistence and forage as it retires, to hang upon his flanks, and retard his progress by every possible means. I am informed the brigades from Southwest Virginia have joined Wheeler. President's dispatch of 23d just received.

BRAXTON BRAGG,
General.

AUGUSTA, *November 25, 1864—8 p. m.*
(Received 26th.)

Col. JOHN B. SALE,
Military Secretary, Richmond:

The enemy has crossed the Oconee; was met this evening in force at Buffalo Creek, near Sandersville. His movements from that point will determine whether he designs attacking here or on Savannah.

BRAXTON BRAGG.

MILLEN, *November 25, 1864.*

General McLAWS:

When it is demonstrated that the enemy is not moving to cross the Savannah River towards Charleston, remove the prisoners to Florence. All prisoners arriving and now in Savannah had better be sent there at once.

W. J. HARDEE,
Lieutenant-General.

TENNILLE, *November 25, 1864.*

Major-General McLAWS:

I am at this place and will receive communications here.

W. J. HARDEE,
Lieutenant-General.

TENNILLE, *November 25, 1864.*

Major-General MCLAWS:

Send two days' of bread and meat for 1,300 men to Millen, and telegraph General Wayne, so that he can send to Millen for it when it arrives.

W. J. HARDEE,
Lieutenant-General.

TENNILLE, *November 25, 1864.*

Major-General MCLAWS,
Savannah:

Wheeler fought the enemy's cavalry three miles and a half from Sandersville and drove them back upon their infantry, taking prisoners, from whom he learned that three corps were crossing Buffalo Creek. It seems certain that the enemy is moving toward Savannah.

W. J. HARDEE,
Lieutenant-General.

TENNILLE, *November 25, 1864.*

Major-General MCLAWS,
Savannah:

Send to No. 12, on the C[entral] railroad, 7,000 army and 5,000 navy-pistol ammunition at once for General Wheeler; it will be needed to-morrow morning.

W. J. HARDEE,
Lieutenant-General.

TENNILLE, *November 25, 1864.*

Major-General MCLAWS:

Send 8,000 rations of bread and meat to Millen for Wheeler's cavalry.

W. J. HARDEE,
Lieutenant-General.

OCONEE, *November 25, 1864.*

Major-General MCLAWS:

Send 1,500 bushels of corn to Millen for Wheeler's cavalry.

W. J. HARDEE,
Lieutenant-General.

OCONEE, *November 25, 1864.*

Major-General MCLAWS,
Savannah:

The enemy are trying to force Ball's Ferry. There is heavy firing below—apparently at Blackshear Ferry. The movements of the enemy are evidently on Savannah.

H. C. WAYNE,
Major-General.

OCONEE, *November 25, 1864.*

General MCLAWS:

The enemy have driven us back from across the bridge. Three heavy columns are across the river, and they have possession of Ball's Ferry, below here.

H. C. WAYNE,
Major-General.

OCONEE, *November 25, 1864.*

Major-General MCLAWS:

Three heavy columns are this side of the river, and to save the men I will retire.

H. C. WAYNE,
Major-General.

OCONEE, *November 25, 1864.*

Capt. R. W. B. ELLIOTT:

The enemy are reported on the right, this side of the river, in large force. We are preparing to meet them. We still hold the bridge, which is burning slowly at the other end.

A. L. HARTRIDGE,
Major, &c.

HEADQUARTERS,
Station No. 13, November 25, 1864—5.30 p. m.

General WHEELER,
Commanding Cavalry Corps:

GENERAL: The information sent me about the movements of the enemy is important. It shows clearly, I think, that the enemy is moving on Savannah. Endeavor to get all the information you can.

Respectfully and truly, yours,

W. J. HARDEE,
Lieutenant-General.

OCONEE, *November 25, 1864.*

General WHEELER:

General Bragg directs me to say to you to stick close to the enemy; to harass him in front and flank; and above all to destroy subsistence and forage in the route over which the enemy advances; also, to keep up and open communication with the forces at this point.

H. C. WAYNE,
Major-General.

HEADQUARTERS CAVALRY DIVISION,
Sandersville, November 25, 1864—4 p. m.

Lieutenant HUDSON,
Acting Assistant Adjutant-General:

LIEUTENANT: From scout reports I locate the enemy, at last reports, as follows: A force on the road from Long Bridge to Warthen's Store, six miles from Warthen's; also, on the road from Long Bridge, exact locality not accurately known, some report only three miles; also, on the Milledgeville road, three miles from Sandersville. I learn from a courier that General Allen is five miles in rear.

Very respectfully, your obedient servant,

ALFRED IVERSON,
Brigadier-General.

AUGUSTA, *November 26, 1864.*

Col. JOHN B. SALE,
Military Secretary, Richmond:

So far we have failed to open communication with Macon, the enemy having interposed his whole force between us—seems to have neglected that point. This leaves us dependent on the force east of him. They are feeble in number, wanting in organization and discipline, and very deficient in equipments. No offensive movement can be undertaken, and but a temporary defense of our scattered posts. If no more means can be had our only policy is to make sacrifices and concentrate. The country is being utterly devastated wherever the enemy move.

BRAXTON BRAGG.

AUGUSTA, *November 26, 1864.*
(Received 27th.)

Col. JOHN B. SALE,
Military Secretary, Richmond:

General Wheeler encountered the enemy's cavalry yesterday three miles west of Sandersville and drove them back to Buffalo Creek, where he found the infantry crossing. Prisoners captured represent four corps. The movement does not indicate whether this or Savannah is the objective point.

BRAXTON BRAGG.

RICHMOND, VA., *November 26, 1864.*

General BRAGG,
Augusta, Ga.:

Yours of the 26th received. I hope you will soon hear from Macon and know of other forces. I do not understand suggestion as to making sacrifices for concentration.

JEFF'N DAVIS.

MACON, GA., *November 26, 1864.*

General J. B. HOOD:

Can you and Lee recommend to me a major-general of Army of Tennessee with sufficient rank to command Wheeler and his cavalry. He must be active, energetic, bold, and a good disciplinarian. His consent for transfer must be had.

G. T. BEAUREGARD,
General.

MACON, GA., *November 26, 1864.*

General J. B. HOOD:

Would not Maj. Gen. Edward Johnson be a good officer for cavalry command referred to this morning? If so, order him, should he consent to transfer, to report forthwith at Montgomery. Cannot Major-General Martin be ordered back to his division?

G. T. BEAUREGARD,
General.

MILLEN, *November 26, 1864.*

President DAVIS:

Enemy entered Sandersville to-day in force. Wheeler says Kilpatrick has gone toward Augusta, and he will pursue him with all of his force, except one brigade, which will be left in this front. Wheeler is uncertain whether Sherman is going to Augusta or Savannah.

W. J. HARDEE,
Lieutenant-General.

SAVANNAH, *November 26, 1864.*

General S. COOPER,
Adjutant and Inspector General:

General Hardee telegraphed last evening—

Send special messenger to Lieutenant-General Taylor, at Macon, to bring all his disposable force to Savannah, as I believe the enemy are marching on that place.

Distances from Macon to Savannah: To Albany by railroad, 107 miles; to Thomasville, to march, sixty-two miles; to Savannah by railroad, 200 miles. The enemy are within 140 miles from Savannah. I have no troops to defend land side.

L. McLAWS,
Major-General.

MILLEN, *November 26, 1864—3.44 p. m.*
(Received 4 p. m.)

General McLAWS:

Send for two companies of cavalry from South Carolina. Wheeler, when I last heard from him, expected to be forced from Sandersville, as he was pressed by a heavy force of cavalry and infantry. I shall be in Savannah to-morrow morning. Please order my carriage to meet me at depot.

W. J. HARDEE,
Lieutenant-General.

MILLEN, *November 26, 1864.*

General McLAWS:

Wheeler says Kilpatrick has gone toward Augusta, and he will follow after him with all his force except one brigade. Enemy entered Sandersville to-day in force.

W. J. HARDEE,
Lieutenant-General.

MILLEN, *November 26, 1864.*

General WHEELER,
Commanding Cavalry:

I send you a dispatch from General Bragg. It will be taken by engine as far as it is deemed safe, and from thence it will be sent to you by courier. It is important that you ascertain in what direction the enemy moves from Sandersville, whether toward Augusta or toward Savannah. Put up your telegraph wires at some point below, so as to communicate with Bragg and myself.

Yours,

W. J. HARDEE,
Lieutenant-General.

RICHMOND, VA., *November 26, 1864.*

Col. W. M. BROWNE,
Augusta, Ga.:

I am very anxious to know progress of operations, and to learn what is known at Macon of our troops, present and expected. Could not a courier go through the country?

JEFF'N DAVIS.

AUGUSTA, *November 26, 1864.*

His Excellency the PRESIDENT:

Enemy's cavalry reported 1,000 strong, but believed not to exceed half that amount, were near Warrenton at midday. Infantry strength not reported, but believed to be 20,000, near Sparta, at same time. Our cavalry in their front barely sufficient to watch roads and drive off stock. Nothing official from Central road. There is good reason to believe the left of the enemy is at Sandersville; the cavalry of that wing said to be 5,000 strong; this is believed to be nearly correct; infantry, 20,000 to 25,000. Dispatch just received says enemy's cavalry, of his right wing, under Kilpatrick, is marching toward Augusta. Wheeler, with nearly equal force, is endeavoring to overtake them. An officer through from Macon to-day says all quiet there; General Taylor in command; enemy devastating country behind him. I have been ordered by General Bragg to take command of local brigade.

W. M. BROWNE,
Colonel, &c.

AUGUSTA, *November 26, 1864.*

Major-General MCLAWS:

Enemy's cavalry near Ogeechee Shoals, Warren County; infantry near Sparta. I have nothing official from Central road.

B. D. FRY,
Brigadier-General.

MILLEN, *November 26, 1864.*

General SAMUEL JONES:

About 10,000 prisoners of war will probably go to Florence. Wheeler says Kilpatrick has gone toward Augusta, and he will follow after him with all his cavalry except one brigade. Enemy entered Sandersville to-day in force.

W. J. HARDEE,
Lieutenant-General.

WAR DEPARTMENT, C. S. A.,
Richmond, Va., November 27, 1864.

General BRAXTON BRAGG,
Augusta:

It was intended your command should extend to the coast and embrace all combinations against the present movements of the enemy. General Hardee will receive instructions from you to insure unity and concert of action.

J. A. SEDDON,
Secretary of War.

AUGUSTA, *November 27, 1864.*

Hon. J. A. SEDDON:

Your dispatch of to-day is received. Unable to decline a responsibility of such magnitude so unexpectedly transferred to me. In assuming it I must candidly express my belief that no practicable combinations of my available men can avert disaster.

BRAXTON BRAGG.

AUGUSTA, *November 27, 1864.*
(Received 28th.)

Col. JOHN B. SALE,
Military Secretary, Richmond:

We have lost communication with the front. A small cavalry raid cut the Savannah railroad and telegraph this morning at Brier Creek, twenty-six miles from here. General Wheeler was yesterday confronting the enemy's infantry at Sandersville. An officer who left Macon on the 23d states that one corps of the enemy was still confronting us there, our force not exceeding 5,000; nearly all militia. The force here, including all available resources, does not exceed 6,000 effectives; only one battery. I am not yet advised from Charleston and Savannah, but know the means are small. Neither point could long resist the enemy's whole force; hence my remark about concentration. General Hardee has gone to Savannah. Wheeler will continue to confront and harass the enemy. I have not learned the strength of his command. He estimates the enemy's force at about 30,000.

BRAXTON BRAGG,
General.

WAR DEPARTMENT, C. S. A.,
Richmond, Va., November 27, 1864.

General HARDEE,
Savannah:

Confer with General Bragg as to combinations against the present movements of the enemy. His command extends over your department.

J. A. SEDDON,
Secretary of War.

SAVANNAH, *November 27, 1864—1 a. m.*

General SAMUEL JONES:

Send Colonel Gonzales to me for a few days. I need intrenching tools; have you any to spare? I need light batteries or light guns; how many can you give me? Answer immediately. It is reported that enemy's cavalry crossed Savannah River twenty miles below Augusta.

W. J. HARDEE,
Lieutenant-General.

SAVANNAH BARRACKS, *November 27, 1864.*

General SAM. JONES:

Have all railroad bridges in your district between Charleston and Savannah thoroughly guarded.

W. J. HARDEE,
Lieutenant-General.

AUGUSTA, *November 28, 1864—5 p. m.*

Col. JOHN B. SALE,
Military Secretary, Richmond:

On 26th enemy started a heavy cavalry force in this direction from his main body near Sandersville, General Wheeler promptly following, leaving a portion of his force to confront Sherman. Kilpatrick reached vicinity of Waynesborough yesterday, where Wheeler overtook and attacked him. A running fight has continued to this time, the advantage with us. We are now driving them toward Millen. Young's command has just arrived, and will go forward to Wheeler, who will, I hope, be able to mount most of them from his captures. Devastation marks the enemy's route. Have nothing from the movements of enemy's infantry since Wheeler left their front. I fear they may cross the Savannah and make for Beaufort; it is perfectly practicable.

BRAXTON BRAGG.

MACON, *November 28, 1864.*
(Received 30th.)

General S. COOPER,
Adjutant and Inspector General:

Forrest's cavalry cannot now be spared from the Army of Tennessee; moreover, it could not reach here in time. The whole of Wheeler's command is operating against Sherman's force. No news from General Hood. Enemy have evacuated Decatur.

G. T. BEAUREGARD,
General.

MACON, *November 28, 1864.*

Lieut. Gen. W. J. HARDEE:

Forrest's cavalry cannot now be spared from the Army of Tennessee; moreover, it could not get here in time. Sherman is doubtless making for sea-coast at Port Royal, Ossabaw Sound, or Darien; thence to re-enforce Grant.

G. T. BEAUREGARD,
General.

AUGUSTA, *November 28, 1864—7 a. m.*

General JOSEPH WHEELER:

GENERAL: Yours of 12.30 yesterday was received last night and gave me great pleasure. I trust you will be able to keep up with the enemy and press him on here. We are fully prepared for him. As soon as possible let me hear what you can learn of the movements of the main column, and endeavor to have my instructions carried out in regard to it. How is enemy provided with subsistence and ammunition?

Very respectfully and truly, yours,

BRAXTON BRAGG.

CHARLESTON, *November 28, 1864.*

General S. COOPER,
Adjutant and Inspector General:

Have you received my telegrams of the 22d and 23d instant asking for re-enforcements? I cannot too strongly urge my need of them. General Hardee informs me, from Savannah, that it was reported yesterday the enemy's cavalry had crossed the Savannah River twenty miles below Augusta.

SAM. JONES,
Major-General.

RICHMOND, *November 28, 1864.*

General SAMUEL JONES,
Charleston, S. C.:

Your dispatches of 22d and 23d were immediately sent to the President and Secretary of War. I have no instructions from either in respect to those dispatches, and you must be as fully aware as the authorities here that there are no re-enforcements that can be sent to you.

S. COOPER.

WAR DEPARTMENT, C. S. A.,
Richmond, Va., November 28, 1864.

General S. JONES,
Charleston, S. C.:

It is impossible to afford re-enforcements. All troops at command of department are being pressed forward to intercept enemy. You must rely on your own resources.

J. A. SEDDON,
Secretary of War.

SAVANNAH, *November 28, 1864.*

Maj. Gen. S. JONES:

Wheeler telegraphs from Waynesborough, at 8.30 p. m. yesterday, that Kilpatrick was there with large cavalry force and had started down on Millen road. General Bragg telegraphs to-day that the enemy had not crossed the Savannah, as reported.

D. H. POOLE,
Assistant Adjutant-General.

AUGUSTA, GA., *November 28, 1864.*

General SAM. JONES:

The report is unfounded; the different ferries are guarded, and all boats are ordered to be destroyed. The enemy's cavalry and our own are near Waynesborough, where fighting has been going on this morning. We are not as well informed about his infantry, but believe it to be between the Ogeechee bridge and Millen.

BRAXTON BRAGG.

HEADQUARTERS DISTRICT OF SOUTH CAROLINA,
Charleston, S. C., November 28, 1864.

Major-General RANSOM,
Commanding:

GENERAL: The major-general commanding directs you to order one company of the Thirty-second Georgia Regiment to Brigadier-General Robertson, without delay. It should go to Adams' Run by the morning train. Please notify the quartermaster as soon as practicable of the strength of the company, that he may furnish the necessary transportation.

CHAS. S. STRINGFELLOW,
Assistant Adjutant-General.

AUGUSTA, *November 29, 1864—12 m.*

Col. JOHN B. SALE,
Military Secretary, Richmond:

It is reported, via Savannah, the enemy with infantry and artillery entered Millen yesterday. Wheeler is rapidly pursuing Kilpatrick, who retreats in that direction from Waynesborough.

BRAXTON BRAGG.

AUGUSTA, *November 29, 1864—6.30 p. m.*

Col. JOHN B. SALE,
Military Secretary, Richmond:

General Jones telegraphs from Charleston:

> Ten gun-boats with transports landing troops at Boykins, on Broad River. Four gun-boats with transports and barges are by this time at Mackay's Point, junction of Pocotaligo with Broad River. I am sending all assistance from here, and think we must make the struggle near the coast.

As the movement relieves Wilmington might not some of the North Carolina reserves be sent to General Jones?

BRAXTON BRAGG.

MACON, *November 29, 1864.*

President JEFFERSON DAVIS:

Having sent General Hardee General Taylor and all aid possible, General Maury reporting Mobile threatened I have sent him General M. L. Smith to command its defenses. I will leave to-day for Montgomery. No news yet from the Army of Tennessee.

G. T. BEAUREGARD,
General.

MACON, *November 29, 1864.*
(Received 30th.)

General S. COOPER:

I have ordered immediate reconstruction of all railroads and telegraph lines destroyed by Sherman's forces. Work reported to be progressing rapidly on Central road.

G. T. BEAUREGARD,
General.

MACON, *November 29, 1864.*
(Received 30th.)

General S. COOPER:

Wheeler's cavalry requires reorganization; one additional major-general is needed. I recommended Brig. Gen. S. W. Ferguson for temporary appointment. Please answer by telegraph.

G. T. BEAUREGARD.

MACON, *November 29, 1864.*
(Received 30th.)

General S. COOPER:

To prevent confusion please inform me if order extending General Hardee's department to south side of Chattahoochee still remains in force.

G. T. BEAUREGARD,
General.

SAVANNAH, *November 29, 1864.*

Hon. J. A. SEDDON,
Secretary of War:

As railroad and telegraphic communications may soon be cut with Charleston I desire you to know that I have, including the local troops, less than 1,000 men of all arms. General Smith is expected with 3,200 men, but has not yet arrived. If railroad communication is cut with Charleston, which is threatened by ten gun-boats and barges, of course no re-enforcements can be sent from Augusta.

W. J. HARDEE,
Lieutenant-General.

HEADQUARTERS,
Savannah, Ga., November 29, 1864—10 p. m.

Maj. Gen. G. W. SMITH,
Commanding, &c.:

GENERAL: Lieutenant-General Hardee directs that you proceed at once with the first two trains of your troops which may arrive at Savannah to-night, and in the same cars to Grahamville and Coosawhatchie, on the Charleston and Savannah Railroad, which places are being threatened by raiding parties of the enemy; and, if you find yourself the ranking officer present, that you command, and drive the enemy back to their gun-boats.

Very respectfully, your obedient servant,

T. B. ROY,
Assistant Adjutant-General.

C. S. NAVAL STATION, COMMANDANT'S OFFICE,
Savannah, Ga., November 29, 1864.

General L. MCLAWS,
Commanding Military District of Georgia, &c., Savannah:

GENERAL: When I consulted with you this morning in relation to the propriety of removing the property of the C. S. Navy Department from this station, in view of the reported approach of the enemy toward this city, and inquired of you as to the time such removal should be effected, you advised me to commence it immediately. Will you do me the favor to suggest the point to which, in your judgment, it will be advisable to remove that property.

I am, sir, respectfully, your obedient servant,

JOSIAH TATNALL,
Flag-Officer, Commanding Naval Station.

SAVANNAH, *November 29, 1864.*

General WAYNE:

Communicate the following information and instructions to Major-General Wheeler:

All the roads leading to Savannah are obstructed. He must operate on the flanks and rear of the enemy.

W. J. HARDEE,
Lieutenant-General.

AUGUSTA, *November 29, 1864.*

Maj. Gen. JOSEPH WHEELER:

Dispatch received. Press closely upon the enemy, and keep me informed.

BRAXTON BRAGG,
General.

HEADQUARTERS,
No. 4½, Central Railroad, November 29, 1864—5.45 p. m.

Major-General WHEELER,
Commanding Cavalry Corps:

GENERAL: I have the honor to forward the following telegram just received from Lieutenant-General Hardee:

SAVANNAH, *November 29, 1864.*

Major-General WAYNE:

Communicate the following [information and] instructions to Major-General Wheeler:

All the roads leading into Savannah are obstructed. He must operate on the flanks and rear of the enemy.

Communicate by courier, if possible, to him along the line of railroad to Savannah.

If possible, please acknowledge the receipt of this dispatch.

Very respectfully, your obedient servant,

H. C. WAYNE,
Major-General.

HEADQUARTERS CAVALRY DIVISION,
Farmer's, November 29, 1864—4.20 p. m.

Lieutenant HUDSON,
Acting Assistant Adjutant-General:

LIEUTENANT: My latest intelligence places the enemy marching toward Waynesborough in heavy force. Captain Humphreys states that a scout on the Pugeley's Bridge road failed to discover the enemy in twelve miles. I stopped Lewis' brigade at Walker's Bridge, with instructions to guard all the bridges from that down. Hannon is at Farmer's Bridge, covering the river above. I will have all General Wheeler's instructions carried out.

Very respectfully, your obedient servant,

ALFRED IVERSON,
Brigadier-General.

AUGUSTA, GA., *November 29, 1864.*

Maj. Gen. SAM. JONES:

Have you any spare arms? Can send you near 1,000 Yankee prisoners, if you can arm and use them. Savannah River should be rigidly patrolled as high up as the mouth of Brier Creek. Pocotaligo will probably be the point aimed at.

BRAXTON BRAGG.

AUGUSTA, *November 29, 1864—11.40 a. m.*

General SAMUEL JONES:

Make every disposition possible to prevent the enemy from ascending Broad River and cutting the Savannah railroad. All your movable force should assemble in that vicinity.

BRAXTON BRAGG.

AUGUSTA, *November 29, 1864—6 p. m.*

General JONES:

One thousand South Carolina reserves have left here, under General Chesnut, to report to General Hardee. A North Carolina brigade of 2,000 is about starting, under General Baker. You are authorized to use them for the defense of your department, subject to General Hardee's instructions. Have transportation ready, and lose no time in making the necessary disposition.

BRAXTON BRAGG.

AUGUSTA, *November 29, 1864.*

General SAM. JONES:

Provide transportation to Savannah for 3,000 men; they leave here this afternoon.

By order of General Bragg:

M. B. McMICKEN,
Lieutenant-Colonel and Chief Quartermaster.

SAVANNAH, *November 29, 1864.*

Major-General JONES:

Lieutenant-General Hardee, temporarily absent, will reply in relation to Kirk's squadron when he returns. Enemy's gun-boats reported coming up Broad River. Latest advices from Augusta report Wheeler driving Kilpatrick from Waynesborough toward Millen. No information of enemy's infantry on Augusta side of Ogeechee. Ferguson crossing Oconee at Milledgeville 26th, following the enemy; reports no enemy near Macon.

T. B. ROY,
Assistant Adjutant-General.

SAVANNAH, *November 29, 1864.*

General S. JONES:

The following dispatch just received from Pocotaligo: "Yankee gun-boats coming up Broad River."

W. J. HARDEE,
Lieutenant-General.

SAVANNAH, *November 29, 1864.*

Maj. Gen. S. JONES:

Send Thirty-second Georgia to Pocotaligo to protect railroad, and instruct the commanding officer to move against any raid of the enemy coming from Broad River.

T. B. ROY,
Assistant Adjutant-General.

CHARLESTON, *November 29, 1864.*
(Received 2.45 o'clock.)

Col. T. B. ROY:

Steamer got aground. Thirty-second Georgia delayed. Forty-seventh Georgia (about 400) at depot, but delayed by train coming from Savannah. Breakdown on the Augusta road 112 miles from here will delay re-enforcements. Will let you know when Forty-seventh Georgia leaves.

H. W. FEILDEN,
Assistant Adjutant-General.

SAVANNAH, *November 29, 1864.*

Maj. Gen. S. JONES:

If any other regiment can be better spared than the Thirty-second Georgia it may be sent to Pocotaligo instead.

T. B. ROY,
Assistant Adjutant-General.

SAVANNAH, *November 29, 1864—7 p. m.*

General SAMUEL JONES:

Hurry forward re-enforcements to Grahamville. The enemy expected there to-morrow morning. Tell Captain Hunt to keep our horses in Charleston.

W. J. HARDEE,
Lieutenant-General.

HEADQUARTERS DISTRICT OF SOUTH CAROLINA,
Charleston, November 29, 1864.

General ROBERT RANSOM:

The major-general commanding directs you to order the Thirty-second Georgia Regiment and Kirk's squadron to Pocotaligo, without delay, to check the enemy advancing on that point.

Very respectfully, your obedient servant,

C. S. STRINGFELLOW,
Assistant Adjutant-General.

POCOTALIGO, *November 29, 1864.*

General S. JONES:

Ten gun-boats with transports and barges are at Boyd's Landing. Troops near Grahamville. Four gun-boats are coming up Broad River to Mackay's Point, which is the approach to Pocotaligo and Coosawhatchie. Re-enforcements needed.

JOHN JENKINS,
Major, Commanding.

GRAHAMVILLE, *November 29, 1864.*

Maj. Gen. SAM. JONES:

It is important that I should be re-enforced to-night. Please hurry Harrison on to Coosawhatchie.

JOHN JENKINS,
Major, Commanding.

HEADQUARTERS ARMIES OF THE CONFEDERATE STATES,
Augusta, November 30, 1864. (Received December 1.)

Col. JOHN B. SALE,
Military Secretary, Richmond:

Following just received from Major-General Wheeler:

FOUR MILES WEST BUCK HEAD CHURCH,
November 29—9 p. m.

We fought General Kilpatrick all night and all day, charging him at every opportunity. Enemy fought stubbornly, and a considerable number of them killed. We stampeded and came near capturing Kilpatrick twice, but having a fleet horse he escaped bare headed, leaving his hat in our hands. Our own loss about 70, including the gallant General Robertson, severely wounded. Our troops all acted handsomely.

General Robertson has arrived here. His left arm is badly broken at the elbow, but he is doing well.

BRAXTON BRAGG.

AUGUSTA, *November 30, 1864.*
(Received December 1.)

Col. JOHN B. SALE,
Military Secretary, Richmond:

To re-establish our communications west, I have ordered the immediate repair of the Georgia railroad to Atlanta. With exception of bridges the damage is reported as slight. We should also have a line of telegraph on that route.

BRAXTON BRAGG.

RICHMOND, *November 30, 1864.*

General BEAUREGARD:
(Care of Col. W. M. Browne, Augusta, Ga.)

Yours of the 24th received. It is probable that the enemy, if short of supplies, may move directly for the coast. When that is made manifest you will be able to concentrate your forces upon the one object, and, I hope, if you cannot defeat his attempt, that you may reduce his army to such condition as to be ineffective for further operations. Until Hood reaches the country proper of the enemy he can scarcely change the plans for Sherman's or Grant's campaigns. They would, I think, regard the occupation of Tennessee and Kentucky as of minor importance.

JEFF'N DAVIS.

SAVANNAH, *November 30, 1864.*

President DAVIS:

Have just reached here. Directed by General Beauregard to send you following dispatch, in his name:

MACON, GA., *November 26—p. m.*

President DAVIS,
Richmond:

I have ordered General Taylor to report forthwith, for present emergency, to General Hardee, but to return soon as practicable. Sherman is evidently moving rapidly to Atlantic coast for purpose of re-enforcing Grant. I have ordered again General Hood to take immediate active offensive operations to relieve General Lee. Railroads in Georgia destroyed by enemy are being repaired expeditiously. I hope to re-establish shortly direct communication with Richmond.

G. T. BEAUREGARD.

[W. M. BROWNE.]

RICHMOND, VA., *November 30, 1864.*

General BEAUREGARD,
Macon:

For the present emergency your command will extend eastward to the sea-coast. Your minute knowledge of the low country will enable you to dispose of the forces operating against Sherman, as well as those defending the coast, so as more effectually to retard the advance of Sherman and the junction of the enemy.

By order of the President:

S. COOPER,
Adjutant and Inspector General.

SAVANNAH, *November 30, 1864.*

General S. COOPER,
Adjutant and Inspector General:

The enemy yesterday landed at two points, threatening Grahamville and Coosawhatchie, on the Charleston and Savannah Railroad. All available forces have been drawn from Charleston for defense of those places, and General Smith, who arrived in the night with 1,200 Georgia State troops, was sent at once to the threatened point. Operator at Grahamville this morning reports enemy 5,000 strong, and still landing from transports.

W. J. HARDEE,
Lieutenant-General.

GRAHAMVILLE, *November 30, 1864.*

Lieutenant-General HARDEE:

The enemy have extended both their wings, and are evidently in force. Fight still progressing. The troops have not arrived. We shall need re-enforcements.

G. W. SMITH,
Major-General.

RICHMOND, VA., *November 30, 1864.*

General TAYLOR,
Savannah, Ga.:

Yours of this date received. When General Beauregard leaves Macon for the East you will be necessary in the West. The enemy's purpose is not so fully developed as to determine his operations.

JEFF'N DAVIS.

NOVEMBER 30, 1864—11.30 A. M.

Maj. Gen. JOSEPH WHEELER:

Thank your gallant old command in my name for their brilliant services. I promised it in advance to the people of your native city, and nobly have you redeemed my pledge. General Robertson has arrived and is doing well, though he will be long disabled.

BRAXTON BRAGG.

FIVE MILES FROM WAYNESBOROUGH,
November 30, 1864. (Via Charleston.)

Lieutenant-General HARDEE:

I am moving toward Walker's Bridge to intercept enemy if they move toward Augusta. Have left scouts to see if they move toward Savannah. Enemy's infantry encamped last night on Sparta road to Augusta, and also on Sparta road to Savannah. It is impossible to tell which direction they will go until it is known what march is made to-day.

JOS. WHEELER,
Major-General.

AUGUSTA, *November 30, 1864—6.45 p. m.*

Major-General WHEELER,
Near Walker's Bridge:

General Bragg wishes you, on approach of the enemy, to destroy all bridges and defend line of Brier Creek. Important to keep telegraph line to Millen standing to last moment.

ARCHER ANDERSON,
Lieutenant-Colonel and Assistant Adjutant-General.

FOUR MILES WEST OF BUCK HEAD CHURCH,
November 30, 1864.

General WAYNE:

GENERAL: The enemy with force of infantry encamped last night at Blount's Mills—Blount's Mills is half-way between Louisville and Walker's Bridge. I cannot learn of the enemy's moving down the railroad toward Savannah. There are rumors to that effect, but my scouts have not yet reported.

Respectfully,

JOS. WHEELER,
Major-General.

N. B.—I am moving with all my force, except one small regiment, to get in front of enemy. Captain Dobbs is in command of regiment left here with orders to report direct to you.

J. W.

ON LOUISVILLE AND AUGUSTA ROAD,
BY FARMER'S BRIDGE, THREE MILES FROM LOUISVILLE,
November 30, 1864—1.30 p. m.

General BRAXTON BRAGG:

GENERAL: I have been on rear and left flank of enemy from Macon here. Colonel Breckinridge, with Kentucky brigade, joined me this morning, and we are operating in concert. The enemy still in Louisville. The Fourteenth Corps is out on this road, and has been encamped here since day before yesterday, when the advance reached Louisville. Their army is detained by the swamp at Rocky Comfort Creek. I have not yet ascertained whether the main force is moving on Waynesborough or down the Ogeechee. I estimate their infantry at about 30,000, or less, and their cavalry at from 3,000 to 3,500. They seem very apprehensive of meeting a large force in front, and are hurrying on as rapidly as possible.

Very respectfully, your obedient servant,

S. W. FERGUSON,
Brigadier-General.

AUGUSTA, *November 30, 1864.*

Maj. Gen. SAMUEL JONES:

With the forces sent you must beat back the enemy and hold the Savannah railroad. Prompt and vigorous measures will accomplish it. Sherman, nevertheless, appears to be advancing very slowly, if at all, with his main force. Wheeler has beaten back his cavalry to the Ogeechee, west of Millen.

BRAXTON BRAGG.

AUGUSTA, *November 30, 1864.*

General SAMUEL JONES:

What is your information from the enemy in your district? Did my troops arrive in time for the action? We have opened communication again from here with Savannah. The enemy's infantry is advancing on this point, and our troops must return at the earliest possible moment.

BRAXTON BRAGG.

SAVANNAH, *November 30, 1864—1 a. m.*

General SAMUEL JONES:

Major-General Smith is ordered to Grahamville and Coosawhatchie, and will command there. Are the points threatened not Pocotaligo ——? Major-General Smith will take 1,500 men with him.

W. J. HARDEE,
Lieutenant-General.

SAVANNAH, *November 30, 1864.*

Maj. Gen. S. JONES:

All the troops coming from Augusta and the regiments from Charleston will be stopped on the Charleston and Savannah Railroad, in vicinity of Coosawhatchie and Grahamville.

By command of Lieutenant-General Hardee:

T. B. ROY,
Assistant Adjutant-General.

SAVANNAH, *November 30, 1864.*

General S. JONES:

Hurry forward the re-enforcements from Augusta. Smith is heavily engaged. Has the Thirty-second Georgia been sent forward?

W. J. HARDEE,
Lieutenant-General.

SAVANNAH, *November 30, 1864.*

General S. JONES:

Have re-enforcements passed through Charleston? Hurry them on to Grahamville to General Smith.

W. J. HARDEE,
Lieutenant-General.

SAVANNAH, *November 30, 1864.*

Major-General JONES:

Dispatch received dated 4 p. m. says eight transports going up Broad River with troops aboard, and seven came down without troops. Enemy re-enforcing by every boat that goes up the river. Hurry forward the troops to Grahamville.

W. J. HARDEE.

[First indorsement.]

GENERAL: I send you all these dispatches without acting on any, because the matters embraced are so important that I have thought you had better see them all, as they may suggest additional orders or modifications of those already given.

C. S. S.

[Second indorsement.]

Major STRINGFELLOW:

Hurry forward the troops now in this city to Grahamville. Send your brother to hurry them up, and see what they need in the way of arms, and have them supplied as far as possible. Major Pringle must hurry and start transportation.

[S. JONES,
Major-General.]

GRAHAMVILLE, *November 30, 1864.*

Maj. Gen. SAMUEL JONES:

General Hardee has directed me to turn over the command to the next officer in rank so soon as enough troops arrive from Charleston to relieve the Georgia militia, and has indicated General Robertson as the officer. I have, therefore, told General Robertson that it is necessary for him to remain here. We repulsed the enemy to-day in every attempt they made on our position. They had largely superior forces, but in repeated attacks during six hours failed to drive us an inch from the position first assumed by us. Hurry up all the forces intended for this section.

G. W. SMITH,
Major-General.

COLUMBIA, *November 30, 1864.*

General SAMUEL JONES:

The battalion of cadets will report to you for service within this State with these conditions: that I shall resume control of them at any moment that I or my successor may think proper. When Colonel De Saussure's forces join them I wish them to compose a part of his command for the present.

M. L. BONHAM.

COLUMBIA, *November 30, 1864.*

Maj. Gen. S. JONES:

By order of the Governor I have directed the State troops who have not rendezvoused at Hamburg, but who are en route for the coast, to report to you to be forwarded. Will you order transportation for them?

A. C. GARLINGTON,
Aide-de-Camp and Inspector-General.

RALEIGH, *November 30, 1864.*

Hon. J. A. SEDDON:

Can you give me any information of affairs in Georgia to lay before the Legislature that would assist in inducing them to authorize sending the State troops beyond the State line? Such a proposition is now before our Legislature, and my total ignorance of the situation prevents my urging it with sufficient force. Answer immediately.

Z. B. VANCE.

WAR DEPARTMENT, C. S. A.,
Richmond, Va., November 30, 1864.

Governor Z. B. VANCE,
Raleigh, N. C.:

There is urgent need for more forces to meet the advance of General Sherman's army, and to prevent its junction with forces being landed and threatening movement at Pocotaligo. Latest accounts make it still doubtful whether Sherman is not marching on Augusta. General Wheeler has just telegraphed that the infantry of the enemy have turned to a road leading to that city. General Bragg has suggested that as the movement near Pocotaligo frees Wilmington from the danger of attack, the reserves from North Carolina should be sent to him, and the matter is now under General Lee's consideration. It would be wise, as well as patriotic, on the part of North Carolina to give all assistance possible to defeat or frustrate the designs of Sherman while remote from her borders. General Beauregard telegraphs his opinion that Sherman's ultimate design is to re-enforce General Grant.

J. A. SEDDON,
Secretary of War.

AUGUSTA, *December 1, 1864—12 m.*

Col. JOHN B. SALE,
Military Secretary, Richmond:

* * * The [enemy's] cavalry having been driven in, the enemy's main force was yesterday found near Louisville, with strong outposts in this direction. They have secured large supplies in the country; but our cavalry is now all up, and it is hoped they will be prevented, to a great extent, in future. The report from Savannah of the enemy's entrance into Millen on 27th was premature. Telegraphic communication was reopened to Savannah by that route yesterday. Enemy is just now reported as at Station 9, on Central railroad, advancing.

BRAXTON BRAGG.

(Extract submitted to the Secretary of War by Colonel Sale.)

AUGUSTA, *December 1, 1864.*

Col. JOHN B. SALE,
Military Secretary, Richmond:

Following received from Lieutenant-General Taylor, at Savannah:

General Hardee is at Grahamville. No fighting there since yesterday evening, when enemy was driven five miles, leaving their dead on the field.

BRAXTON BRAGG.

AUGUSTA, *December 1, 1864.*

General S. COOPER,
Assistant Adjutant-General:

Your dispatch* to General Beauregard has been received and forwarded. I have had no intelligence from him.

BRAXTON BRAGG.

GRAHAMVILLE, *December 1, 1864.*

General MCLAWS:

The enemy are now seriously threatening Coosawhatchie. It is absolutely necessary to keep the two trains here at present.

G. W. SMITH.

HEADQUARTERS ARMIES OF THE CONFEDERATE STATES,
Augusta, Ga., December 1, 1864.

Major-General WHEELER:

GENERAL: General Ferguson reports from Farmer's Bridge road. His note is inclosed,† though it is hoped you have made a junction ere this. The general is instructed to report to you. With this increased force it is hoped you will be able to cover the enemy's front and retard his movements much, whatever may be his line of march. The bridges, causeways, &c., on all creeks should be destroyed; forest trees should be felled at every point where they will obstruct the march; fences may be pulled down and used—indeed, every expedient which ingenuity may suggest should be adopted to retard the enemy's movements. At the same time you should keep your fighting force close in his front, so as to make him work under every disadvantage. To enable you successfully to carry out these orders you are authorized to impress, for temporary use, all the laborers and tools necessary, and to use the means of the people in the country, as far as they may be of advantage. Supplies of all kinds useful to the enemy and not required for your use must be destroyed. You will observe by the map that Rocky Creek still remains to be crossed if the enemy move to Savannah, and Brier Creek should he move here. These swampy streams are represented as impassable, except at the regular bridges, and afford you the means of greatly retarding the enemy. Let it be known through the country generally that we are very largely re-enforced here and at Savannah, and are prepared for any movement on us. We have troops from Virginia, North Carolina, and South Carolina, and the troops from Macon

*Of November 30, p. 911.
†See November 30, 1.30 p. m., p. 912.

commenced arriving in Savannah on 29th ultimo. A good many volunteer and militia companies of cavalry are out about Brier Creek. They should be collected by you and used to obstruct roads and pick up stragglers. Brigadier-General Young, with part of Hampton's cavalry, will join you soon.

I am, general, very respectfully, your obedient servant,

ARCHER ANDERSON,
Lieutenant-Colonel and Assistant Adjutant-General.

P. S.—I inclose a sketch* of the crossings of Brier Creek. A copy of this dispatch has been sent to General Ferguson.

A. A.

HEADQUARTERS ALLEN'S DIVISION OF CAVALRY,
December 1, 1864.

Lieut. M. G. HUDSON,
Acting Assistant Adjutant-General:

LIEUTENANT: I have the honor to report that I have encamped my command on a road leading from the road we came yesterday to Waynesborough, and near the latter road. The intersection is about six miles from our camp of last night. I have sent scouts on all the roads leading toward Louisville, and will also send a scout across the Ogeechee, as directed by General Wheeler.

Very respectfully, your obedient servant,

WM. W. ALLEN,
Brigadier-General, Commanding.

MONTEITH, *December 1, 1864.*
(Received 11 p. m.)

Capt. R. W. B. ELLIOTT,
Assistant Adjutant-General:

A courier has just arrived from No. 2, Central railroad, and reports as follows: That the enemy's cavalry are three miles from Millen, and the infantry seven miles from there. A courier from General Wheeler reports the enemy making for Augusta. General Wheeler wishes 40,000 rounds of ammunition for army and navy pistols sent to Augusta. This courier left his camp yesterday evening.

A. L. HARTRIDGE,
Major, Commanding.

AUGUSTA, *December 1, 1864.*

General SAMUEL JONES:

Send everything you can to Grahamville, so as to crush out the enemy in our front there, and be ready to meet the main army thereafter. Sherman's progress is slow. His main body yesterday at Louisville.

BRAXTON BRAGG.

---

*Not found.

SUMMERVILLE, *December 1, 1864.*

Maj. Gen. SAMUEL JONES:

Will be in Charleston at 1 o'clock to-day with 2,000 men.

L. S. BAKER,
Brigadier-General.

HEADQUARTERS DISTRICT OF SOUTH CAROLINA,
Charleston, December 1, 1864.

General ROBERT RANSOM,
Charleston, S. C.:

GENERAL: Yours of this morning has been laid before the major-general commanding. He directs me to say in reply that no answer was made to the communication referred to because he supposed that you understood, from verbal statements, that it was impossible to give you the men or labor called for. The evils alluded to in connection with the present system of obtaining labor are patent, and have been made the subject of many communications to the Governor of this State and the Department at Richmond. It seems, however, that they are beyond the control or correction of the major-general commanding. By reference to the act of Congress authorizing the impressment of slaves you will observe that it can be done in such States as have legislated on the subject only under the State law, and as South Carolina has provided for this subject her law must govern. By its terms the impressment can be made for thirty days only, and the slaves must be discharged at the expiration of that term. The disregard of this provision in some cases is regarded by Governor Bonham in his late message as one of the main reasons to which he attributed the failure in the execution of the law. He points out the evil arising from the short term of service required, and asks the Legislature to correct them. It is to be hoped that this will be done. Under existing orders from department headquarters the chief engineer has control of and is responsible for the efficient working of these slaves. He was notified this morning that 2,000 would be here during the day, and of that number as many as the exigencies of the service elsewhere allowed will be assigned to your sub-district.

Very respectfully, your obedient servant,

C. S. STRINGFELLOW,
Assistant Adjutant-General.

MONTGOMERY, *December 2, 1864.*
(Via Savannah. Received 4th.)

General S. COOPER,
Adjutant and Inspector General:

Telegram of 30th received here on my way to Mobile. I shall repair forthwith to Atlantic coast.

G. T. BEAUREGARD.

C. S. HEADQUARTERS MILITARY DIVISION OF THE WEST,
Montgomery, Ala., December 2, 1864.

General E. KIRBY SMITH,
Commanding Trans-Mississippi Department:

GENERAL: You are probably aware that the Army of Tennessee, under General J. B. Hood, has penetrated into Middle Tennessee as far as Columbia, and that the enemy is concentrating all his available forces, under General Thomas, to oppose him. It is even reliably reported that the forces under Generals A. J. Smith, in Missouri, and Steele, in Arkansas, have been sent to re-enforce Thomas. It becomes, then, absolutely necessary, to insure the success of Hood, either that you should send him two or more divisions, or that you at once threaten Missouri, in order to compel the enemy to recall the re-enforcements he is sending to General Thomas. I beg to urge upon you prompt and decisive action. The fate of the country may depend upon the result of Hood's campaign in Tennessee. Sherman's army has lately abandoned Atlanta on a venturesome march across Georgia to the Atlantic coast about Savannah. His object is, besides the destruction of public and private property, probably to re-enforce Grant and compel Lee to abandon Richmond. It is hoped that Sherman may be prevented from effecting his object, but should it be otherwise, the success of Hood in Tennessee and Kentucky would counterbalance the moral effect of the loss of Richmond. Hence the urgent necessity of either re-enforcing Hood or making a diversion in Missouri in his favor.

Hoping that you may give us the desired assistance, I remain, your obedient servant,

G. T. BEAUREGARD,
General.

AUGUSTA, *December 2, 1864.*

General S. COOPER:

Following received from Lieutenant-General Hardee, dated yesterday, at Savannah:

I have just returned from the front. The enemy was badly whipped, and has retired. Coosawhatchie, another point on railroad, is threatened, but do not apprehend a serious attack.

BRAXTON BRAGG.

(Copies sent President and Secretary of War.)

GRAHAMVILLE, *December 2, 1864.*

General S. COOPER:

A force of infantry, artillery, and cavalry, under Foster, attempted to gain the railroad at this point, but were met and repulsed. A force of marines, under Dahlgren, attempted to gain the railroad at Coosawhatchie, but were met at Bee's Creek and repulsed.

W. J. HARDEE,
Lieutenant-General.

(Copies sent President, Secretary of War, Generals Lee and Bragg.)

GRAHAMVILLE, *December 2, 1864.*

General MCLAWS:

The enemy is moving upon us. Put about 1,000 men in the cars immediately, and hold them in readiness to come to this point.

W. J. HARDEE,
Lieutenant-General.

GRAHAMVILLE, *December 2, 1864—7.30 a. m.*

Major-General MCLAWS:

The enemy have again retreated. There is no occasion for sending the 1,000 men. What news from up the Central railroad?

W. J. HARDEE,
Lieutenant-General.

GRAHAMVILLE, *December 2, 1864.*

General MCLAWS:

Thirteen hundred troops will leave Augusta this evening for Savannah; 1,000 will leave here this evening for Savannah, and 1,200 more will follow as soon as transportation can be had. I will come to Savannah by first train.

W. J. HARDEE,
Lieutenant-General.

GRAHAMVILLE, *December 2, 1864.*

Major-General MCLAWS.

I have telegraphed superintendent of Charleston and Savannah Railroad for trains to transport 1,200 troops from Coosawhatchie and Grahamville to Savannah immediately. See to it.

W. J. HARDEE,
Lieutenant-General.

NO. 6, CENTRAL RAILROAD, *December 2, 1864.*

General MCLAWS:

Just received following from No. 7:

The scouts from up the railroad left Millen at 6 o'clock this morning. They heard the drums of the enemy at 8.30. Mr. Heard, agent at this place, went to within one mile of Millen at 9 o'clock. The enemy then occupied that place. Three scouts are now coming down the Middle Ground road with dispatches from Colonel Johnson. Will report as soon as they arrive.

E. T. LUDWIG,
Operator.

WAYNE,
Major-General.

NO. 7, CENTRAL RAILROAD, *December 2, 1864.*

Major-General MCLAWS:

At 10 o'clock this a. m. a body of the enemy's cavalry occupied Millen. Colonel Johnson with some of his men and three scouts from this place were at the car-sheds when one of the enemy rode up, about 200 yards in advance. He was taken prisoner, and scouts report that he told Colonel Johnson that their infantry were just above the railroad bridge across Buck Head Creek, half a mile above Millen, and that a body of cavalry were going down the other side of the Ogeechee. Scout just returned from Clifton Ferry, about two miles above this place, reports that a small number [are] already across. He fired on one of their vedettes, and came in to report. He has just gone back for further information.

E. T. LUDWIG,
Operator.

HEADQUARTERS FOURTH BRIGADE, GEORGIA MILITIA,
Altamaha Bridge, December 2, 1864.

R. W. B. ELLIOTT,
Assistant Adjutant-General:

SIR: In accordance with instructions from General McLaws I proceeded on yesterday to this point. I left Colonel Sims, with the Twelfth Regiment, at the west end of Ogeechee bridge, with instructions to hold that and King's Bridge. I have made my headquarters, with two regiments, on the island on the east side of Morgan's Lake. I have a company posted at the eastern trestle-work of this crossing, a guard at the east end of the main bridge. At Johnston Station there is a militia company from McIntosh County, picketing down the river. At Doctor Town, on the west side of the river, there are three small companies of militia; they have sent a scouting party up the river on the east side, and have mounted pickets, one at Clark's Bluff and one at Pinhominy, both below on the west side of the river. My position here is such that I can go easily to either side of the river. My force is, however, not large; the brigade is a small one at best, and many of the men dropped out at home on their way here. I have, aggregate, at Ogeechee, 147 men; at Altamaha, 220 men. I could not make a more equal distribution without breaking the regiments, which, in consequence of the want of field officers, I did not think wise. We are now on the second day without regular rations.

Respectfully,

H. K. McKAY,
Brigadier-General, Commanding.

DOCTOR TOWN, *December 2, 1864.*

Col. T. B. ROY,
Assistant Adjutant-General:

Will arrive at 11 a. m. with 600 men. Please send inspector to point out camping-grounds. Send rations to depot.

L. VON ZINKEN,
Colonel, Commanding Brigade.

AUGUSTA, *December 2, 1864.*

General WHEELER:

The movements of the enemy yesterday indicate a tendency toward Savannah. You should press down upon him, keep in his front, cut off his foraging parties, and skirmish with him hourly. He should not be allowed to get between you and Savannah. The officers who tore up the railroad bridge should be removed.

BRAXTON BRAGG.

AUGUSTA, *December 2, 1864.*

General WHEELER:

Have your scout well to the rear of the enemy, and be prepared to strike. I leave here this evening with 10,000 men; will be followed by portion of General Wade Hampton's cavalry, under General Young. Answer by 9 o'clock, if possible, or have courier meet me at Waynesborough.

BRAXTON BRAGG.

HEADQUARTERS WILLIAMS' KENTUCKY BRIGADE,
Junction of Waynesborough and Warrenton and Farmer's Bridge Roads, December 2, 1864—5 p. m.

ASST. ADJT. GEN., WHEELER'S CAVALRY CORPS:

LIEUTENANT: Since receiving General Wheeler's order to report to General Cobb I have been operating in the rear of the left flank of the enemy; have been engaged several times. I followed Howard's Right Wing, consisting of Fifteenth and Seventeenth Corps, to near McIntyre's, on Central railroad; then moved to Milledgeville, and crossed the Oconee; then by forced march crossed Ogeechee at Fenn's Bridge. I have reason to believe the Fifteenth Corps crossed Oconee at Jackson's Ferry, two miles above Central railroad bridge; the Seventeenth, at Ball's Ferry, six miles below the railroad. I struck the Twentieth Corps on Tuesday a mile and a half from Louisville, on the Fenn's Bridge road; on Wednesday the Fourteenth Corps, two miles and a half from Louisville, on Patterson's Bridge road, and three miles from Louisville, on Farmer's Bridge road; and on yesterday had a very severe fight with a large cavalry force (part of Kilpatrick's corps) nine miles from Louisville, on the Waynesborough road. I have lost many men and valuable officers, and I have captured some prisoners; some I sent to Macon, some turned over to General Ferguson, with whom I have been co-operating, though not under his orders, he thinking it best for us to act independently, but close enough to support each other. A large force of cavalry and at least two divisions of infantry, scouts report, left Louisville yesterday morning. The infantry encamped on the place of Mrs. Netherland, some thirteen miles from Louisville. I think the main force of Slocum have passed down the two Savannah roads—the one to Birdville, the other near the railroad. If I do not receive orders to-night I will move to the Waynesborough road, thence to the Birdville road. I have not definite information of your headquarters.

I am, very respectfully, your obedient servant,

W. C. P. BRECKINRIDGE,
Colonel, Commanding Brigade.

HEADQUARTERS LEWIS' BRIGADE,
Ray's Bridge, December 2, 1864.

Major-General WHEELER:

GENERAL: At the time of receiving your order to halt where I was I had three regiments with me, about three-quarters of a mile from Waynesborough, on Ray's Bridge road, the remaining two regiments on their way from railroad to Ray's Bridge to join me at Waynesborough. Apprehending an attempt of the enemy to reach Ray's Bridge, I left one regiment near Waynesborough and two others disposed and fortified on the road toward the bridge. One regiment is here at this point and the other at railroad bridge. I have sent scouts on all the roads in the direction of Millen. I have not sent scouts in the direction of No. 9 or Louisville, for the reason that I met a scouting party sent by you from Harrison's brigade upon those roads. No enemy have appeared in front of Waynesborough, or nearer than four miles. I have received direct and reliable information that no enemy had been at Millen up to 8 a. m., nor have they been seen anywhere east or below Waynesborough and Millen road. An intelligent gentleman now present, Dr. T. A. Ward, states the first bridge below railroad bridge is Ray's, two miles in air line; Thompson's, six miles below Ray's; Gadby's, six or seven miles below Thompson's; Ellison's, seven or eight miles below Ellison's [Thompson's?]. To each of these bridges I send immediately an officer and five men as you direct. I think, with my brigade in its present disposition, that I can hold the enemy in check for some time.

Respectfully, yours, &c.,

JOS. H. LEWIS,
Brigadier-General.

GRAHAMVILLE, *December 2, 1864.*

General SAMUEL JONES:

Troops coming from Augusta must not stop in Charleston, but be hurried forward to Savannah. I leave for Savannah this afternoon.

W. J. HARDEE,
Lieutenant-General.

GRAHAMVILLE, *December 2, 1864.*

Maj. Gen. SAMUEL JONES:

Send Captain Brooks with the 270 men to Savannah instead of Grahamville.

W. J. HARDEE,
Lieutenant-General.

AUGUSTA, *December 2, 1864.*

General SAMUEL JONES:

Thirteen hundred South Carolina militia, under Colonel De Saussure, will leave here for Savannah at 6 p. m. Provide transportation to Savannah on their arrival.

By command of General Bragg:

M. B. McMICKEN,
Lieutenant-Colonel and Chief Quartermaster.

RICHMOND, *December 2, 1864.*

[General BRAXTON BRAGG:]

GENERAL: I trust you will pardon my presumption in writing you on military subjects, but my knowledge of the country and the railway lines in Georgia and South Carolina emboldens me to offer a suggestion, which I am certain you will receive in the spirit in which it is offered. Of course it will occur to you that the moment the enemy reaches Millen, in Georgia, and any point on the Charleston and Savannah Railroad in South Carolina, Savannah becomes hopelessly isolated, and can neither raise re-enforcements from Augusta or Charleston, nor send any to either of those places. Some place must be given up, however, and it were better Savannah than Charleston. But there is a large amount of most valuable rolling-stock at Savannah, and many locomotives, tools, machine shops, cotton and tobacco. The cotton and tobacco should be destroyed, if necessary, and the rolling-stock, &c.,

run out before the Charleston and Savannah road is cut. Should Sherman reach any point on that road, or a column come out from Beaufort and occupy it, everything of value in Savannah must be lost; for if well out on the Gulf road to Thomasville, a raiding party of 1,000 men would find no difficulty in destroying it. It is impossible for us here to say where Sherman is going. Your last telegram left him at No. 9, ten miles above Millen. Supposing the rear column may reach Grahamville, he may move down the Central road to Savannah, in which case no concentration can be made against him, as he would tear up the road as he advanced, whilst both flanks would be protected, the one by the Savannah and the other by the Ogeechee River. Such forces as might be at Savannah, unable to escape to Charleston and beyond the reach of re-enforcements, would have to retire toward Thomasville. Indeed, if the enemy should establish himself on the Charleston and Savannah road—either by moving up from the sea and down from Georgia—Savannah, Southern Georgia, and all Florida would pass into his hands. This will be evident upon an inspection of the map. It would seem to be of the first importance, therefore, to save the movable railway property at Savannah, of which there is a large amount, and to do this it must be removed before the Charleston and Savannah road is cut, unless Sherman cross the river opposite Millen, in which case it might be moved up the Central road to that point.

Of Sherman's ultimate object there can be but little doubt, viz, the reduction of Savannah or Charleston. If the former, then he will establish a water base there and throw forward his advance to Millen, and thus cut our communications. If Charleston be his object, as it probably is, then his establishment at that place would leave him only sixty miles to march to reach Branchville, where he would place himself astride the only line by which we can communicate with the South. In this event his base would be unassailable and his flanks, admirably protected by a river and swamp on either hand, would be free from attack. For four years the enemy has tried to penetrate the Confederacy from the north and east by land. He reached Atlanta it is true, but found it impossible to keep open his communications, since the further he advanced the longer and more difficult of defense became his base and line of communication. This policy, it now appears, has been changed. Hereafter he will operate from the sea or some of its tributaries. This makes his lease safe, and renders it easy to protect his short communications. This policy reduces the length of his communications to sixty miles from Charleston to Branchville, whereas before it was near 500 miles from Louisville to Atlanta. After Charleston, Wilmington will probably be the next point of attack, and then Richmond. These ideas have been floating through my mind. There may be nothing in them. If so, you will be sure to find it out and no harm will come of them. All I can hope is that you will excuse me for presuming to send them to you. It strikes me that your suggestion of concentration is the only alternative left us, and should be adopted. We must make up our minds to abandon some place and concentrate for a stubborn resistance. There is nothing new here. I do not think Grant has the least idea of attacking Lee. He is only maneuvering to prevent his sending re-enforcements to Georgia. Colonel Forsyth is here and well. The president has disapproved of the finding in the case of his son Charles.

Very truly, yours,

P. W. ALEXANDER.

AUGUSTA, *December 3, 1864—6 p. m.*
(Received 12.30 a. m. 4th.)

Col. JOHN B. SALE,
Military Secretary, Richmond:

A strong force of the enemy's cavalry and infantry advanced from Louisville, and encamped last night six miles from Waynesborough. They turned off this morning toward Savannah. Our cavalry is pressing on the rear, and all available means are being thrown to their front by rail. There is time yet for any assistance which can be spared to be sent by way of Charleston.

BRAXTON BRAGG.

[First indorsement.]

Respectfully submitted to His Excellency the President, as information.

JNO. B. SALE,
Colonel and Military Secretary.

[Second indorsement.]

SECRETARY OF WAR:

What has been or can be done to augment force, &c.?

J. D.

MONTGOMERY, ALA., *December 3, 1864—7 a. m.*

Lieut. Gen. W. J. HARDEE,
Savannah, Ga.:

I leave to-day for Augusta and Savannah. Construct loop-holes and embrasures on defenses of latter city. Works along overflows around city are essential. Obstruct all roads from Millen to Port Royal, Ossabaw Sound, and Brunswick.

G. T. BEAUREGARD.

MONTEITH, *December 3, 1864.*

Capt. R. W. B. ELLIOTT:

The roads are so obstructed between here and Sister's Ferry that I am unable to get a courier to the commander of the C. S. steamer Macon.

A. L. HARTRIDGE,
Major, &c.

SPECIAL ORDERS, No. 7. } HDQRS. ARMIES CONFEDERATE STATES,
Augusta, December 3, 1864.

* * * * * * *

II. Brigadier-General Young will immediately proceed, with all the men he has mounted, in the direction of Waynesborough, join Major-General Wheeler, and receive his orders.

* * * * * * *

By order of General Bragg:

ARCHER ANDERSON,
Assistant Adjutant-General.

HEADQUARTERS,
Augusta, December 3, 1864—10 a. m.

Major-General WHEELER,
Commanding Cavalry Corps:

GENERAL: The commanding general desires me to impress upon you the importance of immediately driving back upon their infantry the enemy's cavalry, now apparently pressing in this direction. Your force, in his opinion, is too much scattered; it should be gathered up; and the enemy's cavalry being pushed back, unremitting effort should be made to harass their main body and impede their march.

I have the honor to be, general, very respectfully, your obedient servant,

ARCHER ANDERSON,
Assistant Adjutant-General.

AUGUSTA, *December 3, 1864—12 m.*

General WHEELER:

In reply to your questions whether you shall operate on Sherman's front or flank, General Bragg cannot instruct. Your own judgment must determine. Main object is to retard and harass enemy.

ARCHER ANDERSON,
Assistant Adjutant-General.

NEAR BEAVER DAM, *December 3, 1864—10 a. m.*

Major-General WHEELER,
Commanding Cavalry:

GENERAL: On yesterday morning the enemy drove me from Buck Head Church, and I fell back to Lawton Station. After remaining at the station some time they came against me in large force of cavalry, and I retreated to Beaver Dam Creek. I have scouts out on the roads, and will dispatch any information they may gain. I destroyed the bridge at the church, but did not get your dispatch in time to destroy the other bridges. I sent a lieutenant with a squad of men to destroy Jones' Bridge, but he has not returned.

Respectfully, general, your obedient servant,

S. P. DOBBS,
Captain, Commanding Ninth Alabama.

P. S.—I sent you two couriers yesterday and neither have returned.

S. P. D.

SAVANNAH, *December 3, 1864.*

General JONES:

Order troops which left Augusta yesterday to stop [at] Coosawhatchie and report to General Chesnut.

W. J. HARDEE,
Lieutenant-General.

SAVANNAH, *December 3, 1864.*

General SAMUEL JONES:

Send the cadets to join the militia at Grahamville

W. J. HARDEE,
Lieutenant-General.

COLUMBIA, *December 3, 1864.*

Maj. Gen. SAMUEL JONES:

Telegram received at 9 p. m. I do not wish the cadets sent to Savannah. I have received no request to send them, and know no reason for it.

M. L. BONHAM.

COLUMBIA, *December 3, 1864.*

Maj. Gen. S. JONES:

If General Bragg has expressed no wish for the cadets to remain at Charleston send them to Grahamville, to report to Colonel De Saussure, at that place. Since I telegraphed you General Bragg telegraphs me that De Saussure's destination was Grahamville, but put Savannah through mistake. He has been halted at the former place.

M. L. BONHAM.

AUGUSTA, *December 4, 1864.*
(Received 1 p. m.)

Col. JOHN B. SALE,
Military Secretary, Richmond:

The column is moving on what is known as "Eastern road to Savannah." There are several ferries from mouth of Brier Creek to Charleston and Savannah Railroad bridge; none below that. General Hardee reports he is patrolling river with a gun-boat. I have had all ferry-boats destroyed, and ordered all roads to and from river to be broken up and blockaded by felling heavy timber. The roads all pass by causeway to the river, on both sides, over dense swamps. None of enemy's forces remain near Macon, and from best information I can obtain it is thought all of ours have left there for Savannah. The Georgia militia who were on Central railroad moved back toward Savannah, and at last accounts were at Station 4½, our cavalry, however, far in advance of them.

BRAXTON BRAGG.

SAVANNAH, *December 4, 1864.*
(Received 5th.)

General S. COOPER,
Adjutant and Inspector General:

Skirmishing with the enemy's infantry this evening at Station 4½, Central railroad, forty-five miles from the city. Two corps of the enemy reported by prisoners to be marching on either side of the Ogeechee. The defense of the South Carolina railroad from Savannah to Charleston requires 3,000 men. Can I expect re-enforcements from Richmond?

W. J. HARDEE,
Lieutenant-General.

SAVANNAH, *December 4, 1864.*

Major-General McLAWS:

Cars will be sent you to-morrow for 3,000 troops. Withdraw to the outer line of defenses, and dispose your troops on that line; remain in charge of them.

By order of Lieutenant-General Hardee:

T. B. ROY,
Assistant Adjutant-General.

No. 3, ATLANTIC AND GULF RAILROAD,
December 4, 1864.

Major-General McLAWS:

The President having ordered my return to my department I cannot remain here longer, unless positively ordered.

R. TAYLOR,
Lieutenant-General.

CIRCULAR.] HEADQUARTERS CAVALRY CORPS,
In the Field, December 4, 1864.

In future, commanders of troops, in falling back before the enemy, will send reliable officers and men, at least one day in advance, to instruct citizens in which direction to drive their stock.

On the enemy's approach all horses, mules, and other stock that citizens have left on the enemy's line of march will be driven off, and proper receipts left for the same. When no owner can be found accurate accounts will be kept so that stock can be reclaimed by the owner.

By order of Major-General Wheeler:

M. G. HUDSON,
First Lieutenant and Aide-de-Camp, Actg. Asst. Adjt. Gen.

HEADQUARTERS WILLIAMS' KENTUCKY BRIGADE,
Dr. Dillard's, three miles from Farmer's Bridge, on Farmer's Bridge and Louisville Roads, December 4, 1864—11 p. m.

Lieutenant HUDSON,
General Wheeler's Aide-de-Camp:

LIEUTENANT: I received your order of 8 a. m. yesterday at 12 m., and moved to strike the enemy's flank. At 12 p. m. last night I received another order to report to you at Thomas' Station, and proceeded this morning at daylight in that direction; but finding it impossible to get there on account of the enemy, I attempted to join you at Waynesborough, and, getting within a mile and a half of town, I was again cut off, and had to fall back to this point. I will report with my command to-morrow morning.

Very respectfully, &c.,

W. C. P. BRECKINRIDGE,
Colonel, Commanding, &c.

SAVANNAH, *December 4, 1864.*

General S. JONES:

I need 600 arms and accouterments for the South Carolina militia now at Grahamville. Send the arms if you have them; also ammunition to suit.

W. J. HARDEE,
Lieutenant-General.

SAVANNAH, *December 4, 1864.*

Maj. Gen. S. JONES:

Make your headquarters at Pocotaligo, or some other convenient point, and take immediate charge of the forces for the defense of the Charleston and Savannah Railroad.

W. J. HARDEE,
Lieutenant-General.

SAVANNAH, *December 4, 1864.*

General JONES:

What troops left Charleston this morning for Savannah? If any, stop them at Pocotaligo.

W. J. HARDEE,
Lieutenant-General.

SAVANNAH, *December 4, 1864.*

General SAMUEL JONES:

Re-enforcements are needed at Pocotaligo immediately; see that they are sent.

W. J. HARDEE.

ADAMS' RUN, *December 4, 1864.*

Major-General JONES:

A regiment of Yankee cavalry is reported moving toward Combahee bridge. I have nothing but some heavy artillery in that sub-district.

B. H. ROBERTSON.
Brigadier-General.

HEADQUARTERS ARMIES OF THE CONFEDERATE STATES,
Augusta, December 5, 1864.

Col. JOHN B. SALE,
Military Secretary:

The following just received from General Wheeler:

NEAR WALKER'S BRIDGE, *December 4, 1864—6 p. m.*

Pursuant to instructions we drove enemy's cavalry upon infantry and attacked about midnight. The infantry was occupied in tearing up railroad near Thomas' Station. At daylight this morning Fourteenth Corps and Kilpatrick's cavalry advanced and attacked my position. My command had been necessarily spread out over two or three miles to procure forage, but was quickly concentrated to resist the attack. Enemy made several charges upon the position which I had taken, all of which were repulsed by fire from behind breast-works and by counter-charges. Enemy's vastly superior forces, which completely enveloped my flanks, compelled me to retire toward Brier Creek. A number of officers and men were killed and wounded, including Colonel Gaines, commanding brigade, severely wounded. Enemy's loss very heavy; General Kilpatrick reported wounded. My officers and men behaved most gallantly.

NEAR WALKER'S BRIDGE, *December 4, 1864—8 p. m.*

Enemy have all moved east of Buck Head Creek. They appear to be encamped on railroad, from Waynesborough to Station 7, on Savannah road. Possibly their advance is nearer Savannah than Station 7. I have had three brigades on enemy's front and rear, and balance of my command on their flank. Seventeenth Corps crossed Ogeechee, from Emanuel to Burke County, opposite 95, on Thursday. On Wednesday Fifteenth Corps moved from Louisville toward Station 90. Enemy's cavalry passed through Waynesborough, stealing horses in Emanuel County. General Sherman in person reported near Thomas' Station to-day.

NEAR WALKER'S BRIDGE, *December 5, 1864—4.30 a. m.*

Enemy's infantry and cavalry left Waynesborough going toward Millen; they were in very large force, both infantry and cavalry. Everything now appears to be moving toward Savannah.

BRAXTON BRAGG.

AUGUSTA, *December 5, 1864.*

General S. COOPER,
Adjutant and Inspector General:

From two sources (unofficial) I learn General Beauregard left Macon on 1st and was in Montgomery on 2d. I again send a copy of your dispatch to him, to be telegraphed from Macon.

BRAXTON BRAGG.

SAVANNAH, *December 5, 1864.*

Major-General JONES:

You are placed in charge of the entire line of the Charleston and Savannah Railroad. It is suggested that there should be a force at Green Pond. You will keep a movable force of 500 infantry and one section of artillery on a train, ready to move at a moment's notice to any threatened points. A train has already been furnished General Chesnut for this purpose.

By command of Lieutenant-General Hardee:

T. B. ROY,
Assistant Adjutant-General.

SAVANNAH, *December 5, 1864.*

Major-General JONES:

Colonel Colcock has been sent up the Savannah River with a battery and a section of artillery and a company of cavalry, and the gun-boat Macon, which has reached Sister's Ferry, has been ordered to patrol as high up the river as practicable. Lee has been ordered to furnish the transportation you need.

T. B. ROY,
Assistant Adjutant-General.

SAVANNAH, *December 5, 1864.*

General S. JONES:

Last information from Wheeler is that all movements of the enemy tend toward Savannah. We still hold Station 4½, Central railroad.

T. B. ROY,
Assistant Adjutant-General.

GRAHAMVILLE, *December 5, 1864.*

Maj. Gen. SAM. JONES:

The gun-boats in position off Dawson's Bluff shelling the works protecting Coosawhatchie. Captain Kanapaux asks for 20-pounder Parrotts; can you furnish them to him?

JAS. CHESNUT, JR.,
Brigadier-General.

COOSAWHATCHIE, *December 5, 1864.*

Major STRINGFELLOW,
Assistant Adjutant-General:

My scouts reported the enemy advancing at 1 o'clock to-day, with artillery and infantry. General Chesnut telegraphed me at 3 o'clock that scouts reported the enemy advancing on the Bee's Creek breastworks in considerable force. Several barges are reported coming up the Coosawhatchie River. They advanced their pickets within 200 yards of Bee's Creek works, four miles distant. We fired on them, and they retired. They are still in our front, four or five miles distant. I have about 1,600 men of all arms. I will dispatch you again as soon as scouts come in. We need more artillery.

L. J. GARTRELL,
Brigadier-General, Commanding.

COOSAWHATCHIE, *December 5, 1864—7 p. m.*

Major STRINGFELLOW,
Assistant Adjutant-General:

Enemy's gun-boats, five in number, retired half a mile lower down the river. Their infantry and artillery have also retired about three miles beyond our outer works. All quiet to-night.

L. J. GARTRELL,
Brigadier-General, Commanding.

AUGUSTA, GA., *December 6, 1864.*

His Excellency JEFFERSON DAVIS,
President of the Confederate States:

SIR: Your letter of the 30th ultimo, acknowledging the receipt of my telegram of 24th of November, was received by me on the road from Macon to this place. With the limited reliable means at our command I believe that all that could be has been done, under existing circumstances, to oppose the advance of Sherman's forces toward the Atlantic coast. That we have not thus far been more successful none can regret more than myself, but he will doubtless be prevented from capturing Augusta, Charleston, and Savannah, and he may yet be made to experience serious loss before reaching the coast.

On the 16th of November, when about leaving Tuscumbia, Ala., on a tour of inspection to Corinth, Miss., I was informed by General Hood of the report just received by him that Sherman would probably move from Atlanta into Georgia. I instructed him at once to repeat his orders to General Wheeler to watch closely Sherman's movements, and should he move as reported, to attack and harass him at all favorable points. I telegraphed to Lieutenant-General Taylor, at Selma, Ala., to call on Governor Watts, of Alabama, and Governor Clark, of Mississippi, for all the State troops that they could furnish, and with all the available movable forces of his department to keep himself in readiness to move at a moment's notice to the assistance of Maj. Gens. Howell Cobb and G. W. Smith, who were then at or about Griffin, Ga., threatening Atlanta. I also telegraphed to General Cobb to call upon Governor Brown, of Georgia, and Governor Bonham, of South Carolina, for all the State troops that could be collected. I made all necessary preparations to repair forthwith to Georgia in the event of Sherman's executing his reported movement.

On my arrival at Corinth, on the 18th of November, having been informed that Sherman had commenced his movement, I issued all necessary orders to meet the emergency, including an order to General Hood to send one division of cavalry (Jackson's) to re-enforce Wheeler, but this order was suspended by him, his objection being that his cavalry could not be reduced without endangering the success of his campaign in Tennessee, and that General Wheeler already had thirteen brigades under his command. I finally instructed him to send only one brigade, if he contemplated taking the offensive at once, as had already been decided upon. I then left Corinth for Macon, where I arrived on 24th of November.

I did not countermand the campaign into Tennessee to pursue Sherman with Hood's army for the following reasons:

First. The roads and creeks from the Tennessee to the Coosa Rivers across Sand and Lookout Mountains had been, by the prevailing heavy rains, rendered almost impassable to artillery and wagon trains.

Second. General Sherman, with an army better appointed, had already the start of about 275 miles, on comparatively good roads. The transfer of Hood's army into Georgia could not have been more expeditious by railway than by marching through the country, on account of the delays unavoidably resulting from the condition of the railroads.

Third. To pursue Sherman the passage of the Army of Tennessee would necessarily have been over roads with all the bridges destroyed, and through a devastated country, affording no subsistence or forage, and, moreover, it was feared that a retrograde movement on our part would seriously deplete the army by desertions.

Fourth. To have sent off the most or the whole of the Army of Tennessee in pursuit of Sherman would have opened to Thomas' forces the richest portion of the State of Alabama, and would have made nearly certain the capture of Montgomery, Selma, and Mobile, without insuring the defeat of Sherman.

Fifth. In October last, when passing through Georgia to assume command of the Military Division of the West, I was informed by Governor Brown that he could probably raise, in case of necessity, about 6,000 men, which I supposed might be doubled in a levy en masse. General Cobb informed me, at the same time, that at Augusta, Macon, and Columbus he had about 6,500 local troops, and that he hoped shortly to have collected at his reserve and convalescent camps near Macon 2,500 more. Of these 9,000 men he supposed about one-half, or 5,000, could be made available as movable troops for an emergency.

To oppose the advance of the enemy from Atlanta the State of Georgia would thus have probably 17,000 men, to which number must be added the thirteen brigades of Wheeler's cavalry, amounting to about 7,000 men. The troops which could have been collected from Savannah, South Carolina, and North Carolina before Sherman's forces could reach the Atlantic coast would have amounted, it was supposed, to about 5,000 men.

Thus it was a reasonable supposition that about 29,000 or 30,000 men could be collected in time to defend the State of Georgia and insure the destruction of Sherman's army, estimated by me at about 36,000 effectives of all arms, their cavalry, about 4,000 strong, being included in this estimate.

Under these circumstances, after consultation with General Hood, I concluded to allow him to prosecute with vigor his campaign into Tennessee and Kentucky, hoping that by defeating Thomas' army, and such other forces as might hastily be sent against him, he would compel Sherman, should he reach the coast of Georgia or South Carolina, to repair at once to the defense of Kentucky, and perhaps Ohio, and thus prevent him from re-enforcing Grant. Meanwhile supplies might be sent to Virginia from Middle and East Tennessee, thus relieving Georgia from the present constant drain upon its limited resources.

I remain, very respectfully, your obedient servant,

G. T. BEAUREGARD,
General.

AUGUSTA, *December 6, 1864—7 p. m.*

General S. COOPER:

Have just arrived and will repair as soon as practicable to Charleston and Savannah.

G. T. BEAUREGARD.

SAVANNAH, *December 6, 1864.*
(Received 7th.)

General S. COOPER,
Adjutant and Inspector General:

The Fifteenth Army Corps is on the right bank of the Ogeechee. Prisoners were captured from it to-day. They are evidently of an intention to recross twenty-five miles above. All recent movements indicate their intention to do so at Jenks' and Wright's Bridges, which have been destroyed.

W. J. HARDEE,
Lieutenant-General.

AUGUSTA, *December 6, 1864.*

General HARDEE:

Wheeler so far off he could not cross river in time. General Young's brigade (250 mounted, 550 dismounted) moves to-day by rail to Pocotaligo, to observe left bank Savannah.

BRAXTON BRAGG.

(Same to Major-General Jones.)

NO. 3, ATLANTIC AND GULF RAILROAD,
December 6, 1864.

Capt. R. W. B. ELLIOTT,
Assistant Adjutant-General:

Lieutenant Baker has just returned from scout. He met the enemy's cavalry yesterday at General Cone's residence, in Bulloch County, and fell back to Jenks' Bridge. Late in the afternoon he was attacked there, and compelled to fall back to Black Creek, in Bryan County, where he made stand until the enemy crossed the creek above, about 2 p. m., and he was ordered by Colonel Prather, Tenth [Eighth] Confederate Cavalry, to retire to Harper's Bridge, on Cannouchee. Movements indicate that a force of the enemy is making its way around headwaters of Cannouchee for this section. He was informed that there was a division of infantry and 500 cavalry at Statesborough on Saturday.

G. P. RANEY,
Acting Assistant Adjutant-General.

AUGUSTA, *December 6, 1864—11.15 a. m.*

Major-General WHEELER,
Alexander:

Press well on enemy's left flank, so that if he crosses Savannah River you will know it immediately, and advise me.

BRAXTON BRAGG.

AUGUSTA, *December 6, 1864—12.45* [*p. m.*].

General SAMUEL JONES:

Three companies South Carolina cavalry militia, under Major Crump, headquarters probably Allendale, Barnwell district, are observing Savannah River and obstructing roads from ferries. Communicate such orders to them as may be proper.

BRAXTON BRAGG.

AUGUSTA, *December 6, 1864—10.30 p. m.*

Maj. Gen. S. JONES:

Organize proper parties to overflow rice lands along Savannah River, to obstruct thoroughly with trees and torpedoes and break up roads from the stream toward Pocotaligo. Fraser Matthewes and Joseph Guss, of engineer department, might superintend.

G. T. BEAUREGARD.

POCOTALIGO, *December 6, 1864—5.30 p. m.*

Lieutenant-General HARDEE,
Savannah:

I cannot answer your question as to the number of troops required to hold this road just at this time, as I have no report yet from Chesnut. Enemy advanced to-day in large force on road from Gregory's, on Tullifinny, to Coosaw. Our troops met and drove them back, but were in return driven back demoralized, and occupied works at Coosaw. General Gartrell has just telegraphed me that he can hold that place. I am endeavoring, and think will succeed, to collect a force of 500 or 600 men to attack in their rear, on road from Old Pocotaligo to Coosaw, at daylight.

SAM. JONES,
Major-General.

CHARLESTON, *December 6, 1864.*

Major STRINGFELLOW:

Forward this through to General Hardee at Savannah: There are two trains with troops from Wilmington and train with light artillery from Augusta on this side of bridge, waiting for the road to be cleared to go on. A train of North Carolina State troops will reach here at 1 a. m.; will hurry them on immediately. There are four trains on Savannah railroad due here, blocking the way.

R. C. GILCHRIST.

ADAMS' RUN, *December 6, 1864.*

General SAMUEL JONES:

General Hardee telegraphs that Wheaton's battery has been ordered to Combahee. Let Webb remain until Wheaton arrives. I have ordered Kemper to Green Pond; communicate with him after his arrival. What is the news this morning?

B. H. ROBERTSON,
Brigadier-General.

COOSAWHATCHIE, *December 6, 1864—10 a. m.*

General SAM. JONES:

Twelve barges are landing troops at Gregory's, on the Tullifinny, about three miles distant. Send Forty-seventh Georgia and section of artillery.

L. J. GARTRELL,
Brigadier-General, Commanding.

COOSAWHATCHIE, *December 6, 1864.*

Major STRINGFELLOW,
Assistant Adjutant-General:

Colonel Daniel, commanding seven companies of Fifth Georgia, reports the enemy about 1,000 strong, and asks for re-enforcements. I have sent him First Reserves, about 200 strong. I have notified him of the movement of troops from Pocotaligo.

L. J. GARTRELL.

COOSAWHATCHIE, *December 6, 1864.*

Major-General JONES:

Are you certain that the telegraph line has not been tapped by a Yankee operator?

L. J. GARTRELL.

COOSAWHATCHIE, *December 6, 1864.*

Major STRINGFELLOW:

The Forty-seventh Georgia just arrived. Section of artillery will come by next train. Send 40,000 rounds ammunition, caliber .69. Some of the boxes have no caps. We have only 35 wounded, most of them slightly.

L. J. GARTRELL.

HEADQUARTERS,
December 6, 1864—2.40 o'clock.

Maj. Gen. S. JONES,
Commanding:

GENERAL: The enemy advanced in heavy force from Gregory's Point. They are now on the road from Old Pocotaligo to this place (Coosawhatchie), and on both sides. We fought them two hours and a half, but had to fall back to our works. If you send a force in their rear, on the road from Old Pocotaligo, it will not only assist us, but probably cut off the enemy. Some provision had better be made to prevent their getting between you and us. I would have communicated with you by telegraph, but the operator says the wires are cut. I must have some old troops; the new ones won't stand.

Very respectfully, your obedient servant,

L. J. GARTRELL,
Brigadier-General, Commanding.

COOSAWHATCHIE, *December 6, 1864.*

General JONES:

The enemy advanced in large force on the road from Gregory's. We met them and drove them back. They were re-enforced, and, portion [of] the troops becoming demoralized, I ordered them to fall back to this side of the river. Enemy not pursuing. The engagement lasted two hours and a half. Loss slight. Send Forty-seventh Georgia Volunteers and any other troops you can spare. The main attack seems to be intended for this point. I would have dispatched you sooner, but being at the front and informed by operator that the line would not work, I sent a courier some time since. We can hold this place. Ammunition is getting short.

L. J. GARTRELL.

POCOTALIGO, *December 6, 1864.*

Col. A. C. EDWARDS,
Commanding Forty-seventh Georgia Regiment:

COLONEL: Brigadier-General Gartrell has been ordered to send your regiment to the position now occupied by the State Cadets, at the Tullifinny trestle, on the railroad, where other troops, under Lieutenant-Colonel Bacon, will be collected before morning. You will be the ranking officer, and will therefore take command. Colonel Bacon's command, with the cadets, will number about 550 men, with two pieces artillery. At the earliest dawn of day you will move down by a plantation road, which crosses the railroad near the Tullifinny trestle and nearly parallel to Tullifinny Creek, until it intersects the road from Old Poco to Coosaw, about 150 yards on the Coosaw side. Lieutenant-Colonel Bacon has a guide with him who knows the road, and you will therefore confer with him. Attack the enemy vigorously at that point and drive him off if possible. The Fifth Georgia will attack in front of Coosawhatchie when your fire is heard. Carry out these instructions promptly and with spirit.

Very respectfully,

C. S. STRINGFELLOW,
Assistant Adjutant-General.

DECEMBER 6, 1864.

Major STRINGFELLOW,
Assistant Adjutant-General:

MAJOR: Courier from Mackay's Point reports the enemy as having landed a regiment of about 500 men at the junction of the Coosawhatchie and Tullifinny.

E. H. BACON,
Lieutenant-Colonel.

POCOTALIGO, *December 6, 1864.*

Lieutenant-Colonel BACON,
Commanding, &c.:

COLONEL: The major-general commanding has ordered Colonel Edwards, of the Forty-seventh Georgia, to the position near the trestle-work on the railroad now occupied by the State Cadets. Leave the cavalry company (Captain Peeples') to picket the road to Coosawhatchie and watch the position at Tullifinny Bridge, and proceed with the rest of your command to report to Colonel Edwards at the place designated. That officer has been ordered to move at the earliest dawn of day to attack the enemy in flank and rear. The guide Craddock left with you knows the road. Inform Major Jackson that the baggage of his command will be at the crossing of the country road over the railroad by the time you reach that point. Move promptly. If you have or can procure any axes carry them with you to clear out the [*sic*] should the enemy blockade it; Captain Bachman has perhaps some with his battery. Direct Captain Peeples to keep the major-general commanding fully informed of any movement on the road to Pocotaligo.

Your obedient servant,

C. S. STRINGFELOW,
Assistant Adjutant-General.

AUGUSTA, *December 7, 1864.*
(Received 11.52 o'clock.)

General S. COOPER:

General Beauregard reached here last evening from Montgomery, where he received your dispatch, and has gone on this morning to Charleston and Savannah. The enemy's rear crossed Beaver Dam Creek yesterday morning south, our cavalry pressing them closely.

BRAXTON BRAGG.

BRANCHVILLE, *December 7, 1864.*

General S. COOPER,
Adjutant and Inspector General:

I cannot return exchanged prisoners to their commands; they will be kept temporarily for defense of Savannah.

G. T. BEAUREGARD.

SAVANNAH, *December 7, 1864.*
(Received 10.45 8th.)

General S. COOPER,
Adjutant and Inspector General:

Considerable fighting at Coosawhatchie to-day without definite results. The enemy hold a position near Coosawhatchie and the railroad. Heavy skirmishing at No. 2, Central railroad, with large force of the enemy, which have crossed the Ogeechee opposite that point. Fighting also at Cannouchee Bridge. Enemy have made their appearance at Hudson's Ferry and Matthews' Point, on the Savannah River. The gunboat Macon is at Sister's Ferry, with orders to patrol the river as high up as Hudson's Ferry. Howard's wing of the Federal army is believed to be on the right bank of the Ogeechee crossing to the left bank.

W. J. HARDEE,
Lieutenant-General.

AUGUSTA, *December 7, 1864—4 o'clock.*

General WHEELER:

No necessity now for further destruction of bridges over Brier Creek. A steamer with two boats has just been ordered to mouth of Brier Creek. Give her orders.

BRAXTON BRAGG.

CHARLESTON, *December 7, 1864—2.30.*

General SAMUEL JONES:

Battery of guns with guard left at 11 a. m. yesterday; train of twenty cars with troops from Augusta left at 10 p. m., and train with Girardey's light battery started at 1 a. m. Train with troops from Wilmington is expected here at 2.30 to-night; also train from Augusta, expected at 4 o'clock, will be sent immediately on. Seventeen cavalry will leave in passenger train to-morrow. Deserters from Morris' Island to-day report that troops are being moved from Morris' Island to Port Royal, where the force is 8,000 strong, mostly black troops.

R. C. GILCHRIST,
Assistant Adjutant-General.

SAVANNAH, *December 7, 1864.*

General SAMUEL JONES:

You must send me at once the Augusta battalion, the Georgia battalion, which arrived to-day, and such other troops as you can spare. Bring part of Chesnut's command to Coosawhatchie; the enemy has left his front. The enemy is advancing on Savannah.

W. J. HARDEE,
Lieutenant-General.

SAVANNAH, *December 7, 1864.*

General JONES:

I do not know how long I shall be able to hold the railroad between this and Savannah railroad bridge. It is therefore all-important that all the re-enforcements I am to receive should be sent forward immediately.

W. J. HARDEE,
Lieutenant-General.

CHARLESTON, *December 7, 1864—12.30.*

General JONES:

A train left at 11 last night with troops; Girardey's battery at 1 a. m.; Shober's (North Carolina) regiment about 3 a. m. Young's brigade had not passed Branchville at 9 a. m. Other troops, under Colonel Brown, are behind Young.

H. W. FEILDEN.

GRAHAMVILLE, *December 7, 1864—11.45.*

General SAM. JONES:

Detachment of cavalry on the road to re-enforce your men at Coosawhatchie.

JAS. CHESNUT, JR.,
Brigadier-General.

GRAHAMVILLE, *December 7, 1864.*

Maj. Gen. S. JONES:

Have the Forty-seventh [Georgia] on the march to you. I am left with the militia only, yet unorganized, and many of them are sick. My reserves relieved the forces at Bee's Creek, who have been sent to Coosawhatchie this afternoon.

JAS. CHESNUT, JR.,
Brigadier-General.

COOSAWHATCHIE, *December 7, 1864—11.30.*

General JONES:

Colonel Daniel has returned with Fifth Georgia Regiment and reports four regiments of the enemy on both sides of the main road in 400 yards of these works. I have put his regiment on the railroad to protect it, and will open upon the enemy with my guns as soon as position can be ascertained. It is impossible to get re-enforcements to Colonel Edwards.

L. J. GARTRELL.

COOSAWHATCHIE, *December 7, 1864—12.30 o'clock.*

General JONES:

This place is seriously threatened by force of four regiments, and several pieces of artillery. I am making disposition to repel any attack and save the railroad and works. Send re-enforcements if possible. They are said to be planting batteries to shell us.

L. J. GARTRELL,
Brigadier-General.

COOSAWHATCHIE, *December 7, 1864—2.50 p. m.*

General JONES:

Captain Kanapaux states that his vedettes report the enemy still landing troops at Gregory's Point.

L. J. GARTRELL.

CHARLESTON, *December 8, 1864—8 a. m.*
(Received 10.50.)

General S. COOPER,
Adjutant and Inspector General:

I arrived here last evening. General Hardee reports considerable fighting yesterday at Coosawhatchie, without definite results; enemy holding a position near there and railroad. Heavy skirmishing at No. 2, Central railroad, with large force of enemy, which has crossed Ogeechee opposite that point. Fighting also at Cannouchee bridge. Enemy has made his appearance at Hudson's Ferry and Matthews' Point, on Savannah River. Gun-boat Macon is at Sister's Ferry, with orders to patrol river as high up as Hudson's Ferry. Howard's wing of Federal Army believed, on right bank of Ogeechee, crossing. Generals Hardee and Jones should be supported with all available force.

G. T. BEAUREGARD.

CHARLESTON, *December 8, 1864—2.30 p. m.*
(Received 9.50 p. m.)

General S. COOPER:

I leave this afternoon for Pocotaligo and Savannah to confer with Generals Jones and Hardee.

G. T. BEAUREGARD.

CHARLESTON, S. C., *December 8, 1864.*

Lieutenant-General HARDEE,
Savannah, Ga.:

Having no army of relief to look to, and your forces being essential to the defense of Georgia and South Carolina, whenever you shall have to select between their safety and that of Savannah, sacrifice the latter, and form a junction with General Jones, holding the left bank of the Savannah River and the railroad to this place as long as possible.

G. T. BEAUREGARD.

SPECIAL FIELD ORDERS, No. 2. } HEADQUARTERS, *Savannah, December 8, 1864.*

* * * * * * *

III. Brooks' foreign battalion is transferred from Cumming's brigade, McLaws' division, to Harrison's brigade, Smith's division.

* * * * * * *

By order of Lieutenant-General Hardee:

D. H. POOLE,
Assistant Adjutant-General.

GRAHAMVILLE, *December 8, 1864.*

[General BRAXTON BRAGG:]

The enemy are still moving on toward Savannah, obstructing the roads in their rear, and resisting warmly this morning. I cannot learn that any force of the enemy have crossed the Savannah River. I hear artillery firing far in my front; do not know what it means. The Fourteenth Corps and Kilpatrick's cavalry are on the river road, Fifteenth on Middle Ground road, and Seventeenth, and probably Twentieth Corps, on Central railroad. I think the force on the right bank of the Ogeechee must be small.

Respectfully, your obedient servant,

JOS. WHEELER.

(Same sent by General Bragg to Col. John B. Sale, military secretary, December 9, 1864.)

SISTER'S FERRY, *December 8, 1864—5 p. m.*

Major-General WHEELER:

GENERAL: Your two dispatches of 10 and 12.30 o'clock have been received. Sister's Ferry is the lowest point at which the enemy can cross the river. There is an old ferry about twenty-five miles lower down which has been discontinued for near thirty years, and I have a strong picket there and an engineer throwing up works. No flats or boats there to cross with. A gun-boat which was up here to protect this crossing has gone down to the railroad bridge to protect that point.

Very respectfully, your obedient servant,

C. J. COLCOCK,
Colonel Third South Carolina Cavalry.

CHARLESTON, *December 8, 1864—11 a. m.*

Maj. Gen. SAM. JONES:

Have measures been adopted for obstructing with torpedoes all roads leading from Savannah River ferry toward Port Royal? Are services of Mr. Fraser Matthewes and about twenty hands required for that object?

G. T. BEAUREGARD.

COOSAWHATCHIE, *December 8, 1864—10.20 a. m.*

Major STRINGFELLOW,
Assistant Adjutant-General:

Enemy occupies same position. All quiet this morning. My effective force this morning (infantry, cavalry, and artillery) is 1,683.

L. J. GARTRELL.

COOSAWHATCHIE, *December 8, 1864—2.35 p. m.*

Major STRINGFELLOW:

I will send morning report by courier. Enemy has constructed works across the main road where it intersects with Gregory's road, one mile distant. We cannot dislodge them with small pieces; it might be done by a movement from the direction of Tullifinny bridge. I have ordered them fired into.

L. J. GARTRELL,
Brigadier-General.

SAVANNAH, *December 9, 1864.*
(Received 6.55.)

General S. COOPER:

I arrived here this morning to confer with General Hardee.

G. T. BEAUREGARD.

SAVANNAH, *December 9, 1864.*
(Received 6.45.)

General S. COOPER:

Enemy's forces are reported to be on river road, Middle Ground road, Central railroad, and Louisville road, about ten miles from city.

G. T. BEAUREGARD,
General.

SAVANNAH, *December 9, 1864.*
(Received 10.55.)

General S. COOPER:

Brigadier-General Elliott, being temporarily in the department, has been assigned to command Third Sub-District of South Carolina during the present emergency.

G. T. BEAUREGARD.

SAVANNAH, GA., *December 9, 1864.*

Lieut. Gen. W. J. HARDEE,
Commanding, &c.:

GENERAL: It is my desire, after the consultation that has taken place, that you should hold this city so long as in your judgment it may be advisable to do so, bearing in mind that should you have to decide between a sacrifice of the garrison or city, you will preserve the garrison for operations elsewhere.

Very respectfully, yours, &c.,

G. T. BEAUREGARD,
General.

SPECIAL FIELD ORDERS, } HEADQUARTERS,
No. 203. } *In the Field, Savannah, December 9, 1864.*

I. Major-General Ransom is placed temporarily in command of the Second and Third Sub-Districts of South Carolina.

II. Col. Alfred Rhett is placed temporarily in command of Second Sub-District of South Carolina.

III. Brig. Gen. Stephen Elliott is assigned to the temporary command of the Third Sub-District of South Carolina, the western limit of which is extended to Rantowles Creek, as formerly existed.

By command of Lieutenant-General Hardee:

T. B. ROY,
Assistant Adjutant-General.

DECEMBER 9, 1864.

Major-General WHEELER,
Commanding Cavalry Corps:

GENERAL: Captain Thomas, of Perrin's regiment, has just got in from the other side of Ogeechee. He reports that about two divisions of infantry, 600 cavalry, and 3,000 beef-cattle were passing down the other side that stream. He followed them twelve miles beyond Swainsborough. Captain Thomas also reports that he saw a dispatch from General Bragg to you going toward Augusta to inform you that a steamer and several small boats were at Augusta subject to your orders. In this connection I would call your attention to the fact that not one of your couriers have brought me a dispatch on this campaign until the circular this morning. Even the dispatch sent yesterday morning, when our headquarters were on the same road and only five miles apart, was handed me to-day by one of my own men.

I am, general, very respectfully, your obedient servant,

S. W. FERGUSON,
Brigadier-General.

SAVANNAH, *December 9, 1864.*

Major-General JONES:

Information is that Yankee scouts, in guise of Wheeler's stragglers, have found means to communicate with enemy on the coast. Tell your subordinates to look to it.

W. J. HARDEE.

CHARLESTON, *December 9, 1864—5.15 a. m.*

General SAM. JONES:

Will send the cavalry company at once by rail unless you wish it to march. Am attending now to torpedoes; will use every exertion to send some during day.

H. W. FEILDEN,
Assistant Adjutant-General.

POCOTALIGO, *December 9, 1864—12 m.*

Lieut. Gen. W. J. HARDEE,
Savannah:

About 9 a. m. the enemy opened a heavy fire from ten or twelve guns on the railroad between Tullifinny trestle and Coosawhatchie, and followed it up by an infantry attack. We still hold the road, and the fire has slackened. General Robertson is commanding there in person. If Generals Chesnut's and Young's [troops] can possibly be spared for a few days I respectfully urge that I be allowed to keep them. They, or some other troops, are absolutely essential to hold this road.

SAM. JONES,
Major-General.

SAVANNAH, *December 9, 1864.*

General SAMUEL JONES:

In addition to General Young's men, which I ordered you to take, apply to General Chesnut to send you the 500 men which I ordered from him to Savannah.

W. J. HARDEE.

POCOTALIGO, *December 9, 1864—6.45 p. m.*

Lieut. Gen. W. J. HARDEE,
Savannah:

The enemy kept up heavy artillery fire on railroad from 9 this morning, occasionally engaging with their infantry. About 4.30 this evening they made vigorous attack, and after two hours and a half hard fighting were repulsed. Their effort to get possession of the road seems more determined and persistent, and I apprehend the attack will be renewed to-night or in the morning. Have ordered up a part of Chesnut's force and Young's dismounted men.

SAM. JONES,
Major-General.

POCOTALIGO, *December 9, 1864—7 p. m.*

Capt. H. W. FEILDEN,
Assistant Adjutant-General, Charleston:

The enemy renewed the attack vigorously near Coosawhatchie about 4.30 o'clock this evening, and after two hours and a half hard fighting were repulsed. Hurry forward any troops coming this way.

SAM. JONES,
Major-General.

COOSAWHATCHIE, *December 9, 1864—9.25 a. m.*

Major STRINGFELLOW:

The enemy opened their batteries on the railroad about 9 o'clock. Nearly all the shells fall short. I am just starting to that side, leaving General Gartrell in command here.

B. H. ROBERTSON.

COOSAWHATCHIE, *December 9, 1864.*

Maj. Gen. SAMUEL JONES:

Enemy seems to have halted as uncertain in his movement. Nothing but desultory cannonading. There is a large extent of railroad unguarded, and I have not force sufficient to protect it. Enemy reported cutting road parallel to the railroad.

B. H. ROBERTSON,
Brigadier-General.

COOSAWHATCHIE, *December 9, 1864—3.45 p. m.*

Maj. Gen. SAMUEL JONES:

The enemy are pressing my men about one mile from Coosawhatchie. I have nothing to defend it there but the Fifth Georgia and a regiment of reserves. General Young informs me that General Hardee has ordered all the troops from Grahamville to Savannah.

B. H. ROBERTSON,
Brigadier-General.

COOSAWHATCHIE, [*December*] *9, 1864—5 p. m.*

Maj. Gen. S. JONES:

Our men are fighting splendid; I think we will hold the road.

B. H. ROBERTSON,
Brigadier-General.

COOSAWHATCHIE, *December 9, 1864—5.40 p. m.*

Major STRINGFELLOW:

The enemy has been signally repulsed in every attempt to get possession of the railroad after two hours and a half hard fighting, in which the enemy lost considerable ground. Everything is again quiet. The extent of casualties not yet known, owing to the inaccessible nature of the ground. Among the wounded is Brigadier-General Gartrell; not dangerously.

B. H. ROBERTSON.

COOSAWHATCHIE, *December 9, 1864—6.20 p. m.*

Major-General JONES:

One of enemy's guns is still shelling the railroad. Would it not be well to send the 20-pounder Parrott guns to Coosawhatchie? I would like to get together the guns of the different batteries now silenced. Can I take the guns from Grahamville and Bee's Creek which belong to Stuart's battery?

B. H. ROBERTSON.

COOSAWHATCHIE, *December 9, 1864—9.40 p. m.*

Major-General JONES:

Send Webb's 20-pounder Parrotts to report before daylight to Brigadier-General Young at the left of my line The enemy must be driven from his breast-works if possible. Have you any more artillery that you can send?

B. H. ROBERTSON.

GRAHAMVILLE, *December 9, 1864—2.40 p. m.*

Major-General JONES:

Eleven vessels of enemy lying off our front. Kirk's squadron cannot be spared without endangering the entire line. Young's command and

500 militia are at depot awaiting a locomotive to move; General Hardee has ordered them to Savannah. Have telegraphed to know if they can be sent to you.

JAS. CHESNUT,
Brigadier-General.

GRAHAMVILLE, *December 9, 1864—5.20 p. m.*

Maj. Gen. S. JONES:

Colonel Griffin with 500 militia has just started for Coosawhatchie. General Young will follow with his command.

JAS. CHESNUT, JR.,
Brigadier-General.

CHARLESTON, *December 10, 1864.*
(Received 11.30 11th.)

General S. COOPER:

Telegraphic and railroad communication interrupted beyond Savannah River; supposed by enemy's forces.

G. T. BEAUREGARD,
General.

SISTER'S FERRY, *December 10, 1864—11 a. m.*

Lieut. M. G. HUDSON,
Aide-de-Camp:

LIEUTENANT: Your dispatch of this morning has been received. Our forces are moving down the river, as the general has directed, leaving a picket at each of the ferries as we pass them. General Anderson's men have been sent lower down this morning. As the rest of the stragglers and detachments from the general's corps are collected, we will send them on to a point lower down and keep opposite to you. Most of the forage below this point has been already consumed, but above there is an abundance. Our forces number about 500 men now. To-morrow we will no doubt have more, as we have heard that there are about 500 of your command at Brown's Ferry, and have sent for them. Colonel Colcock is absent just at this time from headquarters. When he returns will reply more fully.

I have the honor to be, very respectfully, your obedient servant,

THOS. H. COLCOCK,
Adjutant.

The couriers to General Hardee went through from Grahamville, S. C., and would not report to this point, therefore cannot say if they have returned; but as communication was not interrupted up to 10 o'clock yesterday, presume they have.

CIRCULAR.] IN THE FIELD, *December 10, 1864.*

Soldiers! While you have been engaged gallantly fighting the enemy a band of thieves and stragglers have spread over the country robbing and insulting the wives and children of your brother soldiers who are opposing the invaders upon other fields. These soldiers expect protection from you, and I appeal to every officer and soldier of this command to assist in arresting and bringing to justice these depredators, who claim to belong to the command, and by their conduct are bringing disgrace upon you and distress upon citizens, the families of comrades in arms.

JOS. WHEELER,
Major-General.

CHARLESTON, *December 10, 1864.*

Maj. Gen. SAMUEL JONES,
Pocotaligo:

When plans for proposed attack shall have been completed notify me of the fact, as I may be able to send you 500 more troops.

G. T. BEAUREGARD,
General.

POCOTALIGO, *December 10, 1864—5.15 p. m.*

Capt. H. W. FEILDEN,
Assistant Adjutant-General, Charleston:

There has been very little shelling of the road to-day and some slight picket-firing. In other respects all quiet to-day.

SAM. JONES,
Major-General.

COOSAWHATCHIE, *December 10, 1864.*

Maj. Gen. SAM. JONES:

The 20-pounder Parrotts could be very effective from the battery here; can you not send them?

B. H. ROBERTSON,
Brigadier-General.

COOSAWHATCHIE, *December 10, 1864—12.10.*

Major-General JONES:

Nothing has transpired to-day. The enemy seems to be chiefly occupied in felling trees. I have ordered our skirmishers pushed forward.

B. H. ROBERTSON,
Brigadier-General.

COOSAWHATCHIE, *December 10, 1864—2.20 p. m.*

Maj. Gen. S. JONES:

General Young reports enemy in his intrenchments one mile from railroad. Everything has been quiet to-day. I have ordered a reconnaissance on my left and rear. Will report.

B. H. ROBERTSON.

CHARLESTON, *December 11, 1864.*

General S. COOPER,
Adjutant and Inspector General:

General Hardee reports yesterday from Savannah enemy have appeared in force along whole of his main line. Skirmishing and artillery firing throughout the day. No serious attack yet. No report received from General Hood since 28th ultimo.

G. T. BEAUREGARD,
General.

CHARLESTON, *December 11, 1864.*
(Received 3 a. m. 12th.)

General S. COOPER:

No further reports from General Hardee since this morning's telegram. All quiet to-day near Coosawhatchie. Preparations are being made to dislodge enemy at that point.

G. T. BEAUREGARD.

CONFIDENTIAL.] HEADQUARTERS,
Savannah, December 11, 1864.

Major-General McLAWS,
Commanding Division:

GENERAL: Lieutenant-General Hardee directs me to say that the supply of ammunition at this place is limited, especially for artillery, and desires that you take measures to prevent the useless waste of it. He wishes you to impress upon your commanding officers the necessity for economy, and to instruct them to prevent any unnecessary firing.

Respectfully, general, your obedient servant,

D. H. POOLE,
Assistant Adjutant-General.

DECEMBER 11, 1864—1 p. m.

COLONEL: The enemy have little or no cavalry in my front. As far as can be ascertained they have a considerable force of infantry. They are encamped near a creek and beyond it from us. The creek can only be crossed on the bridge, in consequence of swamps on either side. I dismounted a portion of the command and tried to drive them off, but they are too strong. The camp has the appearance of at least a brigade. It is difficult to obtain accurately their force. Pickets have been exchanging shots with them occasionally during the morning. Small arms can be distinctly heard in direction of Savannah.

I am, colonel, respectfully, &c.,

JOS. H. LEWIS,
Commanding.

HEADQUARTERS,
Savannah, Ga., December 11, 1864.

Maj. Gen. JOSEPH WHEELER,
Commanding Cavalry Corps:

GENERAL: Lieutenant-General Hardee asks your special attention to the matter of picketing the Savannah River from the railroad bridge to the city. The enemy have captured some flats on the island plantations, and may cross and strike our line of communication between Screven's Ferry and Hardeeville. The general thinks there should be 1,000 men on this service. He has dispatched Brigadier-General Anderson on the subject, but does not know whether his dispatch has been received.

Very respectfully, your obedient servant,

T. B. ROY,
Assistant Adjutant-General.

HEADQUARTERS,
Savannah, December 11, 1864—6 p. m.

Major-General WHEELER,
Commanding Cavalry:

Lieutenant-General Hardee is apprehensive that the enemy may cross the Savannah River between the railroad bridge and the city on flats captured on the island plantations and get on his line of communication. He considers it important to provide against such a contingency, and desires you to transfer to the left bank of the river a sufficient force to protect his left flank. He also thinks it best that you should cross the river and establish your headquarters at Hardeeville, or some other convenient locality.

Respectfully, general, your obedient servant,

T. B. ROY,
Assistant Adjutant-General.

COLUMBIA, *December 11, 1864.*

President DAVIS:

It is to be feared the force at Coosawhatchie is insufficient to save the road. I have ordered out all the State forces that can be spared. Cannot some of the infantry and cavalry from this State be sent to her assistance? The loss of that road will isolate Savannah.

M. L. BONHAM.

CHARLESTON, *December 11, 1864.*

Maj. Gen. SAMUEL JONES:

General Hardee applies for two of your Georgia regiments to re-enforce or support him. It is essential that you should dislodge enemy in your front soon as possible.

G. T. BEAUREGARD,
General.

CHARLESTON, *December 11, 1864—2.15 p. m.*

Maj. Gen. SAM. JONES:

For [*sic*] movements additional troops could be withdrawn from General C[hesnut] by having trains ready to carry them to and from G[rahamville]. Beware of deserters, and make use of false rumors to conceal your operations.

G. T. BEAUREGARD.

CHARLESTON, *December 11, 1864—6 p. m.*

Maj. Gen. S. JONES:

Should enemy begin to retire from your front send re-enforcements called for by General Hardee and to lines of Fourth and Fifth Sub-Districts, especially the latter; in that event call in time for transportation.

G. T. BEAUREGARD,
General, Commanding.

POCOTALIGO, *December 11, 1864—8 p. m.*

General G. T. BEAUREGARD,
Charleston:

My engineer officer reports enemy strongly intrenched, both flanks and rear of works protected by thickly wooded swamp. I cannot collect more than 1,200 good infantry for the attack, and I have not yet reliable information of their numerical strength. Chesnut reports transport with troops passed down by Hazzard's Point this morning; thinks they are going to Red Bluff or New River bridge. I have directed him to send guard there. General Young has gone to Hardeeville; says General Hardee ordered him to take command of all cavalry on this side of Savannah River. That interferes with brigade organization here and I have ordered him back.

SAM. JONES,
Major-General.

COOSAWHATCHIE, *December 11, 1864—1.40 p. m.*

Major-General JONES:

The enemy is reported throwing out skirmishers down the Coosawhatchie River, with his right a few hundred yards below the county bridge. I have made the proper disposition to meet him.

B. H. ROBERTSON,
Brigadier-General.

[Indorsement.]

A cipher telegram from Charleston needs attention. What you have to do must be executed at once or a considerable part of your means will be taken away.

C. S. S.

COOSAWHATCHIE, *December 11, 1864.*

Major-General JONES:

The enemy was only establishing a picket along the river. When is General Taliaferro coming?

B. H. ROBERTSON,
Brigadier-General.

POCOTALIGO, *December 11, 1864—10.45 a. m.*

Brig. Gen. JAMES CHESNUT,
Grahamville:

So far as yet known position of enemy same as yesterday evening. Pickets in your front and toward Bluffton must be on alert, and give earliest information of any movement of enemy in that direction. Send without delay by special courier return showing name of each organization and its commander, and the effective strength of each.

SAM. JONES,
Major-General.

GRAHAMVILLE, *December 11, 1864—2.45 p. m.*

General SAMUEL JONES:

My pickets report that a transport with troops passed Hazzard's Point this morning, going down the river. I think it well to look to New River bridge and Red Bluff; will make dispositions to that end, if you approve. Please answer at once.

JAS. CHESNUT, JR.

AUGUSTA, *December 12, 1864.*

Col. JOHN B. SALE:

The telegraph having been cut we get nothing from Savannah. A dispatch from Wheeler gives copy of enemy's order for the line of investment around Savannah. It is about eight miles from the city, and was to have been reached on 9th.

BRAXTON BRAGG.

CHARLESTON, *December 12, 1864—11.30 p. m.*
(Received 9.45 13th.)

General S. COOPER,
Adjutant and Inspector General:

Lieutenant-General Hardee reports enemy developed in strong force along his entire front yesterday, and that he has been compelled to extend his lines. He asks for immediate re-enforcements.

G. T. BEAUREGARD,
General.

HEADQUARTERS,
Savannah, Ga., December 12, 1864—10 p. m.

Major-General MCLAWS,
Commanding, &c., Telfair House:

GENERAL: Yours of 9 p. m., inclosing a dispatch from Brigadier-General Mercer, has been received, and I am directed by Lieutenant-General Hardee to say, in reply, that, in case of an attack on General Mercer's right, he hopes you will be able to give him more assistance than that indicated in your dispatch. His impression is that you have the Eighteenth Georgia Regulars in reserve. The general considers it unadvisable to withdraw Miller's company from Thunderbolt. Upon consultation with the engineers it has been decided that neither of the canal bridges would bear the weight of the Blakely gun, and Colonel Jones has sent you two field pieces from Hamilton's battalion instead. Four of the rockets required have been sent to you, and the remainder will be taken by the bearer of this dispatch.

Very respectfully, general, your obedient servant,

T. B. ROY,
Assistant Adjutant-General.

GENERAL FIELD ORDERS, No. 1. } HDQRS. MCLAWS' DIVISION, *Telfair Place, December 12, 1864.*

I. The staff of the major-general commanding is announced as follows: Maj. J. S. Williams, assistant inspector-general; Capt. R. W. B. Elliott, assistant adjutant-general; Capt. M. P. King, assistant inspector-general; Capt. G. B. Lamar, aide-de-camp and acting assistant adjutant-general; Capt. A. Huguenin, aide-de-camp; Capt. J. A. Maxwell, acting chief artillery and ordnance; Surg. John D. Patton, chief surgeon division; Capt. N. B. Brown, chief quartermaster.

II. The headquarters of the division are for the present located at Telfair Place.

By order of Maj. Gen. L. McLaws:

R. W. B. ELLIOTT,
Assistant Adjutant-General.

RICHMOND, VA., *December 12, 1864.*

Governor BONHAM,
Columbia, S. C.:

Yours of the 11th instant received. I have for some time realized the importance of adding veteran troops to the force assembled to resist Sherman, and have corresponded with General Lee on the subject. The recent operations of the enemy have increased the previously entertained estimate of the danger of detaching troops from the Army of Virginia. My anxiety will render me prompt to respond to your request should it become practicable to do so, and General Lee will in no degree withhold any further assistance which he can give consistently with the safety of his position.

JEFF'N DAVIS.

POCOTALIGO, *December 12, 1864.*

General B. BRAGG,
Augusta:

General Jones is out inspecting his lines in front. Will deliver your dispatch on his return. General Beauregard is in Charleston. No news from Savannah to-day. Enemy reported to have burned trestle at Savannah River yesterday. Heavy cannonading heard here. The route to Savannah by Hardeeville and Screven's Ferry was open last evening, and I presume is still. Enemy still in our immediate front in force.

Respectfully,

CHAS. S. STRINGFELLOW,
Assistant Adjutant-General.

CHARLESTON, *December 12, 1864.*

General SAM. JONES:

Have rice fields, as ordered, been overflowed? Send a reliable officer to break and destroy the roads to the Savannah River through the rice fields. He can get negro labor from planters.

G. T. BEAUREGARD,
General.

CHARLESTON, *December 12, 1864.*

General SAMUEL JONES:

If the enemy be too strongly fortified in your front to be dislodged complete your own intrenchments, and send at once re-enforcements to New River, Red Bluff, and points east of Screven's Ferry Causeway where enemy might land. Your action relative to General Young must be referred to General Hardee.

G. T. BEAUREGARD,
General.

CHARLESTON, *December 12, 1864.*

Major-General JONES:

Lieutenant-Colonel Brown's detachment and battery are sent for attack, if it takes place; otherwise, to replace for forty-eight hours troops you may have sent to protect points on New River.

G. T. BEAUREGARD,
General.

CHARLESTON, *December 12, 1864—7 p. m.*

Maj. Gen. SAMUEL JONES:

The boats are completed only for rowing. No track has even [been] made for pontoon, nor can lumber be had without delay. Will send boats and oars as ferries unless I hear further. If lumber can be had will forward. All well.

W. H. ECHOLS,
Major, &c.

HARDEEVILLE, *December 12, 1864.*
(Received 10.55 p. m.)

Major-General JONES:

There is a guard of fifty men at the bridge; the bridge has been destroyed. A party of Yankees from Sherman's army landed at Hayward's plantation to-day; destroyed some houses, and scouts report they have gone. It seems to me that this is the most important place just now. Can you send some troops here, with some artillery? Sherman must be aware that our only communication with Savannah is by Screven's Ferry. He will do all in his power to cut it; I believe he is doing it now. If my opinion is worth anything I should say intrench where you are, and come here with all that can be spared. I hope you will urge upon the railroad men the necessity of keeping at least two trains this side Coosawhatchie. If I had an engine I would run up and have a talk with you. I will execute your orders at once.

Most respectfully,

P. M. B. YOUNG,
Brigadier-General.

AUGUSTA, *December 13, 1864.*

Col. JOHN B. SALE:

I go to Charleston to-morrow to see General Beauregard, at his request. He has assigned me to duty.

BRAXTON BRAGG.

RICHMOND, VA., *December 13, 1864.*

General G. T. BEAUREGARD,
Charleston, S. C.:

I have anxiously desired to send re-enforcements, but events have rendered it impracticable to add to those forwarded some time since. Should a change of circumstances render it possible to do more no time will be lost in doing so. Should the enemy's fleet be detached for operations against Savannah the opportunity will be presented for our squadron at Charleston to assume the offensive, and perhaps to destroy his depot at Port Royal.

JEFF'N DAVIS.

RICHMOND, VA., *December 13, 1864.*

General G. T. BEAUREGARD,
Charleston, S. C.:

Your last dispatch was communicated to General Lee. He replies as follows:

Every available man at the South should now be sent to Savannah. As long as Grant retains his present force here I do not think this army (Northern Virginia) can be weakened. If he withdraws any part I can detach proportionately. If the Department thinks otherwise I will send whatever it directs.

S. COOPER,
Adjutant and Inspector General.

CHARLESTON, *December 13, 1864—9.15 p. m.*
(Received 9.20 14th.)

General S. COOPER:

General Hardee reports to-day from Savannah enemy felt his lines sharply Saturday and Sunday, but was comparatively quiet yesterday and has made no serious demonstration to-day. A battery opened yesterday on Fort McAllister, and Major Anderson expected to be attacked to-day by a column along right bank of Ogeechee. General Jones reports nothing new on line of Savannah railroad. No reports from General Hood since the 28th ultimo.

BEAUREGARD,
General.

CHARLESTON, S. C., *December 13, 1864.*

Lieutenant-General HARDEE,
Savannah, Ga.:

About 450 men will be sent you to-day with instructions to General Jones to divert them, if necessary, to defenses of New River and those east of Screven's Ferry Causeway. These re-enforcements are the last you and Jones, who is subject to your orders, can hope for. Keep yourself well advised, through staff officers and otherwise, of his ability to hold your communication, for Savannah must be held only so long as is consistent with the safety of its garrison.

G. T. BEAUREGARD,
General.

SAVANNAH, *December 13, 1864.*

Maj. Gen. L. MCLAWS:

GENERAL: Your dispatch of to-day in regard to communicating with Fort McAllister reached me this evening. Prior to its reception a telegram had been received from Beaulieu announcing the fall of the fort. It was carried by assault near sundown, after severe and continuous fighting throughout the day. A subsequent dispatch from the commanding officer at Rosedew states that a communication by signal had been received from Fort McAllister, without signature, reporting the loss of the work and representing the officers unhurt, with the exception of Captain Morrison, reported wounded.

Very respectfully, your obedient servant,

EDWARD C. ANDERSON,
Colonel, Commanding.

HEADQUARTERS,
Savannah, Ga., December 13, 1864.

Maj. Gen. JOSEPH WHEELER:

I am instructed by Lieutenant-General Hardee to repeat that he considers it important that a force of your command should be promptly transferred to the vicinity of Hardeeville for the security of that depot and to protect his line of communication, which may be threatened from New River as well as from the Savannah.

Very respectfully, your obedient servant,

T. B. ROY,
Assistant Adjutant-General.

PURYSBURG, *December 13, 1864.*

Maj. Gen. J. WHEELER,
Commanding Cavalry Corps:

I have received your request of this day's date to cross troops of your command over the Savannah River at Sister's Ferry. I will proceed promptly and effect the object of your request.

Very respectfully,

W W. HUNTER,
Flag Officer.

CHARLESTON, *December 13, 1864—1 p. m.*

Maj. Gen. SAMUEL JONES:

Your attention is specially called again to safety of defenses on New River and east of the Screven's Ferry Causeway; they are as essential to safety of forces in Savannah as the position you now hold. Send in time [to] those points any re-enforcements required to hold them; about 450 men are being sent to-day to General Hardee; you are authorized to divert them to those points if necessary.

G. T. BEAUREGARD.

COOSAWHATCHIE, *December 13, 1864.*

Major STRINGFELLOW:

There is no change in immediate front. Enemy is very busy cutting an avenue from his battery on his extreme left to command the railroad just below this point. He was, I think, hauling heavy guns last night, from the noise and the urging on of animals heard all night. It is too foggy to observe the number of vessels.

W. B. TALIAFERRO,
Brigadier-General.

COOSAWHATCHIE, *December 13, 1864.*

Major STRINGFELLOW,
Assistant Adjutant-General:

The enemy are shelling the Dawson Bluff battery and the railroad in vicinity of these headquarters from a battery on Gregory's Neck. Send an engineer to strengthen the works at Dawson Bluff at once.

W. B. TALIAFERRO,
Brigadier-General, Commanding.

POCOTALIGO, *December 13, 1864—4.30 p. m.*

Brig. Gen. W. B. TALIAFERRO,
Coosawhatchie:

General Young has just telegraphed that the enemy has crossed the river at Taylor's, and are eight miles of Red Bluff. Send the men and the three pieces of artillery to Hardeeville, and notify General Young.

By order:

CHAS. S. STRINGFELLOW,
Assistant Adjutant-General.

GRAHAMVILLE, *December 13, 1864.*

Maj. C. S. STRINGFELLOW,
Assistant Adjutant-General:

Fleet report: One ship of the line, one steam frigate, one sloop of war, one cutter, four gun-boats, eight armed vessels, forty-six sail transports, one ocean steamer, five river and tug boats; total transports, fifty-two; grand total, sixty. The river boats actively plying among the fleet off Hilton Head; four schooners going seaward, no troops aboard. No boats passed down Broad River this a. m.

R. J. BROWNFIELD,
Lieutenant and Signal Officer.

GRAHAMVILLE, *December 13, 1864.*

General JONES:

Brigadier-General Young asks for 100 men and a section of artillery to attack some men who have landed on Huger's and Rutledge's plantations, on Savannah River. I earnestly request that you send Captain Heyward's company of cavalry and section of horse artillery now with General Taliaferro. Please answer.

JAS. CHESNUT, JR.,
Brigadier-General.

EIGHT MILES FROM PURYSBURG CROSSING,
December 13, 1864—2 p. m.

General SAMUEL JONES:

The enemy have crossed the river at Taylor's plantation, within eight miles of Red Bluff. Let the troops come at once, with any train you can get, and as many more troops as you can spare. The enemy have cavalry.

P. M. B. YOUNG,
Brigadier-General.

HARDEEVILLE, *December 13, 1864—10.30 p. m.*

General SAMUEL JONES:

Just returned from Taylor's and Rutledge's plantations. The enemy, with a small force, had crossed to the mainland. We easily drove them off. There is a force, I think small, on Argyle Island yet. I will drive them off to-morrow if I can.

P. M. B. YOUNG,
Brigadier-General.

CHARLESTON, *December 13, 1864.*

Maj. Gen. SAMUEL JONES:

Am trying to get the Napoleons for you.

C. K. HUGER,
Major, &c.

CHARLESTON, *December 14, 1864.*
(Received 15th.)

General S. COOPER:

By telegram received to-day Lieutenant-General Hardee reports that enemy carried Fort McAllister by assault yesterday afternoon, and is making preparation to attack Rosedew in reverse. His scouts report an increase in number of steamers and sail vessels about Fort Pulaski and of the force on Tybee Island. All quiet about Coosawhatchie.

G. T. BEAUREGARD,
General.

RICHMOND, VA., *December 14, 1864.*

Col. J. C. IVES,
Aide-de-Camp:

SIR: You will proceed to Charleston and report to General Beauregard. Your familiarity with the defenses and localities now threatened by the enemy will be of service to him. You will keep me advised from there, either by telegraph or mail, of what is transpiring in that quarter.

Very respectfully, your obedient servant,

JEFF'N DAVIS.

SPECIAL FIELD ORDERS, No. 9. } HEADQUARTERS, *Savannah, December 14, 1864.*

* * * * * * *

III. Major-General Wheeler is charged with the defense of the line east of Screven's Ferry Causeway and along New River to Hardeeville. Reports connected with the defense of that line will be made to these headquarters, and also to Major-General Jones, commanding on the Charleston and Savannah Railroad.

By order of Lieutenant-General Hardee:

D. H. POOLE,
Assistant Adjutant-General.

HARDEEVILLE, *December 14, 1864—6.45 p. m.*

General SAMUEL JONES:

There are a good many of the enemy on Argyle Island; several hundred can be seen. They are running all the rice mills on the island. I intended to go down and attack them all along the line with artillery and sharpshooters to-morrow. I will not be able to do much if you take away the section you ordered me to send back; it was six miles off when I got the order, but it is coming back, and will leave here by 10 o'clock, unless you permit me to retain it for two days. We skirmished a little to-day. The enemy were at Chisholm's plantation, two miles from railroad bridge. I could use twelve pieces to great advantage to-morrow if I had them. Answer.

P. M. B. YOUNG,
Brigadier-General.

CHARLESTON, *December 15, 1864.*

Col. JOHN B. SALE,
Military Secretary, Richmond:

My services not being longer needed in this department I shall leave this evening for Wilmington and resume my command. Sherman has opened communication with his new base by the Ogeechee. The means to meet him do not exceed one-half the estimate in yours of the 7th instant. Notify Mrs. B. of my return, and wish for her and Major Cuthbert to join me in Wilmington, the latter temporarily.

BRAXTON BRAGG.

CHARLESTON, *December 15, 1864.*
(Received 12 p. m.)

General S. COOPER:

If enemy take Savannah it is evident that by using the river as a base he may cut the Augusta railroad at many points, and Charleston would then become soon after untenable. I have ordered river obstructed at many points.

G. T. BEAUREGARD,
General.

CHARLESTON, *December 15, 1864.*

General S. COOPER,
Adjutant and Inspector General:

Lieutenant-General Hardee has nothing new to report to-day. There are 5,000 prisoners at Thomasville, Ga., that should be removed to Andersonville. Will you please give the necessary orders.

G. T. BEAUREGARD.

CHARLESTON, *December 15, 1864.*

General S. COOPER:

General Hardee reports at Savannah, on 9th, his effectives of all arms at about 10,000. General Jones reports from Pocotaligo, on 12th, his effectives of all arms at about 5,500. There is no report from General Wheeler, but his forces must be about 3,000.

G. T. BEAUREGARD,
General.

CHARLESTON, *December 15, 1864.*

General S. COOPER:

General Beauregard has ordered rations for 15,000 men for sixty days to be collected in Charleston. Am informed depot commissary has on hand 500,000 pounds of sugar; large portion ordered to Richmond. In present deficiency of meat rations cannot the sugar be detained here for General Hardee?

H. W. FEILDEN,
Assistant Adjutant-General.

CHARLESTON, *December 15, 1864.*
(Received 12 p. m.)

General S. COOPER:

My instructions to Lieutenant-General Hardee are based on the fact that, having no army of relief to look to, it is more important, after proper resistance, to save our troops and material than to sacrifice all by too protracted defense. I desire being informed if these instructions are approved by the War Department, and are applicable to Charleston as well as Savannah.

G. T. BEAUREGARD,
General.

SAVANNAH, *December 15, 1864.*
(Via Hardeeville 16th.)

His Excellency President DAVIS:

Sherman has secured a water base, and Foster, who is already nearly on my communications, can be safely and expeditiously re-enforced. Unless assured that force sufficient to keep open my communications can be sent me, I shall be compelled to evacuate Savannah.

W. J. HARDEE,
Lieutenant-General.

CHARLESTON, S. C., *December 15, 1864—11.30 a. m.*

Lieutenant-General HARDEE,
Savannah, Ga.:

Under no circumstances must you be cut off from junction of your forces with those of General Jones; the safety of Georgia and South Carolina depends upon the results.

G. T. BEAUREGARD,
General.

CHARLESTON, *December 15, 1864.*

Lieutenant-General HARDEE:

Should there be no works at Tunbridge and Mongan's Landings, east of Screven's Ferry Causeway, have them erected forthwith. Rifle pits and batteries for two field pieces might answer for the present. Have creeks leading [to] them obstructed with oak trees or piles and torpedoes. Colonel Clarke, engineer, can inform you.

G. T. BEAUREGARD,
General.

HEADQUARTERS,
Savannah, Ga., December 15, 1864—8 p. m.

Maj. Gen. JOSEPH WHEELER,
Commanding Cavalry Corps, Izard's Place, Savannah River:

GENERAL: Your dispatch of 3.30 p. m. has been received, and I am directed by Lieutenant-General Hardee to say, in reply, that Ferguson's brigade had better be sent over at once. If the need of it should prove to be greater on the left than on the right bank of the river it can be returned to you.

Very respectfully, your obedient servant,

T. B. ROY,
Assistant Adjutant-General.

SAVANNAH, GA., *December 15, 1864—10.15 p. m.*

General WHEELER:

GENERAL: The enemy is reported at Verard's plantation in considable force. It is all important they should be driven from that position without [delay]. For this purpose take any portion of the command you destined for this side of the river.

Respectfully,

W. J. HARDEE,
Lieutenant-General.

HEADQUARTERS CAVALRY COMMAND,
On North Bank Savannah River, Guerard's House,
December 15, 1864.

Lieutenant HUDSON,
Aide-de-Camp:

LIEUTENANT: I have the honor to report to the major-general commanding the state of the forces under my command. I inclose a general order which I issued this afternoon defining the position of each portion of the troops. Colonel Colcock has since come in and reports that but one of his companies has come from the ferries above the railroad bridge; the other companies have remained, owing to an order from a major claiming to belong to General Bragg's staff, who ordered them to remain to keep up a courier line. Thus Colonel Colcock is now commanding thirty men of the South Carolina reserve troops and 165 Kentuckians of Lewis' brigade, under Major Mynheir; Colonel Bird is commanding my brigade, with an effective force of not exceeding 200 men, and Captain Eve commands 130 men of General Young's brigade. With these 500 men I have a river front to guard of thirty miles, every foot of which is accessible to the enemy in the rice flats they are using upon the river. The consequence is that nearly every man is upon picket duty every day, and no force is left to re-enforce the pickets when they are driven in. If the three companies of Colonel Colcock's regiment, the Third South Carolina, and the Eighth and Tenth Confederate Regiments, of my brigade, all of whom are now dismounted and in the trenches around Savannah, could be transferred to this side, the force would be more adequate to the work to be performed. As it is, I dislike very much being responsible for a position such as this, and most earnestly ask to be re-enforced.

I have the honor to be, lieutenant, very respectfully, yours,

R. H. ANDERSON,
Brigadier-General, Commanding.

P. S.—LIEUTENANT: Your dispatch from Beech Hill just received. Please ask the general commanding to bear in mind that the present assignment leaves 130 of General Young's men under my command, which he only let me have by courtesy, and can take away when he pleases. There will be two companies of my command under General Young and one section of artillery—the artillery and one company at Red Bluff, and one company at Bluffton.

[Inclosure.]

GENERAL ORDERS, } HEADQUARTERS CAVALRY FORCES,
No. — } *North Bank of the Savannah, Guerard's House,*
December 15, 1864.

I. Colonel Colcock, Third South Carolina Cavalry, will assume command of Major Mynheir's detachment, and, with it and the rest of his command, will perform the following duty: He will, after leaving a small picket at each of the ferries above the railroad, cover the river well and securely from the railroad bridge to and including Heyward's upper place.

II. Colonel Bird will with his command cover the river well and securely from Smith's to and including Moreland's place.

III. Captain Eve will with his command cover well and securely the river from Moreland's to Screven's Ferry.

The above change will be made successively. When Colcock relieves Colonel Bird's pickets, above Heyward's upper place, Colonel Bird will relieve Captain Eve's pickets, now above Moreland's. Commanding officers will instruct their pickets not to waste their ammunition by firing on the enemy across the river, and to keep themselves concealed behind the river-bank, and make every effort to prevent the enemy landing on this side of the river.

Colonel Colcock and Colonel Bird will establish immediately a courier line between these and their headquarters.

By command of Brig. Gen. R. H. Anderson:

W. W. GORDON,
Assistant Adjutant-General.

CHARLESTON, *December 15, 1864.*

Maj. Gen. SAMUEL JONES:

What is cause of delay in your attack? Increase of tents on Tybee Island may denote reduction of force in your front. Can you not feel enemy's strength without exposing your proposed plans?

G. T. BEAUREGARD.

SAVANNAH, *December 15, 1864.*
(Via Hardeeville 3.30 a. m. 16th.)

Major-General JONES:

Our occupation of Savannah depends on your ability to hold the railroad. Whenever you are unable to hold the road I must evacuate. You must strengthen your position by throwing up works and by making strong abatis. Inform me instantly if Foster is re-enforced by Sherman or otherwise. I feel uneasy about my communications.

W. J. HARDEE,
Lieutenant-General.

SAVANNAH, *December 16, 1864.*

Major-General WHEELER,
Commanding Cavalry:

GENERAL: In assigning Colonel Colcock to the defense of New River it would be well to give him all or as large a part of his regiment as possible. Three companies of his regiment are here and cannot be spared; the remainder might be gotten together. If you can get Colonel Colcock's staff with him I would be glad to have you do so. Your command embraces the country between New River and the Savannah River, and, incidentally, all other points which may be attacked in your neighborhood.

Respectfully, your obedient servant,

W. J. HARDEE,
Lieutenant-General.

CHEVES' PLACE, *December 16, 1864—1.30 a. m.*

Maj. Gen. JOSEPH WHEELER,
Commanding Cavalry Corps, Army of Tennessee:

MY DEAR GENERAL: I have just left General Hardee and all the other generals in a council of war. My orders are (and to give you the same from General Hardee) to go to work at once and get all the flats in the river from the rice canals and float them down to Savannah. I told the general it was my intention to attack at daylight, but he says the attack is of no importance when compared with that of getting the flats into the river and down to Savannah. He suggested that probably we had not better draw the attention of the enemy to our position until we get the flats from the canals into the river. I will be with you by 7 a. m., and will be most happy to serve under your command. General Hardee desires that we use every man that we can to getting out these flats.

I am, general, most respectfully, yours, very truly,

P. M. B. YOUNG.

CHEVES' PLACE, FOUR MILES FROM SCREVEN'S FERRY,
December 16, 1864. (Via Hardeeville 7 p. m. 17th.)

Maj. Gen. SAMUEL JONES:

Did not get your dispatch until early this morning, and as I had to attack to-day, could not come. I was at Savannah last night with a council of war. I will come over to have a talk with you to-morrow, if possible. I think there is about a brigade of the enemy on Argyle Island. They moved up this morning opposite Izard's place, and appeared as if they were going to cross. I attacked with artillery and sharpshooters. They retired after a warm little skirmish. They still occupy the island. I will send up Kanapaux's section early to-morrow morning.

P. M. B. YOUNG.

CHARLESTON, *December 16, 1864.*

Major-General JONES:

Colonel Brown's command, from Second and Third Sub-Districts, including battery, must return to-day if attack is to take place to-morrow. You will call for them when immediately needed. I will be with you at about 2 p. m. to-day.

G. T. BEAUREGARD,
General.

WILMINGTON, *December 17, 1864.*

His Excellency the PRESIDENT:

After a conference with General Beauregard, I determined, as he had no duty to assign me, to return, under the authority of your dispatch, and resume the command of this department.

BRAXTON BRAGG.

RICHMOND, *December 17, 1864.*

General G. T. BEAUREGARD,
Charleston, S. C.:

The spirit of your instructions to General Hardee relative to the defense of Savannah is approved. It is hoped Savannah may be successfully defended, but the defense should not be too protracted to the sacrifice of the garrison. The same remark is applicable to Charleston. We must rely upon your judgment to make the fullest possible defense consistent with the safety of the garrison.

S. COOPER,
Adjutant and Inspector General.

RICHMOND, VA., *December 17, 1864.*

General W. J. HARDEE,
Savannah, Ga.:

Beyond the force sent sometime since to Augusta, General Lee has not thus far found himself able to detach troops from his command. Should a change of circumstances permit further aid to be sent no time will be lost. Whether General Beauregard can secure the communication between Charleston and Savannah in the contingency referred to by you he can best inform you. Close observation will, I hope, enable you to know when the enemy shall send from your front any considerable force, that you may then provide for the safety of your communications and make the dispositions needful for the preservation of your army.

JEFF'N DAVIS.

DECEMBER 17, 1864—12 m.

Maj. Gen. JOSEPH WHEELER,
Commanding, &c., at Cheves' House:

I am informed there is a large canal, known as the Lawrence Canal, passing by Cheves' farm and falling into Tunbridge Creek near the landing. This canal should be thoroughly obstructed, and protected by infantry and artillery if necessary. It is possible that the battery and obstructions at Tunbridge's protect the entrance of said canal. There are several bad places in the main road from Hardeeville to your headquarters; they should be drained and corduroyed before another rain.

Respectfully, your obedient servant,

G. T. BEAUREGARD.

Memorandum for location of Troops.

HEADQUARTERS,
Savannah, Ga., December 18, 1864.

First. Smith's division (about 2,000 men), as soon as it shall reach Hardeeville, to go to Augusta via Charleston (transportation to be provided beforehand).

Second. Wright's division to be sent to Robertson's district as soon as it shall reach Hardeeville, General Robertson to report to Wright temporarily to advise as to dispositions of the troops, and then to be assigned to the command of Gartrell's brigade. Col. G. P. Harrison to be assigned to a brigade wherever his regiment is.

Third. McLaws' division to go, under command of Brigadier-General Taliaferro, to James Island as soon as it can be spared from Hardeeville.

Fourth. Major-General McLaws to relieve General Taliaferro of his present command at Pocotaligo, and to defend the line of the Combahee.

Fifth. Col. E. C. Anderson's brigade to be sent to James Island (Third Sub-District of South Carolina) as soon as it shall reach Hardeeville.

Sixth. Young's brigade to be increased by the Seventh Georgia Cavalry (dismounted), commanded by Col. E. C. Anderson, jr.

Seventh. Wheeler's cavalry corps (that part of it east of the Savannah River) will guard the crossings of the Savannah and New Rivers, also the landings east of Screven's Ferry Causeway, until compelled by the enemy to retire. He will then guard and defend the country between the Savannah and the defensive line in rear of the Combahee. He will also guard the right flank of said line, resting at or near Barnwell, to Augusta.

G. T. BEAUREGARD,
General.

SAVANNAH, *December 18, 1864.*

Savannah: To remain two days after our troops have evacuated the city, to protect the evacuation; then to be ready to proceed to sea by the way of Augustine Creek. Lieutenant McAdams to take two boats from the Savannah to remove the torpedoes at Turner's Rocks.

Isandiga: After the evacuation of our troops will proceed up the river, if there are no enemy's batteries to prevent it, and join Flag-Officer Hunter; otherwise, to try the passage to sea by Augustine Creek.

Fire-Fly: Proceed up the river to join Flag-Officer Hunter.

Georgia: The general commanding will give notice of the time of dismantling Forts Jackson and Lee, when the guns will be spiked and shots jammed in the guns. The crew will leave the ship for Screven's Ferry, at the same time scuttling the ship effectually.

Guns on lower end of Hutchinson's Island: Spike the guns and jam shot in them; break the carriages.

The foregoing plan was adopted on the advice and approval of Generals Beauregard and Hardee.

THOS. W. BRENT,
Commandant Afloat, pro tem.

Morning report.

Command.	Total effective.	Total present.	Aggregate present.	Remarks.
Lewis' brigade	590	641	699	Including First Georgia Regulars.
Baker's brigade	1,922	2,048	2,133	
Cumming's brigade	608	660	711	
Company E, First South Carolina Artillery	80	82	84	
Total	3,200	3,431	3,627	Including light artillery.

R. W. B. ELLIOTT,
Assistant Adjutant-General.

HEADQUARTERS MCLAWS' DIVISION,
Telfair Place, December 18, 1864.

SAVANNAH, *December 18, 1864.*

Maj. Gen. JOSEPH WHEELER:

General Beauregard directs me to inform you that, instead of to-day, he will meet you at Cheves' house about 6 a. m. to-morrow.

Respectfully, your obedient servant,

A. R. CHISOLM,
Aide-de-Camp.

SAVANNAH, *December 18, 1864.*
(Via Hardeeville 19th.)

General SAM. JONES:

Send back to Florence all that part of Brooks' foreign battalion now at Summerville, under guard, and turn them over to the officer commanding Federal prisoners, to be confined as prisoners of war. Order the officers to rejoin their commands.

W. J. HARDEE,
Lieutenant-General.

RICHMOND, VA., *December 19, 1864.*

General R. E. LEE,
Petersburg, Va.:

The following dispatch just received from General Beauregard.

SAVANNAH, *December 18, 1864.*
(Via Hardeeville.)

General Sherman demanded the surrender of Savannah yesterday of General Hardee, which was refused. The loss of Savannah will be followed by that of the railroad from Augusta to Charleston, and soon after of Charleston itself. Cannot Hoke's and Johnson's divisions be spared for the defense of South Carolina and Georgia until part or whole of Hood's army could reach Georgia?

G. T. BEAUREGARD.

I cannot realize the consequences as portrayed. But General Bragg has just returned; if you can have a conference with him you can better judge. Let me have your advice, and, if you choose, communicate with General Beauregard.

JEFF'N DAVIS.

HEADQUARTERS ARMY OF NORTHERN VIRGINIA,
December 19, 1864.

His Excellency JEFFERSON DAVIS:

Dispatch of to-day received. Beauregard and Hardee must judge of necessity of evacuating Savannah. If done troops can be saved, and by uniting all in direction of Branchville any column marching on Charleston would be threatened and communication preserved. I cannot find that any troops have left Grant. He has united to him the Sixth and Nineteenth Corps. If Hoke and Johnson are sent south it will necessitate the abandonment of Richmond with the present opposing force.

R. E. LEE.

CONFIDENTIAL CIRCULAR.] HEADQUARTERS,
Savannah, Ga., December 19, 1864.

1. The troops in and around Savannah will be transferred to-night to the left bank of the Savannah River, and will proceed thence to Hardeeville.

2. At dark the light batteries will, under the direction of Lieutenant-Colonel Jones, chief of artillery, be withdrawn by hand from their positions in line with as little noise as possible, and will be sent over the pontoon bridge to Hardeeville.

3. The troops at Whitemarsh, Forts Jackson and Bartow, will be assembled at Fort Jackson by 9 p. m., and thence will proceed at once, via Screven's Ferry, to Hardeeville.

4. The troops at Rosedew, Beaulieu, &c., will leave their positions at dark, and marching to Savannah, will cross at Screven's Ferry.

5. Major-General Wright's division will be withdrawn from the lines at 8 p. m., and will pass the river on the pontoons.

6. Major-General McLaws' division will be drawn from its position at 10 p. m., and will cross the river on the pontoons.

7. Major-General Smith's division will be withdrawn at 11 o'clock, and will cross on the pontoons.

8. The lines of skirmishers will be left in position as follows: Wright's line until 10.30 o'clock, McLaws' line until 12.30 o'clock, Smith's line until 1 o'clock.

9. The pontoon bridges are placed in charge of Colonel Clarke, chief of engineers, who will destroy the bridges after all the troops shall have crossed; and to enable him to ascertain this the skirmishers of each division will be placed in charge of an intelligent staff officer, who will report to Colonel Clarke, at the pontoon bridge, when the skirmishers of their respective commands shall have passed the river.

10. The chief of artillery will take measures to have the heavy guns in position spiked, or otherwise rendered useless, as follows: On Wright's line at 10 o'clock, on McLaws' line at 11 o'clock, on Smith's line at 12 o'clock.

11. The ammunition will be destroyed by throwing it into the river, or otherwise, and not by blowing it up.

12. The guns on the inner line will be spiked or destroyed, and all powder in the city magazines will be made useless by having water thrown on it.

13. All wagons will be sent into the city in time to cross on the pontoon at dark.

By command of Lieutenant-General Hardee:

T. B. ROY,
Assistant Adjutant-General.

SAVANNAH, *December 19, 1864.*

Major-General McLAWS:

Have you a light battery you can spare for Wheeler, who is pressed by the enemy on the other side of the river near Izard's?

W. J. HARDEE,
Lieutenant-General.

HEADQUARTERS,
Savannah, December 19, 1864.

Major-General McLAWS,
Commanding Division:

GENERAL: Lieutenant-General Hardee directs me to say that the pontoon is completed, and he desires that you will see that your wagons containing cooking utensils and baggage are sent over and on to Hardeeville at daylight in the morning.

Respectfully, general, your obedient servant,

D. H. POOLE,
Assistant Adjutant-General.

CONFIDENTIAL.] HEADQUARTERS MERCER'S COMMAND,
December 19, 1864.

Should orders be issued to move to the rear, commandants of batteries are directed to cut the spokes of the cannon carriages, destroy all the implements, such as sponges, rammers, &c., and sink all handspikes, ammunition, &c., bringing off their haversacks with the priming wires, friction primers, thumb-stalls, &c.

In doing this no noise must be made that will attract the attention of the enemy or give notice of the movements of our troops.

By order of Brigadier-General Mercer:

W. WHEELER,
Captain and Chief of Artillery.

(Commandants Batteries Aminett, Barnes, Simpkins, Wheeler, Barnwell, Elliott, Acee, Richardson, and Lieut. W. Barnwell, commanding Battery No. 4.)

HEADQUARTERS,
Savannah, Ga., December [19], *1864.*

Major-General WHEELER,
Commanding Cavalry Corps:

GENERAL: Lieutenant-General Hardee has received your dispatch in reference to force at Izard's, and asking for a battery of light artillery. He will send you one, and, if possible, two; they can hardly reach you before night, however, as they have to be brought from distant localities. He says oppose the enemy with your utmost ability, and call upon Major-General Jones for re-enforcements if you need them.

Very respectfully,

T. B. ROY,
Assistant Adjutant-General.

SAVANNAH, GA., *December 19, 1864—6.15 p. m.*

General WHEELER,
Commanding Cavalry:

GENERAL: The road to Hardeeville must be kept open at all hazards; it is my only line of retreat. I have sent you about 200 men from Ferguson's brigade and six pieces of artillery. I am about sending in addition to this force about 200 men of the Seventh Georgia, under Colonel Anderson, and about 250 under Major Howard. I have also instructed General Taliaferro to come in person to Hardeeville with some re-enforcements, to keep in communication with you, and to bring to your assistance additional forces, provided they should be needed. The pontoon bridge is not yet completed, but the engineers hope to have it done by morning. Fight the enemy at every step if he attempts to advance, and keep me informed of everything relating to his movements.

Very respectfully, your obedient servant,

W. J. HARDEE,
Lieutenant-General.

CHARLESTON, *December 19, 1864.*

General SAM. JONES:

The following just received from General Bragg, at Wilmington, dated to-day:

A large naval expedition, accompanied by transports and troops, said to have sailed from Hampton Roads on 16th instant; destination reported as Wilmington. As they have had ample time to arrive and we do not hear of them, they may have gone on to Sherman's assistance.

JNO. M. OTEY,
Assistant Adjutant-General.

RICHMOND, VA., *December 20, 1864.*

General G. T. BEAUREGARD,
Charleston, S. C.:

Dispatch of the 18th received. The enemy is concentrating before Wilmington, and the indications are that it will be speedily attacked. Grant has been re-enforced from Sheridan's army, and, so far as known, has not detached any portion of his troops. This sufficiently shows the impracticability of complying with your request for Hoke's and Johnson's divisions. You will be able to judge better than myself, should the necessity arise for the evacuation of Savannah, or of Charleston, and will realize the propriety of postponing such action as long as the safety of the army will permit. In the meantime it is proper that whatever is not needed for the defense of either should be removed to places of greater safety. Non-combatants and all movable property should be sent away as promptly as possible. Should it be necessary to evacuate Savannah it is suggested that by massing principal part of your force so as to threaten route to Charleston its defense as well as communication with Augusta may be maintained, and the final withdrawal from Charleston secured if it should become necessary.

JEFF'N DAVIS.

HEADQUARTERS MILITARY DIVISION OF THE WEST,
Pocotaligo, S. C., December 20, 1864.

Lieutenant-General HARDEE,
Commanding, &c., Hardeeville:

GENERAL: I am directed by the general commanding to forward to you the accompanying memorandum of orders, which he wishes you to issue immediately after the evacuation of Savannah. They are designed to carry out his views as to the best disposition of troops under your command for the defense of Charleston and the State of South Carolina generally, Savannah being in the possession of the enemy.

Maj. Gen. G. W. Smith's command (about 2,000 men) being sent to Augusta, will leave of the troops coming from Savannah about 6,500, which, added to those under the immediate command of Maj. Gen. Sam. Jones, on the line of the Savannah and Charleston Railroad (say about 5,500, exclusive of those in and around Charleston), makes about 12,000 troops. Of these he thinks there should be about 2,500 to guard the left bank of the Combahee, with about 1,000 in reserve at a central point between the Combahee and Ashepoo; about 3,500 in the Fourth Sub-District, with about 1,000 of them in reserve at or near Adams' Run and Green Pond, and about 5,000 in the Second and Third Sub-Districts, in addition to those already there. The cavalry guarding the left (or coast) flank and the front and right flanks may, of course, be used to support the troops to which they are nearest. The orders indicated in the accompanying memorandum will make a distribution approximating as nearly to those numbers as circumstances will permit. In carrying them out it will be necessary that you should send promptly the troops carried to Hardeeville by Brigadier-General Taliaferro to rejoin their respective brigades, and the detached companies or battalions of South Carolina reserves and militia to report to Brigadier-General Chesnut, at Grahamville, and the companies of the Third South Carolina Cavalry, under Colonel Colcock, to unite with those now in front of Grahamville and near Coosawhatchie and Pocotaligo and Kirk's squadron, together with the section of horse artillery attached to the Third South Carolina Cavalry. Endeavor to bring and keep together, as far as practicable, the troops of the same organization.

Very respectfully, your obedient servant,

A. R. CHISOLM,
Aide-de-Camp.

[Indorsement.]

HEADQUARTERS MILITARY DIVISION OF THE WEST,
Charleston, December 24, 1864.

Respectfully forwarded to the War Department for its information. Several lines of defense have been selected from the Savannah River toward Charleston, already more or less fortified. The necessary reconnaissances and defensive works to complete the system have been ordered, and should the enemy give us time it is hoped that his advance on Charleston from that direction will be much retarded, if not altogether prevented. Those defensive lines are—first, the Combahee to Barnwell Court-House; second, the Ashepoo; third, the Edisto; fourth, the Edisto and Ashley. It is not considered advisable to adopt the flanking position recommended by the President in his telegram of the 20th instant, as it could not be carried into effect, with our small force, without abandoning entirely the sea-coast line. This would enable the enemy to approach Charleston from John's Island, or even James Island, with a sea base almost immediately in his rear.

G. T. BEAUREGARD,
General.

[Inclosure.]

Memorandum of orders to be issued by Lieutenant-General Hardee immediately after the evacuation of Savannah.

HEADQUARTERS MILITARY DIVISION OF THE WEST,
Pocotaligo, December 20, 1864.

I. Maj. Gen. G. W. Smith will proceed immediately with his command to Charleston, and thence to Augusta, after being relieved by other troops, as hereinafter directed.

II. Major-General McLaws' division (the senior brigadier commanding) and Colonel Anderson's brigade (preceding) will proceed immediately to Charleston and relieve Maj. Gen. G. W. Smith's division.

III. Major-General Wright's division and Brigadier-General Chesnut's command (about 1,500 men), consisting of South Carolina reserves and Second, Third, and Fourth South Carolina Militia, to the Fourth Military Sub-District, a reserve of about 500 men being stationed at Green Pond and another of like number near Adams' Run. Brigadier-General Robertson will report to Major-General Wright for temporary duty, to advise as to disposition of troops, and then to be assigned to duty as circumstances may require.

IV. Col. George P. Harrison's and Col. A. C. Edwards' brigades to be stationed on the left bank of the Combahee, guarding the several passages (about six) across that river, to Barnwell Court-House; Brigadier-General Young's command to be increased by the Seventh Georgia Cavalry (dismounted), Col. E. C. Anderson, jr., commanding, as reserves at or near Blue House, between the Combahee and Ashepoo Rivers.

V. The Third South Carolina Cavalry and Kirk's squadron will cover the left (or coast) flank of the retiring troops. After crossing the Combahee Maj. John Jenkins, with Captains Seabrook's and Peeples' companies Third South Carolina Cavalry, will take post on John's Island, and Captain Kirk's squadron will proceed, via Charleston, to Christ Church Parish and take post near and northeast of Mount Pleasant.

VI. Major-General Wheeler's corps (that part of it east of Savannah River, and the remainder if it should come up) will guard crossings of the Savannah and New Rivers and the landings east of Screven's Causeway until forced by the enemy to retire. He will then guard and defend the country between the Savannah River and the defensive line of the Combahee and the right flank of that line, resting at or near Barnwell Court-House, and extending by the shortest defensible line to the Savannah River, covering Augusta.

VII. Colonel Gonzales will assign the field artillery now in South Carolina to the most appropriate positions for the defense of the Fourth Sub-District and the line of the Combahee, from Salkehatchie bridge to the coast, taking care to assign the batteries to the positions with which their respective commanders are most familiar. He will assign, subject to General Hardee's approval, the field batteries coming from Savannah, as circumstances may indicate, for the best defense of the line of the Combahee, the Fourth Sub-District, and Augusta.

VIII. As soon as the services of Brigadier-General Taliaferro can be spared from the duty on which he is now engaged, he will proceed to James Island and resume his former command, assigning to their appropriate positions the troops of Major-General McLaws' division and Colonel Anderson's brigade, destined for that island.

IX. As soon as Major-General McLaws' division moves from Hardeeville he will immediately proceed to Pocotaligo and relieve Maj. Gen. Samuel Jones, and take the immediate command of the troops on the line of the Combahee.

X. On being relieved by Major-General McLaws, Major-General Jones will proceed to Charleston and resume his command and enter on the duties designated by Special Orders, No. —, from department headquarters.

XI. As the cavalry retires before the enemy it will drive off all cattle, sheep, and hogs not necessary for its consumption, and impress and send to Charleston, to be turned over to the chief engineer, all negroes capable of bearing arms. It will also destroy all mills, boats, buildings (that may be useful to the enemy for military purposes), and all rice, corn, and other provisions not necessary for its own subsistence beyond such as is absolutely necessary for the consumption of the owners and their families and slaves.

XII. All teams and wagons (with their drivers) on plantations about to fall into the hands of the enemy, not required by their owners, shall be impressed for the use of the army.

CONFIDENTIAL, CIRCULAR No. 2.

HEADQUARTERS,
Savannah, Ga., December 20, 1864.

The movement ordered in confidential circular from these headquarters dated December 19, 1864, will be executed to-night at the hours as originally arranged, and not as subsequently amended—that is, Wright's division will move at 8 o'clock, McLaws' division at 10 o'clock, and Smith's division at 11 o'clock, and Wright's skirmishers will be withdrawn at 10.30 o'clock, McLaws' skirmishers at 12.30 o'clock, and Smith's skirmishers at 1 o'clock.

By command of Lieutenant-General Hardee:

T. B. ROY,
Assistant Adjutant-General.

GENERAL ORDERS, No. 8.

HEADQUARTERS WRIGHT'S DIVISION,
In the Field, December 20, 1864.

* * * * * * *

II. At dark the light batteries under the direction of Capt. John W. Brooks, chief of artillery of division, will be withdrawn by hand from their position in line, with as little noise as possible, and will be sent over the pontoon bridge to Hardeeville.

* * * * * * *

VI. The chief of artillery of this division, Capt. John W. Brooks, will take measures to have the heavy guns in position spiked, or otherwise rendered useless, at 10 p. m. to-night. The ammunition will be destroyed by throwing it into the river, or otherwise, and not by blowing it up.

By order of Maj. Gen. A. R. Wright:

J. V. H. ALLEN,
Captain of Artillery.

[Indorsement.]

DECEMBER 20, 1864.

Respectfully referred to battery commanders, who will execute this order.

The two Napoleons of Lieutenant Richardson's section will immediately move, with their caissons, to the pontoon bridge in Savannah; the other guns will be disabled and ammunition destroyed without noise.

By order of Brigadier-General Mercer:

W. WHEELER,
Chief of Artillery.

NEAR IZARD'S, *December 20, 1864.*
(Via Hardeeville. Received 5.30 p. m.)

General G. T. BEAUREGARD:

The enemy fired upon us at various times to-day until dark with artillery from works near Izard's.

J. WHEELER,
Major-General.

HEADQUARTERS,
Savannah, Ga., December 20, 1864.

Major-General WHEELER, *Commanding Cavalry Corps:*

GENERAL: I am directed by Lieutenant-General Hardee to say that the C. S. steamer Savannah, Capt. Thomas W. Brent, C. S. Navy, commanding, will remain at Screven's Ferry, or in vicinity, for forty-eight hours after the evacuation of Savannah. To enable Captain Brent to save his crew, which will pass on the road from Screven's Ferry to Hardeeville, the general directs that you will keep him well advised of the movements of the enemy, and especially to inform him of any movement threatening the line of communication to Hardeeville in time to save his crew.

Very respectfully, your obedient servant,

T. B. ROY,
Assistant Adjutant-General.

POCOTALIGO, *December 20, 1864.*

Major-General WHEELER:

Enemy reported leaving Tullifinny. Be sharply on the lookout for them on New River line, and inform me promptly if they appear.

SAM. JONES,
Major-General.

(Same to Colonel Colcock.)

POCOTALIGO, *December 20, 1864—3 a. m.*
(Received 9.30 a. m.)

General WHEELER:

I am ordered by General Hardee to Hardeeville, and to place myself in communication with you. Please indicate the least force of infantry which will be needed near Izard's; and if you want light artillery how much.

W. B. TALIAFERRO,
Brigadier-General.

COOSAWHATCHIE, *December 20, 1864.*

Major STRINGFELLOW:

The enemy still occupy the Neck in force. I can ascertain no change in his position on my front.

GEO. P. HARRISON, JR.,
Colonel, Commanding.

HDQRS. DEPT. OF S. CAROLINA, GEORGIA, AND FLORIDA,
Cheves' House, December 21, 1864.

Major-General MCLAWS,
Commanding, &c.:

GENERAL: Lieutenant-General Hardee directs that you assume command of the three divisions en route for Hardeeville—your own, Smith's, and Wright's—and direct and regulate their march to that place.

Very respectfully, your obedient servant,

T. B. ROY,
Assistant Adjutant-General.

POCOTALIGO, *December 21, 1864.*
(Received 1 o'clock 22d.)

President JEFFERSON DAVIS:

General Hardee reports to-day from Hardeeville that evacuation of Savannah was successfully accomplished last night. All light artillery and most of the stores and munitions were brought off; the heavy guns were spiked and otherwise disabled. Line of defense behind Combahee River will be taken soon as practicable.

G. T. BEAUREGARD.

HARDEEVILLE, *December 21, 1864.*
(Received 22d.)

His Excellency JEFFERSON DAVIS:

On the 19th enemy forced a landing on the South Carolina side, so near my communications that to save the garrison it became necessary to give up the city. Its evacuation was successfully accomplished last night. All the light artillery and most of the stores, munitions, &c., were brought off. I learn indirectly that there is a misapprehension as to the force disposable for the defense of Savannah. It summed up, land side and water side, militia, reserves, dismounted cavalry, local and details, 9,089.

W. J. HARDEE,
Lieutenant-General.

SPECIAL FIELD ORDERS, No. 17. } HDQRS. DEPT. OF S. C., GA., AND FLA.,
Hardeeville, S. C., December 22, 1864.

The following disposition of troops will be carried into effect with the least practicable delay:

I. Maj. Gen. G. W. Smith's command, consisting of a division of Georgia militia, and including Pruden's battery, will proceed to Augusta, Ga., via Charleston.

II. Major-General McLaws' division, under command of Brigadier-General Baker, and Col. E. C. Anderson's brigade, the latter taking precedence, will proceed to Charleston and report to Major-General Ransom for duty on James Island.

III. Major-General Wright's division and Brigadier-General Chesnut's command—the latter consisting of South Carolina reserves and the Second, Third, and Fourth South Carolina Militia—will proceed to the Fourth Military Sub-District of South Carolina. Major-General Wright will have command of the district, and will station a reserve force of 500 men at Green Pond, and a like number at Adams' Run Station. Brig. Gen. B. H. Robertson will report to Major-General Wright, to give him such assistance in the disposition of troops as his knowledge of the country will enable him to do, and will afterward be assigned to duty as circumstances may require.

IV. Major-General McLaws, as soon as his division, as heretofore directed, shall move from Hardeeville, will proceed to Pocotaligo and relieve Maj. Gen. S. Jones, and take immediate command of the forces on the line of the Combahee.

V. Maj. Gen. S. Jones, upon being relieved by Major-General McLaws, will proceed to Charleston, assume command of his district, and enter upon the duties designated in ——— from these headquarters.

VI. Major-General Wheeler's cavalry corps (that part of it east of the Savannah River, and the remainder should it come up) will guard the crossing of the Savannah and New Rivers and the landings east of Screven's Causeway until forced by the enemy to retire. General Wheeler will then guard and defend the country between the Savannah River and the defensive line of the Combahee and the right flank of that line, resting at or near Barnwell Court-House.

VII. Cols. G. P. Harrison and A. C. Edwards will report to Major-General McLaws for assignment to brigades, which will be stationed on the left bank of the Combahee, to guard the crossings of that river, to Barnwell Court-House.

VIII. The Seventh Georgia Cavalry (dismounted), Col. E. C. Anderson commanding, is assigned to Young's brigade. The Third South Carolina Cavalry and Kirk's squadron will cover the left (or coast) flank of the retiring troops; and after crossing the Combahee Captains Seabrook's and Peeples' companies Third South Carolina Cavalry, under command of Maj. John Jenkins, will take post on John's Island, and Kirk's squadron will proceed, via Charleston, to Christ Church Parish and take post near and northeast of Mount Pleasant.

IX. The batteries of light artillery will report as follows: Brooks', Barnwell's, and Wagener's batteries to Major-General McLaws, at Hardeeville; Abell's battery for duty at Honey Hill, and Anderson's battery to commanding officer at Coosawhatchie; Daniell's, Hanleiter's, Guerard's, and Maxwell's batteries will report, at Pocotaligo, to Col. A. J. Gonzales, chief of artillery, who will, with the approval of the lieutenant-general commanding, assign them to positions the most appropriate for the defense of the Fourth Military Sub-District and the line of the Combahee, from Salkehatchie bridge to the coast.

X. Brigadier-General Taliaferro will proceed to James Island, resume command of Sub-District No. 3, and will be prepared to put in position the troops of McLaws' division and Anderson's brigade, destined for that island.

XI. As the cavalry retires before the enemy it will drive off all cattle, sheep, and hogs not necessary for its consumption, and impress and send to Charleston, to be turned over to engineer department, all negroes capable of bearing arms; all mills, boats, buildings that may be used by the enemy for military purposes, and all rice, corn, and other provisions not necessary for the subsistence of the cavalry, and not absolutely needed for the consumption of the owners, their families, and slaves, will also be destroyed.

XII. All wagons and teams (with drivers) on plantations about to fall into the hands of the enemy, and which are not required by the owners for the removal of their own property, will be impressed for the use of the army.

By order of Lieutenant-General Hardee:

T. B. ROY,
Assistant Adjutant-General.

SPECIAL FIELD ORDERS, No. 18.

HEADQUARTERS,
Hardeeville, December 22, 1864.

I. Symons' regiment and the Twenty-seventh Battalion Georgia Reserves, and the two companies of Cobb Guards, will not be included in what is known as McLaws' division, but will report to Major-General McLaws for duty on the line to which he has been assigned in Special Field Orders, No. 17, from these headquarters.

By order of Lieutenant-General Hardee:

D. H. POOLE,
Assistant Adjutant-General.

HEADQUARTERS,
Hardeeville, S. C., December 22, 1864.

Major-General McLAWS,
Commanding, &c.:

GENERAL: Lieutenant-General Hardee desires you to send a section of artillery and 200 men to protect the Purysburg Landing from a possible visit of the enemy's steamers. A fatigue party will be furnished from this force to unload the Sampson, a steamer expected at Purysburg to-night with a cargo of corn. This detachment should move at daylight to-morrow.

Very respectfully, your obedient servant,

T. B. ROY,
Assistant Adjutant-General.

HEADQUARTERS,
Hardeeville, S. C., December 22, 1864.

Major-General WHEELER,
Commanding Cavalry:

GENERAL: Lieutenant-General Hardee directs that you will send all the companies of the Third South Carolina Cavalry now serving with you, together with the section of the horse artillery serving with the regiment, to report to Major-General Jones, or other officer commanding at Coosawhatchie, for duty with the other companies of the regiment on duty in that vicinity. He also desires that Guerard's battery and Maxwell's section shall move at once, in compliance with Special Orders, No. 17, of this date.

Very respectfully, your obedient servant,

T. B. ROY,
Assistant Adjutant-General.

HDQRS. GEORGIA RESERVES AND MIL. DIST. OF GEORGIA,
Macon, Ga., December 22, 1864.

Hon. JAMES A. SEDDON,
Secretary of War, Richmond, Va.:

SIR: You will remember that upon the occupation of Atlanta by General Sherman he issued a sweeping order for the removal of men, women, and children from the city. Since the reoccupation of the place by our own people there were found soldiers and citizens who had remained there with the Yankees and had been employed by them in various occupations. When women and children were driven out by the heartless brute Sherman, and were forced to make their way to some place of refuge, those who remained subjected themselves, in my opinion, to the suspicion of treason. Acting upon this opinion I ordered Colonel Glenn, commandant of the post, to arrest all such and send them here. In accordance with these instructions arrests have been made and some eight or ten persons are now here. I deem it important that an example should be made in these cases, not only because they deserve punishment, but as a warning against others tempted hereafter to a similar course. With such as are deserters and absentees from the army I shall deal in the military courts—if I ever get one—and those who are not connected with the army I shall have turned over to the civil authorities. In the absence of the district attorney, who is cut off in Savannah, I have employed Hon. E. A. Nisbet to undertake the prosecution of the cases. I selected Judge Nisbet because of his known ability as a lawyer and his earnest devotion to our cause, and from the fact that he was known to the Department. Judge Nisbet will enter at once upon the duty, and will accept such compensation for his services as the Department shall award him.

I trust that my course in the matter will meet your approval, and that it may result in good to the country.

I am, with sentiments of sincere regard, very truly, yours, &c.,

HOWELL COBB,
Major-General.

[Indorsement.]

DECEMBER 31, 1864.

ADJUTANT-GENERAL:

Inform General Cobb that his course of proceeding is deemed judicious, and meets the approval of the Department. He can better judge than myself what measure of severity is advisable in the state of feeling prevailing in the country, and his judgment is relied on.

J. A. S.,
Secretary.

HDQRS. GEORGIA RESERVES AND MIL. DIST. OF GEORGIA,
Macon, Ga., December 22, 1864.

General S. COOPER,
Adjutant and Inspector General, Richmond, Va.:

GENERAL: I respectfully return the inclosed paper, and beg leave to remark that the circumstances which led to the appointment and assignment of General Gartrell are as well understood by the Department as myself, and I do not see how I am to relieve him from his present position. I am not surprised at the request of General Winder to that effect, for he expressed his regret that General Gartrell should be assigned to that command before he ever entered upon the duties of it, and he has been unceasing in his efforts to get clear of him. If General Gartrell had been the equal in every respect of General R. E. Lee, I have no doubt the same complaints would have been made, for General Winder was determined in advance not to be satisfied with the arrangement. I beg to state frankly to you why, in my opinion, General Winder is so querulous in reference both to the reserves and General Gartrell. Unfortunately there is a mutual dislike and distrust between him and these troops, and each party is conscious of the existence of that feeling on the part of the other. I am not sufficiently acquainted with the facts which gave rise to these feelings to pronounce judgment upon their respective opinions. The objection of General Winder to General Gartrell arises from the respect and confidence of the former in Colonel Forno, whom he prefers in command of the troops. Colonel Forno is an excellent officer and deserves this confidence, and I am not surprised that General Winder is anxious to retain in so important a position one so worthy to hold it.

In the foregoing simple statement you have a solution of the various complaints, suggestions, &c., which are being daily forwarded to you from General Winder. I will add that I have repeatedly called upon General Winder to make his charges and specifications against officers or men of the reserves, and I would have them properly and promptly investigated, but to this hour not one has been made to me.

It is due to General Gartrell to say that he is now temporarily relieved from duty by a dangerous wound received at the head of his troops in a late fight near Savannah, and it is equally due to his troops to say that they have shown themselves in the presence of the enemy worthy of the respect and confidence of their country.

With these remarks I beg leave to say that my relationship, both personal and official, with General Winder has been pleasant in every respect. At the same time I am free to say that he is not more anxious to get rid of the reserves than I am to get rid of his complaints against them, and it will therefore be most acceptable and agreeable to me to have any arrangement made by which the reserves shall no longer be in anywise connected with the general and his prisons.

I am, general, very respectfully, yours, &c.,

HOWELL COBB,
Major-General.

[Inclosure.]

CAMP SUMTER, *Andersonville, Ga., October 8, 1864.*

General S. COOPER,
Adjutant and Inspector General:

GENERAL: Special Orders, No. 108, issued from General Cobb's headquarters, assigns Brig. Gen. L. J. Gartrell to command of the Second Brigade, Georgia Reserves, composed of the First, Second, Third, and Fourth Regiments, and directs him to take command of it wherever it may be. This necessarily brings him to me. An officer of this rank will be embarrassing in a command like this. The officer second in command necessarily has duties to perform that a brigadier-general ought not to be expected to perform. Colonel Forno is an excellent officer, and I would be glad to retain him in his present position. The reserves are not suited to the guarding of prisoners, and I would be glad to change them for other troops. I had some of the militia, and I found them much better suited for the service and much more reliable. Will it be possible to relieve me of the brigadier-general?

Respectfully, your obedient servant,

JNO. H. WINDER,
Brigadier-General.

[First indorsement.]

NOVEMBER 7, 1864.

Respectfully submitted to Secretary of War:

I concur in the views of General Winder, as given within, and ask authority to order as requested.

S. COOPER,
Adjutant and Inspector General.

[Second indorsement.]

NOVEMBER 10, 1864.

ADJUTANT-GENERAL:

General Gartrell cannot be relieved from command of his brigade. This complaint had better be communicated to General Cobb, and he asked to consider and remove it.

J. A. S.,
Secretary.

[Third indorsement.]

ADJUTANT AND INSPECTOR GENERAL'S OFFICE,
November 16, 1864.

Respectfully referred to Major-General Cobb.

His attention is invited to the preceding indorsement.

By command of the Secretary of War:

H. L. CLAY,
Assistant Adjutant-General.

CHARLESTON, *December 23, 1864.*

General S. COOPER,
Adjutant and Inspector General:

Unless Wheeler's command of twelve so-called brigades can be properly organized into divisions, under good commanders, a large portion of it had better be dismounted forthwith; its conduct in front of the enemy, and its depredations on private property, render it worse than useless. I regret being unable to recommend for promotion any of General Wheeler's brigadiers, but hope that if two or three capable major-generals cannot be had, promotions might be made for the purpose indicated from General Hampton's cavalry. Brigadier-General Dearing, of that command, attracted my attention last summer as a promising officer; I would be glad to have him.

G. T. BEAUREGARD,
General.

CHARLESTON, *December 23, 1864.*
(Received 24th.)

General S. COOPER,
Adjutant and Inspector General:

Your attention is respectfully invited to the fact that orders for the collecting of subsistence stores and forage cannot be executed unless the agents of bureau at Richmond be instructed to fill the requisitions of the commissary and quartermaster in this army. Please give this matter your early attention.

G. T. BEAUREGARD,
General.

[First indorsement.]

DECEMBER 24, 1864.

Quartermaster-General and Commissary-General, for special attention. Every effort should be made to fill the requisitions.

J. A. SEDDON,
Secretary of War.

[Second indorsement.]

DECEMBER 24, 1864.

Respectfully returned.

I do not understand the dispatch, as all officers of this department collecting forage in South Carolina and Georgia are instructed to furnish General Beauregard's command, and no complaint has recently come to me. I think the dispatch is not written out as sent by General Beauregard.

A. R. LAWTON,
Quartermaster-General.

[Third indorsement.]

Respectfully returned.

Organic law, as well as the enactments of this Confederacy, warrant the commanding general of an army defending a country to impress subsistence necessary for his troops, and General Beauregard has the power to enforce the impressments made by his order, and it is to be inferred, under present circumstances, that he has the good will of the people generally to aid him. The country his army is depending on is plentiful compared with Virginia, where General Lee's army is operating, and the latter can get nothing except from the collections of this bureau; but the officers of this bureau can no longer impress, because they have no power to enforce it, and the people will not surrender their stores. Virginia is ravaged and drained, and General Lee's army must be supplied from the Carolinas by what the bureau officers can collect. Recently General Beauregard required the chief commissary of subsistence to furnish 15,000 men with sixty days' rations, and the order to assist in supplying Virginia was stated by the chief commissary of subsistence to be impossible. He was directed to send on what had been ordered for here, which would still have left General Beauregard's army in far better condition than was or is General Lee's. General Beauregard can exercise his legal powers to supply his army. The circumstances have arisen for which the law was made. This bureau has for a great while been stating that, under the existing condition of the

Treasury, the absence of legal sanction or power to enforce impressments by bureau officers, the temper of the people, and legal proceedings on the subject, supplies were being consumed much faster than collected. What is now being gathered by officers of this bureau must be distributed in proportion to general necessities in relation to the facilities of armies in different localities for self support, under the authority by law vested in the general commanding.

L. B. NORTHROP,
Commissary-General.

HEADQUARTERS CAVALRY CORPS,
Cheves' House, December 23, 1864.

Major-General MCLAWS,
Commanding Division, &c.:

GENERAL: General Anderson has just returned from flag of truce to Savannah. He saw a number of officers, and from all he could learn he is of the opinion that Sherman will not rest long in Savannah, but advance into South Carolina very soon. He was told that the city would be garrisoned by Foster, who arrived in the city yesterday.

Respectfully, general, your obedient servant,

J. WHEELER,
Major-General.

The State of South Carolina, at a General Assembly, begun and holden at Columbia on the fourth Monday of November, in the year of our Lord one thousand eight hundred and sixty-four, and thence continued by divers adjournments to the twenty-third of December, in the same year.

AN ACT to repeal all acts and parts of acts heretofore passed by the Legislature of this State on the subject of furnishing slave labor on the coast and fortifications within this State, and otherwise to provide for furnishing such labor.

SECTION I. *Be it enacted by the Senate and House of Representatives, now met and sitting in General Assembly, and by the authority of the same,* That, in order to furnish the necessary slave labor to work on the coast of this State and the fortifications within the limits of the same, there shall be organized a force consisting of male slaves between the ages of eighteen and fifty years, liable under existing laws to road duty, not exceeding in number at any one time of one-tenth part of said slaves, to serve for the term of twelve months from the date of their impressment, subject however to the right of their respective owners at the expiration of every three months of the said term of service to substitute other slaves so liable to road duty in their place, and who by such substitution shall constitute a portion or the whole of said force, as the case may be, from the respective dates of such substitution; this force shall be raised by general impressment throughout the whole State whenever His Excellency the Governor may order or direct such agent of the State as he may appoint to make such impressment under the provisions of this act. But if the impressment of a less number than one-tenth would produce should be found to be sufficient, then the impressment shall be made on the State at large according to one uniform rule of equality, to be prescribed in the order of the Governor directing such impressment to be made by the

State agent, and whatever number greater than ten shall be so prescribed as a divisor to make the apportionment of no fractions of slaves either below or above such number selected as a divisor shall be considered or taken into the apportionment unless it is at least one-fifth or more of such divisor, and in such case the fraction of one-fifth shall be taken by requiring the party owning it to furnish one hand for two months, with the same right of substitution as in case of whole numbers, and the same rule as to fractions shall be observed when the number ten is used as the divisor in making the apportionment.

SEC. II. It shall be the duty of His Excellency the Governor to appoint a State agent, such agent to be selected from the class of persons not liable to conscription in the Confederate military service, if the services of a suitable agent can be secured from said class, who shall receive for his services the pay of a lieutenant-colonel of infantry, as allowed by the Confederate Government, during his employment, to be paid to him monthly by the State.

SEC. III. That it shall be the duty of the State agent aforesaid, immediately on the reception of any order from His Excellency the Governor, to make impressment of slaves under this act, to extend such order to the sheriffs of the several judicial districts of the State, whose duty it shall be to execute the same in their respective districts, and it shall be the duty of the commissioners of roads and the authorities of incorporated cities, towns, and villages, and such other person or persons as the State agent may appoint, to furnish to the sheriffs of their respective districts within thirty days after the passage of this act a full and correct return of all male slaves liable to road duty within their respective jurisdictions, which returns shall be based on the statements furnished by the owners of such slaves, sworn to in writing, such statements to be returned to the secretary of the board of commissioners of roads, and by them kept on file; and it shall be the duty of the said sheriffs, upon being notified by the said State agent of any order for the impressment of slaves as aforesaid, thirty days before the summons, all owners liable under such order to furnish slaves to have the slaves so liable at the respective depots and at the proper time, giving ten days' notice thereof to the owners for transportation to the place of labor as may be directed by said order; and the said sheriffs shall in their respective districts, with the assistance of a respectable loyal citizen, to be chosen by the owner of each slave, if he will, and if not, by the sheriff, appraise said slaves on their delivery at said depots, and in case of their disagreement they shall select a third citizen of like qualification, whose decision shall be final, and give receipts to the owners for them, specifying in said receipts the names of the slaves, the valuation put upon them, and term of service for which they are impressed, a duplicate of which receipts shall also be furnished by the several sheriffs to the State agent; and if upon the day and at the place so notified any owner of slaves so liable shall fail to have them in readiness, then the sheriffs of the district where such owner resides shall immediately arrest such slaves, and the cost of such arrests, subsistence of slaves, and transportation to be paid by the defaulting owner, and to be taxed and collected as other costs now are by law, and when there is such default, failure, or refusal to send slaves, after due summons to the owners by the sheriff, the slaves of such defaulters shall labor and serve on the military defenses for twice the period of time specified in the call made by the Governor, provided that the slaves thus furnished shall not be detailed for any other service than such work as is intimately connected with the defense of this State.

SEC. IV. That the State agent may, with the consent of the Governor, appoint such other sub-agents as may be found necessary and proper to the execution of the provisions of this act. But in no case shall he appoint any person as such agent who is liable to conscription in the Confederate service and physically able for active service in the army. Such agents shall be paid by the State eight dollars per day for their services at the end of each month.

SEC. V. The respective sheriffs for their services rendered under the provisions of this act shall be paid by the State eight dollars per day whilst actually engaged in the discharge of said duties, besides their costs for arrests and fees for dieting prisoners so arrested in pursuance thereof, which latter shall be paid by the owners of said prisoners.

SEC. VI. That the pay for such slaves shall be eleven dollars per month, and be furnished with sufficient rations and two suits of clothes during the term of one year, or one suit of clothes every six months, including two pairs of shoes and one hat for the year, by the State, or a fair commutation in money for the clothing if furnished by the owner. And that it shall be the duty of the State agent to certify the pay bills for the pay of the said slaves for their respective owners, specifying the number of said slaves, the time they have been employed, and the names of the owners, which bills so certified shall entitle the owners by themselves, or their order indorsed thereon, to receive the same from the State, and the said bills shall be forwarded to the sheriffs of the respective districts where the owners reside, to be delivered by them to the said owners.

SEC. VII. That the commissioners of roads, city, town, and village authorities, for neglect of any of the duties required of them respectively by this act, shall be liable to indictment, and upon conviction fined in a sum not exceeding one hundred dollars. And that any sheriff who shall neglect or refuse to discharge any of the duties required of him by this act, shall, upon conviction as for a misdemeanor, in addition to liability on his official bond to any person who may have been aggrieved by such default.

SEC. VIII. That it shall be the duty of the State agent to visit all the camps of the laborers, to examine their condition, to observe their treatment and discipline, to examine their food both as to quality and quantity, and to see that it is the proper ration for each, as is allowed by law, as well as their clothing, and especially to inform himself as to their medical and surgical attendance and care, and whenever required to report the same to the Governor, and particularly at the conclusion of the term of service of each levy, it shall be his duty to make such report to the Governor, in whose possession it may be open for examination by the owners of the said slaves; and it shall also be his duty to prohibit the infliction of corporal punishment by one slave upon another, and shall require that if a slave is to be punished for any default of his duty, the punishment shall be administered by a white man in authority. And for the neglect or refusal of said agent to discharge faithfully any of his duties as prescribed by this act, he shall be subject to removal from office by the Governor as well as liable to an action for damages by any individual who has been injured by his negligence or default of duty.

SEC. IX. Transportation shall be furnished by the State agent for slaves impressed under this act, at the expense of the State, going to or returning from the place of labor home and in returning, also with sufficient rations to last them home, and transportation shall be furnished in like manner for substitutes in going to and returning from said place of labor. And an account shall be kept by the said agent of all expenditures incurred and paid by the State in providing the slave labor aforesaid and in carrying this act into full execution, which shall be annually deposited by him in the office of the Governor of the State, to be presented or proffered by him as a claim by this State against the Confederate Government for payment. And that the funds necessary to pay all expenditures incurred under the provisions of this act shall be paid out of the funds of the public treasury, not otherwise appropriated, upon the presentation of the pay bills signed by the State agent.

SEC. X. It shall be the duty of the Governor and the State agent to have all slaves returned to their owners upon the expiration of their term of service for which they were impressed, and the owners of such as may have been killed or died from disease during their term of service shall not be liable to supply their places with other slaves for the unexpired portion of said term of service.

SEC. XI. If the Confederate Government should make any impressment of slave labor over and above what is to be furnished by the provisions of this act, in view of greater emergencies than are contemplated in this act, then and in that event the owners of such slaves shall have credit as for so much labor furnished for coast duty.

SEC. XII. That all acts and parts of acts herebefore passed by the Legislature of this State on the subject of furnishing labor on the coast or fortifications be, and the same are hereby, repealed.

In the Senate and House the twenty-third day of December, in the year of our Lord one thousand eight hundred and sixty-four, and the eighty-ninth year of the sovereignty and independence of the State of South Carolina.

W. D. PORTER,
President of the Senate.
R. B. BOYLSTON,
Speaker of the House of Representatives.

SECRETARY OF STATE'S OFFICE,
Columbia, December 26, 1864.

I hereby certify the foregoing to be a true copy of an act entitled "An act to repeal all acts and parts of acts heretofore passed by the Legislature of this State on the subject of furnishing slave labor on the coast and fortifications within this State, and otherwise to provide for furnishing such labor," ratified the twenty-third day of December, Anno Domini 1864, and now on file in this office.

Given under my hand and the seal of the State.

[SEAL.]

WM. R. HUNTT,
Secretary of State.

CHARLESTON, *December 24, 1864.*
(Received 7 p. m.)

President DAVIS:

The following telegram sent to General Hood yesterday is communicated for your information:

I regret to inform you that no re-enforcements can possibly be sent you from any quarter. General Taylor has no troops to spare, and every available man in Georgia and South Carolina is required to oppose Sherman, who is not on a raid but an important campaign. Should you be unable to gain any material advantage on Tennessee with your present means you must retire at once behind the Tennessee River, and come with or send to Augusta by best and quickest routes all forces not absolutely required to hold defensive line referred to.

G. T. BEAUREGARD,
General.

SPECIAL ORDERS, No. 305.

ADJT. AND INSP. GENERAL'S OFFICE,
Richmond, Va., December 24, 1864.

* * * * * * *

XI. Maj. Gen. D. H. Hill, Provisional Army, C. S., will report without delay to General G. T. Beauregard, commanding, &c., for assignment to duty at or near Charleston, S. C.

* * * * * * *

By command of the Secretary of War:

JNO. WITHERS,
Assistant Adjutant-General.

CHARLESTON, *December 24, 1864.*

Major-General MCLAWS:

March your command without delay to Pocotaligo, leaving only such guards at Hardeeville as you may deem necessary. At Pocotaligo you will receive further instructions. The forces at Grahamville and Coosawhatchie will remain for the present.

W. J. HARDEE,
Lieutenant-General.

SPECIAL FIELD ORDERS, No. 9.

HDQRS. MCLAWS' DIVISION,
Hardeeville, December 24, 1864.

I. Col. J. C. Fiser, Provisional Army, C. S., is assigned to the command of a brigade composed of the following troops: First Georgia Regulars, Col. R. A. Wayne commanding; Symons' Regiment of Reserves, Col. W. R. Symons commanding; Twenty-seventh Georgia Battalion and Cobb Guards, Maj. A. L. Hartridge commanding.

The commanding officers of the above-named organizations will report to Col. J. C. Fiser without delay.

By order of Major-General McLaws:

R. W. B. ELLIOTT,
Assistant Adjutant-General.

POCOTALIGO, *December 24, 1864.*

Major-General MCLAWS:

General Jones left this morning for Charleston. I have orders to resume my old district command [dispatch torn] and locate the troops destined for my command. I do not like to leave here until you come. Deserters report this morning that the enemy contemplated transporting last night part of his force from my immediate front for a landing at Boyd's. I have apprised General Chesnut, and ordered him if he needs them to ask for [re-enforcements]. Please inform me of your movements and when you are likely to be here.

W. B. TALIAFERRO,
Brigadier-General.

NEAR SAVANNAH, *December 24, 1864.*

Lieut. Gen. W. J. HARDEE,
Charleston:

Cannot the order for burning mills and rice, corn, and other provisions be reconsidered? The threats of enemy to burn and destroy all property in South Carolina are of such a character if we commence burning enemy will feel justified in continuing. Will it not be better to give them no provocation to burn? What we would burn in Beaufort District would be of little value to enemy.

J. WHEELER,
Major-General.

CHARLESTON, *December 25, 1864—8 a. m.*

General S. COOPER,
Adjutant and Inspector General:

General Hardee reports that a force of enemy—infantry, artillery, and cavalry—number not known, has moved from Savannah toward the Altamaha River. He has ordered some cavalry to watch and check the column. No report from General Hood since November 28.

G. T. BEAUREGARD,
General.

EXECUTIVE DEPARTMENT, STATE OF SOUTH CAROLINA,
Columbia, December 25, 1864.

His Excellency President DAVIS:

MY DEAR SIR: The accidental circumstance of the delay of Colonel Buist's departure for Richmond enables me to send this note by him. General Preston having informed me that you had been unwell, together with the many matters now pressing upon you, induce me to confine myself at this time to a few brief suggestions. The fall of Savannah has, of course, very much affected the people of this State. The question which naturally presents itself is, why the force which penetrated Georgia cannot penetrate South Carolina. And at this moment it is not an unwillingness to oppose the enemy, but a chilling apprehension of the futility of doing so, which affects the people. I am endeavoring, and I will remove that chill and dispel that apprehension; but upon you must I rely for that material aid which will assist the people of the State to make good their determined opposition. As rapidly as it can be done I am reorganizing the militia; its effective force I cannot yet estimate—I hope larger than has been supposed. If you will send us aid (although for the moment it falls short of effectual aid), if it be that aid which now foreshadows other aid to come, that spirit can be vitalized which when aroused to a certain extent supplies the place of numbers, and is of itself strength.

Of any force which you may send I am very anxious that the brigade of General Conner, a part of General Kershaw's division, should be a part of it, and sent as soon as possible. I would be much rejoiced if General Kershaw with his division could be spared to us. But if that is not practicable I greatly desire the brigade of General Conner. The presence of General Conner with his brigade would greatly tend to inspire confidence and excite hope.

You, of course, are much better informed of the number of troops on our coast and in the city of Charleston than I am. You are also aware of the necessities at other points which may control you; but it is considered that the force on the coast is not sufficient to make effectual resistance to General Sherman. If that is so, Charleston falls; if Charleston falls, Richmond follows. Richmond may fall and Charleston be saved, but Richmond cannot be saved if Charleston falls. If now I urge upon you the concentration of all available strength for the defense of Charleston I will be acquitted of all selfish consideration when I venture to remind you that two years ago, when it seemed as if then a necessity was about to arise in which you would be forced to decide between Charleston and Richmond, I gave you then the assurance of my support, however feeble, in sustaining you in the destruction of Charleston if it would accomplish the end we then desired. Now, however, I presume that, as between these places, there is no doubt that, if unable to save both, Charleston is that which from every consideration we must prefer to save. To save it we must have troops. It is in this connection that I must bring also to your attention the vital consequence of attending at once to Branchville as a place to be fortified and to which troops should be sent. Its strategic importance I am sure is too manifest to require from me any urgency in bringing it to your notice. There are no works there which are of the slightest consequence. I understand surveys are now making; it is difficult to understand why they were not made before this time. You will not understand from this that I wish to indulge in censure or criticism, but to indicate to you that a position of the utmost consequence is not prepared for resistance to the attempt which may be reasonably supposed will be made to possess it. If that attempt should be successful our future will be greatly clouded.

In view of these difficulties I must freely confer with you as to the expediency of adding the services of such State officers as are connected with the State government to those which the engineer officers of the Confederate Government may be now endeavoring to render. I am sure that, with the spirit which prompts me and them, there cannot be conflict or confusion, and that great success will be gained which results from united action. In this connection also suffer me to make another suggestion. The number of detailed men in the State is considerable. It has been supposed that they are not liable to militia duty. It matters little how that may be, except in this respect: that their absence from all appearance of military service by so much diminishes the influences with which I am now attempting to quicken and excite our people not only to effective resistance, but to that confidence in the success of that resistance which will assist me in my efforts and sustain them in their conduct. If when the militia was paraded and inspected the detailed men were also to be paraded, I am quite sure of the effect. It would be no interference with the command of them by Confederate officers; it would not interfere with their business, for it would not occur more than once or twice, and then only for a few hours, and the effect would be, I am sure, beneficial.

These suggestions I make to you with the conviction that you will assist me in every way to develop now all of our resources to aid you in the task that is before you and us. There are other matters concerning which I will at an early day communicate with you.

I have the honor to be, &c.,

A. G. MAGRATH.

CHARLESTON, *December 25, 1864.*

Major-General WHEELER:

Suspend the order for burning mills, corn, rice, and other provisions for the present.

H. W. FEILDEN,
Assistant Adjutant-General.

HEADQUARTERS CAVALRY DIVISION,
Smith's House, December 25, 1864.

Lieut. M. G. HUDSON,
Aide-de-Camp:

LIEUTENANT: General Wheeler told me verbally two days ago that he wished me to take charge of and picket the line between Union Creek and New River bridge, and that he would send me, in addition to my present force, 400 cavalry to perform the duty. Colonel Pointer's regiment, of Allen's brigade, has reported to me, but not the Second Tennessee. General Allen left without telling me what portion of the line was being picketed by his command. I was under the impression that he was covering the river between Izard's and Screven's Ferry, but I have just received a note from General Young asking me to move the left of my line down to Huger's place, as he was picketing six miles with only fifty men. What force is now picketing the line between Screven's Ferry and New River bridge? Please give me all the information you can relative to the manner in which the line from Izard's to New River bridge is being picketed. I would also respectfully request a written order defining exactly the duty I am to perform and when I am to commence performing it. I would also like to be informed what quartermaster at Hardeeville my division quartermaster is to call on for corn. Colonel Pointer has reported to me, and has not a single wagon. How can he subsist his men and horses? Everything for them must come from Hardeeville, and it is absolutely necessary that he should have wagons. I am depending entirely on the major-general commanding to assist me in getting corn for my animals; without his prompt assistance they must suffer. I have ordered Colonel White to extend his line to Clydesdale Creek, and Colonel Pointer to cover the line from Clydesdale Creek to Screven's Ferry. Beyond this I have and shall do nothing until I hear from the major-general commanding and until the Second Tennessee reports. My horses have had no corn for four or five days. Colonel Pointer told me this morning that several horses had already died from eating rice. Please urge upon the general the urgent necessity of supplying my command immediately with corn.

Respectfully requesting an answer at your earliest convenience, I am, lieutenant, very respectfully, your obedient servant,

R. H. ANDERSON,
Brigadier-General.

HDQRS. GEORGIA RESERVES AND MIL. DIST. OF GEORGIA,
Macon, Ga., December 25, 1864.

General G. T. BEAUREGARD, *Charleston, S. C.:*

GENERAL: The telegraphic wires work so badly between Millen and this point that we shall have to rely for the present upon the courier-line. I am using every effort to remedy the difficulties on the line. This morning I learn through the Augusta papers of the evacuation of Savannah. I had hoped to have received earlier and more reliable information of what was occurring with our forces in and about Savannah, but have so far heard nothing except through the newspapers.

The fall of Savannah thus closing that portion of Sherman's campaign, leads to the inquiry of the enemy's next movement. Of this you are far more able to judge than I am, but I venture to call your attention to the probabilities of a movement upon Southwestern Georgia. The removal of the prisoners back to Andersonville, which has been effected, adds to the inducement for a demonstration in that quarter. Kilpatrick's cavalry, being now relieved from Sherman's army, can go in any direction, and already we have reports of its moving in that direction. You are aware that I have no force to meet even a cavalry raid if made in any force, and hence I call your attention to the subject.

In the upper portion of the State I have some cavalry commands, composed principally of militia and deserters and absentees, organized under the authority of General Hood while that section of the State was in the occupancy of the enemy. The strength of these commands I do not know, as they have not yet reported to me, as I have required them to do. When purged of the men who belong to the Confederate service I suppose the various organizations will be about 1,200 strong, and it was with this force, with such aid as I could give from the reserve artillery, that I proposed to drive the enemy from Dalton. I state these facts, and inclose a copy of my general order in reference to these troops, that you may be informed of the condition the State is in, in a military point of view.

About 1,000 men, composed of Colonel Hood's cavalry and a portion of the militia, under General McKay, were at the Altamaha bridge, on the Savannah and Gulf Railroad, at my last advices, on the 19th instant. All the militia that were fit for field service were sent forward to Savannah from this point, and the remainder, composed of old men unable to do field duty, were organized and furloughed by Governor Brown until further orders.

The information from the Army of Tennessee, which I gather from the papers, and the dispatch I forward to you to-day from Colonel Brent containing the curious inquiry of General S. D. Lee, cause apprehensions of serious disasters in that quarter. I am more and more persuaded of the vital importance of increasing our army by the volunteer principle of which I have spoken so freely to you. The number of men whom it seems impossible to obtain by conscription, but who could be got in the way I have proposed, would greatly increase our army.

I should add that General Hood has called for all the arms and ammunition at this place to be forwarded to him, which has been done, reserving a very small portion of each.

I am, general, very respectfully, yours, &c.,

HOWELL COBB,
Major-General.

P. S.—Your boxes received and stored with the depositary here.

H. C.

[Indorsement.]

JANUARY 14, 1865.

Return to the Secretary of War.

Subsequent events answer the main points in this letter.

J. D.

[Inclosure.]

GENERAL ORDERS, } HDQRS. GA. RES. AND MIL. DIST. OF GA.,
No. 30. } *Macon, Ga., December 7, 1864.*

I. The following military organizations, raised under the authority of Governor Brown, and afterward received into the Confederate service by General J. B. Hood—to wit, the regiment commanded by Colonel Findlay, the battalions commanded by Majors Beall, Murkinson, Graham, McCallum, and Ledford, and the battalion lately commanded by Lieutenant-Colonel Glenn, of Pickens County (whose commission was revoked because he was reported to Governor Brown as a deserter), under the person who may have been elected to command it—will be maintained for sixty days from date in discharge of such duties as they may be called upon to perform.

II. After the expiration of the sixty days all men between the ages of eighteen and forty-five subject to conscription will report to the proper enrolling officer for assignment to the army in the field; those liable either to militia duty or to service in the reserves will remain in the present organizations.

III. All persons now in these organizations absent without leave from the Confederate Army will return promptly to their commands with the assurance that their cases will be recommended to the most favorable consideration of their respective commanding generals, in view of the services rendered by them in these organizations; and to carry out this object the officers under whom they have been serving will furnish each one with a statement of his services. After this opportunity further indulgence to absentees will not be granted.

IV. The officers in command of these organizations are enjoined to be vigilant in the arrest of all deserters and absentees, and will forward them without delay to the conscript camp at this place.

By command of Maj. Gen. Howell Cobb:

R. J. HALLETT,
Assistant Adjutant-General.

EXECUTIVE DEPARTMENT,
Macon, Ga., December 7, 1864.

I. The above orders of Major-General Cobb have been submitted to my inspection, and I concur in the order that the persons in said organizations who are subject to my command as militiamen remain in the same organization with those subject to his command as Confederate reserves till further orders, and I direct all such organizations to report to General Cobb, and obey his orders in future as they have heretofore obeyed the orders of General Hood, till further directions from these headquarters.

II. All persons in said organizations who belong to the State Line or the company of State scouts who are now absent without leave will report immediately to their respective commands. Those who obey this order by reporting to their commanding officers, or, if they cannot reach them, to these headquarters, within the next twenty days, will receive a free pardon, except the deduction of their wages for the time they have been absent and one month's additional deduction.

III. All other persons not in said organizations who are so absent without leave will also report to their respective commands within twenty days, and will be excused from any degrading punishment.

JOSEPH E. BROWN.

HDQRS. DEPT. OF S. CAROLINA, GEORGIA, AND FLORIDA,
Charleston, S. C., December 26, 1864.

General S. COOPER,
Adjutant and Inspector General, Richmond:

GENERAL: I have the honor to inclose herewith for your information a copy of a communication of the 17th instant from Maj. Gen. William T. Sherman, U. S. Army, demanding the surrender of Savannah and its dependent forts, and a copy of my reply to that demand.*

Very respectfully, your obedient servant,

W. J. HARDEE,
Lieutenant-General.

CHARLESTON, S. C., *December 26, 1864.*

Major-General MCLAWS,
Pocotaligo:
(Through Major-General Jones.)

Hold your command for the present at Pocotaligo. Take immediate command of the line from Hardeeville to Pocotaligo. Gather in all supplies in the country. Have line of Combahee examined by staff officer.

W. J. HARDEE,
Lieutenant-General.

CHARLESTON, *December 26, 1864.*

Major-General WHEELER,
Hardeeville:

It is intended to hold on to line from Hardeeville to Pocotaligo. It will be necessary for you to hold on to New River.

W. J. HARDEE,
Lieutenant-General.

HEADQUARTERS CAVALRY CORPS,
Hardeeville, December 26, 1864—11.30 a. m.

Col. J. W. CALDWELL,
Commanding Brigade:

COLONEL: The major-general commanding directs that you will move with your command to some point near Robertsville where forage can be procured. This order is given on account of the scarcity of forage here. You will use the most diligent efforts to keep the men from straggling on the march. On selecting a camp you will establish

---

*See p. 737.

and keep constantly a good camp guard. Keep the men closely in camp, enforce the most rigid discipline, use every effort to prevent depredations upon citizens, have regular daily drills, and see that no forage is wasted, requiring your quartermaster to make proper issues regularly. You will draw your subsistence stores from Robertsville.

Respectfully, colonel, your obedient servant,

M. G. HUDSON,
First Lieutenant and Aide-de-Camp.

CIRCULAR ORDERS, No. —. } HEADQUARTERS LEWIS' BRIGADE,
Purysburg, S. C., December 26, 1864.

In obedience to orders from the major-general commanding, the command will be in readiness to move this evening to a point near Robertsville.

Commanding officers are specially enjoined to keep their men in column and allow no straggling whatever. Arriving in camp a good and efficient camp guard will be established and the men required to remain closely in camp, enforcing the most rigid discipline. The regular stated roll-calls will be held in the presence of an officer, and all delinquents faithfully reported.

Depredations of any kind whatever are strictly prohibited, and any one caught committing same will be dealt with accordingly. The commissary will supply subsistence, and the quartermaster make regular issues of forage, and no departure from this order will be made under any circumstances whatever. The colonel commanding feels satisfied that all officers and men will faithfully bear him out in the execution of this order when they are informed that the reputation of themselves and their State is now in question.

It is the wish of the major-general commanding to place us off to ourselves, and see for himself whether it is this brigade that is committing all the depredations reported to him through the country or not.

This order will be read to the command when assembled to move.

By order of John W. Caldwell, colonel commanding brigade:

T. E. STAKE,
Assistant Adjutant-General.

Report of effective strength of General Taliaferro's command, &c., for December 26, 1864.

Command.	Effective strength.	Remarks.
Companies I and K, 3d South Carolina Cavalry, Captain Seabrook.	109	Near Pocotaligo.
Companies A and B, Kirk's Squadron, Captain Kirk.	105	Depot.
Total Major Jenkins' command	214	
5th Georgia Regiment, Major Hundley	222	One mile and a half from Coosaw.
32d Georgia Regiment, Lieutenant-Colonel Bacon.	272	Do.
1st Georgia Reserves, Lieutenant-Colonel Neely	119	Do.
3d Georgia Reserves, Colonel Moore	397	Coosawhatchie.
47th Georgia Regiment, Captain Thompson	232	Tullifinny works.
Detachment 1st South Carolina Cavalry, Captain Trezevant.	131	Do.
7th North Carolina Reserves, Lieutenant-Colonel Hancock.	130	Do.
1st South Carolina Militia, Lieutenant-Colonel Herndon.	403	Do.

Report of effective strength of General Taliaferro's command, &c.—Continued.

Command.	Effective strength.	Remarks.
Anderson's battery, Lieutenant Hurst	112	Coosawhatchie.
Beaufort Artillery, Lieutenant Rhodes	108	Do.
Section De Pass' battery, Lieutenant Manget	53	Do.
Girardey's battery, Captain Girardey	108	Coosawhatchie and Tullifinny.
Detachment 3d South Carolina Cavalry, Captain Campbell.	110	One mile rear of Coosawhatchie.
Detachment Mounted South Carolina Reserves, Captain Kay.	66	Do.
Total Colonel Harrison's command	2,463	
Company B, 8th Battalion, South Carolina Reserves, Captain Fishburne.	40	Work on Coosawhatchie road.
2d Regiment South Carolina Militia, Lieutenant-Colonel Duncan.	138	Honey Hill.
3d Regiment South Carolina Militia, Lieutenant-Colonel Harrington.	290	Do.
4th Regiment South Carolina Militia, Colonel Ligon.	185	Do.
Charles' battery, Sergeant Williamson	81	Do.
Earle's battery, Lieutenant Graham	38	Coosawhatchie and Bolan road.
Companies C and E, 3d South Carolina Cavalry, Lieutenants Farr and Jandon.	110	Courier and picket duty.
1st Battalion South Carolina Reserves, Major Ballinger.	149	Bee's Creek.
6th Battalion South Carolina Reserves, Major Meriwether.	295	Do.
Lafayette Artillery, Captain Kanapaux	102	Do.
Detachment of Charles' battery, Lieutenant Jones.	17	Do.
2d Battalion South Carolina Reserves, Major Barnette.	136	Dawson's Bluff.
Detachment Lafayette Artillery	12	Do.
Total General Chesnut's command	1,593	

RECAPITULATION.

Major Jenkins' command	214
Colonel Harrison's command	2,463
General Chesnut's command	1,593
Grand total	4,270

CHARLESTON, *December 27, 1864.*

General S. COOPER:

General Hood desires me to visit Army of Tennessee. Colonel Brent, my chief of staff, at Montgomery, says my presence is required west, owing to some confusion in various matters and want of supplies and ammunition. Unless otherwise instructed I will leave here as soon as I can make definite arrangements for future operations in this State.

G. T. BEAUREGARD,
General.

CHARLESTON, S. C., *December 27, 1864—11.30 a. m.*

General S. COOPER,
Adjutant and Inspector General, Richmond, Va.:

In event of having to abandon the coast, and enemy's movements will permit a choice of base of operations, shall it be toward North Carolina or Georgia? Latter is true base for forces of this department, but views of War Department may require otherwise.

G. T. BEAUREGARD,
General.

HEADQUARTERS MILITARY DIVISION OF THE WEST,
December 27, 1864.

Lieut. Gen. W. J. HARDEE,
Comdg. Dept. of S. C., Ga., and Fla., Charleston, S. C.:

GENERAL: I am instructed by the commanding general to direct as follows:

First. That you make silently and cautiously all necessary preparations for the evacuation of Charleston should it become necessary, taking at the same time the proper steps to save the garrisons of the different works. Detailed and confidential instructions should be given as to the spiking, by means of rat-tail files, all heavy guns and such others as cannot be moved; for disabling carriages, chassis, and batteries.

Second. That the infantry and cavalry of your command be organized forthwith into brigades and divisions, under good commanders; that all the troops be supplied with knapsacks, haversacks, canteens, blankets, and shoes, and that ample transportation be supplied, as also ammunition for small-arms and light batteries.

Third. That all light batteries be organized into battalions of three batteries each, one battalion being attached to each division, the others in reserve, under the chief of artillery.

The battalions attached to divisions, although under the orders of the division commanders in battle and on the march, will nevertheless make all their returns and reports to the chief of artillery, and all correspondence relative to the organization, equipment, and interior management of battalions will pass through the same channel. Such batteries will only be under the orders of the chief of artillery when in permanent camp or winter quarters. The commanding general also directs that should field officers be needed for the battalions you will apply by telegraph to the War Department and request immediate attention.

I have the honor to be, general, very respectfully, your obedient servant,

JNO. M. OTEY,
Assistant Adjutant-General.

CHARLESTON, *December 27, 1864.*

Hon. J. A. SEDDON,
Secretary of War:

Florida has been cut off in great part from these headquarters, and needs an officer of experience to command there. General Jones can be spared for this purpose. Will you order him?

W. J. HARDEE,
Lieutenant-General.

POCOTALIGO, *December 27, 1864.*

Major-General WHEELER,
Hardeeville:

Direct a detachment from your command, consisting of four commissioned officers and forty men, to proceed at once to Ferebee's place, between Great Swamp and Grahamville, there to meet S. F. O'Neill, of commissary department, to assist in collecting cattle.

L. McLAWS,
Major-General, Commanding.

POCOTALIGO, *December 27, 1864.*

Major-General WHEELER,
Hardeeville:

I am directed by General Hardee to assume command of all the troops between the Savannah River and this point. Order General P. M. B. Young to proceed forthwith to Grahamville with his brigade and take command at that point.

L. McLAWS,
Major-General, Commanding.

HEADQUARTERS CAVALRY CORPS,
Hardeeville, December 27, 1864.

Col. T. B. ROY,
Assistant Adjutant-General:

COLONEL: I dispatched to Lieutenant-General Hardee a day or two past to know if he would permit me to withdraw my picket-line to or near this place. Yesterday I received a dispatch (which suppose was an answer) to hold on to New River, as it was intended to hold the line from Hardeeville to Pocotaligo. I wish to know if it would not answer for my line to extend from New River bridge to Pringle Smith's plantation, on Savannah River? This would shorten my line and enable me to blockade the roads below that line. Please answer by telegraph.

Very respectfully, colonel, your obedient servant,

J. WHEELER,
Major-General.

[Indorsement.]

HDQRS. DEPT. OF S. CAROLINA, GEORGIA, AND FLORIDA,
Charleston, December 29, 1864.

Respectfully returned to Major-General Wheeler:

The authority to shorten his line, within asked for, has been given him by telegraph.

By command of Lieutenant-General Hardee:

T. B. ROY,
Assistant Adjutant-General.

CENTRAL RAILROAD COMPANY,
Macon, Ga., December 27, 1864.

The president reached Macon yesterday. To-day he had a meeting with Mr. Purse, the only director of the company now in Macon. After full conversation with Mr. Adams, superintendent, it was

Resolved, First, in relation to the railroad, that it is expedient and proper that the road be repaired down to Gordon, and thence to Midway, on the Milledgeville Branch, and then that the Eatonton Branch be repaired up to Eatonton. By this means two passages across the State can be secured, viz, one of thirty-five miles, from Midway to Mayfield, and one of twenty-two miles, from Eatonton to Madison. It is expedient to repair the Augusta and Savannah Railroad down to or a little below Thomas' Station. Such portion as above specified to be worked with engines and cars.

Such is the damaged condition of the road below Gordon that it is considered inexpedient at present to attempt the repair of it. In view also of the fact that the enemy with a very large army holds Savannah, it is considered very unsafe to attempt any further repairs of the road.

Resolved, That painful as it is, the employés in the road department must be discharged on the 31st instant, except so many as are indispensably necessary to do the work hereinbefore set forth, and the superintendent is directed to be particular in keeping down the force to the lowest possible point. He is to report to-morrow, or as soon thereafter (before the 31st instant) as he can, the employés who are to be retained.

In relation to the banks:

Resolved, That the only officer to be retained in the service besides the Cooks is Mr. T. M. Cunningham.

Considering the necessary curtailments of expense indicated by the preceding, the president voluntarily relinquishes part of his salary to $8,000 per annum, to begin on the 1st day of January, 1865.

R. R. CUYLER.

RICHMOND, VA., *December 28, 1864.*

General G. T. BEAUREGARD,
Charleston, S. C.:

The Secretary of the Navy represents the value as such, in the Government work-shops at Columbus, Ga., of the naval battalion now at Green Pond, and their rapidly diminishing numbers, that it is suggested the remainder be returned as soon as possible to their former employment at Columbus.

JEFF'N DAVIS.

CHARLESTON, *December 28, 1864.*
(Received 10.30 29th.)

General S. COOPER,
Adjutant and Inspector General:

General Cobb reports railroad from Macon to Milledgeville will be completed to-morrow. He urges completion of telegraph line from Augusta to Atlanta, the one via Millen being unreliable.

G. T. BEAUREGARD,
General.

CHARLESTON, *December 28, 1864.*
(Received 10.30 29th.)

General S. COOPER:

My presence being required immediately in western part of my present command, I respectfully request, on account of interruption in railroad communication, that the order extending the limits of said command to Atlantic coast be recalled. The Department of South Carolina, Georgia, and Florida might be annexed to General Bragg's department.

G. T. BEAUREGARD,
General.

CHARLESTON, *December 28, 1864*.
(Received 10.15 29th.)

General S. COOPER:

The light artillery of this department has been organized into eight battalions of three batteries each, and the following-named artillery officers, the majority of whom are the senior captains in their respective battalions, are recommended for promotion to majors and command the battalions: Capts. G. H. Walter, E. L. Parker, W. K. Bachman, W. E. Earle, H. M. Stuart, J. W. Brooks, J. A. Maxwell, and Lieut. W. H. Kemper. All available artillery officers of rank in this department have been assigned to heavy artillery commands, and will be required with these commands, should they take the field as infantry, except Lieutenant-Colonels Kemper and Jones, to each of whom it is proposed to give two of the above-mentioned battalions as reserves.

W. J. HARDEE,
Lieutenant-General.

SPECIAL ORDERS, No. 311. } HDQRS. DEPT. OF S. C., GA., AND FLA.,
Charleston, S. C., December 28, 1864.

* * * * * * *

IV. Taliaferro's division, Brigadier-General Taliaferro commanding, is hereby constituted as follows:

Rhett's brigade, Col. Alfred Rhett commanding, consisting of First South Carolina Artillery, Colonel Rhett; Second South Carolina Artillery, Colonel Frederick; First South Carolina Infantry, Colonel Butler.

Anderson's brigade, Col. Edward C. Anderson commanding, composed as follows: Regiment consisting of Twenty-second Georgia Battalion (six companies), Cobb Guard (two companies), Mercer Artillery (one company), Hanleiter's battery (one company); Lucas' battalion, Maj. J. J. Lucas, consisting of three companies; Buist's battalion, Maj. G. L. Buist commanding, consisting of Gilchrist's, Melchers', Mathewes', and Johnson's companies; Manigault's battalion, Major Manigault commanding, consisting of Bonaud's battalion (Companies A, B, C, D, E), Smith's company siege train, Zimmerman's company siege train, and Bridges' company siege train.

The several above-named commands will remain as at present assigned, and make their reports as heretofore, until further orders, but commanders will require such reports and returns from their respective commands as may be necessary to acquaint them with their number, condition, &c.

V. The light batteries of this department will be organized into battalions for field service as follows, the senior officers taking command of the battalions for the present; orders for the assembling of the batteries of each battalion will be issued hereafter:

First Battalion—Walter's battery, Kanapaux's battery, Schulz's battery; Second Battalion—Parker's battery, Wheaton's battery, Le Gardeur's battery; Third Battalion—Bachman's battery, Kanapaux's battery, De Pass' battery; Fourth Battalion—Earle's battery, Girardey's battery, Anderson's battery; Fifth Battalion—Stuart's battery, Wagener's battery, Gaillard's battery; Sixth Battalion—Brooks' battery, Barnwell's battery, Abell's battery; Seventh Battalion—Maxwell's battery, Daniell's battery, Guerard's battery; Eighth Battalion—Dunham's battery, Gamble's battery, Villepigue's battery.

The Second Battalion will be assigned to Brigadier-General Taliaferro's division, the Sixth to Major-General McLaws' division, the Seventh to Major-General Wright's division. The First, Third, Fourth, and Fifth Battalions will be the reserve, under command of Lieut. Col. Del. Kemper.

* * * * * * *

By command of Lieutenant-General Hardee:

H. W. FEILDEN,
Assistant Adjutant-General.

HARDEEVILLE, S. C., *December 28, 1864.*

General BRAXTON BRAGG,
Headquarters Armies of the Confederate States:

DEAR GENERAL: The loss of Savannah I presume you anticipated. I felt convinced myself it could not be held, immediately upon my arrival and learning that no re-enforcements could be expected.

I presume you have been mortified to hear the complaints and charges which have been made against my command. The first charge was that my command straggled. This is partially true, but the great cause was the issuing of an illegal order by General Taylor directing General Clanton to organize all absentees from the army into ninety-days' regiments. This order was, of course, abused, as all illegal orders generally are, and his officers enlisted men directly from my ranks, and this nearly ruined one brigade and had a bad effect upon my entire command. After such action on his part he was so unkind as to heap upon me abuse for the very thing which he (General Taylor) has caused. Of course there was other apparent straggling, always incident to rapid movement while watching or engaging an enemy.

With regard to horse stealing, all was charged to me, while the facts are as follows: My command captured a great number of horses from the enemy which were the property of citizens. All of these horses are being restored to their owners as rapidly as possible. As the enemy advanced I sent officers on in advance to advise citizens to take off their horses and mules. When this duty was neglected I had details drive them off and thus saved them from the enemy. This stock has been or is being returned to the owners when it is possible to do so.

You have no doubt heard that I burnt mills after the enemy had passed. This is false. In my anxiety to save property I placed guards at mills, directing them to remain until the enemy drove them off, and only to fire the mill when they saw it was impossible to remain any longer.

I have positive proof that the country swarmed with organized parties who do not and never did belong to my command. Most of these parties were acting under orders from Governor Brown, but in all their stealing they claimed to belong to Wheeler's cavalry. I now have the names of sixteen organized parties who steal on my credit. I have now run them off, and the difficulty has ceased. Captain Conway, who acted so badly, is not and never was in my command. He was acting under orders from Maj. Norman W. Smith.

I make all these explanations to you as I feel grateful for the kindness you have shown me on so many occasions, and I knew you would regret to see me neglectful. I have made two written applications for a board of officers of rank and standing to investigate the entire matter and report the facts. The world is getting worse and worse every day. It is astonishing what false representations are made by some parties. I beg, if any representations are made regarding my command, they will be referred to me and not allowed to rest until I am held accountable or am able to prove the charges incorrect.

We were all much shocked at hearing of the President's death, but were much relieved this morning to hear that the report was incorrect.

I hope Hood will meet with success in Tennessee, but reports indicate that we may be disappointed.

With high regard, your obedient servant and friend,

J. WHEELER.

Field returns showing effective total, total present, and aggregate present, including the troops between Grahamville and the Combahee River.

Command.	Effective total.	Total present.	Aggregate present.	Remarks.
Fiser's brigade				Stationed near Old Pocotaligo.
1st Georgia Regulars	199	209	231	
Symons' regiment reserves	217	219	244	Not numbered.
27th Georgia Battalion	401	447	466	
Total	817	875	941	
Chesnut's brigade				The total present and aggregate present of this command were not reported; this will be rectified. Stationed at Grahamville.
1st Battalion South Carolina Reserves	141			
2d Battalion South Carolina Reserves	136			
6th Battalion South Carolina Reserves	295			
2d Regiment South Carolina Militia	138			
3d Regiment South Carolina Militia	290			
4th Regiment South Carolina Militia	185			
Company B, 8th South Carolina Reserves	40			
Total	1,233			
Harrison's brigade				Stationed at Coosawhatchie.
5th Georgia Regiment	263	313	341	
32d Georgia Regiment	292	304	319	
1st Georgia Reserves	166	175	189	
3d Georgia Reserves	451	519	559	
47th Georgia Regiment	266	304	328	
7th North Carolina Reserves	132	240	263	
1st South Carolina Militia	402	532	585	
1st South Carolina Cavalry	121	140	145	
Detachment South Carolina Cavalry Reserves	76	85	91	
Total	2,169	2,612	2,820	
Cumming's brigade				Stationed at Pocotaligo.
5th Regiment Georgia Reserves	394	425	452	
2d Battalion Georgia Reserves	46	52	58	
Detachment Athens Battalion	28	28	30	
Total	468	505	540	
Hardy's brigade				Stationed at Pocotaligo.
50th North Carolina Regiment	550	627	659	
10th North Carolina Battalion	305	320	332	
Total	855	947	991	
Total infantry	5,542			

Field returns showing effective total, total present, and aggregate present, &c.—Continued.

Command.	Effective total.	Total present.	Aggregate present.	Remarks.
Light artillery:				
Charles' battery	98	....	....	Grahamville.
Section Lafayette Artillery	74	....	....	Do.
Section Earle's battery	38	....	....	Do.
Anderson's battery	119	119	122	Coosawhatchie.
Girardey's battery	112	112	116	Do.
Beaufort artillery	107	121	125	Do.
Section DePass' battery	53	59	60	Do.
Brooks' battery	82	87	100	Pocotaligo.
Barnwell's battery	74	79	83	Do.
Abell's battery	87	88	91	Do.
Section Wagener's battery	45	45	47	Do.
Section Earle's battery	54	72	74	Do.
Section Kanapaux's battery	33	38	39	Do.
Total light artillery	976	....	....	
Cavalry:				
Companies C and E, 3d South Carolina Cavalry.	110	....	....	Grahamville.
Company H and detachments of F, D, and G, 3d South Carolina Cavalry.	110	....	....	Coosawhatchie.
Kirk's squadron	113	137	143	Pocotaligo.
Company I, 3d South Carolina Cavalry	48	60	63	Do.
Company K, 3d South Carolina Cavalry	71	78	81	Do.
Company D, 3d South Carolina Cavalry	60	65	68	Pocotaligo, and employed as couriers to George's Station.
Total cavalry	512	....	....	
Grand total	7,030	....	....	

HEADQUARTERS,
Pocotaligo, December 28, 1864.

CHARLESTON, *December 29, 1864.*

His Excellency President DAVIS:

If you will send us aid we can, with the force here, arrest the progress of invasion. General Beauregard tells me he desires the commands of General Hoke and General Johnson. With these, if no others can be spared, we may hold the lower portion of the State, which is threatened. I write more fully by mail, but time is of the first consequence to us of that we have left to spare.

A. G. MAGRATH.

CHARLESTON, *December 29, 1864.*

General S. COOPER,
Adjutant and Inspector General:

Wheeler's cavalry, I regret to say, is more or less scattered over the country from Alabama to South Carolina. No definite returns can be had. He reports now about 5,000 effective. The number I sent was furnished approximately when [*sic*] I sent to Savannah. Major-

General Martin is in Mississippi in arrest by General Wheeler. Brigadier-General Kelly was killed in Tennessee; Humes is with Wheeler; Jackson's division is with Hood. I will write more fully soon as practicable.

G. T. BEAUREGARD,
General.

RICHMOND, VA., *December 29, 1864.*

General G. T. BEAUREGARD,
Charleston, S. C.:

A telegram just received from Augusta states that General Wright has called for all able-bodied men in the cotton factories. The Secretary of War directs that the artisans shall not be disturbed; they must be kept at work to meet the necessities of the service.

S. COOPER,
Adjutant and Inspector General.

CHARLESTON, *December 29, 1864.*

General S. COOPER,
Adjutant and Inspector General:

Column of enemy which moved a few days since toward Altamaha bridge, on Gulf railroad, is reported to have returned to Savannah, where Kilpatrick is said to be. Nothing of importance reported from that direction. No report of operations from General Hood since 3d instant.

G. T. BEAUREGARD,
General.

WILMINGTON, *December 29, 1864.*

General G. T. BEAUREGARD,
Charleston:

The two battalions I desired to be returned were taken from the regular garrisons of our forts, and their absence embarrasses us much in working the heavy guns. You will observe I do not ask for the infantry. It will be better to send the artillery back, and I have already asked authority to send you other re-enforcements in case you should need them. The fleet has entirely disappeared, and all is quiet here.

BRAXTON BRAGG.

CHARLESTON, *December 29, 1864.*

Major-General WHEELER,
Hardeeville:

Lieutenant-General Hardee approves your proposition to have your advance line run from New River bridge to Izard's, and to blockade the roads below that line.

T. B. ROY,
Assistant Adjutant-General.

CHARLESTON, *December 29, 1864.*

Major-General WHEELER,
Hardeeville, S. C.:

Lose no time in blockading the roads suggested in your telegram of this morning, particularly the road from Screven's Ferry to New River bridge.

W. J. HARDEE,
Lieutenant-General.

CHARLESTON, *December 29, 1864.*

Major-General WHEELER,
Hardeeville:

By direction of General Beauregard you will transfer to the Georgia side of the Savannah River as much of your command as can be dispensed with on Carolina side—say from one-third to one-half.

By command of Lieutenant-General Hardee:

T. B. ROY,
Assistant Adjutant-General.

GENERAL ORDERS, No. 7. } HEADQUARTERS CAVALRY CORPS, *Beaufort District, S. C., December 29, 1864.*

I. The continued and grave complaints made by citizens against this command require that the most stringent efforts be used by all officers to prevent the slightest depredations of any character in future.

II. The requirements of General Orders, Nos. 18 and 21, from army headquarters, and all general orders from these headquarters relating to discipline and depredating upon the property of citizens, will be rigidly enforced.

III. No officer or soldier will be permitted to enter a dwelling under any pretense whatever, unless invited by the occupant. Division, brigade, and regimental commanders will bivouac with their troops, and with assistance of their staff officers will see, by close supervision, that no rails are burned, or depredations of any character whatever committed. They will see that proper and regular issues of forage and subsistence are made and no waste allowed. To this end they will require the most vigorous and energetic efforts on the part of commissaries and quartermasters for the procurement of necessary supplies. When the command is without wagons every detail sent out to procure supplies will be under the command of a commissioned officer, who will be held strictly responsible for depredations committed by the detail.

IV. 1. Each division commander will select a regiment, under a strict officer, which shall be used as a provost guard of the division. This regiment will be selected for its general good conduct, and will be retained on this duty only while its conduct is exemplary. Division commanders may at their option detail men from other regiments for this duty whom they deem specially appropriate for that purpose.

2. When on the march the provost guard shall be kept in advance and will leave a guard at every house on the line of march, under a good officer, which guard will not suffer any soldier of this or any other command to take any species of property whatever from the premises. These guards will be relieved by the provost guard of the division next in rear. The guard of the rear division will remain on duty till the rear guard of the command has passed.

3. When in camp guards from this regiment will be stationed at every house within the lines of the division, of sufficient strength to protect the premises.

V. Each division commander will detail two or more officers to serve upon his staff, whose duty shall be to follow in rear of the command and visit every house on the line of march and every house from which forage or rations are procured. They will examine the vouchers given, see that they are of the proper character, and take a note of every complaint made by citizens. These officers will be required to certify in writing every Sunday morning that this duty has been fully complied with. A complete record of all complaints made by citizens will be kept at division headquarters.

VI. 1. The brave officers and men who for three years have fought with me in this sacred cause, facing every danger and enduring every hardship, are not guilty of horse-stealing and destroying property. Foul aspersions have been thrown upon you by the conduct of a few bad men, some of whom may belong in our ranks, but many of whom, falsely claiming identity with this command, hover around your line of march committing depredations in your name, thus throwing the odium of their bad conduct upon you.

2. Besides being my duty to protect citizens and the families of your fellow soldiers, it is also my duty to protect your honor and your fair names, and I am determined at any cost to accomplish these objects.

3. If the base conduct of a few straggling robbers or the vile tongue of slander has clouded your otherwise bright fame, a course of the most scrupulous and irreproachable conduct on your part can alone relieve you. I therefore appeal to every one of my officers and soldiers to aid to their utmost ability in bringing all offenders to justice.

4. Citizens must also assist in this work. If their property is trespassed upon or their horses stolen, they must follow the culprit until means are acquired to secure his arrest, either by procuring aid or by tracing him to the camp. There complaint should be promptly made to his commanding officer. If full redress is not given, appeal should be made to the next commander, and so on until justice is obtained.

VII. 1. By rigidly enforcing this and other orders from these headquarters on the subject of discipline and depredations, division commanders can render the discipline of their commands perfect. A general court-martial is established in each division, and ample means furnished to relieve the army of disqualified and neglectful officers. Their places can be supplied by meritorious men whom the law admits of being appointed for valor and skill.

2. In holding division commanders strictly responsible for the conduct of their commands, the corps commanders will lend them every aid by assuming the responsibility of ordering any punishment which circumstances may demand. Division will hold brigade commanders strictly responsible; brigade must look to regimental commanders, and they must hold captains to strict account for the conduct of their men. For every breach of discipline some one must be punished. If the officers whose duty it is to punish the offender neglects that duty, his immediate commander must take action against him. Without certain and prompt punishment for every offense or neglect, proper discipline cannot be maintained.

VIII. The spirit of this order will be carried out in all commands less than a division.

J. WHEELER,
Major-General.

HEADQUARTERS CAVALRY CORPS,
Hardeeville, December 29, 1864.

General JOSEPH H. LEWIS,
Commanding Brigade Cavalry:

GENERAL: Inclosed is an order for you to move with your command across the river at Sister's Ferry. General Fry has been requested by telegraph to send a boat from Augusta to assist in crossing your command. Major-General Wheeler desires me to say that the order emanates from General Beauregard, and he presumes has some urgency in it.

Respectfully, general, your obedient servant,

M. G. HUDSON,
First Lieutenant and Aide-de-Camp.

[Inclosure.]

SPECIAL ORDERS, No. 110. } HEADQUARTERS CAVALRY CORPS,
Hardeeville, S. C., December 29, 1864—4 p. m.

* * * * * * *

III. Brigadier-General Lewis, commanding brigade, will move at once with his command across the Savannah River at Sister's Ferry and report to Brigadier-General Iverson.

* * * * * * *

By order of Maj. Gen. Joseph Wheeler:

M. G. HUDSON,
First Lieut., Aide-de-Camp, and Acting Assistant Adjutant-General.

RICHMOND, VA., *December 30, 1864.*

Governor A. G. MAGRATH,
Columbia, S. C.:

Yours of the 25th and 29th received. I have long realized the importance of such action as you suggest, but necessities elsewhere have prevented action in accordance with our wish. I have held several conferences with General Lee on the subject, and will have another, showing him your letter and telegram. The co-operation of the State officers with the engineers of the Confederate States is accepted as proposed. Will write you more fully by mail.

JEFF'N DAVIS.

WAR DEPARTMENT, C. S. A.,
Richmond, Va., December 30, 1864.

General W. J. HARDEE,
Charleston, S. C.:

I have ordered Lieutenant-Colonel Tucker, commanding a battalion, not yet fully organized, of recruits from Federal prisoners, to report to you immediately. The organization not being yet recognized by the Department, but simply formed under an authority, is subject to be modified, divided, or arranged in any way that the interests of the service may require. The existing officers may have some claim to selection, but have not commissions. Will you have special attention given to the battalion, and communicate your conclusions respecting it.

J. A. SEDDON,
Secretary of War.

CHARLESTON, *December 30, 1864.*

General S. COOPER,
Adjutant and Inspector General:

Your telegram ordering all artisans to be returned to their employments has been received. The Naval and Arsenal Battalions had already been returned. Your order will take away all of Wright's division except four small companies. That division is holding an important position. I earnestly urge that you send 1,400 men to replace it. I have already been weakened by the return of the heavy artillerists to Wilmington.

W. J. HARDEE,
Lieutenant-General.

WILMINGTON, *December 30, 1864.*

Brig. Gen. L. S. BAKER,
Goldsborough, N. C.:

If nothing active in your district prevents, proceed to Richmond and report to Colonel Sale, my private secretary. After a full conference with the President on the condition in Georgia and South Carolina return and resume your command.

BRAXTON BRAGG.

WILMINGTON, *December 30, 1864.*

Col. JOHN B. SALE,
Military Secretary, Richmond:

Believing the President will be gratified to know the exact state of affairs in Georgia and South Carolina, I have ordered Brig. Gen. L. S. Baker, who has returned from there disabled for the field by his old wound, to proceed to Richmond and report to you. Obtain an early interview for him. He passed through all the scenes from Augusta to the evacuation of Savannah, and can report fully; and it is very important the exact state of affairs now should be known.

BRAXTON BRAGG.

GENERAL ORDERS, } HDQRS. DEPT. OF S. C., GA., AND FLA.,
No. 92. } *Charleston, S. C., December 30, 1864.*

I. The allowance of field transportation for the troops in this department will be as follows:

1. Division headquarters: For general and all staff officers, two four-horse wagons for baggage, one four-horse wagon for forage, one four-horse forge, one two-horse ambulance.

2. Brigade transportation: For general and staff officers at brigade headquarters, one four-horse wagon for baggage, &c., and one two-horse ambulance; brigade forage, one four-horse wagon; brigade, one four-horse forge; commissary scales and implements for butchering for brigade, one four-horse wagon; field, staff, and company officers of each regiment, one four-horse wagon; cooking utensils for every 300 men, one four-horse wagon; every 300 men, one two-horse ambulance; brigade medical supplies, one four-horse wagon; brigade intrenching tools, one four-horse wagon.

3. To each brigade there will be attached an ordnance train of four-horse wagons sufficient to carry sixty extra rounds of ammunition per man, each wagon carrying fifteen boxes of ammunition. This ordnance train will be in the immediate charge of the brigade ordnance officer, and all the brigade trains of each division in charge of the division ordnance officer.

4. Battalion of light artillery: Battalion headquarters, one two-horse wagon; each battalion, one four-horse forge; officers and men of each battery of light artillery, one four-horse wagon; forage for each battery, two four-horse wagons; extra ammunition for battery, one four-horse wagon; battalion medical supplies, one two-horse wagon; each battery, one two-horse ambulance.

II. This order shall apply to the cavalry of this department, with the following modification: Two four-horse wagons will be allowed to every 100 effective men for forage.

III. The load of a four-horse wagon will not exceed 1,700 pounds.

IV. All transportation and ambulances in excess of the above allowance will be at once turned in to the chief quartermaster.

Requisitions will be made to supply deficiencies.

By order of Lieutenant-General Hardee:

T. B. ROY,
Assistant Adjutant-General.

SPECIAL ORDERS, No. 313. } HDQRS. DEPT. OF S. C., GA., AND FLA.,
Charleston, S. C., December 30, 1864.

* * * * * * *

IX. Maj. Gen. G. W. Smith will have command of a geographical district which will include Augusta and Millen, in Georgia, and Branchville, in South Carolina. He will proceed at once to construct defenses at Branchville.

By command of Lieutenant-General Hardee:

H. W. FEILDEN,
Assistant Adjutant-General.

HEADQUARTERS FISER'S BRIGADE,
Frampton Farm, December 30, 1864.

Major-General McLAWS,
Commanding, &c.:

GENERAL: I sent a regiment at daylight this morning near Tullifinny bridge, and I sent an officer in the direction of the railroad trestle. Found the left of Harrison's line about three-quarters of a mile above Tullifinny bridge. I have connected with the line on my right. Have seen nor heard nothing of the regiment commanded by Colonel Cumming. I suppose you do not intend me to consider myself in command of any line beyond the Tullifinny. If you deem it at all probable that the enemy will advance either by way of Mackay's Point road or the various roads crossing the Tullifinny and leading to the railroad, I would respectfully suggest that you send a regiment or so to occupy from Old Pocotaligo to Frampton farm, and allow me to extend my right, so as to more effectually protect the railroad and Colonel Harrison's rear. Captain Barnwell opened on the enemy this morning from Lawton's farm, but was compelled to withdraw with the loss of 1 man mortally wounded, himself and 2 men slightly. I wish you would ride over, if convenient.

I am, sir, your obedient servant,

JNO. C. FISER,
Colonel, Commanding Brigade.

CHARLESTON, *December 30, 1864.*

Major-General WHEELER,
Hardeeville:

General Hardee desires the two rifled 24-pounders from Red Bluff sent to Adams' Run Station.

A. J. GONZALES,
Colonel and Chief of Artillery, Department.

GENERAL ORDERS, No. 8.

HEADQUARTERS CAVALRY CORPS,
Hardeeville, S. C., December 30, 1864.

I. Until further orders the following will be the allowance of transportation of this corps:

For corps headquarters: For baggage, two four-horse wagons; quartermaster and commissary of subsistence stores, two four-horse wagons; forage, one four-horse wagon; forge, one four-horse wagon; medical supplies, one four-horse wagon; ambulance, one two-horse wagon.

Division headquarters: Baggage, one four-horse wagon; quartermaster and commissary of subsistence stores, one four-horse wagon; forage, one four-horse wagon; transportation for three days' rations for every 600 men, one six-horse wagon; medical supplies, one two-horse wagon.

Brigade headquarters: Baggage, one four-horse wagon; quartermaster and commissary of subsistence stores, one four-horse wagon; medical supplies, one two-horse wagon; forage, one four-horse wagon; ordnance for each 400 muskets, one four-horse wagon.

Regiments: Officers' baggage, including desks, money boxes, and medical supplies, one four-horse wagon; each 400 men present for duty for cooking utensils, one four-horse wagon; each 100 animals for forage, one four-horse wagon; ambulance, one two-horse wagon.

Artillery with cavalry: Each battery, baggage for officers, cooking utensils, and extra harness, one four-horse wagon; forage, one four-horse wagon; forge, one four-horse wagon.

Ordnance: 12-pounder howitzer battery, four guns, two four-horse wagons; Napoleon, three four-horse wagons; battery of rifled guns (four), one four-horse wagon.

Batteries artillery: Extra harness, instead of battery wagons, with wagons, one four-horse wagon; forge, two four-horse wagons; ambulance, two two-horse wagons.

II. All mules and wagons in excess of the above allowance will be immediately turned in to Capt. S. E. Norton, chief quartermaster of this corps.

III. Captain Norton, chief quartermaster, will immediately form the mules and wagons thus turned in with a general supply train, and place the train thus formed in charge of one or more assistant quartermasters as the number of wagons may require to be used as the major-general commanding may direct.

By order of Major-General Wheeler:

HENRY CHAPMAN,
Lieutenant and Acting Assistant Adjutant-General.

HEADQUARTERS CAVALRY DIVISION,
December 30, 1864.

[Lieut. M. G. HUDSON:]

LIEUTENANT: I will move to-morrow morning back to the Statesborough and Hudson's Ferry road. I intend making my headquarters at Doctor Longstreet's. My picket-line will extend from Ebenezer to No. 3, Central railroad. I can forage the command here no longer. Every exertion has been made to keep as close up as possible. No news from the enemy. They are making no movement in this direction. My scouts go within six miles of Savannah.

Very respectfully, your obedient servant,

ALFRED IVERSON,
Brigadier-General.

RICHMOND, VA., *December 30, 1864.*

Lieut. Col. J. G. TUCKER,
Commanding First Foreign Battalion, Columbia, S. C.:

Report immediately with your command to Lieutenant-General Hardee for duty.

S. COOPER,
Adjutant and Inspector General.

CHARLESTON, *December 31, 1864.*

General S. COOPER,
Adjutant and Inspector General:

I respectfully suggest that Augusta be placed in General Hardee's department, owing to breaks in railroad and its immediate connection with defense of South Carolina. I am unable to leave before to-morrow morning.

G. T. BEAUREGARD,
General.

CHARLESTON, *December 31, 1864.*

General S. COOPER,
Adjutant and Inspector General:

I should have stated in telegram of this a. m., in relation to status of Augusta, that General Hardee has now under his command nearly all available forces in Georgia, which he requires also for defense of South Carolina.

G. T. BEAUREGARD,
General.

SPECIAL ORDERS, } ADJT. AND INSP. GENERAL'S OFFICE,
No. 310. } *Richmond, Va., December 31, 1864.*

* * * * * * *

XXVIII. Maj. Gen. Samuel Jones, Provisional Army, C. S., is assigned to the command of the District of Florida, in the Department of South Carolina, Georgia, and Florida.

* * * * * * *

By command of Secretary of War.

JNO. WITHERS,
Assistant Adjutant-General.

CHARLESTON, S. C., *December 31, 1864.*

Lieut. Gen. W. J. HARDEE,
Comdg. Dept. of S. C., Ga., and Fla., Charleston, S. C.:

GENERAL: I inclose herewith a copy of a telegram received to-day from the President, relieving me, at my request, of the general command of the Department of South Carolina, Georgia, and Florida. My presence is absolutely required at this moment at Montgomery and with the Army of Tennessee, and I am unable to inform you when I will be able to return in this direction. The interruption of railroad communication might render it impracticable to get back in time to be of assistance to you, should you require my aid suddenly. The telegram of the President not being explicit as to the status of Augusta, I have requested that it should be included in your department, as you now have under you the whole of Wheeler's cavalry and nearly all the available forces of Georgia, which are also required by you for the defense of South Carolina. The defense of this city is so intimately connected with that of the western portion of this State that you will consider it within the limits of your department until further orders from the War Department.

I have already given you all the verbal instructions possible for the defense of Charleston and this State. The answer of the War Department, not yet received, to my telegram of the 27th instant will determine whether, in the event of evacuating this city, you will retire toward Georgia or North Carolina as a base. The first is your natural base; but should you have reason to expect large re-enforcements from the latter State, you should of course retire in that direction. You will apply to the defense of Charleston the same principle applied to that of Savannah—that is, defend it as long as compatible with the safety of your forces. Having no reason at present to expect succor from an army of relief, you must save your troops for the defense of South Carolina and Georgia.

The fall of Charleston would necessarily be a terrible blow to the Confederacy, but its fall with the loss of its brave garrison would be still more fatal to our cause. You will, however, make all the preparation necessary for the possible evacuation of the city and "clear your decks for action." Should it not take place, the trouble and expense of transportation will amount to little; but should you be compelled to evacuate the city when unprepared, the loss of public property would be incalculable. All the cotton in the city should be removed, and if any be in the city at the time of its evacuation it must be destroyed.

As already instructed, you should organize all your troops for the field, collecting sufficient transportation, ammunition, and provisions for an active campaign. You must have depots of provisions and forage at several points in the interior of the State. Columbia would be a very suitable point; Florence also, if you expect to move in the direction of North Carolina. Augusta, Mayfield, and Milledgeville must be depots for future operations. Your defensive lines from the Savannah River would be, as already explained to you: First, the Combahee and Salkehatchie to Barnwell Court-House, thence to the Savannah River; second, the Ashepoo and Salkehatchie to Barnwell Court-House, thence to Savannah River; third, Edisto to Branchville, thence across toward Barnwell Court-House; fourth, Edisto and Caw Caw Swamp, or Rantowles Creek; fifth, Edisto and Ashley. Wheeler's cavalry must protect your front toward Savannah River, and your right flank from Barnwell Court-House toward Augusta. At least, the larger portion of his cavalry must be south of that river, to watch the movements and check the progress of any force moving toward Augusta or the interior of Georgia, until the rest of the cavalry and other forces could be sent to give battle to the enemy.

Please keep General Cobb and myself advised of your movements and those of the enemy, in order that we may give you in time any assistance in our power.

Hoping that you may be successful in holding Charleston and repelling any advance of the enemy, I remain, respectfully, your obedient servant,

G. T. BEAUREGARD,
General.

[Inclosure.]

RICHMOND, *December 30, 1864.*

General G. T. BEAUREGARD:

Your dispatch of this day received; also a copy of that to General Cooper in relation to assignment of General Bragg. You will leave with General Hardee orders and instructions in regard to the department east of Augusta, and will resume the command of the district west of Augusta as heretofore defined. The change will be more formally announced from the Adjutant-General's Office.

JEFF'N DAVIS.

HARDEEVILLE, *December 31, 1864.*

General McLAWS:

Will send picks and shovels by first train. Brigadier-General Young had been ordered to Georgia side of Savannah River, but orders were countermanded, and he was ordered to you, at Grahamville, on 25th. I earnestly request that company from Eighth Texas ordered to you for temporary duty be returned.

W. Y. C. HUMES,
Brigadier-General.

HARDEEVILLE, *December 31, 1864.*

Major-General McLAWS:

The pickets at Cheves' place report the enemy shelling them from Hutchinson's Island. The enemy attempted to cross the river at same place in three rice boats, but were repulsed. The pickets at Screven's Ferry report five or six transports leaving Savannah this morning heavily loaded with soldiers. Rice boats passing from Savannah side to island loaded with plank.

W. Y. C. HUMES,
Brigadier-General.

COLUMBIA, S. C., *December —, 1864.*

Hon. JAMES A. SEDDON,
Secretary of War:

SIR: The undersigned citizens of South Carolina respectfully request that at least one corps of the army be sent from Virginia to save the States of Georgia and South Carolina from being laid waste by the enemy. There is no force here to prevent it, and it is absolutely necessary to have at least one well-organized corps besides Hardee's on the coast, about which the half-trained citizens may rally. Otherwise, however brave and determined, their efforts will amount to nothing. These two States have, to a large extent, furnished the Army of Virginia with supplies. If they are wasted by raids and their railroads cut, this source of supply is lost. We are sensible of the pressure upon Richmond, and the importance of saving the capital, but it is manifest that its defense must at this moment be made here.

A just regard for the safety of these States and of the common cause in which we are all embarked induces us to press this appeal with great earnestness upon your consideration.

We have the honor to be, with high respect, your obedient servants,

W. F. De Saussure, Andr. Crawford, W. H. Scarborough, Daniel Ravenel, R. S. Bryan, J. L. Clark, James D. Tradewell, James Rose, Edwin I. Scott, J. F. Gourdin, Robt. Bryce, J. W. Hayne, J. S. Guignard, Edward Hope, J. C. Lyons, H. Muller, J. A. Crawford, Campbell R. Bryce, D. W. Ray, Rufus M. Johnston, J. P. Surtlime, J. McKenzie, J. H. Wells, Jacob Levin, Alex. Laughlin, Wm. E. Martin, J. E. Dent, W. B. Johnston, Thos. H. Wade, Wm. Martin, Peter J. Shand, Wm. B. Yates, E. L. Kenison, Alfred Wallace, Jno. Banskett.

[First indorsement.]

JANUARY 5, 1865.

Respectfully submitted, from respect to the signers, to the consideration of the President.

J. A. SEDDON,
Secretary of War.

[Second indorsement.]

SECRETARY OF WAR:

The question presented is one of which General Lee can best judge. I suggest a reference to him.

J. D.

[Third indorsement.]

WAR OFFICE,
February 7, 1865.

ADJUTANT-GENERAL:

Please note the President's suggestion, and refer to General Lee accordingly.

By order of the Secretary of War:

R. G. H. KEAN,
Chief of Bureau of War.

[Fourth indorsement.]

ADJUTANT AND INSPECTOR GENERAL'S OFFICE,
February 9, 1865.

Respectfully referred to General R. E. Lee.

By order of Adjutant and Inspector General:

JNO. WITHERS,
Assistant Adjutant-General.

[Fifth indorsement.]

HEADQUARTERS,
February 11, 1865.

Respectfully returned.

I have sent all the troops from this army that can be spared. The Army of Tennessee is ordered to South Carolina, and a part of it arrived. If the citizens of Georgia and South Carolina will fill up its ranks it will be able to protect the country.

R. E. LEE,
General.

WAR DEPARTMENT, C. S. A., ENGINEER BUREAU,
Richmond, Va., January 3, 1865.

Hon. JAMES A. SEDDON,
Secretary of War:

SIR: I have the honor to report the following injuries to the main railroads in Georgia done by the enemy in General Sherman's advance from Kingston to Savannah, viz:

First. Western and Atlantic road (Georgia State road): Track and bridges from Atlanta to Etowah River, inclusive, are destroyed. Beyond Etowah no injury of moment is reported. Length of track destroyed, about 46 miles; length of bridges at Chattahoochee and Etowah, 1,200 feet. The Governor of Georgia has sent his agents to examine and report as to the extent of injury to this road, the property of the State, but at the time of Captain Grant's report, 16th of December, no portion of the repairs had been made. All the labor and materials that can be obtained by the Government will be first applied to the reconstruction of the Georgia road (from Augusta to Atlanta), and to the Atlanta and West Point road, with a view to get one connection as soon as possible.

Second. Georgia road: The work to be done on this road is comprised in three important bridges—one over the Oconee River, the other two over smaller streams—and thirty-eight miles of track. Of the latter, fifteen miles will require iron rails from other sources. About twenty-three miles of bent rails can be straightened. Cross-ties will be needed for twenty-five to thirty miles. The most favorable estimate as to time for finishing the repairs of this road is the middle of February. All the labor that can be had by temporary impressments and by impressments for twelve months has been assigned to this work, and to,

Third. Atlanta and West Point road: This road at last report was repaired to Palmetto from West Point; it will be finished as soon or sooner than the Georgia road.

Fourth. The Central Railroad of Georgia: This road, which connects Macon with Augusta via Millen, has been repaired to Gordon, where the branch to Milledgeville has its junction with the main road. Cars now run from Macon to Milledgeville. The Central road from Gordon to Millen is very seriously destroyed. Every effort is being made to induce the company to renew the road, but there are about 100 miles seriously injured; they cannot be repaired as soon as the roads leading through Atlanta. The best engineers that could be furnished from the command of General Beauregard are employed in rebuilding the roads; and General Beauregard has assured this bureau that he will give them every support, and that all that is possible will be done to hasten their completion. With every exertion and with all the assistance that can be brought to bear, we can hardly expect the first through line can be repaired before the middle of February next.

I am, sir, very respectfully, your obedient servant,

J. F. GILMER,

Major-General and Chief of Bureau.

ALTERNATE DESIGNATIONS

OF

ORGANIZATIONS MENTIONED IN THIS VOLUME.*

Abell's (Henry F.) **Artillery**. See *Milton Artillery, post, Battery B.*
Acker's (George S.) **Cavalry**. See *Michigan Troops, 9th Regiment.*
Adams' (Edward) **Infantry**. See *Illinois Troops, 48th Regiment.*
Alexander's (Isaac N.) **Infantry**. See *Ohio Troops, 46th Regiment.*
Anderson's (Edward C., jr.) **Cavalry**. See *Georgia Troops, 7th Regiment.*
Anderson's (Ruel W.) **Artillery**. See *Georgia Troops.*
Anderson's (William B.) **Infantry**. See *Illinois Troops, 60th Regiment.*
Andress' (Charles A.) **Infantry**. See *Illinois Troops, 55th Regiment.*
Appel's (Charles A.) **Cavalry**. See *Pennsylvania Troops, 9th Regiment.*
Archer's (Samson M.) **Infantry**. See *Iowa Troops, 17th Regiment.*
Arndt's (Albert F. R.) **Artillery**. See *Michigan Troops, 1st Regiment, Battery B.*
Arsenal Battalion. See *Confederate Troops.*
Ashby's (Henry M.) **Cavalry**. See *Tennessee Troops, Confederate.*
Athens Battalion, Local Defense. See *Georgia Troops.*
Augusta Battalion, Local Defense. See *Georgia Troops.*
Ayres' (Lyman N.) **Infantry**. See *Ohio Troops, 20th Regiment.*
Babbitt's (George S.) **Infantry**. See *Indiana Troops, 23d Regiment.*
Bachman's (William K.) **Artillery**. See *German Artillery, post.*
Bacon's (E. H., jr.) **Infantry**. See *Georgia Troops, 32d Regiment.*
Bailey's (Lyman) **Artillery**. See *Ohio Troops, 15th Battery.*
Bainbridge's (Edmund C.) **Artillery**. See *Union Troops, Regulars, 5th Regiment, Battery K.*
Baird's (George W.) **Infantry**. See *Union Troops, Colored, 32d Regiment.*
Baker's (John J.) **Infantry**. See *Michigan Troops, 19th Regiment.*
Baldwin's (Elbert D.) **Infantry**. See *Indiana Troops, 12th Regiment.*
Baldwin's (Oliver L.) **Cavalry**. See *Kentucky Troops, Union, 5th Regiment.*
Ballinger's Infantry. See *South Carolina Troops, 1st Battalion, Reserves.*
Barnette's Infantry. See *South Carolina Troops, 2d Battalion, Reserves.*
Barnwell's (A. Smith) **Artillery**. See *Georgia Troops.*
Basinger's (William S.) **Infantry**. See *Georgia Troops, 18th Battalion.*
Battey's (Frederick A.) **Infantry**. See *Illinois Troops, 57th Regiment.*
Beach's (Benjamin) **Infantry**. See *Iowa Troops, 11th Regiment.*
Beall's Battalion. (Official designation not of record.) See *Major Beall.*
Beaufort Artillery. See *South Carolina Troops.*
Beck's (Frederick) **Infantry**. See *Ohio Troops, 108th Regiment.*
Beebe's (Yates V.) **Artillery**. See *Wisconsin Troops, 10th Battery.*
Beecher's (James C.) **Infantry**. See *Union Troops, Colored, 35th Regiment.*
Bennett's (Augustus G.) **Infantry**. See *Union Troops, Colored, 21st Regiment.*
Berkey's (John M.) **Infantry**. See *Indiana Troops, 99th Regiment.*
Bertody's (Thomas D.) **Heavy Artillery**. See *Georgia Troops, 22d Battalion.*
Bishop's (Judson W.) **Infantry**. See *Minnesota Troops, 2d Regiment.*

---

* References, unless otherwise indicated, are to index following.

Blanding's (Ormsby) **Heavy Artillery.** See *South Carolina Troops, 1st Regiment.*
Blessingh's (Louis von) **Infantry.** See *Ohio Troops, 37th Regiment.*
Bloodgood's (Edward) **Infantry.** See *Wisconsin Troops, 22d Regiment.*
Boag's (Theodore G.) **Artillery.** See *Gist Guard, Artillery, post.*
Bolton's (C. P.) **Cavalry.** See *A. D. Sparks' Cavalry, post.*
Bonaud's (A.) **Heavy Artillery.** See *Georgia Troops, 28th Battalion.*
Boyd's (Wesley) **Infantry.** See *Illinois Troops, 52d Regiment.*
Boyd's (William S.) **Infantry.** See *Illinois Troops, 66th Regiment.*
Brant's (Jefferson E.) **Infantry.** See *Indiana Troops, 85th Regiment.*
Briant's (Cyrus E.) **Infantry.** See *Indiana Troops, 88th Regiment.*
Bridges' (William M.) **Artillery.** See *Louisiana Troops, Confederate.*
Briggs' (Edward) **Infantry.** See *Ohio Troops, 76th Regiment.*
Bromley's (W. L.) **Cavalry.** See *Tennessee Troops, Confederate, 9th Battalion.*
Brooks' Battalion. (Official designation not of record.) See ——— *Brooks.*
Brooks' (Emerson P.) **Infantry.** See *Ohio Troops, 30th Regiment.*
Brooks' (John W.) **Artillery.** See *Terrell Artillery, post.*
Brown's (Angus P.) **Cavalry.** See *South Carolina Troops, 1st Regiment.*
Brown's (Henry D.) **Infantry.** See *Illinois Troops, 105th Regiment.*
Brown's (Philip P., jr.) **Infantry.** See *New York Troops, 157th Regiment.*
Brown's (Thomas R.) **Infantry.** See *South Carolina Troops, 5th Battalion, Reserves.*
Bruce's (John) **Infantry.** See *Iowa Troops, 19th Regiment.*
Brunner's (John F.) **Artillery.** See *Missouri Troops, Union, 1st Regiment, Battery H.*
Buckingham's (Philo B.) **Infantry.** See *Connecticut Troops, 20th Regiment.*
Buell's (George P.) **Infantry.** See *Indiana Troops, 58th Regiment.*
Bundy's (Henry) **Artillery.** See *New York Troops, 13th Battery.*
Burton's (James E.) **Infantry.** See *Indiana Troops, 33d Regiment.*
Buswell's (Nicholas C.) **Infantry.** See *Illinois Troops, 93d Regiment.*
Butler's (William) **Heavy Artillery.** See *South Carolina Troops, 3d Regiment.*
Cahill's (James B.) **Infantry.** See *Illinois Troops, 16th Regiment.*
Campbell's (Andrew K.) **Infantry.** See *Illinois Troops, 66th Regiment.*
Campbell's (Archibald L.) **Cavalry.** See *South Carolina Troops, 3d Regiment.*
Campbell's (Charles G.) **Siege Artillery.** See *Georgia Troops.*
Campbell's (W. H.) **Cavalry.** See *South Carolina Troops, 3d Regiment.*
Carmichael's (James C.) **Infantry.** See *New York Troops, 157th Regiment.*
Case's (Henry) **Infantry.** See *Illinois Troops, 129th Regiment.*
Caspar's (George R.) **Artillery.** See *Ohio Troops, 15th Battery.*
Catterson's (Robert F.) **Infantry.** See *Indiana Troops, 97th Regiment.*
Channel's (Joseph R.) **Artillery.** See *Illinois Troops, 1st Regiment, Battery C.*
Chapman's (John A.) **Infantry.** See *Illinois Troops, 16th Regiment.*
Charles' (William E.) **Heavy Artillery.** See *South Carolina Troops, 2d Regiment, Battery D.*
Chatfield's (Harvey S.) **Infantry.** See *New York Troops, 102d Regiment.*
Chatham Artillery. See *Georgia Troops.*
Chipman's (Henry L.) **Infantry.** See *Union Troops, Colored, 102d Regiment.*
Chisolm's (Robert) **Cavalry.** See *Florida Troops, Confederate, 5th Battalion.*
Citadel Cadets, Infantry. See *South Carolina Troops.*
Cladek's (John J.) **Infantry.** See *New Jersey Troops, 35th Regiment.*
Clancy's (Charles W.) **Infantry.** See *Ohio Troops, 52d Regiment.*
Clark's (Jeremiah S.) **Artillery.** See *Union Troops, Colored, 2d Regiment, Battery G.*
Clay's (Hiland H.) **Infantry.** See *Illinois Troops, 102d Regiment.*
Clinch's (N. B.) **Artillery.** See *Georgia Troops.*
Clune's (William H.) **Infantry.** See *Iowa Troops, 6th Regiment.*
Cobb Guards, Heavy Artillery. See *Georgia Troops.*
Coe's (Alonzo W.) **Artillery.** See *Illinois Troops, 2d Regiment, Battery I.*
Cogswell's (William) **Infantry.** See *Massachusetts Troops, 2d Regiment.*

Henderson's (Paris P.) **Infantry.** See *Iowa Troops, 10th Regiment.*
Hennessy's (John A.) **Infantry.** See *Pennsylvania Troops, 52d Regiment.*
Henry's (William Clay) **Infantry.** See *Ohio Troops, 81st Regiment.*
Herndon's Infantry. See *South Carolina Troops, 1st Regiment, Militia.*
Heyward's (George C.) **Cavalry.** See *South Carolina Troops, 3d Regiment.*
Hibbets' (Jefferson J.) **Infantry.** See *Ohio Troops, 32d Regiment.*
Hicks' (Lewis E.) **Infantry.** See *Ohio Troops, 69th Regiment.*
Hinson's (Joseph) **Infantry.** See *Ohio Troops, 33d Regiment.*
Hood's (Arthur) **Cavalry.** See *Georgia Troops, 29th Battalion.*
Hooper's (Henry N.) **Infantry.** See *Massachusetts Troops, 54th Regiment, Colored.*
Horn's (Henry) **Infantry.** See *Illinois Troops, 50th Regiment.*
Howard's (Noel B.) **Infantry.** See *Iowa Troops, 2d Regiment.*
Hoyt's (William H.) **Infantry.** See *New York Troops, 134th Regiment.*
Hughes' (Samuel T.) **Infantry.** See *Illinois Troops, 9th Regiment.*
Hundley's (William B.) **Infantry.** See *Georgia Troops, 5th Regiment.*
Hurlbut's (George R.) **Cavalry.** See *Massachusetts Troops, 4th Regiment.*
Hurst's (Samuel H.) **Infantry.** See *Ohio Troops, 73d Regiment.*
Hurst's (William E.) **Artillery.** See *Ruel W. Anderson's Artillery, ante.*
Hurter's (Henry) **Artillery.** See *Minnesota Troops, 1st Battery.*
Hutchins' (Rue P.) **Infantry.** See *Ohio Troops, 94th Regiment.*
Hutchinson's (Frederick S.) **Infantry.** See *Michigan Troops, 15th Regiment.*
Hyzer's (William W.) **Artillery.** See *Michigan Troops, 1st Regiment, Battery C.*
Isaminger's (James) **Infantry.** See *Illinois Troops, 63d Regiment.*
Jackson's (Allan H.) **Infantry.** See *New York Troops, 134th Regiment.*
Jandon's (Henry N.) **Cavalry.** See *South Carolina Troops, 3d Regiment.*
Jayne's (Thomas B.) **Infantry.** See *Pennsylvania Troops, 52d Regiment.*
Jenkins' (Jeremiah W.) **Infantry.** See *Iowa Troops, 31st Regiment.*
Jenkins' (John) **Cavalry.** See *South Carolina Troops, 3d Regiment.*
Johnson's (Edward S.) **Infantry.** See *Illinois Troops, 7th Regiment.*
Johnson's (George W.) **Heavy Artillery.** See *Georgia Troops, 12th Battalion, Battery C.*
Johnson's (Richard) **Artillery.** See *South Carolina Troops.*
Johnson's (Ruel M.) **Infantry.** See *Indiana Troops, 100th Regiment.*
Jones' (Fielder A.) **Cavalry.** See *Indiana Troops, 8th Regiment.*
Jones' (Toland) **Infantry.** See *Ohio Troops, 113th Regiment.*
Jones' (William H.) **Heavy Artillery.** See *South Carolina Troops, 2d Regiment, Battery D.*
Jordan's (Thomas J.) **Cavalry.** See *Pennsylvania Troops, 9th Regiment.*
Jo. Thompson Artillery. See *Georgia Troops.*
Kanapaux's (Charles E.) **Artillery.** See *Palmetto Artillery, post, Battery D.*
Kanapaux's (J. T.) **Artillery.** See *Lafayette Artillery, post.*
Kay's (James D.) **Infantry.** See *South Carolina Troops, 2d Battalion, Reserves.*
Keitt's (Ellison S.) **Cavalry.** See *South Carolina Troops.*
Kellams' (Gideon R.) **Infantry.** See *Indiana Troops, 42d Regiment.*
Kennedy's (Justin C.) **Infantry.** See *Iowa Troops, 13th Regiment.*
Ketcham's (John H.) **Infantry.** See *New York Troops, 150th Regiment.*
Kilcrease Artillery. See *Florida Troops, Confederate.*
Kili's (George F.) **Infantry.** See *Ohio Troops, 54th Regiment.*
Kimmel's (David H.) **Cavalry.** See *Pennsylvania Troops, 9th Regiment.*
King's (Henry) **Infantry.** See *Illinois Troops, 20th Regiment.*
King's (John L.) **Cavalry.** See *Ohio Troops, 4th Company.*
King's (Mitchell) **Heavy Artillery.** See *South Carolina Troops, 3d Regiment.*
King's (Robert H.) **Cavalry.** See *Kentucky Troops, Union, 3d Regiment.*
Kirk's (M. J.) **Partisan Rangers.** See *South Carolina Troops.*
Kirkup's (Robert) **Infantry.** See *Ohio Troops, 5th Regiment.*

Meriwether's (Robert) **Infantry**. See *South Carolina Troops, 6th Battalion, Reserves.*
Merrell's (William) **Infantry**. See *New York Troops, 141st Regiment.*
Merrill's (Samuel) **Infantry**. See *Indiana Troops, 70th Regiment.*
Merriman's (Wheelock S.) **Infantry**. See *Illinois Troops, 12th Regiment.*
Mesereau's (Thomas J.) **Artillery**. See *New York Troops, 3d Regiment, Battery B.*
Metham's (Pren) **Infantry**. See *Ohio Troops, 80th Regiment.*
Meyer's (Edward S.) **Infantry**. See *Ohio Troops, 107th Regiment.*
Meyers' (Charles A.) **Infantry**. See *Missouri Troops, Union, 26th Regiment.*
Miles' (David) **Infantry**. See *Pennsylvania Troops, 79th Regiment.*
Miller's Company. (Official designation not of record.) See ——— *Miller.*
Milton Artillery. See *Florida Troops, Confederate.*
Milton's (William H.) **Cavalry**. See *Florida Troops, Confederate, 5th Battalion.*
Milward's (Hubbard K.) **Infantry**. See *Kentucky Troops, Union, 18th Regiment.*
Mindil's (George W.) **Infantry**. See *New Jersey Troops, 33d Regiment.*
Minter's (William H.) **Infantry**. See *Missouri Troops, Union, 18th Regiment.*
Montague's (Calvin S.) **Infantry**. See *Union Troops, Colored, 102d Regiment.*
Moore's (Albert) **Infantry**. See *Ohio Troops, 14th Regiment.*
Moore's (Israel T.) **Infantry**. See *Ohio Troops, 54th Regiment.*
Moore's (John L.) **Infantry**. See *Georgia Troops, 3d Regiment, Reserves.*
Moore's (Joseph) **Infantry**. See *Indiana Troops, 58th Regiment.*
Morgan's (James) **Infantry**. See *Ohio Troops, 27th Regiment.*
Morgan's (Thomas) **Infantry**. See *Indiana Troops, 74th Regiment.*
Morton's (Quin) **Infantry**. See *Missouri Troops, Union, 23d Regiment.*
Muenscher's (Emory W.) **Infantry**. See *Ohio Troops, 30th Regiment.*
Murkinson's Battalion. (Official designation not of record.) See *Major Murkinson.*
Naval Battalion. See *Confederate Troops.*
Neely's (James J.) **Infantry**. See *Georgia Troops, 1st Regiment, Reserves (Fannin's).*
Newkirk's (Edward P.) **Artillery**. See *New York Troops, 1st Regiment, Battery M.*
Nichols' (Isaac B.) **Reserves**. See *Florida Troops, Confederate.*
Nichols' (Samuel D.) **Infantry**. See *Iowa Troops, 4th Regiment.*
Noble's (William H.) **Infantry**. See *Connecticut Troops, 17th Regiment.*
Orleans Guard, Artillery. See *Louisiana Troops, Confederate.*
Orr's (John W.) **Infantry**. See *Ohio Troops, 39th Regiment.*
Palmer's (Samuel B.) **Artillery**. See *Chatham Artillery, ante.*
Palmer's (Theodoric R.) **Infantry**. See *Michigan Troops, 13th Regiment.*
Palmetto Artillery. See *South Carolina Troops.*
Parker's (Edward L.) **Artillery**. See *Marion Artillery, ante.*
Parrott's (James C.) **Infantry**. See *Iowa Troops, 7th Regiment.*
Parry's (Augustus C.) **Infantry**. See *Ohio Troops, 47th Regiment.*
Patton's (Charles U.) **Cavalry**. See *Indiana Troops, 3d Regiment.*
Pearson's (Robert N.) **Infantry**. See *Illinois Troops, 31st Regiment.*
Pee Dee Artillery. See *South Carolina Troops.*
Peeples' (W. B.) **Cavalry**. See *South Carolina Troops, 3d Regiment.*
Pepper's (F. L.) **Cavalry**. See *Georgia Troops, 29th Battalion.*
Perkins' (George T.) **Infantry**. See *Ohio Troops, 105th Regiment.*
Perrin's (Hector) **Infantry**. See *Illinois Troops, 7th Regiment.*
Philips' (Henry L.) **Infantry**. See *Ohio Troops, 70th Regiment.*
Place's (James E.) **Engineers**. See *New York Troops, 1st Regiment.*
Pointer's (Marcellus) **Cavalry**. See *Alabama Troops, Confederate, 12th Regiment.*
Pomutz's (George) **Infantry**. See *Iowa Troops, 15th Regiment.*
Powell's (Edward) **Reserves**. (Official designation not of record.) See *Edward Powell.*
Powell's (Eugene) **Infantry**. See *Ohio Troops, 66th Regiment.*
Powers' (Edwin H.) **Infantry**. See *Ohio Troops, 55th Regiment.*

INDEX.

Brigades, Divisions, Corps, Armies, and improvised organizations are "Mentioned" under name of commanding officer; State and other organizations under their official designation. (See Alternate Designations, pp. 1015-1024.)

* Composed of clerks, detailed men, etc.
† Composed of employés, detailed men, etc.

*Attached to 18th South Carolina Battalion as Company D.

* Sometimes called 3d Battery.

Page.

Savannah, Ga., Campaign, Nov. 15–Dec. 21, 1864—Continued.

* Also called 1st Regulars.

Page.

Page.

O